Eighth Edition

Business in Action

Courtland L. Bovée

Professor of Business
C. Allen Paul Distinguished Chair
Grossmont College

John V. Thill

Chairman and Chief Executive Officer
Global Communication Strategies

PEARSON

Boston   Columbus   Indianapolis   New York   San Francisco   Amsterdam   Cape Town
Dubai   London   Madrid   Milan   Munich   Paris   Montréal   Toronto   Delhi   Mexico City
São Paulo   Sydney   Hong Kong   Seoul   Singapore   Taipei   Tokyo

Vice President, Business Publishing: Donna Battista
Editor-in-Chief: Stephanie Wall
Acquisitions Editor: Nicole Sam
Editorial Assistant: Olivia Vignone
Vice President, Product Marketing: Maggie Moylan
**Director of Marketing, Digital Services
    and Products:** Jeanette Koskinas
Field Marketing Manager: Lenny Ann Raper
Product Marketing Assistant: Jessica Quazza
Team Lead, Program Management: Ashley Santora
Program Manager: Denise Weiss
Team Lead, Project Management: Jeff Holcomb
Project Manager: Nicole Suddeth
Operations Specialist: Carol Melville
Creative Director: Blair Brown

Art Director: Janet Slowik
**Vice President, Director of Digital Strategy
    and Assessment:** Paul Gentile
Manager of Learning Applications: Paul DeLuca
Digital Editor: Brian Surette
Director, Digital Studio: Sacha Laustsen
Digital Studio Manager: Diane Lombardo
Digital Studio Project Manager: Monique Lawrence
Digital Studio Project Manager: Regina DaSilva
Digital Studio Project Manager: Alana Coles
Digital Studio Project Manager: Robin Lazrus
**Full-Service Project Management, Design, and
    Composition:** Integra
Printer/Binder: RR Donnelley
Cover Printer: Phoenix

Microsoft and/or its respective suppliers make no representations about the suitability of the information contained in the documents and related graphics published as part of the services for any purpose. All such documents and related graphics are provided "as is" without warranty of any kind. Microsoft and/or its respective suppliers hereby disclaim all warranties and conditions with regard to this information, including all warranties and conditions of merchantability, whether express, implied or statutory, fitness for a particular purpose, title and non-infringement. In no event shall Microsoft and/or its respective suppliers be liable for any special, indirect or consequential damages or any damages whatsoever resulting from loss of use, data or profits, whether in an action of contract, negligence or other tortious action, arising out of or in connection with the use or performance of information available from the services.

The documents and related graphics contained herein could include technical inaccuracies or typographical errors. Changes are periodically added to the information herein. Microsoft and/or its respective suppliers may make improvements and/or changes in the product(s) and/or the program(s) described herein at any time. Partial screen shots may be viewed in full within the software version specified.

Microsoft® and Windows® are registered trademarks of the Microsoft Corporation in the U.S.A. and other countries. This book is not sponsored or endorsed by or affiliated with the Microsoft Corporation.

Library of Congress Cataloging-in-Publication Data
Bovée, Courtland L.
    Business in action/Courtland L. Bovée, Grossmont College, John V. Thill,
Global Communication Strategies.—Eighth Edition.
        pages cm
    Includes bibliographical references and index.
    ISBN-13: 978-0-13-412995-2
    1. Business.   2. Commerce.   3. Industrial management.   I. Thill, John V.   II. Title.
    HF1008.B685 2016
    650—dc23
                                                                2015033222

2 16

ISBN 10:   0-13-412995-4
ISBN-13: 978-0-13-412995-2

This book is dedicated to the many instructors and students who have used this text and its predecessors *Excellence in Business* and *Business Today*. We appreciate the opportunity to assist you in your exploration of the world of business, and we wish you great success in this course and in your careers.

Courtland L. Bovée
John V. Thill

Contents in Brief

Contents

Major Changes and Improvements in This Edition

Here are the major changes in the Eighth Edition of *Business in Action:*

- Five new chapter-opening vignettes with chapter-ending case studies:

  Chapter 2: The forecasting challenges faced by Apple when the company was planning the launch of its iPhone 6 models

  Chapter 3: Cisco's successful merger-and-acquisition process, defying the odds when it comes to buying other companies

  Chapter 8: The Mexican building-materials giant Cemex's innovative use of custom collaboration platform to help its global workforce solve pressing business challenges

  Chapter 11: Zappos' unconventional strategies for finding and attracting unconventional employees

  Chapter 16: GoPro's smart use of social media to build awareness of and demand for its rugged action cameras

- More than three dozen new review, analysis, and application questions and student projects
- Fourteen all-new exhibits and 45 updated or redesigned exhibits, further expanding *Business in Action*'s unmatched selection of value-added instructional visuals
- Coverage of the revolution in mobile connectivity and the many ways mobile is reshaping business
- New or substantially revised sections include

  The Technological Environment (Chapter 1), highlighting the disruptive effects of mobile communication and connectivity

  The Trans-Pacific Partnership (PTT) (Chapter 2), highlighting the controversy surrounding this major new trade agreement

  Legal Differences in the Global Business Environment (Chapter 2), updating the European taxation controversy that has forced Google, Amazon, Starbucks, and other U.S. companies to change their business practices

  Blueprint for an Effective Business Plan (Chapter 6), adding a discussion of the contrary view about the value of conventional business plans and the use of *canvases* instead

  Social Networks and Virtual Communities (Chapter 8), adding an overview of Zappos's reliance on social networking to keep its growing workforce connected

  Gamifying for Healthy Competition (Chapter 10), describing how companies are using game principles to motivate employees

  Gender (Chapter 11, in Dimensions of Workforce Diversity), updating the discussion of gender pay imbalance and uncovering the major issues behind the often-quoted statistics about women earning only 70 percent of what men earn

  Test Marketing (Chapter 14), expanding the coverage with the new phenomenon of crowdsourced test marketing and crowdfunding as a way to identify potential hit products

Packaging (Chapter 14), broadening the discussion of how packaging decisions are often a tug-of-war between competing economic and environmental concerns

The Outlook for Wholesaling (Chapter 15), adding discussion of how e-commerce technologies let companies such as Amazon jump into traditional wholesaling and distribution channels because some incumbent players were too slow to adapt

The Outlook for Retailing (Chapter 15), expanding the discussion points of overcapacity, the emergence of mobile commerce, the growth of multichannel retailing, and data security and privacy concerns stemming from personalized marketing efforts

Physical Distribution and Logistics (Chapter 15), using Amazon's new same-day delivery service and experimentation with delivery drones to highlight the importance of competitive physical distribution in the marketing mix.

Public Relations (Chapter 16), explaining how social media have upended the traditional practice of public relations

Business in Action: An Ideal Text for Your Introduction to Business Course

Business in Action is the ideal text for courses that aim to cover the full spectrum of contemporary business topics in the most efficient and successful manner possible.

HIGH-EFFICIENCY LEARNING WITHOUT COMPROMISES

Business in Action offers instructors and students a much-needed alternative to texts that are either overstuffed and overwhelming or so skimpy that they compromise essential coverage. With a full 20 chapters, including chapters dedicated to employee motivation, customer communication, financial markets, and banking, it has the same scope as other comprehensive texts while being up to 20 percent shorter. There is no filler and no fluff, and the examples were chosen carefully to illustrate important points, without overloading the text. We invite you to do side-by-side comparisons with any other business text to see which one will make the best use of students' limited time and energy for studying.

VIGNETTES AND CASE STUDIES THAT BRING BUSINESS CONCEPTS TO LIFE

Every chapter is bookended with a vignette/case study pair that help students grasp the principles covered in the chapter. The chapter-opening vignette introduces a company faced with a major strategic challenge and encourages students to imagine how they would address that challenge. The chapter-closing case study describes the strategic choices the company's leaders made, including how they applied the concepts students just learned in the chapter. Three critical thinking questions require students to apply the concepts covered in the text. Plus, students can find out more about the company featured in the case by completing the "Learn More Online" exercise. In this edition, six of the vignette/case studies are all new, and the rest have been updated to reflect the most recent decisions faced by each featured company.

OBJECTIVE-DRIVEN DESIGN WITH INFORMATION CHUNKING AND INTERIM CHECKPOINTS

Every chapter is divided into six concise segments, each focused on its own learning objective and offering a comprehensive checkpoint to help students review and reinforce what they've learned. With this approach, each learning objective segment is treated almost as a mini-chapter within the chapter, letting students pace their intake and memorization, rather than having to review an entire chapter at once. The consistent six-part structure also simplifies course planning and class time allocation for instructors, and it helps students organize their reading, review, and test preparation.

VISUAL LEARNING FOR A NEW GENERATION OF STUDENTS

Business in Action takes efficiency and student-friendly design to an entirely new level, with more than 150 *Exhibits That Teach*. These unique diagrams, infographics, and other exhibits address the challenge of getting students to read long passages of text by presenting vital concepts visually. The emphasis throughout is on productive learning—on helping students minimize the time they spend reading while maximizing their learning outcome. This value-added approach to visuals is in sharp contrast to books that try to entertain with decorative photos, cartoons, or fractured page designs that disrupt the flow of reading and thereby force students to spend even *more* time reading.

Healthy connection between risk and reward

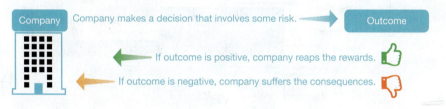

Moral hazard: Link between risk and reward is broken

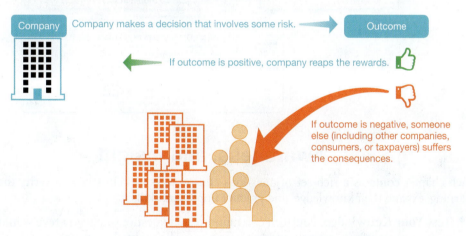

Extending the Value of Your Textbook with Free Multimedia Content

Business in Action's unique Real-Time Updates system automatically provides weekly content updates, including interactive websites, podcasts, PowerPoint presentations, online videos, PDFs, and articles. You can subscribe to updates chapter by chapter, so you get only the material that applies to your current chapter. Visit **http://real-timeupdates .com/bia8** to register.

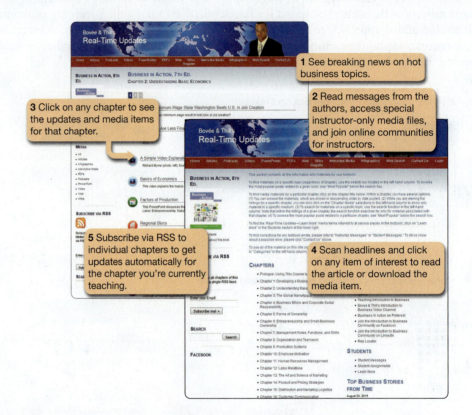

Building Skills, Awareness, and Insight

Each chapter contains a rich set of questions and projects to help students verify their learning, expand their knowledge, and practice important skills:

- **Test Your Knowledge.** Fourteen carefully selected questions help you review information, analyze implications, and apply concepts. Highlighted questions involve ethical considerations and concept integration from other chapters .
- **Expand Your Knowledge.** *Discovering Career Opportunities* tasks give students a chance to explore career resources on campus, observe professionals at their jobs, interview businesspeople, and perform self-evaluations to assess their own career skills and interests. *Improving Your Tech Insights* tasks students to research and summarize an important technical development and explain its business implications; this feature introduces them to such revolutionary developments as nanotechnology, location and tracking technologies, and assistive technologies for people with disabilities.
- **Practice Your Skills.** *Sharpening Your Communication Skills* addresses one of the key skill concerns among today's hiring managers; this exercise lets students practice listening, writing, and speaking in a variety of real-life scenarios. *Building Your Team Skills* teaches important team skills, such as brainstorming, collaborative decision making, developing a consensus, debating, role playing, and resolving conflict. *Developing Your Research Skills* familiarizes students with a wide variety of business reference materials and offers practice in developing research skills.

Full Support for AACSB Learning Standards

The American Association of Collegiate Schools of Business (AACSB) is a not-for-profit corporation of educational institutions, corporations, and other organizations devoted to the promotion and improvement of higher education in business administration and accounting. A collegiate institution offering degrees in business administration or accounting may volunteer for AACSB accreditation review. The AACSB makes initial accreditation decisions and conducts periodic reviews to promote continuous quality improvement in management education. Pearson Education is a proud member of the AACSB and is pleased to provide advice to help you apply AACSB Learning Standards.

Curriculum quality is one of the most important criteria for AACSB accreditation. Although no specific courses are required, the AACSB expects a curriculum to include learning experiences in the following areas:

- Written and oral communication
- Ethical understanding and reasoning
- Analytical thinking
- Information technology
- Interpersonal relations and teamwork
- Diverse and multicultural work environments
- Reflective thinking
- Application of knowledge

Throughout *Business in Action*, you'll find student exercises and activities that support the achievement of these important goals, and the questions in the accompanying test bank are tagged with the appropriate AACSB category.

Course Planning Guide

The structure of *Business in Action* makes it easy to adapt to courses of any length and with any specific instructional goals. The following table suggests one possible sequence and schedule for covering the chapters in the textbook, with time allocations based on the total number of class hours available.

	Hours Devoted to Each Chapter		
Chapter	**30-Hour Course**	**45-Hour Course**	**60-Hour Course**
Chapter 1: Developing a Business Mindset	1	2	3
Chapter 2: Understanding Basic Economics	2	2	3
Chapter 3: The Global Marketplace	1	2	3
Chapter 4: Business Ethics and Corporate Social Responsibility	2	3	3
Chapter 5: Forms of Ownership	1	2	3
Chapter 6: Entrepreneurship and Small-Business Ownership	1	2	3
Chapter 7: Management Roles, Functions, and Skills	2	3	3
Chapter 8: Organization and Teamwork	1	2	3
Chapter 9: Production Systems	1	2	3
Chapter 10: Employee Motivation	1	2	3
Chapter 11: Human Resources Management	1	2	3
Chapter 12: Labor Relations	1	2	3
Chapter 13: The Art and Science of Marketing	2	2	2
Chapter 14: Product and Pricing Strategies	2	2	2
Chapter 15: Distribution and Marketing Logistics	1	1	2
Chapter 16: Customer Communication	1	2	2

Continued on next page

Chapter	Hours Devoted to Each Chapter		
	30-Hour Course	45-Hour Course	60-Hour Course
Chapter 17: Financial Information and Accounting Concepts	2	3	3
Chapter 18: Financial Management	2	2	3
Chapter 19: Financial Markets and Investment Strategies	1	2	3
Chapter 20: The Money Supply and Banking Systems	2	2	3
Appendix A: Business Law	-	1	1
Appendix B: Risk Management	1	1	1
Appendix C: Information Technology	-	-	1
Appendix D: Personal Finance: Getting Set for Life	1	1	1

Resources for Instructors and Students

Instructor's Resource Center

At the Instructor Resource Center, **www.pearsonhighered.com/irc**, instructors can easily register to gain access to a variety of instructor resources available with this text in downloadable format. If assistance is needed, our dedicated technical support team is ready to help with the media supplements that accompany this text. Visit **http://247pearsoned.custhelp.com/** for answers to frequently asked questions and toll-free user-support phone numbers.

The following supplements are available with this text

- **PowerPoints.** A full set of PowerPoint slides is provided. The slides are divided by chapter and are suitable for leading class lectures and discussion. The slides contain the relevant material from each chapter along with reproductions of key tables and figures.
- **Instructor's Resource Manual.** The *Instructor's Resource Manual* makes it easy to plan lectures and incorporate all resources offered with *Business in Action*. Each chapter contains a chapter outline, classroom activities, and answers to all end-of-chapter material.
- **Test Bank.** The test bank contains approximately 100 questions per chapter, including multiple-choice, true/false, and essay questions.
- **TestGen® Computerized Test Bank (and various conversions).** TestGen is a test-generating software program that allows instructors to add, edit, or delete questions from the test bank; analyze test results; and organize a database of exams and student results.

CourseSmart eTextbook

CourseSmart eTextbooks were developed for students looking to save on required or recommended textbooks. Students simply select their eText by title or author and purchase immediate access to the content for the duration of the course using any major credit card. With a CourseSmart eText, students can search for specific keywords or page numbers, take notes online, print out reading assignments that incorporate lecture notes, and bookmark important passages for later review. For more information or to purchase a CourseSmart eTextbook, visit **www.coursesmart.com**.

Customer Service

If you have questions related to this product, please contact our customer service department online at **http://247pearsoned.custhelp.com/**.

About the Authors

Courtland L. Bovée and John V. Thill have been leading textbook authors for more than two decades, introducing millions of students to the fields of business and business communication. Their award-winning texts are distinguished by proven pedagogical features, extensive selections of contemporary case studies, hundreds of real-life examples, engaging writing, thorough research, and the unique integration of print and electronic resources. Each new edition reflects the authors' commitment to continuous refinement and improvement, particularly in terms of modeling the latest practices in business and the use of technology.

Professor Bovée has 22 years of teaching experience at Grossmont College in San Diego, where he has received teaching honors and was accorded that institution's C. Allen Paul Distinguished Chair. Mr. Thill is a prominent business consultant who has worked with organizations ranging from Fortune 500 multinationals to entrepreneurial start-ups. He formerly held positions with Pacific Bell and Texaco.

Courtland L. Bovée

Acknowledgments

A very special acknowledgment goes to George Dovel, whose superb writing and editing skills, distinguished background, and wealth of business experience assured this project of clarity and completeness. Also, we recognize and thank Jackie Estrada for her outstanding skills and excellent attention to details.

The supplements package for *Business in Action* has benefited from the able contributions of numerous individuals. We would like to express our thanks to them for creating a superb set of instructional supplements. We'd like to sincerely thank the following contributors for taking the time to create new content for MyBizLab for this edition: Todd Jamison, Chadron State College; Storm Russo, Valencia College, and Susan C. Schanne, Eastern Michigan University.

John V. Thill

We want to extend our warmest appreciation to the devoted professionals at Pearson. They include Paul Corey, president; Stephanie Wall, editor-in-chief; Nicole Sam; acquisitions editor; Denise Weiss, program manager; Lenny Ann Raper, marketing manager; Jeff Holcomb, senior managing editor of production; Nicole Suddeth, production project manager; all of Prentice Hall Business Publishing; and the outstanding Prentice Hall sales representatives.

Courtland L. Bovée

John V. Thill

Real-Time Updates—Learn More

Real-Time Updates—Learn More is a unique feature you will see strategically located throughout the text, connecting students with dozens of carefully screened online media. These elements—categorized by the icons shown below representing interactive websites, podcasts, PDFs, articles, videos, and PowerPoints—complement the text's coverage by providing contemporary examples and valuable insights from successful professionals.

REAL-TIME UPDATES
Learn More by Reading This Article

REAL-TIME UPDATES
Learn More by Listening to This Podcast

REAL-TIME UPDATES
Learn More by Watching This Video

REAL-TIME UPDATES
Learn More by Reading This PDF

REAL-TIME UPDATES
Learn More by Watching This Presentation

REAL-TIME UPDATES
Learn More by Visiting This Website

REAL-TIME UPDATES
Learn More by Exploring This Interactive Website

REAL-TIME UPDATES
Learn More by Reading This Infographic

Using This Course to Help Launch Your Career

You might not be thinking about your long-term career path as you dive into this business course, but this is actually the perfect time to start planning and preparing. Even though you may not have decided which area of business interests you the most, it's never too early to start accumulating the skills, experiences, and insights that will give you a competitive advantage when it's time to enter (or reenter) the business job market. By thinking ahead about the qualifications you'd like to have on your résumé when you graduate, you can select courses, seek out part-time employment and internship opportunities, and pursue extracurricular activities that will give you the professional profile that top employers look for.

This prologue sets the stage by helping you understand today's dynamic workplace, the steps you can take to adapt to the job market, and the importance of creating an employment portfolio and building your personal brand.

UNDERSTANDING THE CHANGING WORLD OF WORK

Even as the U.S. economy recovers from the Great Recession and employment levels improve, you're likely to encounter some challenges as you start or continue on with your business career. As companies around the world try to gain competitive advantages and cost efficiencies, employment patterns will vary from industry to industry and region to region.

The ups and downs of the economic cycle are not the only dynamic elements that will affect your career, however. The nature of employment itself is changing, with a growing number of independent workers and loosely structured *virtual organizations* that engage these workers for individual projects or short-term contracts, rather than hiring employees. In fact, one recent study predicted that independent workers will outnumber conventional employees in the United States by 2020.[1]

This new model of work offers some compelling advantages for workers and companies alike. Companies can lower their fixed costs, adapt more easily to economic fluctuations and competitive moves, and get access to specialized talent for specific project needs.[2] Workers can benefit from the freedom to choose the clients and projects that interest them the most, the flexibility to work as much or as little as they want, and (thanks to advances in communication technology) access to compelling work even if they live far from major employment centers such as New York City or California's Silicon Valley.[3]

On the other hand, this new approach also presents some significant challenges for all parties. These flexibilities and freedoms can create more complexity for workers and managers, diminished loyalties on both sides, uncertainty about the future, issues with skill development and training, and problems with accountability and liability.[4] Many of these challenges involve communication, making solid communication skills more important than ever.

These changes could affect you even if you pursue traditional employment throughout your career. Within organizations, you're likely to work with a combination of "inside"

Are you comfortable working on your own? Independent workers have become an important part of the global workforce.

Peter Bernik/Shutterstock

employees and "outside" contractors, which can affect the dynamics of the workplace. And the availability of more independent workers in the talent marketplace gives employers more options and more leverage, so full-time employees may find themselves competing against freelancers, at least indirectly.

As you navigate this uncertain future, keep two vital points in mind. First, don't wait for your career to just happen: Take charge of your career and stay in charge of it. Explore all your options and have a plan—but be prepared to change course as opportunities and threats appear on the horizon. Second, don't count on employers to take care of you. The era of lifetime employment, in which an employee committed to one company for life with the understanding it would return the loyalty, is long gone. From finding opportunities to developing the skills you need to succeed, it's up to you to manage your career and look out for your own best interests.

HOW EMPLOYERS VIEW TODAY'S JOB MARKET

From an employer's perspective, the employment process is always a question of balance. Maintaining a stable workforce can improve practically every aspect of business performance, yet many employers want the flexibility to shrink and expand payrolls as business conditions change. Employers obviously want to attract the best talent, but the best talent is more expensive and more vulnerable to offers from competitors, so there are always financial trade-offs to consider.

Employers also struggle with the ups and downs of the economy. When unemployment is low, the balance of power shifts to employees, and employers have to compete in order to attract and keep top talent. When unemployment is high, the power shifts back to employers, who can afford to be more selective and less accommodating. In other words, pay attention to the economy; at times you can be more aggressive in your demands, but at other times you need to be more accommodating.

Companies view employment as a complex business decision with lots of variables to consider. To make the most of your potential, regardless of the career path you pursue, you need to view employment in the same way.

WHAT EMPLOYERS LOOK FOR IN JOB APPLICANTS

Given the complex forces in the contemporary workplace and the unrelenting pressure of global competition, what are employers looking for in the candidates they hire? The short answer: a lot. Like all "buyers," companies want to get as much as they can for the money they spend. The closer you can present yourself as the ideal candidate, the better your chances of getting a crack at the most exciting opportunities.

Specific expectations vary by profession and position, of course, but virtually all employers look for the following general skills and attributes:[5]

- **Communication skills.** Communication is far and away the most commonly mentioned skill set when employers are asked about what they look for in employees. Improving your communication skills will help in every aspect of your professional life.
- **Interpersonal and team skills.** You will have many individual responsibilities on the job, but chances are you won't work alone often. Learn to work with others—and help them succeed as you succeed.
- **Intercultural and international awareness and sensitivity.** Successful employers tend to be responsive to diverse workforces, markets, and communities, and they look for employees with the same outlook.

Communication skills will benefit your career, no matter what path or profession you pursue.

- **Data collection, analysis, and decision-making skills.** Employers want people who know how to identify information needs, find the necessary data, convert the data into useful knowledge, and make sound decisions.
- **Digital, social, and mobile media skills.** Today's workers need to know how to use common office software and to communicate using a wide range of digital media and systems.
- **Time and resource management.** If you've had to juggle multiple priorities during college, consider that great training for the business world. Your ability to plan projects and manage the time and resources available to you will make a big difference on the job.
- **Flexibility and adaptability.** Stuff happens, as they say. Employees who can roll with the punches and adapt to changing business priorities and circumstances will go further (and be happier) than employees who resist change.
- **Professionalism.** Professionalism is the quality of performing at the highest possible level and conducting oneself with confidence, purpose, and pride. True professionals strive to excel, continue to hone their skills and build their knowledge, are dependable and accountable, demonstrate a sense of business etiquette, make ethical decisions, show loyalty and commitment, don't give up when things get tough, and maintain a positive outlook.

Adapting to Today's Job Market

Adapting to the workplace is a lifelong process of seeking the best fit between what you want to do and what employers (or clients, if you work independently) are willing to pay you to do. It's important to think about what you want to do during the many thousands of hours you will spend working, what you have to offer, and how to make yourself more attractive to employers.

WHAT DO YOU WANT TO DO?

Economic necessities and the vagaries of the marketplace will influence much of what happens in your career, of course, and you may not always have the opportunity to do the kind of work you would really like to do. Even if you can't get the job you want right now, though, start your job search by examining your values and interests. Doing so will give you a better idea of where you want to be eventually, and you can use those insights to learn and grow your way toward that ideal situation. Consider these questions:

- **What would you like to do every day?** Research occupations that interest you. Find out what people really do every day. Ask friends, relatives, alumni from your school, and contacts in your social networks. Read interviews with people in various professions to get a sense of what their careers are like.
- **How would you like to work?** Consider how much independence you want on the job, how much variety you like, and whether you prefer to work with products, machines, people, ideas, figures, or some combination thereof.
- **How do your financial goals fit with your other priorities?** For instance, many high-paying jobs involve a lot of stress, sacrifices of time with family and friends, and frequent travel or relocation. If location, lifestyle, intriguing work, or other factors are more important to you, you may well have to sacrifice some level of pay to achieve them.
- **Have you established some general career goals?** For example, do you want to pursue a career specialty such as finance or manufacturing, or do you want to gain experience in multiple areas with an eye toward upper management?
- **What sort of corporate culture are you most comfortable with?** Would you be happy in a formal hierarchy with clear reporting relationships? Or do you prefer less structure? Teamwork or individualism? Do you like a competitive environment?

You might need some time in the workforce to figure out what you really want to do or to work your way into the job you really want, but it's never too early to start thinking about where you want to be. Filling out the assessment in Exhibit 1 might help you get a clearer picture of the nature of work you would like to pursue in your career.

WHAT DO YOU HAVE TO OFFER?

Knowing what you want to do is one thing. Knowing what a company is willing to pay you to do is another thing entirely. You may already have a good idea of what you can offer employers. If not, some brainstorming can help you identify your skills, interests, and characteristics. Start by jotting down achievements you're proud of and experiences that were satisfying, and think carefully about what specific skills these achievements demanded of you. For example, leadership skills, speaking ability, and artistic talent may have helped you coordinate a successful class project. As you analyze your achievements, you may well begin to recognize a pattern of skills. Which of them might be valuable to potential employers?

Next, look at your educational preparation, work experience, and extracurricular activities. What do your knowledge and experience qualify you to do? What have you learned from volunteer work or class projects that could benefit you on the job? Have you held any offices, won any awards or scholarships, mastered a second language? What skills have you developed in nonbusiness situations that could transfer to a business position?

Take stock of your personal characteristics. Are you aggressive, a born leader? Or would you rather follow? Are you outgoing, articulate, great with people? Or do you prefer working alone? Make a list of what you believe are your four or five most important qualities. Ask a relative or friend to rate your traits as well.

If you're having difficulty figuring out your interests, characteristics, or capabilities, consult your college career center. Many campuses administer a variety of tests

EXHIBIT 1	Career Self-Assessment

Consider these 20 questions to help define the sort of career path you would like to pursue.

Activity or Situation	Strongly Agree	Agree	Disagree	No Preference
1. I want to work independently.				
2. I want variety in my work.				
3. I want to work with people.				
4. I want to work with technology.				
5. I want physical work.				
6. I want mental work.				
7. I want to work for a large organization.				
8. I want to work for a nonprofit organization.				
9. I want to work for a small business.				
10. I want to work for a service business.				
11. I want to start or buy a business someday.				
12. I want regular, predictable work hours.				
13. I want to work in a city location.				
14. I want to work in a small town or suburb.				
15. I want to work in another country.				
16. I want to work outdoors.				
17. I want to work in a structured environment.				
18. I want to avoid risk as much as possible.				
19. I want to enjoy my work, even if that means making less money.				
20. I want to become a high-level corporate manager.				

that can help you identify interests, aptitudes, and personality traits. These tests won't reveal your "perfect" job, but they'll help you focus on the types of work best suited to your personality.

HOW CAN YOU MAKE YOURSELF MORE VALUABLE?

While you're figuring out what you want from a job and what you can offer an employer, you can take positive steps toward building your career. First, look for volunteer projects, temporary jobs, freelance work, or internships that will help expand your experience base and skill set.[6] You can look for freelance projects on Craigslist and numerous other websites; some of these jobs have only nominal pay, but they do provide an opportunity for you to display your skills. Also consider applying your talents to *crowdsourcing* projects, in which companies and nonprofit organizations invite the public to contribute solutions to various challenges.

These opportunities help you gain valuable experience and relevant contacts, provide you with important references and work samples for your *employment portfolio*, and help you establish your *personal brand* (see the following sections).

Second, learn more about the industry or industries in which you want to work and stay on top of new developments. Join networks of professional colleagues and friends who can help you keep up with trends and events. Many professional societies have student chapters or offer students discounted memberships. Take courses and pursue other educational or life experiences that would be difficult while working full time.

BUILDING AN EMPLOYMENT PORTFOLIO

Employers want proof that you have the skills to succeed on the job, but even if you don't have much relevant work experience, you can use your college classes to assemble that proof. Simply create and maintain an *employment portfolio*, which is a collection of projects that demonstrate your skills and knowledge. You can create a *print portfolio* and an *e-portfolio*; both can help with your career effort. A print portfolio gives you something tangible to bring to interviews, and it lets you collect project results that might not be easy to show online, such as a handsomely bound report. An e-portfolio is a multimedia presentation of your skills and experiences.[7] Think of it as a website that contains your résumé, work samples, letters of recommendation, relevant videos or podcasts you have recorded, any blog posts or articles you have written, and other information about you and your skills. The portfolio can be burned on a CD or DVD for physical distribution or, more commonly, it can be posted online—whether it's a personal website, your college's site (if student pages are available), a specialized portfolio hosting site such as Behance. To see a selection of student e-portfolios from colleges around the United States, go to **http://real-timeupdates .com/bia8**, click on Student Assignments and locate the link to student e-portfolios.

As you assemble your portfolio, collect anything that shows your ability to perform, whether it's in school, on the job, or in other venues. However, you *must* check with employers before including any items that you created while you were an employee and check with clients before including any *work products* (anything you wrote, designed, programmed, and so on) they purchased from you. Many business documents contain confidential information that companies don't want distributed to outside audiences.

For each item you add to your portfolio, write a brief description that helps other people understand the meaning and significance of the project. Include such items as these:

- **Background.** Why did you undertake this project? Was it a school project, a work assignment, or something you did on your own initiative?
- **Project objectives.** Explain the project's goals, if relevant.
- **Collaborators.** If you worked with others, be sure to mention that and discuss team dynamics if appropriate. For instance, if you led the team or worked with others long distance as a virtual team, point that out.

- **Constraints.** Sometimes the most impressive thing about a project is the time or budget constraints under which it was created. If such constraints apply to a project, consider mentioning them in a way that doesn't sound like an excuse for poor quality. If you had only one week to create a website, for example, you might say that "One of the intriguing challenges of this project was the deadline; I had only one week to design, compose, test, and publish this material."
- **Outcomes.** If the project's goals were measurable, what was the result? For example, if you wrote a letter soliciting donations for a charitable cause, how much money did you raise?
- **Learning experience.** If appropriate, describe what you learned during the course of the project.

Keep in mind that the portfolio itself is a communication project, so be sure to apply everything you'll learn in this course about effective communication and good design. Assume that potential employers will find your e-portfolio site (even if you don't tell them about it), so don't include anything that could come back to haunt you. Also, if you have anything embarrassing on Facebook, Twitter, or any other social networking site, remove it immediately.

To get started, first check with the career center at your college; many schools offer e-portfolio systems for their students. (Some schools now require e-portfolios, so you may already be building one.) You can also find plenty of advice online; search for "e-portfolio," "student portfolio," or "professional portfolio."

BUILDING YOUR PERSONAL BRAND

Products and companies have brands that represent collections of certain attributes, such as the safety emphasis of Volvo cars, the performance emphasis of BMW, or the luxury emphasis of Cadillac. Similarly, when people who know you think about you, they have a particular set of qualities in mind based on your professionalism, your priorities, and the various skills and attributes you have developed over the years. Perhaps without even being conscious of it, you have created a *personal brand* for yourself.

As you plan the next stage of your career, start managing your personal brand deliberately, rather than just letting it happen. Here are the basics of a successful personal branding strategy:[8]

- **Figure out the "story of you."** Simply put, where have you been in life, and where are you going? Every good story has dramatic tension that pulls readers in and makes them wonder what will happen next. Where is your story going next? You might even want to write a brief summary of your story to help clarify your thoughts.
- **Clarify your professional theme.** Volvos, BMWs, and Cadillacs can all get you from Point A to Point B in safety, comfort, and style—but each brand emphasizes some attributes more than others to create a specific image in the minds of potential buyers. Similarly, you want to be seen as something more than just an accountant, a supervisor, a salesperson. What will your theme be? Brilliant strategist? Hard-nosed, get-it-done tactician? Technical guru? Problem solver? Creative genius? Inspirational leader?
- **Reach out and connect.** Major corporations spread the word about their brands with multimillion-dollar advertising campaigns. You can promote your brand for free or close to it. The secret is networking, which you'll learn more about in the next section. You build your brand by connecting with like-minded people, sharing information, demonstrating skills and knowledge, and helping others succeed.
- **Deliver on your brand's promise—every time, all the time.** When you promote a brand, you make a promise—a promise that whoever buys that brand will get the benefits you are promoting. All of this planning and communication is of no value if you fail to deliver on the promises your branding efforts make. Conversely, when you deliver quality results time after time, your talents and professionalism will speak for you.

BUILDING YOUR NETWORK

Networking is the process of making informal connections with mutually beneficial business contacts. Networking takes place wherever and whenever people communicate: at industry functions, at social gatherings, at alumni reunions—and all over the Internet, from LinkedIn to Facebook to Twitter. In addition to making connections through social media tools, you can get yourself noticed by company recruiters.

Networking is more essential than ever because the vast majority of job openings are never advertised to the general public. To avoid the time and expense of sifting through thousands of applications and the risk of hiring complete strangers, most companies prefer to ask their employees for recommendations first.[9] The more people who know you, the better your chance of being recommended for one of these hidden job openings.

Start building your network now, before you need it. Your classmates could end up being some of your most valuable contacts—if not right away then possibly later in your career. Then branch out by identifying people with similar interests in your target professions, industries, and companies. Read news sites, blogs, and other online sources. Follow industry leaders on Twitter. You can also follow individual executives at your target companies to learn about their interests and concerns.[10] Be on the lookout for career-oriented *Tweetups,* in which people who've connected on Twitter get together for in-person networking events. Connect with people on LinkedIn and Facebook, particularly in groups dedicated to particular career interests. Depending on the system and the settings on individual users' accounts, you may be able to introduce yourself via private messages. Just make sure you are respectful of people and don't take up much of their time.[11]

Participate in student business organizations, especially those with ties to professional organizations. Visit *trade shows* to learn about various industries and rub shoulders with people who work in those industries.[12] Don't overlook volunteering, which enables you to meet people, demonstrate your ability to solve problems, manage projects, and lead others. You can do some good while creating a network for yourself.

Remember that networking is about people helping each other, not just about other people helping you. Pay close attention to networking etiquette: Try to learn something about the people you want to connect with, don't overwhelm others with too many messages or requests, be succinct in all your communication efforts, don't give out other people's names and contact information without their permission to do so, never email your résumé to complete strangers, don't assume that you can send your résumé to everyone you meet, and remember to say thank you every time someone helps you.[13]

To become a valued network member, you need to be able to help others in some way. You may not have any influential contacts yet, but because you're actively researching a number of industries and trends in your own job search, you probably have valuable information you can share via your social networks, blog, or Twitter account. Or you might simply be able to connect one person with another who can help. The more you network, the more valuable you become in your network—and the more valuable your network becomes to you.

Finally, be aware that your online network reflects on who you are in the eyes of potential employers, so exercise some judgment in making connections. Also, many employers now contact people in a candidate's public network for background information, even if the candidate doesn't list those people as references.[14]

REAL-TIME UPDATES
Learn More by Visiting This Website

Follow these people to a new career

Alison Doyle maintains a great list of career experts to follow on Twitter. Go to http://real-timeupdates.com/bia8 and click on Learn More in the Students section.

USING ALL THE JOB-SEARCH TOOLS AT YOUR DISPOSAL

As a final note, be sure to use all the job search tools and resources available to you. For example, many companies now offer mobile apps that give you a feel for what it's like to work there and let you search for job openings. A variety of apps and websites can help you find jobs, practice interviewing, and build your professional network (see Exhibit 2).

EXHIBIT 2   **Mobile Job-Search Tools**

A wide variety of mobile apps, such as these from Glassdoor and TheLadders, are available to help you find the ideal job and manage your career path.

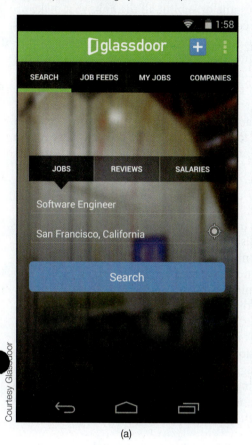

(a)   (b)

Preparing Your Résumé

Although you will create many messages during your career search, your résumé will be the most important document in this process. You will be able to use it directly in many instances, adapt it to a variety of uses such as an e-portfolio or a social media résumé, and reuse pieces of it in social networking profiles and online application forms. Even if you apply to a company that doesn't want to see your résumé, the process of creating it will prepare you for interviewing and preemployment testing.

Before you begin writing a résumé, make sure you understand its true function—as a brief, persuasive business message intended to stimulate an employer's interest in meeting you and learning more about you. In other words, the purpose of a résumé is not to get you a job but rather to get you an interview.[15]

Your résumé is one of the most important documents you'll ever write. You can help ensure success by remembering four things: First, treat your résumé with the respect it deserves. A single mistake or oversight can cost you interview opportunities. Second, give yourself plenty of time. Don't put off preparing your résumé until the last second and then try to write it in one sitting. Experiment with different ideas and phrases until you hit on the right combination. Also, give yourself plenty of time to proofread the résumé when you're finished—and ask several other people to proofread it as well. Third, learn from good models. You can find thousands of sample résumés online at college websites and job sites such as Monster.com. Fourth, don't get frustrated by the conflicting advice you'll read about résumés; they are more art than science. Consider the alternatives and choose the approach that makes the most sense in your specific situation.

Be aware that you will find a wide range of opinions about résumés, regarding everything from appropriate length, content, design, distribution methods, and acceptable degrees of creativity to whether it even makes sense to write a traditional résumé in this age of social media and online applications. For example, you may encounter a prospective employer that wants you to tweet your résumé or submit all the links that make up your online presence, rather than submitting a conventional résumé.[16] You may run across examples of effective résumés that were produced as infographics, interactive videos, simulated search engine results, puzzles, games, graphic novels—you name it, somebody has probably tried it.

By the way, if anyone asks to see your "CV," they're referring to your *curriculum vitae*, the term used instead of *résumé* in some professions and in many countries outside the United States. Résumés and CVs are essentially the same, although CVs can be more detailed. If you need to adapt a U.S.-style résumé to CV format, or vice versa, career expert Alison Doyle offers advice on her website, **www.alisondoyle.com**.

KEEPING YOUR RÉSUMÉ HONEST

Estimates vary, but one comprehensive study uncovered lies about work history in more than 40 percent of the résumés tested.[17] And dishonest applicants are getting bolder all the time—going so far as to buy fake diplomas online, pay computer hackers to insert their names into prestigious universities' graduation records, and sign up for services that offer phony employment verification.[18] "It's becoming common to cheat," observes Professor George Gollin of the University of Illinois, Urbana, mentioning the 200,000 fake college degrees sold every year as one example.[19]

Applicants with integrity know they don't need to stoop to lying. If you are tempted to stretch the truth, bear in mind that professional recruiters have seen every trick in the book, and frustrated employers are working aggressively to uncover the truth. Nearly all employers do some form of background checking, from contacting references and verifying employment to checking criminal records and sending résumés through verification services.[20] Employers are also beginning to craft certain interview questions specifically to uncover dishonest résumé entries.[21]

More than 90 percent of companies that find lies on résumés refuse to hire the offending applicants, even if that means withdrawing formal job offers.[22] And if you do sneak past these filters and get hired, you'll probably be exposed on the job when you can't live up to your own résumé. Given the networked nature of today's job market, lying on a résumé could haunt you for years and could force you to keep lying throughout your career to hide the original misrepresentations on your résumé.[23]

ADDRESSING AREAS OF CONCERN

Many people have gaps in their careers or other issues that could be of concern to employers. Here are some common issues and suggestions for handling them in a résumé:[24]

- **Frequent job changes.** If you've had a number of short-term jobs of a similar type, such as independent contracting and temporary assignments, try to group them under a single heading. Also, if past job positions were eliminated as a result of layoffs or mergers, find a subtle way to convey that information (if not in your résumé then in your cover letter). Reasonable employers understand that many professionals have been forced to job hop by circumstances beyond their control.
- **Gaps in work history.** Mention relevant experience and education you gained during employment gaps, such as volunteer or community work.
- **Inexperience.** Mention related volunteer work and membership in professional groups. List relevant course work and internships.
- **Overqualification.** Tone down your résumé by focusing exclusively on the experience and skills that relate to the position.

- **Long-term employment with one company.** Itemize each position held at the firm to show both professional growth and career growth within the organization and increasing responsibilities along the way.
- **Job termination for cause.** Be honest with interviewers and address their concerns with proof, such as recommendations and examples of completed projects.
- **Criminal record.** You don't necessarily need to disclose a criminal record or time spent incarcerated on your résumé, but you may be asked about it on job application forms. Laws regarding what employers may ask (and whether they can conduct a criminal background check) vary by state and profession, but if you are asked and the question applies to you, you are legally bound to answer truthfully. Use the interview process to explain any mitigating circumstances and to emphasize your rehabilitation and commitment to being a law-abiding, trustworthy employee.[25]

CHOOSING AN INTRODUCTORY STATEMENT

Of all the parts of a résumé, the brief introductory statement that follows your name and contact information probably generates the most disagreement. You can put one of three things here:[26]

- **Career objective.** A career objective identifies either a specific job you want to land or a general career track you would like to pursue. Some experts advise against including a career objective because it can categorize you so narrowly that you miss out on interesting opportunities, and it is essentially about fulfilling your desires, not about meeting the employer's needs. In the past, most résumés included a career objective, but in recent years more job seekers are using a qualifications summary or a career summary. However, if you have little or no work experience in your target profession, a career objective might be your best option. If you do opt for an objective, word it in a way that relates your qualifications to employer needs. Avoid such self-absorbed statements as "A fulfilling position that provides ample opportunity for career growth and personal satisfaction."
- **Qualifications summary.** A qualifications summary offers a brief view of your key qualifications. The goal is to let a reader know within a few seconds what you can deliver. You can title this section generically as "Qualifications Summary" or "Summary of Qualifications," or if you have one dominant qualification, you can use that as the title (see Exhibit 5 on page xxxvii for an example). Consider using a qualifications summary if you have one or more important qualifications but don't yet have a long career history. Also, if you haven't been working long but your college education has given you a dominant professional "theme," such as multimedia design or statistical analysis, you can craft a qualifications summary that highlights your educational preparedness.
- **Career summary.** A career summary offers a brief recap of your career, with the goal of presenting increasing levels of responsibility and performance. A career summary can be particularly useful for executives who have demonstrated the ability to manage increasingly larger and more complicated business operations—a key consideration when companies look to hire upper-level managers.

ORGANIZING YOUR RÉSUMÉ AROUND YOUR STRENGTHS

Although there are a number of ways to organize a résumé, most are some variation of chronological, functional, or a combination of the two. The right choice depends on your background and your goals, as the following sections explain.

The Chronological Résumé

In a *chronological résumé*, the work experience section dominates and is placed immediately after your contact information and introductory statement. Develop your work experience section by listing your jobs in reverse chronological order, beginning with the most recent one and giving more space to the most recent positions. For each job, start by listing the employer's name and location, your official job title, and the dates you held the position (or "to present" if you are still in your most recent job). Next, in a short block of text, highlight your accomplishments in a way that is relevant to your readers. Doing so may require "translating" the terminology used in a particular industry or profession into terms that are more meaningful to your target readers. If the general responsibilities of the position are not obvious from the job title, provide a little background to help readers understand what you did.

The Functional Résumé

A *functional résumé*, sometimes called a *skills résumé*, emphasizes your skills and capabilities, identifying employers and academic experience in subordinate sections. This arrangement stresses individual areas of competence rather than job history. The functional approach has three advantages: (1) Without having to read through job descriptions, employers can see what you can do for them, (2) you can emphasize previous job experience, and (3) you can deemphasize any lengthy unemployment or lack of career progress. However, you should be aware that because a functional résumé can obscure your work history, many employment professionals are suspicious of it.[27] If you don't believe the chronological format will work for you, consider the combination résumé instead.

The Combination Résumé

A *combination résumé* meshes the skills focus of the functional format with the job history focus of the chronological format. The chief advantage of this format is that it lets you highlight particular areas of strength without raising concerns that you might be hiding something about your work history. Using a summary of qualifications or a career summary as your introductory statement is a great way to highlight your ability to contribute to a potential employer.

Exhibits 3 through 5 on the following pages show how a job applicant adapted the combination format to work in three job-search scenarios, each of which you might face in your career as well:

- **Scenario 1: positioning yourself for an ideal opportunity** (when you've found a job opening that aligns closely with your career goals and your academic and professional credentials)
- **Scenario 2: positioning yourself for an available opportunity** (when you can't find a job in your chosen field and need to adapt to whatever opportunities are available)
- **Scenario 3: positioning yourself for more responsibility** (after you have some experience in your field and want to apply for positions of greater responsibility)

PRODUCING YOUR RÉSUMÉ

Producing your résumé is not a simple matter, because you might need to create several formats to satisfy the requirements of various employers. Also, your résumé will be read by a human being in some cases but analyzed by computer-based applicant tracking systems in others. Unfortunately, there is no single format or medium that works for all the situations you will encounter, and employer expectations continue to change as technology evolves. Find out what each employer or job posting website expects and provide your résumé in that specific format; many employers will toss your résumé or application if you don't follow their instructions.

No matter how many media and formats you eventually choose for producing your résumé, a clean, professional-looking design is a must. Unless you have some experience in graphic design and you're applying in a field such as advertising or retail merchandising, where visual creativity is viewed as an asset, resist the urge to "get creative" with your

Even for an ideal job-search scenario, where your academic and professional experiences and interests closely match the parameters of the job opening, you still need to adapt your résumé content carefully to "echo" the specific language of the job description.[45]

The Scenario

You are about to graduate and have found a job opening that is in your chosen field. You don't have any experience in this field, but the courses you've taken in pursuit of your degree have given you a solid academic foundation for this position.

The Opportunity

The job opening is for an associate market analyst with Living Social, the rapidly growing advertising and social commerce service that describes itself as "the online source for discovering valuable local experiences." (A market analyst researches markets to find potentially profitable business opportunities.)

The Communication Challenge

You don't have directly relevant experience as a market analyst, and you might be competing against people who do. Your education is your strongest selling point, so you need to show how your course work relates to the position.

Don't let your lack of experience hold you back; the job posting makes it clear that this is an entry-level position. For example, the first bullet point in the job description says "Become an expert in market data . . .," and the required skills and experience section says that "Up to 2 years of experience with similar research and analysis is preferred." The important clues here are *become* (the company doesn't expect you to be an expert already) and *preferred* (experience would be great if you have it, but it's not required).

Keywords and Key Phrases

You study the job posting and highlight the following elements:

1. Working in a team environment
2. Research, including identifying trendy new businesses
3. Analyzing data using Microsoft Excel
4. Managing projects
5. Collaborating with technical experts and sales staff
6. Creating new tools to help maximize revenue and minimize risks
7. Bachelor's degree is required
8. Natural curiosity and desire to learn
9. Detail oriented
10. Hands-on experience with social media

Emma Gomes
(847) 555–2153
emma.gomes@mailsystem.net
emmawrites.blogspot.com

Address: **Permanent Address:**
860 North 8th Street, Terre Haute, IN 47809   993 Church Street, Barrington, IL 60010

Summary of Qualifications

- In-depth academic preparation in marketing analysis techniques
- Intermediate skills with a variety of analytical tools, including Microsoft Excel and Google Analytics
- Front-line experience with consumers and business owners
- Multiple research and communication projects involving the business applications of social media

Education

B.S. in Marketing (Marketing Management Track), Indiana State University, Terre Haute, IN, anticipated graduation: May 2014

Program coursework

- 45 credits of core business courses, including Business Information Tools, Business Statistics, Principles of Accounting, and Business Finance
- 27 credits of marketing and marketing management courses, including Buyer Behavior, Marketing Research, Product and Pricing Strategy, and seminars in e-commerce and social media

Special projects

- "Handcrafting a Global Marketplace: The Etsy Phenomenon," in-depth analysis of how Etsy transformed the market for handmade craft items by bringing e-commerce capabilities to individual craftspeople
- "Hybrid Communication Platforms for Small Businesses," team service project for five small businesses in Terre Haute, recommending best practices for combining traditional and social-media methods of customer engagement and providing a customized measurement spreadsheet for each company

Work and Volunteer Experience

Independent math tutor, 2009-present. Assist students with a variety of math courses at the elementary, junior high, and high school level; all clients have achieved combined test and homework score improvements of at least one full letter grade, with an average improvement of 38 percent

Volunteer, LeafSpring Food Bank, Terre Haute, IN (weekends during college terms, 2012–present). Stock food and supply pantries; prepare emergency baskets for new clients; assist director with public relations activities, including website updates and social media news releases.

Customer care agent, Owings Ford, Barrington, IL (summers, 2011–2013). Assisted the service and sales managers of this locally owned car dealership with a variety of customer-service tasks; scheduled service appointments; designed and implemented improvements to service-center waiting room to increase guest comfort; convinced dealership owners to begin using Twitter and Facebook to interact with current and potential customers.

Professional Engagement

- Collegiate member, American Marketing Association; helped establish the AMA Collegiate Chapter at Indiana State
- Participated in AMA International Collegiate Case Competition, 2011-2012

Awards

- Dean's List: 2012, 2013
- Forward Youth award, Barrington Chamber of Commerce, 2010

Gomes includes phone and email contacts, along with a blog that features academic-oriented writing.

Using a *summary of qualifications* for her opening statement lets her target the résumé and highlight her most compelling attributes.

Her education is a much stronger selling point than her work experience, so she goes into some detail—carefully selecting course names and project descriptions to echo the language of the job description.

She adjusts the descriptions and accomplishments of each role to highlight the aspects of her work and volunteer experience that are relevant to the position.

The final sections highlight activities and awards that reflect her interest in marketing and her desire to improve her skills.

Notice how Gomes adapts her résumé to "mirror" the keywords and phrases from the job posting:

1. Offers concrete evidence of teamwork (rather than just calling herself a "team player," for example)
2. Emphasizes research skills and experience in multiple instances
3. Calls out Microsoft Excel, as well as Google Analytics, a key online tool for measuring activity on websites
4. Indicates the ability to plan and carry out projects, even if she doesn't have formal project management experience
5. Indicates some experience working in a supportive or collaborative role with technical experts and sales specialists (the content of the work doesn't translate to the new job, but the concept does)
6. Suggests the ability to work with new analytical tools
7. Displays her B.S. degree prominently
8. Demonstrates a desire to learn and to expand her skills
9. Tracking the progress of her tutoring clients is strong evidence of a detail-oriented worker—not to mention someone who cares about results and the quality of her work
10. Lists business-oriented experience with Facebook, Twitter, and other social media

| **EXHIBIT 4** | **Crafting Your Résumé, Scenario 2: Positioning Yourself for Available Opportunities** |

If you can't find an ideal job opening, you'll need to adjust your plans and adapt your résumé to the openings that are available. Look for opportunities that meet your near-term financial needs while giving you the chance to expand your skill set so that you'll be even more prepared when an ideal opportunity does come along.[46]

The Scenario

You are about to graduate but can't find job openings in the field you'd like to enter. However, you have found an opening that is in a related field, and it would give you the chance to get some valuable work experience.

The Opportunity

The job opening is for a seller support associate with Amazon, the online retail giant. Employees in this position work with merchants that sell products through the Amazon e-commerce system to make sure merchants are successful. In essence, it is a customer service job, but directed at these merchants, not the consumers who buy on Amazon.

The Communication Challenge

This isn't the job you ultimately want, but it is a great opportunity with a well-known company.

You note that the position does not require a college degree, so in that sense you might be a bit over-qualified. However, you also see a strong overlap between your education and the responsibilities and required skills of the job, so be sure to highlight those.

Keywords and Key Phrases

You study the job posting and highlight the following elements:

1. Be able to predict and respond to merchant needs; good business sense with the ability to appreciate the needs of a wide variety of companies
2. Strong written and oral communication skills
3. High degree of professionalism
4. Self-starter with good time management skills
5. Logically analyze problems and devise solutions
6. Comfortable with computer-based tools, including Microsoft Excel
7. Desire to expand business and technical skills
8. Customer service experience
9. Collaborate with fellow team members to resolve difficult situations
10. Record of high performance regarding quality of work and personal productivity

---

Emma Gomes
(847) 555–2153
emma.gomes@mailsystem.net
emmawrites.blogspot.com

Address:	**Permanent Address:**
860 North 8th Street, Terre Haute, IN 47809	993 Church Street, Barrington, IL 60010

Summary of Qualifications

- ⑧ • Front-line customer service experience with consumers and business owners
- • Strong business sense based on work experience and academic preparation
- ⑥ • Intermediate skills with a variety of software tools, including Microsoft Excel and Google Analytics
- ⑩ • Record of quality work in both business and academic settings

Education

B.S. in Marketing (Marketing Management Track), Indiana State University, Terre Haute, IN, expected graduation May 2014

<u>Program coursework</u>

- ⑥ • 45 credits of core business courses, including Business Information Tools, Business Statistics, Principles of Accounting, and Business Finance
- ① • 27 credits of marketing and marketing management courses, including Marketing Fundamentals, Buyer Behavior, Marketing Research, Retail Strategies and seminars in e–commerce and social media

<u>Special projects</u>

- ① ② • "Handcrafting a Global Marketplace: The Etsy Phenomenon," in-depth analysis of how the Etsy e-commerce platform helps craftspeople and artisans become more successful merchants
- ① ② ⑨ • "Hybrid Communication Platforms for Small Businesses," team service project for five small businesses in Terre Haute, recommending best practices for combining traditional and social–media methods of customer engagement and providing a customized measurement spreadsheet for each company

Work and Volunteer Experience

- ③ ④ ⑩ **Independent math tutor, 2009-present.** Assist students with a variety of math courses at the elementary, junior high, and high school level; all clients have achieved combined test and homework score improvements of at least one full letter grade, with an average improvement of 38 percent

- ② **Volunteer, LeafSpring Food Bank, Terre Haute, IN (weekends during college terms, 2012–present).** Stock food and supply pantries; prepare emergency baskets for new clients; assist director with public relations activities, including website updates and social media news releases.

- ⑧ ⑤ **Customer care agent, Owings Ford, Barrington, IL (summers, 2011–2013).** Assisted the service and sales managers of this locally owned car dealership with a variety of customer-service tasks; scheduled service appointments; designed and implemented improvements to service-center waiting room to increase guest comfort; convinced dealership owners to begin using Twitter and Facebook to interact with current and potential customers.

Professional Engagement

- ⑦ • Collegiate member, American Marketing Association; helped establish the AMA Collegiate Chapter at Indiana State
- • Participated in AMA International Collegiate Case Competition, 2011-2012

Awards

- ③ ④ ⑩ • Dean's List: 2012, 2013
- ① • Forward Youth award, Barrington Chamber of Commerce, 2010

Gomes modified her summary of qualifications to increase emphasis on customer service.

She adjusts the selection of highlighted courses to reflect the retail and e-commerce aspects of this particular job opening.

She adjusts the wording of this Etsy project description to closely mirror what Amazon is—an e-commerce platform serving a multitude of independent merchants.

She provides more detail regarding her customer support experience.

The final sections are still relevant to this job opening, so she leaves them unchanged.

Notice how Gomes adapts her résumé to "mirror" the keywords and phrases from the job posting:

① Suggests strong awareness of the needs of various businesses

② Examples of experience with written business communication; she can demonstrate oral communication skills during phone, video, or in-person interviews

③ Results-oriented approach to tutoring business suggests high degree of professionalism, as do the two awards

④ The ability to work successfully as an independent tutor while attending high school and college is strong evidence of self-motivation and good time management

⑤ Indicates ability to understand problems and design solutions

⑥ Suggests the ability to work with a variety of software tools

⑦ Demonstrates a desire to learn and to expand her skills

⑧ Highlights customer service experience

⑨ Offers concrete evidence of teamwork (rather than just calling herself a "team player," for example)

⑩ Tracking the progress of her tutoring clients is strong evidence of someone who cares about results and the quality of her work; Dean's List awards also suggest quality of work; record of working while attending high school and college suggests strong productivity

When you have a few years of experience under your belt, your résumé strategy should shift to emphasize work history and accomplishments. Here is how Emma Gomes might reshape her résumé if she had held the two jobs described in Exhibits 3 and 4 and is now ready for a bigger challenge.[47]

The Scenario

Moving forward from Exhibits 3 and 4, let's assume you have worked in both those positions, first for two years as a seller support associate at Amazon and then for almost three years an associate market analyst at LivingSocial. You believe you are now ready for a bigger challenge, and the question is how to adapt your résumé for a higher-level position now that you have some experience in your chosen field. (Some of the details from the earlier résumés have been modified to accommodate this example.)

The Opportunity

The job opening is for a senior strategy analyst for Nordstrom. The position is similar in concept to the position at Living Social, but at a higher level and with more responsibility.

The Communication Challenge

This job is an important step up; a senior strategy analyst is expected to conduct in-depth financial analysis of business opportunities and make recommendations regarding strategy changes, merchandising partnerships with other companies, and important decisions.

You worked with a wide variety of retailers in your Amazon and Living Social jobs, including a number of fashion retailers, but you haven't worked directly in fashion retailing yourself.

Bottom line: You can bring a good set of skills to this position, but your financial analysis skills and retailing insights might not be readily apparent, so you'll need to play those up.

Keywords and Key Phrases

You study the job posting and highlight the following elements:

1. Provide research and analysis to guide major business strategy decisions
2. Communicate across business units and departments within Nordstrom
3. Familiar with retail analytics
4. Knowledge of fashion retailing
5. Qualitative and quantitative analysis
6. Project management
7. Strong communication skills
8. Bachelor's required; MBA preferred
9. Advanced skills in financial and statistical modeling
10. Proficient in PowerPoint and Excel

Emma Gomes
(847) 555–2153
emma.gomes@mailsystem.net
Twitter: www.twitter.com/emmagomes
1605 Queen Anne Avenue North, Seattle, WA 98109

Market and Strategy Analyst

- Five years of experience in local and online retailing, with three years of focus on market opportunity analysis
- Strong business sense developed through more than 60 marketing programs across a range of retail sectors, including hospitality, entertainment, and fashion
- Recognized by senior management for ability to make sound judgment calls in situations with incomplete or conflicting data
- Adept at coordinating research projects and marketing initiatives across organizational boundaries and balancing the interests of multiple stakeholders
- Advanced skills with leading analysis and communication tools, including Excel, PowerPoint, and Google Analytics

Professional Experience

Associate Market Analyst, LivingSocial, Seattle, WA (July 2011-present). Analyzed assigned markets for such factors as consumer demand, merchandising opportunities, and seller performance; designed, launched, and managed marketing initiatives in 27 retailing categories, including fashions and accessories; met or exceeded profit targets on 90 percent of all marketing initiatives; appointed team lead/trainer in recognition of strong quantitative and qualitative analysis skills; utilized both established and emerging social media tools and helped business partners use these communication platforms to increase consumer engagement in local markets.

Seller support associate, Amazon, Seattle, WA (July 2009–June 2011). Worked with more than 300 product vendors, including many in the fashion and accessories sectors, to assure profitable retailing activities on the Amazon e-commerce platform; resolved vendor issues related to e-commerce operations, pricing, and consumer communication; anticipated potential vendor challenges and assisted in the development of more than a dozen new selling tools that improved vendor profitability while reducing Amazon's vendor support costs by nearly 15 percent.

Education

Evening MBA program, University of Washington, Seattle, WA; anticipated graduation: May 2015. Broad-based program combining financial reporting, marketing strategy, competitive strategy, and supply chain management with individual emphasis on quantitative methods, financial analysis, and marketing decision models.

B.S. in Marketing (Marketing Management Track), Indiana State University, Terre Haute, IN, May 2009. Comprehensive coursework in business fundamentals, accounting and finance, marketing fundamentals, retailing, and consumer communications.

Professional Engagement

- Member, American Marketing Association
- Member, International Social Media Association
- Active in National Retail Federation and Retail Advertising & Marketing Association

Awards

- Living Social Top Ten Deals (monthly employee achievement award for designing the most profitable couponing deals); awarded seven times, 2011—2013
- Social Commerce Network's Social Commerce Innovators: 30 Under 30; 2012

Gomes stays with a summary of qualifications as her opening statement but gives it a new title to reflect her experience and to focus on her career path as a market analyst.

Work experience is now her key selling point, so she shifts to a conventional chronological résumé that puts employment ahead of education. She also removes the part-time jobs she had during high school and college.

She updates the Education section with a listing for the MBA program she has started (selecting points of emphasis relevant to the job opening) and reduces the amount of detail about her undergraduate degree.

She updates the Professional Engagement and Awards section with timely and relevant information.

Notice how Gomes adapts her résumé to "mirror" the keywords and phrases from the job posting:

1. Highlights her experience in market and business analysis and her continuing education in this area
2. Mentions skill at coordinating cross-functional projects
3. Lists experiences that relate to the collection and analysis of retail data
4. Emphasizes the work she has done with fashion-related retailing and retailing in general
5. Identifies experience and education that relates to quantitative and qualitative analysis (this point overlaps #1 and #3 to a
6. degree)
7. Mentions project management experience
8. Lists areas that suggest effective communication skills
9. Lists education, with emphasis on coursework that relates most directly to the job posting
10. Mentions work experience and educational background related to these topics

Includes these programs in the list of software tools she uses

résumé layout.[28] Recruiters and hiring managers want to skim your essential information in a matter of seconds, and anything that distracts or delays them will work against you. Moreover, complex layouts can confuse an applicant tracking system, which can result in your information getting garbled.

Fortunately, good résumé design is not difficult to achieve. As you can see in Exhibits 3 through 5, good designs feature simplicity, order, effective use of white space, and clear typefaces. Make subheadings easy to find and easy to read, placing them either above each section or in the left margin. Use lists to itemize your most important qualifications. Color is not necessary by any means, but if you add color, make it subtle and sophisticated, such as a thin horizontal line under your name and address. The most common way to get into trouble with résumé design is going overboard.

Depending on the companies you apply to, you might want to produce your résumé in as many as six formats:

- **Printed traditional résumé.** The traditional paper résumé still has a place in this world of electronic job searches, if only to have a few copies ready whenever one of your networking contacts asks for one. Be sure to use quality paper (white or slightly off-white; avoid gimmicky designs and borders) and a quality printer.

- **Printed scannable résumé.** You might encounter a company that still prefers scannable résumés, a type of printed résumé that is specially formatted to be compatible with optical scanning systems that convert printed documents to electronic text. These systems were quite common just a few years ago, but their use appears to be declining rapidly as more employers prefer email delivery or website application forms.[29] A scannable résumé differs from the traditional format in two major ways: It should always include a keyword summary, and it should be formatted in a simpler fashion that avoids underlining, special characters, and other elements that can confuse the scanning system. If you need to produce a scannable résumé, search online for "formatting a scannable résumé" to get detailed instructions.

- **Digital plain-text file.** A *plain-text file* (sometimes known as an ASCII text file) is a digital version of your résumé that has no font formatting, no bullet symbols, no colors, no lines or boxes, and no other special formatting. The plain-text version can be used in two ways. First, you can include it in the body of an email message, for employers who want email delivery but don't want file attachments. Second, you can copy and paste the sections into the application forms on an employer's website.

- **Microsoft Word file.** In some cases, an employer or job-posting website will want you to upload a Microsoft Word file or attach it to an email message. (Although there are certainly other word processing programs on the market, Microsoft Word is the de facto standard in business these days.)

- **PDF file.** Creating a PDF file is a simple procedure, but you need the right software. Adobe Acrobat (not the free Adobe Reader) is the best-known program, but many others are available, including some free versions and online services.

- **Online résumé.** An online résumé, sometimes known as a social media résumé or multimedia résumé, gives you an opportunity to expand on the information contained in your basic résumé with links to projects, publications, screencasts, online videos, course lists, social networking profiles, and other elements that give employers a more complete picture of who you are and what you can offer.

CONSIDERING PHOTOS, VIDEOS, PRESENTATIONS, AND INFOGRAPHICS

As you produce your résumé in various formats, you will encounter the question of whether to include a photograph of yourself on or with your résumé. For print or electronic documents you will be submitting to employers or job websites, the safest advice is to avoid photos. The reason is that seeing visual cues of the age, ethnicity, and gender of candidates early in the selection process exposes employers to complaints of discriminatory hiring practices. In fact, some employers won't even look at résumés that include photos, and some applicant tracking systems automatically discard résumés with any kind of extra files.[30] However, photographs are acceptable and expected for social media résumés and other online formats where you are not actively submitting a résumé to an employer.

In addition to the six main formats, some applicants create presentations, videos, or infographics to supplement a conventional résumé. Two key advantages of a Prezi or PowerPoint supplement are flexibility and multimedia capabilities. For instance, you can present a menu of choices on the opening screen and allow viewers to click through to sections of interest. (Note that most of the things you can accomplish with presentation software can be done with an online résumé, which is probably more convenient for most readers.)

A video résumé can be a compelling supplement as well, but be aware that some employment law experts advise employers not to view videos, at least not until after candidates have been evaluated solely on their credentials. The reason for this caution is the same as with photographs. In addition, videos are more cumbersome to evaluate than paper or electronic résumés, and some recruiters refuse to watch them.[31] However, not all companies share this concern over videos, so you'll have to research their individual preferences. For example, the online retailer Zappos encourages applicant videos and provides a way to upload videos on its job application webpage.[32]

An infographic résumé attempts to convey a person's career development and skill set graphically through a visual metaphor such as a timeline or subway map or as a poster with an array of individual elements. A well-designed infographic could be an intriguing element of the job-search package for candidates in certain situations and professions because it can definitely stand out from traditional résumés and can show a high level of skill in visual communication. However, infographics are likely to be incompatible with most applicant tracking systems and with the screening habits of many recruiters, so while you might stand out with an infographic, you might also get tossed out if you try to use an infographic in place of a conventional résumé. In virtually every situation, an infographic should complement a conventional résumé, not replace it. In addition, successful infographics require skills in graphic design; otherwise you'll end up with a confusing mess that no recruiter will take time to figure out (you can see many examples of this online). If you lack those skills, you'll need to hire a designer.

PREPARING YOUR APPLICATION LETTER

Whenever you submit a résumé, accompany it with an application letter to let readers know what you're sending, why you're sending it, and how they can benefit from reading it. (Application letters are sometimes called cover letters, and they can be either printed or emailed.) Start by researching the organization and then focus on your audience so that you can show that you've done your homework.

If the name of an individual manager is at all findable, address your letter to that person, rather than something generic such as "Dear Hiring Manager." Search LinkedIn, the company's website, industry directories, Twitter, and anything else you can think of to locate an appropriate name. Ask the people in your network if they know a name. If another applicant finds a name and you don't, you're at a disadvantage.

Remember that your reader's in-box is probably overflowing with résumés and application letters, and respect his or her time. Avoid gimmicks, and don't repeat information that already appears in your résumé. Keep your letter straightforward, fact based, short, upbeat, and professional (see Exhibit 6 on the following page).

FOLLOWING UP AFTER SUBMITTING A RÉSUMÉ

Deciding if, when, and how to follow up after submitting your résumé and application letter is one of the trickiest parts of a job search. First and foremost, keep in mind that employers continue to evaluate your communication skills and professionalism during this phase, so don't say or do anything to leave a negative impression. Second, adhere to whatever instructions the employer has provided. If a job posting says "no calls," for example, don't call. Third, if the job posting lists a *close date*, don't call or write before then because the company is still collecting applications and will not have made a decision about

EXHIBIT 6   Application Letter

In this response to an online job posting, Dalton Smith highlights his qualifications while mirroring the requirements specified in the posting. He grabs attention immediately by letting the reader know he is familiar with the company and the global transportation business.

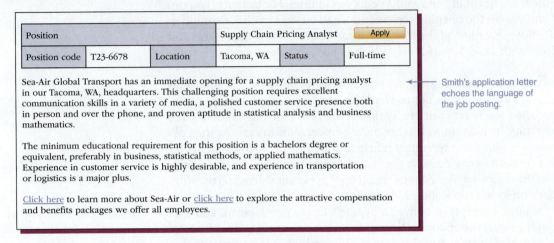

Position			Supply Chain Pricing Analyst		Apply
Position code	T23-6678	Location	Tacoma, WA	Status	Full-time

Sea-Air Global Transport has an immediate opening for a supply chain pricing analyst in our Tacoma, WA, headquarters. This challenging position requires excellent communication skills in a variety of media, a polished customer service presence both in person and over the phone, and proven aptitude in statistical analysis and business mathematics.

The minimum educational requirement for this position is a bachelors degree or equivalent, preferably in business, statistical methods, or applied mathematics. Experience in customer service is highly desirable, and experience in transportation or logistics is a major plus.

Click here to learn more about Sea-Air or click here to explore the attractive compensation and benefits packages we offer all employees.

Smith's application letter echoes the language of the job posting.

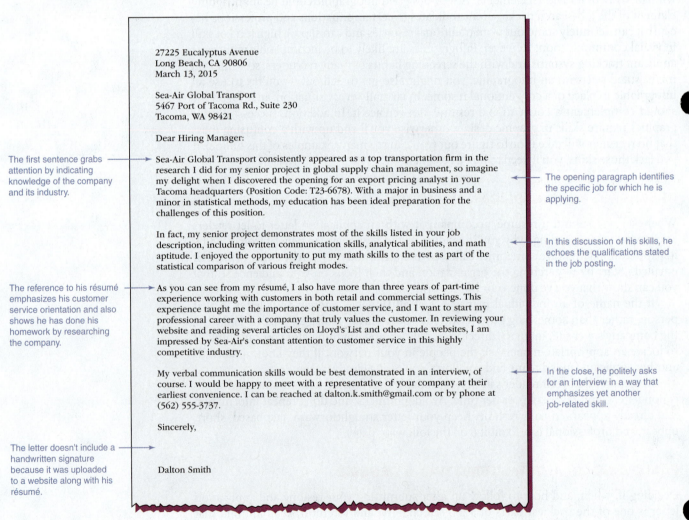

27225 Eucalyptus Avenue
Long Beach, CA 90806
March 13, 2015

Sea-Air Global Transport
5467 Port of Tacoma Rd., Suite 230
Tacoma, WA 98421

Dear Hiring Manager:

Sea-Air Global Transport consistently appeared as a top transportation firm in the research I did for my senior project in global supply chain management, so imagine my delight when I discovered the opening for an export pricing analyst in your Tacoma headquarters (Position Code: T23-6678). With a major in business and a minor in statistical methods, my education has been ideal preparation for the challenges of this position.

In fact, my senior project demonstrates most of the skills listed in your job description, including written communication skills, analytical abilities, and math aptitude. I enjoyed the opportunity to put my math skills to the test as part of the statistical comparison of various freight modes.

As you can see from my résumé, I also have more than three years of part-time experience working with customers in both retail and commercial settings. This experience taught me the importance of customer service, and I want to start my professional career with a company that truly values the customer. In reviewing your website and reading several articles on Lloyd's List and other trade websites, I am impressed by Sea-Air's constant attention to customer service in this highly competitive industry.

My verbal communication skills would be best demonstrated in an interview, of course. I would be happy to meet with a representative of your company at their earliest convenience. I can be reached at dalton.k.smith@gmail.com or by phone at (562) 555-3737.

Sincerely,

Dalton Smith

The first sentence grabs attention by indicating knowledge of the company and its industry.

The reference to his résumé emphasizes his customer service orientation and also shows he has done his homework by researching the company.

The letter doesn't include a handwritten signature because it was uploaded to a website along with his résumé.

The opening paragraph identifies the specific job for which he is applying.

In this discussion of his skills, he echoes the qualifications stated in the job posting.

In the close, he politely asks for an interview in a way that emphasizes yet another job-related skill.

inviting people for interviews. Wait a week or so after the close date. If no close date is given and you have no other information to suggest a time line, you can generally contact the company starting a week or two after submitting your résumé.[33] Keep in mind that a single instance of poor etiquette or clumsy communication can undo all your hard work in a job search, so maintain your professional behavior every step of the way.

When you follow up by email or telephone, you can share an additional piece of information that links your qualifications to the position (keep an eye out for late-breaking news about the company, too) and ask a question about the hiring process as a way to gather some information about your status. Good questions to ask include:[34]

- Has a hiring decision been made yet?
- Can you tell me what to expect next in terms of the hiring process?
- What is the company's timeframe for filling this position?
- Could I follow up in another week if you haven't had a chance to contact me yet?
- Can I provide any additional information regarding my qualifications for the position?

Whatever the circumstances, a follow-up message can demonstrate that you're sincerely interested in working for the organization, persistent in pursuing your goals, and committed to upgrading your skills.

If you don't land a job at your dream company on the first attempt, don't give up. You can apply again if a new opening appears, or you can send an updated résumé with a new unsolicited application letter that describes how you have gained additional experience, taken a relevant course, or otherwise improved your skill set. Many leading employers take note of applicants who came close but didn't quite make it and may extend offers when positions open up in the future.[35]

Interviewing with Potential Employers

An employment interview is a formal meeting during which you and a prospective employer ask questions and exchange information. The employer's objective is to find the best talent to fill available job openings, and your objective is to find the right match for your goals and capabilities.

As you get ready to begin interviewing, keep in mind two vital points. First, recognize that the process takes time. Start your preparation and research early; the best job offers usually go to the best-prepared candidates. Second, don't limit your options by looking at only a few companies. By exploring a wide range of firms and positions, you might uncover great opportunities that you would not have found otherwise. You'll increase the odds of getting more job offers, too.

Most employers interview an applicant multiple times before deciding to make a job offer. At the most selective companies, you might have a dozen or more individual interviews across several stages.[36] Depending on the company and the position, the process may stretch out over many weeks, or it may be completed in a matter of days.[37]

THE TYPICAL SEQUENCE OF INTERVIEWS

The interviewing process starts with a *screening stage*, in which an employer filters out applicants who are unqualified or otherwise not a good fit for the position. Screening can take place on campus, at company offices, or via telephone or computer. If your screening interview will take place by phone, try to schedule it for a time when you can be focused and free from interruptions.[38]

The next stage of interviews helps the organization narrow the field a little further. During this selection stage, show interest in the job, relate your skills and experience to the organization's needs, listen attentively, ask insightful questions that show you've done your research, and display enthusiasm. Typically, if you're invited to visit a company, you will talk with several people in succession, such as a member of the human resources department, one or two potential colleagues, and one or more managers, including your potential supervisor. At Google, for example, recruits talk with at least four interviewers, both managers and potential colleagues.[39]

If the interviewers agree that you're a good candidate, you may receive a job offer, either on the spot or a few days later, by phone, mail, or email. In other cases, you may be invited back for a final evaluation, often by a higher-ranking executive. The objective of this *final stage* is often to sell you on the advantages of joining the organization.

TYPES OF INTERVIEWS

You can expect to encounter several types of interviews. In a *structured interview*, the interviewer (or a computer) asks a series of prepared questions in a set order. In contrast, in an *open-ended interview*, the interviewer adapts his or her line of questioning based on the answers you give and any questions you ask. Many of your interviews will be conventional one-on-one interviews, with just you and a single interviewer. However, in a *panel interview*, you will meet with several interviewers at once. Some organizations perform a *group interview*, in which one or more interviewers meet with several candidates simultaneously. A key purpose of the group interview is to observe how the candidates interact with one another.[40]

Perhaps the most common type of interview these days is the *behavioral interview*, in which you are asked to relate specific incidents and experiences from your past.[41] A *situational interview* is similar to a behavioral interview except that the questions focus on how you would handle various hypothetical situations on the job. A *working interview* is the most realistic of all: You actually perform a job-related activity during the interview. You may be asked to lead a brainstorming session (sometimes with other job candidates), solve a business problem, engage in role playing, or even make a presentation.[42]

Because the interview process takes time, start seeking interviews well in advance of the date you want to start work. Some students start their job search as early as nine months before graduation. Early planning is even more crucial during downturns in the economy because many employers become more selective when times are tough. Whatever shape the economy is in, try to secure as many interviews as you can, both to improve the chances of receiving a job offer and to give yourself more options when you do get offers.

WHAT EMPLOYERS LOOK FOR IN AN INTERVIEW

Interviews give employers a chance to go beyond the basic data of your résumé to get to know you and to answer two essential questions. The first is whether you can handle the responsibilities of the position. Naturally, the more you know about the demands of the position, and the more you've thought about how your skills match those demands, the better you'll be able to respond.

The second essential question is whether you will be a good fit with the organization and the target position. This line of inquiry includes both a general aspect and a specific aspect. The general aspect concerns your overall personality and approach to work. All good employers want people who are confident, dedicated, positive, curious, courteous, ethical, and willing to commit to something larger than their own individual goals. The specific aspect involves the fit with a particular company and position. Just like people, companies have different "personalities." Some are intense; others are more laid back. Some emphasize teamwork; others expect employees to forge their own way and even compete with one another. Expectations also vary from job to job within a company and from industry to industry. An outgoing personality is essential for sales but less so for research, for instance.

WHAT YOU SHOULD LOOK FOR IN AN INTERVIEW

Remember that an interview is a two-way conversation: The questions you ask are just as important as the answers you provide. By asking insightful questions, you can demonstrate your understanding of the organization, you can steer the discussion into areas that allow you to present your qualifications to best advantage, and you can verify for yourself

EXHIBIT 7　　　**Ten Questions to Consider Asking an Interviewer**

Use this list as a starting point when you are planning the questions to ask in a job interview.

Question	Reason for Asking
1. What are the job's major responsibilities?	A vague answer could mean that the responsibilities have not been clearly defined, which is almost guaranteed to cause frustration if you take the job.
2. What qualities do you want in the person who fills this position?	This will help you go beyond the job description to understand what the company really wants.
3. How do you measure success for someone in this position?	A vague or incomplete answer could mean that the expectations you will face are unrealistic or ill defined.
4. What is the first problem that needs the attention of the person you hire?	Not only will this help you prepare, but it can signal whether you're about to jump into a problematic situation.
5. Would relocation be required now or in the future?	If you're not willing to move often or at all, you need to know those expectations now.
6. Why is this job now vacant?	If the previous employee got promoted, that's a good sign. If the person quit, that might not be such a good sign.
7. What makes your organization different from others in the industry?	The answer will help you assess whether the company has a clear strategy to succeed in its industry and whether top managers communicate this to lower-level employees.
8. How would you define your organization's managerial philosophy?	You want to know whether the managerial philosophy is consistent with your own working values.
9. What is a typical workday like for you?	The interviewer's response can give you clues about daily life at the company.
10. What are the next steps in the selection process? What's the best way to follow up with you?	Knowing where the company is in the hiring process will give you clues about following up after the interview and possibly give you hints about where you stand.

Sources: Heather Huhman, "5 Must-Ask Questions at Job Interviews," Glassdoor blog, 7 February 2012, www.glassdoor.com; Joe Conklin, "Turning the Tables: Six Questions to Ask Your Interviewer," *Quality Progress*, November 2007, 55; Andrea N. Browne, "Keeping the Momentum at the Interview; Ask Questions, Do Your Research, and Be a Team Player," *Washington Post*, 29 July 2007, K1.

whether this is a good opportunity. Plus, interviewers expect you to ask questions and tend to look negatively on candidates who don't have any questions to ask. For a list of good questions that you might use as a starting point, see Exhibit 7.

HOW TO PREPARE FOR A JOB INTERVIEW

Thorough preparation is key to success in interviewing. Here are some pointers to help you prepare:

- Learn about the organization, including its operations, markets, and challenges.
- Learn as much as you can about the people who will be interviewing you, if you can find their names.
- Plan for the employer's questions, including questions about tough decisions you've made, your perceived shortcomings, what you didn't like about previous jobs, and your career plans (see Exhibit 8 on the following page).
- Plan questions of your own to find out whether this is really the job and the organization for you and to show that you've done your research.
- Bolster your confidence by removing as many sources of apprehension as you can. Instead of dwelling on your weaknesses, focus on your strengths so that you can emphasize them to an interviewer.
- Polish your interview style by staging mock interviews.
- Present a professional appearance, with appropriate dress and grooming.
- Be ready when you arrive and bring along a pen, paper, a list of questions, copies of your résumé, an outline of your research on the company, and any correspondence you've had regarding the position.
- Double-check the location and time of the interview and map out the route beforehand.
- Relax and be flexible; the schedule and interview arrangements may change when you arrive.

EXHIBIT 8   Twenty-Five Common Interview Questions

Chances are you'll hear many of these questions during your job interviews, so spend some time thinking about your responses.

Questions About College

1. What courses in college did you like most? Least? Why?

2. Do you think your extracurricular activities in college were worth the time you spent on them? Why or why not?

3. When did you choose your college major? Did you ever change your major? If so, why?

4. Do you feel you did the best scholastic work you are capable of?

5. How has your college education prepared you for this position?

Questions About Employers and Jobs

1. Why did you leave your last job?

2. Why did you apply for this job opening?

3. Why did you choose your particular field of work?

4. What are the disadvantages of your chosen field?

5. What do you know about our company?

6. What do you think about how this industry operates today?

7. Why do you think you would like this particular type of job?

Questions About Work Experiences and Expectations

1. What was your biggest failure?

2. Describe an experience in which you learned from one of your mistakes.

3. What motivates you? Why?

4. What do you think determines a person's progress in a good organization?

5. Are you a leader or a follower?

6. What have you done that shows initiative and willingness to work?

7. Why should I hire you?

Questions About Work Habits

1. Do you prefer working with others or by yourself?

2. What type of boss do you prefer?

3. Have you ever had any difficulty getting along with colleagues or supervisors? With instructors? With other students?

4. What would you do if you were given an unrealistic deadline for a task or project?

5. How do you feel about overtime work?

6. How do you handle stress or pressure on the job?

Sources: Alison Green, "The 10 Most Common Job Interview Questions," *U.S. News & World Report*, 24 January 2011, http://money.usnews.com; "Most Common Interview Questions," Glassdoor blog, 29 December 2011, www.glassdoor.com; *The Northwestern Endicott Report* (Evanston, Ill.: Northwestern University Placement Center).

HOW TO FOLLOW UP AFTER AN INTERVIEW

Touching base with a prospective employer after an interview, either by phone or in writing, shows that you really want the job and are determined to get it. It also brings your name to the interviewer's attention again and reminds him or her that you're waiting to know the decision.

Send a follow-up message within two days of the interview, even if you feel you have little chance of getting the job. These messages are often referred to as "thank-you notes," but they give you an important opportunity to go beyond merely expressing your appreciation. You can use the message to reinforce the reasons you are a good choice for the position, modify any answers you gave during the interview if you realisze you made a mistake or have changed your mind, and respond to any negatives that might have arisen in the interview.[43] Email is usually acceptable for follow-up messages, unless the interviewer has asked you to use other media.

If you haven't heard from the interviewer by the promised date or within two weeks after the interview, you have the option of sending a message of inquiry. Such a message is particularly appropriate if you've received a job offer from a second firm and don't want to accept it before you have an answer from the first.

Building Your Career

Even after an employer hires you, you should continue improving your skills to distinguish yourself from your peers and to make yourself more valuable to current and potential employers:[44]

- Acquire as much relevant technical knowledge as you can, build broad-based life experience, and develop your social and communication skills.
- Learn to respond to change in positive, constructive ways; this will help you adapt if your "perfect" career path eludes your grasp.
- Keep up with developments in your industry and the economy at large; read widely and use social media tools to find and follow experts in your chosen field.
- Learn to see each job, even so-called entry-level jobs, as an opportunity to learn more and to expand your knowledge, experience, and social skills.
- Take on as much responsibility as you can outside your job description.
- Share what you know with others instead of hoarding knowledge in the hope of becoming indispensable; helping others excel is a skill, too.
- Understand the big picture; knowing your own job inside and out isn't enough.

Best wishes for success in this course and in your career!

Endnotes

1. Ryan Kim, "By 2020, Independent Workers Will Be the Majority," GigaOm, 8 December 2011, http://gigaom.com.
2. Darren Dahl, "Want a Job? Let the Bidding Begin," *Inc.*, March 2011, 93–96; Thomas W. Malone, Robert J. Laubacher, and Tammy Johns, "The Age of Hyperspecialization," *Harvard Business Review*, July–August 2011, 56–65; Jennifer Wang, "The Solution to the Innovator's Dilemma," *Entrepreneur*, August 2011, 24–32.
3. "LiveOps and Vision Perry Create New Work Opportunities for Rural Tennessee," LiveOps press release, 18 July 2011, www.liveops.com; Malone et al., "The Age of Hyperspecialization."
4. Adapted from Dahl, "Want a Job? Let the Bidding Begin"; Malone et al., "The Age of Hyperspecialization"; Wang, "The Solution to the Innovator's Dilemma"; Marjorie Derven, "Managing the Matrix in the New Normal," *T+D*, July 2010, 42–47.
5. Courtland L. Bovée and John V. Thill, *Business in Action*, 5th ed. (Upper Saddle River, N.J.: Pearson Prentice Hall, 2010), 18–21; Randall S. Hansen and Katharine Hansen, "What Do Employers Really Want? Top Skills and Values Employers Seek from Job-Seekers," QuintCareers.com, accessed 17 August 2010, www.quintcareers.com.
6. Nancy M. Somerick, "Managing a Communication Internship Program," *Bulletin of the Association for Business Communication* 56, no. 3 (1993): 10–20.
7. Jeffrey R. Young, "'E-Portfolios' Could Give Students a New Sense of Their Accomplishments," *The Chronicle of Higher Education*, 8 March 2002, A31.
8. Pete Kistler, "Seth Godin's 7-Point Guide to Bootstrap Your Personal Brand," Personal Branding blog, 28 July 2010, www.personalbrandingblog; Kyle Lacy, "10 Ways to Building Your Personal Brand Story," Personal Branding blog, 5 August 2010, www.personalbrandingblog; Al-Taee, "Personal Branding"; Scot Herrick, "30 Career Management Tips—Marketing AND Delivery Support Our Personal Brand," Cube Rules blog, 8 September 2007, http://cuberules.com; Alina Tugend, "Putting Yourself Out There on a Shelf to Buy," *New York Times*, 27 March 2009, www.nytimes.com.

9. Jessica Dickler, "The Hidden Job Market," CNNMoney.com, 10 June 2009, http://money.cnn.com.

10. Tara Weiss, "Twitter to Find a Job," *Forbes*, 7 April 2009, www.forbes.com.

11. Miriam Saltpeter, "Using Facebook Groups for Job Hunting," Keppie Careers blog, 13 November 2008, www.keppiecareers.com.

12. Anne Fisher, "Greener Pastures in a New Field," *Fortune*, 26 January 2004, 48.

13. Liz Ryan, "Etiquette for Online Outreach," Yahoo! Hotjobs website, accessed 26 March 2008, http://hotjobs.yahoo.com.

14. Eve Tahmincioglu, "Employers Digging Deep on Prospective Workers," MSNBC.com, 26 October 2009, www.msnbc.com.

15. Randall S. Hansen and Katharine Hansen, "What Résumé Format Is Best for You?" QuintCareers.com, accessed 7 August 2010, www.quintcareers.com.

16. Rachel Emma Silverman, "No More Résumés, Say Some Firms,' *Wall Street Journal*, 24 January 2012, http://online.wsj.com.

17. "How to Ferret Out Instances of Résumé Padding and Fraud," *Compensation & Benefits for Law Offices*, June 2006, 1+.

18. "Resume Fraud Gets Slicker and Easier," CNN.com, accessed 11 March 2004, www.cnn.com.

19. "Resume Fraud Still Major Problem HR Needs to Address," *HR Focus*, July 2012, 13–15.

20. Cari Tuna and Keith J. Winstein, "Economy Promises to Fuel Résumé Fraud," *Wall Street Journal*, 17 November 2008, http://online.wsj.com; Lisa Takeuchi Cullen, "Getting Wise to Lies," *Time*, 1 May 2006, 59; "Resume Fraud Gets Slicker and Easier"; Employment Research Services website, accessed 18 March 2004, www.erscheck.com.

21. "How to Ferret Out Instances of Résumé Padding and Fraud."

22. Jacqueline Durett, "Redoing Your Résumé? Leave Off the Lies," *Training*, December 2006, 9; "Employers Turn Their Fire on Untruthful CVs," *Supply Management*, 23 June 2005, 13.

23. Cynthia E. Conn, "Integrating Writing Skills and Ethics Training in Business Communication Pedagogy: A Résumé Case Study Exemplar," *Business Communication Quarterly*, June 2008, 138–151; Marilyn Moats Kennedy, "Don't Get Burned by Résumé Inflation," *Marketing News*, 15 April 2007, 37–38.

24. Kim Isaacs, "Resume Dilemma: Criminal Record," Monster.com, accessed 23 May 2006, www.monster.com; Kim Isaacs, "Resume Dilemma: Employment Gaps and Job-Hopping," Monster.com, accessed 23 May 2006, www.monster.com; Susan Vaughn, "Answer the Hard Questions Before Asked," *Los Angeles Times*, 29 July 2001, W1–W2.

25. John Steven Niznik, "Landing a Job with a Criminal Record," About.com, accessed 12 December 2006, http://jobsearchtech.about.com.

26. Dave Johnson, "10 Resume Errors That Will Land You in the Trash," *BNET*, 22 February 2010, www.bnet.com; Anthony Balderrama, "Resume Blunders That Will Keep You from Getting Hired," CNN.com, 19 March 2008, www.cnn.com; Michelle Dumas, "5 Resume Writing Myths," Distinctive Documents blog, 17 July 2007, http://blog.distinctiveweb.com; Kim Isaacs, "Resume Dilemma: Recent Graduate," Monster.com, accessed 26 March 2008, http://career-advice.monster.com.

27. Katharine Hansen, "Should You Consider a Functional Format for Your Resume?" QuintCareers.com, accessed 7 August 2010, www.quintcareers.com.

28. Rachel Zupek, "Seven Exceptions to Job Search Rules," CNN.com, 3 September 2008, www.cnn.com.

29. Nancy M. Schullery, Linda Ickes, and Stephen E. Schullery, "Employer Preferences for Résumés and Cover Letters," *Business Communication Quarterly*, June 2009, 163–176.

30. John Hazard, "Resume Tips: No Pictures, Please and No PDFs," Career-Line.com, 26 May 2009, www.career-line.com; "25 Things You Should Never Include on a Resume," HR World website, 18 December 2007, www.hrworld.com.

31. John Sullivan, "Résumés: Paper, Please," *Workforce Management*, 22 October 2007, 50; "Video Résumés Offer Both Pros and Cons During Recruiting," *HR Focus*, July 2007, 8.

32. Jobs page, Zappos website, accessed 24 March 2011, http://about.zappos.com/jobs.

33. Lisa Vaas, "How to Follow Up a Résumé Submission," *The Ladders*, 9 August 2010, www.theladders.com.

34. Alison Doyle, "How to Follow Up After Submitting a Resume," About.com, http://jobsearch.about.com; Vaas, "How to Follow Up a Résumé Submission."

35. Anne Fisher, "How to Get Hired by a 'Best' Company," *Fortune*, 4 February 2008, 96.

36. Fisher, "How to Get Hired by a 'Best' Company."

37. Sarah E. Needleman, "Speed Interviewing Grows as Skills Shortage Looms; Strategy May Help Lock in Top Picks; Some Drawbacks," *Wall Street Journal*, 6 November 2007, B15.

38. Scott Beagrie, "How to Handle a Telephone Job Interview," *Personnel Today*, 26 June 2007, 29.

39. "Hiring Process," Google, accessed 2 January 2009, www.google.com.

40. "What's a Group Interview?" About.com Tech Careers, accessed 5 April 2008, http://jobsearchtech.about.com.

41. Fisher, "How to Get Hired by a 'Best' Company."

42. Chris Pentilla, "Testing the Waters," *Entrepreneur*, January 2004, www.entrepreneur.com; Terry McKenna, "Behavior-Based Interviewing," *National Petroleum News*, January 2004, 16; Nancy K. Austin, "Goodbye Gimmicks," *Incentive*, May 1996, 241.

43. Alison Green, "How a Thank-You Note Can Boost Your Job Chances," *U.S. News & World Report*, 27 June 2012, http://money.usnews.com; Joan S. Lublin, "Notes to Interviewers Should Go Beyond a Simple Thank You," *Wall Street Journal*, 5 February 2008, B1.

44. Joan Lloyd, "Changing Workplace Requires You to Alter Your Career Outlook," *Milwaukee Journal Sentinel*, 4 July 1999, 1; Camille DeBell, "Ninety Years in the World of Work in America," *Career Development Quarterly*, Vol. 50, No. 1, September 2001, 77–88.

45. Job description keywords and key phrases quoted or adapted in part from "Associate Market Analyst" job opening posted on LivingSocial website, accessed 9 July 2012, http://corporate.livingsocial.com.

46. Job description keywords and key phrases quoted or adapted in part from "Seller Support Associate" job opening posted on Amazon website, accessed 12 July 2012, https://us-amazon.icims.com/jobs.

47. Job description keywords and key phrases quoted or adapted in part from "Senior Strategy Analyst" job opening posted on Nordstrom website, accessed 17 July 2012, http://careers.nordstrom.com.

PART 1

Setting the Stage: The Business of Business

RYO/a.collectionRF/Getty Images

1

LEARNING OBJECTIVES   After studying this chapter, you will be able to

1 Explain the concept of adding value in a business, and identify the major types of businesses.

2 List three steps you can take to help make the leap from consumer to business professional.

3 Discuss the five major environments in which every business operates.

4 Explain the purpose of the six major functional areas in a business enterprise.

5 Summarize seven of the most important business professions.

6 Identify seven components of professionalism.

BEHIND THE SCENES   YOLANDA DIAZ: BUILDING HER DREAM WITH HARD WORK AND STRONG BUSINESS SENSE

Jim West/Alamy

Yolanda Diaz's hard work, keen business sense, and smart use of available resources turned her dream of business ownership into a multimillion-dollar reality.

www.miradorenterprises.com

Yolanda Diaz's business instincts have been on display since her childhood in El Paso, Texas. To help her mother with household expenses, Diaz approached families in the neighborhood, offering her services at cleaning, cooking, and other chores. In high school, she got formal exposure to business as part of the Vocational Office Education program. Later, while an accounting major at the University of Texas at El Paso, she and her sister launched a part-time clothing company to help cover the cost of tuition.

By the time she graduated with a degree in accounting, Diaz clearly knew the value of hard work—and knew how to create value for customers. She put her degree to good use as an accounting supervisor for several established companies, including the multinational firm United Technologies. After a decade of working for others, though, she was ready to return to her entrepreneurial roots and strike out on her own again.

If you were Diaz, how would you make the transition from employee to business owner? What resources would you use? Which customers would you pursue, and how would you cultivate new opportunities? If you dreamed of starting your own business, how would you make that dream come true?[1]

INTRODUCTION

Like millions of employees before her, Yolanda Diaz (profiled in the chapter opener) made the bold decision to go into business for herself—a decision you might have already made or are contemplating yourself. At the end of the chapter, you can read about how she turned her dream into a successful company. This chapter gets you ready for the whirlwind tour of the business world you'll get in this course, starting with a quick overview of what businesses do and then some advice on making the leap from consumer to business professional.

Understanding What Businesses Do

The term *business* is used in a number of ways:

- As a label for the overall field of business concepts, as in "I plan to major in business."
- As a collective label for the activities of many companies, as in "This legislation is viewed as harmful to American business."
- As a way to indicate specific activities or efforts, as in "Our furniture business earned record profits last year, but our housewares business has lost money for the third year in a row."
- As a synonym for *company*, as in "Apple is a successful business." Other common synonyms here are *firm* and *enterprise*.

In this last sense, a **business** is any profit-seeking organization that provides goods and services designed to satisfy customers' needs.

ADDING VALUE: THE BUSINESS OF BUSINESS

A good way to understand what any business does is to view it as a system for satisfying customers by transforming lower-value inputs into higher-value outputs (see Exhibit 1.1). If you want a loaf of bread, for instance, a silo full of wheat isn't of much value to you.

1   LEARNING OBJECTIVE

Explain the concept of adding value in a business, and identify the major types of businesses.

business
Any profit-seeking organization that provides goods and services designed to satisfy customers' needs.

EXHIBIT 1.1   Adding Value to Satisfy Customers

Every company in this chain adds value for the next customer and for the ultimate consumer.

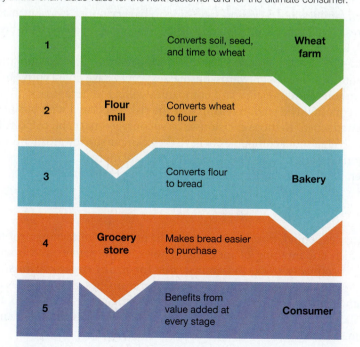

1	Converts soil, seed, and time to wheat	**Wheat farm**
2	**Flour mill** Converts wheat to flour	
3	Converts flour to bread	**Bakery**
4	**Grocery store** Makes bread easier to purchase	
5	Benefits from value added at every stage	**Consumer**

revenue
Money a company brings in through the sale of goods and services.

business model
A concise description of how a business intends to generate revenue.

profit
Money left over after all the costs involved in doing business have been deducted from revenue.

competitive advantage
Some aspect of a product or company that makes it more appealing to target customers.

not-for-profit organizations
Organizations that provide goods and services without having a profit motive; also called *nonprofit organizations*.

After that wheat is milled into flour, it gets one step closer but is valuable only if you want to bake your own bread. A bakery can take care of the baking, but that helps only if you're willing to travel to the bakery instead of going to the supermarket where you normally shop. At every stage, a company adds value to create the product in a way that makes it appealing to the next customer in the chain.

Each company in this chain has made certain choices about what it will do to generate **revenue**: money the company brings in through the sale of goods and services. The result of these decisions is a company's **business model**, which is a clearly stated outline of how the business intends to generate revenue. Of course, generating revenue isn't enough; the business model must also indicate how the company is going to realize **profit**, the amount of money left over after *expenses*—all the costs involved in doing business—have been deducted from revenue.

Competing to Attract and Satisfy Customers

As businesses create value-added products and offer them for sale to customers, they obviously don't do so in a vacuum. Other companies are also trying to sell their products to those same customers, and the result is *competition*. Competition gives customers a wider range of options, and it tends to increase quality, improve customer service, and lower prices.

One of the beauties of a free-market economy is that companies usually have a lot of flexibility in deciding which customers they want to focus on and how they want to compete. For instance, one bakery might decide to compete on price and thus structure its business model in such a way as to mass-produce bread at the lowest possible cost. Another might decide to compete on quality or uniqueness and thus structure its business model around handcrafted "artisan" bread that costs two or three times as much as the mass-produced bread. Each company seeks a **competitive advantage** that makes its products more appealing to its chosen customers. Consumers benefit from better products and more choices, and companies get to focus on what they do best.

Accepting Risks in the Pursuit of Rewards

Take another look at Exhibit 1.1. Notice how every company from the farmer to the grocery store must accept some level of risk in order to conduct its business. Bad weather or disease could destroy the wheat crop. A shift in consumer behavior, such as cash-strapped families in a recession switching to bakery outlet stores instead of regular grocery stores, could leave some bakers, distributors, and retailers with bread nobody wants to buy. Businesses take these risks in anticipation of future rewards.

This linking of risk and reward is critical for two reasons. The first and more obvious is that without the promise of rewards, businesses would have no incentive to take on the risks. And without entrepreneurs and companies willing to accept risk, little would get done in the economy. The second reason that the risk associated with business decisions needs to "stay attached" to those decisions is to encourage smart and responsible decision making. If individuals and companies believe they can pursue rewards without facing the risks that should be attached to those pursuits, they are more likely to engage in irresponsible and even unethical behavior—a situation known as *moral hazard* (see Exhibit 1.2).

IDENTIFYING MAJOR TYPES OF BUSINESSES

The driving forces behind most businesses are the prospects of earning profits and building *assets*, which are anything of meaningful value, from patents and brand names to real estate and company stock. In contrast, **not-for-profit organizations** (also known as *nonprofit organizations*) such as museums, most universities, and charities do not have a profit motive. However, they must operate efficiently and effectively to achieve their goals, and successful nonprofits apply many of the business-management principles you'll learn in this course.

EXHIBIT 1.2 **Risk and Reward**

The relationship between risk and reward is fundamental to every modern economy. A company needs to see some promise of reward before it will decide to accept the risks involved in creating and selling products. However, to ensure responsible behavior, these risks need to stay attached to those decisions, meaning that if the decisions turn out bad, that company should suffer the consequences. If the risk gets disconnected from a decision—meaning someone else will suffer from a bad decision—a situation known as *moral hazard* is created. A significant recent example of this problem involved home-mortgage companies lending money to homeowners who were practically guaranteed to default on their loans, but then selling those loans as investments and thereby transferring the risk of nonpayment to someone else.

Healthy connection between risk and reward

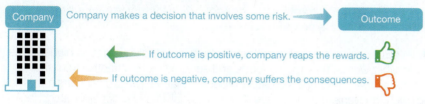

Moral hazard: Link between risk and reward is broken

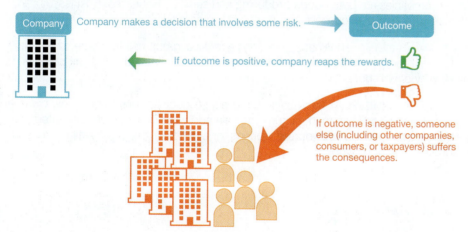

Businesses can be classified into two broad categories. **Goods-producing businesses** create value by making "things," from Pop-Tarts to school furniture to spacecraft. Most goods are *tangible*, meaning they have a physical presence; other goods, such as software, music downloads, and similar digital products, are *intangible*. **Service businesses** create value by performing activities that deliver some benefit to the customer, such as finance, insurance, transportation, construction, utilities, wholesale and retail trade, banking, entertainment, health care, maintenance and repair, and information. Twitter, Jiffy Lube, HBO, and Verizon Wireless are examples of service businesses. Many companies are both goods-producing and service businesses.

Over the past few decades, the U.S. economy has undergone a profound transformation from being dominated by manufacturing to being dominated by services. Although the country remains a manufacturing powerhouse, the service sector now accounts for 70 percent of the economic activity and 80 percent of jobs in the United States.[2]

Because they require large amounts of money, equipment, land, and other resources to get started and to operate, goods-producing businesses are often *capital-intensive businesses*. The capital needed to compete in these industries is a **barrier to entry**, which is a resource or capability a company must have before it can start competing in a given market. Other barriers to entry include government testing and approval, tightly

goods-producing businesses
Companies that create value by making "things," most of which are tangible (digital products such as software are a notable exception).

service businesses
Companies that create value by performing activities that deliver some benefit to customers.

barrier to entry
Any resource or capability a company must have before it can start competing in a given market.

controlled markets, strict licensing procedures, limited supplies of raw materials, and the need for highly skilled employees. Service businesses tend to be *labor intensive*, in that they rely more on human resources than on buildings, machinery, and equipment to prosper. There are exceptions, of course. Airlines require a massive investment in equipment, for example, and the Internet and other technologies have reduced the labor required to operate many types of service businesses.

 Checkpoint

LEARNING OBJECTIVE 1: Explain the concept of adding value in a business, and identify the major types of businesses.

SUMMARY: Businesses add value by transforming lower-value inputs to higher-value outputs. In other words, they make goods and services more attractive from the buyer's perspective, whether it's creating products that are more useful or simply making them more convenient to purchase. Companies fall into two general categories: goods-producing businesses, which create tangible things (except in the case of digital goods), and service businesses, which perform various activities of value to customers. Many companies are both goods-producing and service businesses. Businesses can also be categorized as capital intensive or labor intensive.

CRITICAL THINKING: (1) What inputs does a musical group use to create its outputs? (2) Can not-for-profit organizations benefit from practices used by for-profit companies? Why or why not?

IT'S YOUR BUSINESS: (1) Think back to the last product you purchased; how did the companies involved in its manufacture and sale add value in a way that benefited you personally? (2) Can you see yourself working for a not-for-profit organization after you graduate? Why or why not?

KEY TERMS TO KNOW: business, revenue, business model, profit, competitive advantage, not-for-profit organizations, goods-producing businesses, service businesses, barrier to entry

 2 **LEARNING OBJECTIVE**

List three steps you can take to help make the leap from consumer to business professional.

Making the Leap from Buyer to Seller

Even if this course is your first formal exposure to the business world, you already know a lot about business, thanks to your experiences as a consumer. You understand the impact of poor customer service, for example. You have a sense of product value and why some products meet your needs and others don't. In fact, you're an expert in the entire experience of searching for, purchasing, and owning products.

SEEING BUSINESS FROM THE INSIDE OUT

As you progress through this course, you'll begin to look at things through the eyes of a business professional rather than those of a consumer. Instead of thinking about the cost of buying a particular product, you'll start to think about the cost of making it, promoting it, and distributing it. You'll think about what it takes to make a product stand out from the crowd and recognize the importance of finding opportunities in the marketplace. You'll begin to see business as an integrated system of inputs, processes, and outputs. As Yolanda Diaz did when she launched Mirador Enterprises (see page 22), you'll start to develop a business **mindset** as you gain an appreciation for the many decisions that must be made and the many challenges that must be overcome before companies can deliver products that satisfy customer needs (see Exhibit 1.3).

EXHIBIT 1.3   **The Business Mindset**

Your experiences as a consumer have taught you a great deal about business already. Now the challenge is to turn those experiences around and view the world from a manager's perspective. Here are a few examples of how a business professional approaches some of the questions you've asked as a consumer.

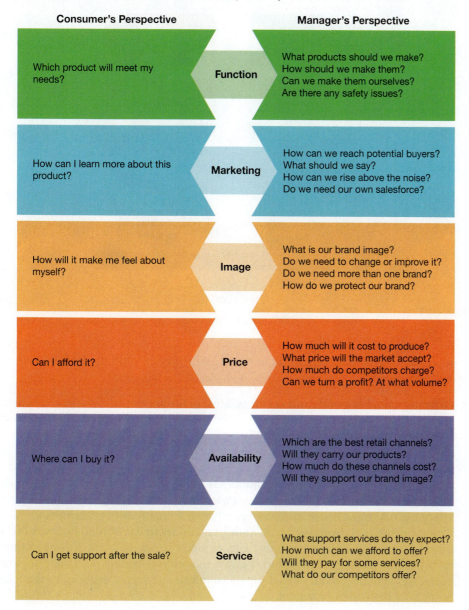

Consumer's Perspective		Manager's Perspective
Which product will meet my needs?	**Function**	What products should we make? How should we make them? Can we make them ourselves? Are there any safety issues?
How can I learn more about this product?	**Marketing**	How can we reach potential buyers? What should we say? How can we rise above the noise? Do we need our own salesforce?
How will it make me feel about myself?	**Image**	What is our brand image? Do we need to change or improve it? Do we need more than one brand? How do we protect our brand?
Can I afford it?	**Price**	How much will it cost to produce? What price will the market accept? How much do competitors charge? Can we turn a profit? At what volume?
Where can I buy it?	**Availability**	Which are the best retail channels? Will they carry our products? How much do these channels cost? Will they support our brand image?
Can I get support after the sale?	**Service**	What support services do they expect? How much can we afford to offer? Will they pay for some services? What do our competitors offer?

APPRECIATING THE ROLE OF BUSINESS IN SOCIETY

Your experiences as a consumer, an employee, and a taxpayer have also given you some insights into the complex relationship between business and society. Chapter 4's discussion of *corporate social responsibility* digs deeper into this important topic, but for now, just consider some of the major elements of this relationship. Business has

REAL-TIME UPDATES

Learn More by Exploring This Interactive Website

Use this powerful search tool for easier online searches

Bovée and Thill Web Search is a custom metasearch engine that automatically formats more than 300 types of searches for optimum results. Go to http://real-timeupdates.com/bia8 and click on Web Search in the navigation bar.

| EXHIBIT 1.4 | Positive and Negative Effects of Business |

The relationship between business and society is complex and far reaching. Individuals, communities, and entire nations benefit in multiple ways from the efforts of businesses, but even responsibly managed companies can at times have negative impacts on society in return.

the potential to contribute to society in many useful ways, including the following (see Exhibit 1.4):

- **Offering valuable goods and services.** Most of the goods and services you consider essential to your quality of life were made possible by someone with a profit motive.
- **Providing employment.** In addition to providing salaries, many companies help their employees meet the costs of health care, child care, education, retirement, and other living expenses.
- **Paying taxes.** U.S. businesses pay hundreds of billions in taxes every year,[3] money that helps build highways, fund education, further scientific research, enhance public safety and national defense, and support other vital functions of government.
- **Contributing to national growth, stability, and security.** Beyond the mere dollars from taxes paid, a strong economy helps ensure a strong country. As one example, by providing job opportunities to the vast majority of people who want to work, businesses help the country avoid the social unrest and family disruptions that often result from high unemployment.

Unfortunately, businesses don't always operate in ways that benefit society. As you progress into positions of increasing responsibility in your career, be aware of the potentially negative effects that business can have on society:

- **Generating pollution and creating waste.** Just like individuals, companies consume resources and produce waste and therefore have an impact on the natural environment and the soil, air, and water on which all living creatures depend.
- **Creating health and safety risks.** Many business operations involve an element of risk to the health and safety of employees and surrounding communities. For instance, some of the products you use every day, from your digital music player to your laptop computer, contain toxic materials. If these materials are not created, handled, and disposed of properly, they can cause serious illness or death.
- **Disrupting communities.** From occupying land to displacing existing businesses to overloading schools and roads with employees and their children,

growing businesses can disrupt communities even as they provide employment and other benefits. And when businesses fall into decline, they can leave behind everything from abandoned buildings to laid-off workers.

- **Causing financial instability.** Irresponsible or poorly managed companies can become a liability to society if they are unable to meet their financial obligations and need assistance from the government, for example.

The potential negative effects of business are serious matters, but the good news is that you have a say in how business operates. Even as an employee early in your career, you can conduct yourself in ways that balance the profit motive with society's shared interests. And as you climb the corporate ladder or perhaps launch your own business, you'll be in a position to make decisions that help your company prosper in an ethical and sustainable manner.

REAL-TIME UPDATES
Learn More by Reading This Article

Managing your career in today's workplace: One expert's view

Read these quick tips on succeeding in the new world of work. Go to http://real-timeupdates.com/bia8 and click on Learn More in the Students section.

USING THIS COURSE TO JUMP-START YOUR CAREER

No matter where your career plans take you, the dynamics of business will affect your work and life in innumerable ways. If you aspire to be a manager or an entrepreneur, knowing how to run a business is vital, of course. If you plan a career in a professional specialty such as law, engineering, or finance, knowing how businesses operate will help you interact with clients and colleagues more effectively. Even if you plan to work in government, education, or some other noncommercial setting, business awareness can help you; many of these organizations look to business for new ideas and leadership techniques. *Social entrepreneurs,* people who apply entrepreneurial strategies to enable large-scale social change, use business concepts as well.

As you progress through this course, you'll develop a fundamental business vocabulary that will help you keep up with the latest news and make better-informed decisions. By participating in classroom discussions and completing the chapter exercises, you'll gain some valuable critical-thinking, problem-solving, team-building, and communication skills that you can use on the job and throughout your life.

This course will also introduce you to a variety of jobs in business fields such as accounting, economics, human resources, management, finance, and marketing. You'll see how people who work in these fields contribute to the success of a company as a whole. You'll gain insight into the types of skills and knowledge these jobs require, and you'll discover that a career in business today is fascinating, challenging, and often quite rewarding.

In addition, a study of business management will help you appreciate the larger context in which businesses operate and the many legal and ethical questions managers must consider as they make business decisions. Government regulators and society as a whole have numerous expectations regarding the ways businesses treat employees, shareholders, the environment, other businesses, and the communities in which they operate.

✓ Checkpoint

LEARNING OBJECTIVE 2: List three steps you can take to help make the leap from consumer to business professional.

SUMMARY: To accelerate your transition from consumer to professional, develop a business mindset that views business from the inside out rather than the outside in, recognize the positive and negative effects that business can have on society, and use this course to develop a business vocabulary and explore the wide variety of jobs in the field of business.

CRITICAL THINKING: (1) How can consumer experiences help a business professional excel on the job? (2) If organized businesses didn't exist and the economy were composed of individual craftspeople, would the result be more or less pollution? Explain your answer.

IT'S YOUR BUSINESS: (1) How might you contribute to society as a business professional? (2) What is your view of business at this point in your life? Negative? Positive? A mixture of both?

KEY TERM TO KNOW: business mindset

3 **LEARNING OBJECTIVE**

Discuss the five major environments in which every business operates.

social environment
Trends and forces in society at large.

Recognizing the Multiple Environments of Business

The potential effects of business, both positive and negative, highlight the fact that no business operates in a vacuum. Every company operates within a number of interrelated environments that affect and are affected by business (see Exhibit 1.5).

THE SOCIAL ENVIRONMENT

Every business operates within the broad **social environment**—the trends and forces in society at large. For instance, all companies are affected by population trends that

EXHIBIT 1.5 **The Multiple Environments of Business**

Every business operates in an overlapping mix of dynamic environments that continuously create both opportunities and constraints.

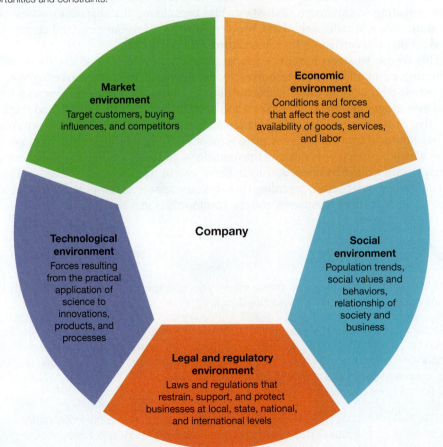

Market environment
Target customers, buying influences, and competitors

Economic environment
Conditions and forces that affect the cost and availability of goods, services, and labor

Technological environment
Forces resulting from the practical application of science to innovations, products, and processes

Company

Social environment
Population trends, social values and behaviors, relationship of society and business

Legal and regulatory environment
Laws and regulations that restrain, support, and protect businesses at local, state, national, and international levels

change the composition of consumer markets and the workforce. One great example is the so-called Baby Boom generation, a population "bulge" made up of people born between 1946 and 1964. This large group of people have affected business in numerous ways as they have moved through childhood, then into adulthood as consumers and workers, and finally back out of the workforce now that the first wave of boomers have reached retirement age. The Baby Boomers have occupied a large number of middle- and upper-management positions, frustrating younger professionals who would like to climb the company ladder and causing many to leave and start their own companies.[4]

Various segments of society also have expectations about the appropriate relationship of business and society. The responsibility of a company to its **stakeholders**—all those groups affected by its activities, from employees to local communities to advocacy groups—is a subject of ongoing controversy. You can read more about stakeholders in Chapter 4's discussion of corporate social responsibility.

stakeholders
Internal and external groups affected by a company's decisions and activities.

THE TECHNOLOGICAL ENVIRONMENT

The **technological environment** stems from the practical application of science to innovations, products, and processes. Technological advances have the potential to change every facet of business, from altering internal processes to creating or destroying market opportunities. *Disruptive technologies*, those that fundamentally change the nature of an industry, can be powerful enough to create or destroy entire companies. Many of the technologies that you use in your academic, personal, and social activities, from digital audio and video to the Internet to social media, are disruptive technologies that have shaken up multiple industries.

technological environment
Forces resulting from the practical application of science to innovations, products, and processes.

One of the newest disruptive technologies to hit the business world is mobile connectivity, including smartphones, tablets, app software, and the networking infrastructure that connects all these devices. Venture capitalist Joe Schoendorf call mobile "the most disruptive technology that I have seen in 48 years in Silicon Valley."[5] Researcher Maribel Lopez calls mobile "the biggest technology shift since the Internet."[6]

Companies recognize the value of integrating mobile technology, from employee collaboration systems to banking to retail. Mobile apps and communication systems can boost employee productivity, help companies form closer relationships with customers and business partners, and spur innovation in products and services (see Exhibit 1.6 on the next page). Given the advantages and the rising expectations of employees and customers, firms on the leading edge of the mobile revolution are working to integrate mobile technology throughout their organizations.[7]

For millions of people around the world, a mobile device is their primary way, if not their only way, to access the Internet. Globally, roughly 80 percent of Internet users access the web at least some of the time with a mobile device.[8] Mobile has become the primary communication tool for many business professionals, including a majority of executives under age 40.[9] Email and web browsing rank first and second in terms of the most common nonvoice uses of smartphones, and more email messages are now opened on mobile devices than on PCs.[10] Roughly half of U.S. consumers use a mobile device exclusively for their online search needs, and many online activities that eventually migrate to a PC screen start out on a mobile screen.[11] For many people, the fact that a smartphone can make phone calls is practically a secondary consideration; data traffic from mobile devices far outstrips voice traffic.[12]

Social media pioneer Nicco Mele coined the term *radical connectivity* to describe "the breathtaking ability to send vast amounts of data instantly, constantly, and globally."[13] Mobile plays a major and ever-expanding role in this

REAL-TIME UPDATES
Learn More by Watching This Video

The mobile business advantage

Hear how leading-edge companies are adapting to take advantage of mobile connectivity and communication. Go to http://real-timeupdates.com/bia8 and click on Learn More in the Students section.

REAL-TIME UPDATES
Learn More by Reading This Infographic

Can you run an entire company from a smartphone?

Mobile apps are powerful enough to enable the mobile small business. Go to http://real-timeupdates.com/bia8 and click on Learn More in the Students section.

EXHIBIT 1.6	Disruptive Technologies: The Mobile Revolution

Mobile connectivity is a classic example of a disruptive technology. Here are some of the many ways it is affecting virtually every aspect of business. Mobile simplifies life in some ways but complicates it in others because it creates opportunities for new business models and threatens some existing models.

Inside the Enterprise   **Outside the Enterprise**

 Mobile presentation tools, such the ability to stream slides to audience members' phones and tablets, give new life to business meetings and conferences.

 Mobile-friendly enterprise communication systems, including collaboration platforms and private Twitter-style microblogging, help colleagues stay in constant contact.

 For many consumers around the world wihtout PCs, mobile devices are their primary way to access the Internet.

 Through services such as Uber, mobile is redefining local transportation options.

Throughout the organization, employees and managers can get vital information wherever they are, whenever they need it.

For many workers today, the office is wherever they need it to be, from their kitchen tables to local coffee shops to customer facilities.

 Business travel no longer forces employees and managers to lose touch with colleagues and customers.

 Location-based services let companies deliver relevant updates, coupons, and digital products to mobile customers, and consumers influence businesses through on-the-spot reviews and social networking

For better or worse, mobile lets employees stay connected to their work around the clock.

With training apps and real-time information delivery, employees can get important advice and data when and where they need it.

 Mobile commerce simplifies life for consumers but disrupts established retail patterns through in-store price comparisons and product research.

 Mobile simplifies transportation and logistics by keeping companies connected to their goods and equipment anywhere in the world.

 Financial apps, from transaction processing to full accounting capabilities, let entrepreneurs take their businesses right to the customer.

 From location scouting to consumer research, mobile devices help researchers collect vital information live and on the spot.

 Through a variety of text-based, audio, and video systems, companies can reach consumers in more ways than ever before.

  Sales and service professionals can use apps for presentations, product configuration, order tracking, troubleshooting, and other in-the-field activities.

phenomenon by keeping people connected 24/7, wherever they may be. Those who've grown up with mobile technology expect to have immediate access to information and the ability to stay connected to their various social and business networks.[14] If *wearable technologies* become mainstream devices, they will contribute even more to this shift in behaviors. You'll read more about mobile in the chapters ahead.

economic environment
The conditions and forces that affect the cost and availability of goods, services, and labor and thereby shape the behavior of buyers and sellers.

THE ECONOMIC ENVIRONMENT

Directly or indirectly, virtually every decision a company makes is influenced by the **economic environment**, the conditions and forces that (1) affect the cost and availability of goods, services, and labor and (2) thereby shape the behavior of buyers and sellers. For example, a growing economy can help companies by increasing demand and supporting higher prices for their products, but it can also raise the costs of labor and the materials the companies need in order to do business. A strong economy can also prompt managers to make decisions that turn out to be unwise in the long term, such as adding costly facilities or employee benefits that the company won't be able to afford when the economy slows down again. A shrinking economy, on the other hand, can damage even well-run, financially healthy companies by limiting demand for their products or the availability of loans or investments needed to expand operations. Chapter 2 explores economic forces in more detail.

THE LEGAL AND REGULATORY ENVIRONMENT

Every business is affected by the **legal and regulatory environment**, the sum of laws and regulations at local, state, national, and even international levels. Some businesses, such as electricity and other basic utilities, are heavily regulated, even to the point of government agencies determining how much such companies can charge for their services. The degree to which various industries should be regulated remains a point of contention, year in and year out.

The policies and practices of government bodies also establish an overall level of support for businesses operating within their jurisdictions. Taxation, fees, efforts to coordinate multiple regulatory agencies, the speed of granting permits and licenses, labor rules, environmental restrictions, protection for assets such as patents and brand names, roads and other infrastructure, and the transparency and consistency of decision making all affect this level of support. Not surprisingly, companies prefer to locate and do business in jurisdictions that offer lower costs, lower complexity, and greater stability and predictability.

legal and regulatory environment
Laws and regulations at local, state, national, and even international levels.

THE MARKET ENVIRONMENT

Within the various other environments just discussed, every company operates within a specific **market environment** composed of three important groups: (1) its *target customers*, (2) the *buying influences* that shape the behavior of those customers, and (3) *competitors*—other companies that market similar products to those customers. The nature and behavior of these groups and their effect on business strategy vary widely from industry to industry.

In commercial aviation, for example, the barriers to entry are extremely high, and the customer decision-making process is lengthy and driven almost entirely by financial considerations. As a consequence, the manufacturers in this industry have to make major investment decisions years in advance of launching new products, but they can do so with the reasonable assumption that a new competitor isn't going to pop up overnight and that their target customers will behave in fairly predictable ways.

In sharp contrast, clothing fashions and fads can change in a matter of weeks or days, and the behavior of celebrities and other buying influences can have a major impact on consumer choices. Moreover, because it is much easier to launch a new line of clothing than a new airplane, competitors can appear almost overnight.

market environment
A company's target customers, the buying influences that shape the behavior of those customers, and competitors that market similar products to those customers.

✔ Checkpoint

LEARNING OBJECTIVE 3: Discuss the five major environments in which every business operates.

SUMMARY: Business influences and is influenced by (1) the social environment—the trends and forces in society at large; (2) the technological environment and its ability to create and destroy markets and alter business processes; (3) the economic environment, the conditions and forces that affect the cost and availability of goods, services, and labor and thereby shape the behavior of buyers and sellers; (4) the legal and regulatory environment, comprising all the rules and regulations relating to business activities; and (5) the market environment, composed of target customers, buying influences, and competitors.

CRITICAL THINKING: (1) Is it wise for cities and states to compete with each other to be more business friendly, specifically with regard to lower tax rates on businesses? Why or why not? (2) Even though it never sells directly to consumers, does a company such as Boeing need to pay attention to population trends? Why or why not?

IT'S YOUR BUSINESS: (1) How has technology made your educational experience in college different from your experience in high school? (2) Have current economic conditions affected your career-planning decisions in any way?

KEY TERMS TO KNOW: social environment, stakeholders, technological environment, economic environment, legal and regulatory environment, market environment

4 **LEARNING OBJECTIVE**

Explain the purpose of the six major functional areas in a business enterprise.

Identifying the Major Functional Areas in a Business Enterprise

Throughout this course, you'll have the opportunity to learn more about the major functional areas within a business enterprise. In the meantime, the following sections offer a brief overview to help you see how all the pieces work together (see Exhibit 1.7).

EXHIBIT 1.7   **Major Functional Areas in a Business Enterprise**

The functional areas in a business coordinate their efforts to understand and satisfy customer needs. Note that this is a vastly simplified model, and various companies organize their activities in different ways.

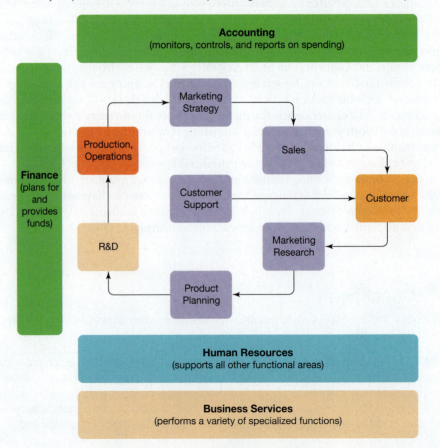

RESEARCH AND DEVELOPMENT

Products are conceived and designed through **research and development (R&D)**, sometimes known as *product design* or *engineering*. Of course, not all companies have an R&D function; many companies simply resell products that other firms make, for example. However, for companies that do develop products, R&D is essential to their survival because it provides the ideas and designs that allow these firms to meet customer needs in competitive markets.

Companies can also engage in *process* R&D to design new and better ways to run their operations. Much of this effort goes into **information technology (IT)** systems that promote communication and information usage through the company or that allow companies to offer new services to their customers.

research and development (R&D)
Functional area responsible for conceiving and designing new products.

information technology (IT)
Systems that promote communication and information usage through the company or that allow companies to offer new services to their customers.

MANUFACTURING, PRODUCTION, AND OPERATIONS

Variously called *manufacturing, production,* or *operations,* this function concerns whatever the company makes (for goods-producing businesses) or does (for service businesses). In addition to supervising the actual production activity, operations managers are responsible for a wide range of other strategies and decisions, including *purchasing* (arranging to buy the necessary materials for manufacturing), *logistics* (coordinating the incoming flow of materials and the outgoing flow of finished products), and *facilities management* (everything from planning new buildings to maintaining them). Chapter 9 explores operations management in more detail.

MARKETING, SALES, DISTRIBUTION, AND CUSTOMER SUPPORT

Your experience as a consumer probably gives you more insight into marketing, sales, distribution, and customer support than any other functional area in business. Although the lines separating these three activities are often blurry, generally speaking, *marketing* is charged with identifying opportunities in the marketplace, working with R&D to develop the products to address those opportunities, creating branding and advertising strategies to communicate with potential customers, and setting prices. The *sales* function develops relationships with potential customers and persuades customers, transaction by transaction, to buy the company's goods and services. Depending on the type of product, a *distribution* function can be involved both before the sale (helping to promote products to retailers, for example) and after the sale (to physically deliver products). After products are in buyers' hands, *customer support* goes to work, making sure customers have the support and information they need.

Perhaps no aspect of business has been changed as dramatically by recent technological advances as these marketing, sales, distribution, and customer support activities. The advent of *social media* has enabled customers to participate in an unstructured conversation with companies and with each other rather than being passive recipients of broadcast advertising messages. The result has been a profound power shift that puts buyers on much more equal footing with sellers, as you'll read about in Chapters 13 through 16.

FINANCE AND ACCOUNTING

The finance and accounting functions ensure that the company has the funds it needs to operate, monitor, and control how those funds are spent and draft reports for company management and outside audiences such as investors and government regulators. Roughly speaking, *financial managers* are responsible for planning, whereas *accounting managers* are responsible for monitoring and reporting.

Accounting specialists work closely with other functional areas to ensure profitable decision making. For instance, accountants coordinate with the R&D and production departments to estimate the manufacturing costs of a new product and then work with the marketing department to set the product's price at a level that allows the company to be competitive while meeting its financial goals. Chapters 17 through 20 address accounting, finance, and related concepts.

HUMAN RESOURCES

As you'll read in Chapter 11, the human resources (HR) function is responsible for recruiting, hiring, developing, and supporting employees. Like finance and accounting, HR supports all the other functional areas in the enterprise. Although managers in other areas are usually closely involved with hiring and training the employees in their respective departments, HR generally oversees these processes and supports the other departments as needed. The HR department is also charged with making sure the company is in compliance with the many laws concerning employee rights and workplace safety.

BUSINESS SERVICES

In addition to these core functions, a wide variety of *business services* exist to help companies with specific needs in law, banking, real estate, and other areas. These services can be performed by in-house staff, external firms, or a combination of the two. For example, a company might have a small permanent legal staff to handle routine business matters such as writing contracts but then engage a specialist law firm to help with a patent application or a major lawsuit. Similarly, all but the smallest companies have accounting professionals on staff to handle routine matters, but companies that sell shares of stock to the public are required to have their financial records *audited* (reviewed) by an outside accounting firm.

 Checkpoint

LEARNING OBJECTIVE 4: Explain the purpose of the six major functional areas in a business enterprise.

SUMMARY: (1) Research and development (R&D) creates the goods and services that a company can manufacture or perform for its customers. (2) Manufacturing, production, or operations is the part of the company where the firm makes whatever it makes or performs whatever services it performs. (3) The related group of functions in marketing, sales, distribution, and customer support are responsible for identifying market opportunities, crafting promotional strategies, and making sure customers are supplied and satisfied with their purchases. (4) Finance and accounting plan for the company's financial needs, control spending, and report on financial matters. (5) Human resources recruits, hires, develops, and supports employees. (6) Various business services provide expertise in law, real estate, and other areas.

CRITICAL THINKING: (1) Do companies that deliver services rather than creating tangible goods ever need to engage in research and development? Why or why not? (2) Why is good customer support essential to the success of marketing and sales activities?

IT'S YOUR BUSINESS: (1) Think of a strongly positive or strongly negative experience you've had with a product or company. What feedback would you like to give the company, and to which functional area would you direct your feedback? (2) Have you already chosen the functional area where you want to work after graduation? If so, what led you to that choice?

KEY TERMS TO KNOW: research and development (R&D), information technology (IT)

5 | **LEARNING OBJECTIVE**

Summarize seven of the most important business professions.

Exploring Careers in Business

Whether you're getting ready to start your career or you've been in the workforce for a while, use this course as an opportunity to explore the many career track options in the world of business. To help stimulate your thinking, this section offers a quick overview of six major business fields.[15] However, don't limit yourself to these six by any means. For just about any professional interest you might have, you can probably find a business-related career to pursue, from entertainment and sports to health care and sciences and everything in between. Also, pay attention to employment trends; as the business environment evolves, employment opportunities in various fields grow and shrink at different rates.

OPERATIONS MANAGER

Operations management encompasses all the people and processes used to create the goods and perform the services that a company sells. The work can involve a wide range of tasks and disciplines, including production engineering, assembly, testing, scheduling, quality assurance, information technology, forecasting, finance, logistics, and customer support. Some degree of technical acumen is always required, and many managers begin their careers in technical positions such as industrial engineering.

The work can be stressful as the organization deals with fluctuating demand levels and with process and supply problems. On the other hand, if you want to balance your business interests with being involved in creating a company's products, one of these management positions might be perfect for you.

HUMAN RESOURCES SPECIALIST

HR specialists and managers plan and direct personnel-related activities, including recruiting, training and development, compensation and benefits, employee and labor relations, and health and safety. In addition, HR managers develop and implement HR systems and practices to accommodate a firm's strategy and to motivate and manage diverse workforces. In the past, top executives and professionals in other functional areas sometimes viewed HR as a tactical function concerned mostly with processing employee records and other nonstrategic duties. However, in many companies, the HR function is becoming more strategic and focused on the global competition to find, attract, and keep the best talent on the market.[16]

INFORMATION TECHNOLOGY MANAGER

Like HR, IT is evolving from a tactical support function into a critical strategic component. Reflecting IT's strategic importance, many midsize and large companies now have a *chief information officer* (CIO) position at the executive level to plot IT strategy. IT specialists design, implement, and maintain systems that help deliver the right information at the right time to the right people in the organization. Jobs in IT typically require a degree in a technical field, but an understanding of business processes, finance, and management is also important, particularly as you move up through the ranks of IT management. Many IT managers and executives also have a business degree, although not all companies require one.[17]

MARKETING SPECIALIST

A wide range of career opportunities exist in the interrelated tasks of identifying and understanding market opportunities and shaping the product, pricing, and communication strategies needed to pursue those opportunities. Whether your interests lie in branding strategy, electronic commerce, advertising, public relations, creative communication, interpersonal relations, or social media, chances are you can find a good fit somewhere in the world of marketing.

Many small companies and virtually all midsize and large companies have a variety of marketing positions, but many of these jobs are also found in advertising agencies, public relations

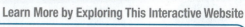

REAL-TIME UPDATES
Learn More by Exploring This Interactive Website

Explore the wide range of career possibilities

The *Occupational Outlook Handbook* gives insider insights and employment projections for hundreds of careers. Go to http://real-timeupdates.com/bia8 and click on Learn More in the Students section.

operations management
Management of the people and processes involved in creating goods and services.

HR specialists help companies recruit and develop the employees who provide essential skills and capabilities.

Racorn/Shutterstock

Sales can be a highly rewarding career path for motivated professionals with solid communication skills.

(PR) firms, and other companies that offer specialized services to clients. Some marketing jobs are highly specialized (advertising copywriter and e-commerce architect, for instance), whereas others encompass many aspects of marketing (brand managers, for example, deal with a variety of marketing and sales functions).

SALES PROFESSIONAL

If you thrive on competition, enjoy solving problems, and get energized by working with a wide range of people, you should definitely consider a career in sales, becoming one of the professionals responsible for building relationships with customers and helping them make purchase decisions. As a consumer, your exposure to sales might be limited to the retail sector of professional selling, but the field is much more diverse. Salespeople sell everything from design services to pharmaceuticals to airliners.

Many salespeople enjoy a degree of day-to-day freedom and flexibility not usually found in office-bound jobs. On the other hand, the pressure is usually intense; few jobs have the immediate indicators of success or failure that sales has, and most salespeople have specific targets, or *quotas*, they are expected to meet.

ACCOUNTANT

If working at the intersection of mathematics and business sounds appealing, a career in accounting or finance could be just right for you. Accounting tasks vary by job and industry, but in general, *management accountants* are responsible for collecting, analyzing, and reporting on financial matters, such as analyzing budgets, assessing the manufacturing costs of new products, and preparing state and federal tax returns. *Internal auditors* verify the work of the company's accounting effort and look for opportunities to improve efficiency and cost-effectiveness. *Public accountants* offer accounting, tax preparation, and investment advice to individuals, companies, and other organizations. *External auditors* verify the financial reports of public companies as required by law, and *forensic accountants* investigate financial crimes.

Accounting professionals need to have an affinity for numbers, analytical minds, and attention to detail. Their work can have wide-ranging effects on investors, employees, and executives, so accuracy and timeliness are critical. Communication skills are important in virtually every accounting function. Computer skills are also increasingly important, particularly for accountants closely involved with the design or operation of accounting systems.

FINANCIAL MANAGER

Financial managers perform a variety of leadership and strategic functions. *Controllers* oversee the preparation of income statements, balance sheets, and other financial reports; they frequently manage accounting departments as well. *Treasurers* and *finance officers* have a more strategic role, establishing long-term financial goals and budgets, investing the firm's funds, and raising capital as needed. Other financial management positions include *credit managers*, who supervise credit accounts established for customers, and *cash managers*, who monitor and control cash flow.

Unlike accounting tasks, for which there is a long tradition of outsourcing, the work of financial managers is generally kept in-house, particularly in midsize and large companies. The work of a financial manager touches every part of the company, so a broad understanding of the various functional areas in business is a key attribute for this position. The ability to communicate with people who aren't financial experts is also vital. Moreover, awareness of information technology developments is important for chief financial officers (CFOs) and other top financial managers, so that they can direct their companies' investments in new or improved accounting systems as needed.

Checkpoint

Achieving Professionalism

As you map out your career, think about what kind of businessperson you want to be. Will you be someone who just puts in the hours and collects a paycheck? Or will you be someone who performs on a higher plane, someone who wants to make a meaningful contribution and be viewed as a true professional? **Professionalism** is the quality of performing at a high level and conducting oneself with purpose and pride. True professionals exhibit seven distinct traits: striving to excel, being dependable and accountable, being a team player, communicating effectively, demonstrating a sense of etiquette, making ethical decisions, and maintaining a positive outlook (see Exhibit 1.8 on the next page).

STRIVING TO EXCEL

Pros are good at what they do, and they never stop improving. No matter what your job might be at any given time—even if it is far from where you aspire to be—strive to perform at the highest possible level. Not only do you have an ethical obligation to give your employer and your customers your best effort, but excelling at each level in your career is the best way to keep climbing up to new positions of responsibility. Plus, being good at what you do delivers a sense of satisfaction that is hard to beat.

In many jobs and in many industries, performing at a high level requires a commitment to continuous learning and improvement. The nature of the work often changes as markets and technologies evolve, and expectations of quality tend to increase over time as well. View this constant change as a positive thing, as a way to avoid stagnation and boredom.

EXHIBIT 1.8	Elements of Professionalism

To develop a reputation as a true professional, develop these seven attributes—and keep improving all the way through your career.

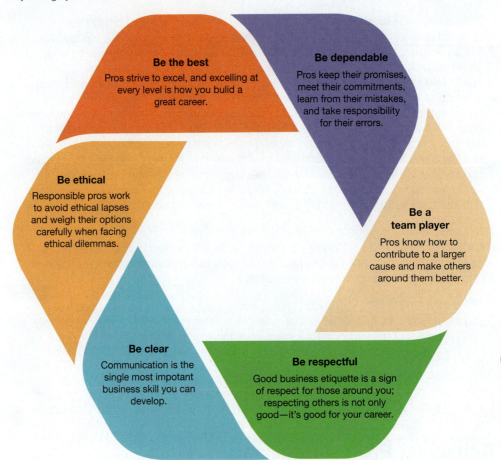

Be the best
Pros strive to excel, and excelling at every level is how you bulid a great career.

Be dependable
Pros keep their promises, meet their commitments, learn from their mistakes, and take responsibility for their errors.

Be ethical
Responsible pros work to avoid ethical lapses and weigh their options carefully when facing ethical dilemmas.

Be a team player
Pros know how to contribute to a larger cause and make others around them better.

Be clear
Communication is the single most impotant business skill you can develop.

Be respectful
Good business etiquette is a sign of respect for those around you; respecting others is not only good—it's good for your career.

BEING DEPENDABLE AND ACCOUNTABLE

Develop a reputation as somebody people can count on. This means meeting your commitments, including staying on schedule and staying within budgets. These are skills that take some time to develop as you gain experience with the amount of time and money required to accomplish various tasks and projects. With experience, you'll learn to be conservative with your commitments. You don't want to be known as someone who overpromises and underdelivers.

Being accountable also means owning up to your mistakes and learning from failure so that you can continue to improve. Pros don't make excuses or blame others. When they make mistakes—and everybody does—they face the situation head on, make amends, and move on.

BEING A TEAM PLAYER

Professionals know that they are contributors to a larger cause, that it's not all about them. Just as in athletics and other team efforts, being a team player in business is something of a balancing act. On the one hand, you need to pay enough attention to your own efforts and skills to make sure you're pulling your own weight. On the other hand, you need to pay attention to the overall team effort to make sure the team succeeds. Remember that if the team fails, you fail, too.

Great team players know how to make those around them more effective, whether it's lending a hand during crunch time, sharing resources, removing obstacles, making introductions, or offering expertise. In fact, the ability to help others improve their performance is one of the key attributes executives look for when they want to promote people into management.

Being a team player also means showing loyalty to your organization and protecting your employer's reputation—one of the most important assets any company has. Pros don't trash their employers in front of customers or in their personal blogs. When they have a problem, they solve it; they don't share it.

COMMUNICATING EFFECTIVELY

If you're looking for a surefire way to stand out from your competition and establish yourself as a competent professional, improving your communication skills may be the most important step you can take. Follow these guidelines to improve your effectiveness as a communicator:

- **Listen actively.** Active listening means making a conscious effort to turn off your own filters and biases to truly hear and understand what someone else is saying.
- **Provide practical information.** Give people useful information that is adapted to their specific needs.
- **Give facts rather than vague impressions.** Use concrete language, specific detail, and supporting information that is clear, convincing, accurate, and ethical.
- **Don't present opinions as facts.** If you are offering an opinion, make sure the audience understands that.
- **Present information in a concise, efficient manner.** Audiences appreciate—and respond more positively to—high-efficiency messages.
- **Clarify expectations and responsibilities.** Clearly state what you expect from your readers or listeners and what you can do for them.
- **Offer compelling, persuasive arguments and recommendations.** Make it clear to people how they will benefit from responding to your messages the way you want them to.

DEMONSTRATING ETIQUETTE

A vital element of professionalism is **etiquette**, the expected norms of behavior in any particular situation. The way you conduct yourself, interact with others, and handle conflict can have a profound influence on your company's success and on your career. Etiquette blunders can have serious financial costs through lower productivity and lost business opportunities.[18] When executives hire and promote you, they expect your behavior to protect the company's reputation. The more you understand such expectations, the better chance you have of avoiding career-damaging mistakes. Moreover, etiquette is an important way to show respect for others and contribute to a smooth-running workplace.

Long lists of etiquette "rules" can be overwhelming, and you'll never be able to memorize all of them. Fortunately, you can count on three principles to get you through any situation: respect, courtesy, and common sense. Moreover, following these principles will encourage forgiveness if you do happen to make a mistake. As you prepare to encounter new situations, take some time to learn the expectations of the other people involved. Travel guidebooks are a great source of information about norms and customs in other countries. Check to see if your library has online access to the CultureGrams database. Don't be afraid to ask questions, either. People will respect your concern and curiosity. You will gradually accumulate considerable knowledge, which will help you feel comfortable and be effective in a wide range of business situations.

etiquette
The expected norms of behavior in any particular situation.

MAKING ETHICAL DECISIONS

True professionals conduct themselves with a clear sense of right and wrong. They avoid committing *ethical lapses,* and they carefully weigh all the options when confronted with *ethical dilemmas.* Chapter 4 discusses these situations in more detail.

MAINTAINING A CONFIDENT, POSITIVE OUTLOOK

Spend a few minutes around successful people in any field, and chances are you'll notice how optimistic they are. They believe in what they're doing, and they believe in themselves and their ability to solve problems and overcome obstacles.

Being positive doesn't mean displaying mindless optimism or spewing happy talk all the time. It means acknowledging that things may be difficult but then buckling down and getting the job done anyway. It means no whining and no slacking off, even when the going gets tough. We live in an imperfect world, no question—jobs can be boring or difficult, customers can be unpleasant, and bosses can be unreasonable. But when you're a pro, you find a way to power through.

Your energy, positive or negative, is contagious. Both in person and online, you'll spend as much time with your colleagues as you spend with family and friends. Personal demeanor is therefore a vital element of workplace harmony. No one expects (or wants) you to be artificially upbeat and bubbly every second of the day, but one negative personality can make an entire office miserable and unproductive. Every person in a company has a responsibility to contribute to a positive, productive work environment.

For the latest information on developing a business mindset and becoming a successful professional, visit **http://real-timeupdates.com/bia8** and click on Chapter 1.

 **Checkpoint**

LEARNING OBJECTIVE 6: Identify seven components of professionalism.

SUMMARY: Professionalism is the quality of performing at a high level and conducting yourself with purpose and pride. Seven key traits of professionalism are striving to excel, being dependable and accountable, being a team player, communicating effectively, demonstrating a sense of etiquette, making ethical decisions, and maintaining a positive outlook.

CRITICAL THINKING: (1) How much loyalty do employees owe to their employers? Explain your answer. (2) Would it be unethical to maintain a positive public persona if you have private doubts about the path your company is pursuing? Why or why not?

IT'S YOUR BUSINESS: (1) In what ways do you exhibit professionalism as a student? (2) You can see plenty of examples of unprofessional business behavior in the news media and in your own consumer and employee experiences. Why should you bother being professional yourself?

KEY TERMS TO KNOW: professionalism, etiquette

 ## BEHIND THE SCENES
YOLANDA DIAZ GROWS MIRADOR ENTERPRISES INTO A MULTIMILLION-DOLLAR SUCCESS STORY

Like millions of people spending their days working for others, Yolanda Diaz of El Paso, Texas, had the dream of striking out on her own. Unlike many dreamers, however, Diaz took the risks and put in the hard work to make her dream a reality. Her

company, Mirador Enterprises, provides facilities maintenance and management services to public-sector customers ranging from local school districts to the U.S. Army and the Department of Homeland Security. A cornerstone of her success is delivering solid value for customers by offering low-risk solutions to everything from routine maintenance to environmental compliance services to archeological site assessments.

As she built her company, Diaz demonstrated principles you read about in this chapter and will study in later chapters. She started with a customer-focused business model and a carefully thought-out business plan—a plan she still follows after more than a decade in business.

To translate those plans into action, she applied good old-fashioned hard work and a valuable combination of work experience and academic preparation. Her degree in accounting from the University of Texas at El Paso and 10 years of experience supervising accounting departments in several other companies taught her what it takes to achieve and maintain profitability. Those jobs also let her hone her management and leadership skills, essential traits for anyone who wants to grow a company.

On the subject of finances, Diaz has a passionate message for anyone who might want to start a company: Take care of your personal finances and your credit score. Banks, investors, strategic partners, suppliers, government agencies, and even customers will investigate your personal credit history to decide whether they want to do business with your company. Even as Mirador grew into a multimillion-dollar operation, banks still wanted evidence that Diaz could manage her personal finances responsibly, taking that as a sign that her business would be able to pay back loans and use lines of credit responsibly. Diaz is particularly keen to make sure college students grasp the importance of smart credit management, because this is the stage in life when many people develop destructive financial habits and set themselves up for years of painful compromises.

Another key message Diaz shares with aspiring entrepreneurs is that you don't have to go it alone. She had years of business experience when she launched Mirador, but she still sought advice and support all along the way, and she continues to network to make connections with potential customers and business partners. She makes a point to help others, too, sharing knowledge and advice with other business owners.

Diaz also took advantage of support offered by the U.S. Small Business Administration (SBA), particularly the SBA's business development assistance for small, disadvantaged businesses. As a minority- and woman-owned company, Mirador qualified for a program that helps entrepreneurs secure contracts to provide goods and services to government agencies. (The SBA has a variety of services available to all entrepreneurs and small business owners. If you're thinking of starting a company, check out what the SBA has to offer at **www.sba.gov**.)

After more than a decade of growth, Diaz's company is well beyond the shaky start-up phase that many new businesses never get past. With several dozen full-time employees and annual revenues exceeding $5 million, Mirador is a testament to the success that hardworking entrepreneurs can achieve with a smart plan, a positive attitude, and the necessary help and resources. Other people think so, too: Diaz and her company have won multiple awards, including recognition from the SBA and the El Paso Hispanic Chamber of Commerce. Perhaps the most important evidence of her success is that most of Mirador's work is repeat business from existing customers—a sure sign that a company is delivering value on competitive terms.

Critical Thinking Questions

1-1. Would Yolanda Diaz have been as successful if she had started her company right out of college, rather than waiting until she'd had a decade of corporate experience? Why or why not?

1-2. If your personal credit is shaky at the moment and you don't have a lot of cash to invest in a new business, what steps could you take to get a new company going?

1-3. Are programs that help specific groups of entrepreneurs, such as the SBA program that helps minority- and woman-owned businesses, fair to those who don't qualify? Explain your answer. (You can read more about this particular program, the "8(a) Business Development Program," on the SBA website.)

LEARN MORE ONLINE

Explore Mirador's website at **www.miradorenterprises.com**. What steps does the company take to present its qualifications to potential customers? What is the purpose of the customer testimonial quotations featured on the website? If you were thinking of starting a business in any industry, what could you learn from Mirador's online presence?

KEY TERMS

barrier to entry (5)
business (3)
business mindset (6)
business model (4)
competitive advantage (4)
economic environment (12)
etiquette (21)
goods-producing businesses (5)
information technology (15)
legal and regulatory
    environment (13)

market environment (13)
not-for-profit organizations (4)
operations management (17)
professionalism (19)
profit (4)
research and development (R&D) (15)
revenue (4)
service businesses (5)
social environment (10)
stakeholders (11)
technological environment (11)

TEST YOUR KNOWLEDGE

Questions for Review

1-4. What is a business model?

1-5. What is moral hazard?

1-6. What are four ways that business can benefit society?

1-7. Do all companies have an R&D function? Explain your answer.

1-8. How does the role of a financial manager differ from the role of an accountant?

1-9. What is professionalism?

Questions for Analysis

⭐ **1-10.** Does a downturn in the economy hurt all companies equally? Provide several examples to support your answer.

1-11. Why is mobile connectivity considered a disruptive technology?

1-12. **Ethical Considerations.** Is managing a business in ways that reflect society's core values always ethical? Explain your answer.

1-13. How can business knowledge and skills help social entrepreneurs reach their goals?

Questions for Application

1-14. How will you be able to apply your experience as a consumer of educational services to the challenges you'll face in your career after graduation?

1-15. What are some of the ways a company in the health-care industry could improve its long-term planning by studying population trends?

⭐ **1-16.** Identify at least five ways in which your life would be different without digital technology. Would it be more or less enjoyable? More or less productive?

⭐ **1-17.** Identify three ways in which the principles of professionalism described in this chapter can make you a more successful student.

EXPAND YOUR KNOWLEDGE

Discovering Career Opportunities

Your college's career center offers numerous resources to help you launch your career. Imagine that you write a blog for students at your college, and you want to introduce them to the center's services. Write a blog post of 300 to 400 words that summarizes what the center can do for students.

Improving Your Tech Insights: Digital Products

The category of digital products encompasses an extremely broad range of product types, from e-books to music and movie files to software and instruction sets for automated machinery. Digital products are commonplace these days, but the ability to remotely deliver product value is quite a staggering concept when you think about it. (As just one example, consider that a single digital music player or smartphone can carry the equivalent of several thousand tapes or CDs.)

Supplying music over the Internet is amazing enough, but today even *tangible* products can be delivered electronically via three-dimensional (3D) printing: The technology that deposits layers of ink in inkjet printers is being adapted to deposit layers of other liquefied materials, including plastics and metals. 3D printers are already being used to "print" product prototypes, architectural models, and a variety of electronic and mechanical components. The price of the technology is dropping far enough that 3D printing is starting to become a possibility for hobbyists, independent inventors, and small businesses. Cubify, maker of the Cube 3D home printer, promotes the ability to make your own toys or jewelry and create parts to repair things around the house.[19]

Choose a category of products that has been changed dramatically by the ability to deliver value digitally. In a brief email message to your instructor, explain how digital technology revolutionized this market segment.

PRACTICE YOUR SKILLS

Sharpening Your Communication Skills

Select a local service business where you have been a customer. How does that business try to gain a competitive advantage in the marketplace? Write a brief summary describing whether the company competes on speed, quality, price, innovation, service, or a combination of those attributes. Be prepared to present your analysis to your classmates.

Building Your Team Skills

In teams assigned by your instructor, each member should first identify one career path (such as marketing or accounting) that he or she might like to pursue and share that choice with the rest of the team. Each team member should then research the others' career options to find at least one significant factor, positive or negative, that could affect someone entering that career. For example, if there are four people on your team, you will research the three careers identified by your three teammates. After the research is complete, convene an in-person or online meeting to give each member of the team an informal career counseling session based on the research findings.

Developing Your Research Skills

Gaining a competitive advantage in today's marketplace is critical to a company's success. Research any company that sounds interesting to you and identify the steps it has taken to create competitive advantages for individual products or the company as a whole.

1-18. What goods or services does the company manufacture or sell?

1-19. How does the company set its goods or services apart from those of its competitors? Does the company compete on price, quality, service, innovation, or some other attribute?

1-20. How do the company's customer communication efforts convey those competitive advantages?

MyBizLab®

Go to the Assignments section of your MyLab to complete these writing exercises.

1-21. If individual accountability is an essential element of professionalism, why is it also important to be an effective team player? Explain your answer.

1-22. Do laws and regulations always restrict or impede the efforts of business professionals, or can they actually help businesses? Explain your answer.

ENDNOTES

1. Mirador Enterprises website, accessed 7 January 2015, www .miradorenterprises.com; "8(a) Business Development Program," U.S. Small Business Administration website, accessed 23 October 2013, www.sba.gov; "Contractor of Year: Mirador Enterprises," *El Paso Times*, 27 May 2010, www.elpasotimes.com; Chris Lechuga, "Entrepreneur Profile: Diaz Knows Hard Work Leads to Success," *El Paso Times*, 7 November 2010, www.elpasotimes.com.

2. "Employment by Major Industry Sector," U.S. Bureau of Labor Statistics, accessed 7 February 2015, www.bls.gov; "Value Added by Industry Group as a Percentage of GDP," accessed 7 February 2015, www.bea.gov.

3. "SOI Tax Stats—Integrated Business Data."

4. Cheryl Winokur Munk, "4 Generations," *Community Banker*, January 2009, 30–33.

5. "The Mobile Revolution Is Just Beginning," press release, World Economic Forum, 13 September 2013, www.weforum.org.

6. Maribel Lopez, "Three Trends That Change Business: Mobile, Social and Cloud," *Forbes*, 28 January 2012, www.forbes.com.

7. Kevin Custis, "Three Ways Business Can Be Successful on Mobile," *Forbes*, 15 November 2013, www.forbes.com; "IBM Survey: Speed and Analytics Key Drivers in Mobile Adoption for Organizations," press release, IBM, 19 November 2013, www.ibm.com.

8. "More Than Nine in 10 Internet Users Will Go Online via Phone," eMarketer, 6 January 2014, www.emarketer.com.

9. Christina "CK" Kerley, *The Mobile Revolution & B2B*, white paper, 2011, www.b2bmobilerevolution.com.

10. Jordie can Rijn, "The Ultimate Mobile Email Statistics Overview," Emailmonday.com, accessed 9 February 2014, www.emailmonday.com.

11. Jessica Lee, "46% of Searchers Now Use Mobile Exclusively to Research [Study]," Search Engine Watch, 1 May 2013, http://searchenginewatch.com.

12. Dennis McCafferty, "10 Awesome Facts About the Mobile Revolution," *CIO Insight*, 6 December 2013, www.cioinsight.com.

13. Nicco Mele, *The End of Big: How the Internet Makes David the New Goliath* (New York: St. Martin's Press: 2013), 1–2.

14. "JWT's 13 Mobile Trends for 2013 and Beyond," J. Walter Thompson website, 2 April 2013, www.jwt.com.

15. Career profiles in this section adapted from U.S. Bureau of Labor Statistics, *Occupational Outlook Handbook, 2008–2009 Edition*, www.bls.gov/oco.

16. Kris Dunn, "The Five Sweetest Jobs in HR and Talent Management," *Workforce*, July 2008, www.workforce.com.

17. Meredith Levinson, "Should You Get an MBA?" *CIO*, 5 July 2007, www.cio.com.

18. Susan G. Hauser, "The Degeneration of Decorum," *Workforce Management*, January 2011, 16–18, 20–21.

19. Cubify website, accessed 7 February 2015, http://cubify.com.

Understanding Basic Economics

LEARNING OBJECTIVES   After studying this chapter, you will be able to

1. Define *economics,* and explain why scarcity is central to economic decision making.

2. Differentiate among the major types of economic systems.

3. Explain the interaction between demand and supply.

4. Identify four macroeconomic issues that are essential to understanding the behavior of the economy.

5. Outline the debate over deregulation, and identify four key roles that governments play in the economy.

6. Identify the major ways of measuring economic activity.

BEHIND THE SCENES COULD YOU PREDICT SALES OF APPLE'S NEXT BESTSELLER?

David Paul Morris/Bloomberg/Getty Images

Apple's Jeff Williams oversees global operations for the company's popular iPod and iPhone product lines.

www.apple.com

Predicting demand for a new product or a new business is one of the toughest decisions managers and entrepreneurs need to make. How can you determine how many people are likely to buy a new car model, business service, industrial machine, or mobile phone? If you guess too high, you could end up losing money after investing in unwanted inventory, underused distribution channels, or overstaffed departments. If you guess too low, you could stress your supply chain and service delivery systems and annoy potential customers who want to buy from you but can't because you aren't prepared to meet demand, and these customers might jump to a competitor who can meet their needs.

Forecasting product demand accurately requires a combination of economic data analysis, experience-driven judgment, and plain old luck. However, even the data analysis component requires a heavy dose of judgment because you have to decide which economic variables are relevant and how to factor them into your forecasting. If you're trying to decide whether to open a coffee shop near campus, for example, and you see that unemployment has dropped in your city, will that mean more demand for your coffee because more people have disposable income or less demand because fewer people have time to hang out in coffee shops?

Now imagine you're in the shoes of Jeff Williams, the senior vice president in charge of operations at Apple. In this role, you oversee production of the company's wildly popular iPhones, and your job includes trying to align production resources with anticipated sales demand. You're responsible for both sides of the equation: Coming up with an accurate idea of demand and making sure the vast Apple supply and manufacturing chain can build enough products to meet that demand in a timely fashion.

Your latest supply-and-demand challenge is the iPhone6. Previous generations of the iPhone have sold many, many millions of units, and surveys indicate that consumer interest in the iPhone6 appears to be through the roof. However, you know from experience that the stated intent to buy a new product doesn't necessarily translate into actual purchases. How can you be sure you've read market demand accurately and lined up the necessary production resources?[1]

INTRODUCTION

From a local coffee shop to a global giant such as Apple (profiled in the chapter-opening Behind the Scenes) economic forces affect every aspect of business. This chapter offers a brief introduction to economics from a business professional's perspective, a high-level look at the study of economics, types of economic systems, and the interaction of supply and demand. Understanding basic economic principles is essential to successful business management, and this knowledge can make you a more satisfied consumer and a more successful investor as well.

What Is This Thing Called the Economy?

The **economy** is the sum total of all the economic activity within a given region, from a single city to a whole country to the entire world. The economy can be a difficult thing to get your mind wrapped around because it is so complex, constantly in motion, a subject of heated dispute, and at times hard to see—even though it's everywhere around us. People who devote their lives to studying it can have a hard time agreeing on how the economy works, when it might be "broken," or how to fix it if it is broken. However, business leaders need to understand and pay attention to some key principles.

Economics is the study of how a society uses its scarce resources to produce and distribute goods and services. Economics is roughly divided into a small-scale perspective and a large-scale perspective. The study of economic behavior among consumers, businesses, and industries that collectively determine the quantity of goods and services demanded and supplied at different prices is termed **microeconomics**. The study of a country's larger economic issues, such as how firms compete, the effect of government policies, and how an economy maintains and allocates its scarce resources, is termed **macroeconomics**.

Although microeconomics looks at the small picture and macroeconomics looks at the big picture, understanding the economy at either scale requires an understanding of how the small and large forces interact. For instance, numerous macro forces and policies determine whether homeowners can afford to install solar energy systems. In turn, the aggregate behavior of all those homeowners at the micro level affects the vitality and direction of the overall economy.

FACTORS OF PRODUCTION

Each society must decide how to use its economic resources, or *factors of production* (see Exhibit 2.1 on the next page). **Natural resources** are things that are useful in their natural state, such as land, forests, minerals, and water. **Human resources** are people and their individual talents and capacities. **Capital** includes money, machines, tools, and buildings that a business needs in order to produce goods and services. **Entrepreneurship** is the spirit of innovation, the initiative, and the willingness to take the risks involved in creating and operating businesses. **Knowledge** is the collective intelligence of an organization. *Knowledge workers*, employees whose primary contribution is the acquisition and application of business knowledge, are a key economic resource for businesses in today's economy.

Traditionally, a business or a country was considered to have an advantage if its location offered plentiful supplies of natural resources, human resources, capital, and entrepreneurs. In today's global marketplace, however, intellectual assets are often the key.

1 **LEARNING OBJECTIVE**

Define *economics,* and explain why scarcity is central to economic decision making.

economy
The sum total of all the economic activity within a given region.

economics
The study of how a society uses its scarce resources to produce and distribute goods and services.

microeconomics
The study of how consumers, businesses, and industries collectively determine the quantity of goods and services demanded and supplied at different prices.

macroeconomics
The study of "big-picture" issues in an economy, including competitive behavior among firms, the effect of government policies, and overall resource allocation issues.

natural resources
Land, forests, minerals, water, and other tangible assets usable in their natural state.

human resources
All the people who work in an organization or on its behalf.

capital
The funds that finance the operations of a business as well as the physical, human-made elements used to produce goods and services, such as factories and computers.

entrepreneurship
The combination of innovation, initiative, and willingness to take the risks required to create and operate new businesses.

knowledge
Expertise gained through experience or association.

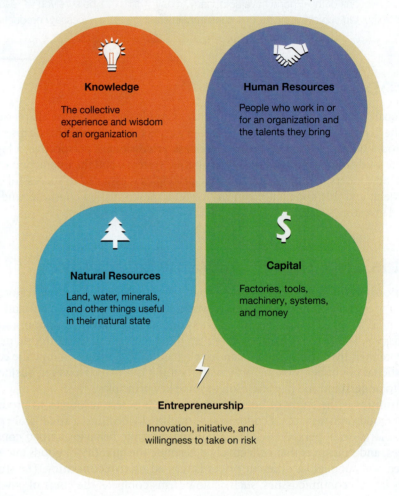

EXHIBIT 2.1   **Factors of Production**

Every good or service is created from some combination of these five factors of production.

Knowledge

The collective experience and wisdom of an organization

Human Resources

People who work in or for an organization and the talents they bring

Natural Resources

Land, water, minerals, and other things useful in their natural state

Capital

Factories, tools, machinery, systems, and money

Entrepreneurship

Innovation, initiative, and willingness to take on risk

Companies can easily obtain capital from one part of the world, purchase supplies from another, and locate production facilities in still another. They can relocate some of their operations to wherever they find a steady supply of affordable workers, or they can assemble virtual teams of knowledge workers from anywhere on the planet. Chapter 3 discusses this issue of economic globalization in more detail.

THE ECONOMIC IMPACT OF SCARCITY

scarcity
A condition of any productive resource that has finite supply.

The impact of **scarcity**, meaning that a given resource has a finite supply, is fundamental to understanding economics.[2] Looking back over the factors of production, you can see that the supply of all these resources is limited. Even entrepreneurial energy is limited in the sense that there are only so many entrepreneurs in the economy, and each entrepreneur can accomplish only so much during a given time span.

Scarcity has two powerful effects: It creates competition for resources, and it forces trade-offs on the part of every participant in the economy. First, at every stage of economic activity, people and organizations compete for the resources they need. Businesses and industries compete with each other for materials, employees, and customers. As a consumer, you compete with other consumers. If you were the only person in town who needed a loaf of bread, you would have tremendous power over the bakeries and grocery stores as the only customer. However, because you compete with thousands of other consumers for a limited supply of bread, you have far less control over the bread market.

Second, this universal scarcity of resources means that consumers, companies, and governments are constantly forced to make *trade-offs*, having to give up one thing to get something else. You have to decide how to spend the 24 hours you have every day, and every choice involves a trade-off: The more time you spend on one activity means less time for every other activity you could possibly pursue. Businesses must make similar trade-offs, such as deciding how much money to spend on advertising a new product versus how much to spend on the materials used to make it, or deciding how many employees to have in sales versus in customer support. Just like you, businesses never have enough time, money, and other resources to accomplish what they'd like to, so success in life and in business is largely a matter of making smart trade-offs.

By the way, economists have a name for the most-attractive option not selected when making a trade-off. **Opportunity cost** refers to the value of the most appealing alternative from all those that weren't chosen.[3] In other words, opportunity cost is a way to measure the value of what you gave up when you pursued a different opportunity.

opportunity cost
The value of the most appealing alternative not chosen.

✓ Checkpoint

LEARNING OBJECTIVE 1: Define *economics*, and explain why scarcity is central to economic decision making.

SUMMARY: Economics is the study of how individuals, companies, and governments use scarce resources to produce the goods and services that meet a society's needs. Scarcity is a crucial concept in economics because it creates competition for resources and forces everyone to make trade-offs.

CRITICAL THINKING: (1) Why is entrepreneurship considered a factor of production? (2) If you had an unlimited amount of money, would you ever need to make trade-offs again? Why or why not?

IT'S YOUR BUSINESS: (1) Did you consider opportunity cost when you chose the college or university you are currently attending? (2) What trade-offs did you make in order to read this chapter at this exact moment in your life? (Think about the decisions you made to get to a point in your life where you're taking a business course.)

KEY TERMS TO KNOW: economy, economics, microeconomics, macroeconomics, natural resources, human resources, capital, entrepreneurship, knowledge, scarcity, opportunity cost

Economic Systems

The roles that individuals, businesses, and the government play in allocating a society's resources depend on the society's **economic system**, the basic set of rules for allocating resources to satisfy its citizens' needs (see Exhibit 2.2 on the next page). Economic systems are generally categorized as either *free-market systems* or *planned systems*, although these are really theoretical extremes; every economy combines aspects of both approaches.

FREE-MARKET SYSTEMS

In a **free-market system**, individuals and companies are largely free to decide what products to produce, how to produce them, whom to sell them to, and at what price to sell them. In other words, they have the chance to succeed—or fail—by their own efforts. **Capitalism** and *private enterprise* are the terms most often used to describe the free-market system, one in which private parties (individuals, partnerships, or corporations) own and operate the majority of businesses and where competition, supply, and demand determine which goods and services are produced.

2   LEARNING OBJECTIVE

Differentiate among the major types of economic systems.

economic system
The policies that define a society's particular economic structure; the rules by which a society allocates economic resources.

free-market system
Economic system in which decisions about what to produce and in what quantities are decided by the market's buyers and sellers.

capitalism
Economic system based on economic freedom and competition.

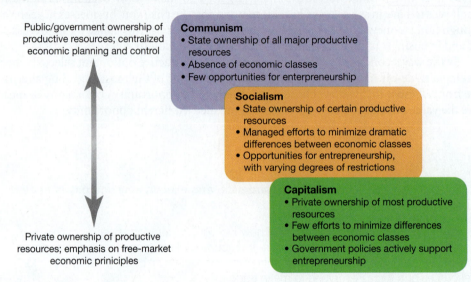

EXHIBIT 2.2   **Economic Systems**

All economic systems are based on certain fundamental principles about how a country should allocate its resources to satisfy the needs of its citizens. Except at the theoretical extremes, the distinctions between systems tend to be blurry, and arguments continue over the precise definition of each system. Most modern economies exhibit a combination of capitalism and socialism. Here are a few of the characteristics that distinguish the three major systems.

Public/government ownership of productive resources; centralized economic planning and control

Communism
- State ownership of all major productive resources
- Absence of economic classes
- Few opportunities for enterpreneurship

Socialism
- State ownership of certain productive resources
- Managed efforts to minimize dramatic differences between economic classes
- Opportunities for entrepreneurship, with varying degrees of restrictions

Capitalism
- Private ownership of most productive resources
- Few efforts to minimize differences between economic classes
- Government policies actively support entrepreneurship

Private ownership of productive resources; emphasis on free-market economic prinicples

In practice, however, no economy is truly "free" in the sense that anyone can do whatever he or she wants to do. Local, state, national, and even international governments such as the European Union intervene in the economy to accomplish goals that leaders deem socially or economically desirable. This practice of limited intervention is characteristic of a *mixed economy* or *mixed capitalism*, which is the economic system of the United States and most other countries. For example, government bodies intervene in the U.S. economy in a variety of ways, such as influencing particular allocations of resources through tax incentives, prohibiting or restricting the sale of certain goods and services, or setting *price controls*. Price controls can involve maximum allowable prices (such as limiting rent increases) and minimum allowable prices (such as supplementing the prices of agricultural goods to ensure producers a minimum level of income or establishing minimum wage levels).[4]

REAL-TIME UPDATES

Learn More by Reading This Article

Is a higher minimum wage really the job killer some claim it to be?

Washington State has the highest minimum wage in the country and some of the strongest job growth. Explore the debate. Go to http://real-timeupdates.com/bia8 and click on Learn More in the Students section.

PLANNED SYSTEMS

planned system
Economic system in which the government controls most of the factors of production and regulates their allocation.

In a **planned system**, governments largely control the allocation of resources and limit freedom of choice in order to accomplish government goals. Because social equality is a major goal of planned systems, private enterprise and the pursuit of private gain are generally regarded as wasteful and exploitive. The planned system that allows individuals the least degree of economic freedom is *communism*, which still exists in a few countries, most notably North Korea and China. As an economic system, communism can't be regarded as anything but a dismal failure. In fact, even as its government remains strongly communist from a political perspective, China has embraced many concepts of capitalism in recent years and has become one of the world's most powerful and important economies as a result.

socialism
Economic system characterized by public ownership and operation of key industries combined with private ownership and operation of less-vital industries.

Socialism lies somewhere between capitalism and communism, with a fairly high degree of government planning and some government ownership of capital resources. However, government ownership tends to be focused on industries considered vital to the common welfare, such as transportation, health care, and communications. Private own-ership is permitted in other industries.

Although "socialism" is sometimes used as a pejorative term in today's heated political and economic dialogues, and many people believe capitalism is inherently superior to socialism, that opinion is not universal. For example, many European countries, including economic heavyweights France and Germany, incorporate vary-ing degrees of socialism.

Moreover, although free-market capitalism remains the foundation of the U.S. econ-omy, some important elements of the U.S. economy are socialized and have been for many years. Public schools, much of the transportation infrastructure, various local and regional utilities, and several major health-care programs all fit the economic definition of socialism. Socialism and capitalism are competing philosophies, but they are not mutu-ally exclusive, and each approach has strengths and weaknesses, which is why most mod-ern economies combine aspects of both.

NATIONALIZATION AND PRIVATIZATION

The line between socialism and capitalism isn't always easy to define, and it doesn't always stay in the same place, either. Governments can change the structure of the economy by **nationalizing**—taking ownership of—selected companies or in extreme cases even entire industries. They can also move in the opposite direction, **privatizing** services once performed by the government by allowing private businesses to perform them instead.

In recent years, governments of various countries have done both, for different rea-sons and in different industries. For example, private companies now own or operate a number of highways, bridges, ports, prisons, and other infrastructure elements in the United States, providing services once provided by the government. The primary reason for this trend is the belief that private firms motivated by the profit incentive can do a more efficient job of running these facilities.[5]

nationalizing
A government's takeover of selected companies or industries.

privatizing
Turning over services once performed by the government to private businesses.

✔ ## Checkpoint

LEARNING OBJECTIVE 2: Differentiate among the major types of economic systems.

SUMMARY: The two basic types of economic systems are free-market systems, in which individuals and companies are largely free to make economic decisions, and planned systems, in which government administrators make all major decisions. The terms *capitalism* and *private enterprise* are often used to describe free-market sys-tems. Communism is the most extreme type of planned system; socialism lies some-where between capitalism and communism and generally refers to government own-ership of fundamental services. The U.S. economy, like virtually all other economies, blends elements of free-market capitalism and government control.

CRITICAL THINKING: (1) Why are no economies truly free, in the sense of having no controls or restrictions? (2) What are some possible risks of privatizing basic services such as the transportation infrastructure?

IT'S YOUR BUSINESS: (1) What are your emotional reactions to the terms *capitalism* and *socialism*? Explain why you feel the way you do. (2) Would you rather pay lower taxes and accept the fact that you need to pay for many services such as health care and education or pay higher taxes with the assurance that the government will provide many basic services for you? Why?

KEY TERMS TO KNOW: economic system, free-market system, capitalism, planned system, socialism, nationalizing, privatizing

demand
Buyers' willingness and ability to purchase products at various price points.

supply
A specific quantity of a product that the seller is able and willing to provide at various prices.

demand curve
A graph of the quantities of a product that buyers will purchase at various prices.

The Forces of Demand and Supply

At the heart of every business transaction is an exchange between a buyer and a seller. The buyer wants or needs a particular service or good and is willing to pay the seller in order to obtain it. The seller is willing to participate in the transaction because of the anticipated financial gains. In a free-market system, the marketplace (composed of individuals, firms, and industries) and the forces of demand and supply determine the quantity of goods and services produced and the prices at which they are sold. **Demand** refers to the amount of a good or service that customers will buy at a given time at various prices. **Supply** refers to the quantities of a good or service that producers will provide on a particular date at various prices. In other words, *demand* refers to the behavior of buyers, whereas *supply* refers to the behavior of sellers. The two forces work together to impose a kind of dynamic order on the free-market system.

UNDERSTANDING DEMAND

The airline industry offers a helpful demonstration of supply and demand. A **demand curve** is a graph that shows the amount of product that buyers will purchase at various prices, all other factors being equal. Demand curves typically slope downward, implying that as price drops, more people are willing to buy. The black line labeled *Initial demand* in Exhibit 2.3 shows a possible demand curve for the monthly number of economy tickets on one airline's Chicago-to-Denver route. You can see that as price decreases, demand increases, and vice versa. If demand is strong, airlines can keep their prices consistent or perhaps even raise them. If demand weakens, they can lower prices to stimulate more purchases. (Airlines use sophisticated *yield management* software to constantly adjust prices in order to keep average ticket prices as high as possible while also keeping their planes as full as possible.)

This movement up and down the demand curve is only part of the story, however. Demand at all price points can also increase or decrease in response to a variety of factors. If overall demand for air travel decreases, the entire demand curve moves to the left (the

EXHIBIT 2.3	**Demand Curve**

The demand curve (black line) for economy seats on one airline's Chicago-to-Denver route shows that the higher the ticket price, the smaller the quantity of seats demanded, and vice versa. Overall demand is rarely static; however, market conditions can shift the entire curve to the left (decreased demand at every price, red line) or to the right (increased demand at every price, green line).

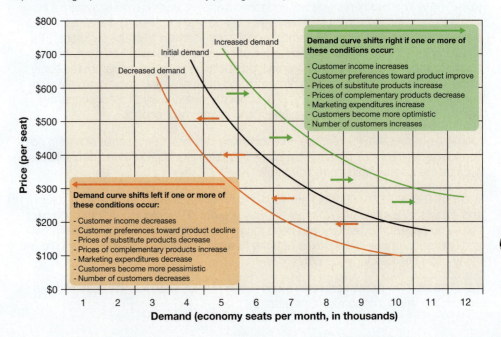

red line in Exhibit 2.3). If overall demand increases, the curve moves to the right (the green line). The bulleted lists in Exhibit 2.3 indicate the effects of some of the major factors that can cause overall demand to increase or decrease:

- Customer income
- Customer preferences toward the product (fears regarding airline safety, for example)
- The price of *substitute products* (products that can be purchased instead of air travel, including rail tickets, automobile travel, or web conferencing)
- The price of *complementary products* (such as hotel accommodations or restaurant dining for the airline industry)
- Marketing expenditures (for advertising and other promotional efforts)
- Customer expectations about future prices and their own financial well-being

For example, if the economy is down and businesses and consumers have less money to spend, overall demand for air travel is likely to shrink. Businesses will seek less-expensive substitutes, such as videoconferencing and online meetings, and consumers may vacation closer to home so they can travel by car. Conversely, if customers have more money to spend, more of them are likely to travel, thereby increasing overall demand.

UNDERSTANDING SUPPLY

Demand alone is not enough to explain how a company operating in a free-market system sets its prices or production levels. In general, a firm's willingness to produce and sell a product increases as the price it can charge and its profit potential per item increase. In other words, as the price goes up, the quantity supplied generally goes up. The depiction of the relationship between prices and quantities that sellers will offer for sale, regardless of demand, is called a **supply curve**.

Movement along the supply curve typically slopes upward: As prices rise, the quantity that sellers are willing to supply also rises. Similarly, as prices decline, the quantity that sellers are willing to supply declines. Exhibit 2.4 shows a possible supply curve for the

supply curve
A graph of the quantities of a product that sellers will offer for sale, regardless of demand, at various prices.

EXHIBIT 2.4	Supply Curve

This supply curve for economy seats on the Denver-to-Chicago route shows that the higher the price, the more tickets (seats) the airline would be willing to supply, all else being equal. As with demand, however, the entire supply curve can shift to the left (decreased supply) or the right (increased supply) as producers respond to internal and external forces.

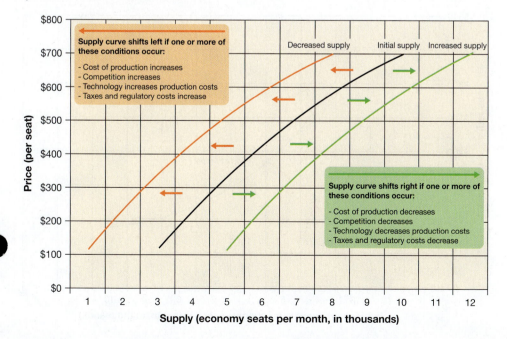

monthly number of economy tickets (seats) supplied on an airline's Chicago-to-Denver route at different prices. The graph shows that increasing prices for economy tickets on that route should increase the number of tickets (seats) an airline is willing to provide for that route, and vice versa.

As with demand, supply is dynamic and is affected by a variety of internal and external factors. They include the cost of inputs (such as wages, fuel, and airport gate fees for the airlines), the number of competitors in the marketplace, and advancements in technology that allow companies to operate more efficiently. A change in any of these variables can shift the entire supply curve, either increasing or decreasing the amount offered at various prices, as Exhibit 2.4 suggests.

UNDERSTANDING HOW DEMAND AND SUPPLY INTERACT

Buyers and sellers clearly have opposite goals: Buyers want to buy at the lowest possible price, and sellers want to sell at the highest possible price. Neither side can "win" this contest outright. Customers might want to pay $100 for a ticket from Chicago to Denver, but airlines aren't willing to sell many, if any, at that price. Conversely, the airlines might want to charge $1,000 for a ticket, but customers aren't willing to buy many, if any, at that price. So the market in effect arranges a compromise known as the **equilibrium point**, at which the demand and supply curves intersect (see Exhibit 2.5). At the equilibrium price point, customers are willing to buy as many tickets as the airline is willing to sell.

equilibrium point
The point at which quantity supplied equals quantity demanded.

Because the supply and demand curves are dynamic, so is the equilibrium point. As variables affecting supply and demand change, so will the equilibrium price. For example, increased concerns about airline safety could encourage some travelers to choose alternatives such as automobile travel or web conferencing, thus reducing the demand for air travel at every price and moving the equilibrium point as well. Suppliers might respond to such a reduction in demand by either cutting the number of flights offered or lowering ticket prices in order to restore the equilibrium level.

REAL-TIME UPDATES
Learn More by Listening to This Podcast

A closer look at the equilibrium point

See how the equilibrium point represents a balance between supply and demand. Go to http://real-timeupdates.com/bia8 and click on Learn More in the Students section.

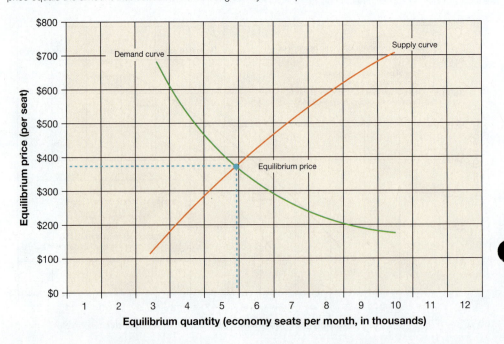

EXHIBIT 2.5   The Relationship Between Supply and Demand

The equilibrium price is established when the amount of a product that suppliers are willing to sell at a given price equals the amount that consumers are willing to buy at that price.

As the iPhone6 story at the beginning of the chapter pointed out, questions of supply, demand, and equilibrium pricing are among the toughest issues managers and entrepreneurs face. For example, imagine you're a concert promoter planning for next year's summer season. You have to balance the potential demand for each performer across a range of prices, in the hope of matching the supply you can deliver (the seating capacity of each venue and the number of shows). You have to make these predictions months in advance and make financial commitments based on your predictions. Predict well, and you'll make a tidy profit. Predict poorly, and you could lose a pile of money.

✓ **Checkpoint**

LEARNING OBJECTIVE 3: Explain the interaction between demand and supply.

SUMMARY: *Demand* is the amount of a good or service that customers will buy at a given time at various prices; it can be shown visually as a *demand curve*. The entire demand curve can shift as market conditions change. Similarly, *supply* is the amount of a good or service that producers will provide on a particular date at various prices; it can be shown with a *supply curve*, which can also shift in response to market forces. In the simplest sense, demand and supply affect price in the following manner: When the price goes up, the quantity demanded goes down, but the supplier's incentive to produce more goes up. When the price goes down, the quantity demanded increases, but the quantity supplied may (or may not) decline. The point at which the demand and supply curves intersect—the point at which demand and supply are equal—is the *equilibrium point*.

CRITICAL THINKING: (1) How does the interaction of demand and supply keep a market in balance, at least approximately and temporarily? (2) If the prices of complementary products for a given product go up, what effect is this increase likely to have on demand for that product?

IT'S YOUR BUSINESS: (1) Are there any products or brands you are so loyal to that you will purchase them at almost any price? Will you accept less-expensive substitutes? (2) Have you ever purchased something simply because it was on sale? Why or why not?

KEY TERMS TO KNOW: demand, supply, demand curve, supply curve, equilibrium point

The Macro View: Understanding How an Economy Operates

All the individual instances of supply and demand and all the thousands and millions of transactions that take place over time add up to the economy. This section explores four "big-picture" issues that are essential to understanding the overall behavior of the economy: competition in a free-market system, business cycles, unemployment, and inflation.

COMPETITION IN A FREE-MARKET SYSTEM

Competition is the situation in which two or more suppliers of a product are rivals in the pursuit of the same customers. The nature of competition varies widely by industry, product category, and geography (see Exhibit 2.6 on the next page). At one extreme is **pure competition**, in which no single firm becomes large enough to influence prices and thereby distort the workings of the free-market system. At the other extreme, in a **monopoly**, one supplier so thoroughly dominates a market that it can control prices and essentially shut out other competitors. Monopolies can happen "naturally," as companies innovate or markets evolve (a *pure monopoly*) or by government mandate (a *regulated monopoly*). However, the lack of competition in a monopoly situation is considered so detrimental

---

4 **LEARNING OBJECTIVE**

Identify four macroeconomic issues that are essential to understanding the behavior of the economy.

competition
Rivalry among businesses for the same customers.

pure competition
A situation in which so many buyers and sellers exist that no single buyer or seller can individually influence market prices.

monopoly
A situation in which one company dominates a market to the degree that it can control prices.

EXHIBIT 2.6　Categories of Competition

Markets vary widely in the nature of competition they exhibit and the choices that buyers have. Here are five major categories of competition and the factors that distinguish them.

Pure Competition	Monopolistic Competition	Oligopoly	Pure Monopoly	Regulated Monopoly
Characteristics: • Many small suppliers • Virtually identical products • Low barriers to entry	**Characteristics:** • Can have few or many suppliers, of varying size • Products can be distinguished but are similar enough to be replacements • Variable barriers to entry but market open to all	**Characteristics:** • Small number of suppliers, even as few as just two (a *duopoly*) • Products can be distinguished in important ways, but replacements are still available • Barriers to entry tend to be high, making entering the market difficult	**Characteristics:** • Only one supplier in a given market • Monopoly achieved without government intervention, by innovation, specialization, exclusive contracts, or a simple lack of competitors • Products are unique, with no direct replacements available • Barriers to entry are extremely high, making entering the market difficult or impossible	**Characteristics:** • Only one supplier in a given market • Monopoly granted by government mandate, such as a license to provide cable TV and Internet service • No product competition is allowed • Barriers to entry are infinitely high; new competitors are not allowed
Price competition: • No single firm can grow large enough to influence prices across the market	**Price competition:** • Firms that excel in one or more aspects can gain some control over pricing	**Price competition:** • Individual firms can have considerable control over pricing	**Price competition:** • Suppliers can charge as much as they want, at least until people stop buying	**Price competition:** • Prices are set by government mandate
Buyers' choices: • Extensive	**Buyers' choices:** • Extensive	**Buyers' choices:** • Limited	**Buyers' choices:** • None	**Buyers' choices:** • None

monopolistic competition
A situation in which many sellers differentiate their products from those of competitors in at least some small way.

oligopoly
A market situation in which a small number of suppliers, sometimes only two, provide a particular good or service.

to a free-market economy that monopolies are often prohibited by law (see "Merger and Acquisition Approvals" on page 41).

Most of the competition in advanced free-market economies is **monopolistic competition**, in which numerous sellers offer products that can be distinguished from competing products in at least some small way. The risk/reward nature of capitalism promotes constant innovation in pursuit of competitive advantage, rewarding companies that do the best job of satisfying customers.

When the number of competitors in a market is quite small, a situation known as **oligopoly** is created. In an oligopoly, customers have some choice, unlike in a monopoly, but not as many choices as in monopolistic competition.

REAL-TIME UPDATES
Learn More by Reading This Article

Why aren't wages rising faster?

Employment in the United States has grown briskly in the past couple of years as the economy recovers from the Great Recession, but economists are having a hard time explaining why wages haven't risen much at all. Go to http://real-timeupdates.com/bia8 and click on Learn More in the Students section.

BUSINESS CYCLES

The economy is always in a state of change, expanding or contracting in response to the combined effects of factors such as technological breakthroughs, changes in investment patterns, shifts in consumer attitudes, world events, and basic economic forces. *Economic expansion* occurs when the economy is growing and consumers are spending more money, which stimulates higher employment and wages, which then stimulate more consumer purchases. *Economic contraction* occurs when such spending declines, employment drops, and the economy as a whole slows down.

If the period of downward swing is severe, the nation may enter into a **recession**, traditionally defined as two consecutive quarters of decline in the *gross domestic product* (see page 44), which is a basic measure of a country's economic output. A deep and prolonged recession can be considered a *depression*, which doesn't have an official definition but is generally considered to involve a catastrophic collapse of financial markets.

When a downward swing or recession is over, the economy enters into a period of recovery. These up-and-down swings are commonly known as **business cycles**, although this term is somewhat misleading because real economies do not expand and contract in regular and predictable "cycles." *Economic fluctuations* is a more accurate way to characterize the economy's real behavior (see Exhibit 2.7).[6]

UNEMPLOYMENT

Unemployment is one of the most serious effects of economic contraction. It is traumatic at a personal level for idle workers and their families, and the decrease in the number of active workers affects the overall economy in terms of lost output.[7] Moreover, unemployed workers increase the financial burden on state governments when they collect unemployment benefit payments.

The **unemployment rate** indicates the percentage of the *labor force* currently without employment. The labor force consists of people ages 16 and older who are either working or looking for jobs.[8] Not all cases of unemployment are the same, however. As Exhibit 2.8 on the next page explains, each of the four types of unemployment—*frictional, structural, cyclical,* and *seasonal*—has unique implications for business and political leaders.

INFLATION

Like almost everything else in the economy, prices of goods and services rarely stay the same for very long. **Inflation** is a steady rise in the average prices of goods and services throughout the economy. **Deflation**, on the other hand, is a sustained fall in average prices. Inflation is a major concern for consumers, businesses, and government leaders

recession
A period during which national income, employment, and production all fall; defined as at least six months of decline in the GDP.

business cycles
Fluctuations in the rate of growth that an economy experiences over a period of several years.

unemployment rate
The portion of the labor force (everyone over 16 who has or is looking for a job) currently without a job.

inflation
An economic condition in which prices rise steadily throughout the economy.

deflation
An economic condition in which prices fall steadily throughout the economy.

EXHIBIT 2.7	Fluctuations in the U.S. Economy

The U.S. economy has a long history of expansion and contraction. This chart shows the year-to-year change (as a percentage of the previous year) in *gross domestic product* (see page 44), a key measure of the country's overall economic output. (Note that because this chart shows *percentage changes*, not absolute output, all the bars above zero represent years of economic expansion, even though a bar might be smaller than the one preceding. All the bars below zero represent years of contraction.)

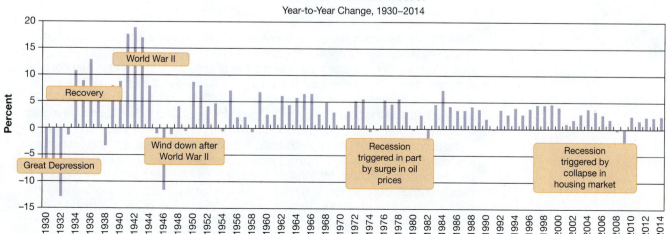

U.S. Gross Domestic Product
Year-to-Year Change, 1930–2014

Source: Data from U.S. Bureau of Economic Analysis, National Income and Product Accounts Tables, 27 February 2015, www.bea.gov.

EXHIBIT 2.8 **Types of Unemployment**

Economists identify four types of unemployment, each with unique causes and concerns.

Frictional Unemployment
- The "natural" flow of workers into and out of jobs, such as when a person leaves one job without first lining up a new job
- Always some level of frictional unemployment in the economy

Structural Unemployment
- A mismatch between workers' skills and current employer needs
- Workers can't find jobs that match their qualifications, and employers can't find employees with the skills their job openings require
- A never-ending concern as changes in the external environments of business make some skills obsolete and create demand for new skills

Cyclical Unemployment
- Caused by economic fluctuations
- Occurs when demand for goods and services drops, businesses reduce production, thereby requiring fewer workers
- An increasing number of people who want to work can't find jobs
- During catastrophic depressions, can run as high as 20 or 25 percent

Seasonal Unemployment
- Predictable increases and decreases in the need for workers in industries with seasonal fluctuations in customer demand
- Common in agriculture, leisure and entertainment, retailing, and accounting services

Source: Data from Roger LeRoy Miller, *Economics Today*, 15th ed. (Boston: Addison-Wesley, 2010), 164–165.

because of its effect on *purchasing power*, or the amount of a good or service you can buy for a given amount of money. When prices go up, purchasing power goes down. If wages keep pace with prices, inflation is less worrisome, but if prices rise faster than wages, consumers definitely feel the pinch.

 Checkpoint

LEARNING OBJECTIVE 4: Identify four macroeconomic issues that are essential to understanding the behavior of the economy.

SUMMARY: First, competition in a free-market system occurs on a spectrum from pure competition to monopolies; most competition in free-market economies is monopolistic competition, meaning that the number of sellers is large enough that none can dominate the market and products can be distinguished in at least some small way. Second, the economy expands and contracts, or fluctuates over time; this activity is commonly called the *business cycle*, although the fluctuations do not follow a regular cyclical pattern. Third, unemployment is a vitally important issue in economics because of the serious effects it has on individuals, families, communities, and the economy as a whole. The types of unemployment include cyclical (from reduced labor needs during an economic contraction), frictional (from the normal inflow and outflow of workers as people change jobs), structural (from the skills workers possess not aligning with the skills employers need), and seasonal (from the ebb and flow of labor demand in certain industries over the course of a year). Fourth, inflation affects every aspect of economic activity because of the effects it has on the prices of goods, services, and labor.

Government's Role in a Free-Market System

For as long as the United States has been in existence, people have been arguing over just how free the free market should be. In the broader view, this argument springs from profound philosophical differences over the role government should play in society as a whole. More narrowly, even professional economists don't always agree on what role the government should play in the economy.

Much of the debate about the government's role can be framed as a question of **regulation** versus **deregulation**—having more rules in place to govern economic activity or having fewer rules in place and relying more on the market to prevent excesses and correct itself over time. Generally speaking, the argument for more regulation asserts that companies can't always be counted on to act in ways that protect stakeholder interests and that the market can't be relied on as a mechanism to prevent or punish abuses and failures. The argument for deregulation contends that government interference can stifle innovations that ultimately help everyone by boosting the entire economy and that some regulations burden individual companies and industries with unfair costs and limitations.

Four major areas in which the government plays a role in the economy are protecting stakeholders, fostering competition, encouraging innovation and economic development, and stabilizing and stimulating the economy.

PROTECTING STAKEHOLDERS

Chapter 1 points out that businesses have many stakeholders, including colleagues, employees, supervisors, investors, customers, suppliers, and society at large. In the course of serving one or more of these stakeholders, a business may sometimes neglect, or at least be accused of neglecting, the interests of other stakeholders in the process. For example, managers who are too narrowly focused on generating wealth for shareholders might not spend the funds necessary to create a safe work environment for employees or to minimize the business's impact on the community.

In an attempt to balance the interests of stakeholders and protect those who might be adversely affected by business, the U.S. federal government has established numerous regulatory agencies (see Exhibit 2.9 on the next page), and state and local governments have additional agencies as well. Chapter 4 takes a closer look at society's concerns for ethical and socially responsible behavior and the ongoing debate about business's role in society.

FOSTERING COMPETITION

Based on the belief that fair competition benefits the economy and society in general, governments intervene in markets to preserve competition and ensure that no single enterprise becomes too powerful. For instance, if a company has a monopoly, it can potentially harm customers by raising prices or stifling innovation and harm potential competitors by denying access to markets. Numerous laws and regulations have been established to

5 LEARNING OBJECTIVE

Outline the debate over deregulation, and identify four key roles that governments play in the economy.

regulation
Relying more on laws and policies than on market forces to govern economic activity.

deregulation
Removing regulations to allow the market to prevent excesses and correct itself over time.

EXHIBIT 2.9	Major Government Agencies and What They Do

Government agencies protect stakeholders by developing and promoting standards, regulating and overseeing industries, and enforcing laws and regulations.

Government Agency or Commission	Major Areas of Responsibility
Consumer Financial Protection Bureau (CFPB)	Educates consumers about and supervises providers of consumer financial services
Consumer Product Safety Commission (CPSC)	Regulates and protects public from unreasonable risks of injury from consumer products
Environmental Protection Agency (EPA)	Develops and enforces standards to protect the environment
Equal Employment Opportunity Commission (EEOC)	Protects and resolves discriminatory employment practices
Federal Aviation Administration (FAA)	Sets rules for the commercial airline industry
Federal Communications Commission (FCC)	Oversees communication by telephone, telegraph, radio, and television
Federal Energy Regulatory Commission (FERC)	Regulates rates and sales of electric power and natural gas
Federal Highway Administration (FHA)	Regulates vehicle safety requirements
Federal Trade Commission (FTC)	Enforces laws and guidelines regarding unfair business practices and acts to stop false and deceptive advertising and labeling
Food and Drug Administration (FDA)	Enforces laws and regulations to prevent distribution of harmful foods, drugs, medical devices, and cosmetics
Interstate Commerce Commission (ICC)	Regulates and oversees carriers engaged in transportation between states: railroads, bus lines, trucking companies, oil pipelines, and waterways
Occupational Safety and Health Administration (OSHA)	Promotes worker safety and health
Securities and Exchange Commission (SEC)	Protects investors and maintains the integrity of the securities markets
Transportation Security Administration (TSA)	Protects the national transportation infrastructure

help prevent individual companies or groups of companies from taking control of markets or acting in other ways that restrain competition or harm consumers.

As the business environment evolves, legislators sometimes consider whether to adjust business regulations in order to maintain a level playing field. The disruptive technology of online commerce provides a good example. Currently, 45 U.S. states collect sales tax on purchases made in physical ("brick-and-mortar") stores, but until recently many of these states have not required online retailers to collect sales taxes from their customers. Combined state and local sales taxes can add anywhere from about 5 percent to nearly 10 percent to the purchase price, which can be a significant amount for major purchases. Brick-and-mortar retailers complain that these inconsistent regulations give online retailers an unfair competitive advantage. In response, about half the states that have sales taxes now require Amazon and other online retailers to collect sales tax.[9]

Antitrust Legislation

Antitrust laws limit what businesses can and cannot do, to ensure that all competitors have an equal chance of succeeding. Some of the earliest government moves in this arena produced such landmark pieces of legislation as the Sherman Antitrust Act, the Clayton Antitrust Act, and the Federal Trade Commission Act, which generally sought to rein in the power of a few huge companies that had financial and management control of a significant number of other companies in the same industry. Usually referred to as *trusts* (hence the label *antitrust legislation*), these huge companies controlled enough of the supply and distribution in their respective industries, such as Standard Oil in the petroleum industry, to muscle smaller competitors out of the way. More recently, government bodies in the United States and Europe have taken action against high-tech firms such as Microsoft and Intel to prevent unfair competitive practices.

Merger and Acquisition Approvals

To preserve competition and customer choice, governments occasionally prohibit companies from combining through mergers or acquisitions (see Chapter 5). In other cases, they may approve a combination but only with conditions, such as *divesting* (selling) some parts of the company or making other concessions.

ENCOURAGING INNOVATION AND ECONOMIC DEVELOPMENT

Governments can use their regulatory and policymaking powers to encourage specific types of economic activity. A good example is encouraging the development and adoption of innovations that governments consider beneficial in some way, such as promoting the growth of alternative energy sources through economic incentives for producers and customers. Governments can also encourage businesses to locate or expand in particular geographic areas by establishing *economic development zones*. These zones typically offer a variety of financial incentives such as tax credits, low-interest loans, and reduced utility rates to businesses that meet specific job-creation and local investment criteria.

STABILIZING AND STIMULATING THE ECONOMY

In addition to the specific areas of regulation and policy just discussed, governments have two sets of tools they can use to stabilize and stimulate the national economy: monetary policy and fiscal policy. **Monetary policy** involves adjusting the nation's *money supply*, the amount of "spendable" money in the economy at any given time, by increasing or decreasing interest rates. In the United States, monetary policy is controlled primarily by the Federal Reserve Board (often called "the Fed"), a group of government officials who oversee the country's central banking system. Chapter 20 discusses the objectives and activities of the Fed in more detail.

monetary policy
Government policy and actions taken by the Federal Reserve Board to regulate the nation's money supply.

Fiscal policy involves changes in the government's revenues and expenditures to stimulate a slow economy or dampen a growing economy that is in danger of overheating and causing inflation. On the revenue side, governments can adjust the revenue they bring in by changing tax rates and various fees collected from individuals and businesses (see Exhibit 2.10). When the federal government lowers the income tax rate, for instance, it does so with the hope that consumers and businesses will spend and invest the money they save from lower tax bills.

fiscal policy
Use of government revenue collection and spending to influence the business cycle.

On the expenditure side, local, state, and federal government bodies constitute a huge market for goods and services, with billions of dollars of collective buying power. Governments can stimulate the economy by increasing their purchases, sometimes even to the point of creating new programs or projects with the specific purpose of expanding employment opportunities and increasing demand for goods and services.

EXHIBIT 2.10	Major Types of Taxes

Running a government is an expensive affair. Here are the major types of taxes that national governments, states, counties, and cities collect to fund government operations and projects.

Type of Tax	Levied On
Income taxes	Income earned by individuals and businesses. Income taxes are the government's largest single source of revenue.
Real property taxes	Assessed value of the land and structures owned by businesses and individuals.
Sales taxes	Retail purchases made by customers. Sales taxes are collected by retail businesses at the time of the sale and then forwarded to state governments. Disputes continue over taxes e-commerce sales made across state lines.
Excise taxes	Selected items such as gasoline, tobacco, and liquor. Often referred to as "sin" taxes, excise taxes are implemented in part to help control potentially harmful practices.
Payroll taxes	Earnings of individuals to help fund Social Security, Medicare, and unemployment compensation. Corporations match employee contributions.

No instance of government spending in recent years has generated more heated controversy than the bailouts made during the financial crisis of 2008 and 2009. The federal government spent billions of dollars in investments and loans to troubled banks to encourage lending after the credit markets had dried up and to prevent several large financial companies from collapsing. The government also stepped in to help save the automakers General Motors and Chrysler during this period.

Debate continues on whether it was wise to intervene by rescuing these ailing companies or whether the government should have let market forces play out. Would the money invested in saving one large company have been better spent in helping a number of small, young companies get off the ground? In general, the rationale for stepping in to rescue any specific company is that its collapse would harm a significant portion of the economy as a whole. However, these decisions hit at the heart of an economic system because they determine how a society chooses to deploy its scarce resources.

 Checkpoint

LEARNING OBJECTIVE 5: **Outline the debate over deregulation, and identify four key roles that governments play in the economy.**

SUMMARY: Proponents of increased regulation assert that companies can't always be counted on to act in ways that protect stakeholder interests and that the market can't be relied on to prevent or punish abuses and failures. Proponents of deregulation contend that government interference can stifle innovations that ultimately help everyone by boosting the entire economy and that some regulations burden individual companies and industries with unfair costs. Four key roles the government plays in the economy are protecting stakeholders, fostering competition, encouraging innovation and economic development, and stabilizing and stimulating the economy.

CRITICAL THINKING: (1) Would it be wise for the government to put price controls on college tuition? Why or why not? (2) Under what conditions, if any, should the federal government step in to rescue failing companies?

IT'S YOUR BUSINESS: (1) How do you benefit from competition among the companies that supply you with the goods and services you need? (2) Does this competition have any negative impact on your life?

KEY TERMS TO KNOW: regulation, deregulation, monetary policy, fiscal policy

6 **LEARNING OBJECTIVE**

Identify the major ways of measuring economic activity.

economic indicators
Statistics that measure the performance of the economy.

Economic Measures and Monitors

Economic indicators are statistics such as interest rates, unemployment rates, housing data, and industrial productivity that let business and political leaders measure and monitor economic performance. *Leading indicators* suggest changes that may happen to the economy in the future and are therefore valuable for planning. In contrast, *lagging indicators* provide confirmation that something has occurred in the past.

Housing starts, for example, are a leading indicator showing where several industries are headed. When housing starts drop, the construction industry contracts, and the effect soon ripples through other sectors of the economy, from the manufacture of plumbing fixtures, carpet, and appliances to a variety of services, including furniture retailing, real estate sales, and other areas that are dependent on housing-related transactions.

Another key leading indicator is *durable-goods orders*, or orders for goods that typically last more than three years (which can mean everything from desk chairs to airplanes). A rise in durable-goods orders is a positive indicator that business spending is turning around. In addition to these indicators, economists closely monitor several *price indexes* and the nation's economic output to get a sense of how well the economy is working.

In contrast, corporate profits and unemployment are among the key lagging indicators.[10] For example, companies tend to reduce their workforces after the economy has slowed down and sales revenues have dropped. Although they don't have the predictive power of leading indicators, lagging indicators give policymakers insights into how the economy is functioning and whether corrective steps might be needed.

PRICE INDEXES

Price changes, especially price increases, are a significant economic indicator. Price indexes offer a way to monitor the inflation or deflation in various sectors of the economy. An index is simply a convenient way to compare numbers over time and is computed by dividing the current value of some quantity by a baseline historical value and then multiplying by 100. Rather than saying something has increased by 28 percent, for example, economists would say the index is at 128.

Government statisticians compute a huge variety of price indexes, each designed to monitor a particular aspect of economic activity. The best known of these, the **consumer price index (CPI)**, measures the rate of inflation by comparing the change in prices of a representative "basket" of consumer goods and services, such as clothing, food, housing, and transportation (see Exhibit 2.11). The CPI has always been a hot topic because the government uses it to adjust Social Security payments, businesses use it to calculate cost-of-living increases for employees, and many use it as a gauge of how well the government is keeping inflation under control.

consumer price index (CPI)
A monthly statistic that measures changes in the prices of a representative collective of consumer goods and services.

EXHIBIT 2.11	**Composition of the Consumer Price Index**

The U.S. Bureau of Labor Statistics computes a variety of consumer price indexes by tracking prices for a representative collection of goods and services, and it periodically adjusts the mix to reflect consumer buying patterns. The particular CPI shown here, often referred to as the "headline CPI" because it is the one usually mentioned in news reports, is officially called the "All Items CPI for All Urban Consumers." The "core CPI," in comparison, excludes the typically volatile categories of food and energy in an attempt to show long-term trends more accurately. The "market basket" of goods and services is adjusted from time to time; this chart reflects the CPI composition in December 2014.

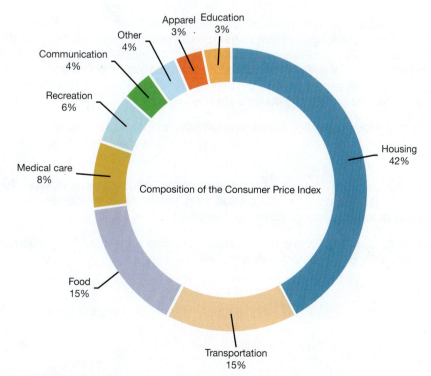

Composition of the Consumer Price Index

Source: Data from U.S. Bureau of Labor Statistics, "Relative Importance of Components in the Consumer Price Indexes: U.S. City Average," December 2014, www.bls.gov.

producer price index (PPI)
A statistical measure of price trends at the producer and wholesaler levels.

In contrast to the CPI, the **producer price index (PPI)** measures prices at the producer or wholesaler level, reflecting what businesses are paying for the products they need. (Like the CPI, the PPI is often referred to as a single index, but it is actually a family of more than 600 industry-specific indexes.) In addition to monitoring economic activity, PPIs have a number of managerial uses, from helping companies place an accurate value on inventories to protecting buyers and sellers with *price-escalation clauses* in long-term purchasing contracts.[11]

NATIONAL ECONOMIC OUTPUT

gross domestic product (GDP)
The value of all the final goods and services produced by businesses located within a nation's borders; excludes outputs from overseas operations of domestic companies.

The broadest measure of an economy's health is the **gross domestic product (GDP)**. The GDP measures a country's output—its production, distribution, and use of goods and services—by computing the sum of all goods and services produced for *final* use in a country during a specified period (usually a year). The products may be produced by either domestic or foreign companies as long as the production takes place within a nation's boundaries. Sales from a Honda assembly plant in California, for instance, would be included in the U.S. GDP, even though Honda is a Japanese company. Monitoring GDP helps a nation to evaluate its economic policies and compare current performance with prior periods or with the performance of other nations.

GDP has largely replaced a previous measure called the *gross national product (GNP)*, which excludes the value of production from foreign-owned businesses within a nation's boundaries and includes receipts from the overseas operations of domestic companies. GNP considers *who* is responsible for the production; GDP considers *where* the production occurs.

For the latest information on economic issues in business, visit **http://real-timeupdates .com/bia8** and click on Chapter 2.

 Checkpoint

LEARNING OBJECTIVE 6: Identify the major ways of measuring economic activity.

SUMMARY: Economic activity is monitored and measured with statistics known as *economic indicators*; leading indicators help predict changes, and lagging indicators confirm changes that have already occurred. Two major indicators are *price indexes,* which track inflation or deflation over time for a fixed "basket" of goods and services, and *gross domestic product (GDP)*, the total value of the goods and services produced for final use in a country during a specified time period.

CRITICAL THINKING: (1) Why would anyone bother to monitor lagging indicators? (2) Why is GDP considered a more accurate measure of a country's economic health than GNP?

IT'S YOUR BUSINESS: (1) In your multiple economic roles as a consumer, employee, and investor, is inflation a good thing, a bad thing, or both? Explain your answer. (2) How have increases in college costs affected your educational plans?

KEY TERMS TO KNOW: economic indicators, consumer price index (CPI), producer price index (PPI), gross domestic product (GDP)

BEHIND THE SCENES
RACING TO SUPPLY ONE OF THE HOTTEST PRODUCTS IN HISTORY

As one of the major forces driving the mobile communications revolution, Apple's involvement in mobile phones has in many ways surpassed its initial identity as a computer company. Its iPhone product launches have almost become cultural events, with the news media covering them like Hollywood movie premiers and consumers lining up outside Apple stores to be the first to get their hands on the latest bit of gadgetry.

From a supply-and-demand perspective, Apple phone launches are massive undertakings, with hundreds of companies and hundreds of thousands of workers involved in producing tens of millions of phones. iPhones are assembled in gargantuan factories in China, primarily those owned by two Taiwanese companies, Foxconn and Pegatron. To give a sense of scale, Foxconn's factory in Zhengzhou employs 200,000 workers. In addition to the assembly factories, the iPhone supply chain involves a host of other companies around the world that provide electrical and mechanical components, from semiconductors to glass touchscreens. Completed products are sold through a global distribution network that includes e-commerce outlets, wireless carriers, and several hundred Apple retail stores.

In other words, estimating the demand for a new Apple product is a decision with far-reaching consequences. Apple and its hundreds of business partners need to figure out how many workers to hire, how many production lines to build or change over to the specific model, how many components to buy, how to structure wireless service contracts, and how many completed phones to have in inventory.

Predicting demand is never a sure thing, but Jeff Williams, Apple's senior vice president in charge of operations, did have one big advantage as Apple readied the iPhone6 for public launch. Unlike a situation with new companies or companies that are introducing an all-new type of product, Williams could analyze the sales histories of the previous generations of iPhones to get at least a pattern of how demand for the iPhone6 might shape up over time. In addition, market researchers cover the smartphone market closely, and buyers have shown a consistent pattern of interest in new iPhone models as each one nears introduction. Williams could also consider the various deals and contracts that wireless carriers would be offering to get a sense of how many current iPhone customers might want to upgrade to the new model and how soon they would be able to do so under their existing contracts.

Of course, even with deep insights into consumer behavior, no one can predict what buyers will do until they actually do it. Moreover, even if Apple can predict demand with great precision, that doesn't mean the company can produce that many phones as fast as consumers want them. Smartphones are amazing devices that incorporate multiple types of radio transceivers, motion sensors, cameras, microphones, special glass for touchscreens, and a powerful computing system. Each of these components has to be designed, manufactured, and delivered to the assembly factories on time for production to stay on schedule.

Perhaps no level of forecasting precision and no amount of planning, however, could've prepared Apple for the crush of demand for the iPhone6. Even before these models were released in the United States in September 2014, eager buyers had preordered 4 million units. By the third day after launch, the sales total hit 10 million, and by the end of the year, iPhone6 sales had topped 75 million.

Whether Apple underestimated demand or simply wasn't able to ramp up production enough to meet that demand isn't known, but it was clear the company had a huge hit on its hands—and a huge backlog. Not long after the launch, as some buyers were waiting up to a month to get their phones, CEO Tim Cook acknowledged that demand and supply were severely out of balance. "We're not close. We're not on the same planet."

By early 2015, supply finally caught up with demand, even as the number of smartphone buyers who said they planned to buy an iPhone6 stayed at a record level. Apple's customer loyalty is legendary, so it's hard to tell if the long wait times damaged the brand or prompted some impatient buyers to switch to Samsung or another competitor. Whatever the long-term outcome, the iPhone6 experience shows that even the world's top companies can struggle to manage the unpredictable nature of supply and demand in today's markets.[12]

Critical Thinking Questions

2-1. If consumers are willing to wait weeks or months for the latest iPhone, why does Apple need to worry about producing enough phones to meet immediate demand?

2-2. If Apply temporarily can't meet demand for a product, should it raise the price to bring supply and demand into balance? Why or why not?

2-3. Apple is famously secretive about the details of upcoming product launches, leaving consumers and industry insiders to speculate on the features and functions of new models. What effect might this have on demand?

Learn More Online

Depending on when you read this, rumors are likely to be swirling online about an upcoming Apple product launch, whether it's the iPhone7 or 8, a new generation of the Apple smartwatch, or another product. Choose one upcoming product and read several articles by industry observers to get a sense of consumer demand for the new product. What products from other companies will be competing with the new Apple product, and what effect will they have on consumer demand? Can you find any worries regarding supply issues? Overall, do you think the new Apple product will be a hit? If not, what factors will account for lower demand?

KEY TERMS

business cycles (37)
capital (27)
capitalism (29)
competition (35)
consumer price index (CPI) (43)
deflation (37)
demand (32)
demand curve (32)
deregulation (39)
economic indicators (42)
economic system (29)
economics (27)
economy (27)
entrepreneurship (27)
equilibrium point (34)
fiscal policy (41)
free-market system (29)
gross domestic product (GDP) (44)
human resources (27)
inflation (37)
knowledge (27)

macroeconomics (27)
microeconomics (27)
monetary policy (41)
monopolistic competition (36)
monopoly (35)
nationalizing (31)
natural resources (27)
oligopoly (36)
opportunity cost (29)
planned system (30)
privatizing (31)
producer price index (PPI) (44)
pure competition (35)
recession (37)
regulation (39)
scarcity (28)
socialism (30)
supply (32)
supply curve (33)
unemployment rate (37)

> **MyBizLab**
> To complete the problems with the ⭐,
> go to EOC Discussion Questions in the
> MyLab.

TEST YOUR KNOWLEDGE

Questions for Review

2-4. Why is the economic concept of scarcity a crucial one for businesspeople to understand?

2-5. How does macroeconomics differ from microeconomics?

2-6. Does the United States have a purely free-market economy or a mixed economy?

2-7. What is the difference between monetary policy and fiscal policy?

2-8. Why might a government agency seek to block a merger or an acquisition?

Questions for Analysis

⭐ **2-9.** Why do governments intervene in free-market systems?

2-10. How do countries know if their economic systems are working?

2-11. Are the fluctuations in the business cycle predictable?

2-12. Is it beneficial for the country as s whole for individual U.S. states to compete with one another to attract companies? (Offering tax breaks in exchange for building new facilities is a common tactic states use to attract commercial investment, for example.)

⭐ **2-13. Ethical Considerations.** The risk of failure is an inherent part of free enterprise. Does society have an obligation to come to the aid of entrepreneurs who try but fail? Why or why not?

Questions for Application

2-14. How might government and education leaders work with businesses to minimize structural unemployment?

2-15. How would a decrease in Social Security benefits to retired persons affect the economy?

⭐ **2-16.** If you wanted to increase demand for your restaurant but are unable to lower prices or increase advertising, what steps might you take?

2-17. Concept Integration. What effect might the technological environment, discussed on page 11 in Chapter 1, have on the equilibrium point in a given market?

EXPAND YOUR KNOWLEDGE

Discovering Career Opportunities

Thinking about a career in economics? Find out what economists do by reviewing the *Occupational Outlook Handbook* in your library or online at www.bls.gov/oco. This is an authoritative resource for information about all kinds of occupations. Search for "economists" and then answer these questions:

2-18. Briefly describe what economists do and their typical working conditions.

2-19. What is the job outlook for economists? What is the average salary for starting economists?

2-20. What training and qualifications are required for a career as an economist? Are the qualifications different for jobs in the private sector than for those in the government?

Improving Your Tech Insights: Data Mining

To find a few ounces of precious gold, you dig through a mountain of earth. To find a few ounces of precious information, you dig through mountains of data, using *data mining*, a combination of technologies and techniques to extract important customer insights buried within thousands or millions of transaction records. (Data mining has many other uses as well, such as identifying which employees are most valuable to a firm. And a related technology, *text mining*, applies similar analysis tools to documents.)

Data mining is an essential part of *business intelligence* because it helps extract trends and insights from millions of pieces of individual data (including demographics, purchase histories, customer service records, and research results). Data mining helps marketers identify who their most profitable customers are, which goods and services are in highest demand in specific markets, how to structure promotional campaigns, where to target upcoming sales efforts, and which customers are likely to be high credit risks, among many other benefits. You may hear the terms *business analytics* and *predictive analytics* used in this context as well, to describe efforts to extract insights from databases.

Research one of the commercially available data-mining or business analytics systems. The list of member companies of the Data Mining Group (www.dmg.org) is a good place to start. In a brief email message to your instructor, describe how the system you've chosen can help companies market their goods and services more effectively.[13]

PRACTICE YOUR SKILLS

Sharpening Your Communication Skills

The subprime mortgage crisis that helped throw the global economy into the Great Recession bewildered a lot of people. In a brief paragraph (no more than 100 words), explain what a subprime mortgage is and why these loans helped trigger the recession.

Building Your Team Skills

Economic indicators help businesses and governments determine where the economy is headed. As part of a team assigned by your instructor, analyze the following headlines for clues to the direction of the U.S. economy:

- "Housing Starts Lowest in Months"
- "Fed Lowers Discount Rate and Interest Rates Tumble"
- "Retail Sales Up 4 Percent Over Last Month"
- "Business Debt Down from Last Year"
- "More Manufacturers Showing Interest in Upgrading Production Equipment"

- "Local Economy Sinks as Area Unemployment Rate Climbs to 9.2 Percent"
- "Computer Networking Firm Reports 30-Day Backlog in Installing Business Systems"

Is each item good news or bad news for the economy? Why? What does each news item mean for large and small businesses? Report your team's findings to the class. Did all the teams come to the same conclusions about each headline? Why or why not? With your team, discuss how these different perspectives might influence the way you interpret economic news in the future.

Developing Your Research Skills

Some career paths have higher unemployment risks during the ups and downs of economic fluctuations. Research three business careers that should be relatively "recession proof" in the coming years, meaning that employment is unlikely to drop dramatically (or may even increase) during a recession. Summarize your findings in a one-page report.

MyBizLab®

Go to the Assignments section of your MyLab to complete these writing exercises.

2-21. When the needs of various stakeholders conflict, how should legislators and regulators approach these dilemmas?

2-22. How might the word "free" affect public and political discussions of free-market systems?

ENDNOTES

1. Louis Bedigian, "iPhone 6 Demand Is Highest Ever 90 Days After Launch … Will This Impact Apple?" *Benzinga*, 27 January 2015, www.benzinga.com; Sam Oliver, "Apple Catches Up with iPhone 6 Demand, US Online Store Lists All Models 'In stock'," AppleInsider, 9 January 2015, http://appleinsider.com; Linda Federico-O'Murchu, "Why Can't Apple Meet Demand for the iPhone 6?" CNBC, 5 December 2014, www.cnbc.com; Jeff Williams executive biography, Apple, accessed 28 March 2015, www.apple.com; "Is Apple's Supply Chain Really the No. 1? A Case Study," Supplychain247, 2 September 2013, www.supplychain247.com; "How & Where iPhone Is Made: Comparison of Apple's Manufacturing Process," CompareCamp.com, 17 September 2014, http://comparecamp.com; Tom Warren, "Apple Sells 10 million iPhones in Opening Weekend Record," *The Verge*, 22 September 2014, www.theverge.com.

2. Roger LeRoy Miller, *Economics Today*, 15th ed. (Boston: Addison-Wesley, 2010), 28.

3. Miller, *Economics Today*, 31.

4. Ronald M. Ayers and Robert A. Collinge, *Economics: Explore and Apply* (Upper Saddle River, N.J.: Pearson Prentice Hall, 2005), 97–103.

5. Emily Thornton, "Roads to Riches," *BusinessWeek*, 7 May 2007, www.businessweek.com; Palash R. Ghosh, "Private Prisons Have a Lock on Growth," *BusinessWeek*, 6 July 2006, www.businessweek.com.

6. Miller, *Economics Today*, 174.

7. Miller, *Economics Today*, 160.

8. Miller, *Economics Today*, 160.

9. Adam Satariano, "Amazon Sales Take a Hit in States with Online Tax," *Bloomberg*, 21 April 2014, www.bloomberg.com; Kevin Drawbaugh, "Congress Expected to Reboot Internet Tax Issues in 2015," *Reuters*, 9 December 2014, www.reuters.com; Scott Drenkard, "State and Local Sales Tax Rates in 2014," Tax Foundation website, 18 March 2014, http://taxfoundation.org.

10. "Lagging Indicator," Investopedia, accessed 22 January 2014, www.investopedia.com.

11. U.S. Bureau of Labor Statistics, Producer Price Indexes; Program Overview, accessed 29 July 2011, www.bls.gov.

12. See Note 1.

13. Data Mining Group website, accessed 19 March 2015, www.dmg.org; James Kobielus, "The Forrester Wave: Predictive Analytics and Data Mining Solutions, Q1 2010," SAS website, accessed 1 August 2011, www.sas.com; Stephen Baker, "How Much Is That Worker Worth?" *BusinessWeek*, 23 March 2009, 46–48; Doug Henschen, "IDC Reports on BI Sales: Which Vendors Are Hot?" *Intelligent Enterprise*, 1 July 2007, www.intelligententerprise.com; Angoss website, accessed 21 May 2009, www.angoss.com.

LEARNING OBJECTIVES   After studying this chapter, you will be able to

1 Explain why nations trade, and describe how international trade is measured.

2 Discuss the nature of conflicts in global business, including free trade and government interventions into international trade.

3 Identify the major organizations that facilitate international trade and the major trading blocs around the world.

4 Discuss the importance of understanding cultural and legal differences in the global business environment.

5 Define the major forms of international business activity.

6 Discuss the strategic choices that must be considered before entering international markets.

BEHIND THE SCENES   H&M: FIRST SWEDEN, THEN THE WORLD

PSL Images/Alamy

As it continues to expand from its home base in Stockholm, Sweden, the fashion retailer H&M has to decide how much to adapt to local markets and how much to maintain a consistent global strategy.

www.hm.com

If you have an eye for fashion and a good sense of value, chances are you already know about H&M. The Swedish company has grown to be the world's second-largest apparel company by pursuing a balance of cutting-edge style, quality, and attractive prices.

H&M started in 1947 as a women's clothing store in Västerås, Sweden. International expansion came slowly at first, with stores in Norway in 1964, Denmark in 1967, and the United Kingdom in 1976. The product range expanded as well, with the addition of men's and children's lines and eventually cosmetics and items for the home. Germany, currently the company's largest market, followed in 1980. The pace accelerated through the 1990s, and by 2013 the company boasted 3,000 stores in more than 50 countries. Even with so many stores in operation, H&M still aims to expand by 10 to 15 percent every year.

To be sure, H&M's global expansion has not gone uncontested. Its biggest competitor overall—and the world's largest clothing retailer—is the multibrand Spanish company Inditex. Inditex's biggest chain, Zara, is still relatively unknown in the United States but has a huge presence in Europe and other markets. Zara is highly regarded as the innovator of "fast fashion," in which high-speed design, production, and distribution systems can jump on trend shifts and get new styles into retail shops in as little as two or three weeks. Inditex isn't sitting still either, with plans to open 1,000 new stores in the next few years.

Imagine you are Karl-Johan Persson, H&M's managing director and chief executive officer. How would you plot the company's continuing global expansion? Would you use the same business strategies in every country or adapt to local markets? Would you present H&M as a consistent global brand or modify the presentation for each country? How would you keep growing when you're already the world's second-largest apparel retailer?[1]

INTRODUCTION

The experience of H&M (profiled in the chapter-opening Behind the Scenes) is a great example of the opportunities and challenges of taking a business international. As you'll read in this chapter, international business has grown dramatically in recent years, and it's no stretch to say this growth affects virtually every company, even those that never reach beyond their own borders. Studying international business is essential to your career, too. The future professionals and managers from Asia and Europe—people you'll be competing with for jobs in the global employment market—take international business seriously.[2]

Fundamentals of International Trade

1   **LEARNING OBJECTIVE**

Explain why nations trade, and describe how international trade is measured.

Wherever you're reading this, stop and look around for a minute. You might see cars that were made in Japan running on gasoline from Russia or Saudi Arabia, mobile phones made in South Korea, food grown in Canada or Mexico or Chile, a digital music player made in China, clothing from Vietnam or Italy, industrial equipment made in Germany— and dozens of other products from every corner of the globe. Conversely, if you or a family member works for a midsize or large company, chances are it gets a significant slice of its revenue from sales to other countries. In short, we live and work in a global marketplace. Moreover, although the United States remains one of the world's most competitive countries, dozens of other countries now compete for the same employees, customers, and investments (see Exhibit 3.1).

EXHIBIT 3.1   **The World's Most Competitive Economies**

According to the World Economic Forum (WEF), these are the 10 most competitive economies in the world, based on their ability to sustain economic growth. (Hong Kong, a Special Administrative Region of the People's Republic of China, is evaluated separately by the WEF.)

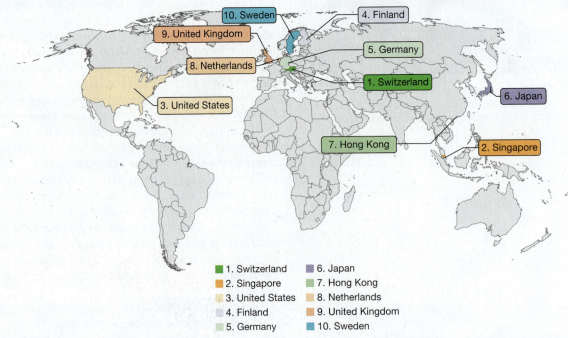

■ 1. Switzerland	■ 6. Japan
■ 2. Singapore	■ 7. Hong Kong
■ 3. United States	■ 8. Netherlands
■ 4. Finland	■ 9. United Kingdom
■ 5. Germany	■ 10. Sweden

Source: Data from Klaus Schwab, *The Global Competitiveness Report 2014–2015*, World Economic Forum, www.weforum.org.

WHY NATIONS TRADE

Commerce across borders has been going on for thousands of years, but the volume of international business has roughly tripled in the past 30 years.[3] One significant result is **economic globalization**, the increasing integration and interdependence of national economies around the world. Six reasons help explain why countries and companies trade internationally:

- **Focusing on relative strengths.** The classic theory of *comparative advantage* suggests that each country should specialize in those areas where it can produce more efficiently than other countries, and it should trade for goods and services that it can't produce as economically. The basic argument is that such specialization and exchange will increase a country's total output and allow both trading partners to enjoy a higher standard of living.
- **Expanding markets.** Many companies have ambitions too large for their own backyards. Well-known U.S. companies such as Microsoft and Boeing would be a fraction of their current size if they were limited to the U.S. marketplace. Similarly, companies based in other countries, from giants such as Toyota, Shell, and Nestlé to thousands of smaller but equally ambitious firms, view the U.S. consumer and business markets as a vast opportunity.
- **Pursuing economies of scale.** All this international activity involves more than just sales growth, of course. By expanding their markets, companies can benefit from **economies of scale**, which enable them to produce goods and services at lower costs by purchasing, manufacturing, and distributing higher quantities.[4]
- **Acquiring materials, goods, and services.** No country can produce everything its citizens want or need at prices they're willing to pay. China's rapidly growing middle class has a voracious appetite for consumer products, but the country has a relatively low concentration of brick-and-mortar stores to meet their needs, and some consumers voice concerns about the quality of locally produced goods. As a result, millions of Chinese shoppers now embrace online retailing—often buying from U.S. companies that are racing to expand their online presence in that country.[5]
- **Keeping up with customers.** In some cases, companies have to expand in order to keep or attract multinational customers. For example, suppose a retailer with stores in 20 countries wants to hire a single advertising agency to manage all its ad campaigns. Any agency vying for the account might need to open offices in all 20 countries in order to be considered.
- **Keeping up with competitors.** Companies are sometimes forced to engage on a global scale simply because their competitors are doing so. Failing to respond can allow a competitor to increase its financial resources and become a greater threat everywhere the companies compete, even on home turf.[6]

These motivations have provided the energy behind the rapid growth in global business, but the level of growth would not have been possible without two key enablers. First, the world's borders are much more open to trade than they were just a few decades ago, thanks to the advent of international trade organizations (see page 56) and a growing awareness by most governments that healthy trade can help their economies. Second, advances in communication and transportation technologies have made global trade safer, easier, and more profitable.[7]

economic globalization
The increasing integration and interdependence of national economies around the world.

economies of scale
Savings from buying parts and materials, manufacturing, or marketing in large quantities.

REAL-TIME UPDATES
Learn More by Exploring This Interactive Website

Do a deep dive into balance of trade data

Explore the overall U.S. balance of trade for any time period and compare trade balances with any other country. Go to http://real-timeupdates.com/bia8 and click on Learn More in the Students section.

HOW INTERNATIONAL TRADE IS MEASURED

Chapter 2 discusses how economists monitor certain key economic indicators to evaluate how well a country's economic system is performing, and several of these indicators measure international trade. As Exhibit 3.2 on the next page illustrates, the United States imports more goods than it exports, but it exports more services than it imports.

EXHIBIT 3.2   **U.S. Exports and Imports Since 1990**

The U.S. trade deficit has been growing dramatically in recent years. Although the United States maintains a trade surplus in services (middle graph), the international market for services isn't nearly as large as the market for goods. Consequently, the trade deficit in goods (*top graph*) far outweighs the trade surplus in services, resulting in an overall trade deficit (*bottom graph*).

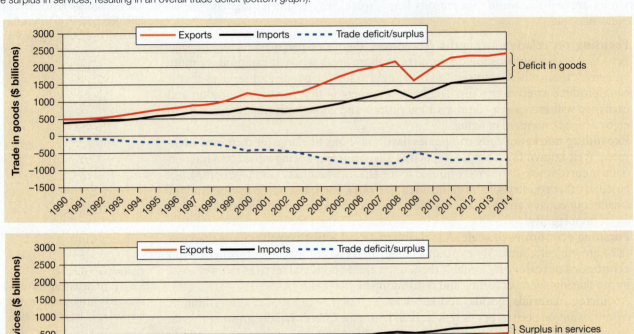

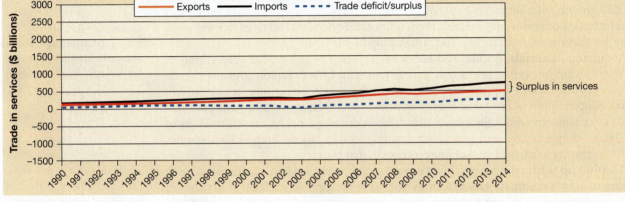

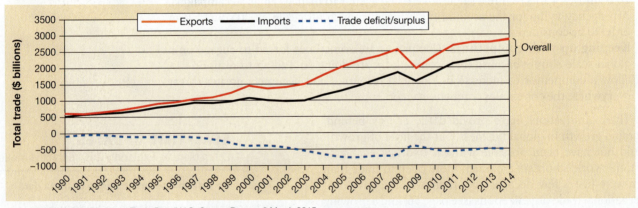

Source: Data from "U.S. International Trade Data," U.S. Census Bureau, 6 March 2015, www.census.gov.

balance of trade

Total value of the products a nation exports minus the total value of the products it imports, over some period of time.

trade surplus

A favorable trade balance created when a country exports more than it imports.

Two key measurements of a nation's level of international trade are the *balance of trade* and the *balance of payments*. The total value of a country's exports *minus* the total value of its imports, over some period of time, determines its **balance of trade**. In years when the value of goods and services exported by a country exceeds the value of goods and services it imports, the country has a positive balance of trade, or a **trade surplus**. The opposite is a **trade deficit**, when a country imports more than it exports.

The **balance of payments** is the broadest indicator of international trade. It is the total flow of money into the country *minus* the total flow of money out of the country over some period of time. The balance of payments includes the balance of trade plus the net dollars received and spent on foreign investment, military expenditures, tourism, foreign aid, and other international transactions. For example, when a U.S. company buys all or part of a company based in another country, that investment is counted in the balance of payments but not in the balance of trade. Similarly, when a foreign company buys a U.S. company or purchases U.S. stocks, bonds, or real estate, those transactions are part of the balance of payments.

FOREIGN EXCHANGE RATES AND CURRENCY VALUATIONS

When companies buy and sell goods and services in the global marketplace, they complete the transaction by exchanging currencies. The process is called *foreign exchange*, the conversion of one currency into an equivalent amount of another currency. The number of units of one currency that must be exchanged for a unit of the second currency is known as the **exchange rate** between the currencies.

Most international currencies operate under a *floating exchange rate system*, meaning that a currency's value or price fluctuates in response to the forces of global supply and demand. The supply and demand of a country's currency are determined in part by what is happening in the country's own economy. Moreover, because supply and demand for a currency are always changing, the rate at which it is exchanged for other currencies may change a little each day.

A currency is called *strong* relative to another when its exchange rate is higher than what is considered normal and called *weak* when its rate is lower than normal ("normal" is a relative term here). Note that "strong" isn't necessarily good, and "weak" isn't necessarily bad when it comes to currencies, as Exhibit 3.3 illustrates. Exchange rates can dramatically affect a company's financial results by raising or lowering the cost of supplies it imports and raising or lowering the price of goods it exports.

trade deficit
An unfavorable trade balance created when a country imports more than it exports.

balance of payments
The sum of all payments one nation receives from other nations minus the sum of all payments it makes to other nations, over some specified period of time.

exchange rate
The rate at which the money of one country is traded for the money of another.

EXHIBIT 3.3	Strong and Weak Currencies: Who Gains, Who Loses?

A strong dollar and a weak dollar aren't necessarily good or bad; each condition helps some people and hurts others.

Source: Based on "Strong Dollar, Weak Dollar: Foreign Exchange Rates and the U.S. Economy," Federal Reserve Bank of Chicago website, accessed 29 January 2005, www.chicagofed.org.

Checkpoint

LEARNING OBJECTIVE 1: Explain why nations trade, and describe how international trade is measured.

SUMMARY: Nations and companies trade internationally for any of six reasons: focusing on their relative strengths (producing the goods and services in which they excel and trading for other products they need); expanding into new markets to increase sales revenues; pursuing economies of scale to achieve lower production costs; acquiring materials, goods, and services not available at home; tending to the needs of multinational customers; and keeping up with competitors that are expanding internationally. Two primary measures of a country's international trade are its *balance of trade*, which is exports minus imports, and its *balance of payments*, a broader measure that includes all incoming payments minus all outgoing payments.

CRITICAL THINKING: (1) Would it be wise for an advertising agency to open offices in Europe and Asia to service a single multinational client? Why or why not? (2) If IBM invests $40 million in a joint venture in China, would that amount be counted in the U.S. balance of trade or the balance of payments?

IT'S YOUR BUSINESS: (1) In the last major purchase you made, did you take into consideration whether the product was made in the United States or another country? (2) Does country of origin matter to you when you shop?

KEY TERMS TO KNOW: economic globalization, economies of scale, balance of trade, trade surplus, trade deficit, balance of payments, exchange rate

---

Conflicts in International Trade

2 LEARNING OBJECTIVE

Discuss the nature of conflicts in global business, including free trade and government interventions into international trade.

Just as employees compete with one another for jobs and companies compete for customers, countries compete with one another for both. Naturally, the U.S. government promotes and protects the interests of U.S. companies, workers, and consumers. Other countries are trying to do the same thing for their stakeholders. As a consequence, international trade is a never-ending tug of war.

FREE TRADE

The benefits of the comparative advantage model are based on the assumption that nations don't take artificial steps to minimize their own weaknesses or to blunt the natural advantages of other countries. For example, if a country cannot produce a particular good at a cost that is competitive on the global market, its government might choose to *subsidize* exporters of this good with financial supports that allow them to charge lower prices than their business operations can naturally support. Trade that takes place without these interferences is known as **free trade**. (Like free-market capitalism, no trade is completely free in the sense that it takes place without regulations of any kind. Instead, international trade should be viewed along a continuum from "more free" to "less free.")

free trade
International trade unencumbered by restrictive measures.

Free trade is not a universally welcomed concept, despite the positive connotation of the word *free*. Supporters claim that it is the best way to ensure prosperity for everyone, and an overwhelming majority of U.S. economists say that the United States should eliminate barriers to trade.[8] Supporters of free trade generally acknowledge that it produces winners and losers but that the winners gain more than the losers lose, so the net effect is positive.[9]

Detractors call free trade unfair to too many people and a threat to the middle class.[10] In addition, some critics argue that free trade makes it too easy for companies to exploit workers around the world by pitting them against one another in a "race to the bottom," in which production moves to whichever country has the lowest wages and fewest restrictions regarding worker safety and environmental protection.[11] This complaint has been at the heart of recent protests over free trade and economic globalization in general. However, some researchers rebut this criticism by saying that companies prefer to do business in countries with stable, democratic governments. Consequently, this camp says, less-developed nations are motivated to improve their economic and social policies, which not only helps business but can raise the standard of living.[12] As one example, from 1981 to 2005, a period during which China became much more actively involved in free-market capitalism and global trade, the country's poverty rate dropped by 68 percent.[13] Of course, such progress might be little comfort to workers in other countries who've lost jobs as the global labor market evolves in the direction of parity.

Free trade agreements are often controversial, with various parties concerned about the effects on jobs, the environment, and other issues.

GOVERNMENT INTERVENTION IN INTERNATIONAL TRADE

When a government believes that free trade is not in the best interests of its national security, domestic industries, workforce, or consumers, it can intervene in a number of ways. Some of these methods are collectively known as **protectionism** because they seek to protect a specific industry or groups of workers. Although they can help some parties in the short term, many protectionist measures actually end up hurting the groups they were intended to help. When an industry is isolated from real-life competition for too long, it can fail to develop and become strong enough to compete efficiently.[14]

The following are the most commonly used ways to intervene in international trade:

- **Tariffs.** Taxes, surcharges, or duties levied against imported goods are known as **tariffs**. Tariffs can be levied to generate revenue, to restrict trade, or to punish other countries for disobeying international trade laws.
- **Quotas. Import quotas** limit the amount of particular goods that countries allow to be imported during a given year.
- **Embargoes.** An **embargo** is a complete ban on the import or export of certain products or even all trade between certain countries.
- **Restrictive import standards.** Countries can assist their domestic producers by establishing restrictive import standards, such as requiring special licenses for doing certain kinds of business and then making it difficult or expensive for foreign companies to obtain such licenses.[15]
- **Export subsidies.** In addition to intervening on imported goods, countries can also intervene to help domestic industries export their products to other countries. **Export subsidies** are a form of financial assistance in which producers receive enough money from the government to allow them to lower their prices in order to compete more effectively in the world market.
- **Antidumping measures.** The practice of selling large quantities of a product at a price lower than the cost of production or below what the company would charge in its home market is called **dumping**. This tactic is most often used to try to win foreign customers or to reduce product surpluses. If a domestic producer can demonstrate that the low-cost imports are damaging its business, most governments will seek redress on their behalf through international trade organizations. Dumping is often a tricky situation to resolve, however; buyers of a product that is being dumped benefit from the lower prices, and proving what constitutes a fair price in the country of origin can be difficult.[16]
- **Sanctions.** Sanctions are politically motivated embargoes that revoke a country's normal trade relations status; they are often used as forceful alternatives short of war. Sanctions can include arms embargoes, foreign-assistance reductions and cutoffs, trade limitations, tariff increases, import-quota decreases, visa denials, air-link cancellations, and more.

protectionism
Government policies aimed at shielding a country's industries from foreign competition.

tariffs
Taxes levied on imports.

import quotas
Limits placed on the quantity of imports a nation will allow for a specific product.

embargo
A total ban on trade with a particular nation (a sanction) or of a particular product.

export subsidies
A form of financial assistance in which producers receive enough money from the government to allow them to lower their prices in order to compete more effectively in the global market.

dumping
Charging less than the actual cost or less than the home-country price for goods sold in other countries.

Checkpoint

LEARNING OBJECTIVE 2: Discuss the nature of conflicts in global business, including free trade and government interventions into international trade.

SUMMARY: The root cause of trade conflict is that every country has a natural interest in protecting its own security and supporting its industries, workers, and consumers. The result is that countries often deviate from the notion of free trade by intervening in various ways, including the use of tariffs, import quotas, embargoes, restrictive import standards, export subsidies, antidumping measures, and sanctions.

CRITICAL THINKING: (1) What would happen to U.S. workers if all trade intervention suddenly disappeared? (2) What would be the effect on U.S. consumers?

IT'S YOUR BUSINESS: (1) Would you be willing to pay more for your clothes in order to keep more apparel manufacturing in the United States? Why or why not? (2) Do you or would you consider purchasing "fair trade" products, for which prices are set high enough to ensure a living wage for everyone involved in their production, even though these higher prices can make them less competitive in world markets?

KEY TERMS TO KNOW: free trade, protectionism, tariffs, import quotas, embargo, export subsidies, dumping

---

3 **LEARNING OBJECTIVE**

Identify the major organizations that facilitate international trade and the major trading blocs around the world.

International Trade Organizations

With international trade such a huge part of the world's economies, organizations that establish trading rules, resolve disputes, and promote trade play an important role in global business.

ORGANIZATIONS FACILITATING INTERNATIONAL TRADE

In an effort to ensure equitable trading practices and to iron out the inevitable disagreements over what is fair and what isn't, governments around the world have established a number of important agreements and organizations that address trading issues, including the WTO, IMF, and World Bank.

The World Trade Organization

The World Trade Organization (WTO), **www.wto.org**, is a permanent forum for negotiating, implementing, and monitoring international trade procedures and for mediating trade disputes among its 160 member countries. The organization's work is guided by five principles: preventing discriminatory policies that favor some trading partners over others or a country's own products over those of other countries; reducing trade barriers between countries; making trade policies more predictable and less arbitrary; discouraging unfair practices; and promoting economic progress in the world's less-developed countries.[17]

Critics of globalization often direct their ire at the WTO, but the organization says these criticisms are unjustified and based on misunderstandings of the WTO's missions and methods. For example, the WTO asserts that contrary to claims by some critics, it does not dictate policies to national governments, does not ignore the special circumstances faced by the world's poorest countries, and does not ignore health and environmental concerns when trying to mediate commercial disputes.[18] One point everyone seems to agree on is that the WTO's work is exceedingly complex and therefore excruciatingly slow. Reaching agreement to eventually eliminate agricultural export subsidies, in which government payments to farmers allowed them to set artificially low prices on the world market, took several decades.[19]

The International Monetary Fund

The International Monetary Fund (IMF), www.imf.org, was established in 1945 to foster international financial cooperation and increase the stability of the international economy. Now with 188 member countries, the IMF's primary functions are monitoring global financial developments, offering technical advice and training to help countries manage their economies more effectively, and providing short-term loans to member countries. These loans can be made for a variety of reasons, from helping a country deal with a natural disaster to stabilizing a country's economy to limit the spread of a financial crisis beyond its borders.[20]

The World Bank

The World Bank (www.worldbank.org) is a group of five financial institutions whose primary goals are eradicating the most extreme levels of poverty around the world and raising the income of the poorest people in every country as a way to foster shared prosperity for everyone. Although it is not as directly involved in international trade and finance on the same scale as the WTO and IMF, the World Bank does indirectly contribute to trade by working to improve economic conditions by investing in education, health care, and other concerns in developing countries.[21]

TRADING BLOCS

Trading blocs, or *common markets*, are regional organizations that promote trade among member nations (see Exhibit 3.4 on the next page). Although specific rules vary from group to group, their primary objective is to ensure the economic growth and benefit of members. As such, trading blocs generally promote trade inside the region while creating uniform barriers against goods and services entering the region from nonmember countries.

trading blocs
Organizations of nations that remove barriers to trade among their members and that establish uniform barriers to trade with nonmember nations.

North American Free Trade Agreement

In 1994, the United States, Canada, and Mexico formed the North American Free Trade Agreement (NAFTA), paving the way for the free flow of goods, services, and capital within the bloc through the phased elimination of tariffs and quotas.[22] NAFTA was controversial when first implemented, and it has remained controversial ever since.[23] Assessing the treaty's full impact is difficult because so many economic factors are involved, and a variety of other forces have affected all three countries' economies over the past two decades.

To a large degree, judging the success of NAFTA depends on what you are trying to measure. Trade between the three nations has increased dramatically in the two decades since NAFTA was instituted, and companies in all three countries have benefitted from easier access to markets. Mexican exports are up dramatically, and U.S. and other foreign companies have invested billions of dollars in Mexico. Some Mexican companies are thriving, thanks to those export opportunities, whereas others, particularly in agriculture, have been hurt severely by low-cost imports from the United States. Many of the manufacturing jobs Mexico hoped to attract wound up in China and other countries instead. In the United States, critics claim that much of the promised benefits of lower consumer prices and steady export markets for small farmers didn't materialize, that benefits of NAFTA have gone mostly to huge agribusiness corporations, and that contrary to promises of job creation in the United States, NAFTA has destroyed many U.S. jobs.[24]

NAFTA illustrates the challenge of analyzing international economic activity and linking measurable effects to specific causes. And, as is often the case with economic change, gains for some groups come at the expense of losses for other groups. The authors of a congressional report issued on NAFTA's 20th anniversary in 2014 summarized its

EXHIBIT 3.4   **Members of Major Trading Blocs**

As the economies of the world become increasingly linked, many countries have formed powerful regional trading blocs that trade freely with one another but place restrictions on trade with other countries and blocs.

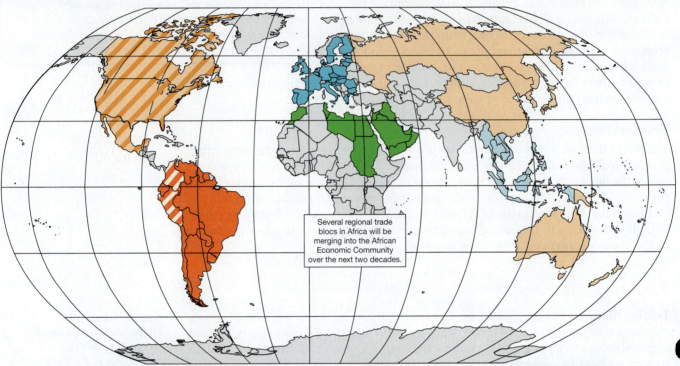

Several regional trade blocs in Africa will be merging into the African Economic Community over the next two decades.

European Union (EU)	North American Free Trade Agreement (NAFTA)	Association of Southeast Asian Nations (ASEAN)	Union of South American Nations	Asia-Pacific Economic Cooperation (APEC)	Greater Arab Free Trade Area (GAFTA)
Austria	Canada	Brunei Darussalam	Argentina	Australia	Bahrain
Belgium	Mexico	Cambodia	Bolivia	Brunei Darussalam	Egypt
Bulgaria	United States	Indonesia	Brazil	Canada	Iraq
Croatia		Laos	Chile	Chile	Jordan
Cyprus		Malaysia	Colombia	China	Kuwait
Czech Republic		Myanmar	Ecuador	Hong Kong	Lebanon
Denmark		Philippines	Guyana	Indonesia	Libya
Estonia		Singapore	Paraguay	Japan	Morocco
Finland		Thailand	Peru	Republic of Korea	Oman
France		Vietnam	Suriname	Malaysia	Palestine
Germany			Uruguay	Mexico	Qatar
Greece			Venezuela	New Zealand	Saudi Arabia
Hungary				Papua New Guinea	Sudan
Ireland				Peru	Syria
Italy				Philippines	Tunisia
Latvia				Russia	United Arab Emirates
Lithuania				Singapore	Yemen
Luxembourg				Chinese Taipei	
Malta				Thailand	
Netherlands				United States	
Poland				Vietnam	
Portugal					
Romania					
Slovakia					
Slovenia					
Spain					
Sweden					
United Kingdom					

Source: Member lists as of 20 March 2015: http://europa.eu; www.asean.org; www.unasursg.org; www.apec.org; www.economy.gov.lb.

overall impact this way: "NAFTA did not cause the huge job losses feared by the critics or the large economic gains predicted by supporters."[25]

The European Union

One of the largest trading blocs is the European Union (EU), **http://europa.eu**, whose membership now encompasses more than two dozen countries and a half billion people. Viewed as a whole, the EU now constitutes the world's largest economy. EU nations have eliminated hundreds of local regulations, variations in product standards, and protectionist measures that once limited trade among member countries. Trade now flows among member countries in much the same way it does among states in the United States. And the EU's reach extends far beyond the borders of Europe; to simplify design and manufacturing for world markets, many companies now create their products to meet EU specifications. If you've seen the "CE" marking on any products you may own, that stands for Conformité Européene and indicates that the product has met EU standards for safety, health, and environmental responsibility.[26]

REAL-TIME UPDATES
Learn More by Exploring This Interactive Website

Explore the latest data on Europe's financial health

This interactive guide shows employment, debt, and other key figures. Go to http://real-timeupdates.com/bia8 and click on Learn More in the Students section.

The EU has taken a significant step beyond all other trading blocs in the area of money by creating its own currency, the *euro*, which has been adopted by more than half the member states of the EU. By switching to a common currency, these countries have made financial transactions simpler and less expensive. According to EU leadership, the euro has simplified commerce for consumers and businesses, lowered inflation and interest rates, improved transparency in pricing, provided a more stable currency, and given the EU a stronger presence in global financial markets.[27] However, with widespread trade imbalances and ongoing financial crises in Greece, Italy, and several other nations weighing down the economies of all Eurozone members, some observers now question whether the currency bloc can continue in its current configuration.

The Asia-Pacific Economic Cooperation

The Asia-Pacific Economic Cooperation (APEC), **www.apec.org**, is an organization of 21 countries working to liberalize trade in the Pacific Rim (the land areas that surround the Pacific Ocean). Member nations represent 40 percent of the world's population and more than 50 percent of the world's gross domestic product. Like other trade blocs, APEC has a long-term goal of liberalizing and simplifying trade and investment among member countries and helping the region as a whole achieve sustainable economic growth. Since APEC's establishment in 1989, trade among member nations has increased sevenfold.[28]

The Trans-Pacific Partnership

The Trans-Pacific Partnership (TPP) is a potentially major trade agreement involving about a dozen countries around the Pacific Rim. After a decade of negotiations, the TPP may be finalized in the near future. Supporters say the TPP is vital to promoting U.S. economic interests in fast-growing countries, but detractors fear it would undermine U.S. laws while giving tremendous legal power to multinational corporations.[29]

✓ Checkpoint

LEARNING OBJECTIVE 3: Identify the major organizations that facilitate international trade and the major trading blocs around the world.

SUMMARY: Major organizations that facilitate trade include the World Trade Organization (WTO), the International Monetary Fund (IMF), and, at least indirectly, the World Bank. Major regional trading blocs include NAFTA (Canada, Mexico, and the United States), the European Union (more than two dozen countries across Europe), and APEC (21 countries around the Pacific Rim).

> **CRITICAL THINKING:** (1) Why do trade disputes sometimes take years to resolve? (2) If a country currently benefits from high tariffs on imports, why might it consider joining a trading bloc that requires it to lower or eliminate those tariffs?
>
> **IT'S YOUR BUSINESS:** (1) Can you identify any ways in which your life as an employee or a consumer has been affected by U.S. membership in trading blocs such as NAFTA and APEC? (2) How can you confirm that the effect was caused by trading bloc membership?
>
> **KEY TERM TO KNOW:** trading blocs

4 **LEARNING OBJECTIVE**

Discuss the importance of understanding cultural and legal differences in the global business environment.

The Global Business Environment

Doing business internationally can be a boon for many companies, but it also presents many challenges. Every country has unique laws, customs, consumer preferences, ethical standards, labor skills, and political and economic forces. Understanding cultural and legal differences is an essential first step for any business contemplating international operations.

CULTURAL DIFFERENCES IN THE GLOBAL BUSINESS ENVIRONMENT

culture
A shared system of symbols, beliefs, attitudes, values, expectations, and norms for behavior.

Culture is a shared system of symbols, beliefs, attitudes, values, expectations, and norms for behavior. Your cultural background influences the way you prioritize what is important in life, helps define your attitude toward what is appropriate in a situation, and establishes rules of behavior.[30] Successful global business leaders recognize and respect differences in language, social values, ideas of status, decision-making habits, attitudes toward time, use of space, body language, manners, religions, and ethical standards. Ignorance of or indifference toward cultural differences is a common cause of communication breakdowns in international affairs. Above all else, businesspeople dealing with other cultures must avoid the twin traps of **stereotyping**, assigning a wide range of generalized (and often superficial or even false) attributes to an individual on the basis of membership in a particular culture or social group, and **ethnocentrism**, the tendency to judge all other groups according to one's own group's standards, behaviors, and customs.

stereotyping
Assigning a wide range of generalized attributes, which are often superficial or even false, to an individual based on his or her membership in a particular culture or social group.

ethnocentrism
Judging all other groups according to the standards, behaviors, and customs of one's own group.

Education and an open mind are the best ways to prepare yourself for doing business with people from another culture. Numerous books and websites offer advice on traveling to and working in specific countries. It is also helpful to sample newspapers, magazines, and even the music and movies of another country. For instance, a movie can demonstrate nonverbal customs even if you don't grasp the language. Learn everything you can about the culture's history, religion, politics, and customs—especially its business customs. Who makes decisions? How are negotiations usually conducted? Is gift giving expected? What is the proper attire for a business meeting? In addition to the suggestion that you learn about the culture, seasoned international businesspeople offer the following tips for improving communication with a person from another culture:

- **Be alert to the other person's customs.** Expect the other person to have values, beliefs, expectations, and mannerisms that may differ from yours.
- **Deal with the individual.** Don't stereotype the other person or react with preconceived ideas. Regard the person as an individual first, not as a representative of another culture.
- **Clarify your intent and meaning.** The other person's body language may not mean what you think, and the person may read unintentional meanings into your message. Clarify your true intent by repetition and examples. Ask questions and listen carefully.

- **Adapt your style to the other person's.** If the other person appears to be direct and straightforward, follow suit. If not, adjust your behavior to match.
- **Show respect.** Learn how respect is communicated in various cultures through gestures, eye contact, social customs, and other actions.

These are just a few tips for doing business in the global marketplace. Successful international businesses learn as much as they can about political issues, cultural factors, and the economic environment before investing time and money in new markets. Exhibit 3.5 can guide you in your efforts to learn more about a country's culture before doing business there.

LEGAL DIFFERENCES IN THE GLOBAL BUSINESS ENVIRONMENT

Differences in national legal systems may not be as immediately obvious as cultural differences, but they can have a profound effect on international business efforts. For instance, the legal systems in the United States and the United Kingdom are based on *common law*,

EXHIBIT 3.5	**Checklist for Doing Business Abroad**

Use this checklist as a starting point when planning business activity in another country.

Action	Details to Consider
Understand social customs	• How do people react to strangers? Are they friendly? Hostile? Reserved? • How do people greet each other? Should you bow? Nod? Shake hands? • How do you express appreciation for an invitation to lunch, dinner, or someone's home? Should you bring a gift? Send flowers? Write a thank-you note? • Are any phrases, facial expressions, or hand gestures considered rude? • How do you attract the attention of a waiter? Do you tip the waiter? • When is it rude to refuse an invitation? How do you refuse politely? • What topics may or may not be discussed in a social setting? In a business setting? • How do social customs dictate interaction between men and women? Between younger people and older people?
Learn about clothing and food preferences	• What occasions require special attire? • What colors are associated with mourning? Love? Joy? • Are some types of clothing considered taboo for one gender or the other? • How many times a day do people eat? • How are hands or utensils used when eating? • Where is the seat of honor at a table?
Assess political patterns	• How stable is the political situation? • Does the political situation affect businesses in and out of the country? • Is it appropriate to talk politics in social or business situations?
Understand religious and social beliefs	• To which religious groups do people belong? • Which places, objects, actions, and events are sacred? • Do religious beliefs affect communication between men and women or between any other groups? • Is there a tolerance for minority religions? • How do religious holidays affect business and government activities? • Does religion require or prohibit eating specific foods? At specific times?
Learn about economic and business institutions	• Is the society homogeneous or heterogeneous? • What languages are spoken? • What are the primary resources and principal products? • Are businesses generally large? Family controlled? Government controlled? • What are the generally accepted working hours? • How do people view scheduled appointments? • Are people expected to socialize before conducting business?
Appraise the nature of ethics, values, and laws	• Is money or a gift expected in exchange for arranging business transactions? • Do people value competitiveness or cooperation? • What are the attitudes toward work? Toward money? • Is politeness more important than factual honesty?

Source: Courtland L. Bovée and John V. Thill, *Business Communication Today*, 13th ed. (c) 2014 p. 75. Reprinted and Electronically reproduced by permission of Pearson Education, Inc" Upper Saddle River, New Jersey.

REAL-TIME UPDATES
Learn More by Reading This Infographic

The staggering scale of international tax havens

See how many trillions of dollars flow through tax havens every year. Go to http://real-timeupdates.com/bia8 and click on Learn More in the Students section.

tax haven
A country whose favorable banking laws and low tax rates give companies the opportunity to shield some of their income from higher tax rates in their home countries or other countries where they do business.

in which tradition, custom, and judicial interpretation play important roles. In contrast, the system in countries such as France and Germany is based on *civil law*, in which legal parameters are specified in detailed legal codes. A third type of legal system, *theocratic law*, or law based on religious principles, predominates in countries such as Iran and Pakistan. Beyond the differences in legal philosophies, the business of contracts, copyrights, and other legal matters can vary considerably from one country to another.

Tax havens and bribery are two serious issues that highlight the challenges and complexities of international business law. A **tax haven** is a country whose favorable banking laws and low tax rates give companies the opportunity to shield some of their income from higher tax rates in their home countries or other countries where they do business.

Although a vast amount of criminal money moves through or is sheltered in certain tax havens, using tax havens isn't necessarily illegal. However, it can be a highly controversial practice, particularly in the case of multinational corporations that use internal transfers or other processes to lower their tax burdens.

For example, Microsoft, Google, and Amazon have lowered their tax burdens in the United Kingdom by recording UK sales through subsidiaries in Ireland or Luxembourg, whose corporate tax rates are much lower than those in the United Kingdom. Similarly, Starbucks has a third of the coffeeshop market in the United Kingdom but in a recent 15-year span avoided paying corporation taxes in 14 of those years through internal transfers that effectively erased the taxable income of its UK stores. Local UK companies complain that they have to pay full UK taxes and are therefore at a competitive disadvantage. Moreover, a rising tide of criticism over the loss of revenue to fund public services is spurring changes in international tax laws that will make it more difficult to avoid taxes through these internal maneuvers. In response to these criticisms and recent moves by government regulators, all three companies have begun changing their accounting practices in ways that will increase the local taxes they pay.[31]

Perhaps no issue in international business law generates as much confusion and consternation as bribery. In some countries, payments to government and business officials are so common that some businesspeople consider them to be standard operating practice—and companies sometimes fear they won't be able to compete if they don't play along. These payments are used to facilitate a variety of actions, from winning contracts for public works projects (such as roads or power plants) to securing routine government services (such as customs inspections) to getting preferential treatment (such as the approval to raise prices).[32]

These payment systems discourage much-needed investment in developing countries, undermine democratic processes and weaken trust in government, raise prices for consumers by inflating business costs, and can even present security risks by essentially putting officials' actions up for the highest bid. Some businesspeople have argued that critics of such payoffs are trying to impose U.S. values on other cultures, but Transparency International, a watchdog group that works to reduce business–government corruption around the world, discredits this argument by saying that "the abuse of power for personal gain—the siphoning off of public or common resources into private pockets—is unacceptable in all cultures and societies."[33]

All U.S. companies operating in other countries and foreign companies doing business in the United States are bound by the Foreign Corrupt Practices Act (FCPA), which outlaws payments with the intent of getting government officials to break the laws of their own countries or to secure "improper advantage" in gaining or retaining sales.[34] The FCPA does allow payments to expedite routine actions such as setting up utilities for a new facility, even though the U.S. and other governments discourage such payments. In addition to banning outright cash payments, the FCPA

REAL-TIME UPDATES
Learn More by Visiting This Website

Working to eradicate corruption around the world

Learn more about the work of Transparency International. Go to http://real-timeupdates.com/bia8 and click on Learn More in the Students section.

also forbids indirect means of influence such as expensive gifts, charitable contributions intended to influence government officials, and travel opportunities (such as company-hosted training seminars) that have little or no legitimate business purpose.[35]

Following the FCPA, the Organisation for Economic Co-Operation and Development (OECD), an international body dedicated to fostering economic prosperity and combating poverty, made bribery of foreign officials a criminal offense for its member nations as well.[36]

✓ Checkpoint

LEARNING OBJECTIVE 4: Discuss the importance of understanding cultural and legal differences in the global business environment.

SUMMARY: Elements of culture include language, social values, ideas of status, decision-making habits, attitudes toward time, use of space, body language, manners, religions, and ethical standards. Awareness of and respect for cultural differences is essential to avoiding communication breakdowns and fostering positive working relationships. Understanding differences in legal systems and specific laws and regulations in other countries is another vital aspect of successful international business. One of the most confusing and frustrating aspects of international trade law is the issue of bribery.

CRITICAL THINKING: (1) What steps could you take to help someone from another country adapt to U.S. business culture? (2) How can you convey respect for another person's culture even if you don't agree with it or even understand it?

IT'S YOUR BUSINESS: (1) When you encounter someone whose native language is different from yours, what steps do you take to make sure communication is successful? (2) How does another person's "foreignness" influence your perceptions of his or her abilities?

KEY TERMS TO KNOW: culture, stereotyping, ethnocentrism, tax haven

Forms of International Business Activity

 LEARNING OBJECTIVE

Define the major forms of international business activity.

Beyond cultural and legal concerns, companies that plan to go international also need to think carefully about the right organizational approach to support these activities. The five common forms of international business are importing and exporting, licensing, franchising, strategic alliances and joint ventures, and foreign direct investment; each has varying degrees of ownership, financial commitment, and risk (see Exhibit 3.6 on the next page).

IMPORTING AND EXPORTING

Importing, the buying of goods or services from a supplier in another country, and **exporting**, the selling of products outside the country in which they are produced, have existed for centuries. Exporting is one of the least risky forms of international business activity. It allows a firm to enter a foreign market gradually, assess local conditions, and then fine-tune its product offerings to meet the needs of local markets. In most cases, the firm's financial exposure is limited to the costs of researching the market, advertising, and either establishing a direct sales and distribution system or hiring intermediaries. Moreover, a variety of intermediaries exist to help companies, even the smallest businesses, get started with exporting.

Many countries now have foreign trade offices to help importers and exporters interested in doing business within their borders. Other helpful resources include professional agents, local businesspeople, and the International Trade Administration of the U.S. Department of Commerce (http://export.gov), which offers several services, including political and credit-risk analysis, advice on entering foreign markets, and financing tips.[37]

importing
Purchasing goods or services from another country and bringing them into one's own country.

exporting
Selling and shipping goods or services to another country.

EXHIBIT 3.6	**Forms of International Business Activity**

Depending on their goals and resources and the opportunities available, companies can choose from five different ways to conduct business internationally.

Importing and exporting
Buying and selling goods and services across national borders, without establishing a physical or legal business presence in other countries

International licensing
Licensing intellectual property such as a design patent to a company in another country, which then produces the product and sells it locally

International franchising
Selling the rights to use an entire business system, such as a fast-food restaurant, including the brand name and internal processes

International strategic alliances and joint ventures
Forming a long-term business partnership with a local company in a new market or creating a new company with a local partner

Foreign direct investment
Buying an established company or launching a new company in another country

INTERNATIONAL LICENSING

licensing
Agreement to produce and market another company's product in exchange for a royalty or fee.

Licensing is another popular approach to international business. License agreements entitle one company to use some or all of another firm's intellectual property (patents, trademarks, brand names, copyrights, or trade secrets) in return for a royalty payment.

Low up-front costs are an attractive aspect of international licensing. Pharmaceutical firms such as Germany's Boehringer Ingelheim routinely use licensing to enter foreign markets.[38] After a pharmaceutical company has developed and patented a new drug, it is often more efficient to grant existing local firms the right to manufacture and distribute the patented drug in return for royalty payments. (Licensing agreements are not restricted to international business, of course; a company can also license its products or technology to other companies in its domestic market.)

INTERNATIONAL FRANCHISING

Some companies choose to expand into foreign markets by *franchising* their operations. Chapter 6 discusses franchising in more detail, but briefly, franchising involves selling the right to use a *business system*, including brand names, business processes, trade secrets, and other assets. For instance, there are more than 18,000 McDonald's restaurants in more than 100 countries outside the United States, and the vast majority of them are run by independent franchisees.[39] Franchising is an attractive option for many companies because it reduces the costs and risks of expanding internationally while leveraging their investments in branding and business processes.

INTERNATIONAL STRATEGIC ALLIANCES AND JOINT VENTURES

Strategic alliances (discussed in Chapter 5), which are long-term partnerships between two or more companies to jointly develop, produce, or sell products, are another important way to reach the global marketplace. Alliance partners typically share ideas, expertise, resources, technologies, investment costs, risks, management, and profits. In some cases, a strategic alliance might be the only way to gain access to a market.

A *joint venture*, in which two or more firms join together to create a new business entity that is legally separate and distinct from its parents, is an alternative to a strategic alliance. In some countries, foreign companies are prohibited from owning facilities outright or from investing in local business, so establishing a joint venture with a local partner may be the only way to do business in that country.

REAL-TIME UPDATES
Learn More by Visiting This Website

Ready to take a business international?

Export.gov can help you at every step, including finding out if your company has what it takes to be a successful exporter. Go to http://real-timeupdates.com/bia8 and click on Learn More in the Students section.

FOREIGN DIRECT INVESTMENT

Many firms prefer to enter international markets through partial or whole ownership and control of assets in foreign countries, an approach known as **foreign direct investment (FDI)**. Some facilities are set up through FDI to exploit the availability of raw materials; others take advantage of low wage rates, whereas still others minimize transportation costs by choosing locations that give them direct access to markets in other countries. Companies that establish a physical presence in multiple countries through FDI are called **multinational corporations (MNCs)**. MNCs can approach international markets in a variety of ways; see "Organizational Strategies for International Expansion" in the next section.

FDI typically gives companies greater control, but it carries much greater economic and political risk and is more complex than any other form of entry in the global market-place. Consequently, most FDI takes place between the industrialized nations with large, stable economies such as the United States, Canada, Japan, and most countries in Europe, which tend to offer greater protection for foreign investors.[40]

foreign direct investment (FDI)
Investment of money by foreign companies in domestic business enterprises.

multinational corporations (MNCs)
Companies with operations in more than one country.

> ## ✓ Checkpoint
>
> **LEARNING OBJECTIVE 5: Define the major forms of international business activity.**
>
> **SUMMARY:** The major forms of international business activity are importing and exporting (buying and selling across national boundaries), licensing (conferring the rights to create a product), franchising (selling the rights to use an entire business system and brand identity), strategic alliances and joint ventures (forming partnerships with other companies), and foreign direct investment (buying companies or building facilities in another country).
>
> **CRITICAL THINKING:** (1) Can a company successfully export to other countries without having staff and facilities in those countries? Why or why not? (2) Why does so much foreign direct investment take place between the industrialized nations?
>
> **IT'S YOUR BUSINESS:** (1) What connotations does the word "imported" have for you? (2) On what do you base your reaction?
>
> **KEY TERMS TO KNOW:** importing, exporting, licensing, foreign direct investment (FDI), multinational corporations (MNCs)

Strategic Approaches to International Markets

 6 **LEARNING OBJECTIVE**

Discuss the strategic choices that must be considered before entering international markets.

Expanding internationally is obviously not a decision any business can take lightly. The rewards can be considerable, but the costs and risks must be analyzed carefully during the planning stage. This section offers a brief look at overall organizational strategies for international expansion, followed by strategic questions in the various functional areas of the business.

ORGANIZATIONAL STRATEGIES FOR INTERNATIONAL EXPANSION

When a firm decides to establish a presence in another country, it needs to consider its long-term objectives, the nature of its products, the characteristics of the markets into which it plans to expand, and the management team's ability to oversee a geographically dispersed operation. These considerations can lead to one of several high-level strategies:[41]

- In the **multidomestic strategy**, a company creates highly independent operating units in each new country, giving local managers a great deal of freedom to run their

multidomestic strategy
A decentralized approach to international expansion in which a company creates highly independent operating units in each new country.

operations almost as though they are independent companies. Although this strategy can help a company respond more quickly and effectively to local market needs, it doesn't deliver the economy-of-scale advantages that other strategies can bring. In addition, the lack of centralized control can lead to situations in which local managers act in ways contrary to corporate strategy or guidelines. For example, when the French grocery retailer Carrefour learned that some of its local store managers in China were luring customers with low advertised prices but then charging more in their stores, the company clamped down on the practice, even though it is apparently widespread in Chinese retailing (despite being illegal).[42]

- In the **global strategy**, a company embraces the notion of economic globalization by viewing the world as a single integrated market. This is essentially the opposite of the multidomestic strategy. Managerial control in the global strategy is highly centralized, with headquarters in the home country making all major decisions.

- In the **transnational strategy**, a company uses a hybrid approach as it attempts to reap the benefits of international scale while being responsive to local market dynamics. This is the essence of the often-heard advice to "think globally, act locally." With this approach, major strategic decisions and business systems such as accounting and purchasing are often centralized, but local business units are given the freedom to make "on-the-ground" decisions that are most appropriate for local markets.

global strategy
A highly centralized approach to international expansion, with headquarters in the home country making all major decisions.

transnational strategy
A hybrid approach that attempts to reap the benefits of international scale while being responsive to local market dynamics.

FUNCTIONAL STRATEGIES FOR INTERNATIONAL EXPANSION

Choosing the right form of business to pursue is the first of many decisions that companies need to make when moving into other countries. Virtually everything you learn about in this course, from human resources to marketing to financial management, needs to be reconsidered carefully when going international. Some of the most important decisions involve products, customer support, pricing, promotion, and staffing:

- **Products.** You face two primary questions regarding products. First, which products should you try to sell in each market? Second, should you *standardize* your products, selling the same product everywhere in the world, or *customize* your products to accommodate the lifestyles and habits of local target markets? Customization seems like an obvious choice, but it can increase costs and operational complexity, so the decision to customize is not automatic. As you'll read at the end of the chapter, for example, H&M follows a strategy of standardized product lines. The degree of customization can also vary. A company may change only a product's name or packaging, or it can modify a product's components, size, and functions. Understanding a country's regulations, culture, and local competition is essential to making smart product design and branding decisions.

- **Customer support.** Cars, computers, and other products that require some degree of customer support add another layer of complexity to international business. Many customers are reluctant to buy foreign products that don't offer some form of local support, whether it's a local dealer, a manufacturer's branch office, or a third-party organization that offers support under contract to the manufacturer.

- **Promotion.** Advertising, public relations, and other promotional efforts also present the dilemma of standardization versus customization. In addition to language differences, companies need to consider nonverbal symbols (the significance of colors and hand gestures, for example), local competition, and a variety of cultural differences.

- **Pricing.** Even a standardized strategy adds to the cost of doing business, from transportation to communication, and customized international strategies add even more. Before moving into other countries, businesses need to make sure they can cover all these costs and still be able to offer competitive prices.

Patrizia Wyss/Alamy

Product branding and packaging are key decisions for international marketers. Notice how Coca-Cola maintains the look of its packaging while translating the product name.

- **Staffing.** Depending on the form of business a company decides to pursue in international markets, staffing questions can be major considerations. Many companies find that a combination of U.S. and local personnel works best, mixing company experience with local connections and lifelong knowledge of the working culture. Staffing strategies can evolve over time, too, as conditions change in various countries. In recent years, for example, U.S. and European countries with operations in China have begun filling more middle- and upper-management positions with local talent, rather than relocating managers from headquarters. The costs of hiring locally are often considerably lower, and there is less risk of a foreign manager failing to adapt to working and living in China.[43] When transferring managers to foreign posts, some U.S. companies have experienced failure rates as high as 50 percent.[44]

Given the number and complexity of the decisions to be made, you can see why successful companies plan international expansion with great care—and adapt quickly if their strategies and tactics aren't working. The consequences of not planning carefully or adapting quickly to missteps can be high. Recognizing the number of Canadian shoppers who crossed the border to shop at its U.S. stores, Target decided to enter the Canadian market to serve these customers on their home turf. The idea seemed to make solid business sense: If people are willing to drive some distance and put up with the hassles of border crossings just to shop at your stores, imagine how much more you could sell to them and their neighbors if you were right down the street.

Target jumped in with both feet, quickly opening more than 100 stores in its first expansion outside the United States. However, after only two years, it shut them all down and left the country. The company admits it tried too much too soon, and shoppers and retailing experts pointed to multiple blunders, including underestimating the strong local competition, opening stores in unappealing locations, setting prices too high, and failing to keep stores stocked with adequate inventory. It was an expensive mistake that cost the company billions of dollars.[45]

For the latest information on internal business, visit **http://real-timeupdates.com /bia8** and click on Chapter 3.

 **Checkpoint**

LEARNING OBJECTIVE 6: Discuss the strategic choices that must be considered before entering international markets.

SUMMARY: The strategic choices a business must make include the basic organizational strategy that defines what kind of company the firm will be in each country and a variety of functional strategies involving such aspects as products, customer support, promotion, pricing, and staffing. Organizational strategies include *multidomestic* (a highly decentralized approach), *global* (a highly centralized approach), and *transnational* (a hybrid approach).

CRITICAL THINKING: (1) If a multidomestic approach gives local managers the most flexibility for responding to local market conditions, why wouldn't every international company use this strategy? (2) How might the choice of overall organizational strategy affect a company's staffing plans in each country?

IT'S YOUR BUSINESS: (1) How does Apple's "Designed in California" product label influence your perceptions of product quality? (2) Do you think it helps counter negative public opinion about U.S. companies that manufacture products in other countries as a way to reduce labor costs? Why or why not?

KEY TERMS TO KNOW: multidomestic strategy, global strategy, transnational strategy

BEHIND THE SCENES
H&M EXPANDS IT GLOBAL FOOTPRINT, BUT NOT WITHOUT COMPETITION AND CHALLENGES

From its humble start in 1947 as a single store in Västerås, Sweden, H&M has grown into a global brand recognized on main streets and in shopping malls around the world. The several brands that make up the H&M family now boast a combined 3,000 stores in more than 50 countries, with the flagship H&M store the leading presence.

Because H&M designs its own clothing lines, manages their production (via outsourcing partners), and retails them in its own branded stores, the company's international expansion strategy is more complicated than it would be for a business that operates strictly on the production side or strictly on the retailing side. However, H&M management has put a lot of thought into its supply chain, creating a system that is both cost-effective and flexible to respond quickly to shifts in consumer demand.

The process starts with the 160 designers and 100 pattern makers who work in the company's Stockholm headquarters. These specialists are members of teams with autonomous responsibility for keeping a finger on the pulse of fashion trends in art, cinema, music, and other cultural influences. When new designs are ready, they are sent to production partners in Europe or Asia, then the finished products are shipped to regional H&M distribution centers for final delivery to stores or e-commerce customers.

With a well-established global network in place, expanding its retail presence is easier than it would be for a younger or smaller company. That retail presence is primarily through company-managed sites, but H&M also works with franchising partners in selected markets such as Indonesia and the Middle East. With its global organizational strategy (see page 56), the company establishes guidelines for merchandising displays, which it develops in a "test store" near company headquarters in Stockholm. Stores themselves are uniquely adapted to local settings and leasing opportunities, but they maintain a consistent and recognizable brand presentation and shopping experience.

H&M's product strategy is fairly consistent worldwide as well, with the same styles generally rolled out on a global scale. The product mix does get adapted to local needs to a degree, such as not selling winter coats in locales that do not experience cold winter temperatures. However, the overall sense of style is consistent all around the globe.

Customer communication is localized to varying degrees. For example, website content is translated into local languages in major markets such as France, Germany, the United States, and Italy. In countries where the company currently has a smaller presence, the websites tend to be in English, with price in the local currency and store-location search engines sometimes presented in the local language. Graphic design and product photography are fairly consistent from country to country, however.

H&M's global expansion strategy has served it well so far, but the company does face serious challenges from two directions. On the one hand, it generally can't beat Zara when it comes to fast turnaround times of new designs, particularly in Europe, because Zara's production facilities are closer to retail outlets. Consequently, H&M can't always present the most cutting-edge fashions to consumers who simply must have the latest styles and are willing to pay for the pleasure. On the other hand, H&M's prices aren't low enough to compete with low-price chains such as Primark in Great Britain or Forever 21 in the United States.

From its position between these two market layers, H&M appears to be pushing both upward and downward. It has opened a small number of stores under the more high-end & Other Stories brand, and it continues to expand its offerings aimed at eco-conscious consumers (such as clothes made of organic cotton). And two other company brands, Monki and Cheap Monday, are aimed at more casual and cost-conscious buyers.

As it expands its brand portfolio, the company shows no intention to ease off from its aggressive global growth, with the aim of increasing the number of stores by 10 to 15 percent every year. Two key markets for near-term expansion are China and the United States, so if you haven't bumped into an H&M store yet, chances are you will soon.

Critical Thinking Questions

3-1. Some companies play up their home-country roots as they expand internationally, such as the way BMW and Mercedes emphasize their German engineering. Should H&M promote some aspect of its "Swedishness"? Why or why not?

3-2. Would H&M have been able to succeed with its consistent global style strategy in the days before mass media and digital communications? Explain your answer.

3-3. H&M's growth, including its international expansion, is entirely self-funded (meaning it doesn't borrow money to launch new stores). How might this influence the company's decision-making and expansion efforts?

LEARN MORE ONLINE

Visit **www.hm.com** and select three of H&M's country websites. How are these sites similar and how are they different? Are the sites translated into the local language for each country? Are the imagery, messaging, and product promotion consistent across all three sites? What does this tell you about H&M's global product strategy?

KEY TERMS

balance of payments (52)
balance of trade (52)
culture (60)
dumping (55)
economic globalization (51)
economies of scale (51)
embargo (55)
ethnocentrism (60)
exchange rate (53)
export subsidies (55)
exporting (63)
foreign direct investment (FDI) (65)
free trade (54)
global strategy (66)

import quotas (55)
importing (63)
licensing (64)
multidomestic strategy (65)
multinational corporations (MNCs) (65)
protectionism (55)
stereotyping (60)
tariffs (55)
tax haven (62)
trade deficit (52)
trade surplus (52)
trading blocs (57)
transnational strategy (66)

MyBizLab®
To complete the problems with the ⭐,
go to EOC Discussion Questions in the
MyLab.

TEST YOUR KNOWLEDGE

Questions for Review

3-4. How can a company use a licensing agreement to enter world markets?

3-5. What two fundamental product strategies do companies choose between when selling their products in the global marketplace?

3-6. What is the balance of trade, and how is it related to the balance of payments?

3-7. What is protectionism?

3-8. What is a floating exchange rate?

Questions for Analysis

3-9. Why would a company choose to work through intermediaries when selling products in a foreign country?

3-10. How do companies benefit from forming international joint ventures and strategic alliances?

3-11. What types of situations might cause the U.S. government to implement protectionist measures?

3-12. How do tariffs and quotas protect a country's own industries?

⭐ **3-13. Ethical Considerations.** Is it unethical for a U.S. company to choose export markets specifically for their less stringent consumer protection standards? Why or why not?

Questions for Application

3-14. Suppose you own a small company that manufactures baseball equipment. You are aware that Russia is a large market, and you are considering exporting your products there. However, you know you need to learn more about Russian culture before making contact with potential business partners. What steps could you take to improve your cultural awareness?

3-15. How has your current employer or any previous employer been affected by globalization? For instance, does your company compete with lower-cost imports? (If you don't have any work experience, ask a friend or family member.)

⭐ **3-16.** Would a major shopping mall developer with experience all across Europe be a good strategic alliance partner for your fast-food chain's first overseas expansion effort? Why or why not?

⭐ **3-17. Concept Integration.** You just received notice that a large shipment of manufacturing supplies that one of your factories in another country has been waiting for has been stuck in customs for two weeks. A local business associate in that country tells you that you are expected to give customs agents some "incentive money" to see that everything clears easily. How will you handle this situation? Evaluate the ethical merits of your decision by considering the approaches listed in Exhibit 4.3 on page 78.

EXPAND YOUR KNOWLEDGE

Discovering Career Opportunities

If global business interests you, consider working for a U.S. government agency that supports or regulates international trade. Search the USAJobs website at **www.usajobs.gov** for an opening in international trade administration, such as an *international trade specialist*.[46] Study the job description and answer the following questions:

3-18. On the basis of this description, what education and skills (personal and professional) would you need to succeed in this job?

3-19. How well does this job description fit your qualifications and interests?

3-20. How important would interpersonal skills be in this position? Why?

Improving Your Tech Insights: Telepresence

Telepresence systems start with the basic idea of videoconferencing but go far beyond, with imagery so real that colleagues thousands of miles apart virtually appear to be in the same room together. The interaction feels so lifelike that participants can forget that the person "sitting" on the other side of the table is actually in another city or even another country. The ability to convey nonverbal subtleties such as facial expressions and hand gestures makes these systems particularly good for developing new relationships and engaging in negotiations, collaborative problem solving, and other complex discussions.[47]

Conduct research to identify a company that has installed a telepresence system. What kinds of meetings does the firm use the telepresence system for? What advantages does the system give the company?

PRACTICE YOUR SKILLS

Sharpening Your Communication Skills

Languages never translate on a word-for-word basis. When doing business in the global marketplace, choose words that communicate a single idea clearly. Avoid using slang or idioms (words that can have meanings far different from their individual components when translated literally). For example, if a U.S. executive tells an Egyptian executive that a change in plans "really threw us a curve ball," chances are that communication will fail.

Team up with two other students and list 10 examples of slang (in your native language) that would probably be misinterpreted or misunderstood during a business conversation with someone from another culture. Next to each example, suggest other words you might use to convey the same message. Make sure the alternatives mean exactly the same as the original slang or idiom. Compare your list with those of your classmates.

Building Your Team Skills

In 2009, eight U.S. steel companies and the United Steelworkers union accused Chinese pipe manufacturers of dumping $2.7 billion worth of a particular type of stainless steel pipe on the U.S. market the previous year. (Specifically, the type of pipe is called "oil country tubular goods" and is used in oil and gas wells.) In a petition to the U.S. International Trade Commission (ITC) and the U.S. Department of Justice (DOJ), the group said 2,000 U.S. employees had lost their jobs as a result of the unfairly priced Chinese imports. The petition asked for tariffs of up to 99 percent on the Chinese steel.[48]

With your team, research the outcome of the steel industry's petition. Did the ITC and DOJ enact tariffs on Chinese steel?

After you have discovered the outcome of the petition, analyze the potential effect of the government's position on the following stakeholders:

- U.S. businesses that buy this type of steel
- U.S. steel manufacturers
- Employees of U.S. steel manufacturers
- The United Steelworkers union
- Chinese steel manufacturers

Present your analysis to the class and compare your conclusions with those reached by other teams.

Developing Your Research Skills

Companies involved in international trade have to watch the foreign exchange rates of the countries in which they do business. Use your research skills to locate and analyze information about the value of the Japanese yen relative to the U.S. dollar. As you complete this exercise, make a note of the sources and search strategies you used.

3-21. How many Japanese yen does one U.S. dollar buy right now? (You can find the foreign exchange rate for the yen at **www.x-rates.com** and many similar sites.)

3-22. Investigate the foreign exchange rate for the yen against the dollar over the past month. Is the dollar growing stronger (buying more yen) or growing weaker (buying fewer yen)?

3-23. If you were a U.S. exporter selling to Japan, how would a stronger dollar be likely to affect demand for your products? How would a weaker dollar be likely to affect demand?

MyBizLab®

Go to the Assignments section of your MyLab to complete these writing exercises.

3-24. How does free trade create situations in which companies can pit the workers of one country against the workers of another?

3-25. Should the U.S. government promote trade policies that benefit some companies or industries while potentially harming others? Why or why not?

ENDNOTES

1. H&M website, accessed 22 March 2015, www.hm.com; Inditex website, accessed 28 October 2013, www.inditex.com; Lydia Dishman, "H&M's Competitive Advantage: Expansion in India," *Forbes*, 29 April 2013, www.forbes.com; John Lynch, "How Fashion Giant Inditex Bucked Trend to Notch €16bn Sales," *Irish Independent*, 28 October 2013, www.independent.ie; "H&M Struggles to Compete in High-Street Fashion," MarketWatch, 15 March 2013, www.marketwatch.com.

2. Ricky W. Griffin and Michael W. Pustay, *International Business*, 6th ed. (Upper Saddle River, N.J.: Pearson Prentice Hall, 2010), 6.

3. Griffin and Pustay, *International Business*, 12.

4. Holley H. Ulbrich and Mellie L. Warner, *Managerial Economics* (New York: Barron's Educational Series, 1990), 190.

5. Janet I. Tu, Seattle-Area Businesses Plug into China's Love of Online Shopping, *Seattle Times*, 2 January 2015, www.seattle times.com.

6. Griffin and Pustay, *International Business*, 13.

7. Griffin and Pustay, *International Business*, 14.

8. Robert Whaples, "The Policy Views of American Economic Association Members: The Results of a New Survey," *Econ Journal Watch*, September 2009, 337–348.

9. Uwe E. Reinhardt, "How Convincing Is the Case for Free Trade?" blog post, 18 February 2011, *New York Times*, www.nytimes.com.

10. "President Bush's Statement on Open Economies," FDCH Regulatory Intelligence Database, 10 May 2007, www.ebsco .com; Vladimir Masch, "A Radical Plan to Manage Globalization," *BusinessWeek*, 24 February 2007, 11; Philip Levy, "Trade Truths for Turbulent Times," *BusinessWeek*, 24 February 2007, 9.

11. "Twelve Myths About Hunger," Institute for Food and Development Policy website, accessed 27 January 2005, www .foodfirst.com.

12. Peter Davis, "Investment and the Development Theory Myth," *Ethical Corporation*, October 2006, 29–30.

13. Moisés Naim, "Globalization," *Foreign Policy*, March–April 2009, 28–34.

14. "Protectionism Fades, So EU Carmakers Must Fight," *Automotive News Europe*, 11 June 2007, 10.

15. "Common Trade Concerns and Problems Experienced by U.S. Textile/Apparel/Footwear/Travel Goods Exporters," U.S. Department of Commerce, International Trade Administration, Office of Textiles and Apparel website, accessed 1 August 2011, http://web.ita.doc.gov.

16. John D. Daniels, Lee H. Radebaugh, and Daniel P. Sullivan, *International Business*, 10th ed. (Upper Saddle River, N.J.: Pearson Prentice Hall, 2004), 182.

17. World Trade Organization website, accessed 22 March 2015, www.wto.org.

18. "10 Common Misunderstandings About the WTO," World Trade Organization website, accessed 6 October 2013, www.wto.org.

19. Joe Chidley, "The WTO at the Brink," *Canadian Business*, 10 April 2009, 35–39.

20. International Monetary Fund website, accessed 22 March 2015, www.imf.org.

21. World Bank Group website, accessed 22 March 2015, www.world bank.org.

22. "North American Free Trade Agreement (NAFTA)," USDA Foreign Agricultural Service website, accessed 29 June 2007, www.fas.usda.gov.

23. Julián Aguilar, "Twenty Years Later, NAFTA Remains a Source of Tension," *New York Times*, 7 December 2012, www.nytimes.com.

24. Armand de Mestral, "NAFTA: The Unfulfilled Promise of the FTA," *European Law Journal*, Vol. 17, No. 5, September 2011, 649–666; "Fool Me Twice? Chamber of Commerce Distorts NAFTA Record, Hides CAFTA Costs," *Public Citizen*, March 2005, www .citizen.org; "North American Free Trade Agreement (NAFTA)," Public Citizen website, accessed 28 January 2005, www.citizen .org; Debra Beachy, "A Decade of NAFTA," *Hispanic Business*, July/August 2004, 24–25; Geri Smith and Cristina Lindblad, "Mexico: Was NAFTA Worth It?" *BusinessWeek*, 22 December 2003, 66–72; Charles J. Walen, "NAFTA's Scorecard: So Far, So Good," *BusinessWeek*, 9 July 2001, 54–56.

25. M. Angeles Villarreal and Ian F. Fergusson, "NAFTA at 20: Overview and Trade Effects," *Congressional Research Service*, 28 April 2014, www.crs.gov.

26. European Community website, accessed 22 March 2015, http://europa.eu.

27. "The Euro," European Community website, accessed 6 October 2013, http://europa.eu.

28. "About APEC," APEC website, accessed 22 March 2015, www .apec.org.

29. "Trans-Pacific Partnership (TPP): Job Loss, Lower Wages and Higher Drug Prices," *Public Citizen*, accessed 22 March 2015, www .citizen.org; "Trans-Pacific Partnership Agreement," Electronic Frontier Foundation, accessed 22 March 2015, www.eff.org; Everett Rosenfeld, "Major Asia-Pacific Trade Pact Enters Final Stages," *CNBC*, 20 March 2015, www.cnbc.com; "Trans-Pacific Partnership," Office of the United States Trade Representative, accessed 22 March 2015, http://ustr.gov.

30. Linda Beamer and Iris Varner, *Intercultural Communication in the Workplace*, 2nd ed. (New York: McGraw-Hill Irwin, 2001), 3.

31. Mathew Ingram, "Amazon to Start Paying More EU Taxes After Pressure from Regulators," *Fortune*, 25 May 2015, www.fortune .com; Peter Campbell and Jay Akbar, "Embarrassment for EU Chief Juncker as Sweetheart Tax Deal Between Amazon and Luxembourg Made When He Was Nation's PM Is Declared Illegal," *Daily Mail*, 16 January 2015, www.dailymail.co.uk; Simon Bowers and Patrick Wintour, "Amazon Told: Time Is Up for Tax Avoidance," *Guardian*, 19 July 2013, www.theguardian .com; Kiran Stacey, Jim Pickard, and Vanessa Houlder, "Coalition Hardens Stance Over Tax," *Financial Times*, 12 February 2013, www.ft.com; "Starbucks Pays UK Corporation Tax for First Time Since 2009," *BBC News*, 23 June 2013, www .bbc.co.uk; Matt Warman, "Google's UK Division Paid £12m in Corporation Tax in 2012," *Telegraph*, 29 September 2013, www .telegraph.co.uk.

32. Daniels, et al., *International Business*, 335.

33. "FAQs on Corruption," *Transparency International*, accessed 8 October 2013, www.transparency.org.

34. "Foreign Corrupt Practices Act," U.S. Department of Justice website, accessed 8 October 2013, www.justice.gov.

35. *A Resource Guide to the U.S. Foreign Corrupt Practices Act*, Criminal Division of the U.S. Department of Justice and the Enforcement Division of the U.S. Securities and Exchange Commission, 2012, 15–17, 25.

36. Organisation for Economic Co-Operation and Development website, accessed 1 August 2011, www.oecd.org.

37. Export.gov, accessed 1 August 2011, http://export.gov.

38. "Partnering for Success," Boehringer Ingelheim, accessed 23 May 2009, www.boehringer-ingelheim.com.

39. Hoovers, accessed 1 August 2011, www.hoovers.com.

40. U.S. Census Bureau, "U.S. Businesses Acquired or Established by Foreign Direct Investors—Investment Outlays by Industry of U.S. Business Enterprise and Country of Ultimate Beneficial Owner," accessed 1 August 2011, www.census.gov; Griffin and Pustay, *International Business*, 170.

41. Griffin and Pustay, *International Business*, 310–311.

42. "Carrefour in China: When the Price Isn't Right," Knowledge @ Wharton, 16 March 2011, www.knowledgeatwharton.com.

43. Griffin and Pustay, *International Business*, 555.

44. Griffin and Pustay, *International Business*, 559.

45. Jordan Weissmann, "Target Is Closing All of Its Stores in Canada. These Pictures Show Why They Were Such a Failure." *Slate*, 15 January 2015, www.slate.com; Anne D'innocenzio and Michelle Chapman, "Litany of Problems Pushes Target into Giving Up on Canada," *Seattle Times*, 16 January 2015, www.seattletimes.com.

46. "International Trade Administration," *USA Jobs*, accessed 22 March 2015, www.usajobs.gov.

47. "Telepresence," ATT, accessed 22 March 2015, www.business.att.com; Steve Lohr, "As Travel Costs Rise, More Meetings Go Virtual," *New York Times*, 22 July 2008, www.nytimes.com.

48. Beth Murtagh, "U.S. Steel Files Trade Complaint Against China for Steel Dumping," *Pittsburgh Business Times*, 11 May 2009, www.bizjournals.com.

4

Business Ethics and Corporate Social Responsibility

LEARNING OBJECTIVES After studying this chapter, you will be able to

1 Discuss what it means to practice good business ethics, and highlight three factors that influence ethical decision making.

2 Define *corporate social responsibility (CSR)*, and explain the difference between philanthropy and strategic CSR.

3 Distinguish among the four perspectives on corporate social responsibility.

4 Discuss the role of business in protecting the natural environment, and define *sustainable development*.

5 Identify four fundamental consumer rights and the responsibility of business to respect them.

6 Explain the responsibilities businesses have toward their employees.

BEHIND THE SCENES NIKE'S GLOBAL PRESENCE PUTS IT ON THE FRONT LINES OF CORPORATE SOCIAL RESPONSIBILITY

Kristopher Skinner/KRTC/Newscom

Nike has taken a leadership role in improving workplace conditions and environmental stewardship in factories around the globe.

www.nike.com

Imagine yourself in this dilemma. Much of the appeal of your products is based on their association with famous athletes, but paying these celebrities to endorse your products adds millions of dollars a year to the cost of doing business. You're also in a ferociously competitive, trend-driven industry, where you can drop off the public radar practically overnight if you don't invest heavily in constant promotion. Plus, many of your products are technically innovative, which requires ongoing research and development. Finally, consumers want to be able to buy your products from thousands of retail outlets, at a moment's notice, wherever they like to shop, so you must keep a vast distribution network supplied with inventory.

Add up all these costs, and you still haven't paid for somebody to actually *make* your products. You could make them in the United States, with its comparatively high labor costs, which would force you to raise prices in order to sustain the profit margin your investors expect in return for the money they have entrusted to you. Of course, if you raise prices too high, consumers will decide that, as cool as your products are, they can get a better deal from your competitors.

Or you could move production to a country with significantly lower labor costs, taking the pressure off your prices and profit margins and allowing you to maintain high levels of investments in other areas. Looks great on paper, but you know that every decision in business involves trade-offs. Moving production overseas and into the hands of other companies entails a significant loss of control over the manufacturing process, materials sourcing, and working conditions.

You can measure financial costs and product quality, providing clear feedback on some important performance parameters. But what about the way your production partners conduct business? Do they conduct themselves in a manner that is consistent with your values and your public image? Do they treat workers humanely? Do they steward shared natural resources in a responsible manner? Do they minimize negative impacts on their communities?

You don't have direct control over how these companies perform, and you don't always know what they're up to, but you know one thing for certain: People are going to hold you accountable for the performance and behavior of these business partners, even if they are independent companies operating in other countries. Big companies make big targets, and you've been the focus of a number of campaigns by advocacy groups and other nongovernmental organizations.

Welcome to a day in the life of Mark Parker, president and CEO of Nike, the athletic footwear and apparel giant based in Beaverton, Oregon. If you were in Parker's Nikes, how would you balance the competing demands of investors, employees, retailers, advocacy groups, and business partners? How would you keep Nike on its path of strong growth while also being a responsible corporate citizen in the more than 160 countries where it does business?[1]

INTRODUCTION

Like Nike's Mark Parker (profiled in the chapter-opening Behind the Scenes), managers in every industry today must balance the demands of running a profitable business with the expectations of running a socially responsible company. As a future business leader, you will face some of the challenges discussed in this chapter, and your choices won't always be easy. You may struggle to find ethical clarity in some situations or even to understand what your choices are and how each option might affect your company's various stakeholders. You may need to muster the courage to stand up to colleagues, bosses, or customers if you think ethical principles are being violated. Fortunately, by having a good understanding of what constitutes ethical behavior and what society expects from business today, you'll be better prepared to make these tough choices. This chapter explores the basic ideas of business ethics and corporate social responsibility and then takes a closer look at business's responsibility toward the natural environment, consumers, and employees.

1   **LEARNING OBJECTIVE**

Discuss what it means to practice good business ethics, and highlight three factors that influence ethical decision making.

Ethics in Contemporary Business

Assessing the ethics of contemporary business is no simple matter, partly because of disagreement over what constitutes ethical behavior and partly because the behavior of individual companies runs the gamut from positive to neutral to negative. However, it is safe to say that there is significant concern about the ethics of current (and future) business leaders. Harvard Business School professor Rakesh Khurana probably speaks for many when he says, "One way of looking at the problem with American business today is that it has succeeded in assuming many of the appearances and privileges of professionalism, while evading the attendant constraints and responsibilities."[2] By and large, the general public seems to agree (see Exhibit 4.1).

The news is not all bad, of course. Most businesses are run by ethical managers and staffed by ethical employees whose positive contributions to their communities are unfortunately overshadowed at times by headline-grabbing scandals. Companies around the world help their communities in countless ways, from sponsoring youth sports teams to raising millions of dollars to build hospitals.

Moreover, even when companies are simply engaged in the normal course of business—and do so ethically—they contribute to society by making useful products, providing employment, and paying taxes. Business catches a lot of flak these days, some of it deserved, but overall, its contributions to the health, happiness, and well-being of society are beyond measure.

REAL-TIME UPDATES
Learn More by Reading This Article

Which companies do U.S. consumers like and loathe the most?

Peruse this ranking of America's most- and least-liked corporations. Go to http://real-timeupdates.com/bia8 and click on Learn More in the Students section.

| EXHIBIT 4.1 | Public Perceptions of Business Ethics |

One can argue whether public perceptions of business ethics accurately reflect the behavior of the entire community of business professionals or simply mirror the behavior of businesses and individuals who make headlines. However, there is no argument on this point: The general public doesn't think too highly of business. This graph shows the percentage of Americans who rate the honesty and ethics of a particular profession as either "high" or "very high." Several business professions are shown, with several nonbusiness professions for comparison.

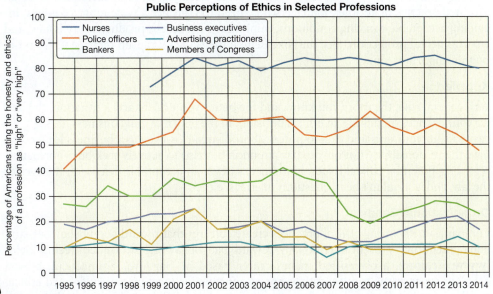

Public Perceptions of Ethics in Selected Professions

Legend: Nurses, Business executives, Police officers, Advertising practitioners, Bankers, Members of Congress

Source: Data from "USA Today/Gallup Poll, December 11–14, 2014—Final Topline," www.gallup.com.

WHAT IS ETHICAL BEHAVIOR?

Ethics are the principles and standards of moral behavior that are accepted by society as right and wrong. Practicing good business ethics involves, at a minimum, competing fairly and honestly, communicating truthfully, being transparent, and not causing harm to others:

- **Competing fairly and honestly.** Businesses are expected to compete fairly and honestly and to not knowingly deceive, intimidate, or misrepresent themselves to customers, competitors, clients, employees, the media, or government officials.
- **Communicating truthfully.** Communicating truthfully is a simple enough concept: Tell the truth, the whole truth, and nothing but the truth. However, matters sometimes aren't so clear. For instance, if you plan to introduce an improved version of a product next year, do you have an obligation to tell customers who are buying the existing product this year? Suppose you do tell them, and so many decide to delay their purchases that you end up with a cash flow problem that forces you to lay off several employees. Would that be fair for customers but unfair for your employees?
- **Being transparent.** Business communication ethics often involve the question of **transparency**, which can be defined as "the degree to which information flows freely within an organization, among managers and employees, and outward to stakeholders."[3]
- **Not causing harm to others.** All businesses have the capacity to cause harm to employees, customers, other companies, their communities, and investors. Problems can start when managers make decisions that put their personal interests above those of other stakeholders, underestimate the risks of failure, or neglect to consider potential effects on other people and organizations. For example, **insider trading**, in which company insiders use confidential information to gain an advantage in stock market trading, harms other investors. (Insider trading is illegal, in addition to being unethical.) Of course, harm can also result even when managers have acted ethically—but they are still responsible for these negative outcomes.

ethics
The rules or standards governing the conduct of a person or group.

transparency
The degree to which affected parties can observe relevant aspects of transactions or decisions.

insider trading
The use of unpublicized information that an individual gains from the course of his or her job to benefit from fluctuations in the stock market.

FACTORS INFLUENCING ETHICAL BEHAVIOR

Of the many factors that influence ethical behavior, three warrant particular attention: cultural differences, knowledge, and organizational behavior.

Cultural Differences

Chapter 3 points out that globalization exposes businesspeople to a variety of cultures and business practices. What does it mean for a business to do the right thing in Thailand? In Nigeria? In Norway? What may be considered unethical in one culture could be an accepted practice in another. Managers may need to consider a wide range of issues, including acceptable working conditions, minimum wage levels, product safety issues, and environmental protection. (See the Nike Behind the Scenes wrap-up on page 91 for more on this important topic.)

Knowledge

As a general rule, the more you know and the better you understand a situation, the better your chances of making an ethical decision. In the churn of daily business, though, it's easy to shut your eyes and ears to potential problems. However, as a business leader, you have the responsibility not only to pay attention but also to actively seek out information regarding potential ethical issues. Ignorance is never an acceptable defense in the eyes of the law, and it shouldn't be in questions of ethics, either.

Organizational Behavior

code of ethics
A written statement that sets forth the principles that guide an organization's decisions.

Companies with strong ethical practices create cultures that reward good behavior—and don't intentionally or unintentionally reward bad behavior.[4] At United Technologies (www.utc.com), a diversified manufacturer based in Hartford, Connecticut, ethical behavior starts at the top; executives are responsible for meeting clearly defined ethical standards, and their annual compensation is tied to how well they perform.[5] To help avoid ethical breaches, many companies develop programs to improve ethical conduct, typically combining training, communication, and a **code of ethics** that defines the values and principles that should be used to guide decisions.

whistle-blowing
The disclosure of information by a company insider that exposes illegal or unethical behavior by others within the organization.

Employees who observe unethical or illegal behavior within their companies and are unable to resolve the problems through normal channels may have no choice but to resort to **whistle-blowing**—expressing their concerns internally through formal reporting mechanisms or externally to the news media or government regulators. However, the decision to "blow the whistle" on one's own employer is rarely easy or without consequences. More than 80 percent of whistle-blowers in one survey said they were punished in some way for coming forward with their concerns.[6] In addition, the laws governing whistle-blowing are a complicated web of federal and state legislation that can be difficult for employees and employers to navigate.[7]

Although whistle-blowing is sometimes characterized as "ratting on" colleagues or managers, it has an essential function. According to international business expert Alex MacBeath, "Often whistle-blowing can be the only way that information about issues such as rule breaking, criminal activity, cover-ups, and fraud can be brought to management's attention before serious damage is suffered."[8]

ETHICAL DECISION MAKING

ethical lapse
A situation in which an individual or a group makes a decision that is morally wrong, illegal, or unethical.

When the question of what is right and what is wrong is clear, ethical decisions are easy to make: You simply choose to do the right thing. (At least making the decision is simple; *implementing* the decision may be another story.) If you choose the wrong course, such as cheating on your taxes or stealing from your employer, you commit an **ethical lapse**. The choices were clear, and you made the wrong one.

ethical dilemma
A situation in which more than one side of an issue can be supported with valid arguments.

However, you will encounter situations in which choices are not so clear. An **ethical dilemma** is a situation in which you must choose between conflicting but arguably valid options, or even situations in which all your options are unpleasant. As Exhibit 4.2 suggests, stakeholders' needs often conflict, requiring managers to make tough decisions about resource allocation.

EXHIBIT 4.2	Stakeholders' Rights: A Difficult Balancing Act

Balancing the individual needs and interests of a company's stakeholders is one of management's most difficult tasks. Consider how these three examples could affect each of five stakeholder groups in a different way. (Note that some people may fall into multiple groups. Employees, for example, are taxpayers and members of the local community, and they may also be shareholders. Also, these scenarios and outcomes offer a simplified view of what is likely to happen in each case, but they illustrate the mixed effects that can result from management decisions.)

Decision	Shareholders (entrust money to the company in anticipation of a positive return on their investment)	Employees (devote time, energy, and creativity to the company's success)	Customers (expect to receive quality products and maximum value for prices paid)	Local Community (can be affected both positively and negatively by the company's presence and actions)	Taxpayers (affected indirectly by the amount of tax revenue that local, state, and federal governments get from the company)
Company decides to *offshore* some of its production to another country with lower labor costs; lays off significant number of employees	⬆ Stand to benefit from lower production costs, which could increase sales, profits, or both, probably leading to increases in share price	⬇ Some employees lose their jobs; morale likely to suffer among those who keep theirs	⬆ Benefit from lower prices	⬇ Suffers from loss of spendable income in the local economy and taxes paid to local government; exodus of employees can drive down home values	⬇⬆ Might be hurt or helped by the move, depending on whether loss of income tax paid by U.S. employees is offset by increased income tax paid by the company, for example
Company institutes a generous pay and benefits increase to improve employee morale	⬇⬆ Might be hurt in the short term as the stock market punishes the company for increasing its cost structure and diverting funds away from development; could help over the long term if the moves boost employee productivity	⬆ Benefit from higher pay and more valuable benefits	⬇⬆ Could be hurt by higher prices if prices are raised to cover the added costs; could benefit from higher levels of employee satisfaction, leading to improved customer service	⬆ Benefits from more spendable income in the local economy and taxes paid to local government; better employee benefits could also mean less drain on community resources such as health clinics	⬆ Benefit from more money paid into government treasuries through higher income taxes
Company installs a multimillion-dollar waste water recirculation system that surpasses regulatory requirements; system will pay for itself in lower water bills, but not for 10 years	⬇⬆ Probably hurt as stock market punishes an investment with no immediate payback; increased goodwill and long-term cost savings help in years ahead	⬇⬆ Probably hurt in the short term as less money is available for raises and benefits; likely to benefit in the long term as the costs are recovered	⬇ Hurt as higher costs are passed along as higher prices	⬆ Helped by the company's efforts to conserve a shared natural resource	⬇ Hurt as the company writes off the cost of the system, thereby lowering the taxes it pays to the government

Consider the following points to help find the right answer whenever you face an ethical dilemma:

- Make sure you frame the situation accurately, taking into account all relevant issues and questions.
- Identify all parties who might be affected by your decision, and consider the rights of everyone involved.

EXHIBIT 4.3	Approaches to Resolving Ethical Dilemmas

These approaches can help you resolve ethical dilemmas you may face on the job. Be aware that in some situations, different approaches can lead to different ethical conclusions.

Approach	Summary
Justice	Treat people equally or at least fairly in a way that makes rational and moral sense.
Utilitarianism	Choose the option that delivers the most good for the most people (or protects the most people from a negative outcome).
Individual rights	To the greatest possible extent, respect the rights of all individuals, particularly their right to control their own destinies.
Individual responsibilities	Focus on the ethical duties of the individuals involved in the situation.
The common good	Emphasize qualities and conditions that benefit the community as a whole, such as peace and public safety.
Virtue	Emphasize desirable character traits such as integrity and compassion.

Sources: Manuel Velasquez, Claire Andre, Thomas Shanks, S. J., and Michael J. Meyer, "Thinking Ethically: A Framework for Moral Decision Making," Markkula Center for Applied Ethics, Santa Clara University, accessed 3 June 2009, www.scu.edu; Ben Rogers, "John Rawls," *The Guardian*, 27 November 2002, www.guardian.co.uk; Irene Van Staveren, "Beyond Utilitarianism and Deontology: Ethics in Economics," *Review of Political Economy*, January 2007, 21–35.

- Be as objective as possible. Make sure you're not making a decision just to protect your own emotions, and don't automatically assume you're viewing a situation fairly and objectively.
- Don't assume that other people think the way you do. The time-honored "Golden Rule" of treating others the way you want to be treated can cause problems when others don't *want* to be treated the same way you do.
- Watch out for **conflicts of interest**, situations in which competing loyalties can lead to ethical lapses. For instance, if you are in charge of selecting an advertising agency to handle your company's next campaign, you would have an obvious conflict of interest if your spouse or partner works for one of the agencies under consideration.

Exhibit 4.3 identifies six well-known approaches to resolving ethical dilemmas.

conflicts of interest
Situations in which competing loyalties can lead to ethical lapses, such as when a business decision may be influenced by the potential for personal gain.

 Checkpoint

LEARNING OBJECTIVE 1: Discuss what it means to practice good business ethics, and highlight three factors that influence ethical decision making.

SUMMARY: Three essential components of good business ethics are competing fairly and honestly, communicating truthfully, and not causing harm to others. Three major influences on ethical decision making are culture, knowledge, and organizational behavior. When facing an ethical dilemma, you can often find clarity by starting with universal standards of justice, considering the rights of everyone involved, being as objective as possible, not assuming that other people think the way you do, and avoiding conflicts of interest.

CRITICAL THINKING: (1) If you go to work tomorrow morning and your boss asks you to do something you consider unethical, what factors will you take into consideration before responding? (2) How can you balance the business need to inspire employees to compete aggressively with the moral need to avoid competing unethically?

IT'S YOUR BUSINESS: (1) In your current job (or any previous job you've held), in what ways does your employer contribute to society? (2) Have you ever encountered an ethical dilemma in your work? If so, how did you resolve it?

KEY TERMS TO KNOW: ethics, transparency, insider trading, code of ethics, whistle-blowing, ethical lapse, ethical dilemma, conflicts of interest.

Corporate Social Responsibility

2 **LEARNING OBJECTIVE**

Define *corporate social respon-sibility (CSR)*, and explain the difference between philanthropy and strategic CSR.

Corporate social responsibility (CSR) is the notion that business has obligations to society beyond the pursuit of profits. There is a widespread assumption these days that CSR is both a moral imperative for business and a good thing for society, but the issues aren't quite as clear as they might seem at first glance.

THE RELATIONSHIP BETWEEN BUSINESS AND SOCIETY

What does business owe society, and what does society owe business? Any attempt to understand and shape this relationship needs to consider four essential truths:

- Consumers in contemporary societies enjoy and expect a wide range of benefits, from education and health care to credit and products that are safe to use. Most of these benefits share an important characteristic: They require money.
- Profit-seeking companies are the economic engine that powers modern society; they generate the vast majority of the money in a nation's economy, either directly (through their own taxes and purchases) or indirectly (through the taxes and purchases made by the employees they support).
- Much of what we consider when assessing a society's standard of living involves goods and services created by profit-seeking companies.
- Conversely, companies cannot hope to operate profitably without the many benefits provided by a stable, functioning society: talented and healthy employees, a legal framework in which to pursue commerce, a dependable transportation infrastructure, opportunities to raise money, and customers with the ability to pay for goods and services, to name just some of them.

Business and society clearly need each other—and each needs the other to be healthy and successful.

PHILANTHROPY VERSUS STRATEGIC CSR

Companies that engage in CSR activities can choose between two courses of action: general philanthropy or strategic CSR. **Philanthropy** involves donating money, employee time, or other resources to various causes without regard for any direct business benefits for the company. For instance, a company might support the arts in its hometown in the interest of enhancing the city's cultural richness. Through a combination of free products, employee time, use of company facilities, and cash contributions, U.S. companies donate billions of dollars to charity every year.[9]

In contrast to generic philanthropy, **strategic CSR** involves social contributions that are directly aligned with a company's overall business strategy. In other words, the company helps itself and society at the same time. This approach can be followed in a variety of ways. A company can help develop the workforce by supporting job training efforts or use volunteering programs to help train employees. For example, in UPS's Community Internship Program, management candidates volunteer in community programs to help them understand the needs and challenges of various population groups while developing essential skills.[10] A company can also make choices that address social concerns while giving it a competitive advantage. As you can read in the "Improving Your Tech Insights" activity on page 94, IBM and Microsoft are among the many companies that invest in *assistive technologies* that help people with disabilities while expanding market opportunities and access to employee talent.

Strategic CSR makes more sense than general philanthropy or an antagonistic business-versus-society mindset, for several reasons. First, because business and society are mutually dependent, choices that weaken one or the other will ultimately weaken both. Second, investments that benefit the company are more likely to be sustained over time. Third, making sizable investments in a few strategically focused areas will yield greater benefits to society than spreading smaller amounts of money around through generic philanthropy.[11]

corporate social responsibility (CSR)
The idea that business has obligations to society beyond the pursuit of profits.

philanthropy
The donation of money, time, goods, or services to charitable, humanitarian, or educational institutions.

strategic CSR
Social contributions that are directly aligned with a company's overall business strategy.

Exactly how much can or should businesses contribute to social concerns? This is a difficult decision because all companies have limited resources that must be allocated to a number of goals, such as upgrading facilities and equipment, developing new products, marketing existing products, and rewarding employee efforts, in addition to contributing to social causes.

 Checkpoint

LEARNING OBJECTIVE 2: Define *corporate social responsibility (CSR),* **and explain the difference between philanthropy and strategic CSR.**

SUMMARY: Corporate social responsibility (CSR) is the notion that business has obligations to society beyond the pursuit of profits. However, there is no general agreement over what those responsibilities are or which elements of society should determine those obligations or benefit from them. Philanthropy involves donating time, money, or other resources, without regard for any direct business benefits. In contrast, strategic CSR involves contributions that are aligned with the company's business needs and strategies.

CRITICAL THINKING: (1) Given that "society" is not an organized entity, how can society decide what the responsibilities of business are in a CSR context? (2) Is philanthropy morally superior to strategic CSR? Why or why not?

IT'S YOUR BUSINESS: (1) How do a company's philanthropic or CSR efforts influence your purchasing behavior? (2) Is it ethical for companies to invest in your college or university in exchange for publicity? Why or why not?

KEY TERMS TO KNOW: corporate social responsibility (CSR), philanthropy, strategic CSR

---

3 **LEARNING OBJECTIVE**

Distinguish among the four perspectives on corporate social responsibility.

Perspectives on Corporate Social Responsibility

To encourage ethical behavior and promote a mutually beneficial relationship between business and society, it is clearly necessary to establish expectations about how businesses should conduct themselves. However, both business and society are still grappling with exactly what those expectations should be. "Social responsibility" certainly sounds admirable, but it's not always clear which segments of society it involves or what those responsibilities are.[12] Approaches to CSR can be roughly categorized into four perspectives (see Exhibit 4.4), from minimalist through proactive.

MINIMALIST CSR

According to what might be termed the *minimalist view,* the only social responsibility of business is to pay taxes and obey the law. In a 1970 article that is still widely discussed today, Nobel Prize–winning economist Milton Friedman articulated this view by saying, "There is only one social responsibility of business: to use its resources and engage in activities designed to increase its profits so long as it stays within the rules of the game, which is to say, engages in open and free competition without deception or fraud."[13]

This view, which tends to reject the stakeholder concept described in Chapter 1, might seem selfish and even antisocial, but it raises a couple of important issues. First, any business that operates ethically and legally provides society with beneficial goods and services at fair prices. One can argue that doing so fulfills a company's primary obligation to society.

Second—and this is a vital point to consider even if you reject the minimalist view— should businesses be in the business of making social policy and spending the public's money? Proponents of the minimalist view claim that this is actually what happens when companies make tax-deductible contributions to social causes. For example, assume that

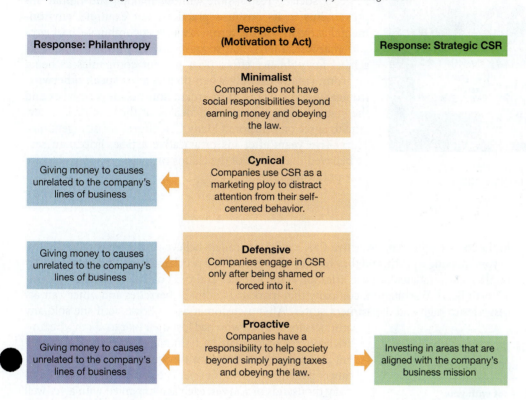

EXHIBIT 4.4   Perspectives on Corporate Social Responsibility

The perspectives on CSR can be roughly divided into four categories, from minimalist to proactive. Companies that engage in CSR can pursue either generic *philanthropy* or *strategic CSR*.

Response: Philanthropy	Perspective (Motivation to Act)	Response: Strategic CSR
	Minimalist Companies do not have social responsibilities beyond earning money and obeying the law.	
Giving money to causes unrelated to the company's lines of business	**Cynical** Companies use CSR as a marketing ploy to distract attention from their self-centered behavior.	
Giving money to causes unrelated to the company's lines of business	**Defensive** Companies engage in CSR only after being shamed or forced into it.	
Giving money to causes unrelated to the company's lines of business	**Proactive** Companies have a responsibility to help society beyond simply paying taxes and obeying the law.	Investing in areas that are aligned with the company's business mission

in response to pressure from activists, a company makes a sizable contribution that nets it a $1 million tax break. That's $1 million taken out of the public treasury, where voters and their elected representatives can control how money is spent, and put it into whatever social cause the company chooses to support. In effect, the corporation and the activists are spending the public's money, and the public has no say in how it is spent. Would it be better for society if companies paid full taxes and let the people (through their elected representatives) decide how their tax dollars are put to work?

REAL-TIME UPDATES
Learn More by Watching This Video

Are corporations putting too much emphasis on shareholder value?

Wharton professor Eric W. Orts discusses the potential harm of focusing too heavily on stock price. Go to http://real-timeupdates .com/bia8 and click on Learn More in the Students section.

DEFENSIVE CSR

Many companies today face pressure from a variety of activists and **nongovernmental organizations (NGOs)**, nonprofit groups that provide charitable services or that promote causes, from workers' rights to environmental protection. One possible response to this pressure is to engage in CSR activities as a way to avoid further criticism. In other words, the company may take positive steps to address a particular issue only because it has been embarrassed into action by negative publicity.

Note that companies can engage in proactive CSR and still receive criticism from advocacy groups. A company and an NGO might disagree about responsibilities or outcomes, or in some cases an NGO might target a company for a problem that the company has already been working on. In other words, it can't immediately be concluded that a company is simply being defensive when it engages in CSR while in the glare of public criticism. (For an example, see the Nike Behind the Scenes wrap-up at the end of the chapter.)

nongovernmental organizations (NGOs)
Nonprofit groups that provide charitable services or promote social and environmental causes.

John Gress/Corbis

Major corporations are often the target of advocacy groups, and the pressure can influence their responses to various CSR issues.

CYNICAL CSR

Another possible approach to CSR is purely cynical, in which a company accused of irresponsible behavior promotes itself as being socially responsible without making substantial improvements in its business practices. For example, environmental activists use the term *greenwash* (a combination of *green* and *whitewash*, a term that suggests covering something up) as a label for publicity efforts that present companies as being environmentally friendly when their actions speak otherwise. Ironically, some of the most ardent anti-business activists and the staunchly pro-business advocates of the minimalist view tend to agree on one point: Many CSR efforts are disingenuous. Thirty-five years after his provocative article, Friedman said he believed that "most of the claims of social responsibility are pure public relations."[14]

PROACTIVE CSR

In the fourth approach, proactive CSR, company leaders believe they have responsibilities beyond making a profit, and they back up their beliefs and proclamations with actions taken on their own initiative. Laurie Erickson is the founder and CEO of The Finest Accessories, a North Bend, Washington, company that markets handmade barrettes and other hair accessories to high-end department stores. After a customer asked Erickson if she sold any products for women who had lost their hair to chemotherapy, Erickson not only created a fashionable scarf that fit the bill but also launched a program of offering a free scarf to any cancer patient who asks for one. The company has now given away thousands of scarves, each accompanied with a get-well card signed by every employee in the company.[15]

See Chapter 5 (page 106) for a discussion of a new type of corporate structure, the *benefit corporation*, which builds proactive CSR into a company's very foundation and legally obligates it to pursue a social or environmental goal.

REAL-TIME UPDATES
Learn More by Visiting This Website

Want to make an impact with your entrepreneurial efforts?

Impact Hub is a global community of local "hubs" that nurture social entrepreneurs. Go to http://real-timeupdates.com/bia8 and click on Learn More in the Students section.

RESOLVING THE CSR DILEMMA

So what's the right answer? Of the four perspectives on CSR, we can instantly eliminate the cynical approach simply because it is dishonest and therefore unethical. Beyond that, the debate is less clear, but the opinions are certainly strong. Some proponents of the minimalist view equate CSR with *collectivism*, a term that suggests socialism and even communism. Some consider CSR demands from activist groups and other outsiders to be little more than extortion.[16] At the other extreme, some critics of contemporary business seem convinced that corporations can never be trusted and that every CSR initiative is a cynical publicity stunt.

A two-tiered approach to CSR can yield a practical, ethical answer to this complex dilemma. At the first tier, companies must take responsibility for the consequences of their actions and limit the negative impact of their operations. This approach can be summarized as "do no harm," and it is not a matter of choice. Just as a society has a right to expect certain behavior from all citizens, it has a right to expect a basic level of responsible behavior from all businesses, including minimizing pollution and waste, minimizing the depletion of shared natural resources, being honest with all stakeholders, offering real value in exchange for prices asked, and avoiding exploitation of employees, customers, suppliers, communities, and investors. Some of these issues are covered by

REAL-TIME UPDATES
Learn More by Exploring This Interactive Website

See how one of the world's biggest energy consumers is reducing, reusing, and recycling

Explore Google's efforts to reduce its energy usage and minimize its impact on the environment. Go to http://real-timeupdates.com/bia8 and click on Learn More in the Students section.

laws, but others aren't, thereby creating the responsibility of ethical decision making by all employees and managers in a firm.

At the second tier, moving beyond "do no harm" becomes a matter of choice. Companies can choose to help in whatever way that investors, managers, and employees see fit, but the choices are up to the company and should not be the result of pressure from outside forces.

For the latest information on CSR, visit **http://real-timeupdates.com/bia8** and click on Chapter 4.

 Checkpoint

LEARNING OBJECTIVE 3: Distinguish among the four perspectives on corporate social responsibility.

SUMMARY: The spectrum of viewpoints on CSR can be roughly divided into minimalist (business's only obligation is to compete to the best of its abilities without deception or fraud), defensive (in which businesses engage in CSR efforts only in response to social pressure), cynical (in which businesses engage in CSR as a public relations ploy), and proactive (in which businesses contribute to society out of a belief that they have an obligation to do so).

CRITICAL THINKING: (1) Do you agree that giving companies tax breaks for charitable contributions distorts public spending by indirectly giving companies and activists control over how tax revenues are spent? Why or why not? (2) If Company A takes a cynical approach to CSR and Company B takes a proactive approach but they make identical contributions to society, is one company "better" than the other? Why or why not?

IT'S YOUR BUSINESS: (1) Have you ever suspected a company of engaging in greenwashing or other disingenuous CSR activities? How would you prove or disprove such a suspicion? (2) If you were the head of a small company and wanted to give back to society in some way, how would you select which organizations or causes to support?

KEY TERM TO KNOW: nongovernmental organizations (NGOs)

CSR: The Natural Environment

In recent years, few issues in the public dialogue have become as politicized and polarized as pollution and resource depletion. Environmentalists and their political allies sometimes portray business leaders as heartless profiteers who would strip the Earth bare for a few bucks. Corporate leaders and their political allies, on the other hand, sometimes cast environmentalists as "tree huggers" who care more about bunnies and butterflies than about jobs and other human concerns. As is often the case, the shouting match between these extreme positions obscures real problems—and opportunities for real solutions.

To reach a clearer understanding of this situation, keep three important points in mind. First, the creation, delivery, use, and disposal of products that society values virtually always generate pollution and consume natural resources. For instance, it's tempting to assume that web-based businesses are "clean" because there is no visible pollution. However, the Internet and all the devices attached to it have a voracious appetite for electricity; Google is one of the largest users of electricity in the world, for example.[17] (See more about Google's energy consumption under "Efforts to Conserve Resources and Reduce Pollution.") Moreover, generation of electricity seriously affects the environment. Although the share of the electricity generated by renewable means in the United States is increasing, and solar is cost-competitive with coal in many locations, two-thirds of the country's electricity is still generated by burning coal, oil, or natural gas (see Exhibit 4.5 on the next page).[18]

4 **LEARNING OBJECTIVE**

Discuss the role of business in protecting the natural environment, and define *sustainable development*.

Sources of Electrical Power in the United States

Most of the electricity generated in the United States is produced by burning fossil fuels. Nuclear and hydroelectric power provide most of the rest. Renewable sources such as wind and solar have grown over the past decade, but they remain minor sources of electricity at this point.

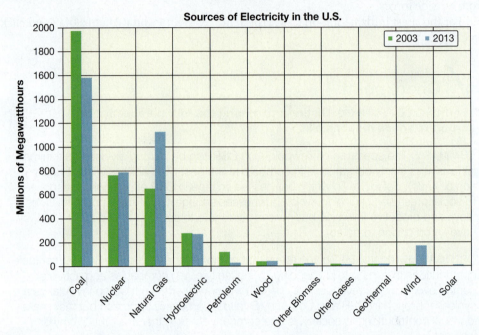

Sources of Electricity in the U.S.

Source: Data from *Electric Power Annual*, 23 March 2015, U.S. Energy Information Administration, www.eia.gov.

Second, "environmental" issues are often as much about human health and safety as they are about forests, rivers, and wildlife. The availability of clean air, water, and soil affects everyone, not just people concerned with wild spaces.

Third, many of these issues are neither easy nor simple. They often require tough trade-offs, occasional sacrifice, disruptive change, and decision making in the face of uncertainty. Meeting these challenges will require people to be clear-headed, open-minded, adaptable, and courageous.

EFFORTS TO CONSERVE RESOURCES AND REDUCE POLLUTION

Concerns over pollution and resource depletion have been growing since the dawn of the Industrial Age in the 19th century. However, widespread concern for the environment really dates to the 1960s, when *ecology*, the study of the relationship between organisms and the natural environment, entered mainstream discussion. In 1963, federal, state, and local governments began enacting laws and regulations to reduce pollution (see Exhibit 4.6). Many states and cities have also passed their own tough clean-air laws.

You've no doubt heard the slogan "reduce, reuse, recycle" as advice for conserving resources and minimizing pollution. Google offers a great example of what businesses can do in this regard. As a major consumer of energy, the company is taking responsibility for that consumption in a number of significant ways, including reducing energy usage in its data centers (massive complexes that house the thousands of computers that make Google searches possible) by more than half, investing in renewable energy in ways that help this fledgling industry sector grow, *repurposing* hundreds of thousands of older computers for new uses, using

REAL-TIME UPDATES
Learn More by Exploring This Interactive Website

Create a more sustainable product with Nike's interactive tool

Nike's Environmental Design Tool measures the environmental impact of a manufactured product and helps design teams improve the sustainability of their products. You can plug in data from your own apparel to see how your clothing scores. Go to http://real-timeupdates.com/bia8 and click on Learn More in the Students section.

EXHIBIT 4.6	Major Federal Environmental Legislation

Since the early 1960s, major federal legislation aimed at the environment has focused on providing cleaner air and water and reducing toxic waste. (Many of these laws have been amended since their original passage dates.)

Legislation	Key Provisions
Clean Air Act (1963) Clean Air Act (1967) Clean Air Act (1970)	Assist states and localities in formulating control programs; set federal standards for auto-exhaust emissions; set maximum permissible pollution levels; authorize nationwide air-pollution standards and limitations to pollutant discharge; require scrubbers in new coal-fired power plants; direct the (Environmental Protection Agency [EPA]) to prevent deterioration of air quality in clean areas; set schedule and standards for cutting smog, acid rain, hazardous factory fumes, and ozone-depleting chemicals
Solid Waste Disposal Act (1965)	Authorizes research and assistance to state and local control programs; regulates treatment, storage, transportation, and disposal of hazardous waste
National Environmental Policy Act (1969)	Establishes a structure for coordinating all federal environmental programs
Resource Recovery Act (1970)	Subsidizes pilot recycling plants; authorizes nationwide control programs
Clean Water Act (1972) Clean Water Act (1977)	Authorizes grant to states for water-pollution control; give federal government limited authority to correct pollution problems; authorize EPA to set and enforce water-quality standards
Noise Control Act (1972)	Requires EPA to set standards for major sources of noise and to advise Federal Aviation Administration on standards for airplane noise
Endangered Species Act (1973)	Establishes protections for endangered and threatened plants and animals
Safe Drinking Water Act (1974)	Sets standards of drinking-water quality; requires municipal water systems to report on contaminant levels; establishes funding to upgrade water systems
Toxic Substances Control Act (1976)	Requires chemicals testing; authorizes EPA to restrict the use of harmful substances
Resource Conservation and Recovery Act (1976)	Gives the EPA authority to control hazardous waste
Comprehensive Environmental Response, Compensation, and Liability Act (1980)	Establishes the "Superfund" program to oversee the identification and cleanup of uncontrolled or abandoned hazardous-waste sites
Nuclear Waste Policy Act (1982)	Establishes procedures for creating geologic repositories of radioactive waste
Marine Protection, Research, and Sanctuaries Act (1988)	Prohibits ocean dumping that could threaten human health or the marine environment
Oil Pollution Act (1990)	Sets up liability trust fund; extends operations for preventing and containing oil pollution
Energy Independence and Security Act (2007)	Aims to reduce U.S. dependence on foreign energy sources by expanding energy production options and improving energy efficiency

Sources: U.S. Environmental Protection Agency website, accessed 23 March 2015, www.epa.gov; "Overview: Key Federal Environmental Laws," FindLaw, accessed 23 March 2015, www.findlaw.com.

its position as a major corporation to help shape energy policy and public awareness, and sharing the results of its considerable research efforts with other companies to help them reduce resource usage.[19]

In addition to technological efforts to reduce pollution and resource consumption, businesses, governments, and NGOs are pursuing a variety of political and economic solutions. For example, **cap and trade** programs try to balance free-market economics with government intervention. Lawmakers first establish a maximum allowable amount of a particular pollutant that a designated group of companies or industries is allowed to emit (the "cap") and then distribute individual emission allowances to all the companies in that group. If a company lowers its emissions enough to stay under its prescribed limit, it can sell, trade, or save leftover allowances (the "trade"). If a company exceeds its emission allowances, it must buy or trade for enough allowances to cover the excess emissions. In this way, companies can choose the lowest-cost means of taking responsibility for their emissions.[20] During the 1990s, a cap-and-trade program to reduce sulfur dioxide emissions from coal-burning power plants, a leading cause of acid rain, reduced emissions by 50 percent.[21]

cap and trade
A type of environmental policy that gives companies some freedom in addressing the environmental impact of specified pollutants, by either reducing emissions to meet a designated cap or buying allowances to offset excess emissions.

When you replaced your smartphone or laptop, where did the old one go?

badmanproduction/Fotolia

REAL-TIME UPDATES
Learn More by Watching This Video

Hear what 1,000 global CEOs think about sustainability

Get the highlights of a comprehensive survey of executive perspectives on business and sustainability issues. Go to http://real-timeupdates.com/bia8 and click on Learn More in the Students section.

sustainable development
Operating business in a manner that minimizes pollution and resource depletion, ensuring that future generations will have vital resources.

THE TREND TOWARD SUSTAINABILITY

Efforts to minimize resource depletion and pollution are part of a broader effort known as *sustainability,* or **sustainable development**, which the United Nations has defined as development that "meets the needs of the present without compromising the ability of future generations to meet their own needs."[22] Notice how this idea expands the stakeholder concept from Chapter 1 by including stakeholders from the future, not just those with an immediate interest in what a company does.

Sustainable development can certainly require changes to the way companies conduct business, but paying attention to a broader scope of stakeholders and managing for the longer term doesn't automatically mean that companies have to take a financial hit to go "green." Many businesses are discovering that taking steps now to reduce consumption and pollution can end up saving money down the road by reducing everything from cleanup and litigation expenses to ongoing production costs. As Xerox CEO Ursula Burns puts it, "The greener we get, the more we can reduce costs and boost efficiency."[23]

In other words, in addition to better stewardship of shared natural resources, sustainable development is also a smart business strategy. By taking a broad and long-term view of their companies' impact on the environment and stakeholders throughout the world, managers can ensure the continued availability of the resources their organizations need and be better prepared for changes in government regulations and shifting social expectations. In fact, a majority of global CEOs now view sustainability as a business opportunity,[24] a viewpoint firmly in line with the concept of strategic CSR.

✓ Checkpoint

LEARNING OBJECTIVE 4: Discuss the role of business in protecting the natural environment, and define *sustainable development*.

SUMMARY: As major users of natural resources and generators of waste products, businesses play a huge role in conservation and pollution-reduction efforts. Many businesses are making an effort to reduce, reuse, and recycle, and governments are trying market-based approaches such as *cap and trade* to encourage businesses to reduce emissions. All these efforts are part of a trend toward *sustainable development,* which can be defined as meeting the needs of the present without compromising the ability of future generations to meet their own needs.

CRITICAL THINKING: (1) Should all industries be required to meet the same levels of pollution control? Why or why not? (2) How would you respond to critics who say that cap-and-trade programs allow polluters to buy their way out of the responsibility of cleaning up their operations?

IT'S YOUR BUSINESS: (1) In what ways could your employer (or your college, if you're not currently working) take steps to reduce resource depletion? (2) How did you dispose of the last electronic product you stopped using?

KEY TERMS TO KNOW: cap and trade, sustainable development

CSR: Consumers

The 1960s activism that awakened business to its environmental responsibilities also gave rise to **consumerism**, a movement that put pressure on businesses to consider consumer needs and interests. (Note that some people use *consumerism* in a negative sense, as a synonym for *materialism*.) Consumerism prompted many businesses to create consumer affairs departments to handle customer complaints. It also prompted state and local agencies to set up bureaus to offer consumer information and assistance. At the federal level, President John F. Kennedy announced a "bill of rights" for consumers, laying the foundation for a wave of consumer-oriented legislation (see Exhibit 4.7).

THE RIGHT TO BUY SAFE PRODUCTS—AND TO BUY THEM SAFELY

As mentioned previously, doing no harm is one of the foundations of CSR. The United States and many other countries go to considerable lengths to ensure the safety of the products sold within their borders. The U.S. government imposes many safety standards that are enforced by the Consumer Product Safety Commission (CPSC), as well as by other

EXHIBIT 4.7   Major Federal Consumer Legislation

Major federal legislation aimed at consumer protection has focused on food and drugs, false advertising, product safety, and credit protection.

Legislation	Major Provisions
Food, Drug, and Cosmetic Act (1938)	Puts cosmetics, foods, drugs, and therapeutic products under Food and Drug Administration's jurisdiction; outlaws misleading labeling
Cigarette Labeling and Advertising Act (1965)	Mandates warnings on cigarette packages and in ads
Fair Packaging and Labeling Act (1966, 1972)	Requires honest, informative package labeling; labels must show origin of product, quantity of contents, uses or applications
Truth in Lending Act (Consumer Protection Credit Act) (1968)	Requires creditors to disclose finance charge and annual percentage rate; limits cardholder liability for unauthorized use
Fair Credit Reporting Act (1970)	Requires credit-reporting agencies to set process for assuring accuracy; requires creditors to explain credit denials
Consumer Product Safety Act (1972)	Creates Consumer Product Safety Commission
Magnuson-Moss Warranty Act (1975)	Requires complete written warranties in ordinary language; requires warranties to be available before purchase
Alcohol Beverage Labeling Act (1988)	Requires warning labels on alcohol products, saying that alcohol impairs abilities and that women shouldn't drink when pregnant
Children's Online Privacy Protection Act (1988)	Gives parents control over the collection or use of information that websites can collect about children
Nutrition Education and Labeling Act (1990)	Requires specific, uniform product labels detailing nutritional information on every food regulated by the Food and Drug Administration (FDA)
American Automobile Labeling Act (1992)	Requires carmakers to identify where cars are assembled and where their individual components are manufactured
Deceptive Mail Prevention and Enforcement Act (1999)	Establishes standards for sweepstakes mailings, skill contests, and facsimile checks to prevent fraud and exploitation
Controlling the Assault of Non-Solicited Pornography and Marketing Act (2003)	Known as CAN-SPAM, attempts to protect online consumers from unwanted and fraudulent email
Consumer Product Safety Improvement Act (2008)	Strengthens standards for lead in children's products; mandates safety testing for imported children's products; creates a searchable database for reporting accidents, injuries, and illnesses related to consumer products
Dodd-Frank Wall Street Reform and Consumer Protection Act (2010)	Amends a number of previous acts and regulations in an attempt to improve the stability of the banking and investment industries; establishes the Consumer Financial Protection Bureau

Sources: www.fda.gov; http://uscode.house.gov; www.ftc.gov; www.cpsc.com; www.ttb.gov; www.consumerfinance.gov.

identity theft
A crime in which thieves steal personal information and use it to take out loans and commit other types of fraud.

federal and state agencies. Companies that don't comply with these rules are forced to take corrective action, and the threat of product-liability suits and declining sales motivates companies to meet safety standards.

Product safety concerns range from safe toys, food, and automobiles to less-tangible worries such as online privacy and **identity theft**, in which criminals steal personal information and use it to take out loans, request government documents and tax refunds, get expensive medical procedures, and commit other types of fraud. Companies play a vital role in fighting this crime because they frequently collect the information that identity thieves use to commit their fraud, including credit card and Social Security numbers. Any company that collects such information has a clear ethical obligation to keep it safe and secure, but the number of massive data-security breaches in recent years indicates how poorly many companies are meeting this obligation.

THE RIGHT TO BE INFORMED

Consumers have a right to know what they're buying, how to use it, and whether it presents any risks to them. They also have a right to know the true price of goods or services and the details of purchase contracts. Accordingly, numerous government regulations have been put in place to make sure buyers get the information they need in order to make informed choices. Of course, buyers share the responsibility here, at least morally if not always legally. Not bothering to read labels or contracts or not asking for help if you don't understand them is no excuse for not being informed.

Fortunately, both consumers and businesses can turn to a wide range of information sources to learn more about the goods and services they purchase. The spread of social media and their use in *social commerce* (see page 300), in which buyers help educate one another, has helped shift power from sellers to buyers. For just about every purchase you can envision these days, you can find more information about it before you choose.

REAL-TIME UPDATES

Learn More by Visiting This Website

Know your rights as a consumer

Get advice on everything from filing a complaint to protecting yourself against fraud. Go to http://real-timeupdates.com/bia8 and click on Learn More in the Students section.

THE RIGHT TO CHOOSE WHICH PRODUCTS TO BUY

Especially in the United States, the number of products available to consumers is staggering, even sometimes overwhelming. But how far should the right to choose extend? Are we entitled to choose products that are potentially harmful, such as cigarettes, alcoholic beverages, guns, sugary soft drinks, or fatty fried foods? Should the government take measures to make such products illegal, or should consumers always be allowed to decide for themselves what to buy?

Consider cigarettes. Scientists determined long ago that the tar and nicotine in tobacco are harmful and addictive. In 1965, the Federal Cigarette Labeling and Advertising Act was passed, requiring all cigarette packs to carry the Surgeon General's warnings. Over the years, tobacco companies have spent billions of dollars to defend themselves in lawsuits brought by smokers suffering from cancer and respiratory diseases. Lawsuits and legislative activity surrounding tobacco products continue to this day—and are likely to continue for years. Meanwhile, consumers can still purchase cigarettes in the marketplace. As one tobacco company executive put it, "Behind all the allegations…is the simple truth that we sell a legal product."[25]

THE RIGHT TO BE HEARD

The final component of consumer rights is the right to be heard. As with the challenge of gathering information, social media give consumers numerous ways to ask questions, voice concerns, provide feedback, and—if necessary—demand attention. Savvy companies monitor Twitter, blogs, and other online venues to catch messages from dissatisfied customers. Companies that fail to respond or that respond in defensive, inward-looking ways are likely to lose business to competitors that embrace this new media environment and the power it gives today's consumers.

✔ Checkpoint

LEARNING OBJECTIVE 5: Identify four fundamental consumer rights and the responsibility of business to respect them.

SUMMARY: Four fundamental consumer rights that form the basis of much of the consumer-related legislation in the United States are the right to safe products, the right to be informed, the right to choose, and the right to be heard. Many specific aspects of these rights are now embodied in government regulations, but others rely on business professionals to practice ethical and responsive decision making.

CRITICAL THINKING: (1) Is there a point at which responsibility for product safety shifts from the seller to the buyer? Explain your answer. (2) If providing full information about products raises prices, should businesses still be required to do so? Why or why not?

IT'S YOUR BUSINESS: (1) How do social media influence your behavior as a consumer? (2) Have you ever lodged a complaint with a business? If so, what was the outcome?

KEY TERMS TO KNOW: consumerism, identity theft

CSR: Employees

6   LEARNING OBJECTIVE

Explain the responsibilities businesses have toward their employees.

The past few decades have brought dramatic changes in the composition of the global workforce and in the attitudes of workers. These changes have forced businesses to modify their recruiting, training, and promotion practices, as well as their overall corporate values and behaviors. This section discusses some key responsibilities that employers have regarding employees.

THE PUSH FOR EQUALITY IN EMPLOYMENT

The United States has always stood for economic freedom and the individual's right to pursue opportunity. Unfortunately, in the past many people were targets of economic **discrimination**, being relegated to low-paying, menial jobs and prevented from taking advantage of many opportunities solely on the basis of their race, gender, disability, or religion.

discrimination
In a social and economic sense, denial of opportunities to individuals on the basis of some characteristic that has no bearing on their ability to perform in a job.

The Civil Rights Act of 1964 established the Equal Employment Opportunity Commission (EEOC), the regulatory agency that addresses job discrimination. The EEOC is responsible for monitoring hiring practices and for investigating complaints of job-related discrimination. It has the power to file legal charges against companies that discriminate and to force them to compensate individuals or groups that have been victimized by unfair practices. The Civil Rights Act of 1991 amended the original act in response to a number of Supreme Court decisions that had taken place in the intervening quarter-century. Among its key provisions are limiting the amount of damage awards, making it easier to sue for discrimination, giving employees the right to have a trial by jury in discrimination cases, and extending protections to overseas employees of U.S. companies.[26]

Affirmative Action

In the 1960s, **affirmative action** programs were developed to encourage organizations to recruit and promote members of groups whose past economic progress has been hindered through legal barriers or established practices. Affirmative action programs address a variety of situations, from college admissions to hiring to conducting business with government agencies. Note that although affirmative action programs address a range of

affirmative action
Activities undertaken by businesses to recruit and promote members of groups whose economic progress has been hindered through either legal barriers or established practices.

population segments, from military veterans with disabilities to specific ethnic groups, in popular usage, "affirmative action" usually refers to programs based on race.

Affirmative action remains a controversial and politicized issue, with opponents claiming that it creates a double standard and can encourage reverse discrimination against white males; proponents say that it remains a crucial part of the effort to ensure equal opportunities for all. One of the key points of contention is whether affirmative action programs are still needed, given the various antidiscrimination laws now in place. Opponents assert that everyone has an equal shot at success now, so the programs are unnecessary and, if anything, should be based on income, not race; proponents argue that laws can't remove every institutionalized barrier and that discrimination going back decades has left many families and communities at a long-term disadvantage.[27]

Policy debates aside, well-managed companies across the country are finding that embracing diversity in the richest sense is simply good business. You'll read more about *diversity initiatives* in Chapter 11.

People with Disabilities

In 1990, people with a wide range of physical and mental difficulties got a boost from the passage of the federal Americans with Disabilities Act (ADA), which guarantees equal opportunities in housing, transportation, education, employment, and other areas for the estimated 50 to 75 million people in the United States who have disabilities. As defined by the 1990 law, *disability* is a broad term that refers not only to those with physical handicaps but also those with cancer, heart disease, diabetes, epilepsy, HIV/AIDS, drug addiction, alcoholism, emotional illness, and other conditions. In most situations, employers cannot legally require job applicants to pass a physical examination as a condition of employment. Employers are also required to make reasonable accommodations to meet the needs of employees with disabilities, such as modifying workstations or schedules.[28]

OCCUPATIONAL SAFETY AND HEALTH

Every year several thousand U.S. workers lose their lives on the job and many thousands more are injured (see Exhibit 4.8).[29] During the 1960s, mounting concern about workplace hazards resulted in the passage of the Occupational Safety and Health Act of 1970, which set mandatory standards for safety and health and also established the Occupational Safety and Health Administration (OSHA) to enforce them. These standards govern everything from hazardous materials to *ergonomics*, the study of how people interact with computers and other machines.

EXHIBIT 4.8	**Fatal Occupational Injuries**

Transportation accidents are the leading cause of death on the job in the United States. Overall, U.S. workers suffer fatal on-the-job injuries at a rate of 3.2 deaths per 100,000 full-time employees per year.

Source: "2013 Census of Fatal Occupational Injuries," U.S. Bureau of Labor Statistics, www.bls.gov.

Concerns for employee safety can extend beyond a company's own workforce, and this concern is particularly acute for the many U.S. companies that contract out production to factories in Asia, Latin America, and parts of the United States to make products under their brand names. Some of these companies have been criticized for doing business with so-called *sweatshops*, a disparaging term applied to production facilities that treat workers poorly. As discussed in the Behind the Scenes wrap-up, Nike is one of many companies taking positive steps to improve conditions in the factories that make its products. U.S. colleges have been influential in this effort, too. Nearly 200 schools have joined the Fair Labor Association (**www.fairlabor.org**) to help ensure that school-logo products are manufactured in an ethical manner.[30]

 Checkpoint

LEARNING OBJECTIVE 6: Explain the responsibilities businesses have toward their employees.

SUMMARY: In addition to the impact a company has on its external stakeholders, CSR applies within the company as well, to the way employees are treated. Major issues include the push for equal opportunity, which includes affirmative action programs and regulations to protect the rights of people with disabilities, and occupational safety and health.

CRITICAL THINKING: (1) Does affirmative action seem like a fair approach? Why or why not? (2) Should employees automatically get paid more to work in hazardous jobs? Why or why not?

IT'S YOUR BUSINESS: (1) Have you ever experienced or observed discrimination on the job? If so, how did you handle the situation? (2) Has this chapter changed your perspective about the relationship between business and society? Why or why not?

KEY TERMS TO KNOW: discrimination, affirmative action

BEHIND THE SCENES
NIKE BUILDS A SUSTAINABLE BUSINESS THROUGH SUSTAINABLE DESIGN AND MANUFACTURING

Nike CEO Mark Parker would surely agree that any examination of Nike's business–society relationship needs to include a look at the massive scale of the company's operations. With annual revenues climbing past $25 billion, a strong presence in every continent except Antarctica, and billions of products sold since its founding in the 1960s, Nike is one of the world's largest and most visible corporations. (Starting right now, see how long you can go without seeing a Nike logo.) In addition to the 40,000 employees who work directly for the company, another million work in hundreds of contract factories across nearly 50 countries that manufacture the company's products. With millions of shoes, garments, sporting goods, and other "Swoosh"-branded products rolling off those production lines every month, the company oversees a vast supply chain that sources a wide variety of natural and synthetic materials and uses almost every mode of transportation imaginable.

It's safe to say that Nike and the global community are stuck with each other—and Nike needs a vibrant, stable world economy as much as the global community needs Nike to be a well-managed and well-behaved corporate citizen.

Workplace conditions and sustainable manufacturing are two issues in particular that highlight the impact Nike has on stakeholders and the considerable investments the company continues to make toward improving its entire "business ecosystem." In the matter of workplace conditions, the first wave of improvement efforts focused on building monitoring systems so that Nike and other companies could get a better sense of how workers were being treated in contract factories. Across a number of industries, some of these "sweatshop" factories had been accused of forcing employees to work 24 hours or more at a time, employing young children in unsafe conditions, or virtually imprisoning workers in conditions that have at times been compared to slavery. Mattel, Reebok, Patagonia, Liz Claiborne, and Gap are among the other industry leaders that have been working at improving monitoring of contract factories.

However, Nike began to realize that setting standards and monitoring operations weren't improving conditions in its contract factories sufficiently, and the company is now working closely with vendors to improve their operations and practices. As the company explains, "What we've learned, after nearly a decade, is that monitoring alone hasn't solved the problems. And many of the problems are recurring in the industry. Our focus now is getting to the root of the problems."

A key part of that effort is an in-depth auditing process conducted by Nike inspectors, who look for evidence of compliance with Nike's own environmental safety and health codes. Nike inspectors examine factory operations and interview supervisors as well as employees to make sure contract manufacturers are living up to the expectations outlined in Nike's *Code of Conduct*. Nike doesn't leave compliance to chance, either. The company's *Code Leadership Standards* is a comprehensive manual that describes exactly what a factory needs to do to meet Nike's standards. If a factory is out of compliance, Nike teams work with local management to help them figure where their processes are breaking down and how to improve.

Sustainable manufacturing has become a strategic imperative for the company, and Nike has sustainability experts working in such areas as reducing the environmental impact of various manufacturing processes and designing new products with more sustainable materials. For example, Nike has worked for years to analyze and document the environmental impact of a wide variety of garment and shoe materials, and its designers now have a handy software tool to help them choose fabrics and other components that maximize product performance and resource sustainability. After spending several million dollars developing it, Nike released this tool for free public use to help other companies improve their design practices. (You can try this software yourself, actually—it's the Environmental Design Tool featured in the Real-Time Updates Learn More item on page 84 in this chapter.)

Recycling is another area of concentration for the company. Nike collects and grinds up millions of pairs of worn-out sneakers every year to produce shock-absorbing materials that are used in running tracks, tennis courts, playgrounds, and other playing surfaces. Nike designers are also ramping up their use of recycled polyester from discarded plastic bottles, keeping hundreds of millions of them out of landfills.

Fabric manufacturing uses enormous volumes of water, and Nike has had a water stewardship program in place since 2001 to help factories minimize water usage and to do a more responsible job of "borrowing" water, as the company phrases it. Given the number of factories it works with worldwide, Nike figures its efforts to improve water stewardship influence the usage of more than 500 billion gallons of water a year.

Even with the considerable investments it has made and the measurable progress that has come from those efforts, the scale of its operations and the visibility of its brand ensure that Nike will continue to attract the attention of stakeholders and advocacy groups. For example, Greenpeace launched a "detox challenge" publicity campaign in which the environmental advocacy group challenged Nike and arch-rival Adidas to reduce the discharge of toxic fabric-treatment chemicals from contract factories in China.

Nike's response included a comprehensive report on its progress toward eliminating toxic chemicals from the manufacturing process—efforts that had been under way for more than a decade. These included the research and chemistry patents it has freely shared with other manufacturers through the GreenXchange intellectual property collaborative and an offer to work with Greenpeace and other NGOs on water usage issues.

Nike also exhibits a remarkable degree of transparency, such as issuing report cards on its progress toward its CSR goals and offering an extensive set of interactive online tools and downloadable files that cover everything from contract employee injury rates to waste management processes to the ethnic and gender composition of its workforce, executive ranks, and board of directors. You can view these files at **www.nikeresponsibility .com/report/downloads**.

Parker talks frankly of the lessons Nike has learned along the way. Reflecting on pressure the company received in the 1990s from worker rights groups, he says, "Our critics were smart (and right) to focus on the industry leader." After first defending conditions in the factories as just the way business was done in those countries, the company realized that change was needed, and it had to be fundamental change affecting every part of the company. Parker now welcomes collaboration with stakeholders and promotes the value of transparency, so that affected groups can see what the company is doing, and the company can learn from anybody who has great ideas to share. "For all the athletic and cultural and financial successes of the company," he says, "I believe our work in sustainable business and innovation has equal potential to shape our legacy."[31]

Critical Thinking Questions

4-1. This chapter covers three factors that influence ethical decisions: cultural differences, knowledge, and organizational behavior. How have these factors shaped Nike's CSR actions over the past two decades?

4-2. How does Mark Parker's phrase "sustainable business" relate to sustainable manufacturing?

4-3. Is it ethical for NGOs to put pressure on just one company in an industry when they are trying to effect change across the entire industry, given that responding to that pressure is likely to cost that company more than its competitors?

LEARN MORE ONLINE

Visit Nike's consumer-oriented website, **www.nike.com**, and its investor-oriented website, **http://investors.nike.com**. Study the messages presented on the two sites. How does Nike reach out to different stakeholder groups using these two separate sites? Read the "Letter to Shareholders" from Nike's latest annual report. How does Nike present itself to this vital stakeholder group? How does the company present its CSR efforts in a way that appeals to a reader whose primary interest is financial investment?

KEY TERMS

affirmative action (89)
cap and trade (85)
code of ethics (76)
conflicts of interest (78)
consumerism (87)
corporate social responsibility (CSR) (79)
discrimination (89)
ethical dilemma (76)
ethical lapse (76)

ethics (75)
identity theft (88)
insider trading (75)
nongovernmental organizations (NGOs) (81)
philanthropy (79)
strategic CSR (79)
sustainable development (86)
transparency (75)
whistle-blowing (76)

MyBizLab®
To complete the problems with the ⭐,
go to EOC Discussion Questions in the
MyLab.

TEST YOUR KNOWLEDGE

Questions for Review

4-4. How does ethics differ from corporate social responsibility?
4-5. What is a conflict of interest?
4-6. What is the difference between defensive and proactive CSR?
4-7. How are businesses responding to the environmental issues facing society?
4-8. What is identity theft, and what responsibilities do businesses have to prevent it?

Questions for Analysis

4-9. Why can't legal considerations resolve every ethical question?
4-10. How do individuals employ philosophical principles in making ethical business decisions? Why is it important for a company to balance its social responsibility efforts with its need to generate profits?
4-11. Why is it important for a company to balance its social responsibility efforts with its need to generate profits?
⭐ **4-12. Ethical Considerations.** Is it ethical for companies to benefit from their efforts to practice CSR? Why or why not? How can anyone be sure that CSR efforts aren't just public relations ploys?

⭐ **4-13.** What effects have social media had on CSR?
⭐ **4-14.** Would it be ethical for U.S. consumers to boycott products made in exploitive, low-wage overseas factories if the employees in those factories are grateful to have their jobs? Why or why not?

Questions for Application

⭐ **4-15.** Based on what you've learned about CSR, what effect will CSR considerations have on your job search?
⭐ **4-16. Concept Integration.** Chapter 2 identified knowledge workers as a key economic resource of the 21st century. If an employee leaves a company to work for a competitor, what types of knowledge would be ethical for the employee to share with the new employer, and what types would be unethical to share?
⭐ **4-17. Concept Integration.** Is it ethical for state and city governments to entice specific businesses to relocate their operations to that state or city by offering them special tax breaks that are not extended to other businesses operating in that area?

EXPAND YOUR KNOWLEDGE

Discovering Career Opportunities

Businesses, government agencies, and not-for-profit organizations offer numerous career opportunities related to ethics and social responsibility. How can you learn more about these careers?

4-18. Search the *Occupational Outlook Handbook* at **www.bls.gov/ooh** for "occupational health and safety specialists and technicians," jobs concerned with a company's responsibility toward its employees. What are the duties

and qualifications of the jobs you have identified? Are the salaries and future outlooks attractive for all of these jobs?
4-19. Select one job from the *Handbook* and search blogs, websites, and other sources to learn more about it. Try to find real-life information about the daily activities of people in this job. Can you find any information about ethical dilemmas or other conflicts in the duties of this position? What role do you think people in this position play within their respective organizations?

4-20. What skills, educational background, and work experience do you think employers are seeking in applicants for the specific job you are researching? What keywords do you think employers would search for when reviewing résumés submitted for this position?

Improve Your Tech Insights: Assistive Technologies

The term *assistive technologies* covers a broad range of devices and systems that help people with disabilities perform activities that might otherwise be difficult or impossible. These include technologies that help people communicate orally and visually, interact with computers and other equipment, and enjoy greater mobility, along with myriad other specific functions.

Assistive technologies create a vital link for thousands of employees with disabilities, giving them opportunities to pursue a greater range of career paths and giving employers access to a broader base of talent. Plus, the economy and society benefit when everyone who can make a contribution is able to, and assistive technologies will be an important part of the solution.

Research some of the technologies now on the market. AssistiveTech.net, **www.assistivetech.ne**t, hosted by the Center for Assistive Technology and Environmental Access at Georgia Tech, is a great place to explore the thousands of assistive products now available. It also provides links to a variety of other sites. The Business Leadership Network (USBLN), **www.usbln.org**, helps companies develop policies and practices to encourage the full participation and advancement of employees with disabilities and to market goods and services to consumers with disabilities. Also visit the Rehabilitation Engineering and Assistive Technology Society of North America (RESNA), **www.resna .org**. (USBLN and RESNA sponsor annual conferences that bring together some of the best minds in the field of assistive technologies, too.) For a look at the federal government's efforts to promote these technologies, visit the National Institute on Disability and Rehabilitation Research, **www2.ed.gov/about/offices/list/ osers/nidrr**. Technology companies such as IBM, **www.ibm .com/able**, and Microsoft, **www.microsoft.com/enable**, also devote significant resources to developing assistive technologies and making information technology more accessible. Choose one assistive technology, and in a brief email message to your instructor, explain how this technology can help companies support employees or customers with disabilities.[32]

PRACTICE YOUR SKILLS

Sharpening Your Communication Skills

Your employer makes a grand show of promoting strong ethics, with regular classes, posters in the hallways, a telephone hotline, and more. However, as the economy has slowed down over the past few months, you've noticed that company managers aren't always practicing what they preach. They're cutting corners on product quality and squeezing suppliers by not paying bills on time. They even launched a frivolous lawsuit against an upstart competitor that will do little more than drain the new firm of funds and delay its entry into the market. This isn't the same company you were once so proud to work for. Write a brief email message to your immediate supervisor, requesting a meeting to discuss your concerns.

Building Your Team Skills

Every organization can benefit from having a code of ethics to guide decision making. But whom should a code of ethics protect, and what should it cover? In this exercise, you and the rest of your team are going to draft a code of ethics for your college or university.

Start by thinking about who will be protected by this code of ethics. What stakeholders should the school consider when making decisions? What negative effects might decisions have on these stakeholders? Then think about the kinds of situations you want your school's code of ethics to cover. One example might be employment decisions; another might be disclosure of confidential student information.

Next, draft your school's code of ethics. Start by identifying general principles and then provide specific guidelines. Write a general introduction explaining the purpose of the code and who is being protected. Next, write a positive statement to guide ethical decisions in each situation you identified previously in this exercise. Your statement about promotion decisions, for example, might read: "School officials will encourage equal access to job promotions for all qualified candidates, with every applicant receiving fair consideration."

Compare your code of ethics with the codes drafted by your classmates. Did all the codes seek to protect the same stakeholders? What differences and similarities do you see in the statements guiding ethical decisions?

Developing Your Research Skills

Articles on corporate ethics and social responsibility regularly appear in business journals and newspapers. Find one or more articles discussing one of the following ethics or social responsibility challenges faced by a business:

- Environmental issues, such as pollution, acid rain, and hazardous-waste disposal
- Employee or consumer safety measures
- Consumer information or education
- Employment discrimination or diversity initiatives
- Investment ethics
- Industrial spying and theft of trade secrets
- Fraud, bribery, and overcharging
- Company codes of ethics

4-21. What is the nature of the ethical challenge or social responsibility issue presented in the article? Does the article report any wrongdoing by a company or agency official? Was the action illegal, unethical, or questionable? What course of action would you recommend the company or agency take to correct or improve matters now?

4-22. What stakeholder group(s) is affected? What lasting effects will be felt by (a) the company and (b) this stakeholder group(s)?

4-23. Writing a letter to the editor is one way consumers can speak their mind. Review some of the letters to the editor in newspapers or journals. Why are letters to the editor an important feature for that publication?

MyBizLab®

Go to the Assignments section of your MyLab to complete these writing exercises.

4-24. What steps could a bookstore take to engage in strategic CSR?

4-25. Why would a company want to make it easy for its own employees to engage in whistle-blowing, even if doing so could subject the firm to legal penalties?

ENDNOTES

1. Nike website, accessed 23 March 2015, www.nikeinc.com; *Nike Sustainable Business Report*, accessed 23 March 2015, www.nikeresponsibility.com; "Nike, Inc.'s Response to Greenpeace Report," 18 July 2011, Nike website, www.nikebiz.com; *Nike 2011 Annual Report*, accessed 4 August 2011, www.nikebiz.com; "Detox Campaign," Greenpeace, accessed 4 August 2011, www.greenpeace.org; *Nike Code Leadership Standard*, Nike website, accessed 7 August 2011, www.nikebiz.com; GreenXchange, accessed 4 August 2011, www.greenxchange.cc; "Workers & Factories: Improving Conditions in Our Contract Factories," Nike website, accessed 4 August 2011, www.nike.com; Abigail Goldman, "Sweat, Fear, and Resignation Amid All the Toys," *Los Angeles Times*, 26 November 2004, A1, A30–A32; Edward Iwata, "How Barbie Is Making Business a Little Better," *USA Today*, 27 March 2006, B1–B2; "Nike Corporate Responsibility/Compliance ESH CLS Audit" worksheet, accessed 4 August 2011, www.nikebiz.com.
2. Rakesh Khurana, "The Future of Business School," *BusinessWeek*, 26 May 2009, www.businessweek.com.
3. James O'Toole and Warren Bennis, "What's Needed Next: A Culture of Candor," *Harvard Business Review*, June 2009, 54–61.
4. O'Toole and Bennis, "What's Needed Next: A Culture of Candor," 59.
5. "Ethics and Business Practices," United Technologies website, accessed 3 August 2011, www.utc.com.
6. Ben Levisohn, "Getting More Workers to Whistle," *BusinessWeek*, 28 January 2008, 18.
7. Alan D. Berkowitz, Claude M. Tusk, J. Ian Downes, and David S. Caroline, "Whistleblowing," *Employee Relations Law Journal*, Vol. 36, No. 4, Spring 2011, 15–32.
8. "Less Than Half of Privately Held Businesses Support Whistleblowing," Grant Thornton website, accessed 13 October 2008, www.internationalbusinessreport.com.
9. "Corporate Giving Restored Since Pre-Global Recession; Non-Cash Contributions Dominate," press release, 16 September 2013, The Conference Board, www.conferenceboard.org.
10. Susan Ladika, "The Responsible Way," *Workforce*, 16 July 2013, www.workforce.com.
11. Michael Porter and Mark Kramer, "Strategy & Society: The Link Between Competitive Advantage and Corporate Social Responsibility," *Harvard Business Review*, December 2006, 78–92.
12. Timothy M. Devinney, "Is the Socially Responsible Corporation a Myth? The Good, the Bad, and the Ugly of Corporate Social Responsibility," *Academy of Management Perspectives*, May 2009, 44–56.
13. Milton Friedman, "The Social Responsibility of Business Is to Increase Its Profits," *New York Times Magazine*, 13 September 1970, SM17.
14. "Social Responsibility: 'Fundamentally Subversive'?" Interview with Milton Friedman, *BusinessWeek*, 15 August 2005, www.businessweek.com.
15. Krisi Heim, "In Person: Laurie Erickson Is a 'Wrap' Star to Cancer Patients," *Seattle Times*, 24 April 2011, www.seattletimes.com.
16. Henry G. Manne, "Milton Friedman Was Right," *WSJ Opinion Journal*, 24 November 2006, www.opinionjournal.com.
17. Kas Thomas, "Google Uses More Electricity Than Most Countries on Earth," assertTrue() blog, 9 March 2009, http://asserttrue.blogspot.com; Rich Miller, "Google Data Center FAQ," Data Center Knowledge website, 26 August 2008, www.datacenterknowledge.com.
18. *Electric Power Annual*, 23 March 2015, U.S. Energy Information Administration, www.eia.gov; Daniel Gross, "Big Solar," *Slate*, 20 February 2015, www.slate.com.
19. Google Green website, accessed 16 October 2013, www.google.com/green; Urs Hölzle, "Energy and the Internet," The Official Google Blog, 11 May 2009, http://googleblog.blogspot.com; eSolar website, accessed 1 June 2009, www.esolar.com; "Google's Green PPAs: What, How, and Why," 29 April 2011, Google website, www.google.com; "Step 5: An Efficient and Clean Energy Future," Google website, accessed 1 June 2009, www.google.com; "Google Data Centers, Best Practices," Google website, accessed 3 August 2011, www.google.com.
20. "Cap and Trade 101," U.S. Environmental Protection Agency website, accessed 1 June 2009, www.epa.gov.
21. John M. Broder, "From a Theory to a Consensus on Emissions," *New York Times*, 16 May 2009, www.nytimes.com.
22. "Report of the World Commission on Environment and Development," United Nations General Assembly, 96th Plenary Meeting, 11 December 1987, www.un.org.
23. Ursula M. Burns, "Is the Green Movement a Passing Fancy?" *BusinessWeek*, 27 January 2009, www.businessweek.com.
24. Accenture and the United Nations Global Compact, "The UN Global Compact-Accenture CEO Study on Sustainability 2013," www.accenture.com.
25. Action on Smoking and Health website, accessed 15 March 2005, www.ash.org; Chris Burritt, "Fallout from the Tobacco Settlement," *Atlanta Journal and Constitution*, 22 June 1997, A14; Jolie Solomon, "Smoke Signals," *Newsweek*, 28 April 1997, 50–51; Marilyn Elias, "Mortality Rate Rose Through '80s," *USA Today*, 17 April 1997, B3; Mike France, Monica Larner, and Dave Lindorff, "The World War on Tobacco," *BusinessWeek*, 11 November 1996; Richard Lacayo, "Put Out the Butt, Junior," *Time*, 2 September 1996, 51; Elizabeth Gleick, "Smoking Guns," *Time*, 1 April 1996, 50.
26. "The Civil Rights Act of 1991," U.S. Equal Employment Opportunity Commission website, accessed 7 August 2011, www.eeoc.gov.

27. Lorraine Woellert, "Anger on the Right, Opportunity for Bush," *BusinessWeek*, 7 July 2003, www.businessweek.com; Roger O. Crockett, "The Great Race Divide," *BusinessWeek*, 14 July 2003, www.businessweek.com; Earl Graves, "Celebrating the Best and the Brightest," *Black Enterprise*, February 2005, 16.

28. "Disability Discrimination," Equal Employment Opportunity Commission website, accessed 12 June 2007, www.eeoc.gov.

29. "Injuries, Illnesses, and Fatalities," Bureau of Labor Statistics, accessed 31 May 2009, www.bls.gov/iif.

30. Fair Labor Association website, accessed 24 March 2015, www.fairlabor.org.

31. See note 1.

32. IBM Accessibility, accessed 23 March 2015, www.ibm.com/able; AssistiveTech.net, accessed 23 March 2015, www.assistivetech.net; Business Leadership Network website, accessed 23 March 2015, www.usblin.org; National Institute on Disability and Rehabilitation Research website, accessed 23 March 2015, www.ed.gov; Rehabilitation Engineering and Assistive Technology Society of North America website, accessed 23 March 2015, www.resna.org; Microsoft Accessibility, accessed 23 March 2015, www.microsoft.com/enable.

WavebreakMediaMicro/Fotolia

5

Forms of Ownership

LEARNING OBJECTIVES After studying this chapter, you will be able to

1. Define *sole proprietorship*, and explain the six advantages and six disadvantages of this ownership model.

2. Define *partnership*, and explain the six advantages and three disadvantages of this ownership model.

3. Define *corporation*, and explain the four advantages and six disadvantages of this ownership model.

4. Explain the concept of *corporate governance*, and identify the three groups responsible for ensuring good governance.

5. Identify the potential advantages of pursuing mergers and acquisitions as a growth strategy, along with the potential difficulties and risks.

6. Define *strategic alliance* and *joint venture*, and explain why a company would choose these options over a merger or an acquisition.

BEHIND THE SCENES CISCO TACKLES THE CHALLENGE OF STAYING ON TOP IN A FAST-MOVING INDUSTRY

Cisco CEO John Chambers oversees the company's successional process for mergers and acquisitions.

www.cisco.com

Across a wide range of industries, from entertainment to clothing to high tech, many customers expect a more-or-less continuous stream of innovations. If the last company they bought from doesn't have something new to enhance their personal lives or improve their business operations, a hoard of ambitious competitors is usually ready to step in and fill the need. To stay in the game, companies in these rapidly changing industries need to be "innovation machines" that can be counted on to offer new ideas and new capabilities. Moreover, any company that wants to grow often has to come up with new product lines to offer existing customers or to move into new markets.

Companies have several options when it comes to churning out fresh, new products on a regular schedule. They can staff a research and development (R&D) department with the right mix of scientists, engineers, industrial designers, artists, and other creative professionals to design their own products. They can partner with other companies in order to offer a more-complete solution to their customers. Or they can take the most complex step of all: buying other companies outright and folding them into their operations.

All three approaches have advantages and disadvantages. Investing in R&D gives you hands-on control of product design, for example, but your staff may not be able to invent all the products you need to stay competitive. At the other extreme, buying entire companies can give you access to critical technology and expertise, but acquisitions are often risky and difficult—and more often than not, they fail to meet their objectives.

San Jose, California-based Cisco Systems is definitely in an industry whose customers require a constant stream of innovations. With annual revenues approaching $50 billion, Cisco is at the center of today's connected world, with networking hardware and software that carries just about every conceivable form of voice, video, and computer data. You may never see a Cisco product up close, but chances are some of your personal

or business communication travels across a Cisco product somewhere along the line. Enabling so many aspects of data networking and staying on top of ever-changing customer needs requires a constant supply of advanced hardware and software.

If you were Cisco CEO John Chambers, how would you address this challenge? Would you try to develop everything in house, partner with other companies, or acquire companies that have invented products that could help Cisco achieve its goals? If you opt for acquisitions, could you do it in a way that minimizes the risks and maximizes the chances of success?[1]

INTRODUCTION

One of the most fundamental decisions you must make when starting a business is selecting a form of business ownership. This decision can be complex and can have far-reaching consequences for owners, employees, and customers. Picking the right ownership structure involves knowing your long-term goals and how you plan to achieve them. Your choice also depends on your desire for control and your tolerance for risk. Then as your business evolves over time, you may need to modify the original structure or join forces with other companies. And even if you have no plans to start a business, knowing the legal structure of the companies where you might work is vital information to have.

The three most common forms of business ownership are sole proprietorship, partnership, and corporation. Each form has its own characteristic internal structure, legal status, size, and fields to which it is best suited. Each also has key advantages and disadvantages for the owners (see Exhibit 5.1 on the next page).

Sole Proprietorships

A **sole proprietorship** is a business owned by one person (although it may have many employees). Many farms, retail establishments, and small service businesses are sole proprietorships, as are many home-based businesses, such as those operated by caterers, consultants, and freelance writers. Many of the local businesses you frequent around your college campus are likely to be sole proprietorships. You may be a sole proprietor yourself: If you are paid for performing any kind of service, from babysitting to website design, without being on a company's payroll, you are legally classified as a sole proprietor.[2]

1 **LEARNING OBJECTIVE**

Define *sole proprietorship*, and explain the six advantages and six disadvantages of this ownership model.

sole proprietorship
A business owned by a single person.

ADVANTAGES OF SOLE PROPRIETORSHIPS

Operating as a sole proprietorship offers six key advantages:

- **Simplicity.** A sole proprietorship is easy to establish and requires far less paperwork than other structures. About the only legal requirement for establishing a sole proprietorship is obtaining the necessary business licenses and permits required by the city, county, and state. Otherwise, just by starting business operations without creating a partnership or a corporation, you legally establish yourself as a sole proprietor.[3]

- **Single layer of taxation.** Income tax is a straightforward matter for sole proprietorships. The federal government doesn't recognize the company as a taxable entity; all profit "flows through" to the owner, where it is treated as personal income and taxed accordingly.

Sole proprietorship can entail significant risks and a lot of work, but the potential rewards entice millions of people to consider it every year.

Moxie Productions/Alamy

EXHIBIT 5.1	Forms of Business Ownership

Each of the major forms of business ownership has distinct advantages and disadvantages.

Structure	Control	Profits and Taxation	Liability Exposure	Ease of Establishment
Sole proprietorship	One owner has complete control	Profits and losses flow directly to the owners and are taxed at individual rates	Owner has unlimited personal liability for the business's financial obligations	Easy to set up; typically requires just a business license and a form to register the company name
General partnership	Two or more owners; each partner is entitled to equal control unless agreement specifies otherwise	Profits and losses flow directly to the partners and are taxed at individual rates; partners share income and losses equally unless the partnership agreement specifies otherwise	All partners have unlimited liability, meaning their personal assets are at risk to mistakes made by others partners	Easy to set up; partnership agreement not required but strongly recommended
Limited partnership	Two or more owners; one or more general partners manage the business; limited partners don't participate in the management	Same as for general partnership	Limited partners have limited liability (making them liable only for the amount of their investment); general partners have unlimited liability	Same as for general partnership
Corporation	Unlimited number of shareholders; no limits on stock classes or voting arrangements; ownership and management of the business are separate (shareholders in public corporations are not involved in management decisions; in private or closely held corporations, owners are more likely to participate in managing the business)	Profits are taxed at corporate rates; profits are taxed again at individual rates when (or if) they are distributed to investors as dividends	Investor's liability is limited to the amount of his or her investment	More complicated and expensive to establish than a sole proprietorship; requirements vary from state to state

- **Privacy.** Beyond filing tax returns and certain other government reports that may apply to specific businesses, sole proprietors generally aren't required to report anything to anyone. Your business is your business. Of course, if you apply for a loan or solicit investors, you will need to provide detailed financial information to these parties.
- **Flexibility and control.** As a sole proprietor, you aren't required to get approval from a business partner, your boss, or a board of directors to change any aspect of your business strategy or tactics. You can make your own decisions, from setting your own hours to deciding how much of the work you'll do yourself and how much you'll assign to employees. It's all up to you (within the limits of whatever contractual obligations you might have, of course, such as a franchising agreement—see page 138). Also, as the sole owner, whatever financial value exists in the business is yours. You can keep the business, sell it, give it away, or bequeath it to your children.

REAL-TIME UPDATES

Learn More by Visiting This Website

Get help from a Small Business Development Center

Thinking of starting a business or already running one? Find out where to get help from a local advisor. Go to http://real-timeupdates .com/bia8 and click on Learn More in the Students section.

- **Fewer limitations on personal income.** As a partner in a partnership or an employee in a corporation, your income is established by various agreements and compensation policies. As a sole proprietor, you keep all the after-tax profits the business generates; if the business does extremely well, you do extremely well. Of course, if the business doesn't generate any income, you don't get a paycheck.
- **Personal satisfaction.** For many sole proprietors, the main advantage is the satisfaction of working for

themselves—of taking the risks and enjoying the rewards. If you work hard, make smart decisions, and have a little bit of luck, you get to see and enjoy the fruits of your labor.

DISADVANTAGES OF SOLE PROPRIETORSHIPS

For all its advantages, sole proprietorship also has six significant disadvantages:

- **Financial liability.** In a sole proprietorship, the owner and the business are legally inseparable, which gives the proprietor **unlimited liability**: Any legal damages or debts incurred by the business are the owner's personal responsibility. If you aren't covered by appropriate insurance and run into serious financial or legal difficulty, such as getting sued for an accident that happened on your premises, you could lose not only the business but also everything else you own, including your house, your car, and your personal investments.

- **Demands on the owner.** There's quite a bit of truth to the old joke that working for yourself means you get to set your own hours—you can work whichever 80 hours a week you want. In addition to the potential for long hours (certainly, not all sole proprietors work crazy hours), you often have the stress of making all the major decisions, solving all the major problems, and being tied so closely to the company that taking time off is sometimes impossible. Plus, business owners can feel isolated and unable to discuss problems with anyone.[4] Fortunately, social media sites have been a huge blessing for sole proprietors in this and many other respects. Business owners can reach out for advice, fresh ideas, useful contacts, or simply the socializing opportunities that are missing for many small-business owners.

- **Limited managerial perspective.** Running even a simple business can be a complicated effort that requires expertise in accounting, marketing, information technology, business law, and many other fields. Few individual owners possess enough skills and experience to make consistently good decisions. To get broader input for important decisions, small-business owners can turn to a variety of sources for input, including networks and support groups designed specifically for proprietors to counsel each other on key decisions.[5]

- **Resource limitations.** Because they depend on a single owner, sole proprietorships usually have fewer financial resources and fewer ways to get additional funds from lenders or investors. This lack of capital can hamper a small business in many ways, limiting its ability to expand, to hire the best employees, and to survive rough economic periods.

- **No employee benefits for the owner.** Moving from a corporate job to sole proprietorship can be a shock for employees accustomed to paid vacation time, sick leave, health insurance, and other benefits that many employers offer. Sole proprietors get none of these perks without paying for them out of their own pockets.

- **Finite life span.** Although some sole proprietors pass their businesses on to their heirs, the owner's death may mean the demise of the business. And even if the business does transfer to an heir, the founder's unique skills may have been crucial to its successful operation.

unlimited liability
A legal condition under which any damages or debts incurred by a business are the owner's personal responsibility.

✓ Checkpoint

LEARNING OBJECTIVE 1: Define *sole proprietorship*, and explain the six advantages and six disadvantages of this ownership model.

SUMMARY: A sole proprietorship is a business owned by a single individual and legally inseparable from that person. The six advantages of this structure are simplicity, a single layer of taxation, privacy, flexibility and control, fewer limitations on personal income, and personal satisfaction. The six disadvantages are unlimited financial liability, demands on the owner, limited managerial perspective, resource limitations, no employee benefits for the owner, and a finite life span.

CRITICAL THINKING: (1) How many sole proprietors do you know? Do they seem satisfied with the choice of working for themselves? Why or why not? (2) Would you ever consider going into business as a sole proprietor? Why or why not?

IT'S YOUR BUSINESS: (1) In your everyday consumer interactions, would you rather do business with a sole proprietorship or a corporation? Why? (2) What would be the potential advantages and disadvantages from a consumer's point of view?

KEY TERMS TO KNOW: sole proprietorship, unlimited liability

2 | **LEARNING OBJECTIVE**

Define *partnership*, and explain the six advantages and three disadvantages of this ownership model.

partnership
An unincorporated company owned by two or more people.

general partnership
A partnership in which all partners have joint authority to make decisions for the firm and joint liability for the firm's financial obligations.

limited partnership
A partnership in which one or more persons act as *general partners* who run the business and have the same unlimited liability as sole proprietors.

limited liability
A legal condition in which the maximum amount each owner is liable for is equal to whatever amount each invested in the business.

master limited partnership (MLP)
A partnership that is allowed to raise money by selling units of ownership to the general public.

limited liability partnership (LLP)
A partnership in which each partner has unlimited liability only for his or her own actions and at least some degree of limited liability for the partnership as a whole.

Partnerships

A **partnership** is a company that is owned by two or more people but is not a corporation. The partnership structure is appropriate for firms that need more resources and leadership talent than a sole proprietorship but don't need the fundraising capabilities or other advantages of a corporation. Many partnerships are small, with just a handful of owners, although a few are immense; the accounting and consulting firm PwC (**www.pwc.com**), for example, has more than 10,000 partners.[6] (Note that some companies refer to their employees as "partners," but that isn't the same thing as legal business partners.)

Partnerships come in two basic flavors. In a **general partnership**, all partners have *joint authority* to make decisions for the firm and *joint liability* for the firm's financial obligations.[7] If the partnership gets sued or goes bankrupt, all the partners have to dig into their own pockets to pay the bills, just as sole proprietors must.

To minimize personal liability exposure, some organizations opt instead for a **limited partnership**. Under this type of partnership, one or more persons act as *general partners* who run the business and have the same unlimited liability as sole proprietors. The remaining owners are *limited partners* who do not participate in running the business and who have **limited liability**—the maximum amount they are liable for is whatever amount each invested in the business.

Two additional types of partnerships have been created in recent years to accommodate the needs of particular industries or professions. A **master limited partnership (MLP)** is allowed to raise money by selling *units* of ownership to the general public, in the same way corporations sell shares of stock to the public. This gives MLPs the fundraising capabilities of corporations without the double-taxation disadvantage (see "Disadvantages of Corporations" on page 105). Strict rules limit the types of companies that qualify for MLP status; most are in the energy industry.[8]

The **limited liability partnership (LLP)** form of business was created to help protect individual partners in certain professions from major mistakes (such as errors that trigger malpractice lawsuits) by other partners in the firm. In an LLP, each partner has unlimited liability only for his or her own actions and at least some degree of limited liability for the partnership as a whole. Restrictions on who can form an LLP—and how much liability protection is offered under this structure—vary from state to state.

ADVANTAGES OF PARTNERSHIPS

Partnerships offer two of the same advantages as sole proprietorship plus four more that overcome some important disadvantages of being a sole owner:

- **Simplicity.** Strictly speaking, establishing a partnership is almost as simple as establishing a sole proprietorship: You and your partners just say you're in business together, apply for the necessary business licenses, and get to work. Although this approach is legal, it is not safe or sensible. Partners need to protect themselves and the company with a partnership agreement (see "Keeping It Together: The Partnership Agreement" on the next page).

- **Single layer of taxation.** Income tax is straightforward for partnerships. Profit is split between or among the owners based on whatever percentages they have agreed to. Each owner then treats his or her share as personal income.
- **More resources.** One of the key reasons to partner up with one or more co-owners is to increase the amount of money you have to launch, operate, and grow the business. In addition to the money that owners invest themselves, a partnership can potentially raise more money because partners' personal assets support a larger borrowing capacity.
- **Cost sharing.** An important financial advantage in many partnerships is the opportunity to share costs. For example, a group of lawyers or doctors can share the cost of facilities and support staff while continuing to work more or less independently.
- **Broader skill and experience base.** Pooling the skills and experience of two or more professionals can overcome one of the major shortcomings of the sole proprietorship. If your goal is to build a business that can grow significantly over time, a partnership can be much more effective than trying to build it up as a sole owner.[9]
- **Longevity.** By forming a partnership, you increase the chances that the organization will endure because new partners can be drawn into the business to replace those who die or retire.

DISADVANTAGES OF PARTNERSHIPS

Anyone considering the partnership structure needs to be aware of three potentially significant disadvantages:

- **Unlimited liability.** All owners in a general partnership and the general partners in a limited partnership face the same unlimited liability as sole proprietors. However, the risk of financial wipeout can be even greater because a partnership has more people making decisions that could end in catastrophe (unless the company is formed as an LLP).
- **Potential for conflict.** More bosses equals more chances for disagreement and conflict. Partners can disagree over business strategy, the division of profits (or the liability for losses), hiring and firing of employees, and other significant matters. Even simple interpersonal conflict between partners can hinder a company's ability to succeed. Given the potential for conflict, some experts recommend against equal ownership splits where everyone has an equal vote in how things are run.[10]
- **Expansion, succession, and termination issues.** Partnerships need to consider how they will handle such issues as expanding by bringing in an additional partner, replacing a partner who wants to sell out or retire, and terminating a partner who is unable or unwilling to meet the expectations of his or her role in the organization. Such issues can destroy partnerships if the owners don't have clear plans and expectations for addressing them.

KEEPING IT TOGETHER: THE PARTNERSHIP AGREEMENT

A carefully written *partnership agreement* can maximize the advantages of the partnership structure and minimize the potential disadvantages. Although state laws (everywhere except Louisiana) specify some basic agreements about business partnerships, these laws are generic and therefore not ideal for many partnerships.[11] At a minimum, a partnership agreement should address investment percentages, profit-sharing percentages, management responsibilities and other expectations of each owner, decision-making strategies, succession and exit strategies (if an owner wants to leave the partnership), criteria for admitting new partners, and dispute-resolution procedures (including dealing with owners who aren't meeting their responsibilities).[12]

A clear and complete agreement is important for every partnership, but it can be particularly important when you are going into business with a friend, a spouse,

REAL-TIME UPDATES

Learn More by Reading This Article

Starting and growing a successful partnership

Get vital advice on making a business partnership work. Go to http://real-timeupdates.com/bia8 and click on Learn More in the Students section.

or anyone else with whom you have a personal relationship. Although you might have a great personal partnership, the dynamics of that relationship could get in the way of a successful business partnership. For instance, a couple who are accustomed to sharing decisions and responsibilities equally in their personal relationship could struggle in a business relationship in which one of them is the clear leader of the company. In addition, stresses and strains in the business relationship can filter into the personal relationship. To protect both the personal and professional partnerships, make sure you start with a clear understanding of what the business relationship will be.

 Checkpoint

LEARNING OBJECTIVE 2: Define *partnership*, **and explain the six advantages and three disadvantages of this ownership model.**

SUMMARY: Partnership is a business structure in which two or more individuals share ownership of the firm. The two basic forms of partnership are *general partnership*, in which all owners play an active role and have unlimited liability, and the *limited partnership*, in which only the general partner or partners have active management roles and unlimited liability. Six key advantages of partnership are simplicity, a single layer of taxation, more resources, cost sharing, broader skill and experience base, and longevity. Three potential disadvantages are unlimited liability for general partners; potential for conflict; and expansion, succession, and termination issues.

CRITICAL THINKING: (1) Would you prefer going into a business with a seasoned professional you don't know well or someone you know, like, and trust but who doesn't have a lot of business experience? Why? (2) What are the three most important qualifications you would look for in a potential business partner?

IT'S YOUR BUSINESS: (1) Would you consider entering into a business partnership with your best friend? Why or why not? (2) Now turn the question around: Would your best friend consider having *you* as a business partner?

KEY TERMS TO KNOW: partnership, general partnership, limited partnership, limited liability, master limited partnership (MLP), limited liability partnership (LLP)

3 **LEARNING OBJECTIVE**

Define *corporation*, and explain the four advantages and six disadvantages of this ownership model.

corporation
A legal entity, distinct from any individual persons, that has the power to own property and conduct business.

shareholders
Investors who purchase shares of stock in a corporation.

public corporation
A corporation in which stock is sold to anyone who has the means to buy it.

private corporation
A corporation in which all the stock is owned by only a few individuals or companies and is not made available for purchase by the public.

Corporations

A **corporation** is a legal entity, distinct from any individual persons, that has the power to own property and conduct business. It is owned by **shareholders**, investors who purchase shares of stock. The stock of a **public corporation** is sold to anyone who has the means to buy it—individuals, investment companies such as mutual funds, not-for-profit organizations, and other companies. Such corporations are said to be *publicly held* or *publicly traded*. In contrast, the stock of a **private corporation**, also known as a *closely held corporation*, is owned by only a few individuals or companies and is not made available for purchase by the public. Corporations can change from private to public ownership or from public to private as their financial needs and strategic interests change.

With their unique ability to pool money from outside investors, corporations can grow to enormous size. The annual revenues of the world's largest corporations, such as Royal Dutch Shell, Walmart Stores, ExxonMobil, and Sinopec Group, are bigger than the entire economies of many countries.[13] However, many small firms and even individuals also take advantage of the unique benefits of corporate organization.

ADVANTAGES OF CORPORATIONS

Corporations have become a major economic force because this structure offers four major advantages over sole proprietorships and partnerships:

- **Ability to raise capital.** The ability to pool money by selling shares of stock to outside investors is the reason corporations first came into existence and remains one of the key advantages of this structure. (As Chapter 18 explains, corporations can also raise money by selling *bonds*.) Some firms have raised a billion dollars or more by selling stock to the public for the first time.[14] The potential for raising vast amounts gives corporations an unmatched ability to invest in research, marketing, facilities, acquisitions, and other growth strategies.

- **Liquidity.** The stock of publicly traded companies has a high degree of **liquidity**, which means that investors can easily and quickly convert their stock into cash by selling it on the open market. In contrast, *liquidating* (selling) the assets of a sole proprietorship or a partnership can be slow and difficult. Liquidity helps make corporate stocks an attractive investment, which increases the number of people and institutions willing to invest in such companies. In addition, because shares have value established in the open market, a corporation can use shares of its own stock to acquire other companies.

- **Longevity.** Liquidity also helps give corporations a long life span; when shareholders sell or bequeath their shares, ownership simply passes to a new generation, so to speak. Finding willing buyers for a corporation's stock is generally much easier than finding willing buyers for a sole proprietorship or stakes in a partnership.

- **Limited liability.** A corporation itself has unlimited liability, but the various shareholders who own the corporation face only limited liability—their maximum potential loss is only as great as the amount they've invested in the company. Like liquidity, limited liability offers protection that helps make corporate stocks an attractive investment.

liquidity
A measure of how easily and quickly an asset such as corporate stock can be converted into cash by selling it.

DISADVANTAGES OF CORPORATIONS

The advantages of the corporate structure are compelling, but six significant disadvantages must be considered carefully:

- **Cost and complexity.** Starting a corporation is more expensive and more complicated than starting a sole proprietorship or a partnership, and "taking a company public" (selling shares to the public) can be extremely expensive for a firm and time-consuming for upper managers. For a large firm, the process can cost many hundreds of thousands of dollars and consume months of executive time.

- **Reporting requirements.** To help investors make informed decisions about stocks, government agencies require publicly traded companies to publish extensive and detailed financial reports. These reports can eat up a lot of staff and management time, and they can expose strategic information that might benefit competitors or discourage investors unwilling to wait for long-term results.

- **Managerial demands.** Top executives must devote considerable time and energy to meeting with shareholders, financial analysts, and the news media. By one estimate, CEOs of large publicly held corporations can spend as much as 40 percent of their time on these externally focused activities.[15]

- **Possible loss of control.** Outside investors who acquire enough of a company's stock can gain seats on the board of directors and therefore begin exerting their influence on company management. In extreme cases, outsiders can take complete control and even replace the company founders if they believe a change in leadership is needed.

- **Double taxation.** A corporation must pay federal and state corporate income tax on its profits, and individual shareholders must pay income taxes on their share of the company's profits received as *dividends* (periodic payments that some corporations opt to make to shareholders).

The board members and officers of a public corporation meet once a year with shareholders.

Sueddeutsche Zeitung Photo/Alamy

- **Short-term orientation of the stock market.** Publicly held corporations release their financial results once every quarter, and this seemingly simple requirement can have a damaging effect on the way companies are managed. The problem is that executives feel the pressure to constantly show earnings growth from quarter to quarter so that the stock price keeps increasing—even if smart, strategic reasons exist for sacrificing earnings in the short term, such as investing in new product development or retaining talented employees instead of laying them off during slow periods. Managers sometimes wind up zigzagging from one short-term fix to the next, trying to prop up the stock price for investors who don't have the patience for strategic, long-term plans to bear fruit. When executive compensation is closely tied to stock prices, managers may have even more incentive to compromise the long-term health of the company in order to meet quarterly expectations.[16] To escape this pressure, corporate leaders sometimes choose to take their companies private, meaning they buy all the shares held by the public and convert them to privately held status.

SPECIAL TYPES OF CORPORATIONS

As with the partnership structure, special types of corporations have been created to aid companies in particular situations. An **S corporation**, or *subchapter S corporation*, combines the capital-raising options and limited liability of a corporation with the federal taxation advantages of a partnership (although a few states tax S corporations like regular corporations).[17] Corporations seeking "S" status must meet certain criteria, including a maximum of 100 investors.[18]

As its name suggests, the **limited liability company (LLC)** structure offers the advantages of limited liability, along with the pass-through taxation benefits of a partnership. Furthermore, LLCs are not restricted in the number of shareholders they can have, and members' participation in management is not restricted as it is in limited partnerships. Given these advantages, the LLC structure is recommended for most small companies that aren't sole proprietorships.[19] Although LLCs are favored by many small companies, they are by no means limited to small firms. A number of multibillion-dollar companies are structured as LLCs.[20]

Finally, an intriguing new type of corporate structure supports the goals of businesspeople who want their companies to pursue social and environmental goals while still pursuing profits as any other corporation does. A **benefit corporation** has most of the attributes of a regular corporation but adds the legal requirement that the company must also pursue a stated nonfinancial goal, such as hiring workers whose life histories make employment difficult to attain or reducing the environmental impact of particular products. The corporation's performance toward meeting that goal must be independently verified as well. These requirements offer key advantages to founders and other stakeholders. Entrepreneurs who launch a corporation with social or environmental objectives in mind are assured that even if they give up or lose voting control of the corporation, the company is still legally required to pursue its social or environmental goal. In addition, the transparency offered by third-party verification provides assurance for customers who want to buy from companies that support causes they value. Roughly half the U.S. states now recognize benefit corporations.[21]

The labels applied to various types of corporations can be a bit confusing. The most important points to remember are the difference between privately and publically held corporations and the basic features of S corporations and LLCs. Exhibit 5.2 summarizes these features, along with some other terms you may run across in the business media.

S corporation
A type of corporation that combines the capital-raising options and limited liability of a corporation with the federal taxation advantages of a partnership.

limited liability company (LLC)
A structure that combines limited liability with the pass-through taxation benefits of a partnership; the number of shareholders is not restricted, nor is members' participation in management.

benefit corporation
A profit-seeking corporation whose charter specifies a social or environmental goal that the company must pursue in addition to profit.

REAL-TIME UPDATES

Learn More by Visiting This Website

Benefit corporations and B Corp certification

B Lab is a nonprofit organization that helped develop the benefit corporation model and offers B Corp certification to companies that emphasize social and environmental values in their operations. Go to http://real-timeupdates.com/bia8 and click on Learn More in the Students section.

EXHIBIT 5.2   **Corporate Structures**

Different types of corporate structures serve different purposes for their owners. The first four terms are the most important to remember.

Structure	Characteristics
Public corporation (also known as *publicly held* or *publicly traded*)	Corporation whose stock is sold to the general public
Private corporation (also known as *closely held*)	Corporation whose stock is held by a small number of owners and is not available for sale to the public
S corporation (also known as *subchapter S corporation*)	Corporation allowed to sell stock to a limited number of investors while enjoying the pass-through taxation of a partnership
Limited liability company (LLC)	Corporate structure with benefits similar to those of an S corporation, without the limitation on the number of investors
Benefit corporation	Profit-seeking corporation whose charter also requires it to pursue a stated social or environmental goal
Subsidiary	Corporation primarily or wholly owned by another company
Parent company	Corporation that owns one or more subsidiaries
Holding company	Special type of parent company that owns other companies for investment reasons and usually exercises little operating control over those subsidiaries
Alien corporation	Corporation that operates in the United States but is incorporated in another country
Foreign corporation (sometimes called an *out-of-state corporation*)	Company that is incorporated in one state (frequently the state of Delaware, where incorporation laws are more lenient) but that does business in several other states where it is registered
Domestic corporation	Corporation that does business only in the state where it is chartered (incorporated)

 Checkpoint

LEARNING OBJECTIVE 3: Define *corporation*, **and explain the four advantages and six disadvantages of this ownership model.**

SUMMARY: A corporation is a legal entity with the power to own property and conduct business. The four primary advantages of this structure are the ability to raise capital by selling shares of ownership, liquidity (meaning it is easy to convert shares of ownership to cash), longevity, and limited liability for owners. Six disadvantages are startup costs and complexity, ongoing reporting requirements, extra demands on top managers, potential loss of control, double taxation, and the short-term orientation of the stock market.

CRITICAL THINKING: (1) Why is the LLC structure recommended for most small companies that aren't sole proprietorships? (2) How can the demands of the stock market affect managerial decision making?

IT'S YOUR BUSINESS: Assume you own stock in a large, publicly traded corporation that is hiring a new CEO. All other things being equal, who would be a better choice: a brilliant strategic thinker who is a weak communicator with poor "people skills" or a gifted public speaker and motivator who is competent but perhaps not brilliant when it comes to strategy? Explain your answer.

KEY TERMS TO KNOW: corporation, shareholders, public corporation, private corporation, liquidity, S corporation, limited liability company (LLC), benefit corporation

board of directors
A group of professionals elected by shareholders as their representatives, with responsibility for the overall direction of the company and the selection of top executives.

corporate governance
In a broad sense, all the policies, procedures, relationships, and systems in place to oversee the successful and legal operation of the enterprise; in a narrow sense, the responsibilities and performance of the board of directors specifically.

proxy
A document that authorizes another person to vote on behalf of a shareholder in a corporation.

shareholder activism
Activities undertaken by shareholders (individually or in groups) to influence executive decision making in areas ranging from strategic planning to social responsibility.

Corporate Governance

Although a corporation's shareholders own the business, few of them are typically involved in managing it, particularly if the corporation is publicly traded. Instead, shareholders who own *common stock* (see page 446) elect a **board of directors** to represent them, and the directors, in turn, select the corporation's top officers, who actually run the company (see Exhibit 5.3). The term **corporate governance** can be used in a broad sense to describe all the policies, procedures, relationships, and systems in place to oversee the successful and legal operation of the enterprise. However, media coverage and public discussion tend to define governance in a more narrow sense, as the responsibilities and performance of the board of directors specifically. Because serious corporate blunders can wreak havoc on employees, investors, and the entire economy, effective corporate governance has become a vital concern for society as a whole, not just for the individual companies themselves.

SHAREHOLDERS

Even though most don't have any direct involvement in company management, shareholders play a key role in corporate governance. All shareholders who own common stock are invited to an annual meeting where top executives present the previous year's results and plans for the coming year and shareholders vote on various resolutions that may be before the board. Those who cannot attend the annual meeting in person can vote by **proxy**, authorizing management to vote on their behalf.

Because shareholders elect the directors, in theory they are the ultimate governing body of the corporation. However, a major corporation may have thousands or even millions of shareholders, so unless they own a large number of shares, individual shareholders usually have little influence. Notable exceptions are *institutional investors*, such as pension funds, insurance companies, mutual funds, religious organizations, and college endowment funds. Those with large holdings of stock can have considerable influence over management. For example, the nearly 300 institutions that make up the Interfaith Center on Corporate Responsibility (ICCR) collectively control more than $100 billion in corporate stock, giving them a powerful voice.[22]

Shareholder activism, in which shareholders pressure management on matters ranging from executive pay to corporate social responsibility to overall company performance, has become an increasingly visible factor in corporate governance. Activist shareholders are becoming better organized and more sophisticated in proposals they

EXHIBIT 5.3	**Corporate Governance**

Shareholders of a corporation own the business, but their elected representatives on the board of directors hire the corporate officers who run the company and hire other employees to perform the day-to-day work. (Note that corporate officers are also employees.)

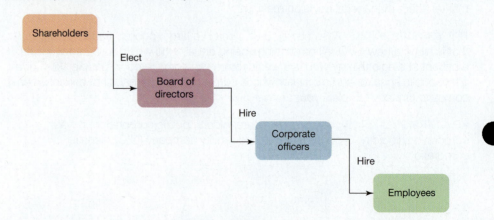

present, forcing boards to pay more attention to the concerns they raise.[23] At the same time, more boards seem to recognize the benefits to be gained by engaging activists and listening to their concerns.[24] However, not everyone is happy with this development. Those who lean toward the minimalist view of corporate social responsibility (see page 80) worry that such activism is beginning to undermine the ability of corporate boards to do their work effectively.[25]

BOARD OF DIRECTORS

As the representatives of the shareholders, the members of the board of directors are responsible for selecting corporate officers, guiding corporate affairs, reviewing long-term plans, making major strategic decisions, and overseeing financial performance. Boards are typically composed of major shareholders (both individuals and representatives of institutional investors), philanthropists, and executives from other corporations. Directors are often paid a combination of an annual fee and *stock options*, the right to buy company shares at an advantageous price.

Much of the attention focused on corporate reform in recent years has zeroed in on boards, with various boards being accused of not paying close enough attention to what their companies were doing, approving management proposals without analyzing them carefully, being allied too closely with management to serve as the independent representatives of shareholders, or simply failing to add enough value to strategy planning. In response to both outside pressure and management's recognition of how important an effective board is, corporations are wrestling with a variety of board-related issues:

Shareholder activism is one of the options available to people who want to influence the decisions and actions of pubic corporations.

Sueddeutsche Zeitung Photo/Alamy

REAL-TIME UPDATES
Learn More by Visiting This Website

Interested in shareholder activism?

This online network offers advice and tools to get you started. Go to http://real-timeupdates.com/bia8 and click on Learn More in the Students section.

- **Composition.** Identifying the type of people who should be on the board can be a major challenge. The ideal board is a balanced group of seasoned executives, each of whom can "bring something to the table" that helps the corporation, such as extensive contacts in the industry, manufacturing experience, insight into global issues, and so on. The ratio of insiders (company executives) to outsiders (independent directors) is another hot topic. Federal law now requires that the majority of directors be independent, but to be effective, these outsiders must have enough knowledge about the inner workings of the organization to make informed decisions. Diversity is also important, to ensure that adequate attention is paid to issues that affect stakeholders who have been historically underrepresented on corporate boards. For example, women hold only 20 percent of all the seats on the boards of the 500 largest U.S. public corporations, although the number of women now being nominated to these boards has increased significantly over the past few years. Members of ethnic minorities currently hold only 17 percent of *Fortune 500* board positions.[26]
- **Education.** Overseeing a modern corporation is an almost unimaginably complex task. Board members are expected to understand everything from government regulations to financial management to executive compensation strategies—in addition to the inner workings of the corporation itself. Various companies offer special training programs or orientation sessions for directors in such areas as financial reporting (to make sure directors who aren't well versed in finance can understand their company's own financial statements), compliance challenges, product research, manufacturing, and human resources issues.[27]
- **Liability.** One of the more controversial reform issues has been the potential for directors to be held legally and financially liable for misdeeds of the companies they oversee and even for simply failing to investigate "red flags" in company financial reports.[28]

- **Independent board chairs.** The *board chair* (or *chairman,* as many companies refer to the position) oversees the other members of the board of directors—who are supposed to oversee the corporate officers who make up the top management team, while the CEO oversees the top management team. However, in many corporations, one person acts as both board chair and CEO (meaning that in a sense, the CEO is his or her own boss), leading critics to ask how effectively such boards can oversee top management. The majority of large European companies now divide these responsibilities between two people, but that trend has not yet caught on widely in the United States. An emerging alternative is a *lead director,* an independent board member who guides the operation of the board and helps maintain its role as an independent voice in governance.[29]
- **Recruiting challenges.** Being an effective director in today's business environment is a tough job—so tough that good candidates may start to think twice about accepting directorships. Well-chosen board members are more vital than ever, though, so corporate and government leaders have no choice but to solve these challenges.

CORPORATE OFFICERS

corporate officers
The top executives who run a corporation.

The third and final group that plays a key role in governance are the **corporate officers**, the top executives who run the company. Because they implement major board decisions, make numerous other business decisions, ensure compliance with a dizzying range of government regulations, and perform other essential tasks, the executive team is the major influence on a company's performance and financial health. The highest-ranking officer is the **chief executive officer (CEO)**, and that person is aided by a team of other "C-level" executives, such as the chief financial officer (CFO), chief information officer (CIO), chief technology officer (CTO), and chief operating officer (COO)—titles vary from one corporation to the next.

chief executive officer (CEO)
The highest-ranking officer of a corporation.

Corporate officers are hired by the board and generally have legal authority to conduct the company's business, in everything from hiring the rest of the employees to launching new products. The actions of these executives can make or break the company, so it is obviously in the board's interest to hire the best talent available, help them succeed in every way possible, and pay attention to what these managers are doing.

✔ Checkpoint

LEARNING OBJECTIVE 4: Explain the concept of *corporate governance*, and identify the three groups responsible for ensuring good governance.

SUMMARY: Corporate governance involves all the policies, procedures, relationships, and systems in place to oversee the successful and legal operation of the enterprise. More narrowly, it refers specifically to the responsibilities and performance of the board of directors. The three groups responsible for good governance are (1) the shareholders, who elect (2) the board of directors, who approve overall strategy and hire (3) the corporate officers who run the company.

CRITICAL THINKING: (1) Why are some shareholder activists pressuring corporations to increase the number of board seats held by women and minorities? (2) Why do so many European corporations now divide board chair and CEO responsibilities between two people?

IT'S YOUR BUSINESS: Should the qualifications of the board of directors play a role in your decision whether to buy the stock of a particular corporation? Why or why not?

KEY TERMS TO KNOW: board of directors, corporate governance, proxy, shareholder activism, corporate officers, chief executive officer (CEO)

Mergers and Acquisitions

If a company determines that it doesn't have the right mix of resources and capabilities to achieve its goals and doesn't have the time or inclination to develop them internally, it can purchase or partner with a firm that has what it needs. Businesses can combine permanently through either *mergers* or *acquisitions*. The two terms are often discussed together, usually with the shorthand phrase "M&A," or are used interchangeably (although they are technically different, and the legal and tax ramifications can be quite different, depending on the details of the transaction).

In a **merger**, two companies join to form a single entity. Companies can merge either by pooling their resources or by one company purchasing the assets of the other.[30] Although not strictly a merger, a *consolidation*, in which two companies create a new, third entity that then purchases the two original companies, is often lumped together with the other two merger approaches.[31] (Adding to the confusion, businesspeople and the media often use the term *consolidation* in two general senses: to describe any combination of two companies, merger or acquisition, and to describe situations in which a wave of mergers and acquisitions sweeps across an entire industry, reducing the number of competitors.)

In an **acquisition**, one company buys a controlling interest in the voting stock of another company. In most acquisitions, the selling parties agree to be purchased; management is in favor of the deal and encourages shareholders to vote in favor of it as well. Because buyers frequently offer shareholders more than their shares are currently worth, sellers are often motivated to sell. However, in some situations, a buyer attempts to acquire a company against the wishes of management. In such a **hostile takeover**, the buyer tries to convince enough shareholders to go against management and vote to sell.

To finance an acquisition, buyers can offer sellers cash, stock in the acquiring company, or a combination of the two. Another option involves debt. A **leveraged buyout (LBO)** occurs when someone purchases a company's publicly traded stock primarily by using borrowed funds, sometimes using the target company's assets as collateral for these loans. The debt is expected to be repaid with funds generated by the company's operations and, often, by the sale of some of its assets. An LBO is an aggressive move and can be quite risky if the buyer takes on so much debt that repayment demands deplete the cash the company has for operations and growth.

ADVANTAGES OF MERGERS AND ACQUISITIONS

A merger or an acquisition is a rare event for many firms, but some other companies use acquisitions as a strategic tool to expand year after year. Companies pursue mergers and acquisitions for a variety of reasons: They might hope to increase their buying power as a result of their larger size, increase revenue by cross-selling products to each other's customers, increase market share by combining product lines to provide more comprehensive offerings, or gain access to new expertise, systems, and teams of employees who already know how to work together. Bringing a company under new ownership can also be an opportunity to replace or improve inept management and thereby help a company improve its performance.[32] In many cases, the primary goal is to reduce overlapping investments and capacities in order to lower ongoing costs. Exhibit 5.4 on the next page identifies the most common types of mergers.

DISADVANTAGES OF MERGERS AND ACQUISITIONS

Although the advantages can be compelling, joining two companies is a complex process because it involves virtually every aspect of both organizations. Here are just some of the daunting challenges that must be overcome:

- Executives have to agree on how the merger will be financed—and then come up with the money to make it happen.
- Managers need to decide who will be in charge after they join forces.
- Marketing departments need to figure out how to blend product lines, branding strategies, and advertising and sales efforts.

5 LEARNING OBJECTIVE

Identify the potential advantages of pursuing mergers and acquisitions as a growth strategy, along with the potential difficulties and risks.

merger
An action taken by two companies to combine as a single entity.

acquisition
An action taken by one company to buy a controlling interest in the voting stock of another company.

hostile takeover
Acquisition of another company against the wishes of management.

leveraged buyout (LBO)
Acquisition of a company's publicly traded stock, using funds that are primarily borrowed, usually with the intent of using some of the acquired assets to pay back the loans used to acquire the company.

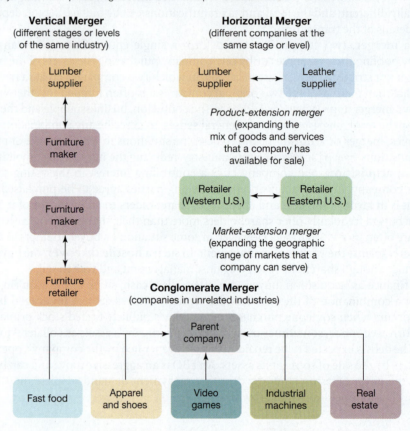

EXHIBIT 5.4   Types of Mergers

A *vertical merger* occurs when a company purchases a complementary company at a different stage or level in an industry, such as a furniture maker buying a lumber supplier. A *horizontal merger* involves two similar companies at the same level; companies can merge to expand their product offerings or their geographic market coverage. In a *conglomerate merger*, a parent company buys companies in unrelated industries, often to diversify its assets to protect against downturns in specific industries.

- Incompatible information systems (including everything from email to websites to accounting software) may need to be rebuilt or replaced in order to operate together seamlessly.
- Companies must often deal with layoffs, transfers, and changes in job titles and work assignments.
- The *organizational cultures* (see page 159) of the two firms must be harmonized somehow, which can result in clashes between different values, management styles, communication practices, workplace atmosphere, and approaches to managing the changes required to implement the merger.[33]

Moreover, while managers and employees are wrestling with all these challenges, they need to continue manufacturing products, satisfying customers, and tending to all the other daily details of business. Mergers can drive customers away if they feel neglected while the two companies are busy with all the internal chores of stitching themselves together.

Because of these risks and difficulties, somewhere between two-thirds and three-quarters of all mergers fail to meet their stated business goals.[34] The worst deals can waste millions or billions of dollars and destroy massive amounts of *market valuation* (the total value of a company's

REAL-TIME UPDATES

Learn More by Listening to This Podcast

Transforming M&A into a strategic advantage

Learn how firms that treat mergers and acquisitions as a strategic corporate capability can gain a key advantage over their competitors. Go to http://real-timeupdates.com/bia8 and click on Learn More in the Students section.

stock). Even with the risks and long odds, though, managers continue to pursue mergers and acquisitions, and some companies have become quite proficient at the process. As you can read in the Behind the Scenes wrap-up on Cisco on page 115, some companies have developed comprehensive processes for evaluating and implementing acquisitions. In fact, "acquisition skill" can be considered a competitive advantage for the companies that do it frequently and do it well.[35]

MERGER AND ACQUISITION DEFENSES

Every corporation that sells stock to the general public is potentially vulnerable to take-over by any individual or company that buys enough shares to gain a controlling interest. However, as mentioned previously, most takeovers are friendly acquisitions welcomed by the acquired company. A hostile takeover can be launched in one of two ways: by tender offer or by proxy fight. In a *tender offer*, the buyer, or *raider*, as this party is sometimes called, offers to buy a certain number of shares of stock in the corporation at a specific price. The price offered is generally more, sometimes considerably more, than the current stock price, so that shareholders are motivated to sell. The raider hopes to get enough shares to take control of the corporation and to replace the existing board of directors and manage-ment. In a *proxy fight*, the raider launches a public relations battle for shareholder votes, hoping to enlist enough votes to oust the board and management.

Corporate boards and executives have devised a number of schemes to defend them-selves against unwanted takeovers. With a *poison pill* defense, a targeted company invokes some move that makes it less valuable to the potential raider, with the hope of discourag-ing the takeover. A common technique is to sell newly issued stock to current stockhold-ers at prices below the market value of the company's existing stock, thereby instantly increasing the number of shares the raider has to buy.[36] With the *white knight* tactic, a third company is invited to acquire a company that is in danger of being swallowed up in a hostile takeover.

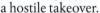

 **Checkpoint**

LEARNING OBJECTIVE 5: Identify the potential advantages of pursuing mergers and acquisitions as a growth strategy, along with the potential difficulties and risks.

SUMMARY: Mergers and acquisitions can help companies reduce costs by eliminating redundancies and increasing buying power, increase revenue by cross-selling goods and services to each other's customers or expanding into new markets, and compete more effectively by adding new technologies or talented employees. However, the difficulties and risks are considerable: coming up with the money, deciding which managers will be in charge, merging marketing and sales efforts, reconciling information systems, dealing with redundant employees, and meshing different corporate cultures.

CRITICAL THINKING: (1) If you were on the board of directors at a company and the CEO proposed a merger with a top competitor, what types of questions would you want answered before you gave your approval? (2) If a CEO has an opportunity to merge with or acquire another company and is reasonably certain that the transaction will benefit shareholders, is the CEO obligated to pursue the deal? Why or why not?

IT'S YOUR BUSINESS: (1) Have you (or someone you know) ever experienced a merger or an acquisition as an employee? Was your job affected? (2) Have you ever experienced a merger or an acquisition as a customer? Did customer service suffer during the transition of ownership?

KEY TERMS TO KNOW: merger, acquisition, hostile takeover, leveraged buyout (LBO)

Define *strategic alliance* and *joint venture*, and explain why a company would choose these options over a merger or an acquisition.

strategic alliance
A long-term partnership between companies to jointly develop, produce, or sell products.

joint venture
A separate legal entity established by two or more companies to pursue shared business objectives.

Strategic Alliances and Joint Ventures

Chapter 3 discusses strategic alliances and joint ventures from the perspective of international expansion, defining a **strategic alliance** as a long-term partnership between companies to jointly develop, produce, or sell products, and a **joint venture** as a separate legal entity established by the strategic partners. Both of these options can be more attractive than a merger or acquisition in certain situations.

STRATEGIC ALLIANCES

Strategic alliances can accomplish many of the same goals as a merger or an acquisition but with less risk and work than permanently integrating two companies.[37] They can help a company gain credibility in a new field, expand its market presence, gain access to technology, diversify offerings, and share best practices without forcing the partners to become permanently entangled. As Behind the Scenes on page 115 explains, strategic alliances are one of the three foundations of Cisco's product-development strategy.

JOINT VENTURES

Although strategic alliances avoid much of the work and risk of formal mergers, they don't create a unified entity that functions with a single management structure, information system, and other organizational elements. In contrast, a joint venture lets companies create an operation that is more tightly integrated than a strategic alliance but without disrupting the original companies to the extent that a merger or acquisition does. In fact, after the spotty record of mergers and acquisitions in recent years, more companies are now considering joint ventures as a more attractive way to collaborate.[38] A good example is clearXchange, a system that enables person-to-person payments via email or text messaging. It was launched by three large banks that compete with one another as a matter of course but that cooperated on the new venture as a way to compete against PayPal.[39]

Exhibit 5.5 offers a quick graphical summary of the major ways businesses can join forces. For the latest information on company structure, corporate governance, and related issues, visit **http://real-timeupdates.com/bia8** and click on Chapter 5.

 Checkpoint

LEARNING OBJECTIVE 6: Define *strategic alliance* and *joint venture*, and explain why companies would choose these options over a merger or an acquisition.

SUMMARY: Strategic alliances can accomplish many of the same goals as a merger or an acquisition but with less risk and work than permanently integrating two companies. A joint venture lets companies create an operation that is more tightly integrated than a strategic alliance but without disrupting the original companies to the extent that a merger or acquisition does.

CRITICAL THINKING: Why are an increasing number of companies considering joint ventures rather than mergers and acquisitions?

IT'S YOUR BUSINESS: Assume that you've worked for years to build up a strong and independent company; would you be comfortable sharing power with another company in a strategic alliance or joint venture? Why or why not?

KEY TERMS TO KNOW: strategic alliance, joint venture

EXHIBIT 5.5 **Options for Joining Forces**

Companies can choose from a variety of ways to combine resources and capabilities.

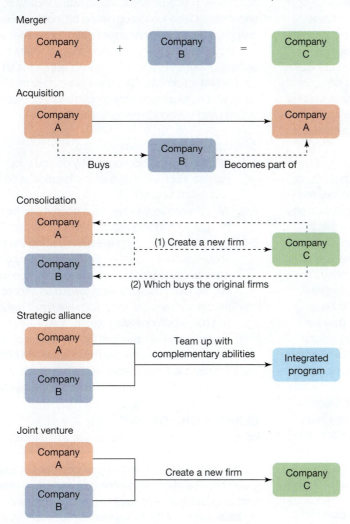

Merger

Company A + Company B = Company C

Acquisition

Company A → Company A

Buys → Company B → Becomes part of

Consolidation

Company A

Company B

(1) Create a new firm → Company C

(2) Which buys the original firms

Strategic alliance

Company A

Company B

Team up with complementary abilities → Integrated program

Joint venture

Company A

Company B

Create a new firm → Company C

BEHIND THE SCENES

CISCO TURNS ONE OF THE TOUGHEST MOVES IN BUSINESS INTO A STRATEGIC ADVANTAGE

Generating $50 billion a year in revenues means having a lot of products to sell, and networking giant Cisco certainly has that. The company sells thousands of hardware and software products and technical services in nearly 40 different categories.

Cisco pursues a three-pronged approach to developing this vast product catalog. First, it maintains a vigorous R&D effort to develop its own designs, spending roughly $6 billion a year on R&D. For comparison, this is nearly the same amount spent by IBM, a company twice the size of Cisco. And in one recent year, Cisco tabulated that it spent as much on R&D as all its direct competitors combined.

Second, Cisco's core business is networking technologies that allow people to share information of all types over the Internet. Because a complete information system usually requires more than just networking, Cisco partners with companies that specialize in computers, mobile phones, software, business consulting, and other products and services. These relationships let Cisco focus on its core strengths while offering customers complete solutions.[40]

Third, Cisco maintains an active acquisitions program, looking for companies that can help it create new markets, develop emerging markets faster, or expand existing markets. Cisco acquires as many as 10 companies a year, a staggering number when you consider how difficult it is to integrate even a single company. Beyond the scale of the activity, though, Cisco's acquisition effort is notable for its above-average success rate.

That success stems from a carefully designed program for selecting targets and merging them into the company. In contrast to the many companies that make only a random acquisition now and then, acquisitions are a core strategic focus for Cisco. CEO John Chambers outlines six rules the company uses to select a company for acquisition and successfully bring it into the Cisco organization. The first rule is making sure the companies have the same vision for where the particular segment of industry is heading, and the second is making sure the target company has a similar culture. Chambers places a high priority on treating employees and customers well, for example, so a company that focuses on generating wealth for its founders at the expense of employees or customers would not be a good fit.

The next two rules focus on the nature of what Cisco is really buying. Chambers wants to acquire not only top-notch products but also the talented employees who design, build, market, and service those products. If key personnel aren't likely to remain after the acquisition, that sends up a major red flag, for example. In addition, Chambers wants acquisitions to be significant strategic additions that have the potential to grow into major business units.

The fifth rule is all about location. Although Chambers doesn't rule out overseas acquisitions, the closer the target company is to Cisco's Silicon Valley headquarters, the better.

His sixth and final rule is to listen to customers. They tell Cisco what products they need and how the company might need to evolve to meet their needs in the future. These insights help the company identify the technologies and products they'll need to remain competitive in key market segments.

After choosing a target and completing the deal, Cisco works carefully to integrate the new employees and new business operations that get picked up in an acquisition. For example, the company's Acquisition Integration Team runs an informational website specifically for employees of acquired companies to make sure these people get the information they need to become productive contributors in their new corporate home.

By following those six rules and a finely tuned process for bringing new companies on board, Cisco has built a reputation as one of the best companies in the world when it comes to acquisitions. However, the methodology is certainly not foolproof,

and Chambers says that as good as Cisco is, its acquisitions succeed only two-thirds of the time. For instance, a couple of notable blunders occurred when the company expanded beyond its core focus of business systems with a move into consumer electronics. Cisco wound up selling off those operations when they proved unable to generate hoped-for revenue and profits.

Occasional missteps aside, in a world where most mergers and acquisitions fail, a two-thirds success rate is an impressive competitive advantage. Chambers plans to retire at the end of 2016, and he expresses strong optimism that Cisco will continue building *and* buying its way to success.

Critical Thinking Questions

5-1. In today's global economy, why do you suppose Cisco puts so much emphasis on the location of potential acquisition targets?

5-2. Would a hostile takeover be a good move for Cisco, given its approach to acquisitions? Why or why not?

5-3. Assume you're a Cisco executive leading the effort to acquire a small software company. The company is interested because it needs more resources to keep growing, but the founders are leaning toward an offer of a 50/50 merger with another small software firm. Neither software firm has experience with mergers or acquisitions, but the key players in both firms are on friendly personal terms. Based on what you've learned in this chapter and Behind the Scenes case study, what would be your pitch to convince them that joining Cisco would be a wiser business decision?

LEARN MORE ONLINE

Imagine that you're one of the founders of a technology startup that Cisco has expressed some preliminary interest in acquiring. You stand to profit nicely if your company is acquired, but you're nervous about transitioning from the free-wheeling life at a startup to being an employee of a huge corporation. Visit the Life at Cisco section of the Cisco website (look for it in the Careers section of **www.cisco.com**). Identify several points about working at Cisco that would or would not appeal to someone in your shoes.

KEY TERMS

acquisition (111)
benefit corporation (106)
board of directors (108)
chief executive officer (CEO) (110)
corporate governance (108)
corporate officers (110)
corporation (104)
general partnership (102)
hostile takeover (111)
joint venture (114)

leveraged buyout (LBO) (111)
limited liability (102)
limited liability company (LLC) (106)
limited liability partnership(LLP) (102)
limited partnership (102)
liquidity (105)
master limited partnership (MLP) (102)
merger (111)
partnership (102)
private corporation (104)

proxy (108)
public corporation (104)
S corporation (106)
shareholder activism (108)

shareholders (104)
sole proprietorship (99)
strategic alliance (114)
unlimited liability (101)

MyBizLab®

To complete the problems with the ⭐,
go to EOC Discussion Questions in the
MyLab.

TEST YOUR KNOWLEDGE

Questions for Review

5-4. What are the three basic forms of business ownership?

5-5. How does unlimited liability put a business owner at risk?

5-6. What is the difference between a general partnership and a limited partnership?

5-7. What is a closely held corporation, and why do some companies choose this form of ownership?

5-8. What is the role of a company's board of directors?

Questions for Analysis

5-9. Why is it advisable for partners to enter into a formal partnership agreement?

5-10. To what extent do shareholders control the activities of a corporation?

⭐ 5-11. How might a company benefit from having a diverse board of directors that includes representatives of several industries, countries, and cultures?

5-12. Why might two companies choose to form a strategic alliance rather than pursue a merger or an acquisition?

⭐ 5-13. **Ethical Considerations.** Are poison-pill defenses ethical? If a potential acquirer buys company stock legally, thereby becoming a part owner of the company, should management be allowed to entrench itself against the wishes of this owner? Explain your answer.

Questions for Application

5-14. Suppose you and some friends want to start a business to take tourists on wilderness backpacking expeditions.

None of you has much extra money, so you plan to start small. However, if you are successful, you would like to expand into other types of outdoor tours and perhaps even open branches in other locations. What form of ownership should your new enterprise take, and why?

5-15. Do you own or have you ever considered owning stock? If so, what steps have you taken to ensure that company management has shareholders' interests in mind?

5-16. Visit Liberty Media's website, **www.libertymedia.com**, and find the company's corporate governance guidelines. Assume that you're going to start a company that you plan to incorporate. Identify at least five principles of good governance from Liberty's website that you will use to guide the board of your new corporation.

⭐ 5-17. **Concept Integration.** You've developed considerable expertise in setting up new manufacturing plants, and now you'd like to strike out on your own as a consultant who advises other companies. However, you recognize that manufacturing activity tends to expand and contract at various times during the business cycle (see Chapter 2). Do you think a single-consultant sole proprietorship or a small corporation with a half dozen or more consultants would be better able to ride out tough times at the bottom of a business cycle?

EXPAND YOUR KNOWLEDGE

Discovering Career Opportunities

Are you best suited to working as a sole proprietor, as a partner in a business, or as an employee or a manager in a corporation? For this exercise, select three businesses with which you are familiar: one run by a single person, such as a web design consultant or a local landscaping firm; one run by two or three partners, such as a small accounting firm; and one that operates as a corporation, such as Target or Walmart.

5-18. Write down what you think you would like about being the sole proprietor, one of the partners, the corporate manager, or an employee in the businesses you have selected. For example, would you like having full responsibility for the sole proprietorship? Would you like being able to consult with other partners in the partnership before making decisions? Would you settle for less autonomy to get the benefits of being a corporate employee?

5-19. Now write down what you might dislike about each form of business. For example, would you dislike the risk of bearing all legal responsibility in a sole proprietorship? Would you dislike having to talk with your partners before spending the partnership's money? Would you dislike having to write reports for top managers and shareholders of the corporation?

5-20. Weigh the pluses and minuses you have identified in this exercise. In comparison, which form of business most appeals to you?

Improving Your Tech Insights: Groupware

Groupware, software that lets people communicate, share files, present materials, and work on documents simultaneously, is changing the way employees interact—and even the way businesses work together. For example, *shared workspaces* are "virtual offices" that give everyone on a team access to the same set of resources and information: databases, calendars, project plans, archived instant messages and emails, reference materials, and team documents. These workspaces (which are typically accessed through a web browser) make it easy for geographically dispersed team members to access shared files anytime, anywhere. Employees no longer need to be in the same office or even in the same time zone. They don't even need to be employees. Groupware makes it easy for companies to pull together partners and temporary contractors on a project-by-project basis. Groupware is often integrated with *web-based meeting systems* that combine instant messaging, shared workspaces, videoconferencing, and other tools.

Pick a company you might like to work for someday, and with that company in mind, conduct research to identify a currently available groupware system. (Groupware systems aren't always identified as such, so you might want to search for "project collaboration systems," "collaboration platforms," or similar terms.) In a brief email message to your instructor, explain how this particular groupware system could help the employees and managers in the company you've chosen be more productive.[41]

PRACTICE YOUR SKILLS

Sharpening Your Communication Skills

You have just been informed that your employer is going to merge with a firm in Germany. Using online or library resources, find information on German business culture and customs and prepare a short report that would help your U.S. colleagues work effectively with your new German colleagues.

Building Your Team Skills

Imagine that the president of your college or university has just announced plans to retire. Your team, playing the role of the school's board of directors, must decide how to choose a new president to fill this vacancy next semester.

First, generate a list of the qualities and qualifications you think the school should seek in a new president. What background and experience would prepare someone for this key position? What personal characteristics should the new president have? What questions would you ask to find out how each candidate measures up against the list of credentials you have prepared?

Now list all the stakeholders that your team, as directors, must consider before deciding on a replacement for the retiring president. Of these stakeholders, whose opinions do you think are most important? Whose are least important? Who will be directly and indirectly affected by the choice of a new president? Of these stakeholders, which should be represented as participants in the decision-making process?

Select a spokesperson to deliver a brief presentation to the class, summarizing your team's ideas and the reasoning behind your suggestions. After all the teams have completed their presentations, discuss the differences and similarities among credentials proposed by all the teams for evaluating candidates for the presidency. Then compare the teams' conclusions about stakeholders. Do all teams agree on which stakeholders should participate in the decision-making process? Lead a classroom discussion on a board's responsibility to its stakeholders.

Developing Your Research Skills

Review recent issues of business newspapers or periodicals (print or online editions) to find an article or series of articles illustrating one of the following business developments: merger, acquisition, hostile takeover, or leveraged buyout.

5-21. Explain in your own words what steps or events led to this development.

5-22. What results do you expect this development to have on (a) the company, (b) consumers, and (c) the industry the company is part of? Write down your answers, along with today's date.

5-23. Follow your story in the business news over the next month (or longer, as your instructor requests). What problems, opportunities, or other results are reported? Were these developments anticipated at the time of the initial story, or did they seem to catch industry analysts by surprise? How well did your answers to question 5-22 predict the results?

MyBizLab®

Go to the Assignments section of your MyLab to complete these writing exercises.

5-24. Why are leveraged buyouts considered risky?

5-25. Is it ethical for special-interest groups to engage in shareholder activism? Explain your answer.

ENDNOTES

1. Peter Burrows, "Cisco CEO Says Company Remains in Hunt for Software Makers," *BloombergBusiness*, 19 February 2015, www.bloomberg.com; Cisco website, accessed 29 March 2015, www.cisco.com; Julie Bort, "Cisco's John Chambers: What I Look For Before We Buy a Startup," *Business Insider*, 23 July 2014, www.businessinsider.com; Julie Bort, "Cisco CEO Opens Up: 'We Want to Change the Standard of Living for Everyone in This World,'" *Business Insider*, 23 July 2014, www.businessinsider.com; "Acquisitions," Cisco website, accessed 29 March 2015, www.cisco.com; "Cisco Acquisition Connection," Cisco website, accessed 29 March 2015, www.cisco.com; Jordan Robertson, "Cisco Sells Linksys Home Router Unit to Belkin," *BloombergBusiness*, 24 January 2013, www.bloomberg.com; Adam Hartung, "Top 20 R&D Spenders—Not Good Investments," *Forbes*, 5 November 2011, www.forbes.com; Padmasree Warrior, "Innovation Engine: Cisco Ranked #1 for R&D Quality by Patent Board," Cisco blog, 19 July 2011, http://blogs.cisco.com.

2. "Sole Proprietorship Basics," *Nolo*, accessed 10 March 2009, www.nolo.com.

3. "Sole Proprietorship Basics," *Nolo*.

4. William Atkinson, "Emotional Exhaustion: When You Have No Energy Left to Give," *LP/Gas*, June 2005, 17–20.

5. "Join the Club," *Entrepreneur*, December 2008, 89.

6. "Facts and Figures," *PwC*, accessed 25 March 2015, www.pwc.com.

7. "Partnership Basics," *Nolo*, accessed 10 March 2009, www.nolo.com.

8. Michael Cumming, "What Is a Master Limited Partnership?" *Morningstar*, 9 August 2007, www.morningstar.com.

9. Kelly K. Spors, "So, You Want to Be an Entrepreneur," *Wall Street Journal*, 23 February 2009, http://online.wsj.com.

10. Stephanie Clifford, "10 Questions to Ask Your Partner (Before You Sign an Agreement)," *Inc.*, November 2006, www.inc.com.

11. "Creating a Partnership Agreement," *Nolo*, accessed 11 March 2009, www.nolo.com.

12. "Creating a Partnership Agreement," *Nolo*.

13. "2014 Fortune Global 500," *Fortune*, accessed 25 March 2015, http://http://fortune.com/global500/; "GDP - Countries - List," *Trading Economics*, accessed 25 March 2015, www.cia.gov.

14. "Largest Global IPOs," Renaissance Capital IPO Center, accessed 25 March 2015, www.renaissancecapital.com.

15. Geoffrey Colvin and Ram Charan, "Private Lives," *Fortune*, 27 November 2006, 190–198.

16. Sanford M. Jacoby and Sally Kohn, "Japan's Management Approaches Offer Lessons for U.S. Corporations," *Seattle Times*, 27 March 2009, www.seattletimes.com.

17. "S Corporation Facts," *Nolo*, accessed 13 March 2009, www.nolo.com

18. "S Corporations," U.S. Internal Revenue Service, accessed 25 March 2015, www.irs.gov.

19. "How to Choose the Right Legal Structure," *Inc.*, January–February 2009, www.inc.com.

20. "The Biggest LLCs in the USA - 2012 Edition," *PRLog*, 21 September 2012, www.prlog.com

21. Benefit Corp website, accessed 25 March 2015, www.benefitcorp.net; Alex Goldmark, "The Benefit Corporation: Can Business Be About More Than Profit?" *Good*, 1 July 2011, www.good.is; "Maryland First State in Union to Pass Benefit Corporation Legislation," B Corporation press release, 14 April 2010, www.crswire.com; B Corporation website, accessed 5 August 2011, www.bcorporation.net.

22. Interfaith Center on Corporate Responsibility, accessed 25 March 2015, www.iccr.org; William J. Holstein, "Unlikely Allies," *Directorship*, 3 October 2006, www.forbes.com.

23. Jena McGregor, "Activist Investors Get More Respect," *BusinessWeek*, 11 June 2007, 34–35.

24. "Posner and Sherman on the Transformation of the Activist Investor," The Deal.com, 11 November 2008, www.thedeal.com.

25. Martin Lipton, "Shareholder Activism and the 'Eclipse of the Public Corporation,'" *The Corporate Board*, May/June 2007, 1–5.

26. "Percentage of New Female Nominees Nearly Doubled in Past Seven Years at Larger U.S. Companies, ISS Research Finds," Institutional Shareholder Services, 25 September 2014, www.issgovernance.com; "Missing Pieces: Women and Minorities on Fortune 500 Boards," fact sheet, Alliance for Board Diversity, accessed 10 October 2013, http://theabd.org; Carol Bowie, "Independent Board Chairs: A Trend Picks Up Speed," *The Corporate Governance Advisor*, March–April 2009, 14–16; Cora Daniels, "Finally in the Director's Chair," *Fortune*, 4 October 2004, 42–44; David A. Nadler, "Building Better Boards," *Harvard Business Review*, May 2004, 102–111; Judy B. Rosener, "Women on Corporate Boards Make Good Business Sense," *Directorship*, May 2003, www.womensmedia.com.

27. Susan Ellen Wolf, Robert J. Bertolini, Thomas J. Colligan, Fred Hassan, and Thomas J. Sabatino, Jr. "The Case for Customized Board Education," *The Corporate Governance Advisor*, January/February 2011, 1–6; Joann S. Lublin, "Back to School," *Wall Street Journal*, 21 June 2004, R3.

28. Bill Baker, Larry West, Brian Cartwright, and Brian Nysenbaum, "Liability of Outside Directors in SEC Enforcement Actions," *The Corporate Governance Advisor*, May/June 2011, 16–21.

29. Jeffrey M. Stein and Parth S. Munshi, "The Changing Role of the Lead Director," *The Corporate Governance Advisor*, November–December 2008, 11–18.

30. "Mergers & Acquisitions Explained," *Thomson Investors Network*, accessed 8 April 2004, www.thomsoninvest.net.

31. *The PSI Opportunity* (online newsletter), PSI website, accessed 8 April 2004, www.psiusa.com.

32. "Spring Merger Fever," *Wall Street Journal*, 22 May 2007, A14.

33. Greta Roberts, "The Soft Things That Make Mergers Hard," *Harvard Business Review* Blog Network, 12 July 2011. http://blogs.hbr.org.

34. Tim Merrifield, "Six Tips for Succeeding with the Art of Acquisition," Cisco website, accessed 5 August 2011, www.cisco.com; "The Contra Team," *Business 2.0*, April 2006, 83.
35. Merrifield, "Six Tips for Succeeding with the Art of Acquisition."
36. Investopedia, accessed 5 August 2011, www.investopedia.com.
37. Michael Hickins, "Searching for Allies," *Management Review*, January 2000, 54–58.
38. "Joint Ventures Overtake M&A," PricewaterhouseCoopers 12th Annual Global CEO Survey, accessed 14 March 2009, www.pwc.com.

39. Aaron Smith and Blake Ellis, "New Cash Transfer Service Rivals PayPal," *CNNMoney*, 25 May 2011, http://money.cnn.com.
40. "Partner Central," Cisco website, accessed 29 March 2015, www.cisco.com.
41. 37Signals website, accessed 2 July 2007, www.37signals.com; Tony Kontzer, "Learning to Share," *InformationWeek*, 5 May 2003, 28; Jon Udell, "Uniting Under Groove," *InfoWorld*, 17 February 2003, www.elibrary.com; Alison Overholt, "Virtually There?" *Fast Company*, 14 February 2002, 108.

Entrepreneurship and Small-Business Ownership

6

LEARNING OBJECTIVES   After studying this chapter, you will be able to

1 Highlight the contributions small businesses make to the U.S. economy.

2 List the most common reasons people start their own companies, and identify the common traits of successful entrepreneurs.

3 Explain the importance of planning a new business, and outline the key elements in a business plan.

4 Identify the major causes of business failures, and identify sources of advice and support for struggling business owners.

5 Discuss the principal sources of small-business private financing.

6 Explain the advantages and disadvantages of franchising.

BEHIND THE SCENES   BRINGING TRADITIONAL HEALING WISDOM TO MODERN CONSUMERS AT SISTER SKY

Monica Simeon and Marina TurningRobe, the sisters behind Sister Sky bath and body products, have turned their business dreams into reality but still face some important challenges as they continue to grow.

www.sistersky.com

For entrepreneurial inspiration, Monica Simeon didn't have to look far. She learned how to run a business by helping her father operate one of the first Native American casinos. She got the inspiration for her business while preparing batches of skin lotions based on traditional herbal remedies after commercial products didn't help with her son's severe eczema. And the opportunity to form a business partnership was as close as her sister, Marina TurningRobe.

Thus was born Sister Sky, which makes natural bath and body products based on recipes and natural plant knowledge handed down from generation to generation. The company is based on the Spokane Indian Reservation in northeast Washington state, where the sisters grew up—and grew into their entrepreneurial lifestyle.

As with many other entrepreneurs, the sisters' vision is much broader than simply earning a living. They emphasize purity and authenticity in their products, whether that means using more-expensive distilled water to avoid risks of contamination, shunning the cheaper petroleum-based ingredients used in many mass-produced bath and body products, or staying true to the wisdom they have inherited from their ancestors. In addition, the sisters believe they have a duty to "promote cultural sharing in a positive way by educating consumers about the indigenous essence and spirit of the plant botanicals contained in our products." Finally, Simeon says, "One of our main goals is to improve the tribal economy by expanding opportunities for jobs beyond the casino."

If you were Simeon or TurningRobe, what steps would you take to make sure your young business made it through the launch stage and onto a path of sustainable growth and profitability? Where might you turn for advice and support if you needed it? How would you stay true to your vision of authentic and purposeful products while pursuing the goal of providing job opportunities—and still meet the unrelenting demands of managing a business in a highly competitive industry?[1]

INTRODUCTION

Because you're studying business, chances are you've already had an idea or two for a new business. Are you ready to commit yourself fully to a business idea, as Monica Simeon and Marina TurningRobe (profiled in the chapter-opening Behind the Scenes) have done? Are you ready to make sacrifices and do whatever it takes to get your company off the ground? Should you start something from scratch or buy an existing business? Being an entrepreneur is one of the most exciting and important roles in business, but it requires high energy and some tough decision making, as you'll discover in this chapter.

1   LEARNING OBJECTIVE

Highlight the contributions small businesses make to the U.S. economy.

The Big World of Small Business

Many businesses start out the way Sister Sky did: with an entrepreneur (or two, in this case), a compelling idea, and the drive to succeed. Small-business ownership gives people like Monica Simeon and Marina TurningRobe the opportunity to pursue their dreams while making lasting and important contributions to their communities. Entrepreneurship also provides the platform for launching companies that grow to be quite large. With the exception of operations spun off from existing companies, even the biggest corporations begin life as small businesses.

Defining just what constitutes a small business is surprisingly tricky, but it is vitally important because billions of dollars are at stake when it comes to such things as employment regulations—from which the smallest companies are often exempt—and government contracts reserved for small businesses.[2] Roughly speaking, a **small business** is an independently owned and operated company that employs fewer than 500 people and "is not dominant in its field of operation," in the words of the U.S. Small Business Administration (SBA). Beyond that general starting point, the SBA defines the maximum size of "small" through either annual revenue or number of employees. The limits vary by industry and are occasionally adjusted to reflect industry changes or inflation.[3]

small business
A company that is independently owned and operated, is not dominant in its field, and employs fewer than 500 people (although this number varies by industry).

ECONOMIC ROLES OF SMALL BUSINESSES

From employing millions of people to creating essential products, small businesses play a vital role in the U.S. economy. Here are some of the major contributions small firms make (see Exhibit 6.1):

- **They provide jobs.** Although most small businesses have no employees, those that do employ about half of the private-sector workforce in this country and create roughly two thirds of all new jobs.[4]
- **They introduce new products.** The freedom to innovate that is characteristic of many small firms continues to yield countless advances: Among all firms that apply for U.S. patents on new inventions, small businesses receive 16 times more patents per employee than larger firms.[5]
- **They meet the needs of larger organizations.** Many small businesses act as distributors, servicing agents, and suppliers to larger corporations and to numerous government agencies (which often reserve a certain percentage of their purchasing contracts for small businesses).
- **They inject a considerable amount of money into the economy.** Small businesses pay nearly half the private-sector payroll in the United States and produce half the country's gross domestic product.[6]

EXHIBIT 6.1 | **The Economic Impact of Small Businesses in the United States**

As these selected statistics show, small businesses are a major force in employment, economic activity, and global exports.

The U.S. Economy: The Impact of Small Business

99.7% of employer firms

48.5% of private-sector employment

46% of private-sector output

37% of high-tech employment

98% of firms that export goods

33% of export value

¥ £ ₩ €

Business Owners by Age

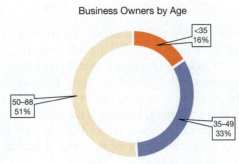

<35 16%
50–88 51%
35–49 33%

Business Owners by Military Service Status

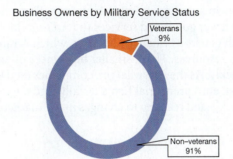

Veterans 9%
Non–veterans 91%

Small Businesses by Employment Status

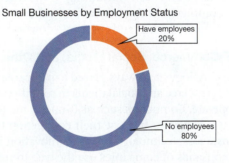

Have employees 20%
No employees 80%

Net Job Creation, 1993–2013 (millions of new jobs)

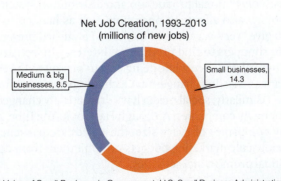

Medium & big businesses, 8.5
Small businesses, 14.3

Source: Frequently Asked Questions: Advocacy the Voice of Small Business in Government, U.S. Small Business Administration, March 2014, www.sba.gov.

- **They take risks that larger companies sometimes avoid.** Entrepreneurs play a significant role in the economy as risk takers—people willing to try new and unproven ideas.
- **They provide specialized goods and services.** Small businesses frequently spring up to fill niches that aren't being served by existing companies.

CHARACTERISTICS OF SMALL BUSINESSES

The majority of small businesses are modest operations with little growth potential, although some have attractive income potential for the solo businessperson. Small businesses such as a self-employed consultant, a local florist, or a small e-commerce venture are sometimes called *lifestyle businesses* because they are built around the personal and financial needs of an individual or a family. In contrast, other firms are small simply because they are young, but they have ambitious plans to grow. These *high-growth ventures* are usually run by a team rather than by one individual, and they expand rapidly by obtaining a sizable supply of investment capital and by introducing new products or services to a large market.

Regardless of their primary objectives, small companies tend to differ from large ones in a variety of important ways. First, most small firms have a narrow focus, offering fewer goods and services to fewer market segments. Second, unless they are launched with generous financial backing, which is rare, small businesses have to get by with limited resources. Third, smaller businesses often have more freedom to innovate and move quickly. As they grow larger, companies tend to get slower and more bureaucratic. In contrast, entrepreneurial firms usually find it easier to operate "on the fly," making decisions quickly and reacting to changes in the marketplace.

FACTORS CONTRIBUTING TO THE INCREASE IN THE NUMBER OF SMALL BUSINESSES

Three factors are contributing to the increase in the number of small businesses today: e-commerce, social media, and other technological advances; the growing diversity in entrepreneurship; and corporate downsizing and outsourcing.

E-Commerce, Social Media, and Other Technologies

Technology has always played a major role in business formation, but the rapid growth of e-commerce and social media in recent years has revolutionized the way many businesses operate. Companies such as Pandora and Facebook couldn't exist without web technologies, of course, because their connection to customers happens entirely online. In other instances, technology enables innovation in one or more functional areas. For example, thousands of companies use the web to replace physical retail stores while continuing to use conventional production and distribution systems in the physical world. Online technology also allows an operation such as handcrafts marketplace Etsy (**www.etsy.com**) to give "very-very small businesses" a unified presence online, as well as making it easier for shoppers to find products of interest.[7] In fact, avoiding the high cost of establishing a physical presence while being able to market to the entire world is one of the most significant and lasting changes that technology has brought to small business.

Similarly, social media have dramatically changed the marketing and selling functions for many companies. Although Facebook, YouTube, and other online media tools are used by companies of every size, these sites are particularly vital to small companies whose minuscule marketing budgets prohibit them from doing much advertising or other traditional promotional activities.

Growing Diversity in Entrepreneurship

Small-business growth is being fueled in part by women, minorities, immigrants, military veterans who want to apply their leadership skills, older workers who can't find employment to fit their interests or skills, and young people who want alternatives to traditional employment. It's never too early to start. Facebook, Google, and Dell are just a few of the significant companies started by college students. In the words of Joseph Keeley, who formed College Nannies and Tutors when he was a freshman at the University of St. Thomas, "As a young entrepreneur, the risk is relatively low. If you have a well-thought-out plan, don't be afraid to execute it. The risk only gets higher as you get older."[8]

Downsizing and Outsourcing

Business start-ups often soar when the economy sours. During hard times, many companies downsize or lay off talented employees, who then have little to lose by pursuing self-employment. Tech titans William Hewlett and David Packard joined forces in Silicon Valley in 1938 during the Great Depression, and Microsoft launched amidst the 1975 recession.[9] During the recent global recession, another wave of entrepreneurs took their turn. As companies were trimming staff, Mark Cannice, who runs the entrepreneurship program at the University of San Francisco, said, "If there is a silver lining, the large-scale downsizing from major companies will release a lot of new entrepreneurial talent and ideas—scientists, engineers, business folks now looking to do other things."[10]

Outsourcing, the practice of engaging outside firms to handle either individual projects or entire business functions (page 202), also creates numerous opportunities for small businesses and entrepreneurs. Some companies subcontract special projects and secondary business functions to experts outside the organization, whereas others turn to outsourcing as a way to permanently eliminate entire departments, and some laid-off employees even become entrepreneurs and sell services to their former employers.

REAL-TIME UPDATES
Learn More by Watching This Video

Young entrepreneurs changing the world

Get insights and inspiration from *Forbes* Under 30 Summit presenters. Go to http://real-timeupdates.com/bia8 and click on Learn More in the Students section.

 ✔ **Checkpoint**

LEARNING OBJECTIVE 1: Highlight the contributions small businesses make to the U.S. economy.

SUMMARY: Small businesses provide jobs, employing about half the private-sector workforce. They introduce new and innovative products, they supply many of the needs of larger organizations, they inject considerable amounts of money into the economy, they often take risks that larger organizations avoid, and they provide many specialized goods and services.

CRITICAL THINKING: (1) Why do you think many companies grow more risk averse as they grow larger? (2) If they wanted to, could large businesses take the place of small businesses in the U.S. economy? For instance, could someone build a nationwide landscaping company? Why or why not?

IT'S YOUR BUSINESS: If you can't land the right job soon after graduation, would you consider starting a business? Why or why not?

KEY TERMS TO KNOW: small business

The Entrepreneurial Spirit

To some people, working for themselves or starting a company seems a perfectly natural way to earn a living. To others, the thought of working outside the structure of a regular company might seem too scary to even contemplate. However, every professional should understand the **entrepreneurial spirit**—the positive, forward-thinking desire to create profitable, sustainable business enterprises—and the role it can play in *every* company, not just small or new firms. The entrepreneurial spirit is vital to the health of the economy and to everyone's standard of living, and it can help even the largest and oldest companies become profitable and competitive.

2 LEARNING OBJECTIVE

List the most common reasons people start their own companies, and identify the common traits of successful entrepreneurs.

entrepreneurial spirit
The positive, forward-thinking desire to create profitable, sustainable business enterprises.

Jim Wilson/The New York Times/Redux

Frustrated in a tough job market, Alex Andon used his expertise in biology and aquarium design to launch Jellyfish Art. The company specializes in the unique and demanding field of aquariums for jellyfish.

WHY PEOPLE START THEIR OWN COMPANIES

Starting a company is nearly always a difficult, risky, exhausting endeavor that requires significant sacrifice. Why do people do it? Some want more control over their future; others are simply tired of working for someone else. Some, such as Monica Simeon and Marina TurningRobe of Sister Sky, have new product ideas that they believe in with such passion that they're willing to risk everything on a start-up enterprise. Some start companies to pursue business goals that are important to them on a personal level. Jennie Baird, cofounder of Generation Grownup, which publishes parenting-related websites, had two important reasons—reasons shared by Simeon, TurningRobe, and many others: "I wanted to take the opportunity to be the one in control of innovation and work on something that I believe in."[11]

Another reason, one that becomes more common during tough job markets, is the inability to find attractive employment anywhere else. Alex Andon searched for months after being laid off from his job in the biotech industry. Out of frustration as much as anything else ("I hate looking for work," he explained), he became an entrepreneur, putting his biology background to work launching Jellyfish Art (**www.jellyfishart.com**) to create and sell jellyfish aquariums.[12]

QUALITIES OF SUCCESSFUL ENTREPRENEURS

Although it's impossible to lump millions of people into a single category, successful entrepreneurs tend to share a number of characteristics (see Exhibit 6.2). If you have many of these traits, successful entrepreneurship could be in your future, too—if you're not already a hard-working entrepreneur.

INNOVATING WITHOUT LEAVING: INTRAPRENEURSHIP

The entrepreneur's innovative spirit is so compelling that many large companies and individuals within companies now try to express it through *intrapreneurship*, a term coined by business consultant Gifford Pinchot to designate entrepreneurial efforts within a larger organization.[13]

However, innovating within a larger organization is often much easier said than done, because companies tend to become more analytical, more deliberate, more structured, and more careful as they mature. Mechanisms put in place to prevent mistakes can also hamper innovative thinking by restricting people to tried-and-true methods. Organizations can develop habits based on behaviors and decisions that made sense in the past but that no longer make sense as the business environment changes. Injecting the entrepreneurial spirit sometimes means going against the accepted wisdom.[14] In other words, it can be risky behavior that may or may not be rewarded. Companies sometimes need to take special steps to encourage, protect, and reward the entrepreneurial spirit.

REAL-TIME UPDATES
Learn More by Reading This Article

The innovation advantage of intrapreneurs

Get advice for entrepreneurs who want to hire game-changing innovators. Go to http://real-timeupdates.com/bia8 and click on Learn More in the Students section.

 Checkpoint

LEARNING OBJECTIVE 2: List the most common reasons people start their own companies, and identify the common traits of successful entrepreneurs.

SUMMARY: People start businesses for a variety of reasons, including gaining more control over their futures, wanting to avoid working for someone else, having

| EXHIBIT 6.2 | Qualities Shared by Successful Entrepreneurs |

Although no single personality profile fits all successful entrepreneurs, here are the qualities that entrepreneurs tend to have.

Confidence
- Like to control their destiny—and believe they can
- Curious and eager to learn to reach their goals
- Learn from mistakes and view failure as a chance to grow
- Highly adaptable and in tune with their markets
- Willing to take sensible risks but are not "gamblers"

Passion
- Love what they do and are driven by a passion to succeed
- Often don't measure success in strictly financial terms
- Have a high degree of confidence and optimism
- Relate well with diverse personalities
- Have a talent for inspiring others

Drive
- Willing to work hard for sustained periods of time
- Extremely disciplined; no one has to motivate them
- Willing to make sacrifices in other areas of their lives

Sources: "Thinking About Starting a Business?," U.S. Small Business Administration website, accessed 2 November 2013, www.sba.gov; Kelly K. Spors, "So, You Want to Be an Entrepreneur," *Wall Street Journal*, 23 February 2009, http://online .wsj.com; Marshall Goldsmith, "Demonstrating the Entrepreneurial Spirit," *BusinessWeek*, 26 August 2008, www.businessweek .com; Sarah Pierce, "Spirit of the Entrepreneur," *Entrepreneur*, 29 February 2008, www.entrepreneur.com; Norman M. Scarborough and Thomas W. Zimmerer, *Effective Small Business Management*, 7th ed. (Upper Saddle River, N.J.: Prentice Hall, 2003), 4.

new product ideas that they are deeply passionate about, pursuing business goals that are important to them on a personal level, or seeking income alternatives during tough employment markets. The entrepreneurial spirit, the positive, forward-thinking desire to create profitable, sustainable business enterprises, is a good way to summarize the entrepreneurial personality. Specifically, successful entrepreneurs tend to love what they do and are driven by a passion to succeed at it, they are disciplined and willing to work hard, they are confident and optimistic, and they like to control their own destiny. Moreover, they relate well to others and have the ability to inspire others, are curious, learn from their mistakes without letting failure drag them down, are adaptable and tuned into their environments, and are moderate but careful risk takers.

CRITICAL THINKING: (1) Would someone who excels at independent entrepreneurship automatically excel at an intrapreneurial effort? Why or why not? (2) Does the inability or unwillingness to work within the constraints of a typical corporation mean someone is naturally suited to entrepreneurship? Why or why not?

IT'S YOUR BUSINESS: (1) If you had to start a business right now and generate profit as quickly as possible, what kind of business would you start? Explain your answer. (2) How would you describe your level of entrepreneurial spirit?

KEY TERMS TO KNOW: entrepreneurial spirit

3 | **LEARNING OBJECTIVE**

Explain the importance of planning a new business, and outline the key elements in a business plan.

The Start-Up Phase: Planning and Launching a New Business

The start-up phase is an exciting time because entrepreneurs and small-business owners love to roll up their sleeves and get to work, but it's also an exhausting time because a lot of work must be done. Focusing that start-up energy and making sure essential tasks get completed calls for careful decision making and planning, starting with choosing the best ownership option and creating an effective business plan.

SMALL-BUSINESS OWNERSHIP OPTIONS

People who have an entrepreneurial urge sometimes jump to the conclusion that starting a new company is the best choice, but it's definitely not the only choice—and not always the right choice. Before you decide, consider all three options: creating a new business, buying an existing business, or buying a franchise. Creating a new business has many advantages, but it can also be the most difficult option (see Exhibit 6.3).

EXHIBIT 6.3 | **Business Start-Up Options**

Creating an all-new, independent business can be an exciting prospect, but this brief comparison highlights how much work it requires and how many risks are involved. (You can read more about franchising on page 138.)

Start-Up Strategy	Financial Outlay at Start-Up	Possibilities for Borrowing Start-Up Capital or Getting Investors	Owner's Freedom and Flexibility	Business Processes and Systems	Support Networks	Workforce	Customer Base, Brand Recognition, and Sales
Create a new, independent business	Some businesses can be started with very little cash; others, particularly in manufacturing, may require a lot of capital	Usually very limited; most lenders and many investors want evidence that the business can generate revenue before they'll offer funds; venture capitalists invest in new firms, but only in a few industries	Very high, particularly during early phases, although low capital can severely restrict the owner's ability to maneuver	Must be designed and created from scratch, which can be time-consuming and expensive	Suppliers, bankers, and other elements of the network must be selected; the good news is that the owner can select and recruit ones that he or she specifically wants	Must be hired and trained at the owner's expense	None; must be built from the ground up, which can put serious strain on company finances until sales volume builds
Buy an existing independent business	Can be considerable; some companies sell for multiples of their annual revenue, for example	Banks are more willing to lend to "going concerns," and investors are more likely to invest in them	Less than when creating a new business because facilities, workforce, and other assets are already in place—more than when buying a franchise	Already in place, which can be a plus or minus, depending on how well they work	Already in place; may need to be upgraded	Already in place, which could a positive or a negative, but at least there are staff to operate the business	Assuming that the business is at least somewhat successful, it has a customer base with ongoing sales and some brand reputation (which could be positive or negative)
Buy into a franchise system	Varies widely, from a few thousand to several hundred thousand dollars	Varies, but many franchisors do not allow franchisees to buy a franchise with borrowed funds, so they must have their own capital	Low to very low; most franchisors require rigid adherence to company policies and processes	One of the key advantages of buying a franchise is that it comes with an established business system	Varies; some franchise companies specify which suppliers a franchisee can use	Must be hired and trained, but a franchisor usually provides training or training support	Customer base and repeat sales must be built up, but one of the major advantages of a franchise is established brand recognition

Compared to starting a new business, buying an existing business can involve less work and less risk—provided, of course, that you check out the company carefully. When you buy a healthy business, you generally purchase an established customer base, functioning business systems, proven products or services, and a known location. In addition, financing an existing business is often much easier because lenders are reassured by the company's history and existing assets and customer base.

Still, buying an existing business is not without disadvantages and risks. You may need a considerable amount of financing to buy a fully functioning company, for example, and you will inherit any problems the company has, from unhappy employees to obsolete equipment to customers with overdue accounts. Thorough research is a must.[15]

The third option, buying a franchise (see page 138), combines many of the benefits of independent business ownership with the support that comes with being part of a larger organization.

BLUEPRINT FOR AN EFFECTIVE BUSINESS PLAN

Although some successful entrepreneurs claim to have done little formal planning, they all have at least *some* intuitive idea of what they're trying to accomplish and how they hope to do it. In other words, even if they haven't produced a formal printed document, chances are they've thought through the big questions, which is just as important. As FedEx founder Fred Smith put it, "Being entrepreneurial doesn't mean [you] jump off a ledge and figure out how to make a parachute on the way down."[16]

A **business plan** summarizes a proposed business venture, communicates the company's goals, highlights how management intends to achieve those goals, and shows how customers will benefit from the company's goods or services. Preparing a business plan serves three important functions. First, it guides the company operations and outlines a strategy for turning an idea into reality. Second, it helps persuade lenders and investors to finance your business if outside money is required. Third, it can provide a reality check in case an idea just isn't feasible.

Business plans can be written before the company is launched, when the founders are defining their vision of what the company will be, when the company is seeking funding, and after the company is up and running, when the plan serves as a monitor-and-control mechanism to make sure operations are staying on track. At any stage, a business plan forces you to think about personnel, marketing, facilities, suppliers, distribution, and a host of other issues vital to a company's success. The specific elements to include in a business plan can vary based on the situation; here are the sections typically included in a plan written to attract outside investors:[17]

- **Summary.** In one or two paragraphs, summarize your business concept, particularly the *business model*, which defines how the company will generate revenue and produce a profit. The summary must be compelling, catching the investor's attention and giving him or her reasons to keep reading. Describe your product or service and its market potential. Highlight some things about your company and its leaders that will distinguish your firm from the competition. Summarize your financial projections and indicate how much money you will need from investors or lenders and where it will be spent.
- **Mission and objectives.** Explain the purpose of your business and what you hope to accomplish.
- **Company overview.** Give full background information on the origins and structure of your venture.
- **Products or services.** Concisely describe your products or services, focusing on their unique attributes and their appeal to customers.
- **Management and key personnel.** Summarize the background and qualifications of the people most responsible for the company's success.

business plan
A document that summarizes a proposed business venture, its goals, and plans for achieving those goals.

Whenever you seek outside funding, investors and lenders will demand to know how they will be repaid and will expect to find this information in your business plan.

68/altrendo images/Ocean/Corbis

- **Target market.** Provide data that will persuade an investor that you understand your target market. Be sure to identify the strengths and weaknesses of your competitors.
- **Marketing strategy.** Provide projections of sales volume and market share; outline a strategy for identifying and reaching potential customers, setting prices, providing customer support, and physically delivering your products or services. Whenever possible, include evidence of customer acceptance, such as advance product orders.
- **Design and development plans.** If your products require design or development, describe the nature and extent of what needs to be done, including costs and possible problems.
- **Operations plan.** Provide information on facilities, equipment, and personnel requirements.
- **Start-up schedule.** Forecast development of the company in terms of completion dates for major aspects of the business plan.
- **Major risk factors.** Identify all potentially negative factors and discuss them honestly.
- **Financial projections and requirements.** Include a detailed budget of start-up and operating costs, as well as projections for income, expenses, and cash flow for the first three years of business. Identify the company's financing needs and potential sources.
- **Exit strategy.** Explain how investors will be able to cash out or sell their investment, such as through a public stock offering, sale of the company, or a buyback of the investors' interest.

REAL-TIME UPDATES
Learn More by Reading This PDF

Want to pitch to investors? Learn from the pros first

Guy Kawasaki and his partners at Garage Technology Ventures offer invaluable advice on presenting a business idea to potential investors. Go to http://real-timeupdates.com/bia8 and click on Learn More in the Students section.

Veteran Silicon Valley entrepreneur and investor Guy Kawasaki advises entrepreneurs to create a concise *executive summary* of their business plan to use when presenting their ideas to investors for the first time. Entrepreneurs often have as little as 20 minutes (and sometimes even less) to make these pitches, so a compelling presentation backed up by an executive summary no longer than 20 pages is ideal. The most important part of the entire package is "the grab," a compelling one- or two-sentence statement that gets an investor's attention. If an investor is intrigued, he or she can then read the executive summary to get a better sense of the opportunity and then review the full business plan before making a decision to provide funds.[18]

Be aware that not all start-up veterans and investors believe in the value of a conventional business plan, at least in a company's early stages. Reasons for the skepticism include the amount of time and energy required to research and write a plan, the reluctance of many target readers to read such lengthy documents, the uncertainty of whether a new product or company idea will even work, and the difficulty of correctly anticipating all the circumstances and obstacles that a young company will encounter. Particularly for companies that are developing new products or new business models before they can launch, some experts recommend that entrepreneurs devote most of their energy to getting a working product or service model in front of potential customers as quickly as possible so they can verify and fine-tune it before proceeding to extensive business planning. Two popular alternatives to conventional business plans are high-level overviews known as the Business Model Canvas and the Lean Canvas. They are essentially one-page business plans that present only the essential ideas that make up an intended business model.[19]

 Checkpoint

LEARNING OBJECTIVE 3: Explain the importance of planning a new business, and outline the key elements in a business plan.

SUMMARY: Planning is essential because it forces you to consider the best ownership strategy for your needs and circumstances (creating a new company, buying an existing company, or buying a franchise), and it forces you to think through the factors that will lead to success. An effective business plan should include your mission and objectives, company overview, management, target market, marketing strategy, design and development plans, operations plan, start-up schedule, major risk factors, and financial projections and requirements.

CRITICAL THINKING: (1) Why is it important to identify critical risks and problems in a business plan? (2) Many experts suggest that you write the business plan yourself, rather than hiring a consultant to write it for you. Why is this a good idea?

IT'S YOUR BUSINESS: (1) Think of several of the most innovative or unusual products you currently own or have recently used (don't forget about services as well). Were these products created by small companies or large ones? (2) Optimism and perseverance are two of the most important qualities for entrepreneurs. On a scale of 1 (lowest) to 10 (highest), how would you rate yourself on these two qualities? How would your best friend rate you?

KEY TERM TO KNOW: business plan

The Growth Phase: Nurturing and Sustaining a Young Business

4 | **LEARNING OBJECTIVE**

Identify the major causes of business failures, and identify sources of advice and support for struggling business owners.

So far, so good. You've done your planning and launched your new enterprise. Now the challenge is to keep going and keep growing toward your goals. To ensure a long and healthy life for your business, start by understanding the reasons new businesses can fail.

THE NEW BUSINESS FAILURE RATE

You may have heard some frightening "statistics" about the failure rate of new businesses, with various sources saying that 70, 80, or even 90 percent of new business ventures fail. Unfortunately, calculating a precise figure that represents all types of businesses across all industries is probably impossible. First, the definition of "failure" can be hard to pin down and varies from one business owner to the next. For example, business owners may retire, return to the corporate workforce to get away from the grind of running a business alone, or simply decide to pursue a different path in life. All of these closures would count as failures in a typical survey, but they wouldn't count as failures to the business owners themselves. Second, establishing a time frame is essential for a failure rate to have any meaning. For example, ill-conceived or undercapitalized businesses often don't survive the first year, so the early failure rate is quite high. However, after the bad ideas collide with reality and disappear, the rate of failure slows down, and the companies that fail do so for a wide variety of reasons, some internal and some external. Third, structural changes in the economy or in a particular industry can cause business closures that don't reflect a general pattern applicable to all companies. For example, since the advent of the online travel shopping, the number of traditional, in-person travel agencies in the United States has plummeted by roughly two-thirds.[20] The fact that so many companies, including many long-established ones, went out of business is the more the result of this structural change in the industry than of some "new business failure" phenomenon.

In other words, view every failure statistic with skepticism unless you can find out how it was calculated. For instance, in the notoriously difficult restaurant industry, "90 percent of new restaurants fail" is repeated so often that many people assume that it must be true. However, one in-depth study showed the rate to be only 60 percent after four years—still a serious number, but considerably less than the near-certain failure rate of 90 percent.[21]

REAL-TIME UPDATES
Learn More by Reading This Article

Learn from the failure of other entrepreneurs

The lessons of failure are just as important as the lessons of success. Go to http://real-timeupdates.com/bia8 and click on Learn More in the Students section.

EXHIBIT 6.4	Why New Businesses Fail

These 12 blunders are among the most common reasons for the failure of new businesses.

Leadership Issues	Marketing and Sales Issues	Financial Issues	Systems and Facilities Issues
Managerial incompetence: Owner doesn't know how to plan, lead, control, or organize.	**Ineffective marketing:** Small companies—especially *new* small companies—face a tremendous challenge getting recognition in crowded markets.	**Inadequate financing:** Being undercapitalized can prevent a company from building the scale required to be successful or sustaining operations until sales revenues increase enough for the firm to be self-funding.	**Poor location:** Being in the wrong place will doom a retail operation and can raise costs for other types of business as well.
Lack of strategic planning: Owner didn't think through all the variables needed to craft a viable business strategy.	**Uncontrolled growth:** Company may add customers faster than it can handle them, leading to chaos, or may even "grow its way into bankruptcy" if it spends wildly to capture and support customers.	**Poor cash management:** A company may spend too much on nonessentials, fail to balance expenditures with incoming revenues, fail to use loan or investment funds wisely, or fail to budget enough to pay its bills.	**Poor inventory control:** Company may produce or buy too much inventory, raising costs too high—or it may do the opposite and be unable to satisfy demand.
Lack of relevant experience: Owner may be experienced in business but not in the particular markets or technologies that are vital to the new firm's success.	**Overreliance on a single customer:** One huge customer can disappear overnight, leaving the company in dire straits.	**Too much overhead:** Company creates too many fixed expenses that aren't directly related to creating or selling products, leaving it vulnerable to any slowdown in the economy.	
Inability to make the transition from corporate employee to entrepreneur: Owner can't juggle the multiple and diverse responsibilities or survive the lack of support that comes with going solo.			

Sources: Brian Hamilton, "The 7 Biggest Financial Mistakes Businesses Make," *Inc.*, 9 August 2011, www.inc.com; Norman M. Scarborough and Thomas W. Zimmerer, *Effective Small Business Management*, 7th ed. (Upper Saddle River, N.J.: Prentice Hall, 2003), 27–29.

Another study—this one a comprehensive analysis using data from the U.S. Census Bureau—found that 50 percent of all new employer firms (those that hire employees) were still in business after four years, and another 17 percent were no longer in operation but had closed "successfully," meaning that the owner retired, sold the company, or otherwise ended the enterprise on a positive note. In other words, averaged across all industries, only 33 percent actually "failed" during this time frame.[22]

Although the statistics may not be quite as gloomy as many people think, even a 33 percent failure rate should demand the careful entrepreneur's attention. To help make sure you don't become a statistic, start by understanding why businesses tend to fail (see Exhibit 6.4) and figure out how to avoid making the same mistakes.

Perhaps one of the most important reasons companies fail is something that doesn't always show up in surveys. It's a simple matter of "motivational collapse," when the would-be entrepreneur encounters one too many setbacks and simply doesn't have the drive to keep going.[23] A truly committed entrepreneur, in contrast, keeps pushing onward, experimenting, making adjustments, and keeping his or her enthusiasm level high until things start to click. One would be hard-pressed to improve on the insight and advice offered by Marina TurningRobe of Sister Sky: "In business, you must have the courage and honesty to admit when you fall short. This helps you refine, reformulate, redesign and come back stronger and better. If you can't admit your shortcomings you will become stagnant, irrelevant, or just plain arrogant. In a competitive business environment, being any of these will be your demise."[24]

ADVICE AND SUPPORT FOR BUSINESS OWNERS

Keeping a business going is no simple task, to be sure. Fortunately, entrepreneurs can get advice and support from a wide variety of sources.

Government Agencies and Not-for-Profit Organizations

Numerous city, state, and federal government agencies offer business owners advice, assistance, and even financing in some cases. For instance, many cities and states have an office of economic development chartered with helping companies prosper so that they might contribute to the local or regional economy. At the federal level, small businesses can apply for loans backed by the Small Business Administration (SBA), get management and financing advice, and learn about selling to the federal government at **www.sba.gov**. The Minority Business Development Agency (**www.mbda.gov**) offers advice and programs to minority-owned businesses. Many state agencies also have offices to help small firms compete.

Some of the best advice available to small businesses is delivered by thousands of volunteers from the Service Corps of Retired Executives (SCORE), a resource partner of the SBA. These experienced business professionals offer free advice and one-to-one counseling to entrepreneurs. You can learn more at **www.score.org**.

Many colleges and universities also offer entrepreneurship and small-business programs. Check with your college's business school to see whether resources are available to help you launch or expand a company. The U.S. Chamber of Commerce (**www.uschamber.com**) and its many local chambers offer advice and special programs for small businesses as well.

Business Partners

Banks, credit card companies, software companies, and other firms you do business with can also be a source of advice and support. For example, the Open Forum, hosted by American Express, offers a variety of videos, articles, and online network tools to help small-business owners, as well as online tutorials and forums where business owners can post questions.[25] As you might expect, the free resources from these companies are part of their marketing strategies and so include a certain amount of self-promotion, but don't let that stop you from taking advantage of all the free advice you can get.

Mentors and Advisory Boards

Many entrepreneurs and business owners take advantage of individual mentors and advisory boards. Mentoring can happen through both formal programs such as SCORE and informal relationships developed in person or online. In either case, the advice of a mentor who has been down the road before can be priceless.

An **advisory board** is a form of "group mentoring" in which you assemble a team of people with subject-area expertise or vital contacts to help review plans and decisions. Unlike a corporate board of directors, an advisory board does not have legal responsibilities, and you don't have to incorporate to establish an advisory board. In some cases, advisors will agree to help for no financial compensation. In other cases, particularly for growth companies that want high-profile experts, advisors agree to serve in exchange for either a fee or a small portion of the company's stock (up to 3 percent is standard).[26]

advisory board
A team of people with subject-area expertise or vital contacts who help a business owner review plans and decisions.

Print and Online Media

Your local library and the Internet offer information to help any small-business owner face just about every challenge imaginable. For instance, blogs written by business owners, investors, and functional specialists such as marketing consultants can offer valuable insights. Websites such as **www.entrepreneurship.org** provide free advice on every aspect of managing an entrepreneurial organization. Also, the websites affiliated with these well-known business magazines should be considered for every small-business owner's regular reading list:

- *Inc.* (**www.inc.com**)
- *Bloomberg Businessweek* (**www.businessweek.com/small-business**)
- *Fortune* and *Money* (**http://money.cnn.com/smallbusiness/**)
- *Harvard Business Review* (**https://hbr.org/topic/entrepreneurship**)
- *Forbes* (**www.forbes.com/entrepreneurs/**)
- *Entrepreneur* (**www.entrepreneur.com/**)
- *Fast Company* (**www.fastcompany.com/**)

Networks and Support Groups

No matter what industry you're in or what stage your business is in, you can probably find a local or an online network of people with similar interests. Many cities across the

EXHIBIT 6.5	Social Networking for Entrepreneurs

Here are just a few of the many online networks that provide advice and vital connections for entrepreneurs. Some of these are not specific to small business, but they've become major resources for business owners. Some also feature public and private groups that focus on specific business issues.

Network	Special Features	URL
StartupNation	Provides articles, forums, blogs, seminars, and podcasts	www.startupnation.com
LinkedIn	So many business professionals and corporate managers are members of this popular network that most entrepreneurs should have a presence as well	www.linkedin.com
Xing	Similar to LinkedIn, with a European focus	www.xing.com
Facebook	Not specifically for entrepreneurs or small business owners but has become a major marketing platform for many small businesses	www.facebook.com
The Funded	Lets entrepreneurs share information on venture capitalists and angel investors, including the amounts and terms they've been offered	http://thefunded.com
Young Entrepreneur	For active entrepreneurs and those considering entrepreneurship	www.facebook.com/YoungEntrepreneurs
Twitter	Not specifically for entrepreneurs or small business owners, but many use it to build connections and conduct research	https://twitter.com
Pinterest	Many consumers use Pinterest to search for product ideas, so it can be a great promotional platform for businesses	www.pinterest.com

country have local networks; search online for "entrepreneur network." Some entrepreneurs meet regularly in small groups to analyze each other's progress month by month. Being forced to articulate your plans and decisions to peers—and to be held accountable for results—can be an invaluable reality check. Some groups focus on helping entrepreneurs hone their presentations to potential investors. In addition to local in-person groups, social networking technology gives entrepreneurs an endless array of opportunities to connect online (see Exhibit 6.5).

Business Incubators

business incubators
Facilities that house small businesses and provide support services during the company's early growth phases.

Business incubators are centers that provide "newborn" businesses with various combinations of advice, financial support, access to industry insiders and connections, facilities, and other services a company needs to get started. Some incubators are not-for-profit organizations affiliated with the economic development agencies of local or state governments or universities, some are for-profit enterprises, some are run by venture capitalists, and some companies have internal incubators to encourage new ventures.

One of the best-known incubators, Y Combinator (http://ycombinator.com), has helped to fund and nurture hundreds of companies in digital media and related industries. In exchange for a small share of ownership, it makes small investments in companies; more important, it helps founders refine their ideas, develop products, polish their pitches to investors, connect with industry experts, handle incorporation issues to avoid legal trouble later on, hire the right kind of employees, and even mediate disputes between company founders. If all this help sounds priceless, Y Combinator would certainly agree with you: "The kind of

REAL-TIME UPDATES
Learn More by Visiting This Website

Find an incubator to nurture your new venture

The National Business Incubation Association has information about incubators and links to one in your area. Go to http://real-time updates.com/bia8 and click on Learn More in the Students section.

advice we give literally can't be bought, because anyone qualified to give it is already rich. You can only get it from investors."[27]

✓ Checkpoint

LEARNING OBJECTIVE 4: Identify the major causes of business failures, and identify sources of advice and support for struggling business owners.

SUMMARY: Ten common reasons for failure are managerial incompetence, inexperience, inadequate financing, poor cash management, lack of strategy planning, ineffective marketing, uncontrolled growth, poor location, poor inventory control, and the inability to make the transition from corporate employee to independent entrepreneur. Another factor that can contribute to any of these explicit reasons is motivational collapse, when the entrepreneur simply gives up. For help and advice, business owners can turn to a variety of government agencies, not-for-profit organizations, business partners, mentors and advisory boards, print and online media, networks and support groups, and business incubators.

CRITICAL THINKING: (1) Why would a state or local government invest taxpayer dollars in a business incubator? (2) Can you think of any risks of getting advice from other entrepreneurs?

IT'S YOUR BUSINESS: (1) Have you ever shopped at a store or eaten in a restaurant and said to yourself, "This place isn't going to make it"? What factors caused you to reach that conclusion? (2) Does your college have an entrepreneur program or participate in a business incubator? If you wanted to start a business, how might such services help you?

KEY TERMS TO KNOW: advisory board, business incubators

Financing Options for Small Businesses

 LEARNING OBJECTIVE

Discuss the principal sources of small-business private financing.

Figuring out *how much* you'll need in order to start a business requires good insights into the particular industry you plan to enter. Figuring out *where* to get the money is a creative challenge no matter which industry you're in. Financing a business enterprise is a complex undertaking, and chances are you'll need to piece together funds from multiple sources, possibly using a combination of *equity* (in which you give investors a share of the business in exchange for their money) and *debt* (in which you borrow money that must be repaid). You'll read more about equity and debt financing in Chapter 18. Exhibit 6.6 on the next page identifies, in broad terms, the major types of financing available to businesses at various stages in their life cycle.

PRIVATE FINANCING

Private financing covers every source of funding except selling stocks and bonds. Nearly all companies start with private financing, even those that eventually "go public." The range of private financing options is diverse, from personal savings to investment funds set up by large corporations looking for entrepreneurial innovations. Many firms get **seed money**, their first infusion of capital, through family loans. If you go this route, be sure to make the process as formal as a bank loan would be, complete with a specified repayment plan. Otherwise, problems with the loan can cause problems in the family.[28]

seed money
The first infusion of capital used to get a business started.

Four common categories of private financing are banks and microlenders, venture capitalists, angel investors, and personal credit cards and lines of credit.

Banks and Microlenders

Bank loans are one of the most important sources of financing for small business, but there's an important catch: In most cases, banks won't lend money to a start-up that hasn't

| EXHIBIT 6.6 | Financing Possibilities over the Life of a Small Business |

The potential funding sources available to a business owner vary widely, depending on where the business is in its life cycle. Note that this is a general map and covers only the most common funding sources. Individual lending opportunities depend on the specific business owner(s), the state of the economy, and the type of business and its potential for growth. For example, venture capital is available only to firms with the potential to grow rapidly and only in a few industries.

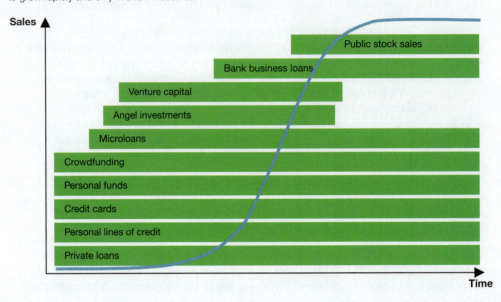

established a successful track record.[29] As your company grows, a bank will usually be a good long-term partner, helping you finance expansions and other major expenses. However, just about your only chance of getting a bank loan is by putting up marketable collateral, such as buildings or equipment, to back the loan.[30]

In response to the needs of entrepreneurs who don't qualify for standard bank loans or who don't need the amount of a regular loan, hundreds of organizations now serve as **microlenders**, offering loans up to $35,000 or so. You can learn more at the Association for Enterprise Opportunity website, at **www.microenterpriseworks.org**.[31]

Venture Capitalists

At the other end of the funding scale are **venture capitalists (VCs)**, investment specialists who raise pools of capital from large private and institutional sources (such as pension funds) to finance ventures that have high growth potential and need large amounts of capital. VC funding provides a crucial stimulus to the economy by making risky, early-stage investments in firms that are likely to become major employers if their products succeed in the marketplace. Because one-third of VC-funded start-ups don't succeed, those that do succeed need to really pay off to compensate. VCs are therefore extremely focused and selective; they invest in only a few thousand companies in the United States every year.[32]

Given the amounts of money involved and the expectations of sizable returns, VCs usually invest in high-potential areas such as information technology, energy, biotechnology, and digital media. Unlike banks or most other financing sources, VCs do more than simply provide money. They also provide management expertise in return for a sizable ownership interest in the business. Once the business becomes profitable, VCs reap the reward by selling their interest to long-term investors, usually after the company goes public.

Angel Investors

Start-up companies that can't attract VC investment (perhaps because they are too early in their product development) often look for **angel investors**, private individuals who put their own money into start-ups, with the goal of eventually selling their interest for a profit.

microlenders
Organizations, often not-for-profit, that lend smaller amounts of money to business owners who might not qualify for conventional bank loans.

venture capitalists (VCs)
Investors who provide money to finance new businesses or turnarounds in exchange for a portion of ownership, with the objective of reselling the business at a profit.

angel investors
Private individuals who invest money in start-ups, usually earlier in a business's life and in smaller amounts than VCs are willing to invest or banks are willing to lend.

These individuals are willing to invest smaller amounts than VCs and often stay involved with the company for a longer period of time. Many of these investors join *angel networks* or *angel groups* that invest together in chosen companies. Angel investing tends to have a more local focus than venture capitalism, so you can search for angels through local business contacts and organizations.

REAL-TIME UPDATES
Learn More by Reading This Article

Looking for an angel?

Find angel investors through the Angel Capital Association. Go to http://real-timeupdates.com/bia8 and click on Learn More in the Students section.

Credit Cards and Personal Lines of Credit

Although they tend to be one of the most expensive forms of financing, credit cards are also widely available and sometimes the only source of funding an entrepreneur has. Consequently, roughly half of all entrepreneurs and small-business owners use their cards to get cash for start-up or ongoing expenses.[33]

Funding a business with credit cards or a personal line of credit might be the only option for many people, but it is extremely risky. Unfortunately, there is no simple answer about whether to use credit cards; some entrepreneurs have used them to launch successful, multimillion-dollar businesses, whereas others have destroyed their credit ratings and racked up debts that take years to pay off.

Small Business Administration Assistance

The SBA offers a number of financing options for small businesses. To get an SBA-backed loan, you apply to a regular bank or credit union, which actually provides the money. The SBA guarantees to repay most of the loan amount (the percentage varies by program) if you fail to do so. In addition to operating its primary loan guarantee program, the SBA also manages a microloan program in conjunction with nonprofit, community-based lenders.[34]

Another option for raising money is the Small Business Investment Companies (SBICs) created by the SBA. These investment firms offer loans, venture capital, and management assistance, although they tend to make smaller investments and are willing to consider businesses that VCs or angel investors may not want to finance. The SBIC program has helped fund some of the best-known companies in the United States, including Apple, FedEx, Jenny Craig, and Outback Steakhouse.[35]

PUBLIC FINANCING

Companies with solid growth potential may also seek funding from the public at large, although only a small fraction of the companies in the United States are publicly traded. Whenever a corporation offers its shares of ownership to the public for the first time, the company is said to be *going public*. The shares offered for sale at this point are the company's **initial public offering (IPO)**. Going public is an effective method of raising needed capital, but it can be an expensive and time-consuming process with no guarantee of raising the amount of money needed. Public companies must meet a variety of regulatory requirements, as you'll explore in more detail in Chapter 18.

initial public offering (IPO)
A corporation's first offering of shares to the public.

CROWDFUNDING

Crowdfunding is an intriguing twist to funding that combines elements of public and private financing. Kickstarter is perhaps the best known of these web services that provide a way for people and organizations to seek money from the public. Crowdfunding services fall into two general categories. Kickstarter and a number of other sites focus on individual projects or charitable endeavors, and people provide money in exchange for the product being created or simply to help people and causes they believe in. In contrast, services such as Crowdfunder (www.crowdfunder.com) and Indiegogo (www.indiegogo.com) help business owners raise money to launch or expand companies, and the people who provide money are investing in or lending to the company. Government regulations regarding investment crowdfunding are still being finalized, but these services have the potential to give entrepreneurs some potent new ways to get their companies off the ground.[36]

crowdfunding
Soliciting project funds, business investment, or business loans from members of the public.

✔ Checkpoint

LEARNING OBJECTIVE 5: Discuss the principal sources of small-business private financing.

SUMMARY: Sources of *private financing* for small businesses include banks and microlenders, venture capitalists, angel investors, credit cards and personal lines of credit, and loan programs from the Small Business Administration. Companies that reach sufficient size with continued growth potential have the additional option of seeking *public financing* by selling shares.

CRITICAL THINKING: (1) Would a profitable small business with only moderate growth potential be a good candidate for venture capitalist funding? Why or why not? (2) Why would angel investors help finance companies privately, rather than buying shares of publicly traded companies?

IT'S YOUR BUSINESS: (1) Would you be willing to take on credit card debt in order to start a company? Why or why not? (2) What would it take to convince you to invest in or contribute to a crowdsourced startup?

KEY TERMS TO KNOW: seed money, microlenders, venture capitalists (VCs), angel investors, initial public offering (IPO), crowdfunding

---

6   **LEARNING OBJECTIVE**

Explain the advantages and disadvantages of franchising.

franchise
A business arrangement in which one company (the franchisee) obtains the rights to sell the products and use various elements of a business system of another company (the franchisor).

franchisee
A business owner who pays for the rights to sell the products and use the business system of a franchisor.

franchisor
A company that licenses elements of its business system to other companies (franchisees).

The Franchise Alternative

An alternative to creating or buying an independent company is to buy a **franchise**, which enables the buyer to use a larger company's trade name and sell its goods or services in a specific territory. In exchange for this right, the **franchisee** (the small-business owner who contracts to sell the goods or services) pays the **franchisor** (the supplier) an initial start-up fee, then monthly royalties based on sales volume. Franchises are a large and growing presence in the U.S. economy, accounting for roughly 10 percent of all employer businesses (those that hire employees).[37]

TYPES OF FRANCHISES

Franchises are of three basic types. A *product franchise* gives you the right to sell trademarked goods, which are purchased from the franchisor and resold. Car dealers and gasoline stations fall into this category. A *manufacturing franchise*, such as a soft-drink bottling plant, gives you the right to produce and distribute the manufacturer's products, using supplies purchased from the franchisor. A *business-format franchise* gives you the right to open a business using a franchisor's name and format for doing business. This format includes many well-known chains, including Taco Bell, Pizza Hut, The UPS Store, and Curves fitness centers.

ADVANTAGES OF FRANCHISING

Franchising is a popular option for many people because it combines at least some of the freedom of working for yourself with many of the advantages of being part of a larger, established organization. You can be your own boss, hire your own employees, and benefit directly from your hard work. If you invest in a successful franchise, you know you are getting a viable business model, one that has worked many times before. If the franchise system is well managed, you get the added benefit of instant name recognition, national advertising programs, standardized quality of goods and services, and a proven formula for success. Buying a franchise also gives you access to a support network and in many cases a ready-made blueprint for building a business. Depending on the system, your initial investment provides you with such services as site-location studies, market research, training, and technical assistance, as well as assistance with building or leasing your structure, decorating the building, purchasing supplies, and operating the business during your initial ownership phase.

DISADVANTAGES OF FRANCHISING

Although franchising offers many advantages, it is not the ideal vehicle for everyone. Perhaps the biggest disadvantage is the relative lack of control, at several levels. First, when you buy into a franchise system, you typically agree to follow the business format, and franchisors can prescribe virtually every aspect of the business, from the color of the walls to the products you can carry. In fact, if your primary purpose in owning a business is the freedom to be your own boss, franchising probably isn't the best choice because you don't have a great deal of freedom in many systems. Second, as a franchisee, you usually have little control over decisions the franchisor makes that affect the entire system. Disagreements and even lawsuits have erupted in recent years over actions taken by franchisors regarding product supplies, advertising, and pricing.[38] Third, if the fundamental business model of the franchise system no longer works—or never worked well in the first place—or if customer demand for the goods and services you sell declines, you don't have the option of independently changing your business in response.

In addition, buying a franchise involves both initial costs associated with buying into a franchise system and regular payments after that, based on a percentage of sales revenue. These costs vary widely, based on the complexity and popularity of the franchise. Many systems require a minimum level of liquid assets (spendable cash, essentially) and personal net worth, in addition to the out-of-pocket costs you'll have. The start-up costs for a simple home-based franchise can be less than $10,000, but a popular fast-food franchise can run from $250,000 to $2 million, and luxury hotels can top $5 million. Most franchises, however, have initial costs in the $50,000 to $200,000 range.[39]

HOW TO EVALUATE A FRANCHISING OPPORTUNITY

With so much at stake, researching a franchising opportunity carefully is vital (see Exhibit 6.7). The Federal Trade Commission (FTC) requires franchisors to disclose extensive information about their operations to prospective franchisees, including background information on the company and its executives, the company's financial status, the history of any litigation involving other franchisees, initial and ongoing costs, all restrictions put on franchisees, the availability and cost of training, procedures for ending the franchise agreement, earnings projections, and the names of current and former franchise owners. Study all this information and talk to as many current and former franchise owners as you can before taking the plunge.[40]

REAL-TIME UPDATES
Learn More by Reading This PDF

Don't sign that franchise agreement before you read this

Before you commit to a franchise, consult "Buying a Franchise: A Consumer Guide," a free publication from the FTC. Go to http://real-timeupdates.com/bia8 and click on Learn More in the Students section.

Buying a new or existing franchise is an attractive alternative for many people who want some of the freedoms of entrepreneurship without all the risks.

RosaBetancourt 0 people images/Alamy Stock Photo

✔ **Checkpoint**

LEARNING OBJECTIVE 6: Explain the advantages and disadvantages of franchising.

SUMMARY: Franchising appeals to many because it combines some of the advantages of independent business ownership with the resources and support of a larger organization. It can also be less risky than starting or buying an independent business

EXHIBIT 6.7	Key Questions to Ask Before Signing a Franchise Agreement

A franchise agreement is a legally binding contract that defines the relationship between a franchisee and a franchisor. Before signing a franchise agreement, be sure to read the disclosure document and consult an attorney.

1. What are the total start-up costs? What does the initial franchise fee cover? Does it include a starting inventory of supplies and products?
2. Who pays for employee training?
3. How are the periodic royalties calculated, and when must they be paid?
4. Who provides and pays for advertising and promotional items? Do you have to contribute to an advertising fund?
5. Are all trademarks and names legally protected?
6. Who selects or approves the location of the business?
7. Are you restricted to selling certain goods and services?
8. Are you allowed to sell online?
9. How much control will you have over the daily operation of the business?
10. Is the franchise assigned an exclusive territory?
11. If the territory is not exclusive, does the franchisee have the right of first refusal on additional franchises established in nearby locations?
12. Is the franchisee required to purchase equipment and supplies from the franchisor or other suppliers?
13. Under what conditions can the franchisor or the franchisee terminate the franchise agreement?
14. Can the franchise be assigned to heirs?

Source: "Buying a Franchise: A Consumer Guide," U.S. Federal Trade Commission website, accessed 31 March 31, 2015, www.ftc.gov.

because you have some evidence that the business model works. The primary disadvantages are the lack of control and the costs, both the initial start-up costs and the monthly payments based on a percentage of sales.

CRITICAL THINKING: (1) Why might a business owner with a successful concept decide to sell franchises rather than expand the company under his or her own control? (2) Why might someone with strong entrepreneurial spirit be dissatisfied with franchise ownership?

IT'S YOUR BUSINESS: (1) Are you a good candidate for owning and operating a franchise? Why or not? (2) Think about a small-business idea you've had or one of the small businesses you patronize frequently. Could this business be expanded into a national or international chain? Why or why not?

KEY TERMS TO KNOW: franchise, franchisee, franchisor

BEHIND THE SCENES
BUILDING AN AUTHENTIC AND PURPOSEFUL BUSINESS AT SISTER SKY

Sisters Monica Simeon and Marina TurningRobe have committed themselves to making products that are both authentic and purposeful and in doing so have created a company that shares those same attributes. Of course, like just about every other small business, Sister Sky has required intense dedication and many, many long days.

After Simeon and TurningRobe decided to turn their first homemade lotions into a real business, they started in a leased manufacturing space in Spokane, Washington. Both of their families would pitch in for 12-hour days, seven days a week—mixing, bottling, and boxing. When sales began to take off, they built their own manufacturing facility on the Spokane Indian

Reservation, as part of their commitment to help reservation economies diversify beyond gaming. Putting their houses up for collateral, they installed a $100,000 automated manufacturing system to replace much of the manual labor and expand their production volume. Beyond employing and mentoring fellow tribal members, including offering job-readiness training for tribal youth, the sisters also made a point of buying goods and services from other Native American–owned companies and serving as entrepreneurial role models in Native American communities.

In addition to scaling up manufacturing, Simeon and TurningRobe had to adjust their original marketing strategy. They initially focused on the general gift market but found that they were a tiny player in a vast market. Realizing that the cultural heritage of their product line gave them a unique advantage, they refocused on hotels and resorts, particularly those with luxury spa services. They also now offer spa consulting services, helping property owners create culturally authentic environments and experiences for their guests.

As is often the case, the challenges don't stop as a business grows, and Simeon and TurningRobe faced several classic small-business dilemmas, including time management. Simeon's husband joined the company as production manager, which freed up the sisters' time for selling, but as Simeon said recently, "We're so busy selling, we have no time to step back and strategize." A consultant who worked with them during a "business makeover" sponsored by *Fortune Small Business* magazine stressed that they really have no choice on this: They simply have to make time for strategizing, forcing themselves to step away from marketing and sales activities every quarter to review and adjust their business plan.

One of the key strategic decisions Simeon and TurningRobe must make is where to expand next. They've already moved beyond spa sales to high-end boutiques and gift shops, where their unique product concept appeals to consumers looking for something out of the ordinary. Being active in social media is helping them make connections with customers and potential business partners, too. Also, having received Minority Business Enterprise (MBE) certification from the National Minority Supplier Development Council, the company has made its first inroads into having its products used by Wyndham and other major hotel and resort chains. Sister Sky's MBE status helps these large customers meet supplier diversity goals.

After more than a decade into their entrepreneurial adventure, the sisters and their company are going strong with expanding sales but also with rewards that go beyond their own business objectives. By employing fellow tribe members and offering both inspiration and practical training, TurningRobe and Simeon are fulfilling their larger purpose, too. "Wealth building in our tribal communities through entrepreneurship is critical if we are going to improve our conditions and solve our own problems," Simeon explains. TurningRobe also speaks for many passionate entrepreneurs when she says, "If you love what you do and strive to create meaning to what you sell or create, and do it on a professional level, then I think you have found your purpose."[41]

Critical Thinking Questions

6-1. Which of the qualities of successful entrepreneurs have Simeon and TurningRobe demonstrated?

6-2. Should Simeon and TurningRobe consider lowering their ingredient costs by switching to petroleum-based ingredients or stopping their use of pure distilled water? Why or why not?

6-3. Would opening their own retail stores be a risky decision for Sister Sky? How would this change the company's business model?

LEARN MORE ONLINE

Explore the Sister Sky website at **www.sistersky.com** and find the company on Facebook and Twitter. How well does the company's online presence reflect its values? Does the information you find encourage you to learn more about the company's products? How could all entrepreneurs, regardless of market niche or company style, learn from Sister Sky's online presence?

KEY TERMS

advisory board (133)
angel investors (136)
business incubators (134)
business plan (129)
crowdfunding (137)
entrepreneurial spirit (125)
franchise (138)
franchisee (138)

franchisor (138)
initial public offering (IPO) (137)
microlenders (136)
seed money (135)
small business (122)
venture capitalists (VCs) (136)

MyBizLab®

To complete the problems with the ⭐, go to EOC Discussion Questions in the MyLab.

TEST YOUR KNOWLEDGE

Questions for Review

6-4. What are three essential functions of a business plan?

6-5. What are the advantages of buying a business rather than starting one from scratch?

6-6. What are the advantages and disadvantages of owning a franchise?

6-7. What are the key reasons for most small-business failures?

6-8. What is a business incubator?

Questions for Analysis

6-9. Why is the entrepreneurial spirit vital to the health of the nation's economy?

6-10. Do you expect that the number of entrepreneurs in the United States will grow in the next 10 years? Why or why not?

6-11. Could writing a conventional business plan every cause more harm than good? Explain your answer?

6-12. What factors should you consider before selecting financing alternatives for a new business?

6-13. **Ethical Considerations.** You're thinking about starting your own chain of upscale, drive-through espresso stands. You have several ideal sites in mind, and you've analyzed the industry and all the important statistics. You have financial backing, and you really understand the coffee market. In fact, you've become a regular at a competitor's operation for over a month. The owner thinks you're his best customer. But you're not there because you love the espresso. No, you're actually spying. You're learning everything you can about the competition so you can outsmart them. Is this behavior ethical? Explain your answer.

Questions for Application

6-14. Briefly describe an incident in your life in which you failed to achieve a goal you set for yourself. What did you learn from this experience? How could you apply this lesson to a future experience as an entrepreneur?

6-15. Based on your total life experience up to this point—as a student, consumer, employee, parent, and any other role you've played—what sort of business would you be best at running? Why?

6-16. **Concept Integration.** Entrepreneurship is one of the five factors of production, as discussed in Chapter 2 (page 27). Review that material and explain why entrepreneurs are an important factor for economic success.

6-17. **Concept Integration.** Pick a local small business or franchise that you visit frequently and discuss whether that business competes on price, speed, innovation, convenience, quality, or any combination of those factors. Be sure to provide some examples.

EXPAND YOUR KNOWLEDGE

Discovering Career Opportunities

Would you like to own and operate your own business? Whether you plan to start a new business from scratch or buy an existing business or a franchise, you need certain qualities to be successful. Start your journey to entrepreneurship by reviewing this chapter's section on entrepreneurs.

6-18. Which of the entrepreneurial characteristics mentioned in the chapter describe you? Which of those characteristics can you develop more fully in advance of running your own business?

6-19. Visit **www.sba.gov** and read the article "Is Entrepreneurship for You?" (look under "Starting & Managing a Business" and then under "Thinking About Starting a Business?"). After considering these aspects of entrepreneurial readiness, how well prepared are you to be an entrepreneur?

6-20. On the SBA website, read the article "Finding a Business Mentor" in the "Finding a Mentor or Counselor" section. With these insights in hand, think about your personal, professional, and academic networks. Assume that you want to start a business right now, before you graduate. Is there anybody you already know who could offer you sound advice? What sort of guidance would this person be able to offer? If you don't know anyone, what steps could you take to meet a mentor or counselor?

Improving Your Tech Insights: Social Networking Technology

One of the biggest challenges small-business owners face is finding the right people and making those connections, whether they're looking for a new employee, an investor, a potential customer, or anyone else who might be important to the future of the business. Using social networking, businesspeople can reach more people than they could ever hope to reach via traditional, in-person networking. In a brief email message to your instructor, describe how you could use social networking to locate potential candidates to serve on the advisory board of your small business. (Make up any details you need about your company.)

PRACTICE YOUR SKILLS

Sharpening Your Communication Skills

Effective communication begins with identifying your primary audience and adapting your message to your audience's needs. This is particularly true for business plans. One of the primary reasons for writing a business plan is to obtain financing. With that in mind, what do you think are the most important things investors will want to know? How can you convince them that the information you are providing is accurate? What should you assume investors know about your specific business or industry?

Building Your Team Skills

The questions shown in Exhibit 6.7 cover major legal issues you should explore before investing money in a franchise. In addition, however, there are many more questions you should ask in the process of deciding whether to buy a particular franchise.

With your team, think about how to investigate the possibility of buying a Burger King franchise. Go to **www.bk.com/ franchising/home** and explore the information the company provides about franchising opportunities.

Next, brainstorm a plan to learn more about the potential positives and negatives of buying a Burger King franchise. Then generate a list of at least 10 questions an interested buyer should ask about this potential business opportunity.

Choose a spokesperson to present your team's ideas to the class. After all the teams have reported, hold a class discussion to analyze the lists of questions generated by all the teams. Which questions were on most teams' lists? Why do you think those questions are so important? Can your class think of any additional questions that were not on any team's list but seem important?

Developing Your Research Skills

Scan issues of print or online editions of business journals or newspapers for articles describing problems or opportunities faced by small businesses in the United States. Clip or copy three or more articles that interest you and then answer the following questions.

6-21. What problem or opportunity does each article present? Is it an issue faced by many businesses, or is it specific to one industry or region?

6-22. What could a potential small-business owner learn about the risks and rewards of business ownership from reading these articles?

6-23. How might these articles affect someone who is thinking about starting a small business?

MyBizLab®

Go to the Assignments section of your MyLab to complete these writing exercises.

6-24. Given the risks involved in starting any company, should an aspiring entrepreneur investigate all possible failure scenarios and develop action plans to avoid these potential outcomes? Explain your answer.

6-25. Is "I don't like having a boss tell me what to do" a good reason to start your own company? Explain your answer.

ENDNOTES

1. Sister Sky website, accessed 28 March 2015, www.sistersky .com; Sister Sky Facebook page, accessed 28 March 2015, www .facebook.com/pages/Sister-Sky/230340194280; "MBDA Helps Sister Sky Tap into a Legacy of Entrepreneurism," *MBDA.gov Newsletter*, March 2011, U.S. Department of Commerce Minority Business Development Agency, accessed 8 August 2011, www .mbda.gov; Patricia Gray, "Conditioning a Firm for Growth," *Fortune Small Business*, 3 December 2007; "Necessity Inspires This Mother's Invention: New Body Lotion Is Nature-Based Eczema Treatment," press release, 2 July 2007, www.theproductrocket .com; A. J. Naff, "Sister Sky: A Perfect Blend of Entrepreneurship and Native Wisdom," *Indian Gaming*, June 2008, 32–33.

2. Bernard Stamler, "Redefinition of Small Leads to a Huge Brawl," *New York Times*, 21 September 2004, G8.

3. "Small Business Size Standards," U.S. Small Business Administration, accessed 31 March 2015, www.sba.gov; "Table of Small Business Size Standards Matched to North American Industry Classification System Codes," U.S. Small Business Administration, effective 14 July 2014, www.sba.gov.

4. "How Important Are Small Businesses to the U.S. Economy?" U.S. Small Business Administration, accessed 30 March 2009, www.sba.gov; Malik Singleton, "Same Markets, New Marketplaces," *Black Enterprise*, September 2004, 34; Edmund L. Andrews, "Where Do the Jobs Come From?" *New York Times*, 21 September 2004, E1, E11.

5. U.S. Small Business Administration, *Frequently Asked Questions: Advocacy the Voice of Small Business in Government*, September 2012.

6. *Frequently Asked Questions: Advocacy the Voice of Small Business in Government*.

7. "About Etsy," Etsy, accessed 11 August 2011, www.etsy.com.

8. College Nannies & Tutors, accessed 2 November 2013, www .collegenanniesandtutors.com; Stacy Perman, "The Startup Bug

Strikes Earlier," *BusinessWeek*, 31 October 2005, www.business week.com.

9. Jim Hopkins, "Bad Times Spawn Great Start-Ups," *USA Today*, 18 December 2001, 1B; Alan Cohen, "Your Next Business," *FSB*, February 2002, 33–40.

10. Matt Richtel and Jenna Wortham, "Weary of Looking for Work, Some Create Their Own," *New York Times*, 13 March 2009, www .nytimes.com.

11. Heather Green, "Self-Help for Startups," *BusinessWeek*, 5 February 2009, www.businessweek.com.

12. Richtel and Wortham, "Weary of Looking for Work, Some Create Their Own."

13. Intrapreneur, accessed 31 March 2009, www.intrapreneur.com.

14. Jeffrey Bussgang, "Think Like a VC, Act Like an Entrepreneur," *BusinessWeek*, 14 August 2008, www.businessweek.com.

15. "Buy a Business," U.S. Small Business Administration, accessed 3 July 2007, www.sba.gov.

16. Joshua Hyatt, "The Real Secrets of Entrepreneurs," *Fortune*, 15 November 2004, 185–202.

17. Heidi Brown, "How to Write a Winning Business Plan," *Forbes*, 18 June 2010, www.forbes.com; Michael Gerber, "The Business Plan That Always Works," *Her Business*, May/June 2004, 23–25; J. Tol Broome, Jr., "How to Write a Business Plan," *Nation's Business*, February 1993, 29–30; Albert Richards, "The Ernst & Young Business Plan Guide," *R & D Management*, April 1995, 253; David Lanchner, "How Chitchat Became a Valuable Business Plan," *Global Finance*, February 1995, 54–56; Marguerita Ashby-Berger, "My Business Plan—And What Really Happened," *Small Business Forum*, Winter 1994–1995, 24–35; Stanley R. Rich and David E. Gumpert, *Business Plans That Win $$$* (New York: Harper & Row, 1985).

18. "Writing a Compelling Executive Summary," Garage Technology Ventures, accessed 9 March 2011, www.garage.com; "Crafting Your Wow! Statement," Garage Technology Ventures, accessed 9 March 2011, www.garage.com; Guy Kawasaki website, accessed 9 March 2011, www.guykawasaki.com.

19. Strategyzer website, accessed 1 March 2015, www.business modelgeneration.com; Ash Maurya, "Why Lean Canvas vs Business Model Canvas?" Practice Trumps Theory blog, 27 February 2012, http://practicetrumpstheory.com

20. Rebecca L. Weber, "The Travel Agent Is Dying, But It's Not Yet Dead," CNN, 10 October 2013, www.cnn.com.

21. Kerry Miller, "The Restaurant-Failure Myth," *BusinessWeek*, 16 April 2007, 19.

22. Brian Headd, "Redefining Business Success: Distinguishing Between Closure and Failure," *Small Business Economics* 21, 51–61, 2003.

23. Joel Spolsky, "Start-Up Static," *Inc.*, March 2009, 33–34.

24. "MBDA Helps Sister Sky Tap into a Legacy of Entrepreneurism."

25. OPEN Forum, accessed 2 November 2013, https://www.open forum.com/explore/.

26. Christine Comaford-Lynch, "Don't Go It Alone: Create an Advisory Board," *BusinessWeek*, 1 February 2007, www.business week.com.

27. "About Y Combinator," Y Combinator, accessed 31 March 2015, http://ycombinator.com.

28. Paulette Thomas, "It's All Relative," *Wall Street Journal*, 29 November 2004, R4, R8.

29. Reed Albergotti, "Long Shot," *Wall Street Journal*, 29 November 2004, R4; Norman Scarborough and Thomas Zimmerer, *Effective Small Business Management* (Upper Saddle River, N.J.: Pearson Prentice Hall, 2002), 439.

30. Bob Zider, "How Venture Capital Works," *Harvard Business Review*, November/December 1998, 131–139.

31. Association for Enterprise Opportunity website, accessed 11 August 2011, www.microenterpriseworks.org.

32. National Venture Capital Association website, accessed 11 August 2011, www.nvca.org.

33. David Port, "APR Hikes Ambush Biz Owners," *Entrepreneur*, 16 March 2009, www.entrepreneur.com; Bobbie Gossage, "Charging Ahead," *Inc.*, January 2004, www.inc.com.

34. U.S. Small Business Administration website, accessed 11 August 2011, www.sba.gov.

35. U.S. Small Business Administration website, accessed 11 August 2011, www.sba.gov.

36. SoMoLend website, accessed 3 November 2013, www.somolend .com; Crowdfunder website, accessed 3 November 2013, http://crowdfunder.com; Steven M. Davidoff, "Trepidation and Restrictions Leave Crowdfunding Rules Weak," *New York Times*, 29 October 2013, www.nytimes.com; Chance Barnettt, "Top 10 Crowdfunding Sites for Fundraising," *Forbes*, 8 May 2013, www .forbes.com.

37. U.S. Census Bureau, "Census Bureau's First Release of Comprehensive Franchise Data Shows Franchises Make Up More Than 10 Percent of Employer Businesses," 14 September 2010, www.census.gov.

38. Douglas MacMillan, "Franchise Owners Go to Court," *BusinessWeek*, 29 January 2007, www.businessweek.com; Jill Lerner, "UPS Store Dispute Escalating," *Atlanta Business Chronicle*, 24 February 2006, www.bizjournals.com.

39. Eddy Goldberg, "The Costs Involved in Opening a Franchise," Franchising.com, accessed 31 March 2015, www.franchising .com; "U.S. Franchising," McDonald's website, accessed 31 March 2015, www.aboutmcdonalds.com; Hayley Peterson, "Here's How Much It Costs to Open Different Fast Food Franchises in the U.S.," *Business Insider*, 4 November 2014. www.businessinsider .com.

40. *Buying a Franchise: A Consumer Guide*, U.S. Federal Trade Commission, accessed 12 August 2011, www.ftc.gov.

41. See Note 1.

PART 3

Guiding the Enterprise: Leadership, Organization, and Operations

WavebreakMediaMicro/Fotolia

Management Roles, Functions, and Skills

LEARNING OBJECTIVES After studying this chapter, you will be able to

1 Explain the importance of management, and identify the three vital management roles.

2 Describe the planning function, and outline the strategic planning process.

3 Describe the organizing function, and differentiate among top, middle, and first-line management.

4 Describe the leading function, leadership style, and organizational culture.

5 Describe the controlling function, and explain the four steps in the control cycle.

6 Identify and explain four important types of managerial skills.

BEHIND THE SCENES WEGMANS SATISFIES CUSTOMERS BY PUTTING EMPLOYEES FIRST

Reprinted with permission from Wegmans Food Markets, Inc.

Wegmans CEO Danny Wegman carries on the family tradition of satisfying customers by paying attention to employees and their needs.

www.wegmans.com

Thousands of companies use slogans such as "The customer is king," proclaiming in various ways that customers are their number-one priority. Not Wegmans, a 100-year-old regional grocery store chain based in Rochester, New York. Wegmans makes a clear statement of its priorities: employees first, customers second.

What do customers think about this, you ask? They love it. Customers routinely drive miles out of their way, past other grocery stores, to shop at Wegmans. The company receives thousands of letters of praise every year from current customers—and several thousand more letters from consumers in cities where it doesn't have stores, begging the chain to open a Wegmans nearby.

Such enthusiasm has helped the company post a solid record of success since its founding in 1915. As a private company, Wegmans isn't required to report its financial results to the public, but the numbers that are available are impressive. Its operating margin (a measure of profitability) is twice as high as that of national chains such as Safeway and Kroger. Sales per square foot, a key measure of selling efficiency, are estimated to be 50 percent higher than the industry average. The *Wall Street Journal* once called Wegmans the "best chain in the country, maybe in the world."

Such results would be impressive in any industry, but they're almost unfathomable in the grocery retailing business, one of the toughest industries on Earth. Most grocery retailers struggle with constant price wars that guarantee paper-thin profit margins (making one or two cents on every dollar of revenue is typical), frequent labor troubles, high employee turnover, and a customer base that views most grocery stores as virtually indistinguishable from one another. As if those problems weren't enough, grocers face the steamrolling cost efficiencies of Walmart and other discount mass merchandisers, which have already captured one-third of the grocery business in the United States.

If you were Danny Wegman, the company's third-generation CEO, how would you sustain the Wegmans way of doing business in the face of relentless competitive pressures? How would you hold your own against the giant discounters that have rampaged through the grocery industry? How would you make sure that Wegmans attracts the best employees in the business and keeps them satisfied and productive?[1]

INTRODUCTION

Whether they are front-line supervisors or top executives such as Danny Wegman (profiled in the chapter-opening Behind the Scenes), managers have tremendous influence over the success or failure of the companies they lead. Leading seems to come naturally to Wegman, but he would probably be the first to tell you that **management**, the interrelated tasks of planning, organizing, leading, and controlling in pursuit of organizational goals,[2] is no easy job. In fact, according to one survey, more than one-third of the people who take on new managerial positions fail within the first 18 months.[3] Even those who eventually succeed can struggle with the transition from individual contributor to manager. If you aspire to become a manager, you can improve your chances of success by gaining a thorough understanding of what being a manager really entails. This chapter explores the roles that managers play, the functions they perform, and the essential skills they need.

management
The process of planning, organizing, leading, and controlling to meet organizational goals.

The Roles of Management

Danny Wegman doesn't buy merchandise from wholesalers, stock shelves, or operate cash registers, but the decisions he makes, the organizational framework he establishes, the expectations he sets, the managers he hires to oversee employees, and the culture he establishes all have an enormous impact on the company's success. Likewise, the managers who report to Wegman, including his daughter, company president Colleen Wegman, aren't directly engaged in the tasks of buying and selling groceries. However, within the scope of his or her own responsibilities, each of these managers also has significant influence on the company's fortunes. Although managers don't usually do the hands-on work in an organization, they create the environment and provide the resources that give employees opportunities to excel in their work.

In addition, given the effect that managerial decisions and behaviors have on employees, customers, investors, and other stakeholders, it's no exaggeration to say that management is one of the most vital professions in the contemporary economy. Managers who effectively and ethically guide their companies contribute greatly to our standard of living and our economic security. By the same measure, managers who fail, through poor planning, misguided decisions, or questionable ethics, can create havoc that extends far beyond the walls of their own companies. In other words, management is one of the most important functions in society, not just within the sphere of business.

All the **managerial roles** that leaders must play can be grouped into three main categories: interpersonal, informational, and decisional.

1 LEARNING OBJECTIVE

Explain the importance of management, and identify the three vital management roles.

INTERPERSONAL ROLES

Management is largely a question of getting work accomplished through the efforts of other people, so a manager must play a number of interpersonal roles, including providing leadership to employees, building relationships, and acting as a liaison between groups and individuals both inside and outside the company (such as suppliers, government agencies, consumers, labor unions, and community leaders). Effective managers tend to excel at networking, fostering relationships with many people within their own companies and within the industries and communities where their companies do business. In fact, the number of connections a person has becomes an increasingly important asset the higher he or she rises in an organization.

INFORMATIONAL ROLES

Managers spend a fair amount of time gathering information from sources both inside and outside an organization. The higher up they are, the more they rely on subordinates to collect, analyze, and summarize information—and the greater the risk that they will fall out of touch with what is happening on "the front lines," where the essential day-to-day work of the organization is performed. Today's companies have devised powerful and clever ways to collect and process information for managers. A good example is the *executive dashboard*, which, just like the dashboard in a car, provides quick-read summaries of vital performance variables (see Exhibit 7.1).

The dashboard analogy is also a good way to think about the information challenges that managers face. As you're driving, making split-second decisions while keeping your eyes on the road, you don't need to know how full the radiator is or how fast the water pump is turning. Such details would overwhelm your decision making and serve no immediate purpose. However, if your engine is in danger of overheating because the water pump is failing, you need enough advance warning to take corrective action before it's too late, so your dashboard provides a quick summary through a temperature gauge or warning light. Similarly, managers must figure out what they need to know and when they need to know it. Generally speaking, as you progress higher up in an organization, you need to monitor more information sources but see fewer details from each one.

Managers also communicate information to employees, other managers, and other stakeholders. This communication involves virtually every form of information, from technical and administrative information to motivational pep talks to strategic planning sessions. And it involves every form of media, from private conversations to videoconferences that connect managers with employees across the country or around the world.

The increasing use of social media for both internal and external communication is changing the nature of the manager's informational role in many companies. In the past, communication was often concentrated in formal channels that tended to flow in only one direction at a time, such as from a manager down to his or her subordinates or from "the company" to customers. With social media, a more conversational model is emerging, in which more people can participate and communication is more immediate and less formal. For example, on the Southwest Airlines Nuts About Southwest blog (**www.blog southwest.com**), a team of employee and manager bloggers from around the company conduct what amounts to multiple ongoing conversations with thousands of Southwest

---

EXHIBIT 7.1	**Executive Dashboards**

To help managers avoid information overload, many companies now use executive dashboards to present carefully filtered highlights of key performance parameters. The latest generation of software makes it easy to customize screens to show each manager the specific summaries he or she needs to see.

Source: Reprinted by permission from Klipfolio Dashboard www.klipfolio.com.

customers. The smart use of social media is helping managers learn more from employees and customers and communicate with stakeholder groups more effectively.

DECISIONAL ROLES

Managers up and down the organizational ladder face an endless stream of decisions. Many of these decisions are fairly routine, such as choosing which of several job candidates to hire or setting the prices of new products. Other decisions, however, might occur only once or twice in a manager's career, such as responding to a product-tampering crisis or the threat of a hostile takeover. Some decisions are made after extensive information gathering and analysis; others have to be made on the spot, with little but judgment and intuition to guide the manager's choice. One of the most significant changes occurring in business management in recent years is the effort to push decision making as far down the organizational pyramid as possible, giving whichever employees face a particular situation the authority to make decisions about it. This approach not only accelerates and improves work flow and customer service but also frees up higher-level managers to work on more strategic matters.

Being able to move among these roles comfortably while performing the basic management functions is just one of the many skills that managers must have. The following sections provide a closer look at those four functions—planning, organizing, leading, and controlling.

✔ Checkpoint

LEARNING OBJECTIVE 1: Explain the importance of management, and identify the three vital management roles.

SUMMARY: Although managers usually don't do the hands-on work in an organization, they create the environment and provide the resources that give employees the opportunities to excel in their work. Managerial responsibilities include creating the organizational framework, fostering a positive culture, setting expectations, and providing resources. The three vital managerial roles are interpersonal (interacting with others), informational (receiving and sharing information), and decisional (making decisions).

CRITICAL THINKING: (1) How are social media changing the nature of a manager's information role? (2) Would managers get more respect from employees if they "rolled up their sleeves" and pitched in with the daily work more often? Why or why not?

IT'S YOUR BUSINESS: (1) Review the process you went through to choose the college you are currently attending. What lessons from your experience could someone apply to managerial decision making? (2) Do you believe you have the right personality for management? If not, what areas would you work on?

KEY TERMS TO KNOW: management, managerial roles

The Planning Function

Managers engage in **planning** when they develop strategies, establish goals and objectives for the organization, and translate those strategies and goals into action plans. **Strategic plans** outline the firm's long-range (often two to five years) organizational goals and set a course of action the firm will pursue to reach its goals. The *strategic planning process* consists of six interrelated steps: defining the organization's mission, vision, and values; performing a SWOT analysis; developing forecasts; analyzing the competition; establishing goals and objectives; and developing action plans (see Exhibit 7.2 on the next page).

---

2 **LEARNING OBJECTIVE**

Describe the planning function, and outline the strategic planning process.

planning
Establishing objectives and goals for an organization and determining the best ways to accomplish them.

strategic plans
Plans that establish the actions and the resource allocation required to accomplish strategic goals; they're usually defined for periods of two to five years and developed by top managers.

EXHIBIT 7.2	The Strategic Planning Process

Specific firms have their own variations of the strategic planning process, but these six steps offer a good general model. The circular arrangement is no coincidence, by the way. Strategic planning should be a never-ending process, as you establish strategies, measure outcomes, monitor changes in the business environment, and make adjustments as needed.

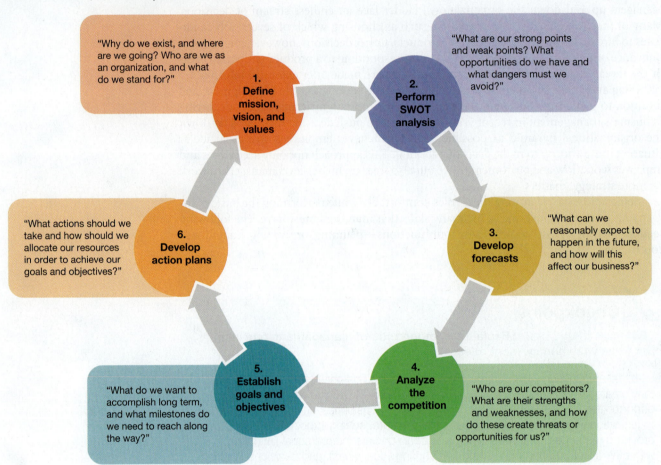

DEFINING THE MISSION, VISION, AND VALUES

mission statement
A brief statement of why an organization exists; in other words, what the organization aims to accomplish for customers, investors, and other stakeholders.

vision statement
A brief and inspirational expression of what a company aspires to be.

To achieve any level of strategic clarity, planners first need to agree on the basic principles that define the organization, and such agreement can be articulated in three interrelated statements. First, a **mission statement** is a brief expression of *why* the company exists.[4] For example, the medical device manufacturer Welch Allyn defines its mission as providing "superlative medical products, services and solutions which are used by healthcare professionals at the point of care in acute and primary settings all around the world."[5] This statement clearly defines the scope of the company's activities and its priorities in serving its target customers. Just as important, it eliminates activities the company could pursue, such as consumer products, but chooses not to.

Second, a **vision statement** is a brief expression of *what* the company aspires to be. The global security company Northrop Gruman puts it this way: "Our vision is to be the most trusted provider of systems and technologies that ensure the security and freedom of our nation and its allies."[6] Notice how this statement differs in both content and tone from the mission statement above. It provides some focus (for example, saying the company wants to be the *most trusted* provider, not necessarily the largest or the most technologically advanced) without getting into the specifics of a mission statement. It also inspires employees with a clear sense of purpose. (Note that these definitions of *mission* and *vision* are not universally agreed upon, and some companies use these terms interchangeably.)

Third, a **values statement** identifies the principles that guide the company's decisions and behaviors and establish expectations for everyone in the organization. For instance, in addition to such attributes as integrity, service, fun, and inclusiveness, Enterprise Holdings (the parent company of Enterprise Rent-a-Car, Alamo, and National Car Rental), identifies hard work as one of its values: "Running a successful business is hard work. Commit to your responsibilities and your future, and you'll receive the accolades and rewards you deserve."[7]

values statement
A brief articulation of the principles that guide a company's decisions and behaviors.

Mission, vision, and values statements are sometimes dismissed as vague "happy talk" that companies spend a lot of time creating but never look at again, and this criticism is sometimes deserved. However, if the statements are (1) crafted with the purpose of truly defining what the company stands for and (2) used in both strategic planning and the ongoing evaluation of the company's performance, they become essential parts of the company's "DNA."

REAL-TIME UPDATES
Learn More by Listening to This Podcast

Bold vision: Dream big and don't back down

Jensen Huang, co-founder and CEO of the video hardware company NVidia, explains why having a big vision is essential to growing a company. Go to http://real-timeupdates.com/bia8 and click on Learn More in the Students section.

ASSESSING STRENGTHS, WEAKNESSES, OPPORTUNITIES, AND THREATS

Before establishing long-term goals, a company needs to have a clear assessment of its strengths and weaknesses relative to the opportunities and threats it faces. This analysis is commonly referred to as SWOT (pronounced "swat"), which stands for strengths, weaknesses, opportunities, and threats.

Strengths are positive internal factors that contribute to a company's success, which can be anything from a team of expert employees to financial resources to unique technologies. *Weaknesses* are negative internal factors that inhibit the company's success, such as obsolete facilities, inadequate financial resources to fund growth, or lack of managerial depth and talent. Identifying a firm's internal strengths and weaknesses helps management understand its current abilities so it can set proper goals.

After taking inventory of the company's internal strengths and weaknesses, the next step is to identify the external opportunities and threats that might significantly affect the firm's ability to attain desired goals. *Opportunities* are positive situations that represent the possibility of generating new revenue. Shrewd managers and entrepreneurs recognize opportunities before others do and then promptly act on their ideas.

Threats are negative forces that could inhibit a firm's ability to achieve its objectives, including such external factors as new competitors, new government regulations, economic contraction, changes in interest rates, disruptions in supply, technological advances that render products obsolete, theft of intellectual property, product liability lawsuits, and even the weather. Depending on the company and the industry, it can also be helpful to consider internal threats if they have the potential to disrupt business.

Exhibit 7.3 on the next page offers a handy visual to remember the four components of a SWOT analysis.

DEVELOPING FORECASTS

By its very nature, planning requires managers to make predictions about the future. Forecasting is a notoriously difficult and error-prone part of strategic planning. Managers need to predict not only *what* will (or will not) occur, but *when* it will occur and *how* it will affect their business. Forecasting is crucial to every company's success because it influences the decisions managers make regarding virtually every business activity, and misreading the future can damage or even destroy a company.

Managerial forecasts fall under two broad categories: *quantitative forecasts*, which are typically based on historical data or tests and often involve complex statistical computations, and *qualitative forecasts*, which are based more on intuitive judgments. Neither method is foolproof, but both are valuable tools and are often used together to help

EXHIBIT 7.3	SWOT Analysis

Identifying a firm's strengths, weaknesses, opportunities, and threats is a common strategic planning technique. Here are some examples of the factors a company might identify during a SWOT analysis.

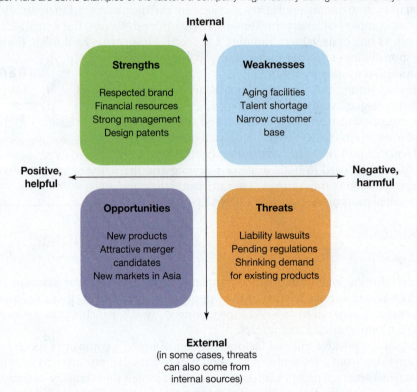

Internal

Strengths

Respected brand
Financial resources
Strong management
Design patents

Weaknesses

Aging facilities
Talent shortage
Narrow customer
base

Positive, helpful   **Negative, harmful**

Opportunities

New products
Attractive merger
candidates
New markets in Asia

Threats

Liability lawsuits
Pending regulations
Shrinking demand
for existing products

External
(in some cases, threats
can also come from
internal sources)

managers fill in the unknown variables that inevitably crop up in the planning process. For example, managers can make statistical projections of next year's sales based on data from previous years while factoring in their judgment about the impact of new competitors, changing regulations, or other external forces.

As important as forecasting is, it represents a vexing paradox because, to a significant degree, the future is simply not predictable. Technology, fashion, and other influential forces often move forward in lurches and leaps that are difficult to predict. Extraordinary events—such as wars, economic meltdowns, or natural disasters can play havoc with the best forecasts. Moreover, a single surprising development can trigger a chain reaction of other developments that might have been impossible to envision before. One key element in the art of management, therefore, is crafting plans that are solid enough to move the company forward in a strategically coherent direction while staying alert to changing conditions and being flexible enough to adapt quickly when things do change.

ANALYZING THE COMPETITION

The competitive context in which a company operates needs to be thoroughly understood and factored into the strategic planning process. Performing a SWOT analysis on each of your major competitors is a good first step. Identifying *their* strengths and weaknesses helps pinpoint *your* opportunities and threats. For instance, if you discover that one of your competitors has been suffering customer satisfaction problems, that could be a sign of financial difficulties, product flaws, or other weaknesses that could be opportunities for you to capture additional market share. Similarly, identifying your competitors' opportunities and threats can give you insight into what they might do next, and you can plan accordingly.

Competitive analysis should always keep the customer's perspective in mind. You may believe you have the best product, the best reputation, and the best customer service, but the only beliefs that matter are the target customer's. Conversely, you might believe that a competitor's less-expensive products are inferior, but those products might well be good enough to meet customers' needs—meaning that the higher cost of your higher-quality products puts you at a disadvantage.

ESTABLISHING GOALS AND OBJECTIVES

Although the terms are often used interchangeably, it helps to think of a **goal** as a broad, long-range accomplishment that the organization wants to attain and to think of an **objective** as a specific, short-range target designed to help reach that goal. For Wegmans, a *goal* might be to capture 15 percent of the grocery market in the mid-Atlantic region over the next five years, and an *objective* in support of that goal might be to open four new stores in Virginia in the next two years.

Businesspeople are often advised to make their goals and objectives "SMART," as in *specific, measurable, attainable, relevant,* and *time limited.* For example, "substantially increase our sales" is a poorly worded statement because it doesn't define what *substantially* means or when it should be measured. This acronym can be a helpful reminder to set meaningful goals, but as with the paradox of forecasting, it's important to use good judgment and be flexible, too.[8] For example, you may not know whether a goal is really attainable until you try to reach it, or you might reach it easily and realize you set your sights too low.

For more on the benefits and risks of goal setting, see pages 233–234.

goal
A broad, long-range target or aim.

objective
A specific, short-range target or aim.

REAL-TIME UPDATES
Learn More by Reading This Article

What makes the digital enterprise effective?

The consulting firm McKinsey & Company offers these tips for companies trying to transform themselves into true digital enterprises. Go to http://real-timeupdates.com/bia8 and click on Learn More in the Students section.

DEVELOPING ACTION PLANS

With strategic goals and objectives in place, the next step is to develop a plan to reach them. Plans are often organized in a hierarchy, just as a company itself is. For instance, the overall strategic plan might be supported at the next level down by a research and development plan, a manufacturing plan, and a marketing plan, describing how each functional area will help the company reach its strategic goals and objectives.

The names and contents of these *tactical plans* or *operational plans* vary widely by industry, company, and business function. Some address all the actions required in a particular department or functional area over a recurring time frame, such as a quarter or a year, whereas others address all the tasks involved in a single project or event. For example, a *launch plan* for a new product might cover a period from several months or a year before the product is introduced to the public on through the launch date and several months afterward. Such a plan would identify all the actions needed to coordinate the launch of the product, including the production ramp-up, promotional activities, sales training, physical distribution, and every other task and resource allocation decision needed to get the new product off to a successful start.

By the way, crafting a solid plan and carrying it through to completion are great ways to make a name for yourself early in your career, even for relatively simple projects. Demonstrate that you can figure out what needs to be done, coordinate all the resources, and then bring it in on schedule and on budget. Upper managers will notice and keep you in mind when they need people to take on more challenging and important projects.

✔ **Checkpoint**

LEARNING OBJECTIVE 2: Describe the planning function, and outline the strategic planning process.

SUMMARY: Planning is the process of developing strategies, establishing goals and objectives for the organization, and translating those strategies and goals into action plans. Plans vary in their time frame and scope, from high-level, long-range strategic plans to lower-level, short-term tactical and operational plans. The strategic planning process consists of six interrelated steps: defining the organization's mission, vision, and values; performing a SWOT analysis; developing forecasts; analyzing the competition; establishing goals and objectives; and developing action plans.

CRITICAL THINKING: (1) Would Boeing and Old Navy develop strategic plans over the same time horizon? Why or why not? (2) How does the vision statement guide the planning process?

IT'S YOUR BUSINESS: (1) What is your personal vision statement for your career and your life? Have you ever thought about your future in this way? (2) Consider a career path that you might pursue upon graduation, and perform a quick SWOT analysis. What are some of your internal strengths and weaknesses and external opportunities and threats?

KEY TERMS TO KNOW: planning, strategic plans, mission statement, vision statement, values statement, goal, objective

---

3 | **LEARNING OBJECTIVE**

Describe the organizing function, and differentiate among top, middle, and first-line management.

organizing
The process of arranging resources to carry out the organization's plans.

management pyramid
An organizational structure divided into top, middle, and first-line management.

top managers
Those at the highest level of the organization's management hierarchy; they are responsible for setting strategic goals, and they have the most power and responsibility in the organization.

The Organizing Function

Organizing, the process of arranging resources to carry out an organization's plans, is the second major function of managers. To organize effectively, managers must think through all the activities that employees perform, as well as all the facilities and equipment employees need in order to complete those activities. Managers also give people the ability to work toward company goals by determining who will have the authority to make decisions, to perform or supervise activities, and to distribute resources. Chapter 8 discusses the organizing function in more detail; for now, it's sufficient to recognize the three levels of management in a typical corporate hierarchy—top, middle, and bottom—commonly known as the **management pyramid** (see Exhibit 7.4).

TOP MANAGERS

Top managers are the upper-level managers, such as Danny Wegman, who have the most power and who take overall responsibility for an organization. This tier includes corporate officers (see page 110) and usually the next layer or two of management beneath

EXHIBIT 7.4	**The Management Pyramid**

Here are some of the typical jobs at the three basic levels of management.

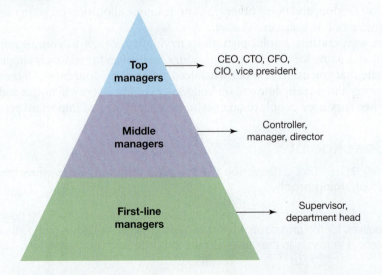

them, depending on the size and structure of the company. The term *executive* applies to top managers. Typical job titles include the "C" level positions, such as chief marketing officer (CMO) and chief financial officer (CFO), and vice presidents (the largest corporations may have dozens of vice presidents overseeing various divisions or functions).

Top managers establish the structure for the organization as a whole, and they select the people who fill the upper-level positions. Top managers also make long-range plans, establish major policies, and often represent the company to the media, the community, and other stakeholders. Two significant ways in which top management differs from lower management tiers are the long time frames with which executives must work and the magnitude of the decisions they need to make. Given the difficulty and importance of these strategic decisions, the ability to make tough judgment calls is highly valued in top executives.

MIDDLE MANAGERS

Middle managers have similar responsibilities but on a smaller scale, such as for an individual division or facility. The term *middle management* is somewhat vague, but in general, managers at this level report upward to top executives, and first-line managers report to middle managers. In other words, they usually manage other managers, not workers. A smaller company might have a single layer of middle management (or none at all, in many cases), whereas a large corporation could have a half dozen or more layers of middle managers.

The term "middle management" is sometimes used disparagingly, giving the impression that middle managers are "bureaucrats" who clog up the works without adding much value. Some highly regarded opinion leaders have gone so far as to blame such managers for much that ails the modern corporation.[9] Many companies have also *flattened* their organizational structures by removing one or more layers of middle management.

However, middle managers play the essential role of translating strategic goals and objectives into the actions that allow the company to meet those targets. Although they may not do the actual day-to-day work, middle managers are the ones who put the systems and resources in place so that front-line teams can work efficiently and with coordinated purpose. They also provide vital coaching and mentoring for first-line managers who are making the transition into management. As leadership consultant Steve Arneson emphasizes, "It's the leaders in the middle who must communicate and execute strategy, solve problems, create efficiencies, and manage performance."[10] In his analysis of the videogame industry, Wharton management professor Ethan Mollick concluded that middle managers who oversaw new game development had a greater impact on company performance than the top managers who set strategy or the developers who designed and created the games.[11]

FIRST-LINE MANAGERS

At the bottom of the management pyramid are **first-line managers** (or *supervisory managers*). They oversee the work of nonmanagerial employees, and they put into action the plans developed at higher levels. Titles at this level include supervisor, department head, and office manager.[12] The types of employees these managers supervise vary widely, from entry-level workers with limited experience and education to advanced experts in engineering, science, finance, and other professional specialties.

Like managers at the levels above them, first-line managers face challenges unique to their position in the hierarchy. As the direct interface between "management" and the employees, they have the most immediate responsibility for ensuring that necessary work is done according to agreed-on performance standards. They must also deal with any friction that exists between employees and management. Supervisors are also usually quite involved in recruiting, hiring, and training of employees. In this role, they perform the vital task of making sure employees acquire the skills they need and adapt to the organization's culture.

middle managers
Those in the middle of the management hierarchy; they develop plans to implement the goals of top managers and coordinate the work of first-line managers.

first-line managers
Those at the lowest level of the management hierarchy; they supervise the operating employees and implement the plans set at the higher management levels.

REAL-TIME UPDATES
Learn More by Reading This Article

A company needs bosses, right?

Supercell, the fast-growing Finnish game maker (Clash of Clans, Hay Day), is organized as autonomous cells with no managers. Go to http://real-timeupdates.com/bia8 and click on Learn More in the Students section.

✔ Checkpoint

SUMMARY: The organizing function involves arranging an organization's resources in the best way possible to help reach its goals and objectives. Top managers grapple with long-range, strategic issues and often must make decisions about events and conditions several years into the future. They also have important communication roles, representing the company to external stakeholders. Middle managers usually have responsibility over individual divisions or facilities and are charged with translating strategic plans into the tactical plans that will allow the company to reach its goals and objectives. First-line managers supervise nonmanagement employees; they have the shortest time horizons and greatest tactical perspective.

CRITICAL THINKING: (1) Why might a manager need to deemphasize skills honed in previous positions as he or she rises through the organizational hierarchy? (2) Would top managers or first-line managers typically have more or less of the information they'd like to have for the decisions they need to make? Why?

IT'S YOUR BUSINESS: (1) Based on your experience leading teams or supervising people at work, how would you rate your performance as a manager? (2) If you were suddenly promoted to manage the department you've been working in, would you change your "work" personality? Why or why not?

KEY TERMS TO KNOW: organizing, management pyramid, top managers, middle managers, first-line managers

---

4 **LEARNING OBJECTIVE**

Describe the leading function, leadership style, and organizational culture.

leading
The process of guiding and motivating people to work toward organizational goals.

The Leading Function

Leading is the process of influencing and motivating people to work willingly and effectively toward common goals. Managers with good leadership skills have greater success in influencing the attitudes and actions of others and motivating employees to put forth their best performance.

All managers have to be effective leaders to be successful, but management and leadership are not the same thing. One way to distinguish between the two is to view management as the rational, intellectual, and practical side of guiding an organization and to view leadership as the inspirational, visionary, and emotional side. Both management and leadership involve the use of power, but management involves *position power* (so called because it stems from the individual's position in the organization), whereas leadership involves *personal power* (which stems from a person's own unique attributes, such as expertise or charisma).[13]

Successful leaders tend to share many of the same traits, but no magical set of personal qualities automatically destines someone for leadership. Nevertheless, in general, good leaders possess a balance of several types of intelligence:

- *Cognitive intelligence* involves reasoning, problem solving, memorization, and other rational skills. Obviously, leaders need a sufficient degree of cognitive intelligence to understand and process the information required for planning and decision making in their jobs.

- *Emotional intelligence* is a measure of a person's awareness of and ability to manage his or her own emotions. People with high emotional intelligence recognize their own emotional states and the effect those emotions have on others, they are able to regulate their emotional responses in order to control or reduce disruptive impulses and moods, and they have a high degree of *empathy* (the ability to understand others' feelings).[14]

REAL-TIME UPDATES
Learn More by Reading This Article

Management is not leadership

Noted management professor John Kotter explains why management is not the same thing as leadership. Go to http://real-timeupdates .com/bia8 and click on Learn More in the Students section.

- *Social intelligence* involves looking outward to understand the dynamics of social situations and the emotions of other people, in addition to your own.[15] Socially adept managers have a knack for finding and building common ground with people of all kinds. Moreover, leaders, in a sense, "infect" their organizations with their own emotions, positive or negative.[16]

All three types of intelligence are essential to building the competencies that lead to success. In fact, various studies suggest that in both leadership and life in general, emotional and social intelligence play a far greater role in success than purely cognitive intelligence.[17]

DEVELOPING AN EFFECTIVE LEADERSHIP STYLE

Leadership style can be viewed as finding the right balance between *what* the leader focuses on and *how* he or she makes things happen in the organization. Every manager has a definite style, although good leaders usually adapt their approach to match the requirements of the particular situation.[18] Across the range of leadership styles, you can find three basic types (see Exhibit 7.5). **Autocratic leaders** control the decision-making process in their organizations, often restricting the decision-making freedom of subordinates. Autocratic leadership generally has a bad reputation, and when it's overused or used inappropriately, it can certainly produce bad results or stunt an organization's growth. However, companies can find themselves in situations where autocratic leadership is needed to guide the firm through challenging situations or to bring uncooperative units in line.

autocratic leaders
Leaders who do not involve others in decision making.

EXHIBIT 7.5	Leadership Styles

Leadership styles fall on a continuum from autocratic (manager makes the decisions) to democratic (manager and subordinates make decisions together) to laissez-faire (subordinates make decisions on their own). Each style has strengths and weaknesses, and effective managers often adapt their style to suit specific situations.

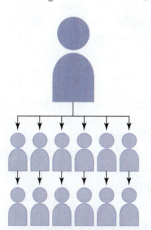

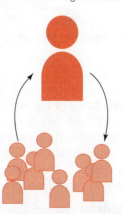

Autocratic Leadership

Manager makes the decisions and issues directives down the chain of command; subordinates have little or no freedom to make decisions, deviate from plans, or provide contrary input.

Democratic Leadership

Manager shares decision-making authority, seeking input and inviting subordinates to participate in a coordinated planning process; group can encourage a change of course if needed.

Laissez-faire Leadership

Manager acts as advisor and supporter, offering input when asked but generally letting subordinates chart and adjust their own course toward meeting agreed-upon goals and objectives.

democratic leaders
Leaders who delegate authority and involve employees in decision making.

participative management
A philosophy of allowing employees to take part in planning and decision making.

laissez-faire leaders
Leaders who leave most decisions up to employees, particularly decisions concerning day-to-day matters.

employee empowerment
Granting decision-making and problem-solving authorities to employees so they can act without getting approval from management.

coaching
Helping employees reach their highest potential by meeting with them, discussing problems that hinder their ability to work effectively, and offering suggestions and encouragement to overcome these problems.

mentoring
A process in which experienced managers guide less-experienced colleagues in nuances of office politics, serving as role models for appropriate business behavior and helping to negotiate the corporate structure.

Democratic leaders, in contrast, delegate authority and involve employees in decision making. Also known as *collaborative* leaders, these managers invite and seek out input from anyone in the organization who can add insight to the decision-making process. For example, after Salesforce installed an internal social networking application that gave everyone in the company the chance to share information, CEO Mark Benioff began monitoring the flow of insights and realized that some of the most valuable information about customers was coming from employees upper management didn't normally communicate with. Inspired by that discovery, he opened the annual strategic planning meeting to the entire company via social networking.[19] This style is often called **participative management**.

The third leadership style takes its name from the French term *laissez-faire*, which can be translated roughly as "hands off." **Laissez-faire leaders** such as Danny Wegman take the role of supporters and consultants, encouraging employees' ideas and offering insights or opinions when asked. After the overall strategic direction and priorities are in place, they emphasize **employee empowerment**—giving employees the power to make decisions that apply to their specific aspects of work. As Wegman puts it, "Once you share a common set of values, you can go and be yourself."[20]

COACHING AND MENTORING

Leaders have an important responsibility for education and encouragement, which may take the form of coaching and mentoring. **Coaching** involves taking the time to meet with employees, discussing any problems that may hinder their ability to work effectively, and offering suggestions and encouragement to help them find their own solutions to work-related challenges. (Note that the term *executive coaching* usually refers to hiring an outside management expert to help senior managers.)

Mentoring is similar to coaching but is based on long-term relationships between senior and junior members of an organization. The mentor is usually an experienced manager or employee who can help guide other managers and employees through the corporate maze. Mentors have a deep knowledge of the business and can explain office politics, serve as role models for appropriate business behavior, and provide valuable advice about how to succeed within the organization. Mentoring programs are used in a variety of ways, such as helping newly promoted managers make the transition to leadership roles and helping women and minorities prepare for advancement.

MANAGING CHANGE

Change presents a major leadership challenge for one simple reason: Many people don't like it, or at least they don't like being told they need to change. They may fear the unknown, may be unwilling to give up current habits or benefits, may not trust the motives of the people advocating change, or may simply have experienced too many change initiatives that didn't yield the promised results.[21] To improve the chances of success when the organization needs to change, managers can follow these steps:[22]

1. **Identify everything that needs to change.** Changes can involve the structure of the organization, technologies and systems, or people's attitudes, beliefs, skills, or behaviors.[23] One particular challenge for managers advocating change is understanding the ripple effect the change will have throughout the organization.[24]

2. **Identify the forces acting for and against a change.** By understanding these forces, managers can work to amplify the forces that will facilitate the change and remove or diminish the negative forces.

3. **Choose the approach best suited to the situation.** Managers can institute change through a variety of techniques, including communication, education, participation in decision making, negotiation, visible support

REAL-TIME UPDATES
Learn More by Watching These Videos

How managers tackle today's leadership challenges

Watch the *Wall Street Journal*'s Boss Talk series. Go to http://real-timeupdates.com/bia8 and click on Learn More in the Students section.

from top managers or other opinion leaders, or coercive use of authority (usually recommended only for crisis situations). When managers engage people in the change, asking for their input and advice so they can help design the changes, they'll be much more likely to embrace the new way of doing things.[25]

4. **Reinforce changed behavior and monitor continued progress.** Once a change has been made, managers need to reinforce new behaviors and make sure old behaviors don't creep back in.

BUILDING A POSITIVE ORGANIZATIONAL CULTURE

Strong leadership is a key element in establishing a productive **organizational culture** (sometimes known as *corporate culture*)—the set of underlying values, norms, and practices shared by members of an organization (see Exhibit 7.6). Culture can be a negative or a positive force in an organization, and managers set the tone by establishing expectations, defining rules and policies that shape behavior, and acting as role models. When employees at Wegmans see Danny Wegman enthusiastically embrace the challenges of the day and treat customers and colleagues with respect, that positive energy radiates throughout the culture. As employee Elaine Danar puts it, "I have an incredible sense of pride to represent this company."[26]

organizational culture
A set of shared values and norms that support the management system and that guide management and employee behavior.

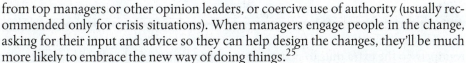

| EXHIBIT 7.6 | **Creating the Ideal Culture in Your Company** |

You can't create a culture directly, but you can establish the behaviors and values that in turn do create a culture. Use this list of questions to explore the many ways you can foster a positive culture—and avoid the growth of a negative culture.

Vision
- Have you articulated a compelling vision for the company?
- Based on that vision, have you defined a mission statement that employees understand and can implement?

Company Values
- Do employees know how their work relates to this vision?
- Is there a common set of values that binds the organization together?
- Do you and other executives or owners demonstrate these values day in and day out?

People
- How are people treated?
- Do you foster an atmosphere of civility and respect?
- Do you value and encourage teamwork, with all ideas welcomed?
- Do you acknowledge, encourage, and act upon (when appropriate) ideas from employees?
- Do you give employees credit for their ideas?
- Have you shown a positive commitment to a balance between work and life?

Community
- Have you clarified how the company views its relationship with the communities it affects?
- Do your actions support that commitment to community?

Communication
- Do you practice and encourage open communication?
- Do you share operating information throughout the company so that people know how the company is doing?
- Do you regularly survey employees on workplace issues and ask for their input on solutions?
- Is there an open-door policy for access to management?

Employee Performance
- Do you handle personnel issues with fairness and respect?
- Do employees receive feedback regularly?
- Are employee evaluations based on agreed-on objectives that have been clearly communicated?

Sources: John Coleman, "Six Components of a Great Corporate Culture," *Harvard Business Review* blogs, 6 May 2013, http://blogs.hbr.org; Andrew Bird, "Do You Know What Your Corporate Culture Is?" *CPA Insight*, February, March 1999, 25–26; Gail H. Vergara, "Finding a Compatible Corporate Culture," *Healthcare Executive*, January/February 1999, 46–47; Hal Lancaster, "To Avoid a Job Failure, Learn the Culture of a Company First," *Wall Street Journal*, 14 July 1998, B1.

Positive cultures create an environment that encourages employees to make smart decisions for the good of the company and its customers. At companies with legendary corporate cultures, such as Wegmans, Nordstrom, and Southwest Airlines, employees routinely go the extra mile to make sure customers are treated well. In contrast, negative, dysfunctional cultures can lead employees to make decisions that are bad for customers and bad for the company.

 Checkpoint

LEARNING OBJECTIVE 4: Describe the leading function, leadership style, and organizational culture.

SUMMARY: Leading is the art and science of influencing and motivating people to work toward common goals. Leaders can exhibit a range of styles in what they choose to focus on (strategic versus operational matters) and how they make things happen (forcing versus enabling). Three specific leadership styles are autocratic, democratic, and laissez-faire. Organizational culture is the set of underlying values, norms, and practices shared by members of an organization.

CRITICAL THINKING: (1) Are management and leadership the same thing? If not, why not? (2) Can a single individual be an autocratic, a democratic, *and* a laissez-faire leader? Why or why not?

IT'S YOUR BUSINESS: (1) What is your natural inclination in terms of the three basic leadership styles—autocratic, democratic, or laissez-faire? Think about times in school, at work, or in social situations in which you played a leadership role. How did you lead? (2) Does leadership experience in school activities such as student government and athletics help prepare you for business leadership? Why or why not?

KEY TERMS TO KNOW: leading, autocratic leaders, democratic leaders, participative management, laissez-faire leaders, employee empowerment, coaching, mentoring, organizational culture

---

The Controlling Function

5   LEARNING OBJECTIVE

Describe the controlling function, and explain the four steps in the control cycle.

controlling
The process of measuring progress against goals and objectives and correcting deviations if results are not as expected.

Controlling is the management function of keeping a company's activities on track toward previously established goals. The nature of control varies widely, from directly intervening in a process to modifying policies or systems in a way that enables employees to reach their objectives.

THE CONTROL CYCLE

A good way to understand managerial control is to envision the *control cycle*, a four-step process of (1) establishing performance standards based on the strategic plan, (2) measuring performance, (3) comparing performance to standards, and (4) responding as needed (see Exhibit 7.7). Of course, the specific steps taken in any situation depend on the industry, the company, the functional area within the company, and the manager's leadership style. In some cases, the control cycle is a formal process with explicit measurements, reports, and other tools. In others, control is subtle.

Establishing Performance Standards

standards
Criteria against which performance is measured.

In the first step of the control cycle, managers set **standards**, the criteria against which performance will be measured. Top managers set standards for the organization as a whole, such as revenue and profitability targets. Then for their individual areas of responsibility, middle and first-line managers set standards based on the overall organizational standards of performance.

The control cycle starts with setting strategic goals and then establishing performance standards that will tell managers and employers whether the company is on track to meet those goals. As the company goes about its business, performance is measured along the way and then compared against the standards. If performance meets or exceeds the standards, no corrective action is required. However, if performance is below the standards, management can either take steps to improve performance (if the standards are still considered achievable) or lower the standards and possibly reset the goals (if they are deemed to be unachievable).

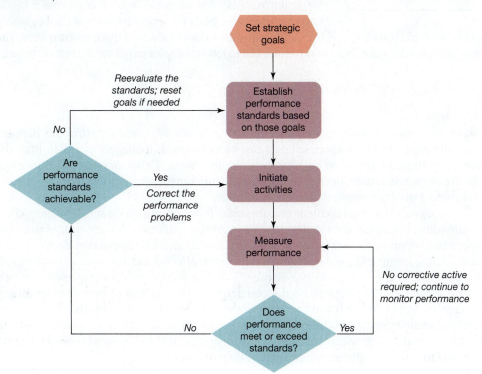

Knowing which variables to use as standards and the values to set as performance targets can require a lot of experience and experimentation. Choosing variables that are truly meaningful rather than just easy to measure can also be a significant challenge. For example, *web analytics* software can deliver lots of data about online traffic, but it might not answer crucial questions such as why website visitors abandon their online shopping carts without buying anything.

A common approach to setting standards is **benchmarking**, comparing a company's key performance attributes with those of industry leaders.[27] For example, a company might discover that its average revenue per employee (total sales divided by the number of employees) is significantly lower than that of the best company in its industry. With this data point in hand, the company could look for ways to make its selling process more efficient, train sales people to go after bigger deals, or find other ways to improve the cost–revenue ratio.

One of the most important performance variables that fall under managerial control is **quality**—a measure of how closely activities or outcomes conform to predetermined standards and customer expectations. You'll learn more about quality in such areas as product and process quality in manufacturing and operations management (see page 214) and quality of hire in human resources (see page 256).

Measuring Performance and Responding as Needed

In the second step of the control cycle, managers assess performance, using both quantitative (specific, numerical) and qualitative (subjective) performance measures. For example, many companies use a **balanced scorecard**, which monitors performance from multiple

benchmarking
Collecting and comparing process and performance data from other companies.

quality
A measure of how closely a product conforms to predetermined standards and customer expectations.

balanced scorecard
A method of monitoring the performance from four perspectives: finances, operations, customer relationships, and the growth and development of employees and intellectual property.

perspectives, including finances, operations, customer relationships, and the growth and development of employees and intellectual property.[28]

In the third step, managers compare performance with the established standards. If the level of performance falls short, the next step is usually to take corrective action to improve performance. However, in some cases, managers might decide that the level of performance originally hoped for is not realistic. For example, a sales department might have set aggressive goals for a new product at the beginning of the year, but then a tough competitor appeared out of nowhere three months later. The department manager may have no choice but to lower the sales target for the rest of the year.

CRISIS MANAGEMENT: MAINTAINING CONTROL IN EXTRAORDINARY CIRCUMSTANCES

No matter how well a company plans for its future, mistakes and catastrophes happen. And although not every specific crisis can be envisioned, managers can plan how the company should respond to each type of possible event. **Crisis management** involves the decisions and actions needed to keep a company functioning smoothly and to tend to stakeholder needs during and after an emergency.

Successful crisis management requires clear thinking and quick action while a crisis is unfolding, but smart companies don't wait until a crisis hits. A *crisis management* plan needs to contain both *contingency plans* to help managers make important decisions in a limited time frame and *communication plans* to reach affected parties quickly and forestall rumors and false information (see Exhibit 7.8). The plan should clearly specify which people are authorized to speak for the company, provide contact information for all key executives, and include a list of the news outlets and social media tools that will be used to disseminate information. In today's media-saturated environment, companies need to begin communicating within minutes after a crisis hits, to reach those who need information and to avoid the appearance of stonewalling or confusion.

crisis management
Procedures and systems for minimizing the harm that might result from some unusually threatening situations.

EXHIBIT 7.8   **Communicating in a Crisis**

Crisis situations test a manager's ability to make decisions and communicate clearly.

When a Crisis Hits:

Do	Don't
Prepare for trouble ahead of time by identifying potential problems, appointing and training a response team, and preparing and testing a crisis management plan.	Blame anyone for anything.
Get top management involved immediately.	Speculate in public.
Set up a news center for company representatives and the media that is equipped with phones, computers, and other electronic tools for preparing news releases and online updates. At the news center, take the following steps:	Refuse to answer questions.
• Issue frequent news updates, and have trained personnel available to respond to questions around the clock.	Release information that will violate anyone's right to privacy.
• Provide complete information packets to the media as soon as possible.	Use the crisis to pitch products or services.
• Prevent conflicting statements, and provide continuity by appointing a single person trained in advance to speak for the company.	Play favorites with media representatives.
• Tell receptionists and other employees to direct all phone calls to the designated spokesperson in the news center.	
• Provide updates when new information is available via blog postings, Twitter updates, text messaging, Facebook, and other appropriate media.	
Tell the whole story—openly, completely, and honestly. If you are at fault, apologize.	
Demonstrate the company's concern by your statements and your actions.	

 **Checkpoint**

LEARNING OBJECTIVE 5: Describe the controlling function, and explain the four steps in the control cycle.

SUMMARY: The controlling function consists of the activities and decisions involved in keeping a company's activities on track toward previously established goals. The four steps in the control cycle are establishing performance standards based on the strategic plan, measuring performance, comparing performance to standards, and responding as needed.

CRITICAL THINKING: (1) Why is it important to meet the needs of internal customers? (2) Is lowering performance standards in response to a failure to meet those standards necessarily a sign of "giving up"? Why or why not?

IT'S YOUR BUSINESS: (1) Do you benchmark your performance in any aspect of your personal or academic life? If yes, does it help you improve? If not, can you identify some aspects that could potentially benefit from benchmarking? (2) Think back over any crises you've faced in your life. How well did you respond? What would you do differently in a future crisis?

KEY TERMS TO KNOW: controlling, standards, benchmarking, quality, balanced scorecard, crisis management

Essential Management Skills

6 | **LEARNING OBJECTIVE**

Identify and explain four important types of managerial skills.

Managers rely on a number of skills to perform their functions and maintain a high level of quality in their organizations. These skills can be classified as *interpersonal, technical, conceptual,* and *decision making*. As managers rise through an organization's hierarchy, they may need to deemphasize skills that helped them in lower-level jobs and develop different skills. For instance, staying closely involved with project details is often a plus for first-line supervisors, but it can lead to serious performance issues for higher-level managers who should be spending time on more strategic issues.[29]

INTERPERSONAL SKILLS

The various skills required to communicate with other people, work effectively with them, motivate them, and lead them are **interpersonal skills**. Because managers mainly get things done through people at all levels of the organization, such skills are essential. Encouraging employees to work together toward common goals, interacting with employees and other managers, negotiating with partners and suppliers, developing employee trust and loyalty, and fostering innovation are all activities that require interpersonal skills.

Communication is the most important and pervasive interpersonal skill that managers use. Effective communication not only increases a manager's and an organization's productivity but also shapes the impressions made on colleagues, employees, supervisors, investors, and customers. In your role as a manager, communication allows you to perceive the needs of these stakeholders (your first step toward satisfying them), and it helps you respond to those needs.[30] Moreover, as the workforce becomes more diverse—and as more companies recognize the value of embracing diversity in their workforces—managers need to adjust their interactions with others, communicating in a way that considers the different needs, backgrounds, experiences, and expectations of their workforces.

interpersonal skills
Skills required to understand other people and to interact effectively with them.

TECHNICAL SKILLS

A person who knows how to operate a machine, prepare a financial statement, or use a web content management system has **technical skills**, the knowledge and ability to perform the tasks required in a particular job. Technical skills are most important at lower

technical skills
The ability and knowledge to perform the mechanics of a particular job.

organizational levels because managers at those levels work directly with employees who are using the tools and techniques.

However, in today's increasingly technology-driven business environment, managers often need to have a solid understanding of the processes they oversee. One obvious reason is that they need to grasp the technical matters if they are to make smart decisions regarding planning, organizing, leading, and controlling. Another key reason for understanding technical matters is that demonstrating a level of technical aptitude gives managers credibility in the eyes of their employees. They may not need to have the hands-on skills that their employees require, but they need to know enough about what they employees do to make insightful decisions.

administrative skills
Technical skills in information gathering, data analysis, planning, organizing, and other aspects of managerial work.

Managers at all levels use **administrative skills**, which are the technical skills necessary to direct an organization, including scheduling, researching, analyzing data, and managing projects. Managers must know how to start a project or work assignment from scratch, map out each step in the process to its successful completion, develop project costs and timelines, and establish checkpoints at key project intervals.

CONCEPTUAL SKILLS

conceptual skills
The ability to understand the relationship of parts to the whole.

Managers need **conceptual skills** to visualize organizations, systems, markets, and solutions—both as complete entities on their own and as interrelated pieces of a whole. For example, the most visible part of a company's accounting system is probably its accounting software and the reports it produces, but the entire system also includes procedures, policies, and the people who process and use financial information. At the same time, the accounting system is also part of an overall business system and needs to integrate seamlessly with sales, purchasing, production, and other functions.

Conceptual skills are especially important to top managers because they are the strategists who develop the plans that guide the organization toward its goals. Managers use their conceptual skills to acquire and analyze information, identify both problems and opportunities, understand the competitive environment in which their companies operate, and develop strategies and plans. The ability to conceptualize solutions that don't yet exist, to see things as they could be rather than simply as how they are, is a vital skill for executives.

DECISION-MAKING SKILLS

decision-making skills
The ability to identify a decision situation, analyze the problem, weigh the alternatives, choose an alternative, implement it, and evaluate the results.

Decision-making skills involve the ability to define problems and opportunities and select the best course of action. To ensure thoughtful decision making, managers can follow a formal process such as the six steps highlighted in Exhibit 7.9:

1. **Recognize and define the problem or opportunity.** Most companies look for problems or opportunities by gathering customer feedback, conducting studies, or monitoring such warning signals as declining sales or profits, excess inventory buildup, or high customer turnover.

2. **Identify and develop options.** The goal of this step is to develop a list of alternative courses of action. A problem that is easy to identify, such as a steady decline in sales revenue, might not have any easy answers. This step requires solid conceptual skills. Managers may need to break old thinking habits and throw away long-held assumptions in order to find promising solutions to tough problems.

3. **Analyze the options.** Once the ideas have been generated, they need to be studied and compared using criteria such as cost, feasibility, availability of resources, market acceptance, potential for revenue generation, and compatibility with the company's mission and vision. Some decisions present a simple yes-or-no choice, but others present multiple options that must be compared.

4. **Select the best option.** For some decisions, quantitative analysis can identify a clear choice from among the available options. For other decisions, however, managers might have to rely on intuition and experience to point the way.

5. **Implement the decision.** After an option has been selected, it's time to implement the decision.

EXHIBIT 7.9	**Steps in the Decision-Making Process**

Following these six steps will help you make better decisions, particularly if you make a habit of applying what you learn from every decision outcome to the next decision you need to make.

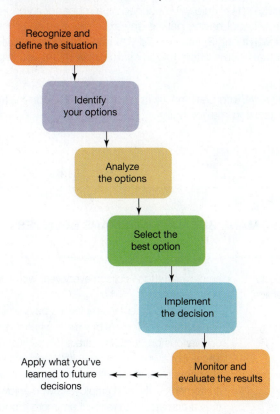

6. **Monitor the results.** Finally, managers monitor the results of decisions over time to see whether the chosen alternative works, whether any new problems or opportunities arise because of the decision, and whether the decision should be modified to meet changing circumstances.

Although this list presents a logical and comprehensive method for decision making, it's important to realize that managers must frequently make decisions with incomplete or imperfect information. In other words, you may not have all the information you need, and you may not have as much time as you'd like to take. In fact, in today's fast-moving markets, the ability to make good decisions with incomplete information has become a highly valued management skill.[31]

For the latest information on managerial skills, visit **http://real-timeupdates.com/ bia8** and click on Chapter 7.

✔ Checkpoint

LEARNING OBJECTIVE 6: Identify and explain four important types of managerial skills.

SUMMARY: Interpersonal skills are the abilities to communicate with, motivate, and lead others. Technical skills involve the "mechanics" of a particular job, including the administrative skills of project management. Conceptual skills are the abilities to visualize organizations, systems, markets, and solutions—even when they may not exist yet. Decision-making skills include defining problems and opportunities and selecting the best course of action to take in each case.

CRITICAL THINKING: (1) Why is trust a vital aspect of a manager's interpersonal skills? (2) What are the risks of poorly defining problems or opportunities before making decisions?

IT'S YOUR BUSINESS: (1) Would you succeed as a manager if you started a company right out of college, without having gained any experience as an employee in another company? Why or why not? (2) How would you rate your conceptual skills? Does "seeing the big picture" come easily to you? If not, how might you improve in this area?

KEY TERMS TO KNOW: interpersonal skills, technical skills, administrative skills, conceptual skills, decision-making skills

BEHIND THE SCENES
CUSTOMERS BELIEVE IN WEGMANS BECAUSE WEGMANS BELIEVES IN ITS EMPLOYEES

The conventional response to all challenges in the retail grocery industry is to just keep squeezing everything—customer service, wages, employee benefits, training, and anything else—to keep prices low and still eke out a profit. However, CEO Danny Wegman and his colleagues are adamant that joining the discounters in a never-ending race to cut, cut, cut is not the Wegmans way. Instead, the company defines its mission as being "the very best at serving the needs of our customers." In pursuit of that mission, the company makes employees its number-one priority and counts on employees to then meet the needs of customers.

To compete successfully against both traditional grocers and discounters such as Walmart, Wegmans's strategy emphasizes a huge selection of products and employees who know food and love serving customers. The cheese department is a good example. Unlike the typical selection of two or three dozen varieties at other stores, Wegmans offers four or five *hundred* varieties—and knowledgeable staff who can help customers select and serve the perfect cheese. In fact, chances are the department manager has been sent on a research tour of cheese-producing areas in Europe to gain firsthand knowledge of the tastes and traditions of each region.

Such training is expensive, to be sure. Add in higher-than-average wages and employee benefits, and Wegmans's labor costs are higher than those of its competitors. Moreover, Wegmans managers exhibit a degree of personal concern for employees not often found in the hectic retail industry. As an example, when one manager whose job required frequent out-of-town travel learned that her mother had been diagnosed with cancer, Wegmans executives modified her responsibilities so that she could stay in town to care for her mother—before she even asked. Another indicator of the company's care for its employees is the investment it makes in their futures, even if those futures take them outside the company. More than 25,000 employees have received company scholarships, and thousands of employees attend college every year with financial assistance from Wegmans.

This investment in employees pays off in important ways. For starters, customers buy more when they understand how to use various products and are successful and satisfied with them. These positive experiences with Wegmans employees also help shoppers build emotional bonds with the store, further increasing customer loyalty. And employees who enjoy their work and feel they are treated with respect are more productive and less likely to leave for other jobs. Employee turnover (the percentage of the workforce that leaves and must be replaced every year) is a major expense for retailers, but turnover at Wegmans is a fraction of the industry average—under 5 percent, compared to retail sector averages of roughly 25 percent for full-time employees and 50 percent or more for part-time employees.

In fact, employee satisfaction is so high that 20 percent of the workers are related, the result of so many employees recommending the company to their relatives. As just one measure of the positive organizational culture at Wegmans, the company has made *Fortune* magazine's list of the 100 Best Companies to Work For every year since the survey began—and it is usually at or near the top of that list.

The mission to be the best at serving consumers extends to the company's decision-making style as well. For day-to-day decisions, laissez-faire management is widespread; executives want front-line employees to make whatever choices are needed to keep customers happy. As a Wegmans executive joked a few years ago, "We're a $3 billion company run by 16-year-old cashiers." The scheme must be working: The company has pushed past $7 billion in sales and shows no signs of slowing down.[32]

Critical Thinking Questions

7-1. Wegmans has always been managed by members of the Wegman family. Do you think the company could continue its winning ways if the next generation doesn't want to take over, forcing the company to hire someone from outside the family as CEO? Explain your answer.

7-2. Would the Wegmans approach work for a car dealer? A bookstore? A manufacturer of industrial goods? Explain your answers.

7-3. How does low employee turnover contribute to the distinct and positive corporate culture at Wegmans?

LEARN MORE ONLINE
Visit the Wegmans website, at **www.wegmans.com**, and click on "Careers." Read the information and watch the videos to learn more about working at Wegmans. Imagine yourself as someone who wants to join the company. Does the information on this website increase your interest in the company? Could you see yourself launching a career at Wegmans?

KEY TERMS

administrative skills (164)
autocratic leaders (157)
balanced scorecard (161)
benchmarking (161)
coaching (158)
conceptual skills (164)
controlling (160)
crisis management (162)
decision-making skills (164)
democratic leaders (158)
employee empowerment (158)
first-line managers (155)
goal (153)
interpersonal skills (163)
laissez-faire leaders (158)
leading (156)
management (147)

management pyramid (154)
managerial roles (147)
mentoring (158)
middle managers (155)
mission statement (150)
objective (153)
organizational culture (159)
organizing (154)
participative management (158)
planning (149)
quality (161)
standards (160)
strategic plans (149)
technical skills (163)
top managers (154)
values statement (151)
vision statement (150)

MyBizLab®
To complete the problems with the ⭐,
go to EOC Discussion Questions in the
MyLab.

TEST YOUR KNOWLEDGE

Questions for Review

7-4. What is management? Why is it so important?

7-5. What is forecasting, and how is it related to the planning function?

7-6. What is the goal of crisis management?

7-7. How does leadership differ from management?

7-8. Why are interpersonal skills important to managers at all levels?

Questions for Analysis

⭐ **7-9.** Why is cognitive intelligence alone insufficient for effective leadership?

7-10. Who provides the leadership in a self-managed team or other organizational unit without an appointed manager? Explain your answer

7-11. How do autocratic, democratic, and laissez-faire leadership styles differ?

7-12. Why are coaching and mentoring effective leadership techniques?

⭐ **7-13.** **Ethical Considerations.** Apart from meeting the company's future talent needs, do managers have a personal ethical obligation to help their employees develop and advance in their careers? Explain your answer.

Questions for Application

7-14. Which would be more difficult to forecast 10 years from now: the number of 60-year-olds or their average disposable income? Why?

7-15. You're the youngest person in your department, and you just got promoted to department manager? What steps could you take to make sure all your employees have confidence in your management and leadership?

7-16. **Concept Integration.** Using Welch Allyn's mission statement on page 150 as a model and the material you learned in Chapter 4, develop a mission statement that balances

the pursuit of profit with responsibility to employees and community. Choose either a manufacturer of musical instruments or a retailer of children's clothing as the company.

7-17. **Concept Integration.** What is the principal difference between a business plan (as discussed in Chapter 6) and a strategic plan?

EXPAND YOUR KNOWLEDGE

Discovering Career Opportunities

If you become a manager, how much of your day will be spent performing each of the four basic functions of management? This is your opportunity to find out. Arrange to shadow a manager (such as a department head, a store manager, or a shift supervisor) for a few hours. As you observe, categorize the manager's activities in terms of the four management functions and note how much time each activity takes. If observation is not possible, interview a manager in order to complete this exercise.

7-18. How much of the manager's time is spent on each of the four management functions? Is this the allocation you expected?

7-19. Ask whether this is a typical workday for this manager. If it isn't, what does the manager usually do differently? During a typical day, does this manager tend to spend most of the time on one particular function?

7-20. Of the four management functions, which does the manager believe is most important for good organizational performance? Do you agree?

Improving Your Tech Insights: Business Intelligence Systems

One of the maddening ironies of contemporary business is that many decision makers are awash in data but starved for true information and insights. *Business intelligence* (BI) systems, also called *business analytics*, aim to harness all that data and turn it into the information and insights that managers need.

Explore the business intelligence or business analytics products offered by several of the leading vendors, IBM (**www.ibm.com**), SAP Business Objects (**www.sap.com**), Information Builders (**www.informationbuilders.com**), Oracle (**www.oracle.com**), and SAS (**www.sas.com**). Research a system offered by one of these vendors, and in a brief email message to your instructor, summarize in your own words the system's benefits for managerial decision makers. (*Business intelligence* is a broad term that describes a variety of approaches, technologies, and specific products, so the field can be a bit confusing. Try several websites, if needed, to find a BI system that you can summarize briefly.)

PRACTICE YOUR SKILLS

Sharpening Your Communication Skills

Potential customers frequently visit your production facility before making purchase decisions. You and the people who report to you in the sales department have received extensive training in etiquette issues because you deal with high-profile clients. However, the rest of the workforce has not received such training, and you worry that someone might inadvertently say or do something that would offend one of these potential customers. In a two-paragraph email, explain to the general manager why you think anyone who might come in contact with customers should receive basic etiquette training.

Building Your Team Skills

With a team of fellow students, perform a SWOT analysis for your college or university, from the perspective of recruiting new students. Identify as many significant strengths and weaknesses as you can think of, being as objective as possible. Next, identify any important opportunities and threats you can find, such as demographic shifts or changes in government funding. Summarize your findings in a chart modeled after Exhibit 7.3.

Finally, evaluate your college's website and other promotional materials, if available, according to how well they present the school's strengths to prospective students.

Developing Your Research Skills

Find two articles in business journals or newspapers (print or online editions) that profile two senior managers who lead a business organization.

7-21. What experience, skills, and business background do the two leaders have? Do you see any striking similarities or differences in their backgrounds?

7-22. What kinds of business challenges have these two leaders faced? What actions did they take to deal with those challenges? Did they establish any long-term goals or objectives for their company? Did the articles mention a new change initiative?

7-23. Describe the leadership strengths of these two people as they are presented in the articles you selected. Is either leader known as a team builder? Long-term strategist? Shrewd negotiator? What are each leader's greatest areas of strength?

MyBizLab®

Go to the Assignments section of your MyLab to complete these writing exercises.

7-24. How does the quality of business management affect society as a whole?

7-25. How will your experiences as an employee affect the leadership style you adopt when you become a manager?

ENDNOTES

1. Wegmans website, accessed 2 April 2015, www.wegmans.com; "100 Best Companies to Work For," *Fortune*, accessed 2 April 2015, http://fortune.com; "Hay Group Study Finds Employee Turnover in Retail Industry Is Slowly Increasing," Hay Group press release, 7 May 2012, www.haygroup.com; Matthew Boyle, "The Wegmans Way," *Fortune*, 24 January 2005, www.fortune.com; William Conroy, "Rochester, N.Y.–Based Grocer Tops Magazine's Best Employer Rankings," *Asbury Park* (NJ) *Press*, 11 January 2005, www.ebsco.com; Matthew Boyle, "The Wegmans Way," *Fortune*, 24 January 2005, 62–68; "UCCNet Designated as U.S. Data Pool of Choice by Leading Retailers," UCCNet website, accessed 8 March 2005, www.uccnet.org; Joy Davis, "Caring for Employees Is Wegmans' Best Selling Point," (Rochester, NY) *Democrat and Chronicle*, 6 February 2005, www.democratandchronicle.com; Michael A. Prospero, "Employee Innovator: Wegmans," *Fast Company*, October 2004, 88; Matt Glynn, "Employees of Rochester, N.Y.–Based Grocer Celebrate Firm's Top Ranking," *Buffalo* (NY) *News*, 11 January 2005, www.ebsco.com.
2. Richard L. Daft, *Management*, 6th ed. (Mason, Ohio: Thompson South-Western, 2003), 5.
3. Anne Fisher, "Starting a New Job? Don't Blow It," *Fortune*, 24 February 2005, www.fortune.com.
4. Daniel S. Cochran, Fred R. David, and C. Kendrick Gibson, "A Framework for Developing an Effective Mission Statement," *Journal of Business Strategies*, Fall 2008, 27–39.
5. Welch Allyn website, accessed 15 July 2015, www.welchallyn.com, Reprinted by permission from Welch Allyn.
6. Northrop Grumman vision statement. Used with permission of Northrop Grumman Corporation.
7. "Our Company," Enterprise Holdings, accessed 2 April 2015, http://http://go.enterpriseholdings.com/our-company/our-values.
8. Alastair Dryburgh, "Don't You Believe It … It's Smart to Have SMART Objectives," *Management Today*, June 2011, 14.
9. Dean Foust, "Speaking up for the Organization Man," *BusinessWeek*, 9 March 2009, 78.
10. Steve Arneson, "Lead from the Middle," *Leadership Excellence*, March 2008, 19.
11. Why Middle Managers May Be the Most Important People in Your Company," Knowledge@Wharton, 25 May 2011, http://knowledge.wharton.upenn.edu.
12. Daft, *Management*, 13.
13. Daft, *Management*, 514–515.
14. "Sometimes, EQ Is More Important Than IQ," CNN.com, 14 January 2005, www.cnn.com; Daniel Goleman, "What Makes a Leader?" *Harvard Business Review*, November–December 1998, 92–102; Shari Caudron, "The Hard Case for Soft Skills," *Workforce*, July 1999, 60–66.
15. James G. Clawson, *Level Three Leadership: Getting Below the Surface*, 2nd ed. (Upper Saddle River, N.J.: Prentice Hall, 2003), 116.
16. Cary Cherniss, "Emotional Intelligence: What It Is and Why It Matters," Consortium for Research on Emotional Intelligence in Organizations website, accessed 4 April 2009, www.eiconsortium.com.
17. Cherniss, "Emotional Intelligence: What It Is and Why It Matters."
18. Daniel Goleman, "Leadership That Gets Results," *Harvard Business Review*, March–April 2000, 78–90.
19. Herminia Ibarra and Morten T. Hansen, "Are You a Collaborative Leader?" *Harvard Business Review*, July/August 2011, 69–74.
20. Wegmans website, accessed 3 April 2009, www.wegmans.com.
21. Jeffrey D. Ford and Laurie W. Ford, "Decoding Resistance to Change," *Harvard Business Review*, April 2009, 99–103; Daft, *Management*, 382; Stephen Robbins and David DeCenzo, *Fundamentals of Management*, 4th ed. (Upper Saddle River, N.J.: Prentice Hall, 2003), 209.
22. Robbins and DeCenzo, *Fundamentals of Management*, 211; Daft, *Management*, 384, 396.
23. Robbins and DeCenzo, *Fundamentals of Management*, 210–211.
24. Ford and Ford, "Decoding Resistance to Change."
25. Paul Hebert, "People Don't Hate Change—They Hate You Trying to Change Them," Fistful of Talent blog, 6 April 2009, www.fistfuloftalent.com.
26. "High Standards," video, Wegmans website, accessed 3 April 2009, www.wegmans.com.
27. "Benchmarking," American Society for Quality, accessed 13 August 2011, http://asq.org.
28. Kevin J. Gregson, "Converting Strategy to Results," *American Venture*, September/October 2004, 16–18.
29. Robert E. Kaplan and Robert B. Kaiser, "Developing Versatile Leadership," *MIT Sloan Management Review*, Summer 2003, 19–26.
30. Courtland L. Bovée and John V. Thill, *Business Communication Today*, 9th ed. (Upper Saddle River, N.J.: Pearson Prentice Hall, 2008), 4.
31. Geoff Gloeckler, "The Case Against Case Studies," *BusinessWeek*, 4 February 2008, 66–67.
32. See note 1.

8 Organization and Teamwork

LEARNING OBJECTIVES   After studying this chapter, you will be able to

1 Explain the major decisions needed to design an organization structure.

2 Define four major types of organization structure.

3 Explain how a team differs from a group, and describe the six most common forms of teams.

4 Highlight the advantages and disadvantages of working in teams, and list the characteristics of effective teams.

5 Review the five stages of team development, and explain why conflict can arise in team settings.

6 Explain the concept of an unstructured organization, and identify the major benefits and challenges of taking this approach.

BEHIND THE SCENES   CEMEX REINVENTS A CENTURY-OLD COMPANY TO COMPETE IN A NEW BUSINESS WORLD

An innovative collaboration platform helps the global cement company Cemex operate with the agility and flexibility of a small company.

Pressmaster/Shutterstock

www.cemex.com

You have probably been on a lab team or other project team that had trouble collaborating. Maybe you couldn't get everyone in the same room at the same time, or important messages got buried in long email threads, or good ideas were lost because the right information didn't get to the right people at the right time.

Imagine trying to collaborate when you have thousands of potential team members spread across dozens of countries. The Mexican company Cemex is one of the world's largest producers of concrete and its two primary components, cement and aggregates (crushed stone, sand, and gravel). Cemex faces teamwork challenges on a global scale, with 44,000 employees in more than 50 countries. After a period of worldwide expansion that began in the 1990s, the century-old company now operates quarries, cement plants, and other facilities on every continent except Antarctica.

Concrete and cement are two of the oldest products on Earth and might not spring to mind when most people think of innovation. However, innovation is key to Cemex's long-term success, for several reasons. First, architects and builders continue to push the envelope by creating designs that require concrete with new performance and handling qualities. Second, Cemex's ability to operate profitably depends on running efficient operations, from raw material extraction to processing to transportation. Third, the production and distribution of concrete-related products have significant environmental impacts, including the acquisition and consumption of heating fuels required by high-temperature cement kilns.

To stay competitive and profitable and to minimize the environmental effects of its operations, Cemex knew it needed to accelerate the pace of innovation. Company leaders figured the way to do that was to enable better collaboration, and the way to do *that* was to enable better communication among its widely dispersed employees.

If you were Gilberto Garcia, Cemex's innovation director, how would you approach this challenge? What procedures and technologies could you put in place to help this mammoth multinational run with the agility and efficiency of a small company?[1]

INTRODUCTION

Individual effort is essential to the success of any business, but professionals rarely work in complete isolation. Most employees are members of one or more departments or teams, and even solo freelancers join virtual teams for many of their projects. The decisions about how to organize all the people involved in a business's operations are some of the most important decisions leaders have to make. Cemex (profiled in the chapter-opening Behind the Scenes) is a great example of how even mature companies have to review and sometimes rethink how they are organized or how their people can best work together. This chapter discusses the most key issues to consider in designing an organization structure, introduces you to the most common ways companies structure themselves, and explores the important matter of teamwork. It concludes with a look at the *unstructured organization*, which may be the structure of the future for many businesses.

Designing an Effective Organization Structure

A company's **organization structure** has a dramatic influence on the way employees and managers make decisions, communicate, and accomplish important tasks. This structure helps the company achieve its goals by providing a framework for managers to divide responsibilities, effectively distribute the authority to make decisions, coordinate and control the organization's work, and hold employees accountable for their work. In contrast, a poorly designed structure can create enormous waste, confusion, and frustration for employees, suppliers, and customers.

When managers design an organization's structure, they use an **organization chart** to provide a visual representation of how employees and tasks are grouped and how the lines of communication and authority flow (see Exhibit 8.1 on the next page). An organization chart depicts the official design for accomplishing tasks that lead to achieving the organization's goals, a framework known as the *formal organization*. Every company also has an *informal organization*—the network of interactions that develop on a personal level among workers. Sometimes the interactions among people in the informal organization parallel their relationships in the formal organization, but often interactions transcend formal boundaries, such as when employees from various parts of the company participate in sports, social, or charitable activities together or use social media to reach across organizational barriers.

In the past, organizations were usually designed around management's desire to control workers, with everything set up in a hierarchy. Today, however, the goal of many companies is an **agile organization** that allows employees to respond quickly to customer needs and changes in the business environment and to bring the best mix of talents and resources to every challenge.

To design the best structure for their organization, managers need to identify the organization's core competencies, clarify job responsibilities, define the chain of command, and organize the workforce in a way that maximizes effectiveness and efficiency.

IDENTIFYING CORE COMPETENCIES

Before they can decide how to organize, companies need to identify which business functions they should focus on themselves and which they should *outsource* (see page 202) to other companies. For instance, many companies outsource the payroll function because it

1   LEARNING OBJECTIVE

Explain the major decisions needed to design an organization structure.

organization structure
A framework that enables managers to divide responsibilities, ensure employee accountability, and distribute decision-making authority.

organization chart
A diagram that shows how employees and tasks are grouped and where the lines of communication and authority flow.

agile organization
A company whose structure, policies, and capabilities allow employees to respond quickly to customer needs and changes in the business environment.

| EXHIBIT 8.1 | **Simplified Organization Chart** |

An organization chart portrays the division of activities and responsibilities across a company.

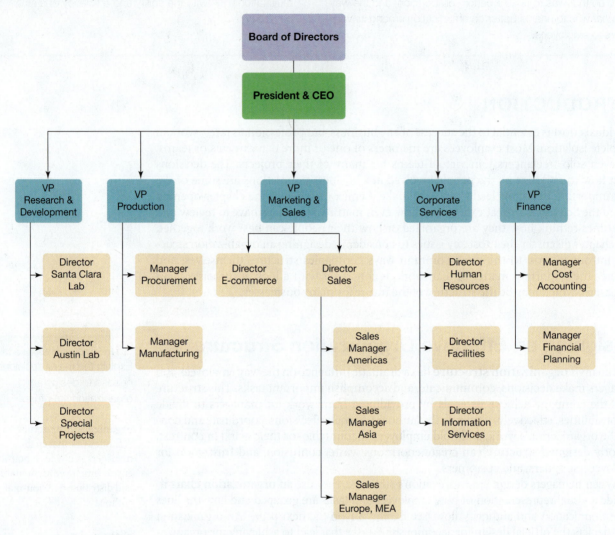

core competencies
Activities that a company considers central and vital to its business.

doesn't make sense for them to invest the time needed to stay on top of frequent changes in income tax laws and related financial matters.[2]

Core competencies are those activities at which a company excels and that give it the potential to create competitive advantages. For example, it's a virtual certainty that you've seen or used a product designed by Frog (**www.frogdesign.com**), a global design consultancy with talents in consumer research, design, and the commercialization phase of bringing new products to market. Frog has worked behind the scenes for many of the world's best-known companies, from Apple to Disney to Sony, but it stays focused on its core competencies in product strategy and design, rather than becoming a manufacturer itself.[3]

IDENTIFYING JOB RESPONSIBILITIES

work specialization
Specialization in or responsibility for some portion of an organization's overall work tasks; also called *division of labor*.

Once a company knows what it wants to focus on, it can design each job needed to deliver those competencies. A key decision here is finding the optimal level of **work specialization**, sometimes referred to as the *division of labor*—the degree to which organizational tasks are broken down into separate jobs.[4] Work specialization can improve organizational efficiency by enabling each worker to perform tasks that are well defined and that require specific skills. When employees concentrate on the same specialized tasks, they can perfect their skills and perform those tasks more quickly. In addition to aligning skills with job tasks, specialization prevents overlapping responsibilities and communication breakdowns.

However, organizations can overdo specialization. If a task is defined too narrowly, employees may become bored with performing the same limited, repetitive job over and over. They may also feel unchallenged and alienated. As you'll see later in the chapter, many companies are adopting a team-based approach to give employees a wider range of work experiences and responsibilities.

DEFINING THE CHAIN OF COMMAND

With the various jobs and their individual responsibilities identified, the next step is defining the **chain of command**, the lines of authority that connect the various groups and levels within the organization. The chain of command helps the organization function smoothly by making two things clear: who is responsible for each task and who has the authority to make decisions.

All employees have a certain amount of *responsibility*—the obligation to perform the duties and achieve the goals and objectives associated with their jobs. As they work toward the organization's goals, employees must also maintain their *accountability*, their obligation to report the results of their work to supervisors or team members and to justify any outcomes that fall below expectations. Managers ensure that tasks are accomplished by exercising *authority*, the power to make decisions, issue orders, carry out actions, and allocate resources. Authority is vested in the positions that managers hold, and it flows down through the management pyramid. *Delegation* is the assignment of work and the transfer of authority, responsibility, and accountability to complete that work.[5]

The simplest and most common chain-of-command system is known as **line organization** because it establishes a clear line of authority flowing from the top down, as Exhibit 8.1 depicts. Everyone knows who is accountable to whom, as well as which tasks and decisions each is responsible for. However, line organization sometimes falls short because the technical complexity of a firm's activities may require specialized knowledge that individual managers don't have and can't easily acquire. A more elaborate system, called **line-and-staff organization**, was developed to address the need to combine specialization with management control. In such an organization, managers in the chain of command are supplemented by functional groupings of people known as *staff*, who provide advice and specialized services but who are not in the line organization's overall chain of command (see Exhibit 8.2 on the next page).

Span of Management

The number of people a manager directly supervises is called the **span of management**, or *span of control*. When a large number of people report directly to one person, that person has a wide span of management. This situation is common in *flat organizations* with relatively few levels in the management hierarchy. In contrast, *tall organizations* have many hierarchical levels, typically with fewer people reporting to each manager than is the case in a flat organization. In these organizations, the span of management is narrow.

To reduce the time it takes to make decisions, many companies are now flattening their organization structures by removing layers of management and pushing responsibilities and authority to lower levels (see Exhibit 8.3 on page 175). Such moves have the additional benefit of putting senior executives in closer contact with customers and the daily action of the business.[6]

However, a flatter structure is not necessarily better in all respects. For example, it increases the demand on individual managers and gives them less time to spend with each employee. The Container Store, for instance, added a layer of management specifically to reduce the span of management in order to give each manager more time "to nurture and develop and train and counsel" his or her employees. "I think it's the best thing we ever did," co-founder Kip Tindell said, noting that even with the added costs, financial performance improved.[7]

chain of command
A pathway for the flow of authority from one management level to the next.

line organization
A chain-of-command system that establishes a clear line of authority flowing from the top down.

line-and-staff organization
An organization system that has a clear chain of command but that also includes functional groups of people who provide advice and specialized services.

span of management
The number of people under one manager's control; also known as *span of control*.

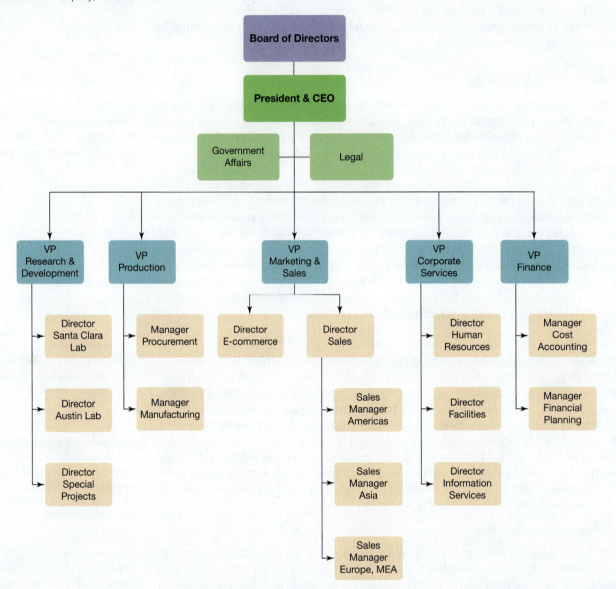

EXHIBIT 8.2 **Simplified Line-and-Staff Structure**

A line-and-staff organization divides employees into those who are in the direct line of command and those who provide staff (support) services to line managers at various levels. In this simplified example, the government affairs and legal departments report to the CEO but would provide support to any department in the company, as needed.

Moreover, the deep experience base that midlevel managers have accrued, regarding both external market dynamics and internal working knowledge of the company itself, can be lost when these positions are eliminated. These managers can be particularly crucial in knowledge-driven industries, where insight and creative thinking are crucial to strategic decision making.[8]

Centralization Versus Decentralization

Centralization
Concentration of decision-making authority at the top of an organization.

Organizations that focus decision-making authority near the top of the chain of command are said to be centralized. **Centralization** can benefit a company by taking advantage of top management's experience and broad view of organizational goals. In addition, it can help companies coordinate large undertakings more efficiently, accelerate decisions that might otherwise get bogged down in discussions and disagreements, and reduce the number of overlapping capabilities.

Flattening an Organization

In this simplified example, a layer of management (the business units) was removed to flatten the organization. In theory, this move reduces costs and speeds communication and decision making. Two obvious downsides are the increased span of management for the two group managers and the loss of knowledge and relationships that the business unit managers brought to the organization.

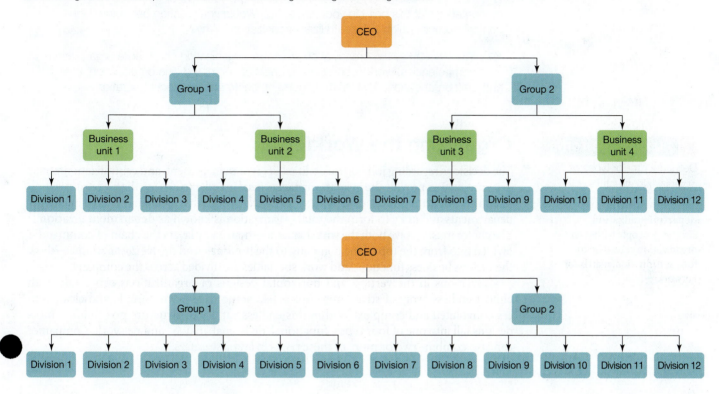

In contrast, **decentralization** pushes decision-making authority down to lower organizational levels—such as department heads—while control over essential companywide matters remains with top management. Implemented properly, decentralization can stimulate responsiveness because decisions don't have to be referred up the hierarchy.[9] However, decentralization does not work in every situation or in every company. At times, strong authority from the top of the chain of command may be needed to keep the organization focused on immediate goals. In other cases, a company may need strong central decision making to coordinate efforts on complex projects or to present a unified image to customers. Decentralization can also lead to inefficiencies if multiple parts of a firm are doing the same basic task or replicating resources such as information systems. Managers should select the level of decision making that will most effectively serve the organization's needs, given the particular circumstances.[10]

decentralization
Delegation of decision-making authority to employees in lower-level positions.

 ✔ **Checkpoint**

LEARNING OBJECTIVE 1: Explain the major decisions needed to design an organization structure.

SUMMARY: The first major decision in designing an organization structure is identifying core competencies, those functions where the company excels and wants to focus. From there, managers can identify job responsibilities (who does what and how much work specialization is optimum), the chain of command, the span of management for each manager, and the degree of centralization or decentralization of decision-making authority.

CRITICAL THINKING: (1) What are the risks of a poorly designed organization structure? (2) How does a flat structure change the responsibilities of individual managers?

IT'S YOUR BUSINESS: (1) What would you say are your two or three core competencies at this point in your career? (2) Would you function better in a highly centralized or in a highly decentralized organization? Why?

KEY TERMS TO KNOW: organization structure, organization chart, agile organization, core competencies, work specialization, chain of command, line organization, line-and-staff organization, span of management, centralization, decentralization

---

2   **LEARNING OBJECTIVE**

Define four major types of organization structure.

departmentalization
Grouping people within an organization according to function, division, matrix, or network.

Organizing the Workforce

The decisions regarding job responsibilities, span of management, and centralization versus decentralization provide the insights managers need in order to choose the best organization structure. The arrangement of activities into logical groups that are then clustered into larger departments and units to form the total organization is known as **departmentalization**.[11] The choice must involve both the *vertical structure*—how many layers the chain of command is divided into from the top of the company to the bottom—and the *horizontal structure*—how the various business functions and work specialties are divided across the company.

Variations in the vertical and horizontal designs of organizations can produce an almost endless array of structures—some flat, some wide; some simple and clear; others convoluted and complex. Within this endless variety of structure possibilities, most designs fall into one of four types: functional, divisional, matrix, and network. Companies can also combine two or more of these types in *hybrid structures*.

FUNCTIONAL STRUCTURES

functional structure
Grouping workers according to their similar skills, resource use, and expertise.

The **functional structure** groups employees according to their skills, resource use, and job requirements. Common functional subgroups include research and development (R&D), production or manufacturing, marketing and sales, and human resources.

Splitting the organization into separate functional departments offers several advantages: (1) Grouping employees by specialization allows for the efficient use of resources and encourages the development of in-depth skills, (2) centralized decision making enables unified direction by top management, and (3) centralized operations enhance communication and the coordination of activities within departments. Despite these advantages, functional departmentalization can create problems with communication, coordination, and control, particularly as companies grow and become more complicated and geographically dispersed.[12] Moreover, employees may become too narrowly focused on departmental goals and may lose sight of larger company goals. Firms that use functional structures often try to counter these weaknesses by using *cross-functional teams* to coordinate efforts across functional boundaries, as you'll see later in the chapter.

DIVISIONAL STRUCTURES

divisional structure
Grouping departments according to similarities in product, process, customer, or geography.

The **divisional structure** establishes self-contained suborganizations that encompass all the major functional resources required to achieve their goals—such as research and design, manufacturing, finance, and marketing.[13] In some companies, these divisions operate with great autonomy and are often called *business units*.

Many organizations use a structure based on *product divisions*—grouping around each of the company's products or family of products. In contrast, *process divisions* are based on the major steps of a production process. For example, Chevron has divisions (including separate companies in some cases) for such process steps as exploration, refining, pipeline distribution, shipping, and marketing.[14] The third approach, *customer divisions*, concentrates activities on satisfying specific groups of customers (see Exhibit 8.4). Finally,

EXHIBIT 8.4	**Customer Division Structure**

Focusing each division on a single type of customer can help a company market its products more efficiently and serve customers more responsively.

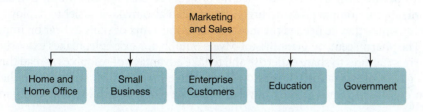

geographic divisions help companies respond more easily to local customs, styles, and product preferences.

Divisional structures offer both advantages and disadvantages. First, because divisions are self-contained, they can react quickly to change, making the organization more flexible. In addition, because each division focuses on a limited number of products, processes, customers, or locations, divisions can often provide better service to customers.

However, divisional departmentalization can also increase costs through duplication (if every product division has its own human resources department, for example). Furthermore, poor coordination between divisions may cause them to focus too narrowly on divisional goals at the expense of the organization's overall goals. Finally, divisions may compete with one another for resources and customers, causing rivalries that hurt the organization as a whole.[15]

MATRIX STRUCTURES

A **matrix structure** is an organizational design in which employees from functional departments form teams to combine their specialized skills (see Exhibit 8.5). This structure

matrix structure
A structure in which employees are assigned to both a functional group and a project team (thus using functional and divisional patterns simultaneously).

EXHIBIT 8.5	**Matrix Structure**

In a matrix structure, each employee is assigned to both a functional group (with a defined set of basic functions, such as production management) and a project team (which consists of members of various functional groups working together on a project, such as bringing out a new consumer product). Even in this simplified model, you can sense how complex matrix management can be, when employees have multiple managers, and managers share employees with other projects and departments.

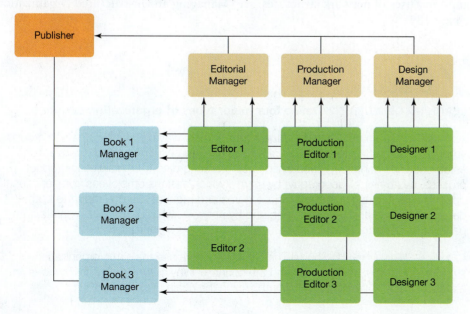

allows the company to pool and share resources across divisions and functional groups. The matrix may be a permanent feature of the organization's design, or it may be established to complete a specific project.

The matrix structure can help big companies function like smaller ones by allowing teams to devote their attention to specific projects or customers without permanently reorganizing the company's structure. A matrix can also make it easier to deploy limited resources where they're needed the most and to bring a mix of skills to bear on important tasks. The pharmaceutical giant Bristol-Myers Squibb, for example, makes extensive uses of matrix structures to share expertise and to take advantage of resources spread throughout its global organization. According to executive Jane Luciano, "The matrix helps us to gain control of issues as they travel around the globe and to leverage economies of scale."[16]

On the downside, people in a matrix structure have to get used to reporting to two bosses, more communication and coordination is usually required, and struggles over resources can foster unhealthy competition between the two sides of the matrix.[17] Strong support from upper management, a culture that values collaboration, and hands-on attention from managers to make sure employees don't get lost in the matrix are essential to using this structural form successfully.[18]

NETWORK STRUCTURES

network structure
A structure in which individual companies are connected electronically to perform selected tasks for a small headquarters organization.

A **network structure** stretches beyond the boundaries of a company to connect a variety of partners and suppliers that perform selected tasks for a headquarters organization. Also called a *virtual organization*, a network organization can outsource engineering, marketing, research, accounting, production, distribution, or other functions. The design of a network structure stems from decisions about core competencies, with executives deciding which functions to focus on internally and which to outsource.

The network structure presents an intriguing blend of benefits and risks. A virtual structure can lower costs and increase flexibility, allowing a company to react more quickly to market demands. It can also boost competitiveness by taking advantage of specific skills and technologies available in other companies. On the other hand, relying too heavily on outsiders can render the company vulnerable to events beyond its control, such as a key supplier going out of business, offering the same goods and services to its competitors, or going into direct competition with the company. Moreover, outsourcing too many fundamental tasks, such as product design, can leave a company without any real competitive distinctions to speak of.[19] For more on contemporary uses of network structures, see "Managing an Unstructured Organization" on page 189.

✓ **Checkpoint**

LEARNING OBJECTIVE 2: Define four major types of organization structure.

SUMMARY: Companies can organize in four primary ways: by function, which groups employees according to their skills, resource use, and expertise; by division, which establishes self-contained departments formed according to similarities in product, process, customer, or geography; by matrix, which assigns employees from functional departments to interdisciplinary project teams and requires them to report to both a department head and a team leader; and by network, which connects separate companies that perform selected tasks for a headquarters organization.

CRITICAL THINKING: (1) Should The Container Store use the same organization structure in each of its stores around the country? Why or why not? (2) Why does a matrix structure create potential problems in the chain of command?

Organizing in Teams

Although the vertical chain of command is a tried-and-true method of organizing for business, it is limited by the fact that decision-making authority is often located high up the management hierarchy while real-world feedback from customers is usually located at or near the bottom. Companies that organize vertically may become slow to react to change, and high-level managers may overlook many great ideas for improvement that originate in the lower levels of the organization. In addition, many business tasks and challenges demand the expertise of people who work in many parts of the company, isolated by the formal chain of command. To combat these issues, organizations can involve employees from all levels and functions in the decision-making process, using a variety of team formats in day-to-day operations.

This section looks at the most common types of teams, and the following two sections address the challenges of improving team productivity and fostering teamwork.

WHAT IS A TEAM?

A **team** is a unit of two or more people who work together to achieve a shared goal. Teams differ from work groups in that work groups interact primarily to share information and to make decisions to help one another perform within each member's area of responsibility. In other words, the performance of a work group is merely the summation of all group members' individual contributions.[20] In contrast, the members of a team have a shared mission and are collectively responsible for their work. By coordinating their individual efforts, the members of a successful team accomplish more together than they could individually, a result known as *synergy*.[21]

Although a team's goals may be set by either the team itself or someone in the formal chain of command, it is the job of the team leader to make sure the team stays on track to achieve those goals. Team leaders are often appointed by senior managers, but sometimes they emerge naturally as the team develops. Some teams complete their work and disband in a matter of weeks or months, whereas those working on complex projects can stay together for years.

team
A unit of two or more people who share a mission and collective responsibility as they work together to achieve a goal.

TYPES OF TEAMS

The type, structure, and composition of individual teams within an organization depend on the organization's strategic goals and the objective for forming the team. Six common forms of teams are problem-solving teams, self-managed teams, functional teams, cross-functional teams, virtual teams, and social networks and virtual communities. Such classifications are not exclusive, of course. A problem-solving team may also be self-managed and cross-functional.

Problem-Solving Teams

A **problem-solving team** is assembled to find ways of improving quality, efficiency, or other performance measures. In some cases, a team attacks a single, specific problem and disbands after presenting or implementing the solution. In other cases, the team continues to meet over time, evaluating trends and fixing new problems as they crop up.

problem-solving team
A team that meets to find ways of improving quality, efficiency, and the work environment.

Self-Managed Teams

self-managed team
A team in which members are responsible for an entire process or operation.

As the name implies, a **self-managed team** manages its own activities and requires minimal supervision. Typically, these teams control the pace of work and determination of work assignments. Fully self-managed teams select their own members. Self-managed teams represent a significant change for organizations and managers accustomed to rigid command-and-control structures. However, the potential advantages include lower costs, faster decision making, greater flexibility and innovation, and improved quality (stemming from the increased pride of ownership that an independent team feels in its work).[22]

Functional Teams

functional team
A team whose members come from a single functional department and that is based on the organization's vertical structure.

A **functional team**, or *command team*, is organized along the lines of the organization's vertical structure and thus may be referred to as a *vertical team*. Such teams are composed of managers and employees within a single functional department, and the structure of a vertical team typically follows the formal chain of command. In some cases, the team may include several levels of the organizational hierarchy within the same functional department.[23]

Cross-Functional Teams

cross-functional team
A team that draws together employees from different functional areas.

In contrast to functional teams, a **cross-functional team**, or *horizontal team*, draws together employees from various functional areas and expertise. Cross-functional teams can facilitate information exchange, help coordinate multiple organizational units, encourage new solutions for organizational problems, and aid the development of new organizational policies and procedures.[24] However, collaborating across organizational boundaries can be challenging, particularly if participation on a cross-functional team conflicts with an individual's regular departmental workload or performance incentives.[25] Cross-functional teams often involve some form of matrix structure, even if temporarily, which brings with it the advantages and challenges of that form.

task force
A team of people from several departments who are temporarily brought together to address a specific issue.

A cross-functional team can take on a number of formats. A **task force** is formed to work on a specific activity with a completion point. Several departments are usually involved so that all parties who have a stake in the outcome of the task are able to provide input. In contrast, a **committee** usually has a long life span and may become a permanent part of the organization structure. Committees typically deal with regularly recurring tasks, such as addressing employee grievances.

committee
A team that may become a permanent part of the organization and is designed to deal with regularly recurring tasks.

Virtual Teams

virtual team
A team that uses communication technology to bring together geographically distant employees to achieve goals.

A **virtual team** is composed of members at two or more geographic locations. Research indicates that virtual teams can be as effective as face-to-face teams, as long as they take steps to overcome the disadvantages of not being able to communicate face to face.[26] For instance, some virtual teams meet in person at least once to allow the members to get to know one another before diving into their work.

To be successful, virtual teams should follow three basic rules. First, a virtual team should take full advantage of the diverse viewpoints, experiences, and skills of the various team members. One of the major benefits of virtual teams, in fact, is the opportunity to assemble teams of experts wherever they may be rather than rely on the people who happen to work in a given geographic location. Second, virtual teams should use technology to overcome the disadvantages of geographic separation. This can include remote access to important digital resources via shared online workspaces, team bonding and communication via social networks and collaboration platforms, project-management systems that clarify task responsibilities and schedules, and wikis and other systems that establish a "group memory" of key information. Third, virtual teams should take extra care to keep functioning effectively. When people work in isolation much of the time and rely on digital media to communication, the potential for

A cross-functional team brings together employees from different parts of the organization. The diversity of skills and experience can help a company address complex, interwoven problems.

Jetta Productions/Blend Images/Corbis

miscommunication increases. For example, the lack of the *nonverbal cues*, such as facial expressions and body language, which people rely on heavily when communicating in person, makes virtual communication especially challenging. Teleconferencing and videoconferencing can help in this regard.[27]

Social Networks and Virtual Communities

Social networking technologies are redefining teamwork and team communication by helping erase the constraints of geographic and organization boundaries. In addition to enabling and enhancing teamwork, social networks have numerous other business applications and benefits (see Exhibit 8.6). Although they are not always teams in the traditional sense, social networks and virtual communities often function as teams, helping people coordinate their efforts in pursuit of a shared goal. In addition, social networking has become an essential tool for many teams, matrix organizations, temporary organizations, and other structures.

Some companies use social networking technologies to form *virtual communities* or *communities of practice* that link employees with similar professional interests throughout the company and sometimes with customers and suppliers as well. The huge advantage that social networking brings is in identifying the best people to collaborate on each problem or project, no matter where they are around the world or what their official roles are

EXHIBIT 8.6	Business Uses of Social Networking Technology

Social networking has emerged as a powerful technology for enabling teamwork and enhancing collaboration in a variety of ways.

Business Challenge	Example of Social Networking in Action
Assembling teams	Identifying the best people, both inside the company and in other companies, to collaborate on projects
Fostering the growth of communities	Helping people with similar—or complementary—interests and skills find each other in order to provide mutual assistance and development
Accelerating the evolution of teams	Accelerating the sometimes slow process of getting to know one another and identifying individual areas of expertise
Maintaining business relationships	Giving people an easy way to stay in contact after meetings and conferences
Supporting customers	Allowing customers to develop close relationships with product experts within the company
Integrating new employees	Helping new employees navigate their way through the organization, finding experts, mentors, and other important contacts
Easing the transition after reorganizations and mergers	Helping employees connect and bond after internal staff reorganizations or mergers with other organizations
Overcoming structural barriers in communication channels	Bypassing the formal communication system in order to deliver information where it is needed in a timely fashion
Brainstorming new ideas, solving problems	Finding "pockets of knowledge" within the organization—the expertise and experience of individual employees
Preparing for major meetings and events	Giving participants a way to meet before an event takes place, helping to ensure that the meeting or event becomes more productive more quickly
Sharing and distributing information	Making it easy for employees to share information with people who may need it—and for people who need information to find employees who might have it
Finding potential customers, business partners, and employees	Identifying strong candidates by matching user profiles with current business needs and linking from existing member profiles
Socializing brands and companies	Making companies more approachable and transparent; today's customers want to interact with the companies they buy from
Responding to crises	Gathering critical details from the field via social media and sharing updates with affected stakeholders

Source: Courtland L. Bovée and John V. Thill, *Business Communication Today*, 13th ed. (Upper Saddle River, N.J.: Pearson Prentice Hall, 2016), 207–208; Christopher Carfi and Leif Chastaine, "Social Networking for Businesses & Organizations," white paper, Cerado website, accessed 13 August 2008, www.cerado.com; "Social Network Websites: Best Practices from Leading Services," white paper, 28 November 2007, FaberNovel Consulting, www.fabernovel.com.

REAL-TIME UPDATES
Learn More by Watching This Video

Building trust in virtual teams

Follow these six tips to build trust with long-distance teams. Go to http://real-timeupdates.com/bia8 and click on Learn More in the Students section.

in the organization. Such communities are similar to teams in many respects, but one major difference is in the responsibility for accumulating organizational knowledge over the long term. For example, the pharmaceutical company Pfizer has a number of permanent product safety communities that provide specialized advice on drug safety issues to researchers across the company.[28]

Social networking can also help a company maintain a sense of community even as it grows beyond the size that normally permits a lot of daily interaction. At the online retailer Zappos, fostering a supportive work environment is the company's top priority. To encourage the sense of community among its expanding workforce, Zappos uses a custom social networking system to track employee connections and encourage workers to reach out and build relationships. In fact, the company is so sold on the idea of networking that it no longer uses traditional job postings and a conventional hiring process. People who are interested in working at Zappos are required to join the social network first. The network lets candidates learn more about what it's like to work at Zappos, and it lets the company learn more about the candidates—including how they interact with other people.[29]

 Checkpoint

LEARNING OBJECTIVE 3: Explain how a team differs from a group, and describe the six most common forms of teams.

SUMMARY: The primary difference between a team and a work group is that the members of a team work toward a shared goal, whereas members of a work group work toward individual goals. The six most common forms of teams are (1) problem-solving teams, which seek ways to improve a situation and then submit their recommendations; (2) self-managed teams, which manage their own activities and seldom require supervision; (3) functional teams, which are composed of employees within a single functional department; (4) cross-functional teams, which draw together employees from various departments and expertise in a number of formats such as task forces and committees; (5) virtual teams, which bring together employees from distant locations; and (6) social networks and virtual communities, which are typically less structured than teams but nonetheless share many aspects of teamwork and promote shared goals.

CRITICAL THINKING: (1) How might the work of a task force or committee disrupt the normal chain of command in an organization? (2) Should new hires with no business experience be assigned to virtual teams? Why or why not?

IT'S YOUR BUSINESS: (1) Would you function well in a virtual team setting that offered little or no chance for face-to-face contact with your colleagues? Why or why not? (2) If you had two similar job offers, one with a company that stresses teamwork and another with a company that stresses independent accomplishment, which would you choose? Why?

KEY TERMS TO KNOW: team, problem-solving team, self-managed team, functional team, cross-functional team, task force, committee, virtual team

---

4 **LEARNING OBJECTIVE**

Highlight the advantages and disadvantages of working in teams, and list the characteristics of effective teams.

Ensuring Team Productivity

Even though teams can play a vital role in helping an organization reach its goals, they are not appropriate for every situation, nor do they automatically ensure higher performance. Understanding the advantages and disadvantages of working in teams and recognizing the characteristics of effective teams are essential steps in ensuring productive teamwork.

ADVANTAGES AND DISADVANTAGES OF WORKING IN TEAMS

Managers must weigh the pros and cons of teams when deciding whether and how to use them. A well-run team can provide a number of advantages:[30]

- **Higher-quality decisions.** Many business challenges require the input of people with diverse experiences and insights, and using teams can be an effective way to bring these multiple perspectives together. Working in teams can unleash new levels of creativity and energy in workers who share a sense of purpose and mutual accountability. Effective teams can be better than top-performing individuals at solving complex problems.[31]
- **Increased diversity of views.** Team members can bring a variety of perspectives to the decision-making process, which can result in more successful actions and decisions, as long as these diverse viewpoints are guided by a shared goal.[32]
- **Increased commitment to solutions and changes.** Employees who feel they've had an active role in making a decision are more likely to support the decision and encourage others to accept it.
- **Lower levels of stress and destructive internal competition.** When people work together toward a common goal rather than competing for individual recognition, their efforts and energies tend to focus on the common good. The sense of belonging to a group and being involved in a collective effort can also be a source of job satisfaction for most people.
- **Improved flexibility and responsiveness.** Because they don't have the same degree of permanence as formal departments and other structural elements, teams are easier to reformulate to respond to changing business needs.

Furthermore, teams fill people's social and emotional needs to belong to a group, reduce employee boredom, increase feelings of dignity and self-worth, and reduce stress and tension among workers. Although the advantages of teamwork help explain the widespread popularity of teams in today's business environment, teams also present a number of potential disadvantages, particularly if they are poorly structured or poorly managed:[33]

- **Inefficiency.** Even successful teams need to be on constant watch for inefficiency—spending more time than necessary on their decisions and activities or simply losing sight of the team's ultimate goal. Potential sources of inefficiency include internal politics, too much emphasis on consensus, and excessive socializing among team members.
- **Groupthink.** Like all social structures, business teams can generate tremendous pressures to conform with accepted norms of behavior. **Groupthink** occurs when these peer pressures cause individual team members to withhold contrary or unpopular opinions. The result can be decisions that are worse than those the team members might have made individually. Overcoming fear of conflict is essential to avoiding groupthink, which may require some coaching from experienced managers and continued attention to rules of engagement when conflict does arise. A particularly insidious aspect of groupthink is that a team suffering from it can appear to be highly functional, given the lack of disagreement, when in fact the team could be failing spectacularly.[34]
- **Diminished individual motivation.** Balancing the need for group harmony with individual motivation is a constant issue with teams. Without the promise of individual recognition and reward, high-performance individuals may feel less incentive to keep working at high levels.
- **Structural disruption.** Teams can become so influential within an organization that they compete with the formal chain of command, in effect superimposing a matrix on the existing structure.
- **Excessive workloads.** The time and energy required to work on teams isn't free, and when team responsibilities are layered on top of individuals' regular job responsibilities, the result can be overload.

REAL-TIME UPDATES

Learn More by Reading This Article

The benefits of mobile collaboration

Going mobile helps teams get work faster and more effectively. Go to http://real-timeupdates.com/bia8 and click on Learn More in the Students section.

REAL-TIME UPDATES

Learn More by Listening to This Podcast

Taking teams to the top

Listen to these hands-on techniques for developing, launching, leading, and evaluating world-class teams. Go to http://real-time updates.com/bia8 and click on Learn More in the Students section.

groupthink
Uniformity of thought that occurs when peer pressures cause individual team members to withhold contrary or unpopular opinions.

CHARACTERISTICS OF EFFECTIVE TEAMS

To be successful, teams need to be designed as carefully as any other part of an organization structure. Establishing the size of the team is one of the most important decisions; the optimal size for teams is generally thought to be between 5 and 12 members. Teams with fewer members may lack the necessary range of skills, whereas members of larger teams may have difficulty bonding properly and communicating efficiently. However, managers sometimes have no choice; complex challenges such as integrating two companies or designing complicated products can require teams of up to 100 people or more.[35]

The types of individuals on a team are also a vital consideration. People who assume the *task-specialist role* focus on helping the team reach its goals. In contrast, members who take on the *socioemotional role* focus on supporting the team's emotional needs and strengthening the team's social unity. Some team members are able to assume dual roles, contributing to the task and still meeting members' emotional needs. These members often make effective team leaders. At the other end of the spectrum are members who are *nonparticpators*, contributing little to reaching the team's goals or to meeting members' socioemotional needs. Obviously, a team staffed with too many inactive members isn't going to accomplish much of anything. Exhibit 8.7 outlines the behavior patterns associated with each of these roles.

Beyond the right number of the right sort of people, effective teams share other characteristics as well:[36]

- **Clear sense of purpose.** Team members clearly understand the task at hand, what is expected of them, and their respective roles on the team.

EXHIBIT 8.7	Team Member Roles

Team members assume one of these four roles. Members who assume a dual role—emphasizing both task progress and people needs—often make the most effective team leaders.

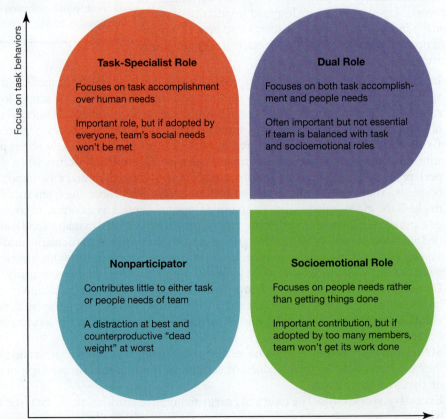

Focus on task behaviors

Task-Specialist Role

Focuses on task accomplishment over human needs

Important role, but if adopted by everyone, team's social needs won't be met

Dual Role

Focuses on both task accomplishment and people needs

Often important but not essential if team is balanced with task and socioemotional roles

Nonparticipator

Contributes little to either task or people needs of team

A distraction at best and counterproductive "dead weight" at worst

Socioemotional Role

Focuses on people needs rather than getting things done

Important contribution, but if adopted by too many members, team won't get its work done

Focus on social behaviors

- **Open and honest communication.** The team culture encourages discussion and debate. Team members speak openly and honestly, without the threat of anger, resentment, or retribution. They listen to and value feedback from others. As a result, all members participate. Conversely, members who either don't share valuable information because they don't understand that it's valuable or, worse, withhold information as a way to maintain personal power can undermine the team's efforts.[37]
- **Empathy and mutual understanding.** Team members can accurately gauge what other members are thinking and feeling. This empathy can function even for virtual teams that communicate solely via text and can't rely on nonverbal cues.[38]
- **Creative thinking.** Effective teams encourage original thinking, considering options beyond the usual.
- **Accountability.** Team members commit to being accountable to each other.
- **Focus.** Team members get to the core issues of the problem and stay focused on key issues.
- **Decision by consensus.** On effective teams, all decisions are arrived at by consensus. But this point comes with a warning: Teams that worry too much about consensus can take a long time to make decisions. In many cases, members need to commit to the group's decision even though they may not support it 100 percent.

For a brief review of characteristics of effective teams, see Exhibit 8.8.

REAL-TIME UPDATES
Learn More by Reading This Article

Three factors that distinguish smart teams

Common sense might tell you that smarter individuals make for a smarter team, but these researchers discovered otherwise. Go to http://real-timeupdates.com/bia8 and click on Learn More in the Students section.

EXHIBIT 8.8   **Characteristics of Effective Teams**

Effective teams practice these good habits.

MAKE EFFECTIVE TEAMWORK A TOP MANAGEMENT PRIORITY

- Recognize and reward group performance where appropriate
- Provide ample training opportunities for employees to develop team skills

SELECT TEAM MEMBERS WISELY

- Involve key stakeholders and decision makers
- Limit team size to the minimum number of people needed to achieve team goals
- Select members with a diversity of views
- Select creative thinkers

BUILD A SENSE OF FAIRNESS IN DECISION MAKING

- Encourage debate and disagreement without fear of reprisal
- Allow members to communicate openly and honestly
- Consider all proposals
- Build consensus by allowing team members to examine, compare, and reconcile differences—but don't let a desire for 100 percent consensus bog the team down
- Avoid quick votes
- Keep everyone informed
- Present all the facts

MANAGE CONFLICT CONSTRUCTIVELY

- Share leadership
- Encourage equal participation
- Discuss disagreements openly and calmly
- Focus on the issues, not the people
- Don't let minor disagreements boil over into major conflicts

STAY ON TRACK

- Make sure everyone understands the team's purpose
- Communicate what is expected of team members
- Stay focused on the core assignment
- Develop and adhere to a schedule
- Develop rules and follow norms

Checkpoint

5 | **LEARNING OBJECTIVE**

Review the five stages of team development, and explain why conflict can arise in team settings.

Fostering Teamwork

Because teams are composed of unique individuals with different perspectives, the interpersonal relationships among team members require careful consideration. Two particularly important issues are team development and team conflict.

TEAM DEVELOPMENT

Teams often require some time and developmental change to reach full productive speed, and team leaders need to understand this process to help groups reach their potential as quickly as possible. Several models of team development have been proposed over the years. One well-known model defined by researcher Bruce Tuckman identifies five stages of development, nicknamed *forming, storming, norming, performing,* and *adjourning*:[39]

- **Forming.** The forming stage is a period of orientation and ice-breaking. Members get to know each other, determine what types of behaviors are appropriate within the group, identify what is expected of them, and become acquainted with each other's task orientation.
- **Storming.** In the storming stage, members show more of their personalities and become more assertive in establishing their roles. Conflict and disagreement often arise during the storming stage, as members jockey for position or form coalitions to promote their own perceptions of the team's mission. Although it is necessary for this storming to occur, team members need to make sure the team doesn't lapse into counterproductive behaviors before it has a chance to resolve these emerging conflicts.
- **Norming.** During the norming stage, conflicts are resolved, and team harmony develops. Members come to understand and accept one another, reach consensus on

who the leader is (if that hasn't already been established formally), and reach agreement on member roles.

- **Performing.** In the performing stage, members are truly committed to the team's goals. Problems are solved, and disagreements are handled in the interest of task accomplishment.
- **Adjourning.** Finally, if the team has a specific task to perform, it goes through the adjourning stage after the task has been completed. In this stage, issues are wrapped up, and the team is dissolved.

As a team moves through these stages, two important developments occur. First, it develops a certain level of **cohesiveness**, a measure of how committed the members are to the team's goals. Cohesiveness is reflected in meeting attendance, team interaction, work quality, and goal achievement. Cohesiveness is influenced by many factors, particularly competition and evaluation. If a team is in competition with other teams, cohesiveness increases as the team strives to excel. In addition, if a team's efforts and accomplishments are recognized by the organization, members tend to be more committed to the team's goals. Strong team cohesiveness generally results in high morale. Moreover, when cohesiveness is coupled with strong management support for team objectives, teams tend to be more productive.

The second development is the emergence of **norms**, informal but often powerful standards of conduct that members share and use to guide their behavior. Norms define acceptable behavior by setting limits, identifying values, and clarifying expectations. By encouraging consistent behavior, norms boost efficiency and help ensure the group's survival. Individuals who deviate from these norms can find themselves ridiculed, isolated, or even removed from the group entirely. (This fear is the leading cause of groupthink, by the way.) Norms can be established in various ways: from early behaviors that set precedents for future actions, from significant events in the team's history, from behaviors that come to the team through outside influences, and from a leader's or member's explicit statements that have an impact on other members.[40]

cohesiveness
A measure of how committed team members are to their team's goals.

norms
Informal standards of conduct that guide team behavior.

TEAM CONFLICT

As teams mature and go about their work, conflicts can arise. Although the term *conflict* sounds negative, conflict isn't necessarily bad. It can be *constructive* if it brings important issues into the open, increases the involvement of team members, and generates creative ideas for solving a problem. Teamwork isn't necessarily about happiness and harmony; even teams that have some interpersonal friction can excel if they have effective leadership and team players committed to strong results. As teamwork experts Andy Boynton and Bill Fischer put it, "Virtuoso teams are not about getting polite results."[41]

In contrast, conflict is *destructive* if it diverts energy from more important issues, destroys the morale of teams or individual team members, or polarizes or divides the team.[42] Destructive conflict can lead to *win-lose* or *lose-lose* outcomes, in which one or both sides lose, to the detriment of the entire team. If you approach conflict with the idea that both sides can satisfy their goals to at least some extent (a *win-win strategy*), you can minimize losses for everyone. For a win-win strategy to work, everybody must believe that (1) it's possible to find a solution that both parties can accept, (2) cooperation is better for the organization than competition, (3) the other party can be trusted, and (4) greater power or status doesn't entitle one party to impose a solution.

Conflict within teams is common as people bring different ideas and expectations to the table. Constructive conflict can help a team generate fresh ideas and devise new solutions, but destructive conflict can divide a team and slow or destroy its progress.

Causes of Team Conflict

Team conflict can arise for a number of reasons. First, individuals may feel they are in competition for scarce or declining resources, such as money, information, and supplies. Second, team members may disagree over responsibilities. Third, poor communication can lead to misunderstandings and misperceptions. In addition, withholding information can undermine trust among members. Fourth, basic differences in values, attitudes, and personalities may lead to clashes. Fifth, power struggles may result when one party questions the authority of another or when people or teams with limited authority attempt to increase their power or exert more influence. Sixth, conflicts can arise because individual team members are pursuing different goals.[43]

Solutions to Team Conflict

As with any other human relationship, the way a team approaches conflict depends to a large degree on how well the team was functioning in the first place. A strong, healthy team is more likely to view a conflict as simply another challenge to overcome—and it can emerge from the conflict even stronger than before. In contrast, a generally dysfunctional team can disintegrate even further when faced with a new source of conflict.

The following seven measures can help team members successfully resolve conflict:

- **Proactive attention.** Deal with minor conflict before it becomes major conflict.
- **Communication.** Get those directly involved in a conflict to participate in resolving it.
- **Openness.** Get feelings out in the open before dealing with the main issues.
- **Research.** Seek factual reasons for a problem before seeking solutions.
- **Flexibility.** Don't let anyone lock into a position before considering other solutions.
- **Fair play.** Insist on fair outcomes and don't let anyone avoid a fair solution by hiding behind the rules.
- **Alliance.** Get opponents to fight together against an "outside force" instead of against each other.

Team members and team leaders can also take several steps to prevent conflicts. First, by establishing clear goals that require the efforts of every member, the team reduces the chance that members will battle over their objectives or roles. Second, by developing well-defined tasks for each member, the team leader ensures that all parties are aware of their responsibilities and the limits of their authority. Finally, by facilitating open communication, the team leader can ensure that all members understand their own tasks and objectives as well as those of their teammates. Communication builds respect and tolerance, and it provides a forum for bringing misunderstandings into the open before they turn into full-blown conflicts.

REAL-TIME UPDATES

Learn More by Listening to This Podcast

Keep small tiffs from escalating into major battles

Dr. Daneen Skube explains how to keep adversarial relationships from going off track. Go to http://real-timeupdates.com/bia8 and click on Learn More in the Students section.

 Checkpoint

LEARNING OBJECTIVE 5: Review the five stages of team development, and explain why conflict can arise in team settings.

SUMMARY: Several models have been proposed to describe the stages of team development; the well-known model defined by researcher Bruce Tuckman identifies the stages as *forming, storming, norming, performing,* and *adjourning.* In the forming stage, team members become acquainted with each other and with the group's purpose. In the storming stage, conflict often arises as coalitions and power struggles develop. In the norming stage, conflicts are resolved and harmony develops. In the performing stage, members focus on achieving the team's goals. In the adjourning stage, the team dissolves on completion of its task. Conflict can arise from competition for scarce resources; confusion over task responsibility; poor communication and misinformation; differences in values, attitudes, and personalities; power struggles; and incompatible goals.

CRITICAL THINKING: (1) How can a team leader know when to step in when conflict arises and when to step back and let the issue work itself out? (2) What are the risks of not giving new teams the time and opportunity to "storm" and "norm" before tackling the work they've been assigned?

IT'S YOUR BUSINESS: (1) Have you ever had to be teammates (in any activity) with someone you simply didn't like on a personal level? If so, how did this situation affect your performance as a team member? (2) Have you ever had to adapt your personality in order to succeed on a particular team? Was this a positive or negative experience?

KEY TERMS TO KNOW: cohesiveness, norms

Managing an Unstructured Organization

Much of the thinking in past decades about organization strategies in business centered on the best way to structure a company to compete effectively and operate efficiently. However, many companies are concluding that the best way to organize might be with little or no structure at all, at least in terms of the traditional forms. Such **unstructured organizations** are using digital technologies—and global socioeconomic changes enabled by these technologies—to rapidly form and re-form work patterns that bear almost no resemblance to the classic structures.

These innovators are experimenting with various combinations of virtual organizations, networked organizations, crowdsourcing, outsourcing, and *hyperspecialization*, the division of work into narrowly focused tasks that can be assigned to specialists who become highly skilled at those discrete tasks.[44] The new "formless forms" are enabled by cloud computing, mobile communication, online collaboration platforms, and all manner of social networking tools. All of these elements have been in use for some time, but the mashup of new thinking and new technology is unleashing them in revolutionary ways. In a sense, by binding together a temporary organization, these technologies take the place of the lines and boxes that define a traditional organization chart.

Just about any category and skill level of work seems a possible candidate for these new approaches—and particularly those that can be expressed digitally. Professions and functions already being affected include software development, product design, visual design, scientific research, legal research, business writing, clerical work, and customer support.[45]

For example, a solo entrepreneur can now quickly assemble a product development team to conceptualize and design a product, then immediately disassemble that team and build a manufacturing team to make the product, and then assemble a sales and customer support team to get the product on the market—all without hiring a single employee. Moreover, this entrepreneur could tap into some of the best technical talent in the world, with top scientists, engineers, and software developers competing to see who can do the best job on the new product. And rather than taking months to establish a company by recruiting employees, leasing office space, hiring supervisors, buying computers, setting up a payroll system, training staffers, and doing all the many other tasks involved in running a conventional company, this entrepreneur could sit at home in his or her pajamas and in a matter of days create an essentially formless company that successfully competes in the global marketplace.

The software development company TopCoder (**www.topcoder.com**) offers a great illustration of the potential of this new way of working. TopCoder boasts a membership of more than a half million computer scientists and software engineers (including many who are still in college), representing virtually every country in the world. Clients such as our pajama-clad entrepreneur present TopCoder with one or more design challenges, and the members then compete to come up with the best solutions.[46] Instead of auditioning several regular vendors and hoping to make the right choice or hiring a small staff of generalists and hoping they'll be able to handle the many specialized tasks involved in developing

6 | LEARNING OBJECTIVE

Explain the concept of an unstructured organization, and identify the major benefits and challenges of taking this approach.

unstructured organization
An organization that doesn't have a conventional structure but instead assembles talent as needed from the open market; the virtual and networked organizational concepts taken to the extreme.

the software for a new product, our entrepreneur could get the best of the best working on each part of the design. And when the design work is completed, the various TopCoder members move on to compete on other client projects, and the entrepreneur moves on to assembling teams of manufacturing and marketing specialists.

Just where these changes are taking the business enterprise is difficult to guess because the revolution is still under way. Some firms may adopt these structureless approaches extensively, while others may use them for specific projects. Even if you spend your career in a conventionally structured company, these changes are likely to affect you because they are accelerating the pace of business, influencing the worldwide talent market, and even changing the nature of work itself in some cases (such as introducing project-by-project talent competition).

The following sections take a look at some of the potential benefits and points of concern that are emerging in relation to these new approaches to organization (see Exhibit 8.9 for a summary).

POTENTIAL BENEFITS OF UNSTRUCTURED ORGANIZATIONS

Unstructured organization promises a number of benefits for firms of all sizes, from entrepreneurs who apply the concept to their entire operations to larger firms that use it for specific parts of the company or individual projects:[47]

- **Increased agility.** In many instances, virtual organizations can be assembled, reconfigured as needed, and disassembled much faster than a conventional employee-based

---

| **EXHIBIT 8.9** | **Benefits and Challenges of Unstructured Organizations** |

The unstructured organization is an extreme version of the virtual and networked models, in which a company assembles freelance talent as needed from the open market rather than hiring and organizing employees in a conventional organizational structure.

Potential Benefits		Potential Challenges	
For Companies	**For Workers**	**For Companies**	**For Workers**
• **Increased agility:** Companies can respond to or create opportunities faster and then reorganize and move on when needed.	• **Performance-based evaluation:** The only thing that matters is getting the job done.	• **Complexity and control issues:** Workers often have competing demands on their time and attention, and managers lack many of the organizational control and incentive "levers" that a regular company has.	• **Uncertainty:** Workers can't be sure they'll have work from one project to the next.
• **Lower fixed costs:** Fewer employees means fewer bills to pay every month.	• **Freedom and flexibility:** Workers have more leeway in choosing which projects they want and how much they want to work.	• **Uncertainty:** Without staff at the ready, companies won't always know if they'll be able to get the talent they need.	• **Loss of meaning and connection:** Independent workers don't get the same sense of working together for a larger, shared purpose that employees get.
• **More flexible capacity management:** Firms can ramp capacity up and down more quickly and with less trauma.	• **Access to more interesting and more fulfilling work:** Workers can connect with opportunities that might be unreachable otherwise.	• **Diminished loyalty:** Managers have to deal with a workforce that doesn't have the same sense of loyalty to the organization that many full-time employees do.	• **Diminished loyalty:** Workers don't have the same sense employees often do that an organization is looking out for them and will reward sacrifices and effort above and beyond contractual obligations.
• **Access to star talent:** Managers can "rent" top talent that is too expensive to hire full time or unwilling to work full time.		• **Management succession:** Companies with fewer employees will find it harder to groom replacement managers and executives.	• **Career development:** Without full-time employers to guide, support, and train them, workers are left to fend for themselves and to keep their skills current at their own expense.
• **Benefiting from competition:** Firms can stage competitions in talent markets to see who can devise the best solutions to problems.		• **Accountability and liability:** Unstructured organizations lack the built-in accountability of conventional structures, and the distribution of work among multiple independent parties could create liability concerns.	

Sources: Darren Dahl, "Want a Job? Let the Bidding Begin," *Inc.*, March 2011, 93–96; Thomas W. Malone, Robert J. Laubacher, and Tammy Johns, "The Age of Hyperspecialization," *Harvard Business Review*, July–August 2011, 56–65; Jennifer Wang, "The Solution to the Innovator's Dilemma," *Entrepreneur*, August 2011, 24–32; Marjorie Derven, "Managing the Matrix in the New Normal," *T+D*, July 2010, 42–47.

organization can be created, changed, or dismantled. This agility makes it easier to jump on emerging market trends and then change course when the market changes again.

- **Lower fixed costs and more flexible capacity management.** Hiring employees to build organizational capacity increases a company's *fixed costs*, those costs that are incurred regardless of production or sales volumes. With the unstructured approach, companies have much more flexibility in adjusting their expense levels to match revenue levels.
- **Access to otherwise unreachable talent.** "Talent markets" such as TopCoder give many more companies access to highly developed and often hyperspecialized talents. Companies that might never be able to attract or afford top experts in a field can essentially rent them project by project instead.
- **Benefits of competition.** Whereas most employees are motivated to do good work most of the time, independent individuals working through TopCoder, Guru (www .guru.com), Upwork (www.upwork.com), and other aggregators must do their best on every single project—and compete with other independents in what is essentially a global marketplace—or risk not getting more assignments. Companies that engage contract talent clearly benefit from this competition. In addition, talent markets such as TopCoder and InnoCentive actually structure projects as competitions, in which potential solution providers compete to offer the best ideas and work products.

For workers, the unstructured model also offers several potential benefits:[48]

- **Performance-based evaluation.** Workers tend to be evaluated almost entirely on measurable performance, project by project—on what they can do for a client, not on who they know in the executive suite, where they went to college, or what they did last year.
- **Freedom and flexibility.** The flip side of agility for companies is extreme flexibility for workers, particularly after they establish themselves in a field. Within the limits of financial need and project availability, of course, independent contractors can often pick and choose the clients and projects that interest them most and decide how much or how little they want to work.
- **Access to jobs that might be otherwise unattainable.** For people geographically removed from major employment centers, finding decent employment can be a serious challenge. The distributed, virtual approach gives people in rural areas and small towns greater access to job opportunities.

POTENTIAL CHALLENGES OF UNSTRUCTURED ORGANIZATIONS

For all its benefits, the unstructured approach presents several potential drawbacks, some of them considerable. These challenges will discourage many companies and workers from taking this route, and they make it more difficult for those who do:[49]

- **Complexity and control issues.** Unstructured organizations can be even more complex than matrix organizations (see page 177) because workers not only have multiple bosses but report to multiple bosses in multiple companies. In addition, even though companies can in effect hire and fire independent contractors more easily, they have less control over this talent than they have over permanent employees.
- **Uncertainty.** Without full-time staff at the ready, companies won't always know if they can get the talent they need for upcoming projects. Conversely, workers won't always know if they'll have a job from one project to the next.
- **Loss of meaning and connection.** Being a full-time employee of an organization means more than just employment to many people. Companies also provide a social structure that is as close as family for some employees. Moreover, the opportunity to help an organization succeed over the long haul, to work with others for a greater purpose, is an important motivator and provides a sense of pride for many employees. Independent contractors who move from project to project don't have the chance to form such bonds.

- **Diminished loyalty.** The bond that develops between employers and employees over time creates a sense of loyalty that can carry both parties through hard times. Employers often make accommodations for employees going through tough personal circumstances, for instance. And many employees are willing to make or at least accept short-term sacrifices that benefit their companies in the long term (such as helping colleagues in addition to doing their own work or accepting pay reductions during periods of slow sales). However, this sense of "all for one and one for all" is not likely to factor heavily in most unstructured scenarios, where workers are more like competing vendors than members of a family.
- **Career development.** Conventional organizations do much more than just put resources in place to tackle one project after another. They invest in employees over months or years, giving them time and opportunities to develop deep knowledge and skills, with the idea that the investment will pay off in the long term. However, independent contractors are responsible for developing themselves, while they're busy making a living, so keeping up with developments in their professions presents a greater burden than it does for typical employees.
- **Management succession.** As companies develop their employees, they also groom future managers and executives who understand both the company internally and its multiple external environments. Without these development channels in place, companies could be hard pressed to replace upper managers when the time comes.
- **Accountability and liability.** Conventional structures tend to have clear lines of accountability up and down the chain of command (meaning who is responsible if things go awry) and clear assignments of legal or financial liability in the event of major foul-ups. However, the situation might not be quite so clear in an unstructured organization that relies on a temporary assemblage of independent companies and contractors.

Although these challenges should not be taken lightly by companies or workers, they are likely to be manageable in enough different scenarios that the unstructured approach will catch on in more and more industries. Exactly where unstructured organizations will take the world of business will be interesting to see.

✔ Checkpoint

LEARNING OBJECTIVE 6: Explain the concept of an unstructured organization, and identify the major benefits and challenges of taking this approach.

SUMMARY: An unstructured organization doesn't rely on conventional organizational structures to assemble the resources needed to pursue business goals. Instead, it assembles independent contractors or companies, as needed, for specific tasks or functions, relying on electronic communications to replace much of the structural linkages in a conventional company. The potential benefits for companies are increased agility, lower fixed costs and more flexible capacity management, access to otherwise unreachable talent, and the benefits of competition among workers or service providers. For workers, the benefits include performance-based evaluation of their efforts, more freedom and flexibility to choose which projects to work on and how much to work, and access to jobs that might be otherwise unattainable. The potential disadvantages of the unstructured approach include complexity and control issues for managers, greater uncertainty for companies and workers, the loss of meaning and connection to a greater purpose for employees, diminished loyalty for both employers and employees, uncertainties in career development and management succession, and concerns over accountability and liability.

CRITICAL THINKING: (1) "Unstructured organization" is something of a contradiction in terms; are such companies still "organized" if they have no permanent structure? Why or why not? (2) How can workers develop marketable skills if they work as independent contractors?

IT'S YOUR BUSINESS: (1) Where do you think you would be most comfortable, as a regular employee in a conventionally structured firm or as an independent contractor, moving from project to project? Why? (2) Assume that you went to work for a conventional employer and then left to work as an independent contractor as soon as you developed enough of a skill set to make it on your own. (Assume as well that you were not violating any sort of employment contract and were free to leave.) Would you have any ethical concerns about leaving an employer who had invested in your professional development? Why or why not?

KEY TERM TO KNOW: unstructured organization

BEHIND THE SCENES
AN INNOVATIVE COLLABORATION PLATFORM AT CEMEX "MAKES A BIG COMPANY LOOK LIKE A SMALL COMPANY"

After an ambitious program of expansion in the 1990s, the Mexican concrete and cement producer Cemex had grown into a global colossus, with facilities in more than 50 countries and business relationships in more than 100. To tackle the strategic challenges of continuous product innovation, improvements in operating efficiency, and reductions in its environmental impact, company leaders knew they needed to get the most from Cemex's 44,000 employees.

To help those far-flung employees learn from one another and work effectively in teams, Cemex created a comprehensive online collaboration platform called Shift. The system combines social networking, wikis, blogs, a Twitter-like microblogging tool, social bookmarking, videoconferencing, a trend-spotting tool called Shift Radar, and more. A custom mobile app lets employees access the system wherever their work takes them.

By connecting people and information quickly and easily, Shift helps overcome the barriers of geography, time zones, and organizational boundaries. Employees and managers can tap into expertise anywhere in the company, workers with similar responsibilities can share ideas on improving operations, and problems and opportunities can be identified and brought to management attention in much less time.

Technology is only part of the solution, however. Many companies that have implemented social platforms struggle to get employees to change ingrained behaviors and use the new tools. By getting top-level executives on board early, Cemex achieved nearly universal adoption, with 95 percent of employees using Shift and forming nearly 3,000 online communities based on technical specialties and shared interests. That level of

engagement is paying off in numerous ways, such as launching a new global brand of ready-mix concrete in one-third the expected time, nearly tripling the company's use of renewable energy, and reducing carbon dioxide emissions by almost 2 million metric tons.

Perhaps most impressive, Shift has lived up to its name by shifting the entrenched hierarchical culture of a large, old-school company to a more agile and responsive social business that is better prepared to face the future in its highly competitive markets. As Gilberto Garcia, Cemex's innovation director puts it, social collaboration "can make a big company look like a small company," by connecting people and ensuring the free exchange of ideas.[50]

Critical Thinking Questions

8-1. Why might it be difficult to implement a system like Shift in a well-established company such as Cemex?

8-2. Should Cemex open Shift up to business partners and customers, in addition to employees? Why or why not? If it did, what factors would the company have to consider first?

8-3. How could Cemex use Shift to recruit new employees?

LEARN MORE ONLINE

Read more about Shift at **http://shiftevolution.cemexlabs.com**. How is Shift similar to the social media and social networking systems you use in your personal life? How does it differ? Would you feel comfortable collaborating with colleagues you've never met using a system like this?

KEY TERMS

agile organization (171)
centralization (174)
chain of command (173)

cohesiveness (187)
committee (180)
core competencies (172)

MyBizLab®

To complete the problems with the ⭐, go to EOC Discussion Questions in the MyLab.

TEST YOUR KNOWLEDGE

Questions for Review

8-4. What is an agile organization?

8-5. What are the characteristics of tall organizations and flat organizations?

8-6. What are the advantages and disadvantages of work specialization?

8-7. What are the advantages and disadvantages of functional departmentalization?

8-8. What are the potential benefits and potential disadvantages of the unstructured organizational model?

Questions for Analysis

8-9. Why is it important for companies to decide on their core competencies before choosing an organization structure?

8-10. How can a virtual organization reduce costs?

8-11. What can managers do to help teams work more effectively?

8-12. How can companies benefit from using virtual teams?

⭐ **8-13.** **Ethical Considerations.** A company executive accidentally emailed you a confidential spreadsheet with the salaries of all the employees in the company. You took only a quick peek before deleting it, but you looked long enough to discover that other managers at your level are earning anywhere from 10 to 40 percent more than you, even though you've been at the company longer than any of them. Based on this discovery, you believe you deserve consideration for a raise. How will you handle the situation?

Questions for Application

8-14. You are the leader of a cross-functional work team whose goal is to find ways of lowering production costs. Your team of eight employees has become mired in the storming stage. The team members disagree on how to approach the task, and they are starting to splinter into factions, each pursuing its own goals. What can you do to help the team move forward?

8-15. You've recently accepted a job as the U.S. sales manager for a German manufacturing company. One of your first assignments is serving on a virtual problem-solving team with colleagues from Germany, France, Japan, and South Korea. Budgets are tight, so you won't have the opportunity to meet with your teammates in person to get to know one another. What steps can you take to help the team develop into a cohesive and efficient unit?

⭐ **8-16.** **Concept Integration.** One of your competitors has approached you with a merger proposal. The economies of scale would be terrific. So are the growth possibilities. There's just one issue to be resolved. Your competitor is organized under a flat structure and uses lots of cross-functional teams. Your company is organized under a traditional tall structure that is departmentalized by function. Using your knowledge about culture clash (see page 112), what are the likely issues you will encounter if these two organizations are merged?

⭐ **8-17.** **Concept Integration.** Chapter 7 discussed several styles of leadership: autocratic, democratic, and laissez-faire. Using your knowledge about the differences in these leadership styles, which style would you expect to find under the following organization structures: (a) tall organization with departmentalization by function, (b) tall organization with departmentalization by matrix, (c) flat organization, and (d) self-directed teams?

EXPAND YOUR KNOWLEDGE

Discovering Career Opportunities

Management jobs require a range of skills and experience, and, not surprisingly, the demands increase with the scope and scale of the opportunity. Use a website such as Indeed or Simply Hired to find three supervisor or management jobs in diff erent companies or industries. Study the listed qualifications, then choose which of the three jobs is the most appealing to you. Compare the requirements of this job with your current qualifications and outline a plan (additional education or stepping-stone positions) you could purse to develop the skills and experience to land your chosen job.

Improving Your Tech Insights: Mobile Collaboration

Mobile devices gives companies a new add another set of options for team projects and other collaborative efforts, particularly when used with cloud computing. Mobility lets workers participate in online brainstorming sessions, seminars, and other formal or informal events from wherever they happen to be at the time. This flexibility can be particularly helpful during the review and production stages of major projects, when deadlines are looming and decisions and revisions need to be made quickly. Find an example of a company that is using mobile devices for team collaboration. In an email to your instructor, identify at least two business benefits that this mobile solution provides.

PRACTICE YOUR SKILLS

Sharpening Your Communication Skills

In group meetings, some of your colleagues have a habit of interrupting and arguing with the speaker, taking credit for ideas that aren't theirs, and shooting down ideas they don't agree with. You're the newest person in the group and not sure if this is accepted behavior in this company, but it concerns you both personally and professionally. Should you go with the flow and adopt their behavior or stick with your own communication style, even though you might get lost in the noise? In two paragraphs, explain the pros and cons of both approaches.

Building Your Team Skills

What's the most effective organization structure for your college or university? With your team, obtain a copy of your school's organization chart. If this chart is not readily available, gather information by talking with people in administration and then draw your own chart of the organization structure.

Analyze the chart in terms of span of management. Is your school a flat or a tall organization? Is this organization structure appropriate for your school? Does decision making tend to be centralized or decentralized in your school? Do you agree with this approach to decision making?

Finally, investigate the use of formal and informal teams in your school. Are there any problem-solving teams, task forces, or committees at work in your school? Are any teams self-directed or virtual? How much authority do these teams have to make decisions? What is the purpose of teamwork in your school? What kinds of goals do these teams have?

Share your team's findings during a brief classroom presentation and then compare the findings of all teams. Is there agreement on the appropriate organization structure for your school?

Developing Your Research Skills

Although teamwork can benefit many organizations, introducing and managing team structures can be a real challenge. Search past issues of business journals or newspapers (print or online editions) to locate articles about how an organization has overcome problems with teams.

8-18. Why did the organization originally introduce teams? What types of teams are being used?

8-19. What problems did each organization encounter in trying to implement teams? How did the organization deal with these problems?

8-20. Have the teams been successful from management's perspective? From the employees' perspective? What effect has teamwork had on the company, its customers, and its products?

MyBizLab®

Go to the Assignments section of your MyLab to complete these writing exercises.

8-21. What are some possible benefits and risks of having teams compete against each other, such as having the sales teams from various regions compete to add the most new customers?

8-22. Review the "Loss of Meaning and Connection" bullet point on page 191 in the discussion of the potential challenges of unstructured organizations. If you were planning to launch an unstructured organization, what steps could you take to help ensure that any independent contractors you hire on a project-by-project basis will have the same pride in their work that a dedicated, full-time employee would have?

ENDNOTES

1. "Company Profile," Cemex website, accessed 6 April 2015, www.cemex.com; "About Shift," Cemex website, accessed 6 April 2015, www.cemex.com; *Cemex: Building the Future*, accessed 11 May 2013, www.cemex.com; Cemex Shift Twitter account, https://twitter.com/CX_Shift, accessed 6 April 2015; Dion Hinchcliffe, "Social Business Success: CEMEX," *ZDNet*, 1 February 2012, www.zdnet.com; "Cemex and Becoming a Social Business with IBM Software," video embedded in Jesus Gilberto Garcia, Miguel Angel Lozano Martinez, and Arturo San Vicente, "Shift Changes the Way Cemex Works," *Management Exchange*, 15 July 2011, www.managementexchange.com; Debra Donston-Miller, "Social Business Leader Cemex Keeps Ideas Flowing," *InformationWeek*, 6 November 2012, www.informationweek.co.uk.

2. "Benefits of Outsourcing Payroll," *Practical Accountant*, November 2008, SR9.

3. Frog Design website, accessed 4 April 2015, www.frogdesign.com.

4. Stephen P. Robbins and David A. DeCenzo, *Management*, 4th ed. (Upper Saddle River, N.J.: Pearson Prentice Hall, 2004), 142–143.

5. Charles R. Greer and W. Richard Plunkett, *Supervision: Diversity and Teams in the Workplace*, 10th ed. (Upper Saddle River, N.J.: Prentice Hall, 2003), 77.

6. Caroline Ellis, "The Flattening Corporation," *MIT Sloan Management Review*, Summer 2003, 5.

7. "Container Store's Hiring Secret," *Fortune* video, accessed 23 August 2011, http://money.cnn.com.

8. "Why Middle Managers May Be the Most Important People in Your Company," Knowledge@Wharton, 25 May 2011, http://knowledge.wharton.upenn.edu.

9. Gareth R. Jones, *Organizational Theory, Design, and Change*, 4th ed. (Upper Saddle River, N.J.: Pearson Prentice Hall, 2004), 109.

10. Jones, *Organizational Theory, Design, and Change*, 109–111.

11. Richard L. Daft, *Management*, 6th ed. (Mason, Ohio: South-Western, 2003), 320.

12. Jones, *Organizational Theory, Design, and Change*, 163.

13. Jones, *Organizational Theory, Design, and Change*, 167.

14. "Our Businesses," Chevron website, accessed 4 November 2013, www.chevron.com.

15. Daft, *Management*, 324–327.

16. Marjorie Derven, "Managing the Matrix in the New Normal," *T+D*, July 2010, 42–47.

17. Jerald Greenberg and Robert A. Baron, *Behavior in Organizations*, 8th ed. (Upper Saddle River, N.J.: Prentice Hall, 2003), 558–560; Daft, *Management*, 329.

18. Derven, "Managing the Matrix in the New Normal."

19. Pete Engardio and Bruce Einhorn, "Outsourcing Innovation," *BusinessWeek*, 21 March 2005, 84–94.

20. Stephen P. Robbins, *Essentials of Organizational Behavior*, 6th ed. (Upper Saddle River, N.J.: Prentice Hall, 2000), 105.

21. Greer and Plunkett, *Supervision*, 293.

22. Steven A. Frankforter and Sandra L. Christensen, "Finding Competitive Advantage in Self-Managed Work Teams," *Business Forum*, 2005, Vol. 27, Issue 1, 20–24.

23. Daft, *Management*, 594; Robbins and DeCenzo, *Fundamentals of Management*, 336.

24. Daft, *Management*, 618; Robbins and DeCenzo, *Fundamentals of Management*, 262.

25. Morten T. Hansen, "When Internal Collaboration Is Bad for Your Company," *Harvard Business Review*, April 2009, 82–88.

26. Jerry Fjermestad, "Virtual Leadership for a Virtual Workforce," *Chief Learning Officer*, March 2009, 36–39.

27. Jenny Goodbody, "Critical Success Factors for Global Virtual Teams," *Strategic Communication Management*, February/March 2005, 18–21; Ann Majchrzak, Arvind Malhotra, Jeffrey Stamps, and Jessica Lipnack, "Can Absence Make a Team Grow Stronger?" *Harvard Business Review*, May 2004, 131–137.

28. Richard McDermott and Douglas Archibald, "Harnessing Your Staff's Informal Networks," *Harvard Business Review*, March 2010, 82–89.

29. Blair Hanley Frank, "Zappos Ditches Job Posts, replaces Them with a Social Network," *GeekWire*, 27 May 2014, www.geekwire.com; Tony Hsieh, "Why I Sold Zappos," *Inc.*, 1 June 2010, www.inc.com.

30. Robbins and DeCenzo, *Fundamentals of Management*, 257–258; Daft, *Management*, 634–636.

31. "Groups Best at Complex Problems," *Industrial Engineer*, June 2006, 14.

32. Max Landsberg and Madeline Pfau, "Developing Diversity: Lessons from Top Teams," *Strategy + Business*, Winter 2005, 10–12.

33. Derven, "Managing the Matrix in the New Normal"; Robert Kreitner, *Management*, 9th ed. (Boston: Houghton Mifflin, 2004), 475–481; Daft, *Management*, 635–636.

34. Liane Davey, "Toxic Teams," *Leadership Excellence*, 2 November 2012, 3.

35. Lynda Gratton and Tamara J. Erickson, "8 Ways to Build Collaborative Teams," *Harvard Business Review*, November 2007, 100–109.

36. Jon R. Katzenbach and Douglas K. Smith, "The Discipline of Teams," *Harvard Business Review*, July/August 2005, 162–171; Laird Mealiea and Ramon Baltazar, "A Strategic Guide for Building Effective Teams," *Public Personnel Management*, Summer 2005, 141–160; Larry Cole and Michael Cole, "Why Is the Teamwork Buzz Word Not Working?" *Communication World*, February/March 1999, 29; Patricia Buhler, "Managing in the 90s: Creating

Flexibility in Today's Workplace," *Supervision*, January 1997, 24+; Allison W. Amason, Allen C. Hochwarter, Wayne A. Thompson, and Kenneth R. Harrison, "Conflict: An Important Dimension in Successful Management Teams," *Organizational Dynamics*, Autumn 1995, 20+.

37. Jared Sandberg, "Some Ideas Are So Bad That Only a Team Effort Can Account for Them," *Wall Street Journal*, 29 September 2004, B1.

38. David Engel, Anita Williams Woolley, Lisa X. Jing, Christopher F. Chabris, and Thomas W. Malone, "Reading the Mind in the Eyes or Reading between the Lines? Theory of Mind Predicts Collective Intelligence Equally Well Online and Face-To-Face," *Plos One*, 16 December 2014, http://journals.plos.org.

39. Mark K. Smith, "Bruce W. Tuckman—Forming, Storming, Norming, and Performing in Groups," Infed.org, accessed 5 July 2005, www.infed.org; Robbins and DeCenzo, *Fundamentals of Management*, 258–259; Daft, *Management*, 625–627.

40. Jones, *Organizational Theory, Design, and Change*, 112–113; Greenberg and Baron, *Behavior in Organizations*, 280–281; Daft, *Management*, 629–631.

41. Andy Boynton and Bill Fischer, *Virtuoso Teams: Lessons from Teams That Changed Their Worlds* (Harrow, UK: FT Prentice Hall, 2005), 10.

42. Thomas K. Capozzoli, "Conflict Resolution—A Key Ingredient in Successful Teams," *Supervision*, November 1999, 14–16.

43. Daft, *Management*, 631–632.

44. Darren Dahl, "Want a Job? Let the Bidding Begin," *Inc.*, March 2011, 93–96; Thomas W. Malone, Robert J. Laubacher, and Tammy Johns, "The Age of Hyperspecialization," *Harvard Business Review*, July–August 2011, 56–65.

45. Malone et al., "The Age of Hyperspecialization."

46. TopCoder website, accessed 4 November 2013, www.topcoder.com.

47. Dahl, "Want a Job? Let the Bidding Begin"; Malone et al., "The Age of Hyperspecialization"; Jennifer Wang, "The Solution to the Innovator's Dilemma," *Entrepreneur*, August 2011, 24–32; Derven, "Managing the Matrix in the New Normal."

48. "LiveOps and Vision Perry Create New Work Opportunities for Rural Tennessee," LiveOps press release, 18 July 2011, www.liveops.com; Malone et al., "The Age of Hyperspecialization."

49. Dahl, "Want a Job? Let the Bidding Begin"; Malone et al., "The Age of Hyperspecialization"; Wang, "The Solution to the Innovator's Dilemma"; Derven, "Managing the Matrix in the New Normal."

50. See Note 1.

LEARNING OBJECTIVES   After studying this chapter, you will be able to

1 Explain the systems perspective, and identify seven principles of systems thinking that can improve your skills as a manager.

2 Describe the *value chain* and *value web* concepts, and discuss the controversy over offshoring.

3 Define *supply chain management*, and explain its strategic importance.

4 Identify the major planning decisions in production and operations management.

5 Explain the unique challenges of service delivery.

6 Define *quality*, explain the challenge of quality and product complexity, and identify four major tools and strategies for ensuring product quality.

BEHIND THE SCENES CUSTOMIZING DREAMS AT KIESEL GUITARS

Vasileios Karafillidis/Shutterstock

Kiesel offers personalized guitars at affordable prices through a combination of sophisticated production systems and old-world handicraft.

www.carvinguitars.com

After beginning guitarists have mastered the nuances of "Mary Had a Little Lamb" and set their sights on making serious music, they often encounter a serious equipment dilemma. Low-cost, beginner guitars lack the materials and workmanship needed to produce top-quality sounds. Some are difficult to keep in tune, and some cannot produce true notes all the way up and down the neck. Plus, they just aren't very cool. Nobody wants to jump on stage in front of 50,000 screaming fans with a guitar purchased at the local discount store.

And so the shopping begins, as the aspiring guitarist looks to find a better "axe." As with just about every product category these days, the array of choices is dizzying. For a few hundred dollars, budding musicians can choose from several imports that offer improved quality. Jumping up toward $1,000 to $2,000, they can enter the world of such classic American brands as Fender, Gibson, and Martin—a world that goes up to $10,000 and beyond for limited-edition models. Musicians with that much to spend and several months to wait can also hire skilled instrument builders known as *luthiers* to create custom guitars that reflect their individual personalities and playing styles. Luthiers can custom-craft just about any attribute a guitarist might want, from the types of wood for the body to the radius of the fingerboard.

But what if our superstar-in-training wants it all: world-class quality, the personalized touch of a custom guitar, and a midrange price tag, without the long delays associated with handcrafted instruments?

That "sweet spot" in the guitar market is the territory staked out by Kiesel Guitars, a San Diego company that has been in the instrument business for nearly 70 years. How can Kiesel profitably do business in this seemingly impossible market segment? How could the company quickly customize guitars and sell them in the $750–$1,500-range without compromising quality?[1]

INTRODUCTION

Kiesel Guitars (profiled in the chapter-opening Behind the Scenes) faced a classic systems challenge: how to design and operate business processes that would enable the company to deliver its unique value to customers. This chapter starts with an overview of systems concepts that every manager can use in any functional area; it then explores systems-related issues in the production function, including value chains and value webs, supply chain management, production and operations management, services delivery, and product and process quality.

The Systems View of Business

1 LEARNING OBJECTIVE

Explain the systems perspective, and identify seven principles of systems thinking that can improve your skills as a manager.

One of the most important skills you can develop as a manager is the ability to view business from a systems perspective. A **system** is an interconnected and coordinated set of *elements* and *processes* that convert *inputs* into desired *outputs*. A company is made up of numerous individual systems in the various functional areas, not only in manufacturing or operations but also in engineering, marketing, accounting, and other areas that together constitute the overall system that is the company itself. Each of these individual systems can also be thought of as a *subsystem* of the overall business.

system
An interconnected and coordinated set of *elements* and *processes* that converts *inputs* to desired *outputs*.

THINKING IN SYSTEMS

To grasp the power of systems thinking, consider a point, a line, and a circle (see Exhibit 9.1 on the next page). If you poked your head into a nearby office building, what would this snapshot tell you? You could see only one part of the entire operation—and only at this one moment in time. You might see people in the advertising department working on plans for a new ad campaign or people in the accounting department juggling numbers in spreadsheets, but neither view would tell you much about what it takes to complete these tasks or how that department interacts with the rest of the company.

If you stood and observed for several days, though, you could start to get a sense of how people do their jobs in a department. In the advertising department, for instance, you could watch as the staff transforms ideas, information, and goals into a plan that leads to the creation of a new online advertising campaign. Your "point" view would thereby extend into a "line" view, with multiple points connected in sequence. However, you still wouldn't have a complete picture of the entire process in action. Was the campaign successful? What did the marketing department learn from the campaign that could help it do even better next time? To see the process operate over and over, you need to connect the end of the line (the completion of this ad campaign) back to the beginning of the line (the start of the next ad campaign) to create a circle. Now you're beginning to form a systems view of what this department does and how its performance can be improved.

This circular view helps you understand the advertising system better, but it still isn't complete, because it doesn't show you how the advertising system affects the rest of the company and vice versa. For instance, did the finance department provide enough money to run the ad campaign? Was the information technology group prepared to handle the surge in website traffic? Was the manufacturing department ready with enough materials to build the product after customers started placing orders? Were the sales and customer service departments ready to handle the increase in their workloads? All of these subsystems connect to form the overall business system. Only by looking at the interconnected business system can you judge whether the ad campaign was a success for the company as a whole.

EXHIBIT 9.1	From Point to Line to Circle: The Systems View

The systems view considers all the steps in a process and "closes the loop" by providing feedback from the output of one cycle back to the input of the next cycle.

Point view: A single task is completed in isolation.

Line view: A series of related tasks are completed in succession.

Circular view: A series of related tasks are completed in succession, the results of the effort are analyzed, and the insights from that analysis are used to improve quality and efficiency of the next cycle of the process.

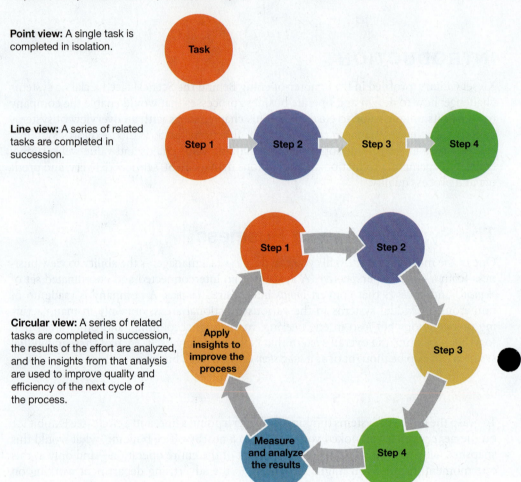

MANAGING SYSTEMS FOR PEAK PERFORMANCE

Much of the art and science of management involves understanding systems or creating new systems and figuring out ways to make them work more efficiently (using fewer resources) and more effectively (meeting goals more successfully). In some instances, systems analysts can run computer simulations to experiment with changes before making any resource decisions (see Exhibit 9.2). However, even without these formal techniques and tools, you can benefit from systems thinking by keeping these principles in mind:[2]

- **Help everyone see the big picture.** It's human nature for individual employees and departments to focus on their own goals and lose sight of what the company as a whole is trying to accomplish. Showing people how they contribute to the overall goal—and rewarding them for doing so—helps ensure that the entire system works efficiently.
- **Understand how individual systems really work and how they interact.** Managers need to avoid the temptation to jump in and try to fix systems without understanding how each one works and how they interact with one another. For instance, as a wholesaling distribution manager, you might notice that delivery drivers are spending more time at retail sites than deliveries really take, so you instruct drivers to reduce the amount of time they spend. However, it might be that drivers are spending that time gathering market intelligence that they turn over to the sales staff. If you're not careful, you might improve the distribution system but damage the sales system.

EXHIBIT 9.2	Systems Diagram and Simulation

Systems modeling software helps managers simulate complex processes in order to test the outcome of various decision possibilities. To find optimum staffing levels, for example, an organization can simulate different rates of hiring, promotion, and retirement to determine how many new people to bring on board.

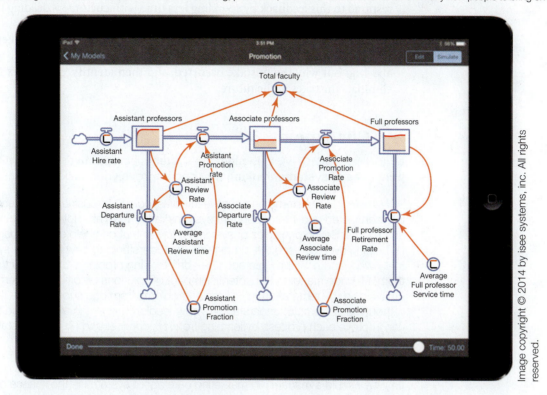

- **Understand problems before you try to fix them.** The most obvious answer is not always the right answer, and poorly conceived solutions often end up causing more harm than good. When you analyze system behavior and malfunctions, make sure you focus on things that are *meaningful*, not merely things that are *measurable*. For instance, it's easy to measure how many reports employees write every month, but that might not be the most meaningful gauge of how well a process is working.

- **Understand the potential impact of solutions before you implement them.** Let's say you manage the customer support department, and to encourage high productivity, you run a weekly contest to see who can handle the most calls. Trouble is, you're essentially rewarding people based on how quickly they can get the customer off the phone, not on how quickly they actually solve customer problems. Customers who aren't happy keep calling back—which adds to the department's workload and *decreases* overall productivity.

- **Don't just move problems around—solve them.** When one subsystem in a company is malfunctioning, its problems are sometimes just moved around from one subsystem to the next, without ever getting solved. For example, if the market research department does a poor job of understanding customers, this problem will get shifted to the engineering department, which is likely to design a product that doesn't meet customer needs. The problem will then get shifted to the advertising and sales departments, which will struggle to promote and sell the product. The engineering, advertising, and sales departments will all underperform, but the real problem is back in the market research department. Market research in this case is a *leverage point*, where a relatively small correction could make the entire company perform better.

- **Understand how feedback works in the system.** Systems respond to *feedback*, which is information from the output applied back to the input. In the case of an ad campaign, the response from target customers is a form of feedback that helps the department understand whether the campaign is working. Feedback can work in unanticipated ways, too. A good example is managers sending mixed signals to their employees, such as telling them that customer satisfaction is the top priority but then criticizing anyone who spends too much time helping customers. Employees will respond to this feedback by spending less time with customers, leading to a decline in customer satisfaction.

- **Use mistakes as opportunities to learn and improve.** When mistakes occur, resist the temptation to just criticize or complain and then move on. Pull the team together and find out why the mistake occurred, and then identify ways to fix the system to eliminate mistakes in the future.

 Checkpoint

LEARNING OBJECTIVE 1: Explain the systems perspective, and identify seven principles of systems thinking that can improve your skills as a manager.

SUMMARY: The systems perspective involves looking at business as a series of interconnected and interdependent systems rather than as a lot of individual activities and events. Seven principles of systems thinking that can help every manager are (1) helping everyone see the big picture, (2) understanding how individual systems really work and how they interact, (3) understanding problems before you try to fix them, (4) understanding the potential impact of solutions before you implement them, (5) avoiding the temptation to just move problems from one subsystem to the next without fixing them, (6) understanding how feedback works in a system so that you can improve each process by learning from experience, and (7) using mistakes as opportunities to learn and improve a system.

CRITICAL THINKING: (1) Why are leverage points in a system so critical to understand? (2) Why should a manager in marketing care about systems in the finance or manufacturing departments?

IT'S YOUR BUSINESS: (1) How could a systems approach to thinking help you get up to speed quickly in your first job after graduation? (2) Think back to your experience of registering for this class. How might you improve that system?

KEY TERMS TO KNOW: system

2 **LEARNING OBJECTIVE**

Describe the *value chain* and *value web* concepts, and discuss the controversy over offshoring.

value chain
All the elements and processes that add value as raw materials are transformed into the final products made available to the ultimate customer.

outsourcing
Contracting out certain business functions or operations to other companies.

Value Chains and Value Webs

As Chapter 1 explains, the essential purpose of a business is adding value—transforming lower-value inputs into higher-value outputs. The details vary widely from industry to industry, but all businesses focus on some kind of transformation like this (see Exhibit 9.3). The **value chain** is a helpful way to consider all the elements and processes that add value as input materials are transformed into the final products made available to the ultimate customer.[3] Each industry has a value chain, and each company has its own value chain as well. (Exhibit 1.1 on page 3 is a simplified example of the value chain in the bread industry.)

REDEFINING ORGANIZATIONS WITH VALUE WEBS

In the decades since Michael Porter introduced the value chain concept, many companies have come to realize that doing everything themselves is not always the most efficient or most successful way to run a business. Many now opt to focus on their core competencies and let other companies handle the remaining business functions—a strategy known as **outsourcing**. Hiring other firms to handle some tasks is not a new concept, to be sure; advertising, public relations, and transportation are among the services that have a long

Business Transformation Systems

All businesses engage in a transformation process of some kind, converting one type of value (inputs) to another type (outputs).

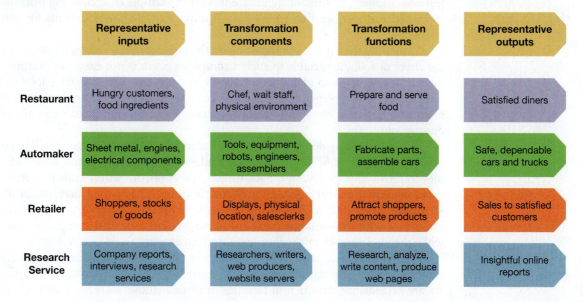

	Representative inputs	Transformation components	Transformation functions	Representative outputs
Restaurant	Hungry customers, food ingredients	Chef, wait staff, physical environment	Prepare and serve food	Satisfied diners
Automaker	Sheet metal, engines, electrical components	Tools, equipment, robots, engineers, assemblers	Fabricate parts, assemble cars	Safe, dependable cars and trucks
Retailer	Shoppers, stocks of goods	Displays, physical location, salesclerks	Attract shoppers, promote products	Sales to satisfied customers
Research Service	Company reports, interviews, research services	Researchers, writers, web producers, website servers	Research, analyze, write content, produce web pages	Insightful online reports

history of being handled by outside firms. The term *outsourcing* is usually applied when a firm decides to move a significant function that was previously done in house, such as information technology or manufacturing, to an outside vendor.

The combination of extensive globalization in many industries and the development of electronic networking has made it easy for companies to connect with partners around the world. Instead of the linear value chain, some businesses now think in terms of **value webs**, multidimensional networks of suppliers and outsourcing partners.[4] Value webs enable the virtual or network organization structures discussed in Chapter 8, and the *unstructured organizations* discussed in that chapter can be viewed as dynamic value webs that grow, shrink, or change as the company's needs change.

The outsourced, value web approach has several key advantages, including speed, flexibility, and the opportunity to access a wide range of talents and technologies that might be expensive or impossible to acquire otherwise. Established companies can narrow their focus to excel at their core competencies; entrepreneurs with product ideas can quickly assemble a team of designers, manufacturing plants, and distributors in far less time than it would take to build an entire company from scratch.

For all its potential advantages, outsourcing does carry some risks, particularly in terms of control. For example, to get its new 787 Dreamliner to market as quickly as possible, Boeing outsourced the manufacturing of many parts of the new plane to other manufacturers. Boeing managers initially decided not to impose the "Boeing way" on these suppliers, so it took a hands-off approach. However, the lack of control eventually came to haunt the company. Many suppliers missed target dates and quality standards, throwing the Dreamliner off schedule by at least three years and costing Boeing billions of dollars in extra work, canceled sales, and delivery penalties.[5]

THE OFFSHORING CONTROVERSY

When companies outsource any function in the value chain, they usually eliminate many of the jobs associated with that function as well. In many cases, those jobs don't go across the street to another local company but rather around the world in pursuit of lower labor costs, a variation on outsourcing known as **offshoring**. (Offshoring can shift jobs to another company or to an overseas division of the same company.)

value webs
Multidimensional networks of suppliers and outsourcing partners.

offshoring
Transferring a part or all of a business function to a facility (a different part of the company or another company entirely) in another country.

Offshoring has been going on for decades, but it began to be a major issue for U.S. manufacturing in the 1980s and then for information technology in the 1990s. Today, offshoring is affecting jobs in science, engineering, law, finance, banking, and other professional areas.[6] The offshoring debate is a great example of conflicting priorities in the stakeholder model; see Exhibit 9.4 for a summary of the key arguments for and against offshoring.

Measuring the impact of offshoring on the U.S. economy is difficult because isolating the effect of a single variable in such a complex system is not easy. For example, economists often struggle to identify the specific reasons one country gains jobs or another loses them. The emergence of new technology, phasing out of old technology, shifts in consumer tastes, changes in business strategies, and other factors can all create and destroy jobs.

As the offshoring debate rages on, the nature of offshoring is changing. The complexities and rising costs of long-distance manufacturing have prompted some U.S. companies to move their production back to U.S. soil, a phenomenon known as *reshoring*. For example, as manufacturing wages in China continue to rise—they increased by more than 70 percent from 2008 to 2013—and the demand for skilled workers outpaces supply, the U.S. states with lowest labor costs are starting to become cost-competitive with China when the total costs of offshoring are taken into account.[7]

Changes in global product demand are also influencing manufacturing location decisions. As developing economies generate more demand for products, some manufacturers are establishing production facilities in or near those markets, a strategy known as *near-shoring*.[8]

Although reshoring might reduce the amount of offshoring done by U.S. companies, globalized manufacturing is here to stay, so it's in everyone's best interest to make it work as well as possible for as many stakeholders as possible. For example, how should U.S. companies be taxed when they have operations all over the world? Also, should unions and regulatory agencies make it more difficult for companies to move jobs overseas, or would it be more beneficial in the long run to let companies compete as vigorously as possible and focus on retraining U.S. workers for new jobs here? These issues are not simple, and you can expect this debate to continue.

REAL-TIME UPDATES
Learn More by Visiting This Website

The effort to bring manufacturing activities back to the United States

See what the Reshoring Initiative is doing to encourage American companies to bring manufacturing back to the United States. Go to http://real-timeupdates.com/bia8 and click on Learn More in the Students section.

 Checkpoint

LEARNING OBJECTIVE 2: Describe the *value chain* and *value web* concepts, and discuss the controversy over offshoring.

SUMMARY: The *value chain* includes all the elements and processes that add value as input materials are transformed into the final products made available to the ultimate customer. The *value web* concept expands this linear model to a multidimensional network of suppliers and outsourcing partners. In the complex argument over *offshoring*—the transfer of business functions to entities in other countries in pursuit of lower costs—proponents claim that (a) companies have a responsibility to shareholder interests to pursue the lowest cost of production, (b) offshoring benefits U.S. consumers through lower prices, (c) many companies don't have a choice once their competitors move offshore, (d) some companies need to offshore in order to support customers around the world, and (e) offshoring helps U.S. companies be more competitive. Those who question the value or wisdom of offshoring raise points about (a) the future of good jobs in the United States, (b) hidden costs and risks, (c) diminished responsiveness, (d) knowledge transfer and theft issues, (e) product safety issues, and (f) national security and public health concerns.

EXHIBIT 9.4	The Offshoring Controversy

Offshoring, or shifting jobs performed by U.S. employees to countries with lower labor costs, is a complex controversy that pits some stakeholders against others. Here are the major arguments for and against the practice, along with some of the key stakeholder groups affected.

Arguments for Offshoring		Arguments Against or Concerns About Offshoring	
Argument	Stakeholders who benefit	Argument/Concern	Stakeholders who suffer
Responsibility to shareholder interests: Companies that engage in offshoring say they have a duty to manage shareholder investments for maximum gain, so it would be irresponsible not to explore cost-saving opportunities such as offshoring.	Shareholders	**Loss of well-paid U.S. jobs:** Opponents of offshoring say that companies are selling out the U.S. middle class in pursuit of profits and pushing a trend that can only harm the country.	Workers
Lower prices for U.S. consumers: For goods in which labor represents a significant portion of production costs, dramatically lowering labor costs lets a company lower its prices to consumers.	Consumers	**Hidden costs and risks:** Says J. Paul Dittman of the University of Tennessee, "Many firms are rethinking the mad rush to outsource . . . the long supply lines, incredibly volatile fuel costs, exchange rates, the geopolitical risks have all come home to roost."	Shareholders
Lack of choice in competitive industries: Given the pricing advantage that offshoring can give U.S. companies, as soon as one company in an industry does it, the others are put under pressure to lower their prices—and offshoring might be the only way for some to lower costs enough to do so.	Shareholders	**Business agility and responsiveness:** When companies rely on operations halfway around the world, they can be slow to respond to marketplace shifts and customer service issues.	Shareholders
Support for local customers around the world: Some companies say that as they expand into other countries, they have no choice but to hire overseas employees in order to support local customers.	Shareholders	**Knowledge transfer and theft risk:** By hiring other companies to perform technical and professional services, U.S. companies transfer important knowledge to these other countries—making them more competitive and depleting the pools of expertise in the United States. Offshoring can also increase the risks of product piracy and theft of intellectual property.	Shareholders, U.S. economy
U.S. competitiveness: Proponents say offshoring is crucial to the survival of many U.S. companies and that it saves other U.S. jobs by making U.S. companies more competitive in the global marketplace.	U.S. economy	**Product safety issues:** Moving more production beyond U.S. borders increases concerns about the ability of regulators to oversee vital health and safety issues.	Consumers
		National security and public health concerns: The weapons and systems used for national defense require lots of steel, semiconductors, and other manufactured materials, and the health-care industry requires a vast supply of materials. What if the United States comes to rely too heavily on other countries for things it needs to protect its borders and its people?	United States, Consumers

Sources: J. Paul Dittmann, "WT100 and the University of Tennessee Supply Chain Survey," *World Trade 100*, July 2011, 42; Hayden Bush, "Reliance on Overseas Manufacturers Worries Supply Chain Experts," *Hospitals & Health Networks*, July 2011, 13; William T. Dickens and Stephen J. Rose, "Blinder Baloney," *The International Economy*, Fall 2007, 18+; "Supply Chain News: The Seven Timeless Challenges of Supply Chain Management," *SupplyChainDigest*, 2 June 2009, www.scdigest.com; Phil Fersht, Dana Stiffler, and Kevin O'Marah, "The Ins and Outs of Offshoring," *Supply Chain Management Review*, March 2009, 10–11; Ajay K. Goel, Nazgol Moussavi, and Vats N. Srivatsan, "Time to Rethink Offshoring?" *McKinsey Quarterly*, 2008 Issue 4, 108–111; Anita Hawser, "Offshoring Industry Faces New Opponent: Its Clients," *Global Finance*, November 2007, 6; Alan S. Brown, "A Shift in Engineering Offshore," *Mechanical Engineering*, March 2009, 24–29; John Ferreira and Len Prokopets, "Does Offshoring Still Make Sense?" *Supply Chain Management Review*, January/February 2009, 20–27; Dan Gilmore, "Can—and Should—Western Manufacturing Be Saved?" *SupplyChainDigest*, 28 May 2009, www.scdigest.com; Geri Smith and Justin Bachman, "The Offshoring of Airplane Care," *BusinessWeek*, 10 April 2008, www.businessweek.com; Susan Carey and Alex Frangos, "Airlines, Facing Cost Pressure, Outsource Crucial Safety Tasks," *Wall Street Journal*, 21 January 2005, A1, A5.

CRITICAL THINKING: (1) Do U.S. companies have an obligation to keep jobs in the United States? Why or why not? (2) Will global labor markets eventually balance out, with workers in comparable positions all over the world making roughly the same wages? Explain your answer.

IT'S YOUR BUSINESS: (1) How vulnerable are your target professions to offshoring? (2) Should such concerns affect your career planning?

KEY TERMS TO KNOW: value chain, outsourcing, value webs, offshoring

3 **LEARNING OBJECTIVE**

Define *supply chain management*, and explain its strategic importance.

supply chain

A set of connected systems that coordinate the flow of goods and materials from suppliers all the way through to final customers.

supply chain management (SCM)

The business procedures, policies, and computer systems that integrate the various elements of the supply chain into a cohesive system.

Supply Chain Management

Regardless of how and where it is structured, the lifeblood of every production operation is the **supply chain**, a set of connected systems that coordinate the flow of goods and materials from suppliers all the way through to final customers. Companies with multiple customer bases can also develop a distinct supply chain to serve each segment.[9]

Supply chain management (SCM) combines business procedures and policies with information systems that integrate the various elements of the supply chain into a cohesive system. As companies rely more on outsourcing partners, SCM has grown far beyond the simple procurement of supplies to become a strategic management function that means the difference between success and failure. Successful implementation of SCM can have a profound strategic impact on companies and the broader economy, in several important ways:[10]

- **Managing risks.** SCM can help companies manage the complex risks involved in a supply chain, risks that include everything from cost and availability to health and safety issues.
- **Managing relationships.** SCM can coordinate the numerous relationships in the supply chain and help managers focus their attention on the most important company-to-company relationships.
- **Managing trade-offs.** SCM helps managers address the many trade-offs in the supply chain. These trade-offs can be a source of conflict within the company, and SCM helps balance the competing interests of the various functional areas. This holistic view helps managers balance both capacity and capability along the entire chain.
- **Promoting sustainability.** As the part of business that moves raw materials and finished goods around the world, supply chains have an enormous effect on resource usage, waste, and environmental impact. A major effort is under way in the field of SCM to develop greener supply chains. A key player in this effort is the giant retailer Walmart, which buys products from more than 100,000 suppliers and has tremendous influence on global supply chains. The company now works with its suppliers to help them meet sustainability targets in the areas of energy and climate, material efficiency, natural resources, and people and community.[11]

REAL-TIME UPDATES
Learn More by Visiting This Website

Sustainability at Walmart

As the world's largest retailer, Walmart is using its considerable influence to increase sustainability in the global supply chain. Go to http://real-timeupdates.com/bia8 and click on Learn More in the Students section.

SUPPLY CHAINS VERSUS VALUE CHAINS

The terms *supply chain* and *value chain* are sometimes used interchangeably, and the distinction between them isn't always clear in everyday usage. One helpful way to distinguish between the two is to view the **supply chain** as the part of the overall value chain that acquires and manages the goods and services needed to produce whatever it is the company produces and then deliver it to the final customer. Everyone in the company is part of the value chain, but not everyone is involved in the supply chain.[12]

Another way to distinguish the two is that the supply chain focuses on the "upstream" part of the process, collecting the necessary materials and supplies with an emphasis on reducing waste and inefficiency. The value chain focuses on the "downstream" part of the process and on adding value in the eyes of customers.[13]

Yet a third way that has recently emerged is talking about value chains as a strategic win-win business partnership rather than the more tactical, deal-driven arrangement of a supply chain. In this usage, "value" also encompasses *values*, including sustainability practices that make products more worthy and appealing in the eyes of customers.[14]

SUPPLY CHAIN SYSTEMS AND TECHNIQUES

The core focus of supply chain management is getting the right materials at the right price in the right place at the right time for successful production. Unfortunately, you can't just pile up huge quantities of everything you might eventually need, because **inventory**, the goods and materials kept in stock for production or sale, costs money to purchase and to store. On the other hand, not having an adequate supply of inventory can result in expensive delays. This balancing act is the job of **inventory control**, which tries to determine the right quantities of supplies and products to have on hand and then tracks where those items are. One of the most important technologies to emerge in inventory control in recent years is *radio frequency identification (RFID)*. RFID uses small antenna tags attached to products or shipping containers; special sensors detect the presence of the tags and can track the flow of goods through the supply chain.

Procurement, or *purchasing*, is the acquisition of the raw materials, parts, components, supplies, and finished products required to produce goods and services. The goal of purchasing is to make sure that the company has all the materials it needs, when it needs them, at the lowest possible cost. A company must always have enough supplies on hand to cover a product's *lead time*—the period that elapses between placing the supply order and receiving materials.

To accomplish these goals, operations specialists have developed a variety of systems and techniques over the years:

- **Material requirements planning (MRP).** MRP helps a manufacturer get the correct materials where they are needed, when they are needed, without unnecessary stockpiling. Managers use MRP software to calculate when certain materials will be required, when they should be ordered, and when they should be delivered so that storage costs will be minimal. These systems are so effective at reducing inventory levels that they are used almost universally in both large and small manufacturing firms.
- **Manufacturing resource planning (MRP II).** MRP II expands MRP with links to a company's financial systems and other processes. For instance, in addition to managing inventory levels successfully, an MRP II system can help ensure that material costs adhere to target budgets.[15] Because it draws together all departments, an MRP II system produces a companywide game plan that allows everyone to work with the same numbers. Moreover, the system can track each step of production, allowing managers throughout the company to consult other managers' inventories, schedules, and plans.
- **Enterprise resource planning (ERP).** ERP extends the scope of resource planning and management even further to encompass the entire organization. ERP software programs are typically made up of modules that address the needs of the various functional areas, from manufacturing to sales to human resources. Some companies deploy ERP on a global scale, with a single centralized system connecting all their operations worldwide.[16]

inventory
Goods and materials kept in stock for production or sale.

inventory control
Determining the right quantities of supplies and products to have on hand and tracking where those items are.

procurement
The acquisition of the raw materials, parts, components, supplies, and finished products required to produce goods and services.

Benjamin Haas/Shutterstock

Tracking and managing inventory levels are essential tasks for ensuring smooth, profitable operations.

REAL-TIME UPDATES
Learn More by Visiting This Website

Interested in a career in supply chain management?

The Council of Supply Chain Management Professionals offers advice on how to launch a career in this important field. Go to http://real-timeupdates.com/bia8 and click on Learn More in the Students section.

✔ **Checkpoint**

LEARNING OBJECTIVE 3: Define *supply chain management*, and explain its strategic importance.

SUMMARY: Supply chain management (SCM) combines business procedures and policies with information systems that integrate the various elements of the supply chain into a cohesive system. SCM helps companies manage risks, relationships, and trade-offs throughout their supply chains, building partnerships that help everyone in the supply chain succeed.

CRITICAL THINKING: (1) Why can't companies just stockpile huge inventories of all the parts and materials they need rather than carefully manage supply from one day to the next? (2) Why would a company invest time and money in helping its suppliers improve their business practices? Why not just dump underperformers and get better suppliers?

IT'S YOUR BUSINESS: (1) In any current or previous job, what steps have supervisors taken to help you understand your role in the supply chain? (2) Is it dehumanizing to your colleagues and business partners to be participants in a supply chain? Why or why not?

KEY TERMS TO KNOW: supply chain, supply chain management (SCM), inventory, inventory control, procurement

---

4 LEARNING OBJECTIVE

Identify the major planning decisions in production and operations management.

production and operations management
Overseeing all the activities involved in producing goods and services.

productivity
The efficiency with which an organization can convert inputs to outputs.

lean systems
Systems (in manufacturing and other functional areas) that maximize productivity by reducing waste and delays.

Production and Operations Management

The term *production* suggests factories, machines, and assembly lines making automobiles, computers, furniture, motorcycles, or other tangible goods. With the growth in the number of service-based businesses and their increasing importance to the economy, however, the term *production* is now used to describe the transformation of resources into both goods and services. The broader term **production and operations management**, or simply *operations management*, refers to overseeing all the activities involved in producing goods and services. Operations managers are involved in a wide range of strategic and tactical decisions, from high-level design of the production system to forecasting and scheduling.

LEAN SYSTEMS

Throughout all the activities in the production process, operations managers pay close attention to **productivity**, or the efficiency with which they can convert inputs to outputs. (Put another way, productivity is equal to the value of the outputs divided by the value of the inputs.) Productivity is one of the most vital responsibilities in operations management because it is a key factor in determining the company's competitiveness and profitability. Companies that can produce similar goods or services with fewer resources have a distinct advantage over their competitors. Moreover, high productivity in the fullest sense also requires low waste, whether it's leftover materials, shoddy products that must be scrapped, or excess energy usage. Consequently, productivity improvements and sustainability improvements often complement each other.

Lean systems, which maximize productivity by reducing waste and delays, are at the heart of many productivity improvement efforts. Many lean systems borrow techniques from Toyota; the *Toyota Production System* is world renowned for its ability to continually improve both productivity and quality (see Exhibit 9.5).[17] Central to the notion of lean systems is **just-in-time (JIT)** inventory management, in which goods and materials are delivered throughout the production process right before they are needed rather than being stockpiled in inventories. Reducing stocks to immediate needs reduces waste and forces factories to keep production flowing smoothly.

just-in-time (JIT)
Inventory management in which goods and materials are delivered throughout the production process right before they are needed.

EXHIBIT 9.5	Conceptual Diagram of the Toyota Production System

The Toyota Production System, one of the most influential production strategies in modern business history, has been studied, duplicated, and adapted by companies in a variety of industries around the world. Toyota refined the system over decades, but it has always been based on the two fundamental principles of just-in-time inventory management, so that expensive inventory doesn't pile up when it isn't being used, and *jidoka*, or "automation with a human touch," whereby the highly automated process can be stopped by any worker any time a problem appears, to avoid making more defective parts or cars. However, as page 215 explains, for all its abilities to reduce manufacturing defects, the system has not been able to prevent all failures— particularly now that cars are vast software systems as well as mechanical systems.

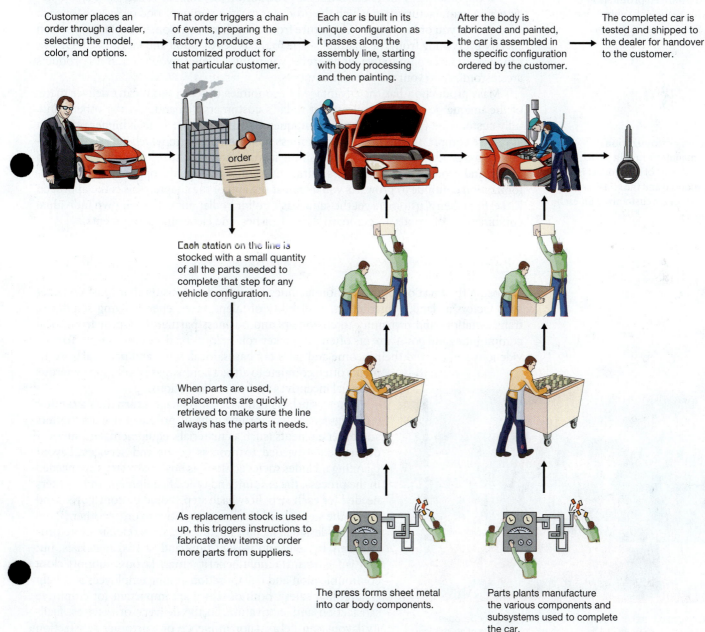

Customer places an order through a dealer, selecting the model, color, and options.

That order triggers a chain of events, preparing the factory to produce a customized product for that particular customer.

Each car is built in its unique configuration as it passes along the assembly line, starting with body processing and then painting.

After the body is fabricated and painted, the car is assembled in the specific configuration ordered by the customer.

The completed car is tested and shipped to the dealer for handover to the customer.

Each station on the line is stocked with a small quantity of all the parts needed to complete that step for any vehicle configuration.

When parts are used, replacements are quickly retrieved to make sure the line always has the parts it needs.

As replacement stock is used up, this triggers instructions to fabricate new items or order more parts from suppliers.

The press forms sheet metal into car body components.

Parts plants manufacture the various components and subsystems used to complete the car.

Source: Data from "Toyota Production System," Toyota Global website, accessed 4 November 2013, www.toyota-global.com.

Achieving such benefits requires constant attention to quality and teamwork because with no spare inventory, there is no room for delays or errors.[18] Without stockpiles of extra parts and materials, each stage in the production process goes idle if the stages before it have not delivered on time.

MASS PRODUCTION, CUSTOMIZED PRODUCTION, AND MASS CUSTOMIZATION

Goods and services can be created through *mass production, customized production,* or *mass customization,* depending on the nature of the product and the desires of target customers. In **mass production**, identical goods or services are created, usually in large quantities, such as when Apple churns out a million identical iPhones. Although not normally associated with services, mass production is also what American Airlines is doing when it offers hundreds of opportunities for passengers to fly from, say, Dallas to Chicago every day: Every customer on these flights gets the same service at the same time.

At the other extreme is **customized production**, sometimes called *batch-of-one production* in manufacturing, in which the producer creates a unique good or service for each customer. If you order a piece of furniture from a local craftsperson, for instance, you can specify everything from the size and shape to the types of wood and fabric used. Or you can hire a charter pilot to fly you wherever you want, whenever you want. Both products are customized to your unique requirements.

Mass production has the advantage of economies of scale, but it can't deliver many of the unique goods and services that today's customers demand. On the other hand, fully customized production can offer uniqueness but usually at a much higher price. An attractive compromise in many cases is **mass customization**, in which part of the product is mass produced and then the remaining features are customized for each buyer. With design and production technologies getting ever more flexible, the opportunities for customization continue to grow. As you'll read at the end of the chapter, this is the approach Kiesel has taken: Customers get the same basic guitar bodies but with their own individual combinations of woods, fingerboard styles, finishes, and electronic components.

mass production
The creation of identical goods or services, usually in large quantities.

customized production
The creation of a unique good or service for each customer.

mass customization
A manufacturing approach in which part of the product is mass produced and the remaining features are customized for each buyer.

FACILITIES LOCATION AND DESIGN

Choosing the location of production facilities is a complex decision that must consider such factors as land, construction, availability of talent, taxes, energy, living standards, transportation, and proximity to customers and business partners. Support from local communities and governments often plays a key role in location decisions as well. To provide jobs and expand their income and sales tax bases, local, state, and national governments often compete to attract companies by offering generous financial incentives such as tax reductions.

After a site has been selected, managers turn their attention to *facility layout,* the arrangement of production work centers and other elements (such as materials, equipment, and support departments) needed to process goods and services. Layout planning includes such decisions as how many steps are needed in the process, the amount and type of equipment and workers needed for each step, how each step should be configured, and where the steps should be located relative to one another.[19]

Well-designed facilities help companies operate more productively by reducing wasted time and wasted materials, but that is far from the only benefit. Smart layouts support close communication and collaboration among employees and help ensure their safety, both of which are important for employee satisfaction and motivation. In the delivery of services, facility layout can be a major influence on customer satisfaction because it affects the overall service experience.[20]

Tyler Olson/Shutterstock

With customized production, such as tailor-made or *bespoke* clothing, each product is created to meet the needs of an individual buyer.

FORECASTING AND CAPACITY PLANNING

Using customer feedback, sales orders, market research, past sales figures, industry analyses, and educated guesses about the future behavior of customers and competitors, operations managers prepare *production forecasts*—estimates of future demand for the company's products. After product demand has been estimated, management must balance that with the company's capacity to produce the goods or services. The term *capacity* refers to the volume of manufacturing or service capability that an organization can handle. **Capacity planning** is the collection of long-term strategic decisions that establish the overall level of resources needed to meet customer demand. When managers at Boeing plan for the production of an airliner, they have to consider not only the staffing of thousands of people but also massive factory spaces, material flows from hundreds of suppliers around the world, internal deliveries, cash flow, tools and equipment, and dozens of other factors. Because of the potential impact on finances, customers, and employees—and the difficulty of reversing major decisions—capacity choices are among the most important decisions that top-level managers make.[21]

capacity planning
Establishing the overall level of resources needed to meet customer demand.

SCHEDULING

In any production process, managers must do *scheduling*—determining how long each operation takes and deciding which tasks are done in which order. Manufacturing facilities often use a *master production schedule (MPS)* to coordinate production of all the goods the company makes. Service businesses use a variety of scheduling techniques as well, from simple appointment calendars for a small business to the comprehensive online systems that airlines and other large service providers use.

To plan and track projects of all kinds, managers throughout a company can use a *Gantt chart*, a special type of bar chart that shows the progress of all the tasks needed to complete a project (see Exhibit 9.6). For more complex projects, the *program evaluation and review technique (PERT)* is useful. PERT helps managers identify the optimal sequencing of activities, the expected time for project completion, and the best use of resources. To use PERT, managers map out all the activities in a network diagram (see Exhibit 9.7 on the next page). The longest path through the network is known as the **critical path** because it represents the minimum amount of time needed to complete the project. Tasks in the critical path usually receive special attention because they determine when the project can be completed.[22] (If anyone ever says *you* are in the critical path, make sure you stay on schedule!)

critical path
In a PERT network diagram, the sequence of operations that requires the longest time to complete.

EXHIBIT 9.6	Gantt Chart

A Gantt chart is a handy tool in project and production management because it shows the order in which tasks must be completed and which tasks are dependent on other tasks. For the new product launch shown here, for example, the analysis task is dependent on all three tasks before it, which means those tasks must be completed before analysis can begin. With periodic updates, it's also easy to show a team exactly where the project stands at any particular moment.

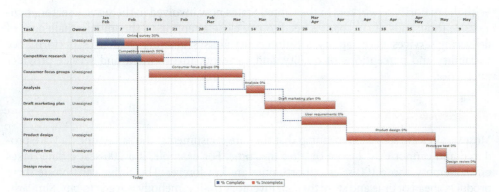

EXHIBIT 9.7   **Simplified PERT Diagram for a Store Opening**

This PERT diagram shows a subset of the many tasks involved in opening a new retail store. The tasks involved in staffing are on the critical path because they take the longest time to complete (51 days), whereas the promotion tasks can be completed in 38 days, and the merchandise tasks can be completed in 39 days. In other words, some delay can be tolerated in the promotion or merchandise tasks, but any delay in any of the staffing tasks will delay the store's opening day.

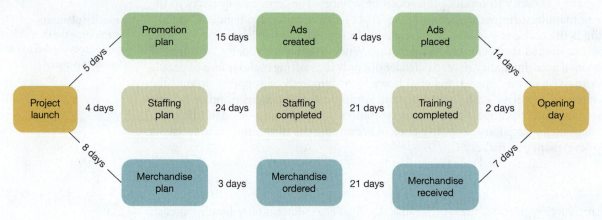

✔ Checkpoint

LEARNING OBJECTIVE 4: Identify the major planning decisions in production and operations management.

SUMMARY: The major decisions in operations management include (1) facilities location and design; (2) forecasting and capacity planning to match resources with demand; (3) scheduling; (4) lean system design to reduce waste and delays; and (5) the choice of mass production, customized production, or mass customization.

CRITICAL THINKING: (1) Why is it essential to identify tasks in the critical path of a project? (2) How does mass customization help a company balance productivity and customer satisfaction?

IT'S YOUR BUSINESS: (1) The phrase "lean and mean" is sometimes used to describe lean systems. What are the risks of using such language? (2) Is this course an example of mass production, customization, or mass customization? Explain.

KEY TERMS TO KNOW: production and operations management, productivity, lean systems, just-in-time (JIT), mass production, customized production, mass customization, capacity planning, critical path

5 **LEARNING OBJECTIVE**

Explain the unique challenges of service delivery.

The Unique Challenges of Service Delivery

With the majority of workers in the United States now involved in the service sector, managers in thousands of companies need to pay close attention to the unique challenges of delivering services: perishability, location constraints, scalability challenges, performance variability and perceptions of quality, and customer involvement and service provider interaction.

PERISHABILITY

Most services are *perishable*, meaning that they are consumed at the same time they are produced and cannot exist before or after that time. For example, if a 200-seat airliner takes off half-empty, those 100 sales opportunities are lost forever. The airline can't create these products ahead of time and store them in inventory until somebody is ready to buy. Similarly, restaurants can seat only so many people every night, so empty tables represent revenue lost forever. This perishability can have a profound impact on the way service businesses are managed, from staffing (making sure enough people are on hand to help with peak demands) to pricing (using discounts to encourage people to buy services when they are available).

LOCATION CONSTRAINTS

Perishability also means that for many services, customers and providers need to be in the same place at the same time. The equipment and food ingredients used in a restaurant can be produced just about anywhere, but the restaurant itself needs to be located close to customers. One of the most significant commercial advantages of the Internet is the way it has enabled many service businesses to get around this constraint. Online retailers, information providers, and other e-businesses can locate virtually anywhere on the planet.

SCALABILITY CHALLENGES AND OPPORTUNITIES

Any business that wants to grow must consider the issue of **scalability**, the potential to increase production by expanding or replicating its initial production capacity. Scaling up always creates some challenges, but service businesses that depend on the skills of specific professionals can be particularly difficult to scale. Examples range from chefs and interior designers to business consultants and graphic designers, particularly when the business is built around the reputation of a single person.

Of course, many goods businesses also rely on highly skilled production workers, but the potential to mechanize goods production can make it easier to scale up manufacturing in some cases. For example, by using computer-controlled routers to carve the bodies of its guitars, Kiesel frees itself from the constraint of hiring enough skilled carvers to do it all by hand.

scalability
The potential to increase production by expanding or replicating its initial production capacity.

PERFORMANCE VARIABILITY AND PERCEPTIONS OF QUALITY

For many types of services, the quality of performance can vary from one instance to the next—and that quality is in the eye of the beholder and often can't be judged until after the service has been performed. If you manufacture scissors, you can specify a certain grade of steel from your suppliers and use automated machinery to produce thousands of identical pairs of scissors of identical quality. Many key attributes such as the size and strength of the scissors are *objective* and measurable, and customers can experience the *subjective* variables such as the feel and action before they buy. In other words, there is little mystery and little room for surprise in the purchase.

However, if you create a haircut using a pair of those scissors, perceptions of quality become almost entirely subjective *and* impossible to judge until after the service is complete. Plus, hair styling is a good example of a service in which *quality of experience* is an important part of customer perceptions as well, which is why, for instance, most salons pay a lot of attention to architecture, interior design, lighting, music, robes, refreshments, and other amenities that have nothing to do with the actual haircut itself.

CUSTOMER INVOLVEMENT AND PROVIDER INTERACTION

Finally, one of the biggest differences between goods and services production is the fact that customers are often involved in—and thereby can affect the quality of—the service delivery. For instance, personal trainers can instruct clients in the proper way to exercise, but if the clients don't follow directions, the result will be unsatisfactory. Similarly, a business consultant relies on accurate

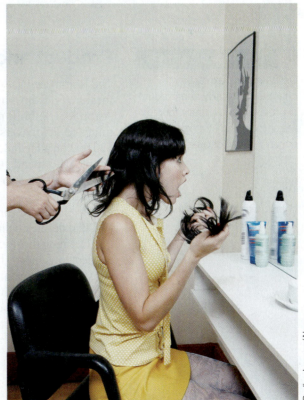

One of the many challenges of providing services is that the evaluation of quality is often subjective.

information from managers in a client organization; lacking that, he or she will be unable to craft the most effective advice.

When customers and service providers interact, the quality of the interpersonal experience also affects customer perceptions of quality. In this sense, service delivery is something of a performance that needs to instill confidence in the client. Weak communication skills or poor etiquette can create dissatisfaction with a service that is satisfactory or even exceptional in all other respects.

 Checkpoint

LEARNING OBJECTIVE 5: Explain the unique challenges of service delivery.

SUMMARY: The delivery of services presents a number of unique challenges, including (1) perishability, which means that services are consumed at the same time they are produced; (2) location constraints, which often require that customers and service providers be in the same place at the same time; (3) scalability challenges, which can make some types of service businesses more difficult to expand; (4) performance variability and perceptions of quality, which heighten the challenge of delivering consistent quality and increase the subjectivity of the customer experience; and (5) customer involvement and service provider interaction, which can put some of the responsibility for service quality on the customer's shoulders and increase the importance of good interpersonal skills.

CRITICAL THINKING: (1) How can technology help some service businesses address the challenge of scalability? (2) If customers are paying for a service, why should they ever have to share in the responsibility of ensuring quality results?

IT'S YOUR BUSINESS: (1) Do you think you have a natural personality for working in a service business? Why or why not? (2) If you're not a "natural," what steps could you take to succeed in a service job anyway?

KEY TERMS TO KNOW: scalability

---

6   LEARNING OBJECTIVE

Define *quality*, explain the challenge of quality and product complexity, and identify four major tools and strategies for ensuring product quality.

quality
The degree to which a product or process meets reasonable or agreed-on expectations.

Product and Process Quality

The term *quality* is often used in a vague sense of "goodness" or "excellence," but to be meaningful from a managerial standpoint, it needs to be defined in context. Hyundai and Aston Martin both make quality automobiles, but quality means dramatically different things to the makers and buyers of these two car brands. People who spend $15,000 or $20,000 on a Hyundai are likely to be satisfied with the quality they receive in return, but people who spend 10 times that much on an Aston Martin have vastly different expectations, even if the two cars are equally safe and reliable. Accordingly, **quality** is best defined as the degree to which a product or process meets reasonable or agreed-on expectations. Within the framework of this general definition, a specific set of parameters can be identified that define quality in each situation.

Defining those expectations of quality and then organizing the resources and systems needed to achieve that level are vital responsibilities in today's competitive, resource-constrained environment. With numerous choices available in most product categories, consumers and business buyers alike tend to avoid or abandon products and companies that can't meet their expectations. Moreover, poor quality wastes time and money, squanders resources, frustrates customers and employees, erodes confidence in companies and their products, and can even put people in danger.

QUALITY AND COMPLEXITY

As many products become increasingly complex, defining and maintaining quality becomes an ever greater challenge. For example, even identical, mass-produced computers immediately become unique when their new owners start adding software, downloading files, and connecting to printers and other devices, each of which is a complex hardware/software system in its own right. All these changes and connections increase the chances that something will go wrong and thereby lower the functional quality of the product. In other words, even though the company verified the quality of the products before they left the factory, it could have thousands of quality issues on its hands over time.

Meeting expectations of quality in complicated, real-world operating conditions over time can present a sizable challenge but one that must be met to ensure buyer satisfaction. Dell, for example, has dozens of customer service specialists who monitor social media conversations for signs of discontent over its products. When they hear complaints, they jump in with advice and offers to help. The team logs more than 25,000 online conversations a day. This effort improves customer satisfaction and creates opportunities to sell additional goods and services—the company figures the program has generated more than $1 billion in additional sales—but it also gives Dell engineers valuable insights into how quality plays out in the messy real world outside the factory.[23]

Even the frequently copied Toyota Production System has proved fallible at times, with several notable safety-related recalls in recent years. According to engineering professor Jeffrey Liker, who has researched and written extensively about Toyota, none of the recalls could be traced to production defects.[24] To improve the design process, though, the company did respond to the criticism that senior engineers in charge of design were isolated at company headquarters in Japan and too insulated from real-world feedback. In response, the company announced that North American engineering teams were being given more control over the development of vehicles designed for the North American market.[25]

REAL-TIME UPDATES
Learn More by Watching This Video

Watch robots build a Tesla electric car

The Tesla factory is as technologically advanced as the electric cars it produces. Go to http://real-timeupdates.com/bia8 and click on Learn More in the Students section.

STRATEGIES FOR ENSURING PRODUCT QUALITY

The traditional means of maintaining quality is called **quality control**—measuring quality against established standards after the good or service has been produced and weeding out any defects. A more comprehensive and proactive approach is **quality assurance**, a holistic system of integrated policies, practices, and procedures designed to ensure that every product meets preset quality standards. Quality assurance includes quality control as well as doing the job right the first time by designing tools and machinery properly, demanding quality parts from suppliers, encouraging customer feedback, training and empowering employees, and encouraging employees to take pride in their work.

Companies can use a variety of tools and strategies to help ensure quality; four of the most significant are continuous improvement, statistical process control, Six Sigma, and ISO 9000.

Continuous Improvement

Delivering quality goods and services is as much a mindset as it is a technical challenge. Companies that excel tend to empower their employees to continuously improve the quality of goods production or service delivery, a strategy often expressed through the Japanese word *kaizen*. By making quality everyone's responsibility, the kaizen approach encourages all workers to look for quality problems, halt production when necessary, generate ideas for improvement, and adjust work routines as needed.[26]

Statistical Process Control

Any quality control or improvement effort depends on reliable feedback that tells workers and managers how well products and processes are performing. Quality assurance often includes the use of **statistical process control (SPC)**, which involves taking samples from the process periodically and analyzing these data points to look for trends and anomalies. One of the most important SPC tools is the *control chart*, which plots measured data over time and helps identify performance that is outside the normal range of operating conditions and therefore in need of investigation.[27]

quality control
Measuring quality against established standards after the good or service has been produced and weeding out any defective products.

quality assurance
A more comprehensive approach of companywide policies, practices, and procedures to ensure that every product meets quality standards.

statistical process control (SPC)
The use of random sampling and tools such as control charts to monitor the production process.

Six Sigma
A rigorous quality management program that strives to eliminate deviations between the actual and desired performance of a business system.

Six Sigma

Whereas *kaizen* is more of a general mindset and SPC is a set of analytical tools, **Six Sigma** is a comprehensive approach that encompasses a philosophy of striving toward perfection, a rigorous methodology for measuring and improving quality, and specific tools such as SPC to track progress.[28] (The term *six sigma* is used in statistics to indicate 3.4 defects per 1 million opportunities—near perfection, in other words.) Six Sigma is a highly disciplined, systematic approach to reducing the deviation from desired goals in virtually any business process, whether it's eliminating defects in the creation of a product or improving a company's cash flow.[29] Six Sigma efforts typically follow a five-step approach, known as DMAIC for short (see Exhibit 9.8).[30]

Many companies now marry the concepts of lean production and Six Sigma, seeking to reduce waste and defects simultaneously. And moving beyond operations, this hybrid approach of *Lean Six Sigma* is also being applied at a strategic level to help identify opportunities in the marketplace and align the resources needed to pursue them.[31]

ISO 9000
A globally recognized family of standards for quality management systems.

ISO 9000

Buyers and business partners often want reassurance that the companies they do business with take quality seriously and have practices and policies in place to ensure quality outputs. **ISO 9000** is a globally recognized family of standards for quality management systems, administered by the International Organization for Standardization (ISO). ISO 9000 is based on eight quality management principles, including customer focus, a systems approach to management, and fact-based decision making.[32]

Hundreds of thousands of organizations around the world have implemented ISO standards, making it a universally recognized indicator of compliance. Achieving ISO certification sends a reassuring signal to other companies that your internal processes meet these widely accepted standards, and many organizations now require that their supplies meet ISO standards. Even without the need to meet this requirement, ISO 9000 provides companies with a "tried and tested framework for taking a systematic approach to managing the organization's processes so that they consistently turn out products that satisfy customers' expectations."[33]

For the latest information on production systems, visit **http://real-timeupdates .com/bia8** and click on Chapter 9.

| EXHIBIT 9.8 | The DMAIC Process in Six Sigma Quality Management |

The five-step process of *define, measure, analyze, improve,* and *control* (DMAIC) is at the heart of Six Sigma quality management efforts. Notice how this is a specific implementation of the control cycle described on page 161.

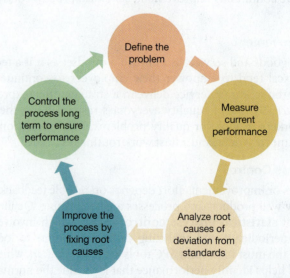

Source: Based on Kelly D. Sloan, "The Path to a Sustainable Playbook," *Industrial Engineer*, April 2011, 41–46.

 **Checkpoint**

LEARNING OBJECTIVE 6: Define *quality*, explain the challenge of quality and product complexity, and identify four major tools and strategies for ensuring product quality.

SUMMARY: Quality is the degree to which a product or process meets reasonable or agreed-on expectations. As products become more complex, the challenges of defining what quality means, ensuring quality production or service performance, and ensuring quality once the product is out in the field all increase. Four major tools and strategies for ensuring product quality are (1) continuous process improvement, enabling employees to search for and correct quality problems; (2) statistical process control (SPC), the use of random sampling and tools such as control charts to monitor the production process; (3) Six Sigma, a rigorous quality management program that strives to eliminate deviations between the actual and desired performance of a business system; and (4) ISO 9000, a globally recognized family of standards for quality management systems.

CRITICAL THINKING: (1) How significant is the role of software in product quality today? (2) How can process simplicity contribute to quality?

IT'S YOUR BUSINESS: (1) Are the grades you get in your various classes an example of quality control or of quality assurance? Explain your answer. (2) Have you ever tried anything like the Six Sigma DMAIC process in your own life, even partially or informally?

KEY TERMS TO KNOW: quality, quality control, quality assurance, statistical process control (SPC), Six Sigma, ISO 9000

 ## BEHIND THE SCENES
KIESEL'S PRODUCTION SYSTEM SATISFIES DEMANDING GUITARISTS

In 1946, Lowell Kiesel founded L. C. Kiesel to manufacture sound pickups for electric guitars, which were gaining popularity in jazz and blues. His timing couldn't have been better as the young company grew, when the new sound of rock and roll in the 1950s set off a tsunami of demand for amplified guitars. Along the way, the company branched out to building its own guitars and over the decades, made a name for itself among serious guitarists by filling the gap between mass-produced and fully custom guitars. (In 1949, the company changed its name to Carvin, but changed back to Kiesel in 2015. It continues to make guitars under both the Kiesel and Carvin brand names.)

The company's secret has been perfecting the art and science of *mass customization*, the ability to adapt standardized products to the tastes of individual customers. In four to six weeks, and for roughly $700 to $1,500, Kiesel can customize one of several dozen models of guitars and basses. All are available in a wide variety of woods, paints, stains, finishes, electronics, and even the slight curvature in the fingerboard; there are so many choices that online discussion boards buzz with debates about which combinations are best for specific styles of music.

Kiesel's factory combines old-world craftsmanship with new-world technologies. Because the custom guitars are built on a standard set of body shapes and styles, Kiesel can use computer-controlled cutting and milling machines that cut and shape the bodies and necks quickly and precisely. A diamond-surface finishing machine mills fingerboards to tolerances of a thousandth of an inch. A dehumidification chamber removes internal stresses from the wood used in the guitar necks to minimize the chance of warping years down the road. Experienced craftspeople with sensitive eyes and ears take over from there, performing such tasks as matching veneer pieces on guitar tops (veneers are thin sheets of wood, often exotic or expensive species), adjusting the action (the feel of the strings against the frets), and listening to the tone quality of finished instruments.

With this blend of automation and human touch, Kiesel produces thousands of instruments a year that win rave reviews from appreciative customers. "Nothing can touch it in terms of sound quality and workmanship" and "I haven't seen anything close to this price that can outperform it" are typical of the comments that Kiesel customers post online. Upon hearing a salesperson in another music store speak disparagingly of the brand, one indignant Kiesel owner retrieved his guitar from his car and put on an impromptu concert for the store's sales staff to demonstrate just how good the Kiesel product sounded. With a proven manufacturing approach and customer loyalty like that, Kiesel will be fulfilling the musical dreams of guitarists for years to come.[34]

Critical Thinking Questions

9-1. If Kiesel experienced an increase in orders from its website over a period of two weeks, should it expand its production capacity to make sure it can handle increased demand in the future? Why or why not?

9-2. Watch some of the video on Kiesel's YouTube channel at **www.youtube.com/user/carvinguitars**. How might this information help convince potential buyers to consider Kiesel or Carvin guitars?

9-3. Wooden musical instruments have been carved by hand for hundreds of years. Why wouldn't Kiesel want to continue this tradition?

LEARN MORE ONLINE

Visit the Kiesel website at **www.carvinguitars.com** (the URL may be changed by the time you read this as the company transitions its branding) and study how the company promotes its customized products. Pretend you're in the market and step through the process of customizing a guitar or bass. Would you feel comfortable purchasing a musical instrument in this manner? Review comments on **www.facebook.com/kieselguitars**. What are employees and customers talking about these days?

KEY TERMS

capacity planning (211)
critical path (211)
customized production (210)
inventory (207)
inventory control (207)
ISO 9000 (216)
just-in-time (209)
lean systems (208)
mass customization (210)
mass production (210)
offshoring (203)
outsourcing (202)
procurement (207)
production and operations management (208)

productivity (208)
quality (214)
quality assurance (215)
quality control (215)
scalability (213)
Six Sigma (216)
statistical process control (215)
supply chain (206)
supply chain management (206)
system (199)
value chain (202)
value webs (203)

MyBizLab

To complete the problems with the ⭐,
go to EOC Discussion Questions in the
MyLab.

TEST YOUR KNOWLEDGE

Questions for Review

9-4. What role does feedback play in a system?

9-5. Why is offshoring controversial?

9-6. What is mass customization?

9-7. What is a lean system?

9-8. What is scalability, in the context of managing a service business?

Questions for Analysis

9-9. Why is it important to monitor performance variables that are the most meaningful, not those that are the most easily measurable?

9-10. Why do some firms now think in terms of value webs instead of value chains?

9-11. How can supply chain management (SCM) help a company establish a competitive advantage?

9-12. How does perishability affect the delivery of services?

9-13. **Ethical Considerations.** How does society's concern for the environment affect a company's decisions about facility location and layout?

Questions for Application

9-14. Business is booming. Sales last month were 50 percent higher than the month before, and so far, this month is looking even better than last month. Should you hire more people to accommodate the increase? Explain your answer.

9-15. If 30 percent of the patrons eating at your restaurant say they won't eat there again, what steps would you take to define the problem(s) that needs to be solved, measure the relevant performance variables, and then analyze the root cause of the problems(s)?

9-16. You've developed a reputation as an outstanding math tutor, and you want to turn your talent into a full-time business after graduation. How will you address the challenge of scalability in your new venture?

9-17. **Concept Integration.** How might supply chain management issues influence your decision on how to expand your vitamin and nutritional supplements company internationally?

EXPAND YOUR KNOWLEDGE

Discovering Career Opportunities

Visit the *Occupational Outlook Handbook* at **www.bls.gov/ooh** and locate "Industrial production managers" in the "Management" section.

9-18. What is the nature of the work for industrial production managers? Does the combination of people management and technical problem solving appeal to you?

9-19. What is the outlook for careers in this profession? If you were interested in this field, would you consider it, given the job outlook?

9-20. If you decide you want to work in a production-related job, what additional classes should you consider taking before you graduate?

Improving Your Tech Insights: Nanotechnology

Think small. Really small. Think about manufacturing products a molecule or even a single atom at a time. That's the scale of *nanotechnology*, a rather vague term that covers research and engineering done at nanoscale, or roughly 1/100,000 the width of a human hair.

The potential uses of nanotechnology range from the practical—smart materials that can change shape and heal themselves, more efficient energy generation and transmission, superstrong and superlight materials for airplanes, better cosmetics, smart medical implants, safer food containers, and ultrasmall computers—to the somewhat wilder: food-growing machines and microscopic robots that could travel throughout your body to cure diseases and fix injuries. (Like any new technology with lots of promise, nanotechnology also suffers from lots of hype.)

More than 1,000 nanotechnology-enabled products have hit the market in a number of industries, from automotive materials to medicine to consumer products. Also, although they're slightly larger than the generally accepted scale of nanotechnology, *microelectromechanical systems (MEMS)* are having a major impact in some industries. These tiny machines (pumps, valves, and so on), some no bigger than a grain of pollen, are used in the nozzles of ink-jet printers, air bag sensors, and ultraprecise miniature laboratory devices.[35]

Conduct research to identify a product currently on the market that uses nanotechnology in some fashion. In an email message to your instructor, describe the product, its target market, the role nanotechnology plays in the product's design, and any known safety concerns regarding the use of nanotechnology in this or similar products.

PRACTICE YOUR SKILLS

Sharpening Your Communication Skills

As the newly hired manager of Campus Athletics, a shop featuring athletic wear bearing logos of colleges and universities, you are responsible for selecting the store's suppliers. Demand for merchandise with team logos and brands can be quite volatile. When a college team is hot, you've got to have merchandise. You know that selecting the right supplier is a task that requires careful consideration, so you have decided to host a series of selection interviews. Think about all the qualities you would want in a supplier, and develop a list of interview questions that will help you assess whether that supplier possesses those qualities.

Building Your Team Skills

Identify a company that has recently decided to offshore some part of its operations. (Search online news sources for "offshore outsourcing" or similar terms.) With the other members of your team, identify all the stakeholder groups that were or might be affected by this decision and speculate on the impact it had on each group. Weighing the effect on all the stakeholders, vote on whether this was a wise decision for the company. Be prepared to present your conclusions to the class.

Developing Your Research Skills

Seeking increased efficiency and productivity, growing numbers of producers of goods and services are applying technology to improve the production process. Find an article in a business journal or newspaper that discusses how one company used computer-aided design (CAD), computer-aided engineering (CAE), computer-integrated manufacturing (CIM), robots, or other technological innovations to refit or reorganize its production operations.

9-21. What problems led the company to rethink its production process? What kind of technology did it choose to address these problems? What goals did the company set for applying technology in this way?

9-22. Before adding the new technology, what did the company do to analyze its existing production process? What changes, if any, were made as a result of this analysis?

9-23. How did technology-enhanced production help the company achieve its goals for financial performance? For customer service? For growth or expansion?

MyBizLab®

Go to the Assignments section of your MyLab to complete these writing exercises.

9-24. How does the offshoring controversy reflect the larger question of balancing the competing demands of stakeholder groups?

9-25. Why might a service business be more selective than a goods-producing business regarding the customers it pursues or accepts?

ENDNOTES

1. Kiesel Carvin Guitars website, accessed 6 April 6, 2015, www.carvinguitars.com; Carvin Facebook page, accessed 6 April 6, 2015, www.facebook.com/Kieselguitars; Kiesel YouTube channel, accessed 6 April 6, 2015, www.youtube.com/user/carvinguitars; Max Mobley, "Builder Profile: Carvin," *PremierGuitar*, 9 August 2011, www.premierguitar.com; "Carvin AW175" (product reviews), Harmony Central website, accessed 18 March 2005, www.harmonycentral.com; "Carvin CT6M California Carved Top," *Guitar Player*, December 2004, www.guitarplayer.com; Rich Krechel, "Some Custom-Made Guitars Can Cost $4,000 to $8,000," *St. Louis Post Dispatch*, 27 September 2001, 16.

2. Based in part on Russell L. Ackoff, "Why Few Organizations Adopt Systems Thinking," Ackoff Center Weblog, 7 March 2007, http://ackoffcenter.blogs.com; Daniel Aronson, "Introduction to Systems Thinking," The Thinking Page website, accessed 21 June 2007, www.thinking.net; "What Is Systems Thinking?" The Systems Thinker website, accessed 21 June 2007, www.thesystemsthinker.com; Peter Senge, *The Fifth Discipline: The Art and Practice of the Learning Organization* (New York: Doubleday, 1994), 57–67.

3. Stephen P. Robbins and David A. DeCenzo, *Fundamentals of Management*, 4th ed. (Upper Saddle River, N.J.: Pearson Prentice Hall, 2004), 405.

4. Peter Fingar and Ronald Aronica, "Value Chain Optimization: The New Way of Competing," *Supply Chain Management Review*, September–October 2001, 82–85.

5. John Gillie, "Boeing Says Dreamliner Testing on Schedule for Third Quarter Delivery," *News Tribune* (Tacoma, Wash.), 25 February 2011, www.thenewstribune.com; Jeffrey Rothfeder, "Bumpy Ride," *Portfolio*, May 2009, www.portfolio.com.

6. Toni Waterman, "Big Name US Firms 'Reshoring' from China," *Channel NewsAsia*, 2 November 2013, www.channelnewsasia.com; Alan S. Brown, "A Shift in Engineering Offshore," *Mechanical Engineering*, March 2009, 24–29.

7. Lisa Harrington, "Is U.S. Manufacturing Coming Back?" *Inbound Logistics*, August 2011, www.inboundlogistics.com.

8. Katy George, "Next-Shoring: A CEO's Guide," *McKinsey Quarterly*, January 2014, www.mckinsey.com.

9. Bruce Constantine, Brian Ruwadi, and Josh Wine, "Management Practices That Drive Supply Chain Success," *McKinsey Quarterly*, no. 2 (2009): 24–26.

10. Tim Laseter and Keith Oliver, "When Will Supply Chain Management Grow Up?" *Strategy+Business*, Fall 2003, 32–36; Robert J. Trent, "What Everyone Needs to Know About SCM," *Supply Chain Management Review*, 1 March 2004, www.manufacturing.net.

11. Ayse Bayat, Sekar Sundararajan, H. Robert Gustafson Jr., and Emory W. Zimmers Jr., "Sustainably Driven Supply Chains," *Industrial Engineer*, August 2011, 26–31; "Sustainability Index," Walmart, accessed 26 August 2011, http://walmartstores.com.

12. Trent, "What Everyone Needs to Know About SCM."

13. Andrew Feller, Dan Shunk, and Tom Callarman, "Value Chains Versus Supply Chains," *BPTrends*, March 2006, www.bptrends.com.

14. Patty Cantrell, "Sysco's Journey from Supply Chain to Value Chain," The Wallace Center, August 2009, www.ngfn.org.

15. Lee J. Krajewski and Larry P. Ritzman, *Operations Management: Processes and Value Chains*, 7th ed. (Upper Saddle River, N.J.: Pearson Prentice Hall, 2005), 744.

16. Malcolm Wheatley and Kevin Parker, "Rise in Global Enterprise Deployments Seen as Response to Far-Flung Supply Networks," *Manufacturing Business Technology*, May 2007, 26–27.

17. Krajewski and Ritzman, *Operations Management: Processes and Value Chains*, 482–483.

18. Roberta A. Russell and Bernard W. Taylor III, *Operations Management: Focusing on Quality and Competitiveness*, 2d ed. (Upper Saddle River, N.J.: Prentice Hall, 1998), 511.

19. Krajewski and Ritzman, *Operations Management*, 299–300.

20. Russell and Taylor, *Operations Management*, 161.

21. Krajewski and Ritzman, *Operations Management*, 244–245.

22. Robert Kreitner, *Management*, 9th ed. (Boston: Houghton Mifflin, 2004), 202–203.

23. "Dell on Social Media,' Dell website, accessed 8 April 2015, www.dell.com; Malcolm Wheatley, "Learning from Failure," *Engineering & Technology*, 11 September–24 September 2010, 56–58.

24. Jeffrey K. Liker, "The Way Back for Toyota," *Industrial Engineer*, May 2010, 28–33; Wheatley, "Learning from Failure."

25. Mark Rechtin, "Toyota Gives Development Clout to N.A.," *Automotive News*, 30 May 2011, 1, 23.

26. Russell and Taylor, *Operations Management*, 131.

27. Keith M. Bower, "Statistical Process Control," *ASQ*, accessed 27 August 2011, http://asq.org.

28. Donald W. Benbow and T. M. Kubiak, "Six Sigma," *ASQ*, accessed 27 August 2011, http://asq.org.

29. Steven Minter, "Six Sigma's Growing Pains," *IndustryWeek*, May 2009, 34–36; Tom McCarty, "Six Sigma at Motorola," *European CEO*, September–October 2004, www.motorola.com.

30. McCarty, "Six Sigma at Motorola"; General Electric, "What Is Six Sigma?" GE website, accessed 21 March 2005, www.ge.com.

31. George Byrne, Dave Lubowe, and Amy Blitz, "Driving Operational Innovation Using Lean Six Sigma," IBM, accessed 27 August 2011, www.ibm.com.

32. Quality Management Principles, *International Organization for Standardization*, 2012, www.iso.org.

33. "ISO 9000 Essentials," International Organization for Standardization website, accessed 27 August 2011, www.iso.org.

34. See note 1.

35. Project on Emerging Nanotechnologies website, accessed 11 April 2015, www.nanotechproject.org; National Nanotechnology Initiative website, accessed 11 April 2015, www.nano.gov; Barnaby J. Feder, "Technology: Bashful vs. Brash in the New Field of Nanotech," *New York Times*, 15 March 2004, www.nytimes.com; "Nanotechnology Basics," Nanotechnology Now website, accessed 16 April 2004, www.nanotech-now.com; Center for Responsible Nanotechnology website, accessed 16 April 2004, www.crnano.org; Gary Stix, "Little Big Science," *Scientific American*, 16 September 2001, www.sciam.com; Tim Harper, "Small Wonders," *Business 2.0*, July 2002, www.business2.com; Erick Schonfeld, "A Peek at IBM's Nanotech Research," *Business 2.0*, 5 December 2003, www.business2.com; David Pescovitz, "The Best New Technologies of 2003," *Business 2.0*, November 2003, 109–116.

PART 4

Supporting the Workforce: Motivation and Human Resources

AIMSTOCK/Getty Images

LEARNING OBJECTIVES After studying this chapter, you will be able to

1 Define *motivation*, and identify the classical motivation theories.

2 Explain why many consider expectancy theory to be the best current explanation of employee motivation.

3 Identify the strengths and weaknesses of goal-setting theory.

4 Describe the *job characteristics model*, and explain how it helps predict motivation and performance.

5 Define *reinforcement theory*, and differentiate between positive and negative reinforcement.

6 List five managerial strategies that are vital to maintaining a motivated workforce.

BEHIND THE SCENES TAKING A SECOND LOOK AT THE CAREER LADDER

Peter Dasilva/The New York Times/Redux

Having followed an unconventional career path herself, Cathy Benko helped redefine career options for Deloitte's employees.

www.deloitte.com

The notion of a business career being a straight vertical ascent from the bottom to the top is so embedded in our thinking that it has its own well-used metaphor: *climbing the corporate ladder*. The basic idea is that you join the workforce after college, you work hard for 30, 40, or 50 years, and you are rewarded along the way with positions of increasing responsibility and reward.

There's just one small problem with this whole ladder idea: It has never been true for millions of business professionals, and it often doesn't work out even for those who believe in the promise of continuous career progress. Simple arithmetic will tell you that the continuous climb simply can't work for most people—there just aren't enough high-level jobs, and the number shrinks dramatically with each step up the ladder. A major corporation with, say, 50,000 employees might have 100 executive positions from the vice president level up to the CEO. Even if only 10 percent of these employees (5,000) aspire to reach the upper levels, 4,900 of them aren't going to make it.

The numbers don't tell the whole story, either. Many employees have other priorities and demands in life, from raising families and dealing with health issues to continuing their education and exploring different career specialties along the way. In other words, millions of employees are unwilling or unable to maintain a straight climb up the ladder, and reward systems built on a steady climb aren't going to do much to motivate these people. As consultant Bruce Tulgan puts it, "Paying your dues, moving up slowly and getting the corner office—that's going away. In 10 years, it will be gone."

Cathy Benko is one of many executives who have been pondering this dilemma. As vice chairman and managing principal of Deloitte LLP, a diversified accounting, consulting, and financial advisory firm, Benko guides company strategy for attracting, developing, and motivating a highly skilled workforce. She realizes that the ladder metaphor has never quite fit many employees and that recent trends make it even less applicable to an ever-growing segment of the workforce. She knows the workplace needs to change to give employees a more satisfying, energizing, and motivating career path.

If you were Benko, what steps would you take to align the workplace with the changing workforce and make sure that every employee, on any career path, has a shot at success?[1]

INTRODUCTION

Deloitte's Cathy Benko (profiled in the chapter-opening Behind the Scenes) knows that a one-size-fits-all approach to managing and motivating employees has never been entirely satisfactory, and it is growing less effective every year as the workplace and the workforce continue to change. She could also tell you that although studying motivation is important, the task is challenging because no single theory or model can explain every motivational situation. The forces that affect motivation can vary widely from person to person and from situation to situation, and some managers and researchers continue to "rely on obsolete and discredited theories."[2] The various theories and models in this chapter each provide some insight into the complicated question of employee motivation, and taken as a whole, they provide an overall picture of the challenges and rewards of motivating employees to higher performance.

What Motivates Employees to Peak Performance?

1 LEARNING OBJECTIVE

Define *motivation*, and identify the classical motivation theories.

Motivating employees is one of the most important challenges every manager faces. No matter how skillful employees may be and how supportive the work environment is, without the motivation to excel, they won't perform at a high level. This section digs into the meaning of motivation and then explores some of the early attempts to provide practical models for motivating employees.

WHAT IS MOTIVATION?

Motivation is a complex subject that defies easy explanation, and some of the brightest minds in the field of management have been working for decades to understand this mysterious force. For one example, things that motivate you might have no effect on other people—or may even *demotivate* them. For another, some of the forces that motivate your behavior stem from deep within your subconscious mind, which means you might be driven by forces that you don't understand and can't even identify.

Starting with a basic definition, **motivation** is the combination of forces that drive individuals to take certain actions and avoid others in pursuit of individual objectives. Pay close attention to *drive* and *actions* in this definition; they are key to understanding motivation.

In a workplace setting, motivation can be assessed by measuring four indicators: *engagement, satisfaction, commitment,* and *rootedness* (see Exhibit 10.1 on the next page).[3] First, **engagement** reflects the degree of energy, enthusiasm, and effort each employee brings to his or her work. If you're "just not into it," chances are you won't perform at your best. Second, *satisfaction* indicates how happy employees are with the experience of work and the way they are treated. Third, *commitment* suggests the degree to which employees support the company and its mission. Fourth,

motivation
The combination of forces that move individuals to take certain actions and avoid other actions.

engagement
An employee's rational and emotional commitment to his or her work.

REAL-TIME UPDATES
Learn More by Reading This Article

Givers, takers, and matchers: How giving can be a source of motivation

Professor Adam Grant explains why being a giver rather than a taker can help your career and your motivation. Go to http://real-time updates.com/bia8 and click on Learn More in the Students section.

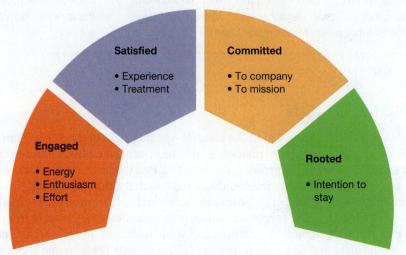

EXHIBIT 10.1   Four Indicators of Motivation

Employees can be said to be fully motivated when they are *engaged*, *satisfied*, *committed*, and *rooted* (meaning they have little or no intention to leave).

Satisfied
• Experience
• Treatment

Committed
• To company
• To mission

Engaged
• Energy
• Enthusiasm
• Effort

Rooted
• Intention to stay

Source: Based on Nitin Nohria, Boris Groysberg, and Linda-Eling Lee, "Employee Motivation: A Powerful New Model," *Harvard Business Review,* July–August 2008, 78–84.

rootedness (or its opposite, the intention to quit) predicts the likelihood that employees will stay or leave their jobs. A person who is engaged, satisfied, and committed and who has no intention of quitting can be safely said to be *motivated*.

These four indicators can identify who is motivated and who isn't, but they don't explain why. For that, it's necessary to dig deeper, looking into what drives people to choose certain actions and avoid others. Contemporary research suggests that motivation stems from four fundamental drives:[4]

- **The drive to acquire.** This includes fulfilling the need for not only physical goods such as food and clothing but also for enjoyable experiences and "psychological goods" such as prestige. Importantly, this drive is relative: Individuals want to know how well they're doing compared to others around them.
- **The drive to bond.** Humans are social creatures, and the need to feel a part of something larger is a vital aspect of employee motivation. This drive can be helpful, such as when it inspires employees to contribute to common goals, but it can also be harmful, such as when it pits groups of employees against one another in an "us-versus-them" mentality.
- **The drive to comprehend.** Learning, growing, meeting tough challenges, making sense of things—these are satisfying outcomes based on the drive to understand the world around us.
- **The drive to defend.** An instinct to protect and a sense of justice can lead human beings to vigorously defend the people, ideas, and organizations they hold dear. This drive is beneficial when it motivates people to fight for what is right, but it can be harmful as well, such as when it motivates people to resist change.

According to Harvard Business School's Nitin Nohria and his colleagues, who helped identify and explain these four drives, satisfying all four is essential to being motivated. When a need goes unsatisfied—or even worse, is betrayed, such as when employees believe an organization they've supported and defended no longer cares about them—poor motivation is the result.[5]

REAL-TIME UPDATES
Learn More by Watching This Presentation

Satisfying the four fundamental drives of employee behavior

Identify techniques that help satisfy the four fundamental drives in any workplace. Go to http://real-timeupdates.com/bia8 and click on Learn More in the Students section.

CLASSICAL THEORIES OF MOTIVATION

The quest to understand employee motivation has occupied researchers for more than a century. This section offers a brief overview of some of the important early theories that helped shape ideas about motivation. Although subsequent research has identified short-comings in all these theories, each contributed to our current understanding of motivation, and each continues to influence managerial practice.

Taylor's Scientific Management

One of the earliest motivational researchers, Frederick W. Taylor, a machinist and engineer from Philadelphia, studied employee efficiency and motivation in the late 19th and early 20th centuries. He is credited with developing **scientific management**, an approach that sought to improve employee efficiency through the scientific study of work. In addition to analyzing work and business processes in order to develop better methods, Taylor popularized financial incentives for good performance. His work truly revolutionized business and had a direct influence on the rise of the United States as a global industrial power in the first half of the 20th century.[6]

Although money proved to be a significant motivator for workers under scientific management, this approach didn't consider other motivational elements, such as opportunities for personal satisfaction. For instance, scientific management can't explain why a successful executive will take a hefty pay cut to serve in government or a nonprofit organization. Therefore, other researchers have looked beyond money to discover what else motivates people.

scientific management
A management approach designed to improve employees' efficiency by scientifically studying their work.

The Hawthorne Studies and the "Hawthorne Effect"

Between 1924 and 1932, a series of pioneering studies in employee motivation and productivity were conducted at the Hawthorne Works of the Western Electric Company in Chicago. The Hawthorne studies are intriguing both for what they uncovered and as an example of how management ideas can get oversimplified and misunderstood over the course of time. The research began as an experiment in scientific management: testing the effect of various levels of electric lighting on worker productivity. The researchers varied the lighting level for one group of workers (the experimental group) and kept it the same for a second group (the control group). Both groups were engaged in the tedious and exacting task of wrapping wire to make telephone coils, so lighting presumably played a key role in eye strain and other factors influencing productivity.[7]

Whatever the researchers expected to find, they surely didn't expect to see productivity increase in *both* groups as the lighting level was increased for the experimental group—and productivity kept increasing in both groups even when the lighting level was then lowered for the experimental group. In other words, no correlation between the level of lighting and the level of productivity was observed, and productivity increased among the control group workers even though their environment hadn't changed at all. This perplexing outcome was followed by a range of tests on other variables in the work environment and in employee rewards. The research team eventually concluded that group norms (see page 183) affected individual performance more than any other factor and that to understand employee performance one needed to understand an employee's total emotional and cultural makeup, on and off the job.[8]

By themselves, these conclusions are important, and the Hawthorne studies helped launch the entire field of industrial psychology and began to enlighten the practice of management in general.[9] Then a couple of decades later, a researcher not connected with the studies suggested the phenomenon of the **Hawthorne effect**, in which the behavior of the Western Electric workers changed because they were being observed and given special treatment as research subjects. In the years that followed, the concept of the Hawthorne effect took on a life of its own and became widely assumed across many fields of research, from management to medicine, even though the original research never reached this conclusion. Moreover, the phenomenon has come to be defined in so many ways that the use of the term could obscure more than it explains. The outcome of the Hawthorne studies has too often been reduced to this oversimplified and uncertain

Hawthorne effect
A supposed effect of organizational research, in which employees change their behavior because they are being studied and given special treatment.

conclusion about the behavior of research subjects; the real and lasting contribution of the studies was to open a lot of eyes about the benefits of understanding human behavior in organizational settings.[10]

Maslow's Hierarchy of Needs

Maslow's hierarchy

A model in which human needs are arranged in a hierarchy, with the most basic needs at the bottom and the more advanced needs toward the top.

In 1943, psychologist Abraham Maslow hypothesized that behavior is determined by a variety of needs, which he organized into categories arranged in a hierarchy. As Exhibit 10.2 shows, the most basic needs are at the bottom of this hierarchy, while the more advanced needs are toward the top. In **Maslow's hierarchy** all of the requirements for basic survival—food, clothing, shelter, and the like—fall into the category of *physiological needs*. These basic needs must be satisfied before the person can consider higher-level needs such as *safety needs, social needs* (the need to give and receive love and to feel a sense of belonging), and *esteem needs* (the need for a sense of self-worth and integrity).[11]

At the top of Maslow's hierarchy is *self-actualization*—the need to become everything one can be. This need is also the most difficult to fulfill—and even to identify in many cases. Employees who reach this point work not just because they want to make money or impress others but because they feel their work is worthwhile and satisfying in itself.

Maslow's hierarchy is a convenient and logical tool for classifying human needs, and many people continue to use it to explain behavior. However, other researchers have not been able to experimentally verify that this is how motivation actually works.[12]

Theory X and Theory Y

Theory X

A managerial assumption that employees are irresponsible, are unambitious, and dislike work and that managers must use force, control, or threats to motivate them.

Theory Y

A managerial assumption that employees enjoy meaningful work, are naturally committed to certain goals, are capable of creativity, and seek out responsibility under the right conditions.

In the 1960s, psychologist Douglas McGregor proposed two radically different sets of assumptions that underlie most management thinking, which he classified as *Theory X* and *Theory Y*. According to McGregor, **Theory X**–oriented managers believe that employees dislike work and can be motivated only by the fear of losing their jobs or by *extrinsic rewards*—those given by other people, such as money and promotions. In contrast, **Theory Y**–oriented managers believe that employees like to work and can be motivated by working for goals that promote creativity or for causes they believe in. Consequently, Theory Y–oriented managers seek to motivate employees through *intrinsic rewards*—which employees essentially give to themselves.[13] As with Maslow's hierarchy, *Theory X* and *Theory Y* seem to have a permanent place in the management vocabulary, but they suffer from the same lack of empirical

EXHIBIT 10.2	**Maslow's Hierarchy of Needs**

Abraham Maslow suggested that needs on the lower levels of the hierarchy must be satisfied before higher-level needs can be addressed (examples are shown to the right). This model offers a convenient way to categorize needs, but it lacks empirical validation.

Source: Based on Andrew J. DuBrin, *Applying Psychology: Individual & Organizational Effectiveness*, 6th ed. (Upper Saddle River, N.J.: Pearson Prentice Hall, 2004), 122–124.

evidence.[14] (However, the distinction between intrinsic and extrinsic rewards remains a valid and essential aspect of many theories of motivation.)

Herzberg's Two Factors

Also in the 1960s, Frederick Herzberg and his associates explored the aspects of jobs that make employees feel satisfied or dissatisfied. The researchers found that two entirely different sets of factors were associated with dissatisfying and satisfying work experiences. In **Herzberg's two-factor theory** (see Exhibit 10.3), so-called *hygiene factors* are associated with dissatisfying experiences, and *motivators* are associated with satisfying experiences. Hygiene factors are mostly extrinsic and include working conditions, company policies, pay, and job security. Motivators tend to be intrinsic and include achievement, recognition, responsibility, and other personally rewarding factors.[15] According to Herzberg's model, managers need to remove dissatisfying elements *and* add satisfying elements—doing one or the other is not enough.[16]

Like Maslow's hierarchy and Theory X/Theory Y, the two-factor theory seems logical and helps explain part of the motivation puzzle. However, it has been criticized because of the methodology used in the original research and the inability of subsequent research to validate the model. Also, although there is a strong causal link between customer satisfaction and profitability, it is far less clear whether satisfied *employees* automatically lead to satisfied *customers*.[17]

Herzberg's two-factor theory
A model that divides motivational forces into satisfiers ("motivators") and dissatisfiers ("hygiene factors").

McClelland's Three Needs

The last of the classical theories to consider is the **three-needs theory** developed by David McClelland. McClelland's model highlights the *need for power* (having—and demonstrating—control over others), the *need for affiliation* (being accepted by others and having opportunities for social interaction), and the *need for achievement* (attaining personally meaningful goals).[18] Unlike with the other classical theories, there is a lot of research

three-needs theory
David McClelland's model of motivation that highlights the needs for power, affiliation, and achievement.

EXHIBIT 10.3	**Herzberg's Two-Factor Theory**

According to Herzberg, *hygiene factors* such as working conditions and company policies can influence employee dissatisfaction. On the other hand, *motivators* such as opportunities for achievement and recognition can influence employee satisfaction.

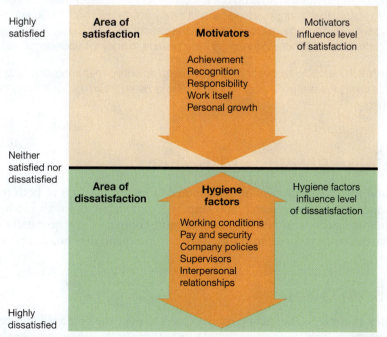

to validate McClelland's ideas and to explain particular outcomes in the workplace. For example, those with a high need for achievement tend to make successful entrepreneurs, but this focus on personal achievement can actually get in the way of managerial effectiveness, which relies on the ability to influence others toward shared goals.[19]

Conversely, managers who are most successful in a conventional organizational structure tend to have a higher need for power and relatively little need for affiliation. They are less concerned with achieving personal goals or being well liked than they are with building up the influence needed to get things done through other people.[20]

Although it helps explain motivation in various contexts, the biggest drawback to McClelland's approach is its limited practicality in terms of identifying needs and crafting motivational programs to harness them in beneficial directions. The three needs are subconscious, according to McClelland, and trained experts are required to help identify them in each individual.[21]

 Checkpoint

LEARNING OBJECTIVE 1: Define *motivation*, and identify the classical motivation theories.

SUMMARY: Motivation is the combination of forces that prompt individuals to take certain actions and avoid others in pursuit of individual objectives. Research suggests that four drives underlie all motivation: the drive to acquire tangible and intangible rewards, the drive to bond with others, the drive to comprehend, and the drive to defend. The classical motivation theories and research that helped shape today's thinking include Taylor's scientific management, the Hawthorne studies, Maslow's hierarchy of needs, McGregor's Theory X and Theory Y, Herzberg's two factors, and McClelland's three needs.

CRITICAL THINKING: (1) How could a manager tap into the drive to defend as a way to help rally employees? (2) Could Herzberg's hygiene factors help explain the significant problem of employee theft and embezzlement? Why or why not?

IT'S YOUR BUSINESS: (1) If you are a typical college student who doesn't have much financial security at the moment but is also trying to fulfill higher-order needs such as social interaction and self-actualization through your education, would it make more sense, according to Maslow, to drop out of college and work seven days a week so you could help ensure that your physiological and safety needs are met? (2) Do you think today's college students more closely match the descriptions of Theory X employees or Theory Y employees? What evidence can you provide to support your conclusion?

KEY TERMS TO KNOW: motivation, engagement, scientific management, Hawthorne effect, Maslow's hierarchy, Theory X, Theory Y, Herzberg's two-factor theory, three-needs theory

---

2 **LEARNING OBJECTIVE**

Explain why many consider expectancy theory to be the best current explanation of employee motivation.

expectancy theory
The idea that the effort employees put into their work depends on expectations about their own ability to perform, expectations about likely rewards, and the attractiveness of those rewards.

Explaining Employee Choices

The classical theories of motivation contributed in important ways to both managerial practices and the ongoing research into employee motivation, but each has been found wanting in some way or another. Starting with more contemporary theories, two models, known as expectancy theory and equity theory, help explain the choices that employees make.

EXPECTANCY THEORY

Expectancy theory, considered by some experts to offer the best available explanation of employee motivation, connects an employee's efforts to the outcome he or she expects from those efforts. Expectancy theory focuses less on the specific forces that motivate

EXHIBIT 10.4	**Expectancy Theory**

Expectancy theory suggests that employees base their efforts on expectations of their own performance, expectations of rewards for that performance, and the value of those rewards.

Source: Based on Stephen P. Robbins and David A. DeCenzo, *Fundamentals of Management,* 4th ed. (Upper Saddle River, N.J.: Pearson Prentice Hall, 2004), 289.

employees and more on the process they follow to seek satisfaction in their jobs. As shown in Exhibit 10.4, the effort employees will put forth depends on (1) their expectations regarding the level of performance they will be able to achieve, (2) their beliefs regarding the rewards that the organization will give in response to that performance, and (3) the attractiveness of those rewards relative to their individual goals.[22]

Exploring these connections from both an employee's and a manager's perspective will give you an idea of how the expectancy model can explain employee behavior and prescribe managerial tactics to help motivate employees. First, as an employee, if you don't believe that the amount of effort you are willing or able to apply to a task will result in an acceptable level of performance, a natural response will be to say, "Well, why bother?" This uncertainty could come from many sources, such as doubts about your skills, confusion about the task, or a belief that "the system" is so broken that no matter how hard you try you can't succeed. Belief in your ability to complete a task is known as *self-efficacy*, and it can be increased by gaining experience, mimicking successful role models, getting encouragement from others, and sometimes even "psyching yourself up."[23] As a manager, your challenges would be to ensure that employees have the skills and confidence they need, that tasks are clearly defined, and that company policies and processes are functional.

Your second concern as an employee is whether the organization will recognize and reward your performance. Knowing you've done great work is its own reward, of course, but for many employees, this isn't enough. As a manager, your challenges include establishing reward systems and expectations to minimize employee uncertainty and taking time from the daily chaos to acknowledge the efforts your employees make.

Finally, if you're confident in your performance and the organization's response, your third concern is whether the promised reward is something you value. What if you are offered a raise but what you really want is for your boss to acknowledge how important your contributions have been to the company? As a manager, aligning rewards with employee priorities is an ongoing challenge; see "Reinforcing High-Performance Behavior" on page 237.

EQUITY THEORY

If you work side by side with someone, doing the same job and giving the same amount of effort, only to learn that your colleague earns more money, will you be satisfied in your work and motivated to continue working hard? Chances are, you will perceive a state of *inequity*, and you probably won't be happy with the situation. **Equity theory** suggests that employee satisfaction depends on the perceived ratio of inputs to outputs. To remedy a

equity theory
The idea that employees base their level of satisfaction on the ratio of their inputs to the job to the outputs or rewards they receive from it.

perception of inequity, you might ask for a raise, decide not to work as hard, try to change perceptions of your efforts or their outcomes, or simply quit and find a new job. Any one of these steps has the potential to bring your perceived input-to-output ratio back into balance.[24] Some of the choices employees can make to address perceived inequity are obviously not desirable from an employer's point of view, so it's important to understand why employees might feel they aren't getting a fair shake.

Equity issues can show up in a number of areas, such as in complaints about gender pay fairness and executive compensation (see page 262) and in many unionizing efforts, whenever employees feel they aren't getting a fair share of corporate profits or are being asked to shoulder more than their fair share of hardships.

Research into equity theory has led to thinking about the broader concept of *organizational justice*, or perceptions of fairness in the workplace. These perceptions relate to outcomes, the processes used to generate those outcomes, and the way employees are treated during the process.[25] No reasonable employee expects to make as much as the CEO, for example, but as long as the process seems fair (both the employee's and the CEO's pay are related to performance, for example), most employees will be satisfied, and the disparity won't affect their motivation. In fact, perceptions of fairness can have as much impact on overall employee satisfaction as satisfaction with pay itself.[26]

 Checkpoint

LEARNING OBJECTIVE 2: Explain why many consider expectancy theory to be the best current explanation of employee motivation.

SUMMARY: Expectancy theory suggests that the effort employees put into their work depends on expectations about their own ability to perform, expectations about the rewards the organization will give in response to that performance, and the attractiveness of those rewards relative to their individual goals. This theory is thought to be a good model because it considers the links between effort and outcome. For instance, if employees think a link is "broken," such as having doubts that their efforts will yield acceptable performance or worries that they will perform well but no one will notice, they're likely to put less effort into their work.

CRITICAL THINKING: (1) What steps could managers take to alleviate the self-doubt employees often feel when they join a company or move into a new position? (2) If you were a human resources manager in a large corporation, how might you respond to employees who complain that the CEO makes two or three hundred times more than they make?

IT'S YOUR BUSINESS: (1) Have you ever given less than your best effort in a college course because you didn't believe you were capable of excelling in the course? (2) Was the outcome satisfying? Would you handle a similar situation the same way in the future?

KEY TERMS TO KNOW: expectancy theory, equity theory

3 **LEARNING OBJECTIVE**

Identify the strengths and weaknesses of goal-setting theory.

goal-setting theory
A motivational theory suggesting that setting goals can be an effective way to motivate employees.

Motivating with Challenging Goals

With the expectancy and equity theories offering some insight into why employees make the choices they do, the next step in understanding motivation is to explore specific leadership strategies that motivate employees. **Goal-setting theory**, the idea that carefully designed goals can motivate employees to higher performance, is one of the most important contemporary theories of motivation. It is both widely used and strongly supported by experimental research.[27] (However, as "Risks and Limitations of Goal-Setting Theory" on page 234 explains, some researchers assert that the benefits of goal setting have been overstated and the risks have been understated, partly because some research studies fail to measure the full consequences of goal-driven behaviors.)

For goals to function as effective motivators, a number of criteria must be met. These criteria include[28]

- Goals that are specific enough to give employees clarity and focus
- Goals that are difficult enough to inspire energetic and committed effort
- Clear "ownership" of goals so that accountability can be established
- Timely feedback that lets people know if they're progressing toward their goals and, if not, how to change course
- Individuals' belief in their ability to meet their goals
- Cultural support for the individual achievement and independence needed to reach the goals

As today's companies face the twin challenges of increasing global competition and a slow economy, goal setting could play an even more important role than it already does.

MANAGEMENT BY OBJECTIVES

Goal-setting theory is frequently implemented through a technique known as **management by objectives (MBO)**, a companywide process that empowers employees and involves them in goal setting and decision making. This process consists of four steps: setting goals, planning actions to meet those goals, implementing the plans, and reviewing performance (see Exhibit 10.5). Because employees at all levels are involved in all four steps, they learn more about company objectives and feel that they are an important part of the companywide team. Furthermore, they understand how their individual job functions contribute to the organization's long-term success.

REAL-TIME UPDATES
Learn More by Exploring This Interactive Website

Plot your career path

See whether you've been on a straight path up the career ladder or have been moving around a career lattice. Go to http://real-time updates.com/bia8 and click on Learn More in the Students section.

management by objectives (MBO)

A motivational approach in which managers and employees work together to structure personal goals and objectives for every individual, department, and project to mesh with the organization's goals.

EXHIBIT 10.5	Management by Objectives

The four steps of the MBO cycle are refined and repeated as managers and employees at all levels work toward establishing goals and objectives, thereby accomplishing the organization's strategic goals

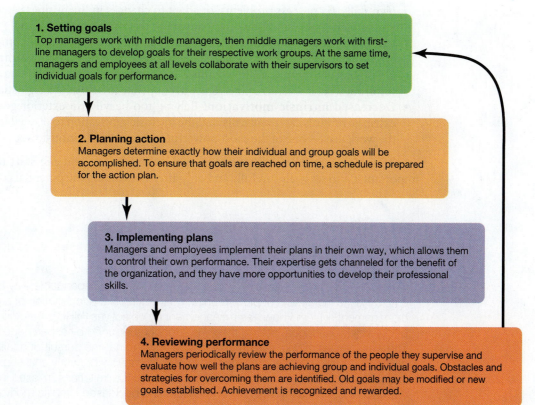

1. Setting goals
Top managers work with middle managers, then middle managers work with first-line managers to develop goals for their respective work groups. At the same time, managers and employees at all levels collaborate with their supervisors to set individual goals for performance.

2. Planning action
Managers determine exactly how their individual and group goals will be accomplished. To ensure that goals are reached on time, a schedule is prepared for the action plan.

3. Implementing plans
Managers and employees implement their plans in their own way, which allows them to control their own performance. Their expertise gets channeled for the benefit of the organization, and they have more opportunities to develop their professional skills.

4. Reviewing performance
Managers periodically review the performance of the people they supervise and evaluate how well the plans are achieving group and individual goals. Obstacles and strategies for overcoming them are identified. Old goals may be modified or new goals established. Achievement is recognized and rewarded.

One of the key elements of MBO is the collaborative goal-setting process. Together, a manager and an employee define the employee's goals, the responsibilities for achieving those goals, and the means of evaluating individual and group performance so that the employee's activities are directly linked to achieving the organization's long-term goals. Jointly setting clear and challenging but achievable goals can encourage employees to reach higher levels of performance, although participation alone is no guarantee of higher performance.[29]

RISKS AND LIMITATIONS OF GOAL-SETTING THEORY

As powerful as goal setting can be, it can misfire in a variety of ways, with results ranging from employee frustration to systematic underperformance to serious ethical and legal problems:[30]

- **Overly narrow goals.** When goals are too narrow, people can miss or intentionally ignore vital aspects of the bigger picture. Salespeople trying to meet their quotas, for example, might be tempted to offer huge discounts or extend credit to customers who can't make the payments.
- **Overly challenging goals.** Lofty goals can inspire great performance, but they can also lead to risky behavior, belligerent negotiating tactics, and ethical lapses as employees cut corners to reach targets.
- **Inappropriate time horizons.** Too much emphasis on short-term performance can degrade long-term performance. A good example is the unhealthy focus that a publicly traded company can place on quarterly performance in order to meet the stock market's expectations. This distorted focus can lead to decisions such as downsizing or cutting back on research that might help the bottom line in the short term but ultimately limit the company's ability to compete and grow.
- **Unintentional performance limitations.** Goals can limit performance potential when employees reach their targets and then stop trying, even though they could go beyond that level if reaching the goal didn't signal that it was acceptable to stop there.
- **Missed learning opportunities.** Employees can get so focused on meeting deadlines and other goals that they overlook opportunities to learn, whether to improve their own skills, fix process problems, or adapt to changes in the business environment— all of which could benefit the company more than meeting the original goal.[31]
- **Unhealthy internal competition.** Goals can pit groups within a company against each other, which can be beneficial if the competition is healthy but ultimately harmful if it is not. For example, healthy competitions among sales regions can be a great motivator, but what if several regions refuse to cooperate to help land a big national client?
- **Decreased intrinsic motivation.** Relying too heavily on exterior goals and their extrinsic rewards can eventually dull the intrinsic motivation to do well for the sake of the work itself—one of the most powerful and sustainable motivators.

As you ponder these limitations of goal-setting theory, you can start to sense how important it is to set goals carefully and only after considering the potential consequences.

 Checkpoint

LEARNING OBJECTIVE 3: Identify the strengths and weaknesses of goal-setting theory.

SUMMARY: Setting challenging goals has proven to be a dependable way to inspire employees to high levels of performance; goal setting is the foundation of a popular management system known as management by objectives (MBO). In addition to being widely used, goal-setting theory is strongly supported by experimental research. The weaknesses of goal setting generally lie in ways that the pursuit of goals can distort behavior. Potential problems include overly narrow or overly challenging goals, inappropriate time horizons, unintentional performance limitations, missed learning opportunities, unhealthy internal competition, and decreased intrinsic motivation.

Redesigning Jobs to Stimulate Performance

4 **LEARNING OBJECTIVE**

Describe the *job characteristics model*, and explain how it helps predict motivation and performance.

Along with setting challenging goals, many companies are exploring ways to redesign the work itself to improve employee satisfaction and motivation.

THE JOB CHARACTERISTICS MODEL

Using the **job characteristics model** proposed by Richard Hackman and Greg Oldman has proven to be a reliable way to predict the effects of five *core job dimensions* on employee motivation and other positive outcomes:[32]

- **Skill variety**—the range of skills and talents needed to accomplish the responsibilities associated with the job. The broader the range of skills required, the more meaningful the work is likely to be to the employee.
- **Task identity**—the degree to which the employee has responsibility for completing an entire task. Greater task identity contributes to the sense of meaning in work.
- **Task significance**—the employee's perception of the impact the job has on the lives of other people.
- **Autonomy**—the degree of independence the employee has in carrying out the job.
- **Feedback**—timely information that tells employees how well they're doing in their jobs.

job characteristics model
A model suggesting that five core job dimensions influence three critical psychological states that determine motivation, performance, and other outcomes.

You can see that some of these dimensions relate to the nature of the work itself and others relate more to management decisions and leadership styles. All of them contribute in one way or another to three *critical psychological states:*

- **Experienced meaningfulness of the work**—a measure of how much employees care about the jobs they are doing.
- **Experienced responsibility for results**—the sense each employee has that his or her efforts contribute to the outcome.
- **Knowledge of actual results**—employees' awareness of the real-life results of their efforts.

As these psychological states increase in intensity, they lead to improvements in motivation, performance, job satisfaction, absenteeism (the amount of time employees miss work), and turnover (the rate at which employees leave their jobs). In other words, if employees believe their work is meaningful, believe their individual efforts are responsible at least in large part for the outcome of that work, and can see evidence of the results of their efforts, they are likely to be more motivated than they would otherwise. It's not hard to see that the reverse is also true. Employees who believe their work is meaningless, who don't feel much responsibility for the outcome, or who never get to see the results of their efforts aren't likely to be terribly motivated or satisfied.

One final aspect of job characteristics research explores how various types of employees respond to changes in the

Companies can boost performance by designing jobs so that employees feel the meaning in their work and a sense of responsibility for results.

Kzenon/Fotolia

core job dimensions. Employees with strong *growth needs*, meaning they feel a strong need to increase self-esteem and self-actualization, respond more dramatically to improvements in job dimensions—and improvements in the critical psychological states will lead to greater increases in their motivation and the other positive outcomes.[33] Conversely, employees who feel little intrinsic need to grow can be among the most difficult to motivate, no matter what steps managers take.

The job characteristics model continues to offer helpful guidance as companies grapple with the challenges in today's work environment. For instance, as more companies increasingly rely on temporary workers to control costs or acquire skills that are needed only for specific projects, managers need to think carefully about the ways they supervise permanent versus temporary employees. As two examples, temporary workers may need to be assigned more discrete tasks that have enough task identity and autonomy to provide a sense of ownership and control, and managers need to make sure they don't take permanent employees for granted and fail to give them adequate feedback about their efforts.[34]

APPROACHES TO MODIFYING CORE JOB DIMENSIONS

The job characteristics model identifies the generic aspects of a job that can be adjusted to improve motivation, but it's up to individual companies and departments to identify and make the specific changes that are relevant to each job in the organization. Three popular approaches are job enrichment, job enlargement, and cross-training:

job enrichment
Making jobs more challenging and interesting by expanding the range of skills required.

- **Job enrichment.** The strategy behind **job enrichment** is to make jobs more challenging and interesting by expanding the range of skills required—typically by expanding upward, giving employees some of the responsibilities previously held by their managers.[35] For example, an employee who had been preparing presentations for his or her boss to give to customers could be asked to give the presentations as well. Job enrichment needs to be approached carefully, however. Some employees respond well, but for others, the increased responsibility is more a source of stress than of inspiration.[36]

- **Job enlargement.** Whereas job enrichment expands vertically, *job enlargement* is more of a horizontal expansion, adding tasks that aren't necessarily any more challenging. If it simply gives workers more to do, job enlargement won't do much to motivate and will more likely demotivate. However, if jobs are enlarged in ways that increase worker knowledge, expansion can improve job satisfaction.[37]

cross-training
Training workers to perform multiple jobs and rotating them through these various jobs to combat boredom or burnout.

- **Cross-training.** Job enrichment and job enlargement expand the scope of an individual job, whereas **cross-training**, or *job rotation*, involves training workers to perform multiple jobs and rotating them through these various jobs to combat boredom or burnout. Cross-training is also valuable in lean manufacturing (see page 208) because it lets companies keep staffs as small as possible and assign people wherever they are needed to handle fluctuations in workflow. And in a tight economy, cross-training helps companies address task needs without adding new staff.[38]

Not all the steps companies can take to improve motivation involve restructuring jobs, providing additional training, or making other explicit changes. Improvements can also come from making changes in management attitudes and practices, such as giving employees more control over their work and providing timely feedback. The best solution is usually a combination of changes that accommodate the nature of the work and the abilities and interests of individual employees and managers.

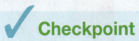 **Checkpoint**

LEARNING OBJECTIVE 4: Describe the *job characteristics model*, and explain how it helps predict motivation and performance.

SUMMARY: The job characteristics model identifies five core job dimensions (skill variety, task identity, task significance, autonomy, and feedback) that create three critical psychological states (experienced meaningfulness of the work, experienced responsibility for results, and knowledge of actual results). Achieving these three states leads to improvements in motivation, job satisfaction, performance, absenteeism, and turnover.

CRITICAL THINKING: (1) Can the job characteristics model be used to motivate employees in such positions as janitors or security guards in a factory? How? (2) Is modifying the five core job dimensions likely to motivate employees who have low growth needs? Why or why not?

IT'S YOUR BUSINESS: (1) Has the requirement of working in teams ever lowered your motivation or satisfaction on a school project? If so, how does the job characteristics model explain this? (2) How does taking elective courses improve your experience of meaningfulness in your college "work"?

KEY TERMS TO KNOW: job characteristics model, job enrichment, cross-training

Reinforcing High-Performance Behavior

5   **LEARNING OBJECTIVE**

Define *reinforcement theory*, and differentiate between positive and negative reinforcement.

Challenging goals and creative job designs can motivate employees to higher levels of performance, but managers also need to make sure that performance can be sustained over time. Employees in the workplace, like people in all other aspects of life, tend to repeat behaviors that create positive outcomes for themselves and to avoid or abandon behaviors that bring negative outcomes. **Reinforcement theory** suggests that managers can motivate employees by shaping their actions through *behavior modification*. Using reinforcement theory, managers try to systematically encourage those actions considered beneficial to the company. Reinforcement is a valuable motivational tool, but it has broad application whenever managers want to shape employee behavior.

reinforcement theory
A motivational approach based on the idea that managers can motivate employees by influencing their behaviors with positive and negative reinforcement.

TYPES OF REINFORCEMENT

Reinforcement can be either *positive* or *negative*. In casual speech, the two terms are usually equated with praise for desirable behavior and criticism or punishment for undesirable behavior, respectively, but they have different and specific meanings in psychological terminology (see Exhibit 10.6). Both positive and negative reinforcement encourage behaviors to be repeated; the difference is in how they do it.

Positive reinforcement offers pleasant consequences for particular actions or behaviors, increasing the likelihood that the behaviors will be repeated. For example, even a simple but sincere "thank you" provides emotional reward and encourages employees

positive reinforcement
Encouraging desired behaviors by offering pleasant consequences for completing or repeating those behaviors.

EXHIBIT 10.6	**Reinforcement and Punishment**

The terminology of reinforcement theory can be confusing because the terms are used differently in everyday speech than in psychology. Three points will help you keep the terms straight in your mind. First, both positive and negative reinforcement encourage a behavior to be repeated—they *reinforce* it, in order words. The difference is in how they work. Second, punishment (not negative reinforcement) is the opposite of positive reinforcement. Third, positive reinforcement can encourage undesirable behaviors, so it isn't necessarily a good thing, despite the "positive" label.

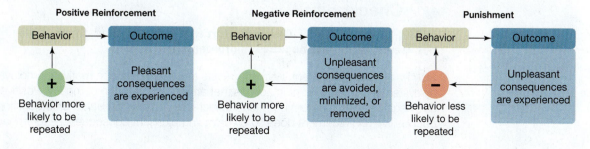

incentives
Monetary payments and other rewards of value used for positive reinforcement.

negative reinforcement
Encouraging the repetition of a particular behavior (desirable or not) by removing unpleasant consequences for the behavior.

to repeat whatever behavior elicited the praise.[39] Positive reinforcement can also have a multiplier effect, in which employees who receive positive reinforcement for one type of behavior are motivated to perform well in other areas, a process known as *chaining*.[40]

Many companies use some form of **incentives**, either monetary payments or other rewards of value, as positive reinforcement to motivate employees to achieve specific performance targets. Like praise and public recognition, incentive programs can become particularly important during economic slowdowns, when many employers can't afford to give big salary increases and companies aren't growing fast enough to create opportunities for career advancement.[41]

Again, don't be misled by the label "positive." Positive reinforcement can encourage bad behavior, so it isn't necessarily good. If an employee gets a compliment after taking credit for someone else's work, this positive feedback might encourage him or her to act unethically again the next time the opportunity arises.

Negative reinforcement also encourages a particular behavior to be repeated, but it does so through the reduction, removal, or absence of an unpleasant outcome. For example, if you initially received some complaints about publicly humiliating your employees after taking over as department manager, but those complaints dwindled over time as people gave up and accepted your poor behavior, their silence would encourage you to continue being a bully. Many people mistakenly use the term *negative reinforcement* when they are actually talking about *punishment*, which refers to actions used to diminish the repetition of unwanted behaviors by adding unpleasant outcomes.[42]

Of these three possibilities, you can see how positive reinforcement is the only one that injects positive energy into the situation. Fear can certainly be a powerful motivator, but it also adds stress and anxiety that can eventually lead to burnout and attrition as employees decide they don't want to deal with the constant pressure. And although punishment can be effective as a way to discourage particular behaviors, the effect isn't always permanent, and it can create serious morale problems.[43]

UNINTENDED CONSEQUENCES OF REINFORCEMENT

Reinforcement sounds like a simple enough concept, but the mechanisms of reinforcement can be subtle and the effects unexpected. Managers must be on constant alert for unintended consequences of incentives and other reinforcement efforts. For example, because they often focus on a single variable, incentive programs can distort performance by encouraging employees to focus on that variable to the detriment of other responsibilities.[44] If your salespeople get a bonus every time they land a new client but receive no penalties whenever an unhappy client leaves for a competitor, sales staffers will naturally tend to focus more on acquiring new clients than on making sure existing clients are satisfied.

Reinforcement doesn't have to involve explicit monetary incentives to distort behavior, either. For instance, imagine that a manager offers enthusiastic praise whenever employees suggest new ideas during meetings but never follows up to see whether those employees actually do any work to implement their great ideas. He or she can be encouraging empty "happy talk" through both positive reinforcement (there are pleasant consequences for spouting out ideas during meetings) *and* negative reinforcement (there are no unpleasant consequences for not doing any of the work, so employees will continue to not do it).

✓ **Checkpoint**

LEARNING OBJECTIVE 5: Define *reinforcement theory*, and differentiate between positive and negative reinforcement.

SUMMARY: Reinforcement theory suggests that managers can motivate employees by systematically encouraging actions that are beneficial to the company. Positive and negative reinforcement both tend to increase the specific behavior in question, but positive reinforcement does so by providing pleasant consequences for engaging in the behavior, whereas negative reinforcement does so by removing unpleasant consequences. The term *negative reinforcement* is sometimes used in casual speech when people are really talking about *punishment,* which is discouraging a particular behavior by offering unpleasant consequences for it.

CRITICAL THINKING: (1) Is demoting an employee for failing to finish a project an attempt at negative reinforcement or punishment? Why? (2) In what ways is reinforcement theory similar to goal-setting theory?

IT'S YOUR BUSINESS: (1) How does your instructor in this course use positive reinforcement to motivate students to higher levels of performance? (2) If you study diligently to avoid being embarrassed when a professor calls on you in class, is this positive or negative reinforcement in action? Why?

KEY TERMS TO KNOW: reinforcement theory, positive reinforcement, incentives, negative reinforcement

Motivational Strategies

Regardless of the specific motivational theories that a company chooses to implement in its management policies and reward systems, managers can improve their ability to motivate employees by providing timely and frequent feedback, personalizing motivational efforts, adapting to circumstances and special needs, tackling workplace problems before they have a chance to destroy morale, and being inspirational leaders.

6 **LEARNING OBJECTIVE**

List five managerial strategies that are vital to maintaining a motivated workforce.

PROVIDING TIMELY AND FREQUENT FEEDBACK

Imagine how you'd feel if you worked for weeks on a complex project for one of your classes, turned it in on time, and then heard … nothing. As days passed with no feedback, doubts would begin to creep in. Was your work so good that your professor is passing it around to other faculty members in sheer astonishment? Was it so bad that your professor is still searching for the words to describe it? Was your project simply lost in the shuffle, and no one cares enough to find it?

No matter which theory of motivation an organization or a manager subscribes to, providing timely and frequent feedback is essential. From the perspective of reinforcement theory, for example, feedback is the mechanism that shapes employee behavior. Without it, opportunities for reinforcement will be missed, and the effort put forth by employees will eventually wane because they'll see little reason to continue.

Feedback "closes the loop" in two important ways: It give employees the information they need in order to assess their own performance and make improvements if necessary, and it serves the emotional purpose of reassuring employees that someone is paying attention. Even if the feedback is constructive criticism, it lets employees know that what they do is important enough to be done correctly.

MAKING IT PERSONAL

A recurring theme in just about every attempt to explain motivation is that motivation is a deeply personal phenomenon. Rewards and feedback that stimulate one employee to higher achievement can have no effect on a second employee and may demotivate a third. As you'll see in Behind the Scenes at the end of the chapter, customizing career paths is an essential aspect of how Cathy Benko and her colleagues at Deloitte help to personalize motivation and rewards.

In an ideal world, managers would be able to personalize motivational efforts completely, giving each employee

REAL-TIME UPDATES

Learn More by Exploring This Interactive Website

Quick summaries of key motivational concepts

These charts offer bite-sized wisdom about what works and what doesn't when it comes to employee motivation. Go to http://real-timeupdates.com/bia8 and click on Learn More in the Students section.

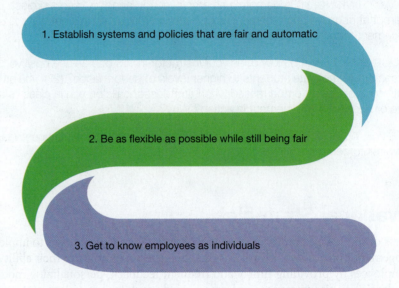

EXHIBIT 10.7 **Personalizing Motivation**

Gearing motivational efforts to the individual makes them more effective, but this approach must be conducted in a way that is fair for everyone. Achieving a balance is not always easy, because various employees are motivated by different things.

1. Establish systems and policies that are fair and automatic

2. Be as flexible as possible while still being fair

3. Get to know employees as individuals

the rewards and feedback that spur him or her to peak achievement. However, the need for fairness and the demands on a manager's time place practical limits on the degree to which motivational efforts can be individualized. The situation calls for a three-pronged approach (see Exhibit 10.7). First, establish systems and policies that are as equitable and as automatic as possible, and explain to employees why they are fair. Second, build in as much flexibility as you can, such as offering employees the cash equivalent of paid time off if they prefer money over time. Third, get to know employees as individuals in order to understand what is important to each person. For example, research suggests that younger employees are more likely to be demotivated by uninteresting work than their older counterparts.[45] (Another possible explanation is that older workers have learned to accept the fact that work can't always be exciting and are more willing to do whatever needs to be done.) If one person craves intellectual challenges, give him or her the tough problems to solve. If another thrives on recognition, give that employee the chance to give presentations to upper management.

Of course, managers need to give everyone an equal shot at opportunities, but as much as possible, they should let employees choose which opportunities and rewards they want to pursue. Employees understand that their managers can't always change "the system," but they do expect their managers to exercise some individual control over how policies are implemented and rewards are given.[46]

GAMIFYING FOR HEALTHY COMPETITION

gamification
Applying game principles such as scorekeeping to various business processes.

One of the newest motivational strategies is **gamification**, applying game principles to various business processes. Importantly, gamification isn't about "playing games" in a business context, but rather applying the motivational power of scorekeeping, competition, and other game-playing mechanics to existing business activities.[47] Companies are now gamifying processes ranging from sales and customer service to employee recruiting, training, and health and fitness. Encouraging participation in and contribution to social networks and other communities is a good example of how gamification can motivate employees and other stakeholders. Depending on the system, members can earn points, badges, and other rewards for anrs.[48]

ADAPTING TO CIRCUMSTANCES AND SPECIAL NEEDS

Just as the dynamics of motivation vary from person to person, they can vary from one situation to the next. For example, a slow economy and rising unemployment introduce a number of stresses into the workplace that need to be considered from a motivational perspective. Employers have less to spend on factors that can help avert employee dissatisfaction (salary, for example) or that can spur motivation (such as bonuses and other incentives). As a result, satisfaction and motivation are in danger of slipping, but employees have fewer options for finding new jobs if they aren't happy. The big exceptions are a company's top performers. When unemployment is rising and money is tight, high performers in any industry can often find new opportunities where average performers cannot. In other words, when companies are struggling, their best employees—the ones they need the most—are the ones most likely to leave. Consequently, managers need to work extra hard to keep these top performers happy and motivated.[49]

The threat of layoffs can motivate some employees but demoralize others. Some will work harder, in the hopes of minimizing their chances of being let go. Others, however, will wonder if there's any point in working hard if the economy is going to wipe out their jobs anyway. If layoffs are already starting to hit, survivors can be demoralized even further if they think the company is treating laid-off employees disrespectfully or unfairly.[50] Clearly, tough economic times put a huge motivational burden on managers, but those who treat employees with honesty and compassion stand the best chance of retaining the best people and keeping them motivated.

When the economy heats up again and unemployment drops, the balance of power shifts back toward workers. Employers who may have counted on job-loss fear as a motivator during the tough times will need to adjust strategies when employees have more options.[51]

ADDRESSING WORKPLACE NEGATIVITY

No workplace is immune to problems and conflicts, but negativity is an emotional "virus" that can infect an entire organization. Just as with physical health, in the workplace managers must address problems and conflicts quickly, before they multiply and erode employee morale. Left to fester long enough, these problems can destroy the sense of community in a company and leave employees feeling hopeless about the future.[52] Jumping on a problem quickly can have a double positive impact: It solves the problem, and it demonstrates to everyone that managers care about the emotional health of the workforce.

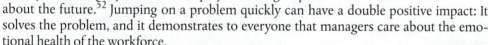

REAL-TIME UPDATES
Learn More by Reading This Article

Eight mistakes that demotivate employees

Leaders need to make sure these motivation poisons don't infect their workplaces. Go to http://real-timeupdates.com/bia8 and click on Learn More in the Students section.

BEING AN INSPIRING LEADER

Theories and systems aside, inspired motivation in a business enterprise requires inspired leadership. To a large degree, good employees come to work already motivated—that's part of what makes them good employees. One of your jobs as a manager is to make sure you don't *demotivate* them. For example, in one survey of U.S. workers, more than one-third of respondents said their supervisors' habits of **micromanaging**—overseeing every small detail of employees' work and refusing to give them freedom or autonomy—were destroying their initiative.[53] Managers with low emotional intelligence (see page 156) can create toxic work environments that demotivate even the most driven employees, so it is essential for managers to understand the effect that their behaviors and attitudes have on employees.

micromanaging
Overseeing every small detail of employees' work and refusing to give them freedom or autonomy.

MOTIVATING YOURSELF

This chapter has focused on systems that organizations can put in place and various steps managers can take to motivate employees. However, this emphasis shouldn't obscure the role and responsibility of employees themselves. Every employee has an ethical obligation to find the motivation to accomplish the tasks for which he or she is getting paid. Managers can foster motivation (and they can certainly diminish it through clumsy leadership), but the motivation has to originate from within each employee.

For the latest information on motivation, visit **http://real-timeupdates.com/bia8** and click on Chapter 10.

✓ Checkpoint

LEARNING OBJECTIVE 6: List five managerial strategies that are vital to maintaining a motivated workforce.

SUMMARY: No matter which motivational theories a company chooses to implement in its management policies and reward systems, managers can motivate employees more effectively by (1) providing timely and frequent feedback, (2) personalizing motivational efforts as much as possible while still being fair to all employees, (3) adapting motivational tactics to circumstances and special needs, (4) addressing workplace negativity before it has a chance to destroy morale, and (5) being inspirational leaders.

CRITICAL THINKING: (1) Referring to the job characteristics model, how does micromanaging destroy motivation? (2) Annual performance reviews are common in many companies; how might they fail to motivate employees?

IT'S YOUR BUSINESS: (1) If you are motivated more by the love of learning than the promised rewards of a grade, how can you motivate yourself when grades play a key role in your success as others perceive it? (2) At work or in academic situations, how do you prevent someone else's negative attitude and behavior from dragging down your own performance?

KEY TERMS TO KNOW: gamification, micromanaging

BEHIND THE SCENES
MOTIVATING INDIVIDUALS BY PERSONALIZING CAREERS AT DELOITTE

As the chief talent officer for a company brimming with talent, Deloitte's Cathy Benko knows how challenging it can be to create stimulating environments and opportunities to motivate a diverse workforce. And having traveled an unconventional path herself ("lots of zigs and zags" is how she describes it), she knows that a relentless 30- or 40-year climb up the corporate ladder is not for everyone.

The conventional ladder concept has never been right for many employees, and it is less appealing to a growing portion of the population. Benko explains that in the time span of just two generations, society and the workforce have been transformed to such an extent that the old ways of work don't work anymore. In studying this lack of fit between workplace and workforce, Benko and her colleagues identified five key issues:

- **A looming talent shortage.** Talk of not enough people to fill jobs might be difficult to fathom in the aftermath of a deep recession and continuing high unemployment in some sectors of the economy, but the long-term trend is unmistakable. By 2025, the shortage of knowledge workers could be as high as 35 million people.

- **A vastly different society.** The corporate ladder—and with it the idea of devoting one's working life to a single company in order to climb one's way to the top—was conceived back in a time when two-thirds of U.S. households consisted of married couples in which one spouse (usually the husband) went to work and the other (usually the wife) stayed home. In a sense, this family structure helped support the corporate ladder by "freeing" the husband to devote himself to his company and career. Today, however, only about 15 percent of households fit that mold, and the old workplace ideals clearly don't fit them.

- **Expanded professional roles for women.** After years of gender imbalance in the workplace, women now hold more than half of all management jobs (although the ratio at the top of the ladder still leans heavily toward men). Plus, women now earn nearly 60 percent of bachelor's and master's degrees, so the presence of women in professional positions is only going to expand.

- **Different desires and expectations from men.** Growing numbers of men are ready to explore a more balanced life with more flexibility and personal time than the constant ladder climb typically offers.

- **A dramatic shift in generational attitudes.** To a large degree, the Baby Boom generation (those born between 1946 and 1964) defined itself by work, and the more of it the better, it seemed for many. However, the two generations that came after, Generation X and Generation Y, have different outlooks, with a much stronger desire to adapt their work to their lives rather than the other way around.

After pondering these tectonic shifts across the social landscape, Benko and Deloitte chose a new metaphor. Instead of a ladder, with its implication of a single path from bottom to top, they now speak in terms of a *lattice*, a crosshatch of horizontal and vertical lines. Just as a rosebush on a garden lattice can grow sideways and even downward for a while if upward isn't the best choice at the moment, a career lattice offers employees much the same flexibility.

Deloitte calls the model "mass career customization," and it mimics the idea of mass customized production described in Chapter 9 (page 210). Employees define where they've been, where they are, and where they'd like to go next, based on four variables: *pace* (from decelerated to accelerated), *workload* (reduced to full), *location/schedule* (restricted to not restricted), and *role* (individual contributor to leader). For example, to take time to have children or go back to college, a manager could step into a nonmanagerial individual contributor role with a reduced workload and less travel. "Our goal is to offer people options to keep their work and personal lives in sync," Benko explains, "and to give employers the loyalty of their best and brightest people. It ends up being a perfect fit."[54]

Critical Thinking Questions

10-1. How might Deloitte's lattice approach help motivate employees and improve job satisfaction and performance?

10-2. How can managers determine whether a Deloitte employee is working at a decelerated pace in the career customization model or simply isn't working very hard?

10-3. What are the potential disadvantages, from the company's point of view, of giving employees this much flexibility?

LEARN MORE ONLINE

Visit the Corporate Lattice/Mass Career Customization website at **www.latticemcc.com**, which offers more information about the Deloitte lattice model. Read "Mass Career Customization at a Glance" and then try the "Interactive Career Exercise," where you can chart your own career (real or imaginary). You can also download two minibooks, *The Corporate Lattice* and *Mass Career Customization*. Does the lattice model sound appealing to you?

KEY TERMS

cross-training (236)
engagement (225)
equity theory (232)
expectancy theory (230)
gamification (240)
goal-setting theory (232)
Hawthorne effect (227)
Herzberg's two-factor theory (229)
incentives (238)
job characteristics model (235)
job enrichment (236)

management by objectives (233)
Maslow's hierarchy (228)
micromanaging (241)
motivation (225)
negative reinforcement (238)
positive reinforcement (237)
reinforcement theory (237)
scientific management (227)
Theory X (228)
Theory Y (228)
three-needs theory (229)

MyBizLab®
To complete the problems with the ⭐, go to EOC Discussion Questions in the MyLab

TEST YOUR KNOWLEDGE

Questions for Review

10-4. What is motivation?
10-5. What is expectancy theory?

10-6. What is management by objectives?
10-7. What are the core job dimensions in the job characteristics model?
10-8. What is negative reinforcement?

Questions for Analysis

10-9. How does expectancy theory explain the effect of self-doubt on employee motivation?

10-10. How might a deadline that is too easy to meet cause someone to work more slowly than he or she might otherwise work?

⭐ **10-11.** What effect will job enhancement likely have on someone with low growth needs? Why?

10-12. Why do managers often find it difficult to motivate employees who remain after downsizing? Explain your answer in terms of one or more motivational theories discussed in the chapter.

10-13. **Ethical Considerations.** Motivational strategies that reward employees for meeting specific performance targets can encourage them to work hard—sometimes too hard. Overwork can contribute to mental and physical health problems as well as interfere with other aspects of employees' lives. As a manager, how do you determine how much work is too much for your employees?

Questions for Application

⭐ **10-14.** You manage the customer service department for an online clothing retailer. Customers tend to call or email with the same types of complaints and problems, day after day, and your employees are getting bored and listless. Some are starting to miss more days of work than usual, and several have quit recently. A few customers have called you directly to complain about poor treatment from your staff. Use the job characteristics model to identify several ways you could improve motivation, job satisfaction, and performance.

⭐ **10-15.** How do you motivate yourself when faced with school assignments or projects that are difficult or tedious? Do you ever try to relate these tasks to your overall career goals? Are you more motivated by doing your personal best or by outperforming other students?

10-16. Imagine yourself in one of the jobs you would like to land after graduation. Thinking about the importance of personalizing motivational tactics whenever possible, identify several steps your manager could take to make sure you stay motivated. Would these steps be fair to other employees as well?

10-17. **Concept Integration.** Chapter 7 discusses several styles of leadership, including autocratic, democratic, and laissez-faire. How do each of these styles relate to Theory X and Theory Y assumptions about workers?

EXPAND YOUR KNOWLEDGE

Discovering Career Opportunities

Careers in sales can be highly rewarding, if you have the right skills, opportunities, and incentives. Search online job postings for a sales position that is related to a career path you might want to pursue (even if you're not interested in sales specifically). Study the job description and identify the circumstances you would need to have in place in order to get motivated to excel in this job. For example, would the opportunity to help customers solve challenging problems motivate you?

Improving Your Tech Insights: Blogging and Microblogging

Blogging and microblogging (of which Twitter is the best-known example) have revolutionized business communication in recent years. Far more than just another communication medium, blogging and microblogging help change the relationship between companies and their stakeholders by transforming communication from the formal mindset of "we talk, you listen" to an informal and interactive conversational mindset.

Identify a company in which one or more managers are regular bloggers or Twitter users. In a brief email to your instructor, explain how the company uses blogging to build relationships with customers and potential customers, employees and potential employees, and other stakeholder groups.

PRACTICE YOUR SKILLS

Sharpening Your Communication Skills

Choose one of the major motivation theories discussed in this chapter: expectancy, goal-setting, job characteristics, or reinforcement theory. Create a brief electronic presentation (three to five slides), using PowerPoint, Keynote, Google Docs, or a similar tool, explaining the theory and identifying its strengths and weaknesses as a practical management approach.

Building Your Team Skills

With your teammates, explore the careers sections of the websites of six companies in different industries. Look for descriptions of the work environment, incentive plans, career paths, and other information about how the company develops, motivates, and supports its employees. After you've compiled notes about each company, vote on the most appealing company to work for. Next, review the notes for this company and identify all the theories of motivation described in this chapter that the company appears to be using, based on the information on its website.

Developing Your Research Skills

Various periodicals and websites feature "best companies to work for" lists. Locate one of these lists and find a company that

does a great job of attracting and motivating high performers. Learn as much as you can about the company's management philosophies. Which of the motivation theories does the company appear to be using? Summarize your findings in a brief email message to your instructor.

MyBizLab®

Go to the Assignments section of your MyLab to complete these writing exercises.

10-18. If a manager does nothing in response to a particular type of employee behavior that the company wants to encourage, is this an instance of reinforcement? Why or why not?

10-19. Do you have an ethical responsibility to motivate yourself at work, no matter the circumstances? Why or why not?

ENDNOTES

1. Cathy Benko profile, LinkedIn, accessed 12 April 2015, www.linkedin.com; Cathy Benko, "Up the Ladder? How Dated, How Linear," *New York Times*, 9 November 2008, www.deloitteandtouche.org; The Corporate Lattice/Mass Career Customization website, accessed 12 April 2015, www.latticemcc.com; Anne Fisher, "When Gen X Runs the Show," *Time*, 25 May 2009, 48–49; Lisa Takeuchi Cullen, "Flex Work Is Not the Answer," Work in Progress blog, 10 October 2007, http://workinprogress.blogs.time.com; Laura Fitzpatrick, "We're Getting Off the Ladder," *Time*, 5 May 2009, 45; "Customizing Your Career," Deloitte website, accessed 17 June 2009, http://careers.deloitte.com; "Mass Career Customization," PBWC Connections website, accessed 17 June 2009, http://www.pbwcconnections.com.

2. Piers Steel and Cornelius J. König, "Integrating Theories of Motivation," *Academy of Management Review*, 31, No. 4, 2006, 889–913.

3. Nitin Nohria, Boris Groysberg, and Linda-Eling Lee, "Employee Motivation: A Powerful New Model," *Harvard Business Review*, July–August 2008, 78–84.

4. Nohria, Groysberg, and Lee, "Employee Motivation."

5. Nohria, Groysberg, and Lee, "Employee Motivation."

6. Stephen P. Robbins and David A. DeCenzo, *Fundamentals of Management*, 4th ed. (Upper Saddle River, N.J.: Prentice-Hall, 2004), 27–29.

7. Augustine Brannigan and William Zwerman, "The Real 'Hawthorne Effect,'" *Society*, January/February 2001, 55–60; Stephen P. Robbins and Mary Coulter, *Management*, 10th ed. (Upper Saddle River, N.J.: Pearson Prentice Hall, 2009), 34.

8. Brannigan and Zwerman, "The Real 'Hawthorne Effect'"; Robbins and Coulter, *Management*, 34.

9. Frank Merrett, "Reflections on the Hawthorne Effect," *Educational Psychology*, February 2006, 143–146; Brannigan and Zwerman, "The Real 'Hawthorne Effect.'"

10. Mecca Chiesa and Sandy Hobbs, "Making Sense of Social Research: How Useful Is the Hawthorne Effect?" *European Journal of Social Psychology*, 38, 2008, 67–74; Brannigan and Zwerman, "The Real 'Hawthorne Effect'"; Robbins and Coulter, *Management*, 34.

11. Andrew J. DuBrin, *Applying Psychology: Individual & Organizational Effectiveness*, 6th ed. (Upper Saddle River, N.J.: Pearson Prentice Hall, 2004), 122–124.

12. Robbins and Coulter, *Management*, 342.

13. Richard L. Daft, *Management*, 6th ed. (Mason, Ohio: Thomson South-Western, 2003), 547; Robbins and DeCenzo, *Fundamentals of Management*, 283–284; DuBrin, *Applying Psychology: Individual & Organizational Effectiveness*, 15–16.

14. Stephen P. Robbins and Timothy A. Judge, *Essentials of Organizational Behavior*, 10th ed. (Upper Saddle River, N.J.: Pearson Prentice Hall, 2010), 64.

15. Daft, *Management*, 552–553.

16. Robbins and Judge, *Essentials of Organizational Behavior*, 66.

17. Rosa Chun and Gary Davies, "Employee Happiness Isn't Enough to Satisfy Customers," *Harvard Business Review*, April 2009, 19; Robbins and Judge, *Essentials of Organizational Behavior*, 66.

18. Saundra K. Ciccarelli and Glenn E. Meyer, *Psychology* (Upper Saddle River, N.J.: Prentice Hall, 2006), 339–340.

19. "Seeking to Hire Strong Leaders? Buyer Beware!" *Compensation & Benefits for Law Offices*, September 2006, 11+.

20. David C. McClelland and David H. Burnham, "Power Is the Great Motivator," *Harvard Business Review*, January 2003, 117–126; Robbins and Judge, *Essentials of Organizational Behavior*, 66–67.

21. Robbins and Judge, *Essentials of Organizational Behavior*, 67.

22. Robbins and DeCenzo, *Fundamentals of Management*, 289.

23. Robbins and Judge, *Essentials of Organizational Behavior*, 72.

24. Daft, *Management*, 554–555.

25. Robbins and Judge, *Essentials of Organizational Behavior*, 75.

26. Deborah Archambeault, Christopher M. Burgess, and Stan Davis, "Is Something Missing from Your Company's Satisfaction Package?" *CMA Management*, May 2009, 20–23.

27. Robbins and Coulter, *Management*, 346.

28. Bill Lycette and John Herniman, "New Goal-Setting Theory," *Industrial Management*, September 2008, 25–30; Robbins and Coulter, *Management*, 346–347.

29. Robbins and Coulter, *Management*, 346.

30. Lisa Ordóñez, Maurice Schweitzer, Adam Galinsky, and Max Bazerman, "Goals Gone Wild: The Systematic Side Effects of Overprescribing Goal Setting," *Academy of Management Perspectives*, February 2009, 6–16.

31. Robert D. Ramsey, "Why Deadlines and Quotas Don't Always Work," *Supervision*, October 2008, 3–5.

32. Richard J. Hackman and Greg R. Oldman, "Motivation Through the Design of Work: Test of a Theory," *Organizational Behavior & Human Performance*, August 1976, 250–279; Robbins and Judge, *Essentials of Organizational Behavior*, 81–82; Jed DeVaro, Robert Li, and Dana Brookshire, "Analysing the Job Characteristics Model: New Support from a Cross-Section of Establishments," *International Journal of Human Resource Management*, June 2007, 986–1003.

33. Robbins and Judge, *Essentials of Organizational Behavior*, 82.

34. Stuart D. Galup, Gary Klein, and James J. Jiang, "The Impacts of Job Characteristics on IS Employee Satisfaction: A Comparison Between Permanent and Temporary Employees," *Journal of Computer Information Systems*, Summer 2008, 58–68.

35. Robbins and Coulter, *Management*, 348.

36. Scott Lazenby, "How to Motivate Employees: What Research Is Telling Us," *Public Management*, September 2008, 22–25.

37. Robbins and Coulter, *Management*, 348.

38. "Caution Urged in Expanding Cross-Training of CU Staff," *Credit Union Journal*, 5 January 2009, 18.

39. Debi O'Donovan, "Motivation Is Key in a Crisis and Words Can Be the Best Reward," *Employee Benefits*, April 2009, 5.

40. Timothy R. Hinkin and Chester A. Schriesheim, "Performance Incentives for Tough Times," *Harvard Business Review*, March 2009, 26.

41. Tom Washington, "Incentives Play Big Part in Motivation During Recession," *Employee Benefits*, April 2009, 14.

42. Ciccarelli and Meyer, *Psychology*, 179.

43. Robbins and Coulter, *Management*, 348.

44. Dan Heath and Chip Heath, "The Curse of Incentives," *Fast Company*, February 2009, 48–49.

45. "Tailor Motivation Techniques to the Worker," *Teller Vision*, March 2009, 5–6.

46. Nohria, Groysberg, and Lee, "Employee Motivation: A Powerful New Model."

47. "What Is Gamification?" Bunchball, accessed 12 April 2015, www.bunchball.com

48. Robert Stanley, "Top 25 Best Examples of Gamification in Business," Clickipedia, 24 March 2014, http://blogs.clicksoftware .com; Brian Burke, "The Gamification of Business," *Forbes*, 21 January 2013, www.forbes.com.

49. Edward E. Lawler III, "Value-Based Motivation," *BusinessWeek*, 27 April 2009, 22.

50. Joan Lloyd, "Threat of Layoffs Demoralizes Employees," *Receivables Report for America's Health Care Financial Managers*, May 2009, 10–11.

51. Lawler, "Value-Based Motivation."

52. Betty MacLaughlin Frandsen, "Overcoming Workplace Negativity," *Long-Term Living: For the Continuing Care Professional*, March 2009, 26–27.

53. "Don't Be a Drag," *CA Magazine*, January–February 2009, 9.

54. See Note 1.

LEARNING OBJECTIVES   After studying this chapter, you will be able to

1 Identify four contemporary staffing challenges, and explain the process of planning for a company's staffing needs.

2 Discuss the challenges and advantages of a diverse workforce, and identify five major dimensions of workforce diversity.

3 Describe the three phases involved in managing the employment life cycle.

4 Explain the steps used to develop and evaluate employees.

5 Describe the major elements of employee compensation.

6 Identify the most significant categories of employee benefits and services.

BEHIND THE SCENES   AN UNCONVENTIONAL APPROACH TO FINDING UNCONVENTIONAL EMPLOYEES

David Becker/UPI/Newscom

Zappos CEO Tony Hsieh makes sure the company's interviewing process finds the candidates who are compatible with an offbeat customer- and colleague-focused culture.

www.zappos.com

When a company communicates its core values with the help of a cartoon amphibian named Core Values Frog, you can guess the company doesn't quite fit the stuffy corporate stereotype. While it is passionately serious about customer satisfaction and employee engagement, the Las Vegas–based online shoe and clothing retailer Zappos doesn't take itself too seriously. In fact, one of the 10 values the frog promotes is "Create fun and a little weirdness."

Fun and a little weirdness can make a workplace more enjoyable, but CEO Tony Hsieh's commitment to employees runs much deeper than that. The company makes frequent reference to "the Zappos Family," and it embraces the ideals of taking care of one another and enjoying time spent together. These activities can range from parades in the workplace and other goofy events to the Wishez program, in which employees can ask one another to fulfill personal wishes, from lighthearted desires such as getting backstage access at concerts to serious matters such as getting help during tough financial times.

Corporate recruiting processes, particularly in this age of *applicant tracking systems*, are often obsessed with facts and figures—of applying standardized templates in an effort find the "ideal" employee. With a focus on measurable line items on a résumé and a risk-averse mindset, these automated systems and the recruiters who rely on them can overlook curiosity, passion, commitment, and other attributes that *really* define a successful employee.

If you were Hsieh, how would you make sure Zappos attracts the kind of employees who can contribute to and excel in the company's unique culture? Would you follow the same strategies that most companies use, or would you carve your own path—even if that means inventing an entirely new way of recruiting employees?[1]

INTRODUCTION

Zappos' Tony Hsieh (profiled in the chapter-opening Behind the Scenes) knows that hiring the right people to help a company reach its goals and then overseeing their training and development, motivation, evaluation, and compensation are critical to a company's success. This chapter explores the many steps companies take to build productive workforces, including solving staffing challenges, addressing workforce diversity, managing the employment life cycle, developing employees, and providing compensation and benefits.

Keeping Pace with Today's Workforce

1 **LEARNING OBJECTIVE**

Identify four contemporary staffing challenges, and explain the process of planning for a company's staffing needs.

human resources (HR) management
The specialized function of planning how to obtain employees, oversee their training, evaluate them, and compensate them.

The field of **human resources (HR) management** encompasses all the tasks involved in attracting, developing, and supporting an organization's staff, as well as maintaining a safe working environment that meets legal requirements and ethical expectations.[2] You may not pursue a career in HR specifically, but understanding the challenges and responsibilities of the HR function will improve your success as a manager.

CONTEMPORARY STAFFING CHALLENGES

Managers in every organization face an ongoing array of staffing challenges, including aligning the workforce with organizational needs, fostering employee loyalty, adjusting workloads and monitoring for employee burnout, and helping employees balance their work and personal lives:

- **Aligning the workforce.** Matching the right employees to the right jobs at the right time is a constant challenge. Externally, changes in market needs, moves by competition, advances in technology, and new regulations can all affect the ideal size and composition of the workforce. Internally, shifts in strategy, technological changes, and growing or declining product sales can force managers to realign their workforces.
- **Fostering employee loyalty.** Most companies can't guarantee long-term employment, but they want employees to commit themselves to the company. With the increasing number of temporary employees and independent contractors, this challenge will continue to grow.
- **Monitoring workloads and avoiding employee burnout.** As companies try to beat competitors and keep workforce costs to a minimum, managers need to be on guard for *employee burnout*, a state of physical and emotional exhaustion that can result from constant exposure to stress over a long period of time. One of the downsides of nonstop electronic connectivity is that many employees struggle to separate work life from personal life, which can create a feeling that work never ends.

work–life balance
Efforts to help employees balance the competing demands of their personal and professional lives.

quality of work life (QWL)
An overall environment that results from job and work conditions.

- **Managing work–life balance.** The concern over workloads is one of the factors behind the growing interest in **work–life balance**, the idea that employees, managers, and entrepreneurs need to balance the competing demands of their professional and personal lives. Many companies are trying to make it easier for employees to juggle multiple responsibilities with on-site day-care facilities, flexible work schedules, and other options designed to improve **quality of work life (QWL)**. Companies such as Zappos also take steps to make the workplace as enjoyable as possible as a way to minimize stress and relieve the monotony of repetitive business tasks.

REAL-TIME UPDATES
Learn More by Visiting This Website

Which companies rank highly in quality of work life?

Fortune's annual "Best Companies to Work For" ranking includes the metric of work–life balance. Go to http://real-timeupdates.com/bia8 and click on Learn More in the Students section.

PLANNING FOR A COMPANY'S STAFFING NEEDS

Planning for staffing needs is a delicate balancing act. Hire too few employees, and you can't keep pace with the competition or satisfy customers. Hire too many, and you raise fixed costs above a level that revenues can sustain. To avoid either problem, HR managers work carefully to evaluate the requirements of every job in the company and to forecast the supply and demand for all types of talent (see Exhibit 11.1). Many companies now rely on **workforce analytics**, a computer-based statistical approach to analyzing and planning for workforce needs.

Evaluating Job Requirements

Through the process of *job analysis*, employers try to identify the nature and demands of each position within the firm as well as the optimal employee profile to fill each position.[3] Once job analysis has been completed, the HR staff develops a **job description**, a formal statement summarizing the tasks involved in the job and the conditions under which the employee will work. In most cases, the staff will also develop a **job specification**, which identifies the type of personnel a job requires, including the skills, education, experience, and personal attributes that candidates need to possess[4] (see Exhibit 11.2 on the next page).

Forecasting Supply and Demand

To forecast demand for the numbers and types of employees who will be needed at various times, HR managers weigh (1) forecasted sales revenues; (2) the expected **turnover rate**, the percentage of the workforce that leaves every year; (3) the current workforce's skill level, relative to the company's future needs; (4) impending strategic decisions; (5) changes in technology or other business factors that could affect the number and type of workers needed; and (6) the company's current and projected financial status.[5]

In addition to overall workforce levels, every company has a number of employees and managers who are considered so critical to the company's ongoing operations that HR managers work with top executives to identify potential replacements in the event of the loss of any of these people, a process known as **succession planning**.[6] A *replacement chart* identifies these key employees and lists potential replacements.

With some idea of future workforce demands, the HR staff then tries to estimate the *supply* of available employees. To ensure a steady supply of experienced employees for new opportunities and to maintain existing operations, successful companies focus heavily on **employee retention**.

If existing employees cannot be tapped for new positions, the HR team looks outside the company for people to join as either permanent employees or **contingent employees** who fulfill many of the responsibilities of regular employees but on a temporary basis. Roughly a third of the U.S. workers fall in this broad category of contractors and freelancers, and all signs are that this portion will continue to grow.[7]

workforce analytics
Computer-based statistical approach to analyzing and planning for workforce needs.

job description
A statement of the tasks involved in a given job and the conditions under which the holder of a job will work.

job specification
A statement describing the kind of person who would be best for a given job—including the skills, education, and previous experience that the job requires.

turnover rate
The percentage of the workforce that leaves every year.

succession planning
Workforce planning efforts that identify possible replacements for specific employees, usually senior executives.

employee retention
Efforts to keep current employees.

contingent employees
Nonpermanent employees, including temporary workers, independent contractors, and full-time employees hired on a probationary basis.

EXHIBIT 11.1	**Steps in Human Resources Planning**

Careful attention to each phase of this sequence helps ensure that a company will have the right mix of talent and experience to meets its business goals.

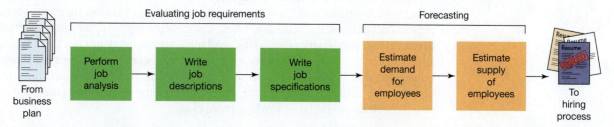

EXHIBIT 11.2	Job Description and Specification

A well-written job description and specification tells potential applicants what to expect from the job and what employers will expect from them.

Job Title
Director of E-Marketing

Location
Denver, CO

Reports to
Vice President of Marketing

Job Detail
Soccer Scope is a leading retailer of soccer equipment, apparel, and accessories based in Denver, Colorado, with retail locations in 23 states. We seek to expand our online presence under the guidance of a director of e-marketing, a new managerial position to be based in our Denver headquarters. The candidate who fills this position will be responsible for all nonstore aspects of our retailing efforts, including Soccer Scope's primary U.S. website and our country and region websites around the world, search-related advertising strategies, search engine optimization strategies, social media strategy and campaigns, email marketing campaigns, clicks-and-bricks integration strategy, affiliate marketing campaigns, customer retention efforts, and all aspects of online marketing research. The director of e-marketing will also work closely with the director of information technology to ensure the successful deployment of e-marketing platforms and with the director of retail operations to ensure a smooth clicks-and-bricks integration of offline and online retailing operations.

In addition to developing e-marketing strategies and directing e-marketing operations, the director is also responsible for leading a team of marketing and technical specialists who will implement and manage various programs.

Responsibilities
- Develop e-marketing strategies and plans consistent with Soccer Scope's overall business strategy and brand imperatives
- Integrate all outbound and inbound media streams to ensure seamless customer contact
- Establish and achieve aggressive customer acquisition and retention goals
- Coordinate efforts with technology and retailing counterparts to ensure successfully integrated online and offline marketing operations
- Assemble, lead, and develop an effective team of e-marketing professionals

Skills and Experience
- BA or BS in business, advertising, marketing, or related discipline required; MBA preferred
- Minimum 8 years of marketing experience, with at least 3 years in e-commerce and social media
- Current and thorough understanding of e-marketing strategies
- Demonstrated proficiency in developing and executing marketing strategies
- Excellent communication skills in all media

ALTERNATIVE WORK ARRANGEMENTS

To meet today's staffing and demographic challenges, many companies are adopting alternative work arrangements to better accommodate the needs of employees—and to reduce costs in many cases. Four of the most popular arrangements are flextime, telecommuting, job sharing, and flexible career paths:

- *Flextime* is a scheduling system that allows employees to choose their own hours, within certain limits. Of course, the feasibility of flextime differs from industry to industry and from position to position within individual companies.
- *Telecommuting*—working from home or another location using electronic communications to stay in touch with colleagues, suppliers, and customers—helps employees balance their professional and personal commitments because they can spend less time in transit between home and work. Telecommuting also plays an important role in efforts to reduce energy use, traffic, and mass transit overload. Telecommuting isn't appropriate for every job, and not every executive believes it is a workable solution, however. Yahoo! and HP, for example, severely curtailed their telecommunicating programs in order to foster better collaboration among workers (and, in Yahoo!'s case, reportedly, to monitor workers more closely).[8]

- *Job sharing*, which lets two employees share a single full-time job and split the salary and benefits, can be an attractive alternative for people who want part-time hours in situations normally reserved for full-time employees.
- Perhaps the most challenging of all alternative work arrangements are situations in which employees want to limit their work time or leave the workforce entirely for an extended period to raise children, attend school, volunteer, or pursue other personal interests. Programs such as Deloitte's mass career customization (see page 242) give employees more freedom in designing their own career paths.

 **Checkpoint**

LEARNING OBJECTIVE 1: Identify four contemporary staffing challenges, and explain the process of planning for a company's staffing needs.

SUMMARY: Four challenges that every HR department wrestles with are aligning the workforce with changing job requirements, fostering employee loyalty, monitoring workloads and avoiding employee burnout, and managing work–life balance. The process of planning for a company's staffing needs includes evaluating job requirements to develop *job descriptions* and *job specifications* and then forecasting the supply of and demand for various types of talent to ensure that the company has the right people in the right positions.

CRITICAL THINKING: (1) How can alternative work arrangements help companies reduce costs and their impact on the environment? (2) How can electronic communication technologies contribute to employee burnout?

IT'S YOUR BUSINESS: (1) Would you prefer to work as an independent contractor or as a permanent employee? What do you see as the advantages and disadvantages of each mode of work? (2) Would you function well as a full-time telecommuter? Why or why not?

KEY TERMS TO KNOW: human resources (HR) management, work–life balance, quality of work life (QWL), workforce analytics, job description, job specification, turnover rate, succession planning, employee retention, contingent employees

Managing a Diverse Workforce

2 **LEARNING OBJECTIVE**

Discuss the challenges and advantages of a diverse workforce, and identify five major dimensions of workforce diversity.

The companies that are most successful at managing and motivating their employees take great care to understand the diversity of their workforces and establish programs and policies that embrace that diversity and take full advantage of diversity's benefits.

DIMENSIONS OF WORKFORCE DIVERSITY

Although the concept is often framed in terms of ethnic background, a broader and more useful definition of *diversity* includes "all the characteristics and experiences that define each of us as individuals."[9] As one example, the pharmaceutical company Merck identifies 19 separate dimensions in its discussions of workforce diversity, including race, age, military experience, parental status, marital status, and thinking style.[10] Over the past few decades, many innovative companies have changed the way they approach workforce diversity, from seeing it as a legal matter to seeing it as a strategic opportunity to connect with customers and take advantage of the broadest possible pool of talent.[11] Smart business leaders such as Ron Glover, IBM's vice president of global workforce diversity, recognize the competitive advantages of a diverse workforce that offers a broader spectrum of viewpoints and ideas, helps companies understand and identify with diverse markets, and enables companies to benefit from a wider range of employee talents. According to Glover, more-diverse teams tend to be more innovative in the long term than more-homogeneous teams.[12]

Differences enrich the workplace but can create managerial challenges. A diverse workforce brings with it a wide range of skills, traditions, backgrounds, experiences,

REAL-TIME UPDATES
Learn More by Visiting This Website

Looking for jobs at diversity-minded companies?

DiversityWorking.com connects job searchers with companies that recognize the value of diverse workforces. Go to http://real-time updates.com/bia8 and click on Learn More in the Students Section.

outlooks, and attitudes toward work—all of which can affect employee behavior on the job. Supervisors face the challenge of communicating with these diverse employees, motivating them, and fostering cooperation and harmony among them. Teams face the challenge of working together closely, and companies are challenged to coexist peacefully with business partners and with the community as a whole. Some of the most important diversity issues today include age, gender, race and ethnicity, religion, and ability.

Age

In U.S. culture, youth is often associated with strength, energy, possibilities, and freedom. In contrast, age is often associated with declining powers and a loss of respect and authority. However, older workers can offer broader experience, the benefits of important business relationships nurtured over many years, and high degrees of "practical intelligence," the ability to solve complex, poorly defined problems.[13]

In contrast, in cultures that value age and seniority, longevity earns respect and increasing power and freedom. For instance, in many Asian societies, the oldest employees hold the most powerful jobs, the most impressive titles, and the greatest degrees of freedom and decision-making authority. If a younger employee disagrees with one of these senior executives, the discussion is never conducted in public. The notion of "saving face"—that is, avoiding public embarrassment—is too strong. Instead, if a senior person seems to be in error about something, other employees will find a quiet, private way to communicate whatever information they feel is necessary.[14]

In addition to cultural values associated with various life stages, the multiple generations within a culture present another dimension of diversity (see Exhibit 11.3). Each of these generations has been shaped by dramatically different world events and social trends, and people's priorities often shift as they grow older, so it is not surprising that they often have different values, expectations, and communication habits.

Gender

Perceptions, roles, and treatment of men and women in the workplace has been a complex and at times contentious issue. The Equal Pay Act of 1963 mandated equal pay for comparable work, and the Civil Rights Act of 1964 made it illegal for employers to practice **sexism**, or discrimination on the basis of gender. The United States has made important strides toward gender equity since then, but significant issues remain. For example, the Equal Employment Opportunity Commission (EEOC) fields 25,000 to 30,000 complaints a year regarding gender discrimination.[15]

Another significant issue is access to opportunities. Although women now hold half of all managerial positions, that ratio shrinks dramatically the higher you look in an organization. For example, among the corporations that make up the S&P 500 stock market index, fewer than 5 percent have women as CEOs.[16] A lack of opportunities to advance into the top ranks is often referred to as the **glass ceiling**, implying that one can see the top but can't get there. The glass ceiling is an important issue for both women and minorities.

One of the most complicated issues of all is the *gender pay gap*, the difference between what women and men earn. Women in the United States earn, on average, about 75 to 80 percent of what men do.[17] While this appears on the surface to be a blatant case of simple discrimination, a closer look at the data reveals a more nuanced picture that requires lots of digging to figure out how much of that 20–25 percent gap is a result of discriminatory practices on the part of employers and how much is attributable to the choices made by individual employees or to subtle but pervasive social forces.

For example, a higher percentage of men choose careers in the lucrative fields of engineering and computer science, whereas a higher percentage of women choose careers in teaching, which pays considerably less. Tellingly, men dominate the ten most-lucrative careers, and women dominate the ten least-lucrative careers.[18]

These numbers help explain the pay gap, but they don't tell the whole story. Within the same profession, men often earn more than women—even in professions such

sexism
Discrimination on the basis of gender.

glass ceiling
An invisible barrier attributable to subtle discrimination that keeps women and minorities out of the top positions in business.

EXHIBIT 11.3		**Generations in the Workplace**

Lumping people into generations is an imprecise science at best, but it helps to know the labels commonly applied to various age groups and to have some idea of their broad characteristics. (Note that these labels are not official, and there is no general agreement on when some generations start and end.)

Common Label	Range of Birth Years	Some Workforce Implications
Radio Generation	1925–1945	People in this group are beyond what was once considered the traditional retirement age of 65, but many want or need to continue working.
Baby Boomers	1946–1964	This large segment of the workforce, which now occupies many mid- and upper-level managerial positions, got its name from the population boom in the years following World War II. The older members of this generation are now past traditional retirement age, but many will continue to work—meaning that younger workers waiting for some of these management spots to open up might have to wait a while longer.
Generation X	1965–1980	This relatively smaller "MTV generation" is responsible for many of the innovations that have shaped today's communication and business habits but sometimes feels caught between the large mass of Baby Boomers ahead of them and the younger Generation Y employees behind them in the workforce. As Generation X takes the reins of corporate leadership, it is overseeing in a vastly different business landscape, one in which virtual and networked organizations replace much of the hierarchy inherited from the Baby Boomers.
Generation Y	1981–1995	Often known as *millennials*, this generation has been noted for its technology-centric approach to communication, impatience with corporate hierarchy, and the desire for a meaningful and personalized work experience. Many in this generation are now managers with power to reshape organizational cultures. New research suggests, however, that millennials aren't dramatically different from their predecessors and generally value the same rewards and express the same career concerns.
Generation Z	1996–	Generation Z, also known as *Generation I* (for Internet) or the *Net Generation*, is the first full generation to be born after the World Wide Web was invented. With a global, socially aware outlook shaped by lifelong networking and media usage, this diverse group appears to be highly entrepreneurial and interested in new ways of approaching business.

Sources: Alexandra Levit, "Make Way for Generation Z," *New York Times*, 28 March 2015, www.nytimes.com; "Workforce 2020: A Millennial Misunderstanding," *SuccessFactors*, accessed 18 April 2015, www.successfactors.com; "How to Manage the Millennials," PwC.com, accessed 7 November 2013; Anne Fisher, "When Gen X Runs the Show," *Time*, 14 May 2009, www.time.com; Deloitte, "Generation Y: Powerhouse of the Global Economy," research report, 2009, www.deloitte.com; "Generation Y," Nightly Business Report website, 30 June 2010, www.pbs.org; Sherry Posnick-Goodwin, "Meet Generation Z," *California Educator*, February 2010, www.cta.org.

as nursing and teaching, where women outnumber men.[19] Several other factors that researchers have found add nuance to the picture. On average, men work more hours per week, take less time off to raise children, and are more likely to try to negotiate pay raises. According to an in-depth statistical analysis released by the U.S. Department of Labor, when adjusted for individual choices, the average pay gap is roughly 5 to 7 percent.[20]

However, even a rigorous statistical investigation doesn't provide all the insights needed to right the imbalance, whatever that figure might be. Important issues that need to be considered include whether girls and young women are being subtly steered away from engineering, computer science, and other lucrative fields, why pay varies so much across different professions, the degree to which the glass ceiling is keeping women out of higher-paying positions, whether women have access to equal work opportunities even when they have the same job titles as men, and how companies should accommodate parents who want or need to step away from work to care for children.[21]

As just one example, consider a case in which a working couple with a newborn child decides that one of them should stay home with the baby for several months. If the mother's employer offers paid maternity leave for new mothers, but the father's employer doesn't offer paid paternity leave for new fathers, the couple will likely make the economic decision for the woman to take time off and the man to continue working. Even if a company's managers make a concerted effort not to penalize employees who take time off for family, extended time away from work can make it difficult for employees

REAL-TIME UPDATES
Learn More by Visiting This Website

Get the facts on gender gaps in corporation leadership

The nonprofit organization Catalyst conducts extensive research around the world to identify and understand opportunities to improve gender inclusivity in business management. Go to http://real-time updates.com/bia8 and click on Learn More in the Students section.

to maintain their skill sets, customer relationships, networking contacts, and other attributes that lead to promotions and pay raises.

Beyond pay and promotional opportunities, many working women also have to deal with **sexual harassment**, defined as either an obvious request for sexual favors with an implicit reward or punishment related to work, or the more subtle creation of a sexist environment in which employees are made to feel uncomfortable by lewd jokes, remarks, or gestures. Even though male employees may also be targets of sexual harassment and both male and female employees may experience same-sex harassment, sexual harassment of female employees by male colleagues or superiors continues to make up the majority of reported cases.[22] Most corporations now publish strict policies prohibiting harassment, both to protect their employees and to protect themselves from lawsuits.[23]

Race and Ethnicity

In many respects, the element of race and ethnicity in the diversity picture involves the same concerns as gender: equal pay for equal work, access to promotional opportunities, and ways to break through the glass ceiling. However, whereas the ratio of men and women in the workforce remains fairly stable year to year, the ethnic composition of the United States has been on a long-term trend of greater and greater diversity.

Grasping this changing situation can be complicated by confusion about the terms *race, ethnicity,* and *minority.* Ethnicity is a broader concept than race, incorporating both the genetic background of race and cultural issues such as language and national origin. Neither term is absolute or precise; millions of people have mixed racial heritage, and ethnicity doesn't always have fixed boundaries that clearly distinguish one group from another. *Minority* is a term often used to designate any race or ethnic segment other than white Americans of European descent. Aside from the negative connotations of *minority*, the term makes less and less sense every year. Caucasian Americans make up less than half the population in a growing number of cities and counties, and in two or three decades will make up less than half of the overall U.S. population.[24]

Labels aside, race remains an important issue in the workforce. The EEOC receives even more complaints about racial discrimination than about gender discrimination.[25] And as with average wages between women and men, disparity still exists along racial lines. Averaging across the entire workforce, Asian Americans earn the most, followed by Caucasian Americans, African Americans, and Hispanic Americans.[26] But as with gender, these aggregate figures need to be viewed in the context of individual decisions and opportunities for advancement.

Religion

The effort to accommodate employees' life interests on a broader scale has led a number of companies to address the issue of religion in the workplace. As one of the most personal aspects of life, of course, religion does bring potential for controversy in a work setting. On the one hand, some employees feel they should be able to express their beliefs in the workplace and not be forced to "check their faith at the door" when they come to work. On the other hand, companies want to avoid situations in which openly expressed religious differences might cause friction between employees or distract employees from their responsibilities.

Religion in the workplace is a complex and contentious issue—and it's getting more so every year, at least as measured by a significant rise in the number of religious discrimination lawsuits.[27] Beyond accommodating individual beliefs to a reasonable degree, as required by U.S. law, companies occasionally need to resolve situations that pit one group of employees against another or against the company's policies.[28] As more companies work to establish inclusive workplaces, and as more employees seek to integrate religious convictions into their daily work, you can expect to see this issue being discussed at many companies in the coming years.

sexual harassment
Unwelcome sexual advance, request for sexual favors, or other verbal or physical conduct of a sexual nature within the workplace.

Tom McCarthy/PhotoEdit

Managers have the responsibility to educate their employees on the definition and consequences of sexual harassment.

REAL-TIME UPDATES
Learn More by Exploring This Interactive Website

Take a closer look at how the United States is changing

The U.S. population is aging and becoming more diverse; dive into the details with this interactive presentation. Go to http://real-timeupdates .com/bia8 and click on Learn More in the Students section.

Ability

People whose hearing, vision, cognitive ability, or physical ability to operate equipment is impaired can be at a significant disadvantage in the workplace. As with other elements of diversity, success starts with respect for individuals and sensitivity to differences. Employers can also invest in a variety of *assistive technologies* (see page 94 for more information) that help people with disabilities perform activities that might otherwise be difficult or impossible. These technologies include devices and systems that help people communicate orally and visually, interact with computers and other equipment, and enjoy greater mobility in the workplace. For example, designers can emphasize *web accessibility*, taking steps to make websites more accessible to people whose vision is limited. Assistive technologies create a vital link for employees with disabilities, giving them opportunities to pursue a greater range of career paths and giving employers access to a broader base of talent.

Diversity Initiatives

To respond to the many challenges—and to capitalize on the business opportunities offered by both diverse marketplaces and diverse workforces—companies across the country are finding that embracing diversity in the richest sense is simply good business. In response, thousands of U.S. companies have established **diversity initiatives**, which can include such steps as contracting with more suppliers owned by women and minorities, targeting a more diverse customer base, and supporting the needs and interests of a diverse workforce. For example, IBM established executive-led task forces to represent women, Asian Americans, African Americans, Hispanic Americans, Native Americans, people with disabilities, and individuals who are gay, lesbian, bisexual, and transgender. As the company puts it, "Our diversity is a competitive advantage and consciously building diverse teams helps us drive the best results for our clients." For instance, women and minorities are a significant presence in the small-business marketplace, and having women and minorities on product development and marketing teams helps IBM understand the needs of these customers.[29]

diversity initiatives
Programs and policies that help companies support diverse workforces and markets.

REAL-TIME UPDATES
Learn More by Watching These Videos

See what Google employees have to say about diversity

The search giant's YouTube channel features employees talking about their experiences working at Google. Go to http://real-timeupdates.com/bia8 and click on Learn More in the Students section.

✔ Checkpoint

LEARNING OBJECTIVE 2: Discuss the challenges and advantages of a diverse workforce, and identify five major dimensions of workforce diversity.

SUMMARY: Differences in everything from religion to ethnic heritage to military experience enrich the workplace and give employers a competitive advantage by offering better insights into a diverse marketplace. A diverse workforce brings with it a wide range of skills, traditions, backgrounds, experiences, outlooks, and attitudes toward work—all of which can affect employee behaviors, relationships, and communication habits. Five major dimensions of workforce diversity addressed in this chapter are age, gender, race, religion, and ability.

CRITICAL THINKING: (1) How could a company benefit by investing in assistive technologies for its workers? (2) How might socioeconomic diversity in a company's workforce create both challenges and opportunities for the company?

IT'S YOUR BUSINESS: (1) What general opinions do you have of the generation that is older than you and the generation that is younger than you? What experiences and observations shaped these opinions? (2) Do you believe that any aspect of your background or heritage has held you back in any way in college or at work? If so, why?

KEY TERMS TO KNOW: sexism, glass ceiling, sexual harassment, diversity initiatives

recruiting
The process of attracting appropriate applicants for an organization's jobs.

Managing the Employment Life Cycle

HR managers oversee employment-related activities from recruiting and hiring through termination and retirement.

HIRING EMPLOYEES

The employment life cycle starts with **recruiting**, the process of attracting suitable candidates for an organization's jobs. The recruiting function is often judged by a combination of criteria known as *quality of hire*, which measures how closely incoming employees meet the company's needs.[30] Recruiters use a variety of resources, including internal searches, advertising, union hiring halls, college campuses and career offices, trade shows, *headhunters* (outside agencies that specialize in finding and placing employees), and social networking technologies. Exhibit 11.4 illustrates the general process that companies go through to hire new employees.

Federal and state laws and regulations govern many aspects of the hiring process. (See Exhibit 11.5 for a list of some of the most important employment-related laws.) In particular, employers must respect the privacy of applicants and avoid discrimination. For instance, any form or test that can be construed as a preemployment medical examination is prohibited by the Americans with Disabilities Act.[31]

termination
The process of getting rid of an employee through layoff or firing.

layoffs
Termination of employees for economic or business reasons.

TERMINATING EMPLOYEES

HR managers have the unpleasant responsibility of **termination**—permanently laying off employees because of cutbacks or firing employees for poor performance or other reasons. **Layoffs** are the termination of employees for economic or business reasons unrelated to employee performance. *Rightsizing* is a euphemism used to suggest that an organization is making changes in the workforce to match its business needs more

---

EXHIBIT 11.4   **The Recruiting Process**

This general model of the recruiting process shows the steps most companies go through to select the best employee for each position.

Step 1: Assemble candidate pool

- Recruiters select a small number of qualified candidates from all the internal and external applicants.
- Many organizations now use computer-based applicant tracking systems to manage the hiring process.

Step 2: Screen candidates

- Recruiters then screen candidates, typically through phone interviews, online tests, or on-campus interviews.
- Interviews at this stage are usually fairly structured, with applicants asked the same questions so that recruiters can easily compare responses.

Step 3: Interview candidates

- Candidates who make it through screening are invited to visit the company for another round of interviews.
- This stage usually involves several interviews with a mix of colleagues, HR specialists, and managers.

Step 4: Compare candidates

- The interview team compares notes and assesses the remaining candidates.
- Team members sometimes lobby for or against individual candidates based on what they've seen and heard during interviews.

Step 5: Investigate candidates

- Recruiters talk to references, conduct background checks, scan social media postings, and in many cases subject applicants to preemployment tests.
- Given the financial and legal risks associated with bad hiring decisions, smart employers research candidates carefully and thoroughly.

Step 6: Make an offer

- With all this information in hand, the hiring manager selects the most suitable person for the job and makes a job offer.

EXHIBIT 11.5	Major Employment Legislation

Here are some of the most significant sets of laws that affect employer–employee relations in the United States.

Category	Legislation	Highlights
Labor and unionization	National Labor Relations Act, also known as the Wagner Act	Establishes the right of employees to form, join, and assist unions and the right to strike; prohibits employers from interfering in union activities
	Labor-Management Relations Act, also known as the Taft-Hartley Act	Expands union member rights; gives employers free speech rights to oppose unions; restricts union's strike options; gives the president the authority to impose injunctions against strikes
	Labor-Management Reporting and Disclosure Act, also known as the Landrum-Griffin Act	Gives union members the right to nominate and vote for union leadership candidates; combats financial fraud within unions
	State right-to-work laws	Give individual employees the right to choose not to join a union
	Fair Labor Standards Act	Establishes minimum wage and overtime pay for nonexempt workers; sets strict guidelines for child labor
	Immigration Reform and Control Act	Prohibits employers from hiring illegal immigrants
Workplace safety	State workers' compensation acts	Require employers (in most states) to carry either private or government sponsored insurance that provides income to injured workers
	Occupational Health and Safety Act	Empowers the Occupational Safety and Health Administration (OSHA) to establish, monitor, and enforce standards for workplace safety
Compensation and benefits	Employee Retirement Income Security Act	Governs the establishment and operation of private pension programs
	Consolidated Omnibus Budget Reconciliation Act (usually known by the acronym COBRA)	Requires employers to let employees or their beneficiaries buy continued health insurance coverage after employment ends
	Federal Unemployment Tax Act and similar state laws	Requires employers to fund programs that provide income for qualified unemployed persons
	Social Security Act	Provides a level of retirement, disability, and medical coverage for employees and their dependents; jointly funded by employers and employees
	Lilly Ledbetter Fair Pay Act	Amends and modifies several pieces of earlier legislation to make it easier for employees to file lawsuits over pay and benefit discrimination
	Patient Protection and Affordable Care Act	Requires companies with more than 50 full-time employees to offer health insurance coverage for employees

Sources: Henry J. Kaiser Family Foundation, *Focus on Health Reform: Summary of the Affordable Care Act*, 23 April 2013; U.S. Department of Labor website, accessed 7 November 2013, www.dol.gov; Henry R. Cheeseman, *Contemporary Business and E-Commerce Law*, 7th ed. (Upper Saddle River, N.J.: Pearson Prentice Hall, 2010), 487–495; "The Lilly Ledbetter Fair Pay Act of 2009," U.S. White House website, accessed 23 June 2009, www.whitehouse.gov.

precisely. Although rightsizing usually involves *downsizing* the workforce, companies sometimes add workers in some areas while eliminating jobs in others.

To help ease the pain of layoffs, many companies provide laid-off employees with job-hunting assistance. *Outplacement* services such as résumé-writing courses, career counseling, office space, and secretarial help are offered to laid-off executives and blue-collar employees alike.

With many companies trimming workforces during a recession, managers need to take care not to discriminate against any segment of the workforce. Older workers appear to be a particularly vulnerable group because they usually have higher salaries and more expensive benefits, making them an inviting target for cost cutting. Age discrimination complaints related to layoffs have been at all-time highs in recent years.[32]

Terminating employment by firing is a complex subject with many legal ramifications, and the line between a layoff and a firing can be blurry. For instance, every state except Montana supports the concept of *at-will employment*, meaning that companies are free to fire nearly anyone they choose. State laws vary, but in general, employers cannot discriminate in firing, nor can they fire employees for whistle-blowing, for filing a worker's compensation claim, or for testifying against the employer in harassment or discrimination lawsuits.[33] If a terminated employee believes any of these principles have been violated, he or she can file a *wrongful discharge* lawsuit against the employer. In addition, employers must abide by the terms of an employment contract, if one has been entered into with the employee (these are much more common for executives than for lower-level employees). Some employers offer written assurances that they will terminate employees only *for cause*, which usually includes such actions as committing crimes or violating company policy.

REPLACING RETIRING EMPLOYEES

Companies can face two dramatically different challenges regarding retiring employees. For companies that are short-handed, the challenge is to persuade older employees to delay retirement. Conversely, companies with too many employees may induce employees to depart ahead of scheduled retirement by offering them *early retirement*, using financial incentives known as **worker buyouts**.

In the past, **mandatory retirement** policies forced people to quit working as soon as they turned a certain age. However, the Age Discrimination in Employment Act now outlaws mandatory retirement based on age alone, unless an employer can demonstrate that age is a valid qualification for "normal operation of the particular business."[34]

worker buyouts
Distributions of financial incentives to employees who voluntarily depart; usually undertaken in order to reduce the payroll.

mandatory retirement
Required dismissal of an employee who reaches a certain age.

 Checkpoint

LEARNING OBJECTIVE 3: Describe the three phases involved in managing the employment life cycle.

SUMMARY: The three phases of managing the employment life cycle are hiring, termination, and retirement. The hiring phase typically involves six steps: selecting a small number of qualified candidates from all of the applications received, screening those candidates to identify the most attractive prospects, interviewing those prospects in depth to learn more about them and their potential to contribute to the company, evaluating and comparing interview results, conducting background checks and pre-employment tests, and then selecting the best candidate for each position and making job offers. Termination can involve firing employees for poor performance or other reasons or laying off employees for financial reasons. Retirement offers a variety of challenges depending on the industry and the company's situation; overstaffed companies may induce some employees to retire early through buyouts, whereas others that face talent shortages may try to induce retirement-age employees to delay retirement.

CRITICAL THINKING: (1) Why would a company spend money on outplacement counseling and other services for laid-off employees? (2) Why would a company spend money to induce retirement-age employees to stay on board for a while, rather than simply hiring younger employees to take their place?

IT'S YOUR BUSINESS: (1) What impression would a potential employer get from studying your current online presence? (2) Have you ever been interviewed over the phone or via computer? If so, did you feel you were able to present yourself effectively without face-to-face contact?

KEY TERMS TO KNOW: recruiting, termination, layoffs, worker buyouts, mandatory retirement

Developing and Evaluating Employees

Another major contribution that HR makes is helping managers throughout the company align employee skill sets with the evolving requirements of each position. This effort includes appraising employee performance, managing training and development programs, and promoting and reassigning employees.

APPRAISING EMPLOYEE PERFORMANCE

How do employees (and their managers) know whether they are doing a good job? How can they improve their performance? What new skills should they learn? Managers attempt to answer these questions by conducting **performance appraisals**, or *performance reviews*, to objectively evaluate employees according to set criteria. The ultimate goal of performance appraisals is not to judge employees but rather to guide them in improving their performance.

performance appraisals
Periodic evaluations of employees' work according to specific criteria.

The worst possible outcome in an annual review is a negative surprise, such as when an employee has been working toward different goals than the manager expects or has been underperforming throughout the year but didn't receive any feedback or improvement coaching along the way.[35] In some instances, failing to confront performance problems in a timely fashion can make a company vulnerable to lawsuits.[36]

To avoid negative surprises, managers should meet with employees to agree on clear goals for the upcoming year and provide regular feedback and coaching as needed throughout the year if employee performance falls below expectations. Ideally, the annual review is more of a confirmation of the past year's performance and a planning session for the next year.

The specific measures of employee performance vary widely by job, company, and industry; Exhibit 11.6 on the next page shows one example of a performance appraisal form. Most jobs are evaluated in several areas, including tasks specific to the position, contribution to the company's overall success, and interaction with colleagues and customers. For example, a production manager might be evaluated on the basis of communication skills, people management, leadership, teamwork, recruiting and employee development, delegation, financial management, planning, and organizational skills.[37]

Many performance appraisals require the employee to be rated by several people (including more than one supervisor and perhaps several coworkers). This practice further promotes fairness by correcting for possible biases. The ultimate in multidimensional reviews is the **360-degree review**[38], in which a person is given feedback from subordinates (if the employee has supervisory responsibility), peers, superiors, and possibly customers or outside business partners. The multiple viewpoints can uncover weaknesses that employees and even their direct managers might not be aware of, as well as contributions and achievements that might have been overlooked in normal reviews.

360-degree review
A multidimensional review in which a person is given feedback from subordinates, peers, superiors, and possibly outside stakeholders such as customers and business partners.

In addition to formal, periodic performance evaluations, many companies evaluate some workers' performance continuously, using **electronic performance monitoring (EPM)**, sometimes called *computer activity monitoring*. For instance, customer service and telephone sales representatives are often evaluated by the number of calls they complete per hour and other variables. Newer software products extend this monitoring capability, from measuring data input accuracy to scanning for suspicious words in employee emails. As you can imagine, EPM efforts can generate controversy in the workplace, elevating employee stress levels and raising concerns about invasion of privacy.[39] Using EPM as a development tool, rather than a disciplinary tool, helps employees accept the practice.[40]

electronic performance monitoring (EPM)
Real-time, computer-based evaluation of employee performance.

TRAINING AND DEVELOPING EMPLOYEES

With the pace of change in everything from government regulations to consumer tastes to technology, employee knowledge and skills need to be constantly updated. Consequently, most successful companies place heavy emphasis on employee training and development efforts, for everyone from entry-level workers to the CEO.

Training usually begins with **orientation programs** designed to ease the new hire's transition into the company and to impart vital knowledge about the organization and its rules, procedures, and expectations. Effective orientation programs help employees

orientation programs
Sessions or procedures for acclimating new employees to the organization.

EXHIBIT 11.6   **Sample Performance Appraisal Form**

This sample form suggests the range of performance variables on which companies typically evaluate their employees.

Name _____   Title _____   Service Date _____   Date _____

Location _____   Division _____   Department _____

Length of Time in Present Position   Period of Review   Appraised by _____

_____   From: _____ To: _____   Title of Appraisor _____

Area of Performance	Comment	Rating
Job Knowledge and Skill Understands responsibilities and uses background for job. Adapts to new methods/techniques. Plans and organizes work. Recognizes errors and problems.		5 4 3 2 1
Volume of Work Amount of work output. Adherence to standards and schedules. Effective use of time.		5 4 3 2 1
Quality of Work Degree of accuracy—lack of errors. Thoroughness of work. Ability to exercise good judgment.		5 4 3 2 1
Initiative and Creativity Self-motivation in seeking responsibility and work that needs to be done. Ability to apply original ideas and concepts.		5 4 3 2 1
Communication Ability to exchange thoughts or information in a clear, concise manner. Ability to deal with different organizational levels of clientele.		5 4 3 2 1
Dependability Ability to follow instructions and directions correctly. Performs under pressure. Reliable work habits.		5 4 3 2 1
Leadership Ability/Potential Ability to guide others to the successful accomplishment of a given task. Potential for developing subordinate employees.		5 4 3 2 1

5. Outstanding   Employee who consistently exceeds established standards and expectations of the job.

4. Above Average   Employee who consistently meets established standards and expectations of the job. Often exceeds and rarely falls short of desired results.

3. Satisfactory   Generally qualified employee who meets job standards and expectations. Sometimes exceeds and may occasionally fall short of desired expectations. Performs duties in a normally expected manner.

2. Improvement Needed   Not quite meeting standards and expectations. An employee at this level of performance is not quite meeting all the standard job requirements.

1. Unsatisfactory   Employee who fails to meet the minimum standards and expectations of the job.

I have had the opportunity to read this performance appraisal.

How long has this employee been under your supervision?

Signature   Date   Signature of Supervisor   Date

skills inventory
A list of the skills a company needs from its workforce, along with the specific skills that individual employees currently possess.

become more productive in less time, help eliminate confusion and mistakes, and can significantly increase employee retention rates.[41] Training and other forms of employee development continue throughout the employee's career in most cases. Many HR departments maintain a **skills inventory**, which identifies both the current skill levels of all the employees and the skills the company needs in order to succeed. (If your employer doesn't maintain one for you, be sure to maintain your own skills inventory so you can stay on top of developments and expectations in your field.)

PROMOTING AND REASSIGNING EMPLOYEES

Many companies prefer to look within the organization to fill job vacancies. In part, this promote-from-within policy allows a company to benefit from the training and experience of its own workforce. This policy also rewards employees who have worked hard and demonstrated the ability to handle more challenging tasks. In addition, morale is usually better when a company promotes from within because other employees see the possibility of advancement. For example, Enterprise Holdings (the parent company of Enterprise Rent-a-Car, Alamo, and National Car Rental) highlights its promote-from-within philosophy and the opportunity to move into managerial responsibilities.[42]

However, a possible pitfall of internal promotion is that a person may be given a job beyond his or her competence. The best salesperson in the company is not necessarily a good candidate for sales manager, because managing requires a different set of skills. If the promotion is a mistake, the company not only loses its sales leader but also risks demoralizing the sales staff. Companies can reduce such risks through careful promotion policies and by providing support and training to help newly promoted employees perform well.

 Checkpoint

LEARNING OBJECTIVE 4: Explain the steps used to develop and evaluate employees.

SUMMARY: The effort to develop and evaluate employees includes providing performance appraisals, managing training and development programs, and promoting and reassigning employees. Managers use performance appraisals to give employees feedback and develop plans to improve performance shortcomings. In a 360-degree review, an employee is evaluated by subordinates (if applicable), peers, and superiors. Training and development efforts begin with orientation for new hires and continue throughout a person's career in many cases. When employees have reached sufficient skill levels to take on new challenges, they may be considered for promotion into positions of more responsibility.

CRITICAL THINKING: (1) How can employers balance the need to provide objective appraisals that can be compared across the company's entire workforce with the desire to evaluate each employee on an individual basis? (2) Beyond increasing their skill and knowledge levels, how can training improve employees' motivation and job satisfaction? (Review Chapter 10 if you need to.)

IT'S YOUR BUSINESS: (1) Have you ever had a performance appraisal that you felt was inaccurate or unfair? How would you change the process as a result? (2) Do the methods your college or university uses to evaluate your performance as student accurately reflect your progress? What changes would you make to the evaluation process?

KEY TERMS TO KNOW: performance appraisals, 360-degree review, electronic performance monitoring (EPM), orientation programs, skills inventory

Administering Employee Compensation

Pay and benefits are of vital interest to all employees, of course, and these subjects also consume considerable time and attention in HR departments. For many companies, payroll is the single biggest expense, and the cost of benefits, particularly health care, continues to climb. Consequently, **compensation**, the combination of direct payments such as wages or salary and indirect payments through employee benefits, is one of the HR manager's most significant responsibilities.

 5 **LEARNING OBJECTIVE**

Describe the major elements of employee compensation.

compensation
Money, benefits, and services paid to employees for their work.

SALARIES AND WAGES

salary
Fixed cash compensation for work, usually by a yearly amount; independent of the number of hours worked.

wages
Cash payment based on the number of hours an employee has worked or the number of units an employee has produced.

Most employees receive the bulk of their compensation in the form of a **salary**, if they receive a fixed amount per year, or **wages**, if they are paid by the unit of time (hourly, daily, or weekly) or by the unit of output (often called "getting paid by the piece" or "piecework"). The Fair Labor Standards Act, introduced in 1938 and amended many times since then, sets specific guidelines that employers must follow when administering salaries and wages, including setting a minimum wage and paying overtime for time worked beyond 40 hours a week. However, most professional and managerial employees are considered exempt from these regulations, meaning, for instance, their employers don't have to pay them for overtime. The distinction between *exempt employees* and *nonexempt employees* is based on job responsibilities and pay level. In general, salaried employees are exempt, although there are many exceptions.[43]

REAL-TIME UPDATES

Learn More by Exploring This Interactive Website

Explore the salary potential for virtually any business career

Curious about salary potential in various business jobs? This free salary wizard has the answers. Go to http://real-timeupdates.com/bia8 and click on Learn More in the Students section.

Defining compensation levels for employees up and down the organization chart is a complex challenge. Companies need to manage compensation in a way that allows them to simultaneously earn a profit, create appealing goods and services, and compete with other companies for the same employees. A firm could attract most of the talent it needs by paying huge salaries, but that probably wouldn't be profitable. Conversely, it could keep salaries low to hold down costs, but then it couldn't attract the talent it needs to be competitive, so it might not generate enough revenue to turn a profit anyway.

In the broadest terms, compensation is dictated by prevailing conditions in the job market and the value each employee brings to the organization. Such variables as geography (locations with higher living expenses tend to have higher salaries), industry, and company size (larger companies tend to pay more) can also factor into the equation. Although it seems like going around in circles to base compensation on prevailing market rates when all the other companies in the market are doing the same thing, the market is the best quasi-independent arbiter available. As executive compensation consultant Russell Miller puts it, "If we don't look to the market to determine if we're paying competitively, where else should we look?"[44]

Judging an employee's worth to an organization is no simple matter, either. Few jobs—sales is a notable exception—have an immediate and measurable impact on revenue, which makes it difficult to say how much most employees are worth to the company. For most positions, companies tend to establish a salary range for each position, trying to balance what it can afford to pay with prevailing market rates. Each employee's salary is then set within that range based on performance evaluations, with higher-performing employees deemed more valuable to the company and therefore deserving of higher pay.

Not surprisingly, people expect to get paid what they believe they are worth—particularly relative to what other people are making. Recall from the discussion of equity theory (page 231) that most employees don't expect to make as much as the CEO, but they do expect the ratio of value provided to rewards gained to be at least reasonable. In the 1950s, CEOs made roughly 20 times more than the average worker pay in their companies, and the ratio has been steadily climbing. Depending on the survey methodology, CEO pay in major corporations is now roughly 200 to 300 times the average employee's.[45] Although it's not really possible to identify exactly how much more valuable a CEO is than an average employee, it is reasonable to ask if today's CEOs are 10 or 15 times more valuable than CEOs were in years past.

INCENTIVE PROGRAMS

As Chapter 10 mentions, many companies provide managers and employees with *incentives* to encourage productivity, innovation, and commitment to work. Incentives are typically cash payments linked to specific goals for individual, group, or companywide performance. In other words, achievements, not just activities, are made the basis for payment.

The success of these programs often depends on how closely incentives are linked to actions within the employee's control:

- For both salaried and wage-earning employees, one type of incentive compensation is a **bonus**, a payment in addition to the regular wage or salary. Paying performance-based bonuses has become an increasingly popular approach to compensation as more companies shift away from automatic annual pay increases.[46]
- In contrast to bonuses, **commissions** are a form of compensation that pays employees in sales positions based on the level of sales they make within a given time frame.
- Employees may be rewarded for staying with a company and encouraged to work harder through **profit sharing**, a system in which employees receive a portion of the company's profits.
- Similar to profit sharing, **gain sharing** ties rewards to profits (or cost savings) achieved by meeting specific goals such as quality and productivity improvement.
- A variation of gain sharing, **pay for performance** requires employees to accept a lower base pay but rewards them with bonuses, commissions, or stock options if they reach agreed-on goals. To be successful, this method needs to be complemented with effective feedback systems that let employees know how they are performing throughout the year.[47]
- Another approach to compensation being explored by some companies is **knowledge-based pay**, also known as *competency-based pay* or *skill-based pay*, which is tied to employees' knowledge and abilities rather than to their job per se. More than half of all large U.S. companies now use some variation on this incentive.[48]

Sales professionals usually earn at least part of their income through commissions; the more they sell, the more they earn.

Jeff Greenberg/The Image Works

bonus
A cash payment, in addition to regular wage or salary, that serves as a reward for achievement.

commissions
Employee compensation based on a percentage of sales made.

profit sharing
The distribution of a portion of the company's profits to employees.

gain sharing
Tying rewards to profits or cost savings achieved by meeting specific goals.

pay for performance
An incentive program that rewards employees for meeting specific, individual goals.

knowledge-based pay
Pay tied to an employee's acquisition of knowledge or skills; also called competency-based pay or skill-based pay.

✔ Checkpoint

LEARNING OBJECTIVE 5: Describe the major elements of employee compensation.

SUMMARY: For most employees, the bulk of their compensation comes in the form of a *salary*, if they receive a fixed amount per year, or *wages*, if they are paid by the unit of time or unit of output. In addition to their base salary or wages, some employees are eligible for a variety of incentive programs, including bonuses, commissions, profit sharing, and gain sharing. In some cases, employers offer pay-for-performance plans that have a lower base salary but allow employees to earn more by hitting specific performance goals. Some companies are also exploring knowledge-based pay, which rewards employees for acquiring information or developing skills related to their jobs.

CRITICAL THINKING: (1) What are some potential risks or limitations of performance-based pay systems? (2) How does equity theory (see Chapter 10) explain the anger some employees feel about the compensation packages their company CEOs receive?

IT'S YOUR BUSINESS: (1) If you worked for a large corporation, would a profit-sharing plan motivate you? Why or why not? (2) What questions would you ask before you accepted a sales position in which most of your compensation would be based on commissions, rather than base salary?

KEY TERMS TO KNOW: compensation, salary, wages, bonus, commissions, profit sharing, gain sharing, pay for performance, knowledge-based pay

Identify the most significant categories of employee benefits and services.

employee benefits
Compensation other than wages, salaries, and incentive programs.

cafeteria plans
Flexible benefit programs that let employees personalize their benefits packages.

Employee Benefits and Services

Companies regularly provide **employee benefits**—elements of compensation other than wages, salaries, and incentives. These benefits may be offered as either a preset package—that is, the employee gets whatever insurance, paid holidays, pension plan, and other benefits the company sets up—or as flexible plans, sometimes known as **cafeteria plans** (so called because of the similarity to choosing items in a cafeteria). The benefits most commonly provided by employers are insurance, retirement benefits, employee stock-ownership plans, stock options, and family benefits.

INSURANCE

Employers can offer a range of insurance plans to their employees, including life, health, dental, vision, disability, and long-term care insurance. Perhaps no other issue illustrates the challenging economics of business today better than health-care costs in general and health insurance in particular. With medical costs rising much faster than inflation in general, companies are taking a variety of steps to manage the financial impact, including forcing employees to pick up more of the cost, reducing or eliminating coverage for retired employees, auditing employees' health claims, monitoring employees' health and habits, dropping spouses from insurance plans, or even firing employees who are so sick or disabled that they are no longer able to work. The situation is particularly acute for small businesses, which don't have the purchasing power of large corporations.[49]

With health-care costs on an unsustainable upward spiral, health-care reform has been a hot political topic in recent years. In aggregate, the United States spends enough to provide adequate care for everyone, but the health-care sector is plagued by waste, inefficiency, and imbalance. Per capita, the United States spends more on health care than any other country, but according to a number of key measures, the quality of care is lower in the United States than in many other countries.[50]

The Affordable Care Act (ACA) of 2010, often referred to informally as Obamacare, sought to tackle one of the thorniest issues in U.S. healthcare: the millions of residents who lacked health insurance. Among other elements in this complex and controversial piece of legislation, the ACA requires that companies with more than 50 workers provide health insurance benefits for the employees, and that people who don't get insurance through work buy individual policies. Millions of previously uninsured people now have coverage, but the ACA also resulted in higher premiums for millions of people who had been buying their own insurance.[51]

RETIREMENT BENEFITS

retirement plans
Company-sponsored programs for providing retirees with income.

pension plans
Generally refers to traditional, defined-benefit retirement plans.

401(k) plan
A defined contribution retirement plan in which employers often match the amount employees invest.

employee stock-ownership plan (ESOP)
A program that enables employees to become partial owners of a company.

Many employers offer **retirement plans**, which are designed to provide continuing income after an employee retires. Company-sponsored retirement plans can be categorized as either *defined-benefit plans*, in which companies specify how much they will pay employees on retirement, or *defined-contribution plans*, in which companies specify how much they will put into the retirement fund (by matching employee contributions, for instance), without guaranteeing specific payout levels during retirement. Although both types are technically **pension plans**, when most people speak of pension plans, they are referring to traditional defined-benefit plans, which are far less common than they were in years past.[52]

Defined-contribution plans are similar to savings plans; they provide a future benefit based on annual employer contributions, voluntary employee matching contributions, and accumulated investment earnings. Employers can choose from several types of defined contribution plans, the most common being the **401(k) plan** (see Exhibit 11.7).

More than 10 million U.S. employees are now enrolled in an **employee stock-ownership plan (ESOP)**, in which a company places some or all of its stock in trust, with each eligible employee entitled to a certain portion. (Most ESOPs are in closely held corporations whose stock isn't available for sale to the public.) Many companies report that ESOPs help boost employee productivity because workers perceive a direct correlation between their efforts and the value of the company stock price.[53]

EXHIBIT 11.7 **The Basics of a 401(k) Plan**

The 401(k) plan is one of the most popular employer-sponsored retirement benefits.

Funding mechanism	• Defined-contribution plan (rather than defined-benefit) • Employees can invest a percentage of their pretax income, up to the amount allowed by law (currently $17,500 with an additional $5,500 allowed for people over 50) • Employers may choose to match some or all of the employee's contributions • Employees make their own investment choices from the mutual funds and other options available in the employer's plan
Advantages for employees	• Potential to significantly increase retirement investment if employer chooses to match employee contributions • Opportunity to reduce immediate tax burden (by reducing taxable income by the amount invested) • Automatic contribution feature makes it a forced savings plan • If the specific employer plan allows it, employees can borrow up to 50 percent of the balance in their plans before reaching retirement age • Plan is portable; employees can take it with them if they leave the company (*vesting* rules apply to any employer matching funds; if employee leaves before matching funds are fully invested, he or she forfeits a portion of those funds)
Potential risks and disadvantages for employees	• As a defined-contribution plan, does not guarantee a specific level of income in retirement • Employer's matching contribution might be in company stock, which might not be a good investment • Account balance vulnerable to changes in stock prices • Can be subject to high and sometimes hidden fees • Investment opportunities under a specific plan may not be desirable or appropriate for every employee • Except for special circumstances, employees cannot begin withdrawing funds until age 59.5 without incurring a penalty

Sources: Mark P. Cussen, "The Basics of a 401(k) Retirement Plan," *Forbes*, 30 July 2013, www.forbes.com; "401(k)s & Company Plans," *CNNMoney*, accessed 7 November 2013, http://money.cnn.com.

STOCK OPTIONS

One method for tying employee compensation to company performance is the stock option plan. **Stock options** grant employees the right to purchase a set number of shares of the employer's stock at a specific price, called the *grant* or *exercise price*, during a certain time period. Options typically *vest* over a number of years, meaning that employees can purchase a prorated portion of the shares every year until the vesting period is over (at which time they can purchase all the shares they are entitled to). The major attractions of stock options from an employer's point of view are that they provide a means of compensation that doesn't require any cash outlay and a means of motivating employees to work hard to make sure the stock price increases.

stock options
A contract that allows the holder to purchase or sell a certain number of shares of a particular stock at a given price by a certain date.

The popularity of stock options has waned somewhat in recent years, following a change in accounting rules that forced companies to account for the value of outstanding options in their annual financial reports. Before that change, investors and regulators argued that companies were hiding the true costs of options and thereby reporting inflated earnings.[54]

Stock options also figure into the controversy about executive compensation, for a couple of reasons. First, from the recipient's point of view, there is no real risk associated with stock options. Second, this lack of risk exposure can lead to riskier decision making. In fact, research suggests that CEOs who are compensated primarily through stock options tend to make poorer decisions regarding acquisitions, and their companies are more likely to experience accounting irregularities.[55]

OTHER EMPLOYEE BENEFITS

Employers offer a variety of other benefits in addition to those just discussed. Some of them are mandated by government regulation and some are offered voluntarily to attract and support employees. Here are some of the most common benefits:

• **Paid vacations and sick leave.** Some companies offer separate vacation and sick days; others combine the paid time off in a single "bucket" and let employees choose how to use the time.
• **Family and medical leave.** The Family Medical Leave Act (FMLA) of 1993 requires employers with 50 or more workers to provide up to 12 weeks of unpaid leave per

Trust Insurance employee Kathy Hatfield gets to spend time with her daughters at the company's on-site day-care center. Such centers reduce costs and stress for employees who have children.

employee assistance program (EAP)
A company-sponsored counseling or referral plan for employees with personal problems.

year for childbirth, adoption, or the care of oneself, a child, a spouse, or a parent with a serious illness.[56]

- **Child-care assistance.** Many companies offer child-care assistance, such as discounted rates at nearby child-care centers or on-site day-care centers.[57]
- **Elder-care assistance.** Many employers offer some form of elder-care assistance to help employees with the responsibility of caring for aging parents.
- **Tuition loans and reimbursements.** U.S. companies contribute billions of dollars every year to continuing education for their employees.[58]
- **Employee assistance programs.** One of the most cost-effective benefits employers can establish is an **employee assistance program (EAP)**, which offers private and confidential counseling to employees who need help with issues related to substance abuse, domestic violence, finances, stress, family issues, and other personal problems.[59]

For the latest information on employee benefits and other human resources topics, visit http://real-timeupdates.com/bia8 and click on Chapter 11.

✓ **Checkpoint**

LEARNING OBJECTIVE 6: Identify the most significant categories of employee benefits and services.

SUMMARY: The major types of employee benefits are insurance and retirement benefits. Companies may help employees with the cost of many types of insurance, including life, health, dental, vision, disability, and long-term care. Retirement programs fall into two basic categories: defined-benefit programs, which promise a specific amount per month after retirement, and defined-contribution programs, in which the company contributes a certain amount per month or year to an investment account but doesn't guarantee payment levels after retirement. Other important benefits are paid vacations and sick leave, family and medical leave, child- and elder-care assistance, tuition reimbursements or loans, and employee assistance programs that deal with personal matters such as substance abuse or domestic violence.

CRITICAL THINKING: (1) Why are stock options a controversial employee benefit, particularly for top executives? (2) What are the risks of investing in an ESOP?

IT'S YOUR BUSINESS: (1) Would you take stock options in lieu of a higher salary? Why or why not? (2) Would you be willing to forgo health insurance or a retirement plan for higher salary or wages? Why or why not?

KEY TERMS TO KNOW: employee benefits, cafeteria plans, retirement plans, pension plans, 401(k) plan, employee stock-ownership plan (ESOP), stock options, employee assistance program (EAP)

BEHIND THE SCENES
FOR ZAPPOS, FINDING THE RIGHT EMPLOYEES MEANS REJECTING THE OLD WAY OF DOING BUSINESS

To a large degree, contemporary employee recruiting practices are all about conformity: identifying the measurable attributes of the ideal employee (education and training, years of experience, technical specialties, job titles, and facts and figures) and then using this template to filter out anyone who isn't a perfect match.

To the dismay of many job seekers, in fact, this is precisely what applicant tracking systems usually do. Candidates who could've turned out to be solid or even superstar employees may never get past this automated screening process if their résumés aren't worded in precisely the way the system expects or they happen to be missing one particular skill they could easily develop on the job if given the chance. People whose résumés aren't "perfect" or who could really shine in an interview may never get the chance to get in front of an interviewer. Moreover, the vigorous screening process offers little opportunity for hiring managers to assess curiosity, passion, and other intangibles that top performers have—or the negative attributes that can make someone a toxic presence in the workplace.

Those positive intangibles are vital to maintaining the upbeat, service-driven culture that Tony Hsieh and his colleagues have fostered. To attract the Zappos kind of candidate, a strict reliance on a facts-and-figures screening simply wouldn't work because it would filter out people with unconventional backgrounds while also passing through people who look good on paper but don't have what it takes to succeed at Zappos.

To find employees who will thrive in and protect the unconventional Zappos culture, the company takes an unorthodox path when it comes to recruiting and interviewing. For example, many companies refuse to look at videos of job candidates early in the recruiting process out of fear of getting slapped with employment discrimination lawsuits appearance, age, race, and other visible factors. In sharp contrast, Zappos encourages applicants to send videos of themselves. And in perhaps its boldest recruiting move yet, the company no longer posts job openings. Instead, it now requires would-be employees to join a customized social network called Inside Zappos. The network lets candidates learn more about what it's like to work at Zappos, and it lets the company learn more about the candidates— including how they interact with other people.

The Zappos interviewing process is designed to find passionate, free-thinking candidates who fit the culture, from the offbeat antics to the serious commitment to customers and fellow employees. Some of the questions interviewees can expect to encounter include "What was the best mistake you made on the job?" and "On a scale of 1 to 10, how weird are you?"

Speaking of offbeat interviews, the company recently screened software engineering candidates using 30-minute coding challenges, in which the first programmer to solve the problem was "fast-tracked to Vegas" for the next round of interviews. Coding contests are not all that unusual for recruiting programmers, but it's unlikely that many feature an open bar, as the Zappos competition did.

A strong customer- and employee-focused culture, a strong commitment to maintaining that culture, and a recruiting strategy that finds the right people for that culture—this relentless focus on doing business the Zappos way keeps paying off. The company continues to grow and to be ranked as one of the best places to work in the United States.[60]

Critical Thinking Questions

11-1. Not all potentially good employees have a bubbly, goofy personality of the type that Zappos likes to attract. Would it be wise for the company to reject a candidate solely on the basis of a shy, introverted personality? Would it be discriminatory to do so?

11-2. What are the potential risks of emphasizing personality, particularly offbeat personality, in the recruiting process?

11-3. How should a positive, upbeat culture handle the inevitable disappointments and tragedies that happen in any company, from the need to terminate low performers to the death of an employee.

LEARN MORE ONLINE

Visit Inside Zappos (**http://jobs.zappos.com**), the careers portion of the Zappos website and read the various department descriptions in the Choose Your Team section. How do these descriptions and the profiles of various team members appeal to potential employees? Could they potentially turn off some job seekers? If so, would this necessarily be a bad thing? Which of the Zappos teams would you choose if you were applying at the company?

KEY TERMS

bonus (263)
cafeteria plans (264)
commissions (263)
compensation (261)
contingent employees (249)
diversity initiatives (255)
electronic performance monitoring (EPM) (259)
employee assistance program (EAP) (266)
employee benefits (264)
employee retention (249)
employee stock-ownership plan (ESOP) (264)
401(k) plan (264)
gain sharing (263)
glass ceiling (252)
human resources (HR) management (248)
job description (249)
job specification (249)
knowledge-based pay (263)
layoffs (256)
mandatory retirement (258)
orientation programs (259)

pay for performance (263)
pension plans (264)
performance appraisals (259)
profit sharing (263)
quality of work life (QWL) (248)
recruiting (256)
retirement plans (264)
salary (262)
sexism (252)
sexual harassment (254)
skills inventory (260)
stock options (265)
succession planning (249)
termination (256)
360-degree review (259)
turnover rate (249)
wages (262)
work–life balance (248)
worker buyouts (258)
workforce analytics (249)

MyBizLab
To complete the problems with the ⭐,
go to EOC Discussion Questions in the
MyLab.

TEST YOUR KNOWLEDGE

Questions for Review

11-4. What do human resources managers do?

11-5. What are some strategic staffing alternatives that organizations use to avoid overstaffing and understaffing?

11-6. What is the purpose of conducting a job analysis? What are some of the techniques used for gathering information?

11-7. How do defined-benefit plans differ from defined contribution plans?

11-8. What is the glass ceiling?

Questions for Analysis

11-9. How do incentive programs encourage employees to be more productive, innovative, and committed to their work?

11-10. Why do some employers offer comprehensive benefits even though the costs of doing so have risen significantly in recent years?

11-11. Why would companies include vesting criteria in their 401(k) retirement plans?

⭐ **11-12.** Why is it in a company's best interests to break down the glass ceiling?

⭐ **11-13.** **Ethical Considerations.** Corporate headhunters have been known to raid other companies of their top talent to fill vacant or new positions for their clients. Is it ethical to contact the CEO of one company and lure him or her to join the management team of another company?

Questions for Application

11-14. Assume that you are the manager of human resources at a manufacturing company that employs about 500 people. A recent cyclical downturn in your industry has led to financial losses, and top management is talking about laying off workers. Several supervisors have come to you with creative ways of keeping employees on the payroll, such as sharing workers with other local companies. Why might you want to consider this option? What other options exist besides layoffs?

11-15. When you begin interviewing as you approach graduation, you will need to analyze job offers that include a number of financial and nonfinancial elements. Which of these aspects of employment are your top three priorities: a good base wage, bonus or commission opportunities, profit-sharing potential, rapid advancement opportunities, flexible work arrangements, good health-care insurance coverage, or a strong retirement program? Which of these elements would you be willing to forgo in order to get your top three?

11-16. What steps could you take as the owner of a small software company to foster "temporary loyalty" from the independent programmers you frequently hire for short durations (one to six months)?

11-17. **Concept Integration.** Of the five levels in Maslow's hierarchy of needs, which is satisfied by offering salary? By offering health-care benefits? By offering training opportunities? By developing flexible job descriptions?

EXPAND YOUR KNOWLEDGE

Discovering Career Opportunities

If you pursue a career in human resources, you'll be deeply involved in helping organizations find, select, train, evaluate, and retain employees. You have to like people and be a good communicator to succeed in HR. Is this field for you? Find ads seeking applicants for positions in the field of human resources, and then answer the following questions.

11-18. What educational qualifications, technical knowledge, or specialized skills are applicants for these jobs expected to have? How do these requirements fit with your background and educational plans?

11-19. Next, look at the duties mentioned in the ad for each job. What do you think you would be doing on an average day in these jobs? Does the work in each job sound interesting and challenging?

11-20. Now think about how you might fit into one of these positions. Do you prefer to work alone, or do you enjoy teamwork? How much paperwork are you willing to do? Do you communicate better in person, on paper, or by phone? Considering your answers to these questions, which of the HR jobs seems to be the closest match for your personal style?

Improving Your Tech Insights: Telecommuting Technologies

Thanks to mobile communications and cloud computing, working without going to the office is easier than ever before.

When they're used successfully, telecommuting technologies can reduce facility costs, put employees closer to customers, reduce traffic and air pollution, give companies access to a wide range of independent talent, and let employees work in higher-salary jobs while living in lower-cost areas of the country. In the future, these technologies have the potential to change business so radically that they could even influence the design of entire cities. With less need to pull millions of workers into central business districts, business executives, urban planners, and political leaders have the opportunity to explore such new ideas as *telecities*—virtual cities populated by people and organizations connected technologically rather than physically.

Telecommuting offers compelling benefits, but it must be planned and managed carefully. Conduct some online research to find out what experts believe are the keys to success. Start with the Telework Coalition, **www.telcoa.org**. You can also find numerous articles in business publications (search for both "telecommuting" and "telework"). In a brief email message to your instructor, provide four or five important tips for ensuring successful telecommuting work arrangements.[61]

PRACTICE YOUR SKILLS

Sharpening Your Communication Skills

Public companies occasionally need to issue news releases to announce or explain downturns in sales, profits, demand, or other business factors. Search the web to locate a company that has issued a press release that recently reported lower earnings or other bad news and access the news release on the firm's website. You can also search for press releases at **www.prnewswire.com** or **www.businesswire.com**. How does the headline relate to the main message of the release? Does the company come right out and deliver the bad news, or build up to it by explaining the circumstances behind it first? What does the company do to present the bad

news in a favorable light, if applicable—and does this effort seem sincere and ethical to you? In a brief message to your instructor, give your assessment of how well the press release conveys the bad news without being overly negative or falsely positive.

Building Your Team Skills

Team up with a classmate to practice your responses to interview questions. Use the list of common interview questions provided on page xliv in the Prologue and take turns posing and responding to those questions. Which questions did you find most difficult to answer? What insights did you gain about your strengths and weaknesses by answering those questions? Why is it a good idea to rehearse your answers before going to an interview?

Developing Your Research Skills

Locate one or more articles in business journals or newspapers that illustrate how a company or an industry is adapting to changes in its workforce. (Examples include retraining, literacy or basic skills training, flexible benefits, and benefits aimed at working parents or people who care for aging relatives.)

11-21. What changes in the workforce or employee needs caused the company to adapt? What did the company do to respond to those changes? Was the company's response voluntary or legally mandated?

11-22. Is the company alone in facing these changes, or is the entire industry trying to adapt? What are other companies in the industry doing to adapt to the changes?

11-23. What other changes in the workforce or in employee needs do you think this company is likely to face in the next few years? Why?

MyBizLab®

Go to the Assignments section of your MyLab to complete these writing exercises.

11-24. How is management likely to change as companies increasingly use contingent workers instead of full-time employees?

11-25. What are some ways that pay-for-performance schemes could backfire if a company doesn't set them up carefully or effectively manage the factors that affect employee performance?

ENDNOTES

1. Zappos Inside Zappos page, accessed 8 August 2014, https://jobs.zappos.com; Blair Hanley Frank, "Zappos Ditches Job Posts, replaces Them with a Social Network," *GeekWire*, 27 May 2014, www.geekwire.com. "Wishez Is Live," Zappos Family blog, 17 November 2010, http://blogs.zappos.com; Tony Hsieh, "Amazon & Zappos, 1 Year Later," Zappos CEO & COO blog, 22 July 2010, http://blogs.zappos.com; Todd Raphael, "7 Interview Questions from Zappos," Todd Raphael's World of Talent blog, 22 July 2010, http://community.ere.net; Jeffrey M. O'Brien, "Zappos Knows How to Kick It," *Fortune*, 22 January 2009, http://about.zappos.com/ press-center; "Zappos Family Seattle Coding Challenge and Tech Tweet Up," Zappos Family blog, 22 March 2011, http://blogs.zappos.com.

2. Gary Dessler, *A Framework for Human Resource Management*, 3rd ed. (Upper Saddle River, N.J.: Pearson Prentice Hall, 2004), 2.

3. Dessler, *A Framework for Human Resource Management*, 66.

4. Dessler, *A Framework for Human Resource Management*, 72.

5. Dessler, *A Framework for Human Resource Management*, 74–75.

6. Shari Randall, "Succession Planning Is More Than a Game of Chance," *Workforce Management*, accessed 1 May 2004, www.workforce.com.

7. Bruce Morton, "Hello New Frontier: The Growing Contingent Workforce," *Allegis Group Services*, 26 March 2013, www.allegisgroupservices.com.

8. Arik Hesseldahl, "Yahoo Redux: HP Says 'All Hands on Deck' Needed, Requiring Most Employees to Work at the Office (Memo)," *AllThingsD*, 8 October 2013, http://allthingsd.com; Ted Samson, "Can a VPN Log Really Point to Employee Slacking?" *InfoWorld*, 5 March 2013, www.infoworld.com.

9. Michael R. Carrell, Everett E. Mann, and Tracey Honeycutt Sigler, "Defining Workforce Diversity Programs and Practices in Organizations: A Longitudinal Study," *Labor Law Journal*, Spring 2006, 5–12.

10. "Dimensions of Diversity—Workforce," Merck website, accessed 4 January 2011, www.merck.com.

11. Nancy R. Lockwood, "Workplace Diversity: Leveraging the Power of Difference for Competitive Advantage," *HR Magazine*, June 2005, special section 1–10.

12. Podcast interview with Ron Glover, *IBM* website, accessed 17 August, 2008, www.ibm.com.

13. Peter Coy, "Old. Smart. Productive." *BusinessWeek*, 27 June 2005, www.businessweek.com; Iris Beamer and Linda Varner, *Intercultural Communication in the Global Workplace*, 3rd ed. (Columbus, Ohio: McGraw-Hill/Irwin, 2004), 107–108.

14. Beamer and Varner, *Intercultural Communication in the Global Workplace*, 107–108.

15. "Sex-Based Charges: FY 1997–FY 2012," EEOC website, accessed 7 November 2013, www.eeoc.gov.

16. "Women CEOs of the S&P 500," Catalyst, 3 April 2015, www.catalyst.org.

17. *Women in America: Indicators of Social and Economic Well Being*, White House Council on Women and Girls, March 2011, iii; *An Analysis of Reasons for the Disparity in Wages Between Men and Women*, U.S. Department of Labor Employment Standards Administration, 12 January 2009, 1.

18. Christina Hoff Sommers, "No, Women Don't Make Less Money Than Men," *The Daily Beast*, 1 February 2014, www.thedailybeast.com.

19. Lydia Dishman, "The Other Wage Gap: Why Men in Female-Dominated Industries Still Earn More," *Fast Company*, 8 April 2015, www.fastcompany.com.

20. *An Analysis of Reasons for the Disparity in Wages Between Men and Women*, 1.

21. Hanna Rosin, "The Gender Wage Gap Lie," *Slate*, 30 August 2013, www.slate.com.

22. "Sexual Harassment Charges: EEOC & FEPAs Combined: FY 1997–FY 2006," EEOC website, accessed 13 August 2007, www.eeoc.gov.

23. Robert Kreitner, *Management*, 9th ed. (Boston: Houghton Mifflin, 2004), 375–377; "One-Fifth of Women Are Harassed Sexually," *HR Focus*, April 2002, 2.

24. Paul Taylor, "The Next America," Pew Research Center, 10 April 2014, www.pewressarch.com; "More Than 300 Counties Now 'Majority–Minority,'" press release, U.S. Census Bureau website, 9 August 2007, www.census.gov; Robert Kreitner, *Management*, 9th ed. (Boston: Houghton Mifflin, 2004), 84.

25. "Race-Based Charges: FY 1997–FY 2012," EEOC website, accessed 7 November 2013, www.eeoc.gov.

26. "Usual Weekly Earnings of Wage and Salary Workers: Third Quarter 2013," *U.S. Bureau of Labor Statistics*, 7 November 2013, www.bls.gov.

27. Mark D. Downey, "Keeping the Faith," *HR Magazine*, January 2008, 85–88.

28. Vadim Liberman, "What Happens When an Employee's Freedom of Religion Crosses Paths with a Company's Interests?" *Conference Board Review*, September/October 2007, 42–48.

29. "Diversity 3.0," IBM website, accessed 21 June 2009, www.ibm.com; Wendy Harris, "Out of the Corporate Closet," *Black Enterprise*, accessed 13 August 2007, http://integrate.factiva.com; May 2007, David A. Thomas, "Diversity as Strategy," *Harvard Business Review*, September 2004, 98–108; Joe Mullich, "Hiring Without Limits," *Workforce Management*, June 2004, 53–58; Mike France and William G. Symonds, "Diversity Is About to Get More Elusive, Not Less," *BusinessWeek*, 7 July 2003, www.businessweek.com; Anne Papmehl, "Diversity in Workforce Paying Off, IBM Finds," *Toronto Star*, 7 October 2002, www.elibrary.com.

30. Samuel Greengard, "Quality of Hire: How Companies Are Crunching the Numbers," *Workforce Management*, July 2004, www.workforce.com.

31. Steven Mitchell Sack, "The Working Woman's Legal Survival Guide: Testing," FindLaw.com, accessed 22 February 2004, www.findlaw.com; David W. Arnold and John W. Jones, "Who the Devil's Applying Now?" *Security Management*, March 2002, 85–88.

32. "Age Discrimination in Employment Act: FY 1997–FY 2010," EEOC website, accessed 30 August 2011, www.eeoc.gov; Russ Banham, "Age Bias Claims Rise," *Treasury & Risk*, May 2009, 14–15.

33. John Jude Moran, *Employment Law: New Challenges in the Business Environment*, 2nd ed. (Upper Saddle River, N.J.: Pearson Prentice Hall, 2002), 127; Dan Seligman, "The Right to Fire," *Forbes*, 10 November 2003, 126–128.

34. "The Age Discrimination in Employment Act of 1967," U.S. Equal Employment Opportunity Commission website, accessed 10 July 2009, www.eeoc.gov; Henry R. Cheeseman, *Contemporary Business and E-Commerce Law*, 7th ed. (Upper Saddle River, N.J.: Pearson Prentice Hall, 2010), 522–523.

35. Kelly Spors, "Why Performance Reviews Don't Work—And What You Can Do About It," Independent Street blog, *Wall Street Journal*, 21 October 2008, http://blogs.wsj.com.

36. Carrie Brodzinski, "Avoiding Wrongful Termination Suits," *National Underwriter Property & Casualty—Risk & Benefits Management*, 13 October 2003, www.elibrary.com.

37. PerformanceNow.com website, accessed 2 May 2004, www.performancenow.com; Dessler, *A Framework for Human Resource Management*, 199.

38. Amy Gallow, "Bouncing Back from a Negative 360-Degree Review," *Harvard Business Review* blogs, 29 July 2010, http://blogs.hbr.org; Tracy Gallagher, "360-Degree Performance Reviews Offer Valuable Perspectives," *Financial Executive*, December 2008, 61.

39. Jeff St. John, "Kennewick, Wash., 'Snoop' Software Maker Also Protects Privacy," (*Kennewick, Wash.*) *Tri-City Herald*, 17 April 2004, www.highbeam.com; Dessler, *A Framework for Human Resource Management*, 204–205.

40. Laurel A. McNall and Sylvia G. Roch, "A Social Exchange Model of Employee Reactions to Electronic Performance Monitoring," *Human Performance*, 22, 2009, 204–224.

41. Carol A. Hacker, "New Employee Orientation: Make It Pay Dividends for Years to Come," *Information Systems Management*, Winter 2004, 89–92.

42. "Enterprise Management Training Program," Enterprise Holdings website, accessed 19 April 2015, http://go.enterpriseholdings.com.

43. Dessler, *A Framework for Human Resource Management*, 223–225.

44. Vadim Liberman, "What About the Rest of Us?" *Conference Board Review*, Summer 2011, 40–47.

45. "Executive Paywatch," AFL-CIO website, accessed 19 April 2015, www.aflcio.org; Elliot Blair Smith & Phil Kuntz, "CEO Pay 1,795-to-1 Multiple of Wages Skirts U.S. Law," Bloomberg, 29 April 2013, www.bloomberg.com.

46. Jeff D. Opdyke, "Getting a Bonus Instead of a Raise," *Wall Street Journal*, 29 December 2004, D1–D2.

47. Paul Loucks, "Creating a Performance-Based Culture," *Benefits & Compensation Digest*, July 2007, 36–39.

48. Dessler, *A Framework for Human Resource Management*, 231–232.

49. Gregory Lopes, "Firms Dock Pay of Obese, Smokers," *Washington Times*, 13 August 2007, www.washingtontimes.com; Joseph Weber, "Health Insurance: Small Biz Is in a Bind," *BusinessWeek*, 27 September 2004, 47–48; Joseph Pereira, "Parting Shot: To Save on Health-Care Costs, Firms Fire Disabled Workers," *Wall Street Journal*, 14 July 2003, A1, A7; Timothy Aeppel, "Ill Will: Skyrocketing Health Costs Start to Pit Worker vs. Worker," *Wall Street Journal*, 17 July 2003, A1, A6; Vanessa Furhmans, "To Stem Abuses, Employers Audit Workers' Health Claims," *Wall Street Journal*, 31 March 2004, B1, B7; Milt Freudenheim, "Employees Paying Ever-Bigger Share for Health Care," *New York Times*, A1, C2; Julie Appleby, "Employers Get Nosy About Workers' Health," *USA Today*, 6 March 2003, B1–B2; Ellen E. Schultz and Theo Francis, "Employers' Caps Raise Retirees' Health-Care Costs," *Wall Street Journal*, 25 November 2003, B1, B11; Vanessa Fuhrmans, "Company Health Plans Try to Drop Spouses," *Wall Street Journal*, 9 September 2003, D1, D2.

50. "Global Health-Care Snapshot," *Wall Street Journal* MarketWatch, accessed 2 December 2011, www.marketwatch.com; Victoria Colliver, "We Spend More, but U.S. Health Care Quality Falls Behind," *San Francisco Chronicle*, 10 July 2007, www.scrippsnews.com; Steve Lohr, "The Disparate Consensus on Health Care for All," *New York Times*, 6 December 2004, C16; Sara Schaefer and Laurie McGinley, "Census Sees a Surge in Americans Without Insurance," *Wall Street Journal*, 30 September 2003, B1, B6; "Half of Health Care Spending Is Wasted, Study Finds," *Detroit News*, 10 February 2005, www.detnews.com.

51. Avik Roy, "3,137-County Analysis: Obamacare Increased 2014 Individual-Market Premiums By Average Of 49%," *Forbes*, 18 June 2014, www.forbes.com.

52. "Choosing a Retirement Plan: Defined Benefit Plan," U.S. Internal Revenue Service, accessed 31 August 2011, www.irs.gov; U.S. Pension Benefit Guaranty Corporation, accessed 31 August 2011, www.pbgc.gov; James H. Dulebohn, Brian Murray, and Minghe Sun, "Selection Among Employer-Sponsored Pension Plans: The Role of Individual Differences," *Personal Psychology*, Summer 2000, 405–432.

53. The ESOP Association website, accessed 19 April 2015, www.esopassociation.org; Dessler, *A Framework for Human Resource Management*, 282.

54. Michelle Kessler, "Fears Subside over Accounting for Stock Options," *USA Today*, 1 January 2006, www.usatoday.com; Robert A. Guth and Joann S. Lublin, "Tarnished Gold: Microsoft Users Out Era of Options," *Wall Street Journal*, 9 July 2003, A1, A9; John Markoff and David Leonhardt, "Microsoft Will Award Stock, Not Options, to Employees," *New York Times*, 9 July 2003, A1, C4.

55. Sydney Finkelstein, "Rethinking CEO Stock Options," *BusinessWeek*, 20 April 2009, 23.

56. Cheeseman, *Contemporary Business and E-Commerce Law*, 626.

57. Patrick J. Kiger, "Child-Care Models," *Workforce Management*, April 2004, 38.

58. Andy Meisler, "A Matter of Degrees," *Workforce Management*, May 2004, 32–38; Stephanie Armour, "More Firms Help Workers Find Home Sweet Home," *USA Today*, 30 August 2004, C1–C2.

59. William Atkinson, "Wellness, Employee Assistance Programs: Investments, Not Costs," *Bobbin*, May 2000, 42; Kevin Dobbs, Jack Gordon, and David Stamps, "EAPs Cheap but Popular Perk," *Training*, February 2000, 26.

60. See Note 1.

61. TelCoa website, accessed 19 April 2015, www.telcoa.org; "Benchmarking Study Finds 'Telework' Has Evolved into a Main- stream Way of Working; Now, 'It's Just Work,'" press release, *TelCoa*, 9 March 2006, www.telcoa.org; Rich Karlgaard, "Outsource Yourself," *Forbes*, 19 April 2004, www.highbeam .com; David Kirkpatrick, "Big-League R&D Gets Its Own eBay," *Fortune*, 3 May 2004, www.highbeam.com; Joseph N. Pelton, "The Rise of Telecities: Decentralizing the Global Society," *The Futurist*, 1 January 2004, www.highbeam.com.

Labor Relations

1 Explain the role of labor unions, and contrast the perspectives of employees and employers on the issue of unionization.

2 Identify the three most important pieces of labor relations legislation enacted in the 20th century.

3 Explain how unions are structured, and describe the organizing process.

4 Describe the collective bargaining process.

5 Explain the procedures for addressing employee grievances and arbitrating disputes.

6 Characterize the ongoing conflict over union organizing efforts.

BEHIND THE SCENES   BOEING AND THE IAM: A HIGH-STAKES BATTLE WITH THOUSANDS OF JOBS ON THE LINE

With tens of thousands of jobs on the line, the International Association of Machinists and Aerospace Workers in the Seattle area faced a tough decision when Boeing Commercial Airplanes demanded wage and benefit concessions in exchange for keeping a major production program in Washington state.

www.boeing.com; www.iam751.org

Few business decisions affect as many people as the decision to build a new airliner. Thousands of jobs are directly at stake, and many thousands more are indirectly affected. Creating something as complex as an airliner also requires an industrial "hub" with a wide variety of technical support services, suppliers, transportation infrastructure, and even educational institutions. Consequently, the decision to build—or not build—a new airplane in a particular location can influence the economic, political, and social life of an entire metropolitan area, from schools to road and rail networks to companies all across the retail sector. The decision about where to build has to be made years before a new plane is brought to market, and the effects of that decision can reverberate for decades.

Boeing has been making airliners in the Seattle area since William Boeing started the company in 1916. The company's footprints are all over Seattle and the Puget Sound region, with huge facilities in Seattle itself and in the nearby cities of Renton and Everett. The company's factory in Everett, where the iconic 747 and the current model 777 are assembled, is the largest enclosed space in the world. Roughly half the company's 170,000 employees work in the region. Boeing is the country's largest exporter, and its presence in Seattle represents a concentration of high-paying manufacturing jobs the likes of which have vanished from many other major U.S. cities.

Although Boeing's presence in the region is massive, the relationship between the company and the various stakeholders

273

in the area has not always been smooth, particularly the contentious contract negotiations with and occasional strikes by District 751 of the International Association of Machinists and Aerospace Workers (IAM). The conflict between the two sides has all the hallmarks of a classic labor-management battle. The company wants labor costs that are low enough to enable it to offer airplanes at competitive prices, the flexibility to outsource aspects of production if needed to achieve its business objectives, and the ability to assure customers that production won't be disrupted by strikes. The union wants the best wages and benefits possible, assurance that jobs won't disappear, and the power to strike if need be to get what it wants.

Relations between the two sides continued to deteriorate when the company outsourced much of the design and production of the 787 Dreamliner to other companies and, in addition to an assembly line at the Everett facility, in 2009 set up a second 787 production line at a new Boeing plant in South Carolina. The fact that South Carolina—unlike Washington—is a *right-to-work* state (meaning it is illegal for unions and employers to establish contracts that require workers to join a union) was particularly galling to the IAM. It accused Boeing of selling out the unionized Washington workers who had helped build the company by moving some operations to a lower-wage, nonunion state.

The conflict flared up again in November 2013, as Boeing was getting ready to announce plans to build its new 777X model. Shortly before the official announcement of the new plane, the company proposed a series of modifications to its existing labor contract with District 751. Boeing management

said that without the savings it could gain from outsourcing, it needed cost concessions from the union to build the 777X in Everett. And even though the first customer deliveries of the 777X won't occur until 2020, Boeing wanted to finalize its long-term cost structure before the official announcement. Company managers were blunt in saying they weren't bluffing, and if they didn't get the concessions, they would be forced to consider other locations to build the plane.

The new terms set off a storm of complaints from union members. Many were vocal in their criticism of the proposed terms, saying the company was trying to force them to give up wage and benefit gains that had taken them years to get through tough contract battles and some expensive strikes. Among the chief complaints were Boeing's proposals to replace a defined-benefit pension plan with a defined-contribution plan and to extend the number of years it took an IAM member to reach the top of the pay scale from 6 years to as long as 20. Members were also furious that Boeing gave them only one week's notice before requiring a take-it-or-leave-it vote that would affect them, their families, and the entire region for years to come.

Some union members, however, said they had to face the realities of a competitive labor market and the company's demonstrated willingness to move production out of state. In their minds, as disagreeable as the new terms were, keeping tens of thousands of jobs in Everett was worth it.

With an estimated 56,000 jobs in the balance, it was a high-stakes, high-stress decision. If you were a member of IAM District 751, would you vote for or against this contract?[1]

INTRODUCTION

At one level, the conflict between Boeing and the IAM (profiled in the chapter-opening Behind the Scenes) is about money. But at a deeper level, the conflict is a fundamental disagreement about rights and responsibilities—about the very purpose of a business.[2] Is the purpose to protect the interests of investors who provide the money to launch and expand a company? Or is the purpose to protect the interests of the employees who get the work done? Balancing those competing ideals and demands is at the heart of labor relations, the subject of this chapter.

1 **LEARNING OBJECTIVE**
Explain the role of labor unions, and contrast the perspectives of employees and employers on the issue of unionization.

labor relations
The relationship between organized labor and management (in its role as the representative of company ownership).

labor unions
Organizations that represent employees in negotiations with management.

The Role of Labor Unions

Perhaps nothing represents the potential for stress in the stakeholder model more than **labor relations**, the relationship between organized labor and business owners. Although they work toward common goals in most cases, managers and employees face an inherent conflict over resources: Company owners and managers want to minimize the costs of operating the business, whereas employees want to maximize salaries and ensure good benefits and safe, pleasant working conditions.

If employees believe they are not being treated fairly and can't get their needs met by negotiating individually with management, they may have the option of joining **labor unions**, organizations that seek to protect employee interests by negotiating with employers for better wages and benefits, improved working conditions, and increased job security. "The Organizing Process," starting on page 282, explains how a group of employees can elect to have a union represent them. As Exhibit 12.1 shows, the role of unions varies

EXHIBIT 12.1   **Union Membership in Selected Industries**

Union membership varies widely by industry, as you can see from this selection of 40 industry sectors.

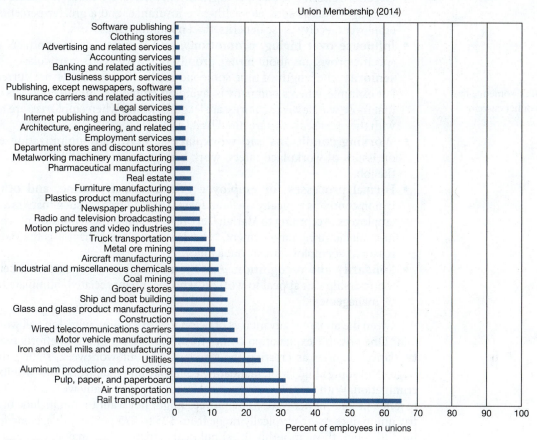

Union Membership (2014)

Source: Data from "Union Membership and Coverage Database from the CPS," Unionstats.com, 24 January 2015, www.unionstats.com.

widely by industry, dominating workforce matters in some industries but having little impact in others.

(A note on terminology: *Labor* can refer to either unions specifically or the workforce as a whole; you can tell by the context which definition is meant. *Organized labor* always refers to unions. And *management* in a discussion of union issues refers to managers in their role as representatives of company ownership.)

UNIONIZATION: THE EMPLOYEE'S PERSPECTIVE

The most fundamental appeal of unionization is strength in numbers, giving workers the opportunity to negotiate on a more equal footing with management. With this negotiating power, union members and supporters point to a number of ways workers benefit from union membership:[3]

- **Higher compensation.** According to the U.S. Bureau of Labor Statistics, union members currently earn about 27 percent more than nonunion workers, taken as an average across the entire workforce.[4] Bear in mind that this is based on averages of all workers in all types of jobs, not a comparison of union and nonunion employees in the same types of jobs. For a breakdown by industries and occupations, see the Real-Time Updates Learn More item on this page. (Note that the 28 percent figure

REAL-TIME UPDATES
Learn More by Reading This PDF

A closer look at union versus nonunion pay

The AFL-CIO offers a comparison of union and nonunion pay and benefits for a variety of demographic groups. Go to http://real-time updates.com/bia8 and click on Learn More in the Students section.

and all data related to organized labor in this chapter refer to the private sector only and do not reflect union membership in the public sector, which includes employees in government, public education, and services such as fire and police).

- **Greater benefits.** As with compensation, on average union members receive better nonwage benefits such as health-care insurance, and a greater percentage of union employees receive these benefits, than nonunion employees.[5]

- **Influence over hiring, promotions, and layoffs.** Union contracts usually have specific provisions about hiring, promotions, and layoffs, particularly with regard to **seniority**, the length of time someone has worked for his or her current employer. For example, when a company is laying off employees, union contracts often specify that those with lowest seniority are let go first, and when employees are rehired, those with the most seniority are hired first.

- **Working conditions and workplace safety.** Many unionization efforts focus on issues of workplace safety, work breaks, training, and other aspects of life on the job.

- **Formal processes for employee grievances, discipline, and other matters.** Union contracts typically spell out formal procedures for such matters as disciplining employees. According to Mariah DeForest, a management consultant who specializes in manufacturing employment, "Unfair supervisory behavior is the most important reason that employees seek out a union."[6]

- **Solidarity and recognition.** Aside from tangible and measurable benefits, union membership can appeal to workers who feel unappreciated, humiliated, or let down by management.

Given the apparent advantages of belonging to a union, why don't all workers want to join? One possible explanation comes from the success of union efforts that led to such legislative victories as creating the standard 40-hour workweek, setting the minimum wage, abolishing child labor, mandating equal pay for equal work, and prohibiting job discrimination. With these improvements already in place, many workers don't feel the need to join a union.[7] Other reasons employees might not want to join include being forced to pay union dues (which typically range from $25 to $75 per month[8]), being forced to help fund (through those monthly dues) political activities they may not support, being held back in their careers by union seniority rules, and being forced to accept the union as the sole intermediary with management rather than negotiating raises, job assignments, and other matters on their own.

UNIONIZATION: MANAGEMENT'S PERSPECTIVE

Either as business owners themselves or as the representatives of owners, managers obviously have an interest in minimizing costs to maximize profits. Although union sympathizers sometimes portray this attitude as simple greed, in general, management's top priority is making sure their firms can remain competitive. For example, by containing the ongoing costs of providing compensation and benefits, a firm is better able to invest in facilities, equipment, and new product development.[9]

In addition to direct costs, other management concerns regarding unions include flexibility and productivity. Union contracts often include **work rules**, or *job rules*, that specify such things as the tasks certain employees are required to do or are forbidden to do. For instance, management might be prevented from having employees cross-trained on a variety of tasks and machines to allow production supervisors more flexibility in responding to changes in product demand without increasing headcount. In the auto industry, for example, an analysis that compared Chrysler, Ford, and GM with Toyota concluded that union work rules forced the U.S. carmakers to create 8,200 more jobs than they would have created otherwise.[10]

The effect of unionization has been studied extensively over the years. In a review of 73 of these studies, professors Christos Doucouliagos and Patrice Laroche found 45 that showed a positive effect of unions on productivity and 28 that showed a negative effect. Their analysis of this research suggests that unions have had a net negative effect

seniority
The length of time someone has worked for his or her current employer.

work rules
A common element of labor contracts that specifies such things as the tasks certain employees are required to do or are forbidden to do.

on productivity in the United Kingdom and Japan but a net positive effect on productivity in the United States. However, those productivity gains are offset by the higher average wages that unionized workers receive. "When the productivity and wage effects are combined, we can conclude that unions have a negative impact on profitability."[11]

Whether this outcome is negative or positive depends on your perspective. It is clearly a negative outcome for shareholders and proprietors, but the higher wages are obviously a positive outcome for workers and, by extension, the communities in which those workers live—including the various businesses they patronize with their paychecks.

 Checkpoint

LEARNING OBJECTIVE 1: Explain the role of labor unions, and contrast the perspectives of employees and employers on the issue of unionization.

SUMMARY: *Labor unions* are organizations that seek to protect employee interests by negotiating with employers for better wages and benefits, improved working conditions, and increased job security. The foundation of unionization is strength in numbers, giving workers the opportunity to negotiate on a more equal footing with company management. From an employee's perspective, unions offer the tangible benefits of greater compensation and benefits and the intangible benefits of solidarity and recognition. From an employer's perspective, unions can present challenges in terms of costs and flexibility, ultimately creating concerns about a firm's ability to compete against companies that have lower costs and greater agility.

CRITICAL THINKING: (1) Why is it so difficult to come up with a single conclusive answer about the effects of unionization on business productivity? (2) How do labor relations demonstrate the stresses inherent in the stakeholder model?

IT'S YOUR BUSINESS: (1) Union supporters often talk about the need for greater democracy in the workplace. Explain why you agree or disagree with this sentiment. (2) Would you rather be promoted on the basis of seniority or of merit? Why?

KEY TERMS TO KNOW: labor relations, labor unions, seniority, work rules

Unionization in Historical Perspective

 LEARNING OBJECTIVE

Identify the three most important pieces of labor relations legislation enacted in the 20th century.

Any attempt to understand labor relations today needs to consider the long history of the labor-management relationship. Although money is usually the core issue at stake, the relationship is a lot more complicated than that. Disputes sometimes take on a pitched emotional tone as the two sides fight for respect, control, and political influence. The division runs deeper than matters of employment and business operations, too: Supporters and opponents of unionism often have profoundly different beliefs about fundamental economic principles and the ideal nature of society itself. This section provides an overview of how the relationship between unions and company ownership has evolved over the years and where the union movement stands today.

Unions can trace their history back nearly 1,000 years, to early guilds in Europe that gave craftspeople bargaining power over merchants. In the United States, the Industrial Revolution in the second half of the 1800s and the Great Depression of the 1930s were formative events in the history of unionization. Violent and even deadly behavior on both sides was not uncommon in those early years, which saw tumultuous riots, attacks by management security forces or government troops on union workers, attacks by union members on nonunion workers, and physical destruction of nonunion building projects, such as the dynamiting of the *Los Angeles Times* building in 1910.[12] After repeated strikes and protests over unsafe working conditions, abusive management practices, long hours, child labor, and other concerns, unions gradually found a sympathetic ear in Congress (see Exhibit 12.2 on the next page).

EXHIBIT 12.2　Major Pieces of Labor Relations Legislation

Most major labor legislation was enacted in the 1930s and 1940s. Subsequent legislation usually amends and clarifies previous laws.

Legislation	Key Provisions
Norris–La Guardia Act of 1932	Limits companies' ability to obtain injunctions against union strikes, picketing, membership drives, and other activities.
National Labor Relations Act of 1935 (Wagner Act)	Established the National Labor Relations Board to supervise union elections and to investigate charges of unfair labor practices by management. Gives employees the right to form, join, or assist labor organizations; the right to bargain collectively with employers through elected union representatives; and the right to engage in strikes, picketing, and boycotts. Prohibits certain unfair labor practices by the employer and union. The *Gale Encyclopedia of American Law* calls it "the most significant piece of federal labor legislation enacted in U.S. history."
Labor-Management Relations Act of 1947 (Taft-Hartley Act)	Amended the Wagner Act to affirm employees' rights to not participate in union activities other than *union shop* provisions, identifies several unfair labor practices, restricts union's strike options, and prohibits strikes in the public sector. Gives states the freedom to pass right-to-work laws.
Labor-Management Reporting Act of 1959 (Landrum-Griffin Act)	Amended the Taft-Hartley Act and Wagner Act to protect members' rights within the union and to control union corruption. Requires all unions to file annual financial reports with the U.S. Department of Labor, making union officials more personally responsible for the union's elections. Also establishes the right to sue unions and the right to attend and participate in union meetings.

Sources: Donna Batten, ed., *Gale Encyclopedia of American Law*, 3rd ed. (Detroit: Gale, 2010) Vol. 7, 290; Vol. 10, 279–280; Henry R. Cheeseman, *Contemporary Business and E-Commerce Law*, 7th ed. (Upper Saddle River, N.J.: Pearson Prentice Hall, 2010), 501; Michael R. Carrell and Christina Heavrin, *Labor Relations and Collective Bargaining: Cases, Practice, and Law*, 9th ed. (Upper Saddle River, N.J.: Pearson Prentice Hall, 2010), 29, 33; "Landrum-Griffin Act," *West's Encyclopedia of American Law*, 2nd ed., Jeffrey Lehman and Shirelle Phelps, eds. (Detroit: Gale, 2005), 200–201.

POWER TO THE UNIONS: THE WAGNER ACT OF 1935

National Labor Relations Act
Legislation passed in 1935 that established labor relations policies and procedures for most sectors of private industry; commonly known as the Wagner Act.

In 1935, Congress passed the **National Labor Relations Act**, also known as the Wagner Act. This landmark legislation established labor relations policies and procedures for most sectors of private industry (railroad and airline unions are addressed separately by the Railway Labor Act[13]), and its provisions remain a topic of ongoing controversy. Key provisions include[14]

- Affirming and protecting the rights of employees to join and assist labor unions, to negotiate with employers through union representatives, and to strike
- Outlawing attempts by employers to interfere with employees' rights to organize, to discriminate against employees on the basis of their union activities or interests, or to interfere with union activities
- Requiring employers to bargain in good faith with unions
- Establishing the National Labor Relations Board (NLRB), **www.nlrb.gov**, which is responsible for preventing and remedying unfair labor practices and overseeing the elections that allow unions to represent particular groups of employees

The Wagner Act profoundly altered the balance of power in U.S. industry. Union membership grew dramatically in the decade that followed, to the point where unions could virtually shut down entire industries through strikes. Not surprisingly, business leaders were vigorously opposed to the Wagner Act and the growing power of unions. The opinion of automotive

Everett Collection/Age Fotostock

The history of labor relations has included heated, sometimes violent, confrontation. Although violence is rare today, a streak of antagonism runs through many labor-management interactions.

pioneer Henry Ford that "labor union organizations are the worst thing that ever struck the earth"[15] is probably an accurate reflection of the mindset of many company owners and managers at the time.

POWER TO THE OWNERS: THE TAFT-HARTLEY ACT OF 1947

During and after World War II, public opinion began to turn against unions, partly in response to union workers striking during wartime. Business organizations—and even some union leaders who felt that the law gave other unions unfair advantages—were furiously lobbying Congress to amend the Wagner Act.[16] Congress eventually passed the **Labor-Management Relations Act** of 1947, also known as the Taft-Hartley Act. This legislation addressed many concerns raised by business owners and shifted the balance of power again. Its key provisions include[17]

- Guaranteeing the right of employees not to join or support unions, except where required by a *union shop* agreement, and granting to each state the right to choose whether it would allow union shops (see "Union Security and Right-to-Work Laws" on the next page)
- Outlawing coercion of or discrimination against employees by unions
- Allowing employers more freedom of speech to dissuade workers from voting for unionization
- Requiring unions to bargain in good faith with employers
- Restricting or outlawing various strike activities by unions, including striking with the intent of forcing an employer to create new jobs for union workers
- Giving the president the authority to outlaw strikes that threaten national security

Unions widely referred to Taft-Hartley as a "slave-labor act," but they were unsuccessful at blocking or changing it.[18] To combat the enlarged power of employers, union leaders made more attempts to cooperate among themselves. This effort eventually led to the merger in 1955 of the two major U.S. labor federations, the American Federation of Labor (AFL) and a group that had splintered off from the AFL in the 1930s, the Congress of Industrial Organizations (CIO).

POWER TO UNION MEMBERS: THE LANDRUM-GRIFFIN ACT OF 1959

In the decade or so following the passage of the Taft-Hartley Act, legislative attention shifted to the internal operation of the major unions. Two major concerns at the time were corruption and communism. New leadership in the AFL-CIO responded by expelling some unions accused of criminal activities or communist domination.[19] Congressional inquiries into financial fraud by union leaders, meanwhile, led to passage of the **Labor-Management Reporting and Disclosure Act** of 1959, commonly known as the Landrum-Griffin Act. The overall intent of this act is to ensure democratic processes and financial accountability within unions, including freedom of speech for union members, the right to secret ballot elections of union leadership, and financial transparency in the use of union funds.[20]

Labor-Management Relations Act
Legislation passed in 1947 that addressed many concerns raised by business owners and shifted the balance of power again; commonly known as the Taft-Hartley Act.

Labor-Management Reporting and Disclosure Act
Legislation passed in 1959 designed to ensure democratic processes and financial accountability within unions; commonly known as the Landrum-Griffin Act.

✔ Checkpoint

LEARNING OBJECTIVE 2: Identify the three most important pieces of labor relations legislation enacted in the 20th century.

SUMMARY: Three major pieces of legislation passed in the 20th century still define many aspects of labor relations and the management of labor unions themselves. The National Labor Relations Act of 1935, better known as the Wagner Act, gives employees the right to unionize and bargain collectively with employers and the right to strike, picket, and boycott. The Labor-Management Relations Act of 1947, better known as the Taft-Hartley Act, affirms employees' rights to not participate in union activities other than *union shop* provisions, identifies several unfair labor practices, restricts unions' strike options, prohibits strikes in the public sector, and gives states the freedom to pass right-to-work laws. The Labor-Management Reporting Act of 1959, better known as the Landrum-Griffin Act, protects members' rights within the union and limits the potential for corruption by union officials.

CRITICAL THINKING: (1) Why are disputes between labor and management often more complicated than just matters of money? (2) Would you agree that the struggle between labor and management has, to at least some degree, been a matter of legislative overcorrection? Why or why not?

IT'S YOUR BUSINESS: (1) Do you believe it is appropriate for unions to be involved in political activities? Why or why not? (2) Given the long and complex history of unionization, some people now have an emotional response to the word *union*. Do you respond positively or negatively when you hear the word? Why?

KEY TERMS TO KNOW: National Labor Relations Act, Labor-Management Relations Act, Labor-Management Reporting and Disclosure Act

3 **LEARNING OBJECTIVE**

Explain how unions are structured, and describe the organizing process.

The Organizing Process

A key element in most labor relations laws is the process of organizing union representation for a particular group of workers. This section looks at the union organizing process, starting with the concepts of union security and right to work, the two main types of unions, and the structure of union organizations.

UNION SECURITY AND RIGHT-TO-WORK LAWS

union security

Measures that protect a union's right to represent workers.

union shop

A unionized workplace in which employees are required to maintain union membership.

When a union negotiates a contract, it usually tries to obtain some degree of **union security**, which consists of measures that protect the union's right to represent workers. The most extreme form is a *closed shop*, in which an employer can hire only union members; Taft-Hartley outlawed closed shops. In a **union shop**, employees don't have to be members when they are hired, but they must join the union within a specified period of time. Any employee who doesn't join the union by that time or maintain union membership after that must be released by the employer. In an *agency shop*, employees aren't required to join the union but must pay the equivalent of union dues.[21] Interestingly, one nationwide survey indicates that most employees, even union members, don't support the concept of a union shop.[22]

right-to-work laws

State laws that prohibit union and agency shops.

One of the most important changes brought about by the Taft-Hartley Act was allowing individual states to pass laws prohibiting union and agency shops. Since the enactment of Taft-Hartley, half the states have passed such **right-to-work laws** (see Exhibit 12.3).[23] These laws remain a strong point of contention between union supporters and opponents. As with many other issues in labor relations, the argument is complex. Businesses and other supporters of right-to-work laws say that compulsory union membership violates individual rights, removes a key reason for unions to stay responsive to member needs, and makes a state less attractive to business. Union leaders and their supporters claim that all workers benefit from union advocacy, and so it is not unreasonable to require all workers to support those efforts through membership; they also point to studies showing that right-to-work states have lower average wages.[24]

REAL-TIME UPDATES

Learn More by Reading This Article

An in-depth tutorial on labor unions

This article offers a closer look at the history and function of labor unions. Go to http://real-timeupdates.com/bia8 and click on Learn More in the Students section.

TYPES OF UNIONS

Unions are of two basic types, with different implications for organizing employees and interacting with management. *Craft unions* offer membership to workers with a specific craft

EXHIBIT 12.3   **Right-to-Work States**

Twenty-fives states currently have some form of right-to-work laws.

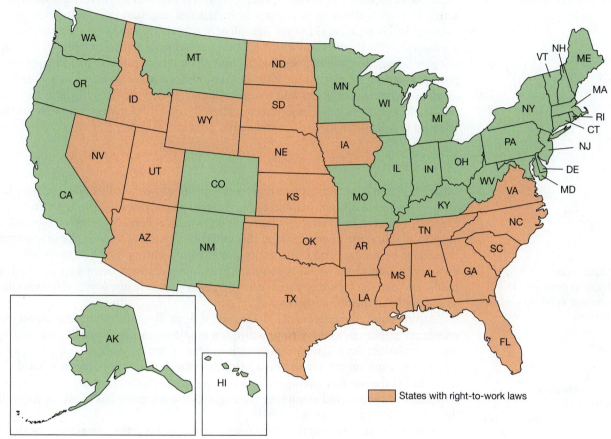

States with right-to-work laws

Source: Based on data from "Right to Work Frequently-Asked Questions," *National Right to Work Legal Defense Fund*, accessed 20 April 2015, www.nrtw.org.

or skill, such as carpentry, masonry, or electrical work. In some instances, craft unions negotiate contracts for certain categories of work at a single employer. In others, particularly in the building trades, these unions often negotiate with a number of employers in a given geographic area. As employees move from one project to another, they remain covered by the same contract.[25] A key feature of craft union membership is the *apprenticeship* model, in which beginners receive training under union auspices. The International Brotherhood of Electrical Workers is an example of a craft union.

In contrast to craft unions, *industrial unions* seek to represent all workers at a given employer or location, regardless of profession or skill level. Rather than belonging to a single union for their entire careers as with craft unions, workers usually join an industrial union because they are required to when they work at a union shop, and they often leave the union if they leave a particular job.[26] The United Auto Workers (UAW) is an example of an industrial union.

HOW UNIONS ARE STRUCTURED

Many unions are organized at local, national, and international levels. **Locals**, or local unions, represent employees in a specific geographic area or facility. Members are informally known as the *rank-and-file*. Each department or facility also elects a *shop steward*, who works in the facility as a regular employee and serves as a liaison with supervisors whenever problems arise. In large locals and in locals that represent employees at several locations, an elected full-time *business agent* visits the various work sites to negotiate with management and enforce the union's agreements with those companies.

locals
Local unions that represent employees in a specific geographic area or facility.

national union

A nationwide organization composed of many local unions that represent employees in specific locations.

A **national union** is a nationwide organization composed of many local unions that represent employees in specific locations; examples include the UAW and the United Steelworkers. *International unions,* such as the Service Employees International Union (SEIU), have members in more than one country. A national union is responsible for such activities as organizing in new areas or industries, negotiating industrywide contracts, assisting locals with negotiations, administering benefits, lobbying Congress, and lending assistance in the event of a strike. Local unions send representatives to the national delegate convention, submit negotiated contracts to the national union for approval, and provide financial support in the form of dues. They have the power to negotiate with individual companies or plants and to undertake their own membership activities. Unions can also be members of a *labor federation* such as the AFL-CIO, giving them a larger, unified voice for political activities and membership drives.

UNION ORGANIZING DRIVES

Unions seek the legal authority to represent a group of workers through a process known as an *organizing drive* (see Exhibit 12.4). A drive starts when workers contact a union expressing interest in joining or when a union organizer contacts workers to promote the benefits of union membership. After this initial expression of interest, the union forms an organizing committee and launches its strategy for securing the right to represent those employees, employees who wish to have the union represent them sign **authorization cards**, and company management usually tries to persuade employees that unionization would not be in their best interest.

authorization cards

Cards signed by employees to indicate interest in having a union represent them.

At this point, the process can go in one of three directions. First, the union and the interested employees can try to pressure the employer into voluntarily recognizing the union as the employees' representative. Boycotts, picketing, strikes, and publicity campaigns are common tactics for this approach.[27] Employers can agree to a "card check," which tallies the number of employees who have signed authorization cards; if more than 50 percent of the affected employees have signed, the company has to accept the union as the employees' representative.

certification election

A secret-ballot election overseen by the NLRB to determine whether a union gains the right to represent a group of employees.

Second, if the employer doesn't voluntarily accept the union, employees or the union can petition the NLRB to conduct a secret-ballot **certification election**. The NLRB

EXHIBIT 12.4	**The Union Organizing Process**

This diagram offers a simplified view of the steps a labor union takes when organizing a group of employees and becoming certified to represent them in negotiations with management. The certification election is necessary only if management is unwilling to recognize the union.

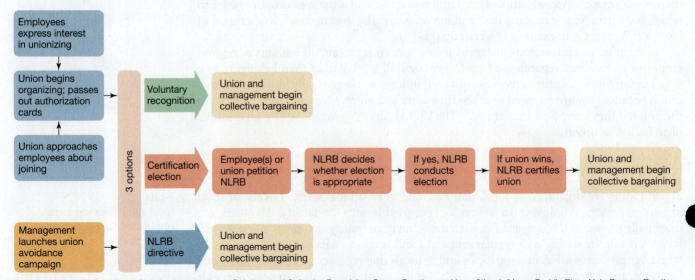

Sources: Michael R. Carrell and Christina Heavrin, *Labor Relations and Collective Bargaining: Cases, Practice, and Law,* 9th ed. (Upper Saddle River, N.J.: Pearson Prentice Hall, 2010), 129–134; "The NLRB Process," U.S. National Labor Relations Board website, accessed 15 November 2013, www.nlrb.gov.

usually requires verification that at least 30 percent of the employees in an appropriate *bargaining unit* are interested in union membership before it will proceed with an election. (Unions typically don't request a vote until they have cards from 60 or 70 percent of the bargaining unit, however, because a significant number of employees who sign cards end up voting against the union.[28]) The NLRB has a number of guidelines for determining which employees are eligible to vote as part of the bargaining unit, but roughly speaking, it requires that employees share the same working conditions.[29] As with almost everything else in labor relations, defining bargaining units can be contentious, given the potential for its effect on election outcomes.[30]

Third, in rare cases, the NLRB can unilaterally direct the employer to bargain with the union if the board determines that a fair election isn't possible.

If a majority of the affected employees vote to make the union their bargaining agent, the NLRB certifies the results and grants the union the authority to begin negotiating with the employer on the employees' behalf. In recent years, unions have won 55 to 60 percent of certification elections.[31] If the union is certified, the employer is then required to negotiate with the union for at least one year on the terms of the contract with employees (covering wages, benefits, work rules, and other factors). These first-time negotiations can be difficult, but they are concluded within the first year most of the time.[32]

Even when a union wins a certification election, there's no guarantee that it will represent a particular group of employees forever. Sometimes employees become dissatisfied with their union and no longer wish to be represented by it. When this happens, the union members can take a **decertification** vote to take away the union's right to represent them. If the majority votes for decertification, the union is removed as the bargaining agent.

MANAGEMENT EFFORTS TO AVOID UNIONIZATION

After a company becomes aware that a union is seeking a certification election, management may launch a campaign to dissuade employees from voting for the union. Reflecting the adversarial nature of labor relations, these campaigns are typically called *union avoidance* from management's perspective and *union busting* from the union's perspective.

Managers and owners are allowed to provide factual information about the union and labor relations laws and to share personal experiences about life in a unionized workplace. However, under the provisions of the Wagner Act, they are not allowed to threaten employees for engaging in union activities or to interrogate employees regarding union sympathies or voting plans. To avoid influencing voting, managers are also not allowed to make any promises (such as raises or promotions) to employees in exchange for voting against the union. In addition, management should refrain from offering new benefits to employees during the organizing drive; such a move can be construed as an attempt to unfairly influence the election.[33]

REAL-TIME UPDATES
Learn More by Visiting This Website

See how the NLRB investigates charges and oversees elections

Follow these flowcharts to see how the NLRB investigates unfair labor practice charges and oversees certification elections. Go to http://real-timeupdates.com/bia8 and click on Learn More in the Students section.

decertification
A vote by employees to take away a union's right to represent them.

✔ **Checkpoint**

LEARNING OBJECTIVE 3: Explain how unions are structured, and describe the organizing process.

SUMMARY: Unions can be structured at local, national, and international levels. A *local* represents employees in a specific area or facility. A union *organizing drive* starts when one or more employees contact a union and express interest in joining or a union organizer contacts employees and gets them to consider the benefits of joining. The organizer then asks employees to sign *authorization cards* to indicate their interest in having a union represent them. At that point, the employer asks for a *card check* count; if more than 50 percent of affected employees have signed, the employer must accept the union as a bargaining agent. If the employer doesn't voluntarily accept the union or agree to a card check, the union can petition the NLRB for a certification election if at least 30 percent of employees have signed. In rare cases, the NLRB can order the employer to bargain with the union if the board believes a fair election is not possible.

CRITICAL THINKING: (1) Why does the concept of an *agency shop* exist, since employees in such facilities aren't required to join the union? (2) Why do union organizers usually gather authorization cards from well over 50 percent of the employees in a bargaining unit before petitioning the NLRB for a certification election?

IT'S YOUR BUSINESS: (1) If you were an entrepreneur ready to start a new company, would state right-to-work laws affect your decision about choosing a location for your business? Why or why not? (2) Union supporters argue that all workers benefit from the improvements in working conditions that unionization has helped bring about over the years; do you agree that all workers are in unions' debt? Why or why not?

KEY TERMS TO KNOW: union security, union shop, right-to-work laws, locals, national union, authorization cards, certification election, decertification

---

4   **LEARNING OBJECTIVE**

Describe the collective bargaining process.

collective bargaining
A negotiation between union and management representatives to forge the human resources policies that will apply to all employees covered by a contract.

collective bargaining agreements (CBAs)
Contracts that result from collective bargaining.

The Collective Bargaining Process

After a union has been recognized as the exclusive bargaining agent for a group of employees, its main job is to negotiate employment contracts with management. In a process known as **collective bargaining**, union and management negotiators work together to forge the human resources policies that will apply to all employees covered by the contract. **Collective bargaining agreements (CBAs)**, the contracts that result from this process, are always a compromise between the desires of union members and those of management. The union pushes for the best possible deal for its members, and management tries to negotiate agreements that are best for the company (and the shareholders, if a corporation is publicly held). Exhibit 12.5 illustrates the collective bargaining process. (*Labor contract* is often used as a synonym for a collective bargaining agreement. Individual employees, particularly in upper management positions, can also have *employment contracts* that aren't associated with union membership.)

Labor agreements usually cover a wide range of issues, often in considerable detail. The current CBA between the National Hockey League and the NHL Players' Association,

---

EXHIBIT 12.5   **The Collective Bargaining Process**

Contract negotiations go through the four basic steps shown here.

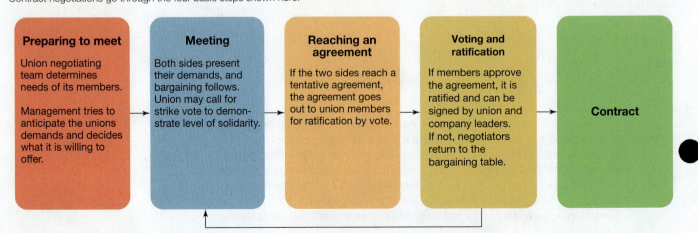

Preparing to meet	Meeting	Reaching an agreement	Voting and ratification	Contract
Union negotiating team determines needs of its members. Management tries to anticipate the unions demands and decides what it is willing to offer.	Both sides present their demands, and bargaining follows. Union may call for strike vote to demonstrate level of solidarity.	If the two sides reach a tentative agreement, the agreement goes out to union members for ratification by vote.	If members approve the agreement, it is ratified and can be signed by union and company leaders. If not, negotiators return to the bargaining table.	

for instance, is longer than this textbook.[34] The agreement details vary widely by industry and profession, but the most common issues addressed included compensation, benefits, working conditions, job security, and worker seniority issues.

NEGOTIATING AN AGREEMENT

When the negotiating teams representing the union and management sit down together, they state their opening positions, and each side discusses its position point by point. The Wagner Act specifies certain topics that must be addressed in collective bargaining, including compensation, working hours, and conditions of employment.[35] Offers and counteroffers are made during *bargaining*, as each side decides how far it is willing to compromise in order to reach agreement. In most cases, union representatives don't have the authority to agree to a contract during these negotiations. Instead, their members authorize them to secure the best offer they can and bring that back to the membership for a vote.[36] These don't always lead to satisfactory outcomes, to be sure. As you'll read at the end of the chapter in the Boeing wrap-up, some members of the IAM found Boeing's proposed contract terms so unappealing that they were furious with their leadership for even bringing the proposal to a vote.

In addition to the actual terms of the contract, an acrimonious long-term relationship between the two sides can sometimes complicate negotiations, creating a "win at all costs" competition or encouraging aggressive stances when sensible compromise would be better for everyone concerned.[37] If negotiations reach an impasse, outside help may be needed. The most common alternative is **mediation**—bringing in an impartial third party to study the situation, explore new options, improve communication, and make recommendations for resolution of the differences. The Taft-Hartley Act established the Federal Mediation and Conciliation Service (FMCS), **www.fmcs.gov**, to provide free mediation services during labor contract disputes. Federal mediators help resolve contract impasses roughly 85 percent of the time.[38] However, mediators can only offer suggestions, and their solutions are not binding.

mediation
Use of an impartial third party to help resolve bargaining impasses.

When a legally binding settlement is needed, the negotiators may submit to **arbitration**—a process in which an impartial referee listens to both sides and then makes a judgment by accepting one side's view. In *compulsory* arbitration, the parties are required by a government agency to submit to arbitration; in *voluntary* arbitration, the parties agree on their own to use arbitration to settle their differences.

arbitration
A decision process in which an impartial referee listens to both sides and then makes a judgment by accepting one side's view.

EXERCISING OPTIONS WHEN NEGOTIATIONS BREAK DOWN

The vast majority of management-union negotiations are settled without the need for either side to take further action. However, negotiations occasionally reach an impasse, and neither side is willing to compromise enough to reach an agreement. Both labor and management are able to draw on many powerful options when negotiations or mediation procedures break down (see Exhibit 12.6 on the next page).

Labor's Options

Strikes and picket lines are perhaps labor's best-known tactics, but other options are also used:

- **Strike.** The most powerful weapon that organized labor can use is the **strike**, a temporary work stoppage aimed at forcing management to accept union demands. The basic idea behind a strike is that, in the long run, it will cost more in lost revenue to resist union demands than to give in. An essential part of any strike is *picketing*, in which union members positioned at entrances to company premises display signs and pass out leaflets, trying to persuade nonstriking employees to join them and to persuade customers and others to stop doing business with the company. Strikes are high-profile events, but they are actually quite rare. For instance, unions affiliated with the AFL-CIO have negotiated some 150,000 agreements over the years, and only 2 percent of those have resulted in strikes.[39]

strike
A temporary work stoppage aimed at forcing management to accept union demands.

EXHIBIT 12.6	When Negotiations Break Down: Labor and Management Options

When negotiations between labor and management reach an impasse, each side has several options at its disposal for putting pressure on the other.

Labor's Options	Management's Options
Strikes: High-pressure, high-profile events; rarely used because of financial impact on workers	**Hiring strikebreakers:** Use of replacement workers to keep operating during strikes
Boycotts: Seek to inflict financial damage by discouraging purchase of company's product	**Lockouts:** Management's version of strikes, pressuring labor by preventing workers from going to work
Publicity campaigns: Attempt to damage company's reputation with investors, communities, and other stakeholders	**Injunctions:** Court orders requiring one side to refrain from or engage in a particular activity
Injunctions: Court orders requiring one side to refrain from or engage in a particular activity	

boycott
A pressure action by union members and sympathizers who refuse to buy or handle the product of a target company.

- **Boycott.** A less direct union weapon than the strike is the **boycott**, in which union members and sympathizers refuse to buy or handle the product of a target company. Millions of union members form an enormous bloc of purchasing power, which may be able to pressure management into making concessions.
- **Publicity.** Labor can press its case by launching publicity campaigns, often called *corporate campaigns*, against the target company and various stakeholders and business partners affiliated with it.[40] These campaigns might include initiating shareholder resolutions aimed at undermining management, recruiting celebrities to speak out against the company, creating websites and using social media to disseminate negative information about the company, sending investors alerts that question the firm's solvency, staging rallies during peak business hours, sending letters to charitable groups questioning executives' motives, alleging safety and health-code violations, and stimulating negative stories in the press.[41]

injunction
A court order that requires one side in a dispute to refrain from or engage in a particular action.

- **Injunctions.** An **injunction** is a court order that requires one side in a dispute to refrain from engaging in a particular action. The NLRB has the authority to ask federal courts to issue injunctions aimed at halting unfair labor practices while a dispute is moving through the board's resolution process.[42]

Labor's other options include *slowdowns*, in which employees continue to do their jobs but at a slow enough pace to disrupt operations, and *sickouts*, in which employees feign illness and stay home.

Management's Options

Management can use a number of legal methods to pressure unions when negotiations stall:

strikebreakers
Nonunion workers hired to do the jobs of striking workers.

- **Strikebreakers.** When union members walk off their jobs, management can legally replace them with **strikebreakers**, nonunion workers hired to do the jobs of striking workers. (Union members refer to them as "scabs.")

- **Lockouts.** The U.S. Supreme Court has upheld the use of **lockouts**, in which management prevents union employees from entering the workplace, in order to pressure the union to accept a contract proposal. A lockout is management's counterpart to a strike. It is a preemptive measure designed to force a union to accede to management's demands. Lockouts are legal only if the union and management have come to an impasse in negotiations and the employer is defending a legitimate bargaining position. During a lockout, the company may hire temporary replacements as long as it has no anti-union motivation and negotiations have been amicable.[43]

- **Injunctions.** Employers can seek injunctions if they believe unions are engaging in unfair labor practices.

lockouts
Decisions by management to prevent union employees from entering the workplace; used to pressure the union to accept a contract proposal.

✔ ## Checkpoint

LEARNING OBJECTIVE 4: Describe the collective bargaining process.

SUMMARY: In collective bargaining, union and management teams negotiate the human resources policies that will apply to all employees covered by the contract, which is known as a collective bargaining agreement (CBA). If the two sides cannot reach agreement, they can seek outside help through mediation or arbitration.

CRITICAL THINKING: (1) Given the history of union-management relations, why do you think mediation tends to be so successful at resolving bargaining impasses? (2) Why would an employer resort to a lockout?

IT'S YOUR BUSINESS: (1) Should U.S. consumers be pressured to buy products made in the United States? Why or why not? (2) Would you refuse to shop at a store that was being picketed by union members? Why or why not?

KEY TERMS TO KNOW: collective bargaining, collective bargaining agreements (CBAs), mediation, arbitration, strike, boycott, injunction, strikebreakers, lockouts

Grievance, Discipline, and Arbitration Procedures

A key element of labor legislation and labor contracts is providing the means to ensure compliance with laws and contract terms. The NLRB acts on complaints of unfair labor practices, and labor contracts contain provisions for handling employee grievances, disciplining employees, and resolving disputes through arbitration.

5 LEARNING OBJECTIVE

Explain the procedures for addressing employee grievances and arbitrating disputes.

UNFAIR LABOR PRACTICES

During organizing campaigns and contract negotiations and through the duration of a completed CBA, unions and management are prohibited from engaging in unlawful acts known as **unfair labor practices**.[44] The NLRB lists the following as examples of unfair practices by employers:[45]

- Threatening employees with termination or cuts in benefits if they vote for a union or engage in any other activity protected by the Wagner Act or other laws
- Threatening to close a facility if employees vote for union representation
- Interrogating employees about union sympathies or activities in ways that could "interfere with, restrain, or coerce" employees trying to exercise their legal rights
- Responding to organizing campaigns by offering wage or benefit improvements as a way to thwart unionization efforts
- Punishing employees for unionization activity by transferring them, giving them more difficult work assignments, or terminating them

unfair labor practices
Unlawful acts made by either unions or management.

The NLRB also responds to complaints about unfair labor practices on the part of unions. Examples include[46]

- Attempting to scare employees into supporting the union by telling them they will lose their jobs otherwise
- Refusing to process grievance claims made by employees who have criticized union officials
- Attempting to get an employee fired for not complying with a union shop agreement when the employee has paid or offered to pay an initiation fee and monthly dues
- Discriminating against employees or giving preferential treatment in union hiring halls (facilities where members of craft unions receive job assignments) because of race or union activities
- Coercing neutral parties into joining labor disputes
- Striking over matters that are not related to working conditions or terms of employment

RESOLVING EMPLOYEE GRIEVANCES

grievance
A formal complaint against an employer.

If an employee or a union believes an employer is not abiding by the terms of a CBA, most agreements specify procedures for filing a **grievance**, a formal complaint against the employer. Grievances can range from the petty to the profound. In some cases, employees may file complaints simply to express frustration, and unions may file grievances as a way to show their power. More substantial reasons include clarifying details of the contract, addressing alleged contract violations by the employer, laying the groundwork for future contract negotiations, and contesting management decisions.[47]

Grievance procedures usually specify a multistep *escalation* process, which typically starts on a small scale with just the employee, his or her supervisor, and the union shop steward. If those parties are unable to resolve the situation, the process escalates, involving higher levels of management on both the employer and union sides. If the highest level of escalation fails to produce an agreeable solution, either party can then decide to submit the grievance to arbitration (see "Arbitrating Disputes").[48]

DISCIPLINING EMPLOYEES

progressive discipline
An escalating process of discipline that gives employees several opportunities to correct performance problems before being terminated.

A CBA also outlines procedures for disciplining employees who violate either the terms of the agreement or company policies. For minor offenses, an escalating process known as **progressive discipline** usually starts with an oral warning for the first offense, followed by a written warning, then another written warning and suspension without pay, and then finally termination after the fourth offense. For serious offenses such as theft, unsafe behavior, or participation in unauthorized strikes, employees can be terminated immediately.[49]

ARBITRATING DISPUTES

In addition to being used to finalize a collective bargaining agreement, arbitration can also be used to interpret or apply the provisions of the agreement.[50] If employee grievances cannot be resolved through the agreed-on grievance procedure or if an employee or his or her union dispute disciplinary action taken by an employer, the next step is usually arbitration. The issues brought to arbitration cover a wide range, including disputes over wages, seniority, terminations, employee discipline, job posting, and the use of subcontractors.[51] (Note that arbitration is not limited to labor contracts. As a prominent form of *alternative dispute resolution*, arbitration is used throughout the business world to resolve consumer complaints, various commercial contracts, health-care claims, and even international trade disputes.[52])

Most labor agreements include provisions for arbitrating disputes that cannot be resolved through normal grievance procedures. However, if one party refuses to submit to arbitration, the other party can either take the matter to court or ask an arbitrator to rule on it. Roughly 10 percent of labor contract cases brought to federal arbitrators involve the determination of *arbitrability*.[53] If the arbitrator determines that the labor contract addresses the issue at hand, he or she will deny the request for arbitration and direct the parties to use the grievance procedures in the contract.

One of the key differences between arbitration and the civil justice system is that in arbitration, the union and the employer get to select the arbitrator. (They also share the cost of the service.) Both the FMCS and organizations such as the American Arbitration Association maintain rosters of approved arbitrators, known in the profession as "neutrals," with experience in labor contract disputes. Most arbitrators are chosen on a case-by-case basis, but in some instances, a union and an employer agree to a permanent arbitrator to hear grievances throughout the life of the contract.[54]

> ## ✔ Checkpoint
>
> **LEARNING OBJECTIVE 5: Explain the procedures for addressing employee grievances and arbitrating disputes.**
>
> **SUMMARY:** The Wagner Act and subsequent legislation identify a number of unfair labor practices, and the NLRB can take action to remedy these whenever a union or an employer files a complaint. In addition, collective bargaining agreements typically include provisions for addressing employee grievances, for disciplining employees who violate the terms of their employment contracts or other workplace rules, and for arbitrating disputes over the interpretation or application of bargain agreements. Grievance procedures usually start on a small scale, involving the employee, the shop steward, and the supervisor. If that group is unable to resolve the complaint, the process escalates, involving higher levels of authority in both the union and the company. If the process is exhausted without resolution, the grievance can be submitted to arbitration, in which an impartial third party makes a decision in the matter.
>
> **CRITICAL THINKING:** (1) Is it in a union's best interest for its members to comply with all the terms of a CBA? Why or why not? (2) What risks do unions and employers take in deciding to use arbitration?
>
> **IT'S YOUR BUSINESS:** (1) How would you respond if you discovered a fellow employee stealing or committing another serious offense on the job (and you were the only other person who knew about it)? (2) Do you believe that employees should be given multiple chances after committing minor offenses in the workplace, as progressive discipline procedures allow? Why or why not?
>
> **KEY TERMS TO KNOW:** unfair labor practices, grievance, progressive discipline

The Future of Labor

LEARNING OBJECTIVE

Characterize the ongoing conflict over union organizing efforts.

Labor relations remains a classic case of stakeholder conflict, with one side pursuing lower costs and more operational flexibility and the other side pursuing higher wages, better benefits, and more stability. Union membership numbers don't tell the whole story of this conflict, because the influence of the labor movement stretches beyond just those workplaces that are unionized. However, one can't avoid looking at membership numbers either, and by that score, unions have been on the losing side of this contest for several decades. From a peak of more than one-third of the U.S. private-sector workforce in the 1950s, only 6.6 percent of private-sector workers now belong to unions.[55]

With their influence based on having a collective voice, unions place a high priority on recruiting and retaining members. Unfortunately for unions, the long-term trend has

How relevant are unions in today's workplace? The answer to that question is critical to the future of the union movement.

not been positive, at least in the private sector. True to the often-combative nature of the relationship, each side blames the decline of organized labor on the other. Some business leaders say unions don't have anything relevant to offer workers in today's environment of more enlightened and supportive management. Union leaders often accuse management of using every tactic they can think of, both legal and illegal, to thwart unionization efforts.

Over the past century, the union movement got its biggest boosts in times of great upheaval, specifically the two world wars and the Great Depression. Labor researcher Rich Yeselson says the wise move for unions might be sit tight until another upheaval, and then try to recruit new workers and new industries on a massive scale.[56]

Do more U.S. workers *want* to be represented by unions? The answer to that question seems to depend on who is doing the asking and how the question is phrased. One 2005 survey said that 53 percent of non-union workers "definitely or probably would vote in favor of union representation in their workplace."[57] However, other surveys produce different figures. Another 2005 survey said that only 16 percent would "definitely" vote for a union and another 20 percent would "probably" vote for a union, for a total positive response of 36 percent.[58] In a 2009 survey that asked the simple yes-or-no question "Would you like to belong to a labor union where you work?" only 9 percent said yes.[59] Clearly, some employees who are not now in unions would like to be in one, but just how many is not clear.

The future of labor could include the new twist of organizing in support of workers without forming unions. This "alt-labor" movement relies on many of the tactics used by unions, including strikes, boycotts, demonstrations, and lawsuits, but does so without the legal force of unionized collective bargaining. More than 200 such groups, sometimes called *worker centers*, are now active in the United States, campaigning on behalf of such diverse groups as restaurant workers, fashion models, and farmworkers.[60]

For the latest information on labor relations topics, visit **http://real-timeupdates.com/bia8** and click on Chapter 12.

✔ Checkpoint

LEARNING OBJECTIVE 6: Characterize the ongoing conflict over union organizing efforts.

SUMMARY: Private-sector union membership has been in a steady decline over the past several decades and is now at historic lows. Both sides tend to blame the other for the decline, with management saying unions don't have anything relevant to offer today's workers, and union leaders saying profit-driven management uses every tool it can to thwart union organizing. Without a major social upheaval, it seems unlikely that unions will be able to reverse the downward trend of union membership. However, the rise of nonunion worker-rights groups in the past few years presents an alternative method of campaigning on behalf of workers.

CRITICAL THINKING: (1) What evidence would you need to reach a solid conclusion about why union membership has declined in the private sector over the past 50 years? (2) Why do you suppose different surveys generate such wildly varying responses to questions about whether nonunion employees would like to join a union?

IT'S YOUR BUSINESS: (1) With everything you've learned about labor relations so far, would you describe yourself as more pro-union or more anti-union? Why? (2) Would you support the efforts of an alt-labor group if attaining its goals would result in higher prices for you as a consumer? Why or why not?

BEHIND THE SCENES
BOEING AND THE IAM: A PROJECT SAVED, BUT STRIFE REMAINS

When Boeing proposed new wage and benefit terms to the members of the International Association of Machinists (IAM) in advance of launching the 777X jetliner, the move reopened some old wounds in the company's relationship with the union—and opened some fresh wounds inside the union organization as well.

The threat of jobs moving out of Washington state had been hanging over the heads of IAM members for years. Boeing has had smaller operations in other states for some time, but when the company moved its corporate headquarters to Chicago in 2001 after being a Seattle-based company for 85 years, many took it as a symbol of the company's lack of loyalty to Seattle and the Puget Sound region and a possible step toward dismantling the company's local airliner-assembly operations and moving those jobs around the country or overseas. The airliner division, Boeing Commercial Aircraft, remains headquartered in Seattle, and the company's stated reason for the Chicago move was to be closer to government decision makers in the *other* Washington (D.C., that is) following its merger with St. Louis–based McDonnell Douglas. However, the departure of the top brass of the most iconic of Seattle companies didn't sit well with many local employees.

In that context, the decision to outsource so much of the 787 Dreamliner stung union members. When the 787 program subsequently fell several years behind schedule and went several billion dollars over budget, union champions viewed that as a "we told you so" moment—as confirmation that the experienced machinists of the IAM in the Seattle area were the best people to be making Boeing airplanes. That sentiment got some strong confirmation from the company, too, when it was forced to bring some of that outsourcing work back in house because outsiders weren't up to the task.

It wasn't too surprising, then, that many IAM members were outraged when Boeing presented them with revised contract terms that would roll back hard-won gains in pensions and wage curves in exchange for the company's agreement to build the upcoming 777X model at the Everett, Washington, facility. Some of the details of the proposal were ironed out behind the scenes by company management and union leaders, but by the time the union rank-and-file knew about it, they had only a week to decide. In fact, some of the local union leaders were dead set against the deal and didn't think it should even be brought to a vote. However, union leaders at the local level were overruled by district and international leaders, and the revised contract was put to a vote of the members of District 751.

Those members soundly rejected the new contract—by a 2-to-1 margin—and many were furious with their own leaders for

putting them in the position of having to vote on it. Boeing said it wasn't bluffing and would open up the 777X competition to other locations, but when forced to vote, the union members apparently believed the company would either have to renegotiate the terms or move ahead with production at Everett anyway.

True to its word, Boeing began sending managers to scout other locations the morning after the vote, asking other states to provide land and facilities at little or no cost to the company in exchange for getting all those jobs. A month later, representatives of Utah, North Carolina, California, and Alabama submitted bids for the program.

While considering those bids, Boeing made a slightly modified offer to the Everett union, but the leaders of IAM District 751 refused to put the revised contract to a vote, saying it was so similar to the rejected deal that there was no point in even voting on it. However, the national leadership of the IAM stepped in and forced a vote in early January 2014. This time, the contract was approved, although by the narrow margin of 51 to 49 percent.

The contract secures 10 years of labor peace for the company and keeps all those jobs in Everett. However, as employers in a variety of industries continue to use their bargaining power with states to find the best deals for locating new facilities, tension between labor and management and within labor unions themselves is likely to continue.[61]

Critical Thinking Questions

12-1. Some union members criticized Washington governor Jay Inslee and the state's U.S. Senator Patty Murray for their role in brokering the contract presented to the IAM. Is this a fair criticism? Why or why not?

12-2. Would it be fair to the residents of Washington state for Boeing to get nearly $9 billion in tax breaks—money that could have been used for schools, roads, and other public needs? Why or why not?

12-3. Is it economically healthy for the United States when individual states compete against one another to attract companies, as Washington and South Carolina have done in the case of Boeing, for example? Why or why not?

LEARN MORE ONLINE
Visit **www.goiam.org** and search for information about the IAM's efforts to unionize Boeing's facility in North Charleston, South Carolina. Has the IAM held an election to unionize this plant? If so, what was the outcome?

KEY TERMS

arbitration (285)
authorization cards (282)

boycott (286)
certification election (282)

MyBizLab

To complete the problems with the ⭐,
go to EOC Discussion Questions in the
MyLab.

TEST YOUR KNOWLEDGE

Questions for Review

12-4. From an employee's perspective, what are the potential benefits of unionization?

12-5. How did the Wagner Act affect the balance of power between unions and employers?

12-6. What is a right-to-work law?

12-7. What is a collective bargaining agreement?

12-8. How does mediation differ from arbitration?

Questions for Analysis

12-9. How does the long history of labor-management relations affect labor relations in today's economy?

12-10. How does the relationship between labor and management reflect the potential for conflict in the stakeholder model?

12-11. What are some of the explanations for the decline in labor union membership in the past 50 years?

12-12. Why have alt-labor groups caught on in the past few years, when the union model is already in place as a way to advocate for workers?

⭐ **12-13.** **Ethical Considerations.** Is it wrong for employees to try to convince each other to vote for or against unionization? How much pressure should employees be allowed to exert on each other during union organizing campaigns?

Questions for Application

12-14. You work as an organizer for a union that is trying to persuade workers in the banking industry to unionize. You've collected authorization cards from 52 percent of the workers at a particular company. Should you file a petition with the NLRB for a secret-ballot election? Why or why not?

12-15. What advice would you give the founders of a new company who want to avoid unionization efforts among their workforce as the company grows?

⭐ **12-16.** A coworker is arguing that the president of the United States should not have the authority to issue an injunction to stop a strike because doing so violates the legal rights of workers. How would you respond?

⭐ **12-17.** **Concept Integration.** Which motivation theory or theories discussed in Chapter 10 help explain the sometimes contentious nature of labor relations?

EXPAND YOUR KNOWLEDGE

Discovering Career Opportunities

Mediation and arbitration are forms of *alternative dispute resolution (ADR)*, so named because they offer alternatives to resolving disputes through lawsuits. Mediate.com (**www.mediate.com**) offers extensive information about mediation, and the American Arbitration Association (**www.adr.org**) offers information about arbitration. The "Arbitrators, Mediators, and Conciliators" section of the *Occupational Outlook Handbook* (**www.bls.gov/ooh**) also provides information on careers in mediation and arbitration. Visit these sites and explore the world of ADR. Is this a career you might want to pursue? What additional education would you need?

Improving Your Tech Insights: Employee Monitoring Software

Who is watching while you work (or don't work)? Chances are good that at least one form of electronic activity will be monitored at whatever company you work for now or will join in the future. The costs of inappropriate behavior can be so high that the majority of employers now monitor or control access to the Internet, telephone conversations (although employers are not allowed to record personal calls), voice mail, email, instant messaging, text messaging (on company-issued phones), and other electronic media. Many employers use keystroke monitoring or screen-image-recording software to keep track of what employees are doing at their computers. Many businesses also use video monitors throughout company facilities.

Employers have a number of concerns, including lost productivity, release of company secrets or confidential customer records, the viewing and sending of inappropriate material, and illegal activities by employees. Privacy advocates may not like all the monitoring, but current laws provide little protection for employee privacy, and courts have ruled that employers have the right to control the use of company-owned systems and to protect confidential information. In a brief email message to your instructor, summarize this dilemma and its possible effects on employee–management relations.[62]

PRACTICE YOUR SKILLS

Sharpening Your Communication Skills

Identify a recent situation in which a labor union went on strike in an attempt to force an employer to drop plans to reduce wages, benefits, or job security. Choose either the union's position or the company's position and do the research necessary to write a compelling one-page argument for your side.

Building Your Team Skills

Form a team with several students who have chosen the same side in the dispute from "Sharpening Your Communication Skills." In a debate against another team that has taken the other side, try to convince the rest of the class that your side is justified in taking its stance. Be prepared to address points likely to be raised by your opponents.

Developing Your Research Skills

Find information about one of the many "alt-legal" groups or worker centers now advocating on behalf of workers in a particular industry. (You can start with InterFaith Worker Justice, **www.iwj.org**; National Day Labor Organizing Network, **www.ndlon.org**; or the Food Chain Workers Alliance, **http://foodchainworkers.org**.) Choose a group or center of interest and outline the workplace issues it is trying to improve on behalf of a particular employee population.

MyBizLab®

Go to the Assignments section of your MyLab to complete these writing exercises.

12-18. If union members strike because of what they perceive to be unfair treatment by managers, would strikebreaking replacements be guilty of an ethical lapse by temporarily filling those positions? Why or why not?

12-19. Should the federal government step in and mandate one set of union laws for all 50 states so that companies can't play states against each other in labor negotiations? Why or why not?

ENDNOTES

1. Dominic Gates, "Four Machinists Ask NLRB to Overturn Last Week's Vote," *Seattle Times*, 7 January 2014, www.seattletimes.com; Dominic Gates, "Machinists Say Yes, Secure 777X for Everett," *Seattle Times*, 3 January 2014, www.seattletimes.com; Boeing website, accessed 16 November 2013, www.boeing.com; Dominic Gates, "A Landmark Vote for Machinists," *Seattle Times*, 12 November 2013, www.seattletimes.com; Dominic Gates, "A Resounding No from Machinists," *Seattle Times*, 13 November 2013, www.seattletimes.com; Guy Norris, "Boeing Opens Up 777X Site Contest After IAM Rejection," *Aviation Week*, 14 November 2013, www.aviationweek.com; Constancy Brooks & Smith, LLP, "Lessons from the NLRB's Boeing Complaint," 10 June 2011, www.constancy.com; Rami Grunbaum, "Machinists Line Up Early, Many Voice Dissatisfaction with Boeing Contract Offer," *Seattle Times*, 13 November 2013, www.seattletimes.com; Loren Thompson, "Boeing Accelerates Shift of Workers Away from Puget Sound Birthplace," *Forbes*, 6 June 2013, www.forbes.com.
2. Robert Brooks, "The Meaning of It All," *Foundry Management & Technology*, March 2008, 4.
3. Based in part on Michael R. Carrell and Christina Heavrin, *Labor Relations and Collective Bargaining: Cases, Practice, and Law*, 9th ed. (Upper Saddle River, N.J.: Pearson Prentice Hall, 2010), 76–81.
4. "Union Members Summary," U.S. Bureau of Labor Statistics news release, 23 January 2013, www.bls.gov.
5. "The Union Advantage: Facts and Figures," Service Employees International Union website, accessed 15 November 2013, www.seiu.org.
6. Mariah DeForest, "Will Your Employees Go Union?" *Foundry Management & Technology*, September 2008, 36–39.
7. Carrell and Heavrin, *Labor Relations and Collective Bargaining*, 79.
8. "Average Dues and Due Growth," data from Labor Management Reporting and Disclosure Act, quoted in Mark Brenner, "Give Your Union a Dues Checkup," *Labor Notes*, accessed 25 June 2009, www.labornotes.org.
9. Carrell and Heavrin, *Labor Relations and Collective Bargaining*, 316–317.
10. Michelle Krebs, "Study: Union Work Rules Cost Big Three," *Edmunds AutoObserver*, 20 June 2007, www.autoobserver.com.

11. Christos Doucouliagos and Patrice Laroche, "What Do Unions Do to Productivity: A Meta-analysis," *Industrial Relations*, October 2003, 650–691.

12. Philip Taft, "Workers of a New Century," U.S. Department of Labor website, accessed 30 June 2009, www.dol.gov.

13. Carrell and Heavrin, *Labor Relations and Collective Bargaining*, 26–27.

14. Carrell and Heavrin, *Labor Relations and Collective Bargaining*, 29; "Overview," U.S. National Labor Relations Board website, accessed, 30 June 2009, www.nlrb.gov; Henry R. Cheeseman, *Contemporary Business and E-Commerce Law*, 7th ed. (Upper Saddle River, N.J.: Pearson Prentice Hall, 2010), 501.

15. Irving Bernstein, "Americans in Depression and War," U.S. Department of Labor website, accessed 30 June 2009, www.dol.gov.

16. Jack Barbash, "Unions and Rights in the Space Age," U.S. Department of Labor website, accessed 30 June 2009, www.dol.gov.

17. Barbash, "Unions and Rights in the Space Age"; Carrell and Heavrin, *Labor Relations and Collective Bargaining*, 33.

18. Barbash, "Unions and Rights in the Space Age."

19. Barbash, "Unions and Rights in the Space Age."

20. "Landrum-Griffin Act," *West's Encyclopedia of American Law*, 2nd ed., Jeffrey Lehman and Shirelle Phelps, eds. (Detroit: Gale, 2005), 200–201.

21. Cheeseman, *Contemporary Business and E-Commerce Law*, 522–523; Carrell and Heavrin, *Labor Relations and Collective Bargaining*, 145–149.

22. Zogby International, *The Attitudes and Opinions of Unionized and Non-Unionized Workers Employed in Various Sectors of the Economy Toward Organized Labor*, August 2005, 17.

23. "Right to Work Frequently-Asked Questions," *National Right to Work Legal Defense Fund*, accessed 20 April 2015, www.nrtw.org.

24. Carrell and Heavrin, *Labor Relations and Collective Bargaining*, 149–151.

25. Carrell and Heavrin, *Labor Relations and Collective Bargaining*, 122–123.

26. Carrell and Heavrin, *Labor Relations and Collective Bargaining*, 123–124.

27. Carrell and Heavrin, *Labor Relations and Collective Bargaining*, 138.

28. James Sherk, "Employee Free Choice Act Effectively Eliminates Secret Ballot Organizing Elections," *Heritage Foundation*, 27 August 2008, www.heritage.org.

29. "Procedures Guide," U.S. National Labor Relations Board website, accessed 28 June 2009, www.nlrb.gov.

30. Steven Greenhouse, "At N.L.R.B., Flurry of Acts for Unions as Chief Exits," *New York Times*, 30 August 2011, www.nytimes.com.

31. DeForest, "Will Your Employees Go Union?"

32. Carrell and Heavrin, *Labor Relations and Collective Bargaining*, 138.

33. "National Labor Relations Act," U.S. National Labor Relations Board website, accessed 28 June 2009, www.nlrb.gov; John Horowitz, "Employee Free Choice Act—Things to Avoid During Union Organizing Campaign," Employee Free Choice Act blog, 4 November 2008, http://employeefreechoiceact.foxrothschild.com; Carrell and Heavrin, *Labor Relations and Collective Bargaining*, 170–171; Cheeseman, *Contemporary Business and E-Commerce Law*, 502–503.

34. "Collective Bargaining Agreement Between National Hockey League and National Hockey League Players' Association, September 16, 2012–September 15, 2022," NHL website, www.nhl.com.

35. "National Labor Relations Act," U.S. National Labor Relations Board website, accessed 28 June 2009, www.nlrb.gov.

36. Carrell and Heavrin, *Labor Relations and Collective Bargaining*, 201–202.

37. "The Strike Zone: How to Defuse Protracted Labor Conflicts," *Negotiation*, March 2008, 6–7.

38. "Using a Third-Party Neutral," U.S. Federal Mediation and Conciliation Service website, accessed 1 September 2011, www.fmcs.gov.

39. Carrell and Heavrin, *Labor Relations and Collective Bargaining*, 107.

40. Jarol B. Manheim, *Trends in Union Corporate Campaigns*, U.S. Chamber of Commerce, 14.

41. Manheim, *Trends in Union Corporate Campaigns*, 16–17.

42. "Injunction Activity Under Section 10(j)," U.S. National Labor Relations Board website, accessed 1 September 2011, www.nlrb.gov.

43. Paul D. Staudohar, "Labor Relations in Basketball: The Lockout of 1998–99," *Monthly Labor Review*, April 1999, 3–9; E. Edward Herman, *Collective Bargaining and Labor Relations*, 4th ed. (Upper Saddle River, N.J.: Prentice Hall, 1998), 61; "NLRB Permits Replacements During Legal Lockout," *Personnel Journal*, January 1987, 14–15.

44. "Fact Sheet," U.S. National Labor Relations Board website, accessed 7 July 2009, www.nlrb.gov.

45. "Employer/Union Rights and Obligations," U.S. National Labor Relations Board website, accessed 1 September 2011, www.nlrb.gov.

46. "Employer/Union Rights and Obligations."

47. Carrell and Heavrin, *Labor Relations and Collective Bargaining*, 483.

48. "Grievance Handling," United Electrical, Radio and Machine Workers of America website, accessed 28 June 2009, www.rankfile-ue.org; Carrell and Heavrin, *Labor Relations and Collective Bargaining*, 481–486.

49. Carrell and Heavrin, *Labor Relations and Collective Bargaining*, 487–491.

50. Carrell and Heavrin, *Labor Relations and Collective Bargaining*, 510.

51. "Federal Mediation and Conciliation Service, 2008 Annual Report," U.S. Federal Mediation and Conciliation Service website, accessed 29 June 2009, www.fmcs.gov.

52. American Arbitration Association website, accessed 29 June 2009, www.adr.org.

53. "Federal Mediation and Conciliation Service, 2008 Annual Report."

54. Carrell and Heavrin, *Labor Relations and Collective Bargaining*, 513.

55. Jon Talton, "Heyday for Unions in the Rearview Mirror," *Seattle Times*, 3 September 2011, www.seattletimes.com; "Union Members Summary," U.S. Bureau of Labor Statistics website, 23 January 2015, www.bls.gov.

56. Rich Yeselson, "Fortress Unionism," *Democracy*, Summer 2013, www.democracyjournal.org.

57. Ian Robinson, "What Explains Unorganized Workers' Growing Demand for Unions?" *Labor Studies Journal*, Vol. 33, No. 3, September 2008, 235–242.

58. Zogby International, "The Attitudes and Opinions of Unionized and Non-Unionized Workers Employed in Various Sectors of the Economy Toward Organized Labor," August 2005, Public Service Research Council website, accessed 30 June 2009, www.psrconline.org.

59. Rasmussen Reports, "Toplines—Unions I—March 13–14, 2009," Rasmussen Reports website, accessed 30 June 2009, www.rasmussenreports.com.

60. Josh Eidelson, "Alt-Labor," *The American Prospect*, 29 January 2013, prospect.org.

61. See note 1.

62. "Electronic Monitoring in the Workplace: Common Law & Federal Statutory Protection," *The National Workrights Institute*, accessed 9 July 2009, www.workrights.org; "Employee Monitoring: Is There Privacy in the Workplace?" *Privacy Rights Clearinghouse*, accessed 9 July 2009, www.privacyrights.org; Brittany Petersen, "Employee Monitoring: It's Not Paranoia—You Really Are Being Watched!" *PC Magazine*, 26 May 2008, www.pcmag.com.

PART 5

Satisfying the Customer: Marketing, Sales, and Customer Support

Raygun/Getty Images

295

LEARNING OBJECTIVES   After studying this chapter, you will be able to

1. Define *marketing*, and explain its role in society.

2. Identify three trends that help define contemporary marketing.

3. Differentiate between consumer buying behavior and organizational buying behavior.

4. Define *strategic marketing planning*, and identify the four basic options for pursuing new marketing opportunities.

5. Identify the four steps in crafting a marketing strategy.

6. Describe the four main components of the marketing mix.

BEHIND THE SCENES RED ANTS PANTS GIVES WORKING WOMEN A CHOICE THAT FITS

Photo by Erik Peterson, Courtesy of Sarah Calhoun

Sarah Calhoun of Red Ants Pants crafted a successful marketing mix to fulfill her mission of providing hardwearing pants for hardworking women.

www.redantspants.com

Something doesn't add up here:

1. Thousands and thousands of women work in heavy labor jobs, from farming and ranching to welding, construction, and pile driving. In fact, a quarter of the workforce in the building trades, agriculture, fishing, and forestry consists of women.
2. The kind of work these women perform quickly shreds regular clothing. They need heavy-duty duds.
3. Carhartt and other work clothing suppliers sell heavy-duty pants that can stand up to the rigors of tough work, but when Sarah Calhoun surveyed the market, these suppliers focused on work pants made for men.
4. Women aren't shaped like men.

Calhoun wasn't a clothing designer, didn't work in the business, and wasn't chasing some lifelong entrepreneurial dream. But she was fed up—with men's work pants that didn't fit or women's regular pants that didn't hold up under the stress and strain of clearing trails, peeling logs, and doing the other sorts of work she took on in her adopted home state of Montana.

Tired of constantly putting down her tools so she could pull up her misfit britches, Calhoun decided to solve the problem herself. She launched Red Ants Pants with the single-minded goal of outfitting women who need rugged workwear.

Why "Red Ants Pants," by the way? In a conversation with a biologist about the social behaviors of ants, she learned that in red ant colonies, females do most of the work. In keeping with the cheeky style she adopted for all her company's communication, she uses the name as a salute to hardworking women everywhere.

Calhoun was convinced she had spotted a business opportunity, but what was the best way to pursue it? How could a total outsider—based in White Sulphur Springs, Montana, no less—break into the clothing industry? How could she design a product that would meet the needs of her target customers? How many choices should she offer in terms of colors, styles, and sizes? What could she do to craft a compelling message and get that message in front of the buying public? How should she price the high-quality product she had in mind? What about distribution and the rest of the marketing mix? If you were in Calhoun's position, how would you go about marketing Red Ants Pants?[1]

INTRODUCTION

Sarah Calhoun's experience in introducing the Red Ants Pants brand (profiled in the chapter-opening Behind the Scenes) illustrates the complex challenge of fashioning an appealing blend of products, prices, distribution methods, and customer communication efforts—the essential elements of marketing. This chapter introduces the basic concepts of marketing; products and pricing are addressed in Chapter 14, distribution and marketing logistics are the topics of Chapter 15, and customer communication is covered in Chapter 16.

Marketing in a Changing World

Marketing requires a wide range of skills, from research and analysis to strategic planning to persuasive communication. On the job and in the media, you will encounter many uses of the term *marketing*, from the broad and strategic to the narrow and tactical. However, noted marketing professors Philip Kotler and Gary Armstrong offer a definition that does a great job of highlighting the contemporary flavor of customer-focused marketing: **Marketing** is "the process by which companies create value for customers and build strong customer relationships in order to capture value from customers in return."[2] The ideas of *value*, the *exchange* of value, and lasting *relationships* are essential elements of successful marketing.

In addition to goods and services, marketing applies to not-for-profit organizations, people, places, and causes. Politicians and celebrities constantly market themselves. So do places that want to attract residents, tourists, and business investments. **Place marketing** describes efforts to market geographic areas ranging from neighborhoods to entire countries. **Cause-related marketing** promotes a cause or a social issue—such as physical fitness, cancer awareness, or environmental sustainability—while also promoting a company and its products.

THE ROLE OF MARKETING IN SOCIETY

Marketing plays an important role in society by helping people satisfy their needs and wants and by helping organizations determine what to produce.

Needs and Wants

Individuals and organizations have a wide variety of needs, from food and water necessary for survival to transaction-processing systems that make sure a retail store gets paid for all the credit card purchases it records. As a consumer, you experience needs any time differences or gaps exist between your actual state and your ideal state. You're hungry and you don't want to be hungry: You need to eat. **Needs** create the motivation to buy products and are, therefore, at the core of any discussion of marketing.

---

1 LEARNING OBJECTIVE

Define *marketing*, and explain its role in society.

marketing
The process of creating value for customers and building relationships with those customers in order to capture value back from them.

place marketing
Marketing efforts to attract people and organizations to a particular geographical area.

cause-related marketing
Identification and marketing of a social issue, cause, or idea to selected target markets.

needs
Differences between a person's actual state and his or her ideal state; they provide the basic motivation to make a purchase.

wants
Specific goods, services, experiences, or other entities that are desirable in light of a person's experiences, culture, and personality.

exchange process
The act of obtaining a desired object or service from another party by offering something of value in return.

transaction
An exchange of value between parties.

utility
The power of a good or service to satisfy a human need.

marketing concept
An approach to business management that stresses customer needs and wants, seeks long-term profitability, and integrates marketing with other functional units within the organization.

Your **wants** are based on your needs but are more specific. Producers do not create needs, but they do try to shape your wants by exposing you to attractive choices. For instance, when you *need* some food, you may *want* a Snickers bar, an orange, or a seven-course dinner at the swankiest restaurant in town. If you have the means, or *buying power*, to purchase the product you want, you create *demand* for that product.[3]

Exchanges and Transactions

When you participate in the **exchange process**, you trade something of value (usually money) for something else of value. When you make a purchase, you encourage the producer of that item to create or supply more of it. In this way, supply and demand tend toward balance, and society obtains the goods and services that are most satisfying. When the exchange actually occurs, it takes the form of a **transaction**. Party A gives Party B $1.29 and gets a medium Coke in return. A trade of values takes place.

Most transactions in today's society involve money, but money is not necessarily required. Bartering or trading, which predates the use of cash, is making a big comeback thanks to the Internet. Hundreds of online barter exchanges are now in operation in the United States alone. Intermediaries such as BizXchange (www.bizx.com) facilitate cashless trading among multiple members through a system of credits and debits. For instance, an advertising agency might trade services to a dairy farm, which then trades products to a catering company, which then trades services to the advertising agency. By eliminating the need for trading partners to have exactly complimentary needs at exactly the same time, these exchanges make it easy for companies to buy and sell without using cash.[4]

The Four Utilities

To encourage the exchange process, marketers enhance the appeal of their goods and services by adding **utility**, which is any attribute that increases the value that customers place on the product. When companies change raw materials into finished goods, they are creating *form utility* desired by consumers. When supermarkets provide fresh, ready-to-eat dishes as an alternative to food ingredients, they are creating form utility. In other cases, marketers try to make their products available when and where customers want to buy them, creating *time utility* and *place utility*. Overnight couriers such as FedEx and UPS create time utility, whereas coffee carts in office buildings and ATMs in shopping malls create place utility. Services such as Apple's iTunes create both time and place utility: You can purchase music any time and from just about anywhere. The final form of utility is *possession utility*—the satisfaction that buyers get when they actually possess a product, both legally and physically. Mortgage companies, for example, create possession utility by offering loans that allow people to buy homes they could otherwise not afford.

THE MARKETING CONCEPT

Business's view of the marketing function has evolved rather dramatically over the decades. In years past, many companies pursued what was known as the *product concept*, which was essentially to focus on the production of goods and count on customers to figure out which products they needed and to take the steps to find and purchase them. In other words, the product concept views the primary purpose of a business as making things, not satisfying customers. As markets evolved and competition heated up, the *selling concept* began to take over, which emphasizes building a business by generating as many sales transactions as possible. The customer features more prominently in the selling concept, but only as a target to be sold to, not as a partner in a mutually satisfying relationship.

In contrast, today's most successful companies tend to embrace the **marketing concept**, the idea that companies should respond to customers' needs and wants while seeking long-term profitability and coordinating their own marketing efforts to achieve the company's long-term goals (see Exhibit 13.1). These *customer-focused* companies build

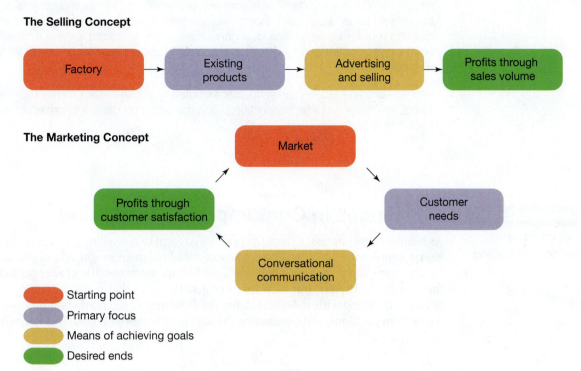

EXHIBIT 13.1   The Selling Concept Versus the Marketing Concept

Firms that practice the selling concept sell what they make rather than making what the market wants. In contrast, firms that practice the marketing concept determine the needs and wants of a market and deliver the desired product or service more effectively and efficiently than competitors do.

Source: Based in part on Philip Kotler and Gary Armstrong, *Principles of Marketing*, 13th ed. (Upper Saddle River, N.J.: Pearson Prentice Hall, 2010), 10.

their marketing strategies around the goal of long-term relationships with satisfied customers.[5] The term **relationship marketing** is often applied to these efforts to distinguish them from efforts that emphasize production or sales transactions. One of the most significant goals of relationship marketing is **customer loyalty**, the degree to which customers continue to buy from a particular retailer or buy the products offered by a particular manufacturer. The payoff from becoming customer-focused can be considerable, but the process of transforming a product- or sales-driven company into one that embraces the marketing concept can take years and may involve changes to major systems and processes throughout the company, as well as the basic culture of the company.[6]

Why all the emphasis on customer service and customer satisfaction in the marketing concept? It's not just about being nice and helpful; satisfying customers is simply smart business. For one thing, keeping your existing customers is usually much cheaper and easier than finding new customers. For another, satisfied customers are the best promotion a company can hope for, particularly given the power of social media and social commerce.

relationship marketing
A focus on developing and maintaining long-term relationships with customers, suppliers, and distribution partners for mutual benefit.

customer loyalty
The degree to which customers continue to buy from a particular retailer or buy the products of a particular manufacturer or service provider.

✓ Checkpoint

LEARNING OBJECTIVE 1: Define *marketing*, and explain its role in society.

SUMMARY: Marketing can be defined as "the process by which companies create value for customers and build strong customer relationships in order to capture value from customers in return." The marketing function guides a company in selecting which products to offer, how much to charge for them, how to distribute them to customers, and how to promote them to potential buyers. Marketing plays an important role in society by helping people satisfy their needs and wants and by helping organizations determine what to produce.

CRITICAL THINKING: (1) Should every company see long-term relationships with customers as vitally important? Why or why not? (2) Would a company that already dominates its markets ever care about the marketing concept? Why or why not?

IT'S YOUR BUSINESS: (1) What is your reaction when you feel as though you're being "sold to" by a company that is clearly more interested in selling products than in meeting your needs as an individual consumer? (2) Do you want to have a "relationship" with any of the companies that you currently patronize as a customer? Why or why not?

KEY TERMS TO KNOW: marketing, place marketing, cause-related marketing, needs, wants, exchange process, transaction, utility, marketing concept, relationship marketing, customer loyalty

---

2   **LEARNING OBJECTIVE**

Identify three trends that help define contemporary marketing.

Challenges in Contemporary Marketing

As business has progressed from the product concept to the selling concept to the marketing concept—with the critical emergence of social commerce—the role of marketing has become increasingly complicated. You'll read about some specific challenges in this and the next three chapters, but here are three general issues that many marketing organizations are wrestling with today: involving the customer in the marketing process, making data-driven decisions, and conducting marketing activities with greater concern for ethics and etiquette.

REAL-TIME UPDATES
Learn More by Visiting This Website

Marketing to the mobile buyer

The Mobile Marketing Association, whose members include many of the biggest consumer brands in the world, is helping refine the art and science of marketing to today's mobile buyers. Go to **http://real-timeupdates.com/bia8** and click on Learn More in the Students section.

INVOLVING THE CUSTOMER IN THE MARKETING PROCESS

A central element in the marketing concept is involving the customer as a partner in a mutually beneficial relationship rather than treating the customer as a passive recipient of products and promotional messages. Involving the customer has always been relatively easy for small, local companies and for large companies with their major customers. For instance, a neighborhood bistro or coffee shop can prepare foods and drinks just the way its regular customers want, and satisfied customers are happy to tell friends and relatives about their favorite places to eat and drink. At the other extreme, a maker of jet engines such as Pratt & Whitney or Rolls-Royce works closely with its airplane manufacturing customers to create exactly the products those customers want.

The challenge has been to replicate this level of intimacy on a broader scale, when a company has thousands of customers spread across the country or around the world. Two sets of technologies have helped foster communication and collaboration between companies and their customers. The first is **customer relationship management (CRM)** systems, which capture, organize, and capitalize on all the interactions that a company has with its customers, from marketing surveys and advertising through sales orders and customer support. A CRM system functions like an institutional memory for a company, allowing it to record and act on the information that is pertinent to each customer relationship.

customer relationship management (CRM)
A type of information system that captures, organizes, and capitalizes on all the interactions that a company has with its customers.

social commerce
The creation and sharing of product-related information among customers and potential customers.

CRM can be a powerful means to foster relationships, but to a certain degree, conventional CRM simply computerizes an existing way of doing business. Companies can also enable **social commerce**, using social networks, *user-generated content* such as online reviews and videos, Twitter updates, and other social media technologies. These tools let customers communicate with companies, with each other, and with

EXHIBIT 13.2	The Social Element in Contemporary Marketing

Social media have dramatically reshaped the practice of marketing in recent years, giving buyers more influence over the success and failure of products and companies. For example, companies such as Indian Motorcycle use social media to build a sense of community among customers and potential customers, and these people help protect and promote the brand.

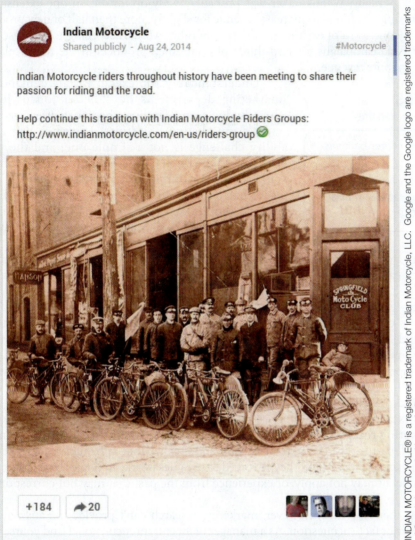

Indian Motorcycle
Shared publicly · Aug 24, 2014   #Motorcycle

Indian Motorcycle riders throughout history have been meeting to share their passion for riding and the road.

Help continue this tradition with Indian Motorcycle Riders Groups:
http://www.indianmotorcycle.com/en-us/riders-group

+184   20

INDIAN MOTORCYCLE® is a registered trademark of Indian Motorcycle, LLC. Google and the Google logo are registered trademarks of Google Inc., used with permission.

other influences in the marketplace such as prominent bloggers and journalists. For example, social networks such as Facebook have the potential to redefine advertising because consumers tend to view friends and peers as more reliable sources of product information than advertising (see Exhibit 13.2).[7]

As Chapter 16 explains, advertisers are learning to enable and participate in these online conversations, rather than blasting out messages to passive audiences as they did in the past. Another valuable use of social media is listening to feedback from customers.[8] Innovative companies are beginning to integrate these two relationship technologies, combining the data capture and retrieval of CRM with the interactivity of social media.[9]

REAL-TIME UPDATES
Learn More by Visiting This Website

New research into consumer-generated content marketing

From brief reviews to online videos, see how content from consumers is reshaping contemporary marketing. Go to **http://real-timeupdates.com/bia8** and click on Learn More in the Students section.

MAKING DATA-DRIVEN MARKETING DECISIONS

Learning more about customers is one aspect of the larger challenge of collecting, analyzing, and using data to make marketing decisions. Marketers in every industry would like to have better insights for making decisions and better ways of measuring the results of every marketing initiative. Pioneering retailer John Wannamaker said 100 years ago that "half the money I spend on advertising is wasted. The trouble is, I don't know which half."[10] Actually, Wannamaker was probably overly optimistic. In one extensive study, advertising was found to increase revenue for slightly more than half of new products but for only one-third of existing products.[11] In other words, according to this research, the advertising campaigns for two-thirds of established products in the marketplace don't bring in more revenue.

Understandably, top executives are demanding that marketing departments do a better job of justifying their budgets and finding the most effective ways of meeting marketing objectives. However, this accountability challenge is not a simple one, and the problem may never be completely solvable for many companies. With so many sources of information in the marketplace, particularly with the continuing growth of online and mobile marketing channels, identifying which sources influence which aspects of buyer behavior can be difficult.

To get a better idea of how well their marketing budgets are being spent, companies can use a class of tools and techniques called *marketing analytics*. For example, Google Analytics helps online advertisers measure the effectiveness of specific search-term keywords, track the behavior of website visitors from their initial landing on an e-commerce site on through to a purchase, and track the results of online videos and social networking efforts.[12] By integrating such tools into an overall measurement system that evaluates both online and offline marketing activities, a company can improve its decision making and focus its time and money in the most productive marketing efforts.

marketing research
The collection and analysis of information for making marketing decisions.

The process of gathering and analyzing *market intelligence* about customers, competitors, and related marketing issues through any combination of methods is known as **marketing research**. As markets grow increasingly dynamic and open to competition from all parts of the globe, today's companies realize that information is the key to successful action. Without it, they're forced to use guesswork, analogies from other markets that may or may not apply, or experience from the past that may not correspond to the future.[13]

At the same time, however, marketing research can't provide the answer to every strategic or tactical question. As a manager or an entrepreneur, you'll find yourself in situations that require creative thinking and careful judgment to make the leap beyond what the data alone can tell you. Research techniques range from the basic to the exotic, from simple surveys to advanced statistical techniques to neurological scanning that tries to discover how and why customers' brains respond to visual and verbal cues about products. You can see a sample of techniques in Exhibit 13.3.

MARKETING WITH GREATER CONCERN FOR ETHICS AND ETIQUETTE

Under pressure to reach and persuade buyers in a business environment that gets more fragmented and noisy all the time, marketers occasionally step over the line and engage in practices that are rude, manipulative, or even downright deceptive. The result is an increasing degree of skepticism of and hostility toward advertising and other marketing activities.[14]

EXHIBIT 13.3	Marketing Research Techniques

Marketers can use a wide variety of techniques to learn more about customers, competitors, and threats and opportunities in the marketplace.

Technique	Examples
Observation	Any in-person, mechanical, or electronic technique that monitors and records behavior, including website usage tracking and monitoring of blogs and social networking websites.
Surveys	Data collection efforts that measure responses from a representative subset of a larger group of people; can be conducted in person (when people with clipboards stop you in a mall, that's called a *mall intercept*), over the phone, by mail or email, or online. Designing and conducting a meaningful survey requires thorough knowledge of statistical techniques such as *sampling* to ensure valid results that truly represent the larger group. For this reason, many of the simple surveys that you see online these days do not produce statistically valid results.
Interviews and focus groups	One-on-one or group discussions that try to probe deeper into issues than a survey typically does. *Focus groups* involve a small number of people guided by a facilitator while being observed or recorded by researchers. Unlike surveys, interviews and focus groups are not designed to collect statistics that represent a larger group; their real value is in uncovering issues that might require further study.
Process data collection	Any method of collecting data during the course of other business tasks, including warranty registration cards, sales transaction records, gift and loyalty program card usage, and customer service interactions.
Experiments	Controlled scenarios in which researchers adjust one or more variables to measure the effect these changes have on customer behavior. For instance, separate groups of consumers can be exposed to different ads to see which ad is most effective. *Test marketing*, the launch of a product under real-world conditions but on a limited scale (such as in a single city), is a form of experimental research.
Ethnographic research	A branch of anthropology that studies people in their daily lives to learn about their needs, wants, and behaviors in real-life settings.
Neuromarketing studies	Research that measures brain activity while customers are viewing or interacting with products, websites, or other elements.

Sources: Ken Anderson, "Ethnographic Research: A Key to Strategy," *Harvard Business Review*, March 2009, 24; Emily R. Murphy, Judy Illes, and Peter B. Reiner, "Neuroethics of Neuromarketing," *Journal of Consumer Behaviour*, July–October 2008, 293–302; Dick Bucci, "Recording Systems Add More Depth When Capturing Answers," *Marketing News*, 1 March 2005, 50; Laurence Bernstein, "Enough Research Bashing!" *Marketing*, 24 January 2005, 10; Naresh K. Malhotra, *Basic Marketing Research* (Upper Saddle River, N.J.: Pearson Prentice Hall, 2002), 110–112, 208–212, 228–229.

To avoid intensifying the vicious circle in which marketers keep doing the same old things, only louder and longer—leading customers to get angrier and more defensive—some marketers are looking for a better way. Social commerce shows a lot of promise for redefining marketing communication from one-way promotion to two-way conversation. Another hopeful sign is **permission-based marketing**, in which marketers invite potential or current customers to receive information in areas that genuinely interest them. Many websites now take this approach, letting visitors sign up for specific content streams with the promise that they won't be bombarded with information they don't care about.

The widespread adoption of social media has also increased the attention given to transparency, which in this context refers to a sense of openness, of giving all participants in a conversation access to the information they need in order to accurately process the messages they are receiving. A major issue in business communication transparency is **stealth marketing**, which involves attempting to promote products and services to customers who don't know they're being marketed to. A common stealth marketing technique is rewarding someone for promoting products to his or her friends without telling them it's a form of advertising. Critics—including the U.S. Federal Trade Commission (FTC) and the Word of Mouth Marketing Association—assert that such techniques are deceptive because they don't give their targets the opportunity to raise their instinctive defenses against the persuasive powers of marketing messages.[15]

Aside from ethical concerns, trying to fool the public is simply bad for business. As LaSalle University professor Michael Smith puts it, "The public backlash can be long, deep, and damaging to a company's reputation."[16]

permission-based marketing
A marketing approach in which firms first ask permission to deliver messages to an audience and then promise to restrict their communication efforts to those subject areas in which audience members have expressed interest.

stealth marketing
The delivery of marketing messages to people who are not aware that they are being marketed to; these messages can be delivered by either acquaintances or strangers, depending on the technique.

Checkpoint

LEARNING OBJECTIVE 2: Identify three trends that help define contemporary marketing.

SUMMARY: Three general issues that many marketing organizations are wrestling with today are involving the customer in the marketing process, making data-driven decisions, and conducting marketing with greater concern for ethics and etiquette. Allowing customers greater involvement is essential to relationship marketing and the marketing concept. Increasingly, this involvement is enabled by *social commerce*—customers using social media to converse with companies and each other. Data-driven decision making is a top priority as many companies struggle to justify and optimize marketing expenditures. Public opinion of business in general and marketing in particular is at a low point these days, prompting many professionals to take a closer look at their business practices and relationships with customers.

CRITICAL THINKING: (1) How can technology help companies replicate the community feel of a small neighborhood business on a global scale? (2) Why do some critics consider stealth marketing to be unethical?

IT'S YOUR BUSINESS: (1) Are you so loyal to any brands or companies that you refuse to accept substitutes—so much so that if you can't have your favorite product, you'll do without? What is it about these products that earns your continued loyalty? (2) Have you ever been a target of stealth marketing? If so, how did you feel about the company after you learned you had been marketed to without your knowledge?

KEY TERMS TO KNOW: customer relationship management (CRM), social commerce, marketing research, permission-based marketing, stealth marketing

---

3 **LEARNING OBJECTIVE**

Differentiate between consumer buying behavior and organizational buying behavior.

consumer market
Individuals or households that buy goods and services for personal use.

organizational market
Companies, government agencies, and other organizations that buy goods and services either to resell or to use in the creation of their own goods and services.

Understanding Today's Customers

To implement the marketing concept, companies must have good information about what customers want. Today's customers, both individual consumers and organizational buyers, are a diverse and demanding group, with little patience for marketers who do not understand them or will not adapt business practices to meet their needs. For instance, consumers faced with complex purchase decisions such as cars can now find extensive information online about products, prices, competitors, customer service rankings, safety issues, and other factors.

The first step toward understanding customers is recognizing the purchase and ownership habits of the **consumer market**, made up of individuals and families who buy for personal or household use, and the **organizational market**, composed of companies and a variety of noncommercial institutions, from local school districts to the federal government.

Exhibit 13.4 models two decision-making paths that buyers can take when they perceive the need to make a purchase, one for routine purchases and one for new, unusual, or highly significant purchases. Consumers and organizations can follow either path, depending on a specific purchase. Broadly speaking, however, organizational buyers tend to approach purchasing in a more rational, data-driven fashion, simply because organizational choices are nearly always about functional and financial value.

THE CONSUMER DECISION PROCESS

Think about several purchase decisions you've made recently. Classical economics suggests that your behavior would follow a rational process of first recognizing a need and then gathering information, identifying alternative solutions, and finally making

EXHIBIT 13.4   **Buyer Decision Making**

The steps buyers go through on the way to making a purchase vary widely, based on the magnitude of the purchase and the significance of the outcome. In general, businesses and other organizations use a more formal and more rational process than consumers, and nonroutine decisions in either sector require more time and energy than routine decisions. Defining routine is not a simple matter, however; a company might make huge resupply purchases automatically while a consumer spends days agonizing over a pair of jeans.

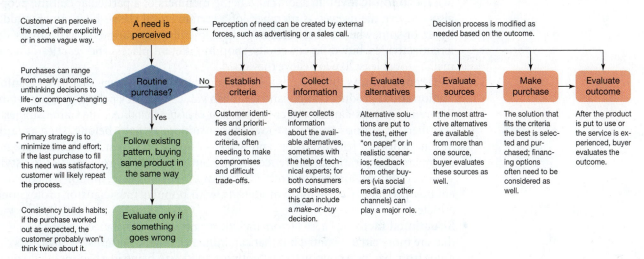

your choice from those alternatives. But how often do you really make decisions in this way? Researchers now understand that consumer behavior tends to be far less logical and far more complicated—and more interesting—than this model suggests. In fact, some research suggests that as much as 95 percent of the decision-making process is sub-conscious and that sensory cues can play a much larger role than objective information.[17] The emerging field of *behavioral economics* is starting to offer better insights into consumer behavior by incorporating a broader (and somewhat less-flattering) view of the way people really make decisions.[18]

Even in situations in which consumers gather lots of information and appear to be making a well-thought-out, rational decision, they often are acting more on gut feelings and emotional responses. For instance, you might see some jaw-dropping sports car glide past you on the street, and in that split second—before you even start "thinking" about it—you've already decided to buy one just like it. Sure, you'll gather brochures, do research on the Internet, test-drive other models, and so on, but chances are you're not really evaluating alternatives. Instead, your rational, conscious brain is just looking for evidence to support the decision that your emotional, semiconscious brain has already made.

Moreover, consumers make all kinds of decisions that are hard to explain by any rational means. We might spend two weeks gathering data on $200 music players but choose a college with a $20,000 annual tuition simply because a best friend is going there. Sometimes we buy things for no apparent reason other than the fact that we have money in our pockets. As a result, at one time or another, all consumers suffer from **cognitive dissonance**, which occurs when one's beliefs and behaviors don't match. A common form of this situation is *buyer's remorse*, in which one makes a purchase and then regrets doing so—sometimes immediately after the purchase.

REAL-TIME UPDATES
Learn More by Visiting This Website

What's hot in global consumer markets?

Follow Trendwatching.com's monthly reports on consumer trends around the world. Go to **http://real-timeupdates.com/bia8** and click on Learn More in the Students section.

cognitive dissonance
Tension that exists when a person's beliefs don't match his or her behaviors; a common example is *buyer's remorse*, when someone regrets a purchase immediately after making it.

You can start to understand why so many decisions seem mysterious from a rational point of view if you consider all the influences that affect purchases:

- **Culture.** The cultures (and subgroups within cultures) that people belong to shape their values, attitudes, and beliefs and influence the way they respond to the world around them.
- **Socioeconomic level.** In addition to being members of a particular culture, people also perceive themselves as members of a certain social class—be it upper, middle, lower, or somewhere in between. In general, members of various classes pursue different activities, buy different goods, shop in different places, and react to different media—or at least like to believe they do.
- **Reference groups.** Individuals are influenced by *reference groups* that provide information about product choices and establish values that they perceive as important. Reference groups can be either *membership* or *aspirational*. As the name suggests, membership groups are those to which consumers actually belong, such as families, networks of friends, clubs, and work groups. In contrast, consumers are not members of aspirational reference groups but use them as role models for style, speech, opinions, and various other behaviors.[19] For instance, millions of consumers buy products that help them identify with popular musicians or professional athletes.
- **Situational factors.** These factors include events or circumstances in people's lives that are more circumstantial but that can influence buying patterns. Such factors can range from having a coupon to celebrating a holiday to being in a bad mood. If you've ever indulged in "retail therapy" to cheer yourself up, you know all about situational factors—and the buyer's remorse that often comes with it.
- **Self-image.** Many consumers tend to believe that "you are what you buy," so they make or avoid choices that support their desired self-images. Marketers capitalize on people's need to express their identity through their purchases by emphasizing the image value of goods and services.

THE ORGANIZATIONAL CUSTOMER DECISION PROCESS

The purchasing behavior of organizations is easier to understand than the purchasing behavior of consumers because it's more clearly driven by economics and influenced less by subconscious and emotional factors. Here are some of the significant ways in which organizational purchasing differs from consumer purchasing:[20]

- **An emphasis on economic payback and other rational factors.** Much more so than with consumer purchases, organizational purchases are carefully evaluated for financial impact, reliability, and other objective factors. Organizations don't always make the best choices, of course, but their choices are usually based on a more rational analysis of needs and alternatives. This isn't to say that emotions play little or no role in the purchase decision, however; organizations don't make decisions, people do. Fear of change, fear of failure, excitement about new technologies, and the pride of being associated with world-class suppliers are just a few of the emotional factors that can influence organizational purchases.
- **A formal buying process.** From office supplies to new factories, most organizational purchases follow a formal buying process, particularly in mid- to large-size companies.
- **Greater complexity in product usage.** Even for the same types of products, organizational buyers have to worry about factors that consumers may never consider, such as user training, compatibility with existing systems and procedures, established purchasing agreements, and compliance with government regulations. In addition, the *network effect*, in which the value of a product increases with the number of customers who use it, can be a key decision driver.[21] A major reason that other software providers have so much trouble putting a dent in Microsoft's dominance of the corporate market is that business users

need compatibility, so it is simpler to select the tools that more people already use. Also, organizations sometimes continue to use products long after better substitutes become available if the costs and complexity of updating outweigh the advantages of the newer solutions.

- **The participation and influence of multiple people.** Except in the very smallest businesses, the purchase process usually involves a group of people. This team can include end users, technical experts, the manager with ultimate purchasing authority, and a professional purchasing agent whose job includes researching suppliers, negotiating prices, and evaluating supplier performance. Multiple family members play a part in many consumer purchases, of course, but not with the formality apparent in organizational markets.
- **Close relationships between buyers and sellers.** Close relationships between buyers and sellers are common in organizational purchasing. In some cases, employees of the seller even have offices inside the buyer's facility to promote close interaction.

✔ Checkpoint

LEARNING OBJECTIVE 3: Differentiate between consumer buying behavior and organizational buying behavior.

SUMMARY: Classical economic theory suggests that consumers follow a largely rational process of recognizing a need, searching for information, evaluating alternatives, making a purchase, and evaluating the product after use or consumption. However, research into behavioral economics and consumer psychology suggests that many consumer purchases are far less rational. Much of this decision making happens subconsciously and is driven to a large degree by emotion, culture, and situational factors. Organizational buying behavior comes much closer to the rational model of classical economics because purchases are usually judged by their economic value to the organization. The most significant ways in which organizational purchasing differs from consumer purchasing are an emphasis on economic payback, a formal buying process, greater complexity in product usage, purchasing groups, and close relationships between buyers and sellers.

CRITICAL THINKING: (1) Can business-to-business marketers take advantage of new insights into consumer buying behavior? Why or why not? (2) How could families and individual consumers benefit from adopting some elements of organizational buying behavior?

IT'S YOUR BUSINESS: (1) Do you read product reviews online before making important purchases? Why or why not? Have you ever contributed to social commerce by posting your own reviews or product advice? (2) Why did you buy the clothes you are wearing at this very moment?

KEY TERMS TO KNOW: consumer market, organizational market, cognitive dissonance

Identifying Market Opportunities

With insights into your customers' needs and behaviors, you're ready to begin planning your marketing strategies. **Strategic marketing planning** is a process that involves three steps: (1) examining the current marketing situation, (2) assessing opportunities and setting objectives, and (3) crafting a marketing strategy to reach those objectives (see Exhibit 13.5 on the next page). Companies often record the results of their planning efforts in a formal *marketing plan*.

4 LEARNING OBJECTIVE

Define *strategic marketing planning*, and identify the four basic options for pursuing new marketing opportunities.

strategic marketing planning
The process of examining an organization's current marketing situation, assessing opportunities and setting objectives, and then developing a marketing strategy to reach those objectives.

EXHIBIT 13.5   **The Strategic Marketing Planning Process**

Strategic marketing planning can involve a range of major decisions that fall into three general steps: (1) examining the current marketing situation, (2) assessing opportunities and setting objectives, and (3) developing a marketing strategy. The nature of these steps can vary widely depending on the products and markets involved; for example, emerging markets and mature markets have very different sets of customer and competitor dynamics.

1. Examine current marketing situation
- Review past performance
- Evaluate competition
- Examine strengths and weaknesses
- Analyze the business environment

2. Assess opportunities and set objectives
- Explore product and market opportunities
- Set sales targets that are invigorating while being realistic

3. Develop marketing strategy
- Divide market into strategically productive segments
- Choose best-fit segments
- Identify ideal position in minds of target customers
- Develop marketing mix

EXAMINING THE CURRENT MARKETING SITUATION

Examining your current marketing situation includes reviewing your past performance (how well each product is doing in each market where you sell it), evaluating your competition, examining your internal strengths and weaknesses, and analyzing the external environment.

Reviewing Performance

Unless you're starting a new business, your company has a history of marketing performance. Maybe sales have slowed in the past year, maybe you've had to cut prices so much that you're barely earning a profit, or maybe sales have been strong and you have money to invest in new marketing activities. Reviewing where you are and how you got there is critical because you want to learn from your mistakes and repeat your successes—without getting trapped in mindsets and practices that need to change for the future, even if they were successful in the past.

Evaluating Competition

In addition to reviewing past performance, you must evaluate your competition. If you own a Burger King franchise, for example, you need to watch what McDonald's and Wendy's are doing. You also have to keep an eye on Taco Bell, KFC, Pizza Hut, and other restaurants, as well as pay attention to any number of other ways your customers might satisfy their hunger—including fixing a sandwich at home. Furthermore, you need to watch the horizon for trends that could affect your business, such as consumer interest in organic foods or in locally produced ingredients.

Examining Internal Strengths and Weaknesses

Successful marketers try to identify sources of competitive advantage and areas that need improvement. They look at such factors as financial resources, production capabilities, distribution networks, brand awareness, business partnerships, managerial expertise, and promotional capabilities. (Recall the discussion of SWOT analysis on page 151.) On the basis of your internal analysis, you will be able to decide whether your business should (1) limit itself to those opportunities for which it possesses the required strengths or (2) challenge itself to reach higher goals by acquiring and developing new strengths.

Analyzing the External Environment

Marketers must also analyze trends and conditions in the business environment when planning their marketing strategies. For example, customer decisions are greatly affected by interest rates, inflation, unemployment, personal income, and savings rates. During recessions, consumers still aspire to enjoy the good life, but they are forced by circumstances to alter their spending patterns.[22] "Affordable luxuries" become particularly appealing during these times, for example. Recessions also create opportunities for agile and aggressive companies to take business away from companies weakened by poor sales and deteriorating finances.[23]

ASSESSING OPPORTUNITIES AND SETTING OBJECTIVES

After you've examined the current marketing situation, you're ready to assess your marketing opportunities and set your objectives. Successful companies are always on the lookout for new marketing opportunities, which can be classified into four options (see Exhibit 13.6).[24] **Market penetration** involves selling more of your existing products into the markets you already serve. **Product development** is creating new products for those current markets, and **market development** is selling your existing products to new markets. Finally, **diversification** involves creating new products for new markets.

Generally speaking, these four options are listed in order of increasing risk. Market penetration can be the least risky because your products already exist and the market has already demonstrated some level of demand for them. At the other extreme, creating new products for new markets is usually the riskiest choice of all because you encounter uncertainties in both dimensions (you may fail to create the product you need, and the market might not be interested in it).

After you've framed the opportunity you want to pursue, you are ready to set your marketing objectives. A common marketing objective is to achieve a certain level of **market share**, which is a firm's portion of the total sales within a market (market share can be defined by either number of units sold or by sales revenue).

market penetration
Selling more of a firm's existing products in the markets it already serves.

product development
Creating new products for a firm's current markets.

market development
Selling existing products to new markets.

diversification
Creating new products for new markets.

market share
A firm's portion of the total sales in a market.

EXHIBIT 13.6	Pursuing Market Opportunities

Every company has four basic options when it comes to pursuing market opportunities. The arrows show the increasing level of risk, from the lowest to the highest.

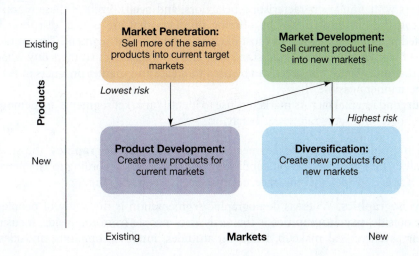

Checkpoint

LEARNING OBJECTIVE 4: Define *strategic marketing planning*, **and identify the four basic options for pursuing new marketing opportunities.**

SUMMARY: Strategic marketing planning involves three steps: (1) examining the current marketing situation (including past performance, competition, internal strengths and weaknesses, and the external environment); (2) assessing market opportunities and setting marketing objectives; and (3) developing a marketing strategy to reach those objectives. The four basic options for pursuing market opportunities are *market penetration* (selling more existing products in current markets), *product development* (creating new products for current markets), *market development* (selling existing products to new markets), and *diversification* (creating new products for new markets).

CRITICAL THINKING: (1) Why is it important to analyze past performance before assessing market opportunities and setting objectives? (2) Why is diversification considered riskier than market penetration, product development, and market development strategies?

IT'S YOUR BUSINESS: (1) Do you see yourself as a trendsetter in any aspect of your life? (2) How could the four options for pursuing market opportunities be applied to your career planning at various stages in your career? (Think of your skills as the products you have to offer.)

KEY TERMS TO KNOW: strategic marketing planning, market penetration, product development, market development, diversification, market share

---

5 LEARNING OBJECTIVE

Describe the four main components of the marketing mix.

marketing strategy
An overall plan for marketing a product; includes the identification of target market segments, a positioning strategy, and a marketing mix.

market
A group of customers who need or want a particular product and have the money to buy it.

market segmentation
The division of a diverse market into smaller, relatively homogeneous groups with similar needs, wants, and purchase behaviors.

demographics
The study of the statistical characteristics of a population.

psychographics
Classification of customers on the basis of their psychological makeup, interests, and lifestyles.

Crafting a Marketing Strategy

Using the current marketing situation and your objectives as your guide, you're ready to develop a **marketing strategy**, which consists of dividing your market into *segments*, choosing your *target markets* and the *position* you'd like to establish in those markets, and then developing a *marketing mix* to help you get there.

DIVIDING MARKETS INTO SEGMENTS

A **market** contains all the customers who might be interested in a product and can pay for it. However, most markets contain subgroups of potential customers with different interests, values, and behaviors. To maximize their effectiveness in reaching these subgroups, many companies subdivide the total market through **market segmentation**, grouping customers with similar characteristics, behaviors, and needs. Each of these market segments can then be approached by offering products that are priced, distributed, and promoted in a unique way that is most likely to appeal to that segment. The overall goal of market segmentation is to understand why and how certain customers buy what they buy so that one's finite resources can be used to create and market products in the most efficient manner possible.[25]

Four fundamental factors marketers use to identify market segments are demographics, psychographics, geography, and behavior:

- **Demographics.** When you segment a market using **demographics**, the statistical analysis of a population, you subdivide your customers according to characteristics such as age, gender, income, race, occupation, and ethnic group.

- **Psychographics.** Whereas demographic segmentation is the study of people from the outside, **psychographics** is the analysis of people from the inside, focusing on their psychological makeup, including attitudes, interests, opinions, and lifestyles.

Psychographic analysis focuses on why people behave the way they do by examining such issues as brand preferences, media preferences, values, self-concept, and behavior.

- **Geography.** When differences in buying behavior are influenced by where people live, it makes sense to use **geographic segmentation**. Segmenting the market into geographic units such as regions, cities, counties, or neighborhoods allows companies to customize and sell products that meet the needs of specific markets and to organize their operations as needed.

- **Behavior. Behavioral segmentation** groups customers according to their relationship with products or response to product characteristics. To identify behavioral segments, marketers study such factors as the occasions that prompt people to buy certain products, the particular benefits they seek from a product, their habits and frequency of product usage, and the degree of loyalty they show toward a brand.[26]

Starting with these variables, researchers can also combine types of data to identify target segments with even greater precision, such as merging geographic, demographic, and behavioral data to define specific types of consumer neighborhoods.

CHOOSING YOUR TARGET MARKETS

After you have segmented your market, the next step is to find appropriate target segments, or **target markets**, on which to focus your efforts. Marketers use a variety of criteria to narrow their focus to a few suitable market segments, including the magnitude of potential sales within each segment, the cost of reaching those customers, the fit with a firm's core competencies, and any risks in the business environment.

Exhibit 13.7 diagrams four strategies for reaching target markets. Companies that practice *undifferentiated marketing* (also known as *mass marketing*) ignore differences among buyers and offer only one product or product line and present it with the same communication, pricing, and distribution strategies to all potential buyers. Undifferentiated marketing has the advantages of simplicity and economies of scale, but it can be less effective at reaching some portions of the market.

By contrast, companies that manufacture or sell a variety of products to several target customer groups practice *differentiated marketing*. This is Toyota's approach, for

geographic segmentation
Categorization of customers according to their geographical location.

behavioral segmentation
Categorization of customers according to their relationship with products or response to product characteristics.

target markets
Specific customer groups or segments to whom a company wants to sell a particular product.

EXHIBIT 13.7	Market-Coverage Strategies

Four alternative market-coverage strategies are undifferentiated marketing, differentiated marketing, concentrated marketing, and micromarketing.

Source: Based on Philip Kotler and Gary Armstrong, *Principles of Marketing*, 13th ed. (Upper Saddle River, N.J.: Pearson Prentice Hall, 2010), 201–207.

example, aiming the Scion brand at young buyers, the Toyota brand at its core audience, and the Lexus brand at those wanting luxury cars. Differentiated marketing is a popular strategy, but it requires substantial resources because the company has to tailor products, prices, promotional efforts, and distribution arrangements for each customer group. The differentiation should be based on meaningful differences that don't alienate any audiences.

Concentrated marketing focuses on only a single market segment. With this approach, you acknowledge that various other market segments may exist but you choose to target just one. The biggest advantage of concentrated marketing is that it allows you to focus all your time and resources on a single type of customer (which is why this approach is usually the best option for start-up companies, by the way). The strategy can be risky, however, because you've staked your fortunes on just one segment.

Micromarketing, or *individualized marketing*, is the narrowest strategy of all, in which firms target a single location or even a single customer.[27] This approach can range from producing customizable products to creating *major accounts* sales teams that craft entire marketing programs for each of their largest customers.

Achieving success in any market segment can take time and significant investment, so embracing market segments for the long term is essential. In fact, many companies now think in terms of *customer lifetime value:* the total potential revenue from each customer over a certain time span minus the cost of attracting and keeping that customer. This approach lets companies focus on their most valuable customers while deciding what to do with their less-profitable customers (such as abandoning those customers or changing marketing strategies to make pursuing them more profitable).[28]

REAL-TIME UPDATES
Learn More by Reading This Article

How established companies are trying to compete against "digital disrupters"

Highly focused start-ups often zero in on one piece of an established company's business or one key weakness. Go to **http://real-timeupdates.com/bia8** and click on Learn More in the Students section.

STAKING OUT A POSITION IN YOUR TARGET MARKETS

positioning
Managing a business in a way designed to occupy a particular place in the minds of target customers.

After you have decided which segments of the market to enter, your next step is to decide what *position* you want to occupy in those segments. **Positioning** is the process of designing a company's offerings, messages, and operating policies so that both the company and its products occupy distinct and desirable competitive positions in your target customers' minds. For instance, for every product category that you care about as a consumer, you have some ranking of desirability in your mind—you believe that certain colleges are more prestigious than others, that certain brands of shoes are more fashionable than others, that one video game system is better than the others, and so on. Successful marketers are careful to choose the position they'd like to occupy in buyers' minds.

In their attempts to secure favorable positions, marketers can emphasize such variables as product attributes, customer service, brand image (such as reliability or sophistication), price (such as low cost or premium), or category leadership (such as the leading online bookseller). For example, BMW and Porsche work to associate their products with performance, Mercedes Benz with luxury, and Volvo with safety.

A vital and often overlooked aspect of positioning is that although marketers take all kinds of steps to position their products, it is *customers* who ultimately decide on the positioning: They're the ones who interpret the many messages they encounter in the marketplace and decide what they think and feel about each product. For example, you can advertise that you have a luxury product, but if consumers aren't convinced, it's not really positioned as a luxury product. The only result that matters is what the customer believes. One auto industry marketing executive put it this way: "Everyone works so hard to control and define what their brand stands for, when they ought to just let the consumer do it."[29]

REAL-TIME UPDATES
Learn More by Reading This Article

Marketing a museum in the social media age

See how the venerated Tate collection of museums in the United Kingdom applies marketing concepts to attract visitors and enhance their museum experiences. Go to **http://real-timeupdates.com/bia8** and click on Learn More in the Students section.

✔ Checkpoint

LEARNING OBJECTIVE 5: Identify the four steps in crafting a marketing strategy.

SUMMARY: Crafting a marketing strategy involves dividing your market into *segments*, choosing your *target markets* and the *position* you *marketing mix* to help you get there. Segmentation (using demographics, psychographics, geography, and behavior) allows a company to select parts of the market most likely to respond to specific marketing programs. Companies can use one of four approaches to selecting target markets: undifferentiated (mass) marketing, differentiated marketing (with a different marketing mix for each segment), concentrated marketing (focusing on a single market segment), and micromarketing or individualized marketing. A *position* refers to the position a company or brand occupies in the mind of the target market segments.

CRITICAL THINKING: (1) Would two companies interested in the same group of customers automatically use the same target market approach (such as differentiated or concentrated)? Why or why not? (2) Why aren't marketers ultimately in control of the positions their products achieve in the marketplace?

IT'S YOUR BUSINESS: (1) Think of three car brands or specific models. How are these products positioned in your mind? What terms do you use to describe them? (2) Given your transportation needs in the near future (assuming you will need a car), which model is the most desirable? The least desirable?

KEY TERMS TO KNOW: marketing strategy, market, market segmentation, demographics, psychographics, geographic segmentation, behavioral segmentation, target markets, positioning

The Marketing Mix

After you've segmented your market, selected your target market, and taken steps to position your product, your next task is to develop a marketing mix. A firm's **marketing mix** consists of product, price, distribution, and customer communication (see Exhibit 13.8). (You might also hear references to "the four Ps" of the marketing mix, which is short for products,

EXHIBIT 13.8	**The Marketing Mix**

The marketing mix consists of four key elements: the products a company offers to potential buyers, the price it asks in return, its methods of distributing those products to customers, and the various efforts it makes to communicate with customers before and after the sale.

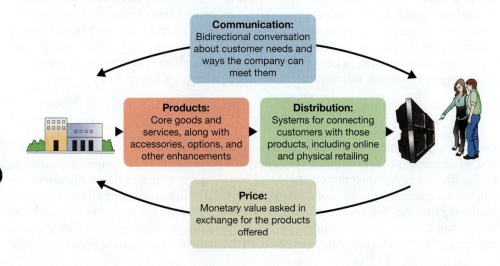

Communication: Bidirectional conversation about customer needs and ways the company can meet them

Products: Core goods and services, along with accessories, options, and other enhancements

Distribution: Systems for connecting customers with those products, including online and physical retailing

Price: Monetary value asked in exchange for the products offered

pricing, place or physical distribution, and promotion. However, with the advent of digital goods and services, distribution is no longer exclusively a physical concern. And many companies now view customer communication as a broader and more interactive activity than the functions implied by *promotion*.)

PRODUCTS

product
A bundle of value that satisfies a customer need or want.

In common usage, *product* usually refers to a tangible good, whereas *service* refers to an intangible performance. However, for the purposes of studying marketing, it is helpful to define **product** as the bundle of value offered for the purpose of satisfying a want or a need in a marketing exchange. In this expanded definition, both tangible goods and intangible services are considered products. The reason for taking this broader view of *product* is that it encourages a more holistic look at the entire offering, which can include the brand name, design, packaging, support services, warranty, ownership experience, and other attributes.

For example, if you buy a pair of $200 Dolce & Gabbana sunglasses with the brand's prominent "DG" initials on the side, you are buying much more than a device that holds a couple of protective lenses in front of your eyes. You are buying a shopping and ownership experience that is distinctly different from that for buying a pair of $5 sunglasses from a discount drugstore. You are buying the opportunity to feel a particular way about yourself and to present a particular image to the world around you. You are buying the right to brand yourself with the Dolce & Gabbana brand and everything that brand means to you. All these elements constitute the Dolce & Gabbana product. You'll explore products in more detail in Chapter 14.

PRICING

price
The amount of money charged for a product or service.

Price, the amount of money customers pay for the product (including any discounts), is the second major component of a firm's marketing mix. Looking back at Kotler and Armstrong's definition of marketing, price is the *value captured* from customers in exchange for the value offered in the product. Setting and managing a product's price is one of the most critical decisions a company must make because price is the only element in a company's marketing mix that produces revenue; all other elements represent costs. Moreover, setting a product's price not only determines income but also can differentiate a product from the competition. Determining the right price is not an easy task, and marketers constantly worry whether they've turned away profitable customers by charging too much or "left money on the table" by charging too little.

A number of factors influence pricing decisions, including marketing objectives, government regulations, production costs, customer perceptions, competition, and customer demand. A company's costs establish the minimum amount it can charge, and the various external forces establish the maximum. Somewhere in between those two extremes lies an optimum price point. Products also exhibit different levels of *price elasticity*, which is a measure of how sensitive customers are to changes in price. If you don't have a smartphone yet and the price of such phones drops by 25 percent, you might well be tempted to buy one. In contrast, if the price of broccoli drops by 25 percent, chances are you won't eat more veggies as a result. You can read more about pricing in Chapter 14.

DISTRIBUTION

distribution channels
Systems for moving goods and services from producers to customers; also known as marketing channels.

Distribution is the third marketing-mix element. It covers the organized network of firms and systems that move goods and services from the producer to the customer. This network is also known as *marketing channels, marketing intermediaries,* or **distribution channels**. As you can imagine, channel decisions are interdependent with virtually everything else in the marketing mix. Key factors in distribution planning include customer needs and expectations, market coverage, distribution costs, competition, positioning, customer support requirements, and sales support requirements. For example, when AstraZeneca introduced a cancer drug with potentially significant side effects, it released the drug through a single specialty pharmacy so that it could manage pharmacist and doctor training more closely.[30]

Marketing intermediaries perform a variety of essential marketing functions, including providing information to customers, providing feedback to manufacturers, providing sales support, gathering assortments of goods from multiple producers to make shopping easier for customers, and transporting and storing goods. These intermediaries fall into two general categories: *wholesalers* and *retailers*. The basic distinction between them is that wholesalers sell to other companies whereas retailers sell to individual consumers. Across industries, you can find tremendous variety in the types of wholesalers and retailers, from independent representatives who sell products from several manufacturers to huge distribution companies with national or international scope to purely digital retailers such as Apple's iTunes service. You can read more about distribution in Chapter 15.

CUSTOMER COMMUNICATION

In traditional marketing thought, the fourth element of the marketing mix is **promotion**, all the activities a firm undertakes to promote its products to target customers. The goals of promotion include *informing*, *persuading*, and *reminding*. Among these activities are advertising in a variety of media, personal selling, public relations, and sales promotion. Promotion may take the form of direct, face-to-face communication or indirect communication through such media as television, radio, magazines, newspapers, direct mail, billboards, transit ads, social media, and other channels.

promotion
A wide variety of persuasive techniques used by companies to communicate with their target markets and the general public.

However, as "Involving the Customer in the Marketing Process" on page 300 points out, forward-thinking companies have moved beyond the unidirectional approach of promotion to interactive customer communication. By talking *with* their customers instead of *at* their customers, marketers get immediate feedback on everything from customer service problems to new product ideas. As you'll read in the Behind the Scenes at the end of the chapter, Sarah Calhoun and her company Red Ants Pants excel at authentic, engaging communication with customers and potential buyers.

Promotion is still a vital part of customer communication, but by encouraging two-way conversations, whether it's two people talking across a desk or an online network spread across the globe, marketers can also learn while they are informing, persuading, and reminding. Moreover, by replacing "sales pitches" with conversations and giving customers some control over the dialogue, marketers can also help break down some of the walls and filters that audiences have erected after years of conventional marketing promotion.[31] Chapter 16 offers a closer look at customer communication.

For the latest information on marketing principles, visit http://real-timeupdates .com/bia8 and click on Chapter 13.

✓ **Checkpoint**

LEARNING OBJECTIVE 7: Describe the four main components of the marketing mix.

SUMMARY: The four elements of the marketing mix are product, price, distribution, and customer communication. Products are goods, services, persons, places, ideas, organizations, or anything else offered for the purpose of satisfying a want or need in a marketing exchange. Price is the amount of money customers pay for the product. Distribution is the organized network of firms that move the goods and services from the producer to the customer. Customer communication involves the activities used to communicate with and promote products to target markets.

CRITICAL THINKING: (1) Why is price sometimes referred to as *captured value*? (2) Why do companies that embrace relationship marketing focus on "customer communication" rather than "promotion"?

IT'S YOUR BUSINESS: (1) If you could buy a product from a website or a store right down the street and the prices were the same, where would you make your purchase? Why? (2) When buying products, do you tend to seek out products with visible logos (such as the Nike swoosh or the Dolce & Gabbana initials), or do you shun such products? Or do you not care one way or the other? Why?

KEY TERMS TO KNOW: marketing mix, product, price, distribution channels, promotion

BEHIND THE SCENES
AGGRAVATION LEADS TO INSPIRATION FOR SARAH CALHOUN OF RED ANTS PANTS

As with many other entrepreneurs, frustration was the source of inspiration for Sarah Calhoun. When she couldn't find rugged work pants designed for women, she decided to fill this unmet market need herself. A chance encounter in a coffee shop with an experienced apparel industry insider (who noticed she was reading *Starting a Business for Dummies*) convinced her that a real opportunity was there and waiting for someone to pursue it.

Calhoun based all three key elements of her marketing strategy—segmentation, target market selection, and positioning—on her mission of pursuing this opportunity. She founded Red Ants Pants with the singular focus on providing hardwearing pants for hardworking women, meeting the needs of customers whose work makes clothing a matter of practical utility and even on-the-job safety.

Red Ants Pants are made from tough, heavy cloth and in both "straight" and "curvy" styles to provide a better fit for more women. In addition, they come in two or three times as many waist/inseam combinations as typical pants, greatly increasing the chance that every woman will find exactly the size she needs.

In keeping with the capacity of a small business and the nature of her product offerings, simplicity is the key word in the product mix. Pants are available in exactly one color: chocolate brown. (It was only after buying $45,000 worth of the practical fabric that Calhoun learned "chocolate brown is the new black" in the fashion world.) A few years after introducing the pants, she expanded the product portfolio with a handful of complementary products, including shirts, hats, and belts.

Calhoun is adamant about keeping production in the United States, too, a rarity in the clothing business, where most production is outsourced to low-cost labor centers in other countries. Instead, she chose a mother/daughter-owned factory two states over, in Seattle, and she views supporting quality jobs in this country as "part of my responsibility as a business owner." Referring to her production partners, she says, "They have 23 employees who are treated well, paid well, and enjoy good working conditions."

At $129 a pair, the pants are not bargain-bin items, to be sure. However, like many purveyors of high-quality products, Calhoun emphasizes value, noting that customers would wear out several pairs of cheaper pants in the time they might wear out a single pair of Red Ants. Plus, the price reflects the structure she has chosen for her business: not offshoring in pursuit of the lowest possible production costs. At the rate her sales are growing, customers apparently agree that it's a fair price to pay for pants that keep them safe and comfortable on the job.

Distribution strategy was one of Calhoun's most important marketing and business decisions. Clothes in general and pants in particular are products for which individual fit and function can't be absolutely confirmed until the customer tries them on. Having her products available in hundreds of retail outlets would let more customers try them on—and give her tremendous visibility in the market. However, it would also put her at the mercy of retailers' demands regarding price and inventory. She opted to function as her own distribution channel, selling from her website, over the phone, and from her storefront operation in White Sulphur Springs, Montana. Having so many sizing options helps ensure that pants fit when customers receive them, but as with most online clothing retailers, she invites customers to exchange pants that don't fit.

Like millions of other small companies in recent years, Red Ants Pants has taken advantage of technology to overcome distribution hurdles. Calhoun explains, "The old quote of retail being location, location, location doesn't hold up as much. I have Internet and I have UPS and mail service, and that's all I need."

Customer communication is another aspect of the marketing mix in which Calhoun demonstrates both the greater flexibility that small companies often have compared to their larger, "more corporate" competitors—and the need to exercise creative brain power over brute-force budget power. Her communication style is more fun and more daring that the typical corporation would attempt, for example, and it seems to resonate with buyers. How many clothing companies would use photographs (discreetly staged, to be sure) to suggest that hardworking women would rather wear no pants than wear pants that don't fit?

Without a significant marketing budget, Calhoun looks for low-cost, high-visibility ways to reach customers. Her most unusual is hitting the highway in an ant-decorated Airstream travel trailer with her sales manager on trips they call the "Tour de Pants." They invite women to stage in-home gatherings, much like old-school Tupperware parties. Through visiting customers in their homes and hearing stories about women working in what are often male-dominated professions, Calhoun also gains invaluable marketing research insights.

Calhoun's most ambitious communication effort so far has been sponsoring the Red Ants Pants Music Festival, which has attracted such major Americana artists as Lyle Lovett and Guy Clark. All profits go to the Red Ants Pants Foundation, which she started to "support family farms and ranches, women in business, and rural initiatives."

The combination of meeting customer needs with quality products and a creative marketing effort is paying off. Red Ants Pants now has customers all across the country and around the world, from Europe to Australia, and even women working the

research stations in Antarctica. Are customers satisfied with the product? "Putting on these pants was a religious experience," is how one phrased it.[32]

Critical Thinking Questions

13-1. How might Calhoun's decision to keep production in the United States help solidify her market position in the minds of her target customers?

13-2. If Red Ants Pants had investors looking for a quick return, how might that influence Calhoun's decision to continue functioning as her own retail channel, rather than going through established retailers?

13-3. How could meeting small groups of women in their homes to talk about pants possibly be an efficient communication strategy?

LEARN MORE ONLINE

Explore the Red Ants Pants website, at **www.redantspants.com**, and follow the links to the company's Facebook page, YouTube channel, and Twitter account. How are the various elements of the marketing mix represented? How does the style of communication help Red Ants Pants connect with customers? What sort of practical information is provided to help customers select and order products?

KEY TERMS

behavioral segmentation (311)
cause-related marketing (297)
cognitive dissonance (305)
consumer market (304)
customer loyalty (299)
customer relationship management (300)
demographics (310)
distribution channels (314)
diversification (309)
exchange process (298)
geographic segmentation (311)
market (310)
market development (309)
market penetration (309)
market segmentation (310)
market share (309)
marketing (297)
marketing concept (298)
marketing mix (313)

marketing research (302)
marketing strategy (310)
needs (297)
organizational market (304)
permission-based marketing (303)
place marketing (297)
positioning (312)
price (314)
product (314)
product development (309)
promotion (315)
psychographics (310)
relationship marketing (299)
social commerce (300)
stealth marketing (303)
strategic marketing planning (307)
target markets (311)
transaction (298)
utility (298)
wants (298)

MyBizLab®

To complete the problems with the ⭐,
go to EOC Discussion Questions in the
MyLab.

TEST YOUR KNOWLEDGE

Questions for Review

13-4. Why are companies pushing for more accountability from the marketing function?

13-5. How does the organizational market differ from the consumer market?

13-6. What is strategic marketing planning, and what is its purpose?

13-7. What external environmental factors affect strategic marketing decisions?

13-8. What are the four basic components of the marketing mix?

Questions for Analysis

13-9. Why would consumers knowingly buy counterfeit luxury brands?

13-10. Should companies open themselves up to criticism by being active on social media? Why or why not?

13-11. Why does a company need to consider its current marketing situation, including competitive trends, when setting objectives for market share?

13-12. Why do companies segment markets?

⭐ **13-13. Ethical Considerations.** Is it ethical to observe shoppers for the purposes of marketing research without their knowledge and permission? Why or why not?

Questions for Application

⭐ **13-14.** How might a retailer use relationship marketing to improve customer loyalty?

13-15. Think of a product you recently purchased and review your decision process. Why did you need or want that product? How did the product's marketing influence your purchase decision? How did you investigate the product before making your purchase decision? Did you experience cognitive dissonance after your decision?

⭐ **13-16.** If you were launching a new manufacturing company, would you draft your marketing plan or design your production processes first? Why?

13-17. Concept Integration. How might the key economic indicators discussed in Chapter 2, including consumer price index, inflation, and unemployment, affect a company's marketing decisions?

EXPAND YOUR KNOWLEDGE

Discovering Career Opportunities

Jobs in marketing cover a wide range of activities, including a variety of jobs such as personal selling, advertising, marketing research, product management, and public relations. You can get more information about various marketing positions by consulting the *Occupational Outlook Handbook* (www.bls.gov/ooh), job-search websites such as Career Builder (www.careerbuilder.com) and Monster (www.monster.com), and other individual company websites resources.

13-18. Select a marketing job that interests you, and use the sites just mentioned to find out more about this career path. What specific duties and responsibilities do people in this position typically handle?

13-19. Find two openings in the field you are researching. What educational background, work experience, and other qualifications are employers seeking in candidates for this position?

13-20. Now think about your talents, interests, and goals. How do your strengths fit with the requirements, duties, and responsibilities of this job? Do you think you would find this field enjoyable and rewarding? Why?

Improving Your Tech Insights: Search Engines

As most every web user knows, search engines identify individual webpages that contain specific words or phrases you've asked for. Search engines have the advantage of scanning millions of individual webpages, and they use powerful ranking algorithms to present the pages that are likely to be the most relevant to your search request. Because each engine uses a proprietary and secret algorithm to rank the displayed results, multiple engines can display different result sets for the same query.

To see how search engines can return markedly different results, search with the phrase "Apple market share" (use the quotation marks) using Google, Yahoo! and Bing. In a brief email message to your instructor, describe the differences and similarities among the three search results. If you were researching a report on Apple's financial prospects, which set of results would be most helpful? Did you see any search results that were more than a year out of date? Based on this one test, which of the three engines would you be most likely to use for your next research project?

PRACTICE YOUR SKILLS

Sharpening Your Communication Skills

In small groups, as assigned by your instructor, take turns interviewing each person in the group about a product that each person absolutely loves or detests. Try to probe for the real reasons behind the emotions, touching on all the issues you read about in this chapter, from self-image to reference groups. Do you see any trends in the group's collective answers? Do people learn anything about themselves when answering the group's questions? Does anyone get defensive about his or her reasons for loving or hating a product? Be prepared to share with the class at least two marketing insights you learned through this exercise.

Building Your Team Skills

In the course of planning a marketing strategy, marketers need to analyze the external environment to consider how forces outside the firm may create new opportunities and challenges. One important environmental factor for merchandise buyers at a retailer such as Target is weather conditions. For example, when merchandise buyers for lawn and garden products think about the assortment and number of products to purchase for the chain's stores, they don't place any orders without first poring over long-range weather forecasts for each market. In particular, temperature and precipitation predictions for the coming

12 months are critical to the company's marketing plan, because they offer clues to consumer demand for barbecues, lawn furniture, gardening tools, and other merchandise.

What other products would benefit from examining weather forecasts? With your team, brainstorm to identify at least three types of products (in addition to lawn and garden items) for which Target should examine the weather as part of its analysis of the external environment. Share your recommendations with the entire class. How many teams identified the same products your team did?

Developing Your Research Skills

From recent issues of business journals and newspapers, select an article that describes in some detail a particular company's attempt to build relationships with its customers (either in general or for a particular product or product line).

13-21. Describe the company's market. What geographic, demographic, behavioral, or psychographic segments of the market is the company targeting?

13-22. How does the company communicate with and learn about its customers?

13-23. According to the article, how successful has the company been in understanding its customers?

MyBizLab®

Go to the Assignments section of your MyLab to complete these writing exercises.

13-24. If you have a product that appeals to the majority of consumers in a given market, would there be any value in segmenting the market before launching the product? Why or why not?

13-25. Is there still any need for traditional marketing techniques in a world of social commerce? Why or why not?

ENDNOTES

1. Red Ants Pants website, accessed 21 April 21, 2015, www.redantspants.com; Becky Warren, "Ants on the Pants," *Country Woman*, February–March 2011, www.countrywomanmagazine.com Dan Testa, "Red Ants Pants: By Working Women, for Working Women," *Flathead Beacon*, 4 March 2010, www.flatheadbeacon.com; Sammi Johnson, "Outdoor Woman: Red Ants Pants," *406 Woman*, April/May 2010, 52–53; Beth Judy, "Fit for Her," *Montana Magazine*, March–April 2010, 14–16; *Montana Quarterly*, Summer 2010, www.redantspants.com; Devan Grote, "Red Ants Pants," *Gettysburg*, Spring 2009, www.redantspants.com.

2. Philip Kotler and Gary Armstrong, *Principles of Marketing*, 13th ed. (Upper Saddle River, N.J.: Pearson Prentice Hall, 2010), 5.

3. Kotler and Armstrong, *Principles of Marketing*, 6.

4. BizXchange website, accessed 21 April 2015, www.bizx.com.

5. June Lee Risser, "Customers Come First," *Marketing Management*, November/December 2003, 22–26.

6. Ranjay Gulati and James B. Oldroyd, "The Quest for Customer Focus," *Harvard Business Review*, April 2005, 92–101.

7. Jonathan L. Yarmis, "How Facebook Will Upend Advertising," *BusinessWeek*, 28 May 2008, www.businessweek.com

8. Paul Gunning, "Social Media Reality Check," *Adweek*, 8 June 2008, 18.

9. Jeremiah Owyang, "When Social Media Marries CRM Systems," Web Strategy blog, 3 June 2008, www.web-strategist.com.

10. "Sorry, John," *Adweek*, 22 June 2009, 9.

11. Dominique M. Hanssens, Daniel Thorpe, and Carl Finkbeiner, "Marketing When Customer Equity Matters," *Harvard Business Review*, May 2008, 117–123.

12. Google Analytics, accessed 11 November 2013, www.google.com/analytics.

13. Eric Almquist, Martin Kon, and Wolfgang Bock, "The Science of Demand," *Marketing Management*, March/April 2004, 20–26; David C. Swaddling and Charles Miller, "From Understanding to Action," *Marketing Management*, July/August 2004, 31–35.

14. "Marketing Under Fire," *Marketing Management*, July/August 2004, 5.

15. Word of Mouth Marketing Association, "WOM 101," http://womma.org; Nate Anderson, "FTC Says Stealth Marketing Unethical," *Ars Technica*, 13 December 2006, http://arstechnica.com; "Undercover Marketing Uncovered," *CBSnews.com*, 25 July 2004, www.cbsnews.com; Stephanie Dunnewind, "Teen Recruits Create Word-of-Mouth 'Buzz' to Hook Peers on Products," *Seattle Times*, 20 November 2004, www.seattletimes.com.

16. Pophal, "Tweet Ethics: Trust and Transparency in a Web 2.0 World."

17. Dan Hill, "Why They Buy," *Across the Board*, November–December 2003, 27–32; Eric Roston, "The Why of Buy," *Time*, April 2004.

18. Dan Ariely, "The End of Rational Economics," *Harvard Business Review*, July/August 2009, 78–84.

19. Michael R. Solomon, *Consumer Behavior*, 6th ed. (Upper Saddle River, N.J.: Pearson Prentice Hall, 2004), 366–372.

20. Based in part on James C. Anderson and James A. Narus, *Business Market Management: Understanding, Creating, and Delivering Value*, 2nd ed. (Upper Saddle River, N.J.: Pearson Prentice Hall, 2004), 114–116.

21. Gerard J. Tellis, Eden Yin, and Rakesh Niraj, "Does Quality Win? Network Effects Versus Quality in High-Tech Markets," *Journal of Marketing Research*, May 2009, 135–149.

22. Eric Beinhocker, Ian Davis, and Lenny Mendonca, "The 10 Trends You Have to Watch," *Harvard Business Review*, July/August 2009, 55–60.

23. Beinhocker et al., "The 10 Trends You Have to Watch."

24. Kotler and Armstrong, *Principles of Marketing*, 43–46.

25. Gordon A. Wyner, "Pulling the Right Levers," *Marketing Management*, July/August 2004, 8–9.

26. Kotler and Armstrong, *Principles of Marketing*, 196–197.

27. Kotler and Armstrong, *Principles of Marketing*, 205–207.

28. Detlef Schoder, "The Flaw in Customer Lifetime Value," *Harvard Business Review*, December 2007, 26.

29. Mark Rechtin, "Scion's Dilemma," *AutoWeek*, 23 May 2006, www.autoweek.com.

30. Caprelsa website, accessed 11 November 2013, www.caprelsarems.com; Ben Comer, "AstraZeneca Signs Exclusive Distribution Deal for Vandetanib," *PharmExec.com*, 27 April 2011, http://blog.pharmexec.com.

31. Paul Gillin, *The New Influencers: A Marketer's Guide to the New Social Media* (Sanger, Calif.: Quill Driver Books, 2007), xi.

32. See Note 1.

LEARNING OBJECTIVES   After studying this chapter, you will be able to

1 Identify the main types of consumer and organizational products, and describe the four stages in the life cycle of a product.

2 Describe six stages in the product development process.

3 Define *brand*, and explain the concepts of brand equity and brand loyalty.

4 Identify four ways of expanding a product line, and discuss two risks that product-line extensions pose.

5 List the factors that influence pricing decisions, and explain break-even analysis.

6 Identify nine common pricing methods.

BEHIND THE SCENES   TRANSFORMING A WORLD-CLASS ATHLETE INTO A WORLD-CLASS BRAND

Marc Serota/Getty Images

Retired professional golfer Annika Sörenstam built a brand image to power her postgolf business career.

www.annikasorenstam.com

Start reading a list of Annika Sörenstam's accomplishments on the golf course, and you might have to stop halfway through and take a nap. Here's the short version: 89 tournament wins worldwide, including 10 major championships, and more than $20 million in prize winnings, with many millions more in product endorsements. Before she stepped away from competitive golf, she dominated the women's professional circuit as no one in recent memory had done before. And she rose high enough to achieve that ultimate badge of celebrity: one-name status. Millions of golf fans don't need to hear a last name; for them, she is simply Annika.

Her career on the course has clearly been a resounding success. But having achieved more before age 40 than most people could hope to achieve in several lifetimes, Sörenstam isn't ready to stop. In fact, she started all over again, this time in a multifaceted business career.

As a competitive athlete, Sörenstam always liked to measure herself against the best of the best. In her new career, she is once again measuring herself against top performers, including such figures as basketball star Michael Jordan. Retired golfers Arnold Palmer, Jack Nicklaus, and Greg Norman are particularly apt role models, as they have built golf-centric business empires and having remained vibrant public figures years after hitting their last competitive shots.

Sörenstam believes it's high time a woman joined their ranks. "Ask a person on the street to name five male athletes who have made a name for themselves outside their sport—no problem," she says. "Ask the same question about women athletes? They can't name one." She plans to be the first. What advice would you give her to make the transition from golf star to business star, from Annika the athlete to Annika the brand?[1]

INTRODUCTION

This chapter explores two of the four elements in the marketing mix, product and price. Annika Sörenstam's challenge in defining the Annika brand (profiled in the chapter-opening Behind the Scenes) is an essential part of product strategy. She also faces another challenge that you'll read more about in this chapter: assembling the right mix of goods and services as part of a firm's overall product mix. Finally, as in every business, Sörenstam has to engage in careful financial analysis and make shrewd pricing decisions to stay both competitive and profitable.

Characteristics of Products

1   **LEARNING OBJECTIVE**

Identify the main types of consumer and organizational products, and describe the four stages in the life cycle of a product.

As the central element in every company's exchanges with its customers, products naturally command a lot of attention from managers who are planning new offerings and coordinating the marketing mixes for existing offerings. To understand the nature of these decisions, it's important to recognize the various types of products and the stages that products go through during their "lifetime" in the marketplace.

TYPES OF PRODUCTS

Think about Doritos tortilla chips, Intel semiconductors, and your favorite musical artist. You wouldn't market these products in the same way, because buyer behavior, product characteristics, market expectations, competition, and other elements of the equation are entirely different.

Classifying products on the basis of tangibility and application can provide useful insights into the best ways to market them. Some products are predominantly tangible; others are mostly intangible. Most products, however, fall somewhere between those two extremes. The *product continuum* indicates the relative amounts of tangible and intangible components in a product (see Exhibit 14.1).

To provide a more complete solution to customer needs, many companies find success by *augmenting* a core product with accessories, services, and other elements (see Exhibit 14.2). In some cases, these enhancements are included in the price of the product,

EXHIBIT 14.1	**The Product Continuum**

Products contain both tangible and intangible components; predominantly tangible products are categorized as goods, whereas predominantly intangible products are categorized as services.

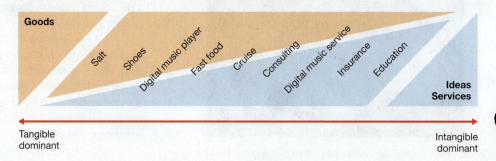

EXHIBIT 14.2 **Augmenting the Basic Product**

Product decisions also involve how much or how little to augment the core product with additional goods and services.

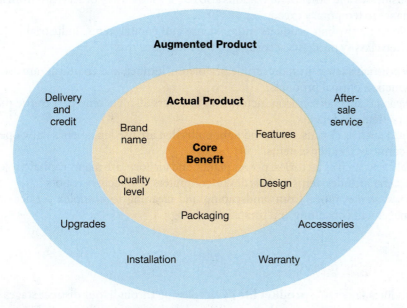

Source: Kotler, Philip R.; Armstrong, Gary, *Principles of Marketing*, 10th ed. © 2004 p.279, 330. Reprinted and electronically reproduced by permission of Pearson Education, Inc., Upper Saddle River, New Jersey.

but product augmentation can also be a way to increase revenue by offering new services and accessories or by charging for enhancements that were previously included at no charge.[2]

Consumer Products

Organizations and consumers use many of the same products, but they can use them for different reasons and in different ways. Products that are primarily sold to individuals for personal consumption are known as *consumer products*. They can be classified into four subgroups, depending on how people shop for them:

- Everyday goods and services that people buy frequently, usually without much conscious planning, are known as **convenience products**.
- **Shopping products** are fairly important goods and services that people buy less frequently, such as computers and college educations. Because the stakes are higher and the decisions more complex, such products require more thought and comparison shopping.
- **Specialty products** are particular brands that the buyer especially wants and will seek out, regardless of location or price, such as Suzuki violin lessons or Bang & Olufsen home entertainment gear.
- When it comes to some products, such as life insurance, cemetery plots, and items that are new to the marketplace, consumers aren't looking for them. The marketing challenges for these *unsought products* include making consumers aware of their existence and convincing people to consider them.

Industrial and Commercial Products

Organizational products, or *industrial and commercial products*, are generally purchased by organizations (including companies, not-for-profit organizations, and governments) in large

convenience products
Everyday goods and services that people buy frequently, usually without much conscious planning.

shopping products
Fairly important goods and services that people buy less frequently with more planning and comparison.

specialty products
Particular brands that the buyer especially wants and will seek out, regardless of location or price.

expense items
Inexpensive products that organizations generally use within a year of purchase.

capital items
More expensive organizational products with a longer useful life, ranging from office and plant equipment to entire factories.

quantities and used to create other products or to operate the organization. **Expense items** are relatively inexpensive goods that are generally used within a year of purchase, such as printer cartridges and paper. **Capital items** are more expensive products with a longer useful life. Examples include computers, vehicles, production machinery, and even entire factories. Businesses and other organizations also buy a wide variety of services, from facilities maintenance to temporary executives.

Aside from dividing products into expense and capital items, industrial buyers and sellers often classify products according to their intended use:

- *Raw materials* such as iron ore, crude petroleum, lumber, and chemicals are used in the production of final products.
- *Components* such as semiconductors and fasteners also become part of the manufacturers' final products.
- *Supplies* such as pencils, nails, and light bulbs that are used in a firm's daily operations are considered expense items.
- *Installations* such as factories, power plants, and airports are major capital projects.
- *Equipment* includes items such as desks, computers, and factory robots.
- *Business services* range from landscaping and cleaning to complex services such as management consulting and financial auditing.

THE PRODUCT LIFE CYCLE

product life cycle
Four stages through which a product progresses: introduction, growth, maturity, and decline.

Most products undergo a **product life cycle**, passing through four distinct stages in sales and profits: introduction, growth, maturity, and decline (see Exhibit 14.3). The marketing challenge changes from stage to stage, sometimes dramatically.

EXHIBIT 14.3	The Product Life Cycle

Most products and product categories move through a life cycle similar to the one represented by the curve in this diagram, with new innovations pushing existing products along the time axis. However, the duration of each stage varies widely from product to product. Automobiles have been in the maturity stage for decades, but faxing services barely made it into the introduction stage before being knocked out of the market by low-cost fax machines that every business and home office could afford—which were themselves pushed along the curve by digital document formats.

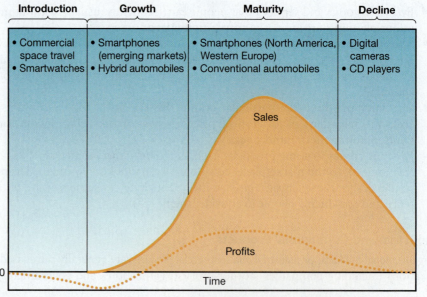

Source: Adapted from Kotler, Philip R.; Armstrong, Gary, *Principles of Marketing*, 10th ed. © 2004 p.279, 330. Reprinted and electronically reproduced by permission of Pearson Education, Inc., Upper Saddle River, New Jersey.

The product life cycle can describe a product class (gasoline-powered automobiles), a product form (sport utility vehicles), or a brand or model (Ford Explorer). Product classes and forms tend to have the longest life cycles, specific brands somewhat shorter life cycles, and individual products even shorter cycles. The amount of time that a product remains in any one stage depends on customer needs and preferences, economic conditions, the nature of the product, and the marketer's strategy. The proliferation of new products, changing technology, globalization, and the ability to quickly imitate competitors is hurtling many product forms and brands through their life cycles much faster today than in the past. In categories such as smartphones, individual models can go through the entire life cycle in as little as nine months.[3]

Introduction

The first stage in the product life cycle is the *introductory stage*, which extends from the research-and-development (R&D) phase through the product's first commercial availability. The introductory stage is a crucial phase that requires careful planning and often considerable investment. For new types of products, companies may need to educate potential customers and *influencers* (such as widely read bloggers) on the uses and benefits of a product.

Speed can be a major concern as well. Some markets offer the luxury of building demand over time if the introduction isn't a blockbuster, but in others a slow introduction can doom a product. The opening weekend for a movie, for instance, often determines its success or failure—a tremendously stressful scenario for people who have invested months or years and many millions of dollars making the film.

Growth

After the introductory stage comes the *growth stage*, marked by a rapid jump in sales—if the product is successful—and, usually, an increase in the number of competitors and distribution outlets. As competition increases, so does the struggle for market share. This situation creates pressure to maintain large promotional budgets and competitive prices. With enough growth, however, a firm may be able to reach economies of scale that allow it to create and deliver its products less expensively than in the introduction phase. The growth stage can reap handsome profits for those products that survive.

Maturity

During the *maturity stage*, usually the longest in the product life cycle, sales begin to level off. Markets tend to get saturated with all the supply that buyers demand, so the only way a firm can expand its sales in this phase is to win sales away from other suppliers. Because the costs of introduction and growth have diminished at this point, most companies try to keep mature products alive so they can use the resulting profits to fund the development of the next generation of new products (often referred to as "milking a cash cow").

Decline

Although maturity can be extended for many years, most products eventually enter the *decline stage*, when sales and profits slip and may eventually fade away. Declines occur for several reasons: changing demographics, shifts in popular taste, overwhelming competition, and advances in technology. For instance, feature-rich smartphones pushed a bunch of other product categories toward or into decline, including personal digital assistants (PDAs), handheld global positioning system (GPS) navigation devices, music players, digital cameras, and portable gaming devices.[4]

When a product begins to decline, the company must decide whether to reduce the product's costs to compensate for declining sales or to discontinue it altogether and focus on developing newer products. Of course, companies can try to make their products more compelling and competitive at any stage. From subtle refinements to complete makeovers, product improvements can sometimes be a way to maintain competitiveness and maximize the returns on the money and effort invested in a product.

Checkpoint

LEARNING OBJECTIVE 1: Identify the main types of consumer and organizational products, and describe the four stages in the life cycle of a product.

SUMMARY: Consumer products can be identified as *convenience, shopping, specialty*, or *unsought*, distinguished primarily by the amount of thought and effort that goes into buying them. Organizational products are divided into *expense items*, less-expensive goods used in production or operations; *capital items*, more expensive goods and facilities with useful lives longer than a year; and *business services*. The product life cycle consists of (1) the introductory stage, during which marketers focus on stimulating demand for the new product; (2) the growth stage, when marketers focus on increasing the product's market share; (3) the maturity stage, during which marketers try to extend the life of the product by highlighting improvements or by repackaging the product in different sizes; and (4) the decline stage, when firms must decide whether to reduce the product's costs to compensate for declining sales or to discontinue it.

CRITICAL THINKING: (1) Do manufacturers have a responsibility to create safe products even if customers don't care and don't want to pay for safety features? Why or why not? (2) Do automobiles ever enter the decline stage of the product life cycle? Explain your answer.

IT'S YOUR BUSINESS: (1) Have you ever had the urge to be "the first one on the block" to buy a new product, try a new fashion, or discover a new musical artist? If so, were you pleased or displeased when "the masses" began to imitate your choice? What does your reaction say about you as a consumer? (2) Have you ever replaced a product (such as a computer or smartphone) that was still functional, just because a newer version had hit the market? What influenced your decision?

KEY TERMS TO KNOW: convenience products, shopping products, specialty products, expense items, capital items, product life cycle

---

2	**LEARNING OBJECTIVE**

Describe six stages in the product development process.

product development process
A formal process of generating, selecting, developing, and commercializing product ideas.

The New-Product Development Process

Mad scientists and basement inventors still create new products, but many of today's products appear on the market as a result of a rigorous, formal **product development process**—a method of generating, selecting, developing, and commercializing product ideas (see Exhibit 14.4).

IDEA GENERATION

The first step in the new-product development process is to come up with some ideas that will satisfy unmet needs. Customers, competitors, and employees are often the best source of new product ideas. Companies can also hire *trend watchers*, monitor social media to spot shifts in consumer tastes, or use *crowdsourcing* to invite the public to submit ideas or product designs. Some ideas are more or less sheer luck: The popular photo-sharing website Flickr started as a feature in a massively multiplayer online game, but the developers soon realized the photo-sharing tool was a better business opportunity than the game they were creating.[5] Of course, many "new" product ideas are simply improvements to or variations on existing products, but even those slight alterations can generate big revenues.

IDEA SCREENING

From all the ideas under consideration, the company selects those that appear to be worthy of further development, applying broad criteria such as whether the product can use

EXHIBIT 14.4	The Product Development Process

The product development process aims to identify the product ideas most likely to succeed in the marketplace. The process varies widely by company, of course; entrepreneurs and start-ups sometimes begin with a single product idea and take it all the way through to commercialization.

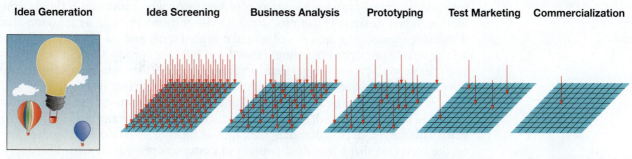

Idea Generation	Idea Screening	Business Analysis	Prototyping	Test Marketing	Commercialization
Brainstorm product concepts that could satisfy unmet market needs or enhance the company's product portfolio	Subject those ideas to *feasibility* or *concept testing* to identify those with the best chance of turning into successful products	Subject those ideas to a *business-case analysis* based on estimates of production costs, sales volumes, and selling price	Develop functioning "pre-release" versions that can be used by target customers to check for design flaws, market appeal, and so on	Release a finished or nearly finished *(beta)* version to selected customers or market segments and measure customer reaction	Fine-tune the product design and the rest of the marketing mix and then officially launch the product and push sales in all target markets

existing production facilities and how much technical and marketing risk is involved. Research suggests that sharply narrowing the possibilities at this stage is better than keeping a large number of ideas alive, as each idea competes for attention or resources until it is abandoned or implemented as a real product.[6] This approach is often referred to as a *feasibility study*, in which the product's features are defined and its workability is tested. In the case of consumer products, marketing consultants and advertising agencies are often called in to help evaluate new ideas. In some cases, potential customers are asked what they think of a new product idea—a process known as *concept testing*. Some companies involve customers early in the design process to make sure new products truly meet customer needs instead of the design team's perception of customer needs. Xerox's Chief Technology Officer Sophie Vandebroek refers to her company's approach as "customer-led innovation" and says that "dreaming with the customer" is essential to creating the right products.[7]

BUSINESS ANALYSIS

A product idea that survives the screening stage is subjected to a business analysis. During this stage, the company reviews the sales, costs, and profit projections to determine whether they meet the company's objectives. In addition, it estimates the costs associated with various levels of production. Given these projections, analysts calculate the potential profit that will be achieved if the product is introduced. If the product meets the company's objectives, it can then move to the prototype development stage.

PROTOTYPE DEVELOPMENT

At this stage, the firm may actually develop a product concept into a functioning "prerelease" product. The firm creates and tests a few samples, or **prototypes**, of the product, including its packaging. These units are rigorously analyzed for usability, durability, manufacturability, customer appeal, and other vital criteria, depending on the type of product. In addition, the company begins to plan for large-scale manufacturing (for tangible goods) or *scalability* (for digital services, for example), then identifies the resources required to bring the product to market.

prototypes
Preproduction samples of products used for testing and evaluation.

TEST MARKETING

test marketing
A product development stage in which a product is sold on a limited basis to gauge its market appeal.

During **test marketing**, the firm introduces the product in selected markets and monitors consumer reactions. Test marketing gives the marketer experience with marketing the product before going to the expense of a full introduction. In a variation on crowdsourcing, a company can let customers vote directly on which products it should bring to market. When Amazon began producing television shows through its Amazon Studios division, it released pilot episodes of several potential series and asked viewers of its Prime service to vote on which ones should move into full series productions.[8] Companies can also release products early to get feedback from potential customers before finalizing features and functions. Software developers often do so through *beta* versions.

Test marketing can be expensive and time-consuming, however, so not all companies choose to take this step with every new product. An alternative that is growing in popularity with the rise of crowdfunding sites such as Kickstarter is to offer a product for sale on the condition that a specified number of customers preorder it first. This approach helps validate market demand before a company moves into the production phase, and it provides vital funding during the startup phase.

COMMERCIALIZATION

commercialization
Large-scale production and distribution of a product.

The final stage of development is **commercialization**, the large-scale production and distribution of products that have survived the testing process. This phase (also referred to as a *product launch*) requires the coordination of many activities—manufacturing, packaging, distribution, pricing, media relations, and customer communication.

Even after following a rigorous process to reduce risk, companies have no guarantee that products will take off when they hit the commercialization phase. Self-inflicted wounds, such as poor advertising, buggy software, or supply shortages, can doom even promising products. And in the external environment, an unexpected new competitor, shifts in consumer tastes, or faltering economic conditions can cause a new product to stall in the marketplace.

 Checkpoint

LEARNING OBJECTIVE 2: Describe six stages in the product development process.

SUMMARY: The first two stages of product development involve generating and screening ideas to isolate those with the most potential. In the third stage, promising ideas are analyzed to determine their likely profitability. Those that appear worthwhile enter the fourth stage, the prototype development stage, in which limited numbers of the products are created. In the fifth stage, the product is test marketed to determine buyer response. Products that survive the testing process are then commercialized, the final stage.

CRITICAL THINKING: (1) Apple claims to never do any marketing research for new product ideas but instead creates products that Apple employees themselves would be excited to have. What are the risks of this approach? Would it work for all consumer and organizational markets? (2) Consumers and government regulators sometimes complain about identical products being sold at different prices to different customers as part of test marketing efforts. Are such tests ethical? Why or why not?

IT'S YOUR BUSINESS: (1) What currently unavailable service can you think of that could be offered on mobile phones? (2) In addition to the mobile phone itself, what other product elements (such as a website or phone accessories) would be required to launch such a service?

KEY TERMS TO KNOW: product development process, prototypes, test marketing, commercialization

Product Identities

3 | **LEARNING OBJECTIVE**

Define *brand*, and explain the concepts of brand equity and brand loyalty.

Creating an identity for products is one of the most important decisions marketers make. That identity is encompassed in the **brand**, which can have meaning at three levels: (1) a unique name, symbol, or design that sets the product apart from those offered by competitors; (2) the legal protections afforded by a trademark and any relevant intellectual property; and (3) the overall company or organizational brand.[9] For instance, the Nike "swoosh" symbol is a unique identifier on every Nike product, a legally protected piece of intellectual property, and a symbol that represents the entire company.

Branding helps a product in many ways. It gives customers a way of recognizing and specifying a particular product so that they can choose it again or recommend it to others. It provides consumers with information about the product. It facilitates the marketing of the product. And it creates value for the product. This notion of the value of a brand is also called **brand equity**. In fact, a brand name can be an organization's most valuable asset, and major brands such as Apple, Google, and IBM are valued at a hundred billion dollars or more.[10] Strong brands simplify marketing efforts because the target audience tends to associate positive qualities with any product that carries a respected brand name—and vice versa.

Customers who buy the same brand again and again are evidence of the strength of **brand loyalty**, or commitment to a particular brand. Brand loyalty can be measured in degrees. The first level is *brand awareness*, which means that people are more likely to buy a product because they are familiar with it. The next level is *brand preference*, which means people will purchase the product if it is available, although they may still be willing to experiment with alternatives if they cannot find the preferred brand. The third and ultimate level of brand loyalty is *brand insistence*, the stage at which buyers will accept no substitute. Some brands, such as Harley-Davidson motorcycles and American Girl dolls, can acquire such a deep level of meaning to loyal consumers that the brands become intertwined with the narratives of the consumers' life stories.[11]

brand
A name, term, sign, symbol, design, or combination of those used to identify the products of a firm and to differentiate them from competing products.

brand equity
The value that a company has built up in a brand.

brand loyalty
The degree to which customers continue to purchase a specific brand.

REAL-TIME UPDATES
Learn More by Watching This Video

Dr. Philip Kotler on the importance of brand equity

The noted marketing professor explains why brand equity is a strategic management imperative. Go to **http://real-timeupdates .com/bia8** and click on Learn More in the Students section.

BRAND NAME SELECTION

Jeep, Levi's 501, and iPod are **brand names**, the portion of a brand that can be spoken, including letters, words, or numbers. Annika Sörenstam (see page 343) uses her first name in all capital letters as her brand name. In contrast, the McDonald's golden arches and the Nike "swoosh" symbol are **brand marks**, the portion of a brand that cannot be expressed verbally. The term **logo** (from *logotype*) once referred to the typesetting treatment of a brand name but is now used more variably to refer to the nonverbal brand mark, the visual treatment of the brand name, or a combination of the two (see Exhibit 14.5 on the next page).

The choice of a brand name and any associated brand marks can be a critical success factor. Imagine if Nike had chosen a cute fuzzy duckling or a balanced, static shape of some kind rather than the dynamic and "athletic" swoosh shape—not to mention naming the brand after the Greek goddess of victory.

In the United States, brand names and brand symbols may be registered with the U.S. Patent and Trademark Office as **trademarks**, brands that have been given legal protection so that their owners have exclusive rights to their use. (Similarly protections exist in other countries.) The Lanham Trademark Act prohibits the unauthorized use of a trademark on goods or services when the use would likely confuse consumers as to the origin of those goods and services.[12] Companies zealously protect their brand names because if a name becomes too widely used in a general sense, it no longer qualifies for protection under trademark laws. Cellophane, kerosene, linoleum, escalator, zipper, and shredded wheat are just a few of the many brand names that have since lost trademark protection and can now be used by anyone.[13]

brand names
The portion of brands that can be expressed orally, including letters, words, or numbers.

brand marks
The portion of brands that cannot be expressed verbally.

logo
A graphical or textual representation of a brand.

trademarks
Brands that have been given legal protection so that their owners have exclusive rights to their use.

EXHIBIT 14.5	Product Identities

The Chevrolet "bowtie" logo, in use for more than a century, is instantly recognizable on the company's cars and trucks.

© Jorgen Udvang / Alamy

REAL-TIME UPDATES
Learn More by Reading This Article

The design choices behind lovable logos

Read how color, font, and shape affect the emotional bond consumers have with brand logos. Go to **http://real-timeupdates .com/bia8** and click on Learn More in the Students section.

national brands
Brands owned by manufacturers and distributed nationally.

private brands
Brands that carry the label of a retailer or a wholesaler rather than a manufacturer.

co-branding
A partnership between two or more companies to closely link their brand names together for a single product.

license
An agreement to produce and market another company's product in exchange for a royalty or fee.

BRAND OWNERSHIP

Brand names may be associated with a manufacturer, a retailer, a wholesaler, or a combination of business types. Brands offered and promoted by a national manufacturer, such as Procter & Gamble's Tide detergent and Pampers disposable diapers, are called **national brands**. **Private brands** are not linked to a manufacturer but instead carry a wholesaler's or a retailer's brand. DieHard batteries and Kenmore appliances are private brands sold by Sears. These *store brands*, as they are also called, have become a major force in the grocery business in recent years as they continue to overcome an early reputation for lower quality and become more widely accepted by consumers.[14]

As an alternative to branded products, retailers can also offer *generic products*, which are packaged in plain containers that bear only the name of the product. Note that "generics" is also a term used in the pharmaceutical industry to describe products that are copies of an original drug (other companies are allowed to make these copies after the patent on the original drug expires).

Co-branding occurs when two or more companies team up to closely link their names in a single product, usually to leverage the brand associations and awareness of one product onto the other. Companies can also **license**, or offer to sell, the rights to well-known brand names and symbols. Mainstream movies, for example, often hit the market with an array of licensing deals with fast-food chains and other consumer products companies.

Companies need to choose such deals carefully, however, to minimize the impact of negative associations in the mind of potential customers to avoid diluting a brand so much that it loses its core meaning to buyers. Annika Sörenstam says she is approached frequently by companies wanting to use her name in branding or endorsement deals, but she rejects most proposals because they wouldn't create an authentic connection with her brand.[15]

PACKAGING

Most tangible products need some form of packaging to protect them from damage or tampering, but packaging can also play an important role in a product's marketing strategy. Packaging makes products easier to display, facilitates the sale of smaller products, serves as a means of product differentiation, and enhances the product's overall appeal and convenience. Packaging can significantly influence buyer perceptions, too, sometimes in surprising ways. For instance, packages with simple geometric lines (such as cylinders or rectangles) are perceived as being larger than geometrically complex packages of the same volume. Package designers can use these perceptual effects to create particular images for their products.[16]

Packaging can also involve decisions about which items to include as the product offering and in what quantities. For example, Costco and other warehouse-style retailers offer many of the same products available through regular grocery stores but in packages of larger quantities. At the other extreme, many food brands offer individual serving-size packages, such as 100-calorie snacks designed to help people limit their calorie intake.

Packaging can be a complex tug-of-war between competing priorities. Consumers are often frustrated by how difficult it can be to open packages—and thousands are injured every year trying to open packages using knives, scissors, hammers, and other tools.[17] Plastic "clamshell" packages can be particularly frustrating and even dangerous to open. Manufacturers and sellers don't set out to antagonize buyers, naturally, but they adopt various packaging methods in order to protect products, reduce shoplifting, and enhance merchandising efforts. Packaging is also a major environmental concern, in both the resources used and waste generated. However, intelligent packaging can also reduce environmental impact, such as by reducing food spoilage. Food production and distribution has considerable environment consequences, and reducing the amount of food that has to be thrown out because of spoilage reduce that environmental impact.[18]

In an effort to balance the competing interests of all parties, a number of companies are working to change their packaging strategies. For example, many manufacturers now participate in Amazon's "Frustration-Free Packaging" program, in which products sold through the online giant use packaging formats that are easier to open, consume fewer materials, and are 100-percent recyclable.[19] Amazon's e-commerce structure is a key element in this effort because the packages don't need to meet the same anti-shoplifting and display considerations as products sold through physical retail channels.

LABELING

Labeling is an integral part of packaging. Whether the label is a separate element attached to the package or a printed part of the container, it serves to identify a brand and communicate multiple types of information, from promotional messages to legally required safety or nutritional data. The labeling of foods, drugs, cosmetics, and many health products is regulated under various federal laws, which often require disclosures about potential dangers, benefits, and other issues consumers need to consider when making a buying decision.

Brands help consumers make confident choices from the often-overwhelming number of products available in today's supermarkets and drugstores.

REAL-TIME UPDATES
Learn More by Reading This Article

The fundamental steps to building your brand

Follow these steps to establish a strong brand for any company. Go to **http://real-timeupdates.com/bia8** and click on Learn More in the Students section.

REAL-TIME UPDATES
Learn More by Exploring This Interactive Website

See the strategies behind the world's strongest brands

Interbrand ranks the world's most valuable brand names—and explains how they got there. Go to **http://real-timeupdates.com/bia8** and click on Learn More in the Students section.

✓ **Checkpoint**

LEARNING OBJECTIVE 3: Define *brand*, **and explain the concepts of brand equity and brand loyalty.**

SUMMARY: *Brand* encompasses the various elements of product identity and meaning. *Brand equity* reflects the value of a brand name based on its strength and appeal in the marketplace and its power as a communication vehicle. *Brand loyalty* can be defined at three levels: brand awareness, in which the buyer is familiar with the product; brand preference, in which the buyer will select the product if it is available; and brand insistence, in which the buyer will accept no substitute.

CRITICAL THINKING: (1) Can a brand with a bad reputation be rescued? Would a company be wiser to just drop a "bad brand" and start fresh with something new? (2) Is staying with the same product only a case of brand "loyalty"? Could other factors be in play that lead consumers or organizations not to switch brands? Explain your answer.

IT'S YOUR BUSINESS: (1) How many visible brand marks are you currently wearing? Are these common brands? (2) What do you think these brands say about you?

KEY TERMS TO KNOW: brand, brand equity, brand loyalty, brand names, brand marks, logo, trademarks, national brands, private brands, co-branding, license

4 | **LEARNING OBJECTIVE**

Identify four ways of expanding a product line, and discuss two risks that product-line extensions pose.

brand managers
Managers who develop and implement the marketing strategies and programs for specific products or brands.

product line
A series of related products offered by a firm.

product mix
The complete portfolio of products that a company offers for sale.

Product-Line and Product-Mix Strategies

In addition to developing product identities, a company must continually evaluate what kinds of products it will offer. To stay competitive, most companies continually add and drop products to ensure that declining items will be replaced by growth products. Companies that offer more than one product also need to pay close attention to how those products are positioned in the marketplace relative to one another. The responsibility for managing individual products, product lines, and product mixes is usually assigned to one or more managers in the marketing department. In a smaller company, the *marketing manager* tackles this effort; in larger companies with more products to manage, individual products or groups of products are usually assigned to **brand managers**, known in some companies as *product managers* or *product-line managers*.

PRODUCT LINES

A **product line** is a group of products from a single manufacturer that are similar in terms of use or characteristics. The General Mills (**www.generalmills.com**) snack-food product line, for example, includes Bugles, Cascadian Farm organic snacks, and Nature Valley Granola Bars. Within each product line, a company confronts decisions about the number of goods and services to offer. On the one hand, offering additional products can help a manufacturer boost revenues and increase its visibility in retail stores. On the other hand, creating too many products and product variations can be expensive for everyone in the supply chain and can be confusing to buyers.

PRODUCT MIX

An organization with several product lines has a **product mix**—a collection of diverse goods or services offered for sale. The General Mills product mix includes cereals, baking products, desserts, snack foods, and entrees (see Exhibit 14.6). Three important dimensions of a product mix are *width, length,* and *depth,* and each dimension presents its own set of challenges and opportunities. A product mix is *wide* if it has several product lines. A product mix is *long* if it carries several items in its product lines. For instance, General Mills produces multiple cereal brands within the ready-to-eat cereal line. A product mix is *deep* if it has a number of versions of *each* product in a product line. The Cheerios brand, for example, currently has more than a dozen different varieties.[20]

When deciding on the dimensions of a product mix, a company must weigh the risks and rewards associated with various approaches. Some companies limit the number of product offerings and focus on selling a few items in higher quantities. Doing so can keep production and marketing costs lower through economies of scale. However, counting too heavily on a narrow set of products leaves a company vulnerable to competitive threats and market shifts. Other companies diversify their product offerings as a protection against shifts in consumer tastes, economic conditions, and technology, or as a way to build marketing synergy by offering complementary products.[21]

Retailers often have considerable influence in manufacturers' product line decisions, particularly in the store-based retail channel. In general, the more revenue a manufacturer represents, the better chance it has of getting all-important shelf space. Consequently, retail store aisles tend to be dominated by a few large brands, and

---

EXHIBIT 14.6   The Product Mix at General Mills (Selected Products)

These selected products from General Mills illustrate the various dimensions of its product mix. The mix is wide because it contains multiple product lines (cereals, fruit snacks, pasta, soup, yogurt, and more). The cereal product line is long because it contains many individual brands (only four of which are shown here). And these four cereal brands show different depths. The Trix brand is a shallow line, whereas the Cheerios brand is deep.

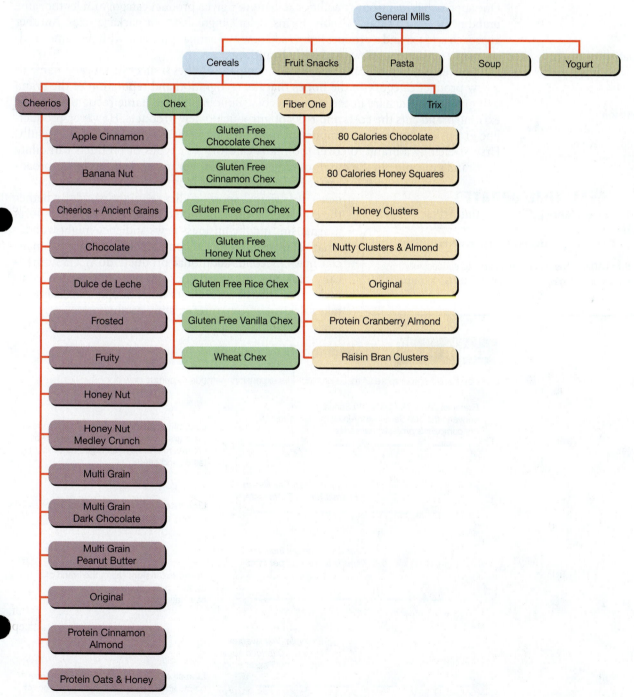

Source: Data from General Mills website, accessed 24 May 2015, www.generalmills.com.

manufacturers look for ways to build portfolios of best-sellers that can command attention at the retail level.

Online retailing presents much better opportunities for large numbers of specialized and low-volume products. Without the physical limitations of a bricks-and-mortar facility, online retailers can offer a much greater variety of products. Although some of these products may individually sell at lower volumes, collectively they represent a substantial business opportunity that has been termed the *long tail* (referring to a sales volume graph in which a vast number of low-volume products stretches out toward infinity).[22]

PRODUCT EXPANSION STRATEGIES

As Exhibit 14.7 shows, you can expand your product line and mix in a number of ways. One approach is to introduce additional items in a given product category under the same brand name—such as new flavors, forms, colors, ingredients, or package sizes. Another approach is to expand a product line to add new and similar products with the same product name—a strategy known as **family branding**.

family branding
Using a brand name on a variety of related products.

brand extension
Applying a successful brand name to a new product category.

Conversely, in a **brand extension**, a company applies a successful brand name to a new product category in the hopes that the recognition and reputation of the brand will give it a head start in the new category. Building on the name recognition of an existing brand cuts the costs and risks of introducing new products. However, product-line extensions present two important risks that marketers need to consider carefully. First, stretching a brand to cover too many categories or types of products can dilute the brand's meaning in the minds of target customers. For instance, if the sports broadcaster ESPN were to branch out into business and financial news, its original sports audience might wonder whether the company is still committed to being a leader in sports journalism, and the business news audience might wonder what value a sports media company could bring to financial news. Second, additional products do not automatically guarantee increased sales revenue. Marketers need to make sure that new products don't simply *cannibalize*, or take sales away from, their existing products.

EXHIBIT 14.7	Expanding a Product Line

Companies use one or more of these product-line expansion methods to pursue new opportunities.

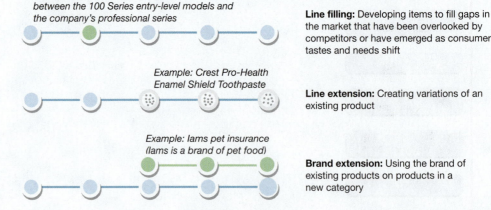

Example: Taylor Guitars's 200 Series, priced between the 100 Series entry-level models and the company's professional series

Line filling: Developing items to fill gaps in the market that have been overlooked by competitors or have emerged as consumer tastes and needs shift

Example: Crest Pro-Health Enamel Shield Toothpaste

Line extension: Creating variations of an existing product

Example: Iams pet insurance (Iams is a brand of pet food)

Brand extension: Using the brand of existing products on products in a new category

Example: Volkswagen Passat CC (priced above the regular Passat models)

Line stretching: Adding items with price points above or below the current product line

PRODUCT STRATEGIES FOR INTERNATIONAL MARKETS

As Chapter 3 notes, product adaptation is one of the key changes that companies need to consider when moving into other countries. First, managers must decide on which products and services to introduce in which countries. When selecting a country, they must take into consideration the type of government, market-entry requirements, tariffs and other trade barriers, cultural and language differences, consumer preferences, foreign-exchange rates, and differing business customs. Then, they must decide whether to standardize the product, selling it everywhere, or to customize the product to accommodate the lifestyles and habits of local target markets. A company might change only the product's name or packaging, or it can modify the product's components, size, and functions.

For example, French consumers have been eating at McDonald's (**www.mcdonalds.fr**) since the company first arrived in 1972, but the burger giant has a unique look in that country. To accommodate a culture known for its cuisine and dining experience, many McDonald's outlets in France have upgraded their decor to a level that would make them almost unrecognizable in the United States. Menus include such variations as Le Croque McDo, a McDonald's take on the traditional French *croque monsieur* grilled ham-and-cheese sandwich.[23]

For the latest information on product and branding strategies, visit **http://real-timeupdates.com/bia8** and click on Chapter 14.

 Checkpoint

LEARNING OBJECTIVE 4: Identify four ways of expanding a product line, and discuss two risks that product-line extensions pose.

SUMMARY: A product line can be expanded by filling gaps in the market, extending the line to include new varieties of existing products, extending the brand to new product categories, and stretching the line to include lower- or higher-priced items. Two of the biggest risks with product-line extensions are losing brand identity and coherence (weakening of the brand's meaning) and cannibalizing sales of other products in the product line.

CRITICAL THINKING: (1) If McDonald's had been relatively unknown to French diners when the company entered that market in 1972, would it have made more sense to use a different and more "French-sounding" brand name? Why or why not? (2) Would a consumer products manufacturer ever want to create more product extensions and variations than it could explain in terms of pure market appeal? Why or why not?

IT'S YOUR BUSINESS: (1) Citing specific examples, how has branding helped you as a consumer? Think about the assurance you have in buying a known and trusted brand, for example. (2) Think about some of the consumer products you buy frequently, such as cereal, painkillers, or snack foods. Do you appreciate the range of choices available to you when you shop for these items, or do you wish that companies would narrow the options to a handful in each category? Why?

KEY TERMS TO KNOW: brand managers, product line, product mix, family branding, brand extension

Pricing Strategies

The second key element in the marketing mix is pricing. Recall from the definition in Chapter 13 that pricing involves *capturing value* back from the customer in exchange for the value provided in the product. Setting and managing prices is a combination of strategic considerations and careful financial analysis.

 LEARNING OBJECTIVE

List the factors that influence pricing decisions, and explain break-even analysis.

STRATEGIC CONSIDERATIONS IN PRICING

Managers must consider a variety of internal and external factors when establishing prices:

- **Marketing objectives.** The first step in setting a price is to match it to the objectives set in the strategic marketing plan. Is the goal to increase market share, increase sales, improve profits, project a particular image, or combat competition? Price is a flexible tool that can help a firm achieve a wide variety of marketing objectives.

- **Government regulations.** To protect consumers and encourage fair competition, governments around the world have enacted various price-related laws over the years. These regulations are particularly important in three areas of prohibited behavior: (1) *price discrimination*, unfairly offering attractive discounts to some customers but not to others; (2) *deceptive pricing*, pricing schemes that are considered misleading; and (3) *price fixing*, an agreement among two or more companies supplying the same type of products as to the prices they will charge. For example, the U.S. government fined 21 airlines more than $1.7 billion—and sent several airline executives to jail—for an extensive price-fixing scheme on flights to and from the United States. The scheme operated for more than five years, until two of the airlines, Lufthansa and Virgin Atlantic, took advantage of an amnesty program and turned themselves in.[24]

- **Customer perceptions.** Another consideration in setting price is the perception of quality and value that a price elicits from customers. An unexpectedly low price can trigger fears of low quality, but a high price can connote quality and even exclusivity. Specific numbers can have a perceptual effect as well, such as the well-known "9 effect." You've probably noticed that many prices end in a 9, such as $9.99 or $5,999. Your conscious mind says, "Gimme a break; we all know that's really $10 or $6,000." However, research suggests that our minds equate that 9 with a bargain—even when it isn't. In one experiment, for example, a dress sold more when priced at $39 than when it was priced at $34.[25] Conversely, companies that want to create a quality or luxury association for their brands sometimes avoid prices that end in 9 specifically to avoid the 9 effect.

- **Market demand.** The discussion of supply and demand in Chapter 2 points out that market demand usually fluctuates as prices fluctuate. However, some goods and services are relatively *insensitive* to changes in price; others are highly *sensitive*. Buyers can also exhibit individual levels of price sensitivity. For instance, brand-loyal customers tend to be less sensitive to price, meaning they will stick with a brand even as the price increases, whereas other buyers will begin switching to cheaper alternatives.[26] Marketers refer to this sensitivity as **price elasticity**—how responsive demand will be to a change in price.

- **Competition.** Competitive prices are obviously a major consideration whenever a firm is establishing or changing its prices. Technology has profoundly shifted the balance of power in this respect from sellers to buyers in recent years, as social commerce websites and mobile Internet access make it easy to find the lowest prices for a wide variety of goods and services. The easier it is for buyers to compare prices, for instance, the more important competitive prices become—particularly when buyers don't perceive much difference among the available products.

price elasticity
A measure of the sensitivity of demand to changes in price.

COST STRUCTURE AND BREAK-EVEN ANALYSIS

Every company has a particular *cost structure* that determines how much it must spend to create and market its products. Some costs remain the same regardless of production and sales volume. Such **fixed costs** include rent or mortgage payments, insurance premiums, real estate taxes, and salaries. These are costs incurred just to "keep the doors open," without creating or selling anything. In contrast, **variable costs**, including raw

fixed costs
Business costs that remain constant regardless of the number of units produced.

variable costs
Business costs that increase with the number of units produced.

materials, supplies consumed during production, shipping, and sales commissions, vary with changes in production and sales volume. Obviously, the more a company can lower its cost structure, the more flexibility it has in setting prices and ensuring desirable levels of profit.

The cost to create and sell each product is a combination of fixed and variable costs. A critical calculation in setting prices is **break-even analysis**, determining the number of units a firm must sell at a given price to recoup both fixed and variable costs—to "break even," in other words. The **break-even point** is the minimum sales volume the company must achieve to avoid losing money. Sales volume beyond the break-even point will generate profits; sales volume below the break-even amount will result in losses.

You can determine the break-even point in number of units with this simple calculation:

$$\text{Break-even point} = \frac{\text{Fixed costs}}{\text{Selling price} - \text{Variable costs per unit}}$$

For example, if you wanted to price haircuts at $20 and you had fixed costs of $60,000 and variable costs per haircut of $5, you would need to sell 4,000 haircuts to break even:

$$\text{Break-even point} = \frac{60,000}{\$20 - \$5} = 4,000 \text{ units}$$

Naturally, $20 isn't your only pricing option. Why not charge $30 instead? At that price, you need to sell only 2,400 haircuts to break even (see Exhibit 14.8 on the next page). Of course, you would have to convince 2,400 people to pay the higher price, and depending on market dynamics and your cost structure, you might make more money selling at the lower price.

Note that break-even analysis doesn't dictate what price you *should* charge; rather, it provides some insight into the price you *can* charge and begin to generate profit. With the break-even point in hand, you can then factor in the various strategic considerations to determine price using one of the methods discussed in the next section.

break-even analysis
A method of calculating the minimum volume of sales needed at a given price to cover all costs.

break-even point
Sales volume at a given price that will cover all of a company's costs.

✔ Checkpoint

LEARNING OBJECTIVE 5: List the factors that influence pricing decisions, and explain break-even analysis.

SUMMARY: Strategic considerations in pricing include marketing objectives, government regulations, customer perceptions, market demand, and competition. *Break-even analysis* is a way to determine how many units (the *break-even point*) a firm needs to produce in order to begin turning a profit by covering its fixed and variable costs. The break-even point is calculated by dividing fixed costs by the difference between the selling price and the variable costs per unit.

CRITICAL THINKING: (1) Why wouldn't a firm just drop any product that isn't selling in high enough volume to reach its break-even point? (2) Is "9" style pricing ethical? Why or why not?

IT'S YOUR BUSINESS: (1) Do you factor in the value of your time when you price-comparison shop? Why or why not? (2) As a consumer taking charge of your own financial future, what lessons could you take from the business concepts of fixed and variable costs?

KEY TERMS TO KNOW: price elasticity, fixed costs, variable costs, break-even analysis, break-even point

EXHIBIT 14.8   **Break-Even Analysis**

The break-even point is the point at which revenues just cover costs. After fixed costs and variable costs have been met, any additional income represents profit. The graphs show that at $20 per haircut, the break-even point is 4,000 haircuts; charging $30 yields a break-even point at only 2,400 haircuts.

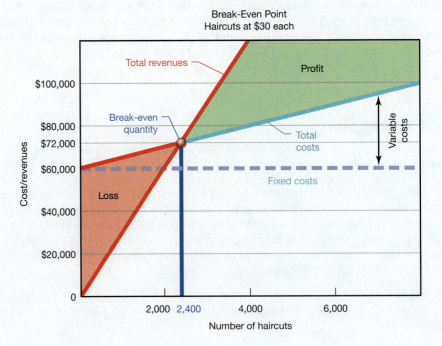

Pricing Methods

6   **LEARNING OBJECTIVE**
Identify nine common pricing methods.

Break-even analysis and the various strategic considerations help managers establish an overall framework of pricing possibilities. You can think of costs as establishing the pricing "floor," whereas demand, competition, and other factors establish the "ceiling." Somewhere between those two limits lies the ideal price for each product. Managers can apply a variety of methods to pinpoint specific prices. Note that some of these methods aren't mutually exclusive; companies can use two or more methods, either in succession or at the same time.

COST-BASED PRICING

Some companies simplify the pricing task by using **cost-based pricing**, also known as *cost-plus pricing*, in which they start with the cost of producing a good or a service and then add a *markup* to arrive at the selling price. Cost-based pricing is simple, but it suffers from a major weakness: It doesn't consider any external factors such as customer demand or competitive prices. The price could be too high for market conditions, leaving the company uncompetitive, or it could be too low, generating less profit than it could otherwise.

cost-based pricing
A method of setting prices based on production and marketing costs, rather than conditions in the marketplace.

VALUE-BASED PRICING

In contrast to cost-based pricing, **value-based pricing** establishes a price on a product's potential or perceived value in the marketplace. In other words, rather than starting with cost and then figuring out a price, this method starts with a target price and works backward to identify a cost structure that will yield acceptable profit margins. The disadvantage of this method is that it requires more information and more analysis because managers need to measure or at least estimate perceptions of customer value in order to establish the price. If a company lacks the information to set a realistic price point based on value, one option is to introduce the product using cost-based pricing and then gradually shift to a value-based model as more is learned about how customers perceive the product.[27]

value-based pricing
A method of setting prices based on customer perceptions of value.

An additional challenge with value-based pricing is that perceptions of value change over time. For example, in a recession or depression, consumers take a much harder look at the value they are receiving for the money they spend. Many want more product value while paying the same price or the same product value at a lower price, whereas others are willing to give up some product value in exchange for lower prices. In all these cases, the perception of value changes, and companies that understand and can deliver on the new perceptions of value stand the best chance of surviving or even thriving during tough times.[28]

REAL-TIME UPDATES
Learn More by Watching This Video

Yield management in the hotel industry

Hear how the Marriott hotel chain uses yield management techniques to maximize revenue. Go to **http://real-timeupdates.com /bia8** and click on Learn More in the Students section.

OPTIMAL PRICING

Optimal pricing attempts to minimize the errors and guesswork of other methods by using computer software to generate the ideal price for every item, at each individual store, at any given time. A price-optimization program feeds reams of data from checkout scanners, seasonal sales figures, competitors, and other sources into probability algorithms to come up with an individual demand curve for each product in each store. From that, retailers can identify which products are the most price sensitive. Then they can adjust prices up or down according to each store's priorities— profit, revenue, or market share. Some systems also let store managers conduct "what if" analyses based on past sales data, helping them see the potential effect of proposed price changes.[29]

optimal pricing
A computer-based pricing method that creates a demand curve for every product to help managers select a price that meets specific marketing objectives.

SKIM PRICING

During the introductory phase of the product life cycle, a company may opt to take advantage of strong demand before competitors can enter the market and exert downward pressure on prices. To achieve this goal, the company can charge a high initial price—a practice known as **skim pricing**—with the intention of dropping the price later. *Early adopters* are often willing to pay a premium to get their hands on new products as

skim pricing
Charging a high price for a new product during the introductory stage and lowering the price later.

EXHIBIT 14.9	**Skim Pricing**

When a product is likely to enjoy high demand at introduction, marketers may decide to charge a premium for it for as long as the demand remains strong.

Apaydin Alain/ABACA/Newscom

soon as possible (see Exhibit 14.9). In consumer markets, some people simply want to have the latest and greatest before anyone else; in organizational markets, new types of equipment can give companies a short-term competitive advantage.

PENETRATION PRICING

penetration pricing
Introducing a new product at a low price in hopes of building sales volume quickly.

Skim prices are set high with the understanding that many customers won't be willing to pay them. In contrast, companies use **penetration pricing** to build sales volume by charging a low initial price. This approach has the added advantage of discouraging competition, because the low price—which competitors would be pressured to match—limits the profit potential for everyone. (If the intent of penetration is to drive competitors out of business, though, companies open themselves up to charges of illegal *predatory pricing*.)

However, penetration pricing doesn't work if the company can't sustain the low price levels profitably, if prices for a particular product are inelastic, or if customers weigh other factors more heavily than price. Moreover, as mentioned previously, prices that are far below the market's expectations can raise concerns about quality, reliability, and safety. Everyone would like to pay less for medical care, but many people would be unwilling to go to cut-rate clinics if they thought their health might be jeopardized.

LOSS-LEADER PRICING

loss-leader pricing
Selling one product at a loss as a way to entice customers to consider other products.

As part of a larger marketing plan, some companies occasionally resort to **loss-leader pricing**, setting a price on one product so low that they lose money on every sale but recoup that loss by enticing customers to try a new product or buy other products. For instance, grocery stores can use milk and other staples as loss leaders to encourage shoppers to visit. (And there's a reason these products are often all the way at the back of the store—you have to walk past hundreds of higher-margin products that you might suddenly decide you can't live without.)

AUCTION PRICING

In an *auction*, the seller doesn't set a firm price but allows buyers to competitively bid on the products being sold. Auctions used to be confined to a few market sectors such as fine art, agricultural products, and government bonds, but that all changed when eBay turned selling and buying via auctions into a new national pastime. Many companies now use eBay and other auction sites to sell everything from modular buildings to tractors to industrial equipment. In *procurement auctions* or *reverse auctions*, potential buyers identify the goods or services they need and the prices they're willing to pay, then suppliers respond with offers at the prices they're willing to charge. The travel website Priceline.com, for example, lets buyers enter a price they're willing to pay and then see whether airlines, hotels, and other providers are willing to sell at that price.[30]

PARTICIPATIVE PRICING

One of the most unusual pricing strategies is **participative pricing**, sometimes known as "pay what you want," in which customers literally get to pay as much as they think a product is worth. Although it might sound like a strategy for financial disaster, with participative pricing buyers sometimes pay *more* than the company would normally charge.[31] When the band Radiohead let buyers name their own price for one of its downloadable albums, the band made more money from that album than from downloads on all their other studio albums combined.[32]

participative pricing
Allowing customers to pay the amount they think a product is worth.

FREE AND FREEMIUM PRICING

Even more radical than participative pricing is no price at all. However, giving away goods and services can make a lot of sense in the right situation, such as when a new company is trying to make a name for itself in the marketplace.[33] Another use of free pricing is when some customers are charged enough to provide free goods and services for other customers, a tactic known as **freemium pricing** (*free + premium*).[34] For example, a number of software products, online services, and smartphone and tablet apps offer a free version with fewer capabilities and one or more paid versions of the full product. Giving away some products while maintaining full prices for others (the common approach of "buy one, get one free") is also a way to effectively offer discounted pricing without the risk of creating expectations of lower prices.[35]

freemium pricing
A hybrid pricing strategy of offering some products for free while charging for others, or offering a product for free to some customers while charging others for it.

PRICE ADJUSTMENT TACTICS

After they've established initial price points, companies need to stay on the lookout for potential advantages that can be gained by adjusting prices up or down over time. They can offer a variety of **discounts**, such as temporary price reductions to stimulate sales, reductions for paying early or paying in cash, or *volume discounts* for buying in bulk.

Although offering discounts is a popular way to boost sales of a product, the downside is that discounts can set off *price wars* between competitors. Price wars can occur when (1) one supplier believes that underpricing the competition is the best way—or perhaps the only way—for it to increase sales volume and (2) customers believe that price is the only meaningful differentiator among the various suppliers. This situation occurs frequently in the air travel industry, which is why it has been wracked with price wars ever since it was deregulated years ago. Price wars present two significant dangers: that customers will begin to believe that price is the only factor to care about in the market and that desperate competitors will cut prices so far that they'll damage their finances—perhaps beyond repair.

discounts
Temporary price reductions to stimulate sales or lower prices to encourage certain behaviors such as paying with cash.

Sometimes sellers combine several of their products and sell them at one reduced price. This practice, called **bundling**, can also promote sales of products consumers might not otherwise buy—especially when the combined price is low enough to entice them to purchase the bundle. Examples of bundled products are season tickets, vacation packages, computer software with hardware, and wrapped packages of shampoo and conditioner. In contrast, a company can also *unbundle* elements of a product and charge separately for the individual elements.

bundling
Offering several products for a single price that is presumably lower than the total of the products' individual prices.

Finally, companies can constantly reprice their products in response to supply and demand fluctuations, a tactic known as **dynamic pricing**. Dynamic pricing not only

dynamic pricing
Continually adjusting prices to reflect changes in supply and demand.

enables companies to move slow-selling merchandise instantly but also allows companies to experiment with different pricing levels. Because price changes are immediately distributed via computer networks, customers always have the most current price information. Airlines and hotels have used this type of continually adjusted pricing for years, a technique often known as *yield management*. However, companies need to be careful not to alienate customers by creating so much pricing uncertainty that purchasing becomes a frustrating cat-and-mouse game. In fact, noted brand strategist Al Ries calls dynamic pricing the "ultimate brand destruction machine" because it rewards buyers for price shopping rather than being loyal to a single brand.[36]

For the latest information on pricing strategies and tactics, visit **http://real-timeupdates .com/bia8** and click on Chapter 14.

 **Checkpoint**

LEARNING OBJECTIVE 6: Identify nine common pricing methods.

SUMMARY: (1) *Cost-based* or *cost-plus pricing* takes the cost of producing and marketing a product and adds a markup to arrive at the selling price. (2) *Value-based pricing* seeks to establish the perceived value of the product in the eyes of target customers and sets a price based on that. (3) *Optimal pricing* is a computer-based method that uses sales data to create a demand curve for every product, allowing managers to select prices based on specific marketing objectives. (4) *Skim pricing* involves setting an initial price that is relatively high in order to capitalize on pent-up demand or the lack of direct competition for a new product. (5) *Penetration pricing* is setting a price low enough to achieve targeted sales volumes. (6) *Loss-leader pricing* is setting the price artificially low on one product in order to attract buyers for other products. (7) *Auction pricing* lets buyers determine the selling price by bidding against one another; in a reverse auction, buyers state a price they are willing to pay and sellers choose whether to match it. (8) *Participative pricing* lets buyers pay whatever they think a product is worth. (9) *Freemium pricing* involves giving away products to some customers (as a means of attracting paying customers, for example) or giving away some products but charging for others.

CRITICAL THINKING: (1) What steps could a company take to determine the perceived value of its products in its target markets? (2) How can patterns of temporary price discounts "train" consumers to stop buying at full price?

IT'S YOUR BUSINESS: (1) Have you ever bid on anything on eBay, another online auction site, or an in-person auction? If so, how did you decide how much to bid? Did you set a maximum price you'd allow yourself to spend? Did you get caught up in the competitive emotions of bidding against someone else? (2) Have you ever purchased a hot new product as soon as it hit the market, only to see the price drop a few months later? If so, did you resolve never to buy so quickly again?

KEY TERMS TO KNOW: cost-based pricing, value-based pricing, optimal pricing, skim pricing, penetration pricing, loss-leader pricing, participative pricing, freemium pricing, discounts, bundling, dynamic pricing

BEHIND THE SCENES
BUILDING THE ANNIKA BRAND

Annika Sörenstam is approaching her second career the same way she approached her first. In golf, she reached the top of her sport by learning from the best, surrounding herself with a supportive team, setting ambitious goals, and working hard to reach those goals.

A central element in her business plan is the role she herself plays as the core of the "Annika" brand. As a young player in her native Sweden, she was so reluctant to step into the limelight that she would falter toward the end of tournaments to avoid winning and facing the media attention that came with it. She clearly fixed that problem, transforming herself into a quietly confident but ferocious competitor who often left other players in the dust as she went on to win nearly 90 tournaments worldwide.

However, as she was nearing retirement from golf and ramping up her business activities, she realized that the persona she had become known for on the course didn't lend itself to her ambitions for the Annika brand. Research by branding consultant Duane Knapp showed that people respected Sörenstam's competitive drive but really had no sense of who she was as a person. Even her own husband says she was viewed by the public as "the stoic Swede who will step on your throat" on the way to victory and not the "humble, pretty, and hilarious" woman he knew off the course.

Transforming Annika the feared competitor into Annika the warm and welcoming brand icon was a top priority. Good examples of this effort are her blog and her Twitter account, which give visitors the chance to know her as she lives off the course, including her love of gourmet cooking, her passion for skiing, and her role as a mother.

Along with crafting an inviting brand image that more accurately reflects her true personality, Sörenstam is busy expanding the Annika product line. She continues to endorse many of the same goods and services she promoted as an active player, including Callaway Golf, Lexus, and Rolex, and she has her own line of clothing in partnership with Cutter & Buck. She chooses deals with great care to preserve the high-quality associations people have on the Annika brand.

A central element in her product portfolio is the Annika Academy, a golf instruction facility in Reunion, Florida, that offers lessons, corporate outings, golf vacations, and the opportunity to train with the same advisors and coaches who work with Sörenstam. For the ultimate golf experience, a few lucky visitors every year can buy the three-day, $12,000 "Sören-Slam" package, which includes nine holes of golf with Sörenstam herself.

Following another path blazed by her golf-business mentors, Sörenstam also launched a golf course design business,

with courses in Turkey, China, and other countries. Having had the opportunity to play some of the finest and most historic golf courses in the world, she combines that experience with her insights as a professional to create challenging but playable courses. Her designs also aim to right an aesthetic wrong shared by too many golf courses: The best views of both the playing area and the surrounding landscape are found on the men's tee boxes. (Golf courses have different sets of tee boxes to reflect the different hitting lengths of average male and female players.) On her courses, women enjoy the same quality of experience as the men.

Sörenstam has had an interest in finance since an early age, and that passion is reflected in yet another part of the product mix, the Annika Financial Group. This small firm helps other professional athletes manage their money and achieve financial security in their postathletic lives.

With a recrafted brand image and a growing product portfolio, Sörenstam is off to a hot start in her quest to be the first woman to join the exclusive club of former athletes who have truly made it big in business. Michael Jordan is "Air Jordan," Arnold Palmer is the "The King," Jack Nicklaus is "The Golden Bear," and Greg Norman, another golf empire builder, is "The Shark." Who knows—perhaps Annika is "The Avenger"?[37]

Critical Thinking Questions

14-1. Golfers who take lessons and purchase other services from the Annika Academy presumably share at least some of Sörenstam's passion for winning. Would toning down the competitive aspect of Sörenstam's public persona negatively affect the Annika brand in the eyes of Academy customers? Explain your answer.

14-2. Sörenstam's charitable efforts include the Annika Foundation, which you can read about on her website. How does her work with the foundation contribute to her brand equity?

14-3. Explain how the brand extension efforts in clothing and financial advice can reasonably fit under the umbrella of the Annika brand.

LEARN MORE ONLINE

Visit Sörenstam's website at **www.annikasorenstam.com** and her accounts on Facebook and Twitter. What is your overall impression of Sörenstam as a businessperson and of the Annika brand as a product identifier? Do these communication efforts help to shift her public image away from that of the fierce competitor?

KEY TERMS

brand (329)
brand equity (329)
brand extension (334)
brand loyalty (329)
brand managers (332)
brand marks (329)
brand names (329)
break-even analysis (337)
break-even point (337)
bundling (341)
capital items (324)
co-branding (330)
commercialization (328)
convenience products (323)
cost-based pricing (339)
discounts (341)
dynamic pricing (341)
expense items (324)
family branding (334)
fixed costs (336)
freemium pricing (341)

license (330)
logo (329)
loss-leader pricing (340)
national brands (330)
optimal pricing (339)
participative pricing (341)
penetration pricing (340)
price elasticity (336)
private brands (330)
product development process (326)
product life cycle (324)
product line (332)
product mix (332)
prototypes (327)
shopping products (323)
skim pricing (339)
specialty products (323)
test marketing (328)
trademarks (329)
value-based pricing (339)
variable costs (336)

MyBizLab®
To complete the problems with the ⭐,
go to EOC Discussion Questions in the
MyLab.

TEST YOUR KNOWLEDGE

Questions for Review

14-4. What are the four stages of the product life cycle?

14-5. What is test marketing?

14-6. What are the functions of packaging?

14-7. How many books will a publisher have to sell to break even if fixed costs are $100,000, the selling price per book is $60, and the variable costs per book are $40?

14-8. How does cost-based pricing differ from value-based pricing?

Questions for Analysis

14-9. How does branding help consumers?

14-10. Why are some well-established brands worth millions or even billions of dollars?

14-11. Given the weaknesses of cost-based pricing, why would any company use this method?

⭐ **14-12.** Why is it important to review the objectives of a strategic marketing plan before setting a product's price?

⭐ **14-13.** **Ethical Considerations.** If your college neighborhood is typical, many companies in the area adorn themselves in your school colors and otherwise seek to identify their names with your school name and thereby encourage business from students. Some of these firms probably have brand licensing agreements with your college or are involved in sponsoring various groups on campus. However, chances are some of them are using school colors and other branding elements without having any formal arrangement with the college. In other words, they may be getting commercial benefit from the association without paying for it.[38] Is this ethical? Why or why not?

Questions for Application

⭐ **14-14.** In what ways might Mattel modify its pricing strategies during the life cycle of a toy product?

⭐ **14-15.** Do you consider yourself an *early adopter* when it comes to trying out new products or new fashions, or do you tend to take a wait-and-see attitude? How does your attitude toward new products and new ideas influence your decision-making as a consumer?

14-16. Concept Integration. Review the theory of supply and demand in Chapter 2 (see pages 32–35). How do skimming and penetration pricing strategies influence a product's supply and demand?

14-17. Concept Integration. Review the discussion of cultural differences in international business in Chapter 3 (see pages 60–61). Which cultural differences do you think Disney had to consider when planning its product strategies for Disneyland Paris? Originally the company offered a standardized product but was later forced to customize many of the park's operations. What might have been some of the cultural challenges Disney experienced under a standardized product strategy?

EXPAND YOUR KNOWLEDGE

Discovering Career Opportunities

Being a marketing manager is a big responsibility, but it can be a lot of fun at the same time. Read what the U.S. Department of Labor has to say about the nature of the work, working conditions, qualifications, and job outlook for marketing managers by accessing the Bureau of Labor Statistics's *Occupational Outlook Handbook*, at www.bls.gov/ooh.

14-18. What does a marketing manager do?

14-19. What are some key questions you might want to ask when interviewing for a job in marketing?

14-20. What training and qualifications should a marketing manager have?

Improving Your Tech Insights: Mobile Location and Tracking Technologies

Businesses use a variety of mobile technologies to locate, identify, and track products, vehicles, and other resources:

- Radio frequency identification (RFID) technology uses small scannable tags attached to products or even people and pets.

- Near-field communication (NFC) uses low-power radio links transfer information between devices (including cards with embedded chips) over short distances. For example, *contactless payment* systems, using either cards or smartphones, using NFC.

- The Global Positioning System (GPS) can pinpoint any location on Earth using a network of satellites and small transceivers. If you've ever used a smartphone or the satnav system in a car to find your way, you've used GPS.

Using online research tools, find a business application of one of these three technologies. In an email message to your instructor or a post on your class blog, describe how the technology is used and explain its business benefits.

PRACTICE YOUR SKILLS

Sharpening Your Communication Skills

Now's your chance to play the role of a marketing specialist trying to convince a group of customers that your product concept is better than the competition's. You're going to wade into the industry battle over digital photo printing. Choose a side: either the photo printer manufacturers, who want consumers to buy printers to print their own digital photos (visit HP, at www.hp.com, for an overview of photo-quality printers), or the service providers, who claim their way is better (visit the website of one of the many retailers that offer a service-based approach, such as www.cvs.com or www.walmart.com). Prepare a short presentation on why the approach you've chosen is better for consumers. Feel free to segment the consumer market and choose a particular target segment if that bolsters your argument.

Building Your Team Skills

Select a high-profile product with which you and your teammates are familiar. Do some online research to learn more about that brand. Then answer these questions and prepare a short group presentation to your classmates summarizing your findings:

- Is the product a consumer product, an organizational product, or both?
- At what stage in its life cycle is this product?
- Is the product a national brand or a private brand?
- How do the product's packaging and labeling help boost consumer appeal?
- How is this product promoted?
- Is the product mix to which this product belongs wide? Long? Deep?
- Is the product sold in international markets? If so, does the company use a standardized or a customized strategy?
- How is the product priced in relation to competing products?

Developing Your Research Skills

Scan recent business journals and newspapers (print or online editions) for an article related to one of the following:

- New product development
- The product life cycle
- Brand extensions
- Pricing strategies
- Packaging

14-21. Does this article report on a development in a particular company, several companies, or an entire industry? Which companies or industries are specifically mentioned?

14-22. If you were a marketing manager in this industry, what concerns would you have as a result of reading the article? What questions do you think companies in this industry (or related ones) should be asking? What would you want to know?

14-23. In what ways do you think this industry, other industries, or the public might be affected by this trend or development in the next five years? Why?

MyBizLab®

Go to the Assignments section of your MyLab to complete these writing exercises.

14-24. What sort of customers should a company target for the introductory phase of a product's life cycle?

14-25. Is it ethical for companies to *split-test* price points by offering different prices to different groups of customers? Why or why not?

ENDNOTES

1. Daniel Roberts, "How Golfer Annika Sorenstam Is Blazing a Profitable Path for Retired Female Athletes," *Fortune*, 24 March 2015, http://fortune.com; Annika Sörenstam website, accessed 22 May 2015, www.annikasorenstam.com; Annika Academy website, accessed 22 May 2015, www.theannikaacademy.com; Jeff Chu, "A New Course for Sörenstam," *Time South Pacific* (Australia/New Zealand edition), 12 January 2009, 46–47; Brian McCallen, "Annika on Course," *Forbes*, 8 October 2007, 68–69; Eben Harrell, "Calling Time," *Time South Pacific* (Australia/New Zealand edition), 26 May 2008, 5; Edward Schmidt, Jr., "Fierce Competition," *Meeting News*, 8 October 2007, 60; Barry Janoff, "Sörenstam Scores with Sponsors; Foul Called on NBA's Offseason," *Brandweek*, 1 October 2007, 12; Jessica Shambora, "Stroke of Genius," *Fortune*, 10 November 2008, 62–64.

2. Werner Reinartz and Wolfgang Ulaga, "How to Sell Services More Profitably," *Harvard Business Review*, May 2008, 90–96.

3. Jung-Ah Lee and Evan Ramstad, "Samsung Pulls Galaxy Tab from Berlin Trade Show," *Wall Street Journal*, 6 September 2011, http://online.wsj.com.

4. Jenna Wortham, "Sending GPS Devices the Way of the Tape Deck?" *New York Times*, 7 July 2009, www.nytimes.com.

5. Michael V. Copeland and Om Malik, "How to Build a Bulletproof Startup," *Business 2.0*, June 2006, www.business2.com.

6. Nicolas Block, Kara Gruver, and David Cooper, "Slimming Innovation Pipelines to Fatten Their Returns," *Harvard Management Update*, August 2007, 3–5.

7. Nanette Byrnes, "Xerox' New Design Team: Customers," *BusinessWeek*, 7 May 2007, 72.

8. Hilary Lewis, "Amazon Orders 5 New Series Including 'Man in the High Castle,'" *Hollywood Reporter*, 18 February 2015, www.hollywoodreporter.com.

9. David Haigh and Jonathan Knowles, "How to Define Your Brand and Determine Its Value," *Marketing Management*, May/June 2004, 22–28.

10. "BrandZ Top 100 Most Valuable Global Brands 2014," *Millward Brown*, www.millwardbrown.com.

11. Nina Diamond, John F. Sherry, Albert M. Muñiz, Mary Ann McGrath, Robert V. Kozinets, and Stefania Borghini, "American Girl and the Brand Gestalt: Closing the Loop on Sociocultural Branding Research," *Journal of Marketing*, May 2009, 118–134.

12. Janell M. Kurtz and Cynthia Mehoves, "Whose Name Is It Anyway?" *Marketing Management*, January/February 2002, 31–33.

13. Dictionary.com, accessed 24 October 2011, www.dictionary.com.

14. Stephanie Strom, "Store-Label Brands Cleaning Up in Supermarket Aisle," *Seattle Times*, 2 October 2013, www.seattletimes.com.

15. Roberts, "How Golfer Annika Sorenstam Is Blazing a Profitable Path for Retired Female Athletes."

16. Lawrence L. Garber Jr., Eva M. Hyatt, and Ünal Ö. Boya, "The Effect of Package Shape on Apparent Volume: An Exploratory Study with Implications for Package Design," *Journal of Marketing Theory & Practice*, Summer 2009, 215–234.

17. Sean Poulter, "The Perils of Opening Impossible Packaging: Four in Ten of Us Have Suffered an Injury While Opening Everyday Goods," *Daily Mail*, 20 August 2013, www.dailymail.co.uk.

18. Kristin Heist, "How Packaging Protects the Environment," *Harvard Business Review*, 14 June 2012, www.hbr.org.

19. "Amazon Certified Frustration-Free Packaging," *Amazon*, accessed 25 May 2015, www.amazon.com.

20. Cheerios website, accessed 25 May 2015, www.cheerios.com.

21. Betsy Morris and Joan L. Levinstein, "What Makes Apple Golden," *Fortune*, 17 March 2008, 68–74; Bharat N. Anand, "The Value of a Broader Product Portfolio," *Harvard Business Review*, January 2008, 20–22.

22. Chris Anderson, "The Long Tail," *Wired*, October 2004, www.wired.com.

23. McDonald's France website, accessed 25 May 2015, www .mcdonalds.fr; Andrew Shanahan, "Why Did France Fall in Love with McDonald's?" *The Guardian*, 24 July 2008, www. guardian.co.uk; Carol Matlack, "What's This? The French Love McDonald's?" *BusinessWeek*, 13 January 2003, 50; Shirley Leung, "Armchairs, TVs and Espresso—Is It McDonald's?" *Wall Street Journal*, 30 August 2002, A1, A6.

24. Alicia A. Caldwell, "21 Airlines Fined for Fixing Passenger, Cargo Fees," *Seattle Times*, 5 March 2011, www.seattletimes.com.

25. Eric Anderson and Duncan Simester, "Mind Your Pricing Cues," *Harvard Business Review*, September 96–103.

26. Edward Ramirez and Ronald E. Goldsmith, "Some Antecedents of Price Sensitivity," *Journal of Marketing Theory & Practice*, Summer 2009, 199–213.

27. Elisabeth A. Sullivan, "Value Pricing: Smart Marketers Know Cost-Plus Can Be Costly," *Marketing News*, 15 January 2008, 8.

28. Peter J. Williamson and Ming Zeng, "Value-for-Money Strategies for Recessionary Times," *Harvard Business Review*, March 2009, 66–74.

29. Revionics website, accessed 27 July 2009, www.revionics.com; Amy Cortese, "The Power of Optimal Pricing," *Business 2.0*, September 2002, 68–70.

30. Priceline website, accessed 14 November 2013, www.priceline .com.

31. Ju-Young Kim, Martin Natter, and Martin Spann, "Pay What You Want: A New Participative Pricing Mechanism," *Journal of Marketing*, January 2009, 44–58.

32. John Varcoe, "Lunatics in Charge," *NZ Marketing Magazine*, June 2009, 10.

33. Don Moyer, "That's Going to Cost You," *Harvard Business Review*, May 2009, 132.

34. Sunil Gupta and Carl F. Mela, "What Is a Free Customer Worth?" *Harvard Business Review*, November 2008, 102–109.

35. "How About Free? The Price Point That Is Turning Industries on Their Heads," Knowledge@Wharton, 4 March 2009, ttp://knowledge.wharton.upenn.edu.

36. Al Ries, "Variable Pricing Is Ultimate Brand-Destruction Machine," *Advertising Age*, 8 June 2009, 11.

37. See note 1.

38. Aubrey Kent and Richard M. Campbell, Jr., "An Introduction to Freeloading: Campus-Area Ambush Marketing," *Sport Marketing Quarterly*, Vol. 16, No. 2 (2007), 118–122.

LEARNING OBJECTIVES   After studying this chapter, you will be able to

1. Explain the role of marketing intermediaries in contemporary business, and list the eight primary functions that intermediaries can perform.

2. Identify the major types of wholesalers, and summarize four trends shaping the future of wholesaling.

3. Identify the major retailing formats, and summarize six trends shaping the future of retailing.

4. Explain the strategic decisions that manufacturers must make when choosing distribution channels.

5. Identify five key attributes of distribution channel design and management.

6. Highlight the major components of physical distribution and logistics.

BEHIND THE SCENES   COSTCO KEEPS CUSTOMERS COMING BACK FOR MORE

Mark Richard/PhotoEdit, Inc.

Costco shoppers have learned to look for great buys on both everyday items and an ever-changing mix of luxury and specialty goods.

www.costco.com

With an unusual mix of low prices and quality goods, Costco Wholesale has become the country's largest and most profitable warehouse club chain. The company knows that low prices on high-quality, high-end merchandise can transcend the common notion of "discount." And, in what amounts to a treasure hunt played out along Costco's cement-floor aisles, the high/low shopping experience is a powerful elixir for today's shoppers.

Once new members get the hang of the treasure hunt mentality, they can get hooked on Costco, because even though they don't know what will be on display, they're sure it will be offered at an appealing price. Like other warehouse clubs, Costco sells a mix of everything from giant boxes of cereal to patio furniture. In fact, Costco often asks vendors to change their factory runs to produce specially built packages that are bigger and less expensive on a per-unit basis. Unlike with other warehouse clubs, however, Costco shoppers can occasionally find $10,000 diamond rings and grand pianos along with mouthwash and laundry detergent.

Must-have merchandise isn't the only reason shoppers keep coming back to Costco. The company also offers a wide array of services, from pharmacies and optical centers to vacation travel packages to home, health, and auto insurance. Small business customers can even sign up to have Costco process their payrolls or provide phone service.

If you were in charge of strategy at Costco, how would you keep Costco on the leading edge of retailing? How would you integrate your physical retail stores with your online e-commerce operation? What could you do to keep your bargain-conscious but demanding customers coming back for more?[1]

INTRODUCTION

Marketing intermediaries such as Costco (profiled in the chapter-opening Behind the Scenes) play an essential role in marketing products created by other companies. This chapter explores the many contributions these intermediaries make, both at the retailing stage that is visible to all consumers and at the less visible but no less important wholesaling stage. Manufacturers and other producers need to understand the distribution process in order to select the right intermediaries and work with them effectively. And, of course, wholesalers and retailers are business entities themselves, with their own strategic questions and operating challenges.

The Role of Marketing Intermediaries

As Chapter 13 points out, a *distribution channel*, or *marketing channel*, is an organized network of firms that work together to get goods and services from producer to customer. Whether you're selling digital music files or scrap iron stripped out of old ships, your **distribution strategy**, or overall plan for moving products to buyers, will play a major role in your success.

Think of all the products you buy: food, cosmetics, clothing, sports equipment, train tickets, gasoline, stationery, appliances, music, books, and all the rest. How many of these products do you buy directly from the producer? For most people, the answer is not many. Most companies that create products do not sell these goods directly to the final users. Instead, producers in many industries work with **marketing intermediaries** to bring their products to market. Even some service companies rely on other firms to perform services on their behalf.

WHOLESALING VERSUS RETAILING

Intermediaries can be grouped into two general types: wholesalers and retailers. **Wholesalers** sell to organizational customers, including other wholesalers, companies, government agencies, and educational institutions. In turn, the customers of wholesalers either resell the products or use them to make products of their own.

Unlike wholesalers, **retailers** primarily sell products to consumers for personal use. Terminology in the distribution field can get a bit confusing, starting with the multiple uses of the term *wholesale*. For instance, even though Costco and other warehouse-type stores often use the "wholesale" label to describe themselves, they function as both wholesalers and retailers simultaneously. Small-business owners, for instance, are enthusiastic Costco shoppers because the store is a low-cost place to buy supplies and equipment. With these shoppers, Costco is functioning as a wholesaler. However, when selling to consumers, Costco is technically operating as a retailer, not a wholesaler. The distinction is important because business strategies for wholesaling and retailing are dramatically different in many ways. Even when they buy the same products, consumers and organizations usually make purchases for different reasons. Because their motivations and expectations are different, consumers (reached by retailers) and organizations (reached by wholesalers) don't respond to marketing programs the same way.

CONTRIBUTIONS OF MARKETING INTERMEDIARIES

Wholesalers and retailers are instrumental in creating three of the four forms of utility mentioned in Chapter 13: They provide the items customers need in a convenient location (place utility), they save customers the time of having to contact each manufacturer to purchase a good (time utility), and they provide an efficient process for transferring products

---

1 **LEARNING OBJECTIVE**

Explain the role of marketing intermediaries in contemporary business, and list the eight primary functions that intermediaries can perform.

distribution strategy
A firm's overall plan for moving products through intermediaries and on to final customers.

marketing intermediaries
Businesspeople and organizations that assist in moving and marketing goods and services between producers and consumers.

wholesalers
Intermediaries that sell products to other intermediaries for resale or to organizations for internal use.

retailers
Intermediaries that sell goods and services to individuals for their own personal use.

from the producer to the customer (possession utility). In addition to creating utility, wholesalers and retailers perform the following distribution functions:

- **Matching buyers and sellers.** By making sellers' products available to multiple buyers, intermediaries such as Costco reduce the number of transactions between producers and customers. In the business-to-business market, the industrial distributor Grainger (www.grainger.com) is a good example of the enormous scale that can be achieved in bringing buyers and sellers together. Boasting a portfolio of nearly 1.5 million products, Grainger connects over 4,000 suppliers with 2 million organizational customers.[2] These customers are saved the time and trouble of working with multiple suppliers, and the product suppliers get access to more customers than all but the very largest of them could ever hope to reach on their own. Although "cutting out the middleman" is sometimes used as a promotional slogan to suggest lower costs, intermediaries such as Grainger can actually make commerce more efficient by reducing the number of contact points between buyers and sellers (see Exhibit 15.1).

- **Providing market information.** Retail intermediaries, such as Amazon and Macy's, collect valuable data about customer purchases: who buys, how often, and how much. For example, e-commerce records and data from "frequent shopper" cards help retailers spot buying patterns, providing vital market information they can then share with producers to optimize product mixes and promotional efforts.

- **Providing promotional and sales support.** Many intermediaries assist with advertising, in-store displays, and other promotional efforts for some or all of the products they sell. Some also employ sales representatives who can perform a number of selling and customer relationship functions.

EXHIBIT 15.1	**How Intermediaries Simplify Commerce**

Intermediaries actually lower the price customers pay for many goods and services because they reduce the number of contacts between producers and consumers that would otherwise be necessary. They also create place, time, and possession utility.

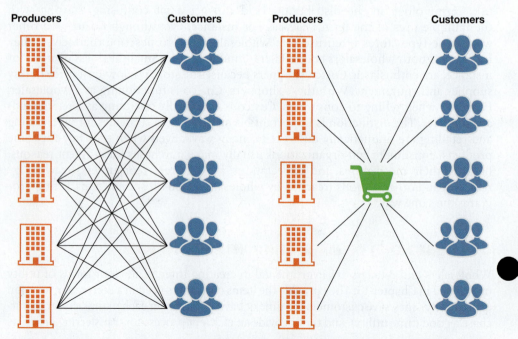

Source: Based on Philip Kotler, *Marketing Management*, 10th ed. (Upper Saddle River, N.J.: Pearson Prentice Hall, 2000), 491.

- **Gathering assortments of goods.** Many intermediaries receive bulk shipments from producers and break them into more convenient units (known as *breaking bulk*) by sorting, standardizing, and dividing bulk quantities into smaller packages.
- **Transporting and storing products.** Intermediaries often maintain inventories of merchandise that they acquire from producers so they can quickly fill customers' orders. In many cases, retailers purchase this merchandise from wholesalers who, in addition to breaking bulk, may also transport the goods from the producer to the retail outlets.
- **Assuming risks.** When intermediaries accept goods from manufacturers, they usually take on the risks associated with damage, theft, product perishability (in the sense of tangible goods that are vulnerable to rotting, for instance), and obsolescence.
- **Providing financing.** Large intermediaries sometimes provide loans to smaller producers.
- **Completing product solutions.** In the information technology sector, manufacturers often rely on a class of intermediaries called *value-added resellers (VARs)* or *system integrators* to complete or customize solutions for customers. These channel partners can bring specialized technical expertise or provide geographic reach into smaller markets.
- **Facilitating transactions and supporting customers.** Intermediaries can perform a variety of functions that help with the selection, purchase, and use of products. Commercial real estate brokers, for example, can negotiate prices and contract terms on behalf of buyers and sellers. In a variety of industries, intermediaries help customers select the products that fit their needs and then provide customer support and technical assistance after the sale.

✔ Checkpoint

LEARNING OBJECTIVE 1: Explain the role of marketing intermediaries in contemporary business, and list the eight primary functions that intermediaries can perform.

SUMMARY: Intermediaries can be responsible for any and all aspects of distribution, one of the key elements in any firm's marketing mix. The two major categories are *wholesalers*, which buy from producers and sell to retailers, to other wholesalers, and to organizational customers such as businesses, government agencies, and institutions; and *retailers*, which buy from producers or wholesalers and sell the products to the final consumers. These marketing intermediaries bring products to market and help ensure that the goods and services are available at the right time, in the right place, and in the right amount. Depending on their position in the channel, intermediaries can perform the eight key functions of matching buyers and sellers; providing market information; providing promotional and sales support; sorting, standardizing, and dividing merchandise; transporting and storing products; assuming risks; providing financing; and completing production solutions.

CRITICAL THINKING: (1) Why wouldn't a computer manufacturer do all the work of customizing systems and thereby keep all the business for itself, rather than relying on value-added resellers? (2) How can Costco be both a wholesaler and a retailer at the same time?

IT'S YOUR BUSINESS: (1) If you had the choice of buying a product directly from the manufacturer or from a local retailer, which would you choose? Why? (2) Have you ever had to work with more than one retailer to get a complete product solution (such as getting car parts or home improvement supplies from multiple stores)? Was the experience satisfactory?

KEY TERMS TO KNOW: distribution strategy, marketing intermediaries, wholesalers, retailers

2 **LEARNING OBJECTIVE**

Identify the major types of wholesalers, and summarize four trends shaping the future of wholesaling.

Wholesaling and Industrial Distribution

Although largely unseen by consumers, wholesaling is a huge presence in the economy. Nearly 6 million people work in wholesaling in the United States, and the sector generates more than 7 trillion dollars in sales every year.[3] By connecting producers with retailers and organizational customers, wholesalers play a vital role in nearly every industry in the world.

MAJOR TYPES OF WHOLESALERS

merchant wholesalers
Independent wholesalers that take legal title to goods they distribute.

Most wholesalers are independent companies that can be classified as *merchant wholesalers, agents,* or *brokers.* The majority of wholesalers are **merchant wholesalers**, independently owned businesses that buy from producers, take legal title to the goods, and then resell them to retailers or to organizational buyers. Most merchant wholesalers are small to midsized businesses, but the field includes a handful of multibillion-dollar firms such as Grainger in industrial supplies, Avnet (**www.avnet.com**) in electronic components, McKesson (**www.mckesson.com**) in health care, and Supervalu (**www.supervalu.com**) in groceries.

Full-service merchant wholesalers provide a wide variety of services, such as storage, sales, order processing, delivery, and promotional support. *Rack jobbers,* for example, are full-service merchant wholesalers that set up displays in retail outlets, stock inventory, and perform other services such as marking prices on merchandise. *Limited-service merchant wholesalers,* on the other hand, provide fewer services. Natural resources such as lumber, grain, and coal are usually marketed through a class of limited-service wholesalers called *drop shippers,* which take ownership but not physical possession of the goods they handle.

distributors
Merchant wholesalers that sell products to organizational customers for internal operations or the production of other goods, rather than to retailers for resale.

Merchant wholesalers can also be distinguished by their customers. Supervalu and others that sell primarily to other intermediaries are usually known in the trade simply as *wholesalers.* In contrast, Avnet and others that sell goods to companies for use in their own products and operations are usually called **distributors**.

agents and brokers
Independent wholesalers that do not take title to the goods they distribute but may or may not take possession of those goods.

Unlike merchant wholesalers, **agents and brokers** never actually own the products they handle, and they perform fewer services. Their primary role is to bring buyers and sellers together; they are generally paid a commission (a percentage of the money received) for arranging sales. Producers of industrial parts often sell to business customers through brokers. *Manufacturers' representatives,* another type of agent, sell various noncompeting products to customers in a specific region. By representing several manufacturers' products, these reps achieve enough volume to justify the cost of a direct sales call.

THE OUTLOOK FOR WHOLESALING

Like all businesses, wholesalers must grapple with changes in the business environment, from changing customer behavior to advances in technology. Here are some key trends that are reshaping the wholesaling sector.

- **E-commerce and new competitors.** Many smaller wholesalers and industrial distributors were slow to embrace e-commerce, and as a result wound up facing new, technologically advanced competitors. Amazon, for example, has grown far beyond its original consumer focus and now offers millions of business, industrial, and scientific products.[4] Wholesalers that haven't already embraced e-commerce are going to have a difficult time competing against the convenience, selection, and prices advantages that Amazon and other online sellers often have.

- **Threat of disintermediation.** As e-commerce continues to disrupt old ways of doing business, some observers have predicted the widespread **disintermediation** of wholesalers, meaning their functions as intermediaries would be taken over by manufacturers on the upstream end or by customers (retailers and other organizational buyers) on the downstream end. Although the share of wholesaling activity performed by independent wholesalers appears to be shrinking somewhat, wholesalers as a group have not disappeared to the extent that some predicted.[5] Intermediaries will continue to play an integral role in the distribution process as long as they can

disintermediation
The replacement of intermediaries by producers, customers, or other intermediaries when those other parties can perform channel functions more effectively or efficiently.

add value and perform essential services more effectively and more efficiently than either manufacturers or customers.[6]

- **Integrated logistics management.** The outsourcing trend discussed in Chapter 9 is definitely having an impact in the wholesaling sector as *third-party logistics (3PL)* firms continue to take over a wide range of tasks in supply chain management, including not only traditional wholesaling activities but also order fulfillment, product repair, customer service, and other functions. These 3PL firms have been growing rapidly in recent years, as more companies look to offload supply chain functions in order to focus on core business activities and to minimize the costs and risks of investing in transportation systems.[7] The emergence of 3PL is coming from two directions, as transportation companies such as UPS and FedEx and wholesalers such as Supervalu and McKesson expand the scope of their services.

- **Industry consolidation.** Consolidation seems likely as large firms with economies of scale buy up or drive out smaller, less-competitive firms. In addition, many customers are pursuing *strategic sourcing*, in which they forge closer relationships with a smaller number of strategic distribution partners.[8]

✔ Checkpoint

LEARNING OBJECTIVE 2: Identify the major types of wholesalers, and summarize four trends shaping the future of wholesaling.

SUMMARY: Most wholesalers can be classified as *merchant wholesalers, agents*, or *brokers*. Merchant wholesalers are independently owned businesses that buy from producers, take legal title to the goods, and then resell them to retailers or to organizational buyers. Merchant wholesalers can be distinguished by level of service (*full service* versus *limited service*) and target customers (*wholesalers* that sell goods to retailers for the purpose of then reselling them to consumers and *distributors* that sell goods to organizations for internal operation use or to make other products). In contrast to merchant wholesalers, agents and brokers do not assume ownership but focus on bringing buyers and sellers together. Key trends shaping wholesaling are e-commerce and new competitors, integrated logistics management, the threat of disintermediation, and industry consolidation.

CRITICAL THINKING: (1) Why does McKesson promote itself as a health-care services company, rather than as a logistics company? (2) Why might a manufacturer choose to hire a third-party logistics firm rather than a conventional wholesaler or distributor?

IT'S YOUR BUSINESS: (1) Considering the forces shaping wholesaling, would you pursue a career in this sector? Why or why not? (2) If your family ran a small industrial products wholesaler that was facing the threat of disintermediation, how would you respond?

KEY TERMS TO KNOW: merchant wholesalers, distributors, agents and brokers, disintermediation

Retailing

3 LEARNING OBJECTIVE

In addition to providing convenient access to products and supporting consumers with a variety of presale and postsale services, retailers play a major role in the buying process because many consumer buying decisions are made in the retail setting (both in-store and online). Consequently, retailing involves a blend of the distribution and customer communication elements of the marketing mix. The term *shopper marketing*, or *in-store marketing*, refers to communication efforts directed at consumers while they are in the retail setting. These efforts can range from printed signs to in-store video screens to smartphone apps

Identify the major retailing formats, and summarize six trends shaping the future of retailing.

that help shoppers find products or stores in a mall, for example.[9] To be sure, the degree to which decision making occurs in the store varies across product categories, consumers, and purchasing situations. For example, consumers engaged in home remodeling projects typically have a clear idea of what they want to buy before they get to the store, so the in-store decisions relate more to specific colors and textures than to broad product categories.[10] In other instances, in-store signs, product labels, and other factors can influence the types of products and specific brands that consumers choose.

Given the importance of the shopping environment, retailers spend considerable time and money crafting physical spaces and shopping experiences that are intended to shape consumer behavior, addressing everything from lighting and color palettes to music, aromas, and employee attire. No detail seems to be too small. For instance, the attractiveness of employees and even other shoppers can influence consumer choices. Although consumers are generally put off by the realization that other shoppers have touched the products on display in a store, if they see an *attractive* person touch a product, people tend to think more highly of that product.[11]

REAL-TIME UPDATES

Learn More by Visiting This Website

Love the retail experience?

Why not make a career of it? Check out the National Retail Foundation's career center. Go to **http://real-timeupdates.com/bia8** and click on Learn More in the Students section.

RETAILING FORMATS

With so much effort directed toward influencing buying decisions across so many categories of products and diverse segments in the consumer market, the retail sector has evolved into a dizzying array of store types and formats. Much of this evolution can be explained by a concept called the **wheel of retailing**. In this model, an innovative retailer with low operating costs attracts a following by offering low prices and limited service. As this store adds more services to broaden its appeal, its prices creep upward, opening the door for a new generation of lower-priced competitors. Eventually, these competitors also upgrade their operations and are replaced by still other lower-priced stores that later follow the same upward pattern.[12]

For instance, Walmart reshaped retailing with low prices enabled by the company's extraordinary abilities at cost control and efficiency but now finds itself facing new low-price competition from the likes of Family Dollar Stores and Dollar General. Family Dollar gained market share during the recent recession as more shoppers turned to it for food and household essentials.[13]

Regardless of product offerings or target markets, all retailing efforts can be divided into *store* formats—based in physical store locations—and *nonstore* formats—which take place anywhere and everywhere outside of physical stores. Exhibit 15.2 summarizes the most important store formats. **Department stores** are the classic major retailers in the United States, with the likes of Bloomingdale's, Macy's, Nordstrom, Dillard's, and Kohl's generally offering a range of clothing, accessories, bedding, and other products for the home. **Specialty stores** such as jewelers and bicycle shops offer a limited number of product lines but an extensive selection of brands, styles, sizes, models, colors, materials, and prices within each line. Huge specialty stores such as The Home Depot and Bed Bath & Beyond that tend to dominate those sectors of retail are known as *category killers*.

Retailers can also be distinguished by their pricing strategies. Family Dollar Stores and Walmart, for example, are **discount stores**, which feature a wide variety of aggressively priced everyday merchandise. **Off-price retailers** such as T.J. Maxx take a slightly different approach, offering more limited selections of higher-end products such as designer-label clothing at steeply discounted prices.[14]

In the nonstore arena, **online retailers** can be either Internet-only operations such as fashion retailer Bluefly (**www.bluefly.com**) or online extensions of store-based operations, such as the sites run by JCPenney (**www.jcpenney.com**) and other department stores. Electronic commerce, or **e-commerce**, is not limited to retailing, to be sure. Companies ranging from small specialty wholesalers to the world's largest distribution firms rely on the Internet as well.

wheel of retailing
An evolutionary process by which stores that feature low prices gradually upgrade until they no longer appeal to price-sensitive shoppers and are replaced by a new generation of leaner, low-price competitors.

department stores
Large stores that carry a variety of products in multiple categories, such as clothing, housewares, gifts, bedding, and furniture.

specialty stores
Stores that carry only a particular type of goods, often with deep selection in those specific categories.

discount stores
Retailers that sell a variety of everyday goods below the market price by keeping their overhead low.

off-price retailers
Stores that sell designer labels and other fashionable products at steep discounts.

online retailers
Companies that use e-commerce technologies to sell over the Internet; includes Internet-only retailers and the online arm of store-based retailers.

e-commerce
The application of Internet technologies to wholesaling and retailing.

EXHIBIT 15.2	Retail Store Formats	

The term *retailer* covers many types of outlets. This table shows some of the most common types.

Retail Format	Key Features	Examples
Department store	Store that offers a wide variety of merchandise under one roof in departmentalized sections, and many customer services	Dillard's, Macy's, Nordstrom
Specialty store	Store that offers a complete selection in a narrow range of merchandise, often with extensive customer services	Payless Shoes, R.E.I.
Category killer	Type of specialty store that focuses on specific products on a massive scale and dominating retail sales in respective product categories	Office Depot, Toys R Us, Lowe's
Discount store	Store that offers a wide variety of merchandise at low prices with relatively fewer services	Dollar General, Target, Walmart
Off-price store	Store that offers designer and name-brand merchandise at low prices and with relatively fewer services	T.J. Maxx, Marshalls
Convenience store	Store that offers a limited range of convenience goods, long service hours, and quick checkouts	7-Eleven, AM-PM
Factory/retail outlet	Large outlet store that sells discontinued items, overruns, and factory seconds	Nordstrom Rack, Nike outlet store
Supermarket	Large, self-service store that offers a wide selection of food and nonfood merchandise	Kroger, Safeway
Hypermarket	Giant store that offers both food and general merchandise at discount prices	Walmart Super Centers, Carrefour
Warehouse club	Large, warehouse-style store that sells food and general merchandise at discount prices; some require club membership	Sam's Club, Costco
Online retailer	Web-based store that offers anything from a single product line to comprehensive selections in multiple product areas; can be web-only (e.g., Amazon.com) or integrated with physical stores (e.g., REI.com)	Amazon.com, REI.com

Meanwhile, the mail-order firms that inspired e-commerce are still going strong in many industries. Attractive catalogs are a powerful marketing tool, but printing and mailing them is expensive, so many mail-order firms are working to integrate their catalog efforts with e-commerce to maximize sales. Vending machines and interactive kiosks are an important format for many food and convenience goods as well. Redbox, for example, now has 35,000 movie rental machines positioned around the United States.[15]

REAL-TIME UPDATES

Learn More by Watching This Video

The future of retail: Some possible innovations

A group of retail strategists brainstormed some intriguing and viable advances in the shopping experience. Go to **http://real-timeupdates .com/bia8** and click on Learn More in the Students section.

THE OUTLOOK FOR RETAILING

As the interface between consumers and the entire supply and manufacturing sector, retailing is a complex and dynamic field. Retailing has always been a challenging field, and with nearly constant innovation and change, it's not getting any easier for many companies. Of course, disruption for some can mean opportunities for others. Here are some significant forces that are reshaping retailing:

- **Physical overcapacity.** In some categories, there are simply too many stores to support current levels of business activity. Shopping malls in particular have been hit hard in recent years. A furious spate of mall building over several decades left the United States with more than a thousand major enclosed malls, far more than the economy could really support. At the same time, the rise of online retailing and the growth of stand-alone discounters were drawing shoppers away from malls, then a major recession in 2008–2010 battered malls even more as consumers cut down on spending. As a result of these forces, more than two dozen major malls have closed in the past several years, and dozens more are considered "dead" because they have such low revenues and high vacancy rates. High-end malls that cater to upper-income shoppers remain economically healthful, but many second- and third-tier malls face a rocky future unless they can reinvent themselves as mixed-use venues with new entertainment options or even apartments or office space.[16]

- **Threat of disintermediation.** Like wholesalers, retailers face the threat of disintermediation if suppliers or customers don't think they add sufficient value or if other types of retailers can do the job better.

- **Continued growth of online retailing.** Online shopping now accounts for nearly 10 percent of all retail sales in the United States.[17] As younger consumers who grew up in the digital era move into the peak earning—and spending—years of middle age, online retailing is going to keep grabbing a larger and larger slice of the pie. Retailers whose business format relies heavily on store-based sales will have to find news ways to attract and retain customers, whether it's superior customer service or a more enjoyable shopping experience.

- **Emergence of mobile commerce.** Mobile commerce is the latest technological wave to reshape the field of retailing. Roughly 80 percent of smartphone-equipped consumers use their devices to get shopping-related information. Around the world, the number of people who shop on their smartphones is rising rapidly.[18] In response to this shift in consumer behavior, retailers are responding with mobile-friendly websites, customized shopping apps, and digital coupons. Mobile is particularly influential in retailing because more than any other technology or communication medium, mobile is the one shoppers have on hand in the store. They can do price comparisons, research products, read reviews from other consumers—and, of course, order from an online retailer while standing in another company's retail store.

- **Growth of multichannel retailing.** Today's consumers increasingly hop across channels as they move through the buying process, such as researching products online and then making the purchase in a physical store, or checking out a product in a retail store and then making the purchase online (a practice known in the trade as "showrooming"). In response to this behavior, many retailers are adopting a **multichannel retailing** strategy, also called *omnichannel retailing*. With this approach, a company builds an integrated online and offline presence so that consumers have a seamless experience throughout the buying process, even if they move from mobile to fixed web to in-store shopping. If a company has any gaps in the chain, such as not having a physical presence or a feature-rich website, it risks losing potential customers who jump to another retailer to get what they need. An integrated retailing system also needs integrated customer support and inventory systems so that customers always feel like they are dealing with a single company.

- **Format innovations.** As companies endlessly search for the magic formula to attract customers and generate profitable sales, they continue to experiment with retailing formats. Two interesting innovations are *hybrid stores* that combine different types of retailers or different retail companies in the same facility and *pop-up stores* that exist for only a short time and are designed more as attention-getting events than as ongoing retail operations.[19]

- **The shopping experience.** Increasingly, retail stores aren't just places to buy things; they're becoming places to research new technologies, learn about cooking, socialize, or simply be entertained for a few minutes while going through the drudgery of picking out the week's groceries. **Retail theater** is an attempt to engage consumers in ways that foster brand loyalty and repeat business. A key area of innovation in the coming years is likely to be personalize the shopping experience through a blend of human and technological interaction. For instance, many household essentials are now available via subscription services, which simplifies the shopping experience by automating the repurchase of

multichannel retailing
Coordinated efforts to reach consumers through more than one retail channel.

retail theater
The addition of entertainment or education aspects to the retail experience.

REAL-TIME UPDATES
Learn More by Visiting This Website

See the hottest new concepts in retailing

Chain Store Age tracks the latest ideas in retailing formats. Go to http://real-timeupdates.com/bia8 and click on Learn More in the Students section.

these "low-thought" items. At the other extreme, retailers can use advanced data analysis to help customers make satisfying decisions for more important purchases. For example, if a clothing store has records of your existing wardrobe, a personal shopper—in the form of either an employee or a smartphone app—can use that information to suggest new items that complement pieces you already own. Similarly, a grocery store app that knows your shopping history can suggest new foods items and recipes or even guide you around the store to find the items you want.[20]

- **Data security and privacy.** A big potential downside of personalization is the amount of data it requires, from intimate personal details to banking and credit card information. Millions of consumer records have been compromised through repeated cyberattacks in recent years, highlighting some fundamental weaknesses in the way retailers and financial institutions process digital information.

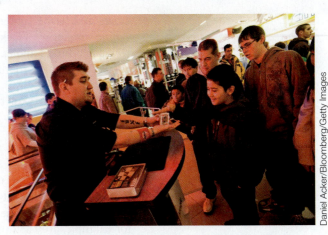

Product demonstrations, in-store classes, and other "retail theater" events help attract shoppers and build store loyalty.

Daniel Acker/Bloomberg/Getty Images

✓ Checkpoint

LEARNING OBJECTIVE 3: Identify the major retailing formats, and summarize six trends shaping the future of retailing.

SUMMARY: Retailers come in many shapes and sizes, but the significant store formats include department stores, specialty stores, category killers, discount stores, and off-price retailers. The two most widely known nonstore retailers are online retailers and mail-order firms. The future of retailing is being shaped by such forces as overcapacity, the threat of disintermediation, the continued growth in online retailing, the emergence of mobile commerce, the growth of multichannel retailing, format innovations such as hybrid stores, emphasis on the shopping experience, and concerns about data security and privacy.

CRITICAL THINKING: (1) Would it ever make sense for Amazon to open retail stores? Why or why not? (2) Moving into the future, what effect is online retailing likely to have on the oversupply of retail store space in the United States?

IT'S YOUR BUSINESS: (1) How have your shopping patterns changed in the past five years, in terms of how you research purchases and where you make those purchases? (2) Roughly what percentage of all your purchases do you make online? What could store-based retailers do to attract a greater portion of your business?

KEY TERMS TO KNOW: wheel of retailing, department stores, specialty stores, discount stores, off-price retailers, online retailers, e-commerce, multichannel retailing, retail theater

Distribution Strategies

Manufacturers and other producers face some critical decisions when selecting marketing channels for their products. Should they sell directly to end users or rely on intermediaries? Which intermediaries should they choose? Should they try to sell their products in every available outlet or limit distribution to a few exclusive outlets? Should they use more than one channel?

The ideal **distribution mix**—number and type of intermediaries—varies widely from industry to industry and even from company to company within the same industry. For example, Black & Decker distributes its power tools through hundreds of hardware

4 **LEARNING OBJECTIVE**

Explain the strategic decisions that manufacturers must make when choosing distribution channels.

distribution mix
A combination of intermediaries and channels a producer uses to reach target customers.

stores and home centers such as Lowe's and Home Depot along with a wide range of online retailers.[21] Black & Decker sells to both consumers and professionals; it wants to reach a broad audience, and its products don't require extensive support from retailers, so these mass-market intermediaries make perfect sense. In contrast, Felder (**www .feldergroupusa.com**), an Austrian company that manufacturers top-of-the line woodworking machines for professional use, makes its products available through only four company-owned stores in the entire United States.[22]

CUSTOMER NEEDS AND EXPECTATIONS

The primary function of distribution channels is delivering value to customers, so channel strategy decisions should start with customer needs and expectations.[23] For instance, how do customers want and expect to purchase your product? If you have a food product, for example, are customers willing to drive to specialty stores to buy it, or does it need to be available in their regular grocery stores if you're to have any hope of selling it? Do customers expect to sample or try on products before they buy? Do they need help from trained product experts? What other goods and services do customers expect to be able to purchase at the same time or from the same supplier? By understanding these needs and expectations, producers can work backward, from their final customers back to their production facilities, to determine the right mix of channel features and functions.

PRODUCT SUPPORT REQUIREMENTS

Products vary widely in the amount of skilled support required before and after a sale. Laboratory instruments such as mass spectrometers require significant technical skills to sell and to support afterward, which is why companies that make them, such as Agilent Technologies (**www.agilent.com**), generally sell them through their own salesforces or through carefully selected and trained channel partners.

SEGMENTATION, TARGETING, AND POSITIONING

Just as producers segment markets, choose target segments, and try to position their products within those segments, marketing intermediaries make strategic marketing decisions regarding their own businesses. For instance, Super Jock'n Jill (**www.superjocknjill.com**) an athletic shoe retailer in Seattle, focuses on quality shoes and clothing for people who are serious about physical fitness. The store offers clinics on nutrition and injury prevention, sponsors races and running clubs, posts race results on its website, and takes other steps to support local walkers and runners.[24]

Super Jock'n Jill doesn't sell shoes from its website, because the company emphasizes individualized analysis and fitting by knowledgeable sales staff—and it offers the almost unheard-of option of letting shoppers lace on shoes and go for a run to test comfort and performance under real-life conditions. In other words, if you produce mass-market sneakers that are more about fashion than performance, this store won't help you reach your target audience.

Ian Shaw/Alamy

Product marketing managers are careful to choose retailers whose position in the marketplace aligns with their product positioning strategies. Manufacturers of luxury products, for example, want retailers with the ability to effectively present their products to higher-income consumers.

COMPETITORS' DISTRIBUTION CHANNELS

Marketing managers must consider the distribution decisions that competitors have already made or are likely to make. For instance, if you are a new producer trying to break into a particular market, you need to encourage buyers to consider your goods along with the products they already know about, so putting your products side by side with the competition in physical or online venues is probably the right choice. In other cases, you might want to distance yourself from competitors, either to make direct comparisons more difficult or to avoid being associated with competitive products.

Of course, marketing intermediaries have their own decisions to make about which products to carry and how to allocate their finite "bandwidth," whether it's the number of sales representatives, physical shelf space in a retail store, or featured pages on a website. Because of these capacity limitations in the channel, producers often compete for the attention and resources of intermediaries. In some industries, channel capacity is at such a premium that retailers can demand payments from producers in exchange for carrying their products for an agreed-upon length of time. These *slotting allowances* are now common in the grocery business, for example, particularly for new products. Retailers are naturally reluctant to give up shelf space to unproven products, so slotting allowances help offset the financial risk of bringing in new products.[25]

ESTABLISHED INDUSTRY PATTERNS AND REQUIREMENTS

Over the years, all industries develop certain patterns of distribution. If you try to "buck the system," you might uncover a profitable new opportunity—or you might fail to reach your target customers entirely. Specific industries have other considerations as well, such as the need to get perishable food items to retail locations quickly or government regulations that dictate how and where certain products (hazardous chemicals and pharmaceuticals, for example) can be sold.

✔ ## Checkpoint

LEARNING OBJECTIVE 4: Explain the strategic decisions that manufacturers must make when choosing distribution channels.

SUMMARY: Defining a distribution strategy requires considering such issues as customer needs and expectations; product support requirements; segmentation, targeting, and positioning objectives; competitors' distribution channels; and established distribution patterns and requirements.

CRITICAL THINKING: (1) Would two manufacturers trying to reach the same customer segment with similar products use identical distribution mixes? Why or why not? (2) Is channel conflict necessarily bad for everyone involved? Explain your answer.

IT'S YOUR BUSINESS: (1) You've probably seen television commercials advertising products that are "not available in stores." How does that lack of availability in stores affect your perception of those products? (2) Would knowing that a manufacturer had to pay a retailer to gain shelf space for a particular product change your perception of that product? Why or why not?

KEY TERM TO KNOW: distribution mix

Considerations in Channel Design and Management

5 **LEARNING OBJECTIVE**

Identify five key attributes of distribution channel design and management.

In addition to the strategic considerations discussed so far in this chapter, marketing managers need to consider five attributes that help define the function and effectiveness of any distribution channel: channel length, market coverage, distribution costs, channel conflict, and channel organization and control.

CHANNEL LENGTH

As you no doubt sense by now, distribution channels come in all shapes and sizes. Some channels are short and simple; others are long and complex. Many businesses purchase goods they use in their operations directly from producers, so those distribution channels are short. In contrast, the channels for consumer goods are usually longer and more complex (see Exhibit 15.3 on the next page).

| EXHIBIT 15.3 | **Common Distribution Channel Models** |

Producers can choose from a variety of distribution channel configurations. Channels in consumer markets tend to be longer (with more participants) than channels in organizational markets.

Consumer Goods and Services

Producer → Consumer

Producer → Retailer → Consumer

Producer → Wholesaler → Retailer → Consumer

Producer → Agent/broker → Wholesaler → Retailer → Consumer

Organizational Goods and Services

Producer → Organization

Producer → Manufacturer's rep → Organization

Producer → Distributor → Organization

Producer → Manufacturer's rep → Distributor → Organization

The four primary channels for consumer goods are

- **Producer to consumer.** Producers that sell directly to consumers through catalogs, telemarketing, infomercials, and the Internet are using the shortest, simplest distribution channel. By selling directly to consumers, Dell, for example, gains more control over pricing, promotion, service, and delivery. Although this approach eliminates payments or discounts to channel members, it also forces producers to handle a variety of distribution and customer supports that they might not otherwise have.

- **Producer to retailer to consumer.** Producers that don't want to be involved in sales to consumers can sell their products to retailers, who then resell them to consumers.

- **Producer to wholesaler to retailer to consumer.** Manufacturers or suppliers of supermarket and pharmaceutical items often rely on two intermediary levels to reach consumers. They sell their products to wholesalers such as Supervalu, which in turn sell to the retailers. This approach works particularly well for small producers that lack the resources to sell or deliver merchandise to individual retail sites. It is also beneficial to retailers that lack the space to store container-size shipments of each product they sell.

- **Producer to agent/broker to wholesaler to retailer to consumer.** Additional channel levels are common in certain industries, such as agriculture, where specialists are required to negotiate transactions or to perform interim functions such as sorting, grading, or subdividing the goods.

MARKET COVERAGE

The appropriate market coverage—the number of wholesalers or retailers that will carry a product—depends on several factors in the marketing strategy. Inexpensive convenience goods or organizational supplies such as computer paper and pens sell best if they are available in as many outlets as possible. Such **intensive distribution** requires wholesalers and retailers of many types. In contrast, shopping goods such as home appliances and autos require different market coverage because customers shop for such products by comparing features and prices. For these items, the best strategy is usually **selective distribution**, selling through a limited number of outlets that can give the product adequate sales and service support. If producers of expensive specialty or technical products do not sell directly to customers, they may choose **exclusive distribution**, offering products in only one outlet in each market area. With any of these approaches, producers need to choose the optimum number of outlets carefully to balance cost and market coverage and then continue to monitor market conditions to maintain a healthy balance.

intensive distribution
A market coverage strategy that tries to place a product in as many outlets as possible.

selective distribution
A market coverage strategy that uses a limited number of carefully chosen outlets to distribute products.

exclusive distribution
A market coverage strategy that gives intermediaries exclusive rights to sell a product in a specific geographic area.

DISTRIBUTION COSTS

Performing all the functions that are handled by intermediaries requires time and resources, so cost plays a major role in determining channel selection. Small or new companies often cannot afford to hire a sales force large enough to sell directly to end users or to call on a host of retail outlets. Neither can they afford to build large warehouses and distribution centers to store large shipments of goods. These firms need the help of intermediaries, which can spread the cost of such activities across a number of products. To cover their costs and turn a profit, intermediaries generally buy products at a discount and then resell them at higher prices.

CHANNEL CONFLICT

Individual channel members naturally focus on running their own businesses as profitably as possible, which can lead to **channel conflict**, or disagreement over the rights and responsibilities of the organizations in a distribution channel. Channel conflict may arise for a number of reasons, such as producers providing inadequate support to their channel partners; markets being oversaturated with intermediaries; producers trying to expand sales by adding additional channels, either on their own or through new intermediaries; or some intermediaries bearing the cost of developing new markets or promoting products only to see the sales revenue go to other intermediaries.

For example, the *showrooming* phenomenon mentioned previously continues to be an issue because shoppers can often take advantage of the opportunity to visit full-service retailers to examine products and get information from product experts and then buy at lower prices from discounters or online stores. The full-service retailers not only lose the sale but end up helplessly assisting their competitors make those sales—and websites and shopping apps on mobile phones are making this problem even worse. Stores such as Best Buy, however, have responded by embracing mobile-enabled shoppers and offering on-the-spot price matching.[26]

channel conflict
Disagreement or tension between two or more members in a distribution channel, such as competition between channel partners trying to reach the same group of customers.

CHANNEL ORGANIZATION AND CONTROL

To minimize costs and the potential for channel conflict, channel partners can take steps to work out issues of organization and control. Without some degree of coordination, the various companies involved will pursue their own economic interests, often to the detriment of the channel as a whole.

Producers and intermediaries can achieve this coordination through **marketing systems**, in which the channel participants agree to operate as a cohesive system under

marketing systems
Arrangements by which channel partners coordinate their activities under the leadership of one of the partners.

EXHIBIT 15.4	Factors That Influence Distribution Channel Choices

Designing a distribution mix is rarely a simple task; here are some of the most important factors to consider.

Factor	Issues to Consider
Customer needs and expectations	Where are customers likely to look for your products? How much customer service do they expect from the channel? Can you make your offering more attractive by choosing an unconventional channel?
Product support requirements	How much training do salespeople need to present your products successfully? How much after-sale support is required? Who will answer questions when things go wrong?
Segmentation, targeting, and positioning	Which intermediaries can present your products to target customers while maintaining your positioning strategy?
Competitors' distribution channels	Which channels do your competitors use? Do you need to use the same channels in order to reach your target customers, or can you use different channels to distinguish yourself?
Established industry patterns and requirements	Which intermediaries are already in place? Can you take advantage of them, or do you need to find or create alternatives? Will retailers demand that you use specific wholesalers or distributors?
Channel length	Do you want to deal directly with customers? *Can* you? Do you need to engage other intermediaries to perform vital functions?
Market coverage	Are you going for intensive, selective, or exclusive distribution? Are the right intermediaries available in your target markets? Can they handle the volumes at which you hope to sell?
Distribution costs	How much will intermediaries add to the price that final customers will eventually pay? Put another way, how much of a discount from the retail price will intermediaries expect from you?
Channel conflict	What are the potential sources of channel conflict, both now and in the future? If such conflict can't be avoided, how will you minimize its effect?
Channel organization and control	How much control do you need to maintain as products move through the channel—and how much can you expect to maintain with each potential intermediary? What happens if you lose control? Who leads the channel?

the leadership of one of the participants.[27] The agreement can be brought about through *ownership* (when the production and distribution firms are owned by a single company), *contracts* (when the participants have formal agreements that specify their rights and responsibilities, such as the franchising agreements discussed in Chapter 6), and *economic power* (when one player is so big that its economic presence is enough to encourage or even force cooperation from the other participants in the channel).[28]

For example, one of the fundamentals of Costco's success is that it sells products in such high volume that many producers can't afford *not* to accommodate Costco's demands for specific price points and packaging configurations. If they don't meet Costco's requirements, they risk missing out on a major source of distribution for their products. Costco, Walmart, and other giant retailers offer enticing opportunities for manufacturers, but playing by their high-volume, low-cost rules can sometimes hurt a manufacturer more than help it.[29]

Exhibit 15.4 offers of a summary of the major factors to consider regarding distribution channels.

 Checkpoint

LEARNING OBJECTIVE 5: Identify five key attributes of distribution channel design and management.

SUMMARY: Five key attributes of channel design and management are channel length (the number of layers between producers and target customers), market coverage needs (intense, selective, or exclusive distribution), distribution costs (all the costs involved in using a particular channel), channel conflict (disagreement and tension between channel partners), and channel organization and control (attempts to coordinate the activities of a channel into a cohesive marketing system).

CRITICAL THINKING: (1) Does exclusive distribution limit the potential size of a manufacturer's market? Why or why not? (2) Is it ethical for one participant in a channel to have power over the marketing system through sheer economic power alone? Why or why not?

IT'S YOUR BUSINESS: (1) How does knowing that a product is available only in selected retail outlets affect your assessment of its quality? (2) Have you ever been skeptical of "shipping and handling" charges added to products you've ordered? Did these charges affect your buying decisions?

KEY TERMS TO KNOW: intensive distribution, selective distribution, exclusive distribution, channel conflict, marketing systems

Physical Distribution and Logistics

In addition to assembling and managing the organizations and systems that make up a distribution channel, any firm that deals in physical goods needs to figure out the best way to move those products so they are available to customers at the right place, at the right time, and in the right amount. **Physical distribution** encompasses all the activities required to move finished products from the producer to the consumer, including forecasting, order processing, inventory control, warehousing, and transportation (see Exhibit 15.5).

Physical distribution may not be the most glamorous aspect of business, but it is one of the most critical. Behind every luxury storefront or cutting-edge e-commerce

6 LEARNING OBJECTIVE
Highlight the major components of physical distribution and logistics.

physical distribution
All the activities required to move finished products from the producer to the consumer.

EXHIBIT 15.5 Steps in the Physical Distribution Process

Managing the physical distribution system is an attempt to balance a high level of customer service with the lowest overall cost.

Order Processing
Order processing systems, which are often linked to e-commerce retailing platforms, need to be fast and accurate to keep customers happy and to avoid expensive mistakes.

Forecasting
One of the biggest challenges in physical distribution is trying to predict demand for each product in the company's product portfolio to make sure those goods are available when and where they are needed.

Inventory Control
Inventory control requires constant balancing between forecasted and actual demand to make sure enough goods are available to ship without stockpiling so much that costs get out of hand.

Warehousing
Warehouses need to be able to house products safely while making them readily available for onward shipping. Modern warehouses use a variety of advanced technologies, from RFID to robotics.

Outboard Transportation
Depending on the type of product and the target market, companies can choose rail, trucks, ships and barges, air, pipelines, and digital networks.

logistics
The planning, movement, and flow of goods and related information throughout the supply chain.

website is a vast network of facilities, vehicles, and information systems that make sure products arrive at their destinations. The secret to making it all happen on time is **logistics**, the planning and movement of goods and information throughout the supply chain. As managers try to squeeze cost efficiencies and competitive advantages everywhere they can, logistics has taken on key strategic importance for many companies.

Two recent moves by Amazon help illustrate the importance of physical distribution in the marketing mix. The first is the introduction of same-day delivery in major metropolitan areas. This helps counters one of the biggest advantages the company's brick-and-mortar competitors still have: the ability to take a desired product home right away.[30] The second is the idea of delivery drones (small, unpiloted aerial vehicles), which the company says could deliver products to customers within 30 minutes.[31] The drone program is still experimental and subject to government approval, but if it is implemented, for selected customers and products it could effectively erase Amazon's remaining disadvantage in the matter of delivery time.

For any mode of transportation, success in physical distribution requires achieving a competitive level of customer service at the lowest total cost. Doing so requires trade-offs because as the level of service improves, the cost of distribution usually increases. For instance, if you reduce the level of inventory to cut your storage costs, you run the risk of being unable to fill orders in a timely fashion. Or, if you use slower forms of transportation, you can reduce your shipping costs, but you might aggravate customers. The trick is to optimize the total cost of achieving the desired level of service. This optimization requires a careful analysis of each step in the distribution process in relation to every other step in the process. Of course, when companies reduce mistakes and eliminate inefficiencies, they can lower costs *and* improve service, which is the goal of every logistics manager.

FORECASTING

To control the flow of products through the distribution system, a firm must have an accurate estimate of demand. To some degree, historical data can be used to project future sales, but despite heavy investments in information technology, forecasting remains a major logistical challenge that is part hard numbers and part managerial judgment.

ORDER PROCESSING

order processing
Functions involved in receiving and filling customer orders.

Order processing involves preparing orders for shipment and receiving orders when shipments arrive. It includes a number of activities, such as checking the customer's credit, recording the sale, making the appropriate accounting entries, arranging for the item to be shipped, adjusting the inventory records, and billing the customer. Because order processing involves direct interaction with the customer, it affects a company's reputation for customer service. To keep buyers happy, companies should establish ambitious standards for accuracy and timeliness in order fulfillment.

INVENTORY CONTROL

As Chapter 9's discussion of just-in-time systems points out, in an ideal world, a company would always have just the right amount of goods on hand to fill the orders it receives. In reality, however, inventory and sales are seldom in perfect balance. For instance, many firms like to keep a ready supply of finished goods on hand so orders can be filled as soon as they arrive. But how much inventory is enough? If your inventory is too large, you incur extra expenses for storage space, handling, insurance, and taxes; you may also run the risk of product spoilage or obsolescence. On the other hand, if your inventory is too low, you may lose sales when the product is not in stock. The objective of inventory control is to resolve these issues. Inventory managers decide how much product to keep on hand and when to replenish the supply of goods in inventory. They also decide how to allocate products to customers if orders exceed supply.

WAREHOUSING

Products held in inventory are physically stored in **warehouses**, which may be owned by the manufacturer, by an intermediary, or by a private company that leases space to others. Some warehouses are almost purely holding facilities, in which goods are stored for relatively long periods. Other warehouses, known as **distribution centers**, serve as command posts for moving products to customers. In a typical distribution center, goods produced at a variety of locations are collected, sorted, coded, and redistributed to fill customer orders. Leading-edge distribution centers use some of the most advanced technologies in business today, including satellite navigation and communication, voice-activated computers, wireless data services, machine vision, robots, radio frequency identification (RFID) tags and scanners, and planning software that relies on artificial intelligence.

warehouses
Facilities for storing inventory.

distribution centers
Advanced warehouse facilities that specialize in collecting and shipping merchandise.

TRANSPORTATION

For any business, transportation is normally the largest single item in the overall cost of physical distribution. When choosing a mode of transportation, managers must also evaluate other marketing issues, including storage, financing, sales, inventory size, speed, product perishability, dependability, flexibility, and convenience. Each of the six major modes of transportation has distinct advantages and disadvantages:

REAL-TIME UPDATES
Learn More by Visiting This Website

See how big Amazon's distribution operations look from the inside

These photos show the scale of the online giant's warehousing and distribution capacity. Go to **http://real-timeupdates.com/bia8** and click on Learn More in the Students section.

- **Rail.** Railroads can carry heavier and more diverse cargo and a larger volume of goods than any other mode of transportation. The obvious disadvantage of trains is that they are constrained to tracks, so they can rarely deliver goods directly to customers.
- **Trucks.** Trucks offer the convenience of door-to-door delivery and the ease and efficiency of travel on public highways. However, large, heavy loads are often better handled by water or rail, and some perishable loads may need to travel by air for the shortest possible delivery time over long distances.
- **Ships and barges.** The cheapest method of transportation is via water; this is the preferred method for such low-cost bulk items as oil, coal, ore, cotton, and lumber. Water transport is slow, however, and, like rail, must be combined with another mode of delivery for most shipments.
- **Air.** Air transport offers the primary advantage of speed across long distances, but it imposes limitations on the size, shape, and weight of shipments. It also tends to be the most expensive form of transportation; however, when speed is a priority, air is usually the only way to go.
- **Pipelines.** For products such as gasoline, natural gas, and coal or wood chips (suspended in liquid), pipelines are an effective mode of transportation. The major downsides are slow speeds and inflexible routes.
- **Digital networks.** Any product that exists in or can be converted to digital format, from books and movies to software to product design files, can be transported over the Internet and other digital networks. The range of digital products is fairly limited, of course, but the Internet has certainly revolutionized industries such as entertainment and publishing.

When companies need to move products quickly over long distances, air transportation is often the best choice.

Shippers can also combine the benefits of multiple modes by using **intermodal transportation**. With *containerized shipping*, for instance, standard-size freight containers can be moved from trucks to railroads to ships for maximum flexibility.

For the latest information on wholesaling, retailing, and marketing logistics, visit http://real-timeupdates.com/bia8 and click on Chapter 15.

intermodal transportation
The coordinated use of multiple modes of transportation, particularly with containers that can be shipped by truck, rail, and sea.

✓ Checkpoint

LEARNING OBJECTIVE 6: Highlight the major components of physical distribution and logistics.

SUMMARY: The major components of a firm's distribution process are order processing, inventory control, warehousing, and outbound transportation. When choosing the best method of outbound transportation, such as truck, rail, ship, airplane, or pipeline, company's should consider cost, storage, sales, inventory size, speed, product perishability, dependability, flexibility, and convenience.

CRITICAL THINKING: (1) Given the huge volume of small packages that Amazon ships every year, should it consider starting its own transportation company instead of giving all that business to UPS and other shippers? Why or why not? (2) If another high-tech company approached Dell with a partnership proposal to build and operate several distribution centers that would ship both companies' products to customers, what would you advise Dell to do? Why?

IT'S YOUR BUSINESS: (1) Online retailers sometimes use free shipping as a promotional appeal. Do you think most consumers really believe the shipping is "free" and not just factored into the product's price? (2) Have you ever paid extra for expedited shipping for an order placed on a website? Was it worth the extra expense?

KEY TERMS TO KNOW: physical distribution, logistics, order processing, warehouses, distribution centers, intermodal transportation

BEHIND THE SCENES
COSTCO PUSHES ITS SUPPLY CHAIN TO SATISFY CUSTOMERS

Much of the merchandise sold at Costco may be similar to that sold at its main competitors—such as the Walmart chain Sam's Club—but Costco aims to be a cut above by offering many unique and unusual items. Its stores also look slightly more upscale than other club stores, the brands it carries have more cachet, and the products are often a bit more expensive, but they still offer extremely good value. And unlike some other discounters, Costco does not have everything under the sun. The stores carry only about 4,000 products each, which is a small fraction of the more than 100,000 items stocked by other warehouse clubs and conventional discounters such as Target and Walmart. About 3,000 of Costco's products are a consistent array of carefully chosen basics, from canned tuna to laundry detergent to printer cartridges. Meat, produce, and bakery items are a major presence in mix as well. The other 1,000 items are a fast-moving assortment of "treasure hunt" goods such as designer-label clothing, watches, and premium wines. These items change from week to week, reinforcing the idea of buying something when you see it because it will probably be gone next week.

Costco prefers to offer name-brand products and has successfully introduced some branded luxury items such as Kate Spade and Coach purses. However, high-end suppliers such as Cartier and Cannondale flinch at the idea of their goods being sold in a warehouse setting, so carrying those brands isn't always possible. Some suppliers, hoping to protect their higher-end retail customers, have been known to spurn Costco's offers "officially," only to call back later to quietly cut a deal. In other cases, Costco goes on its own treasure hunts, using third-party distributors to track down hot products, even though these "gray market" channels can be unpredictable. And if that doesn't work, Costco can commission another manufacturer to create a similar product under its own Kirkland Signature brand, which now accounts for a quarter of annual sales.

To give its millions of members the best prices on everything, Costco negotiates fiercely with suppliers. Aiming to be known as the toughest negotiators in the business, Costco's buyers won't let up until they get their target price on the merchandise. Often, the "right" price is determined by how much less expensively Costco can make a product itself. In addition, because the company stocks far fewer individual products in any given category, suppliers are forced compete with one another to get that precious shelf space, which leads to lower costs for Costco and lower prices for its customers.

Inventory turnover rate is also a key to Costco's financial success. By focusing on fast-selling items, the company moves its merchandise significantly faster than competitors do—so quickly, in fact, that it often sells products to shoppers before it has to pay its suppliers.

The one place Costco doesn't scrimp is its workforce. Costco pays significantly higher wages than competitors and provides employees with a generous array of benefits. This practice is driven by a deeply embedded corporate philosophy that emphasizes taking care of employees, even if that results in somewhat lower profits. And when the economy hit the skids in 2009, many other retailers started laying off employees, but Costco gave its employees a raise instead. In return, Costco employees are highly productive and highly loyal to the company, both of which help keep costs down.

Costco is rolling into its fourth decade with strong financial health, a dominant market position, millions of satisfied customers, and annual sales that have surged past $100 billion. The company is determined not to let the wheel of retailing take Costco for a spin, either. As cofounder Jim Sinegal puts it, "When I started, Sears, Roebuck was the Costco of the country, but they allowed someone else to come in under them. We don't want to be one of the casualties. We don't want to turn around and say, 'We got so fancy we've raised our prices,' and all of a sudden a new competitor comes in and beats our prices." This steadfast strategy is music to the ears of Costco's bargain-hunting customers.[32]

Critical Thinking Questions

15-1. If customers repeatedly ask Costco to carry certain items that the company thinks are outside its price/quality "comfort zone" (because they're too expensive or not of high enough quality), should it give in and carry the items? Why or why not?

15-2. Costco's online sales are growing, but even the company itself says its online presence will never be as fancy as Amazon's. Should the company's online presence be an extension of the brick-and-mortar stores, or should it try to compete more directly with Amazon? Explain your answer.

15-3. If Costco can't find enough land in a particular location to build its usual store format, should it leverage the Costco brand name anyway and build something smaller, such as conventional department stores or grocery stores, in these areas? Why or why not?

LEARN MORE ONLINE

Explore the Costco website, at **www.costco.com**. What evidence do you see of "clicks-and-bricks" integration with the physical stores? Are sales promoted online? How much product information is available? Are nonmembers allowed to make purchases online? How does the online experience at Costco compare to that of another discounter, such as Walmart (**www.walmart.com**), or to a specialty retailer, such as Bluefly (**www.bluefly.com**)?

KEY TERMS

agents and brokers (352)
channel conflict (361)
department stores (354)
discount stores (354)
disintermediation (352)
distribution centers (365)
distribution mix (357)
distribution strategy (349)
distributors (352)
e-commerce (354)
exclusive distribution (361)
intensive distribution (361)
intermodal transportation (365)
logistics (363)
marketing intermediaries (349)

marketing systems (361)
merchant wholesalers (352)
multichannel retailing (356)
off-price retailers (354)
online retailers (354)
order processing (364)
physical distribution (363)
retail theater (356)
retailers (349)
selective distribution (361)
specialty stores (354)
warehouses (365)
wheel of retailing (354)
wholesalers (349)

MyBizLab®
To complete the problems with the ⭐,
go to EOC Discussion Questions in the
MyLab

TEST YOUR KNOWLEDGE

Questions for Review

15-4. What is a distribution channel?

15-5. What are the two main types of intermediaries, and how do they differ from one another?

15-6. What forms of utility do intermediaries create?

15-7. What are some of the main causes of channel conflict?

15-8. How does a specialty store differ from a category killer and a discount store?

Questions for Analysis

15-9. How do marketing systems help avert channel conflict?

15-10. Would it be wise for a brick-and-mortar retailer that wants to stop showrooming to use wireless-jamming technologies to prevent people from using smartphones inside its stores? Why or why not?

15-11. How might a once-valued intermediary find itself threatened with disintermediation?

15-12. How could strategic planning help a discount retailer avoid the pitfalls of the wheel of retailing?

15-13. **Ethical Considerations.** Manufacturers that have been selling to wholesalers and other intermediaries occasionally decide to start selling directly to end customers, which of course puts them in competition with the channel partners that have been selling for them. Even if this is legal, do you think such moves are ethical? Why or why not?

Questions for Application

15-14. Imagine that you own a small specialty store that sells handcrafted clothing and jewelry. What are some of the nonstore retail options you might explore to increase sales? What are the advantages and disadvantages of each option?

15-15. Compare the prices of three products offered at a retail outlet with the prices charged if you purchase those products by mail order (catalog or phone) or over the Internet. Be sure to include extra costs such as handling and delivery charges. Which purchasing format offers the lowest price for each of your products?

15-16. **Concept Integration.** Chapter 9 discussed the fact that supply chain management integrates all the activities involved in the production of goods and services from suppliers to customers. What are the benefits of involving wholesalers and retailers in the design, manufacturing, or marketing of a company's products?

15-17. **Concept Integration.** Which of the four basic functions of management discussed in Chapter 7 would be involved in decisions that establish or change a company's channels of distribution? Explain your answer.

EXPAND YOUR KNOWLEDGE

Discovering Career Opportunities

Retailing is a dynamic, fast-paced field with many career opportunities in both store and nonstore settings. In addition to hiring full-time employees when needed, retailers of all types often hire extra employees on a temporary basis for peak selling periods, such as the year-end holidays.

15-19. Select a major retailer, such as a chain store in your area or an e-commerce retailer. Is this a specialty store, a discount store, a department store, or another type of retailer?

15-20. Visit the website of the retailer you selected. Does the site discuss the company's hiring procedures? If so, what are they? What qualifications are required for a position with the company?

15-21. Research your chosen retailer using library sources or online resources. Is this retailer expanding? Is it profitable? Has it recently acquired or been acquired by another firm? If so, what are the implications of this acquisition for job opportunities?

Improving Your Tech Insights: Mobile Commerce

Mobile connectivity promises to bring nearly as much upheaval to retailing as the Internet did, as more and more consumers around the world use smartphones and tablets for some or all of the steps in the shopping process. As attractive as mobile is for buyers and sellers, however, integrating mobile into existing supply chains, customer support functions, and other business systems is no simple task. Conduct research to find two or three challenges that retailers are facing as they expand mobile shopping opportunities for their customers.

PRACTICE YOUR SKILLS

Sharpening Your Communication Skills

Sales of your DJ equipment (turntables, amplifiers, speakers, mixers, and related accessories) have been falling for months, even as more and more music fans around the world try their hand at being DJs. Magazine reviews and professional DJs give your equipment high marks, your prices are competitive, and your advertising presence is strong. Suspecting that the trouble is in the distribution channel, you and a half dozen fellow executives go on an undercover shopping mission at retail stores that carry your products—and you're appalled by what you see. The salespeople in these stores clearly don't understand your products, so they either give potential customers bad information about your products or steer them to products from your competitors. No wonder sales are falling off a cliff.

The executive team is split over the best way to solve this dilemma; you convince them that retraining your existing channel partners would be less expensive and less disruptive than replacing them. Now you have to convince store managers to let you pull their staffs off the sales floor for a half day so you can train them. Each store will lose a half day's revenue, and each sales rep will lose commissions for that time as well. Draft a short email message for the store managers, explaining why the training would be well worth their time. Make up any details you need to complete the message.

Building Your Team Skills

Complicated or confusing shopping experiences are one of the biggest challenges for online retailing. Customers who can't find what they're looking for or who get lost filling out order forms, for instance, often just click away and leave their virtual shopping carts. Unfortunately, consumers don't always perceive the shopping experience the same way, so it's not always easy for website developers to craft the ideal e-retail experience.

Your team's task is to analyze the shopping experience on three competitive e-retail sites and from that analysis decide how a new competitor in the market could create a better customer experience. First, choose a product that everyone in the group finds interesting but that none of you have purchased online before. Then identify three websites that are likely to offer the product. Next, individually (so you can't guide each other), each person in the group should shop the three sites for your chosen product. (If you can't find the exact model, choose something similar.) Answer the following questions about each site:

15-22. How difficult was it to find the product you wanted?

15-23. How much information was available? Complete product details or just a few highlights? A static photo or a three-dimensional (3D) virtual experience that lets you explore the product from all angles?

15-24. How easy was it to compare this product to similar products?

15-25. Could you find the store's privacy and return policies? Were they acceptable to you?

15-26. How long did it take to get from the site's homepage to the point at which you could place an order for the specific product?

15-27. What forms of help were available in case you had questions or concerns?

15-28. Go ahead and place your item in the shopping cart to simulate placing an order. (Don't actually buy the product, of course!)

15-29. What social commerce and social elements did you encounter on the website? Were they helpful in your search?

15-30. Was the site optimized for mobile devices?

Summarize your impression of each of the three sites and then compare notes with your teammates. Based on the strengths and weaknesses of each site, identify four pieces of advice for a company that wants to compete against these sites.

Developing Your Research Skills

Find an article in a business journal or newspaper that discusses changes a company is making to its distribution strategy or channels. For example, is a manufacturer selling products directly to consumers? Is a physical retailer offering goods via a company website? Is a company eliminating an intermediary? Has a nonstore retailer decided to open a physical store? Is a category killer opening smaller stores? Has a major retail tenant closed its store in a mall?

15-31. What changes in the company's distribution structure or strategy have taken place? What additional changes, if any, are planned?

15-32. What were the reasons for the changes? What role, if any, did e-commerce play in the changes?

15-33. If you were a stockholder in this company, would you view these changes as positive or negative? What, if anything, might you do differently?

MyBizLab®

Go to the Assignments section of your MyLab to complete these writing exercises.

15-34. Other than image, what factors might prompt manufacturers of high-end technical or luxury products to decide not to sell their products through Costco?

15-35. What are the potential consequences of inaccurately forecasting the demand for a particular product?

ENDNOTES

1. *Costco 2014 Annual Report,* www.costco.com; *See What Sets Us Apart,* Costco, www.costco.com; Brad Stone, "Costco CEO Craig Jelinek Leads the Cheapest, Happiest Company in the World," *Bloomberg BusinessWeek,* 6 June 2013, www.businessweek.com; Megan McArdle, "Why Can't Walmart Be More Like Costco?" *The Daily Beast,* 26 November 2012, www.thedailybeast.com; "Costco Wholesale Corp," *Bloomberg BusinessWeek,* accessed 8 September 2011, http://investing.businessweek.com; Mark Brohan, "Web Sales Rebound for Costco in Fiscal 2010," *Internet Retailer,* 8 October 2010, www.internetretailer.com; Datamonitor, "Costco Wholesale Corporation: Company Profile," 12 April 2010, www.ebscohost.com; Costco website, accessed 13 November 2013, www.costco.com.

2. "Company Snapshot," Grainger website, 31 December 2014, www.grainger.com.

3. "Manufacturing & Trade Inventories & Sales," U.S. Census Bureau website, accessed 28 May 2015, www.census.gov; "Wholesale Trade," U.S. Bureau of Labor Statistics website, accessed 28 May 2015, www.bls.gov.

4. Amazon website, accessed 28 May 2015; "Amazon, Google Step into Industrial-Supply E-Commerce Vacuum," *The Future of Commerce,* 8 July 2013, www.the-future-of-commerce.com.

5. Bert Rosenbloom, "The Wholesaler's Role in the Marketing Channel: Disintermediation Vs. Reintermediation," *International Review of Retail, Distribution & Consumer Research,* September 2007, 327–339.

6. Rosenbloom, "The Wholesaler's Role in the Marketing Channel."

7. Joseph O'Reilly, "2013 3PL Perspectives: Drafting a Blueprint for Growth," *Inbound Logistics,* July 2013, www.inboundlogistics.com; Joseph O'Reilly, "3PL Perspectives 2011: The Power of Three," *Inbound Logistics,* July 2011, www.inboundlogistics.com; Philip Kotler and Gary Armstrong, *Principles of Marketing,* 13th ed. (Upper Saddle River, N.J.: Pearson Prentice Hall, 2010), 362–363; Rosenbloom, "The Wholesaler's Role in the Marketing Channel."

8. "Wholesale Trade"; Rosenbloom, "The Wholesaler's Role in the Marketing Channel."

9. Richard Brunelli, "Shopper Marketing? There's an App for That …," *Adweek,* 14 March 2011, S1–S3.

10. Jeneanne Rae, "New Thinking About Consumer Marketing," *BusinessWeek,* 30 June 2009, 16.

11. Jennifer J. Argo, Darren W. Dahl, and Andrea C. Morales, "Positive Consumer Contagion: Responses to Attractive Others in a Retail Context," *Journal of Marketing Research,* December 2008, 690–701.

12. Don E. Schultz, "Another Turn of the Wheel," *Marketing Management,* March/April 2002, 8–9.

13. "Investor Overview," Family Dollar website, accessed 7 September 2011, www.familydollar.com; Kerry Grace Benn, "Family Dollar Earnings Jump 36%, Boosts Fiscal-Year View," *Wall Street Journal,* 8 July 2009, http://online.wsj.com.

14. Teri Agins, "What Is 'Off-Price'?" *Wall Street Journal,* 17 July 2009, http://online.wsj.com.

15. "Facts About Redbox," Redbox website, accessed 28 May 2015, www.redbox.com.

16. "Who Will Survive the Great Mall Shake-Out?" *Knowledge@Wharton,* 31 March 2015, http://knowledge.wharton.unpenn.edu; Nelson D. Schwartz, "The Economics (and Nostalgia) of Dead Malls," *New York Times,* 3 January 2015; Randyl Drummer, "The De-Malling of America: What's Next for Hundreds of Outmoded Malls?" *CoStar Group,* 3 October 2012, www.costar.com; Kate Murphy, "Revitalizing a Dead Mall (Don't Expect Shoppers)," *New York Times,* 30 October 2012, www.nytimes.com; Kris Hudson and Vanessa O'Connell, "Recession Turns Malls into Ghost Towns," *Wall Street Journal,* 22 May 2009, http://online.wsj.com.

17. "Web to Become Top Sales Channel by 2012," *Bookseller,* 24 April 2009, 10; "Quarterly Retail E-Commerce Sales: 1st Quarter 2015," U.S. Census Bureau, www.census.gov.

18. *Achieving Total Retail: Consumer Expectations Driving the Next Retail Business Model,* PwC, February 2014, www.pwc.com; Chris Kelley, "Why You Need a Mobile Website," V2 Marketing Communications, 18 June 2013, http://blog.marketingv2.com.

19. Sharon Edelson, "Pop-ups Offer Retailers Multiple Benefits," *Women's Wear Daily,* 19 May 2009, 12.

20. Puneet Mehta, "Why the Future of Retail Will Blow Your Mind," *Entrepreneur,* 2 June 2014, www.entrepreneur.com.

21. Black & Decker website, accessed 30 May 2015, www.blackanddecker.com.

22. Felder website, accessed 30 May 2015, www.feldergroupusa.com.

23. Kotler and Armstrong, *Principles of Marketing,* 349.

24. Super Jock'n Jill website, accessed 30 May 2015, www.superjocknjill.com.

25. Øystein Foros and Hans Jarle Kind, "Do Slotting Allowances Harm Retail Competition?" *Scandinavian Journal of Economics,* Vol. 110, No. 2, 2008, 367–384; U.S. Federal Trade Commission, "Slotting Allowances in the Retail Grocery Industry: Selected Case Studies in Five Product Categories," November 2003, www.ftc.gov.

26. Heather Somerville, "Retailers Have a New Attitude About Showrooming," *Silicon Beat,* 4 November 2013, www.siliconbeat.com.

27. Kotler and Armstrong, *Principles of Marketing,* 344.

28. Kotler and Armstrong, *Principles of Marketing,* 344–345.

29. Andrew R. Thomas and Timothy J. Wilkinson, "The Devolution of Marketing," *Marketing Management,* Spring 2011, 19–25.

30. Jay Greene, "Amazon Rolls Out Free Same-Day Delivery for Prime Members," *Seattle Times,* 28 May 2015, www.seattletimes.com.

31. Amazon Prime Air, accessed 30 May 2015, www.amazon.com.

32. See note 1.

Customer Communication

LEARNING OBJECTIVES   After studying this chapter, you will be able to

1 Describe the three major tasks in crafting a communication strategy, and identify four important legal aspects of marketing communication.

2 Identify the major types of advertising, the most common advertising appeals, and the most important advertising media.

3 Explain how direct marketing differs from advertising, and identify the major forms of direct media.

4 Describe consultative selling, and explain the personal-selling process.

5 Define *sales promotion*, and identify the major categories of consumer and trade promotions.

6 Explain the uses of social media in customer communication and the role of public relations.

BEHIND THE SCENES   HOW THE QUEST FOR A BETTER CAMERA STRAP TRIGGERED THE GROWTH OF ONE OF TODAY'S HOTTEST COMPANIES

Social media users love to share entertaining videos, and as products designed to capture exciting footage, GoPro's action cameras are readymade for the new world of community-involved marketing.

Eric Millette/Forbes Collection/Corbis

http://gopro.com

If you've watched a daredevil video on YouTube in the past few years, chances are good the video was shot with a GoPro camera. GoPro's digital cameras have captured everything from extreme snowboarders to Felix Baumgartner's epic 24-mile freefall leap from the edge of space. The "adrenaline market" is at the core of the GoPro brand, but the growing population of GoPro users also includes filmmakers, sports and wildlife photographers, oceanographers, atmospheric researchers, and others who need high-quality video footage from a small, rugged, and relatively inexpensive digital camera.

GoPro cameras are practically everywhere these days, but like any company, GoPro's success was not guaranteed and its path was unpredictable. In fact, GoPro didn't even start out to be a camera company. Founder, CEO, and surfing enthusiast Nick Woodman set out to build a strap he could use to attach a disposable camera to his wrist in order to give his pals a "surfer's eye" view of what he saw when he out riding the waves.

The idea of commercializing his surfer's wrist strap took hold. However, after using it himself for a while, he realized he needed to offer an integrated solution that included the camera and a rugged, waterproof housing. He found a suitable low-cost camera made by a manufacturer in China, and combined with a plastic housing he designed himself, the first GoPro was born.

The new action camera looked like a great product, but the business world is littered with great ideas that never get off the ground because not enough people hear about them or can be convinced they are in fact great. If you were Nick Woodman, how would you get the word out about your company's cameras? How would you convince thousands, maybe millions, of people that they needed a new camera to catch life's wild, wacky, or fascinating moments? What steps would you take to convince consumers that the GoPro was a more compelling solution than the alternatives already on the market, and how would you encourage creative new uses for action cameras so you could keep building market demand?[1]

INTRODUCTION

When GoPro (profiled in the chapter-opening Behind the Scenes) wants to generate awareness of and interest in new products, the company and its communication team have a dizzying array of options for reaching out to customers and market influencers. This chapter, our final discussion of the marketing function, explains how marketers set communication goals, define messages, and choose from the ever-growing array of media options to reach target audiences.

1 **LEARNING OBJECTIVE**

Describe the three major tasks in crafting a communication strategy, and identify four important legal aspects of marketing communication.

social communication model
An approach to communication based on interactive social media and conversational communication styles.

Customer Communication: Challenges, Strategies, and Issues

Not long ago, marketing communication was largely about companies broadcasting carefully scripted messages to a mass audience that often had few, if any, ways to respond. Moreover, customers and other interested parties had few ways to connect with one another to ask questions about products, influence company decisions, or offer each other support.

However, various technologies have enabled and inspired a new approach to customer communication. In contrast to the "we talk, you listen" mindset of the past, this new **social communication model** is *interactive* and *conversational*. Today's audiences are no longer passive recipients of messages; instead, they demand to be active participants in a meaningful conversation. On the surface, this approach might look like it has just added a few new electronic media tools to the traditional arsenal of television, radio, newspapers, and magazines. However, as Exhibit 16.1 shows, the changes are much deeper and more profound. "Social Media in the Marketing Process" on page 387 discusses this new model in more detail.

In this new world of interactive communication, it's more vital than ever to have a strategy that (1) establishes *clear communication goals*, (2) defines *compelling messages* to help achieve those goals, and (3) outlines a *cost-effective media mix* to engage target audiences.

ESTABLISHING COMMUNICATION GOALS

Communication activities can help companies meet a wide range of marketing objectives, but only if these activities are crafted with clear and specific goals based on where the target audience is in the purchasing cycle.[2] Marketers take the following steps to move potential customers toward purchases:

- **Generating awareness.** People obviously can't buy things they don't know about, so creating awareness is essential for new companies and new products.
- **Providing information and creating positive emotional connections.** The next step is to build logical and emotional acceptance for the company and its products. Social media can work for or against companies in a significant way at this stage. If customers are pleased with a product, they'll help spread the message through the virtual word-of-mouth communication of social media. But they'll also spread the word if a product does not meet their expectations.
- **Building preference.** If buyers accept a product as a potential solution to their needs, the next step is to encourage them to prefer it over all other products they may be considering.

| EXHIBIT 16.1 | The Social Model of Customer Communication |

The social model of customer communication differs from the conventional promotion model in a number of significant ways.

Conventional Promotion: "We Talk, You Listen"	The Social Model: "Let's Have a Conversation"
Tendencies	**Tendencies**
Publication, broadcast	Conversation
Lecture	Discussion
Intrusion	Permission
Undirectional	Bidirectional, multidirectional
One to many; mass audience	One to one; many to many
Control	Influence
Low message frequency	High message frequency
Few channels	Many channels
Information hoarding	Information sharing
Static	Dynamic
Hierarchical	Egalitarian
Structured	Amorphous
Isolated	Collaborative
Planned	Reactive
Resistive	Responsive

- **Stimulating action.** Now comes the most critical step: convincing a consumer or an organization to act on that product preference to make a purchase, using a compelling *call to action*.
- **Reminding past customers.** Past customers are often the best prospects for future sales, so *reminder advertising* tells these buyers that a product is still available or that a company is ready to serve their needs.

One of the classic approaches to promotional communication is the *AIDA model*, which presents this process in the four steps of getting **A**ttention, building **I**nterest, increasing **D**esire, and prompting **A**ction (see Exhibit 16.2 on the next page). Study the ads and commercials you encounter every day, and you'll be able to spot the AIDA model in action.

DEFINING CUSTOMER MESSAGES

After establishing communication goals, the marketer's next step is to define the **core message**. This is the single most important idea the company hopes to convey to the target audience about a product. This core message is the foundation on which the marketing team can build successive layers of detail and explanation, with each communication effort expanding on the core message. For instance, advertisements try to communicate a few key points quickly, without going into great detail. A sales presentation can then go into more detail, and a technical brochure, online video, or a website can provide extensive information.

As Exhibit 16.1 notes, one of the most significant changes that the social communication model has brought to marketing is that companies now have far less control of their messages. After a message is released into the wild, so to speak, bloggers, reporters, industry analysts, and other parties will begin to repeat it, enhance it, change it, and even refute

core message
The single most important idea a marketer hopes to convey to the target audience about a company or its products.

EXHIBIT 16.2   **The AIDA Model of Persuasive Communication**

With the AIDA model, marketers craft one or more messages to move recipients through four stages of attention, interest, desire, and action.

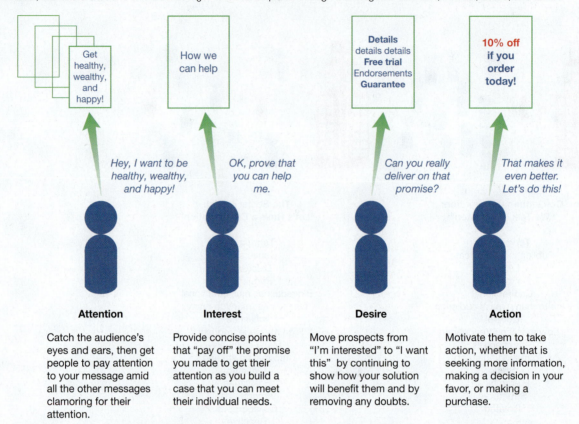

Attention	**Interest**	**Desire**	**Action**
Catch the audience's eyes and ears, then get people to pay attention to your message amid all the other messages clamoring for their attention.	Provide concise points that "pay off" the promise you made to get their attention as you build a case that you can meet their individual needs.	Move prospects from "I'm interested" to "I want this" by continuing to show how your solution will benefit them and by removing any doubts.	Motivate them to take action, whether that is seeking more information, making a decision in your favor, or making a purchase.

it. Starting with a clear and compelling core message increases the chances that it will reach its target audience intact. If the core message is not clear or not credible, it will surely be altered or refuted as it passes from one outside commentator to the next.

ASSEMBLING THE COMMUNICATION MIX

With clear goals and a compelling message, the next step is to share that message using a **communication mix**, also known as a *media mix* or *promotional mix*, through some combination of advertising, direct marketing, personal selling, sales promotion, social media, and public relations. Crafting the optimal mix is one of the toughest decisions marketing managers face and requires constant monitoring as markets and media choices evolve.

To assemble the best mix, companies have to consider a range of product, market, and distribution channel factors. Product factors include the type of product, its price range, and its stage in the product life cycle (see page 324). For example, an innovative technical product may require intensive educational efforts in the introduction and growth stages to help customers understand and appreciate its value. Market factors include the type of intended customers (consumers versus organizations), the nature of the competition, and the size and geographic spread of the target market.

Channel factors include the need for intermediaries, the type of intermediaries available, and the ability of those companies to help with communication. A key decision is whether to focus communication efforts on the intermediaries or on final customers. With a **push strategy**, a producer focuses on intermediaries, trying to persuade wholesalers or retailers to carry its products and promote those products to *their* customers. Conversely, with a **pull strategy**, the producer appeals directly to end customers. Customers learn of the product through these communication efforts and request it from retailers (in the case of consumers) or wholesalers (in the case of business customers). For example, if a television commercial encourages you to "ask your pharmacist" about a specific product,

communication mix
A blend of communication vehicles—advertising, direct marketing, personal selling, sales promotion, social media, and public relations—that a company uses to reach current and potential customers.

push strategy
A promotional strategy that focuses on intermediaries, motivating them to promote, or *push*, products toward end users.

pull strategy
A promotional strategy that stimulates consumer demand via advertising and other communication efforts, thereby creating a *pull* effect through the channel.

EXHIBIT 16.3   Message Integration in Customer Communication

To maximize efficiency and consistency, companies need to integrate their customer communication efforts. However, customers also integrate messages on the receiving end—including messages that might contradict messages from the company.

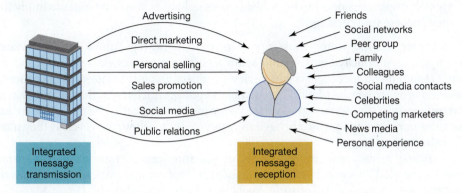

the company is using a pull strategy. Many companies use both push and pull strategies to increase the impact of their promotional efforts.

With the number of communication vehicles continuing to expand, the need for companies to "speak with one voice" becomes even greater. **Integrated marketing communications (IMC)** is a strategy of coordinating and integrating all communication and promotional efforts to ensure clarity, consistency, and maximum communications impact.[3] However, companies obviously can't control all the messages their target audiences receive, particularly now that customers are empowered through social media. While the company is working to integrate its outgoing communication efforts, the customer is also integrating all the incoming messages he or she is receiving (see Exhibit 16.3).

integrated marketing communications (IMC)
A strategy of coordinating and integrating communication and promotion efforts with customers to ensure greater efficiency and effectiveness.

COMMUNICATION LAWS AND ETHICS

As marketing and selling grow increasingly complex, so do the legal ramifications of marketing communication. In the United States, the Federal Trade Commission (FTC) has the authority to impose penalties against advertisers that violate federal standards for truthful advertising. Other federal agencies have authority over advertising in specific industries, such as transportation and financial services. Individual states have additional laws that apply. The legal aspects of promotional communication can be quite complex, and they vary from state to state and from country to country. However, if you are involved in customer communication in any form, at a minimum you need to be aware of these legal issues:[4]

- **Marketing and sales messages must be truthful and nondeceptive.** The FTC considers messages to be deceptive if they include statements that are likely to mislead reasonable customers and are an important part of the purchasing decision. Failing to include important information is also considered deceptive. The FTC also looks at *implied claims*—claims you don't explicitly make but that can be inferred from what you do or don't say.
- **You must back up your claims with evidence.** According to the FTC, offering a money-back guarantee or providing letters from satisfied customers is not enough; you must still be able to support claims for your product with objective evidence such as a survey or scientific study. If you claim that your food product lowers cholesterol, you must have scientific evidence to support that claim.
- **"Bait-and-switch" advertising is illegal.** Trying to attract buyers by advertising a product that you don't intend to sell—and then trying to sell them another (and usually more expensive) product—is illegal.
- **Marketing messages, websites, and mobile apps aimed at children are subject to special rules.** For example, online marketers must obtain consent from parents before collecting personal information about children under age 13.

- **Marketing and sales messages are considered binding contracts in many states.** If you imply or make an offer and then can't fulfill your end of the bargain, you can be sued for breach of contract.
- **In most cases, you can't use a person's name, photograph, or other identity without permission.** Doing so is considered an invasion of privacy. You can use images of people considered to be public figures as long as you don't unfairly imply that they endorse your message.

Moreover, communicators must stay on top of changing regulations, such as the latest laws governing unsolicited bulk email ("spam"), customer privacy, data security, and disclosure requirements for bloggers who review products. Two of the latest ethical concerns that could produce new legislation are *behavioral targeting*, which tracks the online behavior of website visitors and serves up ads based on what they appear to be interested in, and *remarketing* or *retargeting*, in which behaviorally targeted ads follow users even as they move on to other websites.[5]

Regarding privacy and other aspects of communication, responsible companies recognize the vital importance of ethical standards. Professional associations such as the American Association of Advertising Agencies (**www.aaaa.org**), the Direct Marketing Association (**www.the-dma.org**), and the American Marketing Association (**www.ama .org**) devote considerable time and energy to ethical issues in marketing, including ongoing education for practitioners and self-regulation efforts aimed at avoiding or correcting ethical lapses. Several national advertising organizations also coordinate their efforts via the Advertising Self-Regulatory Council (**www.asrcreviews.org**).[6]

 Checkpoint

LEARNING OBJECTIVE 1: Describe the three major tasks in crafting a communication strategy, and identify four important legal aspects of marketing communication.

SUMMARY: The three major tasks in developing a communication strategy are establishing clear communication goals, defining compelling messages to help achieve those goals, and outlining a cost-effective media mix to engage target audiences. Four important issues in communications law are making sure advertising claims are truthful and nondeceptive, supporting claims with real evidence, recognizing that marketing and sales messages are contractual obligations in many cases, and avoiding the unauthorized use of a person's name or image.

CRITICAL THINKING: (1) Why do credit card companies target students even though most of them have little or no income? (2) Would it be wise for a manufacturer that is new to a particular industry (and unknown within it) to invest most of its promotional resources in a pull strategy? Why or why not?

IT'S YOUR BUSINESS: (1) What is your "core message" as a future business professional? How would you summarize, in one sentence, what you can offer a company? (2) Does knowing that advertisers are trying to track your online behavior in order to target you with personalized ads make you want to limit or change your web surfing? Do you think advertisers have the right to do this? Why or why not?

KEY TERMS TO KNOW: social communication model, core message, communication mix, push strategy, pull strategy, integrated marketing communications (IMC)

2   LEARNING OBJECTIVE

Identify the major types of advertising, the most common advertising appeals, and the most important advertising media.

advertising
The delivery of announcements and promotional messages via time or space purchased in various media.

Advertising

Advertising can be defined as the "the placement of announcements and messages in time or space by business firms, nonprofit organizations, government agencies, and individuals who seek to inform and/or persuade members of a particular target market or audience about their products, services, organizations, or ideas."[7] Two key points here are that advertising is paid for and that it is carried by someone else's medium. (Companies sometimes own the media in which they advertise, but this is not the usual case.) This section offers a quick overview of the various types of advertising, the appeals most commonly used in advertising, and the advantages and disadvantages of major advertising media.

TYPES OF ADVERTISING

Companies can use advertising for a variety of purposes. The most common type, *product advertising*, promotes the features and benefits of specific products. The term *comparative advertising* is applied to ads that specifically highlight how one product is better than its competitors. Strong comparative messages can boost sales, but the approach is risky. Competitors are likely to sue if they believe their products have been portrayed unfairly, and sometimes *attack ads* can decrease sales for an entire product category (including the products of the advertiser) by emphasizing the negative aspects of the products in question.[8]

In some countries, comparative ads are tightly regulated and sometimes banned, but that is clearly not the case in the United States. Indeed, the FTC encourages advertisers to use direct product comparisons, with the intent of better informing customers, and even permits disparaging ads, as long as they are truthful and nondeceptive.[9]

Institutional advertising is designed to create goodwill and build a desired image for a company rather than to promote specific products. For example, a firm might promote its commitment to sustainable business practices or workforce diversity. Institutional ads that address public issues are called **advocacy advertising**. Companies with a financial stake in the outcome of public policy decisions can use advocacy ads to persuade voters or legislators to consider a particular point of view.

Advertising can also be classified according to the sponsor. *National advertising* is sponsored by companies that sell products on a nationwide basis, whereas *local advertising* is sponsored by a local merchant. *Cooperative advertising* involves a financial arrangement in which companies with products sold nationally share the costs of local advertising with local marketing intermediaries.

institutional advertising
Advertising that seeks to create goodwill and to build a desired image for a company, rather than to promote specific products.

advocacy advertising
Advertising that presents a company's opinions on public issues such as education or health care.

ADVERTISING APPEALS

A key decision in planning a promotional campaign is choosing the **advertising appeal**, a creative tactic designed to capture the audience's attention and promote preference for the product or company being advertised. Marketers can choose from seven basic appeals (note that these appeals are not limited to advertising; they are used in other types of persuasive communication as well):[10]

advertising appeal
A creative tactic designed to capture the audience's attention and promote preference for the product or company being advertised.

- **Logic.** The basic approach with a logical appeal is to make a claim based on a rational argument supported by solid evidence. Not surprisingly, business-to-business advertising relies heavily on logical appeals because businesses have logical concerns—profitability, process improvements, quality, and other financial and technical concerns (see Exhibit 16.4 on the next page). However, marketers should not ignore the emotional aspects of business purchasing. Managers put their reputations and sometimes their careers on the line when they make major purchase decisions, so advertisers need to consider these emotional elements. Logical appeals are also used in consumer advertising whenever the purchase decision has a rational component and logic might help persuade buyers to consider or prefer a particular product.
- **Emotion.** An emotional appeal calls on audience feelings and sympathies rather than on facts, figures, and rational arguments. Emotional appeals range from sentimental to terrifying. On the lighter side, flowers, greeting cards, and gifts are among the products usually sold with a positive emotional appeal. At the other end of the spectrum are appeals to a broad range of fears: personal and family safety, financial security, social acceptance, and business success or failure. To be effective, appeals to fear must be managed carefully. Laying it on too thick can anger the audience or even cause them to block out the message entirely.

| **EXHIBIT 16.4** | **Emotional and Logical Appeals** |

Depending on the product and the target audience, marketers can emphasize logic or emotions in the advertising appeal by "dialing up" one or the other through specific choices of words, images, and sounds. Even an identical product marketed to consumers and businesses could have dramatically different messages, as these two headlines for an electronic security system suggest.

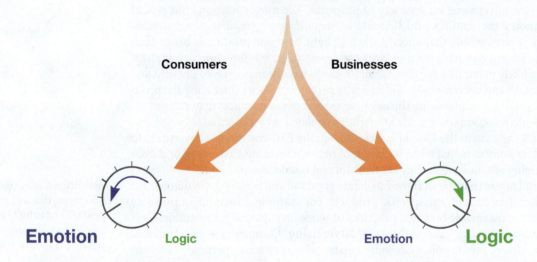

Balancing Emotion and Logic
Example: promoting an electronic security system

Consumers — Emotion / Logic — "Are your loved ones and your most precious possessions safe from intruders?"

Businesses — Emotion / Logic — "Reduce inventory loss and property damage—and get a better deal on your facilities insurance"

- **Humor.** In a world cluttered with advertising, humor is frequently used to capture people's attention. However, humor can be tricky; sometimes it can offend audiences, tainting the brand, or the humor can be so memorable that audiences recall the joke but not the product being advertised.[11]

- **Celebrity.** The thinking behind celebrity involvement in advertising is that people will be more inclined to use products endorsed by a celebrity because they will identify with and want to be like this person (no matter how far-fetched such aspirations might be at a purely logical level). Celebrities can also bring excitement, humor, energy, and even perceived value to a product. In addition to being expensive, however, celebrity endorsements can be risky because the brand's image becomes linked to the celebrity's image, including whatever image problems the celebrity experiences in his or her personal life.[12]

- **Sex.** Sex-oriented appeals are the most controversial type of advertising, in terms of both social reaction and promotional effectiveness. Although the phrase "sex sells" is often repeated, it isn't always true. Sexual appeals can definitely be effective, but the degree of effectiveness varies by product, audience, and the role of the sexual imagery or narrative in the advertising. For example, sexual appeals have been shown to be more effective with audiences that have a low level of emotional or intellectual engagement with the purchase than with audiences that are more involved.[13]

- **Music.** With its ability to create emotional bonds and "embed" itself in listeners' memories, music can be a powerful aspect of advertising. Marketers can take several approaches to integrating music into radio, television, or online advertising, including composing *jingles* specifically for ads, licensing popular songs for use in commercials (although these fees can run into the millions of dollars for hit songs), or working with emerging artists to write songs specifically with advertising use in mind.[14]

- **Scarcity.** If a product is in limited supply or available only for a limited time, advertisers can use this scarcity to encourage consumer responses.

Note that these appeals are not mutually exclusive. For example, ads can use humor to catch an audience's attention and then use an emotional appeal to strengthen the bond with the brand or logic to show the superiority of a product.

ADVERTISING MEDIA

Choosing **advertising media**, or channels of communication, can be as important as selecting the type of advertising and the advertising appeal. As listed in Exhibit 16.5, major advertising media include newspapers, television, radio, magazines, billboards, fixed web (from computers), and mobile web (from mobile phones and other handheld devices). A *media plan* outlines the advertising budget, the schedule of when ads will appear, and a discussion of the **media mix**—the combination of print, broadcast, online, and other media

advertising media
Communication channels, such as newspapers, radio, television, and the World Wide Web.

media mix
A combination of print, broadcast, online, and other media used for an advertising campaign.

EXHIBIT 16.5	Advantages and Disadvantages of Major Advertising Media

Each medium has strengths and weaknesses; companies often combine two or more media in an advertising campaign to maximize their promotional effectiveness.

Medium	Advantages	Disadvantages
Online video	Higher click-through rates than other digital media and can be more effective than television; creative flexibility opens up possibilities for entertaining audiences, leading to greater retention and recall.	Vulnerable to technical glitches; online videos often compete with other website content.
Newspapers	Extensive market coverage; low cost; short lead time for placing ads; good local market coverage; geographic selectivity; credibility	Poor graphic quality; short life span; cluttered pages; visual competition from other ads; printed papers have rapidly declining readership in many cities; lower readership among younger consumer.
Television	Great impact; broad reach; appealing to senses of sight, sound, and motion; creative opportunities for demonstration; high attention; entertainment carryover	High cost for production and air time; less audience selectivity; long preparation time; commercial clutter; short life for message; vulnerability to being skipped or muted; losing ground to new media options
Radio	Low cost; high frequency; immediacy; highly portable; high geographic and demographic selectivity	No visual possibilities; short life for message; commercial clutter; lower attention than television; declining audience share; low level of engagement
Magazines	Good production quality; long life; local and regional market selectivity; authority and credibility; multiple readers extend reach of each issue; close bond with readers	Limited demonstration possibilities; long lead time between placing and publishing ads; lots of ad clutter; high cost; declining readership for many titles
Product placement	Offers a way to get around viewers' advertising filters; chance for high visibility in the right program, movie, or game	Limited choice of vehicles; unpredictable; effectiveness is linked to the popularity of the programming; risk of overuse could reduce effectiveness over time
Fixed web (from stationary computers)	Rich media options and interactivity can make ads more compelling and more effective; changes and additions can be made quickly and easily in most cases; webpages can provide an almost unlimited amount of information; can be measured and personalized through tracking and targeting capabilities; instant links to online retailing and influence on store-based retail sales; growing audiences for Internet radio and video; social media connections can spread marketing messages through word of mouth	Very low click-through rates; extreme degree of audience fragmentation (millions of websites); increasing clutter (such as pop-up ads); not as portable as magazines, newspapers, or mobile web; ad-blocking software can prevent ads from being displayed
Mobile web (from smartphones and tablets)	In addition to almost every advantage of the fixed web other than display size: highly portable; constant, "always-on" presence (most people have their phones with them much of the time); opportunity for location-based advertising; possibilities for narrow targeting	Many users won't tolerate advertising intrusions via mobile phone; small screen size limits display possibilities

Sources: "Media Comparison," *Outdoor Advertising Association of America*, accessed 1 June 2015, www.oaaa.org; Roy H. Williams, "Selecting the Most Effective Advertising Media," *Entrepreneur*, accessed 1 June 2015, www.entrepreneur.com; Davia Temin, "Don't Waste Money—Make Your Social Media Advertising Smarter, More Original, More Effective," *Forbes*, 3 December 2013, www.forbes.com; "Jeffrey M. O'Brien, "The Wizards of Apps," *Fortune*, 5 May 2009, 29–30; Christopher Meyer, "The Year of Marketing Dangerously," *Harvard Business Review*, October 2008, 26–27; Magid Abraham, "The Off-line Impact of Online Ads," *Harvard Business Review*, April 2008, 28; Michael A. Wiles and Anna Danielova, "The Worth of Product Placement in Successful Films: An Event Study Analysis," *Journal of Marketing*, July 2009, 44–63; Kenneth E. Clow and Donald Baack, *Integrated Advertising, Promotion, and Marketing Communications*, 4th ed. (Upper Saddle River, N.J.: Pearson Prentice Hall, 2010), 219–229; "Online Videos More Effective Than TV Advertising," 28 May 2013, http://mashable.com.

REAL-TIME UPDATES
Learn More by Visiting This Website

See the latest ads from all around the world

Ads of the World shows some of the best creative work from the world's advertising professionals. Go to http://real-timeupdates .com/bia8 and click on Learn More in the Students section.

product placement

The paid display or use of products in television shows, movies, and video games.

to be used in the campaign. To create the media mix, advertising experts factor in the characteristics of the target audience, the types of media that will reach the largest audience in the most cost-effective way, and the strengths and weaknesses of the various media as they relate to the product and its marketing message.

Three trends are likely to shape advertising media in the coming years. First, the media landscape will continue to fragment as new online and mobile formats emerge and conventional print and broadcast media fight to hang on to their share of advertisers' budgets. The days when advertisers could reach most consumers through a few television networks and major periodicals are long gone. Figuring out how to reach consumers who spread their attention across a variety of media and delivery platforms is one of the biggest challenges facing marketers today.

Second, the lines between advertising, entertainment, and *value-added content* (such as informative articles and how-to videos) will continue to blur. For example, more advertisers are borrowing storytelling techniques and other methods from the entertainment industry to make their TV commercials, online videos, and other ads more entertaining and thus more likely to be watched.[15]

Product placement, in which companies pay to have their products displayed or used in television shows, movies, and video games, has become a multibillion-dollar business as advertisers respond to the increasing number of ways consumers are able to ignore, skip, or block ads—and as content producers look for more funds to create programming. Product placement ranges from subtle brand displays in the background of a scene to active engagement with a product.[16]

Third, technical innovations will continue to create new advertising tools and techniques. For example, mobile devices are emerging as an enticing platform for advertisers, and the amount of marketing money spent on mobile advertising is likely to increase rapidly in the coming years.[17]

 ## Checkpoint

LEARNING OBJECTIVE 2: Identify the major types of advertising, the most common advertising appeals, and the most important advertising media.

SUMMARY: The major types of advertising based on the type of message are *product* advertising (which promotes the benefits of a product), *comparative* advertising (which compares a product to competitors' products), *institutional* advertising (which promotes a company or other organization), and *advocacy* advertising (which conveys information and opinions about public issues). Advertising can also be categorized by sponsor, including *national, local,* and *cooperative* advertising. The most common advertising appeals are logic, emotion, humor, celebrity, sex, music, and scarcity. Major advertising media include newspapers, television, radio, magazines, billboards, fixed web (from computers), and mobile web (from mobile phones and other handheld devices).

CRITICAL THINKING: (1) Do fragmented media make it easier or harder for marketers to engage in segmented or concentrated marketing? Explain your answer. (2) Why would a company such as McDonald's, which is already well known to virtually all consumers in the United States, continue to spend heavily on advertising?

IT'S YOUR BUSINESS: (1) Have you ever believed that you could create better advertising for a product than the company behind the product created? If so, explain the type of appeal you would've used and why. (2) Do you find that you tend to watch and listen to most television commercials, or do you mute or channel surf during commercials? If you pay attention to commercials, what captures your interest?

KEY TERMS TO KNOW: advertising, institutional advertising, advocacy advertising, advertising appeal, advertising media, media mix, product placement

Direct Marketing

Although it is similar to advertising in many respects, **direct marketing**, defined as direct communication with potential customers other than personal sales contacts, can differ from advertising in three important ways. (The lines continue to blur between types of media, so not all these distinctions hold true for every medium.) First, direct marketing often uses *personally addressable* media such as letters and email messages to deliver targeted messages to individual consumers or organizational purchasers. Second, except for info-mercials, direct marketing doesn't involve the purchase of time or space in other media. The advertiser usually has control over the delivery mechanism and can decide when, where, and how the message is delivered. Third, direct marketing has a *direct response* aspect that often isn't present in advertising. Although effective direct marketing works to build lasting relationships with customers, its primary emphasis is generating sales *now*.

DIRECT MARKETING TECHNIQUES

Direct marketing has evolved dramatically from its early days, when pioneering promotional efforts such as the Sears catalog in the late 1800s helped establish *mail order* on a massive scale.[18] Direct marketing is now a computer-intensive multimedia effort that includes mail, telephone, online, and mobile media. The heart of any direct marketing effort is a customer database that contains contact histories, purchase records, and profiles of each buyer or potential buyer. (Direct marketing is sometimes referred to as *database marketing*.) The data can range from basic demographic information to records of all customer contacts to detailed purchasing records and other behavioral data. Such databases also play a vital role in relationship marketing because they enable a company to personalize its interaction with every customer.

The *measurability* of direct marketing is one of its greatest appeals. If you mail a promotional flyer to 1,000 people and 36 of them call to place an order, you know the campaign had a 3.6 percent response rate. Because direct responses are directly measurable (unlike many advertising efforts), direct marketing lends itself to constant experimentation and improvement. This is particularly true with online direct marketing efforts, where changes can be made cheaply and quickly.

DIRECT MARKETING MEDIA

The catalogs that helped launch direct marketing over a hundred years ago are still a force today, as a peek inside any mailbox in the country will confirm. Here is a brief look at the major media used in direct marketing:

- **Mail.** **Direct mail**, printed material addressed to an individual or a household, has the key advantage of being able to put promotional materials, ranging from simple letters and glossy catalogs to DVDs and product samples, directly into the hands of a target audience.
- **Email.** The ability to send millions of messages in a matter of minutes at almost no cost made email a hit with direct marketers—and practically destroyed email as a viable communication medium in the minds of some users tired of being deluged with unwanted "spam." To minimize the level of annoyance and to help potential customers get the information they really do want, many companies now emphasize *permission-based* email marketing, usually by asking customers or website visitors to *opt-in* to mailing lists.
- **Search engine marketing.** With millions of web and mobile users relying on search engines such as Google and Bing every day, **search engine marketing**, or *search advertising*, has become an important marketing medium. Although it doesn't quite fit the traditional categories of either advertising or direct marketing, search engine marketing comes closer to being a direct medium because it is individualized to each

REAL-TIME UPDATES
Learn More by Visiting This Website

Issues in database marketing

The Data-Driven Marketing Institute is a strong advocate for database marketing techniques. Go to http://real-timeupdates .com/bia8 and click on Learn More in the Students section.

web user. The basic idea of search engine marketing is that advertisers can pay to have small ads presented whenever the keywords they select are used in a search. Web users see these *sponsored results* above or beside the "organic" search results.

- **Direct response online.** The interactive, adaptable nature of websites and mobile apps allows them to go far beyond static advertising media to become direct, personalized communication channels. For example, Sweetwater Sound, a retailer of musical instruments and sound equipment, delivers a variety of personalized website and email messages based on customers' purchase histories and interests. A customer who orders an amplifier for live music production might see messages about cables, speakers, and other equipment that will complement the amplifier purchase. By reaching out to the customer right at the moment of the original purchase decision, Sweetwater can prompt the buyer to consider additional products tailored to his or her individual needs.

- **Telephone.** The telephone is a major promotional tool in consumer and organizational markets and for both *inbound* (when buyers call in to place orders) and *outbound* (when sellers contact potential buyers with sales offers) marketing. Unsolicited marketing calls are not popular with consumers, however. In the United States, the National Do Not Call Registry gives individuals the opportunity to have their landline numbers removed from telemarketers' lists.

- **Direct response television and videos.** More commonly known as *infomercials*, **direct response television** programs have the major advantage of time, allowing companies to demonstrate products and engage viewers in a way that isn't possible with 30- or 60-second commercials.

direct response television
The use of television commercials and longer-format infomercials that are designed to stimulate an immediate purchase response from viewers.

 Checkpoint

LEARNING OBJECTIVE 3: Explain how direct marketing differs from advertising, and identify the major forms of direct media.

SUMMARY: Direct marketing differs from advertising in three important ways: (1) It uses *personally addressable* media such as letters and email messages to deliver targeted messages to individual consumers or organizational purchasers, (2) it doesn't involve the purchase of time or space in other media, and (3) it has a *direct response* aspect that often isn't present in advertising. The major categories of direct marketing media are mail (including catalogs), email, search engine marketing, telephone, and direct response television.

CRITICAL THINKING: (1) Would an iPhone app that streams QVC or another shopping channel to mobile phones be an effective direct marketing medium? Why or why not? (2) If direct marketing has a better return on investment than other forms of promotion, why do companies bother with anything but direct marketing?

IT'S YOUR BUSINESS: (1) As a rough guess, what percentage of the direct marketing messages you receive in a given week are effectively targeted to your needs as a consumer? Identify a recent example that was well targeted and one that was not. (2) Have you ever responded to the offer in a "spam" email message? If so, what enticed you to do so?

KEY TERMS TO KNOW: direct marketing, direct mail, search engine marketing, direct response television

---

4 **LEARNING OBJECTIVE**

Describe consultative selling, and explain the personal-selling process.

personal selling
One-on-one interaction between a salesperson and a prospective buyer.

Personal Selling

Even with the rapid advance of e-commerce and other marketing technologies, **personal selling**, the one-on-one interaction between a salesperson and a prospective buyer, remains a fundamentally important part of the promotional mix in many consumer and organizational markets. Although a sales force can't reach millions of customers at once like a website or a direct marketing program can, today's highly trained sales professionals are able to build relationships and solve problems in ways that impersonal media can't match. Many companies now combine the wide reach and cost efficiencies of online promotion with the individualized touch of personal sales by integrating live chat into their websites. You've probably seen this method in action when you're shopping online and a window pops up with an offer from a sales associate to answer any questions you might have.

CONTEMPORARY PERSONAL SELLING

As with other elements of the communication mix, personal selling has evolved over the years to support the contemporary idea of the customer-oriented marketing concept. In this sense, personal selling has evolved from *peddling products* to *creating partnerships with customers*.[19] One of the most important shifts in the sales profession is the advent of **consultative selling**, in which the salesperson acts as a consultant and advisor who helps current and potential customers find the best solutions to their personal or business needs. And even if a shopper isn't ready to buy something immediately, a good consultative salesperson will view the interaction as a chance to build a long-term relationship that could lead to sales in the future.[20]

consultative selling
An approach in which a salesperson acts as a consultant and advisor to help customers find the best solutions to their personal or business needs.

THE PERSONAL-SELLING PROCESS

Personal selling varies widely from industry to industry, with some sales being completed in a matter of minutes and others taking weeks or months. Time is often the salesperson's most valuable asset, so it must be spent wisely—focusing on the most valuable prospects who are most likely to purchase. The following steps can be adapted to almost any sales situation (see Exhibit 16.6):

- **Step 1: Prospecting.** The process of finding and qualifying potential customers is known as **prospecting**. This step usually involves three activities: (1) *generating sales leads*—names of individuals and organizations that might be likely prospects for the company's product; (2) *identifying prospects*—potential customers who indicate a need or a desire for the seller's product; and (3) *qualifying prospects*—the process of figuring out which prospects have both the authority and the available money to buy.
- **Step 2: Preparing.** With a list of strong prospects in hand, the next step is to prepare for the *sales call* (in person, over the phone, or online via videoconferencing or another method). In this research phase, the sales staff tries to learn more about the people and organizations they will be contacting regarding their buying needs, their motives for buying, and the names of current suppliers. The salesperson then establishes specific objectives to achieve during the sales call, which vary depending on where the

prospecting
The process of finding and qualifying potential customers.

EXHIBIT 16.6	The Personal-Selling Process

The personal-selling process can involve up to seven steps, starting with prospecting for sales leads and ending with following up after the sale has been closed. This diagram gives you a general idea of how salespeople approach major sales opportunities.

1. Prospecting	2. Preparing	3. Approaching the Prospect	4. Aligning with Customer Needs	5. Handling Objections	6. Closing	7. Following Up
Finding and qualifying potential customers; usually involves generating sales leads, identifying prospects, and qualifying prospects	Getting ready for the sales call; researching the customer in more depth, establishing objectives, and preparing a presentation	Taking steps to make a good first impression; crafting the right appearance, maintaining professional behavior, and preparing an engaging introduction	Listening to the prospect describe what is needed and proposing a solution to meet those needs	Addressing any concerns the prospect might raise; exploring the deeper reasons that might be behind the expressed objections	Asking the prospect to choose the solution being offered	Checking in with the customer after the sale to make sure the solution is working out as expected and to keep building a long-term relaionship

buyer is in the decision cycle. Finally, the salesperson often prepares a presentation, which can be as basic as a list of points to discuss or as elaborate as a product demonstration or multimedia presentation.

- **Step 3: Approaching the prospect.** First impressions can make or break a sale, so knowledgeable salespeople take care to (1) craft the appropriate appearance for themselves and for everything that represents them; (2) maintain behaviors and attitudes that are professional, courteous, and confident without being arrogant; and (3) prepare opening lines that include a brief greeting and introduction, followed by a few carefully chosen words that establish a good rapport with the potential customer.

- **Step 4: Aligning with customer needs.** After the conversation has been initiated, the next step is understanding the customer's specific needs. The biggest mistake a salesperson can make at this stage is talking instead of listening. The most extreme form of this error is the *canned sales pitch*, in which the salesperson recites or even reads a stock message, with no regard for the customer's unique circumstances. In contrast, today's enlightened sales professionals focus on questioning and listening before offering a solution that meets each prospect's unique needs.

- **Step 5: Handling objections.** Potential customers can express a variety of objections to the products they are considering, and salespeople need to be ready with answers and alternatives.

- **Step 6: Closing.** Bringing the sales process to a successful conclusion by asking for and receiving an affirmative purchase decision is known as **closing**. Experienced professionals know to look for signs that the prospect is ready to make a decision, and they use a variety of techniques such as offering to write up an order to encourage a definitive answer.[21]

- **Step 7: Following up.** Most companies depend on repeat sales and referrals from satisfied customers, so it's important that salespeople follow up after the sale to make sure customers are satisfied with their purchases. Staying in touch gives a company the opportunity to answer questions, address areas of confusion or dissatisfaction with a purchase, and show customers it is a reliable partner for the long haul.

closing
The point at which a sale is completed.

 Checkpoint

LEARNING OBJECTIVE 4: Describe consultative selling, and explain the personal-selling process.

SUMMARY: Consultative selling is a combination of persuasion and advice, in which the salesperson acts as a consultant and advisor who helps current and potential customers find the best solutions to their personal or business needs. The seven general steps in personal selling are (1) *prospecting*, finding prospects and qualifying them; (2) *preparing*, creating a prospect profile, setting objectives for the call, and preparing a presentation; (3) *approaching* the prospect, with the goal of making a positive first impression; (4) *uncovering* the customer's needs and *presenting* appropriate solutions; (5) *handling objections*, using audience comments as an opportunity to strengthen the presentation; (6) *closing*, focusing on completing the sale; and (7) *following up* after the sale to make sure the buyer is satisfied.

CRITICAL THINKING: (1) Why is the canned approach inadequate for many selling situations? (2) Why should a salesperson take the time to qualify sales leads?

IT'S YOUR BUSINESS: (1) Would you be comfortable in a personal-selling role? Why or why not? (2) What can you learn from professional selling methods to help you in a job interview?

KEY TERMS TO KNOW: personal selling, consultative selling, prospecting, closing

Sales Promotion

Sales promotion consists of short-term incentives to build the reputation of a brand, encourage the purchase of a product, or simply enhance relationships with current and potential customers. Sales promotion consists of two basic categories: consumer promotion and trade promotion.

CONSUMER PROMOTIONS

Companies use a variety of consumer promotional tools and incentives to stimulate repeat purchases and to entice new users:

- **Contests and other audience involvement tactics.** Giving consumers the opportunity to participate in contests, games, sweepstakes, surveys, and other activities, particularly if there is a chance for consumers to demonstrate cleverness or creativity, is a great way to build energy around a brand (see Exhibit 16.7 on the next page).
- **Coupons.** The biggest category of consumer promotion is **coupons**, printed or digital certificates that spur sales by giving buyers a discount when they purchase specified products. And rapid growth of mobile coupons is bringing a new twist to this promotional tactic, with a majority of mobile shoppers now taking advantage of coupons sent to their smartphones via email, text messaging, or apps.[22] Couponing is an inefficient and often risky strategy, however. With paper coupons, consumers redeem only a tiny fraction of the billions of printed coupons distributed every year in the United States.[23] And with all types of coupons, there is always the possibility that the people using the coupons would've purchased the product anyway, so for these shoppers the effort only served to bring in less money for the marketer. Moreover, the rampant use of couponing can train customers to wait for coupons on products they buy regularly, which is effectively offering the products at a permanent discount, or encourage them to abandon brand loyalty and use whatever brand has a coupon that week.
- **Rebates.** With **rebates**, companies offer partial reimbursement of the price as a purchase incentive. Rebates can be an effective tool for boosting sales, but they obviously cut into per-unit profits—and the effect can be more or less permanent when frequent rebates in an industry encourage buyers to delay purchases until a rebate program is available.
- **Point-of-purchase.** A **point-of-purchase (POP) display** is an in-store presentation designed to stimulate immediate sales. POP displays are a vital element in the marketing effort for many products sold at retail stores. Not only do they represent the manufacturer's last chance to communicate with the consumer, but they help capture *impulse purchases*—unplanned purchases that can make up as much as 50 percent of sales in mass merchandise stores and supermarkets.[24]
- **Samples and trial-use versions.** Distributing samples is an effective way to introduce a new product, encourage nonusers to try an existing product, encourage current buyers to use the product in a new way, or expand distribution into new areas. Many software products are also offered as trial versions to let customers try before buying.
- **Special-event sponsorship.** Sponsoring special events has become one of the most popular sales promotion tactics, with thousands of companies spending billions of dollars to sponsor events ranging from golf to opera.
- **Other promotions.** Other popular consumer sales promotion techniques include in-store demonstrations, loyalty and frequency programs such as frequent-flyer programs, and **premiums**, which are free or bargain-priced items offered to encourage the consumer to buy a product. **Specialty advertising** (on pens, calendars, T-shirts, mouse pads, and other items) helps keep a company's name in front of customers for a long period of time.

---

5 LEARNING OBJECTIVE

Define *sales promotion*, and identify the major categories of consumer and trade promotions.

sales promotion
A wide range of events and activities designed to promote a brand or stimulate interest in a product.

coupons
Printed or electronic certificates that offer discounts on particular items and are redeemed at the time of purchase.

rebates
Partial reimbursement of price, offered as a purchase incentive.

point-of-purchase (POP) display
Advertising or other display materials set up at retail locations to promote products to potential customers as they are making their purchase decisions.

premiums
Free or bargain-priced items offered to encourage consumers to buy a product.

specialty advertising
Advertising that appears on various items such as coffee mugs, pens, and calendars, designed to help keep a company's name in front of customers.

EXHIBIT 16.7   Consumer Promotions

Contests and sweepstakes are common tactics for consumer promotions, particularly on social media.

Falken Tire @FalkenTire · 21h
RT to enter to win this Falken Bobblehead! #sundayfunday Rules: bit.ly/18XYTps

Photo courtesy of Falken Tire Corporation

TRADE PROMOTIONS

trade promotions
Sales-promotion efforts aimed at inducing distributors or retailers to push a producer's products.

Although shoppers are more aware of consumer promotions, **trade promotions** aimed at inducing wholesalers or retailers to sell a company's products actually account for the larger share of promotional spending and can be the single largest item in a manufacturer's marketing budget.[25] The most popular trade promotions are **trade allowances**, which involve discounts on product prices, free merchandise, or other payments, such as the retail slotting allowances mentioned in Chapter 15. The intermediary can either pocket the savings to increase profits or pass the savings on to the consumer to generate additional sales. Trade allowances are commonly used when adopting a push marketing strategy because they encourage the intermediaries to carry new products or to sell higher volumes of current products.

trade allowances
Discounts or other financial considerations offered by producers to wholesalers and retailers.

The chief downside of trade allowances is that they can create the controversial practice of *forward buying*, in which customers load up on merchandise while the price is low. For example, if a producer offers retailers a 20 percent discount for a period of 6 weeks, a retailer might choose to buy enough inventory to last 8 or 10 weeks. Purchasing this excessive amount at the lower price increases the retailer's profit, but at the expense of the producer's profit.

In addition to trade allowances, other popular trade promotions are dealer contests and bonus programs designed to motivate distributors or retailers to push particular merchandise. Product samples are also common in many business marketing efforts. For instance, semiconductor manufacturers often provide samples of electronic components to engineers who are designing new products, knowing that if the prototype is successful, it could lead to full-scale production—and orders for thousands or millions of components.

 Checkpoint

LEARNING OBJECTIVE 5: Define *sales promotion*, **and identify the major categories of consumer and trade promotions.**

SUMMARY: The two main types of sales promotion are consumer promotion and trade promotion. Consumer promotions are intended to motivate the final consumer to try new products or to experiment with the company's brands. Examples include contests, coupons, rebates, point-of-purchase displays, samples, special-event sponsorship, premiums, and specialty advertising. Trade promotions are designed to induce wholesalers and retailers to promote a producer's products. Common trade promotions include trade allowances, dealer contests, bonus programs, and samples.

CRITICAL THINKING: (1) If 99 percent of coupons are never used, why do companies keep printing so many? (2) If wholesalers and retailers can make money selling a manufacturer's product, why would the manufacturer need to offer incentives such as sales contests?

IT'S YOUR BUSINESS: (1) How can sales promotions reduce the reluctance that buyers might feel about trying an unfamiliar product? (2) Have you ever participated in a sales promotion without realizing you were doing so? For example, have you ever "liked" a company on Facebook to enter a sweepstakes without realizing that in doing so you were also signing up for all its Wall postings in your Facebook feed?

KEY TERMS TO KNOW: sales promotion, coupons, rebates, point-of-purchase (POP) display, premiums, specialty advertising, trade promotions, trade allowances

Social Media and Public Relations

6 | **LEARNING OBJECTIVE**

Explain the uses of social media in customer communication and the role of public relations.

All the communication methods discussed so far in this chapter involve activities by companies themselves to transmit carefully crafted and controlled messages to target audiences. The final two methods, social media and public relations, differ from the traditional methods in two key respects: They rely on others to forward or create promotional messages, and they don't provide anywhere near the level of control over those messages that conventional marketing methods offer.

SOCIAL MEDIA IN THE MARKETING PROCESS

Social media are any electronic media that transform passive audiences into active participants in the communication process by allowing them to share, revise, or respond to existing content, or to contribute new content. These media include social networks, blogs, microblogging services such as Twitter, wikis, *user-generated content (UGC) sites* such as Flickr and YouTube, *community Q&A sites* such as Get Satisfaction's customer support sites, *community participation websites* such as Yelp, and content curation sites such as Pinterest. To varying degrees, all of these media play a role in contemporary marketing.

social media
Any electronic media that transform passive audiences into active participants in the communication process by allowing them to share content, revise content, respond to content, or contribute new content.

word of mouth
Communication among customers and other parties, transmitting information about companies and products through online or offline personal conversations.

Social media activities combine the newest communication technologies with the oldest form of marketing communication in the world, **word of mouth**—customers and other parties transmitting information about companies and products through personal conversations. As you'll read at the end of the chapter, this online content sharing has been crucial to GoPro's rapid growth.

Word-of-mouth marketing is often called *viral marketing*, in reference to the transmission of messages in much the same way that biological viruses are transmitted from person to person. However, viral marketing is not really an accurate metaphor. As author Brian Solis puts it, "There is no such thing as viral marketing."[26] A real virus spreads from host to host on its own, whereas word-of-mouth marketing spreads *voluntarily* from person to person. The distinction is critical because marketers need to give people a good reason—good content, in other words—to pass along their messages.

The social communication model is by no means limited to the consumer sector. Technical professionals were using the Internet for communication years before the World Wide Web was invented, and now businesspeople in just about every industry use social media to share ideas, conduct research, and evaluate products. In fact, many businesspeople adopted social media to a wider degree before the average consumer.[27]

Communication Strategies for Social Media

Audiences in the social media environment are not willing to be passive recipients in a structured, one-way information delivery process—or to rely solely on promotional messages from marketers. This notion of interactive participation is the driving force behind **conversation marketing**, in which companies *initiate* and *facilitate* conversations in a networked community of customers, journalists, bloggers, Twitter users, and other interested parties. Social media can be a powerful communication channel, but companies should follow these guidelines in order to meet audience expectations:[28]

conversation marketing
An approach to customer communication in which companies initiate and facilitate conversations in a networked community of potential buyers and other interested parties.

- **Remember that it's a conversation, not a lecture or a sales pitch.** One of the great appeals of social media is the feeling of conversation, of people talking *with* one another instead of one person talking *at* everyone else.

- **Offer valuable content to members of your online communities.** People don't join social networks to be sales targets. They join looking for connections, information, and entertainment. *Content marketing* is the practice of providing free information that is valuable to community members but that also helps a company build closer ties with current and potential customers.[29]

- **Facilitate community building.** Make sure customers and other audiences can connect with the company and with each other. If appropriate, encourage user-generated content, in which customers and enthusiasts share videos and other material (see Exhibit 16.8).

- **Initiate and respond to conversations within the community.** Marketers can start or join conversations by providing useful information to current and potential customers.

- **Identify and support champions.** In marketing, *champions* are enthusiastic fans of a company and its products—so enthusiastic that they help spread the company's message, defend it against detractors, and help other customers use its products.

| EXHIBIT 16.8 | **Encouraging Community Participation in the Marketing Process** |

Persuasive communication on social media often avoids overt promotion and instead tries to encourage the target audience to contribute content or participate in a community conversation, as Fezzari Bicycles did with this post on Google+.

- **Restrict conventional promotional efforts to the right time and right place.** Persuasive communication efforts are still valid for specific communication tasks, such as regular advertising and the product information pages on a website, but efforts to inject "salespeak" into social media conversations will be rejected by the audience.

Brand Communities

Another major impact of social media has been the rapid spread of **brand communities**, people united by their interest in and ownership of particular products. These communities can be formal membership organizations, such as the longstanding Harley Owners Group (HOG), or informal networks of people with similar interests. They can be fairly independent from the company behind the brand or can have the active support and involvement of company management, as is the case of Harley-Davidson's support of the motorcycle enthusiasts who are members of HOG (*hog* is an affectionate nickname for a Harley).[30]

Social media are natural communication vehicles for brand communities because these tools let people bond and share information on their own terms. And because a strong majority of consumers now trust their peers more than any other source of product information—including conventional advertising techniques—formal and informal brand communities are becoming an essential information source in consumer buying behavior.[31]

brand communities
Formal or informal groups of people united by their interest in and ownership of particular products.

public relations (PR)
Nonsales communication that businesses have with their various audiences (including both communication with the general public and press relations).

press release
A brief statement or video program released to the press announcing new products, management changes, sales performance, and other potential news items; also called a *news release*.

press conference
An in-person or online gathering of media representatives at which companies announce new information; also called a *news conference*.

PUBLIC RELATIONS

Public relations (PR) encompasses a wide variety of nonsales communications that businesses have with their many stakeholders, including communities, investors, industry analysts, government agencies, and activists. Companies rely on PR to build a favorable corporate image and foster positive relations with all these groups.

PR professionals often work through outside, independent communication channels to reach their target audiences. Historically, these efforts focused on the news media, including newspapers, magazines, radio, and TV. PR staffers "pitch" story ideas to journalists in the hope these journalists find the ideas compelling enough to their readers or listeners to warrant a print article or broadcast segment. To reach a wide number of journalists at once, a company can issue a **press release**, or *news release*, a brief written summary of company news and events such as a factory opening or a new product launch. When a business has significant news to announce, it can arrange a **press conference**, at which reporters can listen to company representatives and ask questions. If the information provided by the PR staff is likely to interest their audiences, journalists will help "spread the word," in the best cases generating high levels of public awareness at a much lower cost than a company could achieve on its own through paid advertising.[32]

With the rise of social media, the scope of PR has expanded to include influential bloggers, Twitter users, and others outside the boundaries of traditional journalism. In fact, many companies now view the press release as a general-purpose tool for communicating directly with customers and other audiences, creating *direct-to-consumer news releases*.[33] Many of these are considered *social media releases* because they include social networking links, "Tweetables" (Twitter-ready statements that can be shared on Twitter at the click of a button), online video links, and other sharable content).

For the latest information on customer communication strategies, techniques, and tools, visit **http://real-timeupdates .com/bia8** and click on Chapter 16.

REAL-TIME UPDATES
Learn More by Reading This Article

How social media changed public relations

Since social media took off, the task of public relations has never been the same. Go to http://real-timeupdates.com/bia8 and click on Learn More in the Students section.

 Checkpoint

LEARNING OBJECTIVE 6: Explain the uses of social media in customer communication and the role of public relations.

SUMMARY: Social media have several potential uses in customer communication, including customer service, rumor control, research, and relationship building. They can also be used for promotion, but that should be done in an indirect, customer-focused manner. Because consumers and investors support companies with good reputations, smart companies use public relations to build and protect their images. They communicate with consumers, investors, industry analysts, and government officials through the media. They pursue and maintain press relations with representatives of newspapers, television, and other broadcast media so that they can provide effective news releases (also known as press releases) and hold effective news conferences.

CRITICAL THINKING: (1) If marketers are advised against blatantly promoting their products in social media, why should they bother using these media at all? (2) Why are press relations critical to the launch of many new products?

IT'S YOUR BUSINESS: (1) Have you ever used social media to ask questions about a product or to criticize or compliment a company? Did anyone from the company respond? (2) Do you consider yourself a member of any brand communities (formal or informal)? If so, what effect do these groups have on your purchasing behavior?

KEY TERMS TO KNOW: social media, word of mouth, conversation marketing, brand communities, public relations (PR), press release, press conference

BEHIND THE SCENES
FANATICAL CUSTOMERS HELP PUSH GOPRO INTO BILLION-DOLLAR TERRITORY

When GoPro founder Nick Woodman wanted to get the word out about his new action camera, he did what committed entrepreneurs with a product to sell often have to do: work the phones, pound the pavement, and keep pitching the product to retailers in the hope they'll give it a try in their stores. One major target, the Seattle-based outdoor retailer REI, took months of persuasion but finally climbed on board and helped GoPro sales ramp up.

Sales kept growing while the company continued to improve the performance and capability of its cameras. After the introduction of high-definition video, sales tripled as a growing base of GoPro fans found new ways to capture must-see video. GoPro cameras are now almost everywhere there is some kind of action, from movie sets to mountain tops to concert stages.

Not surprisingly, GoPro makes extensive use of video in its promotional efforts. Like many companies, it uses video to showcase new products and provide how-to advice for customers. However, GoPro has gone far beyond what many companies do with video by harnessing the amplifying power of social media. The company has taken user-generated content to the extreme, using a variety of recognition and reward mechanisms to encourage GoPro customers to submit video clips. For example, GoPro runs a nonstop contest that recognizes several customers every day for the best footage shot on GoPro cameras. These clips are then highlighted on the company's website and all across the major social media platforms, including YouTube, Facebook, Twitter, Google+, and Instagram. In addition, a daily sweepstakes awards one lucky participant with one of every product the company makes, which maintains a high level of interest among people who don't yet own a GoPro camera.

The company's strategy of building a global video community has been a huge success. When Google (which owns YouTube) announced its first-ever monthly ranking of the highest-performing branded channels on YouTube, it determined that GoPro had the most engaged fan base. To measure engagement, Google factors in such variables as the amount of time visitors spending watching videos, the number of repeat visitors, and the number of times people "like" a video or leave a comment. When you consider that virtually every video on GoPro's YouTube channel functions as an advertisement for the company's cameras, you get an idea of the immense promotional power that this high level of engagement represents.

Thanks to the reach of social media, three-quarters of U.S. consumers are now aware of the cameras, and the company had 70 percent of the action-camera market by 2015. Millions of people view and share GoPro videos and product news on YouTube, Facebook, and other social media platforms.

GoPro's success arc has been impressive by just about any measure. However, Woodman and his company now face two big questions. First, can they stay ahead of the competition in action-camera market? The company has a huge lead, but Sony, JVC, Garmin, and iON, all of whom make action cameras, are working to carve out bigger chunks of the market.

Second, will the action-camera category lose sales to other types of products? One of these contenders is the ubiquitous smartphone, which has plundered a variety of product segments (including digital cameras and camcorders) in the past few years as phones keep adding more and more capability. The other major contender is the aerial drone, one of the newest must-haves for gadget-minded consumers. Market research suggests that some GoPro enthusiasts are now focusing their attention—and budgets—on drones instead. GoPro cameras are frequently used in other manufacturers' drones, and the company launched its own drone in 2016. However, GoPro is several years late to the drone market, so it remains to be seen whether it can become a dominant player in that segment.

Wherever Woodman guides the company in the next few years, though, he can count on a horde of enthusiastic customers to keep spreading the word as they participate in the social marketing of one of the biggest consumer product success stories in history.[34]

Critical Thinking Questions

16-1. Could a company that just introduced an amazing new audio product, say a tiny music player with audiophile-quality sound, hope to replicate the social media success that GoPro has enjoyed? Why or why not?

16-2. GoPro introduced its first camera in 2004, the same year that Facebook was launched. Given the role social media has played in GoPro's success, was it a waste of time and energy for Woodman and his team to spend so much time trying to get their products into retail stores? Why not just use social media exclusively?

16-3. Consumers can be a fickle lot, quickly abandoning a brand if the company behind it stumbles or something new catches their attention. Is it risky for GoPro to rely on social media so heavily? Should it invest more heavily in conventional advertising to guard against a potential cooling off in the social media sphere? Explain your answer.

LEARN MORE ONLINE

Visit GoPro's Facebook page at **www.facebook.com/gopro** and its YouTube channel at **www.youtube.com/user/ GoProCamera**. View a selection of the videos that various users or the company itself have posted. Do these videos make you more interested in buying a GoPro camera? Could a video of an extreme sports event prompt a person who would never engage in such an activity to buy a GoPro?

KEY TERMS

advertising (376)
advertising appeal (377)
advertising media (379)
advocacy advertising (377)
brand communities (389)
closing (384)
communication mix (374)
consultative selling (383)
conversation marketing (388)
core message (373)
coupons (385)
direct mail (381)
direct marketing (381)
direct response television (382)
institutional advertising (377)
integrated marketing communications (375)
media mix (380)
personal selling (382)

point-of-purchase display (385)
premiums (385)
press conference (390)
press release (390)
product placement (380)
prospecting (383)
public relations (PR) (390)
pull strategy (374)
push strategy (374)
rebates (385)
sales promotion (385)
search engine marketing (381)
social communication model (372)
social media (387)
specialty advertising (385)
trade allowances (386)
trade promotions (386)
word of mouth (388)

MyBizLab®

To complete the problems with the ⭐,
go to EOC Discussion Questions in the
MyLab.

TEST YOUR KNOWLEDGE

Questions for Review

16-4. What are two key ways in which the social communication model differs from conventional promotional communication?

16-5. What is the difference between using a push strategy and using a pull strategy to promote products?

16-6. What are the advantages of personal selling over other forms of customer communication?

16-7. What is an advertising appeal?

16-8. What are some common types of consumer promotion?

Questions for Analysis

16-9. Why is it important for sales professionals to qualify prospects?

16-10. What are the potential disadvantages of using celebrity appeals in advertising?

16-11. Why do some companies avoid email marketing, particularly to noncustomers?

16-12. Do marketers have any control over social media? Why or why not?

⭐ 16-13. **Ethical Considerations.** Is your privacy being violated when a website you visit displays ads that are personalized in any way, even if it's just geographically targeted to the local area (based on your computer's Internet address)? Why or why not?

Questions for Application

⭐ 16-14. If you were a real estate agent, how would you determine whether it's worth investing a significant amount of time in a particular prospect?

16-15. Think about an advertisement (in any medium) that had either a strongly positive or strongly negative effect on your attitude toward the product being advertised or the advertiser itself. Why did the ad have this effect? If you responded positively to the ad, do you think you were being manipulated in any way? If you responded negatively—and you are a potential buyer of the product that was advertised—what changes would you make to the ad to make it more successful?

16-16. Would it be a good idea to "repurpose" conventional press releases as posts on your company blog? Why or why not?

⭐ 16-17. **Concept Integration.** Should companies involve their marketing channels in the design of their customer communication programs? What are the advantages and disadvantages of doing so?

EXPAND YOUR KNOWLEDGE

Discovering Career Opportunities

Jobs in customer communication—advertising, direct marketing, personal selling, sales promotion, social media, and public relations—are among the most exciting and challenging in all of marketing. Choose a particular job in one of these areas. Using personal contacts, local directories of businesses or business professionals, or online resources such as company websites or search engines (including Twitter and blog search tools), arrange a brief phone, email, or personal interview with a professional working in your chosen marketing field.

16-18. What are the daily activities of this professional? What tools and resources does this person use most often on the job? What does this professional like most and least about the job?

16-19. What talents and educational background does this professional bring to the job? How are the person's skills and knowledge applied to handle the job's daily activities?

16-20. What advice does the person you are interviewing have for newcomers entering this field? What can you do now to get yourself started on a career path toward this position?

Improving Your Tech Insights: Individualized Advertising

Online advertisers continue to experiment with a variety of technologies that allow them to pinpoint individual audience members with targeted ads or customized messages. One interesting effect of this is that some advertising media or retailing formats are starting to look more like direct marketing media. Amazon.com, for example, personalizes a store front for every one of its customers. Google's behavioral targeting technology, which it refers to as "interest-based advertising," displays ads based on your web-surfing patterns. With the specific technique of *dynamic retargeting*, you might see an ad related to a website you just left, designed to nudge you into returning for another look.[35]

Identify one form of individualized advertising now in use (you can search for "individualized advertising," "personalized advertising," "behavioral targeting," or "interest-based advertising"). In a brief email message to your instructor, describe the technology, explain how it helps businesses reach customers more effectively, and identify any privacy concerns involved with the medium.

PRACTICE YOUR SKILLS

Sharpening Your Communication Skills

The good news: The current events blog you started as a hobby has become quite popular. The bad news: The blog now takes up so much of your time that you've had to quit a part-time job you were using to supplement your regular income. After some discussions with other bloggers, you decide to join Google's AdSense program (www.google.com/adsense) to help pay for the costs of operating your blog. With this program, small ads triggered by keywords in the content you publish will appear on your site. However, you're worried that your audience will think you've "sold out" because you're now generating revenue from your blog. Write a short message that could be posted on your blog, explaining why you consider it necessary to run ads and assuring your readers of your continued objectivity, even if that means criticizing organizations whose ads might appear on your blog.

Building Your Team Skills

In small groups, discuss three or four recent ads or consumer promotions (in any media) that you think were particularly effective. Using the knowledge you've gained from this chapter,

try to come to agreement on which attributes contributed to the success of each ad or promotion. For instance: Was it persuasive? Informative? Competitive? Creative? Did it have logical or emotional appeal? Did it stimulate you to buy the product? Why or why not? Compare your results with those of other teams. Did you mention the same ads? Did you list the same attributes?

Developing Your Research Skills

Choose an article from recent issues of business journals or newspapers (print or online editions) that describes the advertising or promotion efforts of a particular company or trade association.

16-21. Who is the company or trade association targeting?

16-22. What specific marketing objectives is the organization trying to accomplish?

16-23. What role does advertising play in the promotion strategy? What other promotion techniques does the article mention? Are any of them unusual or noteworthy? If so, why?

MyBizLab®

Go to the Assignments section of your MyLab to complete these writing exercises.

16-24. How is the AIDA model incompatible with a social, conversational approach to customer communication?

16-25. What is likely to happen to a company's promotional efforts if it fails to define the core message for a new product before launching it?

ENDNOTES

1. GoPro website, accessed 11 June 2015, www.gopro.com; Akin Oyedele, "Wall Street Analysts Say GoPro Isn't Going Mainstream and Now the Stock Is Falling," *Business Insider*, 20 June 2015, www.businessinsider.com; Nathan Ingraham, "GoPro Will Release a Quadcopter in the First Half of Next Year, *The Verge*, 27 May 2015, www.theverge.com; Ben Popper, "Here's Why GoPro Wants to Make Its Own Drones," *The Verge*, 26 November 2014, www.theverge.com; Ryan Mac, "The Mad Billionaire Behind GoPro: The World's Hottest Camera Company," *Forbes*, 25 March 2013, www.forbes.com; Garett Sloan, "The 10 Best Brand Channels on YouTube," *Adweek*, 2 April 2014, www.adweek.com; Christopher Ratcliff, "A Look Inside GoPro's Dazzling YouTube Strategy," Econsultancy website, 20 February 2014, http://econsultancy.com; GoPro channel on YouTube, accessed 11 June 2015, www.youtube.com/user/GoProCamera; "YouTube Brand Channel Leaderboard January–March 2014," *Google Think Insights*, 31 March 2014, www.thinkwithgoogle.com; Saya Weissman, "GoPro Might Have the Best Brand Content Around," *Digiday*, 6 February 2014, http://digiday.com; Shorty Industry Awards website, accessed 26 April 2014, http://industry.shortyawards.com; Anderson Cooper, "GoPro's Video Revolution," *60 Minutes*, 10 November 2013, www.cbsnews.com.
2. Philip Kotler and Gary Armstrong, *Principles of Marketing*, 13th ed. (Upper Saddle River, N.J.: Pearson Prentice Hall, 2010), 409–140.
3. Kotler and Armstrong, *Principles of Marketing*, 405.
4. "Children's Online Privacy Protection Rule: A Six-Step Compliance Plan for Your Business," U.S. Federal Trade Commission website, 1 June 2015, www.ftc.gov; "Advertising FAQ's: A Guide for Small Business," U.S. Federal Trade Commission website, accessed 1 June 2015, www.ftc.gov.
5. "What Is Retargeting," *AdRoll*, accessed 1 June 2015, www.adroll.com; Miguel Helft and Tanzina Vega, "Retargeting Ads Follow Surfers to Other Sites," *New York Times*, 29 August 2010, www.nytimes.com.
6. National Advertising Review Council website, accessed 1 June 2015, www.asrcreviews.org.
7. "Common Language in Marketing," accessed 1 June 2015, http://marketing-dictionary.org/ama.
8. Emily Bryson York, "The Gloves Are Off: More Marketers Opt for Attack Ads," *Advertising Age*, 25 May 2009, 4.
9. "Statement of Policy Regarding Comparative Advertising," U.S. Federal Trade Commissions website, accessed 1 June 2015, www.ftc.gov.
10. Based in part on Kenneth E. Clow and Donald Baack, *Integrated Advertising, Promotion, and Marketing Communications*, 4th ed. (Upper Saddle River, N.J.: Pearson Prentice Hall, 2010), 153–167.
11. Clow and Baack, *Integrated Advertising, Promotion, and Marketing Communications*, 155–156.
12. Steve McKee, "The Trouble with Celebrity Endorsements," *BusinessWeek*, 17 November 2008, 10.
13. Sanjay Putrevu, "Consumer Responses Toward Sexual and Nonsexual Appeals," *Journal of Advertising*, Summer 2008, 57–69.
14. Clow and Baack, *Integrated Advertising, Promotion, and Marketing Communications*, 162–164.
15. Kotler and Armstrong, *Principles of Marketing*, 436–437.
16. Janet Stilson, "The Clutter Busters," *Adweek*, 2 March 2009, 7.
17. Mark Hoelzel, "Mobile Advertising Is Exploding and Will Grow Much Faster Than All Other Digital Ad Categories," *Business Insider*, 3 April 2015, www.businessinsider.com.
18. "History of the Sears Catalog," Sears Archives, accessed 15 August 2009, www.searsarchives.com.
19. Gerald L. Manning and Barry L. Reece, *Selling Today*, 9th ed. (Upper Saddle River, N.J.: Pearson Prentice Hall, 2004), 7–8.
20. Howard Feiertag, "Build Your Group Sales by Consultative Selling," *Hotel & Motel Management*, 15 June 2009, 10.
21. Kotler and Armstrong, *Principles of Marketing*, 474–475.
22. Rebecca Borison, "75pc of Mobile Shoppers Redeemed Mobile Coupons in 2013: Report," *Mobile Commerce Daily*, 29 January 2014, www.mobilecommercedaily.com.
23. Dan Balaban, "Will Tough Times Spell Greater Opportunity for Mobile Coupons?" *Cards & Payments*, March 2009, 14–17.
24. Clow and Baack, *Integrated Advertising, Promotion, and Marketing Communications*, 284.
25. Clow and Baack, *Integrated Advertising, Promotion, and Marketing Communications*, 340.
26. Brian Solis, *Engage!* (Hoboken, N.J.: Wiley, 2010), 86.
27. Josh Bernoff, "Why B-to-B Ought to Love Social Media," *Marketing News*, 15 April 2009, 20.
28. Christian Pieter Hoffmann, "Holding Sway," *Communication World*, November–December 2011, 26–29; Josh Bernoff, "Social Strategy for Exciting (and Not So Exciting) Brands," *Marketing News*, 15 May 2009, 18; Larry Weber, *Marketing to the Social Web* (Hoboken, N.J.: Wiley, 2007), 12–14; David Meerman Scott, *The New Rules of Marketing and PR* (Hoboken, N.J.: Wiley, 2007), 62.
29. Sonia Simone, "What's the Difference Between Content Marketing and Copywriting?" *Copyblogger*, accessed 4 June 2012, www.copyblogger.com.
30. Susan Fournier and Lara Lee, "Getting Brand Communities Right," *Harvard Business Review*, April 2009, 105–111.
31. Patrick Hanlon and Josh Hawkins, "Expand Your Brand Community Online," *Advertising Age*, 7 January 2008, 14–15.
32. Steve McKee, "Why PR Is the Prescription," *BusinessWeek*, 13 April 2009, 8.
33. David Meerman Scott, *The New Rules of Marketing and PR* (Hoboken, N.J.: Wiley, 2007), 62.
34. See note 1.
35. Anja Lambrecht and Catherine Tucker, "When Personalized Ads Really Work," *Harvard Business Review*, 13 June 2013, http://hbr.org; "Interest-Based Advertising vs. Placement-Targeted Advertising," Google AdSense Help, accessed 11 June 2015, www.google.com;

Micromonkey/Fotolia

LEARNING OBJECTIVES After studying this chapter, you will be able to

1 Define *accounting*, and describe the roles of private and public accountants.

2 Explain the impact of accounting standards such as GAAP and the Sarbanes-Oxley Act on corporate accounting.

3 Describe the accounting equation, and explain the purpose of double-entry bookkeeping and the matching principle.

4 Identify the major financial statements, and explain how to read a balance sheet.

5 Explain the purpose of the income statement and the statement of cash flows.

6 Explain the purpose of ratio analysis, and list the four main categories of financial ratios.

BEHIND THE SCENES REALITY COMES KNOCKING AT THE GOOGLEPLEX

Jin Lee/Bloomberg/Getty Images

Google's chief financial officer Ruth Porat oversees the company's financial planning and management activities.

www.google.com

You may have received some nice employee benefits somewhere along the line, but did an armored truck ever back up to your company's front door to hand out $1,000 to every employee at Christmas time?

As Google's dominance in the profitable search engine market grew in recent years and its stock price soared, the company looked like it just might end up with all the cash in the world. To create one of the world's best places to work, the Mountain View, California, Internet giant sometimes spent money as if it had unlimited cash, too. Employee perks ranged from a companywide ski trip and an annual cash bonus—which really was delivered by armored truck—to free meals cooked by gourmet chefs and on-site doctors, massages, and car service.

Beyond these mere amenities, Google created one of the most interesting and stimulating workplaces imaginable. Engineers were allowed to spend up to 20 percent of their time exploring whatever fascinated them, even if those adventures weren't directly related to the company's current business efforts. Those explorations often did lead to new products and features, though, as Google's product line expanded far beyond its original search engine.

As it launched new projects and business initiatives right and left, Google kept hiring the best and the brightest; by 2008, the company had 20,000 employees and another 10,000 contractors. It had also acquired more than 50 other companies, paying from a few million dollars to get small niche companies on up to $1.65 billion to buy YouTube and $3.1 billion to buy the online advertising company DoubleClick.

Cash was flowing in, cash was flowing out, and all was good in the Googleplex, as the company's headquarters complex is known. But reality has a way of catching up to even the highest-flying companies, and Google would prove no exception. Internally, after a decade of rampant growth, expenses were eating up an ever-larger share of revenue. Externally, the global economy was cooling off quickly, and one company after another began trimming advertising budgets. Despite its many product innovations and explorations, Google still depended on search engine advertising for nearly all its revenue. Online advertising wasn't getting chopped quite as severely as ads for television and other traditional media, but the spending reductions were serious enough to slow Google's sales growth. With expenses growing faster than revenue, something had to give.

If you were in charge of Google's finances, how would you bring spending under control without alienating a workforce that has come to expect a certain level of pampering—and without stifling innovation, the engine behind the company's spectacular growth?[1]

INTRODUCTION

As the chief financial officer of Google (profiled in the chapter-opening Behind the Scenes), Ruth Porat could surely tell you how vital it is to have accurate, up-to-date accounting information. After providing an introduction to what accountants do and the rules they are expected to follow, this chapter explains the fundamental concepts of the accounting equation and double-entry bookkeeping. It then explores the primary "report cards" used in accounting: the balance sheet, income statement, and statement of cash flows. The chapter wraps up with a look at trend analysis and ratio analysis, the tools that managers, lenders, and investors use to predict a company's ongoing health.

Understanding Accounting

Accounting is the system a business uses to identify, measure, and communicate financial information to others, inside and outside the organization. Accurate and timely financial information is important to businesses such as Google for two reasons: First, it helps managers and owners plan and control a company's operations and make informed business decisions. Second, it helps outsiders evaluate a business. Suppliers, banks, and other parties want to know whether a business is creditworthy; shareholders and other investors are concerned with its profit potential; government agencies are interested in its tax accounting.

Because outsiders and insiders use accounting information for different purposes, accounting has two distinct facets. **Financial accounting** is concerned with preparing financial statements and other information for outsiders such as stockholders and *creditors* (people or organizations that have lent a company money or have extended its credit); **management accounting** is concerned with preparing cost analyses, profitability reports, budgets, and other information for insiders such as management and other company decision makers. To be useful, all accounting information must be accurate, objective, consistent over time, and comparable to information supplied by other companies.

WHAT ACCOUNTANTS DO

The work accountants do is sometimes confused with **bookkeeping**, which is the clerical function of recording the economic activities of a business. Although some accountants do perform bookkeeping functions, their work generally goes well beyond the scope of this activity. Accountants prepare financial statements, analyze and interpret financial information, prepare financial forecasts and budgets, and prepare tax returns. Some accountants specialize in certain areas of accounting, such as *cost accounting* (computing and analyzing production and operating costs), *tax accounting* (preparing tax returns and interpreting tax law), *financial analysis* (evaluating a company's performance and the financial implications of strategic decisions such as product pricing, employee benefits, and business acquisitions), or *forensic accounting* (combining accounting and investigating skills to assist in legal and criminal matters).

1 | LEARNING OBJECTIVE

Define *accounting*, and describe the roles of private and public accountants.

accounting
Measuring, interpreting, and communicating financial information to support internal and external decision making.

financial accounting
The area of accounting concerned with preparing financial information for users outside the organization.

management accounting
The area of accounting concerned with preparing data for use by managers within the organization.

bookkeeping
Recordkeeping; the clerical aspect of accounting.

In addition to traditional accounting work, accountants may also help clients improve business processes, plan for the future, evaluate product performance, analyze profitability by customer and product groups, and design and install new computer systems; assist companies with decision making; and provide a variety of other management consulting services. Performing these functions requires a strong business background and a variety of business skills beyond accounting.

PRIVATE ACCOUNTANTS

private accountants
In-house accountants employed by organizations and businesses other than a public accounting firm; also called *corporate accountants.*

controller
The highest-ranking accountant in a company, responsible for overseeing all accounting functions.

certified public accountants (CPAs)
Professionally licensed accountants who meet certain requirements for education and experience and who pass a comprehensive examination.

public accountants
Professionals who provide accounting services to other businesses and individuals for a fee.

Private accountants work for corporations, government agencies, and not-for-profit organizations. Their titles vary by function and include *corporate accountant, managerial accountant,* and *cost accountant.*[2] Private accountants generally work together as a team under the supervision of the organization's **controller**, who reports to the vice president of finance or the chief financial officer (CFO). Exhibit 17.1 shows the typical finance department of a large company. In smaller organizations, the controller may be in charge of the company's entire finance operation and report directly to the president.

Although certification is not required of private accountants, many are licensed **certified public accountants (CPAs)**. Specific requirements vary by state, but to receive a CPA license, an individual must complete a certain number of hours of college-level coursework, have a minimum number of years of work experience in the accounting field, and pass the Uniform CPA Exam.[3] Growing numbers of private accountants are becoming *certified management accountants (CMAs)*; to do so, they must pass an intensive exam sponsored by the Institute of Management Accountants.[4]

PUBLIC ACCOUNTANTS

In contrast to private accountants, **public accountants** are independent of the businesses, organizations, and individuals they serve. Most public accountants are employed by public accounting firms that provide a variety of accounting and consulting

EXHIBIT 17.1	Typical Finance Department

Here is a typical finance department of a large company. In smaller companies, the controller may be the highest-ranking accountant and report directly to the president. The top executive in charge of finance is often called the chief financial officer (CFO).

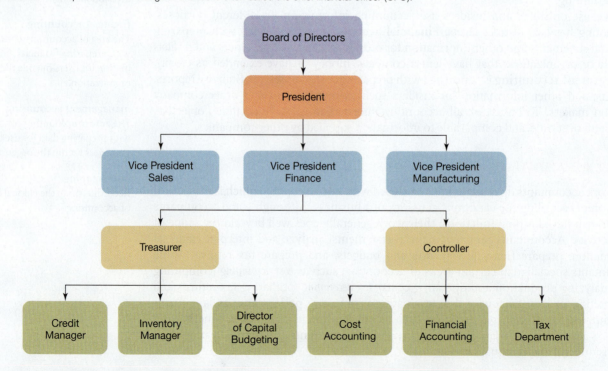

services to their clients. The largest of these, four international networks known as the "Big Four," are Deloitte Touche Tohmatsu (**www.deloitte.com**), Ernst & Young (**www.ey.com**), KPMG (**www.kpmg.com**), and PricewaterhouseCoopers, or PwC (**www.pwc.com**). Whether they belong to one of these giant networks (each of which employs more than 100,000 people) or to a smaller independent firm, public accountants generally are CPAs and must obtain CPA and state licensing certifications before they are eligible to conduct an **audit**—a formal evaluation of a company's accounting records and processes to ensure the integrity and reliability of a company's financial statements.

audit
Formal evaluation of the fairness and reliability of a client's financial statements.

By the way, if you've shied away from accounting as a career choice because of popular stereotypes about it being a dull job fit only for "bean counters," it's time to take another look. Partly as a consequence of financial scandals in recent years and the growing complexity of accounting regulations, accounting specialists are now in demand in many industries. Employment is growing faster than average for all accounting occupations, while salaries and benefits are increasing as everybody from the Big Four to the Federal Bureau of Investigation (FBI) to corporations both large and small actively recruit accountants to help navigate the challenging landscape of contemporary business finance.[5]

REAL-TIME UPDATES
Learn More by Visiting This Website

Considering a career in accounting?

This comprehensive directory can help you explore the profession and find potential employers. Go to http://real-timeupdates.com/bia8 and click on Learn More in the Students section.

✔ Checkpoint

LEARNING OBJECTIVE 1: Define *accounting*, **and describe the roles of private and public accountants.**

SUMMARY: Accounting is the system a business uses to identify, measure, and communicate financial information to others, inside and outside the organization. Accountants perform a wide variety of tasks, including preparing financial statements, analyzing and interpreting financial information, preparing financial forecasts and budgets, preparing tax returns, interpreting tax law, computing and analyzing production costs, evaluating a company's performance, and analyzing the financial implications of business decisions. Private accountants work for corporations, government agencies, and not-for-profit organizations, performing various accounting functions for their employers. Public accountants, in contrast, sell their services to individuals and organizations. One of the most important functions of public accountants is performing audits, a formal evaluation of a company's accounting records and processes.

CRITICAL THINKING: (1) Why would a private accountant bother with becoming a CPA? (2) What effect can unreliable or uncertain accounting have on the economy?

IT'S YOUR BUSINESS: (1) How rigorous are your personal bookkeeping and accounting efforts? Do you keep accurate records, analyze spending, and set budgets? (2) If you don't really account for your personal finances, how might doing so help you, now and in the future?

KEY TERMS TO KNOW: accounting, financial accounting, management accounting, bookkeeping, private accountants, controller, certified public accountants (CPAs), public accountants, audit

---

Major Accounting Rules

In order to make informed decisions, investors, bankers, suppliers, and other parties need some means to verify the quality of the financial information that companies release to the public. They also need some way to compare information from one company to the

2 **LEARNING OBJECTIVE**

Explain the impact of accounting standards such as GAAP and the Sarbanes-Oxley Act on corporate accounting.

next. To accommodate these needs, financial accountants are expected to follow a number of rules, some of which are voluntary and some of which are required by law.

GENERALLY ACCEPTED ACCOUNTING PRINCIPLES (GAAP)

Accounting is based on numbers, so it might seem like a straightforward task to tally up a company's revenues and costs to determine its net profits. However, accounting is often anything but simple. For instance, *revenue recognition*, how and when a company records incoming revenue, is a particularly complex topic.[6] As just one example, should a company record revenue (a) when it ships products to or performs services for customers, (b) when it bills customers, (c) when customers actually pay, or (d) after everyone has paid and any products that are going to be returned for refunds have been returned (because refunds reduce revenue)? If customers are in financial trouble and taking a long time to pay or are not paying at all, or if a poorly designed product is generating a lot of returns, the differences can be substantial.

From booking revenues and expenses to placing a value on assets and liabilities, these decisions affect just about every aspect of a company's stated financial picture. That picture in turn affects how much tax the company has to pay, how attractive it is as an investment opportunity, how creditworthy it is from a lender's point of view, and other significant outcomes.

To help ensure consistent financial reporting so that all stakeholders understand what they're looking at, over the years regulators, auditors, and company representatives have agreed on a series of accounting standards and procedures. **GAAP (generally accepted accounting principles)**, overseen in the United States by the Financial Accounting Standards Board (FASB), aims to give a fair and true picture of a company's financial position and to enable outsiders to make confident analyses and comparisons. GAAP can't prevent every reporting abuse, but it does make distorting financial results in order to fool outsiders more difficult.[7]

As Chapter 18 notes, companies whose stock is publicly traded in the United States are required to file audited financial statements with the Securities and Exchange Commission (SEC). During an audit, CPAs who work for an independent accounting firm, also known as **external auditors**, review a client's financial records to determine whether the statements that summarize these records have been prepared in accordance with GAAP. The auditors then summarize their findings in a report attached to the client's published financial statements. Sometimes these reports disclose information that might materially affect the client's financial position, such as the bankruptcy of a major supplier, a large obsolete inventory, costly environmental problems, or questionable accounting practices. A clean audit report means that to the best of the auditors' knowledge a company's financial statements are accurate.

To assist with the auditing process, many large organizations use *internal auditors*—employees who investigate and evaluate the organization's internal operations and data to determine whether they are accurate and whether they comply with GAAP, federal laws, and industry regulations. Although this self-checking process is vital to an organization's financial health, an internal audit is not a substitute for having an independent auditor look things over and render an unbiased opinion.

Non-GAAP Metrics

U.S. public companies are required to report financial results that meet GAAP standards, but they can also publish "non-GAAP" results. These metrics can range from the number of new customers during a particular period to the widely used but still non-GAAP measure known as EBITDA (see the discussion on page 410). This is typically done when executives believe non-GAAP metrics provide a more compelling or complete picture of the company's performance and prospects. However, the practice is controversial, with some accountants and investors wary that companies really use non-GAAP metrics to obscure poor performance rather than to highlight areas of good performance. Moreover, because the definitions of these measurements are not standardized, companies can

GAAP (generally accepted accounting principles)
Standards and practices used by publicly held corporations in the United States and a few other countries in the preparation of financial statements.

external auditors
Independent accounting firms that provide auditing services for public companies.

change them over time, potentially to make performance look better.[8] In any event, companies must label these figures as non-GAAP data in their financial reports, and securities regulators can ask companies to remove or modify the presentation of non-GAAP data if these figures might mislead investors.[9]

Global Reporting Standards

GAAP has helped standardize accounting and financial reporting for companies in the United States, but the situation is more complex at the international level because GAAP standards are not used in most other countries. The lack of global standardization creates extra work for U.S. multinationals, essentially forcing them to keep two sets of books.[10] In addition, it complicates cross-border transactions, mergers, and investments because companies don't have a single set of tools to compute assets, liabilities, and other vital quantities.

Companies and investors have to deal with different reporting standards in financial markets around the world (*pictured*: the Hong Kong Stock Exchange).

Most other countries use **international financial reporting standards (IFRS)** maintained by the London-based International Accounting Standards Board. After a decade-long effort to harmonize the GAAP and IFRS, the two systems are closer in some respects but still different in some significant ways. In fact, there was a lot of momentum over the years to converge the two systems into a single, global set of standards. However, that convergence effort now appears to be stalled.[11] If the SEC ever does make the switch to IFRS, it could bring extensive changes to the accounting profession, financial management, information systems, stock-based compensation and bonuses, and other aspects of managing a public corporation.[12]

international financial reporting standards (IFRS)
Accounting standards and practices used in many countries outside the United States.

SARBANES-OXLEY

The need for and complexity of financial reporting standards is highlighted in the story of **Sarbanes-Oxley**, the informal name of the Public Company Accounting Reform and Investor Protection Act. (You'll hear it referred to as "Sox" or "Sarbox" as well.) Passed in 2002 in the wake of several cases of massive accounting fraud, most notably involving the energy company Enron and the telecom company WorldCom, Sarbanes-Oxley changed public company accounting in the United States in a number of important ways. Its major provisions include[13]

Sarbanes-Oxley
The informal name of comprehensive legislation designed to improve the integrity and accountability of financial information.

- Outlawing most loans by corporations to their own directors and executives
- Creating the Public Company Accounting Oversight Board (PCAOB) to oversee external auditors, rather than letting the industry regulate itself
- Requiring corporate lawyers to report evidence of financial wrongdoing
- Prohibiting external auditors from providing certain nonaudit services
- Requiring that audit committees on the board of directors have at least one financial expert and that the majority of board members be independent (not employed by the company in an executive position)
- Prohibiting investment bankers from influencing stock analysts
- Requiring CEOs and CFOs to sign statements attesting to the accuracy of their financial statements
- Requiring companies to document and test their internal financial controls and processes

Sarbox generated a lot of criticism initially, particularly from the amount of work involved in documenting internal financial controls. However, after a lot of initial criticism about the costs of compliance and a shift in the PCAOB's stance to let companies focus on monitoring the riskiest financial decisions instead of every mundane transaction, complaints about Sarbox have leveled off in recent years.[14] Opinions vary on whether some aspects went too far or didn't go far enough, but a decade after its implementation, the consensus seems to be that, by and large, the law has improved the quality of financial reporting, increased protections for shareholders, and increased the emphasis on legal compliance and ethical decision making.[15]

Checkpoint

LEARNING OBJECTIVE 2: Explain the impact of accounting standards such as GAAP and the Sarbanes-Oxley Act on corporate accounting.

SUMMARY: Accounting standards such as GAAP help ensure consistent financial reporting, which is essential for regulators and investors to make informed decisions. Sarbanes-Oxley introduced a number of rules covering the way publicly traded companies manage and report their finances, including restricting loans to directors and executives, creating a new board to oversee public auditors, requiring corporate lawyers to report financial wrongdoing, requiring CEOs and CFOs to sign financial statements under oath, and requiring companies to document their financial systems.

CRITICAL THINKING: (1) Should U.S. public companies with no significant overseas business activity be forced to follow international accounting standards? Why or why not? (2) How does requiring CEOs to personally attest to the accuracy of financial statements eliminate errors and misrepresentations?

IT'S YOUR BUSINESS: (1) If you were considering buying stock in a company, would you support rigorous (and potentially expensive) financial accountability such as that called for by Section 404 of Sarbanes-Oxley? Why or why not? (2) Would you consider investing in a privately held company whose financial records had not been reviewed by an external auditor? Why or why not?

KEY TERMS TO KNOW: GAAP (generally accepted accounting principles), external auditors, international financial reporting standards (IFRS), Sarbanes-Oxley

---

3 **LEARNING OBJECTIVE**

Describe the accounting equation, and explain the purpose of double-entry bookkeeping and the matching principle.

assets
Any things of value owned or leased by a business.

liabilities
Claims against a firm's assets by creditors.

owners' equity
The portion of a company's assets that belongs to the owners after obligations to all creditors have been met.

accounting equation
The equation stating that assets equal liabilities plus owners' equity.

Fundamental Accounting Concepts

In their work with financial data, accountants are guided by three basic concepts: the *fundamental accounting equation*, *double-entry bookkeeping*, and the *matching principle*. Here is a closer look at each of these essential ideas.

THE ACCOUNTING EQUATION

For thousands of years, businesses and governments have kept records of their **assets**—valuable items they own or lease, such as equipment, cash, land, buildings, inventory, and investments. Claims against those assets are **liabilities**, or what the business owes to its creditors—such as lenders and suppliers. For example, when a company borrows money to purchase a building, the lender has a claim against the company's assets. What remains after liabilities have been deducted from assets is **owners' equity**:

$$\text{Owners' equity} = \text{Assets} - \text{Liabilities}$$

As a simple example, if your company has $1,000,000 in assets and $800,000 in liabilities, your equity would be $200,000:

$$\$200,000 = \$1,000,000 - 800,000$$

Using the principles of algebra, this equation can be restated in a variety of formats. The most common is the simple **accounting equation**, which serves as the framework for the entire accounting process:

$$\text{Assets} = \text{Liabilities} + \text{Owners' equity}$$
$$\$1,000,000 = \$800,000 + 200,000$$

This equation suggests that either creditors or owners provide all the assets in a corporation. Think of it this way: If you were starting a new business, you could contribute cash to the company to buy the assets you needed to run your business or you could borrow money from a bank (the creditor) or you could do both. The company's liabilities are placed before owners' equity in the accounting equation because creditors get paid first. After liabilities have been paid, anything left over belongs to the owners. As a business engages in economic activity, the dollar amounts and composition of its assets, liabilities, and owners' equity change. However, the equation must always be in balance; in other words, one side of the equation must always equal the other side.

REAL-TIME UPDATES
Learn More by Reading This Article

Introduction to the accounting equation

Get a better feel for the accounting equation with these practical examples. Go to http://real-timeupdates.com/bia8 and click on Learn More in the Students section.

DOUBLE-ENTRY BOOKKEEPING AND THE MATCHING PRINCIPLE

To keep the accounting equation in balance, most companies use a **double-entry bookkeeping** system that records every transaction affecting assets, liabilities, or owners' equity. Each transaction is entered twice, once as a *debit* and once as a *credit*, and they must offset each other to keep the accounting equation in balance. The double-entry method predates computers by hundreds of years and was originally created to minimize errors caused by entering and adding figures by hand; accounting software now typically handles all this behind the scenes.

The **matching principle** requires that expenses incurred in producing revenues be deducted from the revenue they generated during the same accounting period. This matching of expenses and revenue is necessary for the company's financial statements to present an accurate picture of the profitability of a business. Accountants match revenue to expenses by adopting the **accrual basis** of accounting, which states that revenue is recognized when you make a sale or provide a service, not when you get paid. Similarly, your expenses are recorded when you receive the benefit of a service or when you use an asset to produce revenue—not when you pay for it.

Accrual accounting focuses on the economic substance of an event rather than on the movement of cash. It's a way of recognizing that revenue can be earned either before or after cash is received and that expenses can be incurred when a company receives a benefit (such as a shipment of supplies) either before or after the benefit is paid for.

If a business runs on a **cash basis**, the company records revenue only when money from the sale is actually received. Your checking account is a simple cash-based accounting system: You record checks, debit card charges, and ATM withdrawals at the time of purchase and record deposits at the time of receipt. Cash-based accounting is simple, but it can be misleading. It's easy to inflate the appearance of income, for example, by delaying the payment of bills. For that reason, public companies are required to keep their books on an accrual basis.

Depreciation, or the allocation of the cost of a tangible long-term asset over a period of time, is another way that companies match expenses with revenue. (For intangible assets, this allocation over time is known as *amortization*.) When Google buys a piece of real estate, instead of deducting the entire cost of the item at the time of purchase, the company *depreciates* it, or spreads the cost over a certain number of years as specified by tax regulations because the asset will likely generate income for many years. If the company were to expense long-term assets at the time of purchase, its apparent financial performance would be distorted negatively in the year of purchase and positively in all future years when these assets generate revenue.

double-entry bookkeeping
A method of recording financial transactions that requires a debit entry and credit entry for each transaction to ensure that the accounting equation is always kept in balance.

matching principle
The fundamental principle requiring that expenses incurred in producing revenue be deducted from the revenues they generate during an accounting period.

accrual basis
An accounting method in which revenue is recorded when a sale is made and an expense is recorded when it is incurred.

cash basis
An accounting method in which revenue is recorded when payment is received and an expense is recorded when cash is paid.

depreciation
An accounting procedure for systematically spreading the cost of a tangible asset over its estimated useful life.

✓ Checkpoint

LEARNING OBJECTIVE 3: Describe the accounting equation, and explain the purpose of double-entry bookkeeping and the matching principle.

SUMMARY: The basic accounting equation is Assets = Liabilities + Owners' equity. Double-entry bookkeeping is a system of recording every financial transaction as two counterbalancing entries in order to keep the accounting equation in balance. The matching principle makes sure that expenses incurred in producing revenues are deducted from the revenue they generated during the same accounting period.

CRITICAL THINKING: (1) How does double-entry bookkeeping help eliminate errors? (2) Why is accrual-based accounting considered more fraud-proof than cash-based accounting?

IT'S YOUR BUSINESS: (1) Does looking at the accounting equation make you reconsider your personal spending habits? (Think about taking on liabilities that don't create any long-term assets, for example.) (2) How would accrual basis accounting give you better insights into your personal finances?

KEY TERMS TO KNOW: assets, liabilities, owners' equity, accounting equation, double-entry bookkeeping, matching principle, accrual basis, cash basis, depreciation

---

4 **LEARNING OBJECTIVE**

Identify the major financial statements, and explain how to read a balance sheet.

closing the books

Transferring net revenue and expense account balances to retained earnings for the period.

Using Financial Statements: The Balance Sheet

As a company conducts business day after day, sales, purchases, and other transactions are recorded and classified into individual accounts. After these individual transactions are recorded and then summarized, accountants must review the resulting summaries and adjust or correct all errors or discrepancies before **closing the books**, or transferring net revenue and expense items to *retained earnings*. Exhibit 17.2 illustrates the *accounting cycle* that companies go through during a given accounting period, such as a month.

In a way, this is what you do every month when you get your bank statement. You might think you have $50 left in your account but then see your statement and realize with delight that you forgot to record depositing the $100 check your grandmother sent you, and your true balance is $150. Or you might realize with dismay that you forgot to record the $300 ATM withdrawal you made on spring break, and your true balance is −$250. Before you know how much money you'll have available to spend next month— your retained earnings—you have to accurately close the books on this month.

UNDERSTANDING FINANCIAL STATEMENTS

Financial statements consist of three separate but interrelated reports: the *balance sheet*, the *income statement*, and the *statement of cash flows*. These statements are required by law for all publicly traded companies, but they are vital management tools for every company, no matter how large or small. Together, these statements provide information about an organization's financial strength and ability to meet current obligations, the effectiveness of its sales and collection efforts, and its effectiveness in managing its assets. Organizations and individuals use financial statements to spot opportunities and problems, to make business decisions, and to evaluate a company's past performance, present condition, and future prospects.

The following sections examine the financial statements of the hypothetical company Computer Central Services. In the past year, the company shipped more than 2.3 million orders, amounting to more than $1.7 billion in sales—a 35 percent increase in sales over the prior year. The company's daily sales volume has grown considerably over the last decade—from $232,000 to $6.8 million. Because of this tremendous growth and the increasing demand for new computer products, the company recently purchased a new headquarters building.

balance sheet

A statement of a firm's financial position on a particular date; also known as a *statement of financial position*.

BALANCE SHEET

The **balance sheet**, also known as the *statement of financial position*, is a snapshot of a company's financial position on a particular date (see Exhibit 17.3 on page 406). In effect, it freezes all business actions and provides a baseline from which a company can measure

EXHIBIT 17.2 **The Accounting Cycle**

Here are the general steps in the accounting process, or *accounting cycle*, from recording transactions to making sure the books are in balance to closing the books for a particular accounting period (usually a month). Steps 1 through 3 are done as transactions occur; steps 4 through 8 are usually performed at the end of the accounting period.

1. Perform *transactions*
A transaction is any relevant accounting event, including making a sale, making a purchase, or making a debt payment.

2. Analyze and record transactions in a *journal*
Journalizing means analyzing the *source document* (e.g., a sales receipt or a customer invoice) for each transaction, then separating the transaction, into its debit and credit components and recording these chronologically in a journal.

3. *Post* journal entries to the *ledger*
Entries from the chronological journals are moved to the account-based ledger. Over the course of the month or other accounting period, each account (e.g., sales revenue or expenses) in the ledger fills up with the various transaction records posted from the journals. These accounts are considered temporary because they are closed out at the end of the accounting period (see step 8).

4. Prepare a *trial balance*
At the end of the accounting period, the debits and credits in the ledger are totaled, and then the two amounts are compared. If they aren't equal, one or more errors have crept in somewhere in the previous three steps and need to be found and corrected.

5. Make *adjusting entries*, as needed
Not all relevant changes are generated by transaction records during the accounting period, so accountants enter items such as asset depreciation or transactions whose revenues or expenses occur before or after the accounting period.

6. Prepare an adjusted trial balance
This is the same procedure as in step 4 but includes the adjusting entries made in step 5. Again, if the debits total and the credits total don't match, the error needs to be investigated and corrected.

7. Prepare *financial statements*
With the accounts adjusted and in balance for the accounting period, various managerial and government compliance reports can now be generated.

8. *Close the books* for the accounting period
Transfer the balances from temporary ledger accounts to the permanent balance sheet and income statement. Record *reversing entries* as needed to start fresh temporary accounts at the beginning of the next period.

Sources: Jeffery Slater, *College Accounting: A Practical Approach*, 11th ed. (Upper Saddle River, N.J.: Pearson Prentice Hall, 2010), 78, 104, 148; "The Accounting Process," NetMBA, www.netmba.com; Bob Schneider, "Accounting Basics: The Accounting Process," *Investopedia.com*, www.investopedia.com.

change from that point forward. This statement is called a balance sheet because it includes all elements in the accounting equation and shows the balance between assets on one side of the equation and liabilities and owners' equity on the other side.

Every company prepares a balance sheet at least once a year, most often at the end of the **calendar year**, covering January 1 to December 31. However, many business

calendar year
A 12-month accounting period that begins on January 1 and ends on December 31.

EXHIBIT 17.3   Balance Sheet for Computer Central Services

The categories used on the year-end balance sheet for Computer Central Services are typical.

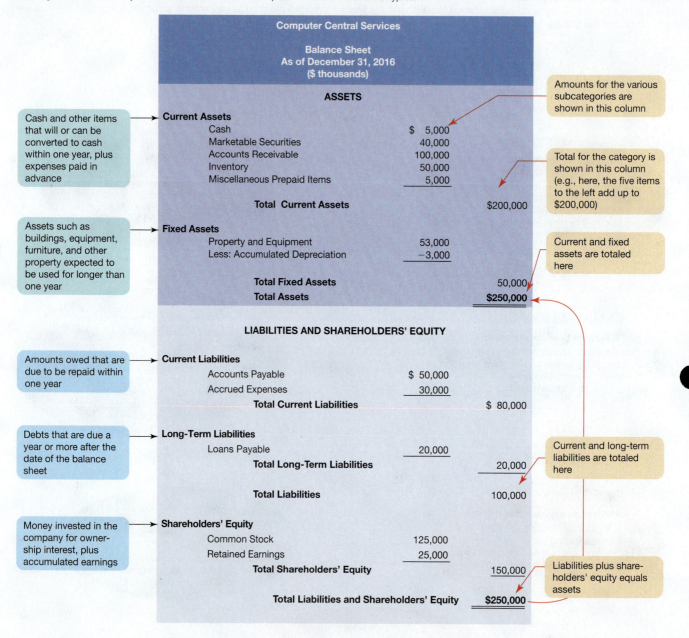

Cash and other items that will or can be converted to cash within one year, plus expenses paid in advance

Assets such as buildings, equipment, furniture, and other property expected to be used for longer than one year

Amounts owed that are due to be repaid within one year

Debts that are due a year or more after the date of the balance sheet

Money invested in the company for ownership interest, plus accumulated earnings

Amounts for the various subcategories are shown in this column

Total for the category is shown in this column (e.g., here, the five items to the left add up to $200,000)

Current and fixed assets are totaled here

Current and long-term liabilities are totaled here

Liabilities plus shareholders' equity equals assets

Computer Central Services
Balance Sheet
As of December 31, 2016
($ thousands)

ASSETS

Current Assets

Cash	$ 5,000	
Marketable Securities	40,000	
Accounts Receivable	100,000	
Inventory	50,000	
Miscellaneous Prepaid Items	5,000	
Total Current Assets		$200,000

Fixed Assets

Property and Equipment	53,000	
Less: Accumulated Depreciation	−3,000	
Total Fixed Assets		50,000
Total Assets		**$250,000**

LIABILITIES AND SHAREHOLDERS' EQUITY

Current Liabilities

Accounts Payable	$ 50,000	
Accrued Expenses	30,000	
Total Current Liabilities		$ 80,000

Long-Term Liabilities

Loans Payable	20,000	
Total Long-Term Liabilities		20,000
Total Liabilities		100,000

Shareholders' Equity

Common Stock	125,000	
Retained Earnings	25,000	
Total Shareholders' Equity		150,000
Total Liabilities and Shareholders' Equity		**$250,000**

fiscal year
Any 12 consecutive months used as an accounting period.

REAL-TIME UPDATES
Learn More by Watching This Presentation

Five tips for reading a balance sheet

This brief presentation explains the key points to look for in a balance sheet. Go to http://real-timeupdates.com/bia8 and click on Learn More in the Students section.

and government bodies use a **fiscal year**, which may be any 12 consecutive months. Some companies prepare a balance sheet more often than once a year, such as at the end of each month or quarter. Every balance sheet is dated to show the exact date when the financial snapshot was taken.

By reading a company's balance sheet, you should be able to determine the size of the company, the major assets owned, any asset changes that occurred in recent periods, how the company's assets are financed, and any major changes that have occurred in the company's debt and equity in recent periods.

Assets

As discussed previously in the chapter, an asset is something owned by a company with the intent to generate income. Assets can be *tangible* or *intangible*. Tangible assets include land, buildings, and equipment. Intangible assets include intellectual property (such as patents and business methods), *goodwill* (which includes company reputation), brand awareness and recognition, workforce skills, management talent, and even customer relationships.[16]

As you might expect, assigning value to intangible assets is not an easy task (and incidentally is one of the major points of difference between GAAP and IFRS), but these assets make up an increasingly important part of the value of many contemporary companies.[17] For instance, much of the real value of a company such as Google is not in its tangible assets but in its search engine algorithms, its software designs, its brand awareness, and the brainpower of its workforce. For example, a recent balance sheet for the company listed nearly $20 billion in goodwill and other intangibles.[18]

The asset section of the balance sheet is often divided into *current assets* and *fixed assets*. **Current assets** include cash and other items that will or can become cash within the following year, such as short-term investments such as money-market funds and *accounts receivable* (amounts due from customers). **Fixed assets** (sometimes referred to as *property, plant, and equipment*) are long-term investments in buildings, equipment, furniture and fixtures, transportation equipment, land, and other tangible property used in running the business. Fixed assets have a useful life of more than one year.

Assets are listed in descending order by *liquidity*, or the ease with which they can be converted into cash. Thus, current assets are listed before fixed assets. The balance sheet gives a subtotal for each type of asset and then a grand total for all assets.

Liabilities

Liabilities may be current or long term, and they are listed in the order in which they will come due. The balance sheet gives subtotals for **current liabilities** (obligations that will have to be met within one year of the date of the balance sheet) and **long-term liabilities** (obligations that are due one year or more after the date of the balance sheet), and then it gives a grand total for all liabilities.

Current liabilities include accounts payable, short-term financing (you'll read more about this in Chapter 18), and accrued expenses. *Accounts payable* include the money the company owes its suppliers as well as money it owes vendors for miscellaneous services (such as electricity and telephone charges). *Accrued expenses* are expenses that have been incurred but for which bills have not yet been received or paid. For example, because salespeople at Computer Central Services earn commissions, the company has a liability to those employees after the sale is made. If such expenses and their associated liabilities were not recorded, the company's financial statements would be misleading and would violate the matching principle because the commission expenses earned at the time of sale would not be matched to the revenue generated from the sale.

Long-term liabilities include loans, leases, and bonds. A borrower makes principal and interest payments to the lender over the term of the loan, and its obligation is limited to these payments (see the section "Debt Financing Versus Equity Financing" in Chapter 18 on page 429). Rather than borrowing money to make purchases, a firm may enter into a *lease*, under which the owner of an item allows another party to use it in exchange for regular payments. Bonds are certificates that obligate the company to repay a certain sum, plus interest, to the bondholder on a specific date. Bonds are traded on organized securities exchanges and are discussed in detail in Chapter 19.

Owners' Equity

The owners' investment in a business is listed on the balance sheet under owners' equity (or *shareholders' equity* or *stockholders' equity* for corporations). Sole proprietorships list owner's equity under the owner's name with the amount (assets minus liabilities). Small

current assets
Cash and items that can be turned into cash within one year.

fixed assets
Assets retained for long-term use, such as land, buildings, machinery, and equipment; also referred to as *property, plant, and equipment*.

current liabilities
Obligations that must be met within a year.

long-term liabilities
Obligations that fall due more than a year from the date of the balance sheet.

retained earnings
The portion of shareholders' equity earned by the company but not distributed to its owners in the form of dividends.

partnerships list each partner's share of the business separately, and large partnerships list the total of all partners' shares. In a corporation, the shareholders' total investment value is the sum of two amounts: the total value of the all the shares currently held, plus **retained earnings**—cash that is kept by the company rather than distributed to shareholders in the form of dividends. As Exhibit 17.3 shows, Computer Central Services has retained earnings of $25 million. The company doesn't pay dividends—many small and growing corporations don't—but rather builds its cash reserves to fund expansion in the future. (Shareholders' equity can be slightly more complicated than this, depending on how the company's shares were first created, but this summary gives you the basic idea of how the assets portion of the balance sheet works.)

 Checkpoint

LEARNING OBJECTIVE 4: Identify the major financial statements, and explain how to read a balance sheet.

SUMMARY: The three major financial statements are the balance sheet, the income statement, and the statement of cash flows. The balance sheet provides a snapshot of the business at a particular point in time. It shows the size of the company, the major assets owned, the ways the assets are financed, and the amount of owners' investment in the business. Its three main sections are assets, liabilities, and owners' equity.

CRITICAL THINKING: (1) Why do analysts need to consider different factors when evaluating a company's ability to repay short-term versus long-term debt? (2) Would the current amount of the owners' equity be a reasonable price to pay for a company? Why or why not?

IT'S YOUR BUSINESS: (1) What are your current and long-term financial liabilities? Are these liabilities restricting your flexibility as a student or consumer? (2) As a potential employee, what intangible assets can you offer a company?

KEY TERMS TO KNOW: closing the books, balance sheet, calendar year, fiscal year, current assets, fixed assets, current liabilities, long-term liabilities, retained earnings

5   LEARNING OBJECTIVE

Explain the purpose of the income statement and the statement of cash flows.

Using Financial Statements: Income and Cash Flow Statements

In addition to the balance sheet, the two other fundamentally important financial statements are the income statement and the statement of cash flows.

INCOME STATEMENT

income statement
A financial record of a company's revenues, expenses, and profits over a given period of time; also known as a *profit-and-loss statement.*

expenses
Costs created in the process of generating revenues.

net income
Profit earned or loss incurred by a firm, determined by subtracting expenses from revenues; casually referred to as the *bottom line.*

If the balance sheet is a snapshot, the income statement is a movie. The **income statement**, or *profit-and-loss statement* or simply "P&L," shows an organization's profit performance over a period of time, typically one year. It summarizes revenue from all sources as well as all **expenses**, the costs that have arisen in generating revenues. Expenses and income taxes are then subtracted from revenues to show the actual profit or loss of a company, a figure known as **net income**—also called *profit* or, informally, the *bottom line.* By briefly reviewing a company's income statements, you should have a general sense of the company's size, its trend in sales, its major expenses, and the resulting net income or loss. Owners, creditors, and investors can evaluate the company's past performance and future prospects by comparing net income for one year with net income for previous years. Exhibit 17.4 shows the income statement for Computer Central Services.

Expenses include both the direct costs associated with creating or purchasing products for sale and the indirect costs associated with operating the business. If a company manufactures or purchases inventory, the cost of storing the product for sale (such as

| | EXHIBIT 17.4 | Income Statement for Computer Central Services |

An income statement summarizes the company's financial operations over a particular accounting period, usually a year.

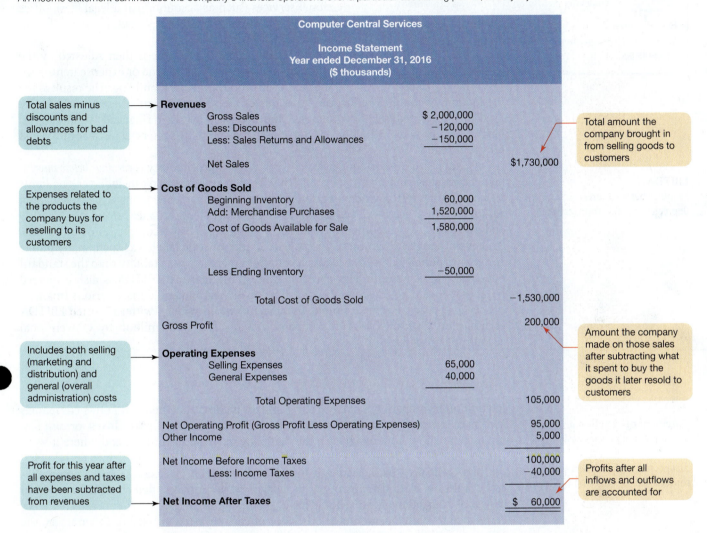

Total sales minus discounts and allowances for bad debts

Expenses related to the products the company buys for reselling to its customers

Includes both selling (marketing and distribution) and general (overall administration) costs

Profit for this year after all expenses and taxes have been subtracted from revenues

Computer Central Services

Income Statement
Year ended December 31, 2016
($ thousands)

Revenues		
Gross Sales	$ 2,000,000	
Less: Discounts	–120,000	
Less: Sales Returns and Allowances	–150,000	
Net Sales		$1,730,000
Cost of Goods Sold		
Beginning Inventory	60,000	
Add: Merchandise Purchases	1,520,000	
Cost of Goods Available for Sale	1,580,000	
Less Ending Inventory	–50,000	
Total Cost of Goods Sold		–1,530,000
Gross Profit		200,000
Operating Expenses		
Selling Expenses	65,000	
General Expenses	40,000	
Total Operating Expenses		105,000
Net Operating Profit (Gross Profit Less Operating Expenses)		95,000
Other Income		5,000
Net Income Before Income Taxes		100,000
Less: Income Taxes		–40,000
Net Income After Taxes		$ 60,000

Total amount the company brought in from selling goods to customers

Amount the company made on those sales after subtracting what it spent to buy the goods it later resold to customers

Profits after all inflows and outflows are accounted for

heating the warehouse, paying the rent, and buying insurance on the storage facility) is added to the difference between the cost of the beginning inventory and the cost of the ending inventory in order to compute the actual cost of items that were sold during a period—or the **cost of goods sold**. The computation can be summarized as follows:

Cost of goods sold = Beginning inventory + Net purchases − Ending inventory

As shown in Exhibit 17.4, cost of goods sold is deducted from sales to obtain a company's **gross profit**—a key figure used in financial statement analysis. In addition to the costs directly associated with producing goods, companies deduct **operating expenses**, which include both *selling expenses* and *general expenses*, to compute a firm's *net operating income*. Net operating income is often a better indicator of financial health because it gives an idea of how much cash the company is able to generate. For instance, a company with a sizable gross profit level can actually be losing money if its operating expenses are out of control—and if it doesn't have enough cash on hand to cover the shortfall, it could soon find itself bankrupt.[19]

Selling expenses are operating expenses incurred through marketing and distributing the product (such as wages or salaries of salespeople, advertising, supplies, insurance for the sales operation, depreciation for the store and sales equipment, and other sales

cost of goods sold
The cost of producing or acquiring a company's products for sale during a given period.

gross profit
The amount remaining when the cost of goods sold is deducted from net sales; also known as *gross margin*.

operating expenses
All costs of operation that are not included under cost of goods sold.

REAL-TIME UPDATES
Learn More by Watching This Video

Essential points on the income statement

See what investors look for in a company's income statement. Go to http://real-timeupdates.com/bia8 and click on Learn More in the Students section.

EBITDA
Earnings before interest, taxes, depreciation, and amortization.

department expenses such as telephone charges). *General expenses* are operating expenses incurred in the overall administration of a business. They include such items as professional services (such as accounting and legal fees), office salaries, depreciation of office equipment, insurance for office operations, and supplies.

A firm's net operating income is then adjusted by the amount of any nonoperating income or expense items such as the gain or loss on the sale of a building. The result is the net income or loss before income taxes (losses are shown in parentheses), a key figure used in budgeting, cash flow analysis, and a variety of other financial computations. Finally, income taxes are deducted to compute the company's after-tax net income or loss for the period.

An alternative—and controversial—measure of profitability is *earnings before interest, taxes, depreciation, and amortization,* or **EBITDA**. Because it doesn't include various items such as the interest payments on loans or the effects of depreciating expensive capital equipment, EBITDA is viewed by some investors as a "purer" measure of profitability and an easier way to compare financial performance across companies or industries. And even though it is a non-GAAP indicator and must be labeled as such, many public companies publish EBITDA because it can suggest greater profitability than the standard operating profit number. However, for those same reasons, EBITDA is also criticized because it doesn't reflect costs that every company has and could mask serious financial concerns. As an extreme example, in a recent year in which Twitter reported EBITDA earnings of $301 million, the company actually *lost* $578 million by conventional accounting measures.[20]

STATEMENT OF CASH FLOWS

statement of cash flows
A statement of a firm's cash receipts and cash payments that presents information on its sources and uses of cash.

In addition to preparing a balance sheet and an income statement, all public companies and many privately owned companies prepare a **statement of cash flows**, or *cash flow statement,* to show how much cash the company generated over time and where it went (see Exhibit 17.5). The statement of cash flows tracks the cash coming into and flowing out of a company's bank accounts. It reveals the increase or decrease in the company's cash for the period and summarizes (by category) the sources of that change. From a brief review of this statement, you should have a general sense of the amount of cash created or consumed by daily operations, the amount of cash invested in fixed or other assets, the amount of debt borrowed or repaid, and the proceeds from the sale of stock or payments for dividends. In addition, an analysis of cash flows provides a good idea of a company's ability to pay its short-term obligations when they become due.

 Checkpoint

LEARNING OBJECTIVE 5: Explain the purpose of the income statement and the statement of cash flows.

SUMMARY: The income statement, also known as the profit-and-loss statement, reflects the results of operations over a period of time. It gives a general sense of a company's size and performance. The statement of cash flows shows how a company's cash was received and spent in three areas: operations, investments, and financing. It gives a general sense of the amount of cash created or consumed by daily operations, fixed assets, investments, and debt over a period of time.

CRITICAL THINKING: (1) How could two companies with similar gross profit figures end up with dramatically different net operating income? (2) How might a statement of cash flows help a turnaround expert decide how to rescue a struggling company?

EXHIBIT 17.5	**Statement of Cash Flows for Computer Central Services**

A statement of cash flows shows a firm's cash receipts and cash payments as a result of three main activities—operating, investing, and financing—for an identified period of time (such as the year indicated here).

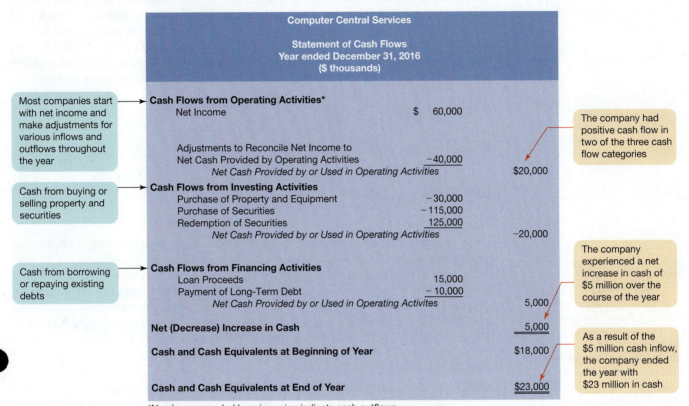

Most companies start with net income and make adjustments for various inflows and outflows throughout the year

Cash from buying or selling property and securities

Cash from borrowing or repaying existing debts

Computer Central Services

Statement of Cash Flows
Year ended December 31, 2016
($ thousands)

Cash Flows from Operating Activities*

Net Income	$ 60,000	
Adjustments to Reconcile Net Income to		
Net Cash Provided by Operating Activities	−40,000	
Net Cash Provided by or Used in Operating Activities		$20,000

Cash Flows from Investing Activities

Purchase of Property and Equipment	−30,000	
Purchase of Securities	−115,000	
Redemption of Securities	125,000	
Net Cash Provided by or Used in Operating Activities		−20,000

Cash Flows from Financing Activities

Loan Proceeds	15,000	
Payment of Long-Term Debt	− 10,000	
Net Cash Provided by or Used in Operating Activites		5,000

Net (Decrease) Increase in Cash	5,000
Cash and Cash Equivalents at Beginning of Year	$18,000
Cash and Cash Equivalents at End of Year	$23,000

The company had positive cash flow in two of the three cash flow categories

The company experienced a net increase in cash of $5 million over the course of the year

As a result of the $5 million cash inflow, the company ended the year with $23 million in cash

*Numbers preceded by minus sign indicate cash outflows.

IT'S YOUR BUSINESS: (1) What would your personal income statement look like today? Are you operating "at a profit" or "at a loss"? (2) What steps could you take to reduce your "operating expenses"?

KEY TERMS TO KNOW: income statement, expenses, net income, cost of goods sold, gross profit, operating expenses, EBITDA, statement of cash flows

Analyzing Financial Statements

After financial statements have been prepared, managers, investors, and lenders use them to evaluate the financial health of the organization, make business decisions, and spot opportunities for improvements by looking at the company's current performance in relation to its past performance, the economy as a whole, and the performance of competitors.

6   LEARNING OBJECTIVE

Explain the purpose of ratio analysis, and list the four main categories of financial ratios.

TREND ANALYSIS

The process of comparing financial data from year to year is known as *trend analysis*. You can use trend analysis to uncover shifts in the nature of a business over time. Of course, when you are comparing one period with another, it's important to take into account the effects of extraordinary or unusual items such as the sale of major assets, the purchase of a new line of products from another company, weather, or economic conditions that may have affected the company in one period but not the next. These extraordinary items are usually disclosed in the text portion of a company's annual report or in the notes to the financial statements.

RATIO ANALYSIS

Unlike trend analysis, which tracks *absolute* numbers from one year to the next, ratio analysis creates *relative* numbers by comparing sets of figures from a single year's performance. By using ratios rather than absolute amounts, analysts can more easily assess a company's performance from one year to the next or compare it with other companies. A variety of commonly used ratios help companies understand their current operations and answer some key questions: Is inventory too large? Are credit customers paying too slowly? Can the company pay its bills? Ratios also allow comparison with other companies within an industry, which helps gauge how well a company is doing relative to its competitors. Every industry tends to have its own "normal" ratios, which act as yardsticks for individual companies.

TYPES OF FINANCIAL RATIOS

Financial ratios can be organized into the following groups, as Exhibit 17.6 shows: profitability, liquidity, activity, and leverage (or debt).

Profitability Ratios

You can analyze how well a company is conducting its ongoing operations by computing *profitability ratios*, which show the state of the company's financial performance or how well it's generating profits. Three of the most common profitability ratios are **return on sales**, or *profit margin* (the net income a business makes per unit of sales); **return on equity** (net income divided by owners' equity); and **earnings per share** (the profit earned for each share of stock outstanding). Exhibit 17.6 shows how to compute these profitability ratios by using the financial information from Computer Central Services.

Liquidity Ratios

Liquidity ratios measure a firm's ability to pay its short-term obligations. As you might expect, lenders and creditors are keenly interested in liquidity measures. A company's **working capital** (current assets minus current liabilities) is an indicator of liquidity because it represents current assets remaining after the payment of all current liabilities. The dollar amount of working capital can be misleading, however. For example, it may include the value of slow-moving inventory items that cannot be used to help pay a company's short-term debts.

A different picture of the company's liquidity is provided by the **current ratio**—current assets divided by current liabilities. This figure compares the current debt owed with the current assets available to pay that debt. The **quick ratio**, also called the *acid-test ratio*, is computed by subtracting inventory from current assets and then dividing the result by current liabilities. This ratio is often a better indicator of a firm's ability to pay creditors than the current ratio because the quick ratio leaves out inventories, which can take a long time to convert to cash. A quick ratio below 1.0 is a sign that the company could struggle to meet its near-time financial obligations and therefore might not be a safe credit risk, a good investment, or possibly a smart place to accept a job. Exhibit 17.6 shows that both the current and quick ratios of Computer Central Services are well above these benchmarks and industry averages.

Activity Ratios

Activity ratios analyze how well a company is managing and making use of its assets. For companies that maintain inventories, the most common activity ratio is the **inventory turnover ratio**, which measures how fast a company's inventory is turned into sales. Inventory is a constant balancing act—hold too little, and you risk being out of stock when orders arrive; hold too much, and you raise your costs. When inventory sits on the shelf, money is tied up without earning interest; furthermore, the company incurs expenses for its storage, handling, insurance, and taxes. In addition, there is often a risk that the inventory will become obsolete or go out of style before it can be converted into finished goods and sold. Car dealers, for example, face the never-ending challenge of

---

return on sales
The ratio between net income after taxes and net sales; also known as the *profit margin*.

return on equity
The ratio between net income after taxes and total owners' equity.

earnings per share
A measure of a firm's profitability for each share of outstanding stock, calculated by dividing net income after taxes by the average number of shares of common stock outstanding.

working capital
Current assets minus current liabilities.

current ratio
A measure of a firm's short-term liquidity, calculated by dividing current assets by current liabilities.

quick ratio
A measure of a firm's short-term liquidity, calculated by adding cash, marketable securities, and receivables, then dividing that sum by current liabilities; also known as the *acid-test ratio*.

inventory turnover ratio
A measure of the time a company takes to turn its inventory into sales, calculated by dividing cost of goods sold by the average value of inventory for a period.

EXHIBIT 17.6   **How Well Does This Company Stack Up?**

Financial ratios offer a quick and convenient way to evaluate how well a company is performing in relation to prior performance, the economy as a whole, and the company's competitors.

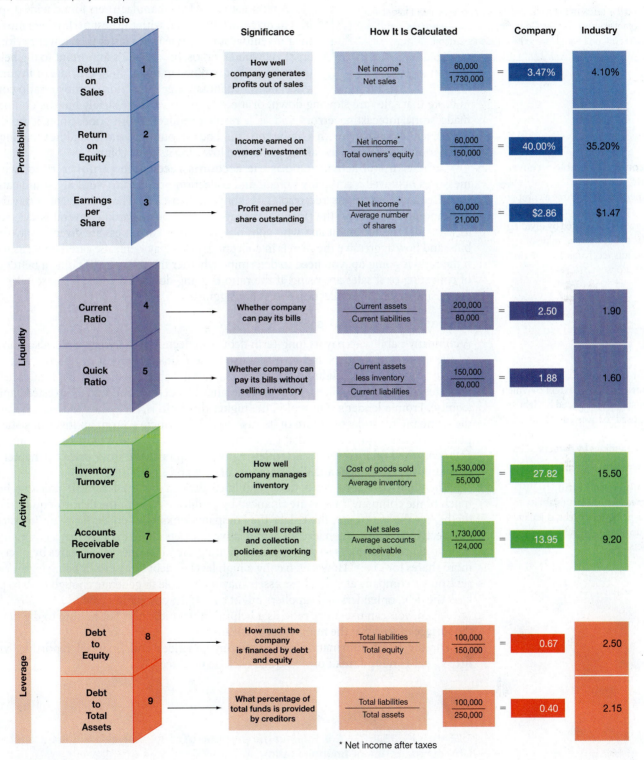

	Ratio		Significance	How It Is Calculated		Company	Industry
Profitability	Return on Sales	1	How well company generates profits out of sales	$\dfrac{\text{Net income}^*}{\text{Net sales}}$	$\dfrac{60,000}{1,730,000}$ =	3.47%	4.10%
	Return on Equity	2	Income earned on owners' investment	$\dfrac{\text{Net income}^*}{\text{Total owners' equity}}$	$\dfrac{60,000}{150,000}$ =	40.00%	35.20%
	Earnings per Share	3	Profit earned per share outstanding	$\dfrac{\text{Net income}^*}{\text{Average number of shares}}$	$\dfrac{60,000}{21,000}$ =	$2.86	$1.47
Liquidity	Current Ratio	4	Whether company can pay its bills	$\dfrac{\text{Current assets}}{\text{Current liabilities}}$	$\dfrac{200,000}{80,000}$ =	2.50	1.90
	Quick Ratio	5	Whether company can pay its bills without selling inventory	$\dfrac{\text{Current assets less inventory}}{\text{Current liabilities}}$	$\dfrac{150,000}{80,000}$ =	1.88	1.60
Activity	Inventory Turnover	6	How well company manages inventory	$\dfrac{\text{Cost of goods sold}}{\text{Average inventory}}$	$\dfrac{1,530,000}{55,000}$ =	27.82	15.50
	Accounts Receivable Turnover	7	How well credit and collection policies are working	$\dfrac{\text{Net sales}}{\text{Average accounts receivable}}$	$\dfrac{1,730,000}{124,000}$ =	13.95	9.20
Leverage	Debt to Equity	8	How much the company is financed by debt and equity	$\dfrac{\text{Total liabilities}}{\text{Total equity}}$	$\dfrac{100,000}{150,000}$ =	0.67	2.50
	Debt to Total Assets	9	What percentage of total funds is provided by creditors	$\dfrac{\text{Total liabilities}}{\text{Total assets}}$	$\dfrac{100,000}{250,000}$ =	0.40	2.15

* Net income after taxes

selling this year's models before next year's arrive. Newer models usually make the older models a lot less attractive in buyers' eyes, often requiring dealers to resort to steep discounts just to get rid of aging inventory.[21]

A recent study of U.S. manufacturers found wide disparities in inventory turnover, with the best performers moving their inventory four or five times faster than lower performers.[22] As with all ratios, however, it's important to dig below the surface after making an initial comparison. For instance, a decline in a manufacturer's inventory turnover ratio could indicate that sales are slowing down, or it could mean sales are steady but the company made some forecasting errors and as a result produced more goods than it needed. Conversely, a company with a high ratio could be discounting heavily and not making as much money as it could by raising prices and lowering its sales volume.

accounts receivable turnover ratio

A measure of the time a company takes to turn its accounts receivable into cash, calculated by dividing sales by the average value of accounts receivable for a period.

Another useful activity ratio is the **accounts receivable turnover ratio**, which measures how well a company's credit and collection policies are working by indicating how frequently accounts receivable are converted to cash. The volume of receivables outstanding depends on the financial manager's decisions regarding several issues, such as who qualifies for credit and who does not, how long customers are given to pay their bills, and how aggressive the firm is in collecting its late payments. Be careful here as well. If the ratio is going up, you need to determine whether the company is doing a better job of collecting or if sales are rising. If the ratio is going down, it may be because sales are decreasing or because collection efforts are lagging.

Leverage, or Debt, Ratios

debt-to-equity ratio

A measure of the extent to which a business is financed by debt as opposed to invested capital, calculated by dividing the company's total liabilities by owners' equity.

A company's ability to pay its long-term debts is reflected in its *leverage ratios*, also known as *debt ratios*. Both lenders and investors use these ratios to judge a company's risk and growth potential. The **debt-to-equity ratio** (total liabilities divided by total equity) indicates the extent to which a business is financed by debt as opposed to invested capital (equity). From a lender's standpoint, the higher this ratio is, the riskier the loan, because the company must devote more of its cash to debt payments. From an investor's standpoint, a higher ratio indicates that the company is spending more of its cash on interest payments than on investing in activities that will help raise the stock price.[23] Chapter 18 compares the advantages and disadvantages of debt and equity financing.

debt-to-assets ratio

A measure of a firm's ability to carry long-term debt, calculated by dividing total liabilities by total assets.

The **debt-to-assets ratio** (total liabilities divided by total assets) indicates how much of the company's assets are financed by creditors. As with the debt-to-equity ratio, the higher this ratio gets, the riskier the company looks to a lender. From an investor's perspective, though, a high level of debt relative to assets could indicate that a company is making aggressive moves to grow without diluting the value of existing shares by offering more shares for sale.[24] However, having a high level of debt to assets, or being *highly leveraged*, puts a company at risk. Those assets may not be able to generate enough cash to pay back the debt, or lenders and suppliers might cut off the company's credit.

Again, you can use every ratio as a helpful initial indicator, but be sure to dig below the surface to see what the number really means.

For the latest information on accounting practices and financial reporting, visit **http://real-timeupdates.com/bia8** and click on Chapter 17.

 Checkpoint

LEARNING OBJECTIVE 6: Explain the purpose of ratio analysis, and list the four main categories of financial ratios.

SUMMARY: Financial ratios provide information for analyzing the health and future prospects of a business. Ratios facilitate financial comparisons among different-size companies and between a company and industry averages. Most of the important ratios fall into one of four categories: profitability ratios, which show how well the company generates profits; liquidity ratios, which measure the company's ability to pay its short-term obligations; activity ratios, which analyze how well a company is managing its assets; and debt ratios, which measure a company's ability to pay its long-term debt.

CRITICAL THINKING: (1) Why is it so important to be aware of extraordinary items when analyzing a company's finances? (2) Why is the quick ratio frequently a better indicator than the current ratio of a firm's ability to pay its bills?

IT'S YOUR BUSINESS: (1) Assume that you are about to make a significant consumer purchase, and the product is available at two local stores, one with high inventory turnover and one with low. Which store would you choose based on this information? Why? (2) If you were applying for a home mortgage loan today, would a lender view your debt-to-assets ratio favorably? Why or why not?

KEY TERMS TO KNOW: return on sales, return on equity, earnings per share, working capital, current ratio, quick ratio, inventory turnover ratio, accounts receivable turnover ratio, debt-to-equity ratio, debt-to-assets ratio

BEHIND THE SCENES
GOOGLE THIS: "COST CONTROL"

By just about any measure you can think of, Google is one of the most spectacular success stories in the history of business. However, even a company as wealthy as Google has to control its spending.

Google's case is unusual in the sense of its sheer scale, but the story is not unique. When a young company is growing quickly and money is pouring in from sales or from investors, the natural tendency is to focus on building the business and capturing market opportunities. The less exciting—but ultimately no less important—task of creating a sustainable cost structure with rigorous expense management often doesn't get as much attention in the early years.

In some companies, rapid growth in a hot economy can mask serious underlying problems that threaten the long-term viability of the enterprise. In the dot-com boom of the late 1990s, for instance, more than a few high-flying companies fell to earth when investors who had enjoyed a rocket ride in the stock market realized the companies didn't have workable business models.

During the mid-2000s, Google's revenue had been increasing at a spectacular pace, from $10.6 billion in 2006, to $16.6 billion in 2007, to $21.8 billion in 2008. However, expenses were growing at an even faster rate. As a result, the company's profit margin dropped from 29 percent in 2006 to around 19 percent in 2008 (still 5 percentage points better than the industry average); 2008 ended with the first-ever drop in quarterly profits in the company's history.

The cooling economy and slowing profits didn't expose any fatal flaws in the Google business model, but the drop certainly was a wake-up call that emphasized the need to transition to the next stage of organizational development. It was time for the accounting and financial management functions to play a more prominent role and to transform a wild and wooly entrepreneurial success story into a major corporation with stable finances.

Back in 2001, Google cofounders Larry Page and Sergey Brin brought in Eric Schmidt, a seasoned technology industry executive, to guide the company's growth beyond its initial start-up stage. Under Schmidt's leadership, Google expanded from 200 employees to more than 20,000 and secured its place as one of the world's most influential companies. Facing the need for a more methodical approach to accounting and financial management, Schmidt brought in another executive with a proven track record in corporate leadership. Patrick Pichette made his name helping Bell Canada reduce operating expenses by $2 billion, and his proven ability to bring expenses in line with revenue was just what Google needed.

Pichette and other executives tackled expenses at three levels: employee perks, staffing, and project investment. Employee benefits have been trimmed and adjusted over time, although it's safe to say they are still better than you'll find just about anywhere, from on-site physicians and nurses and help with medical issues to extra time off and spending money for new parents, tuition reimbursement, and free legal advice. The company's position on benefits now appears to be less about adding fun and possibly frivolous perks and more about "removing barriers so Googlers can focus on the things they love, both inside and outside of work."

At the staffing level, Google began taking a much harder look at hiring practices to better align staffing with project needs. Tellingly, the first layoffs in the company's history, in January

2009, involved 100 recruiters whose services were no longer needed because Google's hiring rate had slowed so dramatically. Thousands of contract workers were let go as well. The vaunted "20 percent time" was adjusted, too, with the company aiming to focus engineers' time more directly on core projects. In some cases, staffers get access to data and computing resources in order to explore new ideas but don't necessarily get the free time during work hours.

At the project and program levels, Google now scrutinizes its investments more carefully and pulls the plug on less-promising activities. Some of the higher-profile shutdowns in the past few years include the Google Buzz social networking capability, the Google Wave collaboration platform, the iGoogle personalizable news page, and Google Reader, one of the most popular RSS newsfeed readers. "More wood behind fewer arrows" is how Google describes its new emphasis on putting its resources into the projects most likely to have sizable long-term success.

Pichette's efforts to install a more sustainable accounting and cost-control system yielded impressive results. After the economy emerged from its deep slump, Google had stockpiled some $50 billion in cash. $50 billion in cash as the economy pulled out of its slump. (Once asked why the company was sitting on so much cash, Pichette explained that in the fast-changing world of search and other digital services, Google might need to jump on an acquisition almost overnight, with potentially billions of dollars of cash in hand.)

Just as with personal finances, however, companies need to stay vigilant year in year out to make sure old habits don't come back. By 2015, Google was once again feeling the pinch after going on a hiring spree to staff up new projects, some of them in such wildly diverse areas as medical research and self-driving cars. Many investors had grown wary of the company's

stock after earnings repeatedly failed to meet analysts' quarterly expectations.

Pichette retired in early 2015 and was replaced by Ruth Porat, a widely respected banking executive with a reputation for prudent financial management. As soon as she came on board, she announced her intention to get Google's expenses back under control. Investors apparently liked what they heard, as the company's stock took a healthy jump after the first quarterly earnings report under Porat's leadership. Now come the challenge of keeping history from repeating itself.[25]

Critical Thinking Questions

17-1. Given the eventual need for rigorous financial management, should every company have extensive cost controls in place from the first moment of operation? Explain your answer.

17-2. Google recently had a debt-to-equity ratio of 0.04. Microsoft, one of its key competitors, had a debt-to-equity ratio of 0.15. From a bank's point of view, which of the two companies is a more attractive loan candidate, based on this ratio? Why?

17-3. Over the course of a recent six-month period, Google's current ratio increased from 8.77 to 11.91. Does this make Google more or less of a credit risk in the eyes of potential lenders? Why?

LEARN MORE ONLINE

Visit Google's "Investor Relations" section, at **http://investor .google.com**. Peruse the latest financial news. How does the company's financial health look at present? What do the trends for revenue, expenses, and income look like? Does the company report both GAAP and non-GAAP financial results? Why would Google report non-GAAP figures?

KEY TERMS

accounting (397)
accounting equation (402)
accounts receivable turnover ratio (414)
accrual basis (403)
assets (402)
audit (399)
balance sheet (404)
bookkeeping (397)
calendar year (405)
cash basis (403)
certified public accountants (CPAs) (398)
closing the books (404)
controller (398)
cost of goods sold (409)
current assets (407)
current liabilities (407)
current ratio (412)
debt-to-assets ratio (414)

debt-to-equity ratio (414)
depreciation (403)
double-entry bookkeeping (403)
earnings per share (412)
EBITDA (410)
expenses (408)
external auditors (400)
financial accounting (397)
fiscal year (406)
fixed assets (407)
GAAP (generally accepted accounting principles) (400)
gross profit (409)
income statement (408)
international financial reporting standards (IFRS) (401)
inventory turnover ratio (412)
liabilities (402)
long-term liabilities (407)

MyBizLab®

To complete the problems with the ⭐, go to EOC Discussion Questions in the MyLab.

TEST YOUR KNOWLEDGE

Questions for Review

17-4. What is GAAP?

17-5. What is an audit, and why are audits performed?

17-6. What is the matching principle?

17-7. What are the three main profitability ratios, and how is each calculated?

17-8. What is the value of an income statement?

Questions for Analysis

17-9. Why were efforts made to converge the GAAP and IFRS standards?

17-10. Why would a company bother with double-entry bookkeeping?

17-11. Why are the costs of fixed assets depreciated?

17-12. Why would a bank lending officer be interested in the cash flow statement of a company that is applying for a loan?

17-13. **Ethical Considerations.** In the process of closing the company books, you encounter a problematic transaction. One of the company's customers was invoiced twice for the same project materials, resulting in a $1,000 overcharge. You immediately notify the controller, whose response is, "Let it go, it happens often.

It'll probably balance out on some future transaction." What should you do now?

Questions for Application

⭐ **17-14.** The senior partner of an accounting firm is looking for ways to increase the firm's business. What other services besides traditional accounting can the firm offer to its clients? What new challenges might this additional work create?

17-15. Visit the websites of Google and Microsoft and retrieve their annual reports. Using these financial reports, compute the working capital, current ratio, and quick ratio for each company. Does one company appear to be more liquid than the other? If so, why?

⭐ **17-16.** If you were asked to lend money to your cousin's clothing store to help her through a slow sales period, would you be more interested in looking at the current ratio or the quick ratio as a measure of liquidity? Why?

⭐ **17-17.** **Concept Integration.** Your appliance manufacturing company recently implemented a just-in-time inventory system (see Chapter 9) for all parts used in the manufacturing process. How might you expect this move to affect the company's inventory turnover rate, current ratio, and quick ratio?

EXPAND YOUR KNOWLEDGE

Discovering Career Opportunities

People interested in entering the field of accounting can choose among a wide variety of careers with diverse responsibilities and challenges. Visit the Accountants and Auditors page at www.bls.gov/ooh to read more about career opportunities in accounting.

17-18. What are the day-to-day duties of this occupation? How would these duties contribute to the financial success of a company?

17-19. What skills and educational qualifications would you need to enter this occupation? How do these qualifications fit with your current plans, skills, and interests?

17-20. What kinds of employers hire people for this position? According to your research, does the number of employers seem to be increasing or decreasing? How do you think this trend will affect your employment possibilities if you choose this career?

Improving Your Tech Insights: GRC Software

The Sarbanes-Oxley Act's requirement that publicly traded companies regularly verify their internal accounting controls spurred the development of software tools to help companies flag and fix problems in their financial systems. In the past few years, some software vendors have gone beyond Sarbox compliance to integrate the monitoring of a wide range of legal and financial issues that require management attention. This new category of software is generally known as *governance, risk, and compliance (GRC) software*. GRC capabilities can either be built into other software packages (such as accounting and finance software, process management software, or business intelligence software) or be offered as stand-alone compliance programs. Vendors that offer GRC capabilities include Oracle (**www.oracle.com**), SAP (**www.sap.com**), and IBM (**www.ibm.com**), among many others [26]

Explore one GRC software solution. In a brief email message to your instructor, describe the benefits of using this particular software package.

PRACTICE YOUR SKILLS

Sharpening Your Communication Skills

Obtain a copy of the annual report of a business and examine what the report shows about finances and current operations.

17-21. Consider the statements made by the CEO regarding the past year: Did the company do well, or are changes in operations necessary to its future well-being? What are the projections for future growth in sales and profits?

17-22. Examine the financial summaries for information about the fiscal condition of the company: Did the company show a profit?

17-23. Obtain a copy of the company's annual report from the previous year and compare it with the current report to determine whether past projections were accurate.

17-24. Prepare a brief written summary of your conclusions.

Building Your Team Skills

Divide into small groups and compute the following financial ratios for Alpine Manufacturing, using the company's balance sheet and income statement. Compare your answers to those of your classmates:

- Profitability ratios: return on sales; return on equity; earnings per share
- Liquidity ratios: current ratio; quick ratio
- Activity ratios: inventory turnover; accounts receivable turnover
- Leverage ratios: debt to equity; debt to total assets

ALPINE MANUFACTURING INCOME STATEMENT YEAR ENDED DECEMBER 31, 2016	
Sales	$1,800
Less: Cost of Goods Sold	1,000
Gross Profit	$ 800
Less: Total Operating Expenses	450
Net Operating Income Before Income Taxes	350
Less: Income Taxes	50
Net Income After Income Taxes	$ 300

ALPINE MANUFACTURING BALANCE SHEET DECEMBER 31, 2016		
ASSETS		
Cash	$ 100	
Accounts Receivable	350	
Inventory	250	
Current Assets (cash + AR + inventory)	700	
Fixed Assets	2,300	
Total Assets		$3,000
LIABILITIES AND SHAREHOLDERS' EQUITY		
Current Liabilities	$ 400	
Long-Term Debts	1,600	
Shareholders' Equity (100 common shares outstanding valued at $10 each)	1,000	
Total Liabilities and Shareholders' Equity		$3,000

Developing Your Research Skills

Select an article from a business journal or newspaper (print or online edition) that discusses the quarterly or year-end performance of a company that industry analysts consider notable for either positive or negative reasons.

17-25. Did the company report a profit or a loss for this accounting period? What other performance indicators were reported? Is the company's performance improving or declining?

17-26. Did the company's performance match industry analysts' expectations, or was it a surprise? How did analysts or other experts respond to the firm's actual quarterly or year-end results?

17-27. What reasons were given for the company's improvement or decline in performance?

MyBizLab®

Go to the Assignments section of your MyLab to complete these writing exercises.

17-28. Should public companies be allowed to publish any non-GAAP performance metrics? Why or why not?

17-29. How could you apply the concept of a balance sheet to your personal financial planning?

ENDNOTES

1. Michael Liedtke, "New CFO Reins in Google Excess, Stock Soars," *Seattle Times*, 16 July 2015, www.seattletimes.com; Antoine Gara, "New Google CFO Ruth Porat Will Get A Massive Raise For Leaving Morgan Stanley," *Forbes*, 26 March 2015, www.forbes.com; Ryan Tate, "Google Couldn't Kill 20 Percent Time Even If It Wanted To," *Wired*, 21 August 2013, www.wired.com; James Manyika, "Google's CFO on Growth, Capital Structure, and Leadership," *McKinsey Quarterly*, August 2011, www.mckinseyquarterly.com; Google financial profile on Trefis, accessed 18 November 2013, www.trefis.com; Bill Coughran, "More Wood Behind Fewer Arrows," Google blog, 20 July 2011, http://googleblog.blogspot.com; Julianne Pepitone, "Google Beats Profit Estimates," *CNNMoney.com*, 16 April 2009, http://money.cnn.com; "Frugal Google," *Fortune*, 22 January 2009, http://money.cnn.com/magazines/fortune; Miguel Helft, "Google's Profit Surges in Quarter," *New York Times*, 16 July 2009, www.nytimes.com; Catherine Clifford, "Layoffs Hit Google: 200 Jobs Cut," *CNNMoney.com*, 26 March 2009, http://money.cnn.com; Adam Lashinsky, "Belt-Tightening at Google," *Fortune*, 22 January 2009, http://money.cnn.com/magazines/fortune; Adam Lashinsky, "The Axman Comes to Google," *Fortune*, 23 March 2009, http://money.cnn.com/magazines/fortune; Google website, accessed 18 November 2013, www.google.com; Jessica E. Vascellaro and Scott Morrison, "Google Gears Down for Tougher Times," *Wall Street Journal*, 3 December 2008, http://online.wsj.com; Abbey Klaassen, "A Maturing Google Buckles Down and Searches for Cost Savings," *Advertising Age*, 1 December 2008, 3, 29.
2. "Accountants and Auditors," *Occupational Outlook Handbook, 2010–11 Edition*, U.S. Bureau of Labor Statistics website, www.bls.gov.
3. "Frequently Asked Questions," American Institute of Certified Public Accountants website, accessed 19 August 2009, www.aicpa.org.
4. "CMA: The Essential Credential," Institute of Management Accountants, accessed 10 September 2011, www.imanet.org.
5. Danielle Lee, "Hiring, Salaries Up for Accounting Graduates," *Accounting Today*, 30 April 2013, www.accountingtoday.com; "Accountants and Auditors," *Occupational Outlook Handbook, 2010–11 Edition*, www.bls.gov/oco/; Nanette Byrnes, "Green Eyeshades Never Looked So Sexy," *BusinessWeek*, 10 January 2005, 44; "Rules Make Accountants Newly Hot Commodity," *Oregonian*, 13 April 2005, www.ebsco.com.
6. Sarah Johnson, "Goodbye GAAP," *CFO*, 1 April 2008, www.cfo.com.
7. "Detecting Two Tricks of the Trade," *Investopedia.com*, accessed 19 August 2009, www.investopedia.com.
8. "Earnings Before Interest, Taxes, Depreciation and Amortization—EBITDA," *Investopedia.com*, accessed 18 November 2013, www.investopedia.com; Jonathan Weil, "Readjusting Black Box's Earnings Adjustments (Adjusted)," *Bloomberg*, 30 January 2013, www.bloomberg.com; Anthony Catanach, "Non-GAAP Metrics: Is It Time to Toss Out the SEC's Reg G?" Grumpy Old Accountants blog, 20 June 2013, http://grumpyoldaccountants.com.
9. Emily Chasan, "New Benchmarks Crop Up in Companies' Financial Reports," *Wall Street Journal*, 13 November 2012, http://online.wsj.com.
10. Johnson, "Goodbye GAAP."
11. Vincent Ryan, "Former SEC Chair Cox Declares IFRS "Bereft of Life," *CFO*, 10 June 2014, www.cfo.com; Paul Pacter, "What Have IASB and FASB Convergence Efforts Achieved?" *Journal of Accountancy*, February 2013, www.journalofaccountancy.com; Tammy Whitehouse, "FASB Looks Inward at Improving GAAP," *Compliance Week*, 1 November 2013, www.complianceweek.com; Anthony Catanach, "The Great IFRS Swindle: Accountants Scamming Accountants" Grumpy Old Accountants blog, 10 November 2013, http://grumpyoldaccountants.com.
12. American Institute of CPAs, "International Financial Reporting Standards (IFRS): An AICPA Backgrounder," 2011, www.ifrs.com; PricewaterhouseCoopers, "IFRS and US GAAP: Similarities and Differences," September 2010, www.pwc.com; KPMG, "IFRS Compared to US GAAP: An Overview," September 2010, www.kpmg.com.
13. "Summary of SEC Actions and SEC Related Provisions Pursuant to the Sarbanes-Oxley Act of 2002," SEC website, accessed 9 May 2004, www.sec.gov; "Sarbanes-Oxley Act's Progress," *USA Today*, 26 December 2002, www.highbeam.com.
14. Sarah Johnson, "PCAOB Chairman Mark Olson to Retire," *CFO*, 9 June 2009, www.cfo.com.
15. "Building Value in Your Sox Compliance Program: Highlights from Protiviti's 2013 Sarbanes-Oxley Compliance Survey," Protiviti, www.protiviti.com; Michael W. Peregrine, "The Law That Changed Corporate America," *New York Times*, 25 July 2012, www.nytimes.com; Kayla Gillan, "It Enhanced Investor Protection," *New York Times*, 25 July 2012, www.nytimes.com.
16. Thayne Forbes, "Valuing Customers," *Journal of Database Marketing & Customer Strategy Management*, October 2007, 4–10.
17. Baruch Lev, "Sharpening the Intangibles Edge," *Harvard Business Review*, June 2004, 109–116.
18. "Google Inc. Financial," Google Finance, accessed 18 November 2013, www.google.com/finance.
19. "How to Spot Trouble in Your Financials," *Inc.*, October 2004, 96.
20. Timothy Green, "How Twitter Tried to Convince Us That It's Doing Really Well," *Money*, 1 May 2015, http://time.com/money; Ben McClure, "A Clear Look at EBITDA," *Investopedia.com*, 17 April 2010, www.investopedia.com; "Bobbie Gossage," Cranking Up the Earnings," *Inc.*, October 2004, 54; Lisa Smith, "EBITDA: Challenging the Calculation," *Investopedia.com*, 20 November 2009, www.investopedia.com.

21. Amy Wilson, "Old Vehicles Clog Dealer Lots," *Automotive News*, 11 May 2009, 4.

22. "Inventory Turnover," *Controller's Report*, October 2008, 13–14.

23. Jeffery Slater, *College Accounting: A Practical Approach*, 11th ed. (Upper Saddle River N.J.: Pearson Prentice Hall, 2010), 741.

24. Slater, *College Accounting: A Practical Approach*, 735.

25. See note 1.

26. Mary Hayes Weier, "Companies Look to Contain Risk with GRC Software," *InformationWeek*, 5 April 2008, www.information week.com; SAP website, accessed 19 June 2015, www.sap.com; IBM website, accessed 19 June 2015, www.ibm.com; Oracle website, accessed 19 June 2015, www.oracle.com; GRC Software Seems to Be Rising," *FierceComplianceIT*, 12 March 2007, www.fiercecomplianceit.com; James Kobielus, "Compliance-Enabling Technologies via SOA on the Rise," *ITWorldCanada*, 8 March 2007, www.itworldcanada.com.

LEARNING OBJECTIVES After studying this chapter, you will be able to

1 Identify three fundamental concepts that affect financial decisions, and identify the primary responsibilities of a financial manager.

2 Describe the budgeting process, three major budgeting challenges, and the four major types of budgets.

3 Compare the advantages and disadvantages of debt and equity financing, and explain the two major considerations in choosing from financing alternatives.

4 Identify the major categories of short-term debt financing.

5 Identify the major categories of long-term debt financing.

6 Describe the two options for equity financing, and explain how companies prepare an initial public offering.

BEHIND THE SCENES CHARGING AHEAD: VISA SEARCHES FOR FUNDS

Chris Hondros/Getty Images

Visa faced the challenge of going public during the worst economic conditions in recent memory. The executive team is shown here at the New York Stock Exchange on the day the company went public.

www.visa.com

The story of Visa, Inc., is a story of big numbers. As the world's largest processor of credit- and debit-card transactions, Visa provides essential services to roughly 15,000 financial institutions, which have issued more than 2 billion Visa-branded cards. The 28 million merchants that accept Visa ring up nearly 80 billion transactions a year—7 trillion dollars' worth.

Visa's history began in 1958, when Bank of America premiered the BankAmericard in Fresno, California, just as the concept of general-purpose credit cards was taking hold across the Unites States. (*Charge cards* issued and accepted by a single company, such as a gas station or department store, had been around for several decades by then.) These new *revolving* credit accounts, which let consumers charge purchases and pay them off over time, revolutionized consumer and business purchasing and changed the way consumers and companies manage their finances.

Over the next 50 years, the business venture that began as BankAmericard grew and transformed into the Visa International Service Association, a global payment-processing system jointly owned by thousands of member banks and other financial institutions. The BankAmericard became the Visa card, and Visa became one of the world's best-known and most valuable brands.

With growth and change came challenges, and by 2007 Visa had more than a few challenges on its hands. Whereas Visa remained a privately held joint venture, archrival MasterCard had become a public company in 2006, raising $2.4 billion with its initial stock offering. MasterCard's stock price continued to climb, giving an already strong competitor more financial power and flexibility, including the ability to attract and motivate top employees with stock options. As competition—and opportunities—grew, Visa needed cash to keep investing in payment-processing technologies, including smart cards with embedded computer chips and phone-based mobile commerce payments. At the same time, Visa was facing several billion dollars in liabilities from lawsuits filed by merchants and rival card companies American Express and Discover. To top it off, the six major banks that were Visa's primary owners were

facing a massive liquidity crisis following a meltdown in the home-mortgage market. They needed cash by the bucketful.

Selling stock for the first time through an initial public offering (IPO) of its own seemed like the obvious answer to Visa's funding challenges. However, did an IPO make sense when the global economy was in the process of falling off a cliff? Did Visa choose the right financing option and the right time to execute it? Would the IPO be another big number in a company history of big numbers, or would it be a big-time failure?[1]

INTRODUCTION

From the coffee shop down the street to the world's largest corporations, every business enterprise needs cash, although not always the billions of dollars that Visa needed. In this chapter, you'll learn more about the major financial decisions companies make, starting with the process of developing a financial plan, then creating and maintaining budgets, and finally comparing ways to finance both ongoing operations and growth opportunities.

1   **LEARNING OBJECTIVE**

Identify three fundamental concepts that affect financial decisions, and identify the primary responsibilities of a financial manager.

financial management

Planning for a firm's money needs and managing the allocation and spending of funds.

The Role of Financial Management

Planning for a firm's money needs and managing the allocation and spending of funds are the foundations of **financial management**, or *finance*. In most smaller companies, the owner is responsible for the firm's financial decisions, whereas in larger operations, financial management is the responsibility of the finance department. This department, which includes the accounting function, reports to a vice president of finance or a chief financial officer (CFO).

No matter what size the company, decisions regarding company finances must consider three fundamental concepts (see Exhibit 18.1). First, if the firm spends too much money meeting short-term demands, it won't have enough to make strategic investments for the future, such as building new facilities, developing the next generation of products,

EXHIBIT 18.1   **Financial Management: Three Fundamental Concepts**

Whether the owner of a small company or the chief financial officer (CFO) of a major corporation, a financial manager must grapple with these three fundamental concepts.

1. Balancing short-term and long-term demands
- Must have ready cash to pay salaries, bills, and taxes
- Need a financial cushion to ride out rough times
- May need money for acquisitions or other extraordinary expenses
- Must make strategic long-term investments

2. Balancing potential risks and potential rewards
- Every decision involves a risk/reward trade-off
- Higher risks may yield higher rewards
- The safest choices aren't always the best choices

3. Balancing leverage and flexibility
- Can use debt strategically and sometimes out of necessity
- Debt can be a tool, but it can also be a trap
- Highly leveraged companies have far less ability to maneuver and are more vulnerable to setbacks

or being able to jump on a strategic acquisition. Conversely, if the firm spends too little in the short term, it can lose key employees to better-paying competitors, compromise product quality or customer service, or create other problems with long-term consequences.

Second, most financial decisions involve balancing potential risks against potential rewards, known as a **risk/return trade-off**. Generally speaking, the higher the perceived risk, the higher the potential reward, and vice versa. However, this situation doesn't always hold true. For example, a company with free cash could (a) invest it in the stock market, which offers potentially high returns but at moderate to high risk; (b) put the money in a bank account, which has little to no risk but low return; or (c) invest in a new facility or a new product, which could yield high returns, moderate returns, or no returns at all. Moreover, the *safest* choice isn't always the *best* choice. For instance, if you're hoarding cash in a safe place while competitors are investing in new products or new stores, you could be setting yourself up for a big decline in revenue.

Third, financial choices can have a tremendous impact on a company's flexibility and resilience. For example, companies that are *highly leveraged* (that is, carrying a lot of debt) are forced to devote more of their cash flow to debt service and therefore can't spend that money on advertising, staffing, or product development. Heavy debt loads and low cash flow make a company especially vulnerable to economic downturns, too. In contrast, companies with lots of cash on hand can weather tough times and make strategic moves that their debt-constrained competitors can't make. In fact, well-funded companies often view recessions as opportunities to take market share from weaker competitors or simply to buy them outright.[2] The semiconductor giant Intel uses downturns to invest in major facility upgrades, enabling it to respond more aggressively when the economy turns around and demand picks up.[3]

DEVELOPING A FINANCIAL PLAN

Successful financial management starts with a **financial plan**, a document that outlines the funds a firm will need for a certain period of time, along with the sources and intended uses of those funds. The financial plan takes its input from three information sources:

- The strategic plan, which establishes the company's overall direction and identifies the need for major investments, expanded staffing, and other activities that will require funds
- The company's financial statements, including the income statement and the statement of cash flows, which tell the finance manager how much cash the company has now and how much it is likely to generate in the near future
- The external financial environment, including interest rates and the overall health of the economy

By considering information from these three sources, managers can identify how much money the company will need and how much it will have to rely on external resources to complement its internal resources over the span of time covered by the financial plan (see Exhibit 18.2 on the next page).

MONITORING CASH FLOW

Overall income, as identified in the income statement, is important, but knowing precisely how much cash is flowing into and out of the company—and when—is critical because cash is necessary in order to purchase the assets and supplies a company needs to operate, to meet payroll, and to pay dividends to shareholders (for those corporations that pay dividends). Cash flow is generally related to net income; that is, companies with relatively high accounting profits generally have relatively high cash flow, but the relationship is not precise.

Companies that don't keep a close eye on cash flow can find themselves facing a *liquidity crisis*, having insufficient cash to meet their short-term needs. In the worst-case scenario, a firm in a liquidity crisis finds itself in a credit crisis, too, meaning it doesn't

risk/return trade-off
The balance of potential risks against potential rewards.

financial plan
A document that outlines the funds needed for a certain period of time, along with the sources and intended uses of those funds.

EXHIBIT 18.2   **Finding and Allocating Funds**

Financial management involves finding suitable sources of funds and deciding on the most appropriate uses for those funds.

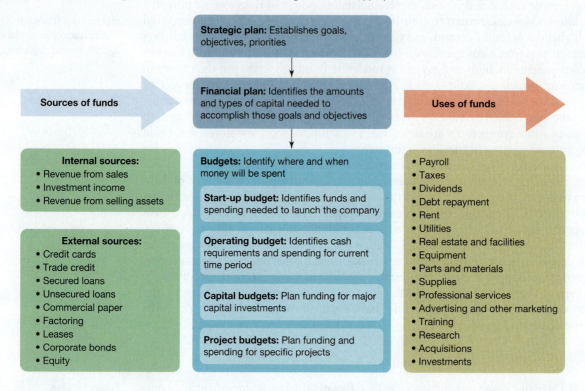

have the cash it needs and can't borrow any more. During the recent recession, many companies caught with no money and no way to borrow had no choice but to reduce their workforces. Whenever economic storm clouds are gathering, financial managers need to jump into action to strengthen balance sheets and do whatever they can to ensure positive cash flow as conditions deteriorate.[4]

A vital step in maintaining positive cash flow is monitoring *working capital accounts*: accounts receivable, accounts payable, inventory, and cash (see Exhibit 18.3).

Managing Accounts Receivable and Accounts Payable

accounts receivable
Amounts that are currently owed to a firm.

Keeping an eye on **accounts receivable**—the money owed to a firm by its customers—is one way to manage cash flow effectively. The volume of receivables depends on a financial manager's decisions regarding several issues: who qualifies for credit and who does not, how long customers are given to pay their bills, and how aggressive the firm is in collecting its debts. In addition to setting guidelines and policies for handling these issues, a financial manager analyzes the firm's outstanding receivables to identify patterns that might indicate problems and establishes procedures for collecting overdue accounts.

accounts payable
Amounts that a firm currently owes to other parties.

The flip side of managing receivables is managing **accounts payable**—the bills that the company owes to its suppliers, lenders, and other parties. Here the objective is generally to postpone paying bills until the last moment, because doing so allows the firm to hold on to its cash as long as possible. However, a financial manager also needs to weigh the advantages of paying promptly if doing so entitles the firm to cash discounts. In addition, paying on time is essential to maintaining a good credit rating, which lowers the cost of borrowing.

Managing Inventory

Inventory is another area in which financial managers can fine-tune the firm's cash flow. As Chapter 9 explains, inventory sitting on the shelf represents capital that is tied up without earning interest. Furthermore, the firm incurs expenses for storage and handling, insurance, and taxes. In addition, there is always a risk that inventory will become

EXHIBIT 18.3 **Monitoring the Working Capital Accounts**

The working capital accounts represent a firm's cash on hand as well as economic value that can be converted to cash (inventory) or is expected from customers (accounts receivable), minus what it is scheduled to be paid out (accounts payable).

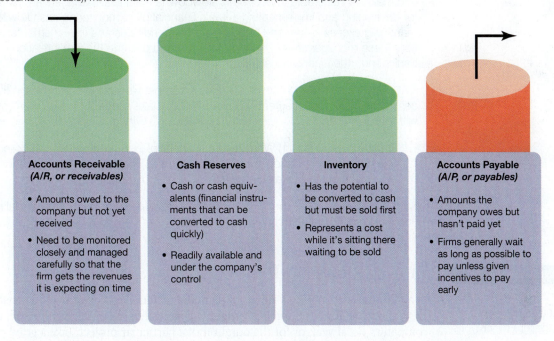

Accounts Receivable (A/R, or receivables)
- Amounts owed to the company but not yet received
- Need to be monitored closely and managed carefully so that the firm gets the revenues it is expecting on time

Cash Reserves
- Cash or cash equivalents (financial instruments that can be converted to cash quickly)
- Readily available and under the company's control

Inventory
- Has the potential to be converted to cash but must be sold first
- Represents a cost while it's sitting there waiting to be sold

Accounts Payable (A/P, or payables)
- Amounts the company owes but hasn't paid yet
- Firms generally wait as long as possible to pay unless given incentives to pay early

obsolete before it can be converted into finished goods and sold. Thus, the firm's goal is to maintain enough inventory to fill orders in a timely fashion at the lowest cost. To achieve this goal, financial managers work with operations managers and marketing managers to determine the *economic order quantity (EOQ)*, or quantity of materials that, when ordered regularly, results in the lowest ordering and storage costs.

MANAGING CASH RESERVES

Financial managers also serve as guardians of a company's cash reserves, whether that cash is from investors that have funded a start-up venture or from profitable product sales in an established company. The nature of this challenge varies widely, depending on the business, the firm's overall financial health, and management's predictions for the economy. For instance, start-ups usually have a finite pool of cash from their investors and need to manage that cash wisely so they don't run out of funds before the new business can start to generate cash on its own. At the other extreme, an established company with many successful and profitable products can generate more cash than it needs for both ongoing operations and "rainy day" emergency funds. Chapter 19 describes many of the investment opportunities that companies have for cash that isn't currently needed.

 **Checkpoint**

LEARNING OBJECTIVE 1: Identify three fundamental concepts that affect financial decisions, and identify the primary responsibilities of a financial manager.

SUMMARY: Decisions regarding company finances must take into account three fundamental concepts. First, every company has to balance short-term and long-term financial demands. Failure to do so can lead to serious cash flow problems and even bankruptcy. Second, most financial decisions involve a *risk/return trade-off* in which, generally speaking, the higher the perceived risk, the higher the potential reward, and vice versa. Third, financial choices can have a tremendous impact on a company's flexibility and resilience. Overburdening a company with debt limits its strategic options and makes it vulnerable to economic slowdowns. Financial managers are responsible for developing and implementing a firm's financial plan, monitoring cash flow and managing excess funds, and budgeting for expenditures and improvements. In addition, these managers raise capital as needed and oversee the firm's relationships with banks and other financial institutions.

CRITICAL THINKING: (1) What role does a company's strategic plan play in the process of financial management? (2) Does it ever make sense for a profitable company with positive cash flow to seek external financing? Why or why not?

IT'S YOUR BUSINESS: (1) What is your financial plan for getting through college? (2) How well do you budget your personal finances? If you don't budget, how do you monitor cash flow to make sure you don't run out of money each month?

KEY TERMS TO KNOW: financial management, risk/return trade-off, financial plan, accounts receivable, accounts payable

---

Describe the budgeting process, three major budgeting challenges, and the four major types of budgets.

budget
A planning and control tool that reflects expected revenues, operating expenses, and cash receipts and outlays.

financial control
The process of analyzing and adjusting the basic financial plan to correct for deviations from forecasted events.

REAL-TIME UPDATES

Learn More by Reading This Article

Build a better budget

These six steps will help any small business improve its budgeting process. Go to http://real-timeupdates.com/bia8 and click on Learn More in the Students section.

hedging
Protecting against cost increases with contracts that allow a company to buy supplies in the future at designated prices.

The Budgeting Process

In addition to developing a financial plan and monitoring cash flow, financial managers are responsible for developing a **budget**, a financial guide for a given period, usually the company's fiscal year, or for the duration of a particular project. Like a good personal or household budget, a company budget identifies where and when money will be spent throughout the year. Particularly in larger organizations, budgeting is often a combination of *top-down mandate,* in which top executives specify the amount of money each functional area can have based on the company's total available budget for the year, and *bottom-up requests,* in which individual supervisors and managers add up the amounts they need based on number of employees, project expenses, supplies, and other costs.

Finalizing a budget is usually a matter of negotiation and compromise in which financial managers try to reconcile the top-down and bottom-up numbers. After a budget has been developed, the finance manager compares actual results with projections to discover variances and recommends corrective action, a process known as **financial control**.

BUDGETING CHALLENGES

The budgeting process might sound fairly straightforward, but in practice, it can be an exhausting, time-consuming chore that everyone dreads and few managers find satisfactory. Budgeting is a challenge for several reasons (see Exhibit 18.4). First, a company always has a finite amount of money available to spend each year, and every group in the company is fighting for a share of it. Consequently, individual department managers can spend a considerable amount of time making a case for their budgetary needs, and top executives frequently need to make tough choices that won't please everybody.

Second, managers often can't predict with complete accuracy how much revenue will come in or how much the various items covered by the budget will cost during the time frame covered by the budget. For instance, some expenses are routine and predictable, but others are variable, and some can be almost impossible to predict. Fixed salaries are easy to predict month to month, but energy costs fluctuate—sometimes wildly so. In some cases, companies can protect themselves against future price increases by **hedging**, arranging contracts that allow them to buy supplies in the future at designated prices. The obvious risk of hedging against rising prices is that prices could instead drop, leaving a company paying more than it would have to otherwise. Chapter 19 addresses hedging in more detail.

EXHIBIT 18.4	**Budgeting Challenges**

Budgeting can be a tough challenge that requires difficult choices; here are three big issues managers usually face.

1. Every company has a limited amount of money to spend.
- Projects and departments are often in competition for resources.
- Managers need to make tough choices, occasionally taking money from one group and giving it to another.

2. Revenues and costs are often difficult to predict.
- Sales forecasts are never certain, particularly for new products or for sales into new markets.
- Fixed costs are easy to predict, but variable costs can be hard to predict, particularly more than a few months out.

3. It's not always clear how much should be spent.
- With some expenses, such as advertising, managers aren't always sure how much is enough.
- Uncertainty leads to budgeting based on past expenditures, which might be out of line with current strategic needs.

Another alternative is *rolling forecasts,* in which the company starts the year with a budget based on revenue and cost assumptions made at that point but then reviews economic performance every month or every quarter to see whether the budget needs to be modified as the year progresses.[5]

Volatile situations can make conventional forecasting a dicey proposition because planners often can't make solid assumptions about major factors in their forecasting models. A useful approach in these circumstances is *scenario planning,* in which managers identify two or more possible ways that events could unfold—different scenarios, that is—and have a budgetary response ready for each one. Scenario planning is particularly valuable for long-range planning because the longer the time frame, the harder it is to pin down revenues and costs with any degree of accuracy.

Third, even if they can predict how much revenue will come in or how much various things will cost, managers can't always be sure how much they *should* spend in each part of the budget. A common practice is to take the amounts spent the previous year and raise or lower them by some amount to arrive at this year's budget. This method is simple, but it can produce seriously flawed numbers by ignoring real-world inputs. It also encourages a mentality of "use it or lose it": At the end of the year, managers hurriedly spend any remaining money in their budgets, even if doing so doesn't make financial sense, because they know that if they don't spend it all, their budgets will be reduced for the next year.

A more responsive approach is **zero-based budgeting**, in which each department starts from zero every year and must justify every item in the budget.[6] This approach forces each department to show how the money it wants to spend will support the overall strategic plan. The downside to zero-based budgeting is the amount of time it takes. One practical alternative is a hybrid approach in which zero-basing is reserved for those areas of the budget with the greatest flexibility, such as advertising and various development projects.[7]

TYPES OF BUDGETS

A company can have up to four types of budgets, depending on the nature and age of its business:

- Before a new company starts business, the entrepreneurial team assembles a **start-up budget**, or *launch budget*, that identifies all the money it will need to "get off the

zero-based budgeting
A budgeting approach in which each department starts from zero every year and must justify every item in the budget, rather than simply adjusting the previous year's budget amounts.

start-up budget
A budget that identifies the money a new company will need to spend to launch operations.

operating budget

Also known as the *master budget*, a budget that identifies all sources of revenue and coordinates the spending of those funds throughout the coming year.

capital budget

A budget that outlines expenditures for real estate, new facilities, major equipment, and other capital investments.

capital investments

Money paid to acquire something of permanent value in a business.

project budget

A budget that identifies the costs needed to accomplish a particular project.

ground." A major concern at this stage is the *burn rate*, which is the rate at which the company is using up the funds from its initial investors. If the burn rate is too high, the firm risks running out of money before it can start generating sustainable sales revenues and become self-funding. Start-up budgets can be the most difficult of all because the company doesn't have any operating history to use as a baseline. Feedback from other entrepreneurs, experienced early-stage investors, and advisors such as SCORE executives or business incubators (see page 132) can be invaluable.

- After a company gets through the start-up phase, the financial manager's attention turns to the **operating budget**, sometimes known as the *master budget*, which identifies all sources of revenue and coordinates the spending of those funds throughout the coming year. Operating budgets help financial managers estimate the flow of money into and out of the business by structuring financial plans within a framework of estimated revenues, expenses, and cash flows. The operating budget incorporates any special budgets, such as *capital* and *project budgets*.

- A **capital budget** outlines expenditures for real estate, new facilities, major equipment, and other **capital investments**. For smaller capital purchases, a company might designate a certain percentage of its annual operating budget for capital items every year. Significant capital investments might require planning over the course of multiple years as the company assembles the necessary funds and makes payments on the purchases while maintaining its ongoing operating budget.

- Another special type of budget that has to be coordinated with the operating budget is the **project budget**, which identifies the costs needed to accomplish a particular project, such as conducting the research and development of a new product or moving a company to a new office building. Project managers typically request funding based on their estimates of the cost to complete the project and its value to the company. They then have the responsibility of making sure the project is completed on budget.

✓ **Checkpoint**

LEARNING OBJECTIVE 2: Describe the budgeting process, three major budgeting challenges, and the four major types of budgets.

SUMMARY: A budget is a financial guide for a given time period or project that identifies how much money will be needed and where and when it will be spent. Budgeting often combines top-down mandates, whereby company executives identify how much money each functional area will have to spend, and bottom-up requests, whereby individual division or department managers add up the funding they'll need to meet their respective goals. Three major budgeting challenges are (1) reconciling the competing demands on the finite amount of money the company has to spend, (2) trying to predict future costs, (3) and deciding how much to spend in each area of the budget. Four major types of budgets are the *start-up budget*, which guides companies during the launch phase of a new company; the *operating* or *master budget*, which outlines all spending during a given time period (typically a year) and incorporates various special budgets; the *capital budget*, which plans expenditures on major capital purchases; and the *project budget*, which guides spending on projects such as new product launches.

CRITICAL THINKING: (1) What are some of the risks of failing to create and manage budgets? (2) How does zero-based budgeting help a company spend its cash in the most effective ways possible?

IT'S YOUR BUSINESS: (1) What steps would you take to identify the costs of a two-week trip to Scotland next summer? (2) Assume that you need to raise $3,000 between now and graduation for a down payment on a car. How would budgeting and financial control help you meet this objective?

KEY TERMS TO KNOW: budget, financial control, hedging, zero-based budgeting, start-up budget, operating budget, capital budget, capital investments, project budget

Financing Alternatives: Factors to Consider

Every firm's need for cash and its ability to get money from various external sources is unique, and it's up to financial executives to find the right source or combination of sources. This section explores the factors that finance managers consider when they are looking for outside funds, and the next three sections cover the three major categories of financing: short-term debt, long-term debt, and equity.

DEBT FINANCING VERSUS EQUITY FINANCING

The most fundamental decision a company faces regarding financing is whether it will obtain funds by **debt financing**, which is borrowing money, or by **equity financing**, which is selling ownership shares in the company. (And as you'll recall from Chapter 6, crowdfunding can have elements of either approach, depending on how it is structured.) To meet their changing needs over time, many firms use a combination of debt and equity financing, and many use several kinds of debt financing at the same time for different purposes.

Note that business debt usually doesn't have the same negative connotations as consumer debt. Whereas consumers are advised to avoid most kinds of debt if at all possible, and being in debt is often a sign of financial trouble or financial mismanagement, robust and well-run businesses of all shapes and sizes use debt as a routine element of financial management. The key difference is that—unlike with nearly all consumer debt other than loans for education—businesses can make money by borrowing money. Of course, companies can get into debt trouble through bad choices and bad luck, just as consumers can, and it's up to financial managers to make smart borrowing choices.

When choosing between debt and equity financing, companies consider a variety of issues, including the prevailing interest rates, maturity, the claim on income, the claim on assets, and the desire for ownership control. Exhibit 18.5 summarizes these considerations.

3 LEARNING OBJECTIVE

Compare the advantages and disadvantages of debt and equity financing, and explain the two major considerations in choosing from financing alternatives.

debt financing
Arranging funding by borrowing money.

equity financing
Arranging funding by selling ownership shares in the company, publicly or privately.

REAL-TIME UPDATES
Learn More by Visiting This Website

The latest coverage of crowdfunding

Inc. magazine can keep you up to date on this emerging funding strategy. Go to http://real-timeupdates.com/bia8 and click on Learn More in the Students section.

EXHIBIT 18.5	Debt Versus Equity Financing

When choosing between debt and equity financing, companies evaluate the characteristics of both types of funding.

Characteristic	Debt Financing	Equity Financing
Maturity	**Specific:** In most cases, specifies a date by which debt must be repaid.	**N/A:** Equity funding does not need to be repaid.
Claim on income	**Nondiscretionary, usually a recurring cost and usually fixed:** Debt obligations must be repaid, regardless of whether the company is profitable; payments can be regular (e.g., monthly), balloon (repaid all at once), or a combination.	**Discretionary cost:** At management's discretion and if company is profitable, shareholders may receive dividends after creditors have been paid; however, company is not required to pay dividends.
Claim on assets	**Priority:** Lenders have prior claims on assets.	**Residual:** Shareholders have claims only after the firm satisfies claims of lenders.
Influence over management	**Usually little:** Lenders usually have no influence over management unless debit vehicles come with conditions or management fails to make payments on time.	**Varies:** As owners of the company, shareholders can vote on some aspects of corporate operations, although in practice only large shareholders have much influence. Private equity holders (such as venture capitalists) can have considerable influence.
Tax consequences	**Deductible:** Debt payments reduce taxable income, lowering tax obligations.	**Not deductible:** Dividend payments are not tax deductible.
Employee benefit potential	**N/A:** Does not create any opportunities for compensation alternatives such as stock options.	**Stock options:** Issuing company shares creates the opportunity to use stock options as a motivation or retention tool.

Of course, not every firm has access to every financing option, and sometimes companies have to take whatever they can get. For instance, only companies that are already public or are prepared to go public (see "Public Stock Offerings" on page 438) can raise funds by selling shares on the open market. Similarly, as you'll read in the sections on debt financing, some debt options are not available to small companies.

LENGTH OF TERM

short-term financing
Financing used to cover current expenses (generally repaid within a year).

long-term financing
Financing used to cover long-term expenses such as assets (generally repaid over a period of more than one year).

Financing can be either short term or long term. **Short-term financing** is financing that will be repaid within one year, whereas **long-term financing** is financing that will be repaid in a period longer than one year. The primary purpose of short-term financing is to ensure that a company maintains its liquidity, or its ability to meet financial obligations (such as inventory payments) as they become due. By contrast, long-term financing is used to acquire long-term assets such as buildings and equipment or to fund expansion via any number of growth options.

COST OF CAPITAL

cost of capital
The average rate of interest a firm pays on its combination of debt and equity.

In general, a company wants to obtain money at the lowest cost and with the least amount of risk. However, lenders and investors want to receive the highest possible return on their investment, also at the lowest risk. A company's **cost of capital** is the average rate of interest it must pay on its debt and equity financing. For any form of financing to make economic sense, the expected returns must exceed the cost of capital. Consequently, financial managers study capital costs carefully in relation to the intended uses of those funds. At the same time, the potential sources of external funds, from banks to stock market investors to suppliers who sell on credit, also analyze a company's plans and prospects to determine whether helping the company is a safe and sensible use of their capital.

During the recent credit crisis, when sources of available credit shrunk dramatically and the limited credit that was available became quite expensive, most companies were forced to rethink their approaches to financing.

Cost of capital depends on three main factors: the risk associated with the company, the prevailing level of interest rates, and management's selection of funding vehicles.

Risk

Lenders that provide money to businesses expect their returns to be in proportion to the two types of risk they face: the quality and length of time of the venture. Obviously, the more financially solid a company is, the less risk investors face and the less money they will demand in compensation. Just as with consumer credit, in which protecting your *credit score* is vital to securing credit at reasonable rates, companies must also guard their reputations as being good credit and investment risks.

In addition to perceived risk, time also plays a vital role. Because a dollar will be worth less tomorrow than it is today, lenders need to be compensated for waiting to be repaid. As a result, for a given type of debt, long-term financing generally costs a company more than short-term financing.

Interest Rates

prime interest rate
The lowest rate of interest that banks charge for short-term loans to their most creditworthy customers.

Regardless of how financially solid a company is, the cost of money will vary over time because interest rates fluctuate. The **prime interest rate** (often called simply the *prime*) is the lowest interest rate offered on short-term bank loans to preferred borrowers. The prime changes irregularly and, at times, quite frequently. Sometimes it changes because of supply and demand; at other times it changes because the prime rate is closely tied to the *discount rate*, the interest rate that the Federal Reserve charges on loans to commercial banks and other depository institutions (see page 474 in Chapter 20).

Companies must take such interest rate fluctuations into account when making financing decisions. For instance, a company planning to finance a short-term project when the prime rate is 3 percent would want to reevaluate the project if the prime rose to 6 percent a few months later. Even though companies try to time their borrowing to take advantage of drops in interest rates, this option is not always possible. A firm's need for money doesn't always coincide with a period of favorable rates. At times, a company may be forced to borrow when rates are high and then renegotiate the loan when rates drop. Sometimes projects must be put on hold until interest rates become more affordable.

Opportunity Cost

Using a company's own cash to finance its growth has one chief attraction: No interest payments are required. Nevertheless, such internal financing is not free; using money for any particular purpose has an *opportunity cost*, defined in Chapter 2 as the value of the most appealing alternative from among those that weren't chosen. For instance, a company might be better off investing its excess cash in external opportunities, such as stocks of other companies, and borrowing money to finance its own growth. Doing so makes sense as long as the company can earn a greater *rate of return* (the percentage increase in the value of an investment) on those investments than the rate of interest paid on borrowed money. This concept is called **leverage** because the loan acts like a lever: It magnifies the power of the borrower to generate profits (see Exhibit 18.6).

However, leverage works both ways: Borrowing may magnify your losses as well as your gains. Because most companies require some degree of external financing from time to time, the issue is not so much whether to use outside money; rather, it's a question of how much should be raised, by what means, and when. The answers to such questions determine the firm's **capital structure**, which is the total mix of debt and equity it uses to meet its short- and long-term needs.

leverage
The technique of increasing the rate of return on an investment by financing it with borrowed funds.

capital structure
A firm's mix of debt and equity financing.

EXHIBIT 18.6   Financial Leverage

Leverage can be your best friend if investments work out well—or it can be your worst enemy if they don't. Assume that you have $10,000 of your own funds to invest in the stock market or some business venture. You also have the opportunity to borrow an additional $50,000 at 6 percent interest. Should you invest just your own $10,000 or leverage your investment by borrowing the $50,000 so you can invest $60,000 instead? If the investment returns 12 percent after a year, you'll earn a healthy $1,200 if you invest just your own money. But with leverage, you would earn more than three and a half times that amount, even after you pay the cost of borrowing the $50,000. However, look at what happens if the investment turns sour. If it loses 12 percent that first year instead, the leveraging will wipe out your entire $10,000.

No leverage; 12% return			5x leverage; 12% return	
Funds	$10,000		Funds	$10,000
Debt	$0		Debt	$50,000
Total to invest	$10,000		Total to invest	$60,000
Annual return (12%)	$1,200		Annual return (12%)	$7,200
Cost of debt	$0		Cost of debt (6%)	($3,000)
Profit (loss)	$1,200		Profit (loss)	$4,200
No leverage; –12% return			**5x leverage; –12% return**	
Funds	$10,000		Funds	$10,000
Debt	$0		Debt	$50,000
Total to invest	$10,000		Total to invest	$60,000
Annual return (–12%)	($1,200)		Annual return (–12%)	($7,200)
Cost of debt	$0		Cost of debt (6%)	($3,000)
Profit (loss)	($1,200)		Profit (loss)	($10,200)

Checkpoint

LEARNING OBJECTIVE 3: Compare the advantages and disadvantages of debt and equity financing, and explain the two major considerations in choosing from financing alternatives.

SUMMARY: Debt financing offers a variety of funding alternatives and is available to a wider range of companies than equity financing. It also doesn't subject management to outside influence the way equity financing does, and debt payments reduce a company's tax obligations. On the downside, except for trade credit, debt financing always puts a demand on cash flow, so finance managers need to consider whether a company can handle debt payments. The major advantages of equity financing are the fact that the money doesn't have to be paid back and the resulting discretionary drain on cash flow (publicly held companies don't have to pay regular dividends if they choose not to). The major disadvantages are the dilution of management control and the fact that equity financing—public equity financing in particular—is not available to many firms. The two major considerations in choosing financing alternatives are *length of term* (the duration of the financing) and *cost of capital* (the average cost to a company of all its debt and equity financing).

CRITICAL THINKING: (1) What factors might lead a company to gain additional funds through debt financing rather than through equity financing? (2) Why does consumer debt have a more negative connotation than business debt?

IT'S YOUR BUSINESS: (1) Do you know your credit score, or have you ever looked at your credit report? To learn more about free credit reports, visit www.ftc.gov/freereports. (2) How should the cost of capital figure into your decisions about attending college, buying cars, and buying housing?

KEY TERMS TO KNOW: debt financing, equity financing, short-term financing, long-term financing, cost of capital, prime interest rate, leverage, capital structure

---

4 LEARNING OBJECTIVE

Identify the major categories of short-term debt financing.

Financing Alternatives: Short-Term Debt

Financial managers have a number of options when it comes to short-term debt financing, including *credit cards, trade credit, secured loans, unsecured loans, commercial paper*, and an alternative to borrowing known as *factoring* (see Exhibit 18.7).

CREDIT CARDS

As Chapter 6 notes, half of all small companies and start-ups use credit cards to help fund their operations. Credit cards are one of the most expensive forms of financing, but they are sometimes the only form available to business owners, particularly in the early stages of a company's growth. If they are used judiciously and only as a short-term measure, credit cards can be a viable way to provide some of the financing a company needs. However, just as with personal use of cards, funding a company this way can quickly spiral out of control and leave an entrepreneur buried under an avalanche of expensive debt.

TRADE CREDIT

trade credit
Credit obtained by a purchaser directly from a supplier.

Trade credit, often called *open-account purchasing*, occurs when suppliers provide goods and services to their customers without requiring immediate payment. Such transactions create the accounts receivable defined on page 407. From the buyer's perspective, trade credit allows a company to get the goods and services it needs without immediately disrupting its cash flow. Trade credit can also lower transaction costs for buyers (as well as sellers) by consolidating multiple purchases into a single payment. In many cases, credit is extended at no interest for a short period (typically 30 days).

From the seller's perspective, offering credit terms is often a competitive necessity, and doing so can allow a supplier to sell more to each customer because purchase levels

EXHIBIT 18.7	Sources of Short-Term Debt Financing

Businesses have a variety of short-term debt financing options, each with advantages and disadvantages.

Source	Funding Mechanism	Length of Term	Advantages	Disadvantages and Limitations
Credit cards	Essentially creates a short-term loan every time cardholder makes purchases or gets a cash advance	Revolving (no fixed repayment date)	Widely available; convenient; no external scrutiny of individual purchases	High interest rates; availability decreasing since the credit crunch; ease of use and lack of external scrutiny can lead to overuse
Trade credit	Allows buyer to make purchases without immediately paying for them	Typically 30 to 90 days	Usually free (no interest) as long as payment is made by due date; enables purchaser to manage cash flow more easily; consolidates multiple purchases into a single payment	Buyer often needs to establish a payment history with seller before credit will be extended; availability and terms vary from seller to seller; some sellers may require promissory note and charge interest
Secured loans	Lender provides cash using borrower's assets (such as inventory or equipment) as collateral; also known as *asset-based loans*	Up to 1 year (for short-term loans)	Can provide financing for companies that don't qualify for unsecured loans or other alternatives	More expensive than some other options
Unsecured loans	Lender provides lump sum of cash via a promissory note or on-demand access to cash via a credit line	Up to 1 year (for short-term loans)	Provides cash or access to cash without requiring borrower to pledge assets as collateral	Cost varies according to borrower's credit rating; often not available to customers with unproven or poor credit history
Commercial paper	Participating in the global *money market*, large institutional investors provide unsecured, short-term loans to corporations	Up to 270 days (longer in special cases)	Less expensive and less trouble to get than conventional loans; can generate very large amounts of cash fairly quickly, from $100,000 to many millions	Available only to large corporations with strong credit ratings; proceeds can only be used to purchase current assets, not fixed assets
Factoring	Company sells its accounts receivable to an intermediary that collects from the customer	N/A	Frees up working capital; makes cash flow more predictable; can provide some protection from bad debts and customer bankruptcies; often can be arranged more quickly than a loan	Expensive (annualized costs can be 30–40 percent)

aren't constrained to buyers' immediate cash balances. However, like all other forms of credit, trade credit involves costs and risks. Allowing customers to delay payments affects the seller's cash flow and exposes it to the risk that some customers won't be able to pay when their bills come due. Extending trade credit can also reduce the company's own credit worthiness because lenders will look at how quickly it is closing its accounts receivable. Companies that offer trade credit should be sure to check the credit worthiness of all buyers, keep credit limits low for new customers until they establish a reliable payment history, and keep a close eye on every customer's payment status.[8]

SECURED LOANS

Secured loans are those backed by something of value, known as **collateral**, that may be seized by the lender in the event that the borrower fails to repay the loan. Common types of collateral include property, equipment, accounts receivable, inventories, and securities.

UNSECURED LOANS

Unsecured loans are ones that require no collateral. Instead, the lender relies on the general credit record and the earning power of the borrower. To increase the returns on such loans and to obtain some protection in case of default, most lenders insist that the borrower maintain some minimum amount of money on deposit at the bank—a **compensating balance**—while the loan is outstanding.

A common example of an unsecured loan is a **line of credit**, which is an agreed-on maximum amount of money a bank is willing to lend a business. Once a line of credit

secured loans
Loans backed up with assets that the lender can claim in case of default, such as a piece of property.

collateral
A tangible asset a lender can claim if a borrower defaults on a loan.

unsecured loans
Loans that require a good credit rating but no collateral.

compensating balance
The portion of an unsecured loan that is kept on deposit at a lending institution to protect the lender and increase the lender's return.

line of credit
An arrangement in which a financial institution makes money available for use at any time after the loan has been approved.

has been established, the business may obtain unsecured loans for any amount up to that limit. The key advantage of a line of credit over a regular loan is that interest (or at least full interest) is usually not charged on the untapped amount.

COMMERCIAL PAPER

commercial paper
Short-term *promissory notes*, or contractual agreements, to repay a borrowed amount by a specified time with a specified interest rate.

When businesses need a sizable amount of money for a short period of time, they can issue **commercial paper**—short-term *promissory notes*, or contractual agreements, to repay a borrowed amount by a specified time with a specified interest rate. Commercial paper is usually sold only by major corporations with strong credit ratings, in denominations of $100,000 or more and with maturities of up to 270 days (the maximum allowed by the Securities and Exchange Commission [SEC] without a formal registration process).[9] Commercial paper is normally issued to secure funds for short-term needs such as buying supplies and paying rent rather than for financing major expansion projects. Because the amounts are generally large, these notes are usually purchased by various investment funds and not by individual investors.

FACTORING AND RECEIVABLES AUCTIONS

factoring
Obtaining funding by selling accounts receivable.

Businesses with slow-paying trade credit customers—some organizational buyers can take months to pay their bills—have the option of selling their accounts receivable, a method known as **factoring**. Factoring can help companies with a variety of cash-flow challenges, including big swings in seasonal revenue, a shortage of working capital relative to growth needs, and long manufacturing cycles that delay the availability of new inventory to sell.[10] Although it's not really a form of borrowing in the conventional sense, factoring is an alternative to short-term debt financing.

Factoring involves several steps. First, a *factor* or *factoring agent* purchases a company's receivables, paying the company a percentage of the total outstanding amount, typically 70 to 90 percent. Second, the factoring agent collects the amounts owed, freeing the company from the administrative tasks of collection. Third, after a customer pays the factor, the factor makes a second payment to the company, keeping a percentage as a fee for its services. Some factors assume the risk that customers won't ever pay (and their fees are naturally higher), whereas others don't, in which case the company has to refund the initial payment it received from the factor.[11]

The use of factoring has increased in recent years, particularly as banks and other lenders have reduced the level of credit that many businesses rely on to manage cash flow. Because it is a comparatively expensive method, factoring is generally best suited for profitable, growing companies with pressing cash flow needs and large, creditworthy customers (businesses or government agencies, not consumers) that are likely to pay their bills but are just slow in doing so.[12] Particularly for companies that sell to retailers, factoring is sometimes a necessity because they have contracts that require them to keep retailers supplied with inventory on a regular schedule and need the cash flow to do so.[13]

An innovative twist on factoring is the *receivables auction*, pioneered by Receivables Exchange (**www.recx.com**). Using an online format somewhat like eBay and other auction sites, companies post their receivables for investors to bid on. Those who offer the best combination of funding amount and fees win the business, and the sellers get their money within a short period of time.[14]

> ## ✔ Checkpoint
>
> **LEARNING OBJECTIVE 4: Identify the major categories of short-term debt financing.**
>
> **SUMMARY:** The major categories of short-term debt financing are *credit cards*, *trade credit* (the option to delay paying for purchases for 30 to 60 days or more), *secured loans* (loans backed by sellable assets such as land, equipment, or inventory), *unsecured loans* (loans and lines of credit extended solely on the borrower's creditworthiness), *commercial paper* (short-term promissory notes issued by major corporations), and *factoring* (selling a firm's accounts payable to a third-party financer; strictly speaking, not a form of debt financing).

CRITICAL THINKING: (1) How does getting a secured loan using accounts receivable as collateral differ from factoring? (2) Why would any seller offer trade financing, since it ties up working capital without generating any income through interest payments?

IT'S YOUR BUSINESS: (1) Would you launch a new company if the only way to finance it was through the use of your personal credit cards? Why or why not? (2) Which of the short-term debt alternatives identified in this section are available to you as a consumer?

KEY TERMS TO KNOW: trade credit, secured loans, collateral, unsecured loans, compensating balance, line of credit, commercial paper, factoring

Financing Alternatives: Long-Term Debt

5 **LEARNING OBJECTIVE**

Identify the major categories of long-term debt financing.

In addition to the various short-term debt alternatives, numerous long-term debt financing options are available as well. Although some of them are similar in concept to short-term debt, the longer time spans create a different set of decisions for both borrowers and lenders. The most common long-term debt alternatives are *long-term loans, leases,* and *corporate bonds* (see Exhibit 18.8).

LONG-TERM LOANS

Long-term loans, sometimes called *term loans,* can have maturities between 1 and 25 years or so, depending on the lender and the purpose of the loan. (Some lenders designate loans with maturities between 1 and 3 years as *intermediate-term loans.*[15]) Common reasons for taking out long-term loans are to buy real estate, to build or expand facilities, to acquire other companies, to purchase equipment or inventory, to refinance existing debt at lower interest rates, or to provide working capital.[16] Long-term loans on real estate are called *mortgages.*

Long-term loans can be an attractive option for borrowers because such loans can provide substantial capital without the need to sell equity in the company. However, because they tie up a lender's capital for a long period of time and usually involve large sums

EXHIBIT 18.8	Sources of Long-Term Debt Financing

Long-term debt financing can provide funds for major asset purchases and other investments needed to help companies grow.

Source	Funding Mechanism	Length of Term	Advantages	Disadvantages and Limitations
Long-term loans	Bank or other lender provides cash; borrower agrees to repay according to specific terms	From 1 to 25 years	Can provide substantial sums of money without diluting ownership through sale of equity; allows company to make major purchases of inventory, equipment, and other vital assets	Not all companies can qualify for loans and acceptable terms; payments tie up part of cash flow for the duration of the loan; purchases made via loans require substantial down payments
Leases	Company earns the right to use an asset in exchange for regular payments; arrangement can be directly between lessor and lessee or can involve a third party such as a bank	Typically several years for equipment and vehicles; longer for real estate	Usually require lower down payments than loans; can provide access to essential assets for companies that don't qualify for loans; let company avoid buying assets that are likely to decline in value or become obsolete; often free company from maintenance and other recurring costs	Can restrict how assets can be used; company doesn't gain any equity in return for lease payments, except in the case of lease-to-own arrangements; can be more expensive than borrowing to buy
Corporate bonds	Company sells bonds to investors, with the promise to pay interest and repay the principle according to a set schedule	Typically from 10 to 30 years	Can generate more cash with longer repayment terms than are possible with loans	Available only to large companies with strong credit ratings

REAL-TIME UPDATES
Learn More by Visiting This Website

Debt financing programs at the Small Business Administration

The Small Business Administration operates several short- and long-term debt financing programs. Go to http://real-timeupdates .com/bia8 and click on Learn More in the Students section.

of money, lending standards tend to be fairly stringent and not all companies can qualify. Lenders usually look at "the five Cs" when considering applications for these loans:[17]

- **Character.** This aspect includes not only the personal and professional character of the company owners but also their experience and qualifications to run the type of business for which they plan to use the loan proceeds.
- **Capacity.** To judge the company's capacity or ability to repay the loan, lenders scrutinize debt ratios, liquidity ratios, and other measures of financial health. For small businesses, the owners' personal finances are also evaluated.
- **Capital.** Lenders want to know how well *capitalized* the company is—that is, whether it has enough capital to succeed. For small-business loans in particular, lenders want to know how much money the owners themselves have already invested in the business.
- **Conditions.** Lenders look at the overall condition of the economy as well as conditions within the applicant's specific industry to determine whether they are comfortable with the business's plans and capabilities.
- **Collateral.** Long-term loans are usually secured with collateral of some kind. Lenders expect to be repaid from the borrower's cash flow, but in case that is inadequate, they look for assets that could be used to repay the loan, such as real estate or equipment.

An old joke about applying for bank loans suggests that the only way to qualify for a loan is to prove you don't need the money. This is an exaggeration, of course, but it is grounded in fact. Before they will part with their capital, responsible lenders want a high degree of assurance that they'll get their money back.

LEASES

lease
An agreement to use an asset in exchange for regular payment; similar to renting.

Rather than borrow money to purchase an asset, a firm may enter into a **lease**, under which the owner of an asset (the *lessor*) allows another party (the *lessee*) to use it in exchange for regular payments. (Leasing is similar to renting; a key difference is that leases fix the terms of the agreement for a specific amount of time.) Leases are commonly used for real estate, major equipment, and vehicles. In some cases, the lease arrangement is made directly between the asset owner and the lessee. In other cases, a bank or other financial firm provides leasing services to its clients and takes care of payments to the lessor.

Leasing may be a good alternative for a company that has difficulty obtaining a loan because of a poor credit rating or that is unwilling or unable to use its working capital for a down payment on a loan. A creditor is more willing to provide a lease than a loan because, should the company fail, the lessor need not worry about a default on loan payments; it can simply repossess the asset it legally owns. Some firms use leases to finance significant portions of their assets, particularly in industries such as airlines, where assets are mostly large, expensive pieces of equipment. Leasing can also provide more flexibility than purchasing through a loan. For instance, a growing company with expanding office space requirements can lease additional space when needed without the cost and delay of buying and selling real estate.

Companies can choose to lease equipment to avoid tying up capital through purchasing.

CORPORATE BONDS

bonds
A method of funding in which the issuer borrows from an investor and provides a written promise to make regular interest payments and repay the borrowed amount in the future.

When a company needs to borrow a large sum of money, it may not be able to get the entire amount from a single source. Under such circumstances, it may try to borrow from many individual investors by issuing **bonds**—certificates that obligate the company to repay a certain sum, plus interest, to the bondholder on a specific date. (Note that although bondholders buy bonds, they are acting as lenders.)

Companies issue a variety of corporate bonds. **Secured bonds**, like secured loans, are backed by company-owned property (such as airplanes or plant equipment) that passes to the bondholders if the issuer does not repay the amount borrowed. *Mortgage bonds*, one type of secured bond, are backed by real property owned by the issuing corporation. **Debentures** are unsecured bonds, backed only by the corporation's promise to pay. Because debentures are riskier than other types of bonds, the companies that issue them must pay higher interest rates to attract buyers. **Convertible bonds** can be exchanged at the investor's option for a certain number of shares of the corporation's common stock. Because of this feature, convertible bonds generally pay lower interest rates.

Of course, organizations that issue bonds must eventually repay the borrowed amount to the bondholders. Normally, this repayment is done when the bonds mature, but the cost of retiring the debt can be staggering because bonds are generally issued in quantity—perhaps thousands of individual bonds in a single issue. To ease the cash flow burden of redeeming its bonds all at once, a company can issue *serial bonds*, which mature at various times, as opposed to *term bonds*, which mature all at the same time.

Another way of relieving the financial strain of retiring many bonds at once is to set up a *sinking fund*. When a corporation issues a bond payable by a sinking fund, it must set aside a certain sum of money each year to pay the debt. This money may be used to retire a few bonds each year, or it may be set aside to accumulate until the issue matures.

With most bond issues, a corporation retains the right to pay off the bonds before maturity. Bonds containing this provision are known as *callable bonds*, or *redeemable bonds*. If a company issues bonds when interest rates are high and then rates fall later on, it may want to pay off its high-interest bonds and sell a new issue at a lower rate. However, this feature carries a price tag: Investors must be offered a higher interest rate to encourage them to buy callable bonds.

Corporate bonds, as well as bonds issued by various government bodies, are discussed from an investor's perspective in Chapter 19.

secured bonds
Bonds backed by specific assets that will be given to bondholders if the borrowed amount is not repaid.

debentures
Corporate bonds backed only by the reputation of the issuer.

convertible bonds
Corporate bonds that can be exchanged at the owner's discretion into common stock of the issuing company.

 Checkpoint

LEARNING OBJECTIVE 5: Identify the major categories of long-term debt financing.

SUMMARY: The three major categories of long-term debt financing are *long-term loans* (substantial amounts of capital for major purchases or other needs, on terms up to 25 years, usually secured by assets), *leases* (similar to renting, conferring the rights to use an asset in exchange for regular payments), and *bonds* (certificates that obligate the company to repay a specified sum, plus interest, to the bondholder on a specific date).

CRITICAL THINKING: (1) How could rates of technological change affect a company's decision about whether to buy or lease equipment, vehicles, and other assets? (2) Why would lenders want to see that a business already has some level of capitalization before giving it access to more capital by means of a loan?

IT'S YOUR BUSINESS: (1) If you have just moved to a new city to start a new job, would you prefer to lease or rent an apartment? Why? (2) Assume you are in the market for a new car. Will you lease or buy? Why?

KEY TERMS TO KNOW: lease, bonds, secured bonds, debentures, convertible bonds

Financing Alternatives: Equity

6   LEARNING OBJECTIVE

Describe the two options for equity financing, and explain how companies prepare an initial public offering.

The most far-reaching alternative for securing funds is to sell shares of ownership in a company. Even the most thorough loan application reviews and strict repayment terms can't match the degree to which selling equity changes the way a company is managed. In the most extreme cases, selling equity can lead to the founders of a firm being ousted from the company. Even when owners retain control, equity financing can complicate operations by adding new layers of public scrutiny and accountability. Moreover, the process of obtaining equity financing is expensive and time-consuming, so even companies that could obtain it don't always choose to do so—and some that sell equity to the public choose to reverse the decision by buying it back.

With all these caveats, why would any company bother with equity financing? The answer is the tremendous upside potential for the company as a whole and for any individual or organization that owns shares. Equity financing has fueled the growth of most of the major corporations in the world, and it has contributed to the financial security of millions of employees (and made millionaires out of thousands of employees, too). Plus, unlike with debt financing, selling stock can continue to generate money for years if share prices continue to increase.

Although this option is available to only a small fraction of companies, it is one of the most powerful forms of financing. Moreover, it directly and indirectly plays a huge role in the economy by giving both individual and institutional investors the opportunity to increase their own capital by investing in company shares. This section takes a quick look at the private and public varieties of equity financing, while Chapter 19 discusses equities from an investor's point of view.

VENTURE CAPITAL AND OTHER PRIVATE EQUITY

As Chapter 6 points out, venture capitalists (VCs), as well as angel investors for companies that aren't yet ready for VC funding, are a key source of equity financing for a certain class of start-up companies. In exchange for a share of ownership, VCs can invest millions of dollars in companies long before those firms can qualify for most other forms of financing, so they represent an essential form of funding for high-growth ventures. VCs also provide managerial expertise and industry connections that can be crucial to new companies.

However, VCs are one of the most specialized and least widely available forms of funding, and most firms have no chance of getting venture capital. VCs typically look for privately held firms that are already well established enough to be able to use a significant amount of money and are positioned to grow aggressively enough to give the VCs a good shot at eventually selling their interests at an acceptable profit. Not all VC-backed firms grow enough to pay back their investors, so to compensate for losses from some investments, VCs rely on getting very high returns from a handful of winners.

private equity
Ownership assets that aren't publicly traded; includes venture capital.

Venture capital is a specialized form of funding known as **private equity** (ownership assets that aren't publicly traded), and other forms of private equity can provide funding for companies that are beyond the start-up stage. For instance, the leveraged buyouts discussed in Chapter 5 are usually done with private equity funds. Other uses of private equity are taking companies private by buying up all publicly held shares and rescuing companies that are on the verge of bankruptcy.

PUBLIC STOCK OFFERINGS

Going public—offering shares of stock to the public through a stock market such as the New York Stock Exchange—can generate millions or even billions of dollars in funding. As you can read in the Behind the Scenes wrap-up starting on page 440, this is the financing path Visa chose, and its initial public offering (IPO) raised a record $19.6 billion.[18]

However, going public is not for the faint of heart. The process takes months of management time and attention, can cost several million dollars, and exposes the company to rigorous scrutiny (which isn't necessarily a bad thing, of course). Complaining that the process had become too difficult in the wake of tighter oversight of public companies, former PayPal CEO Peter Thiel once remarked, "Going public today is a process I wouldn't wish upon my worst enemy."[19] Moreover, companies have no assurance that efforts to go public will pay off. Some offerings fail to sell at the hoped-for share price, and some offerings are withdrawn before going public because their backers don't think the market conditions are strong enough. Like the economy as a whole, the market for IPOs runs in cycles, and timing an IPO is one of the key factors for success (see Exhibit 18.9).

EXHIBIT 18.9   **Global IPO Activity**

The number of initial public offerings (IPOs) tends to track the stock market's ups and downs. This graph compares global IPO activity with the year-end level of the S&P 500 Index, a common composite measure of stock market values.

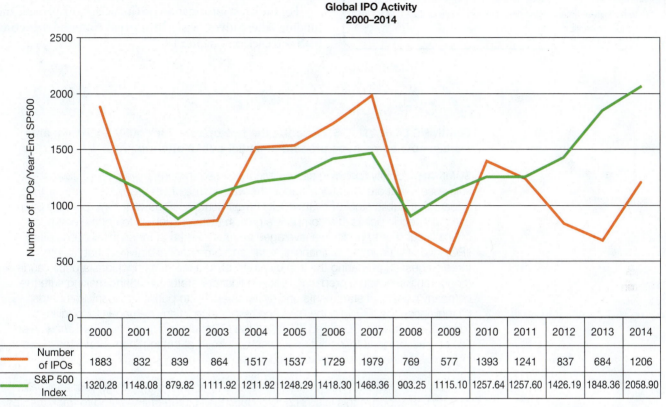

**Global IPO Activity
2000–2014**

	2000	2001	2002	2003	2004	2005	2006	2007	2008	2009	2010	2011	2012	2013	2014
Number of IPOs	1883	832	839	864	1517	1537	1729	1979	769	577	1393	1241	837	684	1206
S&P 500 Index	1320.28	1148.08	879.82	1111.92	1211.92	1248.29	1418.30	1468.36	903.25	1115.10	1257.64	1257.60	1426.19	1848.36	2058.90

Sources: IPO activity from *Global IPO Trends Report 2012, Global IPO Trends Report 2013,* and *Global IPO Trends Report 2014,* Ernst & Young; S&P 500 data from "S&P 500 Index," Google Finance, accessed 21 June 2015, www.google.com/finance.

Despite the costs and risks, the potential rewards are so high that every year thousands of companies around the world attempt to go public. The legal, financial, and promotional steps in the process can be grouped into three phases:[20]

- **Preparing the IPO.** Preparing an offering involves assembling a team of advisors that includes legal experts, a public accounting firm to serve as auditor, and an **underwriter**, a specialized type of bank known as an *investment bank* that buys the shares from the company and sells them to investors. (To spread the risk, a lead underwriter usually assembles a syndicate of other underwriters.) Working with company management, this team prepares required financial statements, organizes a board of directors, hires a public relations firm to begin promoting the upcoming offering, and engages in *due diligence* to make sure the company's financial policies and systems meet the expectations and legal requirements of public ownership.

- **Registering the IPO.** Before a company can sell shares to the public in the United States, it must first register with the SEC. This process includes submitting a **prospectus**, which discloses required information about the company, its finances, and its plans for using the money it hopes to raise. The SEC reviews the information and typically requests modifications and additional information to make the filing conform with all applicable regulations.

- **Selling the IPO.** Before the stock is officially offered for sale, the company and its team promote the offering privately to institutional investors through a series of meetings called the *road show.* Although the IPO is the first "public" offering, shares are usually offered only to institutional investors or selected individual investors before the IPO date. Based on the demand they perceive during the road show, the company and the underwriter decide how to price the IPO shares. After the SEC approves the

underwriter
A specialized type of bank that buys the shares from the company preparing an initial public offering and sells them to investors.

prospectus
A document required by the Securities and Exchange Commission that discloses required information about the company, its finances, and its plans for using the money it hopes to raise.

REAL-TIME UPDATES
Learn More by Visiting This Website

Get the inside scoop on IPO activity

Renaissance Capital is the go-to source for information on IPOs. Go to http://real-timeupdates.com/bia8 and click on Learn More in the Students section.

registration, the stock begins trading on a designated stock exchange, and the company is now officially public.

As with corporate bonds, this chapter's coverage of stocks is from the stock issuer's perspective; Chapter 19 addresses stocks from the investor's perspective.

For the latest information on financial management and funding alternatives, visit **http://real-timeupdates.com/bia8** and click on Chapter 18.

 Checkpoint

LEARNING OBJECTIVE 6: Describe the two options for equity financing, and explain how companies prepare an initial public offering.

SUMMARY: Equity financing can be accomplished through *private equity* (ownership assets that aren't publicly traded the way shares of company stock are) or the issuance of public stock. Private equity investments such as venture capital are often used at specific points in a company's growth history, such as to get the company off the ground or to perform a leveraged buyout. Preparing for an initial public offering (IPO) involves a number of financial, legal, and promotional activities that fall into three stages: (1) preparing the IPO by assembling a team that includes a public auditor and an underwriter, preparing required financial statements, and making sure the company's financial statements and systems are up to public company standards; (2) registering the IPO with the SEC and responding to any demands for additional information from the SEC; and (3) selling the IPO, primarily through a *road show*, a series of presentations to institutional investors aimed at getting them interested in buying blocks of the soon-to-be-released stock.

CRITICAL THINKING: (1) High-tech firms tend to dominate IPO filings year after year; why do you suppose this is so? (2) Why does the volume of IPOs tend to track the ups and downs of the stock market?

IT'S YOUR BUSINESS: (1) If you had the choice between working at a company still in the pre-IPO stage, which is offering a lower salary but a share of ownership that will become shares of company stock after the IPO, or a higher-paying job with no stock, what additional information would you need before you would be comfortable making a choice? (2) Choose any business that you might like to start as an entrepreneur. How would you make a compelling pitch to private equity investors to encourage them to invest in your company?

KEY TERMS TO KNOW: private equity, underwriter, prospectus

BEHIND THE SCENES

VISA FUNDS ITS FUTURE WITH RECORD-SETTING IPO

If ever a company needed a few billion dollars, it was Visa in late 2007. Still operating as a privately held joint venture owned by its member banks, Visa didn't have access to the stock market as a fundraising mechanism. Archrival MasterCard was reaping the benefits of its recent IPO, generating billions of dollars in fresh capital and creating the opportunity to use stock options to recruit and reward employees. Moreover, after settling lawsuits brought against it by merchants and two other credit

card companies, Visa had rung up more than $4 billion in legal liabilities. Plus, the six large banks that made up the primary ownership group within the Visa association were desperately in need of cash to help ride out the recession and credit crunch occurring at the time. On top of these challenges, Visa had to keep investing in new payment-processing systems and technologies as consumers around the world continued to increase their use of conventional credit and debit cards and as promising new opportunities such as mobile commerce were coming up to speed.

An IPO could help solve all these funding dilemmas, but it would prove to be much more complicated than a normal IPO. One of the essential steps was creating a company that could actually go public. In late 2007, Visa Inc. was spun off from the Visa association as a wholly owned subsidiary. This new firm is the company that actually filed the IPO—with the U.S. economy in the depths of the worst downturn since the Great Depression of the 1930s and with the financial services industry in turmoil. One could hardly have picked a worse time to go public, as evidenced by the fact that the normal annual flow of IPOs had slowed to a trickle.

However, Visa had several factors working in its favor. First, with one of the world's best-known brand names and a half-century of growth behind it, Visa didn't need to introduce itself to investors the way most companies do when pitching an IPO. Second, in investor-speak, Visa had a wide "economic moat," meaning its revenue-generating capacity was safeguarded by barriers to entry—including a powerful brand, established relationships with millions of companies worldwide, and a global transaction-processing network—that new market entrants would find hard to overcome. Third, and most important from the timing perspective, Visa isn't really a financial services company in the sense of lending money or issuing credit cards, so it wasn't exposed to the credit meltdown the way banks and credit card companies were. Although it is intertwined with the financial sector, Visa is actually more of a data-processing company than a finance company.

In its prospectus, Visa indicated that it expected to net $16 or $17 billion from the IPO and intended to distribute $10 billion of that to its member institutions, use another $3 billion toward its legal liabilities, and reserve the remaining few billion for general corporate purposes. This was a staggering amount of money to generate in an IPO during the best of times and an almost unimaginable amount to generate during the worst of times.

But that is exactly what Visa did. It went public on March 19, 2008, and broke the record for the largest IPO ever by a U.S. company—more than $19 billion after some optional shares were redeemed by the two lead underwriters on the giant deal, Goldman Sachs and JPMorgan Chase. As both an underwriter earning fees on the IPO and one of the cash-hungry member banks of the Visa association benefiting from the stock sale, JPMorgan Chase made over $1 billion on the deal.

In a turbulent stock market and an even rougher economy over the past several years, Visa's new stock has fared well, all things considered. MasterCard's stock has done slightly better, but both companies were outpacing the overall stock market by a wide margin.

Visa's growth in the coming years stands to benefit from three trends: more transactions are shifting from cash to cards, mobile commerce is on the rise, and credit card use is only just beginning to ramp up in many areas around the world.[21]

Critical Thinking Questions

18-1. How might Visa executives use scenario planning in the budgeting process?

18-2. Could Visa have accomplished its funding goals through short-term or long-term debt financing instead? Why or why not?

18-3. As Visa continues to explore growth opportunities, should it consider becoming a lender by issuing cards itself or lending money to banks that issue cards? Why or why not?

LEARN MORE ONLINE

Visit Visa's website, at **www.visa.com**, and locate the investors section. Has the company reported any significant financial news in the past year? Has it resolved its outstanding legal issues? What were its net income and earnings per share for the more recent fiscal year? Has company management expressed any concerns about ongoing cash flow issues?

KEY TERMS

accounts payable (424)
accounts receivable (424)
bonds (436)
budget (426)
capital budget (428)
capital investments (428)
capital structure (431)
collateral (433)
commercial paper (434)
compensating balance (434)
convertible bonds (437)
cost of capital (430)
debentures (437)
debt financing (429)

equity financing (429)
factoring (434)
financial control (426)
financial management (422)
financial plan (423)
hedging (426)
lease (436)
leverage (431)
line of credit (434)
long-term financing (430)
operating budget (428)
prime interest rate (430)
private equity (438)
project budget (428)

prospectus (439)
risk/return trade-off (423)
secured bonds (437)
secured loans (433)
short-term financing (430)

start-up budget (427)
trade credit (432)
underwriter (439)
unsecured loans (433)
zero-based budgeting (427)

MyBizLab®

To complete the problems with the ⭐,
go to EOC Discussion Questions in the
MyLab.

TEST YOUR KNOWLEDGE

Questions for Review

18-4. What is the primary goal of financial management?

18-5. What types of investments and expenditures are typically considered in the capital budgeting process?

18-6. What is the difference between a secured loan and an unsecured loan?

18-7. What does it mean when someone refers to a company's *capital structure*?

18-8. How can factoring help a company manage its cash flow?

Questions for Analysis

18-9. Would it be wise for a young company that is growing quickly but still hasn't achieved profitability to attempt to issue bonds as a way to expand its working capital? Why or why not?

18-10. Why is careful management of accounts receivable and accounts payable so essential to ensuring positive cash flow?

18-11. Why would a company chose to factor its receivables, given that it will get less money than the receivables are worth?

⭐ **18-12.** Why do lenders often refuse to finance 100 percent of the cost of a purchase, requiring borrowers to make a down payment that covers a portion (typically from 10 to 25 percent) of the purchase price? After all, a lender could potentially earn more by financing the entire purchase amount.

⭐ **18-13.** **Ethical Considerations.** Budget projections always involve a degree of judgment because managers can never predict the future with total accuracy. For instance, one manager with an optimistic view and another with a pessimistic view could look at the same set of facts and arrive at distinctly different conclusions about the company's financial prospects. When budgets will influence decisions made by investors or lenders, how should the people who prepare the budgets deal with the variance between optimistic and pessimistic viewpoints? On the one hand, being too pessimistic could result in lower levels of funding, which could be detrimental to employees, existing investors, existing creditors, and other financial stakeholders. On the other hand, being too optimistic could be detrimental to prospective investors or creditors. How do you find the right balance?

Questions for Application

18-14. The company you cofounded last year is growing rapidly and has strong prospects for an IPO in the next year or two. The additional capital that an IPO could raise would let you hire the brightest people in the industry and continue to innovate with new product research. There is one potential glitch: You and the rest of the executive team have been so focused on launching the business that you haven't paid much attention to financial control. You've had plenty of funds from venture capitalists and early sales, so working capital hasn't been a problem, but an experienced CEO in your industry recently told you that you'll never have a successful IPO unless you clean up the financial side of the house. Your cofounders say they are too busy chasing great opportunities right now, and they want to wait until right before the IPO to hire a seasoned financial executive to put things in order. What should you do and why?

⭐ **18-15.** Why might a company's board of directors decide to lease office space even though it would be more economical to purchase the property and finance it with a long-term loan?

18-16. You're getting ready to expand your woodworking hobby into a full-time business of building custom kitchen cabinets. To create top-quality cabinets, you know you'll need to upgrade from the consumer-grade machinery you have now to industrial-grade equipment. The new equipment will be much more expensive, but, if properly cared for, should last for decades, and you hope to be in business for at least 20 years. If the overall costs of leasing this equipment or borrowing money to buy it are roughly the same, which financing method would you choose? Why?

⭐ **18-17.** **Concept Integration.** Review the definitions of current and fixed assets in Chapter 17 (see page 407). Why would a potential lender be interested in these two classes of assets when reviewing the balance sheet of a company applying for a long-term loan?

EXPAND YOUR KNOWLEDGE

Discovering Career Opportunities

People interested in entering the field of financial management can choose among a wide variety of careers with diverse responsibilities and challenges. Visit the "Financial Managers" page at www.bls.gov/ooh to read more about career opportunities in financial management.

18-18. What are the day-to-day duties of this occupation? How would these duties contribute to the financial success of a company?

18-19. What skills and educational qualifications would you need to enter this occupation? How do these qualifications fit with your current plans, skills, and interests?

18-20. What kinds of employers hire people for this position? According to your research, does the number of employers seem to be increasing or decreasing? How do you think this trend will affect your employment possibilities if you choose this career?

Developing Your Tech Insights: Credit Scoring Software

Credit scoring software is a type of business intelligence software that measures the credit worthiness of applications for credit cards, mortgages, business loans, and other forms of credit. It has the dual objective of filtering out applications that don't meet a lender's criteria and speeding up the process for applications that do meet the criteria.

Using sophisticated mathematical models based on historical records, credit scoring software helps lenders decide which applicants to accept and how much credit to extend to each one. In addition, software with *predictive modeling* or *predictive analytics* helps predict which applicants will make the best customers (lowest risk and highest profit potential) for a given lender. Explore the credit scoring and risk assessment products offered by Fair Isaac (www.fico.com), Equifax (www.equifax.com), or another company in this industry. Choose one product. In a brief email message to your instructor, explain how this tool can help lenders make better decisions.

PRACTICE YOUR SKILLS

Sharpening Your Communication Skills

You've just been hired as the CFO of a start-up company that is a few months away from launching its first products. Unfortunately, the company is running short of cash and doesn't have enough to pay for initial manufacturing costs. Your boss, Connie Washington, is getting frantic. She has worked for several years to get to this point, and she doesn't want the company to collapse before it even starts selling products. She comes to you, asking for ideas to generate some funds—immediately. Several investors have expressed interest in helping with financing, but Washington doesn't want to surrender any control by using equity financing. She wants to start applying for loans, or even stacks of credit cards, if that's what it takes.

However, you don't think piling on debt is a wise idea at this point. The company doesn't have any revenue yet, and there's no guarantee that the new products will be successful. You'd rather share the risk with some equity investors, even if doing so means that Washington will have to give up some of her managerial authority. Draft a short memo to her, explaining why you think equity financing is a better option at this stage (make up any details you need).

Building Your Team Skills

You and your team are going to build an operating expense budget worksheet for a neighborhood Domino's Pizza franchise.

Begin by brainstorming a list of expenses that are typical of a franchise delivery restaurant. One way to do so is to think about the company's process—from making the pizza to delivering it. List the types of expenses and then group your list into categories such as delivery, marketing, manufacturing, financing, and so on. Leave the budget dollar amounts blank. Finally, develop a list of capital investments your company will make over the next three to five years. Compare your budget worksheets to those of the other teams in your class. Which operating and capital expenses did other teams have that your team didn't? Which expenses did your team have that other teams didn't? Did all the teams categorize the expenses in a similar manner?

Developing Your Research Skills

Choose a recent article from a business journal or newspaper that discusses the financing arrangements or strategies of a particular company.

18-21. What form of financing did the company choose? Does the article indicate why the company selected this form of financing?

18-22. Who provided the financing for the company? Was this arrangement considered unusual, or was it routine?

18-23. What does the company intend to do with the arranged financing—purchase equipment or other assets, finance a construction project, finance growth and expansion, or do something else?

MyBizLab®

Go to the Assignments section of your MyLab to complete these writing exercises.

18-24. Assuming the interest rates are roughly the same, would you prefer to finance your new company by getting cash advances on your credit cards or by taking out a second mortgage on your house? Why?

18-25. What is the fundamental difference in the way businesses approach debt and the way consumers approach it?

ENDNOTES

1. "Visa Inc.," Yahoo Finance, accessed 23 June 2015, http:///finance.yahoo.com; "Visa Inc. Posts Strong Fiscal Third Quarter 2011 Earnings Results and Authorizes New $1 Billion Share Repurchase Program," press release, 27 July 2011, http://investor.visa.com; Visa Inc. Annual Reports (2008, 2010, and 2012), Visa website, http://investor.visa.com; "About Visa," Visa website, accessed 20 November 2013, www.visa.com; Michael Kon, "Visa Is Set to Benefit from the Growth in Electronic Payments," Morningstar, 17 August 2011, www.morningstar.com; Katie Benner, "Visa's Record IPO Rings up 28% Gain," *Fortune*, 19 March 2008, http://money.cnn.com; Tami Luhby, "JPMorgan Chase makes $1B-plus on Visa IPO," *CNNMoney.com*, 21 March 2008, http://money.cnn.com; M. J. Stephey, "A Brief History of: Credit Cards," *Time*, 23 April 2009, www.time.com. "Form S-1 Registration Statement, Visa Inc." U.S. Securities and Exchange Commission website, accessed 2 September 2009, www.sec.gov; *Visa Inc.*, Datamonitor, 9 March 2009.

2. Emily Thornton and Frederick Jespersen, "Corporate Cash: Big Stockpiles for Tough Times," *BusinessWeek*, 5 March 2009, 11.

3. David McCann, "For Intel, the Future Is Now," *CFO*, 25 August 2009, www.cfo.com.

4. Janice DiPietro, "Protecting Liquidity in Tough Times," *Financial Executive*, June 2009, 61.

5. Mahmut Akten, Massimo Giordano, and Mari A. Scheiffele, "Just-in-Time Budgeting for a Volatile Economy," *McKinsey Quarterly*, 2009, Issue 3, 115–121.

6. Martin Labbe, "Budgeting the Proper Way," *Fleet Owner*, December 2008, 39.

7. Akten et al., "Just-in-Time Budgeting for a Volatile Economy."

8. "How to Create a Smart Credit Policy," *Inc.*, March 2009, 37–40.

9. "Commercial Paper," Investopedia, accessed 20 November 2013, www.investopedia.com; "Commercial Paper," InvestingAnswers, accessed 20 November 2013, www.investinganswers.com.

10. "Accounts Receivable Factoring Services," CIT website, accessed 20 June 2015, www.cit.com.

11. "Turn Your Receivables into Quick Cash," *CNNMoney.com*, 21 November 2008, http://money.cnn.com/smallbusiness; David Worrell, "Taking the Sting out of Receivables," Investopedia, accessed 28 August 2009, www.investopedia.com.

12. Maureen Farrell, "The Check Is in the Mail," *Forbes*, 11 May 2009, 56–57; "Invoice Factoring Basics," Invoice Factoring Group, accessed 28 August 2009, http://factoring.qlfs.com; "Turn Your Receivables into Quick Cash"; Worrell, "Taking the Sting out of Receivables."

13. "Demand for Factoring High," *The Secured Lender*, April 2009, 26–29.

14. "How It Works," Receivables Exchange, accessed 20 June 20, 2015, www.recx.com.

15. "Bank-Term Loans," *Entrepreneur*, accessed 29 August 2009, www.entrepreneur.com.

16. "Small Business Administration (SBA) Loans," U.S. Bank website, accessed 29 August 2009, www.usbank.com.

17. "Bank-Term Loans"; "Financing for Your Future—The Five C's of Credit," PNC website, accessed 29 August 2009, www.pnc.com.

18. Ben Steverman, "IPOs: Back from the Dead?" *BusinessWeek*, 9 March 2008, 12.

19. Marguerite Rigoglioso, "The Risky Business of Going Public," *Stanford GSB News*, March 2003, www.gsb.stanford.edu.

20. "The Corporate Handbook Series: Going Public," U.S. Securities and Exchange Commission website, accessed 29 August 2009, www.sec.gov; Matt H. Evans, "Excellence in Financial Management: Course 13: Going Public," Excellence in Financial Management website, accessed 29 August 2009, www.exinfm.com.

21. See note 1.

LEARNING OBJECTIVES After studying this chapter, you will be able to

1 Distinguish between common stock and preferred stock, and explain the difference between market value and intrinsic value.

2 Explain the three key variables that distinguish bonds, compare the advantages and disadvantages of owning bonds, and list the major types of bonds.

3 Define *mutual fund*, and explain the advantages and disadvantages of this popular investment vehicle.

4 Define *derivative*, and identify the major types of derivatives.

5 Describe the four major types of financial markets.

6 Describe four major steps required to become an investor.

BEHIND THE SCENES CHESAPEAKE ENERGY SEARCHES FOR STABILITY IN A VOLATILE WORLD

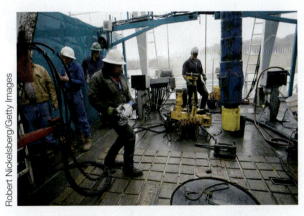

Chesapeake Energy's financial managers are responsible for making sure the company has the funds it needs in order to invest in capital projects and sustain ongoing operations (such as this drilling platform in Fort Worth, Texas).

Robert Nickelsberg/Getty Images

www.chk.com

Imagine trying to run a company when the prices you can charge are subject to wild swings beyond your control and you have no idea in advance how much you'll get for the product you sell. It sells for around $3 for several years, then suddenly jumps to $10, then immediately collapses back to $3, shoots up to $14, bounces around $8 for a couple of years, spikes at $12, then plunges to $3 again. The price triples—then collapses, then quadruples—then collapses; then 15 years later, it's right back where it started.

Meanwhile, your business involves massive capital investments, occasional joint ventures and acquisitions, and high ongoing operating costs. You need a constant stream of cash to run the business, but you can't plan cash flows because you don't know how much revenue you'll receive from one year to the next.

Welcome to the wild world of the natural gas business. Those are actual prices that gas producers received for the standard unit of natural gas, 1,000 cubic feet. (Prices were even more volatile than these selected price points suggest, in fact.)

Now imagine you're Elliot Chambers, vice president of finance of Oklahoma City–based Chesapeake Energy, one of the nation's leading gas producers. Your job is to make sure the company has the funds it needs to pay drilling-rights leases on millions of acres of land, develop new exploration technologies, drill and operate new wells, and support more than 11,000 employees. And you have to do it while your incoming revenue is jumping around like a grasshopper in a frying pan. How can you plan for the long term when income is so volatile? What financial tools can you use to stabilize cash flow and protect the company from price collapses?[1]

INTRODUCTION

Whether you're a corporate financial manager like Chesapeake Energy's Elliot Chambers (profiled in the chapter-opening Behind the Scenes) or an individual investor taking charge of your financial future, you need to understand securities markets and investment strategies. This chapter starts by describing the most common types of securities investments—stocks, bonds, and mutual funds—followed by the more advanced tools that professionals such as Chambers use. The final two sections describe the markets where financial investments are bought and sold and provide an overview of investing strategies.

1 **LEARNING OBJECTIVE**

Distinguish between common stock and preferred stock, and explain the difference between market value and intrinsic value.

stock
Ownership of or equity in a company; a *share* of stock represents a specific portion of ownership.

securities
Investments such as stocks, bonds, options, futures, and commodities.

common stock
Shares of ownership that include voting rights.

capital gains
Increases in the value of a stock or other asset.

preferred stock
Shares of ownership without voting rights but with defined dividends.

Stocks

Stock refers to ownership of or equity in a company, and a *share* of stock represents a specific portion of ownership. Stocks are part of a class of investments known as **securities**, along with bonds, mutual funds, and several others discussed in this chapter. Chapters 5 and 18 discuss the perspective of corporations selling stock; this chapter looks at the perspective of investors (individuals and organizations) buying and owning stock.

TYPES OF STOCK

Companies can issue two major forms of stock: *common stock* and *preferred stock*. **Common stock** is the type of stock people are usually referring to when they talk about stocks. Common stock ownership has three potential benefits. The first is the opportunity to realize significant **capital gains**, or increases in the value of the stock, over time. The second potential advantage is receiving regular income in the form of dividends. However, not all stocks pay dividends, and for those that do, management is under no legal obligation to keep paying dividends. The third benefit of common stock ownership is the right to vote on certain major corporate decisions, including electing the board of directors. (In practice, however, only the very largest stockholders have much influence in the voting.)

The two major disadvantages of owning common stock are risk and volatility. Individual stocks can lose value if the company doesn't meet investor expectations—and can even become worthless if the company declares bankruptcy. And the stock market as a whole can tank, pulling down the value of shares across the board, irrespective of the performance of individual companies. For instance, over the span of just four weeks in the fall of 2008, the U.S. stock market lost one-third of its value.[2] Even when a stock does appreciate in value over the long term, its price will show some degree of *volatility*, or uncertainty, over the short term.

The second major category of stock is **preferred stock**, which can be thought of as a hybrid that combines attributes of common stock and corporate bonds. Preferred stock can be issued in several types, with different rights and obligations for the buyer and seller. But generally speaking, like common stock, preferred stock represents equity in the company. Preferred stock is usually less volatile than common stock, which makes it attractive to risk-averse investors, but it also doesn't appreciate in value to the degree that common stock does. In addition, preferred stock does not come with any voting rights, and it can be *called*, or repurchased on demand, by the issuing company.

Preferred stocks resemble bonds in the sense that they pay fixed dividends—and at higher rates than either common stocks or bonds. Preferred shareholders also have a greater claim to assets than common shareholders, meaning they get paid first in the

EXHIBIT 19.1	Investment Categories of Common Stock

The investing community categorizes stocks according to their particular investment potential. These aren't official definitions, and no central authority decides which.stocks fall in which category, but these labels are an effective way to view potential investments. Of course, a stock can change categories if its appeal to investors changes.

Stock Category	Characteristics
Blue chip	Stocks of major, well-established corporations with demonstrated ability to manage their way through every kind of economic condition; such stocks are usually considered safe, if not necessarily thrilling, choices
Income	Stocks purchased primarily for dividend payouts rather than capital gains potential; companies tend to be older, stable firms with fairly predictable profits but lower prospects for growth
Growth	Stocks from rapidly growing companies that usually reinvest profits (to keep growing) rather than pay dividends; investors buy these stocks for potential capital gains, not income; companies tend to be smaller and younger, and many are in the technology sector
Cyclical	Stocks from companies whose earnings tend to track the ups and downs of the economy in a predictable pattern—in other words, their revenue and profits grow as the economy grows and shrink as the economy shrinks; many of these companies are in basic industries such as housing and transportation
Defensive or counter-cyclical	Stocks of companies that tend to fare better when the economy is doing worse and vice versa; for example, new car sales decline in a falling economy but car repair businesses usually increase revenue as people try to hang onto their automobiles longer
Large cap, mid cap, small cap	General designations for the size of a company's *market capitalization* (the market value of its stock multiplied by the number of shares in circulation); small caps tend to be higher-risk, higher-reward caps than large caps, with mid caps somewhere in between—but these are averages over time, not predictions for specific stocks
Penny	Stocks that sell for less than one dollar per share or, more generally, stocks that are highly speculative (risky, but with upside potential, in other words); tend to be from newer companies or established companies whose stock has plummeted for some reason

Sources: Data from Arthur J. Keown, *Personal Finance: Turning Money into Wealth*, 3rd ed. (Upper Saddle River, N.J.: Pearson Prentice Hall, 2003), 424–425; Jack R. Kapoor, Les R. Dlabay, and Robert J. Hughes, *Personal Finance*, 7th ed. (Boston: McGraw-Hill Irwin, 2004), 460–461.

event of cash-flow problems or bankruptcy. Finally, owning preferred stock has significant tax advantages for U.S. corporations, making it a common investment vehicle for corporate financial managers.[3]

In addition to the legally defined categories of common and preferred stocks, investors also informally divide stock into a variety of categories based on their investment potential (see Exhibit 19.1).

STOCK VALUATION

Determining the value of a stock is obviously important for both sellers and buyers, but it is not a simple matter. At any point in time, each stock has several different values. *Par value*, the value assigned when the stock is first issued, doesn't have much meaning for common stock. However, it is quite important for preferred stock, because it is the value on which dividend percentages are based.

For common stock, you'll hear several terms used to describe its value. **Book value** per share is the difference between the assets and liabilities as listed on the balance sheet, divided by the number of shares in circulation. Book value has two shortcomings: The assets and liabilities (particularly intangibles) might not be valued accurately on the balance sheet, and book value looks backward rather than forward, at what the company might do in the future.[4]

The **market value**, or *market price*, is the price at which a stock is actually selling in the stock market. Market value is forward looking in that it incorporates investor expectations about future earnings. Critically, market value also reflects, particularly in the short term, the emotional reactions of buyers and sellers. This *market sentiment* can range from irrational optimism to irrational pessimism, and it can push prices higher or lower than objective financial analysis would indicate.

book value
The difference between the assets and liabilities as listed on the balance sheet.

market value
The price at which the stock is actually selling in the stock market.

| EXHIBIT 19.2 | How to Read a Stock Quotation |

The formats of stock quotations vary widely, particularly with interactive, online research tools. However, here are the key variables that you are likely to see.

(1)	(2)	(3)	(4)	(5)	(6)	(7)	(8)	(9)	(10)
Stock	SYM	52-Week High	52-Week Low	DIV	YLD %	PE	VOL	HI	Low	Close	Net CHG
Apple	AAPL	404.50	261.40	—	—	14.91	24,230,234	380.88	373.00	376.74	−0.21%
Nordstrom	JWN	59.70	33.06	$0.54	1.12%	18.02	3,155,658	48.21	46.07	46.07	−4.36%
Starbucks	SBUX	40.01	25.22	—	—	32.22	16,806,057	26.95	26.30	26.31	−2.27%
Disney	DIS	36.09	27.99	$0.31	0.90%	15.96	12,642,400	34.62	33.84	33.90	−1.34%

1. **Stock:** The company's name may be abbreviated in some listings.
2. **Symbol:** Symbol under which this stock is traded on stock exchanges.
3. **52-week high/low:** Indicates the highest and lowest trading price of the stock in the past 52 weeks plus the most recent week but not the most recent trading day (adjusted for splits). Stocks are quoted in dollars and cents. In most newspapers, bold-faced entries indicate stocks whose price changed by at least 4% but only if the change was at least $0.75 a share.
4. **Dividend:** Dividends are usually annual payments based on the last quarterly or semiannual declaration, although not all stocks pay dividends. Special or extra dividends or payments are identified in footnotes.
5. **Yield:** The percentage yield shows dividends as a percentage of the share price.
6. **PE:** Price/earnings ratio, calculated by dividing the stock's closing price by the earnings per share for the latest four quarters.
7. **Volume:** Daily total of shares traded. The format of the numbers varies by source; some show exact numbers (as above), but others show hundreds of shares.
8. **High/Low:** The stock's highest and lowest price for that day.
9. **Close:** Closing price of the stock that day.
10. **Net change:** Change in share price from the close of the previous trading day.

intrinsic value
An estimate of what a company is actually worth, independent of book and market values.

Book value is what the balance sheet says the company is worth, and market value is what the stock market says the company is worth, but **intrinsic value** is an attempt to establish what the company is *really* worth. Investors have come up with several ways to estimate intrinsic value by including both quantitative financial factors and such qualitative factors as intangible assets and management capability; as a result, various analysts can arrive at different values for the same stock.[5]

Much of the analysis of stock investing involves deciding whether the current market value is *overpriced* or *underpriced* relative to intrinsic value and other factors. Exhibit 19.2 shows the key variables that investors use to track stocks, including the **price/earnings**

price/earnings ratio
The market value per share divided by the earnings per share.

ratio, or *p/e ratio*, the market value per share divided by the earnings per share. The p/e ratio is often used to assess how a stock is priced, based on company earnings for the previous year (or anticipated earnings for the coming year, in which case it is known as *forward p/e*). A higher-than-average p/e suggests that investors expect the company to grow vigorously, but a p/e that is too high can mean the stock is overpriced and vulnerable to a decline. A lower-than-average p/e might suggest an overlooked stock with upside potential—or a troubled company in which investors have lost confidence. As with all financial ratios, the p/e should be the beginning of an investigation, not the end.

If a company's management team believes that the firm's shares are undervalued, it can opt to repurchase some of the shares through a *stock buyback*, thereby reducing the number of shares outstanding. This move can be a good sign for investors because it usually indicates that management believes strongly in the company's prospects, and doing so tends to drive the share price up by lowering the supply of the stock and improving the p/e ratio. Buybacks are also done to counter the *dilution* effects of employee stock options; when employees exercise stock options, they increase the number of shares outstanding, which can tend to drive market value down.[6]

If a board determines that a stock's price has risen so high that it has become prohibitive for many investors to purchase or has simply gotten out of line with similar stocks, the company may announce a **stock split**. This action divides each share into two or more new shares, and the market value is then reduced by the same ratio. Although a stock split doesn't create more wealth for shareholders, it does give them more shares in order to take advantage of future price increases.

stock split
The act of dividing a share into two or more new shares and reducing the market value by the same ratio.

 **Checkpoint**

LEARNING OBJECTIVE 1: Distinguish between common stock and preferred stock, and explain the difference between market value and intrinsic value.

SUMMARY: Common stock is the type of stock most people are referring to when they speak of stock. It offers the opportunity for significant capital gains, many (but by no means all) common stocks pay dividends, and holders of common stock vote on certain company decisions such as electing directors. The major downsides of common stock are risk and volatility. Preferred stock has some of the attributes of common stock and some attributes of corporate bonds. On the plus side, it pays dividends, is less volatile than common stock, and has tax advantages for corporate investors. On the minus side, it doesn't appreciate as quickly as common stock, it doesn't confer voting rights, and it can be called (repurchased) by the company at any time. Market value is the price at which a stock is currently trading. Intrinsic value is a judgment of how much the company (and therefore its stock) is really worth.

CRITICAL THINKING: (1) Assuming that both can be calculated with reasonable accuracy, does book value or intrinsic value give a more accurate assessment of a company's value? Why? (2) If the average p/e in a particular industry is 16 and you've identified a stock in that industry with a p/e of only 9, does this automatically mean it is a good buy? Why or why not?

IT'S YOUR BUSINESS: (1) As an investor, how well do you think you could handle the volatility of the stock market, knowing that the value of your investments could drop dramatically from time to time? (2) How could you apply your experiences as an employee and as a consumer to determine the intrinsic value of a stock?

KEY TERMS TO KNOW: stock, securities, common stock, capital gains, preferred stock, book value, market value, intrinsic value, price/earnings ratio, stock split

Bonds

Bonds are the second major category of securities investments. Chapter 18 discusses bonds as a fundraising mechanism for corporations; bonds are also issued by various government bodies, from local governments up to the U.S. Treasury. Every bond is characterized by three key variables:

- The **face value**, also called *par value* or *denomination*, is the amount of money, or *principal*, the bond buyer is lending to the bond issuer. Bonds are usually issued in multiples of $1,000, such as $5,000, $10,000, and $50,000. After a bond is in circulation, its *market value* fluctuates over time, primarily as a function of prevailing interest rates, the company's financial performance, and its perceived ability to repay the bond. For instance, if prevailing interest rates drop after a bond is issued, that bond's market value will increase because it pays higher interest than newer bonds are paying.
- The **maturity date** is the date on which the principal will be repaid in full. Corporate bonds typically mature in 3 to 7 years, whereas government bonds mature in anywhere from 30 days to 30 years. Note that bondholders aren't required to keep bonds until maturity; bonds are bought and sold on the open market in much the same way that stocks are.
- The **yield** on a bond is the interest income a purchaser receives from the bond. Yield can get a little confusing, but here are the basics. When a bond is first sold, the issuer

2   LEARNING OBJECTIVE

Explain the three key variables that distinguish bonds, compare the advantages and disadvantages of owning bonds, and list the major types of bonds.

face value
The amount of money, or *principal*, a bond buyer lends to a bond issuer; also known as *par value* or *denomination*.

maturity date
The date on which the principal of a bond will be repaid in full.

yield
Interest income a purchaser receives from the bond.

EXHIBIT 19.3	How to Read a Bond Quotation

Bond quotations usually show some combination of these variables, often in abbreviated form. For instance, the Time Warner bond might be listed as TimeWar 9 1/8 16 (where 9 1/8 is the coupon and 16 represents the year 2016). Some listings also provide such variables as daily volume, change in price from the previous day, and the months in which the bond pays out dividends.

(1)	(2)	(3)	(4)	(5)	(6)	(7)
Issuer	**Coupon**	**Maturity**	**Current Yield**	**Ratings**	**Close**	**CUSIP**
Avnet	6.000	09-01-2018	6.071	Ba1/BBB–	98.836	053807AM5
General Electric	5.000	20-01-2017	4.981	Aaa/AAA	100.390	369604AY9
Morgan Stanley	4.000	01-15-2016	4.078	Aa3/AA–	98.082	61746SBC2
Time Warner	9.125	01-15-2016	7.850	Baa2/BBB +	116.239	887315AK5

1. **Issuer:** Name of company or organization that issued the bond.
2. **Coupon:** The rate of interest that the issuer promises to pay, expressed as an annual percentage of the bond's face value.
3. **Maturity:** Date on which the principle is due and payable to the bondholder.
4. **Current yield:** Annual interest divided by the closing price.
5. **Ratings:** Moody's and S&P ratings for each bond (ratings are provided on some websites).
6. **Close:** Price of the bond at the close of the last day's business; the value shown represents the price per $1,000 expressed in hundreds. The Morgan Stanley bond, for instance, has a price of $980.82 per $1,000.
7. **CUSIP:** A unique identifier for municipal, U.S. government, and corporate bonds assigned by the Committee on Uniform Security Identification Procedures (CUSIP).

offers a specific annual interest rate, known as the *coupon*. A $1,000 bond with an 8 percent coupon, for example, pays $80 a year in interest. If the market value of the bond never fluctuated, the investor's yield would always be equal to this initial coupon rate. However, because market values fluctuate, the *current yield* also fluctuates over time. Current yield is equal to the coupon divided by the current market value; when the market value goes down, the yield goes up, and vice versa. If that $1,000 bond is currently selling for $800, the $80 in interest it continues to pay every year now reflects a current yield of 10 percent.

Bond quotation tables (see Exhibit 19.3) list the key variables to watch when monitoring bonds. When reading these tables, remember that the price is quoted as a percentage of the bond's value. For example, a $1,000 bond shown closing at 65 actually sold at $650.

ADVANTAGES AND DISADVANTAGES OF BONDS

Bonds offer three key advantages to investors. First, most bonds are less risky than stocks and many other investments. Second, bonds offer lower volatility than stocks, which makes them a good choice for investors who need to be able to count on earning a predictable interest rate and receiving their loaned principal back at a specific date. Third, corporate bonds with twice-yearly interest payments can provide a regular source of income. Not all bonds offer regular payments, however. With a *zero-coupon bond*, for example, the purchaser buys the bond at a discount from the face value and then at maturity is repaid the full face value; the difference is the interest earned.[7]

In keeping with the concept of risk/reward trade-off, however, bonds compensate for the safety and predictability with lower average returns, over time, than stocks.[8] The interest rate for each bond reflects its *duration* (that is, how long until it matures) and its *credit quality*. Bonds with longer maturities offer higher interest rates than bonds with shorter maturities, and bonds with lower credit ratings offer higher rates than bonds with higher credit ratings.

The perceived credit quality of a bond is closely tied to the financial stability of the issuing company. *Credit rating agencies* such as Standard & Poor's (S&P) and Moody's rate bonds on the basis of the issuer's financial strength. Exhibit 19.4 shows that the safest corporate bonds are rated AAA (S&P) and Aaa (Moody's). A bond can be *downgraded* if the rating agencies determine that the issuer's finances are deteriorating. *Defaults,* when

EXHIBIT 19.4	Corporate Bond Ratings

Standard & Poor's (S&P) and Moody's Investors Service are among the firms that assess the credit safety of corporate bonds. Low-rated bonds, often known as high-yield bonds or informally as junk bonds, pay higher interest rates to compensate investors for the higher risk.

	S&P Rating	Interpretation	Moody's Rating	Interpretation
Investment Grade	AAA	Highest rating reflects strong analyst confidence in company's ability to meet its commitments	Aaa	Highest quality; lowest level of risk
	AA	High level of analyst confidence	Aa	High quality; very low risk
	A	Good financial strength, but some possibility that the company could be vulnerable to declining circumstances	A	Upper-medium grade; low risk
	BBB	Ability to meet repay looks adequate but more susceptible to economic disruptions than A-rated bonds	Baa	Moderate grade; moderate risk
	BBB–	Lowest investment grade		
Not Investment Grade	BB+	Highest non-investment (speculative) grade	Ba	Somewhat speculative; substantial risk
	BB	Vulnerable to a downturn in business conditions, but less so than "B" grade		
	B	Vulnerable to a downturn in business conditions, more so than "BB"	B	Speculative; high risk
	CCC	Vulnerable; ability to repay contingent on favorable circumstances in the business environment	Caa	Weak standing; high risk
	CC	High probability that the company will not have the capacity to repay	Ca	Highly speculative; often in default or in risk of defaulting
	C	Highly vulnerable to nonpayment, with specific additional circumstances	C	Lowest rated; usually in default; unlikely that principal or interest can be recovered
	D	In default		

Sources. *Rating Symbols and Definitions, March 2015,* Moody's Investors Services, www.moodys.com; "About Credit Ratings," Standard & Poor's, accessed 21 June 2015, www.standardandpoors.com.

companies cannot pay back bondholders at maturity, also increase during economic slowdowns, particularly among riskier *high-yield bonds,* often referred to as *junk bonds.*[9]

Another disadvantage with some bonds is a *call provision,* meaning (as with preferred stocks) that the issuer has the right to call, or repurchase, the bond before maturity.[10] Issuers of such bonds may opt to call them in if interest rates drop after the bonds are issued. This is good news for the issuer (who no longer has to pay at the original rate) but bad news for the bondholder (who no longer receives the anticipated interest income). Callable bonds compensate for this potential loss of income for the bondholder with higher interest rates.

BOND ISSUERS

Unlike stocks, for which corporations are the only issuers, the bond market also includes a wide range of bonds issued by federal, state, and local governments and agencies. To generate funds to operate the federal government, the U.S. Treasury Department offers several types of bonds, primarily classified by maturity. **Treasury bills** (often referred to informally as *T-bills*) are short-term U.S. government bonds that are repaid in less than one year. Like zero-coupon corporate bonds, Treasury bills are sold at a discount and redeemed at face value. The difference between the purchase price and the redemption price is the interest earned for the time period. **Treasury notes** are intermediate-term U.S. government bonds

REAL-TIME UPDATES
Learn More by Visiting This Website

Learn the basics of successful bond investing

Explore the possibilities of corporate, government, municipal, and other types of bonds. Go to http://real-timeupdates.com/bia8 and click on Learn More in the Students section.

Treasury bills
Short-term debt securities issued by the federal government; also referred to as T-bills.

Treasury notes
Debt securities issued by the federal government that are repaid within 1 to 10 years after issuance.

Treasury bonds
Debt securities issued by the federal government that are repaid more than 10 years after issuance.

Treasury Inflation-Protected Securities (TIPS)
Treasury issues in which the principal amount is tied to the Consumer Price Index to protect the buyer against the effects of inflation.

municipal bonds
Bonds issued by states, cities, and various government agencies to fund public projects.

with maturities of 1 to 10 years. **Treasury bonds** are long-term U.S. government bonds with maturities of more than 10 years. With **Treasury Inflation-Protected Securities (TIPS)**, the principal amount is tied to the Consumer Price Index to protect against the erosion of buying power over time.[11] In addition to these Treasury issues, the federal government also sells a variety of *savings bonds* aimed at individual investors.

In general, U.S. government securities pay lower interest than corporate bonds because they are considered safer. They also have tax advantages in that investors pay no state or local income tax on interest earned on these bonds.

Municipal bonds (often informally called *munis*) are issued by states, cities, and various government agencies to raise money for public projects such as building schools, highways, and airports. A *general obligation bond* is a municipal bond backed by the taxing power of the issuing government. When interest payments come due, the issuer makes payments out of its tax receipts. In contrast, a *revenue bond* is a municipal bond backed by the money to be generated by the project being financed.

The appeal of municipal bonds is usually a combination of yield, the potential for tax-exempt income, and relatively low risk. Municipal bonds are generally considered to be safe investments, second only to U.S. Treasury issues, although many municipal bonds did default during the recent recession.[12]

> ## ✔ Checkpoint
>
> **LEARNING OBJECTIVE 2: Explain the three key variables that distinguish bonds, compare the advantages and disadvantages of owning bonds, and list the major types of bonds.**
>
> **SUMMARY:** The three key variables that distinguish bonds are *face value* (the amount the buyer is lending to the issuer), *maturity date* (the date on which the principal will be repaid in full), and *yield* (the interest a bond issuer pays to the buyer). Bonds have three advantages: lower risks than stocks, less volatility, and regular income (with many corporate bonds). The major types of bonds are corporate bonds, U.S. Treasury issues (including Treasury bills, Treasury notes, Treasury bonds, and TIPS), and municipal bonds.
>
> **CRITICAL THINKING:** (1) Why do bonds offer lower average rates of return than stocks? (2) If a company's newest product flops in the marketplace, what effect is that likely to have on the current yield of the company's bonds?
>
> **IT'S YOUR BUSINESS:** (1) If you were approaching retirement age, would you have a higher percentage of bonds or of stocks in your portfolio? Why? (2) Would you ever consider investing in high-yield ("junk") bonds? Why or why not?
>
> **KEY TERMS TO KNOW:** face value, maturity date, yield, Treasury bills, Treasury notes, Treasury bonds, Treasury Inflation-Protected Securities (TIPS), municipal bonds

3   LEARNING OBJECTIVE

Define *mutual fund*, and explain the advantages and disadvantages of this popular investment vehicle.

portfolio diversification
Spreading investments across enough different vehicles to protect against significant declines in any one vehicle.

mutual funds
Financial instruments that pool money from many investors to buy a diversified mix of stocks, bonds, or other securities.

Mutual Funds

As beneficial as they can be, stocks and bonds present three major challenges for individual investors. First, researching, selecting, and monitoring the stocks and bonds in an investment portfolio can be a full-time job. Second, even if they have time, many individuals don't have the expertise needed to fully evaluate many investment alternatives. Third, most individuals don't have enough investment funds to achieve a safe level of **portfolio diversification**—spreading their investment across enough different vehicles to protect against significant declines in any one vehicle.

The financial industry's response to these three challenges is **mutual funds**, financial instruments that pool money from many investors to buy a diversified mix of stocks, bonds, or other securities. By buying shares of a single mutual fund, you can indirectly invest in dozens of securities, depending on the fund's investment profile.

ADVANTAGES AND DISADVANTAGES OF MUTUAL FUNDS

Mutual funds offer three primary advantages. The first is diversification. By pooling money from thousands of clients, a mutual fund can spread its investments across a variety of securities. Doing so decreases the odds of a few poor performers pulling down results—and increases the odds of "catching fire" with a few hot performers. (Not all mutual funds are broadly diversified, however; some specialized funds invest in a single industry or geographic region, for instance.)

The second advantage of mutual funds is professional management. Mutual funds are managed by experienced investors or teams of investors, and you can learn about their backgrounds and amount of experience in managing a fund before you invest in it.

The third advantage of funds is simplifying decision making for individual investors, who don't have to dig into the financial details of various securities. Ironically, though, mutual funds have to some degree been victims of their own success in this regard. So many funds are now available that selecting the right one can seem as complicated as selecting individual stocks and bonds. In fact, Morningstar (**www.morningstar.com**), a popular research service for investors, tracks several thousand more mutual funds than individual stocks.[13]

The primary disadvantage of mutual funds is cost. Mutual funds charge an annual management fee, typically ranging from 1 to 1.5 percent of the amount invested. This might not sound like much, but it can definitely eat into your gains (or add to your losses) over time. More-expensive funds don't necessarily generate better returns than less-expensive funds, so be sure to check the total annual **expense ratio**, or *management expense ratio*, when comparing funds. In addition to annual expenses, funds can charge a variety of "shareholder fees," including a sales commission known as a **load** when a fund is bought or sold. As their name indicates, **no-load funds** do not charge these commissions, although they can charge other fees and still call themselves no-load funds.[14] Unless you can find convincing evidence that a load fund will perform better than a similar no-load fund, the no-load option is probably the better choice.

Another potential disadvantage of mutual funds is their performance relative to the stock market as a whole. Even with full-time professional management, many mutual funds do not perform as well as the overall market. In fact, many investors and securities experts believe it is impossible to consistently "beat the market."[15] This sentiment has fueled the growth of **index funds**, or mutual funds that mirror the composition of a particular **index**, a statistical indicator of the prices of a representative group of securities. For example, the Vanguard 500 fund mirrors the composition of the Standard & Poor's 500, an index based on the stock of 500 large U.S. companies that is frequently used as an indicator of the stock market's overall performance.[16] The Vanguard 500 fund will never outperform the S&P 500, but it will never underperform it, either. The key advantage of index funds is lower cost; with no active management, the cost of running an index fund is lower, and those savings are passed on in the form of lower expense ratios.

Indexing is also commonly used by **exchange-traded funds (ETFs)**, funds that unlike mutual funds are traded on public exchanges in the same way as stocks. Index ETFs combine the advantages of indexing with the flexibility of buying and selling stocks.

CHOOSING MUTUAL FUNDS

With thousands of funds now on the market, choosing the right fund or combination of funds requires some research. The first step is to understand the various types of funds and their investment priorities and strategies. The major categories are

---

REAL-TIME UPDATES
Learn More by Reading This Infographic

Mutual funds: The fundamental concepts

See how mutual funds work and how to invest in them. Go to http://real-timeupdates.com/bia8 and click on Learn More in the Students section.

---

expense ratio
The annual cost of owning a mutual fund, expressed as a percentage.

load
The sales commission charged when buying or selling a mutual fund.

no-load funds
Mutual funds that do not charge loads.

index funds
Mutual funds that mirror the composition of a particular market or index.

index
A statistical indicator of the rise and fall of a representative group of securities.

exchange-traded funds (ETFs)
Mutual funds whose shares are traded on public exchanges in the same way as stocks.

REAL-TIME UPDATES
Learn More by Watching This Video

The basics of exchange traded funds

See how exchange traded funds (ETFs) are created and traded. Go to http://real-timeupdates.com/bia8 and click on Learn More in the Students section.

REAL-TIME UPDATES
Learn More by Exploring This Interactive Website

How much does that fund really cost?

These handy calculators let you compare the real costs of mutual funds. Go to http://real-timeupdates.com/bia8 and click on Learn More in the Students section.

- *Money-market funds,* which invest in high-quality, short-term debt issues from governments and corporations
- *Growth funds,* which invest in stocks of rapidly growing companies
- *Value funds,* which invest in stocks considered to be selling below their true value
- *Income funds,* which invest in securities that pay high dividends and interest
- *Balanced funds,* which invest in a combination of stocks and bonds
- *Sector funds,* also known as *specialty funds,* or *industry funds,* which invest in companies in a particular industry, such as technology or health care
- *Target-date funds,* which attempt to maintain a desirable balance of risk and growth potential based on a target retirement date
- *Global funds,* which invest in foreign and U.S. securities
- *International funds,* which invest strictly in foreign securities
- *Socially responsible funds,* which make investment choices based on criteria related to corporate social responsibility

Within these categories, you can also find subcategories based on company size, such as a large-company value fund or a small-company growth fund. A key decision when selecting the type of funds is to understand your *risk tolerance,* because various funds have more aggressive or more cautious approaches.

Once you have an idea of the fund categories that meet your needs, you can use a *fund screener* (see Exhibit 19.5) to select attractive candidates based on performance, expense ratio, minimum investment, and other criteria.

net asset value (NAV)
A mutual fund's assets minus its liabilities; usually expressed as NAV per share.

Unlike with stocks, where you purchase a specific number of shares at a certain price, the sum of money you invest in a mutual fund is divided into a number of shares based on the fund's **net asset value (NAV)**—its assets minus its liabilities. For instance, if you invest $1,000 in a no-load fund whose NAV per share that day is $47.93, you will receive 20.86 shares ($1,000 divided by $47.93). You can find the current NAV per share and other key variables in a mutual fund quotation (see Exhibit 19.6 on page 456).

REAL-TIME UPDATES
Learn More by Exploring This Interactive Website

Find the funds that are right for you

Mutual fund screeners such as this one help you filter out the worst and find the best funds for your portfolio. Go to http://real-timeupdates.com/bia8 and click on Learn More in the Students section.

✓ Checkpoint

LEARNING OBJECTIVE 3: Define *mutual fund,* **and explain the advantages and disadvantages of this popular investment vehicle.**

SUMMARY: A *mutual fund* is an investment vehicle that pools money from many investors to purchase a diversified mix of securities. The three primary advantages of mutual funds are portfolio diversification, professional management, and relative simplicity. The primary disadvantages of mutual funds are cost and the fact that many funds don't perform as well as the market overall, despite professional management.

CRITICAL THINKING: (1) How might the constant scrutiny and demand for consistent results affect the long-term performance of a mutual fund? (2) If many funds don't outperform the market, why would anybody bother to invest in them, particularly in those funds that lag the market year after year?

IT'S YOUR BUSINESS: (1) Would your inclination be to invest in mutual funds or to do the research yourself and invest in individual stocks and bonds? Why? (2) Would

EXHIBIT 19.5	**Finding the Best Mutual Funds for Your Portfolio**

Mutual fund screeners, such as this one offered by Morningstar (www.morningstar.com), help you find funds by using prebuilt screens or your own your specific investment criteria. For example, Morningstar's "Portfolio Anchors" screen filters by such criteria as fund type, how long the fund manager has been managing the fund, expense ratio, and return. Here are some of the funds it found. (Morningstar is a subscription-based service, but you might be able to access it for free through your library.)

MORNINGSTAR® Investment Research Center℠
Provided by Sno Isle Regional Library
[End Session]

| Home | Companies | Funds | ETFs | Markets | Articles & Videos | Portfolio | Help & Education | Newsletters | 🔍 Enter a Ticker or Name |

Funds

Select from hundreds of criteria to build a list of fund investments.

Click for information on:
⤢ Fund Screener
▸ Fund Favorites
▸ Fund Analyst Reports
⤢ Most Similar Funds
⤢ Fund Compare
▸ International Funds
▯ Funds Summary
▯ CEF Coverage

Screener

View: Snapshot ▾   Find a fund: _____ [Go] Ticker Lookup

Check boxes to: [Delete]

Results: 51 funds   Page: [1] of 3   ◀ Prev 1 2 3 Next ▶

Fund Name	Morningstar Analyst Report	Morningstar Rating	Morningstar Category	YTD Return (%)	Morningstar Analyst Rating
American Century Equity Growth	07-29-11	★★★★	Large Blend	27.73	--
American Century NT Equity Gro		★★★★	Large Blend	28.08	--
American Funds Fundamental Inv	06-18-13	★★★★	Large Blend	25.42	🛡 Gold
Ave Maria Rising Dividend	--	★★★★★	Large Blend	28.33	--
BBH Core Select N	10-23-13	★★★★★	Large Blend	23.46	🛡 Silver
Brown Advisory Value Equity In	--	★★★	Large Blend	32.22	--
Clipper	09-23-13	★★	Large Blend	28.43	🛡 Silver
Columbia Contrarian Core Z	04-01-13	★★★★★	Large Blend	29.87	🛡 Bronze
Dreyfus Basic S&P 500 Stock In	--	★★★★	Large Blend	27.13	--
Dreyfus Fund Incorporated	06-20-12	★★★	Large Blend	26.57	--
Dreyfus S&P 500 Index	05-07-13	★★★	Large Blend	26.77	Neutral
Dreyfus Strategic Value A	07-18-12	★★	Large Blend	31.79	--
DWS S&P 500 Index S	--	★★★	Large Blend	26.88	--
Fidelity Advisor® Diversified	04-16-13	★★★★	Large Blend	28.34	Neutral
Fidelity Dividend Growth	08-06-13	★★★	Large Blend	26.43	🛡 Silver
Fidelity Large Cap Stock	07-09-13	★★★★	Large Blend	32.93	🛡 Silver
Franklin Rising Dividends A	07-25-13	★★★	Large Blend	26.63	🛡 Bronze
Glenmede Large Cap 100	--	★★★★★	Large Blend	31.05	--
Great-West Aggressive Profile	--	★★★	Large Blend	24.35	--
Great-West Aggressive Profile	--	★★★	Large Blend	24.60	--
Hartford Capital Appreciation	--	★★★★	Large Blend	32.66	--
Hartford Disciplined Equity HL	--	★★★★★	Large Blend	30.18	--
Hartford Index HLS IA	--	★★★	Large Blend	26.94	--
ING Corporate Leaders 100 A	--	★★★	Large Blend	28.98	--
Longleaf Partners	06-04-13	★★★	Large Blend	26.77	🛡 Silver
Large Blend Average				26.42	
S&P 500				27.30	

YTD performance is updated daily or with the most recent data available.   Click the button to change screening criteria. ◀

Your Screen (Portfolio Anchors) Summary:

	(Fund Category = Large Blend)
and	(Distinct Portfolio Only = Yes)
and	(Fund Manager Tenure >= 5)
and	(Expense Ratio <= 1.00)
and	(5 Yr Return % Rank Category <= 50)
and	(Minimum Initial Purchase <= 10000)

investing in socially responsible funds that share your personal values be an effective way to support causes you believe in? Why or why not?

KEY TERMS TO KNOW: portfolio diversification, mutual funds, expense ratio, load, no-load funds, index funds, index, exchange-traded funds (ETFs), net asset value (NAV)

EXHIBIT 19.6	**How to Read a Mutual Fund Quotation**

Mutual fund quotations typically show such variables as the net asset value (NAV) of one share, the change in NAV from the previous day, the expense ratio, and returns over various time spans. Some listings also show fund objective or investing style, asset allocation, minimum investment amount, and risk/reward assessments.

(1)	(2)	(3)	(4)		(5)		(6)	(7)	(8)
Fund Name	Symbol	NAV	Change	YTD	3 yr	5 yr	Front load	Expense ratio	Yield
Lord Abbett CA Tax-Free Income	LCFIX	$10.62	−$0.03	−0.51	3.92	3.76	3.25	0.93	4.00
FBR Small Cap	FBRVX	$55.38	−$0.86	2.84	18.00	25.39	None	1.38	—
Janus Contrarian	JSVAX	$19.00	−$0.29	12.89	26.32	24.65	None	1.69	—
Vanguard Mid Cap Index	VIMSX	$20.60	−$0.59	4.17	17.39	17.49	None	0.22	—

1. **Fund name:** Name of mutual fund.
2. **Symbol:** Fund's symbol.
3. **NAV:** Net asset value, the per-share value of the fund.
4. **Change:** Decrease or increase in NAV from previous day.
5. **YTD, 3 yr, 5 yr:** Performance year-to-date, over the past 3 years, over the past 5 years (expressed as a percentage increase or decrease).
6. **Front load:** Percentage of a new investment charged as a sales fee; no-load funds do not charge a front load.
7. **Expense ratio:** Annual cost of owning the mutual fund.
8. **Yield:** Annual yield of income-producing funds, expressed as a percentage.

4	LEARNING OBJECTIVE

Define *derivative*, and identify the major types of derivatives.

derivatives

Contracts whose value is derived from some other entity (usually an asset of some kind, but not necessarily); used to hedge against or speculate on risk.

Derivatives

Most individuals don't venture too far beyond stocks, bonds, and mutual funds, but businesses and other organizations use a wide range of other financial vehicles to meet specific needs. Although you may never be personally involved with any of the financial instruments in this section, it's important to recognize what they are, given their importance to many businesses and their role in the economy.

Derivatives are contracts whose value is derived from some other entity, which is usually an asset of some kind, but not necessarily.[17] Derivatives can be based on stocks, bonds, pools of debt, agriculture products, interest rates, life insurance policies, and even the weather.[18] The basic premise of a derivative is transferring risk from a party that wants to *decrease* its risk exposure to a party that is willing to *increase* its risk exposure in exchange for the opportunity to pursue higher profits. In other words, derivatives can be used defensively, to protect profits by *hedging* a position to guard against the risk of a sudden loss, or offensively, to seek profits by *speculating* on future price changes.

For example, a bank with many home mortgage loans might want to pay someone to shoulder the risk of those loans defaulting, or a grain producer might want to protect itself from a possible drop in grain prices at the point in the future that the crop is harvested and ready to sell. In both cases, a derivative is a tool to accomplish this exchange. An essential point here is that derivatives don't eliminate or even reduce the risk; they simply transfer it from one party to another.[19]

The ability to buy and sell risk is an important part of today's global economy, and derivatives are used by a variety of corporations, banks, governments, not-for-profit organizations, and institutional investors.[20] However, mistakes with derivatives can be quite costly and can magnify financial calamities when the parties involved don't understand the risks, don't manage the risks responsibly, or make decisions based on faulty predictions. All three of these blunders combined to help trigger the global recession in 2008.

Another potential worry with derivatives occurs when *both* parties in a contract are speculating, rather than one party hedging and the other speculating. This situation can happen when a party that doesn't own an asset (such as a portfolio of home loans or a field full of grain, from the previous examples) initiates a derivative on it, purely for the purpose of speculation. When the auto parts maker Delphi defaulted on $2 billion worth of bonds, it was discovered that derivatives equaling more than 10 times that amount had been contracted by multiple speculators.[21]

The field of derivatives is immensely complex, with many types of derivatives across a variety of industries, but the following discussions offer a quick tour of the major types.

OPTIONS AND FINANCIAL FUTURES

An **option** is the purchased right—but not the obligation—to buy or sell a specified number of shares of a stock or other security at a predetermined price during a specified period. Investors who trade options are betting that the price of the stock will either rise or decline. All options fall into two broad categories: *puts* and *calls*; Exhibit 19.7 explains the rights acquired with each type. Like all derivatives, options can be used offensively by speculators hoping to profit from future price changes or defensively by hedgers to protect their existing positions against future losses. In addition to individual stocks, options can also be created using an index of stocks, interest rates, and other financial variables.

An important note here on terminology: *Hedge funds* started in the 1950s as a defensive investment strategy, but the term is now applied to a wide variety of private investment funds—many of which use aggressive and often risky strategies that have nothing to do with hedging.[22] Some of the biggest financial catastrophes in recent years have involved hedge funds whose risky speculation backfired.

Financial futures are similar to options, but they are legally binding contracts to buy or sell a financial instrument (such as stocks, Treasury bonds, and foreign currencies) for a set price at a future date. Options and futures—as with other derivatives—are typically riskier than conventional securities, so they should be considered only by knowledgeable investors who are using capital they can afford to lose. Futures often involve a high degree of leverage, in the sense that you can buy a very large futures contract with a very small "down payment." This leverage can greatly magnify both gains and losses, depending on how prices change over time.

option
The purchased right—but not the obligation—to buy or sell a specified number of shares of a stock at a predetermined price during a specified period.

financial futures
Contracts to buy or sell a financial instrument (such as stocks, Treasury bonds, and foreign currencies) for a set price at a future date.

EXHIBIT 19.7	Types of Options

All stock options fall into two broad categories: puts and calls.

Type	Option Holder's Right	Buyer's Belief	Seller's Belief
Call	The right to buy the stock at a fixed price until the expiration date	Buyer believes the price of underlying stock will increase. Buyer can buy stock at a set price and sell it at a higher price for a capital gain.	Seller believes the price of underlying stock will decline and that the option will not be exercised. Seller earns a premium.
Put	The right to sell the stock at a fixed price until the expiration date	Buyer believes the price of underlying stock will decline and wants to lock in a fixed profit. Buyer usually already owns shares of underlying stock.	Seller believes the price of underlying stock will rise and that the option will not be exercised. Seller earns a premium.

COMMODITIES FUTURES

commodities futures
Contracts to buy or sell specific amounts of commodities for a set price at a future date.

Commodities—agricultural products, petroleum, metals, and other basic goods—are frequently bought and sold through futures contracts as well. **Commodities futures** are an essential hedging tool for many agricultural, industrial, or commercial buyers and sellers of commodities. Buyers use futures contracts to protect against future price *increases*, whereas suppliers use these contracts to protect themselves from future price *decreases*. As you can read in the Behind the Scenes wrap-up at the end of the chapter, Chesapeake Energy uses this hedging technique to try to safeguard its revenue stream from unpredictable price drops. In addition to parties that actually produce or use the commodities, financial speculators who aren't involved with the commodities themselves buy and sell commodities futures in an attempt to profit from price changes.

Jorg Hackemann/Shutterstock

Commodities futures are an important financial management tool for companies such as Chesapeake, whose cash flows and incomes are closely linked to the prices of commodity goods. However, like options and financial futures, commodities can be a risky investment for speculators trying to predict future price changes. Speculators have lost millions of dollars in commodities futures—just a few years ago, a hedge fund manager speculating on natural gas futures singlehandedly lost $6 billion.[23]

Producers, customers, and investors buy and sell futures contracts on dozens of commodities, including agricultural products, metals, and fuels.

CURRENCY FUTURES

currency futures
Contracts to buy or sell amounts of specified currency at some future date.

For companies that conduct business in multiple currencies around the world, variations in exchange rates between two currencies can affect profitability. To hedge against exchange rate shifts that will affect them negatively, these firms can use **currency futures**, contracts to buy or sell amounts of specified currency at some future date. As with other types of futures contracts, the flip side of hedging is speculating, and speculation in the *foreign exchange market*, commonly known as *forex*, is a booming worldwide industry. Currency trading takes place 24 hours a day during the business week, with an average daily volume of several trillion dollars.[24]

CREDIT DERIVATIVES

credit derivatives
Derivatives used to reduce a lender's exposure to credit risk.

Credit derivatives are used to reduce a lender's exposure to credit risk. The most notable type is the *credit default swap*, which works much like an insurance policy. For example, a lender can pay another party to "own" the risk of a loan portfolio without actually transferring the loans themselves. If the loans go bad, that party must absorb the loss. These swaps are a useful concept, but things got messy in recent years because the swap contracts can be bought and sold—and buyers sometimes didn't understand what they were buying or didn't have the capital needed to meet the financial obligations they were taking over.[25]

✔ Checkpoint

LEARNING OBJECTIVE 4: Define *derivative*, **and identify the major types of derivatives.**

SUMMARY: A derivative is a contract whose value is based on some underlying asset or other entity. Except when they are used purely for speculative purposes, derivatives are designed to transfer risk from a party that wants to decrease its risk exposure to a party willing to increase its risk exposure in exchange for the opportunity to generate profits. The major types of derivatives are options, financial futures, commodities futures, currency futures, and credit derivatives.

CRITICAL THINKING: (1) Why would a lender make loans that are so risky that it would consider credit default swaps to protect itself from default? (2) Would options and futures be wise investments for someone getting close to retirement who wants to create a final boost to his or her nest egg before retiring? Why or why not?

IT'S YOUR BUSINESS: (1) Over-the-counter credit derivatives are private contracts between two companies; is it appropriate for the government to force them to be sold on regulated exchanges like commodities are? Why or why not? (2) Should speculating via derivatives be outlawed in the United States, like it is in some countries? Why or why not?

KEY TERMS TO KNOW: derivatives, option, financial futures, commodities futures, currency futures, credit derivatives

Financial Markets

Market is a potentially confusing financial term that is used in a variety of ways in different contexts. For example, when you hear commentators refer to "the market," with no qualifiers, they are probably referring to the stock market and specifically to one or more stock market indexes. Also, a market can be a specific group of organizations or a looser conglomeration of buying and selling activity. Finally, securities markets can be divided into *primary markets*, which handle the initial public offerings of stocks and bonds, and *secondary markets*, which handle all the public buying and selling after that.

THE STOCK MARKET

Organizations that facilitate the buying and selling of stock are known as **stock exchanges**. Some of these are actual physical facilities, whereas others are primarily computer networks. The most famous of the physical variety is the New York Stock Exchange (NYSE; www.nyse.com). The NYSE, often referred to as the "Big Board," is located just off Wall Street in New York City, leading to the frequent use of "Wall Street" as a metaphor for either the stock market or the larger community of financial companies in the immediate area. Tokyo, London, Frankfurt, Paris, Toronto, Shanghai, Hong Kong, and Montreal also have stock exchanges with national or international importance, and smaller regional exchanges play an important role in buying and selling many lesser-known stocks.

The NYSE's major competitor is the NASDAQ (pronounced "NAZZ-dack"), a computerized stock exchange originated by the National Association of Securities Dealers and now owned by NASDAQ OMX Group (www.nasdaq.com). NASDAQ is home to such high-profile stocks as Amazon, Apple, eBay, Intel, and Microsoft.[26]

Stocks that don't meet the listing requirements of an exchange can be sold *over the counter (OTC)*. Together, the various stock exchanges around the world and the OTC market make up the overall "stock market."

THE BOND MARKET

Unlike the stock market, in which most buying and selling is coordinated by organizations such as the NYSE and NASDAQ, most trading in the **bond market** is over the counter, taking place outside organized exchanges. Consequently, the bond market is much more diffuse and decentralized than the stock market, and the processes for buying and selling depends on the type of bond. In the primary market, new issues of Treasury bonds, for example, can be purchased directly from the Treasury Department (www.treasurydirect.gov). In the secondary market, bonds are traded through a wide variety of brokers and

5 **LEARNING OBJECTIVE**

Describe the four major types of financial markets.

stock exchanges
Organizations that facilitate the buying and selling of stock.

REAL-TIME UPDATES
Learn More by Exploring This Interactive Website

Practice your investment skills

Use this portfolio simulator to learn how to buy and sell stocks without risking any money. Go to http://real-timeupdates.com/bia8 and click on Learn More in the Students section.

bond market
The collective buying and selling of bonds; most bond trading is done over the counter, rather than in organized exchanges.

agents (who buy and sell on behalf of customers) and dealers (who buy bonds and then resell them from their own inventories).[27]

THE MONEY MARKET

money market

An over-the-counter marketplace for short-term debt instruments such as Treasury bills and commercial paper.

The **money market** is an over-the-counter marketplace for short-term debt instruments such as Treasury bills and commercial paper. Its purpose is to help corporations and government agencies meet short-term liquidity needs. Unlike with stocks and many bonds, the amounts traded in the money market are far beyond the reach of individual investors, so the money market is used by corporations, governments, banks, and other financial institutions. However, individuals can invest indirectly by purchasing *money-market mutual funds*. These funds generally offer low returns, but they are considered a relatively safe place to keep money that might be needed on short notice.[28]

THE DERIVATIVES MARKET

derivatives market

A market that includes exchange trading (for futures and some options) and over-the-counter trading (for all other derivatives, at least currently).

The **derivatives market** is as diverse as derivatives themselves and includes both exchange-traded and OTC derivatives. Futures and some options are traded on organized exchanges with time-tested financial controls and government regulation. All other derivatives, including the credit default swaps that made headlines in recent years, are traded over the counter.[29] Bringing more of these derivatives under closer regulatory oversight has been an ongoing political battle since the late 1990s.

 Checkpoint

LEARNING OBJECTIVE 5: Describe the four major types of financial markets.

SUMMARY: The *stock market* consists of individual stock exchanges (such as the NYSE and NASDAQ) and the over-the-counter market that facilitate the buying and trading of company stocks. In contrast to the stock market, nearly all trading in the *bond market* is over the counter. The *money market* is where short-term debt instruments such as corporate paper are issued and traded; this is also an over-the-counter market. The derivatives market is a diverse collection of both exchanges (for some options and all futures) and over-the-counter trading (for all other types—although this situation may change in the coming years).

CRITICAL THINKING: (1) What is the difference between the primary market and the secondary market? (2) Why do individual investors participate in the stock and bond markets but not in the money market?

IT'S YOUR BUSINESS: (1) What is your emotional reaction to the term "Wall Street"? Explain your answer. (2) Given all the calamity in the financial markets in recent years, are you now more or less inclined to pursue a career in financial services? Why?

KEY TERMS TO KNOW: stock exchanges, bond market, money market, derivatives market

6   LEARNING OBJECTIVE

Describe four major steps required to become an investor.

Investment Strategies and Techniques

Learning how to make smart investment choices should be high on your life skills to-do list. With many employers cutting back or eliminating retirement plans and with Social Security facing uncertainty, you need to take charge of your financial future. This section offers a basic framework for beginning your education as an investor, whether you're investing for yourself and your family or for your company. Be sure to check out Appendix D as well, which offers a broader view of personal financial planning, and explore the many online tools and apps now available for making investment decisions (see Exhibit 19.8).

EXHIBIT 19.8   *Taking Advantage of New Investing Tools*

Interactive and community-driven research tools such as Trefis (**www.trefis.com**) can help you get insight into where a company's stock might go. One of the key questions Trefis explores is how much of a company's stock price is driven by each of its major product divisions, as shown in this example of Google's stock. By breaking it down this way, you can get a better sense of how market dynamics could affect its overall business and thus its stock price.

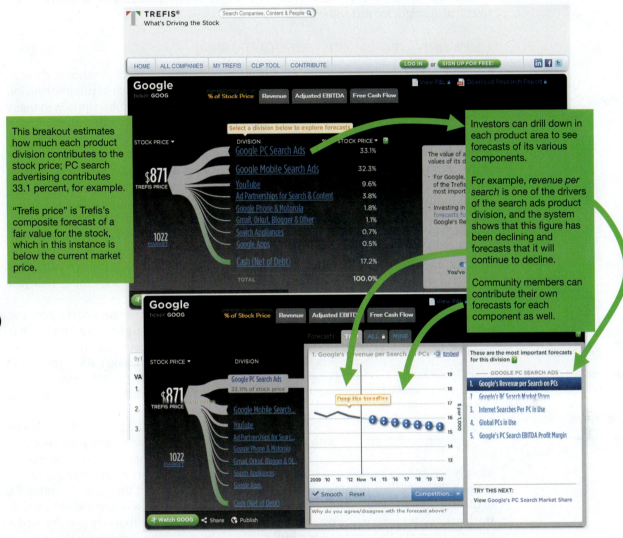

ESTABLISHING INVESTMENT OBJECTIVES

A common mistake in investing is chasing after promising investments without having any long-range goals in mind. Ask yourself the following questions before you invest:

- **Why do you want to get more money?** Simply piling up cash is not a terribly useful goal, because it won't help you make the choices and trade-offs you'll need to make.
- **How much will you need—and when?** Identify how much money you'll need for significant events, from major purchases to college educations to retirement.
- **How much can you invest?** Make a realistic assessment of how much you can invest now and then every month thereafter. You can get started in some mutual funds with as little as $100, so don't let limited cash hold you back.
- **How much risk are you willing to accept?** Identify your tolerance for risk, based on your personality, financial circumstances, and stage in life. As with most everything in finance, risk is inversely related to potential **rate of return**, the gain (or loss) of an investment over time.

rate of return
The gain (or loss) of an investment over time, expressed as a percentage.

- **How much liquidity do you need?** Money that you may need in the short term should not be tied up in long-term investments that are difficult to sell quickly or whose value may fluctuating wildly and leave you facing a loss if you need to sell.
- **What are the tax consequences?** Various investments have different tax ramifications, and some are designed specifically to minimize taxes.

By answering these questions, you'll be able to establish realistic investment objectives that are right for you and your family.

LEARNING TO ANALYZE FINANCIAL NEWS

Knowing how to analyze financial news is essential to making good investment choices. Investors have access to more information than ever before, and much of this information is free (and chances are that your college or community library has subscriptions to many of the sources that aren't free). You can quickly uncover basic information about a company on its website, scan its "financials" on Google Finance (www.google.com/finance) or Yahoo! Finance (http://finance.yahoo.com), read articles from numerous business periodicals online, judge customer sentiment by reading comments on social commerce sites, catch late-breaking news on 24-hour cable TV channels, and monitor the company and its industry using a variety of newsfeeds and social media.

Unfortunately, so much information is available that to avoid being overwhelmed, you almost need to take a defensive posture, filtering out information that is irrelevant and keeping a sharp eye for information that is biased or unreliable. This information overload carries the additional risk of prompting investors to make snap decisions based on something they heard on TV or something that just popped up on Twitter.

Fortunately, the vast majority of the information out there won't apply to you and your investments. Much of it is detailed material aimed at financial specialists, and much of it is short-term "noise" that probably won't affect you in the long term. To make the best use of all this information without getting overwhelmed or sidetracked, start on a small scale. Learn the basic language of investing on a site such as Investopedia (www.investopedia.com), a free website with extensive content written by investment professionals.

You'll gradually pick up on the terminology and start to identify the themes you need to care about and which of the many arcane topics you can leave to the specialists. For instance, you'll soon get familiar with the general conditions of the stock market and learn the terms that define its ups and downs (see Exhibit 19.9). If stock prices have been rising over a long period, for instance, the industry and the media will often describe this situation as a **bull market**. The reverse is a **bear market**, one characterized by a long-term trend of falling prices.

Finally, one more bit of good news: Virtually everything you learn in this course and in other business courses will help you analyze business and financial news and become a more successful investor. When you know what makes companies successful, you can apply this insight to choosing investments with solid growth potential.

CREATING AN INVESTMENT PORTFOLIO

No single investment provides an ideal combination of income, growth potential, safety, liquidity, and tax consequences. For this reason, investors build **investment portfolios**, or collections of various types of investments. Managing a portfolio to balance potential returns with an acceptable level of risk is known as **asset allocation**, dividing investments among *cash instruments* such as money-market mutual funds, *income instruments* such as government and corporate bonds, and *equities* (mainly common stock). In general, younger investors want to focus on *building* capital through equity investments, whereas older investors want to focus on *protecting* capital through income and cash instruments, so they rebalance their portfolios over time.

REAL-TIME UPDATES
Learn More by Reading These Articles

Free tutorials to help you get started in investing

Investopedia helps you understand investment concepts and get started on building a portfolio that's right for your needs. Go to http://real-timeupdates.com/bia8 and click on Learn More in the Students section.

---

bull market
A market situation in which most stocks are increasing in value.

bear market
A market situation in which most stocks are decreasing in value.

investment portfolios
Collections of various types of investments.

asset allocation
Management of a portfolio to balance potential returns with an acceptable level of risk.

| **EXHIBIT 19.9** | **The Stock Market's Ups and Downs** |

The peaks and valleys on this chart represent swings in the Dow Jones Industrial Average (DJIA), a widely used index of U.S. stock prices. Given the volatility that can wipe out substantial gains, you can see why many experts advise against investing in stocks if there's a chance you might need to pull that money out within a few years.

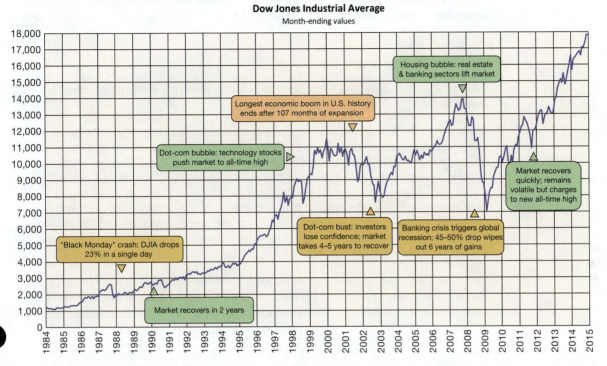

Dow Jones Industrial Average
Month-ending values

- Housing bubble: real estate & banking sectors lift market
- Longest economic boom in U.S. history ends after 107 months of expansion
- Dot-com bubble: technology stocks push market to all-time high
- Market recovers quickly; remains volatile but charges to new all-time high
- Dot-com bust: investors lose confidence; market takes 4–5 years to recover
- Banking crisis triggers global recession; 45–50% drop wipes out 6 years of gains
- "Black Monday" crash: DJIA drops 23% in a single day
- Market recovers in 2 years

Source: DJIA month-end data retrieved from Federal Reserve Bank of St. Louis website, 21 June 2015, www.stlouisfed.org

BUYING AND SELLING SECURITIES

In most cases, buying and selling securities requires using a **broker**, an expert who has passed a series of formal examinations and is legally registered to buy and sell securities on behalf of individual and institutional investors. You pay *transaction costs* for every order, and these fees vary by the level of service you get. A *full-service broker* advises you on selecting investments, for example, whereas a *discount broker* provides fewer services and generally charges lower commissions as a result.

When you buy or sell a stock, you can use a variety of order types to accomplish various goals. The simplest is a **market order**, which tells the broker to buy or sell at the best price that can be negotiated at the moment. Because you can't be sure where prices will finalize with market orders, you can use a **limit order** to specify the highest price you are willing to pay when buying or the lowest price at which you are willing to sell. If you're worried about price declines on a stock you own, you can set a **stop order** that tells the broker to sell if the price drops to a certain level.

More experienced investors can use a number of buying and selling strategies beyond simple cash purchases of stock. With **margin trading**, investors buy stock using a combination of their own cash and money borrowed from their brokers. The appeal of margin trading is leverage, amplifying potential gains by using someone else's money in addition to your own. Margin trading is risky, however, because it also amplifies losses. In fact, with leverage, you can lose more money than you originally invested. And if prices are dropping and you want to hang on until they climb back up, you might not be allowed to. If the stock price drops so low that it violates the maximum leverage allowed in your account, you can be forced to sell immediately.

Most investors buy stock with the anticipation that it will rise in value. However, if you believe that a stock's price is about to drop, you may choose a trading procedure known

broker
A certified expert who is legally registered to buy and sell securities on behalf of individual and institutional investors.

market order
A type of securities order that instructs the broker to buy or sell at the best price that can be negotiated at the moment.

limit order
An order that stipulates the highest or lowest price at which the customer is willing to trade securities.

stop order
An order to sell a stock when its price falls to a particular point, to limit an investor's losses.

margin trading
Borrowing money from brokers to buy stock, paying interest on the borrowed money, and leaving the stock with the broker as collateral.

short selling
Selling stock borrowed from a broker with the intention of buying it back later at a lower price, repaying the broker, and keeping the profit.

as **short selling**, or "going short." With this procedure, you sell stock you borrow from a broker in the hope of buying it back later at a lower price. After you return the borrowed stock to the broker, you keep the price difference. However, selling short can be quite risky because you can lose more than you originally invested. For instance, if the price doubles instead of falling, as you anticipated, you can lose twice as much as you invested.

For the latest information on financial markets and investing, visit http://real-timeupdates.com/bia8 and click on Chapter 19.

 Checkpoint

LEARNING OBJECTIVE 6: Describe four major steps required to become an investor.

SUMMARY: The first step toward becoming an investor is to establish your investment objectives, based on your financial needs and goals, your tolerance for risk, your liquidity requirements, and tax consequences that apply to you. The second step is learning to analyze financial news; the best way is to start with the basics, gradually accumulate information as you need it, and filter out news that is irrelevant or potentially unreliable. The third step is to plan and create an investment portfolio, using asset allocation to maintain an acceptable balance of risk and potential reward. The fourth step is to engage in buying and selling securities, using a broker of your choice and the right trading strategies for your circumstances.

CRITICAL THINKING: (1) If you want to buy a particular stock but are worried that demand from investors could push the price to an unreasonably high level before your order is executed, what type of order would you specify? Why? (2) Does a low p/e ratio mean that a stock is a good buy? Explain your answer.

IT'S YOUR BUSINESS: (1) Do you think you currently have the discipline needed to control your spending in order to free up cash for regular investing? If not, what changes could you make? (2) If someone gave you a "hot tip" on a stock, how would you go about researching the opportunity before making an investment decision?

KEY TERMS TO KNOW: rate of return, bull market, bear market, investment portfolios, asset allocation, broker, market order, limit order, stop order, margin trading, short selling

BEHIND THE SCENES

CHESAPEAKE ENERGY HEDGES, THEN DOESN'T, THEN DOES

In many industries, prices tend to follow reasonably predictable patterns over time, such as rising in line with inflation or declining as a result of new technologies and greater production efficiencies. Commodities such as natural gas are a different beast altogether, with wide and often unpredictable swings. However, producers can't always adjust their ongoing operating expenses to match revenue, at least not with anywhere near the same rapidity at which prices fluctuate. For example, gas companies can spend millions or billions of dollars in exploration and leasing costs (to secure drilling rights from property owners) before production can even begin. If they then decide to limit output because prices are dropping, they can be left with an expensive asset that's generating little or no revenue.

Because operating costs can't be cranked up or down to match revenues, an increasingly common financial strategy for

producers is to even out the revenue stream through the use of commodities futures. By locking in prices months in advance to increase the predictability of their cash flows, companies are better able to manage major capital budgets and their overall operating budgets. At Oklahoma City's Chesapeake Energy, the nation's largest independent producer of natural gas, futures contracts have played an integral part of the company's financial strategy.

Of course, Chesapeake's vice president of finance Elliot Chambers would probably be the first to tell you that even though hedging can reduce a company's risk exposure, it is not without risks. Companies that guess incorrectly about future price shifts can pay dearly. For instance, in the second quarter of 2008, Chesapeake had *paper losses* of $3.4 billion on its hedging contracts because market prices had risen higher than the prices it had previously locked in those contracts.

Such losses are known as paper losses (or *unrealized losses*) because they happen only "on paper" until the futures contract actually comes due. Let's say that in January, Chesapeake signs a futures contract to sell gas at $6 per thousand cubic feet in October. However, if market prices rise to $8 in June, the company has a paper loss at that point of $2 per unit. It hasn't *actually* lost the $2 in June because it doesn't have to settle the contract until October, so the loss is considered to have happened only "on paper."

Interim paper losses might sound like they're not a problem because no money changes hands. After all, the market price in this example could settle back to $6 by October, in which case Chesapeake would essentially break even—or make money if the market price drops below $6 by October. However, the reason paper losses matter is that accounting regulations require companies to treat these losses as real in their ongoing financial statements. In other words, when Chesapeake had paper losses of $3.4 billion on its hedging contracts in the second quarter of 2008, those losses showed up in the quarterly income statement. And because the stock market pays close attention to quarterly income statements, a company's stock can get hammered even though such losses are (as yet) still on paper.

True to the wild nature of the natural gas market, halfway through the third quarter of 2008, Chesapeake's futures contracts had swung around in the positive direction, giving it a paper *gain* at one point of $4.7 billion. Like a paper loss, such a paper gain doesn't involve any money changing hands, but it must be accounted for in the financial statements.

When the contracts come due, losses or gains become quite real. If market prices at that point are higher than the price in the contract, Chesapeake suffers because it is forced to sell product at less than it could have gotten otherwise. Conversely, if market prices are lower than the contract price, the other party loses and Chesapeake wins, because the other party has to pay more than the market price.

Clearly, hedging is not an exact science or a perfect remedy, but it does bring some predictability to a company's cash flow and thereby allow it to plan the massive capital projects needed to bring new production online. Moreover, if a company does well over time, hedging can be a source of revenue. During one three-year period, for instance, Chesapeake increased its revenues by more than $2.4 billion through hedging.

Of course, you have to play to win, and to get the benefits of hedging, a company has to make the decision to hedge. In late 2011, the company pulled back on its hedging strategy in the belief that weather conditions were going to cause a sharp climb in gas demand and therefore gas prices. However, the demand spike never came, and as supplies across the industry continued to expand, prices fell to their lowest point in a decade. By the end of 2012, Chesapeake was nearly out of money after losing more than $2 million a day. At the beginning of 2013, the company reversed course and hedged half its production for the year against further price declines.

By the way, anyone following the use of commodities futures in the natural gas market must wonder *why* gas prices swing up and down so unpredictably—and in ways that aren't always related to supply and demand. After watching the gyrations in energy prices over the past few years and the destruction that derivatives caused in the banking industry, government regulators began to worry that the same financial tools producers use to protect themselves from violent price swings could be contributing to those swings in the first place. The federal Commodity Futures Trading Commission contends that in the hands of speculators, commodities futures contracts are disrupting prices in ways that harm consumers and industrial energy users. Congress has directed the commission to find ways to limit the risk caused by speculators trading commodities futures with no intent of buying or selling the actual commodities themselves.

In response, hedgers such as Chesapeake say they can't run their businesses without the participation of speculators, because they provide the financial predictability necessary to plan budgets in an inherently unstable industry. For instance, Chambers told the commission that without speculators, Chesapeake would never have been able to invest the $3.75 billion it took to discover and develop a major new source of natural gas in Louisiana.

With the United States looking for ways to reduce its dependence on imported oil, the plentiful supply of domestic natural gas is playing an increasingly important role in national policy discussions. It could come down to a tug-of-war between the need to develop more domestic sources in the long term and the need to bring stability to end-user energy prices in the short term.[30]

Critical Thinking Questions

19-1. If speculators are barred from investing in futures contracts, how will that change Chesapeake's approach to financial management? (Assume that natural gas distributors and other major customers would still be able to engage in futures contracts from a commodity buyer's perspective.)

19-2. Why do you suppose accounting regulations require companies to report paper losses or gains from futures contracts in their financial statements?

19-3. Should the government continue to allow speculation in natural gas futures as a way to keep developing domestic energy sources, even if it can be proven that speculation contributes to price volatility for producers and customers? Why or why not?

LEARN MORE ONLINE

Explore Chesapeake's website at **www.chk.com**, particularly the Investors section. How does Chesapeake's financial health look at present? What do the trends for revenue, expenses, and income look like? Read the Letter to Shareholders in the latest annual report. Does it mention hedging? If so, have the company's hedging activities been beneficial in the most recent year?

KEY TERMS

asset allocation (462)
bear market (462)
bond market (459)
book value (447)
broker (463)
bull market (462)
capital gains (446)
commodities futures (458)
common stock (446)
credit derivatives (458)
currency futures (458)
derivatives (456)
derivatives market (460)
exchange-traded funds (ETFs) (453)
expense ratio (453)
face value (449)
financial futures (457)
index (453)
index funds (453)
intrinsic value (448)
investment portfolios (462)
limit order (463)
load (453)
margin trading (463)

market order (463)
market value (447)
maturity date (449)
money market (460)
municipal bonds (452)
mutual funds (452)
net asset value (NAV) (454)
no-load funds (453)
option (457)
portfolio diversification (452)
preferred stock (446)
price/earnings ratio (448)
rate of return (461)
securities (446)
short selling (464)
stock (446)
stock exchanges (459)
stock split (449)
stop order (463)
Treasury bills (451)
Treasury bonds (452)
Treasury Inflation-Protected Securities (TIPS) (452)
Treasury notes (452)
yield (449)

MyBizLab®
To complete the problems with the ⭐,
go to EOC Discussion Questions in the
MyLab.

TEST YOUR KNOWLEDGE

Questions for Review

19-4. What is the difference between a stock's market value and its intrinsic value?

19-5. What is the money market?

19-6. What happens during a two-for-one stock split?

19-7. What is a p/e ratio, and what does it signify to an investor?

19-8. How does buying a commodities future differ from buying a commodity outright?

Questions for Analysis

⭐ **19-9.** If an investor had enough money to diversify adequately through buying individual securities, why might he or she still consider buying mutual funds instead?

19-10. Why is asset allocation recommended as a way to diversify against risk?

⭐ **19-11.** Why may different analysts arrive at different intrinsic values for the same stock?

19-12. When might an investor sell a stock short? What risks are involved in selling short?

⭐ **19-13. Ethical Considerations.** Would it be ethical for you to write in your personal blog about the positive outlook on a stock that you own, without telling readers that you own the stock? Why or why not?

Questions for Application

19-14. If investors want a steady, predictable flow of cash, what types of investments should they seek, and why?

19-15. If you are worried that a panicked market might cause the price of one of your stocks to plunge, what type of sell order could you use with your broker to limit your losses?

19-16. If your bank specializes in lending money to home builders, and the forecast for new home sales is predicting a decline in the coming months, what type of financial instrument could you use to protect against builders defaulting on loans because they are unable to sell the houses they've built?

19-17. Concept Integration. Review the discussion of mission statements on page 150 in Chapter 7. Suppose you were thinking about purchasing 100 shares of common stock in General Electric. Why might you want to first review the company's mission statement? What would you be looking for in the company's mission statement that could help you decide whether or not to invest?

EXPAND YOUR KNOWLEDGE

Discovering Career Opportunities

Think you might be interested in a job in the securities and commodities industry? This industry has one of the most highly educated and skilled workforces of any industry. View the Securities, Commodities, and Financial Services Sales Agents page at www .bls.gov/ooh to read more about these professions.

19-18. What are the licensing and continuing education requirements for securities brokers?

19-19. What is the typical starting position for many people in the securities industry?

19-20. What factors are expected to contribute to the projected long-term growth of this industry?

Improving Your Tech Insights: Online Investing Tools

The Internet has been a boon for individual investors, helping to level the playing field with professional and institutional investors by making in-depth information easily accessible. In addition to information, numerous websites now offer handy interactive tools for investors. Find an online tool that could help you as an investor—anything from a stock screener to an investing tutorial to a portfolio simulator. In a brief email message to your instructor, describe the benefits—and any risks—of using this tool.

PRACTICE YOUR SKILLS

Sharpening Your Communication Skills

Interviewing a full-service broker is one of the most important steps you can take before hiring that broker to execute your trades or manage your funds and investment portfolio. Practice your communication skills by developing two sets of questions:

19-21. Questions you might ask a stockbroker to help you decide whether you would use his or her services.

19-22. Questions you might pose to that broker to help you evaluate the merits of purchasing a specific security.

Building Your Team Skills

You and your team are going to pool your money and invest $5,000. Before you plunge into any investments, how can you prepare yourselves to be good investors? First, consider your group's goals. What will you and your teammates do with any profits generated by your investments? Once you have agreed on a goal for your team's profits, think about how much money you will need to achieve this goal and how soon you want to achieve it.

Next, think about how much risk you personally are willing to take to achieve the goal. Bear in mind that safer investments generally offer lower returns than riskier investments—and certain investments, such as stocks, can lose money. Now hold a group discussion to find a level of risk that feels comfortable for everyone on your team.

After your team has decided how much risk to take, consider which investments are best suited to your group's goals and chosen risk level. Will you choose stocks, bonds, a combination of both, or other securities? What are the advantages and disadvantages of each type of investment for your team's situation? Then come to a decision about specific investment opportunities—particular stocks, for example—that your group would like to investigate further.

Compare your group's goal, risk level, and investment possibilities with those of the other teams in your class and discuss the differences and similarities you see.

Developing Your Research Skills

Stock market analysts advise investors (both individuals and institutions) on which stocks to buy, sell, or hold. Changes in their opinions are called *upgrades* or *downgrades*, depending on the direction of their outlook. Changing a "hold" recommendation to a "buy" recommendation is an upgrade, for example. Find a stock that has been recently upgraded or downgraded (you can use New Ratings, www.newratings.com, or a similar source), and then perform some research on that company so you can answer the following questions.

19-23. Why did the analysts change their rating on this stock? Was it in response to something the company said or did? Is the company performing better or worse than its competitors? Do you think the rating change is fair to the company?

19-24. How did the rating change affect the company's stock price?

19-25. How has the company's stock been performing relative to the Dow Jones Industrial Average (DJIA) and S&P 500 indexes?

MyBizLab®

Go to the Assignments section of your MyLab to complete these writing exercises.

19-26. What are two key reasons investors choose index funds over actively managed mutual funds or individual stocks?

19-27. Assume you are trying to save money for a down payment on a house, and your goal is to have enough within three years. The stock market is raging and has been for nearly four years. Should you invest your current savings in the stock market with an eye toward pulling the money back out when you're ready to buy in three years? Why or why not?

ENDNOTES

1. Stephen Humenik, "CFTC Position Limits: Recent Congressional and Ongoing CFTC Developments," *Inside Energy & Environment*, 26 February 2015, www.insideenergyandenvironment.com; *Chesapeake Energy 2014 Annual Report*, www.chk.com; Joe Carroll, "Chesapeake Increases Hedging as Gas Bull CEO Readies Exit," *Bloomberg*, 12 February 2013, www.bloomberg.com; Dave Michaels, "CFTC to Offer New Take on Speculation-Limits Rule Judge Rejected," *Bloomberg*, 4 November 2013, www.bloomberg .com; *Chesapeake Energy Annual Reports, 2010 and 2012*; Chesapeake Energy website, www.chk.com; Ann Davis, "Hedges Pay Off for Gas Producers," *Wall Street Journal*, 13 August 2009, http://online.wsj.com; Peter Carbonara, "The Folly of Betting Where Oil Will Go," *BusinessWeek*, 6 October 2008, 47; Alan Brochstein, "Natural Gas: Extreme Contango Suggests Caution for E&P Companies," *Seeking Alpha*, 6 September 2009, http:// seekingalpha.com; Christopher Helman, "Would BP Please Buy Chesapeake Energy?" *Forbes*, 29 April 2009, www.forbes.com; Jesse Bogan, "Terrible Twos Near for Natural Gas," *Forbes*, 8 August 2009, www.forbes.com; Jesse Bogan, "Too Much Gas," *Forbes*, 22 May 2009, www.forbes.com; Ben Casselman, "Energy Firms Hedge with an Edge," *Wall Street Journal*, 29 July 2009, http://online.wsj.com; Jack Money, "Chesapeake's Hedging Loss Is More Than Meets the Naked Eye," *The Oklahoman*, 2 August 2008, www.istockanalyst.com; Chesapeake Energy, "September 2009 Investor Presentation," www.chk.com.

2. Ben Steverman, "The Buffett Way: Time for a Rethink?" *BusinessWeek*, 31 March 2009, 27.

3. Tom Drinkard, "A Primer on Preferred Stock," *Investopedia.com*, accessed 5 September 2009, www.investopedia.com.

4. Arthur J. Keown, *Personal Finance: Turning Money into Wealth*, 3rd ed. (Upper Saddle River, N.J.: Pearson Prentice Hall, 2003), 420.

5. Robert G. Hagstrom, Jr., *The Warren Buffett Way* (New York: Wiley, 1995), 36.

6. Cory Janssen, "A Breakdown of Stock Buybacks," *Investopedia.com*, accessed 5 September 2009, www.investopedia.com.

7. Jack R. Kapoor, Les R. Dlabay, and Robert J. Hughes, *Personal Finance*, 7th ed. (Boston: McGraw-Hill Irwin, 2004), 500.

8. Keown, *Personal Finance: Turning Money into Wealth*, 417.

9. "U.S. Junk Bond Default Rate Rises to 10.2 pct—S&P," *Reuters*, 3 September 2009, www.reuters.com.

10. Keown, *Personal Finance: Turning Money into Wealth*, 449.

11. "Treasury Inflation-Protected Securities (TIPS)," U.S. Department of Treasury website, accessed 10 September 2009, www .treasurydirect.gov.

12. Kapoor et al., *Personal Finance*, 506; Jack Colombo, "Muni Bond Default Parade Plays On," *Forbes*, 15 January 2009, www.forbes .com.

13. Morningstar website, accessed 21 November 2013, www .morningstar.com.

14. "Invest Wisely: An Introduction to Mutual Funds," U.S. Securities and Exchange Commission website, accessed 7 September 2009, www.sec.gov

15. Sam Mamudi, "Active Vs. Passive: Indexing Wins '09," *Wall Street Journal*, 5 March 2009, http://online.wsj.com.

16. Vanguard website, accessed 8 September 2009, http://personal .vanguard.com.

17. Mayra Rodriquez Valladares, "Overview of Derivatives," archived presentation, CME Group website, accessed 10 September 2009, www.cmegroup.com.

18. Marcy Gordon, "Behind Obama's Plan to Rein in Derivatives," *BusinessWeek*, 13 August 2009, 12; "'Life Settlements' Bonds Could Be Wall Street's Next Big Act," *MarketWatch*, 6 September 2009, www.marketwatch.com.

19. Carol J. Loomis, "Derivatives: The Risk That Still Won't Go Away," *Fortune*, 24 June 2009, http://money.cnn.com.

20. Valladares, "Overview of Derivatives."

21. Valladares, "Overview of Derivatives."

22. Charles R. Morris, *The Two Trillion Dollar Meltdown* (New York: Public Affairs, 2008), 115.

23. Bethany McLean, "The Man Who Lost $6 Billion," *Fortune*, 21 July 2008, 134–144.

24. *Triennial Central Bank Survey: April 2013*, Bank for International Settlements website, www.bis.org.

25. Wayne Pinsent, "Credit Default Swaps: An Introduction," *Investopedia.com*, accessed 8 September 2009, www.investopedia .com.

26. Datamonitor, "NASDAQ OMX Group, Inc.: Company Profile," 16 July 2008, 19; NASDAQ website, accessed 10 September 2009, www.nasdaq.com.

27. Securities Industry and Financial Markets Association, "Buying and Selling Bonds," investinginbonds.com, accessed 10 September 2009, www.investinginbonds.com.

28. Andrew Beattie, "Money Market Vs. Savings Accounts," *Investopedia.com*, accessed 10 September 2009, www.investopedia .com.

29. Valladares, "Overview of Derivatives."

30. See note 1.

The Money Supply and Banking Systems

20

LEARNING OBJECTIVES   After studying this chapter, you will be able to

1 List the four financial functions of money, and define two key measures of the money supply.

2 Explain the major functions of the Federal Reserve System, and identify other key federal financial institutions.

3 Distinguish investment banks from commercial banks, and identify the three major types of investment banks.

4 Identify the major types of commercial banks, and outline the impact of banking deregulation over the past three decades.

5 Identify the two major sets of economic forces that triggered the meltdown of 2008 and sent the economy into a global recession.

6 Outline the efforts to reform the banking industry in the wake of the subprime crisis.

BEHIND THE SCENES   CAN A NOT-FOR-PROFIT CREDIT UNION COMPETE IN A PROFIT-DRIVEN WORLD?

Credit unions provide many of the same financial services as conventional banks.

ZUMA Press, Inc./Alamy

www.alliantcreditunion.org

In a world of high-glamour high finance, the humble credit union might seem to some people to be out of step, maybe behind the times. When people can manage their finances via smartphone apps and sit behind computer screens in pursuit of nanosecond advantages as day traders in the stock market, aren't these not-for-profit, member-owned cooperatives just a little too quaint to be relevant?

David Mooney isn't buying any of it. As the CEO of Chicago-based Alliant Credit Union, he believes credit unions are in a better position than conventional banks to meet the needs of today's customers. In fact, he believes this so strongly that he left a long and successful career in the mainstream banking industry to take the top job at Alliant, and one of his key reasons was that he believes in the credit union model. Because a credit union is owned by its member/customers and not by shareholders, he can focus on meeting customer needs and not on trying to maximize returns for shareholders.

He's not alone in this sentiment, either. Growing numbers of consumers have expressed frustration at what they see as the reckless behavior of big banks, along with complaints about high fees for basic services, low interest on deposits, and less-than-stellar customer support.

If you were in Mooney's shoes, how would you position Alliant to take advantage of these shifts in consumer sentiment while fending off competition from community banks, online banks, international megabanks—and other credit unions?[1]

INTRODUCTION

Alliant Credit Union's David Mooney (profiled in the chapter-opening Behind the Scenes) works at the heart of an industry that affects everyone in the country and virtually every aspect of business. This chapter explores the role of money in the economy and the banking institutions that manage, protect, and supply the money that all consumers and businesses rely on. After covering the importance and influence of the banking sector, the chapter concludes with a story of banking and financial mismanagement so massive that it brought the global economy to its knees, followed by a discussion of the efforts to ensure a safe and productive banking system.

1 LEARNING OBJECTIVE

List the four financial functions of money, and define two key measures of the money supply.

The Money Supply

Almost every aspect of business you've studied in this course—from understanding the basic economics of supply and demand to paying employees, pricing products, and buying advertising—involves money. Now it's time to explore money itself, along with the organizations that influence how much money is available in the economy, how much it costs to borrow it, and what services these organizations provide to consumers and business customers.

The $10 bill you're carrying around in your pocket and the billions of dollars that a megabank moves around the world are all part of a vast collection known as the *money supply*. The nature of this supply affects virtually every aspect of your financial life, from the size of your car payments to how soon you'll be able to retire.

THE MEANING OF MONEY

money
Anything generally accepted as a means of paying for goods and services; serves as a medium of exchange, a unit of accounting, a store of value, and a standard of deferred value.

Money is anything generally accepted as a means of paying for goods and services. Every country has its own system of money, or currency, except for those that opt to share a currency such as the euro. Money performs four financial functions. First, it serves as a *medium of exchange*, a tool for simplifying transactions between buyers and sellers. Second, it serves as a *unit of accounting*—a measure of value, in other words—so that buyers and sellers don't have to negotiate the relative worth of dissimilar items with every transaction. Third, money serves as a temporary *store of value*—a way of accumulating wealth until it is needed. Fourth, money serves as a standard of *deferred payment*, meaning it can be used to represent debt obligations.[2]

The practical value of money stems from two key properties: liquidity and trust.[3] Money is the most liquid asset because it can be exchanged easily and more or less instantly for something else of value. If you own a million-dollar house but have no money come dinner time, you'll go hungry because your wealth is *illiquid*—you may be "house rich," but you can't very easily exchange part of your house for food.

If you do have a $20 bill to hand to the pizza delivery person, what exactly are you using as payment? A paper rectangle with a bit of ink splashed on it? The only reason the pizza seller will relinquish your dinner is because he or she trusts that the bill you're handing over in exchange represents $20 worth of real economic value. At one point in U.S. history, the value of that paper rectangle would've been tied to the price of gold, and you could exchange your bills for a specific amount of gold, but the value of money is no longer linked to gold. Instead, there is basically a mutual agreement that the bill represents a certain amount of exchangeable value, so the pizza shop can take your $20 and use it to pay its bills, and so on through the entire economy.

MONITORING AND MANAGING THE MONEY SUPPLY

money supply
The amount of money in circulation at any given point in time.

Every economy has a certain amount of money in circulation at any given point in time, a quantity known as the **money supply**, also known as the *money stock*. The money supply can be measured in several ways. Economists focus on two aggregates known as *M1* and *M2* (see Exhibit 20.1). M1 consists of cash held by the public and money deposited in

| EXHIBIT 20.1 | Trends in the Money Supply |

Both M1 and M2 have risen in recent years, which by conventional thinking suggests the risk of inflation. However, inflation has remained under control in recent years, so the presumed causal link with inflation must not be quite so simple.

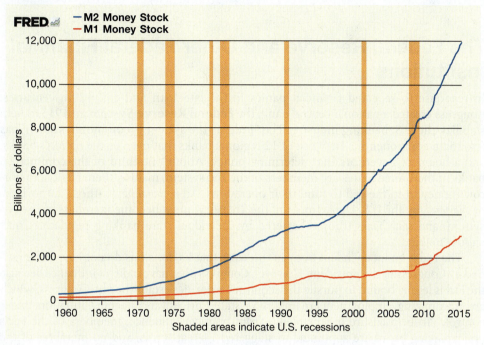

Source: "Economic Research," Federal Reserve Bank of St. Louis website, accessed 22 June 2015, http://research.stlouisfed .org/fred2. Used courtesy of the Federal Reserve Bank of St. Louis.

a variety of checking accounts. M2 is a broader measure, incorporating M1 plus savings accounts, balances in retail money-market mutual funds, and small *time deposits*—money held in interest-paying accounts such as certificates of deposit that may restrict the owner's right to withdraw funds on short notice.[4] In simple terms, M1 is money that is spendable now, and M2 adds money that could be spendable fairly soon.

Policymakers, investors, and others pay attention to the money supply because it affects interest rates, inflation, and other vital aspects of the economy's health.[5] (Just how it affects these variables and to what degree is a matter of ongoing debate and research.) The next section discusses the efforts to maintain a healthy money supply.

✓ Checkpoint

LEARNING OBJECTIVE 1: List the four financial functions of money, and define two key measures of the money supply.

SUMMARY: Money, anything generally accepted as a means of paying for goods and services, performs four financial functions: as a medium of exchange, as a unit of accounting, as a temporary store of value, and as a standard of deferred payment. The money supply is the amount of money in circulation at any given point in time. The aggregate M1 is cash held by the public and money deposited in a variety of checking accounts; M2 includes M1 plus savings accounts, balances in retail money-market mutual funds, and small time deposits such as certificates of deposit.

CRITICAL THINKING: (1) What might happen if people lose trust in their country's currency? (2) Why couldn't you buy your groceries using an amount of gold of equal value to the cost of the items you want to purchase?

2 **LEARNING OBJECTIVE**

Explain the major functions of the Federal Reserve System, and identify other key federal financial institutions.

Federal Reserve System
The central banking system of the United States; responsible for regulating banks and implementing monetary policy.

The Federal Reserve and Other Federal Financial Institutions

In response to repeated financial panics in the late 19th and early 20th centuries, Congress created a national central bank, the **Federal Reserve System**, in 1913 to help stabilize the U.S. banking industry. The "Fed," as the system is commonly known, has two main components: a network of 12 regional banks that oversee the nation's banks, and a board of governors that determine policy. About one-third of the commercial banks in the United States are members of the Fed system, making them eligible to borrow money from the Fed to fund their operations. All *national banks* (those authorized, or *chartered*, by the U.S. Department of the Treasury) must become members of the Fed system, and *state banks* (those chartered by individual state banking regulators) may choose to join.[6]

The Fed is an independent body in the sense that its decisions do not have to be ratified by Congress or the president. However, Congress does have indirect influence because the Fed is legally bound to pursue the economic priorities established by Congress, which are maximizing employment, maintaining stable prices, and keeping inflation under control.[7] To help ensure independence from political influence, members of the Fed's policymaking board are appointed to staggered 14-year terms, and no members of the presidential administration or any elected officials may serve on the board.[8]

THE FED'S MAJOR RESPONSIBILITIES

The work of the Fed can be divided into three broad categories: (1) serving as a bank for the federal government and many commercial banks, (2) supervising and regulating many financial institutions, and (3) managing the nation's money supply by designing and implementing monetary policy. The Fed is also involved in certain aspects of consumer protection, foreign currency exchange trading, and international banking coordination.

As the "bank for banks," the Fed provides many of the services that a commercial bank provides to businesses and consumers, including holding deposits and making loans. It also operates two electronic systems for transferring money between banks, one for large amounts of cash and the smaller *automated clearing house (ACH)* system for routine payments made by check.[9]

As one of the primary supervisory and regulatory bodies, the Fed monitors the operation of state banks that are members of the Fed system, all *bank holding companies* (companies than own multiple banks), and the U.S. operations of foreign banks. The Fed's key objectives in this respect are making sure that banks are financially sound and that customers' accounts are safe, and it has the authority to take formal or informal action against banks that are out of compliance with Fed guidelines. Two other important aspects of the Fed's regulatory mandate are approving bank mergers and acquisitions and implementing finance-related consumer protection laws.[10]

Monetary policy is decided by the Federal Open Market Committee (FOMC), which includes the Fed's board of governors, the president of the New York City Fed, and 4 of the other 11 regional presidents. The three primary goals of maximum employment, stable prices, and moderate inflation are sometimes in conflict, so the FOMC faces a constant balancing act as it tries to optimize the overall results. The FOMC meets eight times a year to assess the nation's economic state and to decide whether changes in monetary policy need to be made.[11]

THE FED'S TOOLS FOR IMPLEMENTING MONETARY POLICY

The Fed has several tools for implementing monetary policy, although "tool" suggests a stronger degree of control than it actually has. The Fed can't forces banks to raise or lower the interest rates they charge businesses or consumers or flip a switch to make the economy heat up or slow down. Instead, it works indirectly, making changes in the economic variables it does control in the hope that those changes will nudge banks and other players in the economy in the desired direction.

The Federal Funds Rate

Much of the Fed's influence is exerted through the **federal funds rate**, which is the rate that member banks charge each other to borrow money overnight from the funds they keep in their Federal Reserve accounts. (You'll often hear this rate referred to as the *overnight rate*.) The federal funds rate is a fundamental driver of economic behavior because it influences short- and long-term interest rates, foreign exchange rates, and inflation.

As important as the federal funds rate is, the Fed doesn't set this rate directly. Instead, it sets a target rate and then tries to push the federal funds rate as close as possible to that target using three mechanisms:[12]

- **Buying and selling Treasury bonds, bills, and notes.** When the Fed buys Treasuries, this injects money into the economy, thereby increasing the money supply, which tends to then decrease the federal funds rate. The opposite effect happens when the Fed sells Treasuries: Selling pulls money out of the economy, decreasing the money supply and increasing the federal funds rate. This buying and selling is the Fed's most powerful tool and is used nearly every day to adjust the level of the Fed's Treasuries holdings. Because these transactions take place on the open market, they are known as *open-market operations*.

- **Adjusting reserve requirements.** All *depository institutions* (those that accept deposits from customers), including commercial banks, savings and loan associations, and credit unions, are required to hold a portion of those deposits in *reserve*. The institutions may keep the reserve as cash in their own vaults or in an account at a regional Federal Reserve bank. By changing the reserve percentage, the Fed allows these institutions to lend out more or less of their deposited amounts, thereby affecting the size of the money supply. In contrast to the frequently used open-market operations, however, the Fed does not change the reserve ratio frequently, because doing so is costly to implement and a small change can have a drastic effect.

- **Lending through the discount window.** The Fed's *discount window* (no longer an actual window) is a process for making short-term loans to depository institutions when they are unable to get funds through normal interbank borrowing. This can happen when the overall supply of funds available has dropped (as happened after the 9/11 terrorist attacks and again during the 2008 credit crisis), an institution did not receive an expected loan from another institution, or a smaller bank needs to even out seasonal fluctuations in its deposits. The volume of lending through the discount window is relatively low, but these loans often play an important role in relieving money supply shortages that might push the federal fund rate up.

Even with these mechanisms at its disposal, however, there are limits to how much the Fed can "move the needle" by changing the federal funds target rate. As you'll read on page 483, during the 2008 credit crisis, the bank lowered its target to essentially zero (0.25 percent) and has kept it there since.[13] In other words, the Fed has pulled on this lever as hard as it can in hopes of stimulating economic growth and employment, but for the time being there's not much more it can do with it.

federal funds rate
The interest rate that member banks charge each other to borrow money overnight from the funds they keep in the Federal Reserve accounts.

discount rate
The interest rate that member banks pay when they borrow funds from the Fed.

prime rate
The interest rate a bank charges its best loan customers.

The Discount Rate

The Fed's other key interest rate is the **discount rate**, which is the rate that member banks pay when they borrow funds through the discount window. Unlike with the federal funds rate, the Fed does set the discount rate directly. When the Fed changes the discount rate, each member bank generally changes its **prime rate**, which is the rate a bank charges its best loan customers. Many other interest rates are also based on the prime rate; some variable rate loans and credit cards adjust their rates over time as the prime fluctuates. Raising the discount rate discourages loans and therefore tightens the money supply; lowering it encourages lending and expands the money supply.

OTHER GOVERNMENT BANKING AGENCIES AND INSTITUTIONS

The Fed shares responsibility for banking oversight and financial activities with a number of other agencies and semi-independent institutions. The most significant at the federal level are these three:

Federal Deposit Insurance Corporation (FDIC)
The federal agency responsible for protecting money in customer accounts and managing the transition of assets whenever a bank fails.

Fannie Mae
The government-sponsored enterprise responsible for guaranteeing and funding home mortgages.

secondary mortgage market
The financial market in which mortgages are bought and sold, providing much of the funds that are loaned to homebuyers.

Freddie Mac
A secondary mortgage institution similar to Fannie Mae.

- **FDIC.** After thousands of banks failed in the United States during the Great Depression, the government established the **Federal Deposit Insurance Corporation (FDIC)**, www.fdic.gov, to protect money in customer accounts and to manage the transition of assets whenever a bank fails. Banks pay a fee to join the FDIC network, and in turn, the FDIC guarantees to cover any losses from bank failure up to a maximum of $250,000 per account.[14] Similar institutions exist for savings and loan associations and credit unions.

- **Fannie Mae.** To spur homeownership after the Depression, Congress established the Federal National Mortgage Association (FNMA), now officially known as **Fannie Mae**. Through its mandate to help low- to middle-income homebuyers by guaranteeing and buying mortgages originated by banks and other lenders, Fannie Mae essentially created the **secondary mortgage market**. This "behind-the-scenes" market provides a good portion of the funds that are loaned to homebuyers. Fannie Mae was spun off as a quasi-independent corporation in 1968 and remains a dominant force in the mortgage business, although some of its practices have come under heavy criticism over the years.[15] The company invested heavily in subprime mortgages and had to be rescued by the federal government in the credit crisis of 2008.

- **Freddie Mac.** Another major player in the secondary market is **Freddie Mac**, created in 1970 as the Federal Home Loan Mortgage Corporation. Like Fannie Mae, Freddie Mac is a quasi-independent corporation—and it also had to be rescued in 2008 after overloading with poor-quality mortgage debt. By the end of 2013, thanks to a modest recovery in the housing market, both Fannie Mae and Freddie Mac had earned enough to repay virtually all of their government bailouts. However, political pressure remains strong to phase out both banks and replace them with a new system for funding home mortgages.[16]

Checkpoint

LEARNING OBJECTIVE 2: Explain the major functions of the Federal Reserve System, and identify other key federal financial institutions.

SUMMARY: The work of the Federal Reserve can be divided into three broad categories. First, it serves as a bank for the federal government and many commercial banks, holding deposits, making loans, and operating electronic transaction systems. Second, it supervises and regulates all financial institutions that are members of the Fed network, bank holding companies, or U.S. operations of foreign banks. Third, it manages the nation's money supply by designing and implementing monetary policy. The Fed's primary tool for implementing monetary policy is influencing the federal funds rate, the interest rate charged by member banks that lend money to each other. The Fed doesn't set this interest rate but rather attempts to influence it by buying and selling Treasuries, adjusting reserve requirements, and lending through its discount window. Other major federal institutions involved in banking include the FDIC and the quasi-government mortgage banks Fannie Mae and Freddie Mac.

CRITICAL THINKING: (1) Why does the Fed want to avoid an "overheating" economy? (2) Why is the Fed's discount window considered the "lender of last resort" for some banks?

IT'S YOUR BUSINESS: (1) In general terms, how might Fed decisions over the next several years affect your life? (2) If you are hoping to get a loan to expand your business, will you welcome the news that the Fed is raising the discount rate? Why or why not?

KEY TERMS TO KNOW: Federal Reserve System, federal funds rate, discount rate, prime rate, Federal Deposit Insurance Corporation (FDIC), Fannie Mae, secondary mortgage market, Freddie Mac

Investment Banking

A wide range of companies help consumers, businesses, and governments with every aspect of banking and financial management. These services can be roughly divided into investment banking (covered in this section) and commercial banking and other financial services (covered in the next section).

3 | LEARNING OBJECTIVE

Distinguish investment banks from commercial banks, and identify the three major types of investment banks.

SERVICES OFFERED BY INVESTMENT BANKS

Investment banks offer a variety of investing and advisory services to organizational customers, including corporations, other financial institutions, pension funds, and governments. Some also cater to wealthy individuals who meet a particular net worth threshold, but they don't provide services to the general public. Investment banks provide some combination of the following services:[17]

- Facilitating mergers, acquisitions, sales, and spin-offs of companies
- Underwriting initial public offerings
- Managing and advising on investments
- Raising capital (such as by selling bonds) on behalf of corporate or government clients
- Advising on and facilitating over complex financial transactions
- Investing in or lending money to companies
- Providing risk management advice
- Providing comprehensive brokerage services to hedge funds and other with complex investing needs
- Enabling clients to trade commodities
- Providing foreign currency exchange trading for clients
- "Making markets" for clients, which involves acting as an interim buyer or seller to help clients acquire or divest assets

investment banks
Firms that offer a variety of services related to initial public stock offerings, mergers and acquisitions, and other investment matters.

Given the scope of many investment banks' activities, there is often the potential for conflicts of interest. For example, the group underwriting a new stock offering is motivated to sell that stock to investors at the highest possible price. Those investors could include clients of the bank's own investment management group, who have a duty to act in their clients' best interests. If the new stock offering isn't the right fit for a particular investment client, the two groups would be in conflict—one wanting to sell that stock to the client, and the other advising the client not to buy it. Similarly, a bank's investment analysts are charged with writing objective, unbiased recommendations about investment possibilities. Most investment banks also actively pursue investments on their own behalf, creating more possibilities for conflict. Banks are bound by a variety of regulations to keep these internal groups from unduly influencing each other to the detriment of the bank's clients, a separation you will sometimes hear referred to as the "Chinese Wall."[18]

Goldman Sachs is one of the biggest and most influential of the "bulge bracket" global investment banks.

Jack Picone/Alamy

TYPES OF INVESTMENT BANKS

Investment banking services can be delivered by institutions that are primarily or exclusive investment banks (meaning they do no commercial banking) or by multifaceted financial services firms that include investment banking as part of an array of services. Whether they are stand-alone or part of a larger firm, investment banks can be divided into three basic categories: *global, regional,* and *boutique.*

Global investment banks are those with international reach and a full menu of client services. The largest of these, a group of about 10, depending on who is counting, comprise what is known informally as the "bulge bracket," because they dominate the industry. However, this number may shrink as some firms get out of the investment banking business in the coming years.[19]

In the United States, these banks were historically the giants of Wall Street, and the names of five in particular overshadowed the history of high finance in the United States: Bear Stearns (founded in 1923), Goldman Sachs (1869), Lehman Brothers (1850), Merrill Lynch (1915), and Morgan Stanley (1935). All five were caught up in the subprime mortgage mess (see pages 478–484), and with a rapidity that shocked the financial world, three of the five ceased to exist as independent investment banks by the end of 2008. (Bear Stearns and Merrill Lynch were taken over by other banks, and Lehman Brothers collapsed in the largest bankruptcy in U.S. history.)[20]

However, even in their revamped forms, whether independent or part of other organizations, Wall Street's major investment banks still dominate the financial sector.

Regional investment banks often provide the same scope of services as the global banks, only with a particular geographic focus. For example, several banks specialize in the Japanese market, several specialize in China, and so on.[21] Boutique investment banks specialize in particular industries or specific services such as mergers and acquisitions.

REAL-TIME UPDATES
Learn More by Exploring This Interactive Website

Interested in working for an investment bank?

This site lists investment banks by type and provides contact details. Go to http://real-timeupdates.com/bia8 and click on Learn More in the Students section.

 Checkpoint

LEARNING OBJECTIVE 3: Distinguish investment banks from commercial banks, and identify the three major types of investment banks.

SUMMARY: Investment banks offer a variety of investing and advisory services to organizational customers, including corporations, other financial institutions, pension funds, and governments. Some also cater to wealthy individuals who meet a particular net worth threshold, but unlike commercial banks they don't provide services to the general public. The three major types of investment banks are global (full palette of services with global reach), regional (full service but in a limited geographic area), and boutique (specializing in specific industries or functions such as mergers and acquisitions).

CRITICAL THINKING: (1) Could efforts to avoid conflicts of interest lead an investment bank to provide poor service to a client? Explain your answer. (2) With the demise or transformation of the great investment banks of Wall Street, has the need for investment banking disappeared? Explain your answer.

IT'S YOUR BUSINESS: (1) Given the opportunity, would you subscribe to buy a newly issued stock from an investment bank or wait until after the initial public offering and see how the market treated the new issue? Explain your reasoning. (2) Investment banks offer some of the highest salaries in the world, but the work can be extremely stressful and the hours are long. Would you be interested in such a career? Why or why not?

KEY TERM TO KNOW: investment banks

Commercial Banking and Other Financial Services

Commercial banks are financial institutions that, generally speaking, accept deposits, offer various types of checking and savings accounts, and provide loans. The terminology can be confusing because some of these institutions don't call themselves banks, and some people use the term *commercial bank* to refer to banks that serve businesses only, not consumers. However, "commercial banking" is a good way to distinguish this class of services from both investment banking and nonbanking financial services. A wide range of services fall under this umbrella, and many banking companies offer multiple services. Here are the major types of commercial banks:

- **Retail banks** serve consumers with checking and savings accounts, debit and credit cards, and loans for homes, cars, and other major purchases.
- **Merchant banks** offer financial services to businesses, particularly in the area of international finance. *Merchant banking* is sometimes more narrowly defined as managing private equity investments, making it more akin to investment banking.[22]
- **Thrift banks**, also called *thrifts*, or *savings and loan associations*, offer deposit accounts and focus on offering home mortgage loans.
- **Credit unions** such as Alliant Credit Union (featured at the beginning of the chapter) are not-for-profit, member-owned cooperatives that offer deposit accounts and lending services to consumers and small businesses. Note that thrifts and credit unions do not refer to themselves as banks, but the broad definition of banking used here distinguishes them from investment banks.
- **Private banking** refers to a range of banking services for high-net-worth (that is, wealthy) individuals and families, such as managing real estate and other investments, setting up trust funds, and planning philanthropic giving.[23]

COMMERCIAL BANKING SERVICES

The range of services that banks and other financial firms are legally allowed to offer has changed over time, and some of these changes have been controversial. For example, some experts blamed risky investment activity by commercial banks (using depositors' funds, in some cases) for the stock market crash that triggered the Great Depression. In response, the Glass-Steagall Act of 1933 (which also established the FDIC) aimed to restore confidence in U.S. financial houses by restricting investment banks and commercial banks from crossing into each others' businesses and potentially abusing their fiduciary duties at the expense of customers. Another key objective of Glass-Steagall was to ensure that a catastrophic failure in one part of the financial services industry would not invade every other part like it did in 1929.[24]

Beginning in 1980, several waves of deregulation dramatically reshaped the banking and financial services industries—and in the eyes of some observers, helped create or worsen the meltdown you'll read about later in this chapter. After several decades of lobbying by the banking industry, piecemeal exemptions to the law, and regulatory changes that chipped away at the wall between commercial and investment banking, the Financial Services Modernization Act of 1999 repealed Glass-Steagall.[25] As a result of this legislation and several other regulatory changes over the past 30 years, many of the barriers that once separated various kinds of banking, investing, and insurance services are now gone, paving the way for colossal, multifaceted firms such as today's JPMorgan Chase and Bank of America.

4 **LEARNING OBJECTIVE**

Identify the major types of commercial banks, and outline the impact of banking deregulation over the past three decades.

commercial banks
Banks that accept deposits, offer various checking and savings accounts, and provide loans.

retail banks
Banks that provide financial services to consumers.

merchant banks
Banks that provide financial services to businesses; can also refer to private equity management.

thrift banks
Banking institutions that offer deposit accounts and focus on offering home mortgage loans; also called *thrifts*, or *savings and loan associations*.

credit unions
Not-for-profit, member-owned cooperatives that offer deposit accounts and lending services to consumers and small businesses.

private banking
Banking services for wealthy individuals and families.

Credit unions are not-for-profit member-owned financial cooperatives that provide deposit and loan services to their members.

REAL-TIME UPDATES
Learn More by Visiting This Website

Free money advice from Mint.com

Manage money and credit wisely with tips from Mint.com's blog. Go to http://real-timeupdates.com/bia8 and click on Learn More in the Students section.

OTHER FINANCIAL SERVICES

independent mortgage companies
Nonbank companies that use their own funds to offer mortgages.

mortgage brokers
Nonbank companies that initiate loans on behalf of a mortgage lender in exchange for a fee.

finance companies
Nonbank institutions that lend money to consumers and businesses for cars and other vehicles, home improvements, expansion, purchases, and other purposes.

credit rating agencies
Companies that offer opinions about the creditworthiness of borrowers and of specific investments.

In addition to commercial banks of all shapes and sizes, various other types of firms provide essential financial services to consumers and businesses. Some complement services offered by commercial banks; others compete with commercial banks in one or more areas. For example, **independent mortgage companies** originate mortgages using their own funds, and **mortgage brokers** initiate loans on behalf of a mortgage lender in exchange for a fee.

A variety of nonbank institutions lend money to consumers and businesses for vehicles, home improvements, expansion, purchases, and other purposes. Some of these **finance companies** are independent; others are affiliated with retailers or manufacturers. For example, Toyota Financial Services, a wholly owned subsidiary of Toyota Motor Corporation, offers car loans to drivers buying Toyota vehicles.[26] Credit cards are another major category of lending; some cards are issued by banks, whereas others are issued by retailers and credit card companies such as American Express.

Credit rating agencies offer opinions about the creditworthiness of borrowers and of specific investments, such as the corporate bonds discussed in Chapter 18 (see page 436). Moody's, Standard & Poor's, and Fitch are the major rating agencies of businesses and securities; Equifax, Experian, and TransUnion are the major agencies that rate consumer creditworthiness. Before any bank or finance company will give you a loan, it will check your *credit rating* to judge the level of risk you represent as a borrower.

 Checkpoint

LEARNING OBJECTIVE 4: Identify the major types of commercial banks, and outline the impact of banking deregulation over the past three decades.

SUMMARY: Commercial banks are financial institutions that, generally speaking, accept deposits, offer various types of checking and savings accounts, and provide loans. Using this definition, the sphere of commercial banking includes retail banks, merchant banks (but not the merchant banking that refers to private equity investing), thrift banks (also known as savings and loans), credit unions, and private banking services for high-net-worth clients. Note that the term *commercial bank* is sometimes used to refer to banks that serve businesses only, not consumers. Banking deregulation removed the barriers between investment and commercial banking and opened the door for huge multifaceted financial services firms.

CRITICAL THINKING: (1) Why might credit unions want to promote themselves as not being banks in the popular usage of the term? (2) Would a credit union have the potential to get into business banking or investment banking? Why or why not?

IT'S YOUR BUSINESS: (1) Does the not-for-profit, member-ownership aspect of credit unions appeal to you? Why or why not?

KEY TERMS TO KNOW: commercial banks, retail banks, merchant banks, thrift banks, credit unions, private banking, independent mortgage companies, mortgage brokers, finance companies, credit rating agencies

5 LEARNING OBJECTIVE
Identify the two major sets of economic forces that triggered the meltdown of 2008 and sent the economy into a global recession.

Banking's Role in the Great Recession

Banks and other financial companies provide vital services for consumers, businesses, and governments. From getting loans to having convenient access to safely stored cash, the quality and convenience of contemporary life would not be possible without these services. At the same time, banking and financial services have such a pervasive presence that problems in the financial sector can spread across the economy, creating widespread havoc. A look back at the housing crisis and credit crisis, key events leading up to the Great Recession of 2007–2009, helps illustrate the role banking and financial services play in everyone's lives.[27]

BUILDING THE PERFECT BUBBLE

The story behind the real estate **bubble** (a term that is used when frenzied demand drives prices of an asset far beyond its intrinsic economic value) and Great Recession of 2007–2009 is complex and not easy to summarize. It involved many forces that took years to develop and then came together in a perfect storm of recklessness, stupidity, fraud, bad luck, and bad outcomes from good intentions. If you hear anyone placing the blame on a single institution, political party, or piece of legislation, you're getting only part of the story:

- All levels of the banking sector contributed to the meltdown—the Fed, Fannie Mae, investment banks, commercial banks, and mortgage companies.
- Choices made by government regulators and elected officials from both political parties contributed.
- Some institutional investors purchased complex, mortgage-based investment products that they didn't understand, which harmed the financial health of some cities and pension funds.
- Credit rating agencies gave investment-quality grades to mortgage-backed securities that really deserved speculative, junk-bond grades.
- The home-building and real-estate industries helped feed the frenzied demand for housing by promoting the idea that buying a home (or two or three) was a low-risk way to wealth and you were missing out if you didn't get your slice of the pie.
- Last, and far from least, through wishful thinking or worse, millions of homebuyers took out mortgages that they had little or no chance of repaying.

The following is a necessarily simplified look at the causes of the Great Recession, with a particular eye on the role of the banking sector.

Recovering from the Dot-Com Bubble

To stimulate the economy after the collapse of the dot-com bubble of the late 1990s and the terrorist attacks of September 11, 2001, the Fed worked to reduce the federal funds rate, which had been as high as 6.5 percent the previous year, to as low as 1 percent.[28] It was an effective stimulant, and the economy began growing again. However, the low rate had two unintended consequences: It helped fuel a new bubble in housing (lower interest rates made home mortgages more attractive), and it prompted a vast pool of institutional investment funds to start looking for something more rewarding than Treasury issues (lower interest rates made those debt instruments less attractive). What made this new bubble so huge and ultimately so destructive was that these two economic forces, Main Street and Wall Street, began feeding off each other, pumping up the bubble from both ends.

Lower interest rates can heat up the housing market in several ways. First, lower rates mean lower monthly payments for a given loan amount, so more people can afford houses, which obviously increases demand. Second, for the same monthly payment, people can afford bigger mortgages, which can spur them to move up to more expensive homes. And third, lower rates coupled with overheated demand and easier access to credit helped transform the humble home from simply a place to live into a mechanism for making money. All these factors drove prices way out of line with actual value in dozens of cities across the country.

Creating a New Bubble in Housing

Before long, houses became the new dot-com stocks. Home prices surged every year from 2002 through 2006 (see Exhibit 20.2 on the next page).[29] Buyers frantic to get in on the boom bid against each other and drove prices sky high. *Flipping*—buying a house, making some quick fixes to raise its value or simply waiting for prices to rise, and reselling it for a big profit—became so popular there were TV shows devoted to it.

The overheated housing market might have just been an "ordinary" bubble that eventually burst and burned the latecomers who got in after all the profits had already been taken out (which happens with every bubble). However, this bubble contained a special poison: millions of risky, foolish, and downright fraudulent mortgages.

Banks and mortgage companies helped pump up the bubble by lowering their standards for writing mortgages, in three key ways. First, in the old days borrowers needed

bubble
A market situation in which frenzied demand for an asset pushes the price of that asset far beyond its true economic value.

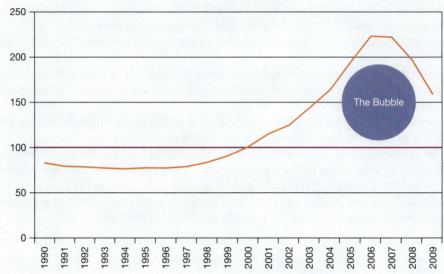

EXHIBIT 20.2 **The Housing Bubble**

Using 2000 as the base year, this graph shows how rapidly home prices grew in the years that followed—far out of line with their fundamental economic value.

U.S. Home Prices
10-city composite index

January 2000 = 100

The Bubble

Source: Data from "S&PCase-Shiller Home Price Indices, September 29, 2009: Historical Values," www.indices.standardand poors.com.

subprime mortgages
Home loans for borrowers with low credit scores.

loan-to-value (LTV)
The percentage of an asset's market value that a lender is willing to finance when offering a loan; the rest of the purchase price has to be paid by the buyer as a down payment.

adjustable rate mortgage (ARM)
A mortgage that features variable interest rates over the life of the loan.

documented proof of sufficient income to make their loan payments, some assets to serve as collateral, and a history of responsible credit use. However, many people couldn't meet those standards, so lenders began writing more **subprime mortgages**, those in which the borrower didn't qualify for a regular "prime" mortgage. Millions of subprime loans were made between 2002 and 2006 (see Exhibit 20.3). Moreover, as the real estate frenzy heated up, documentation standards on all types of loans slipped, and fraud became widespread. At Wachovia, a once-major bank that eventually went bankrupt as the crisis unfolded, 85 percent of the riskiest types of loans it made lacked *any* proof of income or assets.[30]

Second, banks used to have a maximum **loan-to-value (LTV)** ratio of 75 to 80 percent. That was the most they would lend, and borrowers had to come up with the rest in cash as a down payment. However, as the bubble was growing, many new loans were written with LTVs of 90, 95, 100—even 125 percent.[31] In other words, some borrowers were loaned more money than their houses were worth.

Third, in the past, most mortgages had fixed interest rates with monthly payments high enough to pay down part of the principle every month in addition to paying interest. Borrowers knew exactly how much they would have to pay every month, and every month they chiseled away at the principle, increasing their equity. However, this housing boom was fueled in large part by new types of mortgages that were far easier to get but much riskier to have. An **adjustable rate mortgage (ARM)** entices borrowers with low *teaser rates*, which lower their payments in the early years but make them vulnerable to *payment shock* later, when the "real" rates kick in, and even more so if interest rates climb. Even more dangerous was the *option ARM*, which let people choose to pay only the interest on their loans every month (which meant they would never pay off the principle) or even *less* than the interest (which meant the amount they owed increased every month). By the housing boom's peak in 2006, more than 20 percent of all new mortgages were subprime—and half of all those subprimes were ARMs with those time-bomb interest rate hikes.[32]

In hindsight, these practices look like sheer madness. However, as house prices kept rising from 2001 to 2005, they helped mask the danger building up from all these risky

Subprime Lending

This graph shows the number of nonprime home loans created during the housing boom from 2000 through 2007. (Nonprime includes subprime loans and the "Alt-A" category between prime and subprime, which is where many no-documentation loans are categorized.) The graph includes new lending and refinancing, when a homeowner replaces an existing loan with a new loan. Notice the correlation between this graph and the inflation of the housing bubble in Exhibit 20.2.

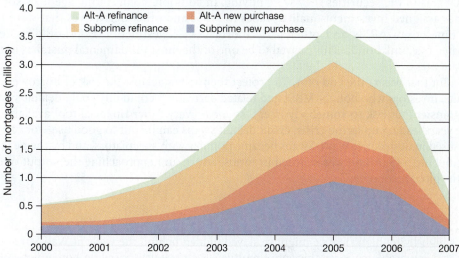

Nonprime Mortgages
(Includes new mortgages and refinancing of existing mortgages)

Source: Data from William B. Shear, Director of Financial Markets and Community Investment, U.S. Government Accountability Office, "Characteristics and Performance of Nonprime Mortgages," 28 July 2009, memo to Representative Carolyn B. Maloney and Senator Charles R. Schumer.

and rotten mortgages.[33] Buyers were getting homes for incredibly low monthly payments, everybody in the banking system was making money, and there was widespread belief (or willing suspension of disbelief) that house prices would just keep climbing. If you had a shaky mortgage, all you had to do was wait for the market value of your house to rise far enough and then you could use the built-up equity to refinance on more sensible terms.

At this point, you're probably wondering why lenders were making loans to people who had little or no chance of ever repaying them. In the old days, whenever a bank lent a homebuyer money, the bank usually kept the loan on its books and therefore kept the risk that the borrower might not repay the money. Because they kept the risk in house, banks maintained those strict lending standards described previously. However, thanks to the growth of the secondary mortgage market, many mortgage lenders no longer carried the risk of borrower default. This is why moral hazard played (see page 4 in Chapter 1) such a huge role in the subprime mess: Lenders could make risky, ridiculous, or even fraudulent loans—and immediately pass the risk on to somebody else.

Securitizing Debt

Meanwhile, far at the other end of the financial galaxy, a large and mostly invisible force from Wall Street had been encouraging the lenders on Main Street to make as many loans as they could—prime, subprime, fixed rate, option ARM, whatever. Institutional investors and hedge funds were looking elsewhere for higher returns than they could get from Treasuries, and they found what they were seeking in *mortgage-backed securities.*

For all types of lenders, the secondary mortgage market is a vital source of funds, because they can sell their loans to investors and use the proceeds to make even more loans. The system has been in place since Fannie Mae's creation in the 1930s and is now an essential part of homeownership in the United States. Although selling loans might sound like an odd concept, every loan represents a stream of future cash flow (the sum of all the payments due from the borrower) and therefore has an identifiable value and can be sold as an asset.

securitization
A process in which debts such as mortgages are pooled together and transformed into investments.

mortgage-backed securities (MBSs)
Credit derivatives based on home mortgages.

In the secondary market, individual loans are often pooled together and transformed into investment products through the process of **securitization**, which allows investors to buy shares of a given pool. **Mortgage-backed securities (MBSs)** are specifically based on home mortgages, and they became spectacularly popular during the housing boom.[34] MBSs and other vehicles derived from them can be good investments, but during the boom years the process got way out of hand. The securitization process can go on through multiple layers, creating derivatives of derivatives and offering a variety of high-, medium-, and low-risk securities for different types of investors.

However, the process was so complicated that investors sometimes had no idea what was in the securities they were buying. In addition, credit rating agencies sometimes assigned investment-quality grades to MBSs and other derivatives that were full of time-bomb ARMs and other toxic mortgages—investments that should've been treated like junk bonds. This proved to be one of the most fundamental mistakes in the entire mess.

But that wasn't the end of it. To protect themselves against the risk of borrower defaults, investors who bought MBSs and related derivatives could buy credit default swaps to transfer that risk to somebody else. Like most every other financial tool available in the years leading up to the crisis, credit default swaps can be put to good use—or can be misused in destructive ways. Swaps became popular with speculators, and by the peak of the bubble, $45 trillion was invested in swaps, an amount approaching the output of the entire global economy.[35]

THE BUBBLE BURSTS: THE MELTDOWN OF 2008

This high-flying high finance might've stayed hidden behind the walls of Wall Street but for two key problems. First, this entire multilevel scheme was based on homeowners being able to pay their mortgages, which for option ARMs and other risky mortgages was based on the notion that surging house prices would keep growing more or less forever. Second, companies that sell credit default swaps are on the hook for those amounts if the underlying investments fail. Many of these speculators didn't have nearly enough cash to cover those obligations, but because the swap market is largely unregulated, there was no one to stop them from loading up on the risk anyway.

In 2006, the four-year run-up in housing prices came to a screeching halt, and to the surprise of everyone who thought home prices could never fall, they did just that. Meanwhile, interest rates had been climbing, doubly shocking ARM borrowers when monthly payments climbed higher than many could handle. And as home prices tumbled, many homeowners lost whatever slim equity they had, if any. Thousands upon thousands couldn't make their payments, couldn't refinance to get lower payments, and couldn't sell as housing demand shriveled. **Defaults**, when borrowers stop making payments, and **foreclosures**, in which lenders take possession of homes after borrowers default on their payments, began to climb.[36]

Before long, the problem spread to derivatives investors who had loaded up on subprime and option ARM mortgages as those securitized investments stopped generating income. The first hit was the investment bank Bear Stearns, when two of its hedge funds collapsed and wiped out the $1.6 billion investors had sunk into them.[37] Not long after, American Home Mortgage, one of the largest mortgage companies in the country, filed for bankruptcy when it could no longer get funds to make new loans. Several dozen lenders had failed by that point, but American Home Mortgage got everybody's attention because it had done almost no subprime lending. The company failed because so many investors were fleeing the secondary mortgage market after getting burned by subprime failures that American Home was left with no access to cash.[38] As Frank Ahrens of the *Washington Post* later put it, "The cascade of failure had begun."[39]

Hoping to ease the pressure on mortgages, the Fed pushed its funds rate down, but property values and home sales continued to plummet as the country fell into a recession so deep that many began to worry about a second Great Depression. Banks continued to fail as the carnage kept spreading through the summer of 2008; then in September the

defaults
Situations in which borrowers stop making payments on their loans.

foreclosures
Situations in which lenders take possession of homes after borrowers default on their mortgage payments.

whole system seemed like it was collapsing. By month's end, some of the biggest names in the banking industry had fallen, the stock market was tumbling, and the worldwide banking system had nearly ground to a halt.

The first to fall that month were Fannie Mae and Freddie Mac, which were late to join the subprime stampede and paid dearly. The federal government seized both institutions and began injecting billions of dollars into each, in the hope of propping up the housing market by ensuring a continued supply of new loans.[40] A week later, under pressure from the federal government, Bank of America bought the struggling Merrill Lynch, the giant brokerage house and investment bank.[41] On the following day came what was perhaps the single biggest psychological blow of the entire crisis: Lehman Brothers, one of the last remaining icons of the Wall Street investment banking establishment, filed for bankruptcy—the largest bankruptcy in U.S. history. Lehman's collapse helped crush investor confidence in financial stocks, triggering a stock market plunge that vaporized trillions of dollars of net worth in a matter of weeks.[42]

The day after Lehman's filing brought the unexpected—and for many people, extremely confusing—announcement that the government was spending $85 billion (an amount that would soon double) to take over the insurance company American International Group (AIG). Banks failing because of bad loans made sense, but what on earth was an insurance company doing in the middle of this mess? The answer was derivatives, derivatives, and more derivatives. AIG had been investing in subprime mortgages itself *and* insuring other subprime investors against losses via credit default swaps. Through these swaps, AIG wound up being responsible for much of the subprime risk across the entire mortgage industry. Fearing that an AIG bankruptcy would bring down the entire banking system, the government felt it had no choice but to bail out the company.[43] (AIG subsequently filed lawsuits against a number of commercial and investment banks for misrepresenting the quality of the mortgage-backed securities it had purchased from them.[44])

The carnage continued, with more stunning bank failures and the largest one-day drop ever in the stock market.[45] As banks failed outright or scrambled for cash to stay open, a **liquidity crisis** rippled through the economy. One hedge fund manager compared it to "an underwater earthquake" as the $4 trillion money market stopped buying the commercial paper on which corporations rely heavily for short-term financing.[46] Before long, businesses of every size found themselves caught in a **credit freeze**, with lines of credit and other vital sources of funding shrinking or disappearing without warning. After years of dishing out cash to anyone with a pulse, lenders suddenly got careful, cutting off credit to almost everyone. The Fed eventually pushed the federal funds rate to essentially zero percent, pushing monetary policy to the limit, but credit remained tight.[47]

THE GREAT RECESSION

Companies that had nothing to do with mortgages or derivatives suffered, and unemployment continued to rise. Cautious businesses and fearful consumers cut back on spending, which reduced business revenues and tax receipts for strained local and state governments even as more people needed government assistance. The positive cycle had reversed with a vengeance, and the negative cycle brought the economy to its knees in the worst economic slowdown since the Great Depression.

Since the beginning of the meltdown, more than 500 U.S. banks have failed.[48] That alone would qualify as a disaster, but far from the poor decision making at the center of the crisis, companies were damaged or destroyed, careers were derailed, families were disrupted, and communities were devastated. People who had saved and invested for years saw the value of their retirement accounts tumble, delaying their retirements— and keeping them in jobs that would have otherwise opened up for younger workers. Whatever stage of life you are in now—student, part-time worker, full-time worker, business owner, parent, whatever—the subprime meltdown affected you directly or indirectly.

liquidity crisis
A severe shortage of liquidity throughout a sector of the economy or the entire economy, during which companies can't get enough cash to meet their operating needs.

credit freeze
A situation in which credit has become so scarce that it is virtually unavailable, at any cost, to most potential borrowers.

Checkpoint

LEARNING OBJECTIVE 5: Identify the two major sets of economic forces that triggered the meltdown of 2008 and sent the economy into a global recession.

SUMMARY: The economic forces that triggered the meltdown can be grouped into the Main Street/real estate side and the Wall Street/investment banking side. On the real estate side, frenzied demand for housing, declining lending standards, and risky new types of mortgages created an unsustainable bubble that drove prices to unrealistic levels and injected a massive number of toxic loans into the Wall Street side via the secondary mortgage market. The securitization of debt resulted in the creation of mortgage-backed securities (MBSs) and other derivatives that were stuffed with those toxic mortgages. To shed the risk of defaults on these derivatives, many of the institutional investors that bought them also bought credit default swaps to transfer the risk to someone else. However, the companies selling those swaps often lacked the resources to make good on them in the event of defaults. When housing prices stopped climbing and then dropped, the entire scheme imploded from both ends. Commercial banks, mortgage companies, and investment banks all began to fail when homeowner defaults rippled through the system and the credit default swaps couldn't pay off. The resulting liquidity crisis rippled through the economy, and thousands of businesses outside finance got caught in a credit freeze after banks stopped lending or cut off lines of credit. Without access to needed funds, many companies began massive layoffs, which damaged the economy even further.

CRITICAL THINKING: (1) Can financial bubbles be avoided? After all, they involve lots of human emotion triumphing over logic. Explain your answer. (2) Assuming you had authority over every aspect of the real estate and banking sectors back in the 2002–2006 time frame, if you could have done one thing to stop the subprime/banking crisis, what would it have been? Explain your choice.

IT'S YOUR BUSINESS: (1) Would you agree to an ARM with low teaser rates if you weren't positive you would be able to afford the higher monthly payments that would kick in after the teaser rate reset to the permanent fixed rate? Why or why not? (2) How does the story of the real estate crash and the banking crisis affect your thoughts about your own financial planning?

KEY TERMS TO KNOW: bubble, subprime mortgages, loan-to-value (LTV), adjustable rate mortgage (ARM), securitization, mortgage-backed securities (MBSs), defaults, foreclosures, liquidity crisis, credit freeze

 6 LEARNING OBJECTIVE

Outline the efforts to reform the banking industry in the wake of the subprime crisis.

Efforts to Regulate and Reform the Banking Industry

Given the destruction that risky or rogue banking practices can wreak on the economy, ensuring a stable banking sector is essential to the country's economic health. Understanding why the banking crisis happened and how it could have been prevented are vital to any effort to avoid repeating these mistakes in the future.

LESSONS TO BE LEARNED

Did anybody see this mess coming? Absolutely. Worries about the housing bubble, risky lending, and unregulated mortgage derivatives began appearing several years before everything collapsed.[49] JPMorgan Chase CEO Jamie Dimon was so worried about a subprime meltdown that he ordered his firm to get out of that market when it was the hottest and most lucrative thing on Wall Street. After earlier encouraging the use of ARMs because they can save buyers thousands of dollars in interest, then-chairman of the Federal Reserve Alan Greenspan began warning bankers about the increasing use of "exotic" forms of ARMs.[50]

However, these voices of caution were often lost in the roar of money making or simply dismissed as being too pessimistic. When economist Nouriel Roubini warned that "the risk of a U.S. recession turning into a systemic financial meltdown cannot be ruled out," he was nicknamed "Dr. Doom."[51] When Brooksley Born, head of the Commodity Futures Trading Commission (CFTC), warned of the risks of the unregulated market in credit default swaps and proposed that her agency be given the authority to regulate swaps, Greenspan and other high-ranking officials convinced Congress to pass a law preventing the CFTC from doing so.[52] Aversion to regulating the financial industry was too high, and too many people were making too much money to pay attention to economic fundamentals.

After the meltdown, bank analyst Chris Whalen said the fact that anyone was surprised by Lehman Brothers's fall just shows how na've people had become. Particularly in the financial profession, he says, people were "convinced that there is no risk. From the collapse of the private mortgage firms in '07, all the way through '08, we were still sleepwalking our way through the crisis . . . it was fantasyland."[53] Fantasyland turned out to be an expensive place to live.

Exhibit 20.4 on the next page summarizes the key lessons that could and should be learned from this catastrophe. Whether they indeed will be learned is up to the consumers, business managers, financial professionals, investors, regulators, and political leaders who control and participate in the banking system. Clay Ewing, an executive with German American Bancorp in Jasper, Indiana, might have summed up the lessons to be learned most succinctly when he observed, "Banking should not be exciting. If banking gets exciting, there is something wrong with it."[54]

EFFORTS TO PREVENT ANOTHER BANKING CRISIS

In the years following the meltdown, Congress and various regulatory agencies put a high priority on instituting changes designed to prevent another calamity of this magnitude. The most significant legislative response to date is the Dodd-Frank Wall Street Reform and Consumer Protection Act of 2010, or the **Dodd-Frank Act** for short. Given the continuing arguments over which of many factors is most to blame for the meltdown and the right and wrong ways to fix each one, it's not surprising that opinions on Dodd-Frank are sharply divided. Some say it didn't go far enough, while others say it went too far; some say it won't accomplish some of its key goals, and some say it will create havoc that will take years to sort out. No one, however, disputes that the multiple provisions of this complex legislation will substantially affect banking and other financial services. Here is a broad outline of the bill's major points of emphasis:[55]

REAL-TIME UPDATES

Learn More by Reading This Article

Did we learn anything from the banking crisis?

Professors from the Wharton School of Business debate. Go to http://real-timeupdates.com/bia8 and click on Learn More in the Students section.

Dodd-Frank Act
Legislation passed in 2010 aimed at reforming the banking industry and offering consumers greater protection.

- **Monitoring for systemic risk.** A key problem in the recent meltdown was the spread of risk from individual companies such as AIG to the rest of the financial sector and from there to the overall economy. Dodd-Frank created the Financial Stability Oversight Council to monitor for such *systemic risks*, those that affect a significant portion of the economy.
- **Protecting consumers.** The new Bureau of Consumer Financial Protection within the Federal Reserve is tasked with making sure consumers get clear and accurate information about financial services and protecting them from "hidden fees, abusive terms, and deceptive practices," according to the bill's sponsors.
- **Closer scrutiny of the derivatives market.** This huge and largely unregulated market played a key role in the crisis. Dodd-Frank aims to provide more transparency and accountability in the markets for derivatives, hedge funds, and other financial products.
- **Ending taxpayer bailouts of companies deemed "too big to fail."** Some financial companies cast such a large shadow over the economy that their failure was considered a threat to the stability of the entire economy, leading to multibillion-dollar

| EXHIBIT 20.4 | **Lessons to Learn from the Subprime Meltdown** |

The subprime meltdown and ensuing credit crisis offer many lessons for consumers, investors, bankers, and regulators. Whether these lessons get learned and stay learned is another thing entirely.

Lesson	Comments
Transferring risk does not reduce or eliminate the risk—and sometimes it can even increase risk.	The risk of subprime defaults moved all the way through the system, from lenders to investment banks to hedge funds and institutional investors, without ever being diminished or successfully managed. Moreover, credit default swaps not only didn't protect investors from subprime defaults in many cases but may have actually increased total risk by making more companies dependent on one another's decision making and financial solvency.
Decoupling risk from responsibility leads to risky and irresponsible behavior.	If people begin to believe there will be no serious consequences for risky, unethical, or even illegal behavior—a condition known as *moral hazard*—they will be more likely to engage in those behaviors. If mortgage brokers can make foolish or fraudulent loans and immediately pass the risk of default to someone else, or if big banks believe the government will bail them out next time they gamble and lose, what's to stop them from behaving that way?
Individual short-term incentives can overpower logic and collective long-term consequences.	The probability of specific, immediate rewards is nearly always going to win out over the possibility of vague, long-term risks. Within companies and across industries, business and political leaders need to understand how reward systems motivate behavior—and fix reward systems that tolerate or encourage foolish behavior.
Unregulated private contracts can have damaging public consequences.	The proper degree of economic regulation is an ongoing debate, but few rational people would argue that if private business dealings (such as credit default swaps) carry significant public risks, then regulators should at least pay attention. The unregulated financial derivatives market created a *shadow banking system* that performed some of the same functions as the real banking system—but without the checks and balances that keep a banking system from spinning out of control.
If something seems too good to be true, it is.	This lesson has been learned, unlearned, and relearned countless times over the years but never seems to stick. There is no magic in the financial markets.
Innovation can be dangerous if it outpaces our ability to understand it or control it.	This danger will always be with us because regulation and other controls always lag innovation. However, leaders need to remember that innovation often creates new and unforeseen risks, so they need to proceed with caution and be ready to react quickly.
Leverage can be dangerous, and massive leverage can be deadly.	Borrowing money to make money is not an inherently bad thing; banks, hedge funds, and individual investors do it all the time and live to tell about it. However, the more you leverage, the more vulnerable you are to declines in the value of the investment. With massive leverage (20 to 1, 30 to 1, and so on), the tiniest blip in asset value can wipe you out.
The past is not always a reliable guide to the future.	The belief that home prices never fall (because they always seemed to go up) was the delusion at the core of this entire mess. However, bubble-inflated prices *always* fall, which is the historical precedent people should have been using instead. The difference between *unlikely* and *impossible* is huge.
Computer models and quantitative analysis must *support* experience and common sense, not *replace* them.	Quantitative analysis is a powerful tool for solving problems—but only those problems that can be accurately quantified. Ignoring experience and common sense in favor of models—and worse yet, distorting your view of reality so that it fits the model's mechanical view of the world—is a recipe for disaster.
Investors must understand the quality of the information they use to make investment decisions.	Many investors in complex financial products relied on flawed information from credit rating agencies—information that was based on faulty assumptions or perhaps even deliberately skewed in some cases.
In every battle between economic theory and reality, reality wins.	The idea that (A) investors behave rationally, so therefore (B) financial markets will behave rationally, so therefore (C) financial markets shouldn't be hampered by regulatory oversight proved to be disastrous. People don't always behave rationally, and even when they do behave rationally they can't always predict the consequences of their decisions.
We can't prevent instability, but we need to get better at preventing full-blown crises	Complex financial systems with many players pursuing individual goals are always going to be unpredictable and therefore at least a little unstable. However, warnings about impending disasters should be listened to carefully and objectively, even if they dispute the prevailing wisdom.

Sources: Justin Fox, "What We've Learned from the Financial Crisis," *Harvard Business Review*, November 2013, 94–101; Stephen Gandel, "Why Your Bank Is Broke," *Time*, 31 January 2009, www.time.com; Eric Gelman, "Fear of a Black Swan," *Fortune*, 3 April 2008, http://money.cnn.com; Frank Ahrens, "Anatomy of a Crisis," webcast, *Washington Post*, accessed 13 September 2009, www.washingtonpost.com; Ryan Barnes, "The Fuel That Fed the Subprime Meltdown," Investopedia.com, accessed 15 September 2009, www.investopedia.com; "Economy in Turmoil," *MSNBC.com*, accessed 15 September 2009, www.msnbc.com; "25 People to Blame for the Financial Crisis," *Time*, accessed 16 September 2009, www.time.com.

government bailouts. Dodd-Frank seeks to prevent bailouts of individual firms, although it allows the government to make moves to support the overall banking industry if needed.

- **Tougher regulation of credit rating agencies.** In an effort to protect investors from unreliable credit ratings, the bill provides for more vigorous rules regarding transparency and accountability of credit rating practices.
- **Prohibiting commercial banks from speculative trading activity.** Known as the "Volcker Rule" after former Fed chairman Paul Volcker, this measure aims to stop banks from making risky trades that could undermine their financial stability and thereby put their customers at risk.

Many of the changes Dodd-Frank calls for have been subject to challenges, intense lobbying by the financial industry, and efforts to repeal or modify some its key requirements. However, some progress is being made toward implementing the bill's many provisions, and reforms such as subjecting derivatives trading to oversight by the CFTC are in place.[56]

The subprime crisis and the ensuing credit crisis will continue to affect the course of the economy for years to come, and the slow, uphill battle to reform the banking industry shows just how pervasive and influential banks are in a modern economy. Amid all the controversy and complexity, though, one point remains clear and beyond dispute: A healthy economy needs healthy banks—and fundamentally sound banking practices.

For the information on developments in the banking industry, visit **http://real-time updates.com/bia8** and click on Chapter 20.

✔ Checkpoint

LEARNING OBJECTIVE 6: Outline the efforts to reform the banking industry in the wake of the subprime crisis.

SUMMARY: The most significant piece of legislation to date is the Dodd-Frank Act of 2010, whose major provisions address monitoring for systemic risk in the financial sector, protecting consumers from unfair banking practices, providing closer scrutiny of the derivatives market, ending taxpayer bailouts of companies deemed "too big to fail," and enacting tougher regulation of credit rating agencies.

CRITICAL THINKING: (1) Should the government limit any company's ability to grow to the point that its failure could seriously damage the overall economy? Why or why not? (2) Do you think those involved in the financial services industry "learned their lessons" and won't repeat the mistakes that led to the 2008 meltdown? Why or why not?

IT'S YOUR BUSINESS: (1) How have the lingering effects of the recession changed the way you manage your personal finances? (2) As a consumer, what lessons can you take away from the subprime mess?

KEY TERM TO KNOW: Dodd-Frank Act

BEHIND THE SCENES
ALLIANT CREDIT UNION: A MEMBER-DRIVEN APPROACH TO MEETING CUSTOMER NEEDS

Alliant Credit Union's humble but bold roots reflect the ethos of "we're all in this together" that powers the credit union philosophy. In 1935, in the depths of the Great Depression with banks failing right and left, a group of United Airlines employees wanted a safe place to put their savings and some way to provide members with loans at reasonable rates. By the end of the year, the

146 members had all of $5,088 in assets, but they had managed to make 38 loans. The United Airlines Employee Credit Union was born.

The credit union served United employees for nearly seven decades, until United filed for bankruptcy in 2002. The credit union then expanded beyond its single-employer focus and became Alliant, which has since grown to become one of the country's largest credit unions. Those 146 founding members might be amazed to know that their group now has more than 270,000 members nationwide and $8 billion in assets. (People in the Chicago area are eligible to join automatically, but anyone in the country can become eligible for membership by making a small donation to the charity Foster Care to Success.)

Alliant promotes its advantage to potential members through simple arithmetic: "All income after operating expenses and reserve allocations is returned to you via higher dividends and great loan rates." In other words, unlike a bank, a credit union doesn't try to profit from its customers so that it can satisfy the demands of the stock market. Alliant's marketing efforts work hard to draw the distinction between banks and credit unions and to convince consumers that a credit union can meet their needs better, with lower fees and loan rates and higher interest rates on deposits.

After 25 years in banking, CEO David Mooney feels right at home at the helm of a credit union. He is not shy about promoting the advantages of the credit union model or advocating for the industry as a whole, and he is not pleased with journalists who create the impression that banks are somehow more advanced or better able to serve customers than credit unions are. Credit unions have access to the same technologies and methods as banks, he counters, and in fact can often innovate faster because they are less encumbered by legacy information systems or the web of interstate banking regulations.

The message appears to be reaching consumers, too. Growing anger at big banks in the wake of the recession, fueled in part by the Occupy Wall Street movement, spurred Bank Transfer Day in 2011, when 600,000 big bank customers shifted their accounts to small community banks or credit unions. And credit union membership has been growing faster than the population, another sign that consumers are choosing credit unions over banks. Having made the move himself, David Mooney is no doubt inspired by the shift.[57]

Critical Thinking Questions

20-1. Why might customers of big banks be reluctant to move to a credit union?

20-2. Should credit unions, even if they are not profit-driven, be given special consideration if they compete in the marketplace with banks that have to pay taxes? Explain your reasoning.

20-3. Could a publicly owned, for-profit bank that truly espoused a customer-first approach successfully compete against both credit unions such as Alliant and other banks? Why or why not?

LEARN MORE ONLINE

Visit the Alliant website at **www.alliantcreditunion.org** and explore the services it offers and the About Alliant section. Does the website do an effective job of presenting the credit union model to potential members? After reading the material, will potential members have a clear distinction in their minds between a credit union and a bank? How do the Alliant mission and values statements support that message?

KEY TERMS

adjustable rate mortgage (ARM) (480)
bubble (479)
commercial banks (477)
credit freeze (483)
credit rating agencies (478)
credit unions (477)
defaults (482)
discount rate (474)
Dodd-Frank Act (485)
Fannie Mae (474)
Federal Deposit Insurance Corporation (FDIC) (474)
federal funds rate (473)
Federal Reserve System (472)
finance companies (478)
foreclosures (482)
Freddie Mac (474)

independent mortgage companies (478)
investment banks (475)
liquidity crisis (483)
loan-to-value (LTV) (480)
merchant banks (477)
money (470)
money supply (470)
mortgage-backed securities (MBSs) (482)
mortgage brokers (478)
prime rate (474)
private banking (477)
retail banks (477)
secondary mortgage market (474)
securitization (482)
subprime mortgages (480)
thrift banks (477)

TEST YOUR KNOWLEDGE

Questions for Review

20-4. What are the primary responsibilities of the Federal Reserve System?

20-5. How do commercial banks differ from investment banks?

20-6. What is a bubble?

20-7. What is a subprime mortgage?

20-8. What does securitization of debt mean?

Questions for Analysis

20-9. How does the money supply affect the cost and availability of credit?

20-10. Generally speaking, what effect did the repeal of the Glass-Steagall Act have on the banking industry?

20-11. How did the decline in lending standards contribute to the financial meltdown of 2008?

20-12. Why would a credit union work to make sure consumers know it is not a bank?

⭐ **20-13.** **Ethical Considerations.** How did the decoupling of risk and reward contribute to the problems in the subprime mortgage industry?

Questions for Application

20-14. If you were in charge of monetary policy and wanted to lower the federal funds rate, would you buy or sell Treasury securities on the open market? Why?

⭐ **20-15.** If a consumer with a relatively low credit score applied for a loan from your bank, what other criteria might you consider before deciding to grant a loan?

⭐ **20-16.** As a corporate financial manager, what steps could you take to protect your company from a liquidity crisis?

⭐ **20-17.** **Concept Integration.** In what ways did the housing bubble and subprime crisis violate the responsibilities suggested by the stakeholder model (see page 11 and pages 75–83)?

EXPAND YOUR KNOWLEDGE

Discovering Career Opportunities

Is a career in community banking for you? Bankers in smaller banks deal with a wide variety of customers, products, transactions, and inquiries every working day. To get a better idea of what community bankers do, explore the Independent Community Bankers of America website, www.icba.org, and visit the websites of several independent community banks in your area.

20-18. How do independent banks seek to differentiate themselves from large banking conglomerates?

20-19. Do the banks you studied serve consumers as well as small businesses? What types of services do they offer each sector?

20-20. What regulatory and political issues does the ICBA currently take an interest in?

Improving Your Tech Insights: Mobile Payment Systems

The *digital wallet* concept, in which consumers can make payments with their smartphones rather than physical credit cards or cash, has been around for a few years but seems finally poised to take off. Research the two leading systems, Apple Pay and Google Pay, to find out the current rates of adoption among smartphone users and any lingering technical or behavioral issues that are discouraging more retailers or consumers to jump on the bandwagon. Report your findings in a brief post on your class blog or an email message to your instructor.

PRACTICE YOUR SKILLS

Sharpening Your Communication Skills

As a loan officer at Long Isle Community Bank, your responsibilities include the unpleasant task of informing some applicants that their loans have not been approved. Today you need to write a letter to Geoff Winders, a customer who applied for a home mortgage but was turned down by the bank's loan committee because his credit score was too low. You can temper the bad news with the suggestion that Mr. Winders attend the free credit repair seminar, Back on Track, that Long Isle offers every Saturday afternoon from 1:00 to 3:00. Write a brief letter that opens by thanking Mr. Winders for being a customer of the bank and for considering the bank for his home mortgage needs. Explain the reason his application was rejected and extend the offer of attending the free seminar.

Building Your Team Skills

With teammates as assigned by your instructor, choose a type of business that you would like to own and manage. Next, identify three institutions in your town or city that could provide the banking services your company would need, based on your growth plans for the first five years. (Make up any details you need.) Choose a branch of a national bank, a smaller community bank, and a credit union. Research the services and capabilities of each and decide which one is the right choice for your company. Present your results using presentation slides, a wiki, or whatever media option your instructor indicates.

Developing Your Research Skills

Many observers criticized the role played by the credit rating agencies Moody's, Standard & Poor's, and Fitch in the subprime crisis. Two particular criticisms are that bond rating agencies are paid by bond issuers, which could lead them to issue biased ratings, and that the agencies gave their top ratings to mortgage-backed securities that contained low-quality debts. Do the research necessary to find answers to the following questions:

20-21. Have any major changes in the debt rating process been proposed or enacted, such as having a not-for-profit organization provide impartial ratings instead of or in addition to the commercial agencies?

20-22. Have any investors or other parties successfully sued a rating agency for providing misleading information?

20-23. Has Congress or any federal agency taken any steps to change the laws and regulations that affect the operation of credit rating agencies?

MyBizLab®

Go to the Assignments section of your MyLab to complete these writing exercises.

20-24. If accepting risk is part of being an entrepreneur or running a business, should the government, taxpayers, or any other entity ever bail out a company that took risks and failed? Explain your answer.

20-25. Should banks that have become "too big to fail" (meaning their collapse would significantly damage the economy) be subject to stricter regulations than smaller banks? Why or why not?

ENDNOTES

1. Alliant Credit union website, accessed 22 June 2015, www.alliantcreditunion.org; "The 8 Least Evil Banks," *CNNMoney*, 28 January 2011, http://money.cnn.com; Adam Mertz, "Former Bankers Embrace CUs," *Credit Union Magazine*, September 2013, 20–22; Mitch Lipka, "Personal Finance: Bank Transfer Day Saw 600,000 Switch," *Reuters*, 27 January 2012, www.reuters.com; "7 Great Credit Unions Anyone Can Join," *Kiplinger*, accessed 27 November 2013, www.kiplinger.com.

2. Roger LeRoy Miller, *Economics Today*, 15th ed. (Boston: Addison-Wesley, 2010), 367–368.

3. Miller, *Economics Today*, 369–370.

4. *The Federal Reserve System: Purposes & Functions*, 9th ed. (Washington, D.C.: Board of Governors of the Federal Reserve System, 2005), 22.

5. Miller, *Economics Today*, 371.

6. *The Federal Reserve System: Purposes & Functions*, 3–12.

7. *The Federal Reserve System: Purposes & Functions*, 15.

8. "How Is the Federal Reserve System Structured?" Federal Reserve System website, accessed 26 November 2013, www.federalreserve.gov.

9. "What We Do," Federal Reserve Bank of New York, accessed 26 November 2013, www.newyorkfed.org.

10. *The Federal Reserve System: Purposes & Functions*, 71–72, 75.

11. *The Federal Reserve System: Purposes & Functions*, 15.

12. *The Federal Reserve System: Purposes & Functions*, 35–50; Joao Santos and Stavros Peristiani, "Why Do Banks Have Discount Windows?" Federal Reserve Bank of New York, 30 March 2011, www.newyorkfed.org.

13. "Federal Funds Target Rate—Upper Bound," *Bloomberg Business*, accessed 22 June 2015, www.bloomberg.com; Michael S. Derby, "Fed's Bullard: Rush to Zero Percent Funds Rate May Have Been Mistake," *Wall Street Journal* blogs, 21 November 2013, http://blogs.wsj.com.

14. "FDIC Deposit Insurance Coverage," FDIC website, 17 October 2013, www.fdic.gov.

15. "Greed and Ambition," *Economist*, 15 October 2011, 99; Fannie Mae website, accessed 27 September 2009, www.fanniemae.com.

16. Margaret Chadbourn, "Taxpayers Close to Breaking Even on Fannie Mae, Freddie Mac Bailout," *Reuters*, 7 November 2013, www.reuters.com; "What the Demise of Fannie Mae and Freddie Mac Means for the Future of Homeownership," Knowledge@Wharton, 16 March 2011, http://knowledge.wharton.upenn.edu.

17. Goldman Sachs website, accessed 25 November 2013, www.goldmansachs.com; J.P. Morgan website, accessed 25 November 2013, www.jpmorgan.com.

18. Lisa Smith, "The Chinese Wall Protects Against Conflicts of Interest," Investopedia, 26 February 2009, www.investopedia.com.

19. Michael J. Moore, "Wall Street's Bulge Bracket May Shrink to 5 Firms, McKinsey Says," *Bloomberg*, 23 January 2013, www.bloomberg.com.

20. Roddy Boyd, "The Last Days of Bear Stearns," *Fortune*, 31 March 2008, http://money.cnn.com; "About Us," Goldman Sachs website, accessed 27 September 2009, www2.goldmansachs.com; "Factbox: A Brief History of Lehman Brothers," *Reuters*, 13 September 2008, www.reuters.com; "Our History," Merrill Lynch website, accessed 27 September 2009, www.ml.com; "Company

History," Morgan Stanley website, accessed 27 September 2009, www.morganstanley.com; Sam Mamudi, "Lehman Folds with Record $613 Billion Debt," *MarketWatch*, 15 September 2008, www.marketwatch.com.

21. "List of Investment Banks," *Wall Street Prep*, accessed 25 November 2013, www.wallstreetprep.com.

22. Valentine V. Craig, "Merchant Banking: Past and Present," U.S. Federal Deposit Insurance Corporation website, accessed 27 September 2009, www.fdic.gov.

23. "Private Banking," JPMorgan website, accessed 27 September 2009, www.jpmorgan.com.

24. Stephan Labaton, "Accord Reached on Lifting Depression-Era Barriers Among Financial Industries," *New York Times*, 23 October 1999, A1, B4.

25. "The Long Demise of Glass-Steagall," *PBS Frontline*, accessed 27 September 2009, www.pbs.org.

26. Toyota Financial Services website, accessed 26 November 2013, www.toyotafinancial.com.

27. In addition to the specific citations that follow, the material in the this section is based on information from the following sources: Frank Ahrens, "Anatomy of a Crisis," webcast, *Washington Post*, accessed 13 September 2009, www.washingtonpost.com; Ryan Barnes, "The Fuel That Fed the Subprime Meltdown," Investopedia.com, accessed 15 September 2009, www.investopedia.com; "Economy in Turmoil," MSNBC.com, accessed 15 September 2009, www.msnbc.com; "25 People to Blame for the Financial Crisis."

28. "Historical Changes of the Target Federal Funds and Discount Rates," Federal Reserve Bank of New York, accessed 20 October 2009, www.newyorkfed.org.

29. Ahrens, "Anatomy of a Crisis."

30. Colin Barr, "WaMu: The Forgotten Bank Failure," *CNN Money*, 10 September 2009, www.money.cnn.com.

31. Barnes, "The Fuel That Fed the Subprime Meltdown."

32. Sumit Agarwal and Calvin T. Ho, "Comparing the Prime and Subprime Mortgage Markets," *Chicago Fed Letter*, August 2007, 1–4.

33. Dennis Capozza and Robert van Order, "Dissecting Defaults," *Mortgage Banker*, August 2009, 34–38.

34. "25 People to Blame for the Financial Crisis."

35. Kimberly Amadeo, "Credit Default Swaps," About.com, 7 May 2012, www.about.com.

36. "The Meltdown in Words," *Newsweek*, accessed 16 September 2009, www.newsweek.com.

37. "Dissecting the Bear Stearns Hedge Fund Collapse," Investopedia.com, accessed 14 October 2009, www.investopedia.com.

38. "American Home Mortgage Seeks Chapter 11 Bankruptcy Protection," *New York Times*, 7 August 2007, www.nytimes.com.

39. Ahrens, "Anatomy of a Crisis."

40. Bill Saporito, "Top 10 Financial Collapses," *Time*, accessed 23 September 2009, www.time.com.

41. Dan Fitzpatrick and Joann S. Lublin, "Bank of America Chief Resigns Under Fire," *Wall Street Journal*, 1 October 2009, http://online.wsj.com.

42. Andy Serwer, Nina Easton, and Allan Sloan, "Geithner: 'We Were Looking at the Abyss,'" *Fortune*, 10 September 2009, http://money.cnn.com; Saporito, "Top 10 Financial Collapses"; "Record Stock Market Falls in 2008," *BBC News*, 31 December 2008, http://news.bbc.co.uk.

43. Michael Lewis, "The Man Who Crashed the World," *Vanity Fair*, August 2009, www.vanityfair.com.

44. Louise Story and Gretchen Morgenson, "AIG to Sue Bank of America over Mortgage-Backed Securities," *Seattle Times*, 7 August 2011, www.seattletimes.com.

45. Binyamin Appelbaum, "U.S. Forces WaMu Sale as Bank Founders," *Washington Post*, 26 September 2008, www.washingtonpost.com.

46. Mohamed El-Erian, "When Wall Street Nearly Collapsed," *Fortune*, accessed 14 October 2009, http://money.cnn.com.

47. "Fed Overnight Rate at 0% for Most of Next Year, Predicts J.P. Morgan Securities," *Financial Week*, 1 December 2008, www.financialweek.com.

48. "Failed Bank List," U.S. Federal Deposit Insurance Corporation, accessed 22 June 2015, www.fdic.gov; "U.S. Banks Post Some of the Worst Losses of Banks Globally in 2008," *Mortgage Banking*, August 2008, 16.

49. Gretchen Morgenson, "Housing Bust: It Won't Be Pretty," *New York Times*, 25 July 2004, www.nytimes.com; Christopher Palmeri and Rich Miller, "ARMed and Dangerous?" *BusinessWeek*, 12 April 2004, 82–84.

50. Palmeri and Miller, "ARMed and Dangerous"; "Greenspan Sharpens Warning About 'Exotic' Mortgages," *Mortgage Banking*, November 2005, 10–11.

51. "The Meltdown in Words."

52. "Interview: Brooksley Born," *Frontline*, 20 October 2009, www.pbs.org.

53. El-Erian, "When Wall Street Nearly Collapsed."

54. David Segal, "We're Dull, Small Banks Say, and Have Profit to Show for It," *New York Times*, 11 May 2009, www.nytimes.com.

55. Silla Brush, "CFTC's Chilton Says He Would Vote Against Current Volcker Rule," *Bloomberg*, 20 November 2013, www.bloomberg.com; U.S. Senate Banking Committee, "Brief Summary of the Dodd-Frank Wall Street Reform and Consumer Protection Act," U.S. Senate Committee on Banking, Housing, and Urban Affairs website, accessed 14 September 2001, http://banking.senate.gov; "The Dodd-Frank Act: A Cheat Sheet," Morrison & Foerster, accessed 14 September 2011, www.mofo.com; Penny Crosman, "Reactions to Dodd-Frank Law Run a Gamut from Enthusiasm to Disgust," *Bank Systems & Technology*, 16 July 2010, www.banktech.com; Gretchen Morgenson, "Strong Enough for Tough Stains?" *New York Times*, 26 June 2010, www.nytimes.com.

56. George Cahlink, "Chances of Changing Dodd-Frank Appear to Rest with Handful of Moderate Democrats," *Roll Call*, 10 June 2015, www.rollcall.com; David Zaring, "Dodd-Frank Is Indeed Taking Root," *New York Times*, 1 November 2013, www.nytimes.com.

57. See note 1.

Business Law

The U.S. Legal System

Federal, state, and local governments work in numerous ways to protect both individuals and other businesses from corporate wrongdoing. Laws also spell out accepted ways of performing many essential business functions—along with the penalties for failing to comply. In other words, like individuals, companies must obey the law or face the consequences.

As you read this material, keep in mind that many U.S. companies also conduct business in other countries, so executives in these firms must also be familiar with **international law**, the laws that govern commerce and other interactions across national boundaries.[1] Successful global business requires an understanding of the domestic laws of trading partners as well as of established international trading standards and legal guidelines.

SOURCES OF LAW

A *law* is a rule developed by a society to govern the conduct of, and relationships among, its members. The U.S. Constitution, including the Bill of Rights, is the foundation for U.S. laws. Because the Constitution is a general document, laws offering specific answers to specific problems are constantly embellishing its basic principles. However, law is not static; it develops in response to changing conditions and social standards. Individual laws originate in various ways: through legislative action (*statutory law*), through administrative rulings (*administrative law*), and through customs and judicial precedents (*common law*). To one degree or another, all three forms of law affect businesses. In situations in which the three forms of law appear to conflict, statutory law generally prevails.

STATUTORY LAW

Statutory law is law written by the U.S. Congress, state legislatures, and local governments. One of the most important elements of statutory law that affects businesses is the **Uniform Commercial Code (UCC)**, designed to reconcile numerous conflicts among state laws in order to simplify interstate commerce.[2] For example, the UCC provides a nationwide standard in many issues of commercial law, such as sales contracts, bank deposits, and warranties.

ADMINISTRATIVE LAW

Once laws have been passed by a state legislature or Congress, an administrative agency or commission typically takes responsibility for enforcing them. That agency may be called on to clarify a regulation's intent, often by consulting representatives of the affected industry. The administrative agency may then write more specific regulations, which are considered **administrative law**.

Administrative agencies also have the power to investigate corporations suspected of breaking administrative laws. A corporation found to be in violation of administrative laws may agree to a **consent order**, which allows the company to promise to stop doing something without actually admitting to any illegal behavior. As an alternative to entering into a consent order, the administrative agency may start legal proceedings against the company, in a hearing presided over by an administrative law judge. During such a hearing, witnesses are called and evidence is presented to determine the facts of the situation. The judge then issues a decision, which may impose corrective actions on the company. If either party objects to the decision, that party may file an appeal to the appropriate federal court.[3]

COMMON LAW

Common law, which originates in courtrooms and judges' decisions, began in England many centuries ago and was transported to the United States by the colonists. It is applied in all states except Louisiana (which follows

Global companies need a thorough understanding of international business law to protect their own interests and to avoid costly mistakes.

EXHIBIT A.1	The U.S. Court System

A legal proceeding may begin in a trial court or an administrative agency. (Examples of both are given here.) An unfavorable decision may be appealed to a higher court at the federal or state level. (The court of appeals is the highest court in states that have no state supreme court; some other states have no intermediate appellate court.) The U.S. Supreme Court, the country's highest court, is the court of final appeal.

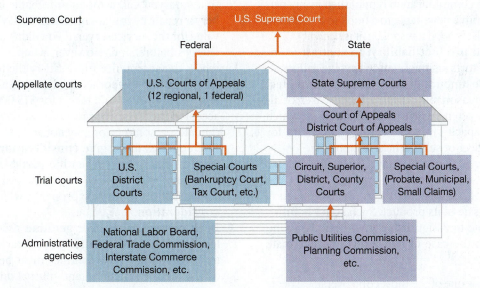

Sources: Bartley A. Brennan and Nancy Kubasek, *The Legal Environment of Business* (New York: Macmillan, 1988), 24; Douglas Whitman and John Gergacz, *The Legal Environment of Business*, 2nd ed. (New York: Random House, 1988), 22, 25.

a French model). Common law is sometimes called the "unwritten law" to distinguish it from legislative acts and administrative-agency regulations, which are written documents. Instead, common law is established through custom and the precedents set in courtroom proceedings.

Despite its unwritten nature, common law has great continuity, which derives from the doctrine of **stare decisis** (Latin for "to stand by decisions"). What the stare decisis doctrine means is that judges' decisions establish a precedent for deciding future cases of a similar nature. Because common law is based on what has gone before, the legal framework develops gradually.

In the United States, common law is applied and interpreted in the system of courts (see Exhibit A.1). Common law thus develops through the decisions in trial courts, special courts, and appellate courts. The U.S. Supreme Court (or the highest court of a state when state laws are involved) sets precedents for entire legal systems. Lower courts must then abide by those precedents as they pertain to similar cases.

Most business cases are heard in standard trial courts. However, a number of cities, counties, and states have established or are considering specialized *business courts* presided over by judges experienced in handling commercial law.[4]

Major Concepts in Business Law

Although businesses must comply with the full body of laws that apply to individuals, a subset of laws can be defined more precisely as **business law**. It includes the elements of law that directly affect business activities. For example, laws pertaining to business licensing, employee safety, and corporate income taxes can all be considered business law. The most important categories of laws affecting business include torts, contracts, agency, property transactions, patents, trademarks, copyrights, negotiable instruments, and bankruptcy.

TORTS

A **tort** is a wrongful act, other than a breach of contract. The victim of a tort is legally entitled to some form of financial compensation, or **damages**, for his or her loss and suffering. This compensation is also known as a *compensatory damage award*. In some cases, the victim may also receive a *punitive damage award* to punish the wrongdoer if the misdeed is deemed particularly bad. Torts can be classified as *intentional*, *unintentional*, or *strict liability*:[5]

- **Intentional torts.** An **intentional tort** is a willful act that results in injury. For example, accidentally hitting

REAL-TIME UPDATES

Learn More by Visiting This Website

Legal advice for small businesses

The Small Business Administration offers free information on some of the key topics in business law. Go to **http://real-timeupdates .com/bia8** and click on Learn More in the Students section.

a softball through someone's window is a tort, but purposely cutting down someone's tree because it obscures your view is an intentional tort. Note that *intent* in this case does not mean the intent to cause harm; it is the intent to commit a specific act. Some intentional torts involve communication of false statements that harm another's reputation. If the communication is published in any permanent form, from a newspaper to a book to a television program, it is called *libel*; if it is spoken, it is *slander*.[6]

- **Negligence and product liability.** In contrast to intentional torts, torts of **negligence** involve failure to use a reasonable amount of care necessary to protect others from unreasonable risk of injury.[7] Cases of alleged negligence often involve **product liability**, which is a product's capacity to cause damages or injury for which the producer or seller is held responsible.

- **Strict liability.** A company may also be held liable for injury caused by a defective product, even if the company used all reasonable care in the manufacture, distribution, or sale of its product. Such **strict liability** makes it possible to assign liability without assigning fault, such as in the case of dangerous but legitimate business activities.[8]

Product liability is one of the most controversial aspects of business law. On one side, advocates for consumers—and particularly patients in the health-care industry—assert that sizable monetary damages in liability cases compensate customers who have been wronged and serve as an incentive for safer products and practices. On the other side, critics of big awards say these payouts lead to higher costs for consumers and can reduce the availability of some goods and services. This battle over *tort reform* has been going on for some years and promises to continue in the years ahead.[9]

CONTRACTS

Broadly defined, a **contract** is an exchange of promises between two or more parties that is enforceable by law. Many business transactions—including buying and selling products, hiring employees, purchasing group insurance, and licensing a technology—involve contracts. Contracts may be either express or implied. An **express contract** is articulated in written or spoken language, whereas an **implied contract** is inferred from the conduct of the parties.[10]

Elements of a Contract

The law of contracts deals largely with identifying the exchanges that can be classified as contracts. The following factors must usually be present for a contract to be valid and enforceable:

- **An offer must be made.** One party must propose that an agreement be entered into. The offer may be oral or written, but it must be firm, definite, and specific enough to make it clear that someone intends to be legally bound by the offer. Finally, the offer must be communicated to the intended party or parties.

- **An offer must be accepted.** For an offer to be accepted, there must be clear intent (spoken, written, or by action) to enter into the contract. An implied contract arises when a person requests or accepts something and the other party has indicated that payment is expected. If, for example, your car breaks down on the road and you call a mobile mechanic and ask him or her to repair it, you are obligated to pay the reasonable value for the services, even if you didn't agree to specific charges beforehand. However, when a specific offer is made, the acceptance must satisfy the terms of the offer. For example, if someone offers you a car for $18,000 and you say you would take it for $15,000, you have not accepted the offer. Your response is a *counteroffer*, which the salesperson may or may not accept.

- **Both parties must give consideration.** A contract is legally binding only when the parties have bargained with each other and have exchanged something of value, such as money or property, which is called the **consideration**.[11]

- **Both parties must give genuine assent.** To have a legally enforceable contract, both parties must agree to it voluntarily. The contract must be free of fraud, duress, undue influence, and mutual mistake.[12] If only one party makes a mistake, it ordinarily does not affect the contract. On the other hand, if both parties make a mistake, the agreement would be void. For example, if both the buyer and the seller of a business believed the business was profitable, when in reality it was operating at a loss, their agreement would be void.

- **Both parties must be competent.** The law gives certain classes of people only a limited capacity to enter into contracts. Minors, people who are senile or insane, and in some cases those who are intoxicated cannot usually be bound by a contract for anything but the bare necessities (food, clothing, shelter, and medical care).

- **The contract must not involve an illegal act.** Courts will not enforce a promise that involves an illegal act. For example, a drug dealer cannot get help from the courts to enforce a contract to deliver illegal drugs at a prearranged price.

- **The contract must be in proper form.** Most contracts can be made orally, by an act, or by a casually written document; however, certain contracts are required, by law, to be in writing. For example, the transfer of goods worth $500 or more must be accompanied by a written document. The written form is also required for all real estate contracts.

Contract Performance

A contract normally expires when the agreed-to conditions have been met—that is, when the parties have *performed* the requirements of the contract. However, not all contracts run their expected course. Both parties involved can agree to back out of a contract, for instance. Or one party may fail to live up to the terms of the contract, a situation called

breach of contract. The other party has several options at that point:

- **Discharge.** When one party violates the terms of the agreement, generally the other party is under no obligation to continue with his or her end of the contract. In other words, the second party is discharged from the contract.
- **Damages.** A party has the right to sue in court for damages that were foreseeable at the time the contract was entered into and that result from the other party's failure to fulfill the contract. The amount of damages awarded usually reflects the amount of profit lost and often includes court costs as well, although figuring out fair amounts is not always easy.
- **Specific performance.** A party can be compelled to live up to the terms of the contract if monetary damages would not be adequate.

To control the increasing costs of litigation, more and more companies are now experimenting with alternatives to the courtroom. One alternative is to work with an independent mediator who sits down with the two parties and tries to hammer out a satisfactory solution to contract problems. Another alternative is mandatory arbitration, in which an impartial arbitrator or arbitration panel hears evidence from both sides and makes a legally binding decision. However, mandatory arbitration has come under fire by consumer groups because it can void a customer's right to sue.

Warranties

The UCC specifies that everyday sales transactions are a special kind of contract (although this provision applies only to tangible goods, not to services), even though they may not meet all the exact requirements of regular contracts. Related to the sales contract is the notion of a **warranty**, a statement that specifies what the producer or seller of a product will do to compensate the buyer if the product fails to meet particular standards of quality and performance. In the event that those standards aren't met, warranties give buyers legal recourse.

Express warranties are specific written statements. Courts may also enforce *implied warranties* that meet a variety of unwritten expectations, such as the expectation that food products are fit for human consumption.[13]

AGENCY

A large body of laws address the legal association known as **agency**, in which a *principal* authorizes an *agent* to act on his or her behalf in contractual matters. Agency relationships can be found in many industries, including sports, entertainment, publishing, and real estate.

All contractual obligations come into play in agency relationships. The principal usually creates such a relationship by explicit authorization. In some cases—such as when a transfer of property is involved—the authorization must be written in the form of a document called a **power of attorney**, which states that one person may legally act for another (to the extent authorized).

Usually, an agency relationship is terminated when the objective of the relationship has been met or at the end of a period specified in the contract between agent and principal. It may also be ended by a change of circumstances, by the agent's breach of duty or loyalty, or by the death of either party.

PROPERTY TRANSACTIONS

Anyone interested in business must know the basics of property law. Most people think of property as some object they own (for example, a book, a car, a house). However, **property** is actually the relationship between the person having the rights to any tangible or intangible object and all other persons. The law recognizes two primary types of property: real and personal. **Real property** is land and everything permanently attached to it, such as trees, fences, or mineral deposits. **Personal property** is all property that is not real property; it may be tangible (cars, jewelry, or anything having a physical existence) or intangible (bank accounts, stocks, insurance policies, customer lists). A piece of marble in the earth is real property until it is cut and sold as a block, when it becomes personal property. Property rights are subject to various limitations and restrictions. For example, the government monitors the use of real property for the welfare of the public, to the point of explicitly prohibiting some property uses and abuses.[14]

Two types of documents are important in obtaining real property for factory, office, or store space: a deed and a lease. A **deed** is a legal document by which an owner transfers the *title*, or right of ownership, to real property to a new owner. A *lease* is used for a temporary transfer of interest in real property. The party that owns the property is commonly called the *landlord*; the party that occupies or gains the right to occupy the property is the *tenant*. The tenant pays the landlord, usually in periodic installments, for the use of the property. Generally, a lease may be granted for any length of time that the two parties agree on.

PATENTS, TRADEMARKS, AND COPYRIGHTS

If you invent a product, write a book, develop some new software, or simply come up with a unique name for your business, you probably want to prevent other people from using or prospering from your **intellectual property** without fairly compensating you. Several forms of legal protection

Trademarked brand names are a valuable element of intellectual property.

are available for your creations. They include patents, trademarks, and copyrights. Which one you should use depends on what you have created. Having a patent, copyright, or trademark still doesn't guarantee that your idea or product will not be copied. However, it does provide you with legal recourse if your creations are infringed upon.

Patents

A **patent** protects the invention or discovery of a new and useful process, an article of manufacture, a machine, a chemical substance, or an improvement on any of these. In the United States, patents are issued by the U.S. Patent and Trademark Office (USPTO). U.S. law grants the owner of a patent the right to exclude others from making, using, or selling the invention for 14, 15, or 20 years (depending on the type of patent and when it was filed).[15] After that time, the patented design becomes available for common use. On the one hand, patent law guarantees the originator the right to use the discovery exclusively for a relatively long period of time, thus encouraging people to devise new devices and processes. On the other hand, it also ensures that rights to the new item will be released eventually, allowing other enterprises to discover even more innovative ways to use it.

Trademarks

A trademark is any word, name, symbol, or device used to distinguish the product of one manufacturer from those made by others. A service mark is the same thing for services. The McDonald's golden arches and Nike's "swoosh"

are two of the most visible of modern trademarks. Brand names can also be registered as trademarks.

If properly registered and periodically renewed as required by the USPTO, a trademark generally belongs to its owner forever. Among the exceptions are popular brand names that have become generic terms, meaning that they describe a whole class of products. A brand name trademark can become a generic term if the trademark has been allowed to expire, if it has been incorrectly used by its owner, or if the public comes to equate the name with the class of products, as in the case of *zipper, linoleum, thermos,* and many other common terms that started out as brand names.[16] Laws also protect *trade dress*, the general appearance or image of a product, as long as the original designer can prove that these visual elements are an important part of the perceived value of the product.[17]

Copyrights

Copyrights protect the creators of literary, dramatic, musical, artistic, scientific, and other intellectual works. Any printed, filmed, or recorded material can be copyrighted. The copyright gives its owner the exclusive right to reproduce, sell, or adapt the work he or she has created.

The U.S. Copyright Office will issue a copyright to the creator or to whomever the creator has granted the right to reproduce the work. (A book, for example, may be copyrighted by the author or the publisher.) The length of time that copyright protection lasts depends on the circumstances of a work's creation and publication. For example, for works created by an individual after 1978, copyright lasts for the duration of the creator's life plus 70 years.[18]

The ability to reproduce and transmit materials digitally has vastly complicated the interpretation and enforcement of copyright law. The No Electronic Theft Act (NET Act) of 1997 criminalized copyright infringement in cases where the retail value of the copyrighted material exceeds $1,000.[19] The Digital Millennium Copyright Act (DMCA) made it illegal to circumvent digital copy-protection schemes often known as *digital rights management*. Critics of the DMCA, such as the Electronic Frontier Foundation (EFF; **www.eff .org**), say it goes too far, restricting free expression, limiting fair use of purchased rights, and restraining competition and innovation.[20] Supporters, however, argue that the DCMA, even if imperfect, has been essential to the explosive growth of the Internet. The DCMA's *safe harbor* provision, which protects service providers from legal liability for content posted by users, enabled the growth of many services (including YouTube and Google) that millions of people use every day.[21]

NEGOTIABLE INSTRUMENTS

A **negotiable instrument** is a transferable document that represents a promise to pay a specified amount. *Negotiable* in this sense means that it can be sold or used as payment of a debt; an *instrument* is simply a written document that expresses a legal agreement. Negotiable instruments include personal and business checks, certificates of deposit, promissory notes, and commercial paper. Negotiable instruments serve several important purposes: substituting for money, extending credit (in some `instances), and providing a record of a transaction.[22]

BANKRUPTCY

When individuals or companies are unable to meet their financial obligations, they have the option of pursuing **bankruptcy** protection to gain some measure of relief from creditors. The federal Bankruptcy Code provides for several types of bankruptcies, each of which is identified by the chapter of the code in which it is described. The three most common forms are[23]

- **Chapter 7 bankruptcy.** In this type of bankruptcy, the debtor's *nonexempt* property is sold, and the proceeds are used to repay creditors, whose claims are then permanently settled (for example, any money debtors earn after settlement is theirs to keep). Debtors are allowed to keep *exempt* property (such as tools used in a profession).
- **Chapter 11 bankruptcy.** In this type of bankruptcy, the debtor is allowed a period of time to reorganize and reestablish financial viability. Chapter 11 protection is sought most frequently by companies, rather than individuals, and usually with the intent to modify capital structures in order to lessen the burden of debt payments.
- **Chapter 13 bankruptcy.** In this type of bankruptcy, individuals who have regular incomes but are unable to meet their recurring debt payments can negotiate new payment plans with their creditors.

MyBizLab®

To complete the problems with the ⭐, go to EOC Discussion Questions in the MyLab.

TEST YOUR KNOWLEDGE

Questions for Review

A-1. What are the three types of U.S. laws, and how do they differ from one another? What additional laws must global companies consider?

A-2. What is the difference between negligence and intentional torts?

A-3. What are the seven elements of a valid contract?

A-4. How can companies protect their intellectual property?

A-5. What criteria must an instrument meet to be negotiable?

Questions for Analysis

A-6. What is precedent, and how does it affect common law?

A-7. What does the concept of strict product liability mean to businesses?

⭐ **A-8.** Why is agency important to business?

⭐ **A-9.** How can intellectual property rights help spur innovation?

⭐ **A-10.** **Ethical Considerations.** Should products that can be used in the commission of a crime be declared illegal? For example, DVD burners can be used to make illegal copies of movies pirated from the Internet. Why wouldn't the government simply ban such devices?

MyBizLab®

Go to the Assignments section of your MyLab to complete these writing exercises.

A-11. Should individual employees or managers of a corporation be penalized (through fines or imprisonment) if they are responsible when their companies commit illegal acts? For example, if a company is fined for polluting, should the people who authorized and carried out the pollution be fined as well? Why or why not?

A-12. Would musicians, artists, writers, and inventors continue to create if they had no patent or copyright protection? Explain your answer.

APPENDIX A GLOSSARY

administrative law Rules, regulations, and interpretations of statutory law set forth by administrative agencies and commissions

agency A business relationship that exists when one party (the principal) authorizes another party (the agent) to enter into contracts on the principal's behalf

bankruptcy A legal procedure by which a person or a business that is unable to meet financial obligations is relieved of debt

breach of contract Failure to live up to the terms of a contract, with no legal excuse

business law The elements of law that directly influence or control business activities

common law Laws based on the precedents established by judges' decisions

consent order A settlement in which an individual or organization promises to discontinue some illegal activity without admitting guilt

consideration A negotiated exchange that is necessary to make a contract legally binding

contract A legally enforceable exchange of promises between two or more parties

damages Financial compensation to an injured party for loss and suffering

deed A legal document by which an owner transfers the title, or ownership rights, to real property to a new owner

express contract A contract derived from words, either oral or written

implied contract A contract derived from actions or conduct

intellectual property Intangible personal property, such as ideas, songs, trade secrets, and computer programs, that are protected by patents, trademarks, and copyrights

intentional tort A willful act that results in injury

international law Principles, customs, and rules that govern the international relationships between states, organizations, and persons

negligence A tort in which a reasonable amount of care to protect others from risk of injury is not used

negotiable instrument A transferable document that represents a promise to pay a specified amount

patent The legal right to exclude others from making, using, or selling an invention or design

personal property All property that is not real property

power of attorney Written authorization for one party to legally act for another

product liability The capacity of a product to cause harm or damage for which the producer or seller is held accountable

property Rights held regarding any tangible or intangible object

real property Land and everything permanently attached to it

stare decisis The concept of using previous judicial decisions as the basis for deciding similar court cases

statutory law Statutes, or laws, created by legislatures

strict liability Liability for injury caused by a defective product or process when all reasonable care is used in its manufacture, distribution, or sale; no fault is assigned

tort A noncriminal act (other than breach of contract) that results in injury to a person or to property

Uniform Commercial Code (UCC) A set of standardized laws, adopted by most states, that govern business transactions

warranty A statement that specifies what the producer of a product will do to compensate the buyer if the product is defective or if it malfunctions

ENDNOTES

1. Henry R. Cheeseman, *Business Law*, 7th ed. (Upper Saddle River, N.J.: Pearson Prentice Hall, 2010), 849.
2. Cheeseman, *Business Law*, 281.
3. George A. Steiner and John F. Steiner, *Business, Government, and Society* (New York: McGraw-Hill, 1991), 149.
4. "Arizona Panel to Study Idea for Business Courts," *Arizona Republic*, 13 May 2014, www.azcentral.com; Lee Applebaum, "The 'New' Business Courts," *Business Law Today*, March/April 2008, www.abanet.org.
5. Cheeseman, *Business Law*, 75.
6. Nancy K. Kubasek, Bartley A. Brennan, and M. Neil Browne, *The Legal Environment of Business*, 3rd ed. (Upper Saddle River, N.J.: Pearson Prentice Hall, 2003), 306.
7. Kubasek et al., *The Legal Environment of Business*, 184.
8. Cheeseman, *Business Law*, 89.
9. Mark A. Hofmann, "Tort Reform Backers Win Some Battles to Reduce Liability Risks," *Business Insurance*, 3 November 2008, 19–21.
10. Cheeseman, *Business Law*, 158–159.
11. Cheeseman, *Business Law*, 154.
12. Kubasek et al., *The Legal Environment of Business*, 128.
13. Cheeseman, *Business Law*, 330.
14. Kubasek et al., *The Legal Environment of Business*, 160; Douglas Whitman and John William Gergacz, *The Legal Environment of Business* (New York: McGraw-Hill, 1990), 260.
15. Cheeseman, *Business Law*, 111; "Patent"; "How Do I Figure Out If a US Patent Is Still in Force?" Brown & Michaels, accessed 22 June 2015, www.bpmlegal.com.
16. Mary Beth Quirk, "15 Product Trademarks That Have Become Victims of Genericization," *Consumerist*, 19 July 2014, http://consumerist.com.
17. Betsy D. Gelb and Partha Krishnamurthy, "Protect Your Product's Look and Feel from Imitators," *Harvard Business Review*, October 2008, 36.
18. "How Long Does Copyright Protection Last?" U.S. Copyright Office, accessed 23 June 2015, www.copyright.gov; Cheeseman, *Business Law*, 116.
19. Cheeseman, *Business Law*, 119.
20. *Unintended Consequences: 12 Years Under the DMCA*, white paper, 2010, Electronic Frontier Foundation, accessed 31 October 2011, www.eff.org.
21. David Kravets, "10 Years Later, Misunderstood DMCA Is the Law That Saved the Web," *Wired*, 27 October 2008, www.wired.com.
22. Cheeseman, *Business Law*, 341.
23. "Bankruptcy Basics," Administrative Offices of the U.S. Courts website, accessed 31 October 2011, www.uscourts.gov.

Risk Management

The Business of Risk

All businesses face the risk of loss. Fire, lawsuits, accidents, natural disasters, theft, illness, disability, interest rate changes, credit freezes, contract defaults, and deaths of key employees can devastate any business if it is not prepared. Misjudging or mismanaging risks can damage careers, companies, and entire economies. For example, referring to the subprime mortgage mess that helped trigger the deepest recession since the Great Depression (see Chapter 20), the editors of the *Harvard Business Review* were blunt: "Of all the management tasks that were bungled in the period leading up to the global recession, none was bungled more egregiously than the management of risk."[1]

In fact, financial risk was so misunderstood and mismanaged that the very tools some banks used to protect themselves from risk often made them more vulnerable instead.[2] Attempts to reduce human error by relying on advanced statistical models and algorithms to predict outcomes sometimes had the unfortunate effect of removing human judgment from the decision making as well. Without experienced minds actively engaged in the process to grapple with uncertainties and the nuances of individual situations, in some cases these algorithms produced disastrous decisions.[3]

UNDERSTANDING RISK

Although the formal definition of **risk** is the variation, based on chance, in possible outcomes of an event, it's not unusual to sometimes hear the term used to mean *exposure to loss*. This second definition is helpful because it explains why people purchase **insurance**, a contractual arrangement whereby one party agrees to compensate another party for losses. In the broadest sense, insurance can range from the home and auto policies that consumers buy to the hedging strategies discussed in Chapter 18 to the credit default swaps you read about in Chapter 19.

Speculative risk refers to exposures that offer the prospect of making a profit or loss—such as investments in stock. **Pure risk**, on the other hand, is the threat of loss without the possibility of gain. Disasters such as an earthquake or a fire at a manufacturing plant are examples of pure risk. Nothing good can come from an exposure to pure risk.

An **insurable risk** is a risk that meets certain requirements in order for the insurer to provide protection, whereas an **uninsurable risk** is one that an insurance company will not cover (see Exhibit B.1). Generally speaking, most speculative risks are not insurable, but many pure risks are. For example, most insurance companies are unwilling to cover potential losses that can occur from general economic conditions such as a recession (although strategies such as financial hedging might help in such scenarios). For a type of loss exposure to present a desirable business opportunity for an insurance company, it needs to meet the following criteria:[4]

- **The potential loss must be accidental.** Replacing an automobile that is totaled in a crash is an insurable event; replacing an automobile that fell apart through neglect is not.
- **The loss must be significant and measurable.** The loss of a building is quantifiable because the property has a measurable market value. In contrast, the pain and suffering associated with a loss may well be significant, but they are not quantifiable and therefore are not insurable.
- **The same threat must be faced by a large number of similar persons or organizations.** For the likelihood of a loss to be predictable, insurance companies must be able to compile data on the frequency and severity of losses posed by a particular threat. For example, by tracking the shipping industry year to year, a provider of marine insurance can collect enough data to be able to predict losses resulting from storms, accidents, piracy, and other threats.
- **The likely frequency of catastrophic losses must be low.** Insurance companies are able to stay in business only if the amounts they pay out in **claims** (customer demands to pay for insured losses) are less than the **insurance premiums** (fees paid by customers to get insurance) they collect. As a simple example, a property insurance company can't survive if it takes in $10 million in premiums every year but 20 or 30 customers lose $1 million buildings every year.

Because not all calamities in life are insurable, businesses can't insure themselves against every potential loss. Even when they can buy coverage, insurance represents a recurring financial burden that must be considered carefully. Consequently, smart companies do everything they can to reduce the financial exposure created by risk through **risk management**, which includes assessing, controlling, and financing risk by shifting it to an insurance company or another outside party or by *self-insuring* to cover possible losses.

EXHIBIT B.1   Insurable and Uninsurable Risk

Some of the risks that businesses and individuals face are insurable, but many others aren't.

Generally Insurable

Property risks: Uncertainty surrounding the occurrence of loss from perils that cause

1. Direct loss of property
2. Loss of use of or benefits of property

Personal risks: Uncertainty surrounding the occurrence of loss due to

1. Premature death
2. Physical disability
3. Old age

Legal liability risks: Uncertainty surrounding the occurrence of loss arising out of

1. Use of automobiles
2. Occupancy of buildings
3. Employment
4. Manufacture of products
5. Professional misconduct

Generally Uninsurable

Market risks: Factors that may result in loss of property or income, such as

1. Price changes, both seasonal and cyclical
2. Consumer indifference
3. Style changes
4. Increased competition

Political risks: Uncertainty surrounding the occurrence of

1. Overthrow of a government
2. Restrictions imposed on free trade
3. Unreasonable or punitive taxation
4. Restrictions of free exchange of currencies

Production risks: Uncertainties surrounding the occurrence of

1. Failure of machinery to function economically
2. Failure to solve technical problems
3. Exhaustion of raw-material resources
4. Strikes, absenteeism, and labor unrest

Personal risks: Uncertainty surrounding the occurrence of

1. Unemployment
2. Poverty from factors such as divorce, lack of education or opportunity, and loss of health from military service

ASSESSING RISK

One of the first steps in managing risk is to identify the source of the threat. Areas of risk in which a potential for loss exists are called **loss exposures**. Some types of exposures are common to all businesses, such as fires, floods, and the death of key personnel. Other risks vary from industry to industry. For example, financial firms have to assess *credit risk* (the risk that borrowers will not repay loans), *market risk* (the risk that investments will lose value), and *operational risk* (the risk that anything from computer hackers to hurricanes will disrupt trading operations). Manufacturers have many of these loss exposures as well, plus such added risks as product liability and inventory losses during storage or transportation. Retailers worry about *shrinkage*, the loss of inventory as a result of shoplifting or internal theft. Medical firms face the possibility of lawsuits from *malpractice* claims.

Risk managers also need to understand the breadth or extent of a risk, because this determines how much control they have—if any. **Systemic risk** exists throughout an entire market or economy, such as the possibility that interest rates might rise and thereby increase capital costs for everyone. In contrast, **nonsystemic risk** threatens only a single company or a single industry. However, nonsystemic risk can become systemic if the scope of the threat grows beyond the single company or industry. This happened during the banking crisis in 2008 after many investment banks transferred their credit default risks to the insurance

company AIG. Eventually, so many companies became dependent on AIG that its instability became a risk for the entire financial sector and eventually for the entire economy.

Finally, managers need to estimate the *probability* that a potential threat could become real and the magnitude of its *impact* if it does become real. For example, chemical spills are much more likely in facilities that use chemicals in processing or manufacturing than in facilities that use chemicals only for cleaning. And the impact of spilling a gallon of cleaning fluid is obviously less severe than the impact of a train derailment that spills the contents of a tanker car.

After managers have characterized a potential for risk, they have three possible responses: accept the risk and go on with business as usual (which can be a reasonable response for low-probability, low-impact risks, for example), take steps to control the risk, or shift some or all of the responsibility for the risk to a third party. Combining the last two steps, controlling and shifting risk, is common.

REAL-TIME UPDATES
Learn More by Reading This Infographic

Outlining a risk management strategy

Review the key steps in crafting a risk management strategy. Go to http://real-timeupdates.com/bia8 and click on Learn More in the Students section.

CONTROLLING RISK

If a risk is controllable and significant enough to warrant attention, managers can use a number of *risk-control techniques* to minimize the organization's losses:

- **Risk avoidance.** A risk manager might try to eliminate the chance of a particular type of loss, such as when a bank chooses not to lend money to new companies that haven't yet proven their ability to sustain profitable sales. The implication of risk avoidance is that it can mean not pursuing particular business opportunities—but that isn't always a bad thing.
- **Loss prevention.** A risk manager may try to reduce (but not totally eliminate) the *chance* of a given loss by removing hazards or taking preventive measures. Security guards at banks, warnings on medicines and dangerous chemicals, and safety locks are examples of physical loss prevention measures. Banks can use tighter lending standards to prevent instances of loan defaults.
- **Loss reduction.** A risk manager may try to reduce the *severity* of losses that do occur. Examples include installing overhead sprinklers to reduce damage during a fire and paying the medical expenses of an injured consumer to reduce the likelihood of litigation and punitive damages.

SHIFTING RISK TO A THIRD PARTY

If a company can't prevent or reduce potential losses to an acceptable level, the next option is to finance the risk by paying another company to assume part or all of it. You do the same thing when you buy an insurance policy for your car: You're paying an insurance company to hold the risk of losses caused by thefts or accidents. (Companies can shift risk in a variety of ways; this appendix focuses on the use of insurance.)

In many cases, though, transferring one type of risk creates another type of risk.[5] For instance, buying an insurance policy against some possible calamity shifts some or all of that risk to the insurer—but then creates a new risk that the insurer won't be able to pay up when disaster strikes. For your personal insurance needs, it's vital to investigate the financial health of an insurer to make sure the company will be around when you need it. Websites such as Insure.com (www.insure.com) let you check on the financial strength ratings of insurance companies.

Insurance companies don't count on making a profit on any particular policy, nor do they count on paying for a single policyholder's losses out of the premium paid by that particular policyholder. Rather, the insurance company pays for a loss by drawing the money out of the pool of funds it has received from all its policyholders in the form of premiums. In this way, the insurance company redistributes the cost of predicted losses from a single individual or company to a large number of policies. To determine premium amounts, insurers rely on **actuaries**—loss-assessment specialists who compile statistics of losses to determine how much income insurance companies need to generate from premiums—to forecast the funds needed to pay claims over a given period.

The types of insurance that a company needs depend on the nature of the business and its ability to withstand specific types of losses. Most companies protect themselves against the loss of property, loss of income, liability, and loss of services of key personnel (see Exhibit B.2).

Property Insurance

Property insurance covers physical damage, destruction, or theft of company property. Policies vary in how much funding is provided. *Replacement-cost coverage* provides enough money to replace or restore property, without any reductions for depreciation in the property's value since it was put into service.[6] In contrast, *actual cash value coverage* pays only what the property is currently worth—which could be far less than the money needed to replace it. Because actual cash value coverage pays less, such policies understandably cost less than replacement-cost policies.

Business Interruption Insurance

In addition to the direct losses they inflict, fires, floods, criminal acts, and other events can cause significant indirect losses if they disrupt business operations. Short-term disruptions cause the loss of immediate sales revenue, and longer-term disruptions can cost a company permanent market share as customers seek out new suppliers.[7] To get

EXHIBIT B.2	Business Risks and Protection

Here are some of the most common types of business insurance.

Risk	Protection
Loss of property	
As a result of destruction or theft	Fire insurance Disaster insurance Marine insurance Automobile insurance
Resulting from dishonesty or nonperformance	Fidelity bonding Surety bonding Credit life insurance Crime insurance
Loss of income	Business interruption insurance Extra-expense insurance
Liability	Comprehensive general liability insurance Automobile liability insurance Workers' compensation insurance Umbrella liability insurance Professional liability insurance
Loss of services of key personnel	Key-person insurance

some level of reimbursement for lost revenue, companies can purchase **business interruption insurance**.

Liability Insurance

A variety of insurance policies are available to protect against **liability losses**, financial losses that occur when companies or their employees are found to be responsible for damage or injury to another party (which can include a company's own employees):

- **Commercial general liability** policies provide financial protection in the event a company is sued for damaging property or causing injury. For some companies, a general liability policy provides adequate coverage for their entire scope of operations, but other companies add specific types of liability coverage as well.[8]
- **Product-liability coverage** provides financial protection in the event that a company's products cause injury, disease, or death. Claims can result from defects in design, packaging, materials, labeling, safety warnings, and user instructions.[9]
- Also known as *malpractice insurance* or *errors and omissions insurance*, **professional liability insurance** covers people who might be found liable for professional negligence. This insurance applies to specialties such as accounting and medicine, as well as top management in public corporations. To protect corporate officers and members of corporate boards from lawsuits stemming from claims of mismanagement, companies can purchase *directors' and officers' liability insurance*, often called *D&O insurance*.[10]
- **Employment practices liability insurance** reimburses employers for a variety of claims related to employment practices, including negligent hiring, wrongful termination, and negligent employee evaluations.[11]
- Finally, just to be safe, businesses sometimes purchase **umbrella policies** to provide coverage for loss exposures not covered by all their other liability policies.[12]

Key-Person Insurance

If an employee or executive is essential to a company's ability to generate revenue, the firm can purchase **key-person insurance** to cushion the financial blow of losing that person's services in the event of death, disability, or unexpected departure. Of course, if a person is that essential to the company, the management team should also take steps to have potential replacements ready to step in if needed.[13]

SELF-INSURING AGAINST RISK

Rather than finance risk through a third party, companies sometimes choose to address risk through **self-insurance**, which attempts to replicate the coverage provided by an independent insurer. The primary advantage of self-insurance is cost, because the company doesn't have to pay for risky behaviors of an insurance company's other clients or

the insurer's own profit margins.[14] When insurance rates climb, more companies typically look to self-insure. For example, when the cost of *windstorm insurance* jumped after a tough hurricane season, many oil drilling companies with platforms in the Gulf of Mexico opted to self-insure rather than renew policies with higher rates.[15]

Companies with strong balance sheets are obviously in the best position to self-insure. Microsoft, for instance, uses self-insurance programs or no insurance at all in many instances because it has so much cash on hand to cover emergencies. In general, the company uses commercial insurers only for potentially catastrophic losses or when it can find great deals on policies.[16]

Insuring the Health and Well-Being of Employees

In addition to protecting company property and assets, many businesses look out for the well-being of employees by providing them with health, disability, workers' compensation, and life insurance coverage. Disease and disability may cost employees huge sums of money unless they are insured. In addition, death carries the threat of financial hardship for an employee's family.

HEALTH INSURANCE

Many employers have long offered health insurance as an employee benefit, and the Affordable Care Act now mandates that all companies with more than 50 full-time employees provide some level of health insurance. Health insurance is available from a variety of sources, including government programs, private not-for-profit organizations, and for-profit commercial providers. Another major source of health coverage is **health maintenance organizations (HMOs)**, which are prepaid, group-practice medical plans in which consumers pay a set fee and, in return, receive many services as needed for either no additional cost or for a modest co-payment. For patients, a key attraction of HMOs is paying the same monthly fees, regardless of usage level. To maintain profitability, therefore, HMOs usually place a high priority on wellness and disease prevention.[17]

As an alternative to HMOs, some employers opt for **preferred-provider organizations (PPOs)**, health-care providers that contract with employers, insurance companies, or other third-party payers to deliver health-care services to employees.[18] The "preferred providers" are medical specialists and medical facilities that have opted to join that particular PPO network. Employees generally aren't required to use in-network providers, but they pay more for using out-of-network services.[19]

Health savings accounts (HSAs) allow people with high-deductible health plans to save a portion of their earnings in a special account that can be used for major medical

REAL-TIME UPDATES
Learn More by Reading This Article

Smart tips for buying life insurance

Before you buy life insurance to protect your loved ones, learn these fundamentals. Go to **http://real-timeupdates.com/bia8** and click on Learn More in the Students section.

expenses when needed.[20] Contributions to HSAs are tax deductible, and any interest or investment gains in an HSA are tax-free as well.[21]

DISABILITY INCOME AND WORKERS' COMPENSATION INSURANCE

Two forms of insurance exist to help employees who are temporarily or permanently unable to work. **Disability income insurance** replaces a portion of an employee's income, typically up to 60 percent or so, with possible supplemental coverage up to 70 or 80 percent.[22] The length of coverage varies widely; some policies are designed only for short-term disabilities, whereas others provide benefits for a number of years.

In contrast to disability insurance, which is provided as part of an employer's overall health insurance package or purchased by individuals, **workers' compensation insurance** programs are administered by state governments. The intent of "workers' comp" is to replace some portion of an employee's income and to pay for some or all necessary medical costs if he or she is unable to work as the result of a job-related accident or illness. Every employer that is required to participate (different states exempt various categories of businesses) pays into an insurance fund based on the number of employees, the types of work those employees perform, and the company's *experience rating*—essentially a running tally of its safety record. Companies with higher accident rates pay higher insurance rates; those with lower accident rates pay lower insurance rates.[23]

MyBizLab®

To complete the problems with the ⭐, go to EOC Discussion Questions in the MyLab.

LIFE INSURANCE

Life insurance provides financial support to family members and others in the event of a person's death. Some employers include life insurance in their benefits packages, and many people buy policies on their own as well. The range of life insurance products is quite varied, from simple term life insurance to more complicated policies that combine investment with insurance:

- The simplest form of life insurance, **term life insurance**, offers coverage for a specific period of time—the *term* of the policy. Unlike other types of life insurance, term life is insurance only, with no savings or investment components. Term life is usually the least expensive, but it must be renewed after the term expires, and renewal rates increase as buyers get older. A great use of term life is investing the money you save (compared to other insurance policies) so that by the time the term is up, you have accumulated enough assets to protect your loved ones without relying on life insurance.[24]

- **Whole life insurance** differs from term in two important ways: It provides coverage until the insured person dies, and part of the premiums paid accumulate in a savings plan. The policyholder can borrow against this amount or cash in the policy, if needed.[25]

- **Universal life insurance** is a combination life insurance and investment product, in which customers purchase an insurance policy and invest additional funds (typically in government bonds). The combination of insurance and investments gives customers some flexibility—depending on the performance of the investments—in the size and frequency of premiums and the size of the death benefits.[26] A similar concept, *variable life insurance*, gives policyholders more control over the investments made with their paid-in premiums.

TEST YOUR KNOWLEDGE

Questions for Review

B-1. What is the difference between pure risk and speculative risk?

B-2. What is risk management?

B-3. What are the four general requirements of insurability?

B-4. What are the three steps to controlling risk?

B-5. What is the difference between workers' compensation insurance and disability income insurance?

Questions for Analysis

B-6. How do insurance companies calculate their premiums?

B-7. Is self-insurance the same as going without insurance? Why or why not?

B-8. Why is it a good idea to purchase business interruption insurance?

B-9. Does every worker or consumer need life insurance? Why or why not?

B-10. Ethical Considerations. Life insurance can be one of the most complex purchases a consumer ever makes. It is also an expensive purchase and often sold by salespeople working on commission, which means they are motivated to make the sale. Whose responsibility is it to make sure purchasers understand the options available to them and understand all the details and ramifications of the specific policies they choose? Why?

MyBizLab®

Go to the Assignments section of your MyLab to complete these writing exercises.

B-11. Should employers be required to provide some level of health insurance to their employees? If not, how should employees get coverage?

B-12. Is the chance that a new product might fail in the marketplace an insurable risk? Why or why not?

APPENDIX B GLOSSARY

actuaries Risk analysts employed by insurance companies to forecast expected losses and to calculate the cost of premiums

business interruption insurance Insurance that covers losses resulting from temporary business closings

claims Demands for payments from an insurance company based on the terms in an insurance policy

commercial general liability Policies that provides protection against all forms of liability not specifically excluded under the terms of the policy

disability income insurance Short-term or long-term insurance that replaces some of the income lost when an individual is unable to perform his or her work as a result of illness or injury

employment practices liability insurance Insurance that reimburses employers for a variety of claims related to employment practices

health maintenance organizations (HMOs) Prepaid medical plans in which consumers pay a set fee to receive a full range of medical care from a group of medical practitioners

health savings accounts (HSAs) Special savings accounts that allow employees to save a portion of their earnings to use for medical expenses when needed

insurable risk Risk that an insurance company might be willing to cover

insurance A written contract that transfers to an insurer the financial responsibility for losses for specific events, up to specified limits and within specified conditions

insurance premiums Fees that insured parties pay insurers for coverage against losses

key-person insurance Insurance that provides a business with funds to compensate for the loss of a key employee by unplanned retirement, resignation, death, or disability

liability losses Financial losses suffered by a business firm or an individual held responsible for property damage or injuries suffered by others

life insurance Insurance that provides financial support to family members and others in the event of a person's death

loss exposures Areas of risk in which a potential for loss exists

nonsystemic risk Risk that threatens only a single company or a single industry

preferred-provider organizations (PPOs) Health-care providers offering reduced-rate contracts to groups that agree to obtain medical care through the providers' organization

product-liability coverage Insurance that protects companies from claims that result from use of a product the company manufactures or distributes

professional liability insurance Insurance that covers claims for damages or injuries caused by professionals in the course of their work

property insurance Insurance that provides coverage for physical damage to or destruction of property and for its loss by theft

pure risk Risk that involves the chance of loss only

risk management A process business firms and individuals use to address their exposures to loss

risk Uncertainty of an event or exposure to loss

self-insurance A financial protection strategy in which a company maintains enough funds to pay for potential losses on its own, rather than purchasing insurance coverage

speculative risk Risk that involves the chance of both loss and profits

systemic risk Risk that exists throughout an entire market

term life insurance Life insurance that provides death benefits for a specified period

umbrella policies Insurance that provides businesses with coverage beyond what is provided by a basic liability policy

uninsurable risk Risk that few, if any, insurance companies will assume because it likely cannot be covered profitably

universal life insurance A combination life insurance and investment product in which customers purchase an insurance policy and invest additional funds

whole life insurance Insurance that provides both death benefits and savings for the insured's lifetime

workers' compensation insurance Insurance that partially replaces lost income and that pays for employees' medical costs and rehabilitation expenses for work-related injuries

ENDNOTES

1. "Spotlight on Risk," *Harvard Business Review*, October 2009, 67.
2. Nassim N. Taleb, Daniel G. Goldstein, and Mark W. Spitznagel, "The Six Mistakes Executives Make in Risk Management," *Harvard Business Review*, October 2009, 78–81.
3. Amar Bhidé, "The Judgment Deficit," *Harvard Business Review*, September 2010, 44–53.
4. Mark S. Dorfman, *Introduction to Risk Management and Insurance*, 8th ed. (Upper Saddle River, N.J.: Pearson Prentice Hall, 2005), 19–24.
5. Robert S. Kaplan, Anette Mikes, Robert Simons, Peter Tufano, and Michael Hofmann, "Managing Risk in the New World," *Harvard Business Review*, October 2009, 69–75.
6. Dorfman, *Introduction to Risk Management and Insurance*, 153.
7. Nick Whitfield, "Business Interruption May Cost More Than Damage," *Business Insurance*, 4 August 2008, 17–19.
8. "Business Liability Insurance: Different Kinds for Different Businesses," Nationwide, accessed 20 December 2011, www.nationwide.com.
9. Karen E. Klein, "Is Liability Insurance a Must to Go Global?" *BusinessWeek*, 18 June 2008, www.businessweek.com.
10. Dorfman, *Introduction to Risk Management and Insurance*, 391.
11. Dorfman, *Introduction to Risk Management and Insurance*, 394.
12. "Understanding General Liability Insurance," Dun & Bradstreet website, accessed 13 October 2009, http://smallbusinessdnb.com
13. "Key Person Insurance Can Help Companies Mourning an Owner or Executive," Insure.com, 28 May 2009, www.insure.com; Dorfman, *Introduction to Risk Management and Insurance*, 51.
14. Nancy L. Bolton, "Self-Insurance Survival: Creating a Health Plan in Unsuccessful Times," *Employee Benefit News*, July 2009, 14–16.
15. Zack Phillips, "In Tight Market Energy Firms Drop Cover, Cross Fingers," Business *Insurance*, 31 August 2009, 1+.
16. Joanne Wojcik, "Microsoft Relies on Self-Insurance for Most Exposures," *Business Insurance*, 20 April 2009, 34–37.
17. Dorfman, *Introduction to Risk Management and Insurance*, 73.
18. Dorfman, *Introduction to Risk Management and Insurance*, 74.
19. "CIGNA Preferred Provider Organization (PPO)," Cigna website, accessed 13 October 2009, www.cigna.com.
20. "Health Savings Accounts (HSAs)," U.S. Department of the Treasury website, accessed 21 November 2013, www.ustreas.gov.
21. Kimberly Lankford, "Know the Facts About Health Savings Plans," *Chicago Tribune*, 27 September 2013, www.chicagotribune.com.
22. Stacey L. Bradford, "Do You Need Disability Insurance?" *SmartMoney*, 10 September 2008, www.smartmoney.com.
23. Dorfman, *Introduction to Risk Management and Insurance*, 461–468.
24. Jack Hough, "Should You Hurry to Buy Life Insurance?" *SmartMoney*, 18 September 2009, www.smartmoney.com; Miriam Gottfried, "Should You Buy Term Life Insurance?" *SmartMoney*, 10 September 2009, www.smartmoney.com; Dorfman, *Introduction to Risk Management and Insurance*, 256–260.
25. Ginger Applegarth, "Term or Permanent Life Insurance?" *MSN Money*, 21 July 2009, http://articles.moneycentral.msn.com.
26. Dorfman, *Introduction to Risk Management and Insurance*, 263–265.

Information Technology

Information Systems

Information represents one of the most intriguing challenges you'll face as both an employee and a manager. A company can find itself drowning in an ocean of data—but struggling to find real insights that can mean the difference between success and failure.

The first step in turning information into a competitive advantage is understanding the difference between **data** (recorded facts and statistics), **information** (useful knowledge, often extracted from data), and **insight** (a deep level of understanding about a particular situation). The transformation of data into insight requires a combination of technology, information-management strategies, creative thinking, and business experience—and companies that excel at this transformation have a huge advantage over their competitors. In fact, entire industries can be created when a single person looks at the same data and information everyone else is looking at but sees things in a new way, yielding insights that no one has ever had before (see Exhibit C.1).

Businesses collect data from a wide array of sources—checkout scanners, website clicks, research projects, and electronic sensors, to name just a few. A single customer order can generate hundreds of data points, from a credit card number to production statistics to accounting totals that end up on a tax form. Even a small business can quickly amass thousands or millions of individual data points; large companies generate billions and even trillions of data points.[1]

To keep all these data points under control and to extract useful information from them, companies rely on **databases**, computerized files that collect, sort, and cross-reference data. In addition to helping with the daily chores of sending out bills, ordering new parts, and doing everything else that keeps the company running, databases can also be used for *data mining*, a powerful computerized analysis technique that identifies previously unknown relations among individual data points.[2]

Most large organizations employ a top-level manager, often called a **chief information officer (CIO)**, whose job is to understand the company's information needs and to create systems and procedures to deliver that information to the right people at the right time. This manager is expected to deliver quality information, which can be defined as *relevant* (directly pertinent to the recipient's needs), *accurate* (both current and free from errors), *timely* (delivered in time to make a difference), and *cost-effective* (costs a reasonable amount of money compared to the value it offers).

HOW BUSINESSES USE INFORMATION

Companies invest heavily in information for the simple reason that they can't live without it. Here's a small sample of the ways managers rely on information:

- **Research and development.** In a sense, the cycle of information use starts with understanding customer needs and then moves to developing new goods and

| EXHIBIT C.1 | From Data to Information to Insight |

Businesses generate massive amounts of data, but a key challenge is transforming all those individual data points into useful information and then applying creative thinking (sometimes with the additional help of computers) to extract deeper insights from the information.

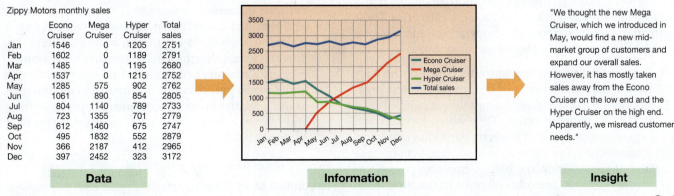

Zippy Motors monthly sales

	Econo Cruiser	Mega Cruiser	Hyper Cruiser	Total sales
Jan	1546	0	1205	2751
Feb	1602	0	1189	2791
Mar	1485	0	1195	2680
Apr	1537	0	1215	2752
May	1285	575	902	2762
Jun	1061	890	854	2805
Jul	804	1140	789	2733
Aug	723	1355	701	2779
Sep	612	1460	675	2747
Oct	495	1832	552	2879
Nov	366	2187	412	2965
Dec	397	2452	323	3172

"We thought the new Mega Cruiser, which we introduced in May, would find a new mid-market group of customers and expand our overall sales. However, it has mostly taken sales away from the Econo Cruiser on the low end and the Hyper Cruiser on the high end. Apparently, we misread customer needs."

Data   **Information**   **Insight**

services to meet those needs. Information is vital at every step, from researching markets to analyzing competitors to testing new products.

- **Planning and control.** Two of the most important functions of management are planning and control—deciding what to do and making sure it gets done. Accounting managers need accurate financial information, sales managers need to know if their teams are meeting their sales goals, human resource managers need to make sure the company has enough of the right kind of employees, and so on.
- **Marketing and sales.** Thanks to technology, marketing and sales have evolved from "gut-feel" activities to more scientific, information-driven functions. "Making Data-Driven Marketing Decisions" on page 302 in Chapter 13 discusses this development in more detail.
- **Communication and collaboration.** Throughout an organization, employees, managers, and teams of every size and shape rely on information to communicate and collaborate. In fact, information technology is changing the very definition of what an organization means, thanks to the Internet's ability to connect people from every corner of the globe.

TYPES OF BUSINESS INFORMATION SYSTEMS

Over the years, the collective label for the technologies used to manage information has changed; what used to be called *data processing* is now called either *information systems (IS)* or *information technology (IT)*, depending on the context. The types of information systems used by a company generally fall into two major categories: (1) operational systems and (2) professional and managerial systems. (The specific systems you'll encounter in various companies are likely to have their own names, often arcane acronyms that make no sense to outsiders.) Some systems meet the information needs of people at specific levels in the organization, whereas *enterprise systems* are designed to connect everyone in the organization, giving each person the information he or she needs to meet specific job responsibilities.

Operational Systems

Operational systems are the "frontline" workhorses of IT, collecting and processing the data and information that represent the day-to-day work of the business enterprise. These systems typically support daily operations and decision making for lower-level managers and supervisors:

- **Transaction processing systems.** Much of the daily flow of data into and out of the typical business organization, particularly regarding sales, is handled by a *transaction processing system (TPS)*, which captures and organizes raw data and converts these data into information. Common transaction processing systems take care of customer orders, billing, employee payroll, inventory changes, and other essential transactions. Such systems are a vital part of supply chain management.

Customer relationship management (CRM) systems help companies capture and organize all the interactions they have with their customers and then use that information to foster positive long-term relationships with customers.

- **Process and production control systems.** Operational systems are also used to make routine decisions that control operational processes. *Process control systems* monitor conditions such as temperature or pressure change in physical processes. *Production control systems* are used to manage the production of goods and services by controlling production lines, robots, and other machinery and equipment.
- **Office automation systems.** *Office automation systems* address a wide variety of typical office tasks. Office automation systems range from a single personal computer with word-processing software to *content management systems* that help companies organize the content on their websites.
- **Customer relationship management systems.** *Customer relationship management (CRM) systems* capture, organize, and capitalize on all the interactions that a company has with its customers, from marketing surveys and advertising through sales orders and customer support. Companies continue to find ways to integrate social media into customer communication, too, such as using Twitter to answer customer support questions and offering coupons and other special deals on their Facebook pages.

Professional and Managerial Systems

In contrast to operational systems, *professional and managerial systems* help with such higher-level tasks as designing new products, analyzing financial data, identifying industry trends, and planning long-term business needs. These systems are used by professionals such as engineers and marketing specialists and by managers up to the top executive and board of directors. An important advance for many professionals is the idea of a *knowledge management (KM) system*, which collects the expertise of employees across an organization.

A **management information system (MIS)** provides managers with information and support for making routine decisions. (Note that *MIS* is sometimes used synonymously with both *IS* and *IT* to describe an overall IT effort.) An MIS takes data from a database and summarizes or restates it into useful information, such as monthly sales summaries, daily inventory levels, product manufacturing schedules, employee earnings, and so on.

Whereas an MIS typically provides structured, routine information for managerial decision making, a *decision support system (DSS)* assists managers in solving highly unstructured and nonroutine problems through the use of decision models and specialized databases. Compared with an MIS, a DSS is more interactive (allowing the user to interact with the system instead of simply receiving information), and it usually relies on both internal and external information. Similar in concept to a DSS is an *executive support system (ESS)*, which helps top executives make strategic decisions.

Employee performance management systems help managers set employee performance goals, develop improvement plans, and reward employees based on measurable performance. By making performance evaluation more transparent and objective, such systems can improve communication, reduce stress, and outline relevant areas for employment development.[3]

One of the most intriguing applications for computers in decision making and problem solving is the development of **artificial intelligence**—the ability of computers to solve problems through reasoning and learning and to simulate human sensory perceptions. For instance, an *expert system* mimics the thought processes of a human expert to help less-experienced individuals make decisions.

Information Systems Management Issues

As a business manager or entrepreneur, you'll be responsible for a variety of legal, ethical, and administrative issues that stem from the use of digital technologies, starting with the challenge of ensuring privacy and security.

ENSURING SECURITY AND PRIVACY

Linking computers and other devices via networking technology creates enormous benefits for businesses and consumers, but there's a dark side to connecting everyone everywhere. Managers need to be constantly vigilant to make sure their computer systems remain secure and that data on them

remain private. In recent years, millions of employee and customer records have been stolen or exposed, and billions of dollars have been lost to damage from computer viruses. The estimated financial damage from computer-based crime is now several hundred billion dollars per year.[4] Moreover, the collection, storage, and use of private information raises a host of legal and ethical issues that managers must consider.

The sources of potential trouble seem to multiply with every passing year and each new technological breakthrough:

- **Malicious software.** **Malware**, short for *malicious software*, is the term often applied to the diverse and growing collection of computer programs designed to disrupt websites, destroy information, or enable criminal activity. **Viruses** are invasive programs that reproduce by infecting legitimate programs; *worms* are a type of virus that can reproduce by themselves. *Trojan horses* allow outsiders to hijack infected devices and use them for purposes such as retransmitting spam email. *Spyware* sneaks onto devices with the intent of capturing passwords, credit card numbers, and other valuable information. Chances are you've also met spyware's less-malicious cousin, *adware*, which creates pop-up ads and other often-unwelcome intrusions.
- **Security breaches.** Any time a device is connected to a wired or wireless network, it becomes vulnerable to security breaches. Given the enormous value of information stored on business information systems, particularly credit card numbers and other personal data that can be used for identity theft, there is financial motivation for outsiders to break in and insiders to sell out.
- **Unauthorized software, services, and devices.** IT departments in many companies face a constant battle with employee use of unauthorized apps, online services, and personal digital devices. Employees not only expose their companies to security risks but also legal risks if they download or transmit inappropriate content on company networks.
- **Social media.** Social media help companies create a more open communication environment for employees, customers, and other communities, but these technologies also create new system vulnerabilities.
- **Misuse of information systems.** As with the use of unauthorized hardware or software, the intentional or unintentional misuse of information systems can create security problems and legal nightmares for managers.
- **Poor security planning and management.** Many viruses and worms are able to wreak their havoc and gain intruders access because devices owners haven't kept their programs or apps up to date or haven't installed *firewalls*, hardware or software devices that block access to intruders. In other cases, companies commit major design blunders, such as creating easily hacked links between high-security financial systems and lower-security building control systems.
- **Lack of physical control.** Software and network security isn't enough. Some of the most egregious security

REAL-TIME UPDATES
Learn More by Watching This Presentation

Simple steps to protect your privacy

Are you following these 10 steps to protect yourself? Go to http://real-timeupdates.com/bia8 and click on Learn More in the Students section.

lapses involve the loss or theft of mobile devices that contain sensitive data such as employee or customer records.

- **Employees' personal devices.** IT departments and managers must also have policies and procedures in place when employees want to connect their own computers, smartphones, and tablets to corporate information networks. These devices can present additional security risks because they don't always have the security controls that equipment designed or customized for business use have.

Whether it's human issues such as background checks on new hires and ongoing security training or technical issues such as firewalls, encryption, or disaster recovery plans, all managers need to devote time and energy to potentially harmful side effects of IT. Sadly, as long as criminals can profit from digital theft and malware writers can amuse themselves by destroying the hard work of others, the problems are likely to get worse.

PROTECTING PROPERTY RIGHTS

Digital technology has increased concerns over the protection of digital products (including software and entertainment products available in digital format) and intellectual property (which includes a wide range of creative outputs with commercial value, such as design ideas, manufacturing processes, brands, and chemical formulas). One of the most controversial issues in this area is *digital rights management (DRM)*, the protection of owners' rights in products that are in digital format. DRM limits the ways consumers can use music files, movies, and other digital purchases, and critics worry that major corporations are using DRM to stifle creativity and control popular culture. Intellectual property protection remains a contentious and complex issue, as copyright owners, privacy advocates, and consumer groups battle over how digital products can or can't be used.

GUARDING AGAINST INFORMATION OVERLOAD

From Twitter feeds to enterprise-wide sales reporting systems, it's not uncommon for businesspeople to be stunned by how quickly their digital systems start piling up data and information. The overuse or misuse of communication technology can lead to *information overload*, in which people receive more information than they can effectively process. Information overload makes it difficult to discriminate between useful and useless information, lowers productivity, and amplifies employee stress both on the job and at home—even to the point of causing health and relationship problems.[5]

Anyone who has sampled today's digital media offerings has probably experienced this situation: You find a few fascinating blogs, a few interesting people to follow on Twitter, a couple of podcast channels with helpful business tips, and then before you know it, your device is overflowing with updates. Even if every new item is useful (which is unlikely), you receive so many that you can't stay ahead of the incoming flood. Between Twitter updates, newsfeeds, email, instant messaging, social networks, and internal systems, today's business professionals could easily spend most of their days just trying to keep up with incoming messages and never get any work done.

To keep social media from turning into a source of stress and information anxiety, consider these tips:

- **Understand what information you really need in order to excel in your current projects and along your intended career path.** Unfortunately, taking this advice is even trickier than it sounds because you can't always know what you need to know, so you can't always predict which sources will be helpful. However, don't gather information simply because it is interesting or entertaining; collect information that is useful or at least potentially useful.
- **Face the fact that you cannot possibly handle every update from every potentially interesting and helpful source.** You have to set priorities and make tough choices to protect yourself from information overload.
- **Add new information sources slowly.** Give yourself a chance to adjust to the flow and judge the usefulness of each new source.
- **Prune your sources vigorously and frequently.** Bloggers run out of things to say; your needs and interests change; higher-priority sources appear.
- **Remember that information is an enabler, a means to an end.** Collecting vast amounts of information won't get you a sweet promotion with a big raise. *Using* information creatively and intelligently will.

MONITORING PRODUCTIVITY

Anyone using digital systems needs to be aware of the "information technology paradox," in which tools designed to save time can waste as much time as they save. For instance, many employers are so concerned about productivity losses from personal use of the Internet at work that they place restrictions on how employees can use it, such as installing software that limits Internet access to business-related sites during working hours.[6]

Managers also need to guide their employees in productive use of information tools. The speed and simplicity of these tools is also one of their greatest weaknesses: It's simply too easy to send too many messages and to subscribe to too many blog feeds, Twitter follows, and other information sources. The flood of messages from an expanding array of digital sources can significantly affect employees' ability to focus on their work. In one study, in fact, workers exposed to a constant barrage of messages experienced an average 10-point drop in their functioning intelligence quotient (IQ).[7]

MANAGING TOTAL COST OF OWNERSHIP

The true costs of IT are a concern for every company. The *total cost of ownership (TCO)* of IT systems, which includes the purchase costs of hardware, software, and networking plus expenses for installation, customization, training, upgrades, and maintenance, can be three to five times higher than the purchase price.[8] And that's for IT that companies really need and actively use. Managers also need to guard against the all-too-common problems of buying technology they don't need and building poorly planned systems that are redesigned or even scrapped before being completed.

DEVELOPING EMPLOYEE SKILLS

With the pervasiveness of IT, virtually everyone from the mailroom to the executive suite is expected to have some level of technology skills. Not only will you need to keep your own skills up to date so that you can manage yourself and others efficiently, but you'll also need to make sure your employees have the skills they need. With so much business communication taking place through digital channels these days, managers and employees need more skills than ever to stay connected.

MAINTAINING THE HUMAN TOUCH

Technology can do wonderful things for business, but it can also get in the way of communication and collaboration. Even in the best circumstances, technology can't

Step away from technology frequently to reconnect with colleagues in person. Interpersonal contact helps build productive working relationships and minimize communication breakdowns.

match the rich experience of person-to-person contact. Let's say you send a text message to a colleague, asking how she did with her sales presentation to an important client, and her answer comes back simply as "Fine." What does *fine* mean? Is an order expected soon? Did she lose the sale and doesn't want to talk about it? Was the client rude, and she doesn't want to talk about it? If you communicate in person, she might provide additional information, or you might be able to offer advice or support during a difficult time. As technological options increase, people seem to need the human touch even more. In fact, some firms have taken such steps as banning email one day a week to force people to communicate in person or at least over the phone.

Moreover, in-person communication is important to your career. You can create amazing apps and documents and presentations without ever leaving your desk or meeting anyone in person. But if you stay hidden behind technology, people won't get to know the real you, and you'll miss opportunities to create and foster helpful and enjoyable working relationships.

MyBizLab®

To complete the problems with the ⭐, go to EOC Discussion Questions in the MyLab.

TEST YOUR KNOWLEDGE

Questions for Review

C-1. What is the difference between data and information?

C-2. What is the key difference between a management information system and a decision support system?

C-3. What is information overload?

C-4. What is the purpose of data mining?

C-5. How do operational information systems differ from managerial systems?

Questions for Analysis

⭐ **C-6.** Why do social media technologies present a potential information security threat?

C-7. What steps can you take to balance the need for relevant, timely information with the need to protect your productivity?

C-8. Why would a firm invest in an expert system if it already employs the experts whose knowledge and experience would be used to develop the system's decision support capabilities?

⭐ **C-9.** Why is new information technology sometimes considered both a benefit and a curse?

⭐ **C-10.** **Ethical Considerations.** Should employees be allowed to use company-owned information technologies for personal use during work hours? Why or why not?

MyBizLab®

Go to the Assignments section of your MyLab to complete these writing exercises.

C-11. Would companies be successful at simply banning the use of personal devices such as smartphones at work in order to protect the integrity of company networks? Why or why not?

C-12. When trying to guard against information overload, what steps can you take to decide whether a particular piece or source of information is worth paying attention to?

APPENDIX C GLOSSARY

artificial intelligence The ability of computers to solve problems through reasoning and learning and to simulate human sensory perceptions

chief information officer (CIO) A high-level executive responsible for understanding a company's information needs and creating systems and procedures to deliver that information to the right people at the right time

data Facts, numbers, statistics, and other individual bits and pieces of data that by themselves don't necessarily constitute useful information

databases Computerized files that collect, sort, and cross-reference data

information Useful knowledge, often extracted from data

insight A deep level of understanding about a particular subject or situation

malware Short for *malicious software*; programs and apps that are designed to disrupt websites, destroy information, or enable criminal activity

management information system (MIS) A computer system that provides managers with information and support for making routine decisions

viruses Invasive programs that reproduce by infecting legitimate programs

---

ENDNOTES

1. Daniel Lyons, "Too Much Information," *Forbes*, 13 December 2004, 110–115.
2. Irma Becerra-Fernandez, Avelino Gonzalez, and Rajiv Sabherwal, *Knowledge Management* (Upper Saddle River, N.J.: Pearson Prentice Hall, 2004), 200.
3. "What is Employee Performance Management?" PeopleStreme, accessed 23 June 2015, www.peoplestreme.com.
4. *Net Losses: Estimating the Global Cost of Cybercrime*, McAfee, 2014, www.mcafee.com.
5. Tara Craig, "How to Avoid Information Overload," *Personnel Today*, 10 June 2008, 31; Jeff Davidson, "Fighting Information Overload," *Canadian Manager*, Spring 2005, 16+.
6. Sushil K. Sharma and Jatinder N. D. Gupta, "Improving Workers' Productivity and Reducing Internet Abuse," *Journal of Computer Information Systems*, Winter 2003–2004, 74–78.
7. Jack Trout, "Beware of 'Infomania,'" *Forbes*, 11 August 2006, www.forbes.com.
8. Kenneth C. Laudon and Jane P. Laudon, *Management Information Systems*, 8th ed. (Upper Saddle River, N.J.: Pearson Prentice Hall, 2004), 208.

Personal Finance: Getting Set for Life

Taking Control of Your Financial Life

In your years as a consumer and a wage earner, even if you've had only part-time jobs so far, you've already established a relationship with money. How would you characterize that relationship? Is it positive or negative? Are you in control of your money, or does money—and a frequent lack of it—control you? Unfortunately, too many people find themselves in the second situation, with heavy debt loads, a constant cycle of struggle from one paycheck to the next, and worries about the future.

The good news is that with some basic information in hand, you can start to improve your financial well-being and take control of your money. The timing might seem ironic, but the best time to establish a positive relationship with money is right now, when you're still a student. If you build good habits now, when money is often scarce, you'll be taking a major step toward getting set for life. Conversely, if you fall into bad habits, you could find yourself struggling and worrying for years to come.

This appendix will help you understand the basic principles of personal finances and give you a solid foundation for managing your money. Before exploring some helpful strategies for each stage of your life, you'll learn three lessons that every consumer and wage earner needs to know and get a brief look at the financial planning process.

THREE SIMPLE—BUT VITAL— FINANCIAL LESSONS

If you've ever read a copy of the *Wall Street Journal* or another financial publication, you might have gotten the sense that money management is complex and jargon infested. However, unless you become a financial professional, you don't need to worry about the intricacies of "high finance." A few simple lessons will serve you well, starting with three ideas that will have enormous impact on your financial future: (1) The value of your money is constantly changing, so you need to understand how time affects your financial health; (2) small sacrifices early in life can have a huge payback later in life; and (3) every financial decision you make involves trade-offs. Taking these three ideas to heart will improve every aspect of your money management efforts, no matter how basic or sophisticated your finances.

The Value of Your Money Is Constantly Changing

If you remember only one thing from this discussion of personal finance, make sure this thought stays with you: A dollar today does not equal a dollar tomorrow. If you've successfully invested a dollar, it will be worth a little more tomorrow. However, if you charged a dollar's worth of purchases on a credit card, you're going to owe a little more than a dollar tomorrow. And even if you hold

REAL-TIME UPDATES
Learn More by Visiting This Website

Money management strategies to get your finances under control

From cars to taxes, take advantage of this free advice. Go to **http://real-timeupdates.com/bia8** and click on Learn More in the Students section.

Piotr Marcinski/Shutterstock

What is your relationship with money? Do you control it, or does it control you?

it tightly in your hand, that dollar will be worth a little less tomorrow, thanks to *inflation*—the tendency of prices to increase over time. When prices go up, your *buying power* goes down, so that dollar will buy less and less with each passing day.

These effects are so gradual that they are virtually impossible to notice from one day to the next, but they can have a staggering impact on your finances over time. Put time to work for you, and you'll join that happy segment of the population whose finances are stable and under control. Let time work against you, and you could get trapped in an endless cycle of stress and debt.

A simple example will demonstrate the power of time. Let's say that 10 years ago you inherited $10,000 and had two choices: hide it under your mattress or invest it in the stock market. Now fast-forward 10 years. If you hid the $10,000 under your mattress, it might now be worth only $7,000 or so. It will still *look* like $10,000, but because of inflation, it'll *spend* like $7,000. On the other hand, if you invested it in the stock market, you might have $15,000 or more. That's a difference of $8,000 between the two choices—almost as much as your inheritance to begin with.

Now let's say you didn't get that inheritance, but you did get the urge to treat your best friends to a relaxing vacation. You didn't have the cash, but lucky you—a shiny new credit card with a $10,000 limit had just arrived in the mail, so away you went, spending right up to your limit. The bill arrived a few days after your return home, and you started paying a modest amount, say $150 a month. At 13 percent interest, which is not unusual for a credit card, it would have taken you these 10 years to pay off the $10,000 you borrowed—and you'll have ended up paying $18,000, nearly twice what you thought that vacation was costing you. Doesn't seem so relaxing now, does it?

Depending on the financial decisions you make, then, time can be your best friend or your worst enemy. The **time value of money** refers to increases in money as a result of accumulating interest.[1] Time is even more powerful when your investment or debt is subject to **compounding**, which occurs when new interest is applied to interest that has already accumulated. Financial planners often talk about the "magic of compounding," and it really can feel like magic—good magic if it's compounded interest on savings or bad magic if it's compounded interest on debt.

Small Sacrifices Early in Life Can Produce Big Payoffs

If you're currently living the life of a typical college student, you probably can't wait to move on and move up in life. You'll land that first "real" job, and then you'll get a nicer apartment, maybe buy a new car, replace those ratty clothes you've been wearing for years, and stop eating ramen seven nights a week. This might be the last thing you want to hear, but if you can convince yourself to continue your frugal ways for a few more years, you'll benefit tremendously in the long run. Keep your expenses down and start saving as aggressively as you can.

Of course, saving during the early years of your career is no easy task, and it may be impossible, depending on your starting salary. In addition to the endless temptations to spend, you may also face the costs of starting a family, for instance. However, you'd be amazed at how much you can save every month by skipping that new car, renting a cheaper apartment, buying fewer clothes, and watching your entertainment expenses closely. A few simple choices may be able to free up hundreds of dollars every month. Even if you can save only small amounts early in your career, the sooner you start, the better off you'll be. Just keep increasing your monthly investment every time your salary increases, and do everything you can to take advantage of the time value of money.

Every Decision Involves Trade-Offs

By now, you've probably noticed that the time value of money and frugal living involve lots of choices. In fact, virtually every financial decision you make, from buying a cup of coffee to buying a house, involves a trade-off, in which you have to give up one thing to gain something else. If your family and friends give you $2,000 for graduation, should you run right out and buy alloy wheels and a custom exhaust system for your car? Or should you invest that $2,000 in the stock market and invest another $200 every month, so that in five or six years you could have enough to buy a new car—in cash, with no monthly payments? If you choose the second option, while your friends are shelling out $400 or $500 in payments for their new cars, you can be investing that amount every month and build up enough money to start your own business or perhaps retire a few years early.

Even the smallest habits and choices have consequences. Addicted to potato chips? Let's say you spend $3.19 for a big bag two or three times a week. Kick that habit now and invest that $400 or so a year instead. Over the course of 40 years, you could earn enough to treat yourself to a new car when you retire. Sounds crazy, but over many years, even tiny amounts of money can add up to large sums.

Not all your choices will be so simple, of course. Most of the examples presented so far have involved trading current pleasures and luxuries for future financial gain—a dilemma you'll be facing most of your life. Other choices involve risks versus rewards. Should you buy life insurance to provide for your family or invest the money and hope it'll grow fast enough to provide your loved ones with enough to get by on in the event of your death? Should you invest your money in a safe but slow-growing investment or an investment that offers the potential for high growth but also high risk of losing everything? As you gain experience with financial choices, you'll recognize your own level of *risk tolerance*. For instance, if you're lying awake at night, worrying about a high-risk stock you just purchased, you may have a lower level of risk tolerance, and you'll probably want to stick with safer, saner investments.

Figuring out the best choice is difficult in many cases but simply recognizing that every decision involves a trade-off will improve your decision making. Too often, people get into trouble by looking at *only* the risk (which can stop them from making choices that might in fact be better for them in the long run) or *only* the potential rewards (which can lure them into making choices that are too risky). Consider all the consequences of every choice you make, and you'll start making better financial decisions.

You'll pick up many other financial tips as you start investing, buying houses, selecting insurance, and making other financial choices, but these three concepts will always apply. With those thoughts in mind, it's time to take a look at the financial planning process.

Creating Your Personal Financial Plan

Creating and following a sensible financial plan is the only sure way to stay in control of your finances. A good plan can help you get the most from whatever amount of money you have, identify the funds you'll need in order to get through life's major expenses, increase your financial independence and confidence, minimize the time and energy needed to manage your finances, and answer a question that vexes millions of people every year: Where did all my money go?

Many people discover they'd rather turn the task over to a professional financial planner. Even if you do most of your planning yourself, you may encounter special situations or major transactions in which you'd like the advice of an expert. The right advice at the right time can make a huge difference. However, before you sign on with anyone, make sure you understand what advice you need and who can provide it. Ask about references, professional credentials, investing strategies, and how the adviser is paid.[2]

Fee-only planners charge you for their services, either an hourly rate or a percentage of the assets they're managing for you. In theory, the major advantage of fee-only planners is complete objectivity because they don't make money on the specific decisions they recommend for you. In contrast, **commission-based planners** are paid commissions on the financial products they sell you, such as insurance policies and mutual funds. Although you can certainly receive good advice from a commission-based planner, make sure he or she has a wide range of offerings for you. Otherwise, you're

likely to be hampered by limited choices.[3] Of course, because these types of planners are selling you something, it's important to make sure their recommendations are really the best choices for your financial needs. If you can't get a good recommendation from family members or colleagues, consider a matchmaker such as **www.wiseradvisor.com**, an impartial service that helps investors find advisers.

Even if you decide to rely on a full-service financial adviser to guide your decisions, you need to stay informed and actively involved. Lawsuits against financial advisers have risen dramatically in recent years, as clients seek compensation for losses in the stock market, for recommendation of *tax shelters* (investments designed primarily to reduce tax obligations) that the Internal Revenue Service (IRS) later ruled "abusive," and for other financial missteps. Keep in mind that even if you get advice, you are ultimately responsible for—and in control of—the choices involving your money. Don't count on anyone else to secure your financial future for you.

Planning can be as simple or as complex as you're inclined to make it, as long as you follow the basic steps shown in Exhibit D.1[4] The following sections discuss each step in more detail.

FIGURE OUT WHERE YOU ARE NOW

Successful financial planning starts with a careful examination of where you stand right now, financially speaking. Before you can move ahead, you need to add up what you own and what you owe, where your money is going, and how you're using credit. You might not like what you see, but if your finances are heading downhill, the sooner you learn that, the sooner you can fix it.

Start by listing your *assets*—the things you own—and your *liabilities*—the amounts of money you owe. Assets include both *financial assets*, such as bank accounts, mutual funds, retirement accounts, and money that people owe you, and *physical assets*, such as cars, houses, and artwork. Liabilities include credit card debts, car loans, home mortgages, and student loans. After you've itemized everything you own and everything you owe, calculate your **net worth** by subtracting your liabilities from your assets. The balance sheet in Exhibit D.2 shows Devon Anderson's net worth. It is currently negative, but that's certainly not uncommon for college students. The important thing for Devon at this

---

EXHIBIT D.1   The Financial Planning Process

The financial planning process starts with an honest assessment of where you are now, followed by setting goals, defining and implementing plans, measuring your progress, then adjusting if needed.

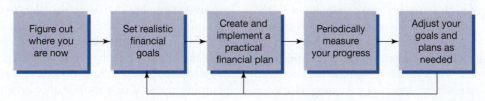

EXHIBIT D.2	Devon Anderson's Balance Sheet

Devon Anderson's net worth is currently negative, driven in large part by her school loans. However, she now knows exactly where she stands and can start working to improve her balance.

Assets

Cash accounts	Checking account	$	450.67
	Savings account		927.89
Investments	50 shares Microsoft		1,802.50
Retirement accounts	(none)		
Automobiles	2006 Escort		5,500.00
Personal property	Jewelry		1,800.00
	Furniture		2,000.00
	Computer		450.00
Total assets			**$ 12,931.06**

Liabilities

Current bills (due within 30 days)	Rent		$650.00
	Utilities		110.00
	Mobile phone		98.00
	Sailing club		78.25
Credit card debt	Visa		1,185.34
	MasterCard		2,431.60
Housing debt	(none)		
Automobile loans	2006 Escort		3,880.10
Other debt	Student loans		22,560.00
Total liabilities			**$ 30,993.29**
Net worth (total assets − total liabilities)			**($ 18,062.23)**

EXHIBIT D.3	Devon Anderson's Income and Expense Statement

Devon was surprised to learn that she has been spending over $800 more every month than she takes in. Because she can't work any more hours without compromising her studies and she is reluctant to ask her parents for more money, the only solution is to cut expenses. After some careful thought, she realizes that by cutting her cell-phone usage in half (or finding a better deal), dropping the sailing club, economizing on groceries, and cutting way back on entertainment, fast food, and new clothes, she can almost break even every month.

Income

Wages (take home, average per month)	$ 1,230.00
Help from the parents	450.00
Total income	$ 1,680.00

Expenses (Average Monthly)

Rent	$ 650.00
Gas bill	34.00
Electric bill	76.00
Mobile phone	98.00
Food	315.00
Misc. household supplies	45.00
School materials & supplies	22.00
Car payment	327.25
Gasoline	38.00
Sailing club	78.25
Clothes	188.00
Entertainment & fast food	325.00
Visa payment	120.00
MasterCard payment	195.00
Total expenses	**$ 2,511.50**
Monthly difference	**($ 831.50)**

point is that she knows how much she's worth, so she has a baseline to build on.

Your balance sheet gives you a snapshot of where you stand at a particular time. The second major planning tool is your **income and expense statement**, or simply *income statement*. This statement answers the all-important question of where your money is going month by month. Start by adding up all your sources of income from jobs, parents, investments, and so on. If you have irregular income, such as a one-time cash infusion from your parents at the beginning of each semester, you can divide it by the number of months it needs to cover to give you an average monthly value. Next, list all your expenses. If you're in the habit of using debit cards, credit cards, or a checkbook for most of your expenses, this task is fairly easy because your statements will show where the money is going. However, if you tend to use cash for a lot of purchases, you'll need to get in the habit of keeping receipts and recording those purchases. (Using cash has the major advantage of limiting your spending to money that you actually have, but it doesn't leave a "paper trail" the way credit and debit cards do, so you have to keep track of the spending yourself.) Exhibit D.3 shows Devon's income and expense statement.

Assembling your balance sheet and your income and expense statement can be a chore the first time around, but updating it as you make progress is much easier. A variety of software programs, websites, and mobile apps can simplify these tasks, but they're not absolutely necessary. You can do all your recordkeeping in a spreadsheet, a financial planning website, or a mobile app, or simply keep records in a notebook. How you record your data is less important than making sure you do it.

SET REALISTIC FINANCIAL GOALS

Now that you've finished assessing your current financial situation, the next step is setting goals. Take some time with this step. Your goals will drive all your financial decisions from here on out, so make sure they're the right ones for you. For instance, saving up for an early retirement requires a different financial strategy than saving up to take a year off in the middle of your career. Think carefully about what you really value in life. Discuss your dreams and plans with family and friends. Is making a million dollars by the time you're 40 your most important goal, and are you willing to work around the clock to get there? Or would you rather accumulate wealth more slowly and live at a more relaxed pace? Do you want to start a family when you're 25? 35? Perhaps being able to take care of an aging relative is important to you. You can't have it all, but you can make trade-offs that are compatible with your personal goals and values.

No matter what they might be, effective financial goals have two aspects in common: They are *specific* and they are *realistic*. "I want to be rich" and "I just don't want to have to worry about money" are not good goal statements because both are too general to give you any guidance. For one person, "not worrying about money" could require $100,000 a year, but another person might get by on $50,000 a year. You can certainly start with a general desire, such as wealth or freedom from worry, but you need to translate that into real numbers so you can craft a meaningful plan.

In addition to making them specific, make sure your goals are realistic. Lots of young people start out life saying they'd like to make a million dollars by age 30 or retire by age 40. These are wonderful desires, but for most people, they simply aren't realistic. The problem with having unrealistic goals is that you'll be repeatedly frustrated by your inability to meet them, and you're more likely to give up on your financial plan as a result.[5] Whereas amassing a million dollars in the first 10 years of your career is unlikely, amassing a million dollars in 40, 30, or sometimes even 20 years is quite attainable for many professional wage earners. A few minutes with a financial calculator will help you assess the various possibilities and determine what is reasonable for you.

You can also visit www.choosetosave.org, which offers a wide variety of online calculators. In fact, just playing around with the many calculators on this site will teach you a fair amount about financial planning.

Many people find it helpful to divide financial objectives into short-, medium-, and long-term goals. Your personal time frame for each might vary, but in general, short-term goals will get you through your current financial situation, medium-term goals will get you into the next stage in your life, and long-term goals will get you completely set for life. The important thing is to consider the

REAL-TIME UPDATES

Learn More by Exploring This Interactive Website

Use these free online financial calculators

Figure out your own finances or just explore the possibilities. Go to http://real-timeupdates.com/bia8 and click on Learn More in the Students section.

phases in your life and establish goals for each phase. Also, think carefully about the type of goals you wish to achieve. For instance, acquiring a ranch might be a significant goal for you, whereas someone who loves to travel may have little interest in real estate. Similarly, if you find that you have a low tolerance for risk or if a number of loved ones depend on you, comprehensive insurance coverage might be a significant goal.

CREATE AND IMPLEMENT A PRACTICAL FINANCIAL PLAN

You've thought about your goals and defined some that are specific and realistic. You're inspired and ready to start. What's next? For all the thousands of books, television shows, magazines, software products, and websites devoted to money, financial success really boils down to one beautifully—and brutally—simple formula: Earn more, spend less, and make better choices with what you have left over. On the plus side, this is an easy concept to understand. On the minus side, it's completely unforgiving. If you're spending more than you're earning or making bad choices with your savings and investments, you're never going to reach your goals until you can turn things around. The sections on life stages later in this appendix explore some of the details of these three components, but here's a brief overview to put it all in context:

- **Earn more.** Particularly in the early stages of your career, pay from your job will probably provide most or all of your income, so be sure to maximize your earning potential. As you get more established and have the opportunity to invest, you can start earning income from real estate, stocks and other investments, and perhaps businesses that you either own yourself or with others. As you move into retirement, your sources of income will shift to returns from your own investments, perhaps along with employer- and government-funded retirement plans.

- **Spend less.** Regardless of how much control you have over your income (and there are times and circumstances in life when you probably can't expect to change your earning power), you always have some control over how you spend your money. The first and most important step to spending less is maintaining a personal budget. For most people, budgeting sounds like about as much fun as having root canal surgery, but it shouldn't be that way. Don't think of budgeting as a straightjacket that crimps your style; think of it as a way to free up more cash so that you can accomplish those wonderful goals you've set for yourself. When you skip a night out at the clubs or squeeze another year out of your car, think of that ranch in Montana you want to buy or that business you want to start. As with dieting, exercise, and other personal improvement regimes, sticking to a budget is difficult at first, but as you start to see some positive results, you'll be motivated to continue. Another important aspect of budgeting is understanding *why* you spend money, particularly on things you don't need and can't afford.[6] Don't try to spend your way out of depression, for instance. "Retail therapy" never solves anything and only makes financial matters worse. If you're prone to budget meltdowns, try to make everything as automatic as possible. For example, have your employer invest part of your salary in a company-sponsored investment program or have a mutual fund company pull money from your checking account every month.

- **Make better choices with what you have left over.** Once you've maximized your income and minimized your expenses, success largely comes down to making better choices with the money you have to save and invest. Investing can be a complex subject, with literally thousands of places to put your money. As with everything else in personal finance, the more you know, the better you're likely to perform (see Chapter 19 for more information). Don't make investments that you don't understand, whether it's some exotic financial scheme or simply the stock of a company that doesn't make sense to you. Proceed at your own pace, such as starting with an *index mutual fund* (which tracks the overall performance of the stock market) instead of trying to pick individual stocks.

In addition to your other healthy financial habits, get in the habit of keeping good records of income, expenses, investments, and other financial matters. Doing so will help you track your progress, and the Internal Revenue Service (IRS) requires you to keep a variety of tax-related records. For a good overview of both suggested and required records, refer to Publication 552 (for personal records) and Publication 583 (for business records), both of which are available online at **www.irs.gov**.

Finally, make sure that anyone who plays a role in your financial plan, whether roommates sharing grocery costs or family members sharing all aspects of finances, buys into the plan. One of the most critical aspects of successful financial planning is discipline, and a plan will fall apart if some people follow it and some don't. Money is one of the most common issues in relationship problems and divorces, so talk things over calmly and honestly with your partner or spouse. Getting everyone to agree to—and commit to—the plan will reduce stress and increase the chances of success.[7]

PERIODICALLY MEASURE YOUR PROGRESS

To make sure you're on track to meet your goals, get in the habit of periodically checking your progress. Is your net worth increasing? (It might still be moving up toward zero, but that's progress!) Are your expenses under control? However, don't obsess over your finances. Life's too short, and there are too many other pleasurable and productive ways to spend your time. You don't need to check your stock portfolio a dozen times a day or lie in bed every night dreaming up new ways to snip nickels and dimes out of your budget. After a while, you'll get a sense of how often you need to measure your progress to make sure you stay on track toward your goals. In general, check your income and expenses at least once a month to make sure you're staying within budget. For larger assets such as your house, you might want to verify approximate values once or twice a year.

However, don't put off checking your financial health so long that you don't notice problems such as poorly performing investments or small expenses that have somehow ballooned into big expenses. If you're using a financial planner, don't wait for an annual statement. Find out where you stand at least once a quarter.

ADJUST YOUR GOALS AND PLANS AS NEEDED

At various points in your life, you'll find that your goals or your financial status have changed enough to require adjustments to your plan. Whenever you pass through one of life's major transitions, such as getting married, having children, changing jobs, or buying a house, you'll need to make some revisions. For instance, many first-time home buyers are surprised by the amount of money it takes to maintain a house, particularly a "fixer-upper" that needs a lot of work. To keep your income and expenses in balance, you may find you need to make sacrifices elsewhere in your budget.

If you're like most college students, you'll go through at least four major stages in your financial life: getting through college, establishing a financial foundation, building your net worth and preparing for life's major expenses, and planning for retirement. (If you're back in college after having been in the workforce for a while, your situation might vary.) The following sections give you an overview of the decisions to consider at each major stage in your life.

REAL-TIME UPDATES

Learn More by Watching These Videos

Free personal investing videos

Investopedia offers a variety of short videos on fundamental investing topics. Go to **http://real-timeupdates.com/bia8** and click on Learn More in the Students section.

Life Stage 1: Getting Through College

With tuition and expenses rising rapidly these days, completing your education can be a mammoth struggle, to be sure. Costs are getting so high that some people are even beginning to wonder if the effort is worth it, particularly if you need to borrow heavily. Consider the eye-opening statistics discussed in the following sections and then think about your specific situation.

FINANCING YOUR EDUCATION

On the plus side, on average, according to one survey, college graduates earn more than 80 percent more per year than people with only high school educations.[8] Over the course of a 40- or 45-year career, this difference can be huge.

However, that doesn't tell the whole story. First, the 80 percent differential is only an average; a college education increases your chances of making more money, but it is by no means a guarantee. Quite a few people with only high school educations make more than people with college educations, and the income variations among graduates with different majors can be dramatic.[9]

Second, while you're in college, people who went to work right out of high school are already earning wages. By the time you graduate, those full-time workers who didn't go to college might be $100,000 or more ahead of you in cumulative earnings to that point.

Third, you're likely to be saddled with some debt when you graduate, setting you even further behind. With costs continuing to climb, more students are forced to borrow in ever-larger amounts to complete their education. Is it a good idea to borrow money to get through college? The only honest answer these days is that it depends. For starters, you need to compare education costs with potential income. Yes, a college education is likely to boost your income, and your education should ideally be about more than simply career training, but the reality of the situation is that your education needs to be paid for somehow. If you take on a lot of debt and need many years to pay off your student loans, you need to think about how doing that will affect your life plans.

Moreover, while education costs have gone up, forcing more students to borrow more, so have the costs of borrowing. Make sure you understand the true cost of any loan before you sign on the dotted line. In general, *private loans*, those that aren't guaranteed by a government agency, are more expensive than those that are. In recent years, some students have been stunned to discover they were paying as much as 18 percent interest or more on student loans.[10] If you're not sure what the true cost of a loan is, ask a financial aid counselor or another trusted adviser before you sign. And remember that a loan is not a gift; it's a serious financial commitment that will affect your life for years.

The worst of all possible outcomes is borrowing a lot of money and then not getting your degree. This situation will saddle you with big loan payments *and* the likelihood of lower income. Once you commit to going for your degree, make sure you get it. Ask for advice—and help—if you need it. Many people find doing so uncomfortable or embarrassing, but you're almost guaranteed to regret it later if you don't ask for help now. Talk to a counselor in your school's financial aid office, and make sure you explore every available option for financial assistance. Ask friends and family members for advice. If you have a job, see whether your employer is willing to help with school expenses.

Our intent here isn't to scare you out of school or reduce a life-enhancing experience to mere dollars and cents, but rather to make sure you understand the reality of the situation so that you can make choices that are best for you, your family, and your future.

STAYING OUT OF THE CREDIT CARD BLACK HOLE

Speaking of borrowing, every college student needs to be aware of the dangers of credit card debt. Far too many students dig themselves into giant holes with such debt. If you find yourself in this situation, don't panic—but stop digging any deeper. Your first step to recovery is to recognize that you're at a make-or-break point in both your college career and your life as a whole. No amount of extracurricular fun is worth the damage that a credit card mess can inflict on your life. Excessive credit card debt from college can follow you for decades and severely limit your financial options.

Don't assume that you can easily pay off those balances when you start working, either. Many graduates entering the workforce are disappointed to find themselves bringing home less and paying out more than they expected. You'll be facing a host of new expenses, from housing to transportation to a business-quality wardrobe. You can't afford to devote a big chunk of your new salary to paying off your beer and pizza bills—with interest—from the previous four or five years.

Your second step is to compile your income and expense statement, as described previously, so you know where all that borrowed money is going. Do a thorough and honest evaluation of your expenses: How much of your spending is going to junk food, clubbing, concert tickets, video games, and other nonessentials? At first, it won't seem possible that these small-ticket items can add up to big trouble, but it happens to thousands of college students every year. Most colleges and college towns offer a wide spectrum of free and low-cost entertainment options. With a little effort and creativity, anyone can find ways to reduce nonessential expenses, often by hundreds of dollars a month. A few sacrifices now can make a big difference.

Life Stage 2: Building Your Financial Foundation

Whew, you made it: You scraped by to graduation, with any luck found a decent job, and now are ready to get really serious about financial planning. First, give yourself a pat

REAL-TIME UPDATES

Learn More by Reading This Infographic

Mint.com's Life After Graduation roadmap

Ponder the key steps and decisions you have in front of you after graduation. Go to **http://real-timeupdates.com/bia8** and click on Learn More in the Students section.

on the back; it's a major accomplishment in life. Second, dust off that financial plan you put together in college. It's time to update it to reflect your new status in life. Third, don't lose those frugal habits you learned in college. Keep your *fixed expenses*, the bills you have to pay every month no matter what, as low as possible. Some of these expenses are mandatory, such as transportation and housing, but others may not be. Such things as gym memberships and added services on your mobile phone have a tendency to creep into your budget and gradually raise your expenses. Before you know it, you could be shelling out hundreds of dollars a month on these recurring but often nonessential expenses. In addition, if your income temporarily drops, the lower your fixed expenses are, the more easily you can handle the setback.

Among the important decisions you may need to make at this stage involve paying for transportation and housing, taking steps to maximize your earning power, and managing your cash and credit wisely.

PAYING FOR TRANSPORTATION

Transportation is likely to be one of your biggest ongoing expenses if that means owning or leasing a vehicle. The *true cost* of owning a vehicle is significantly higher than the price tag. You'll probably have to finance it, you'll definitely need to insure it, and you'll face recurring costs for fuel and maintenance. And, unfortunately, unlike houses, which often *appreciate* in value, cars always *depreciate* in value (except in extremely rare cases, such as with classic cars). In fact, that lovely new ride can lose as much as 20 percent of its value the instant you drive away from the dealership. If you pay $25,000 for a car, for example, your net worth could drop $5,000 before you've driven your first mile. And if you took out a five-, six-, or seven-year loan, you'll probably owe more than the car is worth for the first several years.

There is good news, however: Most cars tend not to depreciate much during their second, third, and fourth years, but their value plummets again after about five years. You can take advantage of this effect by looking for a used car that is about a year old, driving it for three years, and then selling it.[11] Automotive websites such as **www.edmunds.com** offer a wealth of information about depreciation and other costs, including the true cost of owning any given model. Also check with your insurance company before buying any car, as some models cost considerably more to insure.

Negotiating the purchase of a car ranks high on most consumers' list of dreaded experiences. You can level the playing field, at least somewhat, by remembering two important issues. First, most buyers worry only about the monthly payment, which can be a costly mistake. Salespeople usually negotiate with four or even five variables at once, including the monthly payment, purchase price, down payment, value of your trade-in, and terms of your loan. If you don't pay attention to these other variables, you can get a low monthly payment and still get a bad deal. Experts suggest that you arrange your financing ahead of time and then negotiate only the purchase price when you're at the dealership.[12] If you're not comfortable negotiating, consider using a car-buying service such as CarsDirect (**www.carsdirect.com**).

Leasing, rather than buying, is a popular option with many consumers, but it's not always a money-smart option. In general, the biggest advantage of leasing is lower monthly payments than with a purchase (or a nicer car for the same monthly payment, depending on how you look at it). However, leases are even more complicated than purchases and often more expensive, so it's even more important to know what you're getting into. Also, leases usually aren't the best choice for consumers who want to minimize their long-term costs.

PAYING FOR HOUSING

Housing also presents you with a lease-versus-buy decision, although purchasing a house has two huge advantages that purchasing a car doesn't have: Houses *can* appreciate in value over the long term, whereas cars *always* drop in value (unless you have a rare collector's car). The interest on a home mortgage is also tax deductible. And compared to renting, buying your own place also lets you build *equity*, the portion of the house's value that you own. However, there are times when renting makes better financial sense. The **closing costs** for real estate—the fees and commissions associated with buying or selling a house—can be considerable. Depending on how fast your house's value rises, you may need to stay in it several years just to recoup your closing costs before selling.

If you think that a job change, an upcoming marriage, or any other event in your life might require you to move in the near future, plug your numbers into a "rent versus own" calculator to see which option makes more sense. You can find several of these calculators at **www.choosetosave.org**.

When you are ready to buy, take your time. Buying a house is the most complicated financial decision many people will ever make, involving everything from property values in the neighborhood to the condition of the home to the details of the financial transaction. Fortunately, you can learn more about home ownership from a number of sources. Check local lenders and real estate agencies for free seminars. Online sources include the U.S. Department of Housing and Urban Development (**www.hud.gov**) and MSN Real Estate (**www.msn.com**). Buying your own house can and should be a wonderful experience, but don't let emotional factors lead you to a decision that doesn't make financial sense. Keep in mind that a house is both a home and an investment.

MAXIMIZING YOUR EARNING POWER

Why do some people peak at earning $40,000 or $50,000 a year, while others go on to earn 2 or 3 or 10 times that much? Because your salary is likely to be the primary "engine" of your financial success, this question warrants careful consideration. The profession you choose is one of the biggest factors, of course, but even within a given profession, you'll often find a wide range of income levels. A number of factors influence these variations, including education, individual talents, ambition, location, contacts, and good old-fashioned luck. You can change some of these factors throughout your career, but some you can't. However, compensation experts stress that virtually everyone can improve his or her earning power by following these tips:[13]

- **Know what you're worth.** The more informed you are about your competitive value in the marketplace, the better chance you have of negotiating a salary that reflects your worth. Several websites offer salary-level information that will help you decide your personal value, including www.bls.gov, www.salary.com, www.vault.com, and www.salaryexpert.com. (Some of these sites charge a modest fee for customized reports, but the information might be worth many times what you pay for it.)

- **Be ready to explain your value.** In addition to knowing what other people in your profession make, you need to be able to explain to your current employer or a potential new employer why you're worth the money you think you deserve. Collect concrete examples of how you've helped your company or previous employers earn more or spend less in the past—and be ready to explain how you can do so in the future. Moreover, seek out opportunities that let you increase and demonstrate your worth.

- **Don't overlook the value of employee benefits, performance incentives, and perks.** For instance, even if you can't negotiate the salary you'd really like, maybe you can negotiate extra time off or a flexible schedule that would allow you to run a home-based business on the side. Or perhaps you can negotiate a bonus arrangement that rewards you for higher-than-average performance.

- **Understand the salary structure in your company.** If you hope to rise through the ranks and make $200,000 as a vice president, for instance, but the chief executive officer (CEO) is making only $150,000, your goal is obviously unrealistic. Some companies pay top performers well above market average, whereas others stick closely to industry norms.

- **Study top performers.** Some employees have the misperception that top executives must have "clawed their way" to the top or stepped on others on their way

up. However, the employees and managers who continue to rise through an organization often do so because they make people around them successful. Being successful on your own is one thing; helping an entire department or an entire company be successful is the kind of behavior that catches the attention of the people who write the really big paychecks.

MANAGING CASH

When paychecks start rolling in, you'll need to set up a system of **cash management**, a personal system for handling cash and other liquid assets, which are those that can be quickly and easily converted to cash. You have many alternatives for storing cash, from a basic savings account to a variety of investment funds, but most offer interest rates that are below the average level of inflation. In other words, if you were to keep all your money in such places, your buying power would slowly but surely erode over time. Consequently, the basic challenge of cash management is keeping enough cash or other liquid assets available to cover your near-term needs without keeping so much cash that you lose out on investment growth opportunities or fall prey to inflation. Once again, your budget planning will come to the rescue by showing you how much money you need month to month. Financial experts also recommend keeping anywhere from three to six months' worth of basic living expenses in an *emergency fund* that you can access if you find yourself between jobs or have other unexpected needs.

You can choose from several options for holding cash (see Exhibit D.4 for a summary of their advantages and disadvantages):[14]

- **Checking accounts.** Whether it's a traditional checking account from your neighborhood bank, an online account at an Internet bank, or a brokerage account with check-writing privileges, your checking account will serve as your primary cash management tool. A checking account can be either a demand deposit, which doesn't pay interest, or an interest-bearing or *negotiable order of withdrawal (NOW)* account.

- **Savings accounts.** Savings accounts are convenient places to store small amounts of money. Many savings accounts can be linked to a checking account for quick access to your cash. Although they're convenient and safe, savings accounts nearly always offer interest rates below average inflation rates, so the buying power of your account steadily diminishes.

- **Money-market accounts.** Money-market accounts, sometimes called *money-market deposit accounts*, are an alternative to savings accounts; the primary difference is that they have variable interest rates that are usually higher than savings account rates.

- **Money-market mutual funds.** Money-market mutual funds, sometimes called money funds, are similar to stock mutual funds, although they invest in *debt instruments* such as bonds, rather than stocks.

EXHIBIT D.4	**Places to Stash Your Cash**

You can find quite a few places to park your cash, but they're not all created equal. Note that banks and credit unions continue to refine their offerings, so you may find options that don't fit neatly into these categories.

Type of Account	Advantages	Disadvantages
Checking account (demand deposit)	Convenient, usually no minimum balance needed to open, often provides online banking and access via ATMs, insured against losses due to bank failure	Does not earn any interest
Checking account (NOW account)	Convenience of a regular checking account, plus you earn interest on your balance; insured	Some institutions require a minimum balance to open an account; modest interest rates
Savings account	Slightly higher interest rate than on typical checking account, often linked to a checking account for simple transfers; insured	Low interest rates; not as liquid as checking accounts (except for linked accounts, in which you can easily transfer funds to checking)
Money market deposit account	Higher interest rates than checking or savings accounts; insured	High minimum balances; limited check writing; fees can limit real returns
Money market mutual fund	Higher interest rates than many other cash management options	Not insured (but limited exposure to risk); minimum balance requirements; limited check writing
Asset management account	Convenience of having cash readily available for investment purposes; higher interest rates than regular checking or savings accounts; consolidated statements show most of your cash management and investing activity	Expensive (high monthly fees); large minimum balances; restrictions on check writing privileges (such as high minimum amounts) can limit usefulness as regular checking account; not insured against losses
Certificate of deposit	Higher interest rates that are fixed and therefore predictable; insured	Minimum balance requirements; limited liquidity (your money is tied up for weeks, months, or years)

Sources: Lawrence J. Gitman and Michael D. Joehnk, *Personal Financial Planning*, 10th ed. (Mason, Ohio: Thomson South-Western, 2005), 139–143; Jack R. Kapoor, Les R. Dlabay, and Robert J. Hughes, *Personal Finance*, 7th ed. (New York: McGraw-Hill/Irwin, 2004), 141; Arthur J. Keown, *Personal Finance: Turning Money into Wealth*, 3rd ed. (Upper Saddle River, N.J.: Prentice Hall, 2003), 150.

- **Asset management accounts.** Brokerage firms and mutual fund companies frequently offer **asset management accounts** as a way to manage cash that isn't currently invested in stocks or stock mutual funds.
- **Certificates of deposit.** With a certificate of deposit (CD), you are essentially lending a specific amount of money to a bank or another institution for a specific length of time and at a specific interest rate. The length of time can range from a week to several years; the longer the time span and the larger the amount, the higher the interest rate.

No matter which types of accounts you choose, make sure you understand all the associated fees—which might not be clearly labeled as fees. Some accounts charge a fee every month, some charge fees when your balance drops below a certain amount or when you write too many checks, and so on. For accounts with checking capability, **overdraft fees** can chew up hundreds of dollars if you bounce checks frequently. Also, be sure to verify your account statement every month and **reconcile** your checking account to make sure you and the bank agree on the balance.

MANAGING CREDIT

Even if you never want to use a credit card or borrow money, it's increasingly difficult to get by without credit in today's consumer environment. For instance, car rental companies usually require a credit card before you can rent

a car, most hotels require a credit card upon check-in, and landlords want to verify your **credit history**, a record of your mortgages, consumer loans (such as financing provided by a home appliance store), credit card accounts, and bill-paying performance. Banks and other companies voluntarily provide this information to credit rating agencies, businesses that compile **credit reports**. An increasing number of employers are looking into the credit histories of job applicants as well. Moreover, you may find yourself in need of a loan you didn't anticipate, and getting a loan without a credit history is not easy. Consequently, a solid credit history needs to be a part of your lifetime financial plan.

To build a good credit history, apply for a modest amount of sensible credit (a credit card, an auto loan, or a line of credit at a bank, for instance) and use that credit periodically. Also, if you are married or in a domestic partnership where expenses are shared, make sure that at least some credit is being established in your name so that you establish an independent credit record. Most important of all is to pay all your bills on time. If you find that you can't pay a particular bill by the due date, call the company and explain your situation. You may get some leniency by showing that you're making a good-faith effort to pay your bill.

Experts also recommend that you verify the accuracy of your credit report at least once a year. Mistakes do creep into credit reports from time to time, and you also need to make sure you haven't been a victim of identity theft, in which someone illegally applies for credit using your name. Actually, you don't have just one credit report. The three major credit reporting agencies in the United States each keep a file on you and provide their own credit reports to lenders, landlords, and others with a valid need to see them. You are entitled to one free credit report every 12 months from each of the three companies; visit **www.annualcreditreport.com** for more information. You can also directly visit the three bureaus: Experian (**www.experian.com**), TransUnion (**www.transunion.com**), and Equifax (**www.equifax.com**).

Managing your credit wisely will help you avoid one of the most traumatic events that can befall a consumer: **personal bankruptcy**. You have several options for declaring bankruptcy, but none of them is desirable, and all should be avoided by every means possible. Declaring bankruptcy, even if for an unavoidable reason such as medical costs or loss of a spouse, is sometimes called "the 10-year mistake" because it stays on your credit record for 10 years.[15] Bankruptcy is not a simple cure-all, as it is sometimes presented. If you are considering bankruptcy, talk to a counselor first. Start with the National Foundation for Credit Counseling (**www.nfcc.org**). Wherever you turn for advice, make sure you understand it thoroughly and understand why the organization would be motivated to give you that particular advice. You've probably seen ads (and a torrent of spam email) offering ways to get out from under your debt. Many of these schemes involve declaring bankruptcy, which may not be the right choice for you.[16]

After years of growing concern about the number of U.S. consumers filing for personal bankruptcy, Congress modified the bankruptcy filing process in 2005, with the intent of making it considerably more difficult for many people to file. Consumers seeking bankruptcy protection must first submit to credit counseling designed to explore alternatives to bankruptcy. The outcome of credit counseling is likely to depend largely on household income: Those with high incomes will be encouraged to get their spending under control, those with moderate incomes will be encouraged to apply for a *debt-management plan* (an agreement to stop using credit cards and pay off existing balances, possibly in exchange for reduced interest rates), and those with lower incomes and therefore less hope of paying off their debts over time will be directed toward bankruptcy filing.[17]

Life Stage 3: Increasing Your Net Worth and Preparing for Life's Major Expenses

With your basic needs taken care of and a solid foundation under your feet, the next stage of your financial life is to increase your net worth and prepare for both expected and unexpected expenses. Some of the major decisions at this stage include investments, taxes, insurance, your children's education, and emergency planning.

INVESTING: BUILDING YOUR NEST EGG

The various cash management options described previously can help you store and protect money you already have, but they aren't terribly good at generating more money. That's the goal of *investing*, in which you buy something with the idea that it will increase in value before you sell it to someone else. You read about the most common financial investment vehicles in Chapter 19: stocks, mutual funds, and bonds. Real estate is the other major category of investment for most people—not only their own homes but also rental properties and commercial real estate. The final category of investments includes precious metals (primarily gold), gems, and collectibles such as sports or movie memorabilia.

The details of successful investing in these various areas differ widely, but six general rules apply to all of them:

- **Don't invest cash that you may need in the short term.** You may not be able to *liquidate* the investment (selling it to retrieve your cash) in time, or the value may be temporarily down, in which case you'll permanently lose money.
- **Don't invest in anything you don't understand or haven't thoroughly evaluated.** If you can't point to specific reasons that the investment should increase in value, you're simply guessing or gambling.
- **Don't invest on emotion.** You might love eating at a certain restaurant chain, shopping at a particular online retailer, or collecting baseball cards, but that doesn't mean any of these is automatically a good investment.
- **Understand the risks.** Aside from Treasury bills and U.S. savings bonds, virtually no investment can guarantee that you'll make money or even protect the money you originally invested. You could lose most or all of your money, thanks to the risk/reward trade-off discussed previously. To give yourself the opportunity to realize higher gains, you nearly always need to accept higher levels of risk.
- **Beware of anybody who promises guaranteed results or instant wealth.** Chances are that person will profit more by snaring you into the investment than you'll earn from the investment yourself.
- **Given the risks involved, don't put all your eggs in one basket.** Diversify your investments to make sure you don't leave yourself vulnerable to downturns in a single stock or piece of real estate, for instance.

If you plan to invest in a specific area, you would be wise to take a course about it or commit to learning on your own. Most of the websites mentioned throughout this appendix offer information, and some offer formal courses you can take online. Working with an investment club is an increasingly popular way to learn and pool your resources with other individual investors. In the beginning, don't worry about the details of particular stocks or the intricacies of real estate investment trusts and other more advanced concepts. Focus on the fundamentals: Why do stock prices increase or decrease? What effect do interest rates have on bonds? How can a particular house increase in value dramatically while another in the same neighborhood stays flat?

You can also practice investing without risking any money. This is a smart move early in your career, when you're still getting on your feet and may not have much money to invest yet. After you've learned the basics of stock investing, for instance, set up a "mock portfolio" on one of the many online sites that provide free portfolio tracking. Month by month, monitor the performance of your choices. Whenever you see a big increase or decrease, dig deeper to understand why. By practicing first, you can learn from your mistakes before those mistakes cost you any money.

TAXES: MINIMIZING THE BITE

Taxes will be a constant factor in your personal financial planning. You pay *sales tax* on many of the products you buy (in all but five states); you pay federal *excise taxes* on certain purchases, such as gasoline and phone service; you pay *property tax* on real estate; and you pay *income tax* on both earned income (wages, salaries, tips, bonuses, commissions, and business profits) and investment income. The total taxes paid by individuals vary widely, but you can safely assume that taxes will consume 30 to 40 percent of your income.

Your personal tax strategy should focus on minimizing the taxes you are required to pay, without running afoul of the law or harming your financial progress. (For instance, you usually don't want to skip an investment opportunity just because you'll have to pay tax on your gains.) Put another way, you are expected to pay your fair share of taxes, but no one expects you to pay more than your share.

You can reduce taxes in three basic ways: (1) by reducing your consumption of goods and services that are subject to either sales tax or excise taxes, (2) by reducing your *taxable income*, or (3) by reducing your tax through the use of *tax credits*. Reducing consumption is a straightforward concept, although there are obviously limits to how far you can reduce consumption and therefore this portion of your tax obligation.

Reducing your taxable income (the part of your income that is subject to local, state, or federal income tax, not reducing your overall income level) is more complicated but can have a great impact on your finances. Authorities such as the IRS allow a variety of **deductions**, such as interest paid on home mortgages and the costs associated with using part of your home for office space. Qualifying deductions can be subtracted from your *gross income* to lower your taxable income. A portion of your income is also *exempt* from federal income tax, based on the number of dependents in your household. The more **exemptions** you can legally claim, the lower your taxable income. You can also lower your taxable income by investing a portion of your income in *tax-exempt* or *tax-deferred* investments. With **tax-exempt investments** (which are primarily bonds issued by local governments), you don't have to pay federal income tax on any income you earn from the investment. With **tax-deferred investments**, such as 401(k) plans and individual retirement accounts (IRAs), you can deduct the amount of money you invest every year from your gross income, and you don't have to pay tax on income from the investment until you withdraw money during retirement.

Unlike deductions, which only reduce your taxable income and therefore reduce your tax burden by the amount of your tax rate, **tax credits** reduce your tax obligation directly. In other words, a $100 *deduction* reduces your tax bill by $28 (if you're in the 28 percent tax bracket, for instance), whereas a $100 *credit* reduces your tax bill by $100.

Personal tax software can guide you through the process of finding deductions and credits. For more complex scenarios, though, it's always a good idea to get the advice of a professional tax adviser.

INSURANCE: PROTECTING YOURSELF, YOUR FAMILY, AND YOUR ASSETS

Unfortunately, things go wrong in life, from accidents to health problems to the death of an income provider. Insurance is designed to protect you, your family, and your assets if and when these unpleasant events occur. In a sense, insurance is the ultimate risk/reward trade-off decision. If you had an ironclad guarantee that you would never get sick or injured, you would have no need for health insurance. However, there's a reasonable chance that you will need medical attention at some point, and major injuries and illness can generate many thousands of dollars of unplanned expenses. Consequently, most people consider it a reasonable trade-off to pay for health insurance to protect themselves from catastrophic financial blows. Exhibit D.5 on the next page provides a brief overview of your most significant insurance options.

Another vital step to protecting your family—and one that is often overlooked by younger people—is preparing a **will**, a legal document that specifies what will happen to your assets, who will execute your estate (carry out the terms of your will), and who will be the legal guardian of your children, if you have any, in the event of your death.

Life Stage 4: Plan for a Secure, Independent Retirement

Retirement? You're only 25 years old (or 35 or 45). Yes, but as you saw in the discussion of compound interest, it's never too early to start planning for retirement. It's tempting to picture retirement as a carefree time when you can finally ditch your job and focus on hobbies, travel, volunteer work, and the hundreds of other activities you haven't had time for previously in your life. Sadly, the reality for millions of retired people today is much different. Between skyrocketing medical costs, a sluggish economy,

EXHIBIT D.5	Understanding Your Insurance Options

You can buy insurance for every eventuality from earthquake damage to vacation interruptions, but the most common and most important types include medical, disability, auto, homeowner's, and life insurance.

Category	Highlights
Health insurance	Most plans offer a variety of cost and coverage options—for instance, to lower your monthly costs you can select a higher deductible, which is the amount you have to pay before insurance coverage kicks in; selecting the right plan requires a careful analysis of your needs and financial circumstances; all individuals are now required by law to have health insurance: be sure to check www.healthcare.gov or your state's exchange if it doesn't participate in the federal exchange
Disability insurance	Temporarily replaces a portion of your income if you are unable to work; various policies have different definitions of "disability" and restrictions on coverage and payments
Auto insurance	Most states now have *compulsory liability insurance laws*, meaning that you have to prove that you are covered for any damage you might cause as a driver; coverage for your vehicle can be both *collision* (damages resulting from collisions) and *comprehensive* (other damages or theft); you can also buy coverage to protect yourself from illegally uninsured motorists
Homeowner's insurance	Most policies include both *property loss coverage* (to replace or repair the home and its contents) and *liability coverage* (to protect you in case someone sues you); often required by the lender when you have a mortgage
Life insurance	Primary purpose is to provide for others in the event that your death would create a financial hardship for them; common forms are *term life* (limited duration, less expensive, no investment value), *whole life* (permanent coverage, builds cash value over time, more expensive than term life), and *universal life* (similar to whole life but more flexible)

and lower-than-expected company pensions in some cases, retirement for many people is a never-ending financial struggle, with little hope for improvement.

Perhaps the most important step you can take toward a more positive retirement is to shed the misconceptions that people often have about retirement planning, including the following:[18]

- **My living expenses will drop, so I'll need less money.** Some of your expenses may well drop, but rising health-care costs will probably swamp any reductions you have in housing, clothing, and other personal costs.
- **I'll live for roughly 15 years after I retire.** The big advantage of the health care that costs so much today is that people are living longer and longer. You could live for 20 or 30 years after you retire.
- **Social Security will cover my basic living expenses.** Social Security probably won't cover even your basic requirements, and the entire system is in serious financial trouble. Although it's unlikely that political leaders would ever let Social Security collapse, the safest bet is to not count on it at all.

- **My employer will keep funding my pension and health insurance.** Thousands of retirees in recent years have been devastated by former employers either curtailing or eliminating pension and health coverage.
- **I can't save much right now, so there's no point in saving anything at all.** If you find yourself thinking this, remind yourself of the magic of compounding. Over time, small amounts grow into large amounts of money. Do whatever it takes to get started now.
- **I have plenty of time to worry about retirement later.** Unfortunately, you don't. The longer you wait, the harder it will become to ensure a comfortable retirement. If you're not prepared, your only option will be to continue working well into your 70s or 80s.

In other words, the situation is serious. However, that doesn't mean it's hopeless—not by any means. You control your destiny, and you don't need to abandon all pleasures and comforts now to make it happen. But you do need to put together a plan and start saving now. Make retirement planning a positive part of your personal financial planning—part of your dream of living the life you want to live.

MyBizLab®

To complete the problems with the ★, go to
EOC Discussion Questions in the MyLab.

TEST YOUR KNOWLEDGE

Questions for Review

D-1. What does the *time value of money* mean?

D-2. What is compounding?

D-3. What is the major advantage of using a fee-only financial planner?

D-4. What is credit counseling?

D-5. What is the difference between a tax deduction and a tax credit?

Questions for Analysis

★ **D-6.** Should you borrow at any cost to get through college? Explain your answer.

D-7. What are the risks of relying on credit cards for living expenses while in college?

D-8. Why is it essential to keep a close eye on fixed expenses?

★ **D-9.** Why do you need to be able to explain your value to potential employers?

★ **D-10.** **Ethical Considerations.** Is it unethical for lenders to get students to sign up for loans that the students may not fully understand? Why or why not?

MyBizLab®

Go to the Assignments section of your MyLab to complete these writing exercises.

D-11 If you have money to invest but are worried that the stock market could fall soon, is it wise to keep all your investment funds in cash instead? Why or why not?

D-12 Why is it important to understand your risk tolerance before you start investing?

APPENDIX D GLOSSARY

asset management accounts Cash management accounts offered by brokerage firms and mutual fund companies, frequently as tools to manage cash that isn't currently invested elsewhere

cash management All the planning and activities associated with managing your cash and other liquid assets

closing costs Fees associated with buying and selling a house

commission-based planners Financial advisers who are paid commissions on the financial products they sell you, such as insurance policies and mutual funds

compounding The acceleration of balances caused by applying new interest to interest that has already accumulated

credit history A record of your mortgages, consumer loans, credit card accounts (including credit limits and current balances), and bill-paying performance

credit reports Reports generated by credit bureaus, showing an individual's credit usage and payment history

deductions Opportunities to reduce taxable income by subtracting the cost of a specific item, such as business expenses or interest paid on home mortgages

exemptions Reductions to taxable income based on the number of dependents in the household

fee-only planners Financial advisers who charge a fee for their services rather than earning a commission on financial services they sell you

income and expense statement A listing of your monthly inflows (income) and outflows (expenses); also called an *income statement*

net worth The difference between your assets and your liabilities

overdraft fees Penalties charged against your checking account when you write checks that total more than your available balance

personal bankruptcy A condition in which a consumer is unable to repay his or her debts; depending on the type of bankruptcy, a court will either forgive many of the person's debts or establish a compatible repayment plan

reconcile To compare the balance you believe is in your account with the balance the bank believes is in your account

tax credits Direct reductions in your tax obligation

tax-deferred investments Investments such as 401(k) plans and IRAs that let you deduct the amount of your investments from your gross income (thereby lowering your taxable income); you don't have to pay tax on any of the income from these invest-

ments until you start to withdraw money during retirement

tax-exempt investments Investments (usually municipal bonds) whose income is not subject to federal income tax

time value of money The increasing value of money as a result of accumulating interest

will A legal document that specifies what will happen to your assets, who will execute your estate (carry out the terms of your will), and who will be the legal guardian of your children, if you have any, in the event of your death

ENDNOTES

1. Jack R. Kapoor, Les R. Dlabay, and Robert J. Hughes, *Personal Finance*, 7th ed. (New York: McGraw-Hill/Irwin, 2004), 18.
2. "Interview Tips," WiserAdvisor.com, accessed 14 October 2009, www.wiseradvisor.com.
3. Arthur J. Keown, *Personal Finance: Turning Money into Wealth*, 3rd ed. (Upper Saddle River, N.J.: Prentice Hall, 2003), 52–53.
4. Kapoor et al., *Personal Finance*, 11; Lawrence J. Gitman and Michael D. Joehnk, *Personal Financial Planning*, 10th ed. (Mason, Ohio: Thomson South-Western, 2005), 5.
5. Gitman and Joehnk, *Personal Financial Planning*, 15.
6. Deborah Fowles, "The Psychology of Spending Money," About.com, accessed 22 May 2004, www.about.com.
7. Gitman and Joehnk, *Personal Financial Planning*, 15.
8. "Study Puts Dollar Amounts on Earning Power of College Majors," OregonLive.com, 24 May 2011, www.oregonlive.com; Kathy Kristof, "Crushed by College," *Forbes*, 2 February 2009, 60–65.
9. "Study Puts Dollar Amounts on Earning Power of College Majors"; Kristof, "Crushed by College."
10. Ben Elgin, "Study Now—And Pay and Pay and Pay Later," 21 May 2007, *BusinessWeek*, 66–67; Kristof, "Crushed by College."
11. Philip Reed, "Drive a (Nearly) New Car for (Almost) Nothing," Edmunds.com, accessed 22 May 2004, www.edmunds.com.
12. Chandler Phillips, "Confessions of a Car Salesman," Edmunds.com, accessed 22 May 2004, www.edmunds.com.
13. Eryn Brown, "Hot to Get Paid What You're Worth," *Business 2.0*, May 2004, 102–110, 134.
14. Keown, *Personal Finance: Turning Money into Wealth*, 143–148; Gitman and Joehnk, *Personal Financial Planning*, 140–147.
15. Kapoor et al., *Personal Finance*, 222.
16. "Ads Promising Debt Relief May Be Offering Bankruptcy," FTC Consumer Alert, accessed 23 May 2004, www.ftc.gov.
17. Christopher Conkey, "Bankruptcy Overall Means Tougher Choices," *Wall Street Journal*, 22 May 2005, www.wsj.com.
18. Kapoor et al., *Personal Finance*, 582.

Glossary

360-degree review A multidimensional review in which a person is given feedback from subordinates, peers, superiors, and possibly outside stakeholders such as customers and business partners

401(k) plan A defined-contribution retirement plan in which employers often match the amount employees invest

accounting Measuring, interpreting, and communicating financial information to support internal and external decision making

accounting equation The basic accounting equation, stating that assets equal liabilities plus owners' equity

accounts payable Amounts that a firm currently owes to other parties

accounts receivable Amounts that are currently owed to a firm

accounts receivable turnover ratio A measure of the time a company takes to turn its accounts receivable into cash, calculated by dividing sales by the average value of accounts receivable for a period

accrual basis An accounting method in which revenue is recorded when a sale is made and an expense is recorded when it is incurred

acquisition An action taken by one company to buy a controlling interest in the voting stock of another company

actuaries Risk analysts employed by insurance companies to forecast expected losses and to calculate the cost of premiums

adjustable rate mortgage (ARM) A mortgage that features variable interest rates over the life of the loan

administrative law Rules, regulations, and interpretations of statutory law set forth by administrative agencies and commissions

administrative skills Technical skills in information gathering, data analysis, planning, organizing, and other aspects of managerial work

advertising The delivery of announcements and promotional messages via time or space purchased in various media

advertising appeal A creative tactic designed to capture the audience's attention and promote preference for the product or company being advertised

advertising media Communication channels, such as newspapers, radio, television, and the World Wide Web

advisory board A team of people with subject-area expertise or vital contacts who help a business owner review plans and decisions

advocacy advertising Advertising that presents a company's opinions on public issues such as education or health care

affirmative action Activities undertaken by businesses to recruit and promote members of groups whose economic progress has been hindered through either legal barriers or established practices

agency A business relationship that exists when one party (the principal) authorizes another party (the agent) to enter into contracts on the principal's behalf

agents and brokers Independent wholesalers that do not take title to the goods they distribute but may or may not take possession of those goods

agile organization A company whose structure, policies, and capabilities allow employees to respond quickly to customer needs and changes in the business environment

angel investors Private individuals who invest money in start-ups, usually earlier in a business's life and in smaller amounts than VCs are willing to invest or banks are willing to lend

arbitration A decision process in which an impartial referee listens to both sides and then makes a judgment by accepting one side's view

artificial intelligence The ability of computers to solve problems through reasoning and learning and to simulate human sensory perceptions

asset allocation Management of a portfolio to balance potential returns with an acceptable level of risk

asset management accounts Cash management accounts offered by brokerage firms and mutual fund companies, frequently as tools to manage cash that isn't currently invested elsewhere

assets Any things of value owned or leased by a business

audit Formal evaluation of the fairness and reliability of a client's financial statements

authorization cards Cards signed by employees to indicate interest in having a union represent them

autocratic leaders Leaders who do not involve others in decision making

balance of payments The sum of all payments one nation receives from other nations minus the sum of all payments it makes to other nations, over some specified period of time

balance of trade Total value of the products a nation exports minus the total value of the products it imports, over some period of time

balance sheet A statement of a firm's financial position on a particular date; also known as *statement of financial position*

balanced scorecard A method of monitoring the performance from four perspectives: finances, operations, customer relationships, and the growth and development of employees and intellectual property

bankruptcy A legal procedure by which a person or a business that is unable to meet financial obligations is relieved of debt

barrier to entry Any resource or capability a company must have before it can start competing in a given market

bear market A market situation in which most stocks are decreasing in value

behavioral interview Interview in which you are asked to relate specific incidents and experiences from your past

behavioral segmentation Categorization of customers according to their relationship with products or response to product characteristics

benchmarking Collecting and comparing process and performance data from other companies

benefit corporation A profit-seeking corporation whose charter specifies a social or environmental goal that the company must pursue in addition to profit

board of directors A group of professionals elected by shareholders as their representatives, with responsibility for the overall direction of the company and the selection of top executives

bond market The collective buying and selling of bonds; most bond trading is done over the counter, rather than in organized exchanges

bonds A method of funding in which the issuer borrows from an investor and provides a written promise to make regular interest payments and repay the borrowed amount in the future

bonus A cash payment, in addition to regular wage or salary, that serves as a reward for achievement

book value The difference between the assets and liabilities as listed on the balance sheet

bookkeeping Recordkeeping; the clerical aspect of accounting

boycott A pressure action by union members and sympathizers who refuse to buy or handle the product of a target company

brand A name, term, sign, symbol, design, or combination of those used to identify the products of a firm and to differentiate them from competing products

brand communities Formal or informal groups of people united by their interest in and ownership of particular products

brand equity The value that a company has built up in a brand

brand extension Applying a successful brand name to a new product category

brand loyalty The degree to which customers continue to purchase a specific brand

brand managers Managers who develop and implement the marketing strategies and programs for specific products or brands

brand marks The portion of brands that cannot be expressed verbally

brand names The portion of brands that can be expressed orally, including letters, words, or numbers

breach of contract Failure to live up to the terms of a contract, with no legal excuse

break-even analysis A method of calculating the minimum volume of sales needed at a given price to cover all costs

break-even point Sales volume at a given price that will cover all of a company's costs

broker A certified expert who is legally registered to buy and sell securities on behalf of individual and institutional investors

bubble A market situation in which frenzied demand for an asset pushes the price of that asset far beyond its true economic value

budget A planning and control tool that reflects expected revenues, operating expenses, and cash receipts and outlays

bull market A market situation in which most stocks are increasing in value

bundling Offering several products for a single price that is presumably lower than the total of the products' individual prices

business Any profit-seeking organization that provides goods and services designed to satisfy customers' needs

business cycles Fluctuations in the rate of growth that an economy experiences over a period of several years

business incubators Facilities that house small businesses and provide support services during the company's early growth phases

business interruption insurance Insurance that covers losses resulting from temporary business closings

business law The elements of law that directly influence or control business activities

business mindset A view of business that considers the myriad decisions that must be made and the many problems that must be overcome before companies can deliver the products that satisfy customer needs

business model A concise description of how a business intends to generate revenue

business plan A document that summarizes a proposed business venture, goals, and plans for achieving those goals

cafeteria plans Flexible benefit programs that let employees personalize their benefits packages

calendar year A 12-month accounting period that begins on January 1 and ends on December 31

cap and trade A type of environmental policy that gives companies some freedom in addressing the environmental impact of specified pollutants, by either reducing emissions to meet a designated cap or buying allowances to offset excess emissions

capacity planning Establishing the overall level of resources needed to meet customer demand

capital budget A budget that outlines expenditures for real estate, new facilities, major equipment, and other capital investments

capital gains Increases in the value of a stock or other asset

capital investments Money paid to acquire something of permanent value in a business

capital items More expensive organizational products with a longer useful life, ranging from office and plant equipment to entire factories

capital structure A firm's mix of debt and equity financing

capital The funds that finance the operations of a business as well as the physical, human-made elements used to produce goods and services, such as factories and computers

capitalism Economic system based on economic freedom and competition

cash basis An accounting method in which revenue is recorded when payment is received and an expense is recorded when cash is paid

cash management All the planning and activities associated with managing your cash and other liquid assets

cause-related marketing Identification and marketing of a social issue, cause, or idea to selected target markets

centralization Concentration of decision-making authority at the top of an organization

certification election A secret-ballot election overseen by the NLRB to determine whether a union gains the right to represent a group of employees

certified public accountants (CPAs) Professionally licensed accountants who meet certain requirements for education and experience and who pass a comprehensive examination

chain of command A pathway for the flow of authority from one management level to the next

channel conflict Disagreement or tension between two or more members in a distribution channel, such as competition between channel partners trying to reach the same group of customers

chief executive officer (CEO) The highest-ranking officer of a corporation

chief information officer (CIO) A high-level executive responsible for understanding a company's information needs and creating systems and procedures to deliver that information to the right people at the right time

chronological résumé The most common résumé format; it emphasizes work experience, with past jobs shown in reverse chronological order

claims Demands for payments from an insurance company based on the terms in an insurance policy

closing The point at which a sale is completed

closing costs Fees associated with buying and selling a house

closing the books Transferring net revenue and expense account balances to retained earnings for the period

coaching Helping employees reach their highest potential by meeting with them, discussing problems that hinder their ability to work effectively, and offering suggestions and encouragement to overcome these problems

co-branding A partnership between two or more companies to closely link their brand names together for a single product

code of ethics A written statement that sets forth the principles that guide an organization's decisions

cognitive dissonance Tension that exists when a person's beliefs don't match his or her behaviors; a common example is *buyer's remorse*, when someone regrets a purchase immediately after making it

cohesiveness A measure of how committed team members are to their team's goals

collateral A tangible asset a lender can claim if a borrower defaults on a loan

collective bargaining A negotiation between union and management negotiators to forge the human resources policies that will apply to all employees covered by a contract

collective bargaining agreements (CBAs) Contracts that result from collective bargaining

combination résumé A résumé format that includes the best features of the chronological and functional approaches

commercial banks Banks that accept deposits, offer various checking and savings accounts, and provide loans

commercial general liability Policies that provides protection against all forms of liability not specifically excluded under the terms of the policy

commercial paper Short-term *promissory notes*, or contractual agreements, to repay a borrowed amount by a specified time with a specified interest rate

commercialization Large-scale production and distribution of a product

commission-based planners Financial advisers who are paid commissions on the financial products they sell you, such as insurance policies and mutual funds

commissions Employee compensation based on a percentage of sales made

committee A team that may become a permanent part of the organization and is designed to deal with regularly recurring tasks

commodities futures Contracts to buy or sell specific amounts of commodities for a set price at a future date

common law Laws based on the precedents established by judges' decisions

common stock Shares of ownership that include voting rights

communication mix A blend of communication vehicles—advertising, direct marketing, personal selling, sales promotion, social media, and public relations—that a company uses to reach current and potential customers

compensating balance The portion of an unsecured loan that is kept on deposit at a lending institution to protect the lender and increase the lender's return

compensation Money, benefits, and services paid to employees for their work

competition Rivalry among businesses for the same customers

competitive advantage Some aspect of a product or company that makes it more appealing to target customers

compounding The acceleration of balances caused by applying new interest to interest that has already accumulated

conceptual skills The ability to understand the relationship of parts to the whole

conflicts of interest A situation in which competing loyalties can lead to ethical lapses, such as when a business decision may be influenced by the potential for personal gain

consent order A settlement in which an individual or organization promises to discontinue some illegal activity without admitting guilt

consideration A negotiated exchange that is necessary to make a contract legally binding

consultative selling An approach in which a salesperson acts as a consultant and advisor to help customers find the best solutions to their personal or business needs

consumer market Individuals or households that buy goods and services for personal use

consumer price index (CPI) A monthly statistic that measures changes in the prices of a representative collective of consumer goods and services

consumerism A movement that pressures businesses to consider consumer needs and interests

contingent employees Nonpermanent employees, including temporary workers, independent contractors, and full-time employees hired on a probationary basis

contract A legally enforceable exchange of promises between two or more parties

controller The highest-ranking accountant in a company, responsible for overseeing all accounting functions

controlling The process of measuring progress against goals and objectives and correcting deviations if results are not as expected

convenience products Everyday goods and services that people buy frequently, usually without much conscious planning

conversation marketing An approach to customer communication in which companies initiate and facilitate conversations in a networked community of potential buyers and other interested parties

convertible bonds Corporate bonds that can be exchanged at the owner's discretion into common stock of the issuing company

core competencies Activities that a company considers central and vital to its business

core message The single most important idea an advertiser hopes to convey to the target audience about its products or the company

corporate governance In a broad sense, describes all the policies, procedures, relationships, and systems in place to oversee the successful and legal operation of the enterprise; in a narrow sense, refers to the responsibilities and performance of the board of directors specifically

corporate officers The top executives who run a corporation

corporate social responsibility (CSR) The idea that business has obligations to society beyond the pursuit of profits

corporation A legal entity, distinct from any individual persons, that has the power to own property and conduct business

cost-based pricing A method of setting prices based on production and marketing costs, rather than conditions in the marketplace

cost of capital The average rate of interest a firm pays on its combination of debt and equity

cost of goods sold The cost of producing or acquiring a company's products for sale during a given period

coupons Printed or electronic certificates that offer discounts on particular items and are redeemed at the time of purchase

credit derivatives Derivatives used to reduce a lender's exposure to credit risk

credit freeze A situation in which credit has become so scarce that it is virtually unavailable, at any cost, to most potential borrowers

credit history A record of your mortgages, consumer loans, credit card accounts (including credit limits and current balances), and bill-paying performance

credit rating agencies Companies that offer opinions about the creditworthiness of borrowers and of specific investments

credit reports Reports generated by credit bureaus, showing an individual's credit usage and payment history

credit unions Not-for-profit, member-owned cooperatives that offer deposit accounts and lending services to consumers and small businesses

crisis management Procedures and systems for minimizing the harm that might result from some unusually threatening situations

critical path In a PERT network diagram, the sequence of operations that requires the longest time to complete

cross-functional team A team that draws together employees from different functional areas

cross-training Training workers to perform multiple jobs and rotating them through these various jobs to combat boredom or burnout

crowdfunding Soliciting project funds, business investment, or business loans from members of the public

culture A shared system of symbols, beliefs, attitudes, values, expectations, and norms for behavior

currency futures Contracts to buy or sell amounts of specified currency at some future date

current assets Cash and items that can be turned into cash within one year

current liabilities Obligations that must be met within a year

current ratio A measure of a firm's short-term liquidity, calculated by dividing current assets by current liabilities

customer loyalty The degree to which customers continue to buy from a particular retailer or buy the products of a particular manufacturer or service provider

customer relationship management (CRM) A type of information system that captures, organizes, and capitalizes on all the interactions that a company has with its customers

customized production The creation of a unique good or service for each customer

damages Financial compensation to an injured party for loss and suffering

data Facts, numbers, statistics, and other individual bits and pieces of data that by themselves don't necessarily constitute useful information

databases Computerized files that collect, sort, and cross-reference data

debentures Corporate bonds backed only by the reputation of the issuer

debt financing Arranging funding by borrowing money

debt-to-assets ratio A measure of a firm's ability to carry long-term debt, calculated by dividing total liabilities by total assets

debt-to-equity ratio A measure of the extent to which a business is financed by debt as opposed to invested capital, calculated by dividing the company's total liabilities by owners' equity

decentralization Delegation of decision-making authority to employees in lower-level positions

decertification An vote by employees to take away a union's right to represent them

decision-making skills The ability to identify a decision situation, analyze the problem, weigh the alternatives, choose an alternative, implement it, and evaluate the results

deductions Opportunities to reduce taxable income by subtracting the cost of a specific item, such as business expenses or interest paid on home mortgages

deed A legal document by which an owner transfers the title, or ownership rights, to real property to a new owner

defaults Situations in which borrowers stop making payments on their loans

deflation An economic condition in which prices fall steadily throughout the economy

demand Buyers' willingness and ability to purchase products at various price points

demand curve A graph of the quantities of a product that buyers will purchase at various prices

democratic leaders Leaders who delegate authority and involve employees in decision making

demographics The study of the statistical characteristics of a population

department stores Large stores that carry a variety of products in multiple categories, such as clothing, housewares, gifts, bedding, and furniture

departmentalization Grouping people within an organization according to function, division, matrix, or network

depreciation An accounting procedure for systematically spreading the cost of a tangible asset over its estimated useful life

deregulation Removing regulations to allow the market to prevent excesses and correct itself over time

derivatives Contracts whose value is derived from some other entity (usually an asset of some kind, but not necessarily); used to hedge against or speculate on risk

derivatives market A market that includes exchange trading (for futures and some options) and over-the-counter trading (for all other derivatives, at least currently)

direct mail Printed materials addressed to individual consumers, households, or business contacts

direct marketing Direct communication other than personal sales contacts designed to stimulate a measurable response

direct response television The use of television commercials and longer-format infomercials that are designed to stimulate an immediate purchase response from viewers

disability income insurance Short-term or long-term insurance that replaces some of the income lost when an individual is unable to perform his or her work due to illness or injury

discount rate The interest rate that member banks pay when they borrow funds from the Fed

discount stores Retailers that sell a variety of everyday goods below the market price by keeping their overhead low

discounts Temporary price reductions to stimulate sales or lower prices to encourage certain behaviors such as paying with cash

discrimination In a social and economic sense, denial of opportunities to individuals on the basis of some characteristic that has no bearing on their ability to perform in a job

disintermediation The replacement of intermediaries by producers, customers, or other intermediaries when those other parties can perform channel functions more effectively or efficiently

distribution centers Advanced warehouse facilities that specialize in collecting and shipping merchandise

distribution channels Systems for moving goods and services from producers to customers; also known as marketing channels

distribution mix A combination of intermediaries and channels a producer uses to reach target customers

distribution strategy A firm's overall plan for moving products through intermediaries and on to final customers

distributors Merchant wholesalers that sell products to organizational customers for internal operations or the production of other goods, rather than to retailers for resale

diversification Creating new products for new markets

diversity initiatives Programs and policies that help companies support diverse workforces and markets

divisional structure Grouping departments according to similarities in product, process, customer, or geography

Dodd-Frank Act Legislation passed in 2010 aimed at reforming the banking industry and offering consumers greater protection

double-entry bookkeeping A method of recording financial transactions that requires a debit entry and credit entry for each transaction to ensure that the accounting equation is always kept in balance

dumping Charging less than the actual cost or less than the home-country price for goods sold in other countries

dynamic pricing Continually adjusting prices to reflect changes in supply and demand

earnings per share A measure of a firm's profitability for each share of outstanding stock, calculated by dividing net income after taxes by the average number of shares of common stock outstanding

EBITDA Earnings before interest, taxes, depreciation, and amortization

e-commerce The application of Internet technologies to wholesaling and retailing

economic environment The conditions and forces that affect the cost and availability of goods, services, and labor and thereby shape the behavior of buyers and sellers

economic globalization The increasing integration and interdependence of national economies around the world

economic indicators Statistics that measure the performance of the economy

economic system The policies that define a society's particular economic structure; the rules by which a society allocates economic resources

economics The study of how a society uses its scarce resources to produce and distribute goods and services

economies of scale Savings from buying parts and materials, manufacturing, or marketing in large quantities

economy The sum total of all the economic activity within a given region

electronic performance monitoring (EPM) Real-time, computer-based evaluation of employee performance

embargo A total ban on trade with a particular nation (a sanction) or of a particular product

employee assistance program (EAP) A company-sponsored counseling or referral plan for employees with personal problems

employee benefits Compensation other than wages, salaries, and incentive programs

employee empowerment Granting decision-making and problem-solving authorities to employees so they can act without getting approval from management

employee retention Efforts to keep current employees

employee stock-ownership plan (ESOP) A program that enables employees to become partial owners of a company

employment interview Formal meeting during which you and an employer ask questions and exchange information

employment practices liability insurance Insurance that reimburses employers for a variety of claims related to employment practices

engagement An employee's rational and emotional commitment to his or her work

entrepreneurial spirit The positive, forward-thinking desire to create profitable, sustainable business enterprises

entrepreneurship The combination of innovation, initiative, and willingness to take the risks required to create and operate new businesses

equilibrium point The point at which quantity supplied equals quantity demanded

equity financing Arranging funding by selling ownership shares in the company, publicly or privately

equity theory The idea that employees base their level of satisfaction on the ratio of their inputs to the job and the outputs or rewards they receive from it

ethical dilemma A situation in which more than one side of an issue can be supported with valid arguments

ethical lapse A situation in which an individual or a group makes a decision that is morally wrong, illegal, or unethical

ethics The rules or standards governing the conduct of a person or group

ethnocentrism Judging all other groups according to the standards, behaviors, and customs of one's own group

etiquette The expected norms of behavior in any particular situation

exchange process The act of obtaining a desired object or service from another party by offering something of value in return

exchange rate The rate at which the money of one country is traded for the money of another

exchange-traded funds (ETFs) Mutual funds whose shares are traded on public exchanges in the same way as stocks

exclusive distribution A market coverage strategy that gives intermediaries exclusive rights to sell a product in a specific geographic area

exemptions Reductions to taxable income based on the number of dependents in the household

expectancy theory The idea that the effort employees put into their work depends on expectations about their own ability to perform, expectations about likely rewards, and the attractiveness of those rewards

expense items Inexpensive products that organizations generally use within a year of purchase

expense ratio The annual cost of owning a mutual fund, expressed as a percentage

expenses Costs created in the process of generating revenues

export subsidies A form of financial assistance in which producers receive enough money from the government to allow them to lower their prices in order to compete more effectively in the global market

exporting Selling and shipping goods or services to another country

express contract A contract derived from words, either oral or written

external auditors Independent accounting firms that provide auditing services for public companies

face value The amount of money, or *principal*, a bond buyer lends to a bond issuer; also known as *par value* or *denomination*

factoring Obtaining funding by selling accounts receivable

family branding Using a brand name on a variety of related products

Fannie Mae The government-sponsored enterprise responsible for guaranteeing and funding home mortgages

Federal Deposit Insurance Corporation (FDIC) The federal agency responsible for protecting money in customer accounts and managing the transition of assets whenever a bank fails

federal funds rate The interest rate that member banks charge each other to borrow money overnight from the funds they keep in the Federal Reserve accounts

Federal Reserve System The central banking system of the United States; responsible for regulating banks and implementing monetary policy

fee-only planners Financial advisers who charge a fee for their services rather than earning a commission on financial services they sell you

finance companies Nonbank institutions that lend money to consumers and businesses for cars and other vehicles, home improvements, expansion, purchases, and other purposes

financial accounting The area of accounting concerned with preparing financial information for users outside the organization

financial control The process of analyzing and adjusting the basic financial plan to correct for deviations from forecasted events

financial futures Contracts to buy or sell a financial instrument (such as stocks, Treasury bonds, and foreign currencies) for a set price at a future date

financial management Planning for a firm's money needs and managing the allocation and spending of funds

financial plan A document that outlines the funds needed for a certain period of time, along with the sources and intended uses of those funds

first-line managers Those at the lowest level of the management hierarchy; they supervise the operating employees and implement the plans set at the higher management levels

fiscal policy Use of government revenue collection and spending to influence the business cycle

fiscal year Any 12 consecutive months used as an accounting period

fixed assets Assets retained for long-term use, such as land, buildings, machinery, and equipment; also referred to as *property, plant, and equipment*

fixed costs Business costs that remain constant regardless of the number of units produced

foreclosures Situations in which lenders take possession of homes after borrowers default on their mortgage payments

foreign direct investment (FDI) Investment of money by foreign companies in domestic business enterprises

franchise A business arrangement in which one company (the franchisee) obtains the rights to sell the products and use various elements of a business system of another company (the franchisor)

franchisee A business owner who pays for the rights to sell the products and use the business system of a franchisor

franchisor A company that licenses elements of its business system to other companies (franchisees)

Freddie Mac A secondary mortgage institution similar to Fannie Mae

free trade International trade unencumbered by restrictive measures

free-market system Economic system in which decisions about what to produce and in what quantities are decided by the market's buyers and sellers

freemium pricing A hybrid pricing strategy of offering some products for free while charging for others, or offering a product for free to some customers while charging others for it

functional résumé A résumé format that emphasizes your skills and capabilities while identifying employers and academic experience in subordinate sections; many recruiters view this format with suspicion

functional structure Grouping workers according to their similar skills, resource use, and expertise

functional team A team whose members come from a single functional department and that is based on the organization's vertical structure

GAAP (generally accepted accounting practices) Standards and practices used by publicly held corporations in the United States and a few other countries in the preparation of financial statements; on course to converge with IFRS

gain sharing Tying rewards to profits or cost savings achieved by meeting specific goals

general partnership A partnership in which all partners have joint authority to make decisions for the firm and joint liability for the firm's financial obligations

geographic segmentation Categorization of customers according to their geographical location

glass ceiling An invisible barrier attributable to subtle discrimination that keeps women and minorities out of the top positions in business

global strategy A highly centralized approach to international expansion, with headquarters in the home country making all major decisions

goal A broad, long-range target or aim

goal-setting theory A motivational theory suggesting that setting goals can be an effective way to motivate employees

goods-producing businesses Companies that create value by making "things," most of which are tangible (digital products such as software are a notable exception)

grievance A formal complaint against an employer

gross domestic product (GDP) The value of all the final goods and services produced by businesses located within a nation's borders; excludes outputs from overseas operations of domestic companies

gross profit The amount remaining when the cost of goods sold is deducted from net sales; also known as *gross margin*

group interview Interview in which one or more interviewers meet with several candidates simultaneously

groupthink Uniformity of thought that occurs when peer pressures cause individual team members to withhold contrary or unpopular opinions

Hawthorne effect A supposed effect of organizational research, in which employees change their behavior because they are being studied and given special treatment; the validity of the effect is uncertain, and the Hawthorne studies were richer and more influential than this simple outcome would suggest

health maintenance organizations (HMOs) Prepaid medical plans in which consumers pay a set fee in order to receive a full range of medical care from a group of medical practitioners

health savings accounts (HSAs) Special savings accounts that allow employees to save a portion of their earnings to use for medical expenses when needed

hedging Protecting against cost increases with contracts that allow a company to buy supplies in the future at designated prices

Herzberg's two-factor theory A model that divides motivational forces into satisfiers ("motivators") and dissatisfiers ("hygiene factors")

hostile takeover Acquisition of another company against the wishes of management

human resources All the people who work in an organization or on its behalf

human resources (HR) management The specialized function of planning how to obtain employees, oversee their training, evaluate them, and compensate them

identity theft A crime in which thieves steal personal information and use it to take out loans and commit other types of fraud

implied contract A contract derived from actions or conduct

import quotas Limits placed on the quantity of imports a nation will allow for a specific product

importing Purchasing goods or services from another country and bringing them into one's own country

incentives Monetary payments and other rewards of value used for positive reinforcement

income and expense statement A listing of your monthly inflows (income) and outflows (expenses); also called an *income statement*

income statement A financial record of a company's revenues, expenses, and profits over a given period of time; also known as a *profit-and-loss statement*

independent mortgage companies Nonbank companies that use their own funds to offer mortgages

index A statistical indicator of the rise and fall of a representative group of securities

index funds Mutual funds that mirror the composition of a particular market or index

inflation An economic condition in which prices rise steadily throughout the economy

information Useful knowledge, often extracted from data

information systems (IS) A collective label for all technologies and processes used to manage business information

information technology (IT) Systems that promote communication and information usage through the company or that allow companies to offer new services to their customers

initial public offering (IPO) A corporation's first offering of shares to the public

injunction A court order that requires one side in a dispute to refrain from or engage in a particular action

insider trading The use of unpublicized information that an individual gains from the course of his or her job to benefit from fluctuations in the stock market

insight A deep level of understanding about a particular subject or situation

institutional advertising Advertising that seeks to create goodwill and to build a desired image for a company, rather than to promote specific products

insurable risk Risk that an insurance company might be willing to cover

insurance A written contract that transfers to an insurer the financial responsibility for losses for specific events, up to specified limits and within specified conditions

integrated marketing communications (IMC) A strategy of coordinating and integrating communication and promotion efforts with customers to ensure greater efficiency and effectiveness

intellectual property Intangible personal property, such as ideas, songs, trade secrets, and computer programs, that are protected by patents, trademarks, and copyrights

intensive distribution A market coverage strategy that tries to place a product in as many outlets as possible

intentional tort A willful act that results in injury

intermodal transportation The coordinated use of multiple modes of transportation, particularly with containers that can be shipped by truck, rail, and sea

international financial reporting standards (IFRS) Accounting standards and practices used in many countries outside the United States

international law Principles, customs, and rules that govern the international relationships between states, organizations, and persons

interpersonal skills Skills required to understand other people and to interact effectively with them

intrinsic value An estimate of what a company is actually worth, independent of book and market values

inventory Goods and materials kept in stock for production or sale

inventory control Determining the right quantities of supplies and products to have on hand and tracking where those items are

inventory turnover ratio A measure of the time a company takes to turn its inventory into sales, calculated by dividing cost of goods sold by the average value of inventory for a period

investment banks Firms that offer a variety of services related to initial public stock offerings, mergers and acquisitions, and other investment matters

investment portfolios Collections of various types of investments

ISO 9000 A globally recognized family of standards for quality management systems

job characteristics model A model suggesting that five core job dimensions influence three critical psychological states that determine motivation, performance, and other outcomes

job description A statement of the tasks involved in a given job and the conditions under which the holder of a job will work

job enrichment Making jobs more challenging and interesting by expanding the range of skills required

job specification A statement describing the kind of person who would be best for a given job—including the skills, education, and previous experience that the job requires

joint venture A separate legal entity established by two or more companies to pursue shared business objectives

just-in-time (JIT) Inventory management in which goods and materials are delivered throughout the production process right before they are needed

key-person insurance Insurance that provides a business with funds to compensate for the loss of a key employee by unplanned retirement, resignation, death, or disability

knowledge Expertise gained through experience or association

knowledge-based pay Pay tied to an employee's acquisition of knowledge or skills; also called competency-based pay or skill-based pay

Labor-Management Relations Act Legislation passed in 1947 that addressed many concerns raised by business owners and shifted the balance of power again; commonly known as the Taft-Hartley Act

Labor-Management Reporting and Disclosure Act Legislation passed in 1959 designed to ensure democratic processes and financial accountability within unions; commonly known as the Landrum-Griffith Act

labor relations The relationship between organized labor and management (in its role as the representative of company ownership)

labor unions Organizations that represent employees in negotiations with management

laissez-faire leaders Leaders who leave most decisions up to employees, particularly those concerning day-to-day matters

layoffs Termination of employees for economic or business reasons

leading The process of guiding and motivating people to work toward organizational goals

lean systems Systems (in manufacturing and other functional areas) that maximize productivity by reducing waste and delays

lease An agreement to use an asset in exchange for regular payment; similar to renting

legal and regulatory environment Laws and regulations at local, state, national, and even international levels

leverage The technique of increasing the rate of return on an investment by financing it with borrowed funds

leveraged buyout (LBO) Acquisition of a company's publicly traded stock, using funds that are primarily borrowed, usually with the intent of using some of the acquired assets to pay back the loans used to acquire the company

liabilities Claims against a firm's assets by creditors

liability losses Financial losses suffered by a business firm or an individual held responsible for property damage or injuries suffered by others

license, licensing An agreement to produce and market another company's product in exchange for a royalty or fee

life insurance Insurance that provides financial support to family members and others in the event of a person's death

limit order An order that stipulates the highest or lowest price at which the customer is willing to trade securities

limited liability A legal condition in which the maximum amount each owner is liable for is equal to whatever amount each invested in the business

limited liability company (LLC) A structure that combines limited liability with the pass-through taxation benefits of a partnership; the number of shareholders is not restricted, nor is members' participation in management

limited liability partnership (LLP) A partnership in which each partner has unlimited liability only for his or her own actions and at least some degree of limited liability for the partnership as a whole

limited partnership A partnership in which one or more persons act as *general partners* who run the business and have the same unlimited liability as sole proprietors

line of credit An arrangement in which a financial institution makes money available for use at any time after the loan has been approved

line organization A chain-of-command system that establishes a clear line of authority flowing from the top down

line-and-staff organization An organization system that has a clear chain of command but that also includes functional groups of people who provide advice and specialized services

liquidity A measure of how easily and quickly an asset such as corporate stock can be converted into cash by selling it

liquidity crisis A severe shortage of liquidity throughout a sector of the economy or the entire economy, during which companies can't get enough cash to meet their operating needs

load The sales commission charged when buying or selling a mutual fund

loan-to-value (LTV) The percentage of an asset's market value that a lender is willing to finance when offering a loan; the rest of the purchase price has to be paid by the buyer as a down payment

locals Local unions that represent employees in a specific geographic area or facility

lockout A decision by management to prevent union employees from entering the workplace; used to pressure the union to accept a contract proposal

logistics The planning, movement, and flow of goods and related information throughout the supply chain

logo A graphical and/or textual representation of a brand

long-term financing Financing used to cover long-term expenses such as assets (generally repaid over a period of more than one year)

long-term liabilities Obligations that fall due more than a year from the date of the balance sheet

loss exposures Areas of risk in which a potential for loss exists

loss-leader pricing Selling one product at a loss as a way to entice customers to consider other products

macroeconomics The study of "big-picture" issues in an economy, including competitive behavior among firms, the effect of government policies, and overall resource allocation issues

malware Short for *malicious software*; computer programs that are designed to disrupt websites, destroy information, or enable criminal activity

management The process of planning, organizing, leading, and controlling to meet organizational goals

management accounting The area of accounting concerned with preparing data for use by managers within the organization

management by objectives (MBO) A motivational approach in which managers and employees work together to structure personal goals and objectives for every individual, department, and project to mesh with the organization's goals

management information system (MIS) A computer system that provides managers with information and support for making routine decisions

management pyramid An organizational structure divided into top, middle, and first-line management

managerial roles Behavioral patterns and activities involved in carrying out the functions of management; includes interpersonal, informational, and decisional roles

mandatory retirement Required dismissal of an employee who reaches a certain age

margin trading Borrowing money from brokers to buy stock, paying interest on the borrowed money, and leaving the stock with the broker as collateral

market A group of customers who need or want a particular product and have the money to buy it

market development Selling existing products to new markets

market environment A company's target customers, the buying influences that shape the behavior of those customers, and competitors that market similar products to those customers

market order A type of securities order that instructs the broker to buy or sell at the best price that can be negotiated at the moment

market penetration Selling more of a firm's existing products in the markets it already serves

market segmentation The division of a diverse market into smaller, relatively homogeneous groups with similar needs, wants, and purchase behaviors

market share A firm's portion of the total sales in a market

market value The price at which the stock is actually selling in the stock market

marketing The process of creating value for customers and building relationships with those customers in order to capture value back from them

marketing concept An approach to business management that stresses customer needs and wants, seeks long-term profitability, and integrates marketing with other functional units within the organization

marketing intermediaries Businesspeople and organizations that assist in moving and marketing goods and services between producers and consumers

marketing mix The four key elements of marketing strategy: product, price, distribution, and customer communication

marketing research The collection and analysis of information for making marketing decisions

marketing strategy An overall plan for marketing a product; includes the identification of target market segments, a positioning strategy, and a marketing mix

marketing systems Arrangements by which channel partners coordinate their activities under the leadership of one of the partners

Maslow's hierarchy A model in which human needs are arranged in a hierarchy, with the most basic needs at the bottom and the more advanced needs toward the top

mass customization A manufacturing approach in which part of the product is mass produced and the remaining features are customized for each buyer

mass production The creation of identical goods or services, usually in large quantities

master limited partnership (MLP) A partnership that is allowed to raise money by selling units of ownership to the general public

matching principle The fundamental principle requiring that expenses incurred in producing revenue be deducted from the revenues they generate during an accounting period

matrix structure A structure in which employees are assigned to both a functional group and a project team (thus using functional and divisional patterns simultaneously)

maturity date The date on which the principal of a bond will be repaid in full

media mix A combination of print, broadcast, online, and other media used for an advertising campaign

mediation Use of an impartial third party to help resolve bargaining impasses

mentoring A process in which experienced managers guide less-experienced colleagues in nuances of office politics, serving as role models for appropriate business behavior and helping to negotiate the corporate structure

merchant banks Banks that provide financial services to businesses; can also refer to private equity management

merchant wholesalers Independent wholesalers that take legal title to goods they distribute

merger An action taken by two companies to combine as a single entity

microeconomics The study of how consumers, businesses, and industries collectively determine the quantity of goods and services demanded and supplied at different prices

microlenders Organizations, often not-for-profit, that lend smaller amounts of money to business owners who might not qualify for conventional bank loans

micromanaging Overseeing every small detail of employees' work and refusing to give them freedom or autonomy

middle managers Those in the middle of the management hierarchy; they develop plans to implement the goals of top managers and coordinate the work of first-line managers

mission statement A brief statement of why an organization exists; in other words, what the organization aims to accomplish for customers, investors, and other stakeholders

monetary policy Government policy and actions taken by the Federal Reserve Board to regulate the nation's money supply

money Anything generally accepted as a means of paying for goods and services; serves as a medium of exchange, a unit of accounting, a store of value, and a standard of deferred value

money market An over-the-counter marketplace for short-term debt instruments such as Treasury bills and commercial paper

money supply The amount of money in circulation at any given point in time

monopolistic competition A situation in which many sellers differentiate their products from those of competitors in at least some small way

monopoly A situation in which one company dominates a market to the degree that it can control prices

mortgage-backed securities (MBSs) Credit derivatives based on home mortgages

mortgage brokers Nonbank companies that initiate loans on behalf of a mortgage lender in exchange for a fee

motivation The combination of forces that move individuals to take certain actions and avoid other actions

multichannel retailing Coordinated efforts to reach consumers through more than one retail channel

multidomestic strategy A decentralized approach to international expansion in which a company creates highly independent operating units in each new country

multinational corporations (MNCs) Companies with operations in more than one country

municipal bonds Bonds issued by states, cities, and various government agencies to fund public projects

mutual funds Financial instruments that pool money from many investors to buy a diversified mix of stocks, bonds, or other securities

national brands Brands owned by manufacturers and distributed nationally

National Labor Relations Act Legislation passed in 1935 that established labor relations policies and procedures for most sectors of private industry; commonly known as the Wagner Act

national union A nationwide organization composed of many local unions that represent employees in specific locations

nationalizing A government's takeover of selected companies or industries

natural resources Land, forests, minerals, water, and other tangible assets usable in their natural state

needs Differences between a person's actual state and his or her ideal state; they provide the basic motivation to make a purchase

negative reinforcement Encouraging the repetition of a particular behavior (desirable or not) by removing unpleasant consequences for the behavior

negligence A tort in which a reasonable amount of care to protect others from risk of injury is not used

negotiable instrument A transferable document that represents a promise to pay a specified amount

net asset value (NAV) A mutual fund's assets minus its liabilities; usually expressed as NAV per share

net income Profit earned or loss incurred by a firm, determined by subtracting expenses from revenues; casually referred to as the *bottom line*

net worth The difference between your assets and your liabilities

network structure A structure in which individual companies are connected electronically to perform selected tasks for a small headquarters organization

networking The process of making connections with mutually beneficial business contacts

no-load funds Mutual funds that do not charge loads

nongovernmental organizations (NGOs) Nonprofit groups that provide charitable services or promote social and environmental causes

nonsystemic risk Risk that threatens only a single company or a single industry

norms Informal standards of conduct that guide team behavior

not-for-profit organizations Organizations that provide goods and services without having a profit motive; also called *nonprofit organizations*

objective A specific, short-range target or aim

off-price retailers Stores that sell designer labels and other fashionable products at steep discounts

offshoring Transferring a part or all of a business function to a facility (a different part of the company or another company entirely) in another country

oligopoly A market situation in which a very small number of suppliers, sometimes only two, provide a particular good or service

online retailers Companies that use e-commerce technologies to sell over the Internet; includes Internet-only retailers and the online arm of store-based retailers

open-ended interview Interview in which the interviewer adapts his or her line of questioning based on the answers you give and any questions you ask

operating budget Also known as the *master budget*, a budget that identifies all sources of revenue and coordinates the spending of those funds throughout the coming year

operating expenses All costs of operation that are not included under cost of goods sold

operations management Management of the people and processes involved in creating goods and services

opportunity cost The value of the most appealing alternative not chosen

optimal pricing A computer-based pricing method that creates a demand curve for every product to help managers select a price that meets specific marketing objectives

option The purchased right—but not the obligation—to buy or sell a specified number of shares of a stock at a predetermined price during a specified period

order processing Functions involved in receiving and filling customer orders

organization chart A diagram that shows how employees and tasks are grouped and where the lines of communication and authority flow

organization structure A framework that enables managers to divide responsibilities, ensure employee accountability, and distribute decision-making authority

organizational culture A set of shared values and norms that support the management system and that guide management and employee behavior

organizational market Companies, government agencies, and other organizations that buy goods and services either to resell or to use in the creation of their own goods and services

organizing The process of arranging resources to carry out the organization's plans

orientation programs Sessions or procedures for acclimating new employees to the organization

outsourcing Contracting out certain business functions or operations to other companies

overdraft fees Penalties charged against your checking account when you write checks that total more than your available balance

owners' equity The portion of a company's assets that belongs to the owners after obligations to all creditors have been met

panel interview Interview in which you meet with several interviewers at once

participative management A philosophy of allowing employees to take part in planning and decision making

participative pricing Allowing customers to pay the amount they think a product is worth

partnership An unincorporated company owned by two or more people

patent The legal right to exclude others from making, using, or selling an invention or design

pay for performance An incentive program that rewards employees for meeting specific, individual goals

penetration pricing Introducing a new product at a low price in hopes of building sales volume quickly

pension plans Generally refers to traditional, defined-benefit retirement plans

performance appraisals Periodic evaluations of employees' work according to specific criteria

permission-based marketing A marketing approach in which firms first ask permission to deliver messages to an audience and then promise to restrict their communication efforts to those subject areas in which audience members have expressed interest

personal bankruptcy A condition in which a consumer is unable to repay his or her debts; depending on the type of bankruptcy, a court will either forgive many of the person's debts or establish a compatible repayment plan

personal brand The summary perception employers have of your skills, knowledge, and professionalism

personal property All property that is not real property

personal selling One-on-one interaction between a salesperson and a prospective buyer

philanthropy The donation of money, time, goods, or services to charitable, humanitarian, or educational institutions

physical distribution All the activities required to move finished products from the producer to the consumer

place marketing Marketing efforts to attract people and organizations to a particular geographical area

planned system Economic system in which the government controls most of the factors of production and regulates their allocation

planning Establishing objectives and goals for an organization and determining the best ways to accomplish them

point-of-purchase (POP) display Advertising or other display materials set up at retail locations to promote products to potential customers as they are making their purchase decisions

portfolio diversification Spreading investments across enough different vehicles to protect against significant declines in any one vehicle

positioning Managing a business in a way designed to occupy a particular place in the minds of target customers

positive reinforcement Encouraging desired behaviors by offering pleasant consequences for completing or repeating those behaviors

power of attorney Written authorization for one party to legally act for another

preferred stock Shares of ownership without voting rights but with defined dividends

preferred-provider organizations (PPOs) Health-care providers offering reduced-rate contracts to groups that agree to obtain medical care through the providers' organization

premiums (in insurance) Fees that insured parties pay insurers for coverage against losses

premiums (in sales promotions) Free or bargain-priced items offered to encourage consumers to buy a product

press conference An in-person or online gathering of media representatives at which companies announce new information; also called a *news conference*

press release A brief statement or video program released to the press announcing new products, management changes, sales performance, and other potential news items; also called a *news release*

price The amount of money charged for a product or service

price/earnings ratio The market value per share divided by the earnings per share

price elasticity A measure of the sensitivity of demand to changes in price

prime interest rate The lowest rate of interest that banks charge for short-term loans to their most creditworthy customers

prime rate The interest rate a bank charges its best loan customers

private accountants In-house accountants employed by organizations and businesses other than a public accounting firm; also called *corporate accountants*

private banking Banking services for wealthy individuals and families

private brands Brands that carry the label of a retailer or a wholesaler rather than a manufacturer

private corporation A corporation in which all the stock is owned by only a few individuals or companies and is not made available for purchase by the public

private equity Ownership assets that aren't publicly traded; includes venture capital

privatizing Turning over services once performed by the government and allowing private businesses to perform them instead

problem-solving team A team that meets to find ways of improving quality, efficiency, and the work environment

procurement The acquisition of the raw materials, parts, components, supplies, and finished products required to produce goods and services

producer price index (PPI) A statistical measure of price trends at the producer and wholesaler levels

product A bundle of value that satisfies a customer need or want

product development Creating new products for a firm's current markets

product development process A formal process of generating, selecting, developing, and commercializing product ideas

product liability The capacity of a product to cause harm or damage for which the producer or seller is held accountable

product-liability coverage Insurance that protects companies from claims that result from use of a product the company manufactures or distributes

product life cycle Four stages through which a product progresses: introduction, growth, maturity, and decline

product line A series of related products offered by a firm

product mix The complete portfolio of products that a company offers for sale

product placement The paid display or use of products in television shows, movies, and video games

production and operations management Overseeing all the activities involved in producing goods and services

productivity The efficiency with which an organization can convert inputs to outputs

professional liability insurance Insurance that covers claims for damages or injuries caused by professionals in the course of their work

professionalism The quality of performing at a high level and conducting oneself with purpose and pride

profit Money left over after all the costs involved in doing business have been deducted from revenue

profit sharing The distribution of a portion of the company's profits to employees

progressive discipline An escalating process of discipline that gives employees several opportunities to correct performance problems before being terminated

project budget A budget that identifies the costs needed to accomplish a particular project

promotion A wide variety of persuasive techniques used by companies to communicate with their target markets and the general public

property Rights held regarding any tangible or intangible object

property insurance Insurance that provides coverage for physical damage to or destruction of property and for its loss by theft

prospecting The process of finding and qualifying potential customers

prospectus An SEC-required document that discloses required information about the company, its finances, and its plans for using the money it hopes to raise

protectionism Government policies aimed at shielding a country's industries from foreign competition

prototypes Preproduction samples of products used for testing and evaluation

proxy A document that authorizes another person to vote on behalf of a shareholder in a corporation

psychographics Classification of customers on the basis of their psychological makeup, interests, and lifestyles

public accountants Professionals who provide accounting services to other businesses and individuals for a fee

public corporation A corporation in which stock is sold to anyone who has the means to buy it

public relations Nonsales communication that businesses have with their various audiences (including both communication with the general public and press relations)

pull strategy A promotional strategy that stimulates consumer demand via advertising and other communication efforts, thereby creating a *pull* effect through the channel

pure competition A situation in which so many buyers and sellers exist that no single buyer or seller can individually influence market prices

pure risk Risk that involves the chance of loss only

push strategy A promotional strategy that focuses on intermediaries, motivating them to promote, or *push*, products toward end users

quality A measure of how closely a product conforms to predetermined standards and customer expectations

quality assurance A more comprehensive approach of companywide policies, practices, and procedures to ensure that every product meets quality standards

quality control Measuring quality against established standards after the good or service has been produced and weeding out any defective products

quality of work life (QWL) An overall environment that results from job and work conditions

quick ratio A measure of a firm's short-term liquidity, calculated by adding cash, marketable securities, and receivables, then dividing that sum by current liabilities; also known as the *acid-test ratio*

rate of return The gain (or loss) of an investment over time, expressed as a percentage

real property Land and everything permanently attached to it

rebates Partial reimbursement of price, offered as a purchase incentive

recession A period during which national income, employment, and production all fall; defined as at least six months of decline in the GDP

reconcile To compare the balance you believe is in your account with the balance the bank believes is in your account

recruiting The process of attracting appropriate applicants for an organization's jobs

regulation Relying more on laws and policies than on market forces to govern economic activity

reinforcement theory A motivational approach based on the idea that managers can motivate employees by influencing their behaviors with positive and negative reinforcement

relationship marketing A focus on developing and maintaining long-term relationships with customers, suppliers, and distribution partners for mutual benefit

research and development (R&D) Functional area responsible for conceiving and designing new products

résumé A structured, written summary of a person's education, employment background, and job qualifications

retail banks Banks that provide financial services to consumers

retail theater The addition of entertainment or education aspects to the retail experience

retailers Intermediaries that sell goods and services to individuals for their own personal use

retained earnings The portion of shareholders' equity earned by the company but not distributed to its owners in the form of dividends

retirement plans Company-sponsored programs for providing retirees with income

return on equity The ratio between net income after taxes and total owners' equity

return on sales The ratio between net income after taxes and net sales; also known as the *profit margin*

revenue Money a company brings in through the sale of goods and services

right-to-work laws State laws that prohibit union and agency shops

risk Uncertainty of an event or exposure to loss

risk management A process business firms and individuals use to address their exposures to loss

risk/return trade-off The balance of potential risks against potential rewards

S corporation A type of corporation that combines the capital-raising options and limited liability of a corporation with the federal taxation advantages of a partnership

salary Fixed cash compensation for work, usually by a yearly amount; independent of the number of hours worked

sales promotion A wide range of events and activities designed to promote a brand or stimulate interest in a product

Sarbanes-Oxley The informal name of comprehensive legislation designed to improve the integrity and accountability of financial information

scalability The potential to increase production by expanding or replicating its initial production capacity

scarcity A condition of any productive resource that has finite supply

scientific management A management approach designed to improve employees' efficiency by scientifically studying their work

search engine marketing Automated presentation of ads that are related to either the results of an online search or the content being displayed on other webpages

secondary mortgage market The financial market in which mortgages are bought and sold, providing much of the funds that are loaned to homebuyers

secured bonds Bonds backed by specific assets that will be given to bondholders if the borrowed amount is not repaid

secured loans Loans backed up with assets that the lender can claim in case of default, such as a piece of property

securities Investments such as stocks, bonds, options, futures, and commodities

securitization A process in which debts such as mortgages are pooled together and transformed into investments

seed money The first infusion of capital used to get a business started

selective distribution A market coverage strategy that uses a limited number of carefully chosen outlets to distribute products

self-insurance A financial protection strategy in which a company maintains enough funds to pay for potential losses on its own, rather than purchasing insurance coverage

self-managed team A team in which members are responsible for an entire process or operation

seniority The length of time someone has worked for his or her current employer

service businesses Companies that create value by performing activities that deliver some benefit to customers

sexism Discrimination on the basis of gender

sexual harassment Unwelcome sexual advance, request for sexual favors, or other verbal or physical conduct of a sexual nature within the workplace

shareholder activism Activities undertaken by shareholders (individually or in groups) to influence executive decision making in areas ranging from strategic planning to social responsibility

shareholders Investors who purchase shares of stock in a corporation

shopping products Fairly important goods and services that people buy less frequently with more planning and comparison

short selling Selling stock borrowed from a broker with the intention of buying it back later at a lower price, repaying the broker, and keeping the profit

short-term financing Financing used to cover current expenses (generally repaid within a year)

situational interview Similar to a behavioral interview, except the questions focus on how you would handle various hypothetical situations on the job

Six Sigma A rigorous quality management program that strives to eliminate deviations between the actual and desired performance of a business system

skills inventory A list of the skills a company needs from its workforce, along with the specific skills that individual employees currently possess

skim pricing Charging a high price for a new product during the introductory stage and lowering the price later

small business A company that is independently owned and operated, is not dominant in its field, and employs fewer than 500 people (although this number varies by industry)

social commerce The creation and sharing of product-related information among customers and potential customers

social communication model An approach to communication based on interactive social media and conversational communication styles

social environment Trends and forces in society at large

social media Any electronic media that transform passive audiences into active participants in the communication process by allowing them to share content, revise content, respond to content, or contribute new content

socialism Economic system characterized by public ownership and operation of key industries combined with private ownership and operation of less-vital industries

sole proprietorship A business owned by a single person

span of management The number of people under one manager's control; also known as span of control

specialty advertising Advertising that appears on various items such as coffee mugs, pens, and calendars, designed to help keep a company's name in front of customers

specialty products Particular brands that the buyer especially wants and will seek out, regardless of location or price

specialty stores Stores that carry only a particular type of goods, often with deep selection in those specific categories

speculative risk Risk that involves the chance of both loss and profits

stakeholders Internal and external groups affected by a company's decisions and activities

standards Criteria against which performance is measured

stare decisis The concept of using previous judicial decisions as the basis for deciding similar court cases

start-up budget A budget that identifies the money a new company will need to spend to launch operations

statement of cash flows A statement of a firm's cash receipts and cash payments that presents information on its sources and uses of cash

statistical process control (SPC) The use of random sampling and tools such as control charts to monitor the production process

statutory law Statutes, or laws, created by legislatures

stealth marketing The delivery of marketing messages to people who are not aware that they are being marketed to; these messages can be delivered by either acquaintances or strangers, depending on the technique

stereotyping Assigning a wide range of generalized attributes, which are often superficial or even false, to an individual based on his or her membership in a particular culture or social group

stock Ownership of or equity in a company; a *share* of stock represents a specific portion of ownership

stock exchanges Organizations that facilitate the buying and selling of stock

stock options A contract that allows the holder to purchase or sell a certain number of shares of a particular stock at a given price by a certain date

stock split The act of dividing a share into two or more new shares and reducing the market value by the same ratio

stop order An order to sell a stock when its price falls to a particular point, to limit an investor's losses

strategic alliance A long-term partnership between companies to jointly develop, produce, or sell products

strategic CSR Social contributions that are directly aligned with a company's overall business strategy

strategic marketing planning The process of examining an organization's current marketing situation, assessing opportunities and setting objectives, and then developing a marketing strategy to reach those objectives

strategic plans Plans that establish the actions and the resource allocation required to accomplish strategic goals; they're usually defined for periods of two to five years and developed by top managers

strict liability Liability for injury caused by a defective product or process when all reasonable care is used in its manufacture, distribution, or sale; no fault is assigned

strike A temporary work stoppage aimed at forcing management to accept union demands

strikebreakers Nonunion workers hired to do the jobs of striking workers

structured interview Interview in which the interviewer (or a computer) asks a series of prepared questions in a set order

subprime mortgages Home loans for borrowers with low credit scores

succession planning Workforce planning efforts that identify possible replacements for specific employees, usually senior executives

supply A specific quantity of a product that the seller is able and willing to provide at various prices

supply chain A set of connected systems that coordinates the flow of goods and materials from suppliers all the way through to final customers

supply chain management (SCM) The business procedures, policies, and computer systems that integrate the various elements of the supply chain into a cohesive system

supply curve A graph of the quantities of a product that sellers will offer for sale, regardless of demand, at various prices

sustainable development Operating business in a manner that minimizes pollution and resource depletion, ensuring that future generations will have vital resources

system An interconnected and coordinated set of *elements* and *processes* that converts *inputs* to desired *outputs*

systemic risk Risk that exists throughout an entire market

target markets Specific customer groups or segments to whom a company wants to sell a particular product

tariffs Taxes levied on imports

task force A team of people from several departments who are temporarily brought together to address a specific issue

tax credits Direct reductions in your tax obligation

tax-deferred investments Investments such as 401(k) plans and IRAs that let you deduct the amount of your investments from your gross income (thereby lowering your taxable income); you don't have to pay tax on any of the income from these investments until you start to withdraw money during retirement

tax-exempt investments Investments (usually municipal bonds) whose income is not subject to federal income tax

tax haven A country whose favorable banking laws and low tax rates give companies the opportunity to shield some of their income from higher tax rates in their home countries or other countries where they do business.

team A unit of two or more people who share a mission and collective responsibility as they work together to achieve a goal

technical skills The ability and knowledge to perform the mechanics of a particular job

technological environment Forces resulting from the practical application of science to innovations, products, and processes

term life insurance Life insurance that provides death benefits for a specified period

termination The process of getting rid of an employee through layoff or firing

test marketing A product development stage in which a product is sold on a limited basis to gauge its market appeal

Theory X A managerial assumption that employees are irresponsible, are unambitious, and dislike work and that managers must use force, control, or threats to motivate them

Theory Y A managerial assumption that employees enjoy meaningful work, are naturally committed to certain goals, are capable of creativity, and seek out responsibility under the right conditions

three-needs theory David McClelland's model of motivation that highlights the needs for power, affiliation, and achievement

thrift banks Banking institutions that offer deposit accounts and focus on offering home mortgage loans; also called *thrifts*, or *savings and loan associations*

time value of money The increasing value of money as a result of accumulating interest

top managers Those at the highest level of the organization's management hierarchy; they are responsible for setting strategic goals, and they have the most power and responsibility in the organization

tort A noncriminal act (other than breach of contract) that results in injury to a person or to property

trade allowances Discounts or other financial considerations offered by producers to wholesalers and retailers

trade credit Credit obtained by a purchaser directly from a supplier

trade deficit An unfavorable trade balance created when a country imports more than it exports

trade promotions Sales-promotion efforts aimed at inducing distributors or retailers to push a producer's products

trade surplus A favorable trade balance created when a country exports more than it imports

trademarks Brands that have been given legal protection so that their owners have exclusive rights to their use

trading blocs Organizations of nations that remove barriers to trade among their members and that establish uniform barriers to trade with nonmember nations

transaction An exchange of value between parties

transnational strategy A hybrid approach that attempts to reap the benefits of international scale while being responsive to local market dynamics

transparency The degree to which affected parties can observe relevant aspects of transactions or decisions

Treasury bills Short-term debt securities issued by the federal government; also referred to as *T-bills*

Treasury bonds Debt securities issued by the federal government that are repaid more than 10 years after issuance

Treasury Inflation-Protected Securities (TIPS) Treasury issues in which the principal amount is tied to the Consumer Price Index to protect the buyer against the effects of inflation

Treasury notes Debt securities issued by the federal government that are repaid within 1 to 10 years after issuance

turnover rate The percentage of the workforce that leaves every year

umbrella policies Insurance that provides businesses with coverage beyond what is provided by a basic liability policy

underwriter A specialized type of bank that buys the shares from the company preparing an IPO and sells them to investors

unemployment rate The portion of the labor force (everyone over 16 who has or is looking for a job) currently without a job

unfair labor practices Unlawful acts made by either unions or management

Uniform Commercial Code (UCC) A set of standardized laws, adopted by most states, that govern business transactions

uninsurable risk Risk that few, if any, insurance companies will assume because it likely cannot be covered profitably

union security Measures that protect a union's right to represent workers

union shop A unionized workplace in which employees are required to maintain union membership

universal life insurance A combination life insurance and investment product in which customers purchase an insurance policy and invest additional funds

unlimited liability A legal condition under which any damages or debts incurred by a business are the owner's personal responsibility

unsecured loans Loans that require a good credit rating but no collateral

unstructured organization An organization that doesn't have a conventional structure but instead assembles talent as needed from the open market; the virtual and networked organizational concepts taken to the extreme

utility The power of a good or service to satisfy a human need

value-based pricing A method of setting prices based on customer perceptions of value

value chain All the elements and processes that add value as raw materials are transformed into the final products made available to the ultimate customer

value webs Multidimensional networks of suppliers and outsourcing partners

values statement A brief articulation of the principles that guide a company's decisions and behaviors

variable costs Business costs that increase with the number of units produced

venture capitalists (VCs) Investors who provide money to finance new businesses or turnarounds in exchange for a portion of ownership, with the objective of reselling the business at a profit

virtual team A team that uses communication technology to bring together geographically distant employees to achieve goals

viruses Invasive programs that reproduce by infecting legitimate programs

vision statement A brief and inspirational expression of what a company aspires to be

wages Cash payment based on the number of hours an employee has worked or the number of units an employee has produced

wants Specific goods, services, experiences, or other entities that are desirable in light of a person's experiences, culture, and personality

warehouses Facilities for storing inventory

warranty A statement that specifies what the producer of a product will do to compensate the buyer if the product is defective or if it malfunctions

wheel of retailing An evolutionary process by which stores that feature low prices gradually upgrade until they no longer appeal to price-sensitive shoppers and are replaced by a new generation of leaner, low-price competitors

whistle-blowing The disclosure of information by a company insider that exposes illegal or unethical behavior by others within the organization

whole life insurance Insurance that provides both death benefits and savings for the insured's lifetime

wholesalers Intermediaries that sell products to other intermediaries for resale or to organizations for internal use

will A legal document that specifies what will happen to your assets, who will execute your estate (carry out the terms of your will), and who will be the legal guardian of your children, if you have any, in the event of your death

word of mouth Communication among customers and other parties, transmitting information about companies and products through online or offline personal conversations

work–life balance Efforts to help employees balance the competing demands of their personal and professional lives

work rules A common element of labor contracts that specifies such things as the tasks certain employees are required to do or are forbidden to do

work specialization Specialization in or responsibility for some portion of an organization's overall work tasks; also called division of labor

worker buyouts Distributions of financial incentives to employees who voluntarily depart; usually undertaken in order to reduce the payroll

workers' compensation insurance Insurance that partially replaces lost income and that pays for employees' medical costs and rehabilitation expenses for work-related injuries

workforce analytics Computer-based statistical approach to analyzing and planning for workforce needs

working capital Current assets minus current liabilities

working interview Interview in which you perform a job-related activity

yield Interest income a purchaser receives from the bond

zero-based budgeting A budgeting approach in which each department starts from zero every year and must justify every item in the budget, rather than simply adjusting the previous year's budget amounts

Brand, Organization, Name, and Website Index

Subject Index